ANNOTATED

FINANCIAL INSTITUTION

BOND

Third Edition

Michael Keeley

Editor

Cover design by ABA Publishing.

The materials contained herein represent the opinions of the authors and/or the editors, and should not be construed to be the views or opinions of the law firms or companies with whom such persons are in partnership with, associated with, or employed by, nor of the American Bar Association or the Tort Trial and Insurance Practice Section unless adopted pursuant to the bylaws of the Association.

Nothing contained in this book is to be considered as the rendering of legal advice for specific cases, and readers are responsible for obtaining such advice from their own legal counsel. This book is intended for educational and informational purposes only.

© 2013 American Bar Association. All rights reserved.

No part of this publication may be reproduced, stored in a retrieval system, or transmitted in any form or by any means, electronic, mechanical, photocopying, recording, or otherwise, without the prior written permission of the publisher. For permission contact the ABA Copyrights & Contracts Department, copyright@americanbar.org or complete the online form at http://www.americanbar.org/utility/reprint/html.

Printed in the United States of America.

17 16 15 14 13   5 4 3 2 1

Library of Congress Cataloging-in-Publication Data on file.

ISBN: 978-1-62722-435-2

Discounts are available for books ordered in bulk. Special consideration is given to state bars, CLE programs, and other bar-related organizations. Inquire at Book Publishing, ABA Publishing, American Bar Association, 321 N. Clark Street, Chicago, Illinois 60654-7598.

www.ShopABA.org

TABLE OF CONTENTS

Introduction vii

Editor and Authors xi

Past Contributors xviii

Chapter 1 — Insuring Agreements 1

    Section 1 — Insuring Agreement (A)—Fidelity 1
    Michael Keeley, Theresa A. Gooley and Carla C. Crapster

    Section 2 — Insuring Agreement (B)—On Premises 56
    Patricia H. Thompson and Christy L. MacPherson

    Section 3 — Insuring Agreement (C)—In Transit 77
    Brian M. Falcon

    Section 4 — Insuring Agreement (D)—Forgery or
    Alteration 86
    Michele L. Fenice and Adam P. Friedman

    Section 5 — Insuring Agreement (E)—Securities 118
    Gary J. Valeriano and Carleton R. Burch

    Section 6 — Insuring Agreement (F)—Counterfeit Currency 148
    Lisa D. Sparks

    Section 7 — Insuring Agreement (G)—Fraudulent
    Mortgages—2011 Form 150
    Seth Mills and Kevin Mekler

Chapter 2 — General Agreements 155

Section 1 — General Agreement A—Nominees........................... 155
Maura Z. Pelleteri and Amy Malish

Section 2 — General Agreement B—Additional Offices 157
Maura Z. Pelleteri and Amy Malish

Section 3 — General Agreement C—Change of Control—
Notice 161
William T. Bogaert, Stefan Dandelles and Camilla Conlon

Section 4 — General Agreement D—Representation of
Insured 164
William T. Bogaert, Stefan Dandelles and Camilla Conlon

Section 5 — General Agreement E—Joint Insured 179
Maura Z. Pelleteri and Amy Malish

Section 6 — General Agreement F—Notice of Legal
Proceedings Against Insured—Election To Defend....................... 183
Maura Z. Pelleteri and Amy Malish

Section 7 — General Agreement G—Insured's ERISA Plans 204
Seth Mills and Kevin Mekler

Chapter 3 — Conditions and Limitations 209

Section 1 — Definitions 209
Definitions (a)-(l): T. Scott Leo and Brandon G. Hummel
Definitions (m)-(u): Bradford R. Carver and CharCretia DiBartolo

    A. Acceptance 214
    B. Certificate of Deposit 215
    C. Certificate of Origin or Title 216
    D. Certificated Security 217
    E. Counterfeit 218
    F. Document of Title 221
    G. Employee 222
    H. Evidence of Debt 233

TABLE OF CONTENTS iii

    I.   Forgery 234
    J.   Guarantee 238
    K.   Instruction 238
    L.   Letter of Credit 240
    M.   Loan 240
    N.   Money 245
    O.   Negotiable Instrument 249
    P.   Property 251
    Q.   Security Agreement 252
    R.   Statement of Uncertificated Security 254
    S.   Transportation Company 255
    T.   Uncertificated Security 256
    U.   Withdrawal Order 257

Section 2 — Exclusions 259
Exclusions (a)-(l) and Exclusion (aa): Samuel J. Arena, Jr., Daniel T. Fitch and Francis S. Monterosso
Exclusions (m)-(z) and Exclusion (bb): Sam H. Poteet, Jr. and Jeffrey S. Price

    A.   Forgery or Alteration 265
    B.   Riot or Civil Commotion 268
    C.   Nuclear 269
    D.   Acts of Director 270
    E.   Loan Loss 272
    F.   Safe Deposit Box 290
    G.   Travelers' Checks 290
    H.   Employee 292
    I.   Trading Loss 296
    J.   Teller's Cash Shortage 302
    K.   Credit, Debt, Charge Cards 303
    L.   Automated Mechanical Devices 305
    M.   Extortion 306
    N.   Erroneous Entry 307
    O.   Uncollected Funds 309
    P.   Counterfeiting 315
    Q.   Tangible Personal Property 316
    R.   Property In Mail or With Carrier For Hire 318
    S.   Potential Income 319

T. Damages Other Than Direct Compensation
Damages 326
U. Costs, Fees and Expenses 328
V. Indirect or Consequential Loss 330
W. Securities Violation 333
X. Failure of Financial Institution 334
Y. Uncertified Securities 336
Z. Civil, Criminal or Legal Proceeding..............................337
AA. Theft, Disappearance or Destruction of Confidential
Information 338
BB. Dishonest or Fraudulent Acts of an Employee 339

Section 3 — Discovery...341
Toni Scott Reed

Section 4 — Limit of Liability 376
Thomas J. Vollbrecht and Jason Tarasek

Section 5 — Notice/Proof—Legal Proceedings Against
Underwriter 392
Armen Shahinian, Andrew S. Kent and Scott W. Lichtenstein

Section 6 — Valuation 465
Dolores A. Parr

Section 7 — Assignment—Subrogation—Recovery—
Cooperation 470
Dolores A. Parr

Section 8 — Limit of Liability Under This Bond and Other
Insurance 493
Dolores A. Parr

Section 9 — Other Insurance or Indemnity................................495
Lisa D. Sparks

Section 10 — Ownership 497
Seth Mills and Kevin Mekler

Section 11 — Deductible Amount 502
William T. Bogaert, Stefan Dandelles and Camilla Conlon

Section 12 — Termination or Cancellation..................................505
Michael R. Davisson

Chapter 4 — Important Riders and Miscellaneous Topics..............533

Section 1 — A Concise History of the Financial Institution
Bond, Standard Form No. 24...533
Robert J. Duke

Section 2 — Electronic Fraud Insuring Agreement Riders............566
Arthur N. Lambert, Daniel W. White and Victor B. Kao

Section 3 — Retroactive Date Rider 578
Seth Mills and Kevin Mekler

Section 4 — Causation 580
Scott Schmookler and Michael Maillet

Chapter 5 — Loss..610
Peter C. Haley

Section 6 — Construction and Interpretation................................624
James A. Knox, Jr.

Section 7 — Retaliatory Litigation 697
Carol A. Pisano, Richard S. Mills and Ben Zviti

Appendix of Bond Forms 713

Exhibit 1
Financial Institution Bond, Standard Form No. 24
(Revised January, 1986)

Exhibit 2
Statement of Change, Financial Institution Bond, Standard
Form No. 24
(Revised January, 1986)

Exhibit 3
Financial Institution Bond, Standard Form No. 24
(Revised May, 2011)

Exhibit 4
SFAA Electronic Filing Letter for Financial Institution
Bond, Standard Form No. 24
(Revised May, 2011)

Exhibit 5
Financial Institution Bond, Standard Form No. 24
(Revised April 1, 2004)

Exhibit 6
SFAA Filing Letter for Financial Institution Bond, Standard
Form No. 24
(Revised April 1, 2004)

Exhibit 7
Computer Crime Policy for Financial Institutions
(Edition December, 1993)

Exhibit 8
Fraudulent Transfer Instructions Rider
(Revised May, 2011)

Exhibit 9
Retroactive Date Rider/Endorsement
(Revised May, 2011)

Exhibit 10
Bankers Blanket Bond, Standard Form No. 24
(Revised July, 1980)

Exhibit 11
Statement of Change, Bankers Blanket Bond, Standard
Form No. 24
(Revised July, 1980)

Table of Cases..843

Introduction

The current Financial Institution Bond, Standard Form No. 24, had its genesis in 1916, when the first Bankers Blanket Bond, Standard Form No. 1, combined various types of unrelated coverages for financial institutions into a single policy. The form of the bond evolved over time, often changing due to court decisions expanding coverage beyond the drafter's intent, or in light of technological advances. The roots of the current standard form bond date back over forty years to the 1969 version of the Bankers Blanket Bond. Given this lengthy history, it might seem surprising that the bond remains heavily litigated, and that courts often struggle to construe the scope and meaning of various provisions of the policy. For instance, courts continue to grapple with the meaning and application of the manifest intent standard under Insuring Agreement (A), the concept of discovery of loss, and the application of Insuring Agreements (D) and (E) to admittedly complex losses, often involving forged or fraudulent documents.

No single reason exists for the large number of judicial decisions construing the bond. Clearly, some courts simply are not familiar with this type of specialized insurance coverage. The existence of multimillion dollar losses usually assures that cases are handled by talented lawyers for each side, thereby giving courts even more to ponder. And, the often complex nature of bond claims can make the application of the policy difficult, even if the meaning of the relevant provision of the bond otherwise is easily understood. To compound matters even more, the recent soft insurance market has led to many variations of the standard form bond, further challenging courts and the rest of us in the industry.

As a result, a single book collecting each of the cases construing the various sections of the bond is of tremendous value to the industry. The leaders of the Fidelity and Surety Law Committee of TIPS recognized this first in 1980, when they published the original *Annotated Bankers Blanket Bond*.[1] That book was of such value that it was supplemented twice by the Committee, first in 1983, and then again in 1988. A new,

---

[1] ANNOTATED BANKERS BLANKET BOND (Frank L. Skillern, Jr. & Harvey C. Koch eds., 1980).

second edition, the Annotated Financial Institution Bond, was published in 2003.

Since the second edition was published, the industry has again undergone significant change. With the advent of computer technology, it now is easier than ever to counterfeit and create fraudulent and forged documents, leading to a whole new array of bond claims. The increase in electronic commerce has bred a whole new type of electronic thief, thus leading to cyber crime and resulting losses. And, lest we think that old fashioned thievery no longer flourishes, one need only look at recent headlines, including crimes involving Bernie Madoff, Allen Stanford, Lou Pearlman, WorldCom and Enron. In short, fidelity bond claims are as prevalent as ever. Thus, the value of a book of this type remains high.

The earlier versions of this book sought to annotate every case construing the relevant provisions of the standard form Financial Institution Bond. For this third edition, it was decided that many of the older cases contained in the earlier editions were outdated, either because they discussed provisions of the bond no longer in use, or because the weight of authority on certain issues had changed. Therefore, the authors of this new third edition were charged with omitting those annotations that were deemed to be of little or no relevance. This does not mean that all older cases have been omitted. Indeed, *American Surety Co. v. Pauly*[2] and *Guarantee Co. of North America v. Mechanics' Savings Bank & Trust Co.*,[3] each over 100 years old, continue to be highly relevant. These and similar noteworthy older cases remain in this third edition. Additionally, efforts have been made to streamline the annotations to include only those facts important to the stated holding of the case, and to limit the holding of each application to the section of the bond under discussion.

For ease of reference, the annotations follow the structure of the bond. At the end of the book is a separate chapter on important riders and miscellaneous topics, including the history of the bond, loss, causation, construction and interpretation, and retaliatory litigation. An appendix of bond forms and a table of cases is also included.

Each chapter or section begins with the applicable policy language. The 1986 Financial Institution Bond, Standard Form No. 24 is used throughout because it remains the most frequently used form. In some

---

2   170 U.S. 133 (1898).
3   183 U.S. 402 (1902).

instances, language of more recent forms also is included. The annotations begin with any applicable United States Supreme Court decisions, followed by U.S. Circuit Courts of Appeal decisions by circuit and in reverse chronological order, decisions by the U.S. District Courts alphabetically and in reverse chronological order, and then state court decisions alphabetically by state, also in reverse chronological order. In addition to concise annotations, each section also includes a comprehensive list of secondary sources, most of which have been authored by various members of the Fidelity and Surety Law Committee.

Each chapter or section is preceded by a scholarly comment by the author(s) concerning the relevant section of the bond. While most comments are original with this edition of the book, others borrow from the prior edition or its supplements.

Where appropriate, each of the chapters or sections include pertinent subheadings. For instance, the section on Insuring Agreement (A) is divided into the following subheadings: Meaning of Dishonest or Fraudulent Acts; Manifest Intent; Collusion; Financial Benefits; and Benefits of Employment. Other sections are not divided because either the language of the section was more limited or there were a manageable enough number of cases that subdivisions were deemed unnecessary. And, while the various chapters and sections follow a standard format, the authors had discretion to vary from that format where appropriate.

The authors were requested to follow the Chicago Manual of Style and the 19th edition of the Blue Book. While these guides generally were followed, certain exceptions were made in light of industry norms, such as abbreviating the Surety & Fidelity Association of America to SFAA.

As with the two earlier editions of this book, a significant number of the members of the Fidelity and Surety Law Committee have worked tirelessly to make this project possible. On behalf of the Fidelity and Surety Law Committee, I want to thank each of the authors for their significant contributions to this important project. When one realizes the vast number of new cases that were located, read, and summarized, it is easy to understand what a tremendous amount of effort was devoted to this project.

Importantly, special gratitude also must be extended to those individuals involved in the prior editions of this book. Frank L. Skillern, Jr. was the original project Chairman, and along with Harvey C. Koch, served as Editor of the original *Annotated Bankers Blanket Bond*. Mr. Skillern was in charge of the first supplement and edited those annotations, while Mr. Koch assumed these responsibilities in connection with the second supplement. The editor of this third edition served in the same capacity for the second edition. Appreciation also is expressed to each of the authors of the earlier editions. Their names are listed individually following the listing of the contributors to this book. Without the work of all of those before us, this project would not have been practically possible.

Finally, as Editor I also wish to thank all of those at my firm, Strasburger & Price, LLP, who assisted me in editing these materials, over, and over, and over again. Thus, special thanks go out to the following bright lawyers in the firm's Fidelity & Surety Practice Unit: John Riddle, Justin P. Melkus, Jeremy T. Brown, Carla C. Crapster, Clay Cossé, and Ryan B. DeLaune. Additionally, Christine Grey, a genius in our firm's word processing department, deserves special thanks for her considerable efforts in formatting, preparing and proofing the camera-ready copy of this book. Finally, as always, even extra special thanks goes to my incredible Administrative Assistant, Marianna Green, without whose help I might well be working construction, or perhaps working at a winery (hmm). It was the careful eye to detail of all involved that has resulted in the polished look of this book.

MICHAEL KEELEY
Strasburger & Price, LLP
Dallas, Texas
Editor
October 2013

EDITOR

MICHAEL KEELEY • Partner in the Dallas, Texas office of Strasburger & Price, LLP. Mr. Keeley is a graduate of the University of Arizona, B.S. *summa cum laude with honors* 1977, and the University of Arizona School of Law, J.D. *cum laude* 1981. Mr. Keeley is a past Chair of the Fidelity and Surety Law Committee, Editor-in-Chief of the Fidelity Law Journal, Advisor Emeritus to the Fidelity Law Association, Advisor to the Surety & Fidelity Association of America and past Editor-in-Chief of the Tort & Insurance Law Journal.

AUTHORS

SAMUEL J. ARENA, JR. • Partner with Stradley Ronon Stevens & Young, LLP in Philadelphia, Pennsylvania. Mr. Arena is a graduate of Ursinus College, B.A. *magna cum laude* 1979, and Villanova University School of Law, J.D. *cum laude* 1983. Mr. Arena is a past Chair of the Fidelity and Surety Law Committee.

CARLETON R. BURCH • Partner in the Los Angeles, California and Las Vegas, Nevada offices of Anderson, McPharlin & Conners, LLP. Mr. Burch is a graduate of Colorado College B.A., *cum laude*, 1984, and the University of California, Hastings College of Law, J.D. 1987.

WILLIAM T. BOGAERT • Partner in the Boston, Massachusetts office of Wilson, Elser, Moskowitz, Edelman & Dicker, LLP. Mr. Bogaert is a graduate of Clark University, B.A. *with high honors* 1976, and Boston College Law School, J.D. *cum laude* 1985.

BRADFORD R. CARVER • Partner in the Boston, Massachusetts office of Hinshaw & Culbertson LLP. Mr. Carver is a graduate of Colgate University, A.B. 1977, and Western New England College, J.D. *cum laude* 1980.

CAMILLA CONLON • Senior Claims Specialist in the Chicago, Illinois office of ACE North American Professional Risk Claims. Ms. Conlon is a graduate of the University of Michigan B.A. 1988, and Valparaiso Law School, J.D. 1992.

CARLA C. CRAPSTER • Associate in the Dallas, Texas office of Strasburger & Price, LLP. Ms. Crapster is a graduate of Texas A&M University, B.A. *summa cum laude* 2005, and the University of Texas School of Law, J.D. *with high honors* 2008.

STEFAN R. DANDELLES • Partner in the Chicago, Illinois office of Wilson, Elser, Moskowitz, Edelman & Dicker, LLP. Mr. Dandelles is a graduate of the University of Wisconsin, B.A. 1994, and the University of Iowa College of Law, J.D. *with distinction* 1997.

MICHAEL R. DAVISSON • Partner in the Los Angeles, California office of Sedgwick LLP. Mr. Davisson is a graduate of the University of California, B.A. 1975, and the University of California, Hastings College of Law, J.D. 1978.

CHARCRETIA V. DIBARTOLO • Partner in the Boston, Massachusetts office of Hinshaw & Culbertson LLP. Ms. DiBartolo is a graduate of Washington University, B.A. 1988, and Washington University School of Law, J.D. 1991.

ROBERT J. DUKE • Corporate Counsel with The Surety & Fidelity Association of America in Washington, D.C. Mr. Duke is a graduate of Loyola University Maryland, B.B.A. *summa cum laude* 1988 and M.B.A. 1992, and the Columbus School of Law, Catholic University of America, J.D. *summa cum laude* 2005.

BRIAN M. FALCON • Member in the Indianapolis, Indiana office of Frost Brown Todd LLC. Mr. Falcon is a graduate of Ball State University, B.S. 1998, and the Indiana University Robert H. McKinney School of Law, J.D. 2003.

MICHELE L. FENICE • Vice President and Claims Manager of the Employment Practices Liability and Fidelity Claim groups in the Jersey City, New Jersey office of ACE North American Professional Risk Claims Team. Ms. Fenice is a graduate of Albright College, B.A. 1990, and New York School of Law, J.D. 1993.

DANIEL T. FITCH • Partner with Stradley Ronon Stevens & Young, LLP in Philadelphia, Pennsylvania. Mr. Fitch is a graduate of Dickinson College, B.A. *cum laude* 1985, and George Washington University Law School, J.D. *with honors* 1988.

ADAM P. FRIEDMAN • Member in the West Orange, New Jersey office of Wolff & Samson PC. Mr. Friedman is a graduate of Cornell University, B.S. 1988, and Yeshiva University Benjamin N. Cardozo School of Law, J.D. 1991.

THERESA A. GOOLEY • Vice President of Claims with OneBeacon Insurance Group in Minnetonka, Minnesota. Ms. Gooley is a graduate of the University of Minnesota, B.S. 1990, and Drake University Law School, J.D. 1994.

PETER C. HALEY • Partner in the San Rafael, California office of Nielsen Haley & Abbott LLP. Mr. Haley is a graduate of the University of California at Berkeley, A.B. 1964, and Boalt Hall School of Law, University of California, at Berkeley, J.D. 1967.

BRANDON G. HUMMEL • Associate with Leo & Weber, P.C. in Chicago, Illinois. Mr. Hummel is a graduate of The John Hopkins University, B.A. *with honors* 2000, and Northwestern University School of Law, J.D. 2004.

VICTOR B. KAO • Senior Associate in the New York City office of Frenkel Lambert Weiss Weisman & Gordon LLP. Mr. Kao is a graduate of Yale University, B.A. 2000, and the University of Virginia School of Law, J.D. 2004.

MICHAEL KEELEY • Partner in the Dallas, Texas office of Strasburger & Price, LLP. Mr. Keeley is a graduate of the University of Arizona, B.S. *summa cum laude with honors* 1977, and the University of Arizona School of Law, J.D. *cum laude* 1981. Mr. Keeley is a past Chair of the Fidelity and Surety Law Committee, Editor-in-Chief of the Fidelity Law Journal, Advisor Emeritus to the Fidelity Law Association, Advisor to the Surety & Fidelity Association of America and past Editor-in-Chief of the Tort & Insurance Law Journal.

ANDREW S. KENT • Counsel in the West Orange, New Jersey and New York City offices of Wolff & Samson PC. Mr. Kent is a graduate of Rutgers College, B.A. 1989, and Rutgers School of Law, Newark, J.D. 1992.

JAMES A. KNOX • Senior Counsel with Christensen & Ehret, LLP, in Chicago, Illinois. Mr. Knox is a graduate of Southern Methodist University, B.A. 1980, and the University of Texas School of Law, J.D. 1984. Mr. Knox is a former Editor-in-Chief of the Fidelity & Surety Digest and Chair of the Defense Research Institute's Fidelity & Surety Committee.

ARTHUR N. LAMBERT • Senior Partner in the New York City office of Frenkel Lambert Weiss Weisman & Gordon LLP. Mr. Lambert is a graduate of Adelphi University, B.A. *with honors* 1963, and Brooklyn Law School, J.D. *with honors* 1968.

T. SCOTT LEO • Shareholder with Leo & Weber, P.C. in Chicago, Illinois Mr. Leo is a graduate of the University of Illinois, B.A. 1976, and Washington University, J.D. 1980. Mr. Leo is a past Chair of the Fidelity and Surety Law Committee.

SCOTT W. LICHTENSTEIN • Associate in the West Orange, New Jersey and New York City offices of Wolff & Samson, P.C. Mr. Lichtenstein is a graduate of Rutgers College B.A. *magna cum laude* 2006, and Rutgers School of Law, Newark, J.D. 2006.

CHRISTY L. MACPHERSON • Associate in the Atlanta, Georgia office of Carlton Fields. Ms. MacPherson is a graduate of Vanderbilt University, B.S. *summa cum laude* 2004, and the University of North Carolina, J.D. *with honors* 2008.

MICHAEL MAILLET • Assistant Vice-President and Senior Claims Examiner in the New York City office of Chubb & Son. Mr. Maillet is a graduate of Fordham University, B.A. 1974, and Fordham Law School, J.D. 1977.

AMY MALISH • Partner with Krebs, Farley & Pelleteri, PLLC in New Orleans, Louisiana. Ms. Malish is a graduate of the University of Texas,

B.A. *with high honors* 1999, and Loyola University, J.D. *magna cum laude* 2003.

KEVIN MEKLER • Associate in the Tampa, Florida office of Mills Paskert Divers. Mr. Mekler is a graduate of Park University, B.A. *with honors* 2000, and Stetson University, J.D. *with honors* 2004.

RICHARD S. MILLS • Partner in the New York City office of McElroy, Deutsch, Mulvaney & Carpenter, LLP. Mr. Mills is a graduate of The Pennsylvania State University, B.S. 1982, and New York Law School, J.D. 1986.

SETH MILLS • Partner in the Tampa, Florida and Atlanta, Georgia offices of Mills Paskert Divers. Mr. Mills is a graduate of The Citadel, B.A. *with high honors*, 1979 and the University of Florida, J.D. *with honors* 1981. Mr. Mills is a past Chair of the Fidelity & Surety Law Committee.

FRANCIS S. MONTEROSSO • Associate with Stradley Ronon Stevens & Young, LLP in Philadelphia, Pennsylvania. Mr. Monterosso is a graduate of Boston College, B.S. *magna cum laude* 2008, and Villanova University School of Law, J.D. *magna cum laude* 2011.

DOLORES A. PARR • Managing Counsel with Zurich in Baltimore, Maryland. Ms. Parr is a graduate of Towson University, B.A. *magna cum laude* 1974, the University of Baltimore School of Law, J.D. 1977, and John Hopkins University, M.L.A. 2005.

MAURA Z. PELLETERI • Partner with Krebs, Farley & Pelleteri, PLLC in New Orleans, Louisiana. Ms. Pelleteri is a graduate of the University of Maryland, B.S. 1977, and Loyola University, J.D. 1983.

CAROL A. PISANO • Partner in the New York City office of McElroy, Deutsch, Mulvaney & Carpenter, LLP. Ms. Pisano is a graduate of the State University of New York, B.A. *summa cum laude* 1976, and Hofstra University, Maurice A. Deane School of Law, J.D. *with honors* 1979.

SAM H. POTEET, JR. • Principal with Manier & Herod in Nashville, Tennessee. Mr. Poteet is a graduate of Tennessee Technological University, B.S. 1979, and the University of Tennessee College of Law,

J.D. 1982. Mr. Poteet is a Vice-Chair of the Fidelity & Surety Law Committee.

JEFFREY S. PRICE • Principal with Manier & Herod in Nashville, Tennessee. Mr. Price is a graduate of Gardner Webb, B.A. *magna cum laude* 1995, and the University of Tennessee College of Law, J.D. *summa cum laude* 1998.

TONI SCOTT REED • Partner in the Dallas, Texas office of Strasburger & Price, LLP. Ms. Reed is a graduate of Southern Methodist University, B.B.A. and B.A. *summa cum laude* 1990, and J.D. *cum laude* 1993.

SCOTT L. SCHMOOKLER • Partner in the Chicago, Illinois office of Gordon & Rees, LLP. Mr. Schmookler is a graduate of Bradley University, B.A. 1993, and IIT-Chicago Kent College of Law, J.D. 1996.

ARMEN SHAHINIAN • Member of the West Orange, New Jersey and New York City offices of Wolff & Samson PC. Mr. Shahinian is a graduate of Brown University, A.B. 1971, and New York University, J.D. 1974. Mr. Shahinian is a past Chair of the Fidelity and Surety Law Committee, Advisor Emeritus to the Fidelity Law Association, Advisor to the Surety & Fidelity Association of America, and is a member of the Board of Directors of the Surety Claims Institute and Editor-in-Chief of its Newsletter.

LISA D. SPARKS • Associate with Wright, Constable & Skeen, LLP in Baltimore, Maryland. Ms. Sparks is a graduate of the University of Baltimore, B.A. 2005, and J.D. 2007.

JASON TARASEK • Shareholder with Hammargren & Meyer, P.A. in Bloomington, Minnesota. Mr. Tarasek is a graduate of the University of Wisconsin, B.A. *with distinction* 1995, and the University of California, Hastings School of Law, J.D. 2002.

PATRICIA H. THOMPSON • Shareholder in the Miami, Florida office of Carlton Fields. Ms. Thompson is a graduate of Saint Olaf College, B.A. *magna cum laude* 1972, and Vanderbilt University, J.D. 1976. She is a past Chair of the Fidelity and Surety Law Committee.

GARY J. VALERIANO • Partner in the Los Angeles, California office of Anderson, McPharlin & Conners, LLP. Mr. Valeriano is a graduate of the California State University, Northbridge, B.A. 1974, and Loyola University School of Law, J.D. 1979. Mr. Valeriano is Chair Elect Presumptive of the Fidelity & Surety Law Committee.

THOMAS J. VOLLBRECHT • Shareholder with Hammargren & Meyer, P.A. in Bloomington, Minnesota. Mr. Vollbrecht is a graduate of St. John's University, B.A. 1982, and Harvard Law School, J.D. 1986. Mr. Vollbrecht is a Vice-Chair of the Fidelity & Surety Law Committee and Editor-in Chief of the FSLC Newsletter.

DANIEL W. WHITE • Partner in the New York City office of Frenkel Lambert Weiss Weisman & Gordon LLP. Mr. White is a graduate of Vassar College, B.A. 1978, and Brooklyn Law School, J.D. 1984.

BEN ZVITI • Managing Director, Counsel, with Travelers, Bond & Financial Product Claims in New York City. Mr. Zviti is a graduate of New York University, B.A. 2003, and Yeshiva University Benjamin N. Cardozo School of Law, J.D. 2006.

CONTRIBUTORS TO SECOND EDITION

Samuel J. Arena, Jr.
George J. Bachrach
Scott D. Baron
Andrew W. Boczkowski
William T. Bogaert
David M. Burkholder
Bradford R. Carver
Duncan L. Clore
Meredith Constant
Michael R. Davisson
CharCretia D. Bartolo
David T. DiBiase
Jane Landes Foster
Edward G. Gallagher
Julia Blackwell Gelinas
Katherine J. Gibson

Peter C. Haley
Cole S. Kain
Michael Keeley
James A. Knox, Jr.
David J. Krebs
T. Scott Leo
Diane L. Matthews
Thomas H. McNeill
Dolores A. Parr
Martha L. Perkins
Sam H. Poteet, Jr.
Jeffrey S. Price
Gilbert J. Schroeder
Armen Shahinian
Susan Koehler Sullivan
Patricia H. Thompson

CONTRIBUTORS TO FIRST EDITION and 1st and 2nd SUPPLEMENTS

Martin J. Andrew
James A. Black, Jr.
David E. Bordon
R. D. Carnaghan
Duncan L. Clore
Tom Connally
James F. Crowder
David T. DiBiase
David C. Dreifuss
Charles W. Franklin
Bruce Gillman
Peter C. Haley
Patrick E. Hartigan
John R. Hickisch
John W. Hinchey
Charles H. Hoens, Jr.

Alan V. Johnson
David Kerr
Bruce Charles King
Harvey C. Koch
John F. Kruger
R. D. Kuehnle
Robert W. Monaghan
Edgar L. Neel
John P. O'Dea
Eugene R. Preaus
Gary J. Rouse
G. Steven Ruprecht
Gilbert J. Schroeder
Frank L. Skillern
Robin V. Weldy
William H. Woods

Chapter 1

Insuring Agreements

SECTION 1 — INSURING AGREEMENT (A)—FIDELITY*

(A) Loss resulting directly from dishonest or fraudulent acts committed by an Employee acting alone or in collusion with others.

Such dishonest or fraudulent acts must be committed by the Employee with the manifest intent:
  (a) to cause the Insured to sustain such loss; and
  (b) to obtain financial benefit for the Employee or another person or entity.

However, if some or all of the Insured's loss results directly or indirectly from Loans, that portion of the loss is not covered unless the Employee was in collusion with one or more parties to the transactions and has received, in connection therewith, a financial benefit with a value of at least $2,500.

As used throughout this Insuring Agreement, financial benefit does not include any employee benefits earned in the normal course of employment, including: salaries, commissions, fees, bonuses, promotions, awards, profit sharing or pensions.

COMMENT

Financial Institution Bonds have been available to banks in one form or another for over 100 years.[1] As with all forms of insurance, fidelity bonds create a risk-sharing arrangement, with insurers assuming the risk

---

* By Michael Keeley and Carla C. Crapster, Strasburger & Price, LLP, Dallas, Texas. Theresa A. Gooley OneBeacon Insurance Group, Minnetonka, Minnesota.

1 Frank Skillern, Jr., *The New Definition of Dishonesty in Financial Institution Bonds*, 14 FORUM 339 (1978).

of certain losses that are difficult for banks to protect against and banks maintaining the risk of common business losses. For example, banks are in the business of making loans, and thus they are in the best position to avoid the risk of loss due to unpaid loans. As a result, Financial Institution Bonds specifically exclude coverage for loan losses except under very limited circumstances where the loss is caused by employee dishonesty. On the other hand, banks are not as equipped to avoid the risk of loss resulting directly from embezzlement, forged or counterfeit securities, or forged or altered negotiable instruments. As a result, the multi-peril Financial Institution Bond has been providing limited forms of insurance against such losses since 1916.[2]

From the very beginning, coverage for a bank's loss due to employee dishonesty was intended to be narrow, limited to embezzlement and embezzlement-type acts.[3] For just as long, insured banks looking for relief from significant employee dishonesty losses have disagreed over the scope of coverage for such losses. As a result, over the years, insurers, led by the Surety and Fidelity Association of America,[4] have continually modified the standard form Financial Institution Bond to clarify the narrow scope of coverage. In 1976, the industry added a manifest intent requirement by the use of a rider,[5] and then by revision to the standard form Bankers Blanket Bond in 1980,[6] requiring proof that the employee acted with the manifest intent to cause the insured to sustain a loss. The 1980 standard form Bankers Blanket Bond also included a requirement that the employee act with the manifest intent to obtain a financial benefit for either herself or any other person or organization.[7] And, in 1986 the standard form Financial Institution Bond

---

[2] Robin Weldy, *A Survey of Recent Changes In Financial Institution Bonds*, 12 FORUM 895 (1977); *see also* Robin Weldy, *History of Financial Institution Bonds*, in FINANCIAL INSTITUTION BONDS 1 (Harvey Koch ed., 1989).

[3] Weldy, *A Survey of Recent Changes in Financial Institution Bonds*, *supra* note 2, at 896.

[4] Previously known as the Surety Association of America [hereinafter SFAA].

[5] SFAA, Rider No. 6019, *reprinted in* STANDARD FORMS OF THE SURETY ASS'N OF AMERICA [hereinafter Standard Forms].

[6] Bankers Blanket Bond, Standard Form No. 24 (Revised July 1980), *reprinted in* Standard Forms.

[7] *Id.* Insuring Agreement (A).

was revised again, this time to preclude coverage under Insuring Agreement (A) for a loss resulting directly from a loan unless the dishonest employee also acted in collusion with one or more parties to the transaction and received a financial benefit with a value of at least $2,500.[8]

When this chapter was written for the second edition of this book in 2003, the lead author pointed out that much of the controversy in fidelity bond claims had been over the precise meaning and proper application of the manifest intent requirement of Insuring Agreement (A). At that time, certain courts were still applying a wholly objective standard in applying the manifest intent requirement, essentially equating manifest intent with recklessness or negligence, finding that an employee acted with the manifest intent to cause the bank to suffer a loss if the natural and probable consequences of the employee's acts were a loss. Those decisions were fundamentally unsound, either because they were based upon earlier bond forms that were no longer applicable, or because they were based upon inapplicable criminal or tort law cases.

Ten years later, the controversy over the intended scope of coverage under Insuring Agreement (A) has waned, but there continues to be disagreement as to the precise scope of coverage under Insuring Agreement (A). It is safe to say that most, although not all, courts now recognize that losses caused by negligence or recklessness are not covered by the bond. But debate continues over whether an insured must establish that its employee acted with the "specific intent" or "purpose" to cause the insured to sustain a loss, or whether it is adequate to show that the employee knew that a loss was "substantially certain" to follow from his or her actions. A significant minority of courts have applied what the authors have referred to as the "substantial certainty test."[9]

---

[8] Financial Institution Bond, Standard Form No. 24 (Revised to Jan. 1986), *reprinted in* Standard Forms. The SFAA also modified the name of the bond in 1986 from Bankers Blanket Bond to Financial Institution Bond in order to counteract the tendency of some courts to construe the bond broadly because the word "blanket" was contained in the title.

[9] *See, e.g.,* Peoples Bank & Trust Co. v. Aetna Cas. & Sur. Co., 113 F.3d 629, 635 (6th Cir. 1997); FDIC v. Oldenburg, 34 F.3d 1529, 1539 (10th Cir. 1994); FDIC v. United Pac. Ins. Co., 20 F.3d 1070, 1078 (10th Cir. 1994); Heller Int'l Corp. v. Sharp, 974 F.2d 850, 859 (7th Cir. 1992); First Fed. Sav. & Loan Ass'n v. Transamerica Ins. Co., 935 F.2d 1164 (10th Cir. 1991); FDIC v. St. Paul Fire & Marine Ins. Co., 942 F.2d 1032, 1035 (6th

Rather than requiring a showing of specific intent, these courts employ what is tantamount to a fiction, finding that the employee intended a loss if a loss was substantially certain to follow from the employee's conduct, regardless of the employee's true intent. The better-reasoned decisions, however, apply what the lead author has characterized as the specific intent standard, requiring proof that the employee acted with the conscious purpose to cause his or her employer to suffer a loss.[10]

Perhaps the most thorough analysis of the differing standards by courts to date is in *Resolution Trust Corp. v. Fidelity & Deposit Co. of Maryland.*[11] In this case, the Third Circuit adopted the specific intent standard after first reviewing its purpose and history. After carefully considering the distinction between the two standards, including adoption of the general intent and specific intent standards in older criminal law cases and in tort law, as well as under the Model Penal Code, it concluded that the specific intent standard was superior. The court held that the term manifest intent required the insured "to prove that the employee engaged in dishonest or fraudulent acts with the specific purpose, object or desire both to cause a loss and to obtain a financial benefit."[12]

Market forces have caused some insurers to modify the intent requirement of the bond. Thus, while most policies in use today include a manifest intent requirement, various proprietary bond forms include a modified intent standard, using the word "intent" instead of "manifest

---

Cir. 1991); Phillip R. Seaver Title Co., Inc. v. Great Am. Ins. Co., No. 08-CV-11004, 2008 WL 4427582 (E.D. Mich. Sept. 30, 2008); Lynch Properties, Inc. v. Potomac Ins. Co. of Ill., 962 F. Supp. 956, 962 (N.D. Tex. 1996).

10 *See, e.g.,* FDIC v. Nat'l Union Fire Ins. Co., No. 01-2524, 2003 WL 262502 (3d Cir. 2003); FDIC v. Nat'l Union Fire Ins. Co. of Pittsburgh, Pa., 205 F.3d 66, 72 (2nd Cir. 2000); Gen. Analytics Corp. v. CNA Ins. Cos., 86 F.3d 51, 54 (4th Cir. 1996); RTC v. Fid. & Deposit Co. of Md., 205 F.2d 615, 638 (3rd Cir. 2000); First Nat'l Bank of Louisville v. Lustig, 961 F.2d 1162, 1165-67 (5th Cir. 1992); Glusband v. Fittin Cunningham & Lauzon, Inc., 892 F.2d 208, 212 (2nd Cir. 1989); Cont'l Bank v. Aetna Cas. & Sur. Co., No. 024780/91 (N.Y. Sup. Ct. Feb. 17, 1994); J.T. Moran Fin. Corp. v. Nat'l Union Fire Ins. Co. of Pittsburgh, Pa., 147 B.R. 335, 339 (S.D.N.Y. 1992); Verex Assurance, Inc. v. Gate City Mortgage Co., No. C-83-0506W, 1984 WL 2918 (D. Utah Dec. 4, 1984).

11 205 F.3d 615 (3d Cir. 2000).

12 *Id.* at 642.

intent." In 2004, the SFAA issued an updated standard form 24 bond that omitted the term "manifest intent," and instead used the phrase "active and conscious purpose" in its place. The rewording was intended to convey the original purpose behind the manifest intent requirement—a conscious desire to cause a result. However, it became apparent that the market was not ready for such updated language. As a result, in 2011 the SFAA again modified the standard form 24 bond to utilize the "manifest intent" requirement.

While a significant body of case law construes the other important sections of Insuring Agreement (A), they are not as controversial. For instance, it seems well settled that in addition to having the manifest intent to cause the insured to sustain a loss, the employee also must have the same intent to obtain a financial benefit. And if the insured's loss results directly or indirectly from a loan, that portion of the loss is not covered unless the employee both "was in collusion with" one or more parties to the transactions, and also received a financial benefit of at least $2,500. Additionally, while the so-called "employee benefits" exclusion once engendered significant debate, the cases now are well settled that there is no coverage under Insuring Agreement (A) for losses that amount to employee benefits, including salaries, commissions, fees, bonuses, promotions, awards, profit sharing, or pensions.

OUTLINE OF ANNOTATIONS

A. Meaning of Dishonest or Fraudulent Acts
B. Manifest Intent
C. Collusion
D. Financial Benefits
E. Benefits of Employment

ANNOTATIONS

A. Meaning of Dishonest or Fraudulent Acts

2d Cir. 2000 (N.Y.). Bank trustee's failure to disclose knowledge of fraudulent conduct pertaining to a loan constituted a dishonest act under the bond. *FDIC v. Nat'l Union Fire Ins. Co. of Pittsburgh, Pa.*, 205 F.3d 66, 70-71.

2d Cir. 1988 (N.Y.). Under New York law, different standards of proof applied to the terms "dishonest acts" and "fraudulent acts" in fidelity bond issued to investment firm. Fraud had to be proven by "clear and convincing" evidence; dishonesty, by a "preponderance of the evidence." Trial judge erroneously required "clear and convincing" evidence of dishonesty to establish coverage. The error was harmless, however, because the record failed to show that the employee acted with the manifest intent to cause a loss and to obtain a financial benefit for himself or others, even under the lower evidentiary standard. *Leucadia, Inc. v. Reliance Ins. Co.*, 864 F.2d 964, 972.

3d Cir. 2002 (Penn.). Nurses employed by drug-testing firm falsified patient records during clinical trials. The court of appeals held that submitting falsified patient records was irrefutably dishonest. *Scirex Corp. v. Fed. Ins. Co.*, 313 F.3d 841, 849.

4th Cir. 1979 (S.C.). An employee of insured mortgage broker admitted that he advanced construction monies to contractors without the required prior approval of HUD and falsely certified the dates and amounts of the advances to HUD. The employee's conduct was held to be dishonest as a matter of law. The court noted that: (1) fraudulent or dishonest conduct need not amount to a crime and need only involve bad faith or a want of integrity or untrustworthiness or a disposition to lie or cheat or a faithlessness to a trust; and (2) there need not be an intent to profit or cause a monetary loss to the employer. *C. Douglas Wilson & Co. v. Ins. Co. of N. Am.*, 590 F.2d 1275, 1278-79.

4th Cir. 1934 (N.C.). The making of an unauthorized loan, approved by directors, was not a dishonest act. Directors repeatedly approved loan renewals and, though the conduct at issue involved a technical violation of the banking laws, it was not dishonest. *Fid. & Deposit Co. of Md. v. People's Bank of Sanford*, 72 F.2d 932, 937.

5th Cir. 1995 (La.). Bank did not have to prove a dishonest act for each loan; instead, a general pattern of dishonesty, whereby employee was motivated by separate instances of bribery to make multiple loans, was sufficient. *FDIC v. Fid. & Deposit Co. of Md.*, 45 F.3d 969, 976.

5th Cir. 1985 (Tex.). Bank president's act of embezzling loan-commitment fee was held to be dishonest and fraudulent. *Cont'l Sav. Ass'n v. USF&G,* 762 F.2d 1239, 1243-44.

5th Cir. 1981 (La.). Bank president permitted borrowers to collect the proceeds of life insurance policies pledged as collateral for two loans made by the bank. These acts were found to be dishonest, but no coverage existed. *Cent. Progressive Bank v. Fireman's Fund Ins. Co.,* 658 F.2d 377, 380-81.

5th Cir. 1981 (Tex.). To constitute a dishonest or fraudulent act under Texas law, the employee must have some degree of intent to perform a wrongful action, though the intent need not be to the extent required by criminal law. There must be a physical act plus a mental state. Mere negligence, carelessness, or incompetence is insufficient. *Merch. & Farmers State Bank of Weatherford, Tex. v. Fid. & Cas. Co. of N.Y.,* 791 F.2d 1141, 1144-45.

5th Cir. 1981 (Tex.). Lawsuits were filed against the bank alleging conspiracy to defraud through forgery and check kiting perpetrated by a bank director and facilitated by the bank's president. The allegations were held to fall within the bond's fidelity clause. *First Nat'l Bank of Bowie v. Fid. & Cas. Co. of N.Y.,* 634 F.2d 1000, 1004.

5th Cir. 1978 (Fla.). An employee's acts do not need to be criminal, nor is it necessary that the employee personally benefit or intend to benefit, for acts to be dishonest. However, willfulness and an intent to deceive are necessary elements for acts to be dishonest and fraudulent. More than negligence, mistake, carelessness or incompetence must be present. *Eglin Nat'l Bank v. Home Indem. Co.,* 583 F.2d 1281, 1282-87.

5th Cir. 1977 (La.). Insured suffered trading losses when an employee-broker speculated in the commodities market. The broker used the insured's membership in the Chicago Board of Trade to gain access to the floor of the exchange. The court held that the broker's conduct was dishonest. The employee used the insured's credit, knew that the insured would have to pay any loss sustained and gave the insured bad checks to allow deception to continue. *Howard, Weil, Labouisse, Friedrichs, Inc. v. Ins. Co. of N. Am.,* 557 F.2d 1055, 1058.

5th Cir. 1970 (Tex.). Bank director placed the interests of third parties ahead of the interests of the bank in various real estate transactions. The director's actions were dishonest because he disregarded his responsibilities to the bank and concealed his conflict of interest. *FDIC v. Aetna Cas. & Sur. Co.,* 426 F.2d 729, 737-39.

5th Cir. 1956 (Fla.). There must be an element of moral turpitude or want of integrity for an act to be dishonest under a fidelity bond. *Glenn Falls Indem. Co. v. Nat'l Floor & Supply Co.,* 239 F.2d 412, 413-14.

5th Cir. 1950 (Tex.). Action of employee in purchasing steel in insured's name and diverting it to the open market at a secret personal profit was fraudulent and dishonest conduct. *Eagle Indem. Co. v. Cherry,* 182 F.2d 298, 299-300.

5th Cir. 1934 (Tex.). Insured claimed that its president had insolvent persons execute notes and secretly used the proceeds to finance his stock-market operations. President's acts were dishonest as a matter of law. The court noted that "[i]nsurance against dishonest acts is insurance of fidelity; it is intended to, it does, guarantee openness and fair dealing on the part of the bank's officers. It is intended to, it does, underwrite that the bank's officers shall act with common honesty and an eye single to its interests. It guarantees that the bank shall at all times have the benefit of the unbiased, critical, and disinterested judgment of the president in regard to the loans it makes." *Md. Cas. Co. v. Am. Trust Co.,* 71 F.2d 137, 138-39.

7th Cir. 1983 (Ill.). Although the facts of an employee's conduct were undisputed, the characterization of that conduct was a separate question of fact. Because the inferences to be drawn from the employee's conduct could reasonably show dishonesty, on the one hand, or error of judgment, incompetence, or negligence, on the other hand, summary judgment was reversed. *Rock Island Bank v. Aetna Cas. & Sur. Co.,* 706 F.2d 219, 222-24.

7th Cir. 1980 (Ill.). A jury should determine whether an act is dishonest or fraudulent. *Cent. Nat'l Life Ins. Co. v. Fid. & Deposit Co. of Md.,* 626 F.2d 537, 541.

7th Cir. 1979 (Ill.). The words "dishonest" and "fraudulent" used in a fidelity bond are to be given broad meaning. They are broader than their "criminal" meaning and include acts that show a want of integrity or breach of trust. The following conduct of a bank president was held to be dishonest and fraudulent as a matter of law: (1) approving seventy-two loans to eight friends, relatives, and business associates, most without security, and all of whom were out of the territory and were refinancing the loans when they came due; (2) continuing to purchase participations from another bank owned by his brother-in-law in violation of the instructions of the board of directors; and (3) diverting monies to himself that belonged to the bank from credit life commissions. *First Nat'l Bank Co. v. Ins. Co. of N. Am.*, 606 F.2d 760, 768-69.

7th Cir. 1971 (Ind.). Whether an employee's conduct constitutes dishonesty is a question of fact. The words "dishonest" and "fraudulent" are to be given a broad meaning, and it is not necessary to show that an employee benefited personally for the act to be dishonest. Bank vice president's fraudulent entries and failure to charge back dishonored checks were sufficient evidence of dishonesty. *Citizens State Bank v. Transamerica Ins. Co.*, 452 F.2d 199, 203-04.

8th Cir. 1993 (S.D.). Jury instruction correctly included broad definition of "dishonest" and "fraudulent" that permitted jury to find dishonesty where employee acts in disregard of employer's interest, subjecting employer to a likelihood of loss. *First Dakota Nat'l Bank v. St. Paul Fire & Marine Ins. Co.*, 2 F.3d 801, 814.

8th Cir. 1975 (Mo.). Bank president's acts in creating a "check floating" operation involving his bank and two other banks were held to constitute dishonest and fraudulent conduct. Conduct does not have to involve a criminal offense to be dishonest. Conduct is dishonest and fraudulent if an employee creates a conflict of interest and acts in his own interest or in disregard of his employer's interest, subjecting the employer to the likelihood of a loss. *First Nat'l Bank of Sikestown v. Transamerica Ins. Co.*, 514 F.2d 981, 987.

8th Cir. 1971 (Mo.). Office manager of a small loan company falsified credit applications to improve the apparent financial condition of applicants and received a kickback for referring potential customers to other lenders. The receipt of kickbacks was dishonest within terms of bond, as such conduct was inimical to best interests of the employer. *Boston Sec., Inc. v. United Bonding Ins. Co.,* 441 F.2d 1302, 1303-04.

8th Cir. 1971 (S.D.). President of insured used insured's funds to make advances to another corporation of which he was also president in violation of the bylaws of the insured. The president's actions were dishonest as a matter of law. The words "fraudulent or dishonest" are to be given a broad meaning, and may be inferred from the facts, but must be proven by a preponderance of the evidence. It is not necessary that the employee benefit. *Gen. Fin. Corp. v. Fid. & Cas. Co. of N.Y.,* 439 F.2d 981, 985-86.

9th Cir. 1991 (Or.). Production credit association made loans to a cattle company whose president and principal stockholder was also a director of the production credit association. The director had falsified the loan documents by inflating the cattle inventory. The director disappeared and the loans were never repaid. The director's failure to disclose his fraud and dishonesty to the production credit association was conduct covered by the association's fidelity bond. *Interstate Prod. Credit Ass'n v. Fireman's Fund Ins. Co.,* 944 F.2d 536, 539-40.

9th Cir. 1981 (Cal.). When determining whether employees of a bank acted dishonestly in accepting deposits with the knowledge of the bank's insolvency, courts should not look to the definition of dishonesty set forth in the National Bank Act. *Fid. Sav. & Loan Ass'n v. Aetna Life & Cas. Co.,* 647 F.2d 933, 936-37.

9th Cir. 1979 (Cal.). An employee who knowingly pays more for an item than it is worth with the intention of enriching the person from whom the purchase is made is guilty of theft, and thus is dishonest. *Research Equity Fund, Inc. v. Ins. Co. of N. Am.,* 602 F.2d 200, 204.

9th Cir. 1963 (Wash.). The dictionary definitions of "dishonesty" and "fraud" have similar meanings. Implicit in each is the concept of bad faith or an intent to accomplish some wrongdoing. The court approved a jury instruction that emphasized the wrongful intent and affirmed a trial court judgment for the bonding company. *Sherwood & Roberts-Kennewick, Inc. v. St. Paul Fire & Marine Ins. Co.,* 322 F.2d 70, 73-76.

10th Cir. 1972 (N.M.). Employee authorized overdisbursement on interim construction loans resulting in loss to the insured and, on instruction from the president of the insured, lied to a member of the board of directors concerning the extent and condition of the insured's construction-financing program. The jury could have reasonably concluded that the employee and president did not act dishonestly, but had the best interests of the insured in mind. Even though there was ample evidence to conclude that they exercised poor judgment, made serious mistakes and were generally negligent in handling the affairs of the insured, the jury's verdict in favor of the insured was supported by substantial evidence. *N.M. Sav. & Loan Ass'n v. USF&G,* 454 F.2d 328, 330.

10th Cir. 1971 (Okla.). Four employees of the insured made disbursements to another company pursuant to a contract. Insured argued that interlocking directorates between the companies made the contract invalid, and that the disbursements were dishonest and fraudulent acts within the meaning of the bond. The court found that the contract was valid and made in good faith and that therefore, the employees' conduct was not dishonest. *W. Fid. Corp. v. Ins. Co. of N. Am.,* 437 F.2d 752, 752-53.

10th Cir. 1969 (Okla.). A fidelity bond indemnified against loss "through the fraudulent or dishonest misapplication, misappropriation or conversion committed by any one or more of the Employees...." Coverage under the quoted language was not limited to employee embezzlement for direct personal benefit but included loss that resulted from fictitious assignments and conversion of trust fund monies paid upon valid accounts. *Ins. Co. of N. Am. v. Greenberg,* 405 F.2d 330, 332.

D.C. Cir. 1988. The actions of a labor union's officers in planning and executing an air traffic controller strike did not constitute "fraudulent or dishonest acts" within the meaning of a fidelity bond. *Skirlick v. Fid. & Deposit Co.,* 852 F.2d 1376, 1378-80.

D.C. Cir. 1970. The court approved a jury instruction on the issue of dishonesty that stated "there must be found to exist a compelling sense of conscious wrong rather than a mere omission or act amounting to negligence or mere lack of judgment." *Imperial Ins., Inc. v. Emp'r's Liab. Assurance Corp.,* 442 F.2d 1197, 1202-03.

N.D. Cal. 1994. Court held that dishonest acts must be against insured employer in order to trigger coverage under "dishonesty" provision of general liability policy. There was no evidence that any employee committed dishonest acts against the employer. Dishonest acts against third-party claimant and assignee of employer did not trigger employer's dishonesty coverage. *Fireman's Fund Ins. Co. v. Nat'l Bank for Coops.,* 849 F. Supp. 1347, 1362.

D. Del. 1977. The court discussed the meaning of dishonest acts as used in the policy. After quoting Webster ("not honest, lying, cheating, etc.") and Black's Law Dictionary ("disposition to lie, cheat or defraud; untrustworthiness, lack of integrity;"), the court applied these definitions to the several fact situations involved in securities cases decided against the insured. *Stargatt v. Avenell,* 434 F. Supp. 234, 243-44.

D.D.C. 1962. Insured brought action on Brokers Blanket Bond. The court found that employee was himself duped by friends who used him in fraudulent scheme and, therefore, the employee's conduct was not dishonest or fraudulent. The court held that "there must exist a compelling sense of conscious wrong rather than a mere omission or act amounting to negligence." *Sade v. Nat'l Sur. Corp.,* 203 F. Supp. 680, 683-84.

S.D. Fla. 1970. Insured's vice president allowed a customer to exceed the authorized and statutory loan limits and allowed lessees of customer to be shown as a borrower. The officer's acts were dishonest and fraudulent. The court noted: (1) the terms "dishonest" and "fraudulent" are broader and more comprehensive than "criminal" and include acts which show a want of integrity or breach of trust; (2) acts or a course of conduct demonstrating an intentional breach of trust or a reckless disregard for the interests of employer are dishonest or fraudulent within bond; (3) knowingly making unauthorized loans is a breach of trust that constitutes fraud or dishonesty within bond. *Miami Nat'l Bank v. Penn. Ins. Co.,* 314 F. Supp. 858, 860-63.

N.D. Ill. 1988. Credit union sought reimbursement under a fidelity bond for losses resulting from investments made by credit union's treasurer. The terms "fraud" and "dishonesty" in a fidelity bond are given a broad meaning. Dishonesty includes a reckless, willful and wanton disregard for the interests of the employer. A fact question precluding summary judgment is raised if an act is manifestly unfair to the employer or subjects the employer to a likelihood of loss. *N. Side "L" Fed. Credit Union v. Cumis Ins. Soc'y, Inc.,* No. 87 C 7150, 1988 U.S. Dist. LEXIS 12010, at *4-7.

E.D. Ill. 1926. Cashier requested stockholders and directors to sign accommodation notes upon agreement that notes would be limited in amount and used only as collateral for bank's loans from correspondent banks. After bank closed and cashier disappeared, these notes were found in the records of the bank as part of its assets. The cashier was guilty of fraud and dishonesty. The word "dishonesty" was given a broad significance and taken most strongly against bonding company. *Aetna Cas. & Sur. Co. v. Commercial State Bank,* 13 F.2d 474, 477-78.

D. Kan. 1989. Under Kansas law, the words "dishonest" and "fraudulent" in a fidelity bond are to be given a broad meaning. Their connotation is broader than the word "criminal" and includes acts that show a want of integrity or breach of trust. Employee acted dishonestly by arranging to receive kickbacks from customers. *Koch Indus., Inc. v. Nat'l Union Fire Ins. Co. of Pittsburgh, Pa.*, No. 89-1158-K, 1989 U.S. Dist. LEXIS 15703, at *40-44.

W.D. La. 1993. Bank employee issued letter of credit to borrowers without authority and agreed to release collateral on a loan they already owed, knowing that they were in financial trouble. When the bank later refused to release the collateral, borrowers sued the bank. Bank sued bonding company for costs to defend borrowers' suit, claiming the suit was caused by employee's dishonest acts. Court disagreed, finding that any connection between borrowers' suit and employees' acts was too tenuous and that issuing letter of credit without authority may not be a dishonest act. *Farm Credit Bank of Tex. v. Fireman's Fund Ins. Co.*, 822 F. Supp. 1251, 1255-57.

D.N.J. 1977. Ship loans were made without the prior approval of the insured's board of directors or executive committee and in violation of lending limits and collateral requirements set by the board. The loans were regularly renewed without reduction and renewals were disguised as new loans in monthly reports to the board. The president of the insured and its attorney handled the loans and concealed from the board the true facts. The court held that the acts of the president and attorney were dishonest and fraudulent within the meaning of the bond. The court noted that: (1) fidelity bonds are to be broadly construed; (2) the clear intent of the bond is to protect the insured against wrongful acts of employees which, though not criminal, display significant lack of probity, integrity or trustworthiness; (3) coverage does not extend to acts which constitute mere negligence, mistake, error in judgment or incompetence. *Midland Bank & Trust Co. v. Fid. & Deposit Co. of Md.*, 442 F. Supp. 960, 971.

D.N.J. 1971. President of a bank made a loan allegedly in violation of the orders of the board of directors. The president's acts were not dishonest or fraudulent. No reason for the alleged violation of the board's orders was shown, the president had nothing to gain, and did nothing to conceal the transaction or alter the records and brought the loan up for board review in a routine way. *Essex County State Bank v. Fireman's Fund Ins. Co.*, 331 F. Supp. 931, 933-34.

D.N.M. 1979. President of a bank made loans in excess of the bank's legal lending limit to cover overdrafts, which were not reported to the bank's board of directors. The president acted with the intent to injure the bank, and his actions were dishonest and fraudulent as defined in the bonds. *Plaza Del Sol Nat'l Bank v. Firemen's Ins. Co.*, No. 78-073-B, 1979 U.S. Dist. LEXIS 12876, at *15-19.

W.D. Okla. 1973. Employee of insured made loans to another company and pledged insured's assets as collateral. The acts of the employee were unwise but not dishonest, where the loans were approved in advance or subsequently ratified by insured's board of trustees. The fact that the board of trustees may not have understood all that it approved at a time when it had all of the facts at its disposal did not make the acts dishonest. Dishonesty does not include good faith business judgment that results in financial disaster. *Alfalfa Elec. Coop., Inc. v. Travelers Indem. Co.,* 376 F. Supp. 901, 913.

D.P.R. 1991. The words "fraud or dishonesty" in a fidelity bond are given a broad meaning and are ordinarily held to extend beyond acts that are criminal. The words include any act showing a lack of integrity, breach of trust, or abstraction of funds together with deceit and concealment. Mere negligence, mistake, or error in judgment does not suffice, however, and an intent to deceive must be present in order for employee's actions to be dishonest. *FDIC v. CNA Cas. of P.R.,* 786 F. Supp. 1082, 1087-89.

D.P.R. 1972. Shortage in correspondent account was held to have been sustained through the dishonest and fraudulent conduct of employees, despite lack of sufficient evidence to convict the principal employee in a criminal proceeding and the lack of records due to their destruction. Evidence of fraud and dishonesty was found to be "clear and convincing no matter what standard of proof [was] applied." *Banco de San German, Inc. v. Md. Cas. Co.,* 344 F. Supp. 496, 508.

M.D. Tenn. 1990. Bank director authorized unsound loans to third parties to enable the third parties to purchase shares in his company. Director failed to adequately check the borrowers' financial statements, failed to reveal his conflict of interest to the board, and violated bank policy by failing to recuse himself from voting on the loans. After a review of many opinions, the court determined that the paradigmatic case of dishonesty exists where an employee has cheated and deceived his employer by furthering his own interests at the employer's expense and covered up his misdeeds. Such was the case here, and the director's conduct was held dishonest. *FDIC v. St. Paul Fire & Marine Ins. Co.,* 738 F. Supp. 1146, 1156-59, *aff'd in part, vacated in part by,* 942 F.2d 1032, 1035-37.

E.D. Va. 1969. The court noted that: (1) the terms "dishonest" and "fraudulent" as used in policy are broader than term "criminal" and include acts which show a want of integrity or breach of trust; (2) knowingly making unauthorized loans is such a breach of trust;

(3) intent to deceive is an essential element of fraud or dishonesty, but such intent may be inferred from officer's reckless disregard; and (4) knowingly making false reports to superiors constitutes evidence of intent to deceive. *Arlington Trust Co. v. Hawkeye Sec. Ins. Co.,* 301 F. Supp. 854, 857-59.

S.D. W. Va. 1973. Assistant cashier filed false reports concerning collateral in connection with floor-plan financing for a car dealer resulting in judgment against the insured in favor of a bank that purchased some of the loans. The conduct of the employee was dishonest and fraudulent as a matter of law. The evidence established that the employee made representations of fact purportedly based upon personal knowledge when he did not know if they were true or not. *First Nat'l Bank of West Hamlin v. Md. Cas. Co.,* 354 F. Supp. 189, 194.

Ariz. Ct. App. 1971. Though a criminal act is not required to prove dishonesty, there must be some conduct from which can be implied an intent to deceive, cheat or defraud. *Md. Cas. Co. v. Clements,* 487 P.2d 437, 441-42.

Cal. Ct. App. 1940. Bank president secretly borrowed money from insured knowing that he could not repay. The president's acts were dishonest. Fidelity insurance is intended to, and does, guarantee openness and fair dealing on the part of the bank's officials with the bank. *Pac. Indem. Co. v. Hargreaves,* 98 P.2d 217, 221.

Ill. App. Ct. 1998. An employee's act need not be technically criminal nor benefit him personally to qualify as dishonest. *Oxford Bank & Trust v. Hartford Accident & Indem. Co.,* 698 N.E.2d 204, 210.

Ill. App. Ct. 1979. Dishonesty includes an act that is manifestly unfair to the employer, palpably subjects it to a likelihood of loss, indicates a reckless, willful, and wanton disregard for the interest of the employer, and constitutes wrongful acts which, although not criminal, nevertheless display a significant lack of probity, integrity, or trustworthiness. *Reserve Ins. Co. v. Gen. Ins. Co.,* 395 N.E.2d 933, 936.

Ill. App. Ct. 1963. The solicited sale of unregistered securities was a criminal misdemeanor under Illinois law without regard to the person's intent. However, the jury could have found the requisite intent to make the act of the employees dishonest as well as criminal, pointing out that the question of dishonesty is one of fact for the jury. *Home Indem. Co. v. Reynolds & Co.,* 187 N.E.2d 274, 282.

Iowa 1979. Evidence that a bank officer transferred funds from one account to another without authorization, made false records and false reconciliation of accounts with other banks, credited checks to improper accounts, falsely reconstructed checking accounts, and held overdrafts as cash items supported a finding that the bank officer was guilty of fraudulent and dishonest acts. The terms were held to include acts that show a want of integrity or breach of trust and acts in disregard of employer's interest that are likely to subject the employer to loss. Knowingly making unauthorized loans in excess of authority was held to constitute dishonest and fraudulent conduct. *FDIC v. Nat'l Sur. Corp.,* 281 N.W.2d 816, 818-20.

Kan. 1989. Bank director secured several loans from the bank. The loans were allegedly secured by cattle that the bank later discovered did not exist. The director also deposited several insufficient funds checks with the bank. The words "dishonest" and "fraudulent" in a fidelity bond were given a broad meaning, and the director's actions manifestly represented a series of dishonest and fraudulent acts. *First Hays Banshares, Inc. v. Kan. Bankers. Sur. Co.,* 769 P.2d 1184, 1192.

Kan. Ct. App. 2005. An employee's surreptitious and unauthorized act of raising her personal credit limit constituted dishonest conduct. The court adopted a broad definition of dishonest and concluded that conduct may be dishonest even if the employee does not intend to harm the insured. The terms "dishonest" and "fraudulent" are not ambiguous and are therefore not subject to rules of construction. *Troy State Bank v. Bancinsure, Inc.,* No. 92,115, 2005 Kan. App. Unpub. LEXIS 120, at *8-11.

La. Ct. App. 1972. Employee owed customer $500 and made a loan to the same customer on behalf of insured. There was no evidence that the personal debt had any influence on employee in making loan. The employee was liable to insured for violating instructions, but the conduct was held not to be dishonest or fraudulent. *W.H. Hodges & Co. v. Hartford Accident & Indem. Co.,* 262 So. 2d 542, 543.

Md. 1975. Bank employee allegedly concealed and misrepresented the financial condition of a borrower. The employee was a "financial consultant" to the borrower and attended meetings of its board. The court noted that fraud and dishonesty, as used in the policy, included any act showing a want of integrity or breach of trust but not acts done in actual good faith, without intentional fault, or technically fraudulent acts innocently done, even though they constitute a breach of obligation by the person whose fidelity is insured. An insurer is not liable for loss occasioned by mere negligence, carelessness, inattention to business, mistake, errors in judgment, incompetency, or other acts or omissions not denoting conscious wrongdoing or involving moral turpitude. *First Nat'l Bank of S. Md. v. USF&G,* 340 A.2d 275, 280-284.

Mich. Ct. App. 2011. Court refused to carefully construe the phrase "dishonest or fraudulent" but noted that "whatever else it may mean, any reasonable reading" of that phrase includes acts that result in the employee pleading guilty to a felony offense involving elements of fraud or dishonesty. The employee's conviction of forgery and uttering and publishing a false, forged, or altered document was enough to prove dishonesty, despite that this criminal record was later expunged. *Alcona County v. Mich. Mun. League Liab. & Prop.*, No. 292155, 2011 Mich. App. LEXIS 473, at *20-22.

Minn. 1957. Coverage for acts of fraud and dishonesty extends beyond acts that are criminal. Dishonesty can be established by circumstantial evidence. *Prior Lake State Bank v. Nat'l Sur. Corp.,* 80 N.W.2d 612, 619-20.

Minn. 1953. Employee involved was the manager of liquor store. It was discovered that cash and liquor were missing from the store. This evidence provided only a conjectural basis for an inference that any dishonest act was attributable to the accused employee. Evidence of dishonesty was insufficient to submit to jury and the court directed verdict for bonding company, which was affirmed. The court noted that dishonesty is not established by proof of employee's mistakes or negligence. *Village of Plummer v. Anchor Cas. Co.,* 61 N.W.2d 225, 226.

Neb. 1981. Insuring Agreement (A) in the Bankers Blanket Bond issued to a group of banks does not insure the banks against the consequences of their own torts. *Omaha Bank for Coops. v. Aetna Cas. & Sur. Co.*, 301 N.W.2d 564, 569.

N.J. 1978. A branch manager knowingly misrepresented the value of an insured's collateral on a large loan. This conduct was dishonest and fraudulent. The subjective intent of the employee may have been blameless but the nature of his acts indicated that he put the interests of the customer above those of the insured. *Nat'l Newark & Essex Bank v. Am. Ins. Co.*, 385 A.2d 1216, 1222-23.

N.Y. App. Div. 2012. The phrase "dishonest or fraudulent acts" must be given its ordinary meaning and broadly include acts that demonstrate a want of integrity or a breach of trust or moral turpitude affecting the official fidelity or character of the employee. It was dishonest for an employee to sign the name of another without consent in order to approve transactions that the employee forging the signatures lacked authority to approve. *Capital Bank & Trust Co. v. Gulf Ins. Co.*, 91 A.D.3d 1251, 1253.

Tex. 1964. To constitute fraudulent and dishonest conduct, the employee must have some degree of intent to perform the wrongful act. There must be the physical act, plus the mental state, though the intent need not be of the degree required for criminal conduct. Mere negligence, carelessness, or incompetence is insufficient. If the employee has knowledge of and aids in concealing another person's wrongful conduct, the employee is guilty of the same wrongful conduct. *Great Am. Ins. Co. v. Langdeau*, 379 S.W.2d 62, 65.

Tex. Civ. App. 1977. Employee's use of union funds for personal expenses was a "misappropriation" as a matter of law despite the intent of the employee to repay. The wrongful intent was established by the employee's intent to use the funds personally. *Downer v. Amalgamated Meatcutters and Butcher Workmen of N. Am.*, 550 S.W.2d 744, 746.

Tex. Civ. App. 1976. Insurance agent failed to remit the rightful share of premium payments that came into his hands, and made unauthorized personal expenditures out of a bank account into which premiums were deposited. The agent's conduct was dishonest and fraudulent within the meaning of the bond because it involved his intent to perform the wrongful act. *Lawyers Sur. Corp. v. Am. Pub. Life Ins. Co.,* 540 S.W.2d 842, 845.

Wash. 1993. Escrow company obtained a fidelity bond as required by Washington's Escrow Agent Registration Act. The vice president of the escrow company diverted funds from escrow trust accounts to the company's operating account in order to cover general operating expenses. To avoid detection, he occasionally shifted money back from the general operating account to the trust account, and he filed false operating reports. The resulting losses were covered by the company's fidelity bond. A fraudulent or dishonest act was held to be any act showing a want of integrity, breach of trust, or abstraction of funds together with deceit and concealment. *Estate of K.O. Jordan v. Hartford Accident & Indem. Co.,* 844 P.2d 403, 410-12.

Wash. 1935. Bank president made loans in violation of a statute requiring approval of the board of directors. The president's acts were dishonest and fraudulent within the meaning of the bond. The court noted that: (1) dishonesty is to be given a broad and comprehensive meaning; and (2) the question of dishonesty is a question of fact. The court also found that violation of state banking law is also the "violation of a public, as well as a private, trust" and therefore is not innocent of a dishonest motive or intent. *Hansen v. Am. Bonding Co.,* 48 P.2d 653, 656.

B. Manifest Intent

1st Cir. 2003 (Mass.). Court affirmed summary judgment for the insurer on the ground that the employee lacked the manifest intent to cause the insured a loss. He intended to cheat donors but not the charity. This case thoroughly discusses the point that there can be no coverage when the employee intended to benefit himself but not to cause the insured a loss. *Fireman's Fund Ins. Co. v. Special Olympics Int'l, Inc.,* 346 F.3d 259, 262-63.

2d Cir. 2000 (N.Y.). The Second Circuit held that the trustee's failure to inform the bank of the fraud and theft established manifest intent as a matter of law. Reviewing the various approaches employed by different courts, the Second Circuit concluded that the test was essentially a subjective inquiry into the employee's state of mind with a necessary objective requirement in that the employee's actions can circumstantially establish that the employee acted with the manifest intent to cause the insured a loss. To establish manifest intent, the insured must show that the employee acted with the specific purpose to harm the insured. Reckless behavior alone does not suffice, and actions that will possibly benefit the employer do not establish manifest intent as a matter of law. Reckless disregard for a substantial risk of loss to the insured or proof of the employee's knowledge that a result was substantially certain to occur are sufficient. *FDIC v. Nat'l Union Fire Ins. Co. of Pittsburgh, Pa.*, 205 F.3d 66, 72-76.

2d Cir. 1989 (N.Y.). Trial court erroneously refused to give an instruction on "manifest intent." A new trial was not necessary, however, because the evidence was insufficient to establish either element of the manifest intent requirement. First, investment firm owner's conduct in making risky investments was reckless and imprudent, but there was no evidence that he intended to cause a loss. Second, there was no evidence that he intended to obtain a financial benefit or that he misappropriated funds. *Glusband v. Fittin Cunningham & Lauzon, Inc.*, 892 F.2d 208, 210-11.

3d Cir. 2004 (Pa.). Insured bank loaned customers money to pay insurance premiums for auto policies. Part of the bank's collateral was the right to cancel the policy and receive the return premium. It was therefore critical that the bank identify a default and cancel the defaulted policy promptly. A third-party operator had responsibility for identifying defaults but failed to do so. The insured bank sought coverage for the nonpayment of loans, but coverage was denied because the operator lacked intent to confer a financial benefit on itself. The operator received only normal payments such as bonuses and commissions in exchange for its performance—no additional funds for failing to catch defaults as it had promised. *Hudson United Bank v. Progressive Cas. Ins. Co.*, 112 F. App'x 170, 173-75.

3d Cir. 2003 (N.J.). Loan officer who advised bank to make an uncreditworthy loan did not act with the manifest intent to obtain a financial benefit for himself or for a third party. Court applied a specific intent standard. *FDIC v. Nat'l Union Fire Ins. Co. of Pittsburgh, Pa.*, 57 Fed. Appx. 965, 967.

3d Cir. 2000 (N.J.). The case includes a brief discussion of the history of the "manifest intent" requirement of Insuring Agreement (A), and contrasts the two different approaches—general intent versus specific intent—adopted by various jurisdictions. The Third Circuit predicted that the Supreme Court of New Jersey would conclude that the "specific intent" standard more closely comports with the bond drafters' intent. According to the Third Circuit, manifest intent is characterized by the mental state "purposefully" and is analogous to the Model Penal Code's definition of "specific intent." An employee's manifest intent could be established by proof that the employee acted recklessly, knowing that it was substantially certain that his or her conduct would cause the insured to sustain a loss that would inure to the employee's benefit. *RTC v. Fid. & Deposit Co. of Md.*, 205 F.3d 615, 636-646.

4th Cir. 1996 (Va.). Insured's employee altered customer purchase orders resulting in the shipment of useless products to customer. Insured sustained losses when customer refused to accept delivery. To satisfy manifest intent requirement, insured must demonstrate that employee had specific intent to accomplish a particular purpose, analogous to intent required by criminal law. Summary judgment was inappropriate because fact issues remained as to whether employee possessed manifest intent to benefit employee or a third person. *Gen. Analytics Corp. v. CNA Ins. Cos.*, 86 F.3d 51, 53-54.

4th Cir. 1993 (N.C.). President of securities firm pleaded guilty to fraud and to embezzling from firm's clients. The president's guilty plea and other statements established his manifest intent to defraud, which satisfied the bond's requirement of manifest intent to cause the insured a loss. *In re Waddell Jenmar Sec., Inc.*, 991 F.2d 792, No. 92-2158, 1993 WL 128018, at *3 (unpublished table opinion).

4th Cir. 1934 (N.C.). The making of an unauthorized loan, approved by directors, was not a dishonest act. Directors repeatedly approved renewals of loan and, though it involved a technical violation of the banking laws, the employee involved did not intend to injure the bank.

Fid. & Deposit Co. of Md. v. People's Bank of Sanford, 72 F.2d 932, 937.

5th Cir. 1996 (Ky.). Insurers defeated bank's bad faith claim that was based upon insurer's denial of coverage under Bankers Blanket Bond for dishonest acts committed by a loan officer. Coverage was "fairly debatable" because the definition of "manifest intent" had not yet been determined under Kentucky law. Though the majority of courts have adopted a subjective test, Kentucky law was unclear on whether manifest intent was based on the subjective intent of the loan officer or the objective result of his conduct. Furthermore, the insurers reasonably contested coverage based on factual questions regarding loan officer's intent. *First Nat'l Bank of Louisville v. Lustig (Lustig II)*, 96 F.3d 1554, 1564-67.

5th Cir. 1992 (La.). This case presents a thorough discussion of the manifest intent issue and implicitly recognizes the specific intent standard. According to the Fifth Circuit, there is a continuum of dishonest acts: at one end are acts of embezzlement that benefit the employee at the expense of the employer; and at the other end are acts that benefit both the employer and the employee. The court also held that when determining the employee's purpose, all surrounding circumstances must be considered, including the employee's conduct, not just the employee's explanation. Though the court held that manifest intent could be inferred from reckless conduct, the standard is nevertheless a subjective standard that seeks to determine the employee's intent. *First Nat'l Bank of Louisville v. Lustig (Lustig I)*, 961 F.2d 1162, 1165-67.

6th Cir. 2012 (Ohio). Bank employee transferred funds from client's brokerage accounts into his own account. Employee had manifest intent to cause the bank a loss because it was "absolutely certain" that a loss would result from his theft. The court noted: "An insured meets the requirement [of proving manifest intent] where 'a particular result is substantially certain to follow from conduct.'" The court also noted that the employee's actions could not have benefited the bank—bank-embezzlement is a zero-sum game; the employer must lose for the employee to win. *First Defiance Fin. Corp. v. Progressive Cas. Ins. Co.*, 688 F.3d 265, 271-72.

6th Cir. 1998 (Ky.). Bond did not cover certain fraudulent acts of the insured's employees. However, the court of appeals disavowed any language in the district court's opinion that could be construed as meaning that "manifest intent" requires an employee to actually receive a personal monetary benefit. The law of the circuit requires only that the employee intended to receive such a benefit. *Ins. Co. of N. America v. Liberty United Bancorp., Inc.*, 142 F.3d 434, No. 96-6502, 1998 U.S. App. LEXIS 3781, at *2-3 (unpublished table opinion).

6th Cir. 1997 (Ky.). Bank employees defrauded bank customers by inducing customers to take out a loan to purchase a fake business. Bond did not cover damages resulting from lawsuit filed against bank by customers who had been defrauded by bank employees. Bond covers loss suffered by a third party only if dishonest employees know or expect loss will migrate to bank. Too many contingencies intervened between fraud and eventual loss to bank to conclude dishonest employees had the manifest intent to cause the bank's loss. *Peoples Bank & Trust Co. of Madison Cnty. v. Aetna Cas. & Sur. Co.*, 113 F.3d 629, 634-635.

6th Cir. 1991 (Tenn.). The court rejected a purely objective standard for manifest intent, noting that the principle that a person is presumed to intend the natural and probable consequences of his actions had been undermined in recent years. Manifest intent does not necessarily require that the employee actively wish for or desire a particular result, but exists when a particular result is substantially certain to follow. *FDIC v. St. Paul Fire & Marine Ins. Co.*, 942 F.2d 1032, 1035-37.

6th Cir. 1987 (Tenn.). Broker dealer's trader violated company policy by making trades in excess of her inventory limit. No coverage for the resulting losses under the broker dealer's fidelity bond because the trader lacked the manifest intent to cause her employer a loss. Instead, her evident motive initially was to make money for her employer and then to cover up and recoup any losses. *Mun. Sec., Inc. v. Ins. Co. of N. America*, 829 F.2d 7, 9-10.

7th Cir. 1992 (Ill.). Failure to instruct the jury on the definition of "manifest intent" was reversible error because the term has a technical legal meaning. Court followed cases holding that manifest intent exists when a particular result is substantially certain to follow and that manifest intent does not require that the employee actively wish for or desire a particular result. The court held that the jury should not inquire solely into the subjective motive or purpose of the employee and that manifest intent could be inferred from reckless conduct. *Heller Int'l Corp. v. Sharp*, 974 F.2d 850, 856-59.

7th Cir. 1983 (Ill.). Although the facts of an employee's conduct were undisputed, the characterization of that conduct was a separate question of fact. Because the employee's conduct could reasonably show dishonesty, on the one hand, or error of judgment, incompetence, or negligence on the other hand, summary judgment was reversed. *Rock Island Bank v. Aetna Cas. & Sur. Co.*, 706 F.2d 219, 223-24.

8th Cir. 2001 (N.D.). Bank employee made loans to her husband and her husband's company based on false documents. Noting that North Dakota courts had not ruled upon the definition of "manifest intent," the court adopted the dictionary definition to conclude that "manifest intent" means "clearly evident intent," and held that it is reasonable to infer that a person intends the natural and probable consequences of his acts. Manifest intent to cause a loss was present where the employee represented to the bank that she would hold her husband's company's funds in the bank to pay off a line of credit but did not do so. *BancInsure, Inc. v. BNC Nat'l Bank, N.A.*, 263 F.3d 766, 771.

8th Cir. 1993 (S.D.). Jury instruction on manifest intent, which stated that a "person is deemed to intend the natural consequences of his actions," was not erroneous because any potential adverse effect of this language was cured by qualifying language stating that the jury could choose whether or not to infer manifest intent from employee's conduct. *First Dakota Nat'l Bank v. St. Paul Fire & Marine Ins. Co.*, 2 F.3d 801, 813-14.

8th Cir. 1989 (Minn.). Banker's special bond contained duty to defend clause. The court held there was no duty to defend and no coverage for customer's claim that bank president forged customer's signature on a mortgage deed and note. The bond's manifest intent provision required that the employee have the intent to both benefit himself and cause the bank a loss. Bank president's alleged forgery could only have been done with the intent to benefit the bank, and thus there was no coverage. *Red Lake Cnty. State Bank v. Emp'rs Ins. of Wausau*, 874 F.2d 546, 549.

9th Cir. 1991 (Cal.). Employees of insured government contractor falsified test results on products supplied by the contractor. Fines and penalties incurred by the contractor were not covered by employee dishonesty policy. The employees lacked manifest intent to cause the employer a loss but apparently intended to benefit their employer by falsifying the test results. *Genisco Tech. Corp. v. Seaboard Sur. Co.*, No. 90-55480, 1991 WL 78151, at *2-4.

10th Cir. 1994 (Utah). Court reviewed cases from other jurisdictions to determine that manifest intent exists when a particular result is substantially certain to follow from an employee's conduct, and that manifest intent may be inferred from recklessness and other circumstantial evidence. *FDIC v. Oldenburg*, 34 F.3d 1529, 1539-42.

10th Cir. 1994 (Utah). The Tenth Circuit rejected insurer's argument that jury should have been instructed that "manifest intent" requires that the employee actively wish for or desire a particular result. Jury was properly instructed that "manifest intent" exists when a particular result is substantially certain to follow from the employee's conduct and that manifest intent may be inferred from an employee's reckless conduct. *FDIC v. United Pac. Ins. Co.*, 20 F.3d 1070, 1076-79.

10th Cir. 1991 (Utah). Loan officer made loans without approval of loan committee. Losses resulted and the insured savings and loan association sued to recover under fidelity bond. Affirmed summary judgment for insurer, holding that the possibility that the loan officer used poor judgment in making loans did not establish manifest intent to cause a loss. *First Fed. Sav. & Loan Ass'n of Salt Lake City v. Transamerica Ins. Co.*, 935 F.2d 1164, 1166-67.

N.D. Ill. 2000. Insured's salesman allegedly bribed a customer's purchasing agent to purchase parts at inflated prices. The customer successfully sued the insured for disgorgement of profits. The loss was not covered by the insured's Crimeguard policy, which covered losses resulting from "dishonesty." The court found that the salesman lacked manifest intent to cause his employer to lose the profits obtained through his scheme. Such intent would require the absurd assumption that the salesman intended for his conduct to be discovered. *Williams Elecs. Games, Inc. v. Barry*, No. 97 C 3743, 2000 WL 106672, at *6.

N.D. Ill. 1992. The district court rejected a specific intent standard and held that to establish manifest intent the bank need only show that the loan officer acted with the same degree of intent as required by the law of intentional torts. According to the district court, the purpose of the Bankers Blanket Bond is to insure the bank from losses stemming from intentional torts committed by bank employees. *Affiliated Bank/Morton Grove v. Hartford Accident & Indem. Co.*, No. 9 C 4446, 1992 WL 91761, at *8-14.

S.D. Iowa 2005. Former bank employee made loans that were not repaid. An Iowa statute controlled, but manifest intent (which could be found according to court if the loss is substantially certain to result from the employee's conduct) was consistent with the statute's requirement of coverage for fraud and dishonesty. The court did not rule on whether the employee had manifest intent to cause a loss, stating: "Where an individual's conduct falls somewhere between the two extremes of embezzlement and simple poor judgment, intent becomes a question of fact." *Kan. Bankers Sur. Co. v. Farmers State Bank*, 408 F. Supp. 2d 751, 756-57.

D. Mass. 2010. Employee deposited the paycheck of the bank's CEO into his own account, instead of his own pay. He then complained that he was not receiving his own pay (without mentioning that he was receiving the CEO's pay). The employee received his own pay and the CEO's. The court granted summary judgment for the insured which necessarily required a conclusion that the employee had the manifest intent to cause the bank a loss. *FundQuest Inc. v. Travelers Cas. & Sur. Co.*, 715 F. Supp. 2d 202, 212.

D. Minn. 2001. The district court held that an employee manifestly intends to cause loss when such loss is a natural consequence of the employee's actions. Under this standard, the bank failed to show that employee's actions at issue in the litigation were part of the embezzlement scheme. *First Nat'l Bank of Fulda, Minn. v. BancInsure, Inc.*, No. Civ. 00-2002 DDA/FLN, 2001 WL 1663872, at *4-8.

D.N.J. 2012. Court granted summary judgment for insured, finding that the employee had the manifest intent to cause loss where employee stole funds from client accounts and diverted clients' funds to his personal use. *Sperry Assocs. Fed. Credit Union v. Cumis Ins. Soc'y, Inc.*, No. 10-00029 (DRD), 2012 U.S. Dist. LEXIS 26839, at *31-33.

D.N.J. 2001. Loan officer concealed from the bank his knowledge that loans made to a large construction project were uncollectible and that construction project was in danger of being unprofitable. The court applied a subjective standard to determine that the losses were not covered by the bank's Financial Institution Bond. The court held that even if the loan officer was substantially certain that the bank would suffer a loss, there was no evidence that his specific purpose was to cause the loss. *FDIC v. Nat'l Union Fire Ins. Co. of Pittsburgh, Pa.*, 146 F. Supp. 2d 541, 549-53.

D.N.J. 1991. Predicting how the Supreme Court of New Jersey would rule, the court rejected the insured's argument that bond covered actions that were reckless or wanton but taken without the subjective intent to cause a loss. The term "manifest intent" unambiguously required employee to act with "some degree of dishonest intent" to obtain a benefit and to cause a loss to the insured. *Oritani Sav. & Loan Ass'n v. Fid. & Deposit Co. of Md.*, 821 F. Supp. 286, 290-91.

D.N.J. 1983. Under Insuring Agreement (A), the question of intent to cause the insured a loss is one of fact, precluding summary judgment. *Liberty Nat'l Bank v. Aetna Life & Cas. Co.*, 568 F. Supp. 860, 868.

S.D.N.Y. 2009. Court adhered to the "substantial certainty" test and found that actions can circumstantially establish that an employee acted with the manifest intent to cause the insured a loss. *U.S. Alliance Fed. Credit Union v. Cumis Ins. Soc'y, Inc.*, No. 03 Civ. 10317 (PGG), 2009 U.S. Dist. LEXIS 83047, at *23-36.

Bankr. S.D.N.Y. 1992. Stockbroker employee violated securities firm's policy by trading from his own account without sufficient liquid assets to cover potential losses. Resulting losses were not covered by the firm's security dealer blanket bond. The court held that fidelity bonds cover losses due to embezzlement or embezzlement-like acts, not losses resulting from reckless or improvident trading. Though the employee intended to make money, he lacked the manifest intent to cause his employer a loss. *In re J.T. Moran Fin. Corp.*, 147 B.R. 335, 339-40.

N.D. Ohio 2010. Bank employee transferred funds from clients' brokerage accounts into his own account. The court used a "substantially certain to result" test for manifest intent and concluded that the route from the employee's thefts to the bank's loss was short, certain, and obvious, and thus the court granted summary judgment to the bank. *First Defiance Fin. Corp. v. Progressive Cas. Ins. Co.*, 688 F. Supp. 2d 703, 708-09.

S.D. Ohio 1998. Bank's CEO made a loan in excess of his lending authority. Evidence that the CEO was angry at the chairman of the board for failure to pay bonuses and that the CEO had made the unauthorized loan to "get back at the bank" was sufficient to raise a genuine issue of material fact that the CEO intended to harm the bank. *First Bank of Marietta v. Hartford Underwriters Mut. Ins. Co.*, 997 F. Supp. 934, 937, *aff'd on different grounds*, No. 98-4284, 1999 WL 1021852 (Mar. 6, 1998).

Bankr. N.D. Ohio 1988. Court applied an objective standard to find that an employee of a brokerage firm who falsely represented to customers his authority to sell shares at discounted prices had the manifest intent to cause his employer a loss. An employee has the manifest intent to cause a loss when he knows to a substantial certainty that his employer will sustain a loss, and an individual is presumed to intend the natural consequences of his acts. Thus, there was coverage under a fidelity bond because it strained credulity to believe that the employee did not know his employer would be responsible to compensate investors whose funds had been converted. *In re Baker & Getty Fin. Servs., Inc. v. Nat'l Union Fire Ins. Co. of Pittsburgh, Pa.*, 93 B.R. 559, 565-66.

W.D. Pa. 2001. The district court adopted the analysis of the Third Circuit because the Pennsylvania Supreme Court had not ruled on the meaning of "manifest intent." According to the Third Circuit, "manifest intent" means the employee acted with the specific purpose, object or desire to cause the loss to the insured. Manifest intent may be proven by circumstantial evidence indicating that the employee acted with reckless disregard for a substantial risk of loss, but mere recklessness or knowledge that a result was substantially certain to occur would not satisfy the policy language. The district court found that, although the former administrator may have intended to cause a loss to the estate, there was no evidence that former administrator intended to cause a loss to his employer. *Shoemaker v. Lumbermens Mut. Cas. Co.*, 176 F. Supp. 2d 449, 453-57.

E.D. Pa. 1995. The court predicted that the Pennsylvania Supreme Court would reject a purely objective test of manifest intent and hold that manifest intent under employee dishonesty coverage is determined by the external indicia of the employee's subjective intent. Deviating from a Pennsylvania Superior Court case, however, the court also predicted that the Pennsylvania Supreme Court would find that manifest intent could be established if the employee either desires the loss to result from her actions or knows that the loss is substantially certain to result. *Good Lad Co. v. Aetna Cas. & Sur. Co.*, No. 92-5678, 1995 WL 393964, at *11-26.

E.D. Pa. 1992. Court applied an objective standard to determine that losses caused by a salesman's violation of his employer's policy restricting credit sales were covered by a fidelity bond. The court held that manifest intent requires more than a mere probability of loss but does not require that an employee wish for or desire the result. *Keystone Floor Prods., Inc. v. Home Ins. Co.*, No. 92-1988, 1992 WL 94918, at *11-13.

Bankr. E.D. Pa. 1992. Former employee's guilty plea to mail fraud was sufficient to establish coverage under a fidelity bond. Though it did not appear that specific intent to defraud was sufficient to establish coverage, it nevertheless appeared that employee engaged in embezzlement or embezzlement-like acts. The employee removed and utilized employer's funds in a manner that permitted the inference that he intended to benefit himself at his employer's expense. Employee's behavior demonstrated the requisite manifest intent to trigger coverage. *In re Lloyd Sec., Inc.*, No. 91-1090S, 1992 WL 236162, at *23-29.

D.P.R. 2008. Where an employee knows that his actions will naturally or probably cause consequences, he is deemed to have acted with intent to cause those consequences. *Oriental Fin. Group, Inc. v. Fed. Ins. Co.*, 598 F. Supp. 2d 199, 214-15.

D.P.R. 2004. A group of employees manipulated the reconciliations of cash accounts and concealed the true cash account balances, causing a loss to the bank. The court refused to grant summary judgment to the insurer, holding that the three crucial questions (whether a "loss" resulted; whether the employees had engaged in dishonest or fraudulent acts; and whether the acts were committed intentionally to obtain a benefit or to cause the financial group a loss) were properly left for trial as they were imbued with questions of intent. *Oriental Fin. Grp. v. Fed. Ins. Co.*, 309 F. Supp. 2d 216, 227-28.

N.D. Tex. 2004. Employees of the insured securities broker executed risky trades in their own accounts in violation of the insured's rules. The trades were unsuccessful, and the employees were unable to cover the negative position in the accounts. The court granted summary judgment to the insurer because the employees entered into the trades with the intent to make money and not to cause a loss. There was no manifest intent to cause the insured a loss. *Investors Trading Corp. v. Fid. and Deposit Co. of Md.*, No. 3:02-CV-2176-P 2004 U.S. Dist. LEXIS 25906, 2004 WL 3045196, at *3-6.

N.D. Tex. 1996. Manifest intent does not require that the employee actively wish for or desire a particular result; manifest intent exists when a particular result is substantially certain to follow from the employee's conduct. Employee's intent should be determined from her subjective motive and purpose and inferences from tangible manifestations of behavior. Under this standard, there was no coverage under the insured's crime policy because the funds embezzled by the employee did not belong to the insured. Thus, the employee did not intend to cause her employer a loss as a matter of law. *Lynch Props., Inc. v. Potomac Ins. Co. of Ill.*, 962 F. Supp. 956, 962.

S.D. Tex. 1993. Bank president employed poor banking practices, failed to follow internal procedures, and misrepresented the condition of borrowers and the value of their collateral. The loss was not covered under a standard bankers bond because there was no evidence that the bank president intended to cause a loss, and no evidence that the loss was the result of anything other than incompetence and bad judgment. *Progressive Cas. Ins. Co. v. First Bank*, 828 F. Supp. 473, 474-45.

W.D. Va. 1989. Bank's CEO made loans in excess of his lending authority and deposited participation funds into borrower's account rather than using the funds to reduce the bank's liability. The court applied an objective standard to determine that the CEO had the manifest intent to cause the bank a loss, and that the loss was covered. Referring to the criminal law, the court noted that it can be inferred that a person intends the natural and probable consequences of his acts. *USF&G v. Citizens Bank of Tazewell*, 718 F. Supp. 471, 474.

W.D. Wash. 2012. Manifest intent language could not be enforced because it went beyond state statute requiring that escrow agency bond cover "any fraudulent or dishonest acts resulting in a loss." *Ritchie v. Capitol Indem. Corp.*, No. C11-1903RAJ, 2012 U.S. Dist. LEXIS 106804, at *10-12.

Ala. 1986. A directed verdict on the bond claims should not have been entered because there was conflicting evidence regarding the president's "manifest intent" to cause the bank a loss. *Ins. Co. of N. Am. v. Citizensbank of Thomasville,* 491 So. 2d 880, 884.

Conn. Super. Ct. 1997. Insurance agency's employee retained premium payments due to customers of the insurance company. The insurance company reimbursed its customers and sought reimbursement from the agency. Agency's employee dishonesty policy did not apply because acts were not intended to cause the agency a loss—instead, the acts caused direct loss to the insurance company, and only indirect loss to the agency. *ITT Hartford Life Ins. Co. v. Pawson Assocs., Inc.*, No. 940361910S, 1997 WL 345345, at *4-6.

Ill. App. Ct. 1998. Bank employee embezzled funds from the bank and failed to report suspicious activity that indicated a check kiting scheme, even though employee had been charged with the responsibility of monitoring accounts for check kiting. The court held the that employee had the manifest intent to harm the bank because he desired the consequences of his action or believed that the consequences were substantially certain to result. *Oxford Bank & Trust v. Hartford Accident & Indem. Co.*, 698 N.E.2d 204, 210.

Ill. App. Ct. 1998. Insurers moved to stay lawsuit filed by insured pending resolution of insurers' prior-filed action in England, which was subject to English law. A stay of the coverage proceedings was appropriate, in part, because a potential key issue—the meaning of "manifest intent"—was an issue of first impression in England and an issue of intense debate among American courts. Thus, it would be difficult for an Illinois court to predict how an English court would decide the matter. *Philips Elecs., N.V. v. N.H. Ins. Co.*, 692 N.E.2d 1268, 1278.

Ill. App. Ct. 1983. Summary judgment was granted to the insurer under Brokers Blanket Bond with 1976 rider adding manifest intent requirement because no manifest intent to cause the insured a loss was shown and because the employee received no financial benefit from the unauthorized trading, except commissions. *Mortell v. Ins. Co. of N. Am.*, 458 N.E.2d 922, 929.

Ind. Ct. App. 1937. Act of bank cashier in paying checks of bank's president who had insufficient funds to cover checks was held not to constitute dishonesty under cashier's fidelity bond in absence of showing of some intent or purpose of cashier. Term "dishonesty" was held to include an element of deceit or bad faith on the part of the person charged and not to include error of judgment or injudicious exercise of discretion. *State v. Jay,* 10 N.E.2d 737, 741.

Mich. Ct. App. 2006. The court held that an insured was not entitled to recover under a policy that covered the loss of Business Personal Property resulting from dishonest acts committed by an employee with the manifest intent to cause a loss. The court found that the insured failed to meet its burden of proving that a claim fell within the terms of the policy because it did not show that the dishonest acts at issue were manifestly intended to cause a loss. *Five Star Real Estate, LLC v. Kemper Cas. Ins. Co.*, No. 258602, 2006 WL 1294238, at *7.

Minn. Ct. App. 1995. Bank's employee coerced a customer into signing a promissory note and giving the loan proceeds to the employee. Both the employee and customer declared bankruptcy, and that the bank did not receive payments on the debt. These facts supported the conclusion that the employee had the intent to cause the bank a loss. The evidence in the record also supported the conclusion that the employee acted with the intent to benefit himself. *Citizens State Bank of Big Lake v. Capitol Indem. Corp.*, No. C1-95-321, 1995 WL 421672, *at 2-3.

Minn. Ct. App. 1991. Bank's president, who was also the majority shareholder, disregarded regulators' instructions to write off problem loans and instead cashed certificates of deposits and used the proceeds to pay off the loans. President also took the bank's money for his own personal use and falsified the bank's records. The resulting losses were covered by the bank's fidelity bond because the bank president's conduct demonstrated an intolerable disregard for established banking rules, regulations, and laws, and because a person is deemed to intend the natural consequences of his actions. The natural consequences of the president's fraud was a loss to the bank, thus, there could be no dispute that the loss was covered by the bond. *Transamerica Ins. Co. v. FDIC*, 465 N.W.2d 713, 716, *rev'd in part on other grounds*, 489 N.W.2d 224.

Minn. Ct. App. 1985. Employer sued under a Commercial Blanket Bond containing a clause similar to Insuring Agreement (A) to recover losses incurred when a sales manager submitted false orders, ordered unnecessary merchandise, and misused the company credit card. There was no evidence of manifest intent to harm the employer or to obtain financial benefit for the employee other than benefits earned in the normal course of employment. *Benchmark Crafters, Inc. v. NW. Nat'l Ins. Co.*, 363 N.W.2d 89, 91.

N.J. Super. Ct. App. Div. 2003. Salesperson for insured car dealership engaged in credit scheme that fraudulently induced a third-party lender to finance car purchases to high risk customers. Lender brought suit against employer when customers defaulted on their loans. The court held that car dealership's policy provided no coverage because salesperson did not intend to harm his employer. Instead, car dealership became the unintended beneficiary of the fraud because it received the proceeds of the illicit sales. *Auto Lenders Acceptance Corp. v. Gentilini Ford, Inc.*, 816 A.2d 1068, 1071-73.

N.J. Super. Ct. Law Div. 1993. Senior loan officer of a savings and loan took certain actions without board approval, causing his employer to acquire unenforceable mortgage loans. The resulting losses were not covered because the employee's conduct was consistent with an intent to benefit his employer, not to cause it a loss. The court rejected the insured's argument that intent to cause a loss could be inferred from recklessness or from the loss itself. *N.J. Sav. & Loan Ass'n v. Fid. & Deposit Co. of Md.*, 660 A.2d 1287, 1293.

N.Y. Sup. Ct. 2006. The insured broker dealer's client was running a Ponzi scheme. The insured's employees helped the client cover up the truth by falsifying documents. The insured itself pleaded guilty to securities fraud. The court agreed with the insurer that the bond did not cover the loss. The dishonest employees were stealing for, rather than from, the insured. *HSBC USA Inc. v. Gulf Ins. Co.*, Index No. 603413/04 (no published opinion).

N.Y. App. Div. 1998. Insured broker dealer sought coverage for payments made to settle class actions filed by shareholders of public companies that were the subject of various insider trading schemes perpetrated by insured's employee. Coverage is trigged by acts of embezzlement, at one end of a continuum of dishonest employee conduct, but not triggered by dishonest acts that, though they result in loss, were intended to benefit the employer. There was no coverage in this case because there was no evidence that the employee had the manifest intent to cause his employer a loss. *Aetna Cas. & Sur. Co. v. Kidder, Peabody & Co.*, 676 N.Y.S.2d 559, 563.

N.Y. Sup. Ct. 1995. Stock brokers made unauthorized trades on customers' accounts, without the customers' knowledge, as part of a scheme to artificially raise a publicly-traded company's stock prices. The securities firm sustained losses when the scheme was detected by regulators and the firm was unable to meet margin calls. The manifest intent provision limits protection under the bond to losses due to embezzlement or embezzlement-like acts. Thus, coverage was not triggered because the employees intended to make money, not cause a loss. *Cont'l Bank, N.A. v. Aetna Cas. & Sur. Co.*, 626 N.Y.S.2d 385, 387-88.

N.Y. App. Div. 1988. Bank employee allowed a customer to receive immediate credit for five checks from certain drawers, even though the employee knew that checks from these drawers had previously been dishonored. When the five checks likewise were dishonored, the employee attempted to conceal the loss by debiting an unrelated account. The loss was covered. The employee acted with the requisite manifest intent because he knew that the bank would ultimately bear responsibility for the loss. The dissent, by contrast, stated that the employee may not have acted with manifest intent. According to the dissent, the employee's plea allocution indicated that the employee's initial crediting of the customer's account demonstrated an error in judgment that the employee later attempted to conceal from his superiors. *Nat'l Bank of Pakistan v. Basham*, 531 N.Y.S.2d 250, 251.

Ohio Ct. App. 1993. Bank vice president used his access to bank computers to create fictitious loans. He converted the funds to his personal use and also applied the funds from the fictitious loans to pay off actual delinquent loans. Insurer relied on testimony of vice president that he did not intend to cause bank a loss, but merely to create the appearance that he was doing a good job by bringing past-due accounts current. Court of appeals determined that under natural and probable consequences test, the jury could infer that the vice president intended to cause bank a loss and to obtain a financial benefit for himself. *First Nat'l Bank of Dillonvale v. Progressive Cas. Ins. Co.*, 640 N.E.2d 1147, 1149.

Pa. Super. Ct. 1995. Court adopted substantial certainty test and held that the factfinder could consider the employee's testimony as well as external indicia or circumstantial evidence in determining which employee had the subjective intent to cause a loss. *Susquehanna Bancshares, Inc. v. Nat'l Union Fire Ins. Co. of Pittsburgh, Pa.*, 659 A.2d 991, 993-98.

Pa. Ct. of Common Pleas 1988. Bank employee was convicted of a criminal statute under which guilt could be established by proof of reckless disregard of the bank's interests. The court held that the conviction was not sufficient to conclusively establish coverage under the bond. While reckless disregard might have been sufficient to establish coverage under older bonds, the current requirement of manifest intent means that conduct amounting to reckless disregard would not be covered. *Luzerne Nat'l Bank v. Hanover Ins. Co.*, 49 Pa. D. & C.3d 399, 403-05.

Wash. 1993. Vice president of escrow company diverted funds from escrow trust accounts to the company's operating account. The apparent purpose of the diversion was to cover general expenses. The resulting losses were covered by the company's fidelity bond. According to the court, a person acts with manifest intent when the person desires to achieve the particular consequences of the act or knows that the consequences are substantially certain to follow from the act. The vice president knew that his embezzlement of funds from the trust account was substantially certain to result in a loss because the company would be unable to meet its obligations as trustee of the escrow funds. *Estate of K.O. Jordan v. Hartford Accident & Indem. Co.*, 844 P.2d 403, 412-13.

Wash. Ct. App. 1990. Employee of meat-processing company knowingly overpaid supplier of raw materials. Supplier had allegedly threatened employee that supply of materials would be cut off if employee failed to pay the inflated prices. The resulting losses were covered. According to the court, an employee has the manifest intent to cause his employer a loss when he desires to cause the consequences of his act or believes that they are substantially certain to result. The court determined that the jury could have found that the employee desired or was substantially certain that the supplier would obtain a benefit at his employer's expense. *Hanson PLC v. Nat'l Union Fire Ins. Co. of Pittsburgh, Pa.*, 794 P.2d 66, 71-73.

Wis. Ct. App. 2003. Bank employees schemed to fraudulently obtain mortgage loans for insufficiently funded borrowers who did not otherwise qualify for the loans. The court noted in a footnote that the employees lacked manifest intent to cause the bank a loss because the losses did not result from the scheme but from the defaults on the loans. *Tri City Nat'l Bank v. Fed. Ins. Co.*, 674 N.W.2d. 617, 626 n. 8.

C. Collusion

4th Cir. 1930 (W. Va.). A cashier worked in the bank with his children. Together, they misappropriated bank funds and used the funds in a business the family owned. The Fourth Circuit held that the word "connivance" in the bond meant "an agreement or consent, indirectly given, that something unlawful be done by another." The evidence was sufficient to establish that the cashier connived with his family and that the loss was covered by the fidelity bond. *Brandon v. Holman,* 41 F.2d 586, 587-88.

6th Cir. 1992 (Tenn.). The district court approved the following jury instruction: "In determining whether a director or officer was in collusion with [the employee], you may consider the silence of that person or his or her failure to report the dishonesty to the Board of Directors or regulatory authorities as evidence of collusion." The Sixth Circuit agreed with the district court's finding that the instruction did not "equate silence with collusion: it simply states the logical conclusion that silence may be considered as evidence of such collusion." *FDIC v. Aetna Cas. & Sur. Co.*, 947 F.2d 196, 210.

10th Cir. 1994 (Utah). President and general counsel of a bank were accused of making fraudulent loans to a company that the president of the bank owned. Some bank employees knew of those loans, but the insurer failed to establish that those employees were not in collusion with the president and general counsel. Because the insurer admitted that the employees who were alleged to have made the discovery worked on the loans with the dishonest employees, the court upheld the finding of collusion made by the trial court. *FDIC v. Oldenburg*, 34 F.3d 1529, 1548-49.

10th Cir. 1991 (Okla.). Vice president's silence after learning of chairman of board's check kiting scheme, which allowed chairman to continue scheme, was sufficient to uphold finding of collusion. *Adair State Bank v. Am. Cas.*, 949 F.2d 1067, 1074-76.

S.D. Ala. 2006. There was not enough evidence to support an inference of collusion between two employees where one employee set up a dummy account for another. *Cont'l Cas. Co. v. Compass Bank*, No. 04-0766-KD-C, 2006 U.S. Dist. LEXIS 13009, at *28-29.

D. Ariz. 1994. Upheld summary judgment for insurer as to collusion (for purposes of discovery/termination) because the mere fact that bank officers followed the president's orders in funding and documenting an illegal loan was not sufficient to create a fact issue on collusion. *RTC v. Aetna Cas. & Sur. Co.*, 873 F. Supp. 1386, 1388-89.

D. Ariz. 1990. "Collusion" is synonymous with "conspiracy." The fact that loans were allegedly supported by worthless collateral or that loans were made negligently or recklessly did not create an inference of conspiracy. *Standard Chartered Bank v. Milus*, 826 F. Supp. 310, 312-13.

D. Mont. 1990. Two employees who actively attempted to disclose the wrongdoing of one another to the other board members were not in a collusive relationship but instead were adverse to one another. *Fed. Sav. & Loan Ins. Corp. v. Aetna Cas. & Sur. Co.*, 785 F. Supp. 867, 870.

S.D. Tex. 1993. Bank president made numerous unsound loans. The loss was not covered because there was no evidence of collusion. In order to trigger coverage, there must be more than evidence of a borrower's gain; there must be some evidence of banker's secret personal gain from which collusion may be inferred. *Progressive Cas. Ins. Co. v. First Bank*, 828 F. Supp. 473, 474-75.

Ill. App. Ct. 1991. Two employees rented post office boxes and opened checking accounts under the auspices of nonexistent companies and then submitted fraudulent invoices to their employer. They also diverted the insured's funds by fraudulently submitting personal expenses for payment. The scheme was accomplished by mutual approval of each other's expense reports. Collusion does not require the employees to jointly initiate a common scheme. Collusion is established if each employee begins stealing independently, but later become sufficiently concerned and implicated in each other's fraud. The employees are deemed to have acted in collusion when they discovered or became aware of each other's scheme and overtly assisted in perpetrating the scheme, not merely in concealing it. *Purdy Co. of Ill. v. Transp. Ins. Co., Inc.*, 568 N.E.2d 318, 321.

D. Financial Benefit

5th Cir. 1995 (La.). Chief lending officer had engaged in a pattern of dishonest conduct. He received bribes and kickbacks in connection with loans and failed to disclose business relationships with borrowers. The evidence supported an inference that chief lending officer would not have approved risky loans that would probably cause the bank a loss had he not had a personal stake in the outcome. *FDIC v. Fid. & Deposit Co. of Md.*, 45 F.3d 969, 975.

6th Cir. 1998 (Ky.). Bond did not cover certain fraudulent acts of the insureds' employees. However, the court disavowed any language in the district court's opinion that could be construed as meaning that "manifest intent" requires an employee to actually receive a personal monetary benefit. The law of the circuit requires only that the employee intended to have received such a benefit. *Ins. Co. of N. Am. v. Liberty United Bancorp., Inc.*, 142 F.3d 434, No. 96-6502, 1998 U.S. App. LEXIS 3781, at *3 (unpublished table opinion).

8th Cir. 1993 (S.D.). Bank's successor sued insurer under fidelity bond for dishonest acts of bank president. The unrealized gain on stock purchased by bank president did not constitute a financial benefit for purposes of the bond. *First Dakota Nat'l Bank v. St. Paul Fire & Marine Ins. Co.*, 2 F.3d 801, 808-10.

D. Colo. 2008. Bank officers caused a loss by re-aging delinquent accounts using non-existent funds. The court refused to grant summary judgment to the insured because the plaintiff had presented evidence that nonemployees received a financial benefit from the scheme (meaning that the benefit could not qualify as wages or bonuses as to those nonemployees). The court found that the plaintiff might prevail on the financial benefit issue before a jury. *FDIC v. St. Paul Cos.*, 634 F. Supp. 2d 1213, 1221-22.

S.D. Fla. 2011. Employee was convicted of various criminal charges for his role in fraudulent loan transactions. Insurer argued that there was no evidence of any financial benefit to the employee in connection with the loan transactions. The FDIC argued that sales of bank stock held by trusts for the employee's children was a financial benefit. The court reviewed details of the trusts and found that they were valid and enforceable, but held that benefit to the trusts would not be a benefit to the employee. *St. Paul Mercury Ins. Co. v. FDIC*, No. 08-21192-CIV-GARBER, 2010 U.S. Dist. LEXIS 30930, at *14-16.

N.D. Ga. 2010. Insured's motion for summary judgment denied because there was conflicting evidence as to whether an employee received compensation for his illegal participation in a Ponzi-like scheme or for the legal services and surveying he provided. *Fed. Ins. Co. v. United Cmty. Banks, Inc.*, No. 2:08-cv-0128-RWS, 2010 U.S. Dist. LEXIS 101646, at *41.

N.D. Ill. 1992. Bank alleged that loan officer acted dishonestly by attempting to conceal bank customer's overdrawn and delinquent accounts. The overdrafts that the loan officer attempted to conceal were "loans" within meaning of Insuring Agreement (A), but there was an issue of material fact regarding whether loan officer obtained a financial benefit in excess of $2,500. *Affiliated Bank/Morton Grove v. Hartford Accident & Indem. Co.*, No. 9 C 4446, 1992 WL 91761, at *8-14.

S.D. Iowa 2005. Former bank employee made loans that were not repaid. Bank made an Insuring Agreement (A) claim. Court found that the bond was given to comply with an Iowa statute and that the statute controlled, but followed precedent in holding that the financial benefit provision of the bond did not conflict with the statute. The court held that where a series of fraudulent loans is shown, it is not necessary to prove a financial benefit from each individual loan. It concluded that there was arguably a financial benefit where an employee received an interest in a farm operation. *Kan. Bankers Sur. Co. v. Farmers State Bank, Yale, IA*, 408 F. Supp. 2d 751, 756-57.

E.D. La. 2007. Employees participated in a fraudulent mortgage scheme. Insurer moved for summary judgment and argued that the bank had not shown any financial benefit to the employee. Bank, however, argued that one of the employees received a free property appraisal from one of the appraisers allegedly involved in the scheme. The court found that the alleged free appraisal raised an issue of fact and denied the insurer's motion as to Insuring Agreement (A). *First Guar. Bank v. BancInsure, Inc.*, No. 06-3497, 2007 U.S. Dist. LEXIS 30934, at *6.

M.D. La. 2008. Employee was misrepresenting that apartments were being rented so that he would receive commissions that he was not entitled to. Employer sought coverage under its Commercial Crime Policy for the lost rents it believed it was receiving. The court granted the insurer summary judgment. It concluded that the employee received no financial benefit other than commissions, which were not considered financial benefits under the policy. Thus, the lost rent did not result from covered employee dishonesty. *Palm Hills Props., L.L.C. v. Cont'l Ins. Co.*, No. 07-668-RET-SCR, 2008 WL 4303817, at *4.

S.D. Miss. 2010. Bank customer borrowed money from several banks and gave first liens on a single piece of real estate as collateral. An attorney schemed with the customer and certified to each bank that the property was unencumbered. The customer defaulted causing the insured bank a loss. Insurer denied coverage because there was no showing of an improper financial benefit to the attorney (also the insured's employee). The court disagreed and pointed to the many perks that the customer/borrower provided to the attorney in exchange for providing false statements to banks. The court considered whether those perks and payments were "in connection with" the improper statements or whether they were in connection with legitimate services that the attorney provided. The word "connection" was broad, and there was clearly some connection between the improper benefits the customer was paying to the attorney and his provision of fraudulent documents to the banks. *Peoples Bank of the S. v. Bancinsure, Inc.*, 753 F. Supp. 2d 649, 653-57.

D.N.J. 1983. The question of intent to cause the insured a loss is one of fact, precluding summary judgment. If an intent to benefit anyone financially is shown, the bank's loss is covered. *Liberty Nat'l Bank v. Aetna Life & Cas. Co.*, 568 F. Supp. 860, 868.

S.D. Ohio 1998. Bank's CEO made a loan in excess of his lending authority. The district court rejected the bank's argument that alleged enhancement of CEO's prestige in the community and enhancement of CEO's performance at the bank constituted financial benefits sufficient to trigger coverage. *First Bank of Marietta v. Hartford Underwriters Mut. Ins. Co.*, 997 F. Supp. 934, 937-39.

Bankr. E.D. Pa. 1987. Debtor's president and other high-level employees borrowed substantial sums through debtor, and then fraudulently attempted to liquidate the obligations upon which they were personally liable. Employees invaded debtor's escrow accounts and used the funds to retire debt obligations that were personally guaranteed by the employees. The retirement of personally-guaranteed debts constituted a financial benefit to the employees. *In re Leedy Mortgage Co.*, 76 B.R. 440, 456-57.

S.D. Tex. 1993. Bank president employed poor banking practices, failed to follow internal procedures, and misrepresented the condition of borrowers and the value of their collateral. The loss was not covered under the bond because there was no evidence that the bank president intended to obtain a financial benefit. *Progressive Cas. Ins. Co. v. First Bank*, 828 F. Supp. 473, 474-75.

Cal. Ct. App. 2002. Court affirmed summary judgment for insurer. Burden was on insured mortgage lender to demonstrate that employees who allegedly participated in fraudulent loan scheme acted with intent to receive financial benefit. Mortgage lender failed to prove that the value of the benefit received by employees exceeded $2,500. *Mortgage Assocs., Inc. v. Fid. & Deposit Co. of Md.*, 129 Cal. Rptr. 2d 365, 369-70.

Ill. App. Ct. 1983. Summary judgment was granted to insurer because the employee received no financial benefit from the unauthorized trading, except commissions. *Mortell v. Ins. Co. of N. Am.*, 458 N.E.2d 922, 929.

Minn. Ct. App. 1995. Bank's employee coerced a customer into signing a promissory note and giving the loan proceeds to the employee. Both the employee and customer declared bankruptcy, and that the bank did not receive payments on the debt. These facts supported the conclusion that the employee had the intent to cause the bank a loss. The evidence in the record also supported the conclusion that the employee acted with the intent to benefit himself. *Citizens State Bank of Big Lake v. Capitol Indem. Corp.*, No. C1-95-321, 1995 WL 421672, *at 2-3.

Minn. Ct. App. 1985. Employer sued insurer on a Commercial Blanket Bond containing a fidelity clause similar to Insuring Agreement (A) to recover losses incurred when a sales manager submitted false orders, ordered unnecessary merchandise, and misused the company credit card. There was no coverage for the loss. The court rejected the insured's argument that the employee's four months of employment before the fraud was discovered satisfied the financial benefit requirement of the bond. *Benchmark Crafters, Inc. v. NW. Nat'l Ins. Co.*, 363 N.W.2d 89, 91.

N.J. 2004. Insured automobile dealer had an employee who fabricated credit information of purchasers, allowing them to buy cars that they otherwise could not have afforded. Court held that a reasonable jury could conclude from this fact that the employee knew that his conduct was substantially certain to result in a benefit to the purchasers. The court thus denied insurer's motion for summary judgment. *Auto Lenders Acceptance Corp. v. Gentilini Ford, Inc.*, 854 A.2d 378, 395-96.

Ohio Ct. App. 1993. Bank vice president used his access to bank computers to create fictitious loans. He converted the funds to his personal use and also applied the funds from the fictitious loans to pay off actual delinquent loans. Insurer relied on testimony of vice president that he did not intend to cause bank a loss, but merely to create appearance that he was doing a good job by bringing past due accounts current. Court of appeals determined that under natural-and-probable-consequences test, the jury could infer that the vice president intended to cause bank a loss and to obtain a financial benefit for himself. *First Nat'l Bank of Dillonvale v. Progressive Cas. Ins. Co.*, 640 N.E.2d 1147, 1149.

Pa. Super. Ct. 1999. Bank employee colluded with a bank customer to defraud the bank by manipulating a floor-plan-financing system in order to obtain financing for nonexistent vehicles. The court affirmed summary judgment for insurer. Bank failed to show that an employee who colluded with bank customer in the fraudulent loan scheme obtained a financial benefit in excess of $2,500. Unrealized gain on stock purchase and sale did not constitute financial benefit. *First Philson Bank, N.A. v. Hartford Fire Ins. Co.*, 727 A.2d 584, 589-90.

Wash. 1993. The vice president of an escrow company diverted funds from escrow trust accounts to the company's operating account in order to cover general operating expenses, including payments on debts for which vice president was personally liable. The diversion of funds constituted a financial benefit to the vice president. Furthermore, to the extent the diversions kept the company afloat, the vice president benefited in his role as a shareholder. *Estate of K.O. Jordan v. Hartford Accident & Indem. Co.*, 844 P.2d 403, 413.

E. Benefits of Employment

3d Cir. 2004 (Pa.). Insured bank loaned the money to pay premiums for auto policies. Part of the bank's collateral was the right to cancel the policy and receive the return premium. It was therefore critical that the bank identify a default and cancel the defaulted policy promptly. A third-party operator had responsibility for identifying defaults, but failed to do so. Insured bank sought coverage for the nonpayment of loans, but coverage was denied because the operator lacked intent to confer a financial benefit on itself. The third party had received only normal payments such as bonuses and commissions in exchange for its performance—no additional funds for failing to catch defaults as it had promised. *Hudson United Bank v. Progressive Cas. Ins. Co.*, 112 F. App'x 170, 173-75.

3d Cir. 2000 (N.J.). Dishonestly obtained "golden handcuff payments" were not covered by the bond. The bond does not provide coverage when employee's purpose is to obtain the type of financial benefit that the insured provides knowingly to its employees as part of its compensation scheme and as a result of the employment relationship. Exclusionary language "earned in the course of employment" describes the character of the payment at issue rather than the frequency with which the payment is received by the employee. The opinion includes a collection of cases interpreting the employee benefits language of the bond. *RTC v. Fid. & Deposit Co. of Md.*, 205 F.3d 615, 644-49

5th Cir. 2003 (Tex.). Unauthorized pay increases that controller of car dealership gave herself and another employee were not covered by car dealership's commercial crime policy. The language of the policy unambiguously exempted from coverage salaries obtained due to employee dishonesty. *Performance Autoplex II LTC. v. Mid-Continent Cas. Co.*, 322 F.3d 847, 857-58.

6th. Cir. 1987 (Tenn.). Broker dealer's trader violated company policy by making trades in excess of her inventory limit. The commissions paid to the trader (to which she was not entitled) were not covered because the language of the policy explicitly excluded dishonest or fraudulent acts intended to enhance the employee's regular compensation. *Mun. Sec., Inc. v. Ins. Co. of N. Am.*, 829 F.2d 7, 9-10.

8th Cir. 2010 (Iowa). The court affirmed summary judgment for the insurer in a padded payroll case. The employee overstated his time and allegedly was paid more than $100,000 in excess of the wages to which he was entitled. The court interpreted the provision as excluding all wages from coverage, even those that were not earned or normal, because the provision would be meaningless if interpreted as urged by the insured. "The employee dishonesty provision does not cover losses resulting from overpaid employee benefits of the type earned in the normal course of business." *R & J Enterprizes v. Gen. Cas. Co. of Wis.*, 627 F.3d 723, 727-28.

9th Cir. 1986 (Cal.). Employee of a stereo equipment manufacturer perpetrated a complex fraud that enabled him to collect commissions on fraudulent sales of stereo equipment. The insured brought suit for the commissions and other losses incurred as a result of the scheme. The insured argued that the commissions were covered because fraudulent sales were not its normal course of business. The court rejected the argument and held that the policy unambiguously excluded commissions. The court reasoned that, if the insured were correct, the exclusion of commissions would have no meaning or effect because fraud or dishonest acts are not usually part of the normal course of business. The court also rejected the argument that the commission payments qualified as "other property" covered by the policy. *James B. Lansing Sound, Inc. v. Nat'l Union Fire Ins. Co. of Pittsburgh, Pa.*, 801 F.2d 1560, 1567.

M.D. Ala. 1997. Car salesman dishonestly obtained commissions by allegedly manipulating a government price discount program. Insured car dealership suffered losses resulting from chargebacks to the

SECTION 1 — INSURING AGREEMENT (A)—FIDELITY   47

manufacturer because of the improper discounts. The district court rejected the insured's argument that the policy was ambiguous. The unearned commissions were excluded because they were received "in the normal course of business," a term that the court construed as merely defining the type of excluded benefit. *Auburn Ford Lincoln Mercury, Inc. v. Universal Underwriters Ins. Co.*, 967 F. Supp. 475, 478-79.

N.D. Ill. 1986. Life insurance salesmen perpetrated a fraudulent scheme to sell life insurance policies with the intent to obtain greater commissions. The district court predicted that the Illinois Supreme Court would find that the fidelity bond language was unambiguous and excluded coverage for all types of commissions, whether earned or unearned, if obtained dishonestly. *Hartford Accident & Indem. Ins. Co. v. Wash. Nat'l Ins. Co.*, 638 F. Supp. 78, 80-81.

M.D. La. 2008. Dishonest employee embezzled money by misrepresenting that apartments had been rented in order to receive commissions. The insured claimed lost rent for the apartments. Insurer entitled to summary judgment because the bond required a financial benefit to the employee or someone else and provided that employee benefits, including commissions, were not a financial benefit. *Palm Hills Props., L.L.C. v. Cont'l Ins. Co.*, No. 07-668-RET-SCR, 2008 WL 4303817, at *4.

S.D. Miss. 2010. Bank customer borrowed money from several banks and gave first liens on a single piece of real estate as collateral. An attorney schemed with the customer and certified to each bank that the property was unencumbered. The customer defaulted causing the insured bank a loss. Insurer denied coverage because there was no showing of an improper financial benefit to the attorney (also the insured's employee). The court disagreed and pointed to the many perks that the customer/borrower provided to the attorney in exchange for providing false statements to banks. The court considered whether those perks and payments were "in connection with" the improper statements or whether they were in connection with legitimate services that the attorney provided. The word "connection" was broad, and there was clearly some connection between the improper benefits the customer was paying to the attorney and his provision of fraudulent documents to the banks. *Peoples Bank of the S. v. Bancinsure, Inc.*, 753 F. Supp. 2d 649, 653-57.

S.D.N.Y. 1986. Employee entered into an agreement with a third party involving stock loan transactions which resulted in an artificial increase in the department's net profits, ultimately increasing the employee's income under a profit sharing formula. The employee's acts did not meet the employee fidelity bond's definition of "fraudulent and dishonest acts" because the gain sought was associated with his employment. As long as the financial benefits to him were in the form of salary, commissions, fees, or other emoluments of his employment, it was irrelevant whether they were honestly or dishonestly earned. *Morgan, Olmstead, Kennedy & Gardner, Inc. v. Fed. Ins. Co.*, 637 F. Supp. 973, 978-79.

Bankr. E.D. Pa. 1987. Debtor's president and other high-level employees borrowed substantial sums through debtor, and then fraudulently attempted to liquidate the obligations upon which they were personally liable. The employees' actions had no connection to their compensation and thus, the bond's exclusionary clause for salary did not apply. *In re Leedy Mortgage Co.*, 76 B.R. 440, 456-57.

M.D. Tenn. 1990. Bank director caused the bank to issue checks to a company in which the director was stockholder. A portion of the funds was used to buy a life insurance policy for the director. The director designated the payment as "fees" in the monthly financial statement reviewed by the board. The director also instructed the bank's controller to issue monthly checks payable to the director for "executive committee fees;" though the director performed no services in return for these payments and admitted that the designation was for the purpose of concealing the payments. The district court held that recovery is barred by the "employee benefits" provision when two conditions are satisfied: (1) the employer knowingly pays the funds to the employee; and (2) the employee defrauds the employer into believing the employee has earned the funds as compensation for his work. Neither condition was satisfied and the payments to the company and the "executive committee fees" constituted pure embezzlement, which the FDIC was entitled to recover under a Bankers Blanket Bond. *FDIC v. St. Paul Fire & Marine Ins.*

Co., 738 F. Supp. 1146, 1156-57, *aff'd in part, vacated in part by*, 942 F.2d 1032, 1035-37.

D. Utah 1984. Loan officers made loans to persons of questionable credit in order to collect the commissions. The fidelity bond unambiguously excluded coverage for commissions. *Verex Assurance, Inc. v. Gate City Mortgage Co.*, No. C-83-0506W, 1984 WL 2918, 1984 U.S. Dist. LEXIS 21545, at *2-7.

Ala. 2002. Employees of transit authority issued payroll checks to themselves in excess of their salaries. The losses were covered by the transit authority's fidelity policy. According to the court, the embezzled funds were not "salaries" because the funds exceeded the fixed compensation that the employees were entitled to be paid. *Cincinnati Ins. Co. v. Tuscaloosa Cnty. Parking & Transit Auth.*, 827 So. 2d 765, 767-68.

Ill. App. Ct. 1983. Salesmen employed by a licensed futures commodity merchant allegedly used fraud and deception to induce customers to purchase commodity options. The customers sued the merchant and the merchant sought coverage under a Brokers Blanket Bond. It was undisputed that the salesmen did not gain anything except a commission from the unauthorized trading alleged in the customer complaints. Thus, there was no coverage with respect to the customer claims. *Mortell v. Ins. Co. of N. Am.*, 458 N.E.2d 922, 929.

Md. Ct. Spec. App. 2003. Employee was substantially overpaid during several payroll periods due to a data entry error. Employee ran from the building when confronted and never returned the overpaid funds. The "salary and benefits exclusion" clearly and unambiguously excluded coverage. The "salary and benefits" exclusion has been in standard fidelity bonds since 1980, and its purpose is two-fold: (1) to avoid involving insurers in employer-employee disputes over salary, commissions, and benefits when the conduct of the employee is within the internal control of the employer, and (2) to counteract a trend in court decisions expanding coverage beyond the limit intended by insurers. *ABC Imaging of Wash., Inc. v. Travelers Indem. Co. of Am.*, 820 A.2d 628, 631-35.

Mich. Ct. App. 2012. Insured's controller issued herself a duplicate paycheck each month (in addition to the check she received legitimately). Insurer argued that the checks were not a financial benefit because they were part of a salary earned in the normal course of employment. The court reviewed cases on both sides of the padded payroll-type loss and thought they could best be rationalized by an analysis based on whether the employer knowingly paid the money. Because the insured did not knowingly issue the duplicate checks, the court held that they were an improper financial benefit. The fact that the account happened to be the payroll account did not convert the embezzled money into salary. *Amerisure Ins. Co. v. Debruyn Produce Co.*, 825 N.W.2d 666, 668-69.

Minn. Ct. App. 1985. Employer sued Insurer on a Commercial Blanket Bond containing a fidelity clause similar to Insuring Agreement (A) to recover losses incurred when a sales manager submitted false orders, ordered unnecessary merchandise, and misused the company credit card. There was no coverage for the loss. It was uncontroverted that employee did not gain anything except his regular salary and expenses from the fraudulent acts. *Benchmark Crafters, Inc. v. Northwestern Nat'l Ins. Co.*, 363 N.W.2d 89, 91.

Miss. Ct. App. 2005. Crooks used an altered power of attorney to lease a car from the insured dealership. The person who executed the power of attorney sued the crooks, the insured, and others. Insured sought to compel the insurer to provide a defense. The court affirmed summary judgment for the insurer in part because the only benefit to an employee was a commission, which was not a financial benefit under the policy. *Watson Quality Ford v. Great River Ins. Co.*, 909 So. 2d 1196, 1200.

N.J. Super. Ct. Law Div. 1993. A savings and loan sought to recover under Servicing Contractor Rider commissions and fees it had paid to a mortgage debt servicing contractor. Contractor, who had also procured the mortgages and sold them to the savings and loan, defaulted on its obligations and was later found to have engaged in criminal conduct in connection with the mortgages. The Rider excluded coverage for commissions and fees earned in the normal course of business. The commissions and fees were excluded from coverage because the contractor would have been entitled to receive them had it properly performed the services it had contracted to provide. The court noted that cases interpreting similar bond language did not require the commissions and fees to be earned honestly for the exclusion to apply. *N.J. Sav. & Loan Ass'n v. Fid. & Deposit Co. of Md.*, 660 A.2d 1287, 1296-97.

N.Y. App. Div. 2002. Employee of a clothing manufacturer created fake purchase orders. Though the insured did not pay bonuses to its employees, the employee apparently was motivated by the hope of obtaining some form of extra compensation for generating a large sales volume. The insured sustained a loss after it manufactured the garments and then was only able to sell them below cost. The exclusion for employee benefits did not depend on the employee's receipt or entitlement to a bonus or other normal form of financial benefit, but on the employee's intent to obtain such benefit. *Jamie Brooke, Inc. v. Zurich-Am. Ins. Co.*, 748 N.Y.S.2d 5, 6.

N.Y. App. Div. 2000. Insured's comptroller allegedly embezzled funds from a payroll account by secretly and fraudulently paying himself unauthorized and excessive salary, commissions and bonuses. The court held that, if the allegations were true, the insured's employee dishonesty policy endorsement would provide coverage because the insured did not knowingly make the payments and because the policy provided protection from embezzlement or theft. *Klyn v. Travelers Indem. Co.*, 709 N.Y.S.2d 780, 781.

Pa. Super. Ct. 1999. Bank employee colluded with bank customer to defraud the bank by manipulating a floor-plan-financing system in order to obtain financing for nonexistent vehicles. Court of appeals affirmed summary judgment for insurer. Shares of bank's stock received by employee through employee stock option plan (ESOP), salaries, and bonuses were benefits earned in the normal course of business and thus were not covered. *First Philson Bank, N.A. v. Hartford Fire Ins. Co.*, 727 A.2d 584, 589-90.

Tex. App. 1997. Employee dishonesty policy did not cover losses incurred when two employees manipulated the time card system to obtain compensation for time they did not work. *Dickson v. State Farm Lloyds*, 944 S.W.2d 666, 668.

Wash. 1993. Vice president of an escrow company diverted funds from escrow trust accounts to the company's operating account in order to cover general operating expenses. The Supreme Court of Washington held that, to the extent the diversions kept the company afloat, the diversion of funds constituted a financial benefit to the vice president in his role as a shareholder, and such benefit was not an excluded as employee benefit earned in the normal course of business. *Estate of K.O. Jordan v. Hartford Accident & Indem. Co.*, 844 P.2d 403, 409-13.

SECONDARY SOURCES

SAMUEL J. ARENA, JR. ET AL., THE MANIFEST INTENT HANDBOOK (Samuel J. Arena, Jr. et al. eds., American Bar Association 2002).

George Biancardi, *Underwriting and Claim Issues in a Changing Market: A Commercial Crime Perspective* (unpublished paper presented at ABA TIPS FLSC, Toronto, Can., Aug. 1998, on file at the Stradley Library, No. 2870).

Thomas J. Burnside, *When Crime and Fraud Benefit the Employer: "Manifest Intent" or "Business as Usual"* (unpublished paper presented at the Northeast Surety & Fidelity Claims Association Claims Conference, Iselin, N.J., Oct. 1993, on file at the Stradley Library, No. 3064).

Norman R. Carpenter, *The Catch 22 of the Manifest Intent: Inferring the Obvious* (unpublished paper presented at ABA TIPS FSLC, Chicago, Ill., Aug. 1995, on file at the Stradley Library, No. 2467).

Gary M. Case, *"Manifest Intent": The Search for an Evidentiary Standard* (unpublished paper presented at the Northeast Surety & Fidelity Claims Association Claims Conference, Hartford, Conn., Nov. 1992, on file at the Stradley Library, No. 2150).

Michael R. Davisson & Lawrence S. DeVos, *The Forgotten Insuring Agreement: Coverage for Loss Arising From Dishonest Acts by Servicing Contractors*, 17 FID. L.J. 117 (2011).

Robert J. Duke, *A Brief History of the Financial Institution Bond*, in FINANCIAL INSTITUTION BONDS 1 (Duncan L. Clore ed., 3d ed. 2008).

Jeffrey A. Ford & John S. Torkelson, *The Current Status of Manifest Intent Requirement in Fidelity Bonds* (unpublished paper presented at Surety Claims Institute, Lansdowne, Va., June 1997, on file at the Stradley Library, No. 2686).

Glenn R. Kazlow, *Division Among the Circuits: The Courts Wrestle with the Meaning of "Manifest Intent"* (unpublished paper presented at NBCA, Pinehurst, N.C., Oct. 2000, on file at the Stradley Library, No. 3064).

Michael Keeley & Christopher A. Nelson, *Critical Issues in Determining Employee Dishonesty Coverage*, 44 TORT & INS. L.J. 933 (2009).

Michael Keeley & Christopher A. Nelson, *Employee Dishonesty: The Essential Elements of Coverage Under Insuring Agreement (A)*, in FINANCIAL INSTITUTION BONDS 39 (Duncan L. Clore ed., 3d ed. 2008).

Michael Keeley & Lisa Block, *Loan Loss Coverage Under Insuring Agreement (A)*, in LOAN LOSS COVERAGE UNDER FINANCIAL INSTITUTION BONDS 1 (Gilbert J. Schroeder & John J. Tomaine eds., 2007).

Michael Keeley & Sean Duffy, *Investigating the Employee Dishonesty Claim: Interviewing Witnesses, Obtaining Documents, and Other Important Issues*, in HANDLING FIDELITY BOND CLAIMS 153 (Michael Keeley & Sean Duffy eds., 2d ed. 2005).

Michael Keeley & Lisa Block, *"Manifest Intent"—The Waters Are Clearing; Or Are They?*, Fidelity & Surety Law Committee Newsletter (ABA TIPS Fidelity & Surety Law Comm. Fall 2000).

Michael Keeley, *Employee Dishonesty Claims: Discerning the Employee's Manifest Intent*, 30 TORT & INS. L.J. 915 (1995).

Michael Keeley, *Critical Loan Loss Issues Under Insuring Agreement (A) of the Financial Institution Bond* (unpublished paper presented at ABA TIPS FSLC Mid-Winter Conference, New York, N.Y., Nov. 1993, on file at the Stradley Library, No. 2120).

Christopher Kirwan, *Mischief or "Manifest Intent"? Looking for Employee Dishonesty in the Uncharted World of Fiduciary Misconduct,* 30 TORT & INS. L.J. 183 (1994).

Jane Landes et. al., *Does a Criminal Conviction Equal Dishonesty? Criminal Intent Versus Manifest Intent,* 24 TORT & INS. L.J. 785 (1989).

Robert L. Lawrence, *Manifest Intent and Insuring Agreement (A)—Where Are We Now?* (unpublished paper presented at ABA TIPS FSLC, Atlanta, Ga., Sept. 1994, on file at the Stradley Library, No. 1143).

Ronald G. Mund, *"Dishonesty v. Business Judgement v. Negligence: The Bankers Blanket Bond v. The Directors' and Officers' Liability Policy"* (unpublished paper presented at ABA TIPS FSLC, New York, N.Y., Jan. 1986, on file at the Stradley Library, No. 57).

Dolores A. Parr & Gail K. Donovon, *Back to the Future: Proposed Fidelity Coverage for Financial Institution Bonds and Commercial Crime Policies* (unpublished paper presented to the ABA Fidelity and Surety Law Committee Mid-Winter Meeting, New York, N.Y., Jan. 22, 1999, on file at the Stradley Library, No. 2932).

Martha L. Perkins & Robert K. Grennan, *Coverage for Losses Resulting From Association Property Manger Dishonesty,* XVII FID. L.J., 2d ed., 77 (2011).

Sam H. Poteet & H. Rowan Leathers, III, *Financial Institution Bond, Standard form 24)—Common Law or Statutory Bond? and Consequences of Such a Decision on Surety Defenses Such as Manifest Intent and Notice Requirements* (unpublished paper presented at the Third Annual Conference of the Southern Surety & Fidelity Claims Association, Atlanta, Ga., May 1992, on file at the Stradley Library, No. 2093).

Toni Scott Reed, *Commercial Crime Coverage for the Twenty-First Century: Does a "Theft" Standard in Traditional Insuring Agreement (A) Broaden or Narrow Coverage for Employee Dishonesty?*, XIV FID. L.J. 137 (2008).

Toni Scott Reed, *Employee Theft v. Manifest Intent: The Changing Landscape of Commercial Crime Coverage*, 36 TORT & INS. L.J. 43 (2000).

Toni Scott Reed, *Recurring Questions in Loan Loss Coverage Cases*, 5 FID. L.J. 103 (1999).

Paul H. Robinson & Jane A. Grail, *Element Analysis in Defining Criminal Liability: The Model Penal Code and Beyond*, 35 Stan. L. Rev. 681 (1983).

Roger P. Sauer & Eric B. Levine, *Excluding Expert Testimony in Fidelity Bond Cases: A Practical Guide for Defense Counsel*, THE BRIEF, Summer 2002, at 66 (publication of the American Bar Association).

Frank L. Skillern, Jr., *Fidelity Coverage: What is Dishonesty?*, in BANKERS AND OTHER FINANCIAL INSTITUTION BONDS (1979).

Sandra M. Stone & Barry F. MacEntee, *Defining Employee Dishonesty Within the Framework of the Automatic Termination Provision and the Fidelity Insuring Agreement*, XVII FID. L.J., 2d ed., 143 (2011).

Ron A. Yarbrough & Gregory L. Kennedy, *"Thou Shall Not Steal"— Manifest Intent and the Eighth Commandment in the New Millennium* (unpublished paper presented at ABA TIPS FSLC, San Francisco, CA, January 2000, on file at Stradley Library No. 3024).

SECTION 2 — INSURING AGREEMENT (B)—ON PREMISES*

(B) (1) Loss of items enumerated in the definition of Property resulting directly from
    (a) robbery, burglary, misplacement, mysterious unexplainable disappearance and damage thereto or destruction thereof, or
    (b) theft, false pretenses, common-law or statutory larceny, committed by a person physically present in an office or on the premises of the Insured at the time the enumerated items of Property are surrendered,
while such enumerated items of Property are lodged or deposited within offices or premises located anywhere.
(2) Loss of or damage to furnishings, fixtures, supplies or equipment within an office of the Insured covered under this bond resulting directly from larceny or theft in, or by burglary or robbery of, such office, or attempt thereat, provided that:
    (a) the Insured is the owner of such furnishings, fixtures, supplies, equipment, or office or is liable for such loss or damage, and
    (b) the loss is not caused by fire.

COMMENT

Insuring Agreement (B) provides coverage for three categories of risk. Section 2(B)(1)(a) covers loss of items enumerated in the bond's definition of "Property," when the loss results directly from certain named perils, provided the items are "lodged or deposited within offices or premises located anywhere." Section 2(B)(1)(b) focuses on the location of the person directly causing the loss and covers only loss of items enumerated in the bond's definition of "Property" caused by a specific list of risks, provided the loss is the direct result of wrongful acts committed while the actor is physically present on the insured's

---

* By Patricia H. Thompson and Christy L. MacPherson, Carlton Fields, P.A., Miami, Florida and Atlanta, Georgia.

premises.[1] Finally, section 2(B)(2) provides a limited, but more traditional form of property damage coverage, insuring loss of or damage to fixtures, furniture, supplies, or equipment resulting directly from certain listed perils, such as larceny or burglary, provided that the insured is the owner of or is liable for such fixtures, furniture, and other items, and the loss is not caused by fire.

This insuring agreement is the result of a series of revisions to the 1969 standard form Bankers Blanket Bond. The revisions were intended to shorten and simplify the insuring agreement and to clearly limit the coverage provided thereby, in reaction to court decisions that expanded coverage beyond that originally contemplated by the underwriters. As a result of the revised language of this insuring agreement and the addition of several new exclusions, many of the older cases should be reviewed carefully to determine whether the policy language being construed is the same as the bond form at issue.

One important earlier revision to Insuring Agreement (B) is also found in each of the other insuring agreements: the insured is required to show that the alleged loss resulted *directly* from a named peril. This requirement is intended to limit coverage to loss that resulted immediately, without any intervening cause, from a covered risk, rather than from other causes, such as the insured's own error, breach of contract, or failure to follow proper banking practices.[2]

The requirement that the loss result directly from a covered peril is underscored by the deletion of language in the 1980 bond form which allowed coverage for loss, even if "occurring with . . . negligence," and by the addition of Exclusion 2(h), which eliminates coverage for loss caused by the insured's employees (subject to certain exceptions). The Eighth Circuit has observed that this exclusionary language bars coverage for losses caused by bank employees, whether they were acting negligently or not.[3]

Several other exclusions are crucial to a proper understanding of the scope of coverage provided by Insuring Agreement (B). The two most frequently cited are Exclusion 2(e), which excludes losses related to

---

1 *See, e.g.,* Private Bank & Trust Co. v. Progressive Cas. Ins. Co., 409 F.3d 814, 817 (7th Cir. 2005).

2 *See, e.g.,* Empire Bank v. Fid. & Deposit Co. of Md., 27 F.3d 333, 334 (8th Cir. 1994); Lynch Props., Inc. v. Potomac Ins. Co., 962 F. Supp. 956, 961 (N.D. Tex. 1996).

3 *Empire Bank*, 27 F.3d at 335.

loans, and Exclusion 2(o), which excludes losses resulting from uncollected funds. These exclusions make it clear that the bond is not credit insurance. Therefore, any losses caused by the extension of credit in the broadest sense, whether by paying on uncollected funds, allowing overdrafts, check kiting, or more traditional lending transactions, are not covered by Insuring Agreement (B), even though the extension of credit might have been induced by false pretenses, fraud, or larcenous intent on the part of the "borrower."[4]

Some of the less often cited exclusions to coverage under this insuring agreement include Exclusion 2(m), which eliminates coverage for extortionate threats that induce a bank employee to surrender bank funds away from bank offices; Exclusion 2(f), which limits the insurer's liability for the contents of customer safe-deposit boxes; and Exclusion 2(l), which excludes coverage for vandalized or malfunctioning ATMs and for ATMs that are not located inside the insured's offices.

Finally, to the extent certain types of property damage or loss are covered by other insurance, coverage may be excluded by Exclusion 2(q).

OUTLINE OF ANNOTATIONS

A. Robbery
B. Larceny, Theft, and False Pretenses
C. Misplacement Mysterious Unexplained Disappearance
D. Customer Losses
E. "On Premises" Requirement
F. Direct Loss

ANNOTATIONS

A. Robbery

5th Cir. 1973 (Ga.). Insured bank made a Bankers Blanket Bond claim for a loss resulting when its president paid the bank's money to an

---

[4] *See, e.g.,* First Tex. Sav. Ass'n v. Reliance Ins. Co., 950 F.2d 1171, 1177-78 (5th Cir. 1992); First Nat'l Bank & Trust Co. v. Cont'l Ins. Co., 510 F.2d 7, 12 (10th Cir. 1975).

extortionist who was holding the president's family captive off the insured bank's premises. The court found the loss to be a robbery by extortion, which was covered by the on premises insuring agreement because the extortionist's demands caused the president to take the bank's money from the bank's premises. This bond did not have extortion exclusion. *Bank of Dade v. Fid. & Deposit Co. of Md.,* 483 F.2d 735, 738.

B. Larceny, Theft, and False Pretenses

3d Cir. 1993 (N.J.). Savings and loan association sued to recover losses resulting from wire transfers induced by a fraudulent telephone call scheme. The insured could not prove that the persons making the telephone calls were physically present in its offices or on its premises. The court stated that it was undisputed that the telephone fraud involved false pretenses. *Oritani Sav. & Loan Ass'n v. Fid. & Deposit Co. of Md.,* 989 F.2d 635, 638.

4th Cir. 1989 (N.C.). Insured bank sought to recover for losses suffered when it was fraudulently induced by telephone to wire funds directly into securities broker's account in New York. The Fourth Circuit stated that the broker's misrepresentation constituted "false pretenses" for purposes of the blanket bond. *S. Nat'l Bank of N.C. v. United Pac. Ins. Co.,* 864 F.2d 329, 332.

4th Cir. 1980 (Va.). The insured, a company engaged in the business of factoring, sought to recover for a loss sustained when it bought fictitious accounts receivable. The district court granted summary judgment to the insured, finding coverage under the false pretenses coverage of Insuring Agreement (B). The Fourth Circuit reversed, holding that because the loss resulted from non-payment of the purchased accounts, the loan exclusion applied. *United Va. Factors Corp. v. Aetna Cas. & Sur. Co.,* 624 F.2d 814, 815-18.

5th Cir. 1976 (La.). Insured bank advanced funds to its customer against an uncollected sight draft and expected to charge interest for the funds advanced between the time of crediting the account of its customer and collecting the proceeds of the sight draft. When the sight draft was dishonored, the bank claimed coverage for theft. The court found the transaction to be a "de facto loan," subject to the loan exclusion. The court observed that a note is not a prerequisite for a loan transaction and that the issue of whether a transaction constitutes a loan is to be determined from the surrounding facts in each particular case. *Calcasieu-Marine Nat'l Bank v. Am. Emp'rs Ins. Co.*, 533 F.2d 290, 297-98.

5th Cir. 1973 (Tex.). Insured bank made claim under a Bankers Blanket Bond for loss suffered from loans secured by phone collateral. The Court found that the loss was subject to the loan exclusion, even though the loans were obtained under false pretenses. *Bank of the Sw. v. Nat'l Sur. Co.*, 477 F.2d 73, 76.

5th Cir. 1970 (Tex.). Insured bank claimed that the loss it suffered due to customer loan secured by worthless warehouse receipts was theft by false pretenses and not subject to the loan exclusion. The court found that customer who obtained money through an otherwise bona fide loan transaction did not procure the loan through theft, despite his subjective intent not to repay the money. The court noted that the exclusionary clause of the bond cannot be nullified by the subjective fraudulent intent of the borrower. *Md. Cas. Co. v. State Bank & Trust Co.*, 425 F.2d 979, 981-82.

6th Cir. 1971 (Ky.). Insured bank claimed a loss by false pretenses when it discovered it had paid a check which had been altered to increase the amount of the check, which, under Kentucky law, constituted a forgery. The policy contained a forgery exclusion rider. Therefore, even though false pretenses were involved, the loss was found to be excluded from coverage under the forgery rider. *Am. Nat'l Bank & Trust Co. of Bowling Green v. Hartford Acc. & Indem. Co.*, 442 F.2d 995.

7th Cir. 2009 (Ill.). Bad actor obtained money orders from insured bank in exchange for checks drawn on bad actor's account at another bank, which did not contain sufficient funds to pay the checks. The other bank eventually froze the account, and the insured bank was left with $307,000 of worthless checks. The court held that the insured bank's loss resulted directly from false pretenses. *First State Bank of Monticello v. Ohio Cas. Ins. Co.*, 555 F.3d 564, 568-70.

7th Cir. 1970 (Ill.). Insured bank claimed false pretenses loss under its Bankers Blanket Bond when it discovered it had advanced funds against forged retail installment sales contracts assigned to it as collateral. The court concluded that because the bank customer had forged the documents, the forgery exclusion precluded coverage for false pretenses. The court allowed recovery under Clause E, which provided coverage for losses based on taking forged security. *Roodhouse Nat'l Bank v. Fid. & Deposit Co. of Md.*, 426 F.2d 1347, 1349-51.

7th Cir. 1970 (Ill.). Check-kiting scheme carried on by insured bank's customer was held to be within the scope of the state's deceptive practices statute and, thus, covered under Insuring Agreement (B) of a pre-1969 Bankers Blanket Bond. *First Nat'l Bank of Decatur v. Ins. Co. of N. Am.*, 424 F.2d 312, 317.

8th Cir. 1979 (Ark.). Vendors sued purchaser and escrow agent for losses suffered when purchaser allegedly fraudulently induced escrow agent to release escrow documents. The court held that the bank employee's negligent failure to comprehend the significance of the fact that the release of originally escrowed documents was inconsistent with the escrow agreement did not preclude the loss from being an insured event because the bond covered losses sustained as result of false pretenses even if insured negligently released insured property. *Perkins v. Clinton State Bank*, 593 F.2d 327, 334-35.

8th Cir. 1954 (Mo.). Insured bank that lost money under a check kiting scheme made claim for loss due to false pretenses. The court found coverage, holding that the scheme practiced by the customer fell within the Missouri statutory definition of false pretenses and, further, that the check kiting scheme constituted a series of acts which together were a studied device tantamount to false pretenses under the ordinary meaning of the term. *Fid. & Cas. Co. v. Bank of Altenburg*, 216 F.2d 294, 302-03.

8th Cir. 1953 (Mo.). Coverage was found for loss caused by a check kiting scheme under the insured bank's false pretenses coverage. The court rejected the insurer's defense that the loss fell within the loan exclusion because the bank allowed the customer credit against uncollected checks. The court held that it was inconceivable that any disinterested banker, insurance underwriter or lawyer would construe the word "loan," as used in the loan exclusion, to cover the obligation imposed by law to reimburse a bank for money or credit obtained through the use of worthless checks. It should be noted that the policy in this case did not have an uncollected funds exclusion. *Hartford Acc. & Indem. Co. v. FDIC*, 204 F.2d 933, 936-37.

9th Cir. 2000 (Cal.). Bank customer's husband wrongfully altered a check and withdrew money from wife's account. The court found that although the husband may have committed false pretenses on the bank's premises, the bank's liability to the wife was the direct result of its breach of her contractual relationship with the bank rather than the husband's fraud. Thus, the court found no recovery. *Cal. Korea Bank v. Va. Sur. Co.,* No. 98-56778, 2000 WL 713798, at *1-2.

9th Cir. 1967 (Idaho). False pretenses coverage was established from loss to bank which cashed counterfeit sight drafts for employees of dairy company. The customary course of dealing between the dairy company and the bank constituted a representation by the company that its sight drafts would be honored upon presentment. *United Pac. Ins. Co. v. Idaho First Nat'l Bank*, 378 F.2d 62, 65-67.

10th Cir. 1975 (Okla.). Insured bank was alerted to possibility of a check kiting scheme and, in response to depositor's explanation, loaned the depositor additional sums, crediting the depositor's checking account with the loaned funds. In return, the depositor executed promissory notes to the bank secured by pledges of individual and personal assets. The depositor defaulted on the loans and the collateral proved worthless. The bank sought recovery of its losses under its blanket bankers bond. The court found that application of the loan exclusion was not altered by the fact that the depositor may have made false statements in securing the loan and pledging worthless collateral. *First Nat'l Bank & Trust Co. v. Cont'l Ins. Co.,* 510 F.2d 7, 12.

N.D. Ala. 1974. Insured bank claimed false pretenses coverage for loss of money it advanced on premises to customer based on phony sight drafts. Court found for insured holding 1969 revision of loan exclusion clause only applied to check kiting which was not part of the facts before it. Further, because money was paid on premises, the transaction fell within the exception to loan exclusion. *Shoals Nat'l Bank of Florence v. Home Indem. Co.,* 384 F. Supp. 49, 51-52, 55.

C.D. Cal. 1987. FSLIC, as assignee of insured savings and loan association, brought action against insurer for loss of securities due to the fraudulent acts of the insured's broker/dealer. The court held that federal book entry securities constituted "property" under Insuring Agreement (B) of the bond even though the securities were in the possession of the broker. Construing the phrase "lodged or deposited within offices or premises located anywhere," the court broadly construed "premises" to mean any premises, not simply premises of the insured. *FSLIC v. Transamerica Ins. Co.,* 661 F. Supp. 246, 249-50.

S.D. Ill. 1975. Insured bank that lost money on loans to customer based on false information claimed that syntax and punctuation of loan exclusion clause in an early bond form made it applicable only to coverage for offices and equipment loss and not to remainder of Clause B. The court found the exclusionary language to be unambiguous, and the only reasonable construction was that losses based on loans were not covered, even though loans were obtained by false pretenses. *Cmty. Nat'l Bank in Monmouth v. St. Paul Fire & Marine Ins. Co.,* 399 F. Supp. 873, 876-78.

E.D. La. 1970. The insured bank made a claim for loss as a result of a classic check kiting scheme. Under a pre-1969 bond, the court found coverage because the insured suffered the loss of property through false pretenses when the customer presented checks for deposit on premises. The court flatly rejected the idea that monies advanced under a check kiting scheme could be interpreted as an excluded loan transaction. *Nat'l Bank of Commerce v. Fid. & Cas. Co. of N.Y.,* 312 F. Supp. 71, 74-75.

W.D. Mo. 1980. Where insured bank knew that accounts which two companies had created were being used so that checks made payable to one company were being deposited in account of another, but where the bank did not know of its customers' underlying fraudulent transfers in anticipation of one company's bankruptcy, the existence of the customers' scheme to defraud creditors did not constitute a "false pretense" practiced on the bank for purposes of its bond coverage.

Columbia Union Nat'l Bank v. Hartford Acc. & Indem. Co., 496 F. Supp. 1263, 1273.

W.D. Mo. 1969. Insured bank, which as transfer agent was sued for improper issuance of stock based upon fraudulent instructions by its customer's president, was entitled to recover under its Bankers Blanket Bond's on premises false pretenses coverage for all amounts it had paid in settlement of all resulting suits filed against it. *Merchs.-Produce Bank v. USF&G,* 305 F. Supp. 957, 961-67.

S.D. Ohio 1990. Insured bank purchased residential mortgage loans from a mortgage company based on the company's false representations that the mortgages constituted first liens on the borrowers' property. When the mortgages proved to be junior to other liens, the bank sought coverage for loss caused by the mortgage company's false pretenses. However, the court found coverage was excluded by the loan exclusion. *Liberty Sav. Bank v. Am. Cas. Co. of Reading,* 754 F. Supp. 559, 561-63.

S.D. Ohio 1954. Insured bank sustained loss due to reliance on fictitious documents presented to it by customer to obtain credit cards to his account. Court held transaction was covered loss under the larceny or false pretenses provisions of an early bond form and that the transaction was not excluded as a loan. *Nat'l Bank of Paulding v. Fid. & Cas. Co.,* 131 F. Supp. 121, 124.

E.D. Va. 1975. Under rather complex facts involving automobile sales financing, the insured bank advanced funds to its customer against sight drafts and uncollected checks. The insured claimed loss based on forgery or false pretenses when the uncollected checks were returned by the drawee bank as bearing unauthorized signatures. The court concluded that money was obtained by false pretenses and not as part of an excluded check kiting scheme. The court found that the check kiting exclusion in that bond referred only to the classic "fraud device aimed at playing deposits against the calendar." *Clarendon Bank & Trust v. Fid. & Deposit Co. of Md.,* 406 F. Supp. 1161, 1166-68.

W.D. Wis. 1983. The insured bank had a policy of allowing a particular customer immediate credit on checking account deposits. Subsequently, the bank suffered a loss when the customer fraudulently withdrew funds against worthless checks. The customer was not physically present on the bank premises when he withdrew the funds. The court held that the customer's check kiting constituted a loss of money by false pretenses, clearly covered by Insuring Clause (B), but that it was equally clear that the uncollected funds exclusion applied. Therefore, the loss was not covered. *Bradley Bank v. Hartford Acc. & Indem. Co.*, 557 F. Supp. 243, 246.

D. Utah 2012. Insured credit union made claim under bond's on premises coverage for "checks deposited with improper endorsement, losses from the fraudulent invoices and the deposits made from accounts with insufficient funds," arguing that the bond provided coverage because customer's actions took place on premises of the credit union and involved false pretenses. The court held there was no coverage under the on premises provision based on "check cashing," "uncollected funds," and "missing endorsement" exclusions. *Cyprus Fed. Credit Union v. CUMIS Ins. Soc'y, Inc.*, No. 2:10CV00550, 2012 WL 1952460, at *2-3.

Ala. 1966. A customer submitted falsified invoices to the insured bank to secure a series of loans, causing a substantial loss. The court held that there could be no recovery under the portion of the policy insuring against losses caused by false pretenses because the exclusion for loan losses applied. The insured unsuccessfully argued that under the particular wording of the bond in question, the loan loss exclusion applied only if a loan loss were caused by actual forgery. *Tiarks v. First Nat'l Bank of Mobile*, 182 So. 2d 366, 374.

Fla. Dist. Ct. App. 1985. The insured bank's customer deposited checks from various other banks into his savings account at the insured bank. These deposits were given immediate credit and were then transferred by the customer to his checking accounts at the insured bank or, in some cases, were withdrawn completely. Subsequently, the deposited checks were dishonored, and the insured bank suffered a loss. The court held that the losses were ultimately incurred as a result of an overall check kiting scheme, notwithstanding the "somewhat unique" transfer of money within one bank between a savings and checking account, and were therefore covered as losses brought about by false pretenses. *NCNB Nat'l Bank v. Aetna Cas. & Sur. Co.*, 477 So. 2d 579, 581-83.

Iowa 1986. The insured bank's customer purported to give the bank first liens on several pieces of heavy construction equipment to secure the bank's loans. When the customer defaulted, the bank learned that in several instances the customer did not own the equipment on the date of the loan or the equipment was encumbered by prior liens. The bank's claim for coverage for its resulting losses was denied by the court, which stated succinctly, "[t]he policy clearly and explicitly excludes a claim under Clause B for a loss resulting from the default on a loan even when it was procured by false pretenses." Thus, the court stated that it need not decide whether the bank's loss resulted from false pretenses. *Gateway State Bank v. N. River Ins. Co.,* 387 N.W.2d 344, 347.

Minn. 1978. Insured bank's borrower secured a loan from the insured bank with the subjective intent not to repay the loan. The court held that the borrower's subjective intent did not avoid the policy provision excluding coverage for loss resulting from nonpayment of any loan obtained from the bank, "whether procured in good faith or through trick, artifice, fraud or false pretenses." *Franklin Nat'l Bank v. St. Paul Fire & Marine Ins. Co.,* 266 N.W.2d 718, 718.

Minn. Ct. App. 1989. Insured bank brought claim for losses incurred through a customer's deposit of invalid credit card sales slips. The court denied coverage based on the loan exclusion, finding the sales slips to be evidences of debt. *Suburban Nat'l Bank v. Transam. Ins. Co.,* 438 N.W.2d 119, 121.

Mo. 1966. Bank that sustained loss when it allowed customer funds to be diverted to another's account by honoring unauthorized endorsements was entitled to recover for on premises loss caused by false pretenses. *Jefferson Bank & Trust Co. v. Cent. Sur. & Ins. Corp.,* 408 S.W.2d 825, 828-29.

N.Y. App. Div. 1968. Insured bank was allowed coverage for check kiting losses, despite the insurer's argument that the resulting overdraft was treated as a loan on certain bank records and, therefore, subject to the loan loss exclusion. The court also found that check kiting constitutes "false pretenses," notwithstanding the fact that the depositor made no representation as to the deposited checks' value. The court ruled that false pretenses exist whenever both the drawer and payee of the check know that there are insufficient funds and where they intend thereby to obtain the use of the bank's money. Also, the check kiting scheme constitutes a "larceny" by false pretenses under criminal statutes and, accordingly, is covered by the bond. It should be noted that the subject bond pre-dated the uncollected funds exclusion. *Liberty Nat'l Bank & Trust Co. v. Travelers Indem. Co.,* 295 N.Y.S.2d 983, 985-86.

N.Y. App. Div. 1964. Loss resulting when a municipal official misappropriated municipal funds on deposit with the insured bank by diverting them to other accounts he controlled was held to be covered as an on premises loss caused by larceny. *St. Lawrence Cnty. Nat'l Bank v. Am. Motorists Ins. Co.,* 544, 21 A.D.2d 702.

N.Y. App. Div. 1958. The insured bank sought coverage for losses resulting from the assignment of worthless conditional sales contracts from a car dealer. The insurer argued, unsuccessfully, that the contracts were loans and, therefore, excluded from coverage. The court found coverage, describing the contracts as a "series of larcenies." The court held that "a conditional sales agreement is not usually considered a loan," essentially because a loan would be "negotiable in form." *Johnstown Bank v. Am. Sur. Co. of N.Y.,* 6 A.D.2d 4, 6-7.

Tex. Ct. App. 1978. The insured bank negligently permitted funds to be withdrawn by a depositor for his own purposes and to the detriment of his business associate where the deposit contract provided that the funds could not be withdrawn unless the depositor's business associate also signed-off on the withdrawal. The bank settled the negligence and breach of contract suit brought against it by the business associate and then sought recovery of its loss under the "on premises" coverage of its blanket bond. The court found no such coverage because there had been no allegation that property had been removed from the premises by false pretenses. The court rejected the argument that the "crux" of this claim was the theft by the depositor of his associate's funds from the insured bank's premises. *White Rock Nat'l Bank of Dallas v. U.S. Fire Ins. Co.,* 562 S.W.2d 268, 272-74.

Ver. 1967. A regular customer of the insured bank cashed a relatively small check at the insured bank drawn on the customer's account at another bank, then issued a stop-payment order on the check and filed a petition in bankruptcy. The insured bank sued for coverage for loss caused by false pretenses. A directed verdict for the insured bank was reversed, and the case was sent back for further proceedings to determine whether the customer had the requisite fraudulent intent under Vermont law at the time he cashed the check. *Lyndonville Sav. Bank & Trust Co. v. Peerless Ins. Co.,* 234 A.2d 340, 343.

Wis. 1973. Insured bank's borrower persuaded the bank to return to him securities held as collateral on a loan, promising to provide insured with replacement securities which were never provided. The court denied coverage based on the loan exclusion, finding that while there may have been false representations vis-à-vis the securities, it was the failure to repay the loan that caused the loss. *Racine Cnty. Nat'l Bank v. Aetna Cas. & Sur. Co.,* 203 N.W.2d 145, 148-49.

C. Misplacement Mysterious Unexplainable Disappearance

6th Cir. 1990 (Ohio). Insured bank filed action against its insurer to recover for lost securities that were being held for the insured at a trust company. Because the securities merely secured repurchase agreements, the insured did not own them. Nevertheless, the lost securities were held to be the insured's property for purposes of this insuring agreement. The court, however, remanded for further consideration of the applicability of the loan exclusion. *First Fed. Sav. & Loan Ass'n of Toledo v. Fid. & Deposit Co. of Md.,* 895 F.2d 254, 258-60.

7th Cir. 1994 (Ill.). RTC sued to recover losses sustained in repurchase transactions for which the underlying securities were missing. The RTC argued that the securities dealer "misplaced" the securities because it deliberately put the securities in the wrong place when it improperly moved them from safekeeping accounts into clearing accounts. The court held that the loan loss exclusion applied and, therefore, did not address whether the losses would fall within the language of Insuring Agreement (B). *RTC v. Aetna Cas. & Sur. Co.,* 25 F.3d 570, 577-78.

7th Cir. 1970 (Ill.). Insured bank claimed loss through misplacement for money inadvertently placed by a teller in a metal locker and stolen while being transported by a moving company to new banking premises. The court found that the loss occurred because of the misplacement of the money regardless of the subsequent theft off the premises by one of the moving company's employees. *Bremen State Bank v. Hartford Acc. & Indem. Co.,* 427 F.2d 425, 427-28.

M.D. La. 1975. Insured bank improperly credited corporate account with another customer's funds, which the corporate president promptly withdrew and then absconded. After reimbursing the other customer, the insured made claim for loss due to misplacement. The court found coverage, despite the insurer's argument that the loss was caused by the president's wrongful withdrawal off premises. The deposit receipt was held to be evidence of debt owed to the depositor. Therefore, the mistaken credit was a covered misplacement of property. *Aetna Cas. & Sur. Co. v. La. Nat'l Bank,* 399 F. Supp. 54, 56-57.

S.D.N.Y. 1984. Insured credit union sought to recover losses sustained when the bank that issued certificates of deposit to credit union failed. Coverage was denied because the insured could not show that the money on deposit with the failed bank was property owned by the credit union. Further, the credit union's investment in the bank's certificates of deposit was in the nature of a loan. Therefore, the loss was excluded from coverage by the loan exclusion. *IBM Poughkeepsie Emps. Fed. Credit Union v. Cumis Ins. Soc'y, Inc.,* 590 F. Supp. 769, 775-77.

Ind. Ct. App. 2003. Mortgage company sought coverage for loss sustained when title company deposited mortgage company's check into the wrong account. The court agreed that the funds might have been misplaced, but not while the property was "lodged or deposited within... offices of any financial institution" as required under the specific language of the insured's policy. The loss, therefore, was not covered. *Utica Mut. Ins. Co. v. Precedent Cos.,* 782 N.E.2d 470, 475-76.

Mo. Ct. App. 1975. Savings and loan association sought recovery for funds the association negligently paid in violation of certain court-ordered restrictions on an account. The court concluded that the bond did not cover a loss due to negligence involving normal banking operations. Further, a voluntary payment made by the association did not constitute a "loss" of property. *Hamiltonian Fed. Sav. & Loan Ass'n v. Reliance Ins. Co.,* 527 S.W.2d 440, 442-45.

N.Y. 1927. Insured bank made claim for funds improperly paid to customer due to temporary misplacement of a subscription warrant entitling customer to subscribe to convertible debenture bonds. The court held the bond covered loss of specified property caused by permanent misplacement of that property, but not, as in this case, loss of funds caused by the temporary misplacement of the warrant. *Mfr. Nat'l Bank of Troy v. USF&G,* 156 N.E. 94, 94-96.

N.Y. App. Div. 1967. Insured savings and loan wrongfully surrendered customer's account proceeds to an execution creditor because the "red flag" file jacket on the customer's file which would have provided notice that the account was assigned was missing. The insured sought coverage, claiming its loss was caused by mysterious disappearance of the notice of assignment. The court found that misplacement or mysterious disappearance of the notice of assignment was not a loss of covered property. Because the notice of assignment was later found, it was never really lost, and the bond does not cover consequences of temporarily mislaying property. *Metro. Sav. & Loan Ass'n v. Hanover Ins. Co.,* 286 N.Y.S.2d 129, 131-35.

N.Y. App. Div. 1931. Insured bank delivered stock certificate to wrong person and, after making its error good to the rightful owner, claimed under blanket bond for loss due to misplacement. Court held insured knew where certificates were, even though they were out of insured's possession. Also, the loss resulted through employee mistake, which was excluded. *N.Y. Trust Co. v. Royal Indem. Co.,* 233 A.D. 408, 410-11.

D. Customer Losses

Mo. 1964. Under a specific Bankers Blanket Bond provision that gave the insured the option to include customer losses on insured's proof of loss, court held insurer liable for customer money (loan proceeds) stolen in parking lot, finding the customer to be a third-party beneficiary of the bond. *Brugioni v. Md. Cas. Co.,* 382 S.W.2d 707, 710-13.

E. "On Premises" Requirement

3d Cir. 1993 (N.J.). Savings and loan association sued to recover losses resulting from wire transfers induced by fraudulent telephone-call scheme could not prove that the persons making the telephone calls were physically present in its offices or on its premises. The district court used a finding of "constructive presence" to find coverage under the bond. Reversing the district court holding, the court of appeals found that the word "present" in subsection (b)(i) was unambiguous, thereby denying coverage to the bank. *Oritani Sav. & Loan Ass'n v. Fid. & Deposit Co. of Md.,* 989 F.2d 635, 638-43.

4th Cir. 1989 (N.C.). Insured bank sought to recover for losses suffered when it was fraudulently induced by telephone to wire funds directly into securities broker's account in New York. The court of appeals held that the bond did not cover the bank's loss because the securities broker was never physically in the same location in which the bank's money was deposited when he made the misrepresentations that prompted the bank to wire the money to New York. The crucial factor in determining whether the on premises requirement has been satisfied is not the defrauder's location when criminal liability attaches, but rather his location when he engages in misrepresentations. *S. Nat'l Bank of N.C. v. United Pac. Ins. Co.,* 864 F.2d 332-33.

5th Cir. 1996 (Miss.). A wrongdoer stole and forged law firm trust account checks, most of which he then used to launch a check kite. However, the depositor negotiated a few of the forged checks at the insured bank where the law firm maintained its trust account. Because the checks were negotiated on the premises of the insured bank, the loss was covered by the on premises insuring agreement. Because the firm's trust account legitimately had sufficient funds on deposit at the time customer negotiated and cashed the forged checks, the loss from these particular checks did not fall within the uncollected funds exclusion. *USF&G v. Planters Bank & Trust Co.,* 77 F.3d 863, 868.

5th Cir. 1973 (Ga.). Insured bank made a Bankers Blanket Bond claim for a loss resulting when its president paid the bank's money to an extortionist who was holding the president's family captive off the insured bank's premises. The court found that even though the extortionist did not have actual possession of the funds until the funds had been paid to him at a location off the bank's premises, the bank's loss occurred while the money was on the bank's premises, because the bank had no control over the funds once the president began collecting them from the bank's premises. *Bank of Dade v. Fid. & Deposit Co. of Md.*, 483 F.2d 735, 737.

7th Cir. 2013 (Wis.). Employee of third-party defrauded the third-party by telephonic transactions in which she purchased cashier's checks from insured bank with third-party's funds and named her personal creditors as payees. The court found that the employee caused an actual loss to the third-party when bank personnel complied with her request and issued a cashier's check, not when her couriers obtained possession of the cashier's checks. No larceny was committed on premises because the employee did not set foot in the insured bank. *Bankmanagers Corp. v. Fed. Ins. Co.*, 712 F.3d 1163, 1163.

7th Cir. 2009 (Ill.). Bad actor went on the premises of the insured bank and obtained money orders in exchange for checks drawn on bad actor's account at another bank, which did not contain sufficient funds to pay the checks. The other bank eventually froze the account, and the insured bank was left with $307,000 of worthless checks. The court held that there was coverage under the bond because the insured bank's loss resulted directly from the bad actors on premises false pretenses. *First State Bank of Monticello v. Ohio Cas. Ins. Co.*, 555 F.3d 564, 568-70.

7th Cir. 1991 (Ill.). Insured bank's dishonest customer deposited misappropriated checks drawn to the order of his employer into his own account and then withdrew the cleared funds. The bank sought coverage for its liability to the wronged employer under Insuring Agreement (B). The court found no coverage because the customer was not physically present in the bank at the time he withdrew the stolen funds. Further, any withdrawals made while physically present did not exceed the $10,000 deductible. *Alpine State Bank v. Ohio Cas. Ins. Co.*, 941 F.2d 554, 560-61.

9th Cir. 1989 (Wash.). The court ruled that the mere depositing of a subsequently dishonored check by a customer who is on bank premises at the time of the deposit does not satisfy the on premises requirement of this insuring agreement. Therefore, unless the bank's customer receives payment on the deposited check while at the bank, a loss resulting from the check subsequently being dishonored is subject to the uncollected funds exclusion. *Am. Sav. Bank, F.S.B. v. Hartford Acc. & Indem. Co.,* No. 88-3512, 1989 WL 76912, at *1-2.

9th Cir. 1986 (Cal.). Depositary bank suffered losses from deposits that were credited to a customer's account, but were not collected because the endorsements on the deposited checks were forged. The bank argued that when its operations officer initialed the deposit slip and allowed immediate credit against the checks, a constructive payment or withdrawal actually occurred on premises. The appellate court denied coverage, finding no actual payment or withdrawal occurred at the time the operations officer initialed the deposit slip. *Mitsui Mfrs. Bank v. Fed. Ins. Co.,* 795 F.2d 827, 831-32.

N.D. Cal. 1986. Insured bank sought to recover losses sustained when credit card sales drafts proved uncollectable due to a massive credit card fraud scheme. Coverage was denied because depositor was not physically present in the bank when actual payment was made on checks drawn against the account, despite the bank's argument that its agreement to allow withdrawals constituted "constructive payment," thereby satisfying the on premises requirement. *Bay Area Bank v. Fid. & Deposit Co. of Md.,* 629 F. Supp. 693, 696-97.

E.D. La. 1970. Where insured bank made claim under a pre-1969 bond for loss as a result of a classic check kiting scheme, the court found coverage because the insured suffered the loss of property through false pretenses when the customer presented checks for deposit on premises. The court reasoned that when the bank's customer mailed a deposit to the bank, he intended the bank to believe the check was good, and the act of depositing the check in the bank constituted a false representation there. *Nat'l Bank of Commerce v. Fid. & Cas. Co. of N.Y.,* 312 F. Supp. 71, 76.

W.D. Wis. 1983. The court held that the customer's check kiting constituted a loss of money by false pretenses, clearly covered by Insuring Agreement (B), but that it was equally clear that the uncollected funds exclusion applied. Accordingly, the issue on cross-motions for summary judgment was whether or not the "within the office" exception to the uncollected funds exclusion for false pretenses coverage would apply. It was held that the "within the office" exception was not ambiguous and required the physical or constructive presence of the customer in the office at the time of the withdrawal. Therefore the loss was not covered. *Bradley Bank v. Hartford Acc. & Indem. Co.,* 557 F. Supp. 243, 246-48.

D. Wyo. 1974. Money stolen when a customer's money bag became lodged in the insured bank's night depository chute rather than passing into bank's vault was held to be covered as larceny of customer property which is (or ought to be) deposited on the insured bank's premises, whether or not the insured is liable to its customer for the loss. *W. Nat'l Bank of Casper v. Hawkeye-Sec. Ins. Co.,* 380 F. Supp. 508, 511-512.

Minn. 1975. In an unusual fact situation involving insured airline, in response to demands by plane hijacker, insured airline obtained money from bank and delivered it to a stewardess who brought it aboard the hijacked plane. Denying the insurer's contention that the wrongful taking did not occur 'within the premises' as defined in the policy, the court found coverage under the blanket crime policy, noting that there was little reason for distinction between money that the insured had on hand, that it borrowed, or that it could readily borrow. The court also noted that "mere unforseeability of the manner in which the loss was sustained will not per se constitute grounds for the insurer to deny coverage." *Nw. Airlines, Inc. v. Global Indem. Co.,* 225 N.W.2d 831, 834-37.

Tex. 1976. Loss caused by officer delivering bank funds to an extortionist off premises held to be covered under Insuring Agreement (B) because once the threat of extortion is communicated to the officer, the thief effectively exerts control over the funds through the officer's decision to comply with extortionist's instructions, depriving the insured of its property. It should be noted that this bond did not have an extortion exclusion. *U.S. Fire Ins. Co. v. First State Bank of El Paso,* 538 S.W.2d 209, 211-12.

F. Direct Loss

7th Cir. 2009 (Ill.). Bad actor presented worthless checks at insured bank in exchange for money orders drawn on the insured bank. By providing money orders, the insured disbursed immediately available funds to the bad actor, and the checks given to the insured as payment for the money orders were returned unpaid. The court found that the bad actor's on premises fraud was the actual and direct cause of the bank's loss, and that the slight gap in time between the money-order transactions and the non-payment of the checks made no difference. *First State Bank of Monticello v. Ohio Cas. Ins.*, 555 F.3d 564, 571.

7th Cir. 2005 (Ill.). The insured bank argued that it was the fraudulent deposit made on bank premises, not the subsequent telephonic withdrawal called in from off bank premises, that "directly caused" the bank's loss. The court of appeals rejected this contention, and denied the insured's argument that its losses were covered provided "the 'principal' fraudulent acts or 'most' of the fraudulent scheme occurs on the bank's premises." Accordingly, the court upheld summary judgment for the insurer. *Private Bank & Trust Co. v. Progressive Cas. Ins. Co.*, 409 F.3d 814, 815-18.

Del. Ch. 2010. The insured life insurance company and its affiliates invested over $3 billion with Bernard Madoff, and sought coverage for the cost to defend and any liability in underlying suits by investors whose money was lost. The insurers moved to dismiss, arguing that any such losses could not result directly from a covered cause. The court rejected the insurer's categorical position that a third party claim can never be a direct loss and denied the motion to dismiss. *Mass. Mut. Life Ins. Co. v. Certain Underwriters at Lloyd's of London*, No. 4791-VCL, 2010 WL 2929552, at *15.

Kan. Ct. App. 2007. Customer of insured bank deposited checks drawn on account of family trust of which he was a trustee into his personal and business accounts at insured bank and used the funds for his own purposes. The trust's attorney sued the insured bank, and the bank sued its insurer. The court held that this was not a loss resulting directly from theft on the bank's premises. Rather, the loss was caused by the failure of the bank's employees to follow ordinary standards of banking practice. *Citizens Bank, N.A. v. Kan. Bankers Sur. Co.*, 149 P.3d 25, 2007 WL 45946, at *2-5.

SECONDARY SOURCES

Samuel J. Arena, Jr. & David M. Burkholder, *Insuring Agreement (B)— On Premises*, in FINANCIAL INSTITUTION BONDS (Duncan L. Clore ed., 3d ed., 2008).

James F. Crowder & Patricia H. Thompson, *What is "On Premises" Under Clause B of the Bankers Blanket Bond In 1976?*, 11 FORUM 1185 (1976).

James A. Knox, *The Outer Limits of the Extension of Clause (B) Coverage of Bankers Blanket Bonds*, 2 FORUM 238 (1967).

Edgar L. Neel, *Financial Institution and Fidelity Coverage for Loan Losses*, 21 TORT & INS. L.J. 590 (1986).

Hugh M. Palmer, *Is There a Mystery to Mysterious, Unexplainable Disappearance Coverage?*, 16 FORUM 988 (1981).

SECTION 3 — INSURING AGREEMENT (C)—IN TRANSIT*

(C) Loss of Property resulting directly from robbery, common-law or statutory larceny, theft, misplacement, mysterious unexplainable disappearance, being lost or made away with, and damage thereto or destruction thereof, while the Property is in transit anywhere in the custody of
- (a) a natural person acting as a messenger of the Insured (or another natural person acting as messenger or custodian during an emergency arising from the incapacity of the original messenger), or
- (b) a Transportation Company and being transported in an armored motor vehicle, or
- (c) a Transportation Company and being transported in a conveyance other than an armored motor vehicle provided that covered Property transported in such manner is limited to the following:
  - (i) records, whether recorded in writing or electronically, and
  - (ii) Certificated Securities issued in registered form and not endorsed, or with restrictive endorsements, and
  - (iii) Negotiable Instruments not payable to bearer, or not endorsed, or with restrictive endorsements.

Coverage under this Insuring Agreement begins immediately upon the receipt of such Property by the natural person or Transportation Company and ends immediately upon delivery to the designated recipient or its agent.

COMMENT

Published cases interpreting and applying this coverage are relatively rare. However, the ubiquitous nature of both ATMs and payroll tax

---

* By Brian M. Falcon, Frost Brown Todd LLC, Indianapolis, Indiana.

services—and the need to keep both flush with money—has provided fertile ground for increased litigation in recent years.

The primary purpose of this insuring agreement is to protect the insured against loss of property during gaps in transportation and specifically while its property is being transported from the insured bank to a designated destination. The substantive terms of coverage under this agreement have not changed since its revision in 1986. The current version provides for coverage in one of three situations: (1) loss while the property is in the custody of a messenger; (2) loss while the property is in the custody of a Transportation Company *and* being transported in an armored motor vehicle; and (3) loss for certain types of property (including records, Certificated Securities and specified Negotiable Instruments not in readily transferable form) in the custody of a Transportation Company *and* being transported in something other than an armored motor vehicle.

Pursuant to the final sentence of this agreement, coverage is afforded for a very discreet and definite period of time. It is not triggered until the messenger or Transportation Company receives the property. It terminates immediately upon delivery by the messenger or Transportation Company to the insured's designated recipient. Accordingly, the most frequently litigated issue under this section of the Financial Institution Bond has been whether the lost property was truly in the hands of a "messenger," versus the insured's authorized representative.

For purposes of coverage under this insuring agreement, a "Transportation Company" is defined by Section 1(s) as "any organization which provides its own or leased vehicles for transportation or which provides freight forwarding or air express services." "Certificated Securities" are defined by Section 1(d) to include "share[s]" of "a type commonly dealt in on securities exchanges or markets." "Negotiable Instruments" are defined by Section 1(o) to include "any writing signed by the maker... containing any unconditional promise or order to pay a sum certain in Money... payable on demand or at a definite time... and payable to order or bearer."

Based on this insuring agreement's plain language and purpose, the standard exclusion under Section 2(r)(2), precluding coverage for loss of property while in the custody of a Transportation Company, does not bar coverage under Insuring Agreement (C). However, the exclusion under Section 2(r)(1) for the loss of Property in the mail remains applicable.

Finally, under Section 9 of the Financial Institution Bond, coverage under this section applies only as excess over any valid and collectible insurance or indemnity obtained by the insured, the Transportation Company having custody over the property, or by another entity on whose premises the loss occurred or which employed the person causing the loss or the messenger who conveyed the property at issue. The insurer and its counsel should always exercise due care to identify the existence of any such primary coverage.

OUTLINE OF ANNOTATIONS

A. Property in the Custody of a Messenger
B. Property in the Custody of a Transportation Company
C. "In Transit" Defined
D. "Negotiable Instruments" Defined
E. Exclusions for Loss Caused by Dishonest Acts of Authorized Representatives
F. Miscellaneous Exclusions

ANNOTATIONS:

A. Property in the Custody of a Messenger

5th Cir. 1973 (Tex.). Insured bank made loan in part on stocks that borrower converted for his own use. In holding that Bankers Blanket Bond (1969 version) In Transit coverage did not cover loss, court noted that there were no facts to support claim that stocks were in transit to banks when converted by borrower. If there had been such evidence, borrower would have been acting on his own behalf and not as messenger within meaning of Bond clause. *Bank of the Sw. v. Nat'l Sur. Co.*, 477 F.2d 73, 76.

10th Cir. 1976 (Col.). The court held that Insuring Agreement (C) (1969 version of Bankers Blanket Bond, modified) covered a cash letter that was taken by force from the insured bank's messenger. Purpose of coverage is to cover gaps in transportation of property—intervals when property is not in possession of carrier or in mail, as in this case. "Delivery at destination" means inside the bank's premises. "Messenger" need not be an employee or partner of insured and can even be, as in this case, employee of another bank acting for insured in completing delivery. *United Bank of Pueblo v. Hartford Acc. & Indem. Co.,* 529 F.2d 490, 494-95.

Ind. Ct. App. 2003. Insured mortgage lender issued a check payable to the title company that was to conduct the closing on a residential real estate purchase. The loan did not close and was never funded. Instead of destroying the check or returning it to the lender, the title company deposited the check and ceased operations, essentially converting the funds. The lender made a claim on its Financial Institution Bond. The insurer denied the claim. The court found that In Transit coverage was not applicable because the check, payable to the title company, was not misplaced in transit from the lender to the title company. The court also found that the title company was a corporation, not a natural person acting as a messenger on the lender's behalf to deliver the check to the borrowers. *Utica Mut. Ins. Co. v. Precedent Cos.*, 782 N.E.2d 470, 476-77.

N.Y. App. Div. 1977. Under a Public Employees Honesty Blanket Bond and a Comprehensive Dishonesty, Disappearance and Destruction Policy, school district made a claim for a shortage in a teacher-employee's student activity fund account. The teacher claimed $6,500 of the fund was stolen from his car while parked by a tavern. Reversing a finding for the insured school district, the court found that the social activities of the teacher at the time of the theft were not related to nor incidental to the conveyance of the funds and, therefore, they were not "being conveyed by a messenger," as required for coverage. *Cent. Sch. Dist. v. Ins. Co. of N. Am.*, 391 N.Y.S.2d 492, 495 *aff'd,* 374 N.E.2d 393 (N.Y. 1978).

B. Property in the Custody of a Transportation Company

C.D. Cal. 2007. A bank that supplied "vault cash" to ATMs sought coverage under its Financial Institution Bond after discovering that the armored car company that serviced and transported the money to and from the ATMs had stolen approximately $50 million. The armored car company sorted the money at its local office for distribution to ATMs and, where appropriate, for return of residual funds to bank. The armored car company failed to deposit all of the residual funds with the bank. The court granted summary judgment for the insurer, holding that the property was not "in transit" because it was converted at the armored car company's local office, not while it was being transported. Although the money still had to be conveyed to the bank, the concept of "transit" had been broken by the stop at the armored car company's office. *Palm Desert Nat'l. Bank v. Fed. Ins. Co.*, 473 F. Supp. 2d 1044, 1051, *aff'd*, 300 F. App'x. 554 (9th Cir. 2008).

C. "In Transit" Defined

2d Cir. 1967 (N.Y.). The insured was engaged in the sale of securities. The insured's messenger delivered the stock certificates to one of the insured's customers and picked up and delivered to the insured's bank uncertified checks for the purchase of the certificates. When a stop payment was placed on the checks and the funds were deemed uncollectible, the insured sought coverage under its Brokers Blanket Bond. The insured argued that, until the checks were validly paid for, the certificates and checks were still "in transit." The district court disagreed and determined that there was no coverage. The district court held that "in transit" is not ambiguous, and its plain, ordinary, and popular sense means only the transportation of certificates by a messenger to and including the physical delivery to the customer. The Second Circuit affirmed the district court's ruling, finding that the bond's "in transit" provision is primarily concerned with any perils that might thwart delivery. In this case, all of the securities had been delivered to the customer and the checks issued in payment for the securities had been delivered to the insured's bank. Nothing was lost from the moment of receipt by the insured's messenger until the delivery to the intended destination. Because all securities and funds had been delivered, the property was no longer "in transit." *Sutro Bros. & Co. v. Indem. Ins. Co. of N. Am.*, 386 F.2d 798, 801.

Minn. Ct. App. 2000. The insured wired funds to its mortgage loan originator, which diverted over $5 million that should have been forwarded to banks. The insured made a claim under the transit coverage provision of its Mortgage Bankers Bond, claiming that the wired funds constituted property in transit and that its originator was acting as a messenger. The court found that the insured should have paid the money directly to the banks as requested by the bailee letters and held that the insured's reliance on the originator to allocate the money appropriately did not transform the originator into a "messenger." At the time of misappropriation, the funds were not property in transit in the custody of a person acting as messenger; therefore, the loss was not covered. *KMC Mgmt. Corp. v. Certain Underwriters*, No. C7-00-1148, 2000 WL 1742096, at *2.

Tenn. Ct. App. 2000. Insured sought coverage for loss of cargo while stored within insured's truck and trailer, which were driven by the insured's employee. After leaving a trade show, the employee disconnected the trailer and parked it at the insured's location. While parked, the trailer and the cargo were stolen. The court held that the insured's lawsuit was properly dismissed because the property was not "in transit" when stolen. At the time of the theft, the cargo was not in the process of being shipped and the trailer was not merely parked overnight in the course of a delivery. It had been left on the insured's lot for a week and was therefore not "in transit." *Williams v. Berube & Assocs.*, 26 S.W.3d 640, 644.

D. "Negotiable Instruments" Defined

D. Kan. 1987. Insured bank made claim under a Bankers Blanket Bond (1980 version) for the loss of treasury receipts. The treasury receipts were restrictively endorsed to the insured bank. The court held that the term "negotiable instrument" in Exclusion (s) was to be defined by reference to the definitional section of the bond. Applying this definition to the facts, the court found that the treasury receipts were not negotiable instruments, and thus coverage for the loss of the treasury receipts under Insuring Agreement (C) was not excluded under Exclusion (s). *Kan. State Bank & Trust v. Emery Air Freight*, 656 F. Supp. 200, 204.

E. Exclusions for Loss Caused by Dishonest Acts of Authorized Representatives

1st Cir. 1998 (Mass.). The insured's payroll tax service provider wrongfully diverted money earmarked for the insured's payroll taxes by (1) lifting payroll tax checks out of mailboxes while they were being conveyed to the taxing authorities, and (2) abstracting funds sent by the insured to cover payroll taxes by means of computer from the banking premises. The district court found these losses to be covered under both the "premises" and "transit" clauses of the insured's Crime Insurance Policy. However, the First Circuit reversed the ruling, holding that the policy's "authorized representative" exclusion barred coverage. The "authorized representative" exclusion could be applied to either a person or a company empowered to act on an entity's behalf. The court rejected the insured's argument that executives acting on behalf of an authorized representative—but for their own benefit—should not qualify. In fact, the court noted that the authorized representative can only act through its officers and employees. Therefore, who actually benefitted from the misappropriation—the authorized representative or its executives—was irrelevant. *Stop & Shop Cos. v. Fed. Ins. Co.*, 136 F.3d 71, 76-77.

9th Cir. 1999 (Cal.). Officers and employees of a payroll tax service embezzled funds from the insured corporation by removing checks that were to be sent to the proper taxing authority from the mailing system and electronically transferring funds from the checks to other company accounts. The insured brought suit for the losses under its Crime Insurance Policy's "premises" and "in transit" provisions. The court held that the insured was barred from recovering for the losses because the policies excluded coverage for losses caused by dishonest acts committed by the insured's "authorized representative." The payroll tax service was authorized to possess and disburse the insured's funds on the premises and in transit, rendering it the insured's "authorized representative." *Stanford Univ. Hosp. v. Fed. Ins. Co.*, 174 F.3d 1077, 1083-84.

F. Miscellaneous Exclusions

N.Y. App. Div. 1996. The court reversed the trial court's determination that the bond's "uncollected funds" exclusion barred recovery under the "in transit" coverage part. The property was lost when the insured's messenger was robbed. The trial court relied upon the "uncollected funds" exclusion, which excluded losses from payments made to, or withdrawals from, a depositor's account involving items of deposit not finally paid for any reason. The court held that the exclusion explicitly addressed losses due only to uncollected funds and that the "in transit" coverage was equally explicit in its coverage of losses to property that was lost or destroyed while in transit. The two provisions were deemed mutually exclusive and the "in transit" bond coverage was the only provision that applied to the loss. *Flushing Sav. Bank v. Hartford Fire Ins. Co.,* 650 N.Y.S.2d 727, 728.

SECONDARY SOURCES

Peter I. Broeman, *An Overview of the Financial Institution Bond, Standard Form No. 24*, 110 BANKING L.J. 439 (1993).

Leo J. Fogary & Linda A. Klein, *Handling Fidelity Bond Litigation*, 47 AM. JUR. TRIALS 411 (2013) (originally published in 1993).

Edward G. Gallagher et al., *Riders SR 6145b, SR 5976c and SR 6110e to Standard Form No. 24 (rev'd Jan. 1986)*, COMPLETE GUIDE TO THE ERISA BONDING REQUIREMENT, App. C (1994).

Mark A. Gamin, Armen Shahinian & Andrew S. Kent, *The Subtleties of Insuring Agreement (C) of the Financial Institution Bond*, IX FID. L.J. 115 (2003).

EGON GUTTMAN, 28A MODERN SECURITIES TRANSFERS APPENDIX B (4th ed. 2012).

Peter C. Haley, *The Power of Defined Terms and Causation Theories Under Insuring Agreement (E) of the Financial Institution Bond*, 31 TORT & INS. L.J. 609 (1996).

Toni Scott Reed, *Bond Claims and the Impact of the Uniform Electronic Transactions Act, the Uniform Computer Information Transactions Act, and Other Technological Developments*, 36 TORT & INS. L.J 735 (2001).

J. Kelly Reyher, *A Brief Review of the Financial Institution Bond Standard Form No. 24 and Commercial Crime Policy*, Practicing Law Institute, Litigation and Administrative Practice Course Handbook Series Litigation (1997).

SECTION 4 — INSURING AGREEMENT (D)—FORGERY OR ALTERATION*

(D) Loss resulting directly from
 (1) Forgery or alteration of, on or in any Negotiable Instrument (except an Evidence of Debt), Acceptance, Withdrawal Order, receipt for the withdrawal of Property, Certificate of Deposit or Letter of Credit;
 (2) transferring, paying or delivering any funds or Property or establishing any credit or giving any value on the faith of any written instructions or advices directed to the Insured and authorizing or acknowledging the transfer, payment, delivery or receipt of funds or property, which instructions or advices purport to have been signed or endorsed by any customer of the Insured or by any banking institution but which instructions or advices either bear a signature which is a Forgery or have been altered without the knowledge and consent of such customer or banking institution. Telegraphic, cable or teletype instructions or advices, as aforesaid, exclusive of transmissions of electronic funds transfer systems, sent by a person other than the said customer or banking institution purporting to send such instructions or advices shall be deemed to bear a signature which is a Forgery.
 A mechanically reproduced facsimile signature is treated the same as a handwritten signature.

(1986 version)

(D) Loss resulting directly from the Insured having, in good faith, paid or transferred any Property in reliance on any Written, Original:

---

[*] By Michele L. Fenice, ACE North American Professional Risk Claims, New York, New York. Adam P. Friedman, Wolff & Samson PC, West Orange, New Jersey.

SECTION 4 — INSURING AGREEMENT (D)—FORGERY OR ALTERATION

(1) Negotiable Instrument (except an Evidence of Debt),
(2) Certificate of Deposit,
(3) Letter of Credit,
(4) Withdrawal Order,
(5) receipt for the withdrawal of Property, or
(6) instruction or advice directed to the Insured and purportedly signed by a customer of the Insured or by a banking institution

which (a) bears a handwritten signature which is a Forgery; or (b) is altered, but only to the extent the Forgery or alteration causes the loss.

Actual physical possession of the items listed in (1) through (6) above by the Insured is a condition precedent to the Insured's having relied on the items.

A reproduction of a handwritten signature is treated the same as the handwritten signature. An electronic or digital signature is not treated as a reproduction of a handwritten signature.

(2004/2011 version)

COMMENT

Insuring Agreement (D) is one of the more litigated insuring agreements in the Financial Institution Bond. Its thrust is coverage for losses resulting directly from the forgery or alteration of negotiable instruments (primarily checks, but not an Evidence of Debt) and the like—documents that readily can be turned into cash.

Form 24 has been the subject of various revisions, including in 1980, 1986, 2004, and 2011. The 2004 revision updated Insuring Agreement (D) in an attempt to better conform it to modern banking practices. In particular, the 2004 revision removed references to "[t]elegraphic, cable or teletype instructions or advices." It also clarified that a covered forgery be of a "handwritten signature" and that an "electronic or digital signature" does not qualify for coverage, and added the requirement of "actual physical possession" of the original document. Quoted above are both the 1986 and 2004/2011 versions of Insuring Agreement (D). The

1986 version remains popular and most of the cases cited below involve the 1986 version. The 2011 revision did not alter Insuring Agreement (D) from the 2004 revision.

The 1980 revision of the Financial Institution Bond added "forgery" as a defined term. Cases litigating whether an act constitutes a "forgery" may not be as prevalent today as they were prior to the addition of the defined term, but the issue of whether a document does or does not contain a forgery remains fertile ground for litigation.

Another common topic in today's litigation of Insuring Agreement (D) is whether a loss results "directly" from a covered risk. Courts have adopted two primary standards to determine "direct loss": the "direct means direct" standard, which is the intended meaning of the insuring agreement, and the "proximate cause" standard, which inappropriately brings tort concepts into the contractual milieu of the insuring agreement. While the trend seems to be in favor of the "direct means direct" standard, the "proximate cause" standard retains vitality in a minority of jurisdictions. As reflected below, the "proximate cause" standard allows some courts to take an overly broad view of "direct" causation.

Because they both provide similar, but not overlapping, coverages, cases involving Insuring Agreement (E) address many of the same issues and principles as those involved in cases under Insuring Agreement (D). In fact, cases involving Insuring Agreement (E) may provide much of the case law addressing these issues, as Insuring Agreement (E), by its nature, may be more subject to litigation. In addition, the "actual physical possession" requirement now found in Insuring Agreement (D), as a result of the 2004 revision, has been in Insuring Agreement (E) for much longer. While research did not locate any reported decisions addressing "actual physical possession" under Insuring Agreement (D), this requirement has been well-litigated in connection with Insuring Agreement (E). Consequently, a practitioner must consider decisions addressing Insuring Agreement (E) when evaluating many claims under Insuring Agreement (D).

Similarly, many claims for coverage under Insuring Agreement (D) turn on the application of an exclusion. These exclusions are addressed separately in this book, and the practitioner should consult those chapters as well.

OUTLINE OF ANNOTATIONS

A. Forgery
B. Alteration
C. Loss "Resulting Directly" From a Covered Risk
D. Negotiable Instrument
E. Written Instructions and Advices
F. Other Covered Documents
G. The "on the Faith of" Requirement

ANNOTATIONS

A. Forgery

2d Cir. 1978 (N.Y.). The insured bank brought an action under a Brokers Blanket Bond for losses stemming from its president's issuance of a series of cashier's checks, which he drew and signed without authority as part of a scheme to embezzle money from the insured. The court reversed judgment for the insurer, holding that while at one time the unauthorized but otherwise genuine signature of a corporate officer would not have constituted a forgery under New York law, "recent developments" under New York law supported the argument that such a signature might constitute a forgery. The court held that the term "forgery" as undefined in the bond was ambiguous and accordingly construed it against the insurer. *Filor, Bullard & Smyth, Inc. v. Ins. Co. of N. Am.*, 605 F.2d 598, 603-04.

2d Cir. 1939 (N.Y.). The insured's employee presented fraudulent payment vouchers to the insured. In reliance on the vouchers, the insured issued checks, signed by both the employee and a co-drawer, both of whose endorsements were genuine. The employee then endorsed his own name on the checks and converted the proceeds for his personal use, thereby causing the insured a loss. The court first held that the fraudulent vouchers were not "written instructions or advices" because they did not direct the payment of money within the meaning of the forgery provision of a depositors or commercial forgery policy. The court also held that the insured's loss was not covered because the employee's endorsement was genuine and did not constitute a forgery. The mere fact that the employee acted outside the scope of his authority did not render his endorsement on the checks forgeries. *Fitzgibbons Boiler Co. v. Employers' Liab. Assur. Corp.,* 105 F.2d 893, 896.

3d Cir. 2004 (N.J.). The insured's customer opened a business account in the name of "TCS New Jersey." The customer deposited a check made payable to "TCS America" into that account. She endorsed the check "Deposit Only TCS" and then signed her name underneath. After she withdrew the funds by issuing a variety of checks, the TCS check eventually was dishonored and the insured was obligated to indemnify the issuing bank, by which time the insured was unable to recover the check's proceeds. The insured made a claim under, *inter alia,* Insuring Agreement (D) of its Financial Institution Bond to recover its loss, and the court upheld the insurer's rejection of this portion of the claim. Because the customer signed her own name in the endorsement, there was no "forgery" and thus no coverage under Insuring Agreement (D). *Lusitania Sav. Bank, FSB, v. Progressive Cas. Ins. Co.,* No. 04-3503, 2005 WL 1586618, at *3.

3d Cir. 1943 (Pa.). The insured loaned money to a customer secured by fraudulent warehouse receipts representing both non-existent and encumbered collateral. When the borrower defaulted, the insured sought coverage under a Bankers Blanket Bond, which provided coverage for loss through credit extensions based on "the faith of forged or altered written instructions or advices from any customers...." Finding coverage under the bond, the court held that the warehouse receipts were forgeries under Pennsylvania law because they contained false statements of fact. The court further held that the warehouse receipts constituted "written instructions or advices" because they notified the insured that the warehouse held the goods identified in the warehouse receipts. *Provident Trust Co. v. Nat'l Sur. Corp.,* 138 F.2d 252, 254.

5th Cir. 2008 (Tex.). The insured bank sought coverage under Insuring Agreement (D) for a settlement payment made to its customer. The bank allowed a principal of one of its customers to negotiate checks made out to the customer and deposit them into a personal account. The person who negotiated the checks was authorized to do so on behalf of the customer, but exceeded that authority by depositing them into his personal account. A rider expanded the definition of "forgery" under Insuring Agreement (D) to include "unauthorized endorsements," which was a defined term. The appellate court reversed summary judgment for the insured bank. With respect to Insuring Agreement (D), it held that the trial court incorrectly looked to the UCC definition of "unauthorized endorsement" when it should have used the bond's definition, and under the bond's definition, the endorsements were not "unauthorized," as the definition did not include where the endorser is authorized to endorse but misuses that authority. *Citibank Texas, N.A. v. Progressive Cas. Ins. Co.,* 522 F.3d 591, 595-96.

5th Cir. 1986 (Tex.). The insured sustained losses when its customer failed to repay loans secured by a pledge of altered CDs representing amounts far in excess of the sums actually deposited with the bank that issued the CDs. The signatures on the CDs were not forged. The insured sought coverage under Insuring Agreement (D) of its "non-standard comprehensive blanket bond," which covered forged or altered securities, but did not define forgery or limit coverage to documents "forged as to signature," as Form 24 then provided. The court held that the insured's loss resulted not from forgery or alteration of the CDs but from the misrepresentation of fact made in the CDs, a risk allocated to the insured under the loan exclusion clause of the bond. The court looked to Texas criminal law, under which one signing his own name without an intent to defraud does not commit forgery. *Charter Bank NW v. Evanston Ins. Co.,* 791 F.2d 379, 382.

6th Cir. 1962 (Tenn.). The insured sustained losses when it made a loan secured by fictitious warehouse receipts representing non-existent collateral. The court held the insured's losses were not covered under, *inter alia,* Insuring Clause (D) of a Bankers Blanket Bond because, although the warehouse receipts contained false statements of fact, they were signed and issued by authorized officers of the warehouse and thus were not "forged" for purposes of the bond. *First Nat'l Bank of Memphis v. Aetna Cas. & Sur. Co.,* 309 F.2d 702, 705.

7th Cir. 1994 (Ind.). A lending bank made a loan to its customer, who forged the endorsement of a fictitious payee on the loan check. The customer deposited the check into his personal account at another bank (the insured), and used the proceeds to pay off personal loans with the insured. The insurer issued a Depository Institutions Blanket Bond to the insured, which defined forgery as "the signing of the name of another with the intent to deceive; it does not include the signing of one's own name with or without authority, in any capacity, for any purpose . . . ." The lending bank sought to recover from the insured for paying on a forged endorsement, and the insured asserted a claim against the insurer's bond for the potential loss resulting from the lending bank's claim. The insurer argued that there was no forgery because the customer did not have an intent to deceive, as the proceeds of the loan were intended for his benefit. The court held that by signing the name of a fictitious payee, the customer had signed the name of another, but concluded that there was an issue of fact with respect to whether the customer acted with an "intent to deceive," and vacated the entry of judgment for the insured, remanding to the trial court. *Cincinnati Ins. Co. v. Star Fin. Bank,* 35 F.3d 1186, 1190.

7th Cir. 1991 (Ill.). The insured's employee misappropriated checks payable to the insured by endorsing the checks with a rubber stamp reading "for deposit only—account number 58-070-8." He did not sign the checks. After the insurer denied liability, the insured brought a declaratory judgment action, seeking coverage under, *inter alia,* Insuring Agreement (D). The court held the insured's loss was not covered because the employee's use of the rubber stamp was not a forgery. The employee had not signed the name of another person or entity. *Alpine State Bank v. Ohio Cas. Ins. Co.,* 941 F.2d 554, 560.

7th Cir. 1938 (Wis.). The insured's employee fraudulently induced the insured to sign several blank checks as drawer, convincing the insured that the checks would be used for legitimate business purposes. The employee then completed the checks by making them payable to "cash" in amounts that exceeded his authority, countersigning each check below the signature of the insured and its vice-president, and signing his own name on the back as endorser. The employee presented the checks for payment and misappropriated the proceeds. The insurer contended that the checks were not forgeries because they did not contain forged signatures. The court held that the insured's losses were covered under a "Blanket Forgery Bond" because the common-law definition of "forgery" included any alteration of a writing with the intent to defraud (the bond did not define "forgery"). Making or signing an instrument in disobedience of instructions or in the improper exercise of authority, so long as done with intent to defraud, fit within the common-law definition of "forgery." *Quick Serv. Box Co. v. St. Paul Mercury Indem. Co.,* 95 F.2d 15, 16-17.

8th Cir. 1970 (Mo.). An insurance company's agent fraudulently induced his employer to issue checks payable to a policyholder who purportedly wanted to take a loan against his policies. The agent then forged the policyholder's endorsements on the checks issued by the insurance company. The bank that accepted the deposit of the checks suffered a loss due to the forged endorsements and sought coverage under Insuring Agreement (D) of a Bankers Blanket Bond. The court held the agent's endorsement of the policyholder's name was a forgery, and that the loss was covered by the bond. Because the agent had no intention of giving the proceeds of the check to the policyholder, the court reasoned that the check was payable to a fictitious payee, and that losses caused by payments to fictitious payees were expressly covered by the bond. *Delmar Bank of Univ. City v. Fid. & Deposit Co. of Md.,* 428 F.2d 32, 36.

8th Cir. 1961 (Mo.). The insured financed automobiles and was fraudulently induced to take chattel mortgages representing non-existent vehicles to secure loans made to a customer. When the customer failed to repay the loan, the insured brought a claim under, *inter alia,* Insuring Agreement (D) of its Bankers Blanket Bond, arguing that forgery was not confined to a signature but included the false representations in the chattel mortgages. The court held that the fact the terms "forgery or alteration" were not defined in the Bankers Blanket Bond did not render the bond ambiguous. The notes and chattel mortgages were not forgeries because they contained genuine signatures. The only falsity was in the extrinsic fact that the debtor did not actually own the automobiles identified in the notes and mortgages. Although a fraud was perpetrated on the insured, the court held the loss did not result from a forgery within the meaning of the bond. *State Bank of Poplar Bluff v. Md. Cas. Co.,* 289 F.2d 544, 548.

9th Cir. 1958 (Cal.). The insured's treasurer, who was authorized to sign certain types of checks, signed and issued checks from an account on which he was not authorized to do so to finance his check cashing business. His signature on the checks was genuine. The court held that the insured's losses were not covered under Insuring Agreement (D) because, under California law, an instrument signed by the one purporting to have executed it is not a forgery. *Torrance Nat'l Bank v. Aetna Cas. & Sur. Co.,* 251 F.2d 666, 668-69.

10th Cir. 2011 (Okla.). The insured sought coverage under Insuring Agreement (E) of its Financial Institution Bond for a loss resulting from a default on a loan and the failure of the collateral, a corporate guaranty. The insurer obtained summary judgment dismissing the claim on the ground that the claim did not involve a forged or altered document. On appeal, the insured argued that Insuring Agreement (E) was ambiguous because Insuring Agreement (D) also provided coverage for forgeries and alterations. The appellate court rejected this argument, noting that Insuring Agreement (D) and Insuring Agreement (E) cover different types of forgeries and alterations, and thus there is no ambiguity in the bond. *First Nat'l Bank of Davis v. Progressive Cas. Ins. Co.,* 415 F. App'x 867, 870.

M.D. Ga. 1996. An attorney presented a draft made payable to his client, "Knight's Furniture Company, and Ernest Yates, its attorney" for deposit into his firm's trust account with the insured bank, endorsing the draft as "Knight's Furniture Company, Inc. by Ernest J. Yates, its attorney, and Ernest J. Yates." The attorney converted the proceeds for his own use. When the client discovered that the funds were missing, it filed a conversion action against the insured bank, alleging that the insured had wrongly accepted the check for deposit. The client recovered a judgment against the insured, which then sought coverage under Insuring Agreement (D), claiming it had suffered a loss due to the attorney's forged endorsement of his client's name on the check. The bond provided that "a signature which consists in whole or in part of one's own name signed with or without authority, in any capacity, for any purpose" is not a forgery. The court held that the insured's loss thus was not covered. Because the attorney signed his own name to the instrument, the loss was not caused by a "forgery" as defined by the Insuring Agreement. *Reliance Ins. Co. v. First Liberty Bank,* 927 F. Supp. 448, 450.

N.D. Ill. 2006. The insured asserted a claim under Insuring Agreement (D) of a Securities Dealer Fidelity Bond, which mimicked Insuring Agreement (D) of the Financial Institution Bond. The insured held and administered the funds of its customer's profit-sharing plan. An employee of the customer embezzled funds that were being held by the insured, through, *inter alia,* forged checks and instructions. The customer sued the insured, which in turn, tendered its defense to its insurer. The insurer declined to provide a defense, disclaiming liability under the bond. The insured ultimately settled with the customer. In ruling that the insurer was obligated to defend, the court said that coverage under Insuring Agreement (D) appeared to be implicated because the fraud involved checks and written instructions bearing the forged signatures of the plan's authorized signatories. The court also rejected the insurer's argument that the loss was not direct, applying a proximate cause standard and rejecting the "direct means direct" standard adopted previously by Illinois state court because one of the cases upon which the state court relied (from another jurisdiction) had been overturned. *Rothschild Inv. Corp. v. Travelers Cas. & Sur. Co.,* No. 05 C 3041, 2006 WL 1236148, at *4-5.

D. Mass. 1974. The insured credit union issued checks on its own preprinted form. The insured had an agreement with State Street Bank, its depository bank, pursuant to which State Street was authorized to pay checks issued by the insured. The insured discovered that certain persons opened bank accounts at other banks with checks purporting to have been drawn by the insured and made payable to fictitious payees. The checks were presented to State Street and paid, with a corresponding charge made to the insured's account. The insured sought coverage for its losses under Insuring Agreement (D) when State Street refused to re-credit its account. The insurer denied coverage on the grounds that the checks were counterfeit, rather than forged, and because the actual cause of the insured's loss was State Street's refusal to credit its account. The court rejected both arguments. It held that the insured's loss was covered because there is no distinction between a forgery and a counterfeit when dealing with private checks, since it is the genuineness of the signature that determines whether a check is valid. The court further held that the insured's loss was caused directly by the forgery and not by State Street's failure to credit its account. *MBTA Employees Credit Union v. Employer's Mut. Liab. Ins. Co. of Wis.,* 374 F. Supp. 1299, 1302.

D. Neb. 1992. The insured's customer presented a certified check, which was purportedly drawn on the account of J.A. Becker, P.C., at

Packers National Bank, for deposit to an account with the insured. The certified check, which had been accepted for deposit by the insured, bore a stamp which stated it was "certified" by "Ellen Davis, Cashier," without any reference to Packers National Bank in the stamp. After accepting the check for deposit, the insured immediately issued a number of cashier's checks to the depositor in reliance on the certified check. The insured sustained a loss when Packers National Bank informed the insured that it had not certified the check, and that the alleged drawer did not have an account with it. The court held the insured's loss was not covered under Insuring Agreement (D) because the insured failed to offer any evidence that the stamp was a forgery. Because the insured could not prove who "Ellen Davis" was, it could not prove that her signature was a forgery. *Ralston Bank v. Kan. Bankers Sur. Co.,* 794 F. Supp. 896, 898.

E.D.N.Y. 2012. CU National serviced mortgage loans for Suffolk, the lender. Without authorization, CU National sold certain of Suffolk's mortgage loans to Fannie Mae, without Suffolk's knowledge. Suffolk perpetrated the scheme by creating a fraudulent Allonge and Assignment. Suffolk's employees signed their own names, but falsely represented that they were an officer or employee of Suffolk. After discovering the loss, Suffolk sought recovery under, *inter alia,* the "Forgery and Alteration" coverage of its Credit Union Bond. The court rejected this aspect of the claim. The Allonges and Assignments did not contain forgeries as defined in the bond, since the employees signed their own names. The documents also were not alterations, since they were fraudulent *ab initio,* and "alteration" contemplates a genuine document that has been fraudulently changed. *Suffolk Fed. Credit Union v. CUMIS Ins. Soc'y, Inc.,* 910 F. Supp. 2d 446, 460.

E.D. Va. 1975. The insured's customer was given authority to sign checks by a third party in connection with a financing arrangement. The third party cancelled the financing plan, but an employee of the customer continued to sign the third-party checks by signing the third party's name and placing his own initials next to the signature. The court held the insured's losses were not covered by Insuring Agreement (D) because they were not caused by forgery. While the customer's employee had forged the third party's signature, the addition of his own initials after the forged signature "establishe[d] the necessary agency relationship to take this case outside the ambit of forgery." *Clarendon Bank & Trust v. Fid. & Deposit Co. of Md.,* 406 F. Supp. 1161, 1166.

Ala. 1970. The insured extended credit to a borrower, who executed a note in favor of the insured secured by invoices the borrower purported to have sent to its customers for goods. Rather than submit genuine invoices representing actual amounts owing, the borrower submitted duplicates of old invoices that did not contain any signatures, and packing slips that were created and signed by the borrower's employee. When the insured did not receive payment from the borrower's customers, it contacted the customers and discovered that the borrower never made the shipments represented by the invoices and packing slips. The insured sought coverage for its loss under Insuring Agreement (D) of a Bankers Blanket Bond. The court held the insured's loss was not covered by the bond. Under Alabama law, forgery is defined as the making or altering of the signature of another with the intent to deceive. The invoices were not forgeries because they did not contain any signatures. In addition, the packing slips were not forgeries because, while they contained false statements, they did not contain any false signatures, as they had been signed by the person whose name appeared on them. *Fid. & Cas. Co. v. Bank of Commerce,* 234 So. 2d 871, 876.

Cal. Ct. App. 1949. The insured purchased discounted contracts from a customer, which the customer had forged. The insured sought coverage for its losses under the forgery provision of a Bankers Blanket Bond (similar to Insuring Agreement (D)), which provided coverage for losses arising from the insured's extension of credit based on written instructions or advices that "have been altered without the knowledge and consent of the customer" of the insured. The court held that the insured's losses were not covered because the bond required that the forgery or alteration occur without the customer's knowledge. Because the customer committed the forgery, the customer could not be said to be without knowledge of the forgery. *First Thrift of Los Angeles v. Pac. Indem. Co.,* 212 P.2d 560, 561.

Ohio Ct. App. 1996. Gail Smith Development managed the day-to-day operations of O'Mara Enterprises. To facilitate its operations, O'Mara entrusted a Gail Smith employee with the use of its facsimile signature stamp to issue checks for O'Mara's obligations. The employee used the stamp to draw checks on O'Mara's accounts, ostensibly for the payment of O'Mara's federal payroll taxes. Gail Smith converted the proceeds of the O'Mara checks. The insured suffered a loss after O'Mara obtained a judgment against it for honoring the forged checks. The insured sought coverage under Insuring Agreement (D). The court held that the insured's loss was covered, reasoning that Gail Smith's unauthorized use of a facsimile signature stamp with intent to deceive the insured constituted forgery and that the forgery was the proximate cause of insured's loss. *Bank One, Steubenville v. Buckeye Union Ins. Co.,* 683 N.E.2d 50, 53.

B. Alteration

D. Minn. 2006. The insured bank's customer issued a check to Ruddy. It requested that the Ruddy check be stopped, and the insured complied. Two weeks later, someone called the insured, purporting to be from the customer, and directed a wire transfer to Ruddy in an amount similar to the check. It was subsequently learned that the wire transfer was unauthorized. The insured bank asserted a claim under, *inter alia,* Insuring Agreement (D), which the insurer denied. The insured then sued, and the insurer moved to dismiss. The court denied the motion as to the Insuring Agreement (D) claim. It held that because on a motion to dismiss it was required to resolve all questions in favor of the insured and because it found the term "alteration" to be ambiguous, it was possible that the insured could prove that the telephone call directing the wire transfer constituted an alteration of the check. *First Integrity Bank, N.A. v. Ohio Cas. Ins. Co.,* No. 05-2761 (MJD/RLE), 2006 WL 1371674, at *4.

D. Or. 2001. The insured, a national discount securities brokerage firm, accepted three checks from a customer and credited the customer's account for the amount of the checks. The customer subsequently wired money out of the account. The checks were later dishonored, and the insured suffered a loss by allowing the customer to draw upon the proceeds of the checks. With respect to the first check, the customer intercepted the check, which was made payable to a different payee, endorsed her own name on the back of the check, and deposited it with the brokerage firm. The court held that this check was not altered within the meaning of Insuring Agreement (D) because the customer had simply signed her own name to it. With respect to the two other checks, the customer altered the name of the payee to her own name, and then endorsed her own name on the checks. As to these checks, the court held the insured's loss was covered because the names of the payees on the checks had been changed and thus had been altered within the meaning of bond. *Bidwell & Co. v. Nat'l Union Fire Ins. Co. of Pitt., Pa.,* No. CV-00-89-HU, 2001 WL 204843, at *4-5.

E.D.N.Y. 2012. CU National serviced mortgage loans for Suffolk, the lender. Without authorization, CU National sold certain of Suffolk's mortgage loans to Fannie Mae, without Suffolk's knowledge. Suffolk perpetrated the scheme by creating a fraudulent Allonge and Assignment. Suffolk's employees signed their own names, but falsely represented that they were an officer or employee of Suffolk. After discovering the loss, Suffolk sought recovery under, *inter alia,* the "Forgery and Alteration" coverage of its Credit Union Bond. The court held that the documents were not alterations, since they were fraudulent *ab initio,* and "alteration" contemplates a genuine document that has been fraudulently changed. *Suffolk Fed. Credit Union v. CUMIS Ins. Soc'y, Inc.,* 910 F. Supp. 2d 446, 460.

Ind. Ct. App. 2003. The insured mortgage company drew and delivered a check for a residential mortgage to Fidelity Title Company. The closing never occurred, but Fidelity Title deposited the check into its account anyway, in violation of a voucher attached to the check that instructed that the check was to be returned if the closing did not occur. Fidelity Title went out of business, and the insured sought coverage for its loss under Insuring Agreement (D). The court held that the insured's loss was not covered because even though Fidelity Title may have negotiated the instrument in breach of the voucher's instructions, it did not alter the check as required for coverage. *Utica Mut. Ins. Co. v. Precedent Cos.,* 782 N.E.2d 470, 477.

Ind. Ct. App. 1980. A depository bank sought coverage under Insuring Agreement (D) after it suffered losses resulting from its payment of a check on which the amount in words had been erroneously imprinted by a check writing machine for $100,000 more than intended, and the amount in figures had been "rather crudely" altered by the payee to match the erroneous amount in words. Prior to the drawer's attempted stop payment, the insured applied a portion of the proceeds in satisfaction of several antecedent note obligations owing by the payee. The court held that the insured did not sustain a loss as a result of any alteration because, under the UCC, the words spelling out the amount of the check govern, so any alteration of the numerical statement of the amount was not material. The court further held that the loss did not result from any alteration but from the stop payment placed on the check. *St. Paul Fire & Marine Ins. Co. v. State Bank of Salem,* 412 N.E.2d 103, 113.

C. Loss "Resulting Directly" From a Covered Risk

2d Cir. 1965 (N.Y.). The insured made loans to a borrower, evidenced by a promissory note signed by the borrower's president and secured by an assignment of accounts receivable, certain of which were non-existent. The court held that the insured's losses resulted from the borrower's default on the loans, not from any forgery or alteration of the accounts receivable. Thus, the insured's losses were not covered by Insuring Agreement (D). *Exch. Nat'l Bank of Olean v. Ins. Co. of N. Am.,* 341 F.2d 673, 676.

4th Cir. 1962 (Va.). The insured sustained a loss when a borrower went bankrupt and could not repay a loan made by the insured for a construction project. The borrower's contractor forged the borrower's endorsement on the checks issued by the insured (a portion of the loan's proceeds) which were ultimately intended for the contractor's benefit. The court held that the insured's loss was caused by the borrower's failure to repay the loan and not by the contractor's forgery of the borrower's endorsement on the checks. *Piedmont Fed. Sav. & Loan Ass'n v. Hartford Acc. & Indem. Co.,* 307 F.2d 310, 314.

5th Cir. 1986 (Tex.). The insured sustained losses when its customer failed to repay loans secured by a pledge of altered CDs representing amounts far in excess of the sums actually deposited with the bank that issued the CDs. The signatures on the CDs were not forged. The insured sought coverage under Insuring Agreement (D) of its "non-standard comprehensive blanket bond," which covered forged or altered securities, but did not define forgery or limit coverage to documents "forged as to signature," as standard Form 24 then provided. The court held that the insured's loss resulted not from forgery or alteration of the CDs but from the misrepresentation of fact made in the CDs—a risk allocated to the insured under the loan exclusion clause of the bond. The court looked to Texas criminal law, under which one signing his own name without an intent to defraud does not commit forgery. *Charter Bank NW v. Evanston Ins. Co.,* 791 F.2d 379, 383.

5th Cir. 1974 (Fla.). The insured credited a customer's account when the customer deposited a check bearing the forged signature of the drawer and allowed the customer to draw on the amounts deposited. The insured sustained a loss when the signature proved to be forged and there were insufficient funds in the customer's account to cover the checks. The court found that an ambiguity existed between Insuring Agreement (D)'s forgery coverage (which seemed to afford coverage) and Exclusion 1(d) (which excluded losses resulting from the extension of credit on an uncollected item of deposit). The court reasoned there was an ambiguity because the insured's loss resulted from both the forged drawer's signature and the lack of funds in the customer's account and construed that ambiguity against the insurer. The court reversed the entry of summary judgment in favor of the insurer and remanded. *First Nat'l Bank of Miami v. Ins. Co. of N. Am.,* 495 F.2d 519, 522.

6th Cir. 2013 (Ky.). The insured bank sought coverage under Insuring Agreement (D) for a loss resulting from a loan default. As collateral for the loan, the borrower purported to assign a life insurance policy to the insured bank. The borrower substantially overstated the policy's value and, unbeknownst to the insured, had assigned it to multiple other banks. As proof of the supposed value of the policy, the borrower supplied the insured with a purported letter from the life insurance company. The letter was addressed to "Client" and not the insured bank and contained a forgery. The court affirmed summary judgment to the fidelity insurer on the ground that Insuring Agreement (D) did not apply because the forged letter was not directed to the insured. The court also relied upon the separate ground that the loss was not direct because the policy, the underlying collateral, was in essence worthless since it previously had been assigned to multiple other banks. *Forcht Bank, N.A. v. BancInsure, Inc.,* No. 11-6328, 2013 WL 518405, at *6.

6th Cir. 2008 (Mich.). The insured bank sustained a loss as a result of a scheme involving fraudulent mortgages. The insured asserted a claim for its loss under the bond's version of Insuring Agreement (D), contending that coverage existed because the promissory notes involved in the transactions were forged. While the signatures on the notes purported to be of real people, these people had no interest in the property that was the subject of the notes. The appellate court affirmed summary judgment for the insurer. Assuming that the promissory notes were negotiable instruments and not evidences of debt, the insured did not sustain a loss directly as a result of the forgeries. Even if the signatures on the notes had been legitimate, the notes would not have had any real value because the collateral underlying them was fictitious. *Flagstar Bank, F.S.B. v. Fed. Ins. Co.,* 260 F. App'x 820, 822-25.

8th Cir. 1993 (Mo.). The insured sought coverage under Insuring Agreement (D) for losses sustained when its agent engaged in a series of dishonest transactions involving a bogus annuity contract and forged deposit fund certificates which he created. The court held the loss was not covered because the annuity contract was entirely bogus, rather than forged as to signature, and the forged signatures on the deposit fund certificates were not a substantial factor in causing the loss on the certificates. *Ks. Life Ins. Co. v. Am. Ins. Co.,* 12 F.3d 1102 (unpublished), 1993 WL 497073, at *1.

9th Cir. 2000 (Cal.). The insured suffered a loss when it settled a customer's lawsuit arising from the insured's handling of her CDs. The court held that the insured's loss was not covered under the forgery provision of a "bankers special bond," which limited coverage to "loss resulting directly from forgery or alteration of, on or in any check." The court held that while the customer's husband may have wrongfully altered the amount of the customer's check and withdrawn funds from her account, his actions were not the cause of the insured's loss; rather, the insured's loss was the direct result of its unauthorized transfer of and failure to return the customer's funds. *Cal. Korea Bank v. Virginia Sur. Co.,* 2000 WL 713798, at *1.

N.D. Ill. 2006. The insured asserted a claim under Insuring Agreement (D) of a Securities Dealer Fidelity Bond, which mimicked Insuring Agreement (D) of the Financial Institution Bond. The insured held and administered the funds of a profit-sharing plan of its customer. An employee of the customer embezzled funds that were being held by the insured through, *inter alia,* forged checks and instructions. The customer sued the insured, which in turn tendered its defense to its insurer. The insurer declined to provide a defense, disclaiming liability under the bond. The insured ultimately settled with the customer. In ruling that the insurer was obligated to defend, the court said that coverage under Insuring Agreement (D) appeared to be implicated because the fraud involved checks and written instructions bearing the forged signatures of the plan's authorized signatories. The court also rejected the insurer's argument that the loss was not direct, applying a proximate cause standard and rejecting the "direct means direct" standard adopted previously by Illinois state court because one of the cases upon which the state court relied (from another jurisdiction) had been overturned. *Rothschild Investment Corp. v. Travelers Cas. & Sur. Co.,* No. 05 C 3041, 2006 WL 1236148, at *5, *9-10.

N.D. Ill. 1989. The insured made a loan to a customer secured by a CD and the assignment of a savings account. The CD was fabricated by the customer, and bore a forged signature purporting to be that of an officer the bank which supposedly issued the CD. The customer also forged the endorsement of the same bank officer on the assignment of his savings account. When the customer defaulted on the loan and the collateral proved defective, the insured sought coverage for the loss under Insuring Agreement (D). The insurer argued that the loss resulted directly from the worthlessness of the collateral and not from the forgery. The insured argued that it would not have made a loan to the insured had it known that documents representing the collateral were forged. The court held that Insuring Agreement (D) provided coverage for the insured's losses, on the ground that the Insuring Agreement reflected the insurer's intent to insure against loss resulting from the forgery of instruments provided as collateral for the extension of credit. (The Illinois Court of Appeals has since rejected the rationale of this decision.) *M.G. Bancorporation, Inc. v. Reliance Ins. Co.,* No. 87 C 10470, 1989 WL 20774, at *4.

D. Mass. 1974. The insured credit union issued checks on its own preprinted form. The insured had an agreement with State Street Bank, its depository bank, pursuant to which State Street was authorized to pay checks issued by the insured. The insured discovered that certain persons opened bank accounts at other banks with checks purporting to have been drawn by the insured and made payable to fictitious payees. The checks were presented to State Street and paid, with a corresponding charge made to the insured's account. The insured sought coverage for its losses under Insuring Agreement (D) when State Street refused to re-credit its account. The insurer denied coverage on the grounds that the checks were counterfeit, rather than forged, and because the actual cause of the insured's loss was State Street's refusal to credit its account. The court rejected both arguments. It held that the insured's loss was covered because there is no distinction between a forgery and a counterfeit when dealing with private checks, since it is the genuineness of the signature that determines whether a check is valid. The court further held that the insured's loss was caused directly by the forgery and not by State Street's failure to credit its account. *MBTA Employees Credit Union v. Employer's Mut. Liab. Ins. Co. of Wis.,* 374 F. Supp. 1299, 1302.

D.N.J. 1983. The insured suffered a loss resulting from a customer's default on two loans secured by CDs purportedly issued by an entity which held a British West Indies banking charter but had no assets, depositors, offices, or employees. The insured sought coverage under, *inter alia,* Insuring Agreement (D). The court held that the insured's loss was not covered because the loss was directly caused by the fact that the CDs were worthless, not by the forgery of any signature on the CDs. Even if the CDs contained genuine signatures, the insured still would have suffered a loss because the CDs represented non-existent collateral. *Liberty Nat'l Bank v. Aetna Life & Cas. Co.,* 568 F. Supp. 860, 865-66.

N.D.N.Y. 2010. The insured's customer deposited a fraudulent cashier's check into his account. Before the check finally cleared, the customer instructed the insured to wire most of the check's proceeds to an account in China. The insured complied with the instructions. The insured sustained a loss when the check ultimately was not paid, and it was unable to stop or recall the wire. The insured sought coverage under the bond's version of Insuring Agreement (D). Based on the undisputed facts, the court upheld the insurer's denial based on the bond's exclusion (q), which excluded loss resulting from a withdrawal from a customer's account involving a deposit item that has not finally been paid, for any reason. *Adirondack Trust Co. v. St. Paul Mercury Ins. Co.,* No. 1:09-cv-1313 (GLS/DRH), 2010 WL 2425915, at *2.

S.D. Ohio 2008. The proceeds of a cashier's check, which either was a forgery or a counterfeit, were debited from the insured's account. When the insured bank reconciled its cashier's checks, it learned that the check was fraudulent. It returned the check to the Federal Reserve, which credited the insured bank's account and debited the depositary bank's account. The depositary bank then sued the insured bank, alleging that the insured failed to return the check within the time provided by the applicable regulations. The insured ultimately settled the depositary bank's claim for fifty percent, and asserted a claim under, *inter alia,* its Financial Institution Bond's version of Insuring Agreement (D). The court upheld the insurer's denial of the claim under Insuring Agreement (D) on the ground that the insured did not sustain a "direct" loss. The insured was made whole by the Federal Reserve and did not sustain a loss until it settled with the depositary bank. *Merchants Bank & Trust Co. v. Cincinnati Ins. Co.,* No. 1:06cv561, 2008 WL 728332, at *3-4.

Ga. Ct. App. 2000. The insured approved a loan to a customer that was secured by a non-existent credit union bank account. The customer had forged a letter from the credit union that purported to confirm the existence of the account and its balance. The insured sustained a loss when the customer defaulted on the loan and was unable to collect from the purported security. The insured sought coverage under Insuring Agreement (D), claiming that its loss resulted directly from the forged letter. The court rejected the claim, holding that the bond did not provide coverage for the insured's loss because the forged letter was not the direct cause of the insured's loss. Even if the signature on the confirmation letter had been authentic, the insured still would have suffered the same loss because the purported collateral did not exist. *Ga. Bank & Trust v. Cincinnati Ins. Co.,* 538 S.E.2d 764, 766.

Ind. Ct. App. 1980. A depository bank sought coverage under Insuring Agreement (D) after it suffered losses resulting from its payment of a check on which the amount in words had been erroneously imprinted by a check writing machine for $100,000 more than intended, and the amount in figures had been "rather crudely" altered by the payee to match the erroneous amount in words. Prior to the drawer's attempted stop payment, the insured applied a portion of the proceeds in satisfaction of several antecedent note obligations owing by the payee. The court held that the insured did not sustain a loss as a result of any alteration because, under the UCC, the words spelling out the amount of the check govern, so any alteration of the numerical statement of the amount was not material. The court further held that the loss did not result from any alteration but from the stop payment placed on the check. *St. Paul Fire & Marine Ins. Co. v. State Bank of Salem*, 412 N.E.2d 103, 113.

La. Ct. App. 1972. The insured made a loan to a borrower. Six days later, the insured requested that the borrower secure its indebtedness with collateral. The borrower submitted several promissory notes purportedly executed by others, payable to the borrower. When the borrower defaulted on the loan, the insured tried to collect on the promissory notes, only to discover that many of the promissory notes had been forged by the borrower. The insured sought coverage for its loss under Insuring Agreement (D), which limited coverage to losses sustained through the forgery or alteration of certain enumerated instruments, not including promissory notes. The court therefore held that the insured's loss was not covered. The court also stated that the real cause of the loss was the borrower's failure to repay the loan, not any fraud perpetrated upon the bank at the time the loan was made. *Allen State Bank v. Traveler's Indem. Co.*, 270 So. 2d 270, 273.

Mass. Super. Ct. 2005. The bookkeeper of Vulcan issued checks from Vulcan's checking account payable to the insured bank, at which she maintained a loan, for purposes of paying off her loan. The proceeds of the checks were, in fact, credited against her loan. When Vulcan learned of the embezzlement, it sent a letter to the insured demanding reimbursement and then sued the insured. The insured asserted a claim under, *inter alia,* Insuring Agreement (D), for its potential liability to Vulcan. The court upheld the insurer's rejection of the claim, holding that liability to a third party is not a direct loss. *Commerce Bank & Trust v. St. Paul Mercury Ins. Co.*, No. 04-1264B, 2005 WL 4881101, at *4-5.

Minn. Ct. App. 2012. This case involves the relatively well-known fraud committed by Louis Pearlman. The insureds made substantial loans to Pearlman in reliance upon purported stock certificates and board resolutions that were forgeries. When Pearlman defaulted on the loans, the insureds sought coverage under, *inter alia,* Insuring Agreement (D).

The appellate court affirmed the lower court's award of summary judgment to the insurers. Insuring Agreement (D) did not provide coverage because the insured's loss was caused directly by the fact that the underlying collateral was worthless, not by any forgery. The appellate court did not disturb the lower court's conclusion that the stock certificates and board resolutions also were not "negotiable instruments" or "instructions or advices." *Alerus Fin. Nat'l Ass'n v. St. Paul Mercury Ins. Co.*, No. A11-680, 2012 WL 254484, at *6.

D. Negotiable Instrument

D. Minn. 2012. The insured sustained a loss as a result of the default on a loan to finance the lease of sound and lighting equipment for a nightclub. The collateral for the loan included a written guaranty of repayment from the borrower's mother. After default, the mother claimed that her signature on the guaranty was a forgery. The insurer obtained summary judgment dismissing the insured's claim under Insuring Agreement (D). The court held that the guaranty was not a "Negotiable Instrument" as defined, as the guaranty contained promises other than a promise to pay and was not payable to order or bearer. *Highland Bank v. BancInsure, Inc.*, No. 10-4107 (SRN/AJB), 2012 WL 3656523, at *2.

Minn. Ct. App. 2012. This case involves the relatively well-known fraud committed by Louis Pearlman. The insureds made substantial loans to Pearlman in reliance upon purported stock certificates and board resolutions that were forgeries. The appellate court did not disturb the lower court's conclusion that the stock certificates and board resolutions were not "negotiable instruments" or "instructions or advices." *Alerus Fin. Nat'l Ass'n v. St. Paul Mercury Ins. Co.*, No. A11-680, 2012 WL 254484, at *6.

N.Y. 1930. The insured's customer deposited several checks and drafts into his account with the insured. The insured allowed the customer to draw on the amounts deposited, but later discovered he had forged both the checks and the drafts. The coverage afforded by Insuring Agreement (D) was limited to losses resulting from the insured's payment of forged checks. The court held that the losses that resulted from the insured's payment of forged checks were covered but that the losses caused by the forged drafts were not covered. The bond's coverage was limited to those documents the insured reasonably believed to constitute checks. Because the drafts were issued by a mortgage company and not a bank, the insured could not reasonably have believed that the drafts were checks, so its resulting loss from payment on the drafts was not covered. *World Exch. Bank v. Commercial Cas. Ins. Co.,* 173 N.E. 902, 904-05.

E. Written Instructions and Advices

2d Cir. 1939 (N.Y.). The insured's employee presented fraudulent payment vouchers to the insured. In reliance on the vouchers, the insured issued checks, signed by both the employee and a co-drawer, both of whose endorsements were genuine. The employee then endorsed his own name on the checks and converted the proceeds for his personal use, thereby causing the insured a loss. The court first held that the fraudulent vouchers were not "written instructions or advices" because they did not direct the payment of money within the meaning of the forgery provision of a depositors or commercial forgery policy. The court also held that the insured's loss was not covered because employee's endorsement was genuine and did not constitute a forgery. The mere fact that the employee acted outside the scope of his authority did not render his endorsement on the checks forgeries. *Fitzgibbons Boiler Co. v. Employers' Liab. Assur. Corp.,* 105 F.2d 893, 896.

3d Cir. 1943 (Pa.). The insured loaned money to a customer secured by fraudulent warehouse receipts representing both non-existent and encumbered collateral. When the borrower defaulted, the insured sought coverage under a Bankers Blanket Bond, which provided coverage for loss through credit extensions based on "the faith of forged or altered written instructions or advices from any customers...." Finding coverage under the bond, the court held that the warehouse receipts were forgeries under Pennsylvania law because they contained false statements of fact. The court further held that the warehouse receipts constituted "written instructions or advices" because they notified the insured that the warehouse held the goods identified in the warehouse receipts. *Provident Trust Co. v. Nat'l Sur. Corp.,* 138 F.2d 252, 254.

6th Cir. 2013 (Ky.). The insured bank sought coverage under Insuring Agreement (D) for a loss resulting from a loan default. As collateral for the loan, the borrower purported to assign a life insurance policy to the insured bank. The borrower substantially overstated the policy's value and, unbeknownst to the insured, had assigned it to multiple other banks. As proof of the supposed value of the policy, the borrower supplied the insured with a purported letter from the life insurance company. The letter was addressed to "Client," not the insured bank, and contained a forgery. The court affirmed summary judgment to the fidelity insurer, on the ground that Insuring Agreement (D) did not apply because the forged letter was not directed to the insured. *Forcht Bank, N.A. v. BancInsure, Inc.*, No. 11-6328, 2013 WL 518405, at *6.

6th Cir. 1964 (Ky.). The insured sustained losses when it purchased discounted notes secured by forged automobile chattel mortgages and leasing agreements. The court held the insured's losses were not covered under Insuring Agreement (D). The chattel mortgages and leasing agreements were not "advices and instructions" because they were neither commercial paper nor were they "directed to the insured and authorizing or acknowledging the transfer, payment, delivery or receipt of funds or Property." *Liberty Nat'l Bank & Trust Co. of Louisville v. Nat'l Sur. Corp.*, 330 F.2d 697, 699-700.

7th Cir. 1936 (Ill.). The insured engaged in the purchase of notes secured by chattel mortgages on automobiles. An automobile dealer with whom the insured did business forged the signatures on a number of notes purchased by the insured. Each note was accompanied by what the court described as a "forged instrument," which was essentially a letter in which the purported maker of the note requested that the insured purchase his note. The insured conceded that the forged notes and mortgage documents were not covered by under its "Combined Depositors-Commercial Forgery and Alteration Policy," which contained a forgery provision similar to that in Insuring Agreement (D). Rather, the insured argued that the "forged instruments" constituted written directions or orders to pay within the meaning of the policy. The court disagreed, finding that the "forged instrument" was not an order to pay but simply a letter requesting that the insured purchase the note. Accordingly, the court held that insured's loss was not covered. *Tenant Fin. Corp. v. Md. Cas. Co.*, 86 F.2d 789, 790-91.

8th Cir. 2012 (Mo.). The insured bank sought coverage for a loss resulting from a wire transfer request received via fax from an imposter. The signatures on the transfer request were forgeries. The insurer denied the claim, asserting that the faxed transfer request was an "electronic record" and not a "writing" as defined by the bond. The court affirmed summary judgment for the insured, holding that a fax constitutes a "writing" and not an "electronic record" under the bond's definitions. The court explained that under the bond's language an "electronic record" is something stored on a hard drive or a disk. The court also commented that the language of the bond "has simply not kept pace with the digital revolution . . . ." *Mo. Bank & Trust Co. v. OneBeacon Ins. Co.,* 688 F.3d 943, 947-48.

9th Cir. 2001 (Cal.). The court held that a signature on an instruction or advice can be covered under a forgery provision in a "fiduciary" bond similar to that contained in Insuring Agreement (D) only where the signature purports to be that of the insured's customer but is not. The court also held that purchase orders and escrow instructions are not "instructions" or "advices." *Universal Bank v. Northland Ins. Co.,* 8 F. App'x 784, 786.

N.D. Cal. 2013. The bond's Insuring Agreement (D) included an additional coverage called a "Fraudulent Instructions Insuring Clause," which insured against loss resulting from the insured "having in good faith . . . transferred funds on deposit in a Customer's account in reliance upon a fraudulent telephonic voice instruction" transmitted to the insured purporting to be from "an individual person who is a Customer of" the insured. The court rejected the insured's claim under this coverage because it could not establish that the accountholder who supposedly requested the subject wire transfer satisfied the bond's definition of "Customer." *First Nat'l Bank of Northern Cal. v. St. Paul Mercury Ins. Co.,* No. C 11-6631 PJH, 2013 WL 61026, at *4-5.

N.D. Fla. 1967. The insured extended a loan to a customer based on the strength of a "Program Certificate and Advices of Dreyfus Investment Program of the Bank of New York," which was allegedly altered. This certificate evidenced the ownership of shares in the investment program. The insured suffered a loss when the customer defaulted on the loan and sought coverage under, *inter alia,* Insuring Agreement (D). The court held the insured's loss was covered because the certificate was altered without the knowledge or consent of the Bank of New York (the issuer of the certificate) and constituted an "instruction or advice" to the insured. *First Nat'l Bank of Fort Walton Beach v. United States Fid. & Guar. Co.,* 274 F. Supp. 305, 306.

W.D. Tenn. 1997. The insured, a mortgage company, loaned $450,000 to a customer who signed a promissory note, which was secured by an assignment of a bonus purportedly due the customer from his employer. The customer submitted several forged documents, including a forged letter purporting to be from his employer stating that he received a bonus of $811,500, and that $410,000 of that bonus would be paid to the insured. When the customer defaulted on the loan, the bank sought to enforce the assignment of the bonus, at which time it learned that the customer forged the letter from his employer and that he was not entitled to receive a bonus. The court held that the insured had failed to establish its right to recover under Insuring Agreement (D) of a Savings and Loan Blanket Bond. The forged letter could not be construed as a "written instruction or advice" because the letter neither ordered nor directed the insured to do anything. *K.W. Bancshares, Inc. v. Syndicates of Underwriters at Lloyd's,* 965 F. Supp. 1047, 1052.

Md. Ct. Spec. App. 1999. Reiners, purporting to be an agent for Phillip Morris, informed the insured that Phillip Morris needed a large loan for a secret project to be conducted by a subsidiary corporation called World Wide Regional Export. Reiners submitted an incumbency certificate, on which he forged the name of a Phillip Morris executive. The certificate falsely represented that Reiners was a high-ranking Phillip Morris official with authority to act on Phillip Morris's behalf. Over the next twenty-eight months, the insured loaned $300 million to World Wide. The insured eventually discovered the fraud and was able to recover all but $35 million of its losses. It sought coverage for that amount from its insurer, claiming that the forged incumbency certificate was a "written instruction," qualifying for coverage under Insuring Agreement (D). The court held that the forged incumbency certificate (which simply purported to identify that Reiners was authorized to act on Phillip Morris' behalf) was not an "instruction" or "advice" within the meaning of Insuring Agreement (D) because it did not authorize or direct the insured to pay any money and did not mention loans, funds, or payments. *First Union Corp. v. USF&G,* 730 A.2d 278, 283-84.

Minn. Ct. App. 2012. This case involves the relatively well-known fraud committed by Louis Pearlman. The insureds made substantial loans to Pearlman in reliance upon purported stock certificates and board resolutions that were forgeries. The appellate court did not disturb the lower court's conclusion that the stock certificates and board resolutions were not "negotiable instruments" or "instructions or advices." *Alerus Fin. Nat'l Ass'n v. St. Paul Mercury Ins. Co.,* No. A11-680, 2012 WL 254484, at *6.

F. Other Covered Documents

E.D. Ark. 2004. The insured bank extended credit to its customer based on leases of copy machines. The amount of credit the bank extended was calculated by multiplying the monthly lease payment by the lease term. The customer defrauded by the bank by providing forged leases which exaggerated their term, thereby leading the bank to extend greater credit to the customer than it would have had it received legitimate leases. The credit line ultimately fell into default, and the insured bank asserted a claim under, *inter alia,* Insuring Agreement (D) of its Financial Institution Bond. The insurer's rejection of the claim under Insuring Agreement (D) was upheld by the court, as the lease documents were not "negotiable instruments" or any other type of document enumerated in Insuring Agreement (D). The court, however, denied the insurer summary judgment under Insuring Agreement (E), rejecting its contention that the forged leases were not the direct cause of the loss. *Pine Bluff Nat'l Bank v. St. Paul Mercury Ins. Co.,* 346 F. Supp. 2d 1020, 1026.

N.D. Ill. 2009. The insured loaned money to its customer based on the customer's receivables, which served as security for the advances. The customer altered its invoices to reflect greater receivables than it actually had, thereby enticing the insured to make advances to the customer that it would not have made otherwise. The insured claimed coverage under the bond's version of Insuring Agreement (D), contending that its advance requests and invoices constituted Withdrawal Orders. The court rejected the contention, noting that the documents were not authorizations to debit the customer's account; they were requests for financing. *Metro Fed. Credit Union v. Fed. Ins. Co.*, 607 F. Supp. 2d 870, 876.

D. Kan. 1991. The insured sustained losses when a customer defaulted on two construction loans. To obtain the loan proceeds, the customer was required to submit monthly draw requests which had to be approved by the insured. The insured required that the customer submit site inspection reports, subcontractor agreements, lien waivers, and checks drawn on the customer's bank account at another bank to support its draw requests. The customer either created or altered the documents submitted in support of the draw requests. The court held that the bond did not provide coverage for losses caused by the forged site inspection reports, subcontractor agreements, and lien waivers. They were not Withdrawal Orders within meaning of Insuring Agreement (D) because they did not direct or order the payment of money. With respect to the checks, however, the court noted that the customer had altered many checks to contain different amounts and found that some of the checks had never been sent to or negotiated by the named payees. Thus, the court held that the insured's losses resulted directly from the forged or altered checks and were covered under Insuring Agreement (D), which provided coverage for loss resulting directly from the forgery or alteration of *any* Negotiable Instrument or Withdrawal Order. *First Fed. Sav. Bank of Newton v. Cont'l Cas. Co.*, 768 F. Supp. 1449, 1453-54.

E.D. Mich. 2013. The insured bank sought coverage for a loss resulting from a wire transfer request received via fax from someone purporting to be the insured's customer. The signature on the wire transfer request, which sought disbursement from a home equity line of credit, was forged. The insurer denied the claim, relying on the loan loss exclusion. The district court held that the claim was covered under the plain language of Insuring Agreement (D). It concluded that the loan loss exclusion did not apply because the exclusion bars coverage resulting from a customer's default on a loan or extension of credit, and the loss at issue did not result from such a default. *Bank of Ann Arbor v. Everest Nat'l Ins. Co.*, No. 12-11251, 2013 WL 665067, at *3-4.

D. Minn. 2006. The insured bank's customer issued a check to Ruddy. It requested that the Ruddy check be stopped, and the insured complied. Two weeks later, someone called the insured, purporting to be from the customer, and directed a wire transfer to Ruddy in an amount similar to the check. The insured subsequently learned that the wire transfer was unauthorized. The insured bank asserted a claim under, *inter alia*, Insuring Agreement (D), which the insurer denied. The insured then sued, and the insurer moved to dismiss. The court denied the motion as to the Insuring Agreement (D) claim. It held that because on a motion to dismiss it was required to resolve all questions in the insured's favor, and because it found the term "alteration" to be ambiguous, it was possible that the insured could prove that the telephone call directing the wire transfer constituted an alteration of the check. *First Integrity Bank, N.A. v. Ohio Cas. Ins. Co.,* No. 05-2761 (MJD/RLE), 2006 WL 1371674, at *4.

Ala. 1970. The insured extended credit to a borrower, who executed a note in favor of the insured secured by invoices the borrower purported to have sent to its customers for goods. Rather than submit genuine invoices representing actual amounts owing, the borrower submitted duplicates of old invoices that did not contain any signatures, and packing slips that were created and signed by the borrower's employee. When the insured did not receive payment from the borrower's customers, it contacted the customers and discovered that the borrower never made the shipments represented by the invoices and packing slips. The insured sought coverage for its loss under Insuring Agreement (D) of a Bankers Blanket Bond. The court held the insured's loss was not covered by the bond. The invoices were not forgeries under Alabama law because they did not contain any signatures. In addition, the packing slips were also not forgeries because, while they contained false statements, they did not contain any false signatures, as they had been signed by the person whose name appeared on them. *Fid. & Cas. Co. v. Bank of Commerce,* 234 So. 2d 871, 875-76.

La. Ct. App. 1972. The insured made a loan to a borrower. Six days later, the insured requested that the borrower secure its indebtedness with collateral. The borrower submitted several promissory notes purportedly executed by others, payable to the borrower. When the borrower defaulted on the loan, the insured tried to collect on the promissory notes, only to discover that many of the promissory notes had been forged by the borrower. The insured sought coverage for its loss under Insuring Agreement (D), which limited coverage to losses sustained through the forgery or alteration of certain enumerated instruments, not including promissory notes. The court therefore held that the insured's loss was not covered. The court also stated that the real cause of the loss was the borrower's failure to repay the loan, not any fraud perpetrated at the time the loan was made. *Allen State Bank v. Traveler's Indem. Co.*, 270 So. 2d 270, 273.

G. The "on the Faith of" Requirement

Md. Ct. Spec. App. 1999. Reiners, purporting to be an agent for Phillip Morris, informed the insured that Phillip Morris needed a large loan for a secret project to be conducted by a subsidiary corporation called World Wide Regional Export. Reiners submitted an incumbency certificate, on which he forged the name of a Phillip Morris executive. The certificate falsely represented that Reiners was a high-ranking Phillip Morris official with authority to act on Phillip Morris's behalf. Over the next twenty-eight months, the insured loaned $300 million to World Wide. The insured eventually discovered the fraud and was able to recover all but $35 million of its losses. It sought coverage for that amount from its insurer. In addition to holding that the incumbency certificates were not instructions or advices, the court held that the insured did not rely "on the faith of" the certificates in making the loans because it had not received the certificates when it made the loans. *First Union Corp. v. USF&G*, 730 A.2d 278, 283-84.

SECONDARY SOURCES

Charles L. Armstrong, Thomas H. McNeill & James E. Reynolds, *Warehouse Lending Losses under the Financial Institution Bond*, XII FID. L.J. 1 (2006).

Elizabeth S. Carley, Jeffrey S. Price & Justin D. Wear, *Who Should Pay for the Bank's Mistakes? A Discussion of Loss Causation Under Insuring Agreement D and Insuring Agreement E of the Standard Form No. 24 Financial Institution Bond* (2009) (unpublished paper presented Twentieth Annual Southern Surety and Fidelity Claims Conference) *available at* http://www.forcon.com/papers/ssfcc/2009/12.%20Price.pdf.

Bradford R. Carver, *Loss and Causation, in* HANDLING FIDELITY BOND CLAIMS 363 (Michael Keeley & Sean Duffy eds., 2d ed. 2005).

Bogda M.B. Clarke, Patricia H. Thompson & Michael A. Shafir, *"Loss Resulting Directly From...": Causation Under The Financial Institution Bond And Similar Insurance Forms*, IX FID. L.J. 25 (2003).

Stefan Dandelles, David Brown & Barbara Leone, *Funds Transfer Fraud: How Simplified Banking Impacts Financial Institution Bond Coverage* (unpublished paper presented at the ABA TIPS FSLC Mid-Winter Conference, New York, N.Y., Jan. 2011).

David T. DiBiase, Carleton R. Burch & David J. Billings, *The ABC's of Insuring Agreement (D) Under the Financial Institution Bond*, XVII FID. L.J., 2d ed., 1 (2011).

Sean W. Duffy, *Fighting Check Forgery in the New Economy: Is Computer-Generated Check Fraud Covered Under the Financial Institution Bond?*, VI FID. L.J. 1 (2000).

Richard E. Elsea, Jeffrey S. Price & Justin D. Wear, *Specific Types of Claims (Accounts Receivable Financing, Loan Participation and Syndication, Subprime Lending, Floor Plan Financing, Equipment Lease Financing, Mortgage Warehouse Lending) and Riders (Fraudulent Mortgage Rider, and Servicing Contractor Rider), in* LOAN LOSS COVERAGE 283 (Gilbert J. Schroeder & John J. Tomaine eds., 2007).

Melissa L. Gardner & Jason Glasgow, *Check Exposures in Today's Electronic Banking Age: Is The Financial Institution Bond Keeping Stride With a Looming Paperless Society?*, XIII FID. L.J. 13 (2007).

Maura Z. Pelleteri & Diane L. Matthews, *Stealth Loans, Rogue Banking Officers, and Poor Banking Practices Under Insuring Agreements (A), (D), and (E)*, VI FID. L.J. 39 (2000).

Scott L. Schmookler, *Insuring Agreement (D)*, in FINANCIAL INSTITUTION BONDS 313 (Duncan Clore ed., 3d ed. 2008).

Scott L. Schmookler, *The Compensability of Warehouse Lending Losses*, in LOAN LOSS COVERAGE 355 (Gilbert J. Schroeder & John J. Tomaine eds., 2007).

Gail D. Spielberger, *Construction and Application of Insuring Agreement D* (unpublished paper presented at the Fifteenth Annual Northeast Surety and Fidelity Claims Conference 2004), *available at* http://www.forcon.com/ papers/nesfcc/2004/05.Spielberger.pdf.

Susan K. Sullivan & Teresa Jones, *The Question of Causation in Loan Loss Cases*, XI FID. L.J. 89 (2005).

Daniel E. Tranen & Stefan R. Dandelles, *Are Financial Institution Bonds Susceptible? Warehouse Lending Losses Due to Forged Promissory Notes*, 51 FOR THE DEF. 36 (2009).

Gary J. Valeriano, *Handling Forgery Claims and Articles 3 and 4 of the Uniform Commercial Code*, in HANDLING FIDELITY BOND CLAIMS 223 (Michael Keeley & Sean Duffy eds., 2d ed. 2005).

SECTION 5 — INSURING AGREEMENT (E)—SECURITIES*

(E) Loss resulting directly from the Insured having, in good faith, for its own account or for the account of others,
  (1) acquired, sold or delivered, or given value, extended credit or assumed liability, on the faith of, any original
    (a) Certificated Security,
    (b) Document of Title,
    (c) deed, mortgage or other instrument conveying title to, or creating or discharging a lien upon, real property,
    (d) Certificate of Origin or Title,
    (e) Evidence of Debt,
    (f) corporate, partnership or personal Guarantee,
    (g) Security Agreement,
    (h) Instruction to a Federal Reserve Bank of the United States or
    (i) Statement of Uncertificated Security of any Federal Reserve Bank of the United States, which
      (i) bears a signature of any maker, drawer, issuer, endorser, assignor, lessee, transfer agent, registrar, acceptor, surety, guarantor, or of any person signing in any other capacity which is Forgery, or
      (ii) is altered, or
      (iii) is lost or stolen;
  (2) guaranteed in writing or witnessed any signature upon any transfer, assignment, bill of sale, power of attorney, Guarantee, endorsement or any items listed in (a) through (h) above;
  (3) acquired, sold or delivered, or given value, extended credit or assumed liability, on the faith

---

* By Gary J. Valeriano and Carleton R. Burch, Anderson, McPharlin & Conners LLP, Los Angeles, California.

of any item listed in (a) through (d) above which is a Counterfeit.

Actual physical possession of the items listed in (a) through (i) above by the Insured, its correspondent bank or other authorized representative, is a condition precedent to the Insured's having relied on the faith of such items.

A mechanically reproduced facsimile signature is treated the same as a hand-written signature.

COMMENT

Insuring Agreement (E) provides indemnity for specified losses from certain classes of paper-based risks faced by financial institutions. Case law generally continues to limit the coverage to traditional paper-based risks, rejecting efforts to expand it to include electronic or digital transactions except where specifically modified to include such coverage.

The standard insuring agreement provides indemnity for losses sustained directly by financial institutions: (1) from having bought, sold, or loaned money; (2) in good faith; (3) on a specified, listed class of documents; (4) which bear a Forgery, or are altered, lost, stolen, or Counterfeit; and (5) where the "Originals" of such documents are in the insured's "actual physical possession."

Insuring Agreement (E) has remained relatively stable over time. The listed perils in particular have remained largely consistent over time, as has the requirement of "actual physical possession" of the enumerated documents as a "condition precedent" to coverage. Some courts have concluded that if the physical possession condition is satisfied, then the "on the faith of" requirement is necessarily satisfied. This was not the apparent intent of the bond. Possession of an "Original" provides the insured with the opportunity to examine the document, which may result in the discovery of obvious defects. The physical possession requirement was added merely to foreclose an insured's attempt to argue that it relied on the document, even though it did not possess an "Original." In other words, it reflects a conclusion that it is impossible for an insured to have relied on the faith of a defective document if it did not even have possession of the "Original" because in that situation it did not have the opportunity to examine the "Original."

Some courts have concluded that the "on the faith of" requirement requires the insured to take minimal steps to verify the authenticity of the signature or instrument, but most have held that verification is not required. Although verification is arguably not required, the "on the faith of" requirement imposes, at an absolute minimum, the obligation to examine the original. Otherwise, the inclusion of the actual physical possession requirement would serve no practical purpose.

Disputes have occasionally arisen as to whether documents not listed in the classes of covered documents, but bearing a covered defect, can be linked to or "bundled" with a covered document not bearing a covered defect to create a covered "bundled" document bearing a covered defect. This was never the intent of the drafters, and permitting such bundling very clearly expands the scope of Insuring Agreement (E) beyond its intended scope. In response to this argument, in 2004, Form 24 was revised to include an anti-bundling provision in Section 9 of the Conditions and Limitations section of the bond, which was retained when the bond was revised in 2011. The most common issues litigated under Insuring Agreement (E) are whether a bank's claim arose "directly" from a defective covered document, and whether the insured had "actual physical possession" of the original of the alleged covered document.

OUTLINE OF ANNOTATIONS

A. Cases Interpreting the Term "Forgery"
B. Types of Covered Documents
C. Cases Interpreting the Term "Counterfeit"
D. The "on the Faith of" Requirement
E. The "Original Documents" and "Actual Physical Possession" Requirements
F. Other Cases

ANNOTATIONS

A. Cases Interpreting the Term "Forgery"

5th Cir. 1986 (Tex.). The court held that certificates of deposit that misrepresented the deposited amounts were not forgeries because the bank president actually signed the certificates. The court reasoned that there is no forgery when the signor intends to sign their true name and not the name or identity of another. *Charter Bank Nw. v. Evanston Ins. Co.*, 791 F.2d 379, 382.

5th Cir. 1983 (La.). On appeal, the circuit court affirmed the trial court's finding in favor on the bonding company based on the bank's "bad faith." Because bank's bad faith was sufficient for ruling for the insurer, it did not further explore the issue of forgery. *Marsh Inv. Corp. v. Langford*, 721 F.2d 1011, 1015.

5th Cir. 1973 (Tex.). Bank issued an auto loan secured in part by a fraudulent Tax Collector's Receipt for Title Application, or white slip. However, the white slip did not contain an actual or facsimiled signature. The court found that the typed name of the official did not serve as a signature, but rather as an identification of Tax Assessor/Collector. The court held that the white slip was not a forgery under Agreement (E) because it did not bear a "non-genuine signature." *Bank of the Sw. v. Nat'l Sur. Co.*, 477 F.2d 73, 76.

6th Cir. 1991 (Tenn). Circuit court vacated the district court's holding that, under Insuring Clause (E), an insured bears the burden of proving that a signature is a forgery. Before trial, the insurer and insured stipulated that the document at issue was not executed or authorized by the purported signatory. The trial court was therefore bound by the parties' stipulation, and it was not necessary for the bank to present evidence that the signature was inauthentic. *FDIC v. St. Paul Fire & Marine Ins. Co.*, 942 F.2d 1032, 1038-39.

7th Cir. 1991 (Ill.). The court held that a depositor that misappropriated checks by endorsing with a corporate "for deposit only" stamp did not constitute a forgery because the stamp was not the signing of another's name. The court also ruled that even if the stamp was to be considered a signature, it also included the purported forger's first name and therefore could not be a "forgery" under the bond. *Alpine State Bank v. Ohio Cas. Ins.*, 941 F.2d 554, 559-60.

8th Cir. 1961 (Mo.). Bank issued loan secured in part by promissory note and chattel mortgages covering automobiles that the borrower did not own at the time of execution. The court followed the majority rule that "forgery is the fraudulent making or altering of a writing to the prejudice of another's right." The court held that the documents were not forged because they were genuinely executed by the borrower, which therefore prejudiced his own right and not the right of another. *State Bank of Poplar Bluff v. Md. Cas. Co.*, 289 F.2d 544, 548-49.

9th Cir. 1958 (Cal.). Insured bank sought coverage by arguing that an agent's unauthorized signing of his own name as agent constituted a forgery. The court held that there was no coverage because there is no forgery when the instrument is actually signed by the person purporting to have executed the signature. *Torrance Nat'l Bank v. Aetna Cas. & Sur. Co.*, 251 F.2d 666, 668-69.

S.D.N.Y. 1990. The bond defined forgery as "signing the name of another with intent to deceive." The court held that bills of lading containing illegible signatures were not forgeries because the bank failed to prove that the signer signed the name of another person. *French Am. Banking Corp. v. Flota Mercante Grancolombiana S.A.*, 752 F. Supp. 83, 88-90.

Colo. 1961. Insured issued a loan in reliance on invoices for goods and services never furnished. Despite the misrepresentation of services, the invoices were genuinely executed and genuine in form and appearance. The court held that there is no forgery for false representations in otherwise genuine and genuinely executed documents. Because the invoice was not a forgery, the resulting loss was not covered. *USF&G v. First Nat'l Bank of Fort Morgan*, 364 P.2d 202, 205-06.

N.Y. App. Div. 1987. The insured sought coverage for losses sustained from advancing funds based on forged bills of lading and counterfeit invoices. Insurer argued that there was no forgery because the bill of lading contained a stamped, printed signature and not a handwritten or facsimile signature. The court rejected the insurer's argument and held that an unauthorized use of a corporate name stamp on otherwise covered documents can constitute a forgery. *William Iselin & Co. v. Fireman's Fund Ins. Co.*, 117 A.D.2d 86, 89-90.

Wis. 1964. Bank issued loans secured by assignments of accounts receivable that were based on unsigned false invoices. The court determined that the unsigned false invoices and subsequent assignments were not forgeries because forgery related to the "genuineness of execution." The assignments were validly signed by the borrower. Although the invoices were unsigned, they were prepared by or under the direction of the borrower. There was no issue as to genuineness of execution, thus no coverage. *First Am. State Bank v. Aetna Cas. & Sur. Co.*, 130 N.W.2d 824, 826.

B. Types of Covered Documents

4th Cir. 1984 (N.C.). In funding a loan, the bank relied on a certificate of title that stated that the deed of trust securing the loan was a valid first lien on the real property. In fact the certificate was forged and the loan was junior to a prior deed of trust. The district court found that the certificate was not a covered document under the 1969 version of Agreement (E) because it was not transferable. The appellate court reversed and held that the certificate was covered as a securities document. The court reasoned that the certificate was an integral part of the loan packet because it assured the identity of the loan security. *Home Sav. & Loan Ass'n v. Fid. & Deposit Co. of Md.*, 742 F.2d 831, 833.

5th Cir. 1997 (Tex.). Although mortgage documents were defective in that they had little or no value, the defect was not the result of the forged signatures. The court held that in order for coverage to exist for a defective instrument, the defect must have resulted from the forgery. If the forgery has no impact on the value of the instrument, it is not a covered document under Insuring Agreement (E). *FDIC v. Fireman's Ins. Co. of Newark, N.J.*, 109 F.3d 1084, 1089.

5th Cir. 1970 (Tex.). Bank issued a loan in reliance upon a false telegram that acknowledged the loan between bank and borrower and stated that the broker would sell borrower's stocks to repay loan. Court held that the telegram was a covered document because the phrase "securities, documents, or other written instruments" was sufficiently broad to include the telegram and it was common to rely on telegrams as evidence of debts or property rights. *Snyder Nat'l Bank v. Westchester Fire Ins. Co.,* 425 F.2d 849, 852.

5th Cir. 1969 (Fla.). Bank issued a loan in reliance upon altered "Dividend Reinvestment Advices" and "Confirmation of Dividend Reinvested" forms. These forms were held to be covered documents because the terms "securities, documents, or other written instruments" were deemed ambiguous and interpreted against the insurer. *First Nat'l Bank of Fort Walton Beach v. USF&G,* 416 F.2d.52, 56.

6th Cir. 1979 (Ky.). Bank issued loans secured in part by invoices and accounts receivable forged by borrower. Policy expressly excluded coverage for losses resulting from false documents with no value. Court held the invoices to have sufficient value because the receipt portions of the invoices were evidences of debt acknowledged by the purchasers. *First Nat'l Bank v. Aetna Cas. & Sur. Co.,* 610 F.2d 424, 425.

6th Cir. 1977 (Mich.). Bank loaned money for construction of federally subsidized housing. Before each advance, bank required a separate FHA certificate of mortgage to insure against default. After developer defaulted, it was discovered that some of the certificates contained forged signatures. Court held that certificates were "securities, documents, or other written instruments" under five component definition. *Union Inv. Co. v. Fid. & Deposit Co.,* 549 F.2d 1107, 1110.

6th Cir. 1964 (Ky.). Insured purchased discounted notes that were secured by automobile chattel mortgages and automobile leasing agreements containing forged signatures. The court held that the documents were covered as "securities, documents or other written instruments" under Insuring Clause (E). *Liberty Nat'l Bank & Trust Co. v. Nat'l Sur. Corp.,* 330 F.2d. 697, 698-99.

7th Cir. 2007 (Wis.). Bank extended credit to a used-car dealership. Credit was secured in part by fabricated lease agreements for nonexistent cars and altered, valid lease agreements bearing lessee signatures forged by the dealership's president. Insurer argued that Insuring Agreement (E) did not cover losses based on forged documents describing nonexistent or fictitious assets and transactions. The court affirmed the district court's finding that coverage applied, reasoning that but for the forged documents purporting the existence of collateral, credit would not have been extended and therefore, no loss would have occurred. *First Nat'l Bank of Manitowoc v. Cincinnati Ins. Co.*, 485 F.3d 971, 978.

8th Cir. 1969 (Mo.). Insured, as loan participant with another bank, advanced loan proceeds in reliance upon, in part, carbon copies of bills of lading containing forged signatures acknowledging receipt. The court held that coverage applied to resulting loss because: (a) the carbon copy of the bill of lading was one of the "securities, documents, or other written instruments" defined by Insuring Clause (E); (b) the insured extended credit on the basis of a forged document, and thus could recover; and (c) reliance on photostatic copies did not preclude coverage when copies were accurate reproductions. *Am. Ins. Co. v. First Nat'l Bank in St. Louis*, 409 F.2d. 1387, 1390-91.

11th Cir. 2011 (Fla.). The insured bank made a loan secured in part by a personal guaranty from the customer's wife. When the customer defaulted, the bank tried and failed to collect on the wife's guaranty because wife had few assets. The wife later claimed and proved that her signature was forged. The bank notified insurer of its loss and sought coverage. The district court granted summary judgment for insurer because the loss did not result directly from reliance on the forgery. The purported guarantor had few assets when default occurred, and the bank could not have recovered even if the signature was authentic. However, the Eleventh Circuit reversed and held that the guaranty would have had value even in the absence of assets because the guaranty imposed a legal obligation on the guarantor. *Beach Cmty. Bank v. St. Paul Mercury Ins. Co.*, 635 F.3d 1190, 1196-97.

E.D. Ark. 2004. Bank extended a revolving line of credit to a customer in exchange for a general assignment of the customer's assets, which included an assignment of a stream of payments due to the customer under equipment lease contracts. It was later discovered that the bank received falsified leases containing misrepresented lease lengths and amounts. The district court found that the lease was not a certified security or a document of title, but it was a security agreement because it had provisions in common with instruments that secured payment of an obligation. *Pine Bluff Nat'l Bank v. St. Paul Mercury Ins. Co.*, 346 F. Supp. 2d 1020, 1026-28.

N.D. Cal. 2012. As collateral, the bank's customer provided PDF copies of broker account statements representing securities that the customer claimed to own. The customer also executed various loan documents, including an Account Control Agreement ("ACA"). After the customer defaulted, it was discovered that the customer altered the broker account statements of others and he did not own the securities represented therein. Court found that the broker account statements were not security agreements because they neither created a security interest nor secured performance or payment from the customer. However, the court found that the ACA was a security agreement when read in connection with the promissory note, commercial pledge, and commercial security agreement. The ACA secured the payment or performance obligation created by the other documents by placing restrictions on the portfolio's assets to ensure that the assets were available if the bank wished to collect on the loan. *Valley Cmty. Bank v. Progressive Cas. Ins. Co.*, 854 F. Supp. 2d 697, 704-05.

N.D. Ill. 2011. Bank funded a loan secured in part by a lease listing two mechanical chemical polishers as collateral. After the customer defaulted, it was discovered that the serial numbers on the chemical polishers were fraudulent. The fraudulent transaction involved a lease that constituted an evidence of debt, a corporate guarantee, and a security agreement, which were all covered under Insuring Agreement (E). However, none of the documents were forged, altered, lost, or stolen. Because plaintiff did not allege forgery as to the lease, the court granted the insurer's motion to dismiss. *First McHenry Corp. v. BancInsure, Inc.*, No. 10 C 50256, 2011 U.S. Dist. LEXIS 64589, at *3-4, *11, *14.

N.D. Ind. 1996. Insurer argued that forged, uncovered, supporting documents must be viewed separately from the unforged, covered instrument. However, court held that the documents were to be "bundled" together and construed as a single instrument because the supporting documents were required to bind the bank. Loss directly resulting from the bundled documents was therefore covered. *Ominsource Corp. v. CNA Ins. Co.*, 949 F. Supp. 681, 687-88.

D. Kan. 1991. Court held that Insuring Agreement (E) did not cover loss based on checks payable to subcontractors where checks contained forged lien waiver stamps. The checks were not a document creating a lien on real property because the lien was created by the subcontractor's performance. Although the forged lien waiver stamps could be considered a document discharging a lien, the insured received copies of the lien waivers and therefore could not have acted upon the original of a document bearing a forged signature as required for coverage. *First Fed. Sav. Bank v. Cont'l Cas. Co.*, 768 F. Supp. 1449, 1455-56.

M.D. La. 1993. Bank approved loan relying, in part, on a public ordinance that purported to grant the customer a cable television franchise. The bank argued that the ordinance was a "certificate of origin or title." To prove that the ordinance was a covered document, the bank needed to show that the ordinance was a document by which ownership was transferred. The court found that the mere possession or ownership of the ordinance did not transfer the cable franchise. The ordinance expressly required prior approval by the city council before ownership could be transferred. Thus, the ordinance was not a "certificate of origin or title" because the customer could not pledge to transfer any rights it had under the ordinance without the approval of the city council. *FDIC v. Fid. & Deposit Co.*, 827 F. Supp. 385, 395-96.

S.D. Ohio 2008. Insured bank failed to return a fraudulent cashier's check before the midnight deadline. The insured settled with the depository bank and sought to recover the settlement from the insurer. The court rejected the insurer's argument that Insuring Agreement (E) did not apply to cashier's checks. The court found nothing in the language of Insuring Agreement (E) to exclude a cashier's check from coverage. *Merchs. Bank & Trust Co. v. Cincinnati Ins. Co.*, No. 1:06cv561, 2008 U.S. Dist. LEXIS 20151, at *10-11.

D. Or. 2011. The insured bank made a loan that was secured in part by forged guaranties from the borrower's parents. The court found that the bank's loss resulted directly from its extension of credit in reliance on the forged guaranties because the bank would not have extended credit without the forged guaranties. The court distinguished the forged guaranties from cases involving fictitious or worthless collateral, reasoning that at the time of the forgery, the guarantors had sizeable assets. Furthermore, if the signatures were authentic, the guaranty would have had value and imposed a legal obligation on the guarantors. *Columbia Cmty. Bank v. Progressive Cas. Ins. Co.*, No. 10-817-AA, 2011 U.S. Dist. LEXIS 64004, at *13-15.

W.D. Tenn. 1997. Lender issued personal loan in reliance, in part, upon a forged employer letter that purported to evidence a future bonus. Court held that the letter was not an original security agreement under Insuring Agreement (E) because the loss would have occurred even if the signature was genuine. The loss did not result directly from having relied on the letter since the promised bonus did not exist. *K.W. Bancshares, Inc. v. Syndicates of Underwriters at Lloyd's*, 965 F. Supp. 1047, 1055.

N.D. Tex. 1977. As loan collateral, borrower presented fake documents that described nonexistent vehicles and contained forged dealers' signatures. The court held that the fake documents had value and thus were "securities, documents, or other written instruments." Court reasoned that the concocted instrument, if genuine, would have transferred "value," therefore "value" was present. The court also held that the documents were not counterfeit under the bond because there were no original instruments and they did not imitate "a security, document, or other written instrument," but rather created one. *Richardson Nat'l Bank v. Reliance Ins. Co.*, 491 F. Supp. 121, 123, *aff'd*, 619 F.2d 557 (5th Cir. 1980).

Cal. 1971. Insured accepted a "treaty of reinsurance" that guaranteed the casualty company's payment upon the borrower's default. The signature was genuine but unauthorized. Even though the document was not a forgery under California criminal law, "forgery" was held subject to a broad interpretation under the doctrine of reasonable expectations in the insurance context. The bond did not contain the modern definition of "forgery" and therefore covered the resulting loss. *Century Bank v. St. Paul Fire & Marine Ins. Co.*, 93 Cal. Rptr. 569, 570-71.

Cal. Ct. App. 1969. The court held that a continuing loan guaranty, on which one of the signatures was forged, was a "written instrument" covered by Insuring Clause (E). *Jones v. Fireman's Fund Ins. Co.*, 76 Cal. Rptr. 97, 100-01.

Ill. App. Ct. 1989. In order to receive loan funds on behalf of the trustee, an individual delivered to the bank a power of attorney, purportedly executed by the trustee appointing the individual as agent. The bank tendered the funds after the individual executed a promissory note. The power of attorney was forged. The trial court found coverage because the promissory note, which was an evidence of debt, was executed at the same time the power of attorney was presented. The appellate court affirmed, stating that instruments executed for the same purpose and in the course of the same transaction will be construed as a single instrument. The forged power of attorney bundled with the evidence of debt therefore created coverage. *Cmty. State Bank v. Hartford Ins. Co.*, 542 N.E.2d 1317, 1320.

Iowa 1980. Bank made loan to customer secured in part by an account receivable that was evidenced by a photocopy of the settlement agreement between the customer and the account debtor. The customer crudely altered the settlement amount. The court held that the photocopy of a settlement agreement did not constitute "securities, documents or other written instruments," because the 1969 amendment definition included only originals or counterparts of originals. *First Nat'l Bank, Colfax v. Hartford Acc. & Indem. Co.*, 295 N.W.2d 425, 429-30.

Mass. 1959. Bank issued a loan in reliance upon a forged certified financial statement. The court held that "securities, documents or other written instruments" referred only to documents executed as the expression of some act, contract, or proceeding connected with or in the nature of securities, thus disqualifying forged certified financial statement from Insuring Clause (E) coverage. *Rockland-Atlas Nat'l Bank v. Mass. Bonding & Ins. Co.*, 157 N.E.2d 239, 243-45.

Md. Ct. App. 1999. Borrower submitted two forged incumbency certificates to establish his authority to act for company. The court affirmed summary judgment for insurer. The court held that the certificates were not an "evidence of debt" because they simply represented a person's authority to act on behalf of a company. Furthermore, the bank did not receive the certificates before it approved the loan, so the loan was not made in reliance upon the forged certificates. *First Union Corp. v. USF&G*, 730 A.2d 278, 282-83.

Minn. Ct. App. 2012. Customer obtained five loans using guarantees and stock from one of his businesses as collateral. However, the corporation existed only on paper and had no actual business or assets. District court granted summary judgment for insurer as to insureds' claims under Insuring Agreements (D) and (E) because the loan losses were not directly caused by the bank's reliance on the collateral and the forged corporate documents were not "guaranties." The appellate court affirmed, concluding that the loan losses were not covered because the losses resulted from the worthlessness of the guaranties and stock, not directly from the forgeries. *Alerus Fin. Nat'l Ass'n v. St. Paul Mercury Ins. Co.*, No. A11-680, 2012 WL 254484, at *14-17.

Minn. Ct. App. 1989. Bank invested money to participate in a corporate loan. Bank entered into two non-transferable certificates of participation, signed by the lender's vice-president. The vice-president later admitted to misappropriating the bank's investment for his own use. The court held that the certificates were not securities because they were not "in bearer or registered form," they were "not part of a class or series of instruments," and they were not "capable of division into a class or series of instruments." Additionally, there was no forgery because the vice-president signed his own name. *Empire State Bank v. St. Paul Fire & Marine Ins. Co.*, 441 N.W.2d 811, 813-14.

Minn. Ct. App. 1987. Before issuing commercial loan, bank required customer to present and assign to the bank fully executed construction contracts. Bank issued funds in reliance on two fictitious contracts containing forged signatures. The court held that the contracts were not "evidences of debt," because they were not "primary indicia of debt." The contracts, at best, showed prospective financial obligations to the contractor. The contracts were not "security agreements," because they did not "create an interest in personal property or fixtures." The contracts and the assignments them had no value and created no interest in property. *Merchs. Nat'l Bank of Winona v. Transamerica Ins. Co.*, 408 N.W.2d 651, 653-54.

C. Cases Interpreting the Term "Counterfeit"

2d Cir. 1965 (N.Y.). A borrower assigned accounts receivable to the insured as loan security. The invoices evidencing the accounts receivable reflected nonexistent transactions. The invoices were not "counterfeited" because they did not simulate another authentic document. False factual representations contained in otherwise genuine documents were held not covered by Insuring Clause (E). *Exch. Nat'l Bank of Olean v. Ins. Co. of N. Am.,* 341 F.2d 673, 676.

3d Cir. 1973 (N.J.). The bank accepted warehouse receipts as loan security. However, the receipts grossly misrepresented the amount of product that was stored in the warehouse. The court held that coverage under Insuring Clause (E) did not apply because the receipts were not counterfeit. They contained a misrepresentation of facts, which was distinguishable from the spurious or imitative execution of a document. *Whitney Nat'l Bank v. Transam. Ins. Co.,* 476 F.2d 632, 634-35.

3d Cir. 1959 (Pa.). The insured accepted as loan security duplicate invoices purportedly representing assigned accounts receivable. However, the underlying transactions never took place. The court stated that general business usage would indicate that "counterfeit" is something that purports to be something that it is not, which is "precisely" what the spurious invoices were held to be. Therefore, the insured could recover under Insuring Clause (E). *Fid. Trust Co. v. The Am. Sur. Co.,* 268 F.2d 805, 806.

4th Cir. 1963 (N.C.). As security for a loan, borrower pledged copies of fictitious invoices containing genuine signatures. The court held that the loss was not covered because Insuring Clause (E) covered losses arising from reliance on false pretenses only if the fraud was accompanied by the use of a counterfeited or forged signature. *N.C. Nat'l Bank v. U.S. Cas. Co.,* 317 F.2d 304, 307.

4th Cir. 1962 (S.C.). Insured issued loan to borrower in reliance upon unsigned invoices for goods never furnished. The words "counterfeit" and "forged" were both held to be modified by the words "as to the signatures." Thus, Insuring Clause (E) coverage applies only if there is a non-genuine signature contained in the documents. The court found no

Insuring Clause (E) coverage because the invoices were unsigned. *First Nat'l Bank of S.C. v. Glens Falls Ins. Co.*, 304 F.2d 866, 869-70.

5th Cir. 1990 (Tex.). The court held that fabricated stock certificates were not counterfeit because the owner never owned the stock and thus the certificates did not imitate a genuine existing document. The court reasoned that the loss did not result directly from the forgery because the loss would have resulted had the signatures been genuine. *Reliance Ins. Co. v. Capital Bancshares, Inc.*, 912 F.2d 756, 757.

5th Cir. 1970 (Fla.). As loan security, borrower pledged a fake stock certificate containing genuine and authorized signatures. The fake stock certificate was an imitation of genuine stock owned by other banks. The phrase "counterfeited or forged as to the signatures" was interpreted disjunctively, thus affording coverage for documents that: (a) attempt to simulate other documents which are authentic, but (b) are not forged as to their signatures. The court held that the stock certificate was "counterfeited." *Am. Nat'l Bank v. Fid. & Cas. Co. of N.Y.*, 431 F.2d 920, 921, 923.

5th Cir. 1970 (Tex.). Borrower pledged warehouse receipts for cotton as security for loan. At the time the receipts were pledged, the cotton had been sold and shipped, but the borrower had not cancelled the receipts. The court held that there was no Insuring Clause (E) coverage for insured's resulting loss because the receipts were not "counterfeited," but genuine. The failure to cancel them prior to their collaboration did not make them "counterfeited" within Insuring Clause (E). *Md. Cas. Co. v. State Bank & Trust Co.*, 425 F.2d 979, 983.

6th Cir. 1974 (Ohio). Bank issued loan in reliance upon financial statements containing false data. The court held that under Insuring Clause (E), documents are "counterfeited" only when they imitate genuine documents "having a resemblance intended to deceive and to be taken for the original." Here, the statements were genuine as to form because they did not attempt to imitate a genuine document. There was no coverage for false representations of fact in otherwise genuine documents. *Richland Trust Co. v. Fed. Ins. Co.*, 494 F.2d 641, 642.

6th Cir. 1962 (Tenn.). As loan security, Bank accepted validly issued and executed warehouse receipts that contained false representations of fact. The court found no coverage for insured's resulting loss because false representations contained in otherwise genuine documents were not within the ambit of Insuring Clause (E). *First Nat'l Bank of Memphis v. Aetna Cas. & Sur. Co.,* 309 F.2d 702, 705.

7th Cir. 2012 (Wis.). Customer borrowed money to purchase a luxury motor home. Loan was secured in part by the motor home's certificate of origin. After customer's default, the bank learned that the certificate was a fake, the motor home's VIN plate had been altered, and the manufacturer had never produced a motor home with the purported VIN. The court affirmed summary judgment for the insurer because the certificate of origin was not a "counterfeit" under Insuring Agreement (E). The fabricated certificate of origin could not be an imitation of "an actual, valid Original" because the customer's fabricated certificate did not correspond to any actually existing certificate of origin or motor home. *N. Shore Bank FSB v. Progressive Cas. Ins. Co.,* 674 F.3d 884, 888-89.

7th Cir. 2003 (Ill.). The bank loaned funds to marina owner to finance its boat inventory. In exchange, the bank retained the Manufacturer's Statements of Origin ("MSOs"). When the owner failed, the insurer discovered that the owner had created duplicate or fake MSOs for certain boats to obtain loans from multiple sources against the same collateral. Some of the duplicate or fake MSOs were submitted signed and others were submitted unsigned. Court affirmed the district court's holding that the bank was entitled to coverage for the unsigned MSOs, reasoning that the unsigned documents may be "an imitation which is intended to deceive and to be taken as an original" within the bond's definition of a counterfeit. Nothing in the bond required that a document be signed. *State Bank of the Lakes v. Kan. Bankers Sur.,* 328 F.3d 906, 908.

7th Cir. 1969 (Ill.). Insured accepted as loan security an assignment of accounts receivable, which were evidenced by invoices. The invoices contained genuine signatures, but identified nonexistent transactions. The court held that there was no forgery because the signatures on the invoices were genuine. The documents were held not to be counterfeit because they were not imitations of other documents such that a party was deceived on the basis of the quality of the imitation. Invoices representing nonexistent transactions were not counterfeit and thus, were not covered. *Capitol Bank of Chicago v. Fid. & Cas. Co. of N.Y.,* 414 F.2d 986, 988-89.

9th Cir. 1967 (Idaho). Bank incurred loss resulting from a counterfeit cashier's check. The court noted if an individual signs their own name it is not a forgery, even if he misrepresented his authority. The court, however, found the cashier's check to be counterfeit because it was an instrument purporting to be something that it was not. Thus the bank could recover for its resulting loss because under Insuring Clause (E) counterfeit instruments need not be forged to be covered. *United Pac. Ins. Co. v. Idaho First Nat'l Bank,* 378 F.2d 62. 69.

10th Cir. 1965 (Okla.). Borrower assigned accounts receivable to insured as loan security. The assignment was genuine, however, the invoices purporting to evidence the accounts receivable reflected fictitious transactions. The invoices were not "counterfeited" under Insuring Clause (E) because, though falsely representing certain facts, they were not imitations of genuine documents intended to deceive and to be taken for the original. *First Nat'l Bank and Trust Co. v. USF&G,* 347 F.2d 945, 947.

M.D. La. 1993. The court held that there was no coverage under Insuring Agreement (E) because the city ordinance submitted to the insured was not a counterfeit. The court reasoned that the ordinance submitted did not imitate an authentic original document because the genuine city ordinance pertained to voting districts, not a cable television franchise as presented. The court also denied coverage because the bogus ordinance did not transfer ownership. *FDIC v. Fid. & Deposit Co. of Md.,* 827 F. Supp. 385, 393-94.

D.N.J. 1983. The word "counterfeited" within the meaning of the bond means a spurious or imitative execution of a document as distinguished from the document's explicit or implicit misrepresentation of facts. The court held that genuine certificates of deposit issued by a bank that had no assets were not counterfeit under Insuring Agreement (E). *Liberty Nat'l Bank v. Aetna Life & Cas. Co.,* 568 F. Supp. 860, 864.

S.D.N.Y. 1985. The bank extended credit that was secured by fictitious bills of lading. When the bank issued a new loan, a portion of the proceeds of the new loan were used to pay off the earlier loan. The balance of the new loan was secured by the fictitious bills of lading. The court held that the bank's loss was covered whether it resulted from the old loan or the new loan. *French Am. Bank Corp. v. Flota Mercante Grancolombiana S.A.,* 609 F. Supp. 1352, 1356-57.

D.N.D. 2008. The bank advanced funds to a customer in reliance on a faxed copy of an unsigned "Buyer's Bill," which purportedly evidenced the purchase of cattle. However, the Buyer's Bill did not contain the signature of the seller or buyer, an inspector's certification, or identifying information of the cattle that the customer purchased. After customer's default, the bank discovered that the customer had never purchased the cattle. The bank argued that the Buyer's Bill was a counterfeit because it was an imitation made with the intent to deceive. The court found that the Buyer's Bill was not a counterfeit document because it was not an imitation or alteration of a preexisting genuine Buyer's Bill. *Dakota W. Credit Union v. CUMIS Ins. Soc'y,* 532 F. Supp. 2d 1110, 1115-17.

Ala. 1970. A borrower pledged as loan security: (a) an invoice, which was a duplicate of an old invoice; and (b) packing slips. The invoice contained no signature. The packing slips contained a genuine signature. The court held that there was no coverage because Insuring Clause (E) only covered situations where there were genuine signatures on the documents. *Fid. & Cas. Co. v. Bank of Commerce,* 234 So. 2d 871, 877-87.

Ala. 1966. Insured accepted, as loan security, invoices reflecting nonexistent sales. The court found no Insuring Clause (E) coverage because invoices did not bear forged signatures, and were not counterfeited because they were not imitations of other genuine documents. Insuring Clause (E) did not cover loss caused by false representation of facts contained in genuine documents. *Tiarks v. First Nat'l Bank of Mobile,* 182 So. 2d 366, 370-71.

Cal. Ct. App. 1978. A bank loaned money to a borrower pursuant to an "Accounts Receivable Financing Arrangement." Many of the invoices reflected nonexistent transactions, and others overstated the amount and value of the goods and services. The court held that bank could not recover for the resulting losses under Insuring Clause (E). The 1969 revised definition of "counterfeited" was not ambiguous, and the documents in question were not counterfeit because they were not imitations of other documents intended to deceive and to be taken for the original. *Hinkson v. Fireman's Fund Ins. Co.,* 146 Cal. Rptr. 669, 671-72.

La. Ct. App. 1995. The bank made a loan based upon a pledge of phony stock certificates. The court noted that while the certificates first appeared to be legitimate, "there were various differences between the real certificates and those presented to the bank, such as the color and width of borders." Nonetheless, the court held that the certificates were covered under Insuring Clause (E) because they "were imitations, were intended to deceive and were meant to be accepted as originals." *One Am. Corp. v. Fid. & Deposit Co. of Md.,* 658 So. 2d 23, 24-25.

N.Y. App. Div. 1986. Insured entered into an accounts receivable financing agreement with a business, and later discovered that it had been purchasing fictitious accounts receivable. The court held that the fictitious accounts receivable were counterfeit because the prior invoices and delivery documents imitated those from real accounts and customers, despite reflecting fictitious transactions. *William Iselin & Co., Inc. v. Fireman's Fund Ins. Co.,* 117 A.D.2d 86, 91-92.

N.Y. App. Div. 1965. The bank loaned funds in reliance on an assignment of accounts receivable based on invoices for nonexistent transactions. The court agreed that a document or writing is "counterfeit" if it is an imitation or attempt to simulate an authentic document or writing. However, court held that Insuring Agreement (E) did not cover losses resulting from accounts receivable that were nonexistent. *State Bank of Kenmore v. Hanover Ins. Co.,* 267 N.Y.S.2d 672, 674-75.

Ohio Ct. App. 1965. Insured loaned money in reliance upon duplicate certificates of title, which were procured by borrower through false representations of fact to the court clerk. Thus, two or more titles had been obtained for each automobile identified in the certificates of title. The court found no Insuring Clause (E) coverage for insured's resulting loss because loans were procured through trick, artifice, fraud, or false pretenses, within exclusion of Bankers Blanket Bond. The court also found that there was no forgery and that the documents were not counterfeited because they were not imitations of a genuine document. *Union Banking Co. v. USF&G*, 213 N.E.2d 191, 196-98.

D. The "on the Faith of" Requirement

5th Cir. 2012 (La.). Bank gave customer a revolving line of credit in exchange for security interest in the customer's home loan packages, pursuant to a longstanding "warehouse lending arrangement." The bank sustained losses resulting from three loan packages containing forged or falsified documents. The district court interpreted "on the faith of" and "actual possession" to require only reliance and physical possession. The district court did not find any indication that the bond required the bank to review or verify the signatures on the home loan packages before relying on the document. Additionally, the bank had satisfied the "on the faith of" requirement as evidenced by the extension of credit on the three loans. The court affirmed summary judgment for the bank. *Peoples State Bank v. Progressive Cas. Ins. Co.*, 478 F. App'x 858, 859.

5th Cir. 1976. (La.). As security, the bank accepted invoices and receipts purportedly evidencing the sale and shipment of product. The invoices contained forged signatures. The court held that despite the forgery, there could be no recovery under Insuring Clause (E). The bank had relied upon its prior dealings with the borrower, not on the forged documents, in extending credit. Therefore, the loan was not made "on the faith of" the forged documents. *Calcasieu-Marine Nat'l Bank v. Am. Emp'rs Ins. Co.*, 533 F.2d 290, 294.

7th Cir. 1994. (Ill.). The court held that actual physical possession of the covered document is required under Insuring Clause (E). *RTC v. Aetna Cas. & Sur. Co.*, 25 F.3d 570, 581.

10th Cir. 1990 (Okla.). Bank extended loan based on counterfeit securities, however, the policy in question was issued after the transaction. The court held that the bank's loss was not covered because the policy required the transaction to occur after policy was issued and while policy was in force. *United Bank & Trust Co. v. Kan. Bankers Sur. Co.*, 901 F.2d 1520, 1524.

11th Cir. 1990 (Fla.). The court held that actual physical possession of a forged document is required in order to find the insured's reliance upon the forged document in extending credit. The loss was not covered under Insuring Clause (E) because the bank extended credit before it actually possessed the forged bills of lading. The court opined that it would be rare to find a loss covered under Insuring Clause (E) for forged bills of lading because in practice, credit is customarily extended before the bills of lading are actually provided to the entity extending the credit. *Republic Nat'l Bank v. Fid. & Deposit Co. of Md.*, 894 F.2d 1255, 1262-63.

D. Minn. 2013. Court held that bank did not extend credit "on the faith" of forged guaranty because it never obtained a legal interest in the guaranty when it made a loan to fund an equipment leasing transaction. The bank was not a party to the guaranty; the guarantors did not guarantee payment to the bank but only to the lessor; and although the bank was assigned the rights to the underlying lease payments, it was never assigned any rights to the guaranty. Because bank did not actually receive legal interest, its references to the guaranty in its financing checklist or transaction summary were irrelevant. *BancInsure, Inc. v. Highland Bank,* No. 11-cv-2497 (SRN/JSM), slip op. at 15-18.

D. Minn. 2012. In exchange for a loan, the bank received assignment of a lease and guarantees from the borrower and his mother. The mother later claimed that her signature on the guaranty was forged and that she had not agreed to guarantee the loan. None of the bank employees who had authority to approve loans saw the original lease documents or guarantees when the loan was funded and the bank had only received e-mail copies of the documents. Additionally, the bank president confirmed that the bank would not have had the originals of the documents in the normal course of its loan approval process. Because those with loan approval authority did not see the original documents, the bank could not have relied on the original documents when extending the loan and Insuring Agreement (E) did not cover the loss. *Highland Bank v. BancInsure, Inc.*, No. 10-4107 (SRN/AJB), 2012 U.S. Dist. LEXIS 119940, at *7-11.

SECTION 5 — INSURING AGREEMENT (E)—SECURITIES

Cal. Ct. App. 1972. Bank loaned money and required, as security, financial statements and personal guarantees from partners and their wives. However, one of the partner's financial statements was forged and listed only his assets, not his liabilities. Additionally, a wife's signature was forged on the guarantee. The court held that despite the forgery, there was no Insuring Clause (E) coverage because the loan was not made "on the faith of" the forged documents. The paucity of information in the financial statement, and the comparative wealth of the guarantors, excluding the wife, precluded a finding of reliance by the insured. *Cont'l Bank v. Phoenix Ins. Co.,* 24 Cal. App. 3d 909, 913-14.

Iowa 1980. A bank alleged its reliance on a photocopy of a settlement agreement given as loan collateral. The customer falsely represented that more money was due him under the agreement, which had actually been satisfied in full. The court held no recovery could be had under Insuring Clause (E). The bank did not extend credit on the "faith of" the agreement because the agreement specifically stated that no further money was to be paid to customer and strong circumstantial evidence indicated a lack of reliance. Additionally, the photocopy did not constitute a "security document or other written instrument" under Insuring Clause (E). *First Nat'l Bank, Colfax v. Hartford Acc. & Indem. Co.,* 295 N.W.2d 425, 428.

La. Ct. App. 1972. A borrower pledged 51 third-party promissory notes as collateral for two loans. The loans were not repaid, and the bank eventually determined that some of the notes had been forged. The court held no coverage under Insuring Clause (E) existed because the notes had been pledged six months after the loans had been made. *Allen State Bank v. The Traveler's Indem. Co.,* 270 So. 2d 270, 273.

N.H. 1981. Contrary to customer's direction, the bank issued checks to a payee without an escrow provision. The payee converted the funds and failed to fulfill its obligation to the customer. The court held that the phrase "on the faith of" limits coverage to losses incurred when the insured gives value or extends credit "in reliance upon" the instrument in question. The bank neither gave value nor extended credit in reliance upon any instrument. Therefore, there was no coverage under Insuring Clause (E). *Exeter Banking Co. v. N.H. Ins. Co.,* 438 A.2d 310, 315.

Tex. Civ. App. 1975. After three separate loans to borrower went into default, the insured threatened to "call" borrower's loans unless security was pledged. The borrower then pledged stock certificates that were later discovered to be both forged and worthless. The court held no Insuring Clause (E) coverage because the insured had already sustained the loss before any forged securities were accepted. Accordingly, there was no loss "through" acceptance of the forged securities as loan collateral. *Tex. Nat'l Bank of Dallas v. Fid. & Deposit Co. of Md.*, 526 S.W.2d 770, 774.

E. The "Original Documents" and "Actual Physical Possession" Requirements

8th Cir. 2006 (Minn.). In exchange for a loan, the bank required two personal guarantees from its customer's business associates. The bank disbursed the funds before it had actual, physical possession of the original guarantees. It was later discovered that the customer forged the signatures on the guarantees. The court rejected the bank's argument that the bond's reference to "mechanically reproduced facsimile signature" meant that possessing the faxed personal guarantees was the same as possessing the original. While Insuring Agreement (E) provides that a mechanically reproduced signature is treated the same as a handwritten signature, the mechanical reproduction does not transform a reproduced signature into an "original" signature, nor does it transform the document that contains the signature into an "original" document. Because the bank did not have actual physical possession of the original guarantees before it disbursed the funds, there was no coverage under Insuring Agreement (E). *BancInsure, Inc. v. Marshall Bank, N.A.*, 453 F.3d 1073, 1075-76.

9th Cir. 2010 (Mont.). The insured banks participated in several bad loans. The insurer denied the claim because Insuring Agreement (E) requires the banks to have physical possession of the original security document before extending credit. The court affirmed summary judgment for the insurer because the banks did not prove that they or an authorized representative had "[a]ctual physical possession" of the original security documents before credit was extended. *Bank of Bozeman v. BancInsure, Inc.*, 404 F. App'x 117, 118-119.

N.D. Cal. 2012. As collateral, the bank's customer provided PDF copies of broker account statements representing securities that the customer supposedly owned. The court found that the broker account statements were not security agreements because they neither created a security interest nor secured performance or payment from the customer. However, even if the statements were security agreements under the bond, the PDF statements failed to meet the "original" document requirement because the bond explicitly prevented the bank from relying on electronic versions as originals. *Valley Cmty. Bank v. Progressive Cas. Ins. Co.*, 854 F. Supp. 2d 697, 706-07.

E.D. Wis. 2005. Owner of used car dealership obtained a "line" of credit based on the auto leases. After the dealer called or faxed the lease terms to the bank, the bank would approve the loan if it found the lease terms acceptable. A number of the leases were for nonexistent cars and contained forged customers' signatures. Although the bank had orally approved the loans before receiving the leases, the court held that there was coverage because funds were not disbursed until after the insured had received the lease agreements. *First Nat'l Bank v. Cincinnati Ins. Co.*, No. 03-C-241, 2005 U.S. Dist. LEXIS 42823, at *7-9.

Minn. 1989. A bank extended a loan on the faith of fake stock certificates, which had earlier been used to defraud another local bank. The court held that Insuring Clause (E)'s physical possession requirement is strictly enforced, reasoning that "[i]f a bank, such as respondent, chooses not to follow sound business practices and fails to investigate, verify, examine, or even possess securities before remitting loan proceeds, it cannot successfully claim this is an insured risk and not an ordinary business loss." The court also held that, under Insuring Clause (E) a counterfeit document must directly imitate in detail—i.e., be an exact imitation of—another preexisting document. *Nat'l City Bank of Minn. v. St. Paul Fire & Marine Ins. Co.*, 447 N.W.2d 171, 175-76, 180.

Pa. Super. Ct. 1989. A bank extended credit in reliance on forged bills of lading. The insurer denied coverage under the Bankers Blanket Bond because the bank did not possess the original bills of lading, but only photocopies. The court held that only original documents suffice in an Insuring Clause (E) claim. The court applied Black's Law Dictionary's definition of "original" as "the first copy or archetype; that from which another instrument is transcribed, copied, or imitated." The court also held that original forged documents are subject to the "actual physical possession" clause and that physical possession of original documents is a condition precedent to recovery. *Hamilton Bank v. Ins. Co. of N. Am.*, 557 A.2d 747, 750-51.

F. Other Cases

3d Cir. 1992 (Penn.). The court applied a "proximate cause" test to determine whether a loss based on a forged notary's signature on a mortgage document resulted directly from the forgery. In finding that the loss resulted directly from the forged document, the court held that the issue was whether the forged signature was a substantial factor in causing the loss. *Jefferson Bank v. Progressive Cas. Ins. Co.*, 965 F.2d 1274, 1280-81, 1285.

6th Cir. 2013 (Ky.). Bank made $1 million loan to borrower secured by an assignment of a life insurance policy with a purported net cash surrender value of $1.8 million. When borrower defaulted, bank discovered that the actual value of the policy was $65,000. Bank sought indemnity for its loss under Insuring Agreements (D) and (E), which insurer denied. The court granted the insurer's summary judgment because Insuring Agreement (E) only covered losses "resulting directly from" forged documents, not from losses caused by the bank's acceptance and reliance on collateral that was nearly worthless, regardless of whether the signatures on the assignment documents were genuine. *Forcht Bank, NA v. BancInsure, Inc.*, No. 11-6328, 2013 U.S. App. LEXIS 3193, at *14-15.

6th Cir. 2008 (Mich.). The bank entered into a warehouse-lending agreement with borrower. Consistent with the Bank's policies, it required the borrower to submit documents to obtain the advances, including original promissory notes. It was later discovered that 39 of the promissory notes were forged and evidenced nonexistent mortgage transactions. The court found that the collateral that the bank had received was entirely fictitious. Because the promissory notes would have been worthless even if they contained authentic signatures, the court affirmed the district court's holding that the bank's loss did not directly result from the forgery. *Flagstar Bank, FSB v. Fed. Ins. Co.*, 260 F. App'x 820, 823, 825.

7th Cir. 2007 (Wis.). Bank extended credit to a used-car dealership. Credit was secured in part by fabricated lease agreements for nonexistent cars and altered valid lease agreements bearing forged lessee signatures. The circuit court affirmed the district court's finding that the loss was covered under Insuring Agreement (E), reasoning that but for the forged documents purporting the existence of collateral, credit would not have been extended and therefore, no loss would have occurred. *First Nat'l Bank of Manitowoc v. Cincinnati Ins. Co.*, 485 F.3d 971, 980.

8th Cir. 2008 (Minn.). Insured bank funded several mortgage refinances by advancing the funds to a closing agent, who stole them. The bank sought coverage under Insuring Agreement (E) because the original mortgage documents were "lost" preventing the bank from recording the mortgages. The lower court concluded that "lost" refers to a document that was lost by its true owner before the bank came into possession of the document. The court affirmed the district court's decision that there was no coverage because the original securities were not "lost or stolen" when assigned to the bank, but rather lost after the loan was made. *Ohio Sav. Bank v. Progressive Cas. Ins. Co.*, 521 F.3d 960, 964-65.

8th Cir. 1971 (Mo.). The borrower pledged shares of stock as loan security and executed two promissory notes. The notes were not paid when due, and the bank allowed the borrower to "replace" the earlier notes with two new promissory notes, secured by third-party promissory notes. Two of the third party promissory notes contained forged signatures. The court held that the loss was covered under Insuring Clause (E). The court rejected the insurer's argument that there was no loss because the insured did not prove that the original loan security, the stock, ever had any value. The value of the stock was immaterial because there was a novation, which substituted a new legal obligation for an old one. *Baltimore Bank & Trust Co. v. USF&G*, 436 F.2d 743, 746.

11th Cir. 2011 (Fla.). Bank made a loan to customer secured in part by a personal guaranty from customer's wife. When customer defaulted, the bank tried and failed to collect on wife's guaranty. Wife proved that her signature was forged. The district court granted summary judgment for insurer because loss did not result directly from reliance on forgery. The purported guarantor had few assets when default occurred, and bank could not have recovered even if the signature was authentic. The circuit court reversed and held that the guaranty would have had value even in the absence of assets because the guaranty imposed a legal obligation on the guarantor. *Beach Cmty. Bank v. St. Paul Mercury Ins. Co.*, 635 F.3d 1190, 1196-97.

E.D. Ark. 2004. Bank extended a revolving line of credit to a customer in exchange for a general assignment of the customer's assets, which included payments due to the customer under lease contracts. It was later discovered that the bank received falsified lease forms. The court found that "loss resulting directly from" was equivalent to proximate cause as defined by Black's Law Dictionary. The court held that Insuring Agreement (E) does not expressly require that the forgery be the sole cause of loss. *Pine Bluff Nat'l Bank v. St. Paul Mercury Ins. Co.*, 346 F. Supp. 2d 1020, 1030.

N.D. Cal. 2012. As collateral, the bank's customer provided PDF copies of broker account statements representing securities that the customer supposedly owned. The customer also executed various loan documents, including an Account Control Agreement ("ACA"). The court found that the ACA was a security agreement when read in connection with the promissory note, commercial pledge, and commercial security agreement. However, the court also found that the plaintiff's loss was not directly caused by the forged signature on the ACA because a validly signed ACA would not have prevented the loss. Rather, the loss was directly caused by the customer's misrepresentations regarding ownership of the securities. *Valley Cmty. Bank v. Progressive Cas. Ins. Co.*, 854 F. Supp. 2d 697, 708-09.

W.D. Okla. 2010. Bank funded a loan that was secured by a business performance guaranty. There was no evidence that the guaranty or any other qualifying document that the bank relied on to fund the loan bore any forgeries, or were altered, lost, or stolen. The loan went into default. The bank sought coverage under Insuring Agreement (E), arguing that the "forgery," "alterations," and "lost or stolen" requirements did not apply to Uncertified Securities under E(1)(i). The court disagreed and found that the bond's language was not ambiguous and that the requirements within the subparagraphs applied to all of the covered documents described in E(1). The court reasoned that the Uncertified Securities Rider supported its finding. Because there was no evidence to suggest that the bank relied on documents that bore any forgeries or were altered, lost, or stolen, the bank's loss was not covered under Insuring Agreement (E). *First Nat'l Bank of Davis v. Progressive Cas. Ins. Co.*, No. CIV-09-546-F, 2010 U.S. Dist. LEXIS 141769, at *10, *13-14, *aff'd*, 415 F. App'x 867 (10th Cir. Feb. 1, 2011).

D. Or. 2011. The insured bank made a loan that was secured in part by forged guaranties from the customer's parents. The court found that the bank's loss resulted directly from its extension of credit in reliance on the forged guaranties because the bank would not have extended credit without the forged guaranties. The court distinguished the forged guaranties from fictitious or worthless collateral, reasoning that at the time of the forgery, the guarantors had sizeable assets. Furthermore, if the signatures were authentic, the valid guaranty would have had value and imposed a legal obligation on the guarantors. *Columbia Cmty. Bank v. Progressive Cas. Ins. Co.*, No. 10-817-AA, 2011 U.S. Dist. LEXIS 64004, at *12-14.

D. Or. 1968. The insured bank participated with another bank in a loan, which was secured by forged and counterfeit stock certificates. The security was provided to the other bank, but not to the insured bank. The court held that the insured could recover under Insuring Clause (E) because (a) the insured had constructive possession of the stock; (b) the insured suffered "loss" under Insuring Clause (E); and (c) the negligence of insured did not negate bond coverage, because the insured could have acted "in good faith" as defined by Insuring Clause (E), and still have been negligent. *Citizens Bank of Or. v. Am. Ins. Co.*, 289 F. Supp. 211, 213-14.

Ga. Ct. App. 2000. The bank approved a loan secured by a credit union bank account. After the default, the bank discovered that the letters confirming the existence of the credit union account were false and contained a forged signature of the credit union representative. Court held that bank could not recover under the bond because the loss was caused by nonexistent assets. The bond did not relieve the bank from its responsibility to investigate its borrower's assets and "did not protect the bank from its bad business deal." *Ga. Bank & Trust v. Cincinnati Ins. Co.*, 538 S.E.2d 764, 766.

Miss. 1966. The insured bank made loans to a borrower based upon stolen warehouse receipts. The court held that bank could recover under Insuring Clause (E) because it had no title to the product referred to by the receipts and was not required to sue the warehouse before seeking bond coverage. *St. Paul Fire & Marine Ins. Co. v. Lefiore Bank & Trust Co.*, 181 So. 2d 913, 918-19.

Minn. Ct. App. 2012. Customer obtained five loans using guarantees and stock from one of his businesses as collateral. The customer's business existed only on paper and had no assets. The appellate court affirmed no coverage under Insuring Agreement (E) because the losses resulted from the worthlessness of the guarantees and stock, not directly from the forgeries. *Alerus Fin. Nat'l Ass'n v. St. Paul Mercury Ins. Co.*, No. A11-680, 2012 WL 254484, at *14-17.

Ohio 1966. The insurer was granted a decree reforming a Bankers Blanket Bond, where: (a) the insured's previous Bankers Blanket Bond contained no Insuring Clause (E) coverage; and (b) the insured's insurance agent did not request Insuring Clause (E) coverage when applying for the bond at issue. The court held that the inclusion of Insuring Clause (E) coverage, under the circumstances, did not constitute a correct integration of the parties' agreement. *Ohio Farmers Ins. Co. v. Clinton County Nat'l Bank,* 220 N.E.2d 381, 385-86.

SECONDARY SOURCES

Samuel J. Arena, Jr. & Marianne Johnston, *Determining the Amount of Loan Loss and the Potential Income Exclusion, in* LOAN LOSS COVERAGE UNDER FINANCIAL INSTITUTION BONDS 153 (Gilbert J. Schroeder & John J. Tomaine eds., 2008).

Peter C. Haley & Sarah Mubashir, *Loan Loss Coverage Under Insuring Agreement (E), in* LOAN LOSS COVERAGE UNDER FINANCIAL

INSTITUTION BONDS 73 (Gilbert J. Schroeder & John J. Tomaine eds., 2008).

Peter C. Haley & Dolores Parr, *On Coverage Under Insuring Agreement E of the Financial Institution Bond, in* FINANCIAL INSTITUTION BONDS 385 (Duncan L. Clore ed., 3d ed., 2008).

Peter Haley & Sarah Mubashir, *How to Combine Fact Finding and Legal Research in the Investigation of Clause (E) Claims, in* HANDLING FIDELITY BOND CLAIMS 275 (Michael Keeley & Sean Duffy eds., 2d ed., 2005).

Michael Keeley, Michele L. Fenice & J. Will Eidson, *Insuring Agreement (E)—Revisited,* XVII FID. L.J. 2d ed., 203 (2011).

John J. McDonald, Jr., Joel T. Wiegert & Michelle M. Carter, *The Loan Loss Exclusion, in* LOAN LOSS COVERAGE UNDER FINANCIAL INSTITUTION BONDS 123 (Gilbert J. Schroeder & John J. Tomaine eds., 2008).

Edgar Neal, *Financial Institution and Fidelity Coverage for Loan Losses,* 21 TORT & INS. L.J. 590 (1986).

Maura Z. Pelleteri, *Causation in Loan Loss Cases in,* LOAN LOSS COVERAGE UNDER FINANCIAL INSTITUTION BONDS 217 (Gilbert J. Schroeder & John J. Tomaine eds., 2008).

Jean E. K. Prem, Jeffrey M. Paskert & James A. Black, Jr., *On the Loan Loss Exclusion: Assuring that Credit and Business Risks Remain with the Financial Institution, in* FINANCIAL INSTITUTION BONDS 443 (Duncan L. Clore ed., 3d ed. 2005).

SECTION 6 — INSURING AGREEMENT (F)—COUNTERFEIT CURRENCY*

(F) Loss resulting directly from the receipt by the Insured, in good faith, of any Counterfeit Money of the United States of America, Canada or of any other country in which the Insured maintains a branch office.

COMMENT

This provision is substantially the same as that found in the 1980 version of the Financial Institution Bond. However, it adds coverage for "Counterfeit Money of . . . any country in which the Insured maintains a branch office." The bond defines "Counterfeit" as "an imitation which is intended to deceive and to be taken as an original." The bond defines "Money" as "a medium of exchange in current use authorized or adopted by a domestic or foreign government as part of its currency." This insuring agreement was not changed as part of the 2004 or 2011 revisions.

While this provision has not been expressly addressed by the courts, and the nature of counterfeit currency is usually different from other counterfeited instruments, opinions regarding other counterfeit provisions may nevertheless be helpful in interpreting Insuring Agreement (F), such as the annotations in Chapter 1, Section 5 — Insuring Agreement (E)—Securities and Chapter 3, Section 1 — Definitions.

ANNOTATIONS

D. Kan. 1991. Checks made payable to subcontractors but never delivered to them were not counterfeit documents under Insuring Agreement (E) because the contractor presented copies of the original checks to the lender to induce the lender to release funds. Although undelivered, the original checks were genuine, not imitations of original genuine documents. *First Fed. Sav. Bank of Newton v. Cont'l Cas. Co.*, 768 F. Supp. 1449, 1456.

---

*   By Lisa D. Sparks, Wright, Constable & Skeen, LLP, Baltimore, Maryland.

W.D. Penn. 1959. Notwithstanding genuine and unnecessary signatures, false instruments purporting to reflect accounts receivable pledged as collateral were "counterfeited" under Insuring Agreement (E). This definition of counterfeit in Insuring Agreement (E) refers to written instruments other than and different from currency, which is covered by Insuring Agreement (F). *Fid. Trust Co. v. Am. Sur. Co. of N.Y.*, 174 F. Supp. 630, 632-33.

SECONDARY SOURCES

NONE

SECTION 7 — INSURING AGREEMENT (G)—FRAUDULENT MORTGAGES—2011 FORM*

(G) Loss resulting directly from the Insured's having, in good faith and in the normal course of business in connection with any Loan, accepted or received or acted upon the faith of any Written, Original:

(1) real property mortgages, real property deeds of trust or like instruments pertaining to realty, or

(2) assignments of such mortgages, deeds of trust or instruments

which prove to have been defective by reason of the signature thereon of any person having been obtained through trick, artifice, fraud or false pretenses or the signature on the recorded deed conveying such real property to the mortgagor or grantor of such mortgage or deed of trust having been obtained by or on behalf of such mortgagor or grantor through trick, artifice, fraud or false pretenses.

COMMENT

Insuring Agreement (G) was added to the Financial Institution Bond in 2011. This section adopted in large part the language of what was formerly known as the Fraudulent Mortgages Insuring Agreement Rider.[1] Insuring Agreement (G) provides a narrow exception to Exclusion (e), the loan loss exclusion, which excludes loss resulting directly or indirectly from the complete or partial nonpayment of, or default upon, any loan or transaction involving the insured as a lender or borrower, or extension of credit, whether procured in good faith or through trick, artifice, fraud, or false pretenses.

Although there is little case law applying the language of current Insuring Agreement (G), cases interpreting the rider remain applicable because the majority of the language from the rider was incorporated into Insuring Agreement (G), with few modifications. Courts addressing the rider held that the coverage required proof that: (1) the insured acted in good faith and in the normal course of business; (2) the insured suffered

---

* By Seth Mills and Kevin Mekler, Mills Paskert Divers, Tampa, Florida.

[1] For purposes of this section, the Fraudulent Mortgages Insuring Agreement Rider will hereinafter be referred to as the "Rider."

a loss; (3) the loss must have been caused by the insured's reliance on a real property mortgage or certain specified instruments relating to mortgages; (4) the mortgage or instrument must be defective; and (5) the defect must be caused by a signature on that mortgage or instrument being obtained by fraud.

Generally, the most frequently litigated issues under the rider have been: (1) the type of instrument; (2) whether the signature was procured by fraud; and (3) whether the "defect" directly caused the loss. Under this general framework, the courts strictly construed the types of instruments that were covered under the rider. For example, a title commitment was found not to be a covered instrument because it is not a mortgage, deed of trust, or equivalent document.

The courts conducted significantly more detailed analysis with regard to whether the signature was procured by fraud and whether the "defect" directly caused the loss. To determine whether the signature was procured by fraud, the courts looked at whether the mortgagors knew that they were signing a mortgage or were caused to believe that the mortgage did not or would not have the effect of encumbering the property. A mortgage that is defective by reason of the signature thereon is one that fails to provide the promised security interest in real property because the mortgagor was tricked or defrauded as to the nature of the document being signed. Similarly, the courts routinely held that there was no coverage under the Rider where the signatory was part of the fraudulent scheme because the defect was not obtained by fraud. Rather, the signature was part of the fraud.

Courts typically addressed the last issue, whether the "defect" directly caused the loss, in connection with claims for coverage under other insuring agreements. In conducting this analysis, the courts continued to wrestle with whether to apply "direct" versus "proximate" causation. However, the majority of courts have found no coverage where the fact that the signature was fraudulently obtained had no impact on the instrument's value to the insured. This analysis is similar to the analysis of worthless or fictitious collateral under Insuring Agreements (D) and (E).

One primary difference between the Rider and Insuring Agreement (G) is the inclusion of the requirement for a "Written, Original" mortgage, deed of trust, or like instrument. This language was not included in the Rider, and there is no case law interpreting this requirement under Insuring Agreement (G). The courts are therefore likely to interpret this requirement by looking to cases construing other insuring agreements that require presentation or possession of original documents, like Insuring Agreement (E).

ANNOTATIONS

3rd Cir. 1992 (Penn.). Summary judgment entered for the insurer where bank alleged coverage under Fraudulent Mortgages Insuring Agreement Rider for losses associated with borrower who defaulted on obligation to repay loan advanced by bank. The bank alleged that the loss was covered because the mortgage was acknowledged by an imposter posing as a notary, and the mortgage was never recorded. The court held that the signature of the imposter notary was "not obtained by fraud; rather it was part of the fraud" thus, there was no coverage. Additionally, the bank argued that the title commitment contained three fraudulently obtained signatures of bank officers. The court held that there was no coverage because a title commitment is not a mortgage, deed of trust, or like instrument. *Jefferson Bank v. Progressive Cas. Ins. Co.*, 965 F.2d 1274, 1278-79.

5th Cir. 1997 (Tex.). Summary judgment entered for insurer on FDIC's claim that defunct savings association was fraudulently induced to enter mortgage swap transactions that involved impaired mortgages. The court held that although the mortgages may have been defective, the defects were not caused by a signature obtained through fraud. The court reasoned that an instrument is only defective under the Fraudulent Mortgages Insuring Agreement Rider if the defect results from a signature being obtained through fraud. However, when the fact that the signature is fraudulently obtained has no impact on the instrument's value to the insured, the rider does not provide coverage. The signature at issue, fraudulently obtained or not, had no effect on the values of the assignment or underlying mortgage. *FDIC v. Firemen's Ins. Co. of Newark, N.J.*, 109 F.3d 1084, 1088-89.

8th Cir. 2008 (Minn.). The court upheld a summary judgment for the insurer related to a claim asserted by the assignee of a mortgage lender, alleging that the president of its closing agent stole funds advanced by the assignee to "table fund" several mortgages. The insured alleged that borrowers were fraudulently induced to sign notes and mortgages by representations that the loan proceeds would be used to satisfy their existing mortgages. The court held that the borrowers knew that they were signing mortgages that would encumber their property, thus the signatures were not defective. The court reasoned that "a mortgage defective by reason of the signature thereon is one that fails to provide the promised security interest in real property because the mortgagor was tricked or defrauded as to the nature of the document." *Ohio Sav. Bank v. Progressive Cas. Ins. Co.*, 521 F.3d 960, 963-64.

D. Neb. 2008. Warehouse lender sought coverage under Financial Institution Bond that contained a Fraudulent Mortgages Insuring Agreement Rider for alleged losses arising from a fraudulent conveyance of certain parcels of land. The insured alleged that the borrower was defrauded into thinking he had obtained title to the properties and that his signature on the deeds of trust conveyed an interest in the property to the insured. The court held that fraudulent inducement alone does not establish coverage. There must also be some showing that the signature is defective because the signatory was defrauded as to the nature of the document signed. Ultimately, the court granted summary judgment for the insurer because the borrower's signature was authentic, and he knew that he was signing deeds of trust. *TierOne Bank v. Hartford Fire Ins. Co.*, No. 4:07-CV-3199, 2008 WL 5170579, at *6-7.

N.J. Super. Ct. Law Div. 1993. Partial summary judgment entered for insurer under Fraudulent Mortgage Insuring Agreement Rider on claim by insured bank related to failed transactions to purchase second mortgages. The bank alleged that the purchase was nothing more than a "criminal racketeering enterprise" that misappropriated funds earmarked to pay the mortgages. The court held that the loss was not covered under the Fraudulent Mortgage Insuring Agreement Rider because the bank failed to establish either that the mortgagors did not know they were signing a mortgage or that they were caused to believe that the mortgage did not or would not have the effect of encumbering the property. Additionally, the court held that the bank's losses resulted not from a "defective" mortgage, but rather from the over-valuation of the mortgaged properties. *N. Jersey Sav. and Loan Ass'n. v. Fid. & Deposit Co. of Md.*, 660 A.2d 1287, 1299-1300.

SECONDARY SOURCES

David T. DiBiase & Jacqueline Kirk, *Riders On The Storm: An Examination Of Industry Trends Relative To Special Fidelity Bond Riders And Endorsements*, III FID. L.J. 115 (1997).

Jason Glasgow & Elizabeth F. Staruck, *The Bubble Burst: The Fraudulent Mortgage Rider In The Current Mortgage Crisis*, XVI FID. L.J. 179 (2010).

Chapter 2

General Agreements

SECTION 1 — GENERAL AGREEMENT A—NOMINEES*

A. Loss sustained by any nominee organized by the Insured for the purpose of handling certain of its business transactions and composed exclusively of its Employees shall, for all the purposes of this bond and whether or not any partner of such nominee is implicated in such loss, be deemed to be loss sustained by the Insured.

COMMENT

Nominees are often used by financial institutions to act on their behalf in a limited capacity or in a specific manner. Organized as a separate institution, the nominee may have the added benefit of limiting a bank's liability regarding the functions it performs.

While expanding coverage to losses sustained by a bank's nominee, the Financial Institution Bond, in truth, does not enlarge the insurer's risk. General Agreement A limits coverage to those nominees that the insured organizes and who are wholly comprised of the insured's employees. Thus, General Agreement A merely provides coverage for acts of employees it would otherwise insure if the nominee were not organized.

ANNOTATIONS

8th Cir. 1970 (Mo.). In action against bond providing coverage for insured company and forty-seven named associated, subsidiary, and affiliated companies, the court held that Bankers Blanket Bond covered

---

* By Maura Z. Pelleteri and Amy Malish, Krebs, Farley & Pelleteri, PLLC, New Orleans, Louisiana.

losses sustained by a former subsidiary that had been sold. The defendant insurer argued that the bond only covered companies that were associates, subsidiaries, or affiliates of the insured company and that when the former subsidiary ceased to be a member of that class, coverage for the subsidiary terminated. The court rejected the insurer's contention, ruling that fidelity coverage continued for the former subsidiary because it was a named insured, not because of its membership in a stated class. *Okla. Morris Plan Co. v. Sec. Mut. Cas. Co.*, 455 F.2d 1209, 1211.

S.D. Miss. 1998. The insured's general agent asserted that its losses, which had been caused by a dishonest employee's malfeasance, were covered by the bond. The insurer moved to dismiss because the agent was not an insured under the bond. The court rejected the agent's position and held that the agent's agency agreement with the insured evidenced that the agent was an independent company, not a nominee "organized by the insured." *Nationalcare Corp., Inc. v. St. Paul Prop. & Cas. Ins. Co.*, 22 F. Supp. 2d 558, 565.

SECONDARY SOURCES

NONE

SECTION 2 — GENERAL AGREEMENT B—ADDITIONAL OFFICES*

B. If the Insured shall, while this bond is in force, establish any additional offices, other than by consolidation or merger with, or purchase or acquisition of assets or liabilities of, another institution, such offices shall be automatically covered hereunder from the date of such establishment without the requirement of notice to the Underwriter or the payment of additional premium for the remainder of the premium period.

If the Insured shall, while this bond is in force, consolidate or merge with, or purchase or acquire assets or liabilities of, another institution, the Insured shall not have such coverage as is afforded under this bond for loss which

(a) has occurred or will occur in offices or premises, or

(b) has been caused or will be caused by an employee or employees of such institution, or

(c) has arisen or will arise out of the assets or liabilities acquired by the Insured as a result of such consolidation, merger, or purchase or acquisition of assets or liabilities unless the Insured shall

  (i) give the Underwriter written notice of the proposed consolidation, merger or purchase or acquisition of assets or liabilities prior to the proposed effective date of such action and

  (ii) obtain the written consent of the Underwriter to extend the coverage provided by this bond to such additional offices or premises, Employees and other exposures, and

  (iii) upon obtaining such consent, pay to the Underwriter an additional premium.

---

* By Maura Z. Pelleteri and Amy Malish, Krebs, Farley & Pelleteri, PLLC, New Orleans, Louisiana.

COMMENT

General Agreement B describes how coverage may be extended when the insured's business expands. It is important to note that not all expansions are treated the same. Where the insured's expansion merely includes the establishment of additional offices, the new offices and their employees will automatically be covered under the bond, without notifying the underwriter, obtaining its consent, or paying an additional premium for this additional coverage. In contrast, where the insured expands its business by combining with another institution, whether by consolidation, merger, or the purchase of another company's assets or liabilities, coverage will not be extended to the new offices, employees, or claims arising out of newly acquired assets or liabilities unless all conditions of this general agreement are met.

To obtain coverage where the insured's business combines with another, the insured must provide written notice to the underwriter in advance of the effective date of the proposed consolidation, merger, or purchase. Additionally, the insured must obtain the underwriter's written consent to expand coverage to the newly obtained offices, employees, and other exposures acquired by the insured. Finally, where the underwriter's consent is obtained, the insured will almost always have to remit an additional premium to expand coverage.

ANNOTATIONS

9th Cir. 1975 (Cal.). Litigation expenses incurred by acquiring company in defending actions for losses sustained before merger with another company were found not to be covered by the bond. The court ruled that the litigation expenses were not recoverable because the underlying losses occurred before the merger, and thus, were sustained not by the acquiring company, but by the company that was acquired, a non-insured party. Although the acquiring company argued that it sustained a loss at the time of and by virtue of the merger, the court explained that acquisition of a company and its liabilities did not amount to a new loss for the acquiring company. The court further found the acquiring company's argument that it was ignorant of the lawsuits against the acquired company until after the merger to be irrelevant because the acquiring company never sustained a loss within the meaning of the bond. *Fid. Sav. & Loan Ass'n v. Republic Ins. Co.,* 513 F.2d 954, 956.

M.D.N.C. 1959. The insured bank sustained losses due to employee dishonesty prior to its merger with another bank, at which time coverage under its bond expired. The insured bank knew of irregularities and discrepancies but did not know the cause thereof before the merger. The court held that the losses had not been discovered during the policy period. *Wachovia Bank & Trust Co. v. Mfrs. Cas. Ins. Co.,* 171 F. Supp. 369, 375.

W.D. Pa. 2012. The insured, a newly formed company, hired its president in connection with an asset purchase agreement with another company, whereby the insured obtained the latter's workforce, operating systems, equipment, and office. After the insured's president was discovered to have engaged in unauthorized account transfers and disbursements, the insured sought coverage under a special mortgage bankers bond. The insurer denied coverage because the bond did not cover losses caused by employees of acquired institutions. The court agreed with the insured's contention that the asset purchase agreement did not qualify as a "merger, consolidation or purchase of another institution" under the bond. The court reasoned that the terms used in the bond uniformly indicated situations in which there is a total acquisition of a target company that ceases to exist after the transaction. Review of the asset purchase agreement, however, indicated that a total acquisition had not been accomplished, as evidenced by the agreement's application only to "certain assets" and that operations of the acquired company had not terminated after the transaction. *K2 Settlement, LLC v. Certain Underwriters at Lloyd's,* No. 11-0191, 2012 U.S. Dist. LEXIS 170832, at *16.

N.C. 2003. Insured's subsidiary merged with another company, resulting in the addition of 6,000 new agents. Neither the insured nor its broker advised the fidelity insurer of the merger before its consummation. Approximately seven months later, the broker notified the fidelity insurer of the merger. Two months after that, the insured filed a claim under the bond because one of the newly acquired agents was discovered to have embezzled funds. The court held that notice of the merger and the insurer's consent were prerequisites to coverage of the acquired entity's employees. Since neither of these conditions occurred before the merger, the court granted summary judgment for the insurer. *Jefferson Pilot Fin. Ins. Co. v. Marsh USA, Inc.,* 582 S.E.2d 701, 707.

SECONDARY SOURCES

NONE

SECTION 3 — GENERAL AGREEMENT C—CHANGE OF CONTROL—NOTICE*

C. When the Insured learns of a change in control, it shall give written notice to the Underwriter.

As used in this General Agreement, control means the power to determine the management or policy of a controlling holding company or the Insured by virtue of voting stock ownership. A change in ownership of voting stock which results in direct or indirect ownership by a stockholder of an affiliated group of stockholders of ten percent (10%) or more of such stock shall be presumed to result in a change of control for the purpose of the required notice.

Failure to give the required notice shall result in termination of coverage for any loss involving a transferee, to be effective upon the date of the stock transfer.

COMMENT

General Agreement C has undergone multiple changes since it first appeared in the 1980 standard form Bankers Blanket Bond. As stated in the Surety Association of America's Statement of Change in connection with the 1980 form, this general agreement was an incorporation of a "Change of Control" rider that had been in use for several years. Rider SR 6014 added a new General Agreement C that required the insured to notify the underwriter within thirty days after a change of control.[1] The purpose of such a notice requirement has been explained as follows:

---

*   By William T. Bogaert and Stefan R. Dandelles, Wilson Elser Moskowitz Edelman & Dicker LLP, Boston, Massachusetts and Chicago, Illinois, and Camilla Conlon, ACE North American Professional Risk Claims, Chicago, Illinois.
1   Robin V. Weldy, *History of Financial Institution Bonds, in* BANKERS AND OTHER FINANCIAL INSTITUTION BLANKET BONDS 1, 10 (Frank L. Skillern, Jr. ed. 1979). This "notice of change of control" requirement followed one promulgated by the FDIC, codified at Section 7, Subsection (j) of the FDIC Act, 12 U.S.C. §§ 1811-31 (1989). *Id.* at 10-11. Rider SR 6037 provided

Most bank bond underwriters make a painstaking examination of a bank before issuing a Bankers Blanket Bond. A later merger, with a questionable institution or change of ownership and control, unknown to the underwriter, may render such an examination worthless. The surety industry feels that it is well within its rights to demand reasonable information relating to all aspects of bank operations and conditions.[2]

A change in ownership of ten percent of the outstanding voting stock was presumed to change control of the institution.

There were further revisions in 1986 involving three provisions: first, a change of power to determine the management of a controlling bank holding company (as opposed to just the insured) must be reported to the underwriter; second, the thirty-day time limit for giving notice of the change of control was deleted; and third, the reference to the names of owners and total number of shares was deleted.

In 2004, additional revisions were made that included a change in the title of the provision from "Change of Control" to "Change of Ownership." This change in title reflects the focus of the revised provision, which requires notice to the underwriter when a change in ownership of more than ten percent of the insured's stock (or that of a parent or holding company that controls the insured) has occurred. In addition, the 2004 revision re-institutes the thirty-day reporting period after a triggering event. In a related revision in the 2004 bond, the Termination condition of the bond was revised to provide "immediate" termination upon a "Change in Control," which is defined to mean a change in ownership of more than fifty percent of the voting stock of the insured or of a parent or holding company that controls the insured. These revisions set out a clear protocol: a reporting requirement upon "Change of Ownership" with a ten percent threshold and automatic termination upon a "Change in Control" with a fifty percent threshold.

Finally, the bond was again revised in May 2011. The changes contemplate different organizational structures of insureds, rather than merely the traditional "corporation" with stockholders and voting shares; in other words, partnerships, LLCs, and other similar non-corporate

---

for similar change-of-control requirements in the Savings and Loan Association Blanket Bond. *Id.* at 11.

2   *Id.* at 10.

entities. Thus, while the 2011 revision maintains the thirty-day reporting period and the ten percent ownership threshold, it expands the scope to include partners or members of an organization in addition to stockholders, and clarifies that the ten percent threshold involves either "voting stock" or the "total ownership interest" of the insured (or a controlling holding or parent company).

ANNOTATIONS

11th Cir. 2002 (Ga.). The Financial Institution Bond terminated immediately upon the taking over of the insured by another institution. The Eleventh Circuit held that the term "taking over" was not ambiguous and occurred when more than fifty percent of the insured's stock was acquired, regardless of whether the purchaser exercised any control over the insured's core functions. The court distinguished the provision of the bond concerning a "take over," which occurred with the acquisition of one hundred percent of the stock of the insured, and the provision concerning a "change in control," which would occur when ten percent of the insured's stock was acquired. Because the bond terminated upon the taking over of the insured, the insurer was not liable for any losses discovered after that taking over. *Am. Cas. Co. v. Etowah Bank,* 288 F.3d 1282, 1285-88.

SECONDARY SOURCES

NONE

SECTION 4 — GENERAL AGREEMENT D—REPRESENTATION OF INSURED*

> D. The Insured represents that the information furnished in the application for this bond is complete, true and correct. Such application constitutes part of this bond.
>
> Any misrepresentation, omission, concealment or any incorrect statement of a material fact, in the application or otherwise, shall be grounds for the rescission of this bond.

(1986 version)

> D. The Insured represents that the information furnished in the application for this bond is complete, true and correct. Such application constitutes part of this bond.
>
> Any intentional misrepresentation, omission, concealment or incorrect statement of a material fact, in the application or otherwise, shall be grounds for the rescission of this bond.

(2004 version)

> D. The Insured represents that the information furnished in the application for this bond is complete, true and correct. Such application constitutes part of this bond.
>
> Any omission, concealment or incorrect statement, in the application or otherwise, shall be grounds for the rescission of this bond, provided such omission, concealment or incorrect statement is material.

(2011 version)

---

* By William T. Bogaert and Stefan R. Dandelles, Wilson Elser Moskowitz Edelman & Dicker LLP, Boston, Massachusetts and Chicago, Illinois, and Camilla Conlon, ACE North American Professional Risk Claims, Chicago, Illinois.

COMMENT

General Agreement D memorializes in writing the insured's representation that the information it has supplied to the insurer in applying for a Financial Institution Bond is complete, true, and correct. The provision further reflects the parties' agreement that the bond may be rescinded by the insurer if the insured has provided incorrect or incomplete information that is material to the bond's issuance.

General Agreement D was revised in 1986, 2004, and 2011. Each of these bond forms are currently in use. Each contains slightly different language, which may impact an effort by the insurer to rescind the contract in circumstances in which it issued the bond based on false information concerning the risk.

The first substantial revision to General Agreement D was in 1986. At that time, the title of the agreement changed from "Warranty" to "Representation of the Insured." The provision stating that the insured represents that the information supplied in applying for the bond is true, correct, and accurate was also added to General Agreement D as part of the 1986 revision. This change expressly incorporated into the bond the insured's legal duty to provide the insurer with all information that would influence the insurer into entering into the insurance contract. Accordingly, if the insured provides information that is false, or conceals or fails to disclose information material to the insurer's decision to issue the bond, General Agreement D (1986 revision) provides that the bond may be rescinded by the insurer and considered void from its inception.

The 1986 revision also added the agreement that the application constitutes part of the bond. This addition addressed the requirement, found in some states, that the application must be part of the insurance contract in order for an insurer to rescind the insurance contract based upon misrepresentations in the application. Further, the insurer's reliance upon the information supplied in the application is confirmed in the bond's consideration clause, which states that the bond has been issued by the underwriter "in reliance upon all statements made and information furnished to the underwriter by the insured, in applying for the bond . . . ."

Collectively, the provisions added in 1986 reflect the agreement between the insurer and the insured that the insured represents that it has provided truthful information in applying for the bond, and that the insurer has relied upon that information in issuing the bond. If the insured supplies false material information, the parties acknowledge that the insurer has a basis to rescind the bond and that the bond is considered to be void ab initio. The justification for this remedy is that the insurer would not have agreed to issue the bond at the agreed upon terms (if at all) had the true information been disclosed. Under General Agreement D, as revised in 1986, it is irrelevant whether the misrepresentation or omission was intentionally or negligently made, as long as it was material. When a misrepresentation or omission in the application process results in the rescission of the bond, the insured will have no coverage for a loss that, but for rescission, may have been covered.

The 2004 revision to General Agreement D—through the mere insertion of the word "intentional"—significantly altered the legal significance of the representations made by the insured in applying for the bond. The 2004 revision provides that a misrepresentation, omission, or incorrect statement of material fact by the insured in applying for the bond shall be grounds for rescission if *intentionally* made. This revised language requires the insurer to demonstrate that the insured intentionally provided false information or intentionally omitted truthful information in applying for the bond as a requirement for rescission. An innocent or negligent misrepresentation does not provide a basis for rescission.

The 2011 revision of General Agreement D deleted the words, "intentional misrepresentation," clarifying that an insurer may rescind if it has relied upon false information material to the risk, regardless of whether the insured provided inaccurate information innocently.

Notwithstanding General Agreement D, an insurer's right to rescind the bond may be modified or restricted by statute or case law. The requirements for rescission vary from state to state, so the law of the applicable state must be reviewed in evaluating rescission.

ANNOTATIONS

U.S. 1902. Court denied recovery to bank on Cashier's Bond due to bank president's misrepresentation in the application, where the bank's president had received reports of cashier's unlawful speculation. The bank breached the bond stipulation because it failed to investigate or give notice of the reports. In finding for the insurer, the Supreme Court relied on a bond provision "that any written answers [in the application] . . .

shall be held to be a warranty." *Guar. Co. of N. Am. v. Mechs.' Sav. Bank & Trust Co.*, 183 U.S. 402, 423.

2d Cir. 1999 (N.Y.). Chapter 11 trustee appealed judgment for insurers that CEO's material misrepresentations on application regarding diverting funds for personal use could be imputed to corporation so as to void policies *ab initio*. The court found the adverse domination and adverse interest doctrines inapplicable. The policies were void *ab initio* because of materially false answers given by the CEO regarding "whether there was any other information material to the proposed insurance." *In re Payroll Express Corp.*, 186 F.3d 196, 210.

3rd Cir. 1994 (N.J.). Insurers brought declaratory judgment action against receiver of insolvent financial institution seeking to rescind a Financial Institution Bond. The court held that Financial Institutions Reform, Recovery and Enforcement Act of 1989 did not create jurisdictional bar to the affirmative defense of rescission. *Nat'l Union Fire Ins. Co. v. City Sav. Bank*, 28 F.3d 376, 392-93.

5th Cir. 1919 (Ala.). Receiver of bank brought action for recovery under bond that was subject to a provision that all of the obligee's statements are hereby warranted to be true. Despite evidence that the cashier was in default, the bank certified in subsequent renewals that the books and accounts were correct and that the cashier was not in default. Court held that the bank had notice of the terms of the original bond, including the warranty provision, and that therefore, "there is no room for holding the surety company bound by a continuation certificate issued on the faith of a statement which was warranted to be true, but was false . . . ." *Green v. Interstate Cas. Co.*, 256 F. 81, 83.

6th Cir. 1991 (Tenn.). Insurer refused payment under a Bankers Blanket Bond due to alleged misrepresentations on application relating to whether the insured was under investigation in connection with its banking practices. Sixth Circuit held that the D'Oench doctrine, or 12 U.S.C. §1823(e) (1988), was inapplicable to the Bankers Blanket Bond and that the FDIC acquires such a bond with knowledge of the recognized defenses available under insurance law. *FDIC v. Aetna Cas. & Sur. Co.*, 947 F.2d 196, 208.

8th Cir. 1935 (Ark.). Insured brought action against insurer to recover upon a fidelity bond after insured's collecting agent embezzled funds. Bank stated on bond application that it checked the account of the bank's collecting agent on a monthly basis. In fact, the account was never checked and the bank's noncompliance with this warranty prevented recovery. The court relied on a bond provision and application that expressly made the bank's statements warranties and not mere representations. *Emp'rs' Liab. Assurance Corp. of London, England v. Wasson*, 75 F.2d 749, 755.

8th Cir. 1924 (Ark.). In a two-part question on a bond application, the bank responded that account examinations would be performed monthly but did not respond to the question about who would perform such examinations. The court held that the bank's failure to answer the full question and the casualty company's acceptance of the application and execution of the bond constituted a waiver as to the portion of the question left unanswered. This gave the bank the freedom to have anyone, except the applicant-employee, conduct the monthly examination. However, in reversing the lower court, the court held that the two-part question actually dealt with separate issues such that a waiver as to the second part of the answer was not a waiver as to the first part. Because the bank failed to perform monthly examinations as warranted and because such requirement was not waived, the bank was precluded from recovery. *Md. Cas. Co. v. Bank of England*, 2 F.2d 793, 795-96.

9th Cir. 2001 (Idaho). Court refused to rescind a commercial crime policy despite the insured's failure to disclose loss history information in its renewal application form. There was an issue of fact regarding whether the insured suffered a material loss. The court reasoned that if the insured had not suffered a material loss, then its failure to include the circumstance on the application would not have constituted a material misrepresentation justifying rescission. *Gulf USA Corp. v. Fed. Ins. Co.*, 259 F.3d 1049, 1061.

9th Cir. 1925 (Wash.). The court affirmed the lower court's decision that insurer issued fidelity bond in reliance on continuation certificate, which constituted a contract between the bank and the insurer. "If it made false material representations or warranties relied upon by defendant, the contract... is subject to avoidance." The bond provision stated that the misrepresentations at issue were "warranties and form part of and be [sic] conditions precedent to the issuance." *Duke v. Fid. & Deposit Co.*, 5 F.2d 305, 306.

9th Cir. 1904 (Wash.). Insured savings and loan association brought action to recover upon a fidelity bond after the insured's secretary embezzled funds. Insurer defended on grounds that answers in application relating to being short on account were false. Court held that provision in fidelity bond "[t]hat all the representations made by the employer... to the surety... are warranted by the employer to be true..." was not a warranty. Court reasoned that other language requiring knowledge of the employer qualified this statement. *Am. Bonding Co. of Baltimore v. Spokane Bldg. & Loan Soc.*, 130 F. 737, 741.

10th Cir. 1994 (Utah). Court held that the D'Oench doctrine, or 12 U.S.C. § 1823(e) (1988), applied to fidelity bonds. Therefore, the insurer's misrepresentation defense based on untruthful assertions made in the bond application failed. *FDIC v. Oldenburg*, 34 F.3d 1529, 1554.

10th Cir. 1930 (Okla.). In action to recover on bond executed by cashier of the bank, bond provision stated that representations on application were warranties by bank. The court held that answers to questions concerning whether applicant was in debt to the bank were not false. However, the court found that the bond should have terminated after discovery of defalcation. *USF&G v. Shull*, 43 F.2d 532, 536-37.

E.D. Ky. 2011. The court refused to rescind a bond, holding that material misrepresentations made by the President and CEO in the application were not imputed to the corporation, due to the adverse-interest doctrine. *BancInsure, Inc. v. U.K. Bancorporation Inc.*, 830 F. Supp. 2d 294, 305.

D. Mass. 1998. Court granted the insurer's motion for summary judgment and held that misrepresentations in application rendered bond void *ab initio*. FDIC, as receiver for the insured bank, brought action against the insurer to recover on a Bankers Blanket Bond. The insurer argued that it was entitled to rescind the bond due to material misrepresentations by the insured on its application. The court found that the insured bank made misrepresentations by withholding critical information about the misconduct of two discharged loan officers when it answered "no," to an application question asking the insured to state any irregularities in banking or financial operations known to the bank. *FDIC v. Underwriters of Lloyd's of London,* 3 F. Supp. 2d 120, 141.

D.N.J. 2005. "A misrepresentation by the insured, whether contained in the policy itself or in the application for insurance, will support a forfeiture of the insured's rights under the policy if it is untruthful, material to the particular risk assumed by the insurer, and reasonably relied upon by the insurer issuing the policy." *TIG Ins. Co. v. Privilege Care Mktg.*, No. 03-03747, 2005 U.S. Dist. LEXIS 7428, at *17.

Bankr. D.N.J. 2005. The bankruptcy court rescinded the insurance contract, holding that debtor's claims and loss history responses on insurance renewal applications were false and material and that the insurer reasonably relied upon them. Rescission was therefore justified on grounds of equitable fraud. *Great Am. Ins. Cos. v. Subranni (In re Tri-State Armored Servs.)*, 332 B.R. 690, 710.

D.N.J. 1996. Court granted insurer's summary judgment motion on grounds that the insured misrepresented material information on the application with respect to whether the insured had received criticism from regulators. Interpreting New Jersey law and citing General Agreement D, the court held that the insured knowingly and falsely misrepresented that regulators had not criticized its operations. The misrepresentation materially affected the insurer's decision to issue the bond. *FDIC v. Moskowitz,* 946 F. Supp. 322, 330-31.

S.D.N.Y. 2001. Receiver of investment firm brought a third-party action against the firm's London insurers, who had issued blended fidelity and professional liability policies. Both parties sought summary judgment based on the insurers' claim that they were induced to sell policies by misrepresentations on an unsigned Bankers Blanket Bond application and in the underwriting process. Court held that where the insurers had knowledge of the basis to rescind after the policy was issued (but prior to the claim), but chose not to, they were deemed to have ratified the coverage. *SEC v. Credit Bancorp, Ltd.*, 147 F. Supp. 2d 238, 256.

E.D. Pa. 1993. Court erred in determining that fidelity bond was subject to rescission for failure of insured to list all losses sustained by officers in past three years. Under Pennsylvania law, the insurer must establish that (1) the declaration by the insured was false; (2) the false declaration was material to the risk; and (3) the insured knew it to be false. Court concluded that there was no evidence to support the materiality element. *Fid. Fed. Sav. & Loan Ass'n v. Felicetti,* 813 F. Supp. 332, 335.

Bankr. E.D. Pa. 1992. Trustee in a securities fraud case brought an action against the insurer to collect on a Securities Dealers Bond. In its summary judgment motion, the insurer argued that the insured's principals failed to disclose in the bond application their participation in fraudulent activity and that this justified rescission. The bankruptcy court denied the insurer's motion, holding that the principals' knowledge of their own fraudulent acts could not be imputed to the corporate insured. However, the court also denied the trustee's summary judgment motion because "[i]t appears grossly unfair to allow the principal of a corporation, knowing not only of his own fraud, but also that his actions cannot be imputed to his corporation, to load up on purchases of fidelity bonds in order to replenish the corporation at the expense of an innocent and ignorant insurance company." *In re Lloyd Sec., Inc.,* Nos. 90-0985S, 91-1090S, 1992 WL 119362, at *11.

W.D. Tenn. 1986. Insured bank moved for summary judgment on the insurer's affirmative defense that fidelity bond was void because of the insured's misrepresentations in the application. The court held that the insurer's misrepresentation defense was not valid to the extent the insurer conducts an in-depth inquiry and the insured's non-disclosure pertains to a subject about which the insurer did not inquire. However, the court stated that the insurer's misrepresentation defense would not be stricken to the extent that it was based on alleged affirmative representations by the insured in connection with its fidelity bond application. The insurer's failure to inquire about certain subjects on the application does not permit an insured to affirmatively misrepresent information. *United Am. Bank in Memphis v. Aetna Cas. & Sur. Co.,* No. 84-2225, 1986 U.S. Dist. LEXIS 27619, at *10-11.

Ark. 1909. Court held that statements by the insured that are made part of the basis of the Cashier's Bond issued by the insurer are treated as representations if not labeled as warranties and will not avoid the bond except for fraud or misrepresentation. Court found that statements representing condition of the bank, the accounts of the bank, and the character of the employees were mere representations, which were made honestly. They thus did not vitiate the bond because the provision did not state that it was a warranty; rather, such representations only constituted part of the basis and consideration of the contract. *Title Guar. & Sur. Co. v. Bank of Fulton,* 117 S.W. 537, 541.

Ark. 1908. Court held that the employer's representations in bond application concerning the frequency with which it checked employee's account constituted a warranty that was breached. Bond provided that statements by the employer were warranted to be true, were considered conditions precedent, and would void the policy if untrue. *USF&G v. Bank of Batesville,* 112 S.W. 957, 958.

Ark. 1906. A fidelity bond contained a provision stating "[t]hat all the representations made by the employer . . . are warranted by the employer to be true," and the application for the bond contained similar language. However, the court found that the bank did not breach any conditions or warranties of the bond because the alleged misstatements were not material. *Am. Bonding Co. of Baltimore v. Morrow,* 96 S.W. 613, 615.

Cal. Ct. App. 1914. Statements and answers in letter containing employer's responses to insurer's questions for purposes of procuring the bond were made warranties and part of the contract by way of a policy stipulation. Court held that policy was void *ab initio* because warranties were false and policy was issued in reliance upon them. Court reasoned that when a warranty is broken at its inception, the policy never attaches to the risk that it purports to cover. *Wolverine Brass Works v. Pac. Coast Cas. Co.,* 146 P. 184, 184-85.

Colo. 1907. Court reversed ruling for insured on action to recover on bond. Insured's secretary answered application questions that bond deemed "to be considered warranties, and they shall form the basis of the guarantee hereby applied for." Court held that the insured's misrepresentation regarding checking accounts and financial books was an absolute breach of contract made to induce the insurer to issue the bond. Court reasoned that the bond made the answers material to the risk and that insurer would not have issued the bond had the insured not given the answers that it did. *USF&G v. Downey,* 88 P. 451, 452.

Colo. 1906. Court explained that a material misrepresentation made in response to a specific inquiry upon which the insurer relies avoids the policy whether or not the questions were warranties or representations. Court held that answers in connection with questions relating to examination of accounts/books and shortages were false, material to the risk, and within the knowledge of the officer who completed the application. *Am. Bonding & Trust Co. v. Burke,* 85 P. 692, 694-95.

Ky. Ct. App. 1918. Employer's fraudulent misrepresentation in application for renewal of Cashier's Bond—which were made knowingly, were material to the risk, were relied upon by the insurer, and induced execution of the bond—prevented recovery upon the bond. Bond provision provided that the bank's representations were warranted to be true and that bond was executed upon that condition. Court reasoned that where the employer fails to use due diligence to learn the truth of his application answers, recovery upon bond is not permitted if the insurer relies upon the answer. *Fid. & Deposit Co. v. Kane,* 206 S.W. 888, 892.

Ky. Ct. App. 1903. Court deemed employer's false statements in application to be warranties and fatal to an action upon the bond. Bond recited that employer's statements constitute an essential part of the bond and form the basis of the contract. Court held that the application of the statute was irrelevant because the misrepresentations were material to the risk. *Warren Deposit Bank v. Fid. & Deposit Co.,* 74 S.W. 1111, 1114.

La. Ct. App. 1937. Bank answered in statement that bank would systematize its books and check employee's books on a bi-annual basis, and that the last check of the accounts showed all accounts to be correct in every respect. Bond provision stated: "statements ... are warranted by the employer to be true, and shall constitute part of the basis and consideration of the contract . . . ." Court held that the bank's false answers made it impossible for the bond to be effective because the answers were warranties, the questions asked were highly material to the interest of the insurer, and the truth of the answers were indispensable prerequisites to the issuance of the bond. *City Bank & Trust Co. v. Commercial Cas. Co.,* 176 So. 27, 30.

Minn. 1919. Employer stated on its bond application that to the best of its knowledge, no employee had committed a dishonest act. The bond provided that all employer-furnished statements concerning the employee and his accounts were warranted to be true. Evidence established that employer knew of dishonest acts by the employee and made misrepresentations in the application regarding its knowledge. The employer claimed that its misrepresentations were not made with the intent to deceive. The court stated that the misrepresentations avoided the contract regardless of intent because the misrepresentation increased the risk of loss. *W.A. Thomas Co. v. Nat'l Sur. Co.,* 172 N.W. 697, 698.

Neb. 1909. Bond provided that "it is issued ... upon the faith of said statements, which plaintiff warrants to be true, and as a condition precedent to the employer's right to recover upon the bond; that if said written statement is in any respect untrue, the bond shall be void." Court affirmed district court's judgment for insurer because insured made no effort to examine accounts and permitted cashier to perform tasks that it warranted the cashier would not perform. Court explained that common honesty dictates that the insured should neither be untruthful nor negligent in answering questions propounded to it for the purpose of securing material information concerning the risk that a bonding company is asked to assume. *Sunderland Roofing & Supply Co. v. USF&G,* 122 N.W. 25, 27.

Okla. 1914. Court held that insurer was estopped from denying liability on a Cashier's Bond based on alleged misrepresentations on application question regarding frequency of examinations of cashier's account. Court cited bond provision that stipulated that representations of the employer were expressly warranted to be true. Although it considered these representations warranties for the sake of argument, court found representations relating to frequency of examination and examiner to be true. *USF&G v. Boley Bank & Trust Co.,* 144 P. 615, 617.

Okla. 1911. Court held that the answers to questions submitted by the insured in connection with the bond constituted warranties. Bond provision stated that "representations are hereby expressly warranted to be true" and "Employer's Statement" showed that it was the express intention of the parties that the answers relating to examination of accounts were warranties and conditions precedent. However, court failed to find evidence to establish that there were any false representations establishing a breach of the bond. *S. Sur. Co. v. Tyler & Simpson Co.,* 120 P. 936, 940-41.

Okla. 1906. Court found that "where statements and representations have been used by the insured as the basis for the insurance, and by the terms of the policy . . . said statements are made part of the policy itself, [and] any material, false, and fraudulent statement made by the insured will avoid the policy." Court ultimately held that representations of assistant cashier that president was not indebted to bank were "outrageously untrue," and were known to be untrue, thereby avoiding liability of the insurer. *Willoughby v. Fid. & Deposit Co.,* 85 P. 713, 715.

Or. 1917. Finding for insurer, the court held that the plaintiff's written answers to the insurer's questions regarding custody of securities and examinations of books were warranties based on express declaration contained in the application and bond. The application stated that the answers were warranted to be true, and the bond stated that it was executed in reliance upon the faith of the plaintiff's written statements, which were warranties and conditions precedent to recovery on the bond. *Bissinger & Co. v. Mass. Bonding & Ins. Co.,* 163 P. 592, 593.

Pa. 1933. Insurer issued a Bankers Blanket Bond to title company based on a written application completed by the company's secretary/treasurer, who was embezzling money from the company at the time he signed the application. At trial, the lower court excluded the application from evidence because it was not attached to the bond at issuance. The Pennsylvania Supreme Court held that the rule excluding the application did not exclude other proof. The bond provision stated that "no statement . . . made in the application for this bond or otherwise submitted by or on behalf of the insured shall be deemed a warranty of anything except the fact that the statement is true to the best of the knowledge . . . of the person making it." The court stated that the warranty was broken as soon as it was made. Court also stated that the misstatement which was "otherwise submitted" may be a complete defense to the suit on the bond if the statement as to the honesty of the employees whose fidelity was to be insured was applied. *Gordon v. Cont'l Cas. Co.,* 166 A. 557, 558.

S.D. 1939. Insured brought action under Cashier's Bond for its cashier's alleged misappropriation of bank funds during the bond's term. The original bond had been continued "in reliance upon the statements contained in the Clearance Certificate [which] are to be deemed warranties and a part of this contract." The court held that statements in certificate were intended to be warranty representations and that such warranty was breached pursuant to statute and case law when an examination of the books was not made and shortages were known in the cashier's account. *FDIC v. W. Sur. Co.,* 285 N.W. 909, 912.

Tenn. 1914. Employer's continuation certificate to insurer to renew Cashier's Bond certifying that books of the cashier were examined and found correct was held not to be a warranty of the correctness of such accounts, but only that such examinations were made and no errors were discovered. Bond provision stating "[w]hereas the employer has heretofore delivered to the company certain representations and promises relative to the duties and accounts of the employee and other matters, it is hereby understood and agreed that those representations and such promises ... shall constitute part of the basis and consideration of the contract" did not defeat coverage under the bond. *Hunter v. USF&G,* 167 S.W. 692, 693.

Utah Ct. App. 1991. The insurer appealed the trial court ruling that employee dishonesty loss was covered by a Savings and Loan Blanket Bond, arguing that coverage should be barred because the insured failed to reveal an employee's dishonesty and pending lawsuits when it applied for the bond. The majority held that because the omitted material information was not asked for in the bond application and because the insured did not intentionally withhold information from the insurer, the bond could not be voided under Utah Code Ann. § 31-19-8 (1974). The bond provision read: "[m]isrepresentations ... shall not prevent recovery ... unless (a) fraudulent; or (b) material either to acceptance of risk, or to hazard assumed by the insurer; or (c) the insurer in good faith either would not have either issued contract ... , or would not have provided coverage with respect to hazard resulting in the loss, if the true facts had been made known to the insurer as required...." *Home Sav. & Loan v. Aetna Cas. & Sur. Co.,* 817 P.2d 341, 358-59.

Wash. 1910. Court overruled lower court's ruling for insured allowing recovery on fidelity bond. President of the insured answered in application for bond that accounts were examined and in every respect correct with funds on hand to balance the accounts. Bond recited that "[i]f the employee's written statement herein before referred to shall be found in any respect untrue this bond shall be void." Court held that the representation that the books were examined and found to balance was a warranty of a material fact; that it was known, or should have been known, by the respondent that the representation was false; and without it appellant would not have assumed the risk. *Poultry Producers' Union v. Williams,* 107 P. 1040, 1042.

Wis. 1942. Court held that an application question relating to examination and checking of accounts prevented recovery where the insured failed in its duty to examine and check accounts for a period of more than seven years. The court relied, in part, on bond provision that "[a]ll written statements made ... by the employer in connection with this bond ... are warranted ... to be true" and on the application stipulation that "[i]t is agreed that the above answers ... constitute the basis of and form a part of the consideration of the bond." *Bloedow v. Nitschke,* 1 N.W.2d 762, 764.

Wis. 1911. Bond provision stated that all "the representations made by the employer ... are warranted to be true." However, court stated that whether representations on the application concerning frequency of inspection of agent's books were warranties was not material. Court held that provisions in bond regarding supervision of agent and inspection of accounts superseded application and were conditions subsequent and not conditions precedent, which must be pleaded by the insurer to defeat the employer's recovery. *United Am. Fire Ins. Co. v. Am. Bonding Co. of Baltimore,* 131 N.W. 994, 997.

SECONDARY SOURCES

Bogda M.B. Clarke, James D. Ferrucci & Armen Shahinian, *Fraud in the Inducement as a Defense to Fidelity and Surety Claims*, 42 Tort & Ins. L.J. 181 (2006).

Robert M. Horkovich, Adam A. Reeves & Peter J. Andrews, *Insurance Coverage for Employee Theft Losses: A Policyholder Primer on Commonly Litigated Issues,* 29 U. MEM. L. REV. 363 (1999).

David J. Krebs & Diane L. Matthews, *Judicial Rescission of Fidelity Coverage,* VII FID. L.J. 89 (2001)

Joseph Powers, *Pulling the Plug on Fidelity, Crime, and All Risk Coverage: The Availability of Rescission as a Remedy or Defense,* 32 TORT & INS. L.J. 905 (1997).

7 LEE RUSS AND THOMAS F. SEGALLA, COUCH ON INSURANCE 3d § 100.1 (3d ed. 2007).

J.F. Rydstrom, Annotation, *Obligee's Concealment or Misrepresentation Concerning Previous Defalcation as Affecting Liability on Fidelity Bond or Contract,* 4 A.L.R.3d 1197 (1998).

Cynthia H. Young, *Misrepresentations in the Financial Institution Bond Application*, II FID. L. ASS'N J. 21 (1996).

SECTION 5 — GENERAL AGREEMENT E—JOINT INSURED*

E. **If two or more Insureds are covered under this bond, the first named Insured shall act for all Insureds. Payment by the Underwriter to the first named Insured of loss sustained by any Insured shall fully release the Underwriter on account of such loss. If the first named Insured ceases to be covered under this bond, the Insured next named shall thereafter be considered as the first named Insured. Knowledge possessed or discovery made by any Insured shall constitute knowledge or discovery by all Insureds for purposes of this bond. The liability of the Underwriter for loss or losses sustained by all Insureds shall not exceed the amount for which the Underwriter would have been liable had all such loss or losses been sustained by one Insured.**

COMMENT

The provisions within this general agreement create an organized procedure by which the insurer can make payment under the bond where there are multiple named insureds. Because the first named insured is given the power to act for others, the insurer can discharge its liability by making payment to the first named insured where multiple insureds sustain a loss under the bond. Not only does this procedure help reduce the amount of paperwork the insurer is burdened with, it also obviates any need for the insurer to allocate losses amongst insureds. At the same time, this agreement provides that knowledge of each insured covered by the bond is to be imputed to the others. As a result, discovery and all provisions triggered by discovery will be deemed to have occurred at the same time for each insured. While multiple insureds may be covered under the bond, this general agreement makes clear that the insurer's liability will not exceed the limits of liability set forth under the bond.

---

* By Maura Z. Pelleteri and Amy Malish, Krebs, Farley & Pelleteri, PLLC, New Orleans, Louisiana.

ANNOTATIONS

5th Cir. 1954 (Tex.). Insurer contended that trial court had erred in ruling that plaintiff, who was not first named insured under the bond, had a right to bring action. Relying on Federal Rule of Civil Procedure 17 and without citing to terms of the bond, the court held that "whatever might have been the purpose of inserting that clause in the bond," under the facts of the case, the plaintiff was entitled to maintain the action. The court further noted that no rights of the defendant or the first named insured under the bond were jeopardized thereby. *New Amsterdam Cas. Co. v. W.D. Felder & Co.*, 214 F.2d 825, 826.

8th Cir. 1972 (Mo.). Under the Bankers Blanket Bond, the named insured finance company was the designated party to act on behalf of any of the other named insureds. After named insured transferred assets of subsidiary to a loan company, a loss was discovered. Thereafter, the named insured finance company dissolved. Under the terms of the merger, the loan company stepped into named insured's shoes and assumed the rights under the bond to sue for the loss on behalf of a subsidiary company. The right of the loan company to sue was found to hinge not on the substantive right to sue as a named insured under the policy, but simply as named insured finance company's assigned designee. While noting that the bond contemplates only one party, the parent or subsidiary, to act for all, the court recognized the subsidiary as the real party in interest. There can only be one loss and one recovery; thus the fact that the judgments ran jointly to the loan company and subsidiary was found not to create any prejudice to the insurer. *Okla. Morris Plan Co. v. Sec. Mut. Cas. Co.*, 455 F.2d 1209, 1212.

8th Cir. 1965 (Mo.). Issuer of blanket bond argued that the trial court erred in ruling that plaintiff, a subsidiary of first named insured who acquired right to bring suit for subject loss through an assignment, had the right to maintain the action. Insurer contended that because the first named insured had not actually joined the lawsuit until three years after the subject loss was discovered, the claim was barred under the provisions of the bond. Rejecting the insurer's position, the court ruled that the suit for recovery under the policy did not necessarily have to be instituted by first named insured and that suit was timely filed. *Lumberman's Mut. Cas. Co. v. Norris Grain Co.*, 343 F.2d 670, 689.

N.D. Ga. 2010. Trustee for bankrupt bank holding and parent company sought recovery for losses sustained by a subsidiary bank against issuer of blanket bond. Under the bond, only the bank holding company was listed as an insured. Thereafter, the FDIC, as receiver for the subsidiary bank, intervened in trustee's action, seeking reformation of the bond to include the subsidiary as a named insured on grounds of mutual mistake and for declaratory judgment that it had the exclusive right to assert claims against the bond. Following its finding that the bond should be reformed based on evidence that all parties intended for the subsidiary bank to be listed as an insured, the court held that the FDIC could bring an action under the bond on behalf of the subsidiary bank. The court further noted that because the bank holding company was in bankruptcy, it could no longer act on behalf of the subsidiary. The court noted that under these facts, the bond permitted the next named insured to bring a claim on its own behalf. *Lubin v. Cincinnati Ins. Co.*, No. 09-2985, 2010 U.S. Dist. LEXIS 133794, at *34-39, *aff'd*, 677 F.3d 1039 (11th Cir. 2012).

N.Y. App. Div. 2012. Defendant moved to dismiss plaintiffs' complaint on grounds that plaintiffs, alleged victims of Bernie Madoff's Ponzi scheme, did not sustain any losses under fidelity bonds at issue. Defendant contended that plaintiffs sustained no actual loss because the aggregate amount of plaintiffs' net account balances were greater than the amount invested with Madoff. In addition to the bond's single loss provision, the defendant asserted that the bond's joint insured provision compelled aggregation of plaintiffs' net wins and losses. In rejecting defendant's position, the court held that the joint insured provision, like the single loss provision, refers to losses, not "net" losses, and thus defendant could not add terms to create a limitation of coverage. The court further noted that the joint insured language made clear that the main purpose of the provision was to create an organized procedure to make claims under the bond and that assigning one of the insureds the power to act for others resolved the insurer's problem of having significant paperwork where multiple insureds file claims under one bond. *Jacobson Family Invs., Inc. v. Nat'l Union Fire Ins. Co.*, No. 601325/10, 2012 N.Y. Misc. LEXIS 5752, at *11-13.

SECONDARY SOURCES

NONE

SECTION 6 — GENERAL AGREEMENT F—NOTICE OF LEGAL PROCEEDINGS AGAINST INSURED—ELECTION TO DEFEND*

F. The Insured shall notify the Underwriter at the earliest practical moment, not to exceed 30 days after notice thereof, of any legal proceeding brought to determine the Insured's liability for any loss, claim or damage, which, if established, would constitute a collectible loss under this bond. Concurrently, the Insured shall furnish copies of all pleadings and pertinent papers to the Underwriter.

The Underwriter, at its sole option, may elect to conduct the defense of such legal proceeding, in whole or in part. The defense by the Underwriter shall be in the Insured's name through attorneys selected by the Underwriter. The Insured shall provide all reasonable information and assistance required by the Underwriter for such defense.

If the Underwriter elects to defend the Insured, in whole or in part, any judgment against the Insured on those counts or causes of action which the Underwriter defended on behalf of the Insured or any settlement in which the Underwriter participates and all attorneys' fees, costs and expenses incurred by the Underwriter in the defense of the litigation shall be a loss covered by this bond.

If the Insured does not give the notices required in subsection (a) of Section 5 of this bond and in the first paragraph of this General Agreement, or if the Underwriter elects not to defend any causes of action, neither a judgment against the Insured, nor a settlement of any legal proceeding by the Insured, shall determine the existence, extent or amount of coverage under this bond for loss sustained by the Insured, and the Underwriter shall not be liable for any attorneys' fees, costs and expenses incurred by the Insured.

With respect to this General Agreement, subsections (b) and (c) of Section 5 of this bond apply upon the entry of such judgment or the occurrence of such settlement instead of upon discovery of loss. In addition, the Insured must notify the Underwriter within 30 days after such judgment is

---

* By Maura Z. Pelleteri and Amy Malish, Krebs, Farley & Pelleteri, PLLC, New Orleans, Louisiana.

entered against it or after the Insured settles such legal proceeding, and, subject to subsection (e) of Section 5, the Insured may not bring legal proceedings for the recovery of such loss after the expiration of 24 months from the date of such final judgment or settlement.

COMMENT

Coverage for defense costs and expenses incurred in defending third-party claims has been offered under fidelity bonds for over sixty years. The predecessors to General Agreement F—Notice of Legal Proceedings against Insured—Election to Defend, were the "Court Costs and Attorneys' Fees" provisions found in earlier Bankers Blanket Bonds. Significant changes to this defense-cost provision were introduced with the Financial Institution Bond's 1986 revision.

While varying slightly in their respective terms and coverage, each of the earlier defense-cost provisions premised coverage on whether the third party's claims against the insured alleged facts that if proven, would constitute a valid and collectible loss under the bond. These bonds provided that the insurer had the option, but not the duty, to defend the insured in the action brought against it. Although some courts mistakenly held to the contrary by confusing fidelity coverage with liability coverage, most courts now recognize that the fidelity insurer does not owe a duty to defend. Under earlier forms, the insurer, however, was obligated to provide indemnification for attorneys' fees and costs where there was a covered claim. Case law interpreting these earlier forms focused on whether the insurer's liability for litigation costs was evaluated solely on the face of the third-party's complaint or whether consideration should be given to matters outside of the parties' pleadings.

The 1986 revision introduced several significant changes with respect to coverage for litigation expenses and costs incurred in defending third-party claims, as well as the insured's obligations under the bond. First, with respect to proceedings brought against the insured, General Agreement F provides that the insured is obligated to notify the insurer of such proceeding "at the earliest practical moment" and not more than "30 days after notice thereof," a clarification of earlier versions that stated that the insured was required to provide notice "promptly." Another change introduced in the 1986 revision makes it obligatory for the insured to provide the insurer copies of pleadings and "pertinent papers," whether requested by the insurer or not. Under earlier bonds, the insured was only required to provide such materials when the insurer requested them.

Probably the most significant change introduced with the 1986 revision related to the insurer's discretion to provide coverage for defense costs. Under this revision, the insurer's liability hinges upon whether the insurer "at its sole option" elects to defend the insured. General Agreement F grants the insurer the option of defending the insured in "whole or in part," providing the insurer the option of defending the whole action or only certain claims. If the insurer elects to defend, then it is liable for the defense costs incurred in defending the action. Electing to defend also renders the insurer liable for any judgment rendered against the insured with respect to those claims the insurer elects to defend. Similarly, the insurer's election renders it liable for the amount of the settlements in which it participates for those claims it elects to defend. However, if the insurer declines to provide a defense or if the insured fails to comply with notice requirements under Section 5(a) or General Agreement F, the insurer will have no liability for any attorneys' fees, costs, or expenses incurred by the insured. Further, any judgment rendered against the insured or any settlement entered by the insured will have no effect on determinations regarding the existence, extent, or amount of coverage owed under the bond.

The 1986 revision also introduced slight changes and clarifications of the requirements for filing a proof of loss and the time period for filing suit against the insurer for third-party claims, which are governed by Sections 5(b) and (d), respectively. Earlier versions of the bond required the insured to file a proof of claim within six months of discovery of the loss. Under the 1986 revision, the time period for filing a proof of loss was extended. The insured's obligations under Sections 5(b) and (c) do not apply upon discovery of loss, but upon entry of judgment or the occurrence of settlement. Thus, the insured need now only submit a proof of loss within six months after entry of a judgment in the underlying action, or after a settlement thereof. In addition to the foregoing requirements, General Agreement F obligates the insured to notify the insurer within thirty days after a judgment is entered against the insured or after the insured settles the legal proceeding. With respect to the time periods for filing suit against the insurer, General Agreement

F provides that the insured may initiate a lawsuit no later than twenty-four months after such settlement or final judgment.

Coverage for defense costs remains part of the bond's applicable limit of liability. Under the 1959 and 1961 versions, coverage for defense costs was in addition to the otherwise applicable limit of liability. In 1980, coverage was changed to make liability for defense costs part of, and not an addition to, the coverage limits. The 1986 revision removed any reference to applicable limits of liability under this agreement. The issue is now addressed under Section 4 "Limits of Liability," which specifically provides that defense costs paid by the insurer are to be included towards exhaustion of the bond's aggregate limit. Once the limit is exhausted, the insurer has no further liability for defense costs.

Predecessor versions, such as the 1969 edition, provided for the proration of defense costs based upon coverage of the loss compared to uncovered losses, accounting both for the deductible and the limits of liability. However, this proration feature was not consistently applied, leading to much confusion. The 1980 version clarified the proration clause and further added a requirement that the insured reimburse the insurer to the extent the insurer paid defense costs in excess of its pro rata share. The 1986 version went further and eliminated the proration of defense costs altogether. The changes made in the 1986 version remained intact in the bond's revisions in 2004 and 2011.

OUTLINE OF ANNOTATIONS

A. Notice of Legal Proceedings Against Insured
B. Election Not to Defend
C. Liability for Defense Costs and Attorneys' Fees

ANNOTATIONS

A. Notice of Legal Proceedings Against Insured

1st Cir. 1997 (Mass.). The court held that the FDIC was precluded from recovery under the Financial Institution Bond because the insured bank failed to give timely notice within the thirty-day time period set forth in the bond. The bond required notice to the insurer upon a claim of employee dishonesty and did not permit the insured to wait until the claim was proven. The court found that two lawsuits alleging knowing acts of dishonesty or fraud by bank employees plainly constituted discovery of the loss and that the harm caused by the alleged acts would qualify as loss under the bond. As further support, the court noted that General Agreement F independently required the bank to provide the insurer all pleadings and pertinent papers within thirty days of notice of the suit. *FDIC v. Ins. Co. of N. Am.*, 105 F.3d 778, 782-83.

2nd Cir. 1981 (N.Y.). On appeal, insured argued that summary judgment for insurer on claim for reimbursement of attorneys' fees and litigation costs was erroneous, arguing that insurer's denial of coverage relieved it of obligation under attorneys' fees provision to promptly notify the insurer of any such suit. In response, the insurer argued that the district court had properly ruled that the insured's delay of nine months violated the contractual requirement that the insured notify it promptly of suits against it. Citing precedent that a repudiation of liability by an insurer for lack of coverage operates as a waiver of notice requirements, the court remanded the matter for a determination of facts concerning the denial of liability. *H.S. Equities, Inc. v. Hartford Acc. & Indem. Co.*, 661 F.2d 264, 270.

9th Cir. 1992 (Cal.). In response to action by insured to recover for judgment awarded against it, the insurer argued that the insured had not sustained a "loss" during the bond period because the third party litigation only became a "loss" when final judgment was entered, which occurred several years after the expiration of the bond period. In interpreting the bond's Court Costs and Attorneys' Fees clause, the court noted that the bond provision twice used the word "loss." The second loss—the valid and collectible loss—is a subset of the first loss, and in the instant matter, was represented by the judgment entered against the insured. The court held that it is the first loss—the employee's fraudulent conduct—that must be discovered during the bond period. The court held that the only reasonable interpretation is that fraudulent acts creating a prospective collectible loss, which conclude in a judgment against the insured, are covered by the bond. Finding that the fraud was discovered and reported to the insurer before the expiration of the bond period, coverage was afforded for the underlying loss and for attorneys' fees and court costs associated with the third-party action. *First Am. Title Ins. Co. v. St. Paul Fire & Marine Ins. Co.*, 971 F.2d 215, 217-18.

5th Cir. 1985 (Tex.). The court found that the insured had complied with the bond's notice provision, which merely required the insured to "promptly give notice to the underwriter of the institution of" suit. The court held that the insured's oral notification to the insurer of the lawsuit against it was sufficient because the bond did not require that notice be in writing or that pleadings be submitted to the underwriter unless they were requested. *Cont'l Sav. Ass'n. v. U.S. Fid. & Guar.*, 762 F.2d 1239, 1243.

Conn. 1999. Insured bank brought suit against its fidelity carrier after it settled a lawsuit asserted against the bank. The lawsuit alleged that the bank had improperly paid checks lacking proper endorsements. Notice of the claim was not provided to the insurer until over three years after the initial discovery of the loss, but was provided within thirty days of the insured's settlement. The court held that General Agreement F does not extinguish the underwriter's obligation to indemnify the insured due to late notice. The court reasoned that the only practical effect of the insured's failure to give General Agreement F notice was that the settlement did not determine "the existence, extent or amount" of the insurer's coverage obligations to the insured under the bond. *Webster Bank v. Travelers Cas. & Sur. Co.*, No. 960476078, 1999 Conn. Super. LEXIS 1218, at *12-17.

B. Election Not to Defend

5th Cir. 2008 (Tex.). Insured bank brought suit against fidelity carrier for losses sustained in prior state court action filed against it by a depositor on a claim of unauthorized endorsement. The insurer declined to defend the insured in the state court action, in which summary judgment was subsequently granted against bank because it had permitted unauthorized signatures as defined under the UCC. Thereafter, the bank settled with the depositor and sought to recover its losses from the fidelity carrier. The district court granted summary judgment for the insured because collateral estoppel precluded the insurer from attacking the state court's liability determination. The Fifth Circuit reversed, ruling that the district court failed to properly distinguish between the ubiquitous general liability policy, under which an insurer is duty bound to defend the insured, but may do so under a reservation of rights, and a Financial Institution Bond, under which the insurer had the option but not the duty to defend. Under the bond, the insurer had no legal ability to defend its insured in state court under a reservation of rights. If it had elected to defend its insured, it would have committed itself not only to pay its insured's defense costs but also to pay the full amount of the judgment. *Citibank Tex. v. Progressive Cas. Ins. Co.*, 522 F.3d 591, 593-95.

8th Cir. 1982 (Mo.). The insured bank was sued by the trustee in bankruptcy seeking recovery on checks deposited in an account at the insured bank. The underwriter declined the insured's defense on grounds that the trustee's complaint did not allege a loss under the "Loss of Property" coverage. However, the stipulated extrinsic facts showed that the employees of the insured may have had knowledge that coverage could apply. Although finding that the insurer's refusal to defend was not vexatious as a result of the insured's late notice, the court held that, before declining to defend, an underwriter has an obligation to look beyond the allegations made in the complaint against its insured to facts known to the underwriter or facts which can be discovered through a reasonable investigation. *Columbia Union Nat'l Bank v. Hartford Acc. & Indem. Co.*, 669 F.2d 1210, 1215.

E.D. Mich. 1992. Reasoning that the Sixth Circuit construes surety bonds in a similar fashion to insurance contracts and plainly ignoring the bond language that states that the insurer has the option to defend, the court held that the insurer's duty to defend is the same as the duty to indemnify for defense costs. The court further held that the clear implication from the bond's "Court Costs and Attorneys' Fees" provision is that indemnification for defense costs will be provided even in situations of potential coverage, which is triggered by the allegations contained in the action brought against the insured. *Manley Bennett, McDonald & Co. v. St. Paul Fire & Marine Ins. Co.*, 792 F. Supp. 1070, 1073.

W.D. Mo. 1984. The district court rejected insured bank's contention that issuer of a blanket bond had a duty to defend action brought against it even if only the possibility of coverage existed. Finding no evidence indicating that the bond covered any third-party claims brought against insured bank, the court held that the insurer had no duty to defend and no duty to indemnify bank for its defense expenses. The court noted that the bond does not create a duty to defend but only a duty to indemnify. *Shearson v. First Cont'l Bank & Trust Co.*, 579 F. Supp. 1305, 1314.

N.D. Ill. 2006. Under a securities dealers' fidelity bond, an employee of a client of the insured, for whom the insured held and administered employee benefit plans, embezzled millions of dollars from the plans. After being sued by the client, the insured settled and made a claim under the bond for payment of the settlement amount and the attorneys' fees and costs incurred in defending the underlying action. The insurer declined to defend the action on the basis that any alleged loss would not be a direct loss as required for bond coverage and that coverage was precluded by the exclusion for transactions in a customer's account. The district court held that the insurer had a "duty to defend" the suit because the allegations in the complaint implicated coverage under the Forgery Insuring Agreement. Having refused to reimburse the insured's defense fees, the insurer had breached its duty to defend, rendering it liable for the insured's defense costs and the amount paid in settlement. *Rothchild Inv. Corp. v. Travelers Cas. & Sur. Co.*, No. 05-3041, 2006 U.S. Dist. LEXIS 30033, at *11-34.

D. Minn. 2003. After it was sued for losses sustained by inventory financing company due to worthless certification of deposit scheme, insured made demand on fidelity insurer for indemnification for its liability for over $12 million loss, interest, and defense costs. Insured attempted to tender its defense to carrier. The fidelity carrier denied liability for indemnification under Insuring Agreement (A) and refused to defend the insured. Insured sued insurer for, *inter alia*, breach of contract, breach of fiduciary duty, and declaratory judgment in connection with the duty to defend. In granting the fidelity carrier's motion to dismiss, the court held that the bond plainly did not create a duty to defend, but rather gave the carrier the contractual right to defend. *RBC Dain Rauscher, Inc. v. Fed. Ins. Co.*, No. 03-2609, 2003 U.S. Dist. LEXIS 26475, at *13-32.

Cal. Ct. App. 1987. The court held that the insurer was under an obligation to either defend its insured or reimburse it for its defense costs because the insurer allegedly learned of facts extrinsic to the complaint in the underlying action that suggested potential employee dishonesty. The court reasoned that inadequate allegations of a third-party's complaint are not determinative of the insurer's obligation to defend if the insurer learns from the insured or other sources facts that give rise to potential liability under the bond. *Downey Sav. & Loan Ass'n v. Ohio Cas. Ins. Co.*, 234 Cal. Rptr. 835, 842-43.

Ill. App. Ct. 1983. Recognizing that the bond's general agreement gave the defendant insurer the right to defend "at the underwriter's election," the court held that the underwriter had no duty to defend under the bond. *Mortell v. Ins. Co. of N. Am.*, 458 N.E.2d 922, 1028.

C. Liability for Defense Costs and Attorneys' Fees

2nd Cir. 1981 (N.Y.). Insured was sued by third party for alleged securities violations by one of insured's employees. Fidelity insurer declined to defend the insured and denied the claim on grounds that the securities law violations were not dishonest within the meaning of brokers blanket bond. The insured eventually settled the underlying lawsuit and then sought recovery for the settlement costs and attorneys' fees incurred. The trial ruled in favor of the insured, finding that the insured's settlement of the action was conclusive evidence of employee dishonesty. On appeal, the court reversed, finding that the trial court had erred in finding that the settlement was conclusive evidence of coverage under the bond. *H.S. Equities, Inc. v. Hartford Acc. & Indem. Co.*, 661 F.2d 264, 269.

5th Cir. 2004 (Tex.). Bank sued the issuer of its Financial Institution Bond to recover (1) loss under a certificate of deposit issued to operator of Ponzi scheme; (2) settlement paid to investors of Ponzi scheme; and (3) attorneys' fees and expenses incurred in defending a forfeiture action to protect interest in certificate of deposit and in intervening in lawsuit against firm accused of conspiring with operator of Ponzi scheme. Upon review of the district court's grant of summary judgment for bank, the court agreed that the losses associated with the certificates of deposit were afforded coverage under the bond's "Securities" provision and further held that because that loss was covered, the loss attributable to the bank's settlement of the investor's claims was a covered loss. *Brady Nat'l Bank v. Gulf Ins. Co.*, 94 F. App'x. 197, 204-06.

5th Cir. 1996 (La.). Court applied the "pleadings only rule" in finding that sureties had a duty to reimburse the insured for the cost of litigating claims which potentially stated a cause of action within the terms of bond. Although the same complaint alleged facts that may have provided a defense to the sureties, the court only looked to the potentiality of coverage to determine the duty to indemnify. *First Nat'l Bank of Louisville v. Lustig*, 96 F.3d 1554, 1570.

5th Cir. 1985 (Tex.). In evaluating insured savings association's claim for attorneys' fees and court costs it expended in defending an action for fraud brought against it, the court held that the insured had demonstrated that its liability was "on account of any loss claim or damage," which if established, would have constituted a valid and collectible loss under Insuring Agreement (A). The court expressed that the bond's terms do not require the insured to suffer an actual collectible loss, only that it at least be threatened with a potential collectible loss. Additionally, the court permitted the insured to recover all fees expended in defense of the action brought against it, even though the original state court action did not allege fraud against the insured. Although the state court petition primarily alleged breach of contract, it did not exclude the "potentiality" that the basis of the breach was the savings association president's embezzlement, a covered loss. Finally, the court found that the proration clause was not triggered. Consequently, the insured was entitled to the full amount of fees and costs expended in defending the lawsuit brought against it. *Cont'l Sav. Ass'n v. USF&G*, 762 F.2d 1239, 1243-45.

5th Cir. 1981 (Tex.). Insured defended seven lawsuits alleging a conspiracy to defraud by means of a forgery and check kiting scheme perpetuated by its director and its president. The bank successfully defended the suits and sought indemnity from the underwriter for its costs and attorneys' fees. The appellate court upheld the trial court's finding that if the facts alleged in the complaint were proven, the bank would have been liable as principal for the actions of the president. Further, the court found that the bond would have provided coverage for the bank's liability. The insurer argued that the facts outside of the pleadings showed that the bank's president's actions did not amount to dishonesty under the bond because the bank acquiesced. The court found this argument "frivolous." The determinative factor was whether the facts as alleged in the complaint would constitute a valid claim under the bond. *First Nat'l Bank of Bowie v. Fid. & Cas. Co. of N.Y.*, 634 F.2d 1000, 1003-04.

5th Cir. 1966 (Tex.). Insured brought suit against insurer for attorneys' fees and costs expended in defending lawsuit, which was subsequently settled by insured. The court observed that the "duty to defend" is fixed by the allegations of the complaint. The appellate court affirmed the district court's finding that the underlying loss fell within the coverage of brokers blanket bond, thereby obligating insurer to pay plaintiff its defense costs, as well as losses plaintiff sustained. *Nat'l Sur. Corp. v. Rauscher, Pierce & Co.*, 369 F.2d 572, 575-78.

6th Cir. 1994 (Mich.). The appellate court affirmed the district court's finding that the bond's duty to indemnify defense costs was the equivalent to a duty to defend under a general liability insurance policy. The court further held that the duty to indemnify for defense costs is triggered by a potential covered loss. *Manley, Bennett, MacDonald & Co. v. St. Paul Fire & Marine Ins. Co.*, No. 93-1664, 1994 U.S. App. LEXIS 20429, at *1-2.

7th Cir. 1994 (Ind.). While noting that the district court ruled that the insurer had no duty to defend its insured in underlying action, the appellate court reversed the district court's finding that insurer was required to indemnify its insured for losses sustained for defense costs and amounts paid in settlement in defending action. The court found that genuine issues of material fact remained as to whether dishonest employee's endorsement of money order was a "forgery" within meaning of bond, and there were insufficient facts to determine as a matter of law that an adverse judgment in the underlying state action would not result in the insured sustaining an actual loss. *Cincinnati Ins. Co. v. Star Fin. Bank*, 35 F.3d 1186, 1188-92.

7th Cir. 1989 (Wis.). Indemnification for amounts paid in settlement and expenses incurred in defending racketeering case filed against insured by a competitor were not compensable under blanket fidelity bond. The court held that the policy by its express terms does not purport to promise indemnification for losses resulting from dishonest acts of former employees committed several months after they leave the insured's employ. Because the racketeering case sought recovery for matters which did not constitute a covered loss, insured was not entitled to indemnification. *Cont'l Corp. v. Aetna Cas. & Sur. Co.*, 892 F.2d 540, 549.

8th Cir. 1990 (Iowa). Insured sustained losses as a result of settlements reached with two bank customers in connection with fraudulent loan scheme committed by insured's employee. The insured reached settlement agreements prior to the initiation of litigation with both customers to avert potentially staggering compensatory and punitive damages awards. Court agreed that the settled claims constituted valid, collectible losses under the bond. The court further agreed that the attorneys' fees incurred by the insured during settlement negotiations were recoverable because the negotiations constituted a "legal proceeding" within the meaning of the bond. However, the appellate court held that the award of attorneys' fees incurred should have been apportioned between the fidelity carrier and the insured's D&O insurer, which had previously been dismissed from litigation. *First Am. State Bank v. Cont'l Ins. Co.*, 897 F.2d 319, 326.

8th Cir. 1989 (Minn.). Bank brought complaint against insurer for attorneys' fees incurred in defending action brought by bank customer who alleged that bank president forged customer's signature on mortgage deed and promissory note. In upholding the dismissal of bank's complaint against insurer, the court recognized that the terms of the bond do not require the insurer to provide a defense or pay the costs of defense unless the allegations made against the bank, if proven, constitute a loss under the bond. *Red Lake Cnty. State Bank v. Emp'rs' Ins. of Wausau*, 874 F.2d 546, 548.

8th Cir. 1971 (Mo.). The insurer admitted liability for certain defense costs, but disputed others. The court found that the insured's claim for defense costs was inflated and refused to impose statutory penalties for the insurer's alleged unreasonable refusal to pay the insured. *USF&G v. Empire State Bank*, 448 F.2d 360, 368.

9th Cir. 2000 (Cal.). Insured bank settled third-party suit alleging that bank had improperly handled certificates of deposit. In affirming summary judgment for insurer, the court held that losses sustained due to settlement and litigation expenses resulted from bank's breach of contract and were not proximately caused by dishonest employee's fraud. Court found third party's separate claim relating to bank's acceptance of check with a forged endorsement covered because the bond embraced the total amount and costs expended on all claims in third-party's lawsuit. *Cal. Kor. Bank v. Va. Sur. Co.*, Nos. 98-56778, 98-56806, 2000 U.S. App. LEXIS 12306, at *5-9.

9th Cir. 1991 (Cal.). Bankruptcy trustee appealed award of Rule 11 sanctions imposed by district court for opposing summary judgment motion filed by insurer. Insurer was one of three sureties sued on grounds that it had violated its duty to defend lawsuit against stockbroker. Trustee had argued that no loss was "sustained" until insurer's bond period. The court ruled that trustee's reliance on the attorneys' fees and costs provision was unavailing. Bond language clearly provided that coverage would only be provided for those losses discovered during the bond period and that his attempts to imbue the word "sustained" with significance were unjustified. *Schwaber v. Hartford Acc. & Indem. Co.*, No. 89-55736, 1991 U.S. App. LEXIS 14095, at *5-12.

9th Cir. 1980 (Cal.). Plaintiff was a financial service company that operated a retail securities business. Bond covered losses resulting from dishonest or fraudulent trading of securities. The bond specifically excluded any loss not discovered prior to its termination. Sometime after plaintiff discontinued its retail brokerage operations and modified the bond, it sought to recover for losses it had incurred when an employee engaged in a number of dishonest and fraudulent practices in the handling of a customer account. In affirming summary judgment for insurer, the court agreed that the language of the bond was not ambiguous. The insured was not covered unless the fraudulent nature of the loss was discovered before the bond's termination. That requirement was not met, so defendants had no duty to defend or indemnify. *F.S. Smithers & Co., Inc. v. Fed. Ins. Co.*, 631 F.2d 1364, 1368.

9th Cir. 1975 (Cal.). Litigation expenses incurred by acquiring company in defending actions for losses sustained before merger with another company were found not to be covered by the bond. The court ruled that the litigation expenses were not recoverable because the underlying losses occurred prior to the merger, and thus, were sustained not by the insured, but the company that was acquired, a non-insured party. Although the acquiring company argued that it sustained a loss at the time and by virtue of the merger, the court explained that acquisition of a company and its liabilities did not amount to a new loss for the insured. The court further found the acquiring company's argument that it was ignorant of the lawsuits against the acquired company until after the merger to be irrelevant because the acquiring company never sustained a loss within the meaning of the bond. *Fid. Sav. & Loan Ass'n v. Republic Ins. Co.,* 513 F.2d 954, 956.

S.D. Fla. 1986. In using a duty to defend analysis, the court found that the duty is invoked solely by the allegations of the complaint. Finding that complaint alleged no claim that would be covered, the court held that there was no duty to defend and no liability for defense costs or attorneys' fees incurred in defending third-party action. *Great Am. Bank of Fla. Keys v. Aetna Cas. & Sur. Co.,* 662 F. Supp. 363, 364-65.

N.D. Ill. 1992. The court recognized that Exclusion (u)(2) in a 1986 Financial Institution Bond excluded the recovery of attorneys' fees as part of the insured's primary loss. *Beverly Bancorp., Inc. v. Cont'l Ins. Co.,* No. 92 C 4823, 1992 WL 345420, at *2.

D. Kan. 1994. Insured bank asserted that its fidelity insurer had breached its duty to indemnify its attorneys' fees and costs incurred in defending against the bankruptcy trustee's adversary proceeding. The court noted that insurer had a duty to indemnify insured for its defense costs if the claim would constitute a collectible loss under the bond. The trustee's claim, which sought to set aside three transfers of ten percent participation interests in three loans, was found not to be a collectible loss under Insuring Clause (K). Consequently, the court held that St. Paul had not breached its duty to indemnify bank. *Lyons Fed. Sav. & Loan v. St. Paul Fire & Marine Ins. Co.,* 863 F. Supp. 1441, 1448-49.

W.D. Ky. 1996. Court found that none of the allegations in third-party actions brought by the insured bank's loan customer against the bank, if established, would constitute a collectible loss under the bond. Court held that the insured bank's claim for attorneys' fees incurred in defending such actions and amounts paid in settlement were not covered. *Ins. Co. of N. Am. v. Liberty Nat'l Bancorp.*, No. 93-0624, 1996 U.S. Dist. LEXIS 22825, at * 25-31.

W.D. La. 1993. The court held that the express language of fidelity bond made clear that defense costs are covered if the suit is on account of an act covered elsewhere in the bond. Offering no evidence in support of claim, plaintiff's claim for cost of defense was denied. *Farm Credit Bank of Tex. v. Fireman's Fund Ins. Co.*, 822 F. Supp. 1251, 1258.

W.D. Mo. 1969. Third-party complaint, if established, would have constituted a valid and collectible loss under Insuring Agreement (B). Insurer was therefore liable to indemnify insured for court costs and attorneys' fees in defending action. That the insured settled did not relieve defendant from liability. *Merchs.-Produce Bank v. USF&G*, 305 F. Supp. 957, 965-66.

D.N.J. 1990. In an action not involving defense costs, the court held the insured was entitled to recover, as its primary loss, attorneys' fees it incurred in collection actions against parties that caused the loss. However, the insured was not entitled to recover its fees incurred in the coverage action against its insurer. *Oritani Sav. & Loan Ass'n v. Fid. & Deposit Co. of Md.*, 744 F. Supp. 1311, 1320.

S.D.N.Y. 1987. The insured's receiver brought an action seeking to recover under two bonds issued to the insured, described as a "employee fidelity bond" and Brokers Blanket Bond. The court held that the insurer was liable for the receiver's defense costs incurred in an action by a creditor of the insured because defendant's agreement to indemnify the insured for "any loss of money" under employee fidelity bond was broad enough to cover attorneys' fees. In contrast, the court held that the Brokers Blanket Bond insurer's liability could not be established until its liability for coverage was established. *Glusband v. Fitten Cunningham Lauzon, Inc.*, No. 80 Civ. 7387, U.S. Dist. LEXIS 1867, at *7-9.

S.D.N.Y. 1969. The court held, without discussion, that the insurer was liable for defense costs. The opinion addresses what constitutes "costs." *Oscar Gruss & Son v. Lumbermens Mut. Cas. Co.*, 46 F.R.D. 635, 637.

E.D. Wis. 2012. Following finding that plaintiff's losses did not amount to a covered loss under the fidelity bond's "on premises" insuring agreement, the court held that insurer did not owe indemnification for court costs and attorneys' fees. The plain wording of the bond made clear that entitlement to indemnification for court costs and attorneys' fees is conditioned upon the matter being one for which the plaintiff would be entitled to recover under the bond. *Bankmanagers Corp. v. Fed. Ins. Co.*, No. 11-871, 2012 U.S. Dist. LEXIS 129647, at *24.

Bankr. N.D. Ohio 1988. In interpreting 1980 edition of Court Costs and Attorneys' Fees provision, the court found that the bankruptcy trustee was not entitled to amounts in excess of the single loss limit of liability for court costs and attorneys' fees since such amounts were included within the single loss limitation. *In re Baker & Getty Fin. Servs., Inc.*, 93 B.R. 559, 569.

Cal. Ct. App. 1978. Insured brought action to recover under successive Brokers Blanket Bonds for attorneys' fees and costs incurred after successfully defending claim. The court held that when the loss is discovered for purposes of primary coverage was ambiguous, and as a result, both bonds covered the insured's attorneys' fees and costs incurred in defending the action. The court instructed that the insurers' liability was to be allocated according to their respective coverages. *Cont'l Ins. Co. v. Morgan, Olmstead, Kennedy & Gardner, Inc.*, 83 Cal. App. 3d. 593, 608.

Ga. Ct. App. 1970. The court held that under the bond's attorneys' fees provision, indemnity is only provided in those situations of a defensive nature and not in an affirmative suit by the insured. As such, bond did not provide indemnity for expenses incurred in filing suit seeking to set aside cancellation of deed obtained through fraud, although court left open that insurer admitted liability for such expenses. *Rossville Fed. Sav. & Loan Assoc. v. Ins. Co. of N. Am.*, 174 S.E.2d 204, 207.

Ill. App. Ct. 1989. Insured bank sought to recover expenses incurred in defending action brought by customer who alleged that the bank's employee had acted intentionally and negligently, but not fraudulently, with respect to conduct in calling of a loan. The court affirmed summary judgment for insurer due to the absence of allegations of fraud or dishonesty, as well as evidence in the record indicating that the bank's officers knew of and participated in the employee's conduct. *State Street Bank & Trust v. USF&G*, 539 N.E.2d. 779, 781-82.

Iowa 1986. Upon finding that the insured's loss was not afforded coverage under the bond's On Premises or Securities Insuring Agreements, the court ruled that there was no basis for a recovery of attorneys' fees or court costs. *Gateway State Bank v. The N. River Ins. Co.*, 387 N.W.2d. 344, 348.

Iowa 1963. Insured sought declaration that the insurer was liable for $2,500 for each of eight forgeries and $1,500 for ninth forgery, as well as attorneys' fees and costs in connection with defending an action against it. Despite the insurer's contention that its liability was limited to a total of $2,500, the court found that the bond covered up to $2,500 for each forgery. The insurer argued that it was liable for defense only to the extent of the proportionate share to which it was liable under the bond. Without citing to any bond language, the court rejected the insurer's position, finding that there was no basis for reducing the insurer's liability. *Humboldt Trust & Sav. Bank v. Fid. & Cas. Co. of N.Y.*, 122 N.W.2d 358, 360.

Kan. Ct. App. 1979. Insured brought action against insurer for recovery of attorneys' fees incurred in defending action. The insured had been insured by two policies. The first insurer agreed to defend the insured but the second refused to do so. In denying plaintiff's claim for attorneys' fees and costs brought against insurer who declined to defend, the court found that the policy created a duty to defend, but the defendant had not acted in bad faith in refusing to defend because the insured had been adequately defended by first insurer. *Southgate State Bank & Trust Co. v. United Pac. Ins. Co.*, 588 P.2d 486, 488-90.

La. Ct. App. 1970. Insured under Brokers Blanket Bond claimed entitlement to expenses and attorneys' fees incurred in defending third-party action and for those fees expended in coverage suit. Plaintiff's losses were excluded by trading loss exclusion, so plaintiff was found to have no claim for court costs or attorneys' fees. *Hepler v. Fireman's Fund Ins. Co.*, 239 So. 2d 669, 678.

Minn. 1989. Without citing to relevant bond language, the court ruled that because plaintiff bank was not entitled to indemnification, bank's request for attorneys' fees must be denied as well. *Nat'l City Bank of Minn. v. St. Paul Fire & Marine Ins. Co.*, 447 N.W.2d 171, 180.

Minn. 1976. On appeal, the Supreme Court of Minnesota found that the issuer of a fidelity bond was not obligated to indemnify the insured bank for legal expenses incurred in defense and settlement of a customer's suit for damages resulting from fraudulent acts on the part of the bank and three officer/directors. The court held that the stipulated facts, as shown by the complaint and facts outside the complaint known to the insurer, demonstrated that the acts giving rise to the bank's liability were known acts of the officer/directors. The court noted that it was undisputed that the board of directors had knowledge of the conflict of interest giving rise to the customer's complaint. Because there could be no coverage under the bond, the insured was not entitled to recover its legal expenses. *Farmers & Merchs. State Bank of Pierz v. St. Paul Fire & Marine Ins. Co.*, 242 N.W.2d 840, 841-44.

Mo. 1966. Plaintiff sought recovery of the amount it paid in third-party litigation, plus costs and expenses incident to suit. After insured was sued, plaintiff sought protection and indemnity from defendant and a second insurer, which also had provided a blanket bond to plaintiff. After finding that plaintiff's loss was covered under defendant's bond, the court remanded the matter to ascertain whether second insurer had paid plaintiff $1,000 in exchange for a covenant not to sue. If so, plaintiff's recovery from second insurer would be credited against amount sought from defendant, who would be liable for net amount of loss and attorneys' fees incurred. *Jefferson Bank & Trust Co. v. Cent. Sur. & Ins. Co.*, 408 S.W.2d 825, 832-33.

Neb. 1979. Action brought by insured bank against fidelity carrier for litigation expenses was found to be barred by res judicata. In prior garnishment action, judgment creditor brought action against bank and its fidelity carrier on grounds that insurer was obligated to indemnify plaintiff under Bankers Blanket Bond. In prior action, the court ruled that the defendant fidelity carrier was not liable to the plaintiff or its insured. Since the court had previously determined that the action against the insured was not a valid and collectible loss under the bond, an issue that could not be re-litigated, the insurer was excused from liability for costs and attorneys' fees expended by the bank in defense of the prior action. *Bank of Mead v. St. Paul Fire & Marine Ins. Co.*, 275 N.W.2d 822, 825.

N.H. 1981. Plaintiff brought declaratory judgment to determine extent of coverage under bond and for attorneys' fees and court costs incurred in defending action alleging negligence and breach of fiduciary duty. Finding that the third-party's claims were beyond the scope of the policy's coverage, the court held that insurer was not liable for attorneys' fees or court costs. *Exeter Banking Co. v. N.H. Ins. Co.*, 438 A.2d 310, 315.

N.J. Super. Ct. App. Div. 1993. Finding that savings and loan association could not demonstrate that the claims asserted against it by third parties fell within coverages of the bond or its riders, the court ruled that the insured was not entitled to indemnification for reasonable court costs or attorneys' fees under the bond. *N. Jersey Sav. & Loan Ass'n v. Fid. & Deposit Co. of Md.*, 660 A.2d 1287, 1300.

N.Y. App. Div. 1998. Fidelity insurer brought declaratory judgment action that it was not obliged to indemnify the defendant insured under bond for losses sustained by insured in connection with third-party claims arising out of the misconduct of its employee. The insured argued that the attorneys' fees provision inferred broad third-party coverage, or alternatively, was so inconsistent with the statement of risk covered that the inconsistency must be construed in favor of coverage. The court found that the attorneys' fee provision is carefully couched in terms of the bond's basic coverage, providing coverage for costs and fees incurred in defending a suit against a third party only if there is a "collectible loss under this bond." As such, the court ruled that the attorneys' fees provision neither extends the covered risk to third-party claims carte blanche, nor is inconsistent with the general terms of coverage. *Aetna Cas. & Sur. Co. v. Kidder, Peabody & Co.*, 676 N.Y.S.2d 559, 565-65.

N.Y. App. Div. 1993. The court noted that fidelity bonds are not liability policies, and as such, do not provide coverage for defense costs or indemnification for all third-party claims. The court held that no coverage is afforded with respect to an employee's fraudulent conduct in which the insured knowingly participates. *Drexel Burnham Lambert Group, Inc. v. Vigilant Ins. Co.*, 595 N.Y.S.2d 999, 1010.

N.Y. App. Div. 1964. Insured was found not to be entitled to recovery for amounts expended in defending third-party action because loss was not covered. In reaching this result, the court looked to evidence beyond the pleadings that the insured's partners were aware of employee's misconduct. *Atkin v. Hill, Darlington, & Grimm*, 254 N.Y.S.2d 867, 869-76.

Tex. 1969. Court upheld summary judgment dismissing insured's claim for attorneys' fees and court costs incurred in defending a prior suit because allegations did not fall within coverage of any insuring agreements. In determining whether coverage was afforded under the bond, the court held that recourse must be had to the pleadings and papers in the suit that insured had defended. Although the insured argued that the liability alleged would have constituted a covered loss under the bond's On Premises or Forgery or Alteration Insuring Agreements, the court found that neither of these provisions were triggered, warranting dismissal of the insured's claim for litigation expenses. *Aetna Cas. & Sur. Co. v. S. Brokerage Co.*, 443 S.W.2d. 45, 47-49.

Tex. 1968. Court reversed summary judgment for bank that brought suit against fidelity carrier for attorneys' fees expended in successfully defending a lawsuit. The court disagreed that the bond required the insured to sustain an actual loss before being entitled to reimbursement for court costs and attorneys' fees incurred and paid in successfully defending a claim. Finding that the allegations against the bank did not allege liability that would have caused it a loss subject to indemnification, the court entered summary judgment for the insurer. *Nat'l Sur. Co. v. First Nat'l Bank of Midland*, 431 S.W.2d. 353, 355-57.

Tex. Ct. App. 1978. Court gave pleadings liberal interpretation and found that pleadings did not allege a loss under the On Premises coverage of the bond. *White Rock Nat'l Bank of Dallas v. U.S. Fire Ins. Co.*, 562 S.W.2d 268, 273.

Utah Ct. App. 1991. A third party filed a seven-count complaint against the insured on which it was ultimately successful, including obtaining an award of attorneys' fees. The insured then sought to recover the amount of the judgment and its own defense costs. The insurer argued that only one-seventh of defense costs were covered since only one of the seven counts allegedly constituted a covered loss. The court, however, allowed for recovery for the entire loss, including attorneys' fees and the full amount of insured's defense costs. *Home Sav. & Loan v. Aetna Cas. & Sur. Co.*, 817 P. 2d 341, 365-66.

SECONDARY SOURCES

Lisa A. Block & Scott L. Schmookler, *The Compensability of Third Party Loss*, in HANDLING FIDELITY BOND CLAIMS 389 (Michael Keeley and Sean Duffy eds., 2d ed. 2005).

William F. Haug, *Effect of Decision by Insurer Not to Defend Insured Against Claims Cognizable under Bonds,* XII THE FORUM 410 (1976).

Frank Mays Hull, *Surety's Liability for Attorneys' Fees and Court Costs Under Fidelity Bonds*, XIV THE FORUM 634 (1979).

Donald L. Mrozek & Sandra M. Stone, *General Agreement F Notice of Legal Proceedings Against Insured—Election to Defend*, in FINANCIAL INSTITUTION BONDS 537 (Duncan L. Clore ed., 3d ed. 2008).

Gilbert J. Schroeder, *Court Costs and Attorneys' Fees*, in FINANCIAL INSTITUTION BONDS 351 (Duncan L. Clore ed., 2d ed. 1998).

SECTION 7 — GENERAL AGREEMENT G—INSURED'S ERISA PLANS*

If any Employee or director of the Insured is required to provide a bond to a health, welfare or pension plan subject to the Employee Retirement Income Security Act of 1974 (ERISA) (hereinafter the Plan), the majority of whose beneficiaries are Employees or former Employees of the Insured, the Plan shall be deemed an insured under this bond for the purposes of Insuring Agreement (A) only and subject, in addition to all other terms and conditions of this bond, to the following:
(1) the deductible required by Section 12 of the Conditions and Limitations of this bond shall be applicable to a loss suffered by the Plan only after the Plan has received from the Underwriter
   a. the lesser of $500,000 or 10% of the assets of the Plan at the beginning of the fiscal year of the Plan in which the loss is discovered, if the Plan does not hold "employer securities" within the meaning of section 407(d)(1) of ERISA; or
   b. the lesser of $1,000,000 or 10% of the assets of the Plan at the beginning of the fiscal year of the Plan in which the loss is discovered, if the Plan holds "employer securities" within the meaning of section 407(d)(1) of ERISA,
(2) notwithstanding Section 3 of the Conditions and Limitations of this bond, loss suffered by the Plan is covered if discovered during the term of this bond or within one year thereafter, but if discovered during said one year period, the loss payable under this bond shall be reduced by the amount recoverable from any other bond or insurance protecting the assets of the Plan against loss through fraud or dishonesty; and

---

* Seth Mills and Kevin Mekler, Mills Paskert Divers, Tampa, Florida.

(3) if more than one Plan subject to ERISA is an Insured pursuant to this General Agreement, the Insured shall purchase limits sufficient to provide the minimum amount of coverage required by ERISA for each Plan and shall distribute any payment made under this bond to said Plans so that each Plan receives the amount it would have received if insured separately for the minimum coverage which ERISA required it to have.

COMMENT

The "Insured's ERISA Plans" provision was added as General Agreement G of the Financial Institution Bond in the 2004 revisions. Previously, insurers typically provided specific coverage for an Insureds' ERISA plans by way of an endorsement. The Employee Retirement Income Security Act of 1974[1] is the governing legislation requiring qualified plans to obtain coverage against loss of plan funds caused by the fraudulent or dishonest acts of persons who handle plan funds. ERISA governs not only who must be bonded, but also the scope of coverage and certain specific terms, including the amount of the bond, the term of the bond, the discovery period, and use of overlapping or supplemental bonds/policies.

The scope of coverage for ERISA Plans under General Agreement G is limited to the coverage afforded under Insuring Agreement (A) only, and is subject to all other terms and conditions of the bond. Thus, for purposes of coverage, the Plan is limited to claims for loss resulting directly from dishonest or fraudulent acts committed by an employee, acting alone or in collusion with others, with the manifest intent to cause the insured to sustain such loss, and to obtain an improper financial benefit for the employee or another person or entity. This limitation is important when analyzing a claim under General Agreement G because this section expressly incorporates all other terms and conditions of the bond; that is, the myriad of factual defenses applicable to claims under Insuring Agreement (A).

---

[1] 29 U.S.C. 1001 (2012).

General Agreement G also addresses the primary statutory requirements for coverage expressed by ERISA. Initially, this section identifies that the Plan shall be deemed an insured under the bond if "any Employee or director of the Insured is required to provide a bond under [ERISA]." Section G(1) provides for the application of the deductible on a sliding scale, dependent upon the size of the plan, and whether the Plan includes "employer securities" within the meaning of section 407(d)(1) of ERISA. Section G(2) provides an expansion of the "Discovery" definition contained in Section 3 of the bond, to permit discovery within one year from the expiration of the bond, subject to setoff for amounts recoverable (not recovered) from any other bond or insurance covering the Plan. Finally, Section G(3) addresses insureds with more than one Plan covered under the bond. This section requires the insured to purchase the minimum amount required under ERISA for each Plan and provides a methodology for allocating payments made under the bond to each Plan.

Because General Agreement G only was added by the 2011 revisions, no case has yet analyzed the application of this section. However, the ERISA cases arising prior to the 2011 revision generally focused on whether ERISA's requirements expanded coverage. Historically, the courts have been unwilling to expand or judicially reform the scope of the bond because ERISA does not mandate that all requirements be fulfilled by a single bond or policy. Instead, the courts have placed the burden on the Insured to obtain the required coverage, and have allowed insureds to do so by procuring the requisite number of bonds or policies.

ANNOTATIONS

9th Cir. 1996 (Cal.). Summary judgment affirmed for insurer under employee dishonesty bond containing ERISA endorsement. The bond identified specific categories of individuals whose dishonest acts were covered. Subsequently, the insured invested plan proceeds in second mortgages through a third party ("defalcator") who was using the plan funds to run a Ponzi scheme. When the Ponzi scheme failed and the insured discovered the loss, it sought coverage under the fidelity bond. The insured claimed, in part, that the defalcator was a fiduciary that was required to be bonded under ERISA, and that the bond was designed to cover anyone who was required to be bonded under ERISA, therefore coverage existed regardless of whether the bond expressly included coverage. The court rejected the insured's argument, and held that the insurer's endorsement "does not bond everyone who must be bonded. It bonds only those classes of persons it designates." The court further clarified that there is nothing in ERISA that requires a single bond to cover everyone who must be bonded under ERISA, and the insured is responsible for ensuring that the sufficient bond(s) are obtained. *Joseph Rosenbaum, M.D., Inc. v. Hartford Fire Ins. Co.*, 104 F.3d 258, 262-63.

Oregon Ct. App. 2009. Summary judgment affirmed for insurers under Welfare and Pension Plan ERISA Compliance endorsements to two commercial crime policies. Insureds entered into agreements with an investment management company, and subsequently filed proofs of loss claiming that they incurred losses as result of dishonest acts committed by the investment company's principals. The court determined that the investment company was considered an administrator under ERISA. However, because the policies specifically excluded from the definition of covered employees "independent contractor administrators or managers," there was no coverage. The court also rejected the insured's argument that because administrators must be bonded under ERISA, the crime policies coverage is illusory. *Emp'rs-Shopmens Local 516 Pension Trust v. Travelers Cas. and Sur. Co. of Am.*, 235 P. 3d 689, 697-700.

SECONDARY SOURCES

David T. DiBiase & Jacqueline Kirk, *Riders On The Storm: An Examination Of Industry Trends Relative To Special Fidelity Bond Riders And Endorsements*, III FID. L.J. 115 (1997).

Edward G. Gallagher, *ERISA Bonding Requirements And The Fidelity Insurer*, XIV FID. L.J. 247 (2008).

G. Kevin Kiely & Carla Scott, *Litigating The ERISA Fidelity Bond Claim*, XV FID. L.J. 221 (2009).

Patrick J. O'Connor, Thomas J. Vollbrecht, Paul W. Heiring & Barbara Haley, *ERISA Bond Claims Over Employer Stock Losses: The Landscape In A Post-Enron World*, X FID. L.J. 19 (2004).

Chapter 3

Conditions and Limitations

SECTION 1 — DEFINITIONS*

Section 1. As used in this bond:
(a) Acceptance means a draft which the drawee has, by signature written thereon, engaged to honor as presented.
(b) Certificate of Deposit means an acknowledgment in writing by a financial institution of receipt of Money with an engagement to repay it.
(c) Certificate of Origin or Title means a document issued by a manufacturer of personal property or a governmental agency evidencing the ownership of the personal property and by which ownership is transferred.
(d) Certificated Security means a share, participation or other interest in property of or an enterprise of the issuer or an obligation of the issuer, which is:
  (1) represented by an instrument issued in bearer or registered form;
  (2) of a type commonly dealt in on securities exchanges or markets or commonly recognized in any area in which it is issued or dealt in as a medium for investment; and
  (3) either one of a class or series or by its terms divisible into a class or series of shares, participations, interests or obligations.
(e) Counterfeit means an imitation which is intended to deceive and to be taken as an original.

---

* Definitions (a) through (l) by T. Scott Leo and Brandon G. Hummel, Leo & Weber, P.C., Chicago, Illinois. Definitions (m) through (u) by Bradford R. Carver and CharCretia DiBartolo, Hinshaw & Culbertson, LLP, Boston, Massachusetts.

(f) Document of Title means a bill of lading, dock warrant, dock receipt, warehouse receipt or order for the delivery of goods, and also any other document which in the regular course of business or financing is treated as adequately evidencing that the person in possession of it is entitled to receive, hold and dispose of the document and the goods it covers and must purport to be issued by or addressed to a bailee and purport to cover goods in the bailee's possession which are either identified or are fungible portions of an identified mass.

(g) Employee means
   (1) an officer or other employee of the Insured, while employed in, at, or by any of the Insured's offices or premises covered hereunder, and a guest student pursuing studies or duties in any of said offices or premises;
   (2) an attorney retained by the Insured and an employee of such attorney while either is performing legal services for the Insured;
   (3) a person provided by an employment contractor to perform employee duties for the Insured under the Insured's supervision at any of the Insured's offices or premises covered hereunder;
   (4) an employee of an institution merged or consolidated with the Insured prior to the effective date of this bond; and
   (5) each natural person, partnership or corporation authorized by the Insured to perform services as data processor of checks or other accounting records of the Insured (not including preparation or modification of computer software or programs), herein called Processor. (Each such Processor, and the partners, officers and employees of such Processor shall, collectively be deemed to be one Employee for all the purposes of this bond, excepting, however, the second paragraph of Section 12. A Federal Reserve Bank or clearing house shall not be construed to be a processor.)

(h) Evidence of Debt means an instrument, including a Negotiable Instrument, executed by a customer of the Insured and held by the Insured which in the regular course of business is treated as evidencing the customer's debt to the Insured.
(i) Forgery means the signing of the name of another person or organization with intent to deceive; it does not mean a signature which consists in whole or in part of one's own name signed with or without authority, in any capacity, for any purpose.
(j) Guarantee means a written undertaking obligating the signer to pay the debt of another to the Insured or its assignee or to a financial institution from which the Insured has purchased participation in the debt, if the debt is not paid in accordance with its terms.
(k) Instruction means a written order to the issuer of an Uncertificated Security requesting that the transfer, pledge or release from pledge of the Uncertificated Security specified be registered.
(l) Letter of Credit means an engagement in writing by a bank or other person made at the request of a customer that the bank or other person will honor drafts or other demands for payment upon compliance with the conditions specified in the Letter of Credit.
(m) Loan means all extensions of credit by the Insured and all transactions creating a creditor relationship in favor of the Insured and all transactions by which the Insured assumes an existing creditor relationship.
(n) Money means a medium of exchange in current use authorized or adopted by a domestic or foreign government as part of its currency.
(o) Negotiable Instrument means any writing
    (a) signed by the maker or drawer; and
    (b) containing an unconditional promise or order to pay a sum certain in Money and no other promise, order, obligation or power given by the maker or drawer; and
    (c) is payable on demand or at a definite time; and
    (d) is payable to order or bearer.

(p) Property means Money, Certified Securities, Uncertified Securities of any Federal Reserve Bank of the United States, Negotiable Instruments, Certificates of Deposit, Documents of Title, Acceptances, Evidences of Debt, Security Agreements, Withdrawal Orders, Certificates of Origin or Title, Letters of Credit, insurance policies, abstracts of title, deeds and mortgages on real estate, revenue and other stamps, tokens, unsold state lottery tickets, books of account and other records whether recorded in writing or electronically, gems, jewelry, precious metals in bars or ingots, and tangible items of personal property which are not herein above enumerated.

(q) Security Agreement means an agreement which creates an interest in personal property or fixtures and which secures payment or performance of an obligation.

(r) Statement of Uncertificated Security means a written statement of the issuer of an Uncertificated Security containing:
   (a) A description of the Issue of which the Uncertificated Security is a part;
   (b) The number of shares or units:
      (i) transferred to the registered owner;
      (ii) pledged by the registered owner to the registered pledges;
      (iii) released from pledge by the registered pledgee;
      (iv) registered in the name of the registered owner on the date of the statement; or
      (v) subject to pledge on the date of the statement;
   (c) The name and address of the registered owner and registered pledgee;
   (d) A notation of any liens and restrictions of the issuer and any adverse claims to which the Uncertificated Security is or may be subject or a statement that there are none of those liens, restrictions or adverse claims; and
   (e) The date:

(i) the transfer of the shares or units to the new registered owner of the shares or units was registered;
(ii) the pledge of the registered pledgee was registered, or
(iii) of the statement, if it is a periodic or annual statement.

(s) Transportation Company means any organization which provides its own or leased vehicles for transportation or which provides freight forwarding or air express services.

(t) Uncertificated Security means a share, participation or other interest in property of or an enterprise of the issuer or an obligation of the issuer, which is:
   (a) not represented by an instrument and the transfer of which is registered upon books maintained for that purpose by or on behalf of the issuer;
   (b) of a type commonly dealt in on securities exchanges or markets; and
   (c) either one of a class or series or by its terms divisible into a class or series of shares, participations, interests or obligations.

(u) Withdrawal Order means a non-negotiable instrument, other than an Instruction, signed by a customer of the Insured authorizing the Insured to debit the customer's account in the amount of funds stated therein.

COMMENT

Definitions have accumulated in the standard form Financial Institution Bond over the years. The 1969 Bankers Blanket Bond contained only two definitions, "Employee" and "Property." The fifteen definitions in the 1980 Bankers Blanket Bond increased to twenty-one definitions in the 1986 Financial Institution Bond. Many of these terms are drawn from the Uniform Commercial Code, while others, by design, do not follow the Code. A number of the definitions are narrower than what some might believe are their common, everyday meanings or their definitions under various state laws. Through the definitions, the provisions of the bond—especially Insuring Agreements (D) and (E) and the exclusions—are now more concisely and narrowly defined.

The most recent definition, added in the 1986 Financial Institution Bond, is definition (m), "Loan." There are no cases directly discussing the application of the definition of "Loan" to coverage issues. In contrast there are a number of cases that address whether a transaction or group of transactions constitute loans or extensions of credit under earlier bond forms that did not define the term loan.

The definitions that are the subject of most of the reported decisions are: (g) Employee, (f) Forgery, and (e) Counterfeit. But the number of decisions addressing these definitions decreased in the past decade, and those decisions tend to rely directly on the language of the definitions found in the bond. The definitions that have not been the subject of reported decisions generally describe a document or action in unambiguous terms or do not relate to issues essential to determining coverage.

A. Acceptance

(a) Acceptance means a draft which the drawee has, by signature written thereon, engaged to honor as presented.

COMMENT

The definition of "Acceptance" is drawn from the Uniform Commercial Code, which defines this term as the drawee's signed agreement to pay a draft as presented.[1] The term is applied in Insuring Agreement (D) (Forgery or Alteration). This definition has not been applied in any decision relating to the Financial Institution Bond.

ANNOTATIONS

NONE

---

1 U.C.C. § 3-409(a) (2003).

SECONDARY SOURCES

David T. DiBiase, Carleton R. Burch & David J. Billings, *The ABC's of Insuring Agreement (D) Under the Financial Institution Bond*, XVII FID. L.J., 2d ed., 1 (2011).

B. Certificate of Deposit

(b) Certificate of Deposit means an acknowledgment in writing by a financial institution of receipt of Money with an engagement to repay it.

COMMENT

The definition of "Certificate of Deposit" is virtually identical to the Uniform Commercial Code definition, which also defines it as a "note of the bank."[2] The definition has not been applied in any case construing the Financial Institution Bond.

ANNOTATIONS

NONE

SECONDARY SOURCES

David T. DiBiase, Carleton R. Burch & David J. Billings, *The ABC's of Insuring Agreement (D) Under the Financial Institution Bond*, XVII FID. L.J., 2d ed., 1 (2011).

Michael Keeley, Michele L. Fenice & J. Will Eidson, *Insuring Agreement (E)—Revisited*, XVII FID. L.J., 2d ed., 203 (Dec. 2011).

---

2 U.C.C. § 3-104 (2003).

C. Certificate of Origin or Title

(c) Certificate of Origin or Title means a document issued by a manufacturer of personal property or a governmental agency evidencing the ownership of the personal property and by which ownership is transferred.

COMMENT

This defines the term as used in Insuring Agreement (E). Both Certificates of Origin and Certificates of Title are documents evidencing ownership. A Certificate of Origin is used where an item is newly manufactured or imported and not previously titled. The Uniform Commercial Code does not define the term but provides that a security interest may be perfected for certain property only by appearing on the certificate of title.[3]

ANNOTATIONS

M.D. La. 1993. A city ordinance is not a "Certificate of Origin or Title" where the ordinance itself does not purport to transfer ownership. Mere possession of the ordinance did not transfer title, and the terms of the ordinance required prior approval by the city council. *FDIC v. Fid. & Deposit Co. of Md.*, 827 F. Supp. 385, 394-96.

SECONDARY SOURCES

Michael Keeley, Michele L. Fenice & J. Will Eidson, *Insuring Agreement (E)—Revisited*, XVII FID. L.J., 2d ed., 203 (2011).

---

[3] U.C.C. § 9-102 (2003).

D. Certificated Security

(d) Certificated Security means a share, participation or other interest in property of or an enterprise of the issuer or an obligation of the issuer, which is:
  (1) represented by an instrument issued in bearer or registered form;
  (2) of a type commonly dealt in on securities exchanges or markets or commonly recognized in any area in which it is issued or dealt in as a medium for investment; and
  (3) either one of a class or series or by its terms divisible into a class or series of shares, participations, interests or obligations.

COMMENT

This is the definition of the term found in Insuring Agreement (E). The definition is considerably more detailed than the Uniform Commercial Code definition, which defines a "certificated security" as a security represented by a certificate.[4] Until the 1986 revision of the Financial Institution Bond—which added "Statement of Uncertificated Security" to the list of documents covered by Insuring Agreement (E)—coverage under Insuring Agreement (E) required that any security be certificated. This was consistent with the physical possession requirement of Insuring Agreement (E). The change in Insuring Agreement (E) was necessary after 1986 when certain United States Treasury obligations were only issued as book entry securities without certificates. With the exception of book entry securities that can be documented through a statement of an uncertificated security from the Federal Reserve Bank, the definition still requires that a security be represented by an instrument.

---

[4] U.C.C. § 8-102 (2003).

ANNOTATIONS

E.D. Ark. 2004. Falsified leases furnished to obtain a revolving line of credit were not Certificated Securities because they were not represented by an instrument issued in bearer or registered form, were not the type of document commonly utilized on securities exchanges or markets, and were not commonly recognized or dealt in as a medium for investment. *Pine Bluff Nat'l Bank v. St. Paul Mercury Ins. Co.,* 346 F. Supp. 2d 1020, 1026-28.

SECONDARY SOURCES

Peter Haley, *The Power of Defined Terms and Causation Theories Under Insuring Agreement (E) of the Financial Institution Bond*, 31 TORT & INS. L.J. 609 (1996).

Michael Keeley, Michele L. Fenice & J. Will Eidson, *Insuring Agreement (E)—Revisited,* XVII FID. L.J., 2d ed., 203 (2011).

E. Counterfeit

(e) Counterfeit means an imitation which is intended to deceive and to be taken as an original.

COMMENT

"Counterfeit" is a term used in Insuring Agreement (E). For purposes of determining whether something is Counterfeit under this definition, it is important that the defective document imitate an original, genuine document. The cases dealing with whether there is a Counterfeit document within the definition of the bond tend to look to whether the purported Counterfeit was an attempt to imitate an actual document or was entirely a fabrication. The definition requires an imitation of an original. The distinction between an imitation and an invention out of whole cloth is not always easily discernible, but the more variations there are between the imitated document and the original, the less likely the document will be considered a Counterfeit. If a document merely resembles a genuine document, it is not a Counterfeit. The Uniform Commercial Code does not define this term, but describes the term "genuine" to mean "free of forgery or counterfeiting."[5]

ANNOTATIONS

5th Cir. 1990 (Tex.). Bogus stock certificates that were not imitations of genuine stock certificates were not "Counterfeit" as defined by the Financial Institution Bond. *Reliance Ins. Co. v. Capital Bancshares, Inc./Capital Bank,* 912 F.2d 756, 757.

7th Cir. 2012 (Wis.). A fake certificate of origin for a motor home presented as collateral to secure a loan was not a counterfeit as defined under Form 24. The bond defined "Counterfeit" as "a written imitation of an actual, valid Original which is intended to deceive and to be taken as the Original." Because the certificate was not "an imitation or duplicate of a preexisting genuine original document" for the specific motor home presented as collateral for the loan, the court found that the insured's claim did not fall within the case law's well-established understanding of the term "Counterfeit." *N. Shore Bank, FSB v. Progressive Cas. Ins. Co.,* 674 F.3d 884, 888-89.

7th Cir. 2003 (Ill.). The court affirmed the district court and concluded that signatures on fake manufacturers certificates of origin ("MCOs") furnished to secure loans were not required in order to satisfy the definition of "Counterfeit" under a fidelity bond. The unsigned MCOs may have passed in the trade as official. Further, currency does not have to be signed in order to be "counterfeit" under federal law. *State Bank of the Lakes v. Kan. Bankers Sur. Co.,* 328 F.3d 906, 908-09.

N.D. Ill. 1999. Duplicate statements of origin used to induce a bank to extend a line of credit to a customer to purchase a boat were counterfeit because they were intended to be imitations of the originals. *State Bank of the Lakes v. Kan. Bankers Sur. Co.,* No. 98 C 3212, 1999 WL 674739 at *3-4.

---

5   U.C.C. § 1-201(19) (2003).

M.D. La. 1993. A fake city ordinance is not a "Counterfeit" as defined by the bond because it is not an imitation of a specific original. Although there was an actual ordinance issued bearing the same public ordinance number as the fake ordinance, the real ordinance differed from the fake ordinance substantially. The court found that there was no attempt to imitate an original as required by the definition. *FDIC v. Fid. & Deposit Co. of Md.*, 827 F. Supp. 385, 394-96.

D.N.D. 2008. A credit union issued a loan secured by a faxed, unsigned buyer's bill purporting to document the sale of 1,276 heads of livestock to the borrower. The loan went into default, and the credit union asserted a claim against its fidelity insurer alleging counterfeit. The court rejected the insured's claim on summary judgment and found that the buyer's bill was not an imitation or duplicate of a preexisting original document as required by the bond. The court also concluded that it was not reasonable for the insured to rely on the faxed, unsigned bill. *Dakota W. Credit Union v. CUMIS Ins. Soc'y*, 532 F. Supp. 2d 1110, 1115-18.

D.N.J. 1983. In a case involving claims of forgery, counterfeiting, and employee dishonesty under the 1969 form Bankers Blanket Bond, the court held that losses from loans secured by worthless certificates of deposit ("CDs") issued by an entity that had been chartered as a bank in the British West Indies, but which had no assets, were not losses under either Insuring Agreement (D) or (E). The loss occurred because the CDs implicitly misrepresented the amounts available to issuing bank for its own account, and therefore were not counterfeited or forged within the meaning of the bond. Court concluded that bank would be expected to protect itself against the risk posed by the possible worthlessness of CDs through its normal credit evaluation procedures. *Liberty Nat'l Bank v. Aetna Life & Cas. Co.*, 568 F. Supp. 860, 864.

Minn. 1989. Fake stock certificates that were not imitations of genuine certificates were not "Counterfeits" as defined in the Financial Institution Bond. *Nat'l City Bank of Minneapolis v. St. Paul Fire & Marine Ins. Co.*, 447 N.W.2d 171, 177-80.

SECONDARY SOURCES

Peter C. Haley & Dolores Parr, *Coverage Under Insuring Agreement (E) of the Financial Institution Bond*, in FINANCIAL INSTITUTION BONDS 385 (Duncan Clore ed., 3d ed. 2008).

F. Document of Title

(f) **Document of Title means a bill of lading, dock warrant, dock receipt, warehouse receipt or order for the delivery of goods, and also any other document which in the regular course of business or financing is treated as adequately evidencing that the person in possession of it is entitled to receive, hold and dispose of the document and the goods it covers and must purport to be issued by or addressed to a bailee and purport to cover goods in the bailee's possession which are either identified or are fungible portions of an identified mass.**

COMMENT

The definition of "Document of Title" first appeared with the rewriting of Insuring Agreement (E) in the 1980 revisions to the Bankers Blanket Bond, where it appeared in Section 1(e) of the Conditions and Limitations section of that bond. The 1986 revisions only added the definition of the term "Certificated Security." In 2004, the defined term "Written" was added to make clear that Insuring Agreement (E) did not cover electronic transactions, which are covered, if at all, by separate rider.[6] Because the term is so specifically defined, its interpretation has been the subject of only two significant decisions, which upheld the plain language of the definition without submitting the matter to a jury.

---

[6] Surety Association of America, Form & Rider Filing Letter, Financial Institution Bond, Standard Form No. 24 § III (Dec. 24, 2003).

ANNOTATIONS

E.D. Ark. 2004. Falsified leases furnished to obtain a loan were not "documents of title" as defined under a fidelity bond because as long as the lessee fulfilled its obligations under the leases and the leases remained in effect, the lessee—the borrower or bank—was entitled to hold the leased property. *Pine Bluff Nat'l Bank v. St. Paul Mercury Ins. Co.,* 346 F. Supp. 2d 1020, 1026-28, 1033.

D.N.D. 2008. A credit union issued a loan secured by a faxed, unsigned buyer's bill purporting to document the sale of 1,276 heads of livestock to the borrower. The loan went into default, and the credit union asserted a claim against its fidelity insurer alleging counterfeit. The court rejected the insured's claim on summary judgment and found that the buyer's bill was not an imitation or duplicate of a preexisting original document as required by the bond. In addition, the court concluded that it was not reasonable for the insured to rely on the faxed, unsigned bill. *Dakota W. Credit Union v. CUMIS Ins. Soc'y,* 532 F. Supp. 2d 1110, 1117-18.

SECONDARY SOURCES

Michael Keeley, Michele L. Fenice & J. Will Eidson, *Insuring Agreement (E)—Revisited,* XVII FID. L.J., 2d ed., 203 (2011).

G. Employee

    (g) Employee means
        (1) an officer or other employee of the Insured, while employed in, at, or by any of the Insured's offices or premises covered hereunder, and a guest student pursuing studies or duties in any of said officers or premises;
        (2) an attorney retained by the Insured and an employee of such attorney while either is performing legal services for the Insured;
        (3) a person provided by an employment contractor to perform employee duties for the Insured under

the Insured's supervision at any of the Insured's offices or premises covered hereunder;
(4) an employee of an institution merged or consolidated with the Insured prior to the effective date of this bond; and
(5) each natural person, partnership or corporation authorized by the Insured to perform services as data processor of checks or other accounting records of the Insured (not including preparation or modification of computer software or programs), herein called Processor. (Each such Processor, and the partners, officers and employees of such Processor shall, collectively be deemed to be one Employee for all the purposes of this bond, excepting, however, the second paragraph of Section 12. A Federal Reserve Bank or clearing house shall not be construed to be a processor.)

COMMENT

This definition is the subject of more decisions than any other definition. Insuring Agreement (A) provides certain coverage for acts committed by an "Employee," as that term is defined in the bond. The 1980 form expanded the definition of "Employee" to include temporary employees or loaned employees in subparagraph (3). The inclusion of contract employees is consistent with the Uniform Commercial Code, which for purposes of determining an employer's responsibility for a fraudulent endorsement by an employee, defines "Employee" to include an independent contractor or an employee of an independent contractor retained by the employer.[7]

Many of the cases examining the term "Employee" deal with non-traditional employment relationships or service vendors and independent contractors who might be deemed to fall within the insured's control and direction. A number of cases address the control and domination of the insured institution by the Employee and discuss whether the individual is

---

[7] U.C.C. § 3-405(a)(1) (2003).

an alter ego of the insured or subject to the insured's control and direction. An alter ego who controls the corporation—rather than being controlled by the corporation—and causes the loss is not an Employee. This follows from the principle that the insured itself should not benefit from its own misconduct. While the definition of "Employee" does not reference or expressly exclude alter egos as Employees, the alter-ego cases reveal the type of control and direction that the insured must exercise over its Employees. In Exclusion (d), the bond itself excludes actions of directors of the insured, except when the directors are acting in the capacity of Employees. Between the definition of "Employee" and this exclusion, the alter-ego cases provide a map for drawing the line between acts of Employees and the level of control and domination that makes the person the insured's alter ego. These cases will not be discussed in detail or exhaustively below because they do not directly interpret or apply the definition of Employee. These cases are set forth in Chapter 1, Section 1 — Insuring Agreement (A)—Fidelity.

A couple of the more recent decisions address whether the wrongdoing party in question falls within the definition of Employee as a loan servicer, examining whether the party's employment activities relate to actual loan servicing.

OUTLINE OF ANNOTATIONS

A. Employee Generally
B. Alter-Ego Decisions
C. Attorneys as Employees
D. Servicers as Employees

ANNOTATIONS

A. Employee, Generally

4th Cir. 1942 (N.C.). The company's president was not an employee of the insured bank where the bank lent money to a company and agreed to turn over for collection the notes payable to the company's president, which had been deposited with the bank as collateral security for the indebtedness. *Nat'l Bank of Burlington v. Fid. & Cas. Co. of N.Y.,* 125 F.2d 920, 923-24.

5th Cir. 1977 (La.). The insured's commodity solicitor and registered representative had a personal commodity account and, while on the floor of the Chicago Board of Trade, wrote his own order tickets or asked other employee of the insured to write order tickets for him. Broker/customer was found to be an employee of the insured. *Howard v. Ins. Co. of N. Am.,* 557 F.2d 1055, 1058.

6th Cir. 1977 (Ohio). Court found that worker was not insured's employee, where he maintained an office for work as a real estate broker and appraiser in his home worked chiefly for the insured but also did work for others, was paid an agreed-upon sum for each appraisal and inspection for the insured, was not furnished with an employee's withholding statement, was not listed by the insured as an employee for purposes of workmen's compensation or unemployment compensation, was not entitled to fringe benefits, did not have income tax withheld or social security employer contributions paid by the insured, paid all of the expenses concurred in connection with inspections and appraisals, and had no set working hours. *Third Fed. Sav. & Loan Ass'n v. Fireman's Fund Ins.,* 548 F.2d 166, 171-72.

6th Cir. 1969 (Mich.). Where the insured established a branch office in the office of a real estate broker and placed the broker in charge as an assistant vice president, the broker became an employee of the insured. *William H. Sill Mortgs., Inc. v. Ohio Cas. Ins. Co.,* 412 F.2d 341, 344-47.

8th Cir. 1971 (S.D.). Where the majority shareholder served as a director and president of the insured, the district court determined that he was not an employee because the board of directors served only to rubberstamp his actions. The court of appeals reversed and held that the majority shareholder/director/president was an employee because the insured asked that he be included as a covered employee, and the insurer charged an additional premium and voided the provision specifically excluding him. Also, while the board of directors generally served only as a rubberstamp, it had the "right to govern and direct." *Gen. Fin. Corp. v. Fid. & Cas. Co. of N.Y.,* 439 F.2d 981, 984-86.

8th Cir. 1967 (Iowa). Where the president of the insured engaged in a separate general contracting business and all jobs requiring posting of a performance bond were fully subcontracted to the president's business, the president was an employee of the insured since he performed definite services and was subject to the control, direction, and ultimate discharge of the insured and its board of directors. *Wooddale, Inc. v. Fid. & Deposit Co. of Md.,* 378 F.2d 627, 632.

9th Cir. 1979 (Cal.). Although the individual alleged to have caused the losses to the insured company was not its employee as defined in the bond, the court nevertheless found that the insured was covered for the individual's conduct because he was an employee of another insured. The insured company itself had no employees and was named on the bond as one of several insured companies, one of which employed the individual responsible for the loss. The court reasoned that there would be no coverage at all for the company having no employees and that the intent of the bond must have been to offer coverage for the acts of the employees of the other insured companies. *Research Equity Fund, Inc. v. Ins. Co. of N. Am.,* 602 F.2d 200, 202-03.

Bankr. Ga. 1995. In determining whether an individual is an "employee" as defined in a crime policy, the court ruled that the mere fact that the individual in question owned a majority of the shares of the corporation did not in itself prove that he dominated the corporation, and thus, could not be an employee. The court looked to whether the individual's actions were unilateral and not subject to the control of anyone else within the corporation in determining that the individual dominated the company and was not an employee. *In re Prime Commercial Corp.,* 187 B.R. 785, 797-98.

D.N.J. 1977. Where a New York attorney served as a director of the insured bank and arranged, in collusion with the president of the insured bank, to ship loans without sufficient collateral and in excess of what had been allowed by the board of directions, the attorney was an employee of the insured since he prepared the necessary documentation for the loans. *Midland Bank & Trust Co. v. Fid. & Deposit Co. of Md.,* 442 F. Supp. 960, 970.

E.D.N.Y. 1977. One of several mortgage-servicing contractors employed by the insured to collect monthly mortgage payments owed to the insured embezzled some of the funds he collected. The court held that coverage was provided by a Service Contractors Rider, but the mortgage-servicing contractor was not an employee under the usual definition. *Hudson City Sav. Inst. v. Hartford Acc. & Indem. Co.,* 440 F. Supp. 41, 43-44.

S.D.N.Y. 2001. A court granted a motion to strike an insurer's affirmative defense in a suit relating to a combined coverages policy that included fidelity coverage. The definition of "employee" in the policy in question did not require that the individual be subject to the insured's direction or control. Like many combined coverage policies, the language was similar to the standard form bonds but also contained manuscript terms. The definition in the policy described an employee as "[t]he Assured's officers, clerks, servants, and other employees while employed by the Assured and guest students pursuing studies or duties at the Assured's premises." *SEC v. Credit Bancorp, Ltd.,* 147 F. Supp. 2d 238, 259-60.

E.D. Pa. 2001. In a suit alleging coverage under Insuring Agreement (A) of a Financial Institution Bond for losses resulting from fraudulent computer entry, the court denied an insurer's motion for summary judgment on the ground that company retained by the bank to enter data and track information related to the bank's premium finance division could be an employee within the definition of the bond. The bond language defining the term employee to include "each natural person, partnership or corporation authorized to perform services as data processor of checks or other accounting records of the Insureds," was broad enough to include a data servicing company. The court, in denying the motion, noted the language of the bond which defined the term "employee." *Hudson United Bank v. Progressive Cas. Ins. Co.,* 152 F. Supp. 2d 751, 754.

E.D. Pa. 1998. The district court granted summary judgment in favor of an insurer defending a suit on a commercial crime policy that defined "employee" as a person in the service of the insured and subject to the insured's direction and control. The court found that the undisputed facts established that the insured had no right to direct the individual that allegedly caused the loss. *Omni Servs. Group v. Hartford Ins. Co.,* 2 F. Supp. 2d 714, 715-18.

Ark. Ct. App. 1981. Although temp agency paid bookkeeper and provided other benefits of her employment, temporary bookkeeper was found to be an employee of the insured because of the insured's control over her work. *Radiology Assocs., P.A. v. Aetna Cas. & Sur. Co.,* 613 S.W.2d 106, 107-08.

Ind. App. Ct. 2003. Title company that wrongfully deposited mortgage company's check was not an "employee" of mortgage company as defined under fidelity bond. The bond defined employee to include "each natural person, partnership or corporation authorized by the Insured to perform services as data processor of checks or other accounting records of the Insured . . . ." The court ruled that the insured's claim was not covered because the check was issued to the title company, the title company was instructed to but failed to return the check, and the title company's function in the transaction could not be considered that of a data processor of the check. *Utica Mut. Ins. Co. v. Precedent Cos., LLC,* 782 N.E.2d 470, 474-75.

N.J. Super. Ct. App. Div. 2000. In two related New Jersey cases, the court determined that the principals were in fact alter egos of the insured and not employees. In the *Premier* case, the individual causing the loss was the sole director, president, and shareholder, and was not an employee because the insured could not control him. In the *Hartford* case, the alleged wrongdoer installed his wife as the sole director and shareholder of the insured. The court found that the wrongdoer was not an employee subject to the control and direction of the insured corporation. *Conestoga Title Ins. Co. v. Premier Title Agency, Inc.,* 746 A.2d 462, 464-65; *Hartford Fire Ins. Co. v. Conestoga Title Ins. Co.,* 746 A.2d 460, 461-62.

N.Y. App. Div. 1983. Conflicting affidavits on the duties performed by an individual created a factual dispute as to employment status, precluding summary judgment. The court said that a three-pronged test determines whether one is an employee of an insured: individual must be compensated by insured; subject to insured's right to control; and not a broker, agent, factor, commission merchant, consignee, contractor, or other agent or representative of the same general character. *175 Check Cashing Corp. v. Chubb Pac. Indem. Group,* 464 N.Y.S.2d 118, 119-21.

N.Y. App. Div. 1983. A security guard paid by a security services firm was robbed at gunpoint. The insured paid security guard directly for some overtime work. The court held that there was a question of fact whether the individual was an employee within policy definition. An individual must be compensated by the insured, subject to the insured's right to control, and may not be a broker, agent, factor, commission merchant, consignee, contractor, or other agent or representative of the same general character. *Fortunoff Silver Sales, Inc. v. Hartford Acc. & Indem. Co.,* 459 N.Y.S.2d 866, 867.

N.Y. App. Div. 1980. The court applied a three pronged test for determining whether an individual was an employee of the insured. Factual questions regarding the manner of compensation of the individual, the level of control the insured exercised over the individual, and whether the individual was acting in the capacity of an agent, broker, or contractor precluded summary judgment. *Gross Veneer Co. v. Am. Mut. Ins. Co.,* 424 N.Y.S.2d 743, 744.

Wash. Ct. App. 1979. The president of the insured company who held the right to vote all of the corporation's stock was found to be an employee. The court reasoned that if the right to control voting was an unacceptable risk for coverage, the policy could have excluded individuals exercising such control. *Seattle Int'l Corp. v. Commerce & Indus. Ins. Co.,* 600 P.2d 612, 614.

W. Va. App. 2001. A construction manager may be an employee of the owner for purposes of fidelity coverage. The court ruled that the primary factor in determining whether an individual is an independent contractor or an employee is whether the hiring party retains the right to control or direct the work. In reversing summary judgment for the insurer, the court found a question of fact with regard to whether the construction manager was an employee. *Mt. Lodge Ass'n v. Crum & Forster Indem. Co.,* 558 S.E.2d 336, 344-46.

B. Alter-Ego Decisions

4th Cir. 1970 (Md.). The court reversed summary judgment for the insurer, holding that there was a question of fact as to whether the principals held substantial control of the insured. *Phoenix Sav. & Loan, Inc. v. Aetna Cas. & Sur. Co.,* 427 F.2d 862, 871-74.

4th Cir. 1965 (S.C.). Men who controlled all of the stock of a corporation and acted as its sole directors and chief executive officers were not employees under the terms of the bond. *Kerr v. Aetna Cas. & Sur. Co.,* 350 F.2d 146, 154-55.

5th Cir. 1976 (Ala.). The purchasers of the controlling stock of the insured's parent company, who elected themselves officers and directors of the insured and then misappropriated insured's assets, were not employees of the insured. *First Nat'l Life Ins. Co. v. Fid. & Deposit Co. of Md.,* 525 F.2d 966, 968-70.

5th Cir. 1972 (Tex.). Where controlling shareholder and president of the insured defrauded the insured, he was not the insured's alter ego, and his knowledge of his own actions could not be imputed to the insured because of his adverse interests. *FDIC v. Lott,* 460 F.2d 82, 87-88.

7th Cir. 1973 (Ill.). For purposes of deciding a summary judgment motion, the court found there was a genuine issue of fact whether two officers of a corporation were employees, where there were three owners, including the two officers, and a six member board of directors. *Charm Promotions, Ltd. v. Travelers Indem. Co.,* 489 F.2d 1092, 1097-98.

8th Cir. 1971 (S.D.). Although evidence indicated that the board rubber stamped the actions of the insured's majority shareholder, president, and director, the court held that he was an employee because the insured, for an additional premium, asked that he be covered as an employee. The court also noted the board possessed a duty to direct and govern his activities. *Gen. Fin. Corp. v. Fid. & Cas. Co. of N.Y,* 439 F.2d 981, 985-87.

N.D. Ga. 1962. Members of a board who took control of the insured by electing themselves officers at a board meeting where a quorum was not present were not employees of the insured. *Ga. Cas. & Sur. Co. v. Seaboard Sur. Co.,* 210 F. Supp. 644, 651-54.

Ariz. Ct. App. 1985. In a suit brought by a receiver of a corporation on a fidelity bond, the corporation's two officers, who were directors and sole shareholders, were held to be alter egos of the corporation. They were not employees of the corporation and their acts were not covered by the bond. *Emp'rs Admin. Servs., Inc. v. Hartford Acc. & Indem. Co.,* 709 P.2d 559, 206-07.

N.D. 1996. In deciding whether a shareholder was an "employee," the court looked to whether the individual's control or ownership of the company was overwhelming. The fidelity coverage endorsement to the errors and omissions policy, which was the subject of this decision, did not define "employee." The mere fact that the individual in question owned substantial shares in the insured did not eliminate that individual as a covered "employee." *Emp'rs Reinsurance Corp. v. Landmark,* 547 N.W.2d 527, 535-39.

C. Attorneys As Employees

5th Cir. 1972 (Ga.). An attorney approved to perform closings for a title company, who failed to remit the full amount of the payments for the property, was an employee of the title company for the purpose of determining coverage for his actions under a fidelity bond. *Pioneer Nat'l Trust Ins. Co. v. Am. Cas. Co. of Reading Pa.,* 459 F.2d 963, 965-67.

D.N.J. 1977. An attorney serving as a director of an insured bank—who, in collusion with the president of the insured, arranged for ship loans without adequate collateral and in excess of the limits established by the board—was an employee of the insured because his duties included preparing the documentation for the loans. *Midland Bank & Trust Co. v. Fid. & Deposit Co. of Md.,* 442 F. Supp. 960, 970.

D. Servicers as Employees

D. Colo. 2008. Financial services company that had joined with insured bank in fraudulent credit card venture was not covered "employee" under fidelity bond, which defined "employee" in part as "corporation authorized by the insured to perform services as data processor of checks or other accounting records." Although financial services company had agreed to perform all processing services for the card program relating to applications, card issuance, etc., the services contract stated "[insured] shall select an independent processing operation to process card transactions." As a result, the court rejected the insured's argument that the services company was an "employee" under the bond. *FDIC v. St. Paul Cos.,* 634 F. Supp. 2d 1213, 1220-21.

E.D.N.Y. 2012. Credit union brought an action against its fidelity bond insurer to recover losses it suffered when its loan servicer sold mortgage loans to the secondary market that the insured did not approve for sale. The insured claimed that its losses were covered because a servicing contractor constitutes an "employee" under the bond. The court looked to the servicer's contractual duties and noted that the servicer was not engaged to sell loans to the secondary market, but only to collect loan amounts, remit payments to the insured, etc. Thus, on summary judgment the court partially rejected the insured's claim to the extent the servicer performed functions for which it did not contract. The court concluded, however, that there were disputed material fact issues with regard to losses tied to the servicer's concealment of improperly sold loans. *Suffolk Fed. Credit Union v. CUMIS Ins. Soc'y, Inc.,* 910 F. Supp. 2d 446, 456-59.

SECONDARY SOURCES

Peter Broeman, *An Overview of the Financial Institution Bond, Standard Form 24*, 110 BANKING L.J. 439 (1993).

Michael R. Davisson & Lawrence S. DeVos, *The Forgotten Insuring Agreement: Coverage for Loss Arising From Dishonest Acts by Servicing Contractors*, XVII FID. L.J., 2d ed., 117 (2011).

Peter Haley, *Clause (E): The Continued Importance of Defined Terms and Causation Requirements*, in FINANCIAL INSTITUTION BONDS (Duncan L. Clore ed., 1998).

Carol A. Pisano, *The Outsourcer's Apprentice*, 26 THE BRIEF 12 (1997).

Armen Shahinian & Scott D. Baron, *Who Is a Covered "Employee" Under the Financial Institution Bond*, in FINANCIAL INSTITUTION BONDS (Duncan L. Clore ed., 1998).

H. Evidence of Debt

(h) Evidence of Debt means an instrument, including a Negotiable Instrument, executed by a customer of the Insured and held by the Insured which in the regular course of business is treated as evidencing the customer's debt to the Insured.

COMMENT

This is the definition of the term in Insuring Agreements (D) and (E). "Evidence of Debt" generally is construed as referring to some primary indicia of a debt, such as a promissory note. A document that merely references a debt, such as a security agreement, is not an Evidence of Debt.

ANNOTATIONS

E.D. Ark. 2004. Falsified leases furnished to obtain loan did not constitute "evidence of debt" as defined under fidelity bond because the leases were evidence of the lessee's debt to the borrower, not the borrower's debt to the insured bank. *Pine Bluff Nat'l Bank v. St. Paul Mercury Ins. Co.,* 346 F. Supp. 2d 1020, 1026-27.

N.D. Ill. 2009. Under Illinois law, applications for advances on line of credit, submitted to credit union together with allegedly fraudulent invoices purportedly evidencing the borrower's accounts receivable, were not "evidences of debt" within meaning of fidelity bond because the advance requests and invoices were evidence of collateral, not debt. *Metro Fed. Credit Union v. Fed. Ins. Co.,* 607 F. Supp. 2d 870, 875, 878-79.

Md. App. 1999. Incumbency certificates representing an agent's authority to act for a corporation were not "evidences of debt." *First Union Corp. v. USF&G,* 730 A.2d 278, 283-84.

Minn. Ct. App. 1989. A bank brought an action against its Bankers Blanket Bond insurer for losses in connection with a credit card financing program resulting from a customer's deposit of invalid credit card sales slips. The Blanket Bond excluded loss from "Evidences of Debt." The bank purchased credit card sales slips at a discount from the merchants, and collected the full amount charged from the purchasers through a program administrator. The sales slips purchased at a discount were deemed to be "evidences of debt" and were excluded under the policy. *Suburban Nat'l Bank v. Transamerica Ins. Co.,* 438 N.W.2d 119, 121.

Minn. Ct. App. 1987. Fictitious construction contracts bearing forged signatures were assigned to the insured bank to induce it to make loans to a customer. The court rejected the bank's claim that construction contracts were "evidences of debt" under Insuring Agreement (E) of the bond. Construction contracts are not primary indicia of debt. *Merchs. Nat'l Bank of Winona v. Transamerica Ins. Co.,* 408 N.W.2d 651, 653.

SECONDARY SOURCES

Michael Keeley, Michele L. Fenice & J. Will Eidson, *Insuring Agreement (E)—Revisited,* XVII FID. L.J., 2d ed., 203 (2011).

I. Forgery

(i) Forgery means the signing of the name of another person or organization with intent to deceive; it does not mean a signature which consists in whole or in part of one's own name signed with or without authority, in any capacity, for any purpose.

COMMENT

What constitutes a Forgery is generally determined by reference to state law. The cases examining whether a Forgery exists within the definition of the bond often address whether another party's signature was signed with an intent to deceive. A scheme perpetrated with one's own signature does not involve a Forgery. The cases note that while a Forgery might exist under the law of the particular state, the bond's narrower definition of Forgery will determine coverage. The recent cases consistently apply the bond definition in requiring that a Forgery be an imitation of someone else's signature.

ANNOTATIONS

2nd Cir. 1978 (N.Y.). Under a Brokers Blanket Bond, failure to exclude unauthorized signatures from definition of "forgery" rendered the term ambiguous in light of the current law. Construing the term in favor of insured, the court held that the bond covered the loss due to dishonored cashier's checks bearing unauthorized but genuine signature of the bank's president. *Filor, Bullard & Smyth v. Ins. Co. of N. Am.,* 605 F.2d 598, 602.

3rd Cir. 2005 (N.J.). The appellate court affirmed the district court's finding that there was no "forgery" under a fidelity bond where the endorser received a check not payable to her, incorporated a business to match the payee on the check, opened a bank account in the payee's name, and signed her own name to the check upon depositing the check. *Lusitania Sav. Bank, FSB v. Progressive Cas. Ins. Co.,* No. 04-3503, 2005 WL 1586618, at *2-3.

5th Cir. 1982 (La.). A bank sued borrower's mother for outstanding loans and borrower offered to be responsible for his mother's indebtedness by giving new collateral and restructuring his own indebtedness to the bank. The new collateral consisted of a mortgage on property owned by a third party. The borrower signed the collateral mortgage and note as agent for the third party even though he was not. The bank contended this was a forgery. The court, in denying the claim of forgery, pointed out that under Louisiana law, in direct contrast to New York law, signing one's own name and representing that one has authority to give writing is not forgery. Court noted that under the U.C.C., forgeries include authorized signatures but they are not functional equivalents. *Marsh Inv. Corp. v. Langford,* 554 F. Supp. 800, 805-07.

7th Cir. 1991 (Ill.). A bank customer deposited his employer's checks into his personal account at the insured bank by using a rubber stamp endorsement that stated the checks were for "deposit only" to the personal account. The stamp endorsement did not constitute a forgery under the definition in the Financial Institution Bond. Forgery is the signing of the name of another with intent to deceive. *Alpine State Bank v. Ohio Cas. Ins. Co.,* 941 F.2d 554, 559-60.

9th Cir. 2001 (Cal.). Under the definition of "forgery" in a fiduciary bond, the court held that a signature was not a forgery because it did not purport to be the signature of a customer. *Universal Bank v. Northland Ins. Co.,* 8 F. App'x 784, 785-86.

M.D. Ga. 1996. A forgery within the meaning of the Financial Institution Bond definition did not include the endorsement by an attorney of a draft payable to the attorney and his client. The attorney endorsed his own name and forged the client's endorsement to deposit the proceeds of a draft into his trust account, from which the attorney apparently converted the funds. The bank sought recovery for the loss it incurred after the attorney's client obtained a judgment against the bank for conversion. Although the client's endorsement was apparently forged, the definition of forgery excludes a signature consisting, in whole or in part, of one's own name. *Reliance Ins. Co. v. First Liberty Bank,* 927 F. Supp. 448, 449-50.

D. Minn. 2005. Insured who relied on faxed copies of forged personal guarantees furnished to issue a loan filed suit to recover under a Form 24 Financial Institution Bond. The bond stated that the insured must have actual physical possession of the original document at the time of funds disbursal in order to assert a claim. Because the insured failed to demonstrate that it had actual physical possession of the guarantees at the time of funds disbursal, the court granted the insurer's motion for summary judgment. *BancInsure, Inc. v. Marshall Bank, N.A.,* 400 F. Supp. 2d 1140, 1143-45.

D. Neb. 1992. Absent evidence that someone signed a check with another party's name with intent to deceive, there is no forgery as that term is defined in the Financial Institution Bond. There was no evidence that an individual signing a corporate check was either signing as a representative of the corporation or that someone other than the individual signed the check with intent to deceive. *Ralston Bank v. Kan. Bankers Sur. Co.,* 794 F. Supp. 896, 898.

D.N.J. 1983. In a case involving claims of forgery, counterfeiting, and employee dishonesty under the 1969 form of the Bankers Blanket Bond, the court held that losses from loans secured by worthless certificates of deposit issued by an entity which had been chartered as a bank in the British West Indies, but which had no assets, were not losses under either Insuring Agreement (D) or (E). The loss occurred because the CDs implicitly misrepresented fact of amounts available to the issuing bank for its own account. They were not counterfeited nor forged within the meaning of the bond. The court concluded that the bank would be expected to protect itself against the risk posed by the possible worthlessness of CDs through its normal credit evaluation procedures. *Liberty Nat'l Bank v. Aetna Life & Cas. Co.,* 568 F. Supp. 860, 866-67.

S.D.N.Y. 1990. Fictitious bills of lading that bore no signature were not forgeries within the meaning of the bond. To prove forgery, one must show the use of the name to falsely represent that another person signed the document in question. Fictitious bills of lading were not counterfeit because they did not imitate genuine, specific original documents. *French Am. Banking Corp. v. Flota Mercante Grancolombiana, S.A.,* 752 F. Supp. 83, 89-91.

Ind. Ct. App. 2003. A title company that wrongfully deposited a mortgage check did not commit an act of forgery as defined in the Financial Institution Bond. The act of improperly negotiating an instrument is not an alteration of the instrument. *Utica Mut. Ins. Co. v. Precedent Cos.,* 782 N.E.2d 470, 476.

SECONDARY SOURCES

David T. DiBiase, Carleton R. Burch & David J. Billings, *The ABC's of Insuring Agreement (D) Under the Financial Institution Bond*, XVII FID. L.J., 2d ed., 1 (2011).

Sean W. Duffy, *Fighting Check Forgery in the New Economy: Is Computer Generated Check Fraud Covered Under the Financial Institution Bond*, VI FID. L.J. 1 (2000).

J. Guarantee

(j) **Guarantee means a written undertaking obligating the signer to pay the debt of another to the Insured or its assignee or to a financial institution from which the Insured has purchased participation in the debt, if the debt is not paid in accordance with its terms.**

COMMENT

The term "Guarantee" unambiguously refers to written loan guarantees on loans made directly by the insured or on loans for which the insured purchased participation. The term appears in Insuring Agreement (E).

ANNOTATIONS

NONE

SECONDARY SOURCES

Michael Keeley, Michele L. Fenice & J. Will Eidson, *Insuring Agreement (E)—Revisited,* XVII FID. L.J., 2d ed., 203 (2011).

K. Instruction

(k) **Instruction means a written order to the issuer of an Uncertificated Security requesting that the transfer, pledge or release from pledge of the Uncertificated Security specified be registered.**

COMMENT

"Instruction" is a defined term appearing in Insuring Agreement (E). Insuring Agreement (D) refers to "written instructions," which is arguably broader than the defined term "Instruction." The bond definition is virtually identical to the Uniform Commercial Code definition, except that the Code does not appear to require that the instruction be "written" as required by the bond's definition.[8]

ANNOTATIONS

8th Cir. 2012 (Mo.). Faxed wire transfer instructions amounted to a written instruction as defined under fidelity bond. Under the bond, the instruction had to be "printed, typewritten or otherwise intentionally reduced to tangible form" and could "not include an Electronic Record." "Electronic record" included "information which is created, generated, sent, communicated, received, or stored by electronic means and is retrievable in perceivable form." Court concluded that once the fax was printed out, it was no longer perceivable, but was possessed. Therefore, the instruction met the written requirement of the bond's instruction language. *Mo. Bank and Trust Co. of Kan. City v. OneBeacon Ins. Co.,* 688 F.3d 943, 946-48.

9th Cir. 2001 (Cal.). Neither purchase agreements nor escrow instructions met the bond's definition of "Instruction." *Universal Bank v. Northland Ins. Co.,* 8 F. App'x 784, 785.

W.D. Tenn. 1997. A forged letter from a mortgage company comptroller advised a bank that an executive seeking a loan was entitled to an annual bonus of $800,000. The letter was not an "instruction" within the meaning of Insuring Agreement (D) because the letter did not direct the bank to do anything. *KW Bancshares, Inc. v. Syndicates of Underwriters at Lloyd's,* 965 F. Supp. 1047, 1051-53.

Md. App. 1999. Incumbency certificates representing an agent's authority to act for a corporation were not "instructions or advices" because they were not commercial paper and did not acknowledge the payment or transfer of money. *First Union Corp. v. U.S. Fid. & Guar.,* 730 A.2d 278, 283-84.

---

8 U.C.C. § 8-102(12) (2003).

SECONDARY SOURCES

NONE

L. **Letter of Credit**

(l) **Letter of Credit means an engagement in writing by a bank or other person made at the request of a customer that the bank or other person will honor drafts or other demands for payment upon compliance with the conditions specified in the Letter of Credit.**

COMMENT

The definition of "Letter of Credit" is virtually identical to the definition found in the Uniform Commercial Code.[9] The defined term is found in Insuring Agreement (D). There are no cases discussing the Financial Institution Bond definition.

ANNOTATIONS

NONE

SECONDARY SOURCES

David T. DiBiase, Carleton R. Burch & David J. Billings, *The ABC's of Insuring Agreement (D) Under the Financial Institution Bond*, XVII FID. L.J., 2d ed., 1 (2011).

M. **Loan**

(m) **Loan means all extensions of credit by the Insured and all transactions creating a creditor relationship in favor**

---

[9] U.C.C. § 5-103(a) (2003).

of the insured and all transactions by which the Insured assumes an existing credit relationship.

COMMENT

The definition of "Loan" was added to the standard form Financial Institution Bond in 1986. This definition addresses the use of the term in Insuring Agreement (A), requiring the receipt of a financial benefit if a "Loan" is involved, and relates to Exclusion (e), the loan loss exclusion. The definition in the bond is not limited to circumstances where there is a "meeting of the minds" between a customer and the bank. Any transaction whereby one owes money to a financial institution, including overdrafts, advancing credit on a check returned for insufficient funds, and overdraft protection, should be regarded as a Loan under the Bond.

The annotations below include the cases that actually apply the definition set forth above to determine whether a transaction constitutes a "Loan." They also include a few landmark decisions that thoroughly explore the meaning of the term "Loan" in the context of fidelity bonds. Though those cases do not interpret the definition set forth above, they are nonetheless instructive in a dispute over whether a transaction qualifies as a loan in fidelity cases, particularly because there are so few cases actually applying the bond's definition of "Loan." Section 2 of this chapter, which addresses application of the loan loss exclusion, includes many more cases deciding whether a transaction constitutes a "Loan." The reader may find it helpful to review those annotations, as well.

ANNOTATIONS

5th Cir. 1976 (La.). Transactions involving advances to a customer based on deposits of drafts were de facto loans because the bank could have no reasonable expectation that the drafts would be paid in the normal course of business. Thus, extension of credit on the understanding that there is assumption of risk of nonpayment, but with expectation of repayment, was treated as a loan. *Calcasieu-Marine Nat'l Bank v. Emp'rs Ins. Co.,* 533 F.2d 290, 299-301.

6th Cir. 1990 (Ohio). In a claim by a savings and loan for losses on a blanket bond that did not define loan, the court applied a number of factors to determine whether the repurchase agreements that the savings and loan invested in were loans. Factors included whether the seller could require the purchaser to resell, whether the purchaser could require the seller to repurchase, whether collateral was pledged or interest charged. Court ultimately remanded for further determination on the issue. *First Fed. Sav. & Loan Assoc. of Toledo v. Fid. & Deposit Co. of Md.,* 895 F.2d 254, 261.

7th Cir. 1994 (Ill.). Savings and loan sought recovery from insurer on a blanket bond for losses related to securities repurchase and reverse repurchase agreements. The bond did not define the term "loan." The court held that repurchase transactions between savings and loan and securities broker were in the "nature of a loan" because they were "in economic substance collateralized lending" and found the loan loss exclusion applied. *RTC v. Aetna Cas. & Sur. Co. of Ill.,* 25 F.3d 570, 580.

7th Cir. 1970 (Ill.). A transaction involving a check kiting scheme was held not to involve a loan and, therefore, the loss was not excluded. The court stated that it was not conceivable to construe "loan" to cover obligation imposed by law to reimburse a bank for money or credit obtained through the use of worthless checks. *First Nat'l Bank of Decatur v. Ins. Co. of N. Am.,* 424 F.2d 312, 316.

N.D. Cal. 2004. Theft of currency by ATM owner was not covered by the bond and that the ATM cash program was "in the nature of a loan" or "an extension of credit" and subject to Exclusion (e). *Humboldt Bank v. Gulf Ins. Co.,* 323 F. Supp. 2d 1027, 1033.

N.D. Ill. 1992. Insured bank brought a claim against insurer on Financial Institution Bond for losses resulting from check kiting, unpaid overdrafts, and certain intra bank transfers of funds. Insurer moved for summary judgment on the grounds that Exclusions (o) and (e) precluded coverage. The court determined that the overdrafts were transactions that created a "creditor relationship in favor of the Insured" inasmuch as the employee used the bank's money to write checks and had a legal obligation to repay that money. Thus, the employee's over-drafted account constituted a loan within the bond's definition. *Affiliated Bank/Morton Grove v. Hartford Acc. & Indem. Co.*, No. 91-C-4446, 1992 WL 91761, at *6.

E.D. Mich. 2013. Bank, based on a fraudulently procured signature and phone number, made a wire transfer to South Korea of $190,000 from a customer's home equity line of credit. Bank later realized that the transfer was fraudulent and reimbursed customer's account for the full amount. It then made a claim on the bond. The insurer denied coverage, claiming the loss was excluded by Exclusion (e) as a loan loss. The court rejected the insurer's argument that the loan loss exclusion applied such that the transaction involved the insured as a lender on the home equity line of credit. The court stated, "[i]t is undisputed that [the customer] did not borrow the money from the Bank; he did not receive the funds and he did not agree to repay the debt. [The customer] was unaware of these transactions until he was notified of the fraud by the Bank. The loss at issue here is not the result of a loan. The risk at issue was the risk of forgery—a risk that is expressly covered by the FIB." *Bank of Ann Arbor v. Everest Nat'l Ins. Co.*, No. 12-11251 2013 WL 665067, at *4.

E.D. Mich. 1993. The insured bank brought suit against the insurer under a fidelity bond for losses incurred as a result of the defalcation of a bank employee. The employee embezzled funds by creating false loan accounts. The court denied insurer's motion for summary judgment finding that the employee's transactions did not constitute Loans. The court found that because the bond defined "Loans" as "extensions of credit," the policy definition of "Letter of Credit" was relevant and dispositive. The court held that the policy defined "Letter of Credit" as an engagement "made at the request of a customer." Because the "loans" were to fictitious customers, no such request could have been made and no loan existed. *Peoples State Bank v. Am. Cas. Co. of Reading, Pa.*, 818 F. Supp. 1073, 1077.

S.D. Miss. 2012. Insurer brought action seeking declaration that it had no obligation under the bond to indemnify bank for losses caused by bank employee's dishonest and/or fraudulent conduct. Bank employee conducted multiple fraudulent transfers, forged signatures, made unauthorized withdrawals, and released collateral without authority. The court held credit was not extended to any of the individuals whose identities the bank employee fraudulently used, and thus the actions by bank employee did not extend "loans" to the defrauded individuals so as to trigger Exclusion (e). *BankInsure, Inc. v. Peoples Bank of the S.*, 866 F. Supp. 2d 577, 588.

S.D. Ohio 1954. The insured bank engaged in a procedure where it would credit customer's account upon receiving bills of lading. The bank customer obtained credits to account by presenting fictitious papers. The court held that this transaction was not a loan because a loan of money was a contract requiring a meeting of the minds. The court reasoned that no meeting of the minds was present even though the insured bank expected a return of its money in the same manner that it received its money back in previous transactions. *Nat'l Bank of Paulding v. Fid. & Cas. Co.*, 131 F. Supp. 121, 123-24.

E.D. Penn. 2003. Insured bank sued fidelity insurer seeking indemnification for losses sustained in automobile insurance premium finance business. Bank entered into a profit-sharing arrangement with K-C Insurance Premium Finance Company ("K-C"). Under the terms of the agreement, K-C was to operate and market an automobile insurance premium finance business that would loan funds for insurance premiums to high risk automobile drivers. K-C was responsible for administering the program and the bank supplied the funding. K-C's computer program generated incomplete data which it supplied to the bank. As a result, the bank made overpayments to K-C under the profit sharing agreement. The court held that the bank failed to show that it had sustained losses resulting directly from dishonest or fraudulent conduct by an employee. Instead, the court found that the losses in question resulted "directly or indirectly" from the non-payment of loans, which rendered the loan loss exclusion applicable. *Hudson United Bank v. Progressive Cas. Ins. Co.*, 284 F. Supp. 2d 249, 255.

Ill. App. Ct. 1998. A bank sued its fidelity insurer seeking coverage for losses from a check kiting scheme in which its employee had participated with a customer. The court held that overdrafts in the accounts were not "loans" within the policy definition. The court held that a "meeting of the minds" between the customer and the bank was necessary in order for the losses to be "Loans" as defined by the policy. *Oxford Bank & Trust v. Hartford Acc. & Indem. Co.*, 698 N.E.2d 204, 212.

Kan. 2010. A bank employee of the bank cashed checks for three customers resulting in significant insufficient funds in each account. This practice of allowing overdrafts was held to be a "Loan" by the bank to the customer allowed to overdraft his account. *Nat'l Bank of Andover v. Kan. Bankers Sur. Co.*, 225 P.3d 707, 722-23.

Ohio Ct. App. 1993. A former employee of the insured used his access to bank computers to create numerous fictitious loans in order to convert funds to his personal use. The jury found that all losses suffered by the bank were the result of the employee's theft and not of "Loans." The court stated that the purpose of excluding coverage for "Loans" in this type of insuring agreement is to eliminate coverage for bad loans. Here, that was not the case. The court upheld the jury's finding. *First Nat'l Bank v. Progressive Casualty Ins. Co.*, 640 N.E.2d 1147, 1151.

Pa. Super. Ct. 1999. The bank brought an action against its fidelity insurer seeking to recover losses incurred due to an employee's alleged fraudulent acts in connection with a floor plan financing system set up between the bank and an automobile dealer. The court granted the insurer's motion for summary judgment, in part, on the grounds that the check kiting scheme was a "loan" within the bond's definition because the unpaid drafts constituted extensions of credit to an existing customer. *First Philson Bank, N.A. v. Hartford Fire Ins. Co.*, 727 A.2d 584, 589.

SECONDARY SOURCES

Michael Keeley, Michele Fenice & J. Will Eidson, *Insuring Agreement (E)—Revisited,* XVII FID. L.J., 2d ed., 203 (2011).

Edgar L. Neel, *Financial Institution and Fidelity Coverage for Loan Losses*, 21 TORT & INS. L.J. 590 (1986).

N. Money

(n) **Money means a medium of exchange in current use authorized or adopted by a domestic or foreign government as part of its currency.**

COMMENT

This definition relates to Insuring Agreement (F) (Counterfeit Currency), and is based on Section 1-201(24) of the Uniform Commercial Code. The comment to Section 1-201(24) of the Uniform Commercial Code specifically notes that the test is that of "a sanction of government, whether by authorization before issue or adoption afterward, which recognizes the circulating medium as a part of its official currency of that government." The Uniform Commercial Code rejects the "narrow view that money is limited to legal tender." It should be noted, however, that the bond definition does not incorporate entirely Section 1-201(24), leaving out that portion of the definition that includes "monetary unit of account established by an intergovernmental organization or by agreement between two or more countries."

ANNOTATIONS

D.C. Cir. 1970. Imperial Insurance Company ("Imperial") sought to recover under its commercial crime policy for consequential losses resulting from payments made under surplus risk policies as a result of fraudulent or dishonest acts of its general manager. The fidelity carrier argued that Imperial's loss was not covered as a third party loss. "Money" under the policy was defined as "currency, coins, bank notes and bullion, travelers checks, register checks, and money orders held for sale to the public." Finding for the insured, the court reasoned that the "loss here was a pecuniary depletion of Imperial's monetary assets. In that sense, it was a loss of property." The court held that the definition of "money" as "currency, coins, bank notes and bullion," when followed by the general expression "other property" does not clearly exclude liability to compensate for payments made from the insured's funds, if due to the misconduct described. *Imperial Ins. Inc. v. Emp'r's Liab. Assurance Corp.*, 442 F.2d 1197, 1199.

4th Cir. 1992 (N.C.). Insured brought suit against its insurer seeking coverage for lost interest on sums stolen by its former president. The policy defined "money" as "currency, coins, bank notes and bullion, and travelers' checks, register checks and money orders held for sale to the public." The court held that "[i]nterest on stolen currency, coins, etc. is not included in the definition of 'money.'" Accordingly, the court reasoned that the fidelity policy only provided coverage for the principal amount stolen by the plaintiff's former president. *Empire of Carolina, Inc. v. Cont'l Cas. Co.*, N.C. App. 675, 678.

9th Cir. B.A.P. 2011. U.S. Trustee objected to compensation sought by Chapter 7 trustee as allegedly exceeding statutory cap if court did not include the amount credit bid by creditor in order to acquire real property securing its claim among "monies disbursed" in case. Bankruptcy court construed the statutory term "Money" in accordance with its ordinary or natural meaning. The court referenced the Oxford English Dictionary to define money as "[a]ny generally accepted medium of exchange which enables a society to trade goods without the need for barter; any objects or tokens regarded as a store of value and used as a medium of exchange." Additionally, the court held that a "medium of exchange is something commonly accepted in exchange for goods and services and recognized as representing a standard of value." *U.S. Trustee v. Tamm (In re Hokulani Square, Inc.)*, 460 B.R. 763, 770.

9th Cir. 1990. The Portland Federal Credit Union brought an action against CUMIS, seeking to recover under its fidelity bond losses suffered because of its loan officer's disbursement of proceeds from an improper loan on the construction of a new building. Under the bond, "Money" was further defined as "currency, coin, bank notes, Federal Reserve notes, revenue stamps and postage stamps." The court held that the loan loss did not qualify as a loss of money because it did not involve loss of "currency, coin, bank notes, Federal Reserve Notes, revenue stamps or postage stamps." *Portland Fed. Emps. Credit Union v. Cumis Ins. Soc'y*, 894 F.2d 1101, 1104.

Cal. Ct. App. 1983. An insured brought an action against his homeowner's insurer for a loss resulting from a burglary of his silver coin collection. The insurance policy contained an exclusion limiting the insurer's liability to $100 for a loss by theft of "money, bullion, numismatic property and bank notes." The plaintiff argued that his silver coins were not money because they were taken out of circulation and were an investment on his part. The court disagreed, holding that "silver coins are most reasonably regarded as "money," and whether kept out of circulation by plaintiff or not, maintain their monetary character." *McKee v. State Farm Fire & Cas. Co.*, 145 Cal. App. 3d 772, 776.

Conn. Super. Ct. 2010. The plaintiff, a law firm, sought coverage under a commercial crime policy's computer fraud coverage for a loss suffered by way of an e-mail scam in which the law firm thought a Chinese company had retained it to collect a debt from a Connecticut company. The law firm deposited a fraudulent check, which was later rejected by the bank, and sought coverage for the loss. The insurer denied coverage, claiming that the alleged loss fell within Exclusion (F), for a loss resulting directly or indirectly from the plaintiff's acceptance of money orders or counterfeit money. The policy defined "counterfeit money" as "an imitation of money that is intended to deceive and to be taken as genuine." "Money" under the policy was defined as "a medium of exchange in current use and authorized or adopted by a domestic or foreign government, including currency, coins, bank notes, bullion, travelers checks, registered checks and money orders held for sale to the public." The court held that a "bank check" does not fall within the recognized definition of money as listed in the policy or in the recognized definitions of money in its usual and ordinary meanings. Therefore, the fraudulent bank check did not constitute a "money order" or "counterfeit money" as provided in the exclusion. *Owens, Schine & Nicola, P.C. v. Travelers Cas. and Sur. Co. of Am.,* No. CV095024601, 2010 WL 4226958, at *9.

N.Y. Civ. Ct. 1967. The plaintiff suffered a loss resulting from a theft of his rare coin collection and sought recovery from insurer which denied the claim because collectable coins were not "money" as defined in the policy. The court found that "[m]oney is a generic and comprehensive term. It is not a synonym of coin. It includes coin, but is not confined to it. It includes whatever is lawfully and actually current in buying and selling, of the value and as the equivalent of coin." "Moreover, 'money' is any matter, whether metal, paper, beads, shells, rocks, etc., which has a currency as a medium in commerce." The court held for the insurer, reasoning that the essential and natural functions of money are: (1) a commodity having a value of its own; (2) a common measure of value; (3) as having a general exchangeability; and (4) as having a general medium of exchange. The stolen coins were no longer considered a medium of exchange. Accordingly, the rare coin collection was not money in accordance with the limitation of liability provision. *DeBaise v. Commercial Union Ins. Co.*, 53 Misc. 2d 45, 46.

SECONDARY SOURCES

Scott S. Spearing & Kevin P. Polansky, *What is Money in Today's Financial System?*, XVIII FID. L.J. 83 (2012).

U.C.C. § 1-201(24), cmt. 24 (2001).

O. Negotiable Instrument

(o) **Negotiable Instrument means any writing**
   (a) **signed by the maker or drawer;**
   (b) **containing an unconditional promise or order to pay a sum certain in Money and no other promise, order, obligation or power given by the maker or drawer;**
   (c) **is payable on demand or at a definite time; and**
   (d) **is payable to order or bearer.**

COMMENT

The Financial Institution Bond's definition of "Negotiable Instrument" was specially drafted for purposes of the bond, and it is not identical to all elements of or definitions used in Section 3-104 of the Uniform Commercial Code. The drafters of the bond purposefully designed the definition of "Negotiable Instrument" to be more narrow under the bond than under the UCC. By way of example, the bond definition does not allow "other" promises, orders, obligations, or powers that are described in and permitted by Article 3 of the UCC. The definition used in the bond is a contractual definition, not one produced wholly from statute or otherwise. Very importantly then, certain documents that may be a "negotiable instrument" under the UCC do not fit the definition specially crafted for the bond.

ANNOTATIONS

D. Kan. 1987. A bank that had shipped treasury receipts through air freight corporation brought action against air freight corporation and insurer after treasury receipts were lost in transport. The insured sought coverage under Insuring Agreement (C), "In Transit" coverage. On cross motions for summary judgment, the court held in favor of the insured, finding that the bond's definition of "Negotiable Instrument" was applicable and controlling in interpreting the term "non-negotiable instrument" contained in Exclusion (s). The lost treasury receipts did not fall within the policy definition of "Negotiable Instrument," because the treasury receipts did not include "order" or "bearer" language. Thus, the treasury receipts were "non-negotiable" and the exception to Exclusion (s) applied. *Kan. State Bank & Trust Co. v. Emery Air Freight Corp.,* 656 F. Supp. 200, 204.

N.Y. 1928. Action to recover upon promissory notes made by defendant to a corporation and delivered to plaintiff as security for a loan. Each promissory note bore an endorsement stating, "[t]his note is given in accordance with the terms of a conditional sales agreement between the payee and the market hereof." The back of the notes stated, "[t]he within notes [sic] is subject to the terms of a conditional sales agreement executed by the maker thereof upon this date." The court held that the provision in the note stating, in effect, that it was subject to the terms of another agreement not attached thereto precluded the promise of payment from being absolute on its face and thus destroyed negotiability. *Old Colony Trust Co. v. Stumpel,* 161 N.E. 173, 173.

W. Va. 1986. Upon default of borrower, bank brought action against guarantors of promissory notes. The circuit court entered judgment in favor of guarantors, and bank appealed. The court held that (1) guaranty agreements were not negotiable instruments subject to UCC provisions concerning negotiable instruments, and (2) bank's extension of time for payment and release of certain security did not discharge obligations of guarantors. *Gregoire v. Lowndes,* 342 S.E. 2d 264, 266.

SECONDARY SOURCES

Thomas M. Geisler, Jr. *Proof of Fraud In The Making of Commercial Paper And The Resulting Consequences*, AM. JUR. PROOF OF FACTS 3d 141 (2007).

Jay M. Zitter, Annotation, *What Constitutes "Fixed Amount of Money" For Purposes of [Rev] §3-104 of Uniform Commercial Code Providing That Negotiable Instrument Must Contain Unconditional Promise to Pay Fixed Amount of Money*, A.L.R. 5th 289 (2000).

U.C.C. § 3-104, cmt. 1 (2002).

P. Property

(p) **Property means Money, Certified Securities, Uncertified Securities of any Federal Reserve Bank of the United States, Negotiable Instruments, Certificates of Deposit, Documents of Title, Acceptances, Evidences of Debt, Security Agreements, Withdrawal Orders, Certificates of Origin or Title, Letters of Credit, insurance policies, abstracts of title, deeds and mortgages on real estate, revenue and other stamps, tokens, unsold state lottery tickets, books of account and other records whether recorded in writing or electronically, gems, jewelry, precious metals in bars or ingots, and tangible items of personal property which are not hereinbefore enumerated.**

COMMENT

This definition incorporates numerous other defined terms which should be referenced in order to understand this definition completely. The definition also includes the catch-all, "tangible items of personal property which are not hereinbefore enumerated."

ANNOTATIONS

C.D. Cal. 2000. The insured filed a declaratory judgment action against its insurer seeking coverage under its commercial crime policy for losses suffered from its employees' criminal misconduct. The insured's employee allegedly disclosed insured's trade secrets to a third party in exchange for a cash payment. The court was asked to determine whether the loss of "trade secrets" was covered under the policy. The policy defined "property other than money and securities" to mean "any tangible property other than 'money' and 'securities' that has intrinsic value but does not include any property listed in any Coverage Form as Property Not Covered." The court reasoned that generally "tangible" means "corporeality" and held that "[t]angible property does not encompass trade secrets." *Avery Dennison Corp. v. Allendale Mut. Ins. Co.*, No. CV 99-09217CM (cwx), 2000 WL 33964136, at *4.

SECONDARY SOURCES

Scott S. Spearing & Kevin P. Polansky, *What is Money in Today's Financial System?*, XVIII FID. L.J. 83 (2012).

Q. Security Agreement

(q) Security Agreement means an agreement which creates an interest in personal property or fixtures and which secures payment or performance of an obligation.

COMMENT

This definition incorporates Section 1-201(35) of the Uniform Commercial Code, which defines "security interest" as "an interest in personal property or fixtures which secures payment or performance of an obligation." Both the comment to Section 1-201(35) of the Uniform Commercial Code and the few cases construing the definition confirm that, in order for a document to qualify as a Security Agreement, the document must confer real value to the holder of the agreement. The parties' belief that the document secures an obligation is not enough to create a Security Agreement as defined by the bond.

ANNOTATIONS

6th Cir. 1964. Bank sustained losses of $798,715.93 when it was swindled by two different companies. In both instances, the companies presented to the bank for its purchase at discount notes secured by automobile chattels mortgages and auto leasing agreements made out in the company's favor and signed by ostensible lessor or purchasers of said automobiles. The fundamental fraud in the transaction was forgery of the names of these automobile purchasers or lessors. Once the bank realized the fraud, it notified the bonding company. The bonding company paid its full obligation under Clause (E) (Securities), but denied coverage under Clause (D) (Forgery or Alterations). The court held that the losses sustained by bank were covered under Clause (E), which provided for coverage of only $500,000, and which dealt principally with losses resulting from purchase and extension of credit on fact of any securities, documents, or other written documents, but were not covered under Clause (D), which provided for coverage of $1,500,000 and dealt with forgery or alteration of commercial paper. *Liberty Nat'l Bank & Trust Co. of Louisville v. Nat'l Sur. Corp.*, 330 F.2d 697, 700.

W.D. Tenn. 1997. A bank sued its insurer seeking a declaratory judgment that coverage for loss existed under a Bankers Blanket Bond. The bank's loss arose out of customer's default on personal loans obtained by representing to the bank, through a forged letter from employer, that he was to receive a substantial bonus. The court denied coverage under Insuring Agreement (E), in part because the letter did not constitute a security agreement as defined in the bond. The letter held no real value and created no interest in property. *K.W. Bancshares, Inc. v. Syndicate of Underwriters at Lloyd's,* 965 F. Supp. 1047, 1055.

Minn. Ct. App. 1987. A bank brought suit seeking a declaration that fictitious construction contracts containing forged signatures, which were assigned to bank as a condition for obtaining loans, were either evidence of debt or security agreements as defined by the policy issued to the bank. The court held that Insuring Agreement (E) necessarily refers only to documents that have real value to insured bank in the event of the borrower's default. The mere fact that the bank took construction contracts as security for its loans did not mean contracts were "security agreements" as defined by the policy because construction contracts, in and of themselves, absent performance, were of no value. *Merch. Nat'l Bank of Winona v. Transam. Ins. Co.*, 408 N.W.2d 651, 654.

SECONDARY SOURCES

Dag E. Yterberg, Annotation, *What are "Securities, Documents or Other Written Instruments" Within Terms of Bankers Blanket Bond Insuring Against Losses from Counterfeiting or Forgery*, 38 A.L.R. 3d 1437 (1971).

U.C.C. § 1-201(37), § 9-102, cmt. 3(b).

R. Statement of Uncertificated Security

(r) **Statement of Uncertificated Security means a written statement of the issuer of an Uncertificated Security containing:**
 (a) a description of the Issue of which the Uncertificated Security is a part;
 (b) the number of shares or units:
  (i) transferred to the registered owner;
  (ii) pledged by the registered owner to the registered pledgee;
  (iii) released from pledge by the registered pledgee;
  (iv) registered in the name of the registered owner on the date of the statement; or
  (v) subject to pledge on the date of the statement;
 (c) the name and address of the registered owner and registered pledgee;
 (d) a notation of any liens and restrictions of the issuer and any adverse claims to which the Uncertificated Security is or may be subject or a

SECTION 1 — DEFINITIONS 255

  statement that there are none of those liens, restrictions or adverse claims; and
(e) the date:
  (i) the transfer of the shares or units to the new registered owner of the shares or units was registered;
  (ii) the pledge of the registered pledgee was registered, or
  (iii) of the statement, if it is a periodic or annual statement.

COMMENT

This definition relates to Exclusion (y), which excludes loss involving any Uncertificated Security. There are no cases construing or applying this definition.

ANNOTATIONS

NONE

SECONDARY SOURCES

NONE

S. Transportation Company

(s) **Transportation Company** means any organization which provides its own or leased vehicles for transportation or which provides freight forwarding or air express services.

COMMENT

This definition replaces the previously used term "carrier for hire" and is relevant to Insuring Agreement (C)(b) and (c), which provide coverage for loss of Property in transit where the Property is in the possession of a Transportation Company. The definition confirms that, under the limited circumstances of Insuring Agreement (C)(b) and (c), the Transportation Company must be a legitimate entity involved in the business of transportation services. This definition is also relevant to Exclusion (r), which excludes coverage for loss of Property while in the custody of a Transportation Company, unless covered by Insuring Agreement (C).

ANNOTATIONS

NONE

SECONDARY SOURCES

NONE

T. Uncertificated Security

(t) **Uncertificated Security means a share, participation or other interest in property of or an enterprise of the issuer or an obligation of the issuer, which is:**
  - **(a) not represented by an instrument and the transfer of which is registered upon books maintained for that purpose by or on behalf of the issuer;**
  - **(b) of a type commonly dealt in on securities exchanges or markets; and**
  - **(c) either one of a class or series or by its terms divisible into a class or series of shares, participations, interests or obligations.**

COMMENT

This definition relates to Exclusion (y), which excludes coverage for loss involving an Uncertificated Security.

ANNOTATIONS

NONE

SECONDARY SOURCES

NONE

U. Withdrawal Order

(u) Withdrawal Order means a non-negotiable instrument, other than an Instruction, signed by a customer of the Insured authorizing the Insured to debit the customer's account in the amount of funds stated therein.

COMMENT

This definition specifically relates to Insuring Agreement (D)(1), covering loss resulting directly from Forgery or alteration. The definition is specifically limited to non-negotiable instruments. Therefore, definition (o), "Negotiable Instrument," should be consulted. Similarly, the definition specifically excludes an "Instruction," defined in definition (k), which relates specifically to Uncertificated Securities.

ANNOTATIONS

N.D. Ill. 2009. The insured loaned money to its customer based on the customer's receivables, which served as security for the advances. The customer altered its invoices to reflect greater receivables than it actually had, thereby enticing the insured to make advances to the customer that it would not have made otherwise. The insured claimed coverage under the bond's version of Insuring Agreement (D), contending that its advance requests and invoices constituted Withdrawal Orders. The court rejected the contention, noting that the documents were not authorizations to debit the customer's account; they were requests for financing. *Metro Fed. Credit Union v. Fed. Ins. Co.,* 607 F. Supp. 2d 870, 876.

D.C. Kan. 1991. Insured sought coverage under a Savings and Loan Blanket Bond after suffering losses in connection with loan advances made toward a construction project. The insured contended that various documents submitted with the monthly draw requests (lien waivers stamped on the back of checks, a site inspection report, and subcontractor agreements) were forged, altered, or counterfeit and constituted Withdrawal Orders, an undefined term in the bond. The court relied on the UCC's definition of "order" and found that the site inspection report and the subcontractor agreements were not Withdrawal Orders because they did not "order" or "direct" the payment of money. Any other conclusion "would transfer virtually any document, having even the most remote bearing upon the disbursement of funds," into a Withdrawal Order. The court held, however, that the lien waivers could give rise to coverage under Insuring Agreement (D) because they were stamped on checks—documents which were undisputedly Withdrawal Orders. Because there was a forgery *on* a Withdrawal Order, as required by Insuring Agreement (D), the court denied the insurer's motion for summary judgment as to Insuring Agreement (D). *First Fed. Sav. Bank v. Cont'l Cas. Co.*, 768 F. Supp. 1449, 1454-55.

E.D. Mich. 2013. The court granted summary judgment in insured's favor where it was undisputed that a wire transfer request was a Withdrawal Order. *Bank of Ann Arbor v. Everest Nat'l Ins. Co.*, No. 12-11251, 2013 U.S. Dist. LEXIS 24999, at *9.

SECONDARY SOURCES

NONE

SECTION 2 — EXCLUSIONS*

Section 2. This bond does not cover:

(a) loss resulting directly or indirectly from forgery or alteration, except when covered under Insuring Agreements (A), (D), (E) or (F);

(b) loss due to riot or civil commotion outside the United States of America and Canada; or loss due to military, naval or usurped power, war or insurrection unless such loss occurs in transit in the circumstances recited in Insuring Agreement (C), and unless, when such transit was initiated, there was no knowledge of such riot, civil commotion, military, naval or usurped power, war or insurrection on the part of any person acting for the insured in initiating such transit;

(c) loss resulting directly or indirectly from the effects of nuclear fission or fusion or radioactivity; provided, however, that, this paragraph shall not apply to loss resulting from industrial uses of nuclear energy;

(d) loss resulting directly or indirectly from any acts of any director of the Insured other than one employed as a salaried, pensioned or elected official or an Employee of the Insured, except when performing acts coming within the scope of the usual duties of an Employee, or while acting as a member of any committee duly elected or appointed by resolution of the board of directors of the Insured to perform specific, as distinguished from general, directorial acts on behalf of the Insured;

(e) loss resulting directly or indirectly from the complete or partial non-payment of, or default upon, any Loan or transaction involving the Insured as a lender or borrower, or extension of credit, including the purchase, discounting or other acquisition of false or genuine accounts, invoices, notes, agreements or Evidences of Debt, whether such Loan, transaction or

---

* Exclusions (a) through (l) and Exclusion (aa) by Samuel J. Arena, Jr., Daniel T. Fitch, and Francis S. Monterosso, Stradley, Ronon, Stevens & Young, LLP, Philadelphia, Pennsylvania. Exclusions (m) through (z) and Exclusion (bb) by Sam H. Poteet, Jr. and Jeffrey S. Price, Manier & Herod, P.C., Nashville, Tennessee.

extension was procured in good faith or through trick, artifice, fraud or false pretenses, except when covered under Insuring Agreements (A), (D) or (E);

(f) loss of Property contained in customers' safe deposit boxes, except when the Insured is legally liable therefor and the loss is covered under Insuring Agreement (A);

(g) loss through cashing or paying forged or altered travelers' checks or travelers' checks bearing forged endorsements, except when covered under Insuring Agreement (A); or loss of unsold travelers' checks or unsold money orders placed in the custody of the Insured with authority to sell, unless (a) the Insured is legally liable for such loss and (b) such checks or money orders are later paid or honored by the drawer thereof, except when covered under Insuring Agreement (A);

(h) loss caused by an Employee, except when covered under Insuring Agreement (A) or when covered under Insuring Agreement (B) or (C) and resulting directly from misplacement, mysterious unexplainable disappearance or destruction of or damage to Property;

(i) loss resulting directly or indirectly from trading, with or without the knowledge of the Insured, whether or not represented by any indebtedness or balance shown to be due the Insured on any customer's account, actual or fictitious, and notwithstanding any act or omission on the part of any Employee in connection with any account relating to such trading, indebtedness, or balance, except when covered under Insuring Agreements (D) or (E);

(j) shortage in any teller's cash due to error, regardless of the amount of such shortage, and any shortage in any teller's cash which is not in excess of the normal shortage in the teller's cash in the office where such shortage shall occur shall be presumed to be due to error;

(k) loss resulting directly or indirectly from the use or purported use of credit, debit, charge, access, convenience, identification or other cards
   (1) in obtaining credit or funds, or

SECTION 2 — EXCLUSIONS 261

(2) in gaining access to automated mechanical devices which, on behalf of the Insured, disburse Money, accept deposits, cash checks, drafts or similar written instruments or make credit card loans, or

(3) in gaining access to point of sale terminals, customer-bank communication terminals, or similar electronic terminals of electronic funds transfer systems,

whether such cards were issued, or purport to have been issued, by the Insured or by anyone other than the Insured, except when covered under Insuring Agreement (A);

(l) loss involving automated mechanical devices which, on behalf of the Insured, disburse Money, accept deposits, cash checks, drafts or similar written instruments or make credit card loans, unless such automated mechanical devices are situated within an office of the Insured which is permanently staffed by an Employee whose duties are those usually assigned to a bank teller, even though public access is from outside the confines of such office, but in no event shall the Underwriter be liable for loss (including loss of Property)

(1) as a result of damage to such automated mechanical devices from vandalism or malicious mischief perpetrated from outside such office, or

(2) as a result of failure of such automated mechanical devices to function properly, or

(3) through misplacement or mysterious unexplainable disappearance while such Property is located within any such automated mechanical devices,

except when covered under Insuring Agreement (A);

(m) loss through the surrender of Property away from an office of the Insured as a result of a threat

(1) to do bodily harm to any person, except loss of Property in transit in the custody of any person acting as messenger provided that when such transit was initiated there was no knowledge by the Insured of any such threat, or

(2) to do damage to the premises or property of the Insured, except when covered under Insuring Agreement (A);

(n) loss resulting directly or indirectly from payments made or withdrawals from a depositor's account involving erroneous credits to such account, unless such payments or withdrawals are physically received by such depositor or representative of such depositor who is within the office of the insured at the time of such payment or withdrawal, or except when covered under Insuring Agreement (A);

(o) loss resulting directly or indirectly from payments made or withdrawals from a depositor's account involving items of deposit which are not finally paid for any reason, including but not limited to Forgery or any other fraud, except when covered under Insuring Agreement (A);

(p) loss resulting directly or indirectly from counterfeiting, except when covered under Insuring Agreements (A), (E) or (F);

(q) loss of any tangible item of personal property which is not specifically enumerated in the paragraph defining Property and for which the Insured is legally liable, if such property is specifically insured by other insurance of any kind and in any amount obtained by the Insured, and in any event, loss of such property occurring more than 60 days after the Insured shall have become aware that is liable for the safekeeping of such property,
except when covered under Insuring Agreements (A) or (B)(2);

(r) loss of Property while
(1) in the mail, or
(2) in the custody of any Transportation Company, unless covered under Insuring Agreement (C) except when covered under Insuring Agreement (A);

(s) potential income, including but not limited to interest and dividends, not realized by the Insured;

SECTION 2 — EXCLUSIONS

(t) damages of any type for which the Insured is legally liable, except compensatory damages, but not multiples thereof, arising directly from a loss covered under this bond;

(u) all fees, costs and expenses incurred by the Insured
   (1) in establishing the existence of or amount of loss covered under this bond, or
   (2) as a party to any legal proceeding whether or not such legal proceeding exposes the Insured to loss covered by this bond;

(v) indirect or consequential loss of any nature;

(w) loss resulting from any violation by the Insured or by any Employee
   (1) of law regulating (i) the issuance, purchase or sale of securities, (ii) securities transactions upon security exchanges or over the counter market, (iii) investment companies, or (iv) investment advisers, or
   (2) of any rule or regulation made pursuant to any such law, unless it is established by the Insured that the act or acts which caused the said loss involved fraudulent or dishonest conduct which would have caused a loss to the Insured in a similar amount in the absence of such laws, rules or regulations;

(x) loss resulting directly or indirectly from the failure of a financial or depository institution, or its receiver or liquidator, to pay or deliver, on demand of the Insured, funds or Property of the Insured held by it any capacity, except when covered under Insuring Agreements (A) or (B)(1)(a);

(y) loss involving any Uncertificated Security except an Uncertificated Security of any Federal Reserve Bank of the United States or when covered under Insuring Agreement (A);

(z) damages resulting from any civil, criminal or other legal proceeding in which the Insured is alleged to have engaged in racketeering activity except when the Insured establishes that the act or acts giving rise to such damages were committed by an Employee under circumstances which result directly in a loss to the Insured covered by Insuring Agreement (A). For the purposes of this exclusion, "racketeering activity" is defined in 18 United States Code 1961 et seq., as amended.

(aa) loss resulting directly or indirectly from the theft, disappearance or destruction of confidential information including, but not limited to, trade secrets, customer lists, and intellectual property.

(bb) loss resulting directly or indirectly from the dishonest or fraudulent acts of an Employee if any Insured, or any director or officer of an Insured who is not in collusion with such Employee, knows, or knew at any time, of any dishonest or fraudulent act committed by such Employee at any time, whether in the employment of the Insured or otherwise, whether or not of the type covered under Insuring Agreement (A), against the Insured or any other person or entity and without regard to whether knowledge was obtained before or after the commencement of this bond. Provided, however, that this exclusion does not apply to loss of any Property already in transit in the custody of such Employee at the time such knowledge was obtained or to loss resulting directly from dishonest or fraudulent acts occurring prior to the time such knowledge was obtained.

COMMENT

The 1980 standard form Bankers Blanket Bond contained twenty-three exclusions. The introduction of the Financial Institution Bond in 1986 increased the number of exclusions to twenty-six. This increase resulted from the addition of four exclusions and the deletion of one. Former Exclusion (r), which provided for the exclusion of "loss or loss of Property in or from an office or premises" listed in the declarations, was eliminated from the bond. Exclusion (w) (securities law violation), Exclusion (x) (failure to pay or deliver), Exclusion (y) (uncertificated securities) and Exclusion (z) (racketeering activities—RICO) were added. A number of other changes, some of which had been added by rider to the Bankers Blanket Bond, were incorporated in the 1986 bond form. The standard form has been updated twice since 1986, in 2004 and 2011. Since the publishing of the Second Edition of the Annotated Financial Institution Bond, two additional exclusions have been included: Exclusion (aa) (theft, disappearance or destruction of confidential information) and (bb) (dishonest or fraudulent acts of an employee). These changes are discussed in the comments following the separate treatment of each exclusion below.

Although several of the exclusions have been the subject of much litigation, many are not the subject of any reported decisions. From this, the inference can be that either such exclusions are so clearly and unambiguously worded that they would not likely be the subject of a dispute, or that the circumstances under which such exclusions would come into play have not yet resulted in a reported case. Exclusions such as Exclusion (f) (safe deposit box) and Exclusion (j) (teller's cash shortage) fall within the former category, whereas, Exclusion (b) (riot or civil commotion) and Exclusion (c) (nuclear) fall within the latter category. Exclusion (e) (loan loss), Exclusion (i) (trading loss), Exclusion (o) (uncollected funds), and Exclusion (s) (potential income) have been the subject of the most reported decisions.

A. Forgery or Alteration

(a) **loss resulting directly or indirectly from forgery or alteration, except when covered under Insuring Agreements (A), (D), (E) or (F);**

COMMENT

This exclusion has been included in the bond since its earliest forms. The changes from the 1969 version of the Bankers Blanket Bond, Standard Form No. 24 to the 1980 version largely were stylistic in nature. There were no changes to this exclusion in Form 24 in 1986 other than the removal of the initial capital letter in the word "Forgery." The definition of "Forgery" remained in the 1986 form. One commentator has conjectured that this change indicates that the term "forgery" is being used in the 1986 form in its generic sense and not as the term is defined in the policy.[1] The 2004 version added the "or indirectly" language and removed Insuring Agreement (F) from the exclusion. In 2011, although no substantive changes were made, "Forgery" was capitalized to refer to the defined meaning.

By its clear and unambiguous terms, this exclusion removes from coverage loss resulting directly or indirectly from "forgery or alteration" except where such loss otherwise would be covered under certain enumerated Insuring Agreements. The basic forgery coverages are set forth in Insuring Agreement (D) (Forgery or Alteration) and Insuring Agreement (E) (Securities). Forgery losses otherwise covered under Insuring Agreement (A) (Fidelity) and Insuring Agreement (F) (Counterfeit Currency) also are carved out of this exclusion. Even if forgery losses fall within the scope of Insuring Agreement (B) (On Premises) or Insuring Agreement (C) (In Transit), they are not covered by operation of this exclusion.

ANNOTATIONS

5th Cir. 1986 (Tex.). A bank sued its insurer for coverage under a professional and directors and officers liability and comprehensive blanket bond for losses resulting from making loans on $200,000 certificates of deposit that had been issued on actual deposits of $2,000. The court ruled that "Charter Bank's loss in this case occurred not because customer's certificates of deposit were forged or altered, but because they contained fraudulent misrepresentations of fact. The risk of such a loss was allocated to Charter Bank under Exclusion 2(e) of the bond and was outside the bond's coverage." *Charter Bank N.W. v. Evanston Ins. Co.,* 791 F.2d 379, 383.

6th Cir. 2013 (Ky.). An insured bank sought coverage under a Financial Institution Bond. The bank made loans to a third party, secured by an alleged life insurance policy. The assignment of the life insurance policy was forged and the policy had been assigned to numerous banks. The forged document was worthless from the time the loan was made and the

---

[1] *See* James A. Black, *Section 2—Exclusions*, ANNOTATED FINANCIAL INSTITUTION BOND (Formerly BANKERS BLANKET BOND), Ch. 6 (Harvey C. Koch ed., 2nd Supp. 1998).

bank was unable to recover. The Sixth Circuit affirmed the trial court's finding for the defendant insurance company because "the contractual stipulations for indemnity were not met," without reaching the question of whether the situation fell within the scope of the forgery or loan loss exclusions. *Forcht Bank, N.A. v. BancInsure, Inc.*, No. 11-6328, 2013 WL 518405, at *5-6.

6th Cir. 1982 (Tenn.). A bank made a claim for recovery for losses arising out of a fraudulent sale-leaseback transaction. The insured bank had lent money based on representations by a customer that certain equipment served as collateral for loans. There was no equipment. The Sixth Circuit found no forgery and upheld the insured's application of the loan loss exclusion. *Farmers Bank & Trust Co. of Winchester v. Transam. Ins. Co.*, 674 F.2d 548, 552-53.

6th Cir. 1971 (Ky.). The insured bank's teller accepted a cashier's check originally issued for $20.00 but altered to read in the amount of $20,000. Court found that forgery exclusion applied to bar coverage. The material alteration with intent to defraud of the amount payable of an otherwise valid cashier's check is forgery. *Am. Nat'l Bank & Trust Co. of Bowling Green v. Hartford Acc. & Indem. Co.*, 442 F.2d 995, 998.

9th Cir. 1967 (Idaho). A creamery impliedly misrepresented to the insured bank that drafts, which were later dishonored, were issued in the ordinary course of company business; that company had funds or credit to assure payment; and that drafts would be honored upon presentment. The court held that the bank's loss on drafts was not excluded under the forgery exclusion. The court noted that while it may be correct to say that a forgery connotes a false pretense, which is covered under the bond, not every false pretense is forgery. The court also found that the counterfeit "cashier check" was not covered due to the forgery exclusion. Instead the loss was covered under the primary insuring agreement's false pretenses and/or counterfeited instrument coverage. *United Pac. Ins. Co. v. Idaho First Nat'l Bank*, 378 F.2d 62, 67.

Mass. Super. Ct. 2005. A bookkeeper used one of her company's officer's signature stamps to sign checks made payable to herself. She deposited the checks in payment of her HELOC account at various branches of a bank. When the company discovered the embezzlement, it informed the bank. The court granted summary judgment in favor of the insurance company because, regardless of the "forgery or alteration" exclusion, the bank's loss was neither a direct or indirect result of the fabricated documents, and the loss was not covered under the policy. *Commerce Bank & Trust v. St. Paul Mercury Ins. Co.*, No. 04-1264B, 2005 WL 4881101, at *5-6.

SECONDARY SOURCES

Samuel J. Arena, Jr. & Jason W. Glasgow, *"On Premises" Coverage: The Bad Exchange Scam* (unpublished paper presented at the Fall 2010 Meeting of the American Bar Association, FSLIC).

B. Riot or Civil Commotion

(b) **loss due to riot or civil commotion outside the United States of America and Canada; or loss due to military, naval or usurped power, war or insurrection unless such loss occurs in transit in the circumstances recited in Insuring Agreement (C), and unless, when such transit was initiated, there was no knowledge of such riot, civil commotion, military, naval or usurped power, war or insurrection on the part of any person acting for the insured in initiating such transit;**

COMMENT

Except for capitalizing "Insured" to refer to the definition of the term, this exclusion is in the same form that it appeared in the 1969 and 1980 versions of the Bankers Blanket Bond, Standard Form No. 24. It excludes from coverage loss due to "riot or civil commotion" provided that such is outside the United States or Canada. It also excludes from coverage loss due to "military, naval or usurped power, war or insurrection." Earlier versions of the Bankers Blanket Bond included within the scope of this exclusion any loss that resulted from "wind storm, tornado, earthquake, volcanic eruption or similar disturbance of nature."

Carved out of this exclusion are otherwise excluded losses that occur while the property is in transit provided that there is coverage under Insuring Agreement (C) and the person acting for the insured who initiated such transit had no knowledge of the subject "riot, civil commotion, military, naval or usurped power, war or insurrection."

ANNOTATIONS

NONE

SECONDARY SOURCES

Mark A. Gamin, Armen Shahinian & Andrew S. Kent, *The Subtleties of Insuring Agreement (C) of the Financial Institution Bond*, IX FID. L.J. 115 (2003).

C. Nuclear

(c) loss resulting directly or indirectly from the effects of nuclear fission or fusion or radioactivity; provided, however, that this paragraph shall not apply to loss resulting from industrial uses of nuclear energy;

COMMENT

This exclusion was added to the Bankers Blanket Bond, Standard Form No. 24 in 1969. Minor changes were made in 1980. There were no changes made to Form 24 in 1986. Excluded from coverage is loss resulting directly or indirectly from the effects of "nuclear fission or fusion or radioactivity." Loss resulting from "industrial uses" of nuclear energy is expressly carved out of this exclusion. Changes in 2004 were made to include "chemical" and "biological contamination" to the exclusion.

ANNOTATIONS

NONE

SECONDARY SOURCES

NONE

D. Acts of Director

(d) **loss resulting directly or indirectly from any acts of any director of the Insured other than one employed as a salaried, pensioned or elected official or an Employee of the Insured, except when performing acts coming within the scope of the usual duties of an Employee, or while acting as a member of any committee duly elected or appointed by resolution of the board of directors of the Insured to perform specific, as distinguished from general, directorial acts on behalf of the Insured;**

COMMENT

In 2004, this exclusion was significantly revised from the bond's 1986 version to, "loss resulting directly or indirectly from any acts of any director of the Insured, except when covered under Insuring Agreement (A)." In 2011, the exclusion's language was revised to account for the updated definition of "Employee." Earlier changes to this exclusion came in the 1980 version of Form 24 when the words "directly or indirectly" were inserted between the words "resulting" and "from." The 1969 version of Form 24 expanded the scope of this exclusion by changing the focus of the exclusion from the title or position of the person performing the acts in question to the nature of the acts being performed by that individual. The 1946 version of this bond excluded "[a]ny loss resulting from any act or acts of any director of the Insured, other than one employed as a salaried, pensioned or elected official or an Employee of the Insured."

The rationale for this exclusion is simple: the bond is intended to protect the insured financial institution from the dishonesty of its employees. The bond is not intended to protect the insured from its "own" dishonesty, including from the dishonesty of its directors when they are performing general directorial acts on behalf of the insured financial institution.

ANNOTATIONS

4th Cir. 1970 (Md.). The insured's losses arose from defalcations of two individuals who served as directors of the insured from time to time. The insurer argued that the two individuals acted in the complained-of transactions as directors of the insured. The court reasoned that the acts of directors who were salaried employees of the insured, like the two individuals at issue, rendered them more like corporate officers than directors. Thus, the "directors" exclusion did not apply to preclude coverage. *Phoenix Sav. & Loan, Inc. v. Aetna Cas. & Sur. Co.,* 427 F.2d 862, 873-74.

5th Cir. 1976 (Ala.). The insured suffered losses when purchasers of controlling stock in the insured's parent company manipulated the stocks and assets of the insured. The court noted that the "director" exclusion covers the unfaithful activity that breaches the confidence of an insured in regular officials who serve as its directors, but it does not include the acts of outside directors not in the service of the insured. *First Nat'l Life Ins. Co. v. Fid. & Deposit Co. of Md.,* 525 F.2d 966, 970-71.

6th Cir. 1992 (Ky.). The insured sustained losses when a member of the insured's board of directors caused the insured to become insolvent by purposefully making poor recommendations for out-of-territory loans. The court noted that the insured's control over the director was insufficient to establish that the director was an employee. No evidence showed that any officer or supervisory agent of the insured gave instructions, directions, or supervision to the director regarding the performance of his duties, thereby leaving the reasonable conclusion that he was an independent contractor. Thus, the "director" exclusion was found to be inapplicable. *Bank of Cumberland v. Aetna Cas. & Sur. Co.,* 956 F.2d 595, 597-98.

Kan. 1989. A director caused the insured to sustain losses when he fraudulently obtained several loans and deposited insufficient funds checks in substantial amounts with the insured. The court held that the "director" was an "Employee" only for acts committed while he acted as a member of a committee of the insured, not merely because he was a member of a committee. *First Hays Bancshares, Inc. v. Kan. Bankers Sur. Co.,* 769 P.2d 1184, 1191-92.

Minn. 1976. The court held that the insured's losses arising from allegedly fraudulent acts of the bank were not covered under the bond. The directors of the bank knew of the transactions at issue. The acts of the directors constituted the acts of the bank. The court concluded that because the bond was not intended to insure the bank against the acts taken by its directors, there was no coverage for the claimed losses under the bond. *Farmers & Merch. State Bank of Pierz v. St. Paul Fire & Marine Ins. Co.,* 242 N.W.2d 840, 843-44.

SECONDARY SOURCES

Howard Marks, *The "Other" Exclusions of Commercial Blanket Bonds and Dishonesty Policies* (unpublished paper presented at National Institute Program of the American Bar Association Tort and Insurance Practice Section, Fidelity and Surety Law Committee, New York, N.Y., Nov. 1991).

E. Loan Loss

(e) **loss resulting directly or indirectly from the complete or partial non-payment of, or default upon, any Loan or transaction involving the Insured as a lender or borrower, or extension of credit, including the purchase, discounting or other acquisition of false or genuine accounts, invoices, notes, agreements or Evidences of Debt, whether such Loan, transaction or extension was procured in good faith or through trick, artifice, fraud or false pretenses, except when covered under Insuring Agreements (A), (D) or (E);**

COMMENT

Under the loan loss exclusion, loss resulting from the complete or partial non-payment of, or default upon, a "Loan" or "transaction involving the Insured as a lender or borrower, or extension of credit," is excluded unless it otherwise would be covered by Insuring Agreement (A) (Fidelity), Insuring Agreement (D) (Forgery or Alteration), or Insuring Agreement (E) (Securities). By its clear and unambiguous terms, the exclusion applies regardless of whether the subject loan transaction or extension of credit was procured in good faith or through "trick, artifice, fraud or false pretenses." The underlying rationale of this exclusion is that the making of loans and the extension of credit in any form (such as honoring checks before they "clear") is the business of the financial institution and, therefore, part of its "business risk," which the bond is not meant to cover.

Exclusion (e) was significantly expanded in 1969 to make clear that the term "loan" meant any transaction "in the nature of, or amounting to, a loan."[2] Before 1969, the standard bond form covered losses resulting from "the complete or partial non-payment of or default upon any loan made by or obtained by the Insured, whether procured in good faith or through trick, artifice, fraud or false pretenses, except when covered by Insuring Clause (A) or (D)."[3] It did not include any language making clear that the term "loan" should be broadly interpreted. The 1969 statement of change does not explain the reasons for revising the exclusion.[4] But it is likely that the expansion was a response to cases such as *Fidelity & Casualty Co. of New York v. Bank of Altenburg*[5] and *Johnstown Bank v. American Surety Co. of New York*,[6] both discussed in the annotations below. *Altenburg* was a check kiting case, and *Johnstown* involved conditional sales agreements. Both cases involved transactions that were in the nature of a loan, but the courts nonetheless refused to apply the exclusion. The former Director of Fidelity at the SFAA stated, in an article presented to the Fidelity & Surety Law Committee in 1969, that both of these cases led to the expansion of the

---

2 Bankers Blanket Bond, Standard Form No. 24 (April 1969).
3 Bankers Blanket Bond, Standard Form No. 24 (March 7, 1941).
4 Analysis of Changes, Bankers Blanket Bond, Standard Form No. 24, revised to April, 1969.
5 216 F.2d 294, 304 (8th Cir. 1954).
6 174 N.Y.S.2d 385, 387-88 (N.Y. S. Ct. App. Div. 1958).

loan loss exclusion to make sure that the exclusion would not be narrowly interpreted as it had been before.[7] The article noted that the 1969 revision was an effort to "eliminate the credit risk from the bond since the very reason [that a bank] exists is to extend credit."[8]

The 1986 Financial Institution Bond, Standard Form No. 24, introduced the term "Loan" as a defined term and thereby simplified the loan loss exclusion. Since that time, "Loan" has been defined as "all extensions of credit by the Insured and all transactions creating a creditor relationship in favor of the Insured and all transactions by which the Insured assumes an existing creditor relationship." Additionally, Insuring Agreement (A) was revised to make coverage for employee dishonesty in connection with a Loan contingent on the dishonest employee's colluding with one or more parties to the transaction and receiving a financial benefit worth at least $2,500 in connection with that transaction. The 2004 changes included removing Insuring Agreement (D) from, and adding Insuring Agreement (G) to, the exclusion's carve-out. In 2011, "but not limited to" was added to the exclusion to indicate that the exclusion does not present an exhaustive list.

ANNOTATIONS

3d Cir. 1992. Bank loaned money to a lawyer who arranged for an imposter to acknowledge the mortgage. The lawyer had borrowed money from another bank using the same property as security the day before. Bank realized that it did not have priority and could not recover from the lawyer's personal possessions and filed a claim with its insurance company. The Third Circuit found that the bank could recover if the losses resulted directly from an extension of credit in good faith reliance on a mortgage that bore a forged signature. But there was a fact issue as to whether the reliance on the forged signature (versus the lack of collateral) was the proximate cause of the loss. The court therefore reversed entry of summary judgment in favor of the insurer and

---

[7] John F. Fitzgerald, *Comments on Current Changes in Financial Institution Bonds* 5-6 (unpublished paper presented to the Committee on Fidelity & Surety Law, Section of Insurance, Negligence and Compensation, American Bar Association, August 8-14, 1969, New York, New York).

[8] *Id.*

remanded. *Jefferson Bank v. Progressive Cas. Ins. Co.*, 965 F.2d 1274, 1282-85.

4th Cir. 1993 (S.C.). The insured suffered losses from the misrepresentations of a customer in the business of offering mortgages to sellers of secondary mortgages and mortgage pools. The court affirmed lower court jury's verdict in favor of the defendants, concluding that the loan exclusion applied because the insured's losses resulted from the customer's failure to collect on the loans. *First Sav. Bank, FSB v. Am. Cas. Co. of Reading, Pa.*, No. 92-1320, 1993 WL 27403, at *5-6.

4th Cir. 1980 (Va.). The insured sought recovery for losses sustained by misrepresentations of a third-party in connection with the insured's purchase of accounts receivable. The accounts receivable, however, turned out to be non-existent, and the insured suffered losses when it tried to collect on the accounts. Section 2(e) of the bond precluded coverage for "(1) any loan or transaction in the nature of, or amounting to a loan made by or obtained from the Insured, or (2) any note, account, agreement or other evidence of debt assigned or sold to, or discounted or otherwise acquired by, the Insured whether procured in good faith or through trick, artifice, fraud or false pretenses unless such loss is covered under Insuring Agreement (A), (D) or (E)." The Fourth Circuit determined that section 2(e)(1) of the loan exclusion was inapplicable because the transactions did not qualify as loans. The court also noted that section 2(e)(2) excluded coverage for losses resulting from the non-payment of accounts purchased by the insured, regardless of whether the purchase was procured through trick, artifice, fraud or false pretenses. The only exception to this general exclusion is a transaction involving forged or counterfeited documents, which was not present. Because the insured's losses resulted from the purchase of the fictitious accounts, the exclusion precluded recovery by the insured under the bond. *United Va. Factors Corp. v. Aetna Cas. & Sur. Co.*, 624 F.2d 814, 816-18.

4th Cir. 1964 (N.C.). The insured bank made loans based on false and counterfeit invoices. The Fourth Circuit noted that "[w]hile the document employed to pass the invoice to the Bank speaks of a sale, in actuality and in law it was obviously nothing more than a pledge of the invoice as security for the note evidencing a loan." Thus, because the transaction was a loan, the Fourth Circuit determined that the loan loss exclusion precluded recovery for the insured. *N.C. Nat'l Bank v. Lumbermen's Mut. Cas. Co.,* 335 F.2d 486, 487.

5th Cir. 1992 (Tex.). The insured bank allowed a customer who misrepresented his wealth and obtained special privileges to access funds immediately from deposits even when the funds were insufficient to cover the withdrawals. The customer conducted a check kiting scheme to use insured's money to finance major securities investments. The court held that the bank's reliance on customer's promise to repay overdrafts when it granted the customer immediate access to the funds represented by his deposits constituted a "loan or transaction in the nature of a loan or extension of credit" as a matter of law. Therefore, the loan loss exclusion applied. *First Tex. Sav. Ass'n v. Reliance Ins. Co.,* 950 F.2d 1171, 1174-78.

5th Cir. 1986 (Tex.). In furtherance of a fraudulent loan-pyramiding scheme, an individual borrowed $200,000 from the insured bank, pledging two certificates of deposit payable to the individual for $100,000 each. The individual defaulted on the bank loans. Coverage was not governed by the Bankers Blanket Bond Standard Form No. 24, but under a similar loan loss exclusion, Exclusion 2(E), of a Professional and Directors and Officers Liability and Comprehensive Blanket Bond. The Fifth Circuit held that the risk of such a loss was allocated to the insured bank under the loan exclusion of the bond and was outside the bond's coverage. *Charter Bank Nw. v. Evanston Ins. Co.,* 791 F.2d 379, 381-83.

5th Cir. 1976 (La.). This is a landmark case which distinguishes between checks and drafts, holding that transactions involving advances to a customer based on deposits of drafts were de facto loans, as bank could have no reasonable expectation that the drafts would be paid in the normal course of business. The Fifth Circuit further held that the loan exclusion applies to de facto loans as well as true loans, noting that the Bankers Blanket Bond does not provide credit insurance. The court distinguished this case from check kiting cases because the insured bank can reasonably expect checks to be paid in the normal course of business. Court further noted that checks are usually handled as "cash" items, whereas drafts are usually handled as "collection" items. *Calcasieu-Marine Nat'l Bank v. Emp'rs Ins. Co.,* 533 F.2d 290, 299-301.

5th Cir. 1973 (Tex.). A loan exclusion was held to be applicable even if the loans were obtained under false pretenses. *Bank of the Sw. v. Nat'l Sur. Co.,* 477 F.2d 73, 76-77.

5th Cir. 1970 (Tex.). The insured lent money on a note secured by warehouse receipts for cotton which had not been cancelled as required by law. The court held that the basic transaction was a loan, and the transaction was squarely within the exclusion irrespective of the intent to repay. *Md. Cas. Co. v. State Bank & Trust Co.,* 425 F.2d 979, 980-82.

5th Cir. 1969 (Ala.). A loan exclusion was held applicable to a claim involving a customer who agreed to bring to the insured bank checks payable to himself and the bank jointly so that the bank could apply proceeds on the loan. The customer deposited some of these checks in his account and withdrew the funds so deposited. The court noted that the bonding company did not provide a policy of credit insurance, and the real cause of the loss was the customer's failure to repay the loans. *E. Gadsden Bank v. USF&G,* 415 F.2d 357, 359-60.

6th Cir. 2013 (Ky.). An insured bank sought coverage under a Financial Institution Bond. The bank made loans to a third party, secured by an alleged life insurance policy. The assignment of the life insurance policy was forged and the policy had been assigned to numerous banks. The forged document was worthless from the time the loan was made and the bank was unable to recover. The Sixth Circuit affirmed the trial court's finding for insurer because "the contractual stipulations for indemnity were not met," without reaching the question of whether the situation fell within the scope of the forgery or loan loss exclusions. *Forcht Bank, N.A. v. BancInsure, Inc.,* No. 11-6328, 2013 WL 518405, at *5-6.

6th Cir. 1990 (Ohio). A loan exclusion was inapplicable insofar as the re-purchase agreements at issue were not in the nature of a loan but, rather, a sale that included collateral. However, the non-payment or default upon any "note, account, agreement or other evidence of debt assigned or sold to" the insured was not addressed by the district court, necessitating remand. *First Fed. Sav. & Loan Ass'n of Toledo v. Fid. & Deposit Co. of Md.,* 895 F.2d 254, 260.

6th Cir. 1982 (Tenn.). The insured bank sustained loss as a result of a fraudulent sale-leaseback transaction. The insurer refused to indemnify the loss based on the loan exclusion and argued that although there was a fraud on the bank, there could be no coverage unless it was accompanied by a forgery. The Sixth Circuit found that the insured did not carry its burden of proof on whether forgery occurred and, thus, could not recover under bond. *Farmers Bank & Trust Co. of Winchester v. Transam. Ins. Co.,* 674 F.2d 548, 550-51.

6th Cir. 1977 (Ohio). The insured sustained losses on several loans due to the misrepresentations made by an inspector hired by the insured. The Sixth Circuit stated that the bond was not credit insurance and that the loss on the loan induced by fraud did not result from employee dishonesty or forgery, the exceptions to operation of exclusion clause 2(d). The actual cause of the insured's loss, according to the court, was a defect in the purchaser's title, which was mortgaged to the insured as security for the loan to the purchaser and which made the loan uncollectible. The court determined that the language of exclusion clause 2(d) stated that the exclusion applied to a loss on a loan induced by fraud if the loss actually results from a default. The customer's actions did not remove the claimed losses from the loan exclusion, and, thus, the losses were not covered. *Third Fed. Sav. & Loan Ass'n of Cleveland v. Fireman's Fund Ins. Co.,* 548 F.2d 166, 171-72.

6th Cir. 1962 (Tenn.). The customer gave the insured bank worthless warehouse receipts as security for loan. The insured later sustained loss when it settled with customer's trustee in bankruptcy on a claim that payment of loans constituted a voidable preference. The loan exclusion was held to be applicable. *First Nat'l Bank of Memphis v. Aetna Cas. & Sur. Co.,* 309 F.2d 702, 704-05.

7th Cir. 1994 (Ill.). Bank transferred securities to securities dealer in exchange for cash on the agreement that the securities dealer would return the securities to the bank in exchange for more cash (a repurchasing transaction). The securities dealer wrongfully used the securities in other transactions for its own benefit. The bank was unable to collect the cash it had expected. The court held that the repurchasing transactions were in the nature of a loan and that the loan loss exclusion (exclusion (e)) therefore applied. The repurchasing transactions were, in essence, collateralized loans. *RTC v. Aetna Cas. & Sur. Co.*, 25 F.3d 570, 577-80.

7th Cir. 1986 (Ill.). An individual engaged in a check kiting scheme, writing checks on account with the bank, and then presenting them to insured savings and loan in exchange for the insured's treasurer checks made payable to the individual. The Seventh Circuit held that the loan exclusion under the bond did not apply because the evidence did not demonstrate that the insured and an individual engaged in a credit transaction. The court found that when the insured issued the treasurer checks, the insured presumed that it was receiving, in turn, a thing of like value. *Fid. & Deposit Co. of Md. v. Reliance Fed. Sav. & Loan Ass'n*, 795 F.2d 42, 44-45.

7th Cir. 1970 (Ill.). A transaction involving a check kiting scheme was held not to involve a loan and, therefore, the loss was not excluded. The court stated that it was not conceivable to construe "loan" to cover obligation imposed by law to reimburse a bank for money or credit obtained through the use of worthless checks. *First Nat'l Bank of Decatur v. Ins. Co. of N. Am.*, 424 F.2d 312, 316.

7th Cir. 1969 (Ill.). A loss was sustained in connection with a loan secured by accounts receivable to which the underlying transactions had not taken place. The court found the loan exclusion applied and affirmed trial court's granting of summary judgment in favor of the insurer. *Capitol Bank of Chicago v. Fid. & Cas. Co. of N.Y.*, 414 F.2d 986, 989.

8th Cir. 1965 (Iowa). A loss in connection with a check kiting scheme was held to be covered by Insuring Agreement (B). The court held that the transaction did not constitute a loan and, therefore, the loan exclusion did not apply. There was evidence that the insured bank knew that there were insufficient funds to cover the checks written by the customer. *Indem. Ins. Co. of N. Am. v. Pioneer Valley Sav. Bank*, 343 F.2d 634, 652-53.

8th Cir. 1965 (Neb.). The insured allowed the customer to draw against deposit of checks which were subsequently dishonored. The loss to the insured was held to be covered under Insuring Agreement (B) and the loan exclusion was not applicable. *U.S. ex rel. First Cont'l Bank & Trust Co. v. W. Contracting Corp.,* 341 F.2d 383, 390-91.

8th Cir. 1954 (Mo.). The bank sustained a loss from a check kiting scheme when it relied on depositor's implied representation that checks offered for deposit were good. The Eighth Circuit found the loan exclusion inapplicable and held the bank's loss was covered under coverage for losses through false pretenses. *Fid. & Cas. Co. of N.Y. v. Bank of Altenburg,* 216 F.2d 294, 304.

8th Cir. 1953 (Mo.). This was the first reported appellate case holding that the loan loss exclusion was not applicable to a check kiting scheme. The bank involved failed, and, thus, the FDIC became involved. This case is generally known as the *Brazeau Bank* case, after the name of the bank involved. *Hartford Acc. & Indem. Co. v. FDIC,* 204 F.2d 933, 936-37.

9th Cir. 1990 (Or.). The insured suffered losses from an under-collateralized loan that defaulted and from bad deals made by its employee in connection with the construction of a new credit union building. The Ninth Circuit predicted that an Oregon court would find that the insured's losses would not be excluded by the loan exclusion because the loans at issue probably fell under the bond's definition of securities and, consequently, were covered under an insuring clause that was exempted from the exclusion. *Portland Fed. Emps. Credit Union v. Cumis Ins. Soc'y, Inc.,* 894 F.2d 1101, 1105.

10th Cir. 1975 (Okla.). The insured was alerted to the possibility of a check kiting scheme. After talking to the customer, the insured loaned the customer sufficient sums to cover an overdraft on his account, for which the customer signed two notes to the insured. The court held that the real cause of insured's loss was the failure to repay the loan and not from the check kiting. The court further held that losses on other promissory notes which were part of an overall scheme by the customer to defraud the bank also were excluded from coverage by operation of the loan exclusion. *First Nat'l Bank & Trust Co. v. Cont'l Ins. Co.,* 510 F.2d 7, 11-13.

11th Cir. 1990 (Fla.). A bank lost money by relying on a forged letter of credit. The court did not discuss the loan loss exclusion, but refused to apply coverage under a Bankers Blanket Bond because the loss was the type of bad business judgment that bonds generally do not insure. The court noted that to find coverage in a case like this would harm insurers and insureds in the long run because insurers are simply unwilling to offer broad coverage for poor credit choices. *Republic Nat'l Bank of Miami v. Fid. & Deposit Co. of Md.*, 894 F.2d 1255, 1263.

N.D. Ala. 1974. An auto dealer opened an account at the insured bank and deposited sight drafts, which provided that they were void unless certain documents were enclosed, including the title to the car involved. The dealer was allowed to draw against deposits. The drafts were returned because the enclosed documents were fictitious. The court held that the loss was covered by Insuring Agreement (B) and that the carve-out to Exclusion 2(e) was applicable because the withdrawal of funds from the account was made within the insured's office and there was no expectation by the insured bank of repayment of the money withdrawn. Thus, the "loan" loss exclusion did not apply. *Shoals Nat'l Bank of Florence v. Home Indem. Co.*, 384 F. Supp. 49, 52-55.

E.D. Ark. 2004. The insured bank suffered losses as a result of a borrower's default on a loan. The borrower sold copy machines, and the borrower's loan with the bank was partially based on the assignment of the stream of payments owed to the borrower by his customers. The bank learned that the customer forged a number of the lease agreements he showed the bank for advance funds against his line of credit. The bank made insurance claims under Insuring Clauses (D) and (E). The court explained that "in a loan loss case, the insured must show 'loss causation' as well as 'transaction causation.' . . . [T]he insured must show that (a) it would not have made the loan in question had it been aware that forged documents were being pledged as loan security, and (b) absent the forgery, the documents would have had real monetary value, thus causing an economic loss to the insured as a direct result of the forgery." The court determined that the loan loss exclusion did not exclude coverage here, because the exclusion "does not apply to Insuring Clause (E) . . . ." *Pine Bluff Nat'l Bank v. St. Paul Mercury Ins. Co.*, 346 F. Supp. 2d 1020, 1032-33.

N.D. Cal. 2004. $5.25 million was stolen from the insured bank and the insurance company claimed that the theft was not covered by the bank's Financial Institution Bond. The bank supplied cash to a company that owned or leased automated teller machines. When the company refused to hire an armored carrier service to transport the money, the bank gave its 120-day notice of termination. During those 120 days, the bank continued to supply the company with cash, and the company's owner stole most of the $5.25 million. The court explained that although the bank did not consider providing cash to the company as a loan, the exclusion includes more than just a "loan" as defined by banking standards. It includes everything "in the nature of a loan" or an "extension of credit." The loan loss exclusion prevented the bank from recovering under the bond. *Humboldt Bank v. Gulf Ins. Co.*, 323 F. Supp. 2d 1027, 1033-35.

M.D. Fla. 1967. Without citing any authority, the court held that losses resulting from a check kiting scheme were covered by the loan exclusion. *Citizens Nat'l Bank of St. Petersburg v. Travelers Indem. Co.*, 296 F. Supp. 300, 300-01.

N.D. Ill. 1992. The insured bank suffered losses as a result of check kiting, unpaid overdrafts, and intra-bank transfers of funds. The loan exclusion was held applicable to overdrafts on a demand deposit. "[O]verdraft by a bank depositor is treated as a loan from the bank to the depositor just as depositors with positive balances are considered creditors." *Affiliated Bank/Morton Grove v. Hartford Acc. & Indem. Co.*, No. 91-C-4446, 1992 WL 91761, at *9-10.

S.D. Ill. 1975. The insured bank made loans based on false information. The loans were not repaid and the bank sustained a loss. The court held that the loan exclusion applied to bar coverage. The court rejected the bank's argument that the loan exclusion only applied to the insuring clause related to office and equipment loss or damage, reasoning that such interpretation was so strained and technical as to be wholly invalid. *Cmty. Nat'l Bank in Monmouth v. St. Paul Fire & Marine Ins. Co.*, 399 F. Supp. 873, 876-79.

D. Kan. 1994. The loan exclusion was held applicable to the borrower's failure to pay on loans. The servicing contractor's misrepresentations to the insured were not the cause of the insured's losses. *Lyons Fed. Sav. & Loan v. St. Paul Fire & Marine Ins. Co.,* 863 F. Supp. 1441, 1446-48.

D. Kan. 1982. Under the 1969 bond form, the court applied Exclusion 2(e) to a check kiting scheme relying upon the "uncollected items of deposit" language of the exclusion. *Sec. Nat'l Bank of Kansas City v. Cont'l Ins. Co.,* 586 F. Supp. 139, 150-51.

E.D. La. 1970. The loan exclusion did not apply to bar coverage for a loss incurred by the insured bank through check kiting scheme. The court reasoned that "loan" does not include money advanced in good faith on worthless checks. *Nat'l Bank of Commerce in New Orleans v. Fid. & Cas. Co. of N.Y.,* 312 F. Supp. 71, 75-76.

E.D. Mich. 2013. A bank received a wire request from a purported customer for $196,000 to be wired to a South Korean bank, with all of the necessary account information—name, handwritten signature, email address, etc. Pursuant to its procedures, the bank compared the signature to the customer's signature in his file. The bank verified the wire via a telephone call. After a second similar request, the bank discovered that the person requesting the wire transfer was not actually the bank's customer. The bank did not suffer a loss as a result of the nonpayment of a loan. The customer "did not borrow the money from the Bank; he did not receive the funds and he did not agree to repay the debt." Therefore, the "loan loss" exclusion did not prevent the bank from recovering under the FIB for the alleged forgery. *Bank of Ann Arbor v. Everest Nat'l Ins. Co.,* No. 12-11251, 2013 WL 665067, at *3-4.

E.D. Mich. 2006. Bank extended credit based on collateral that turned out to be completely fictional. The bank was unable to collect the funds extended and sought coverage under a Financial Institution Bond that contained an exclusion highly analogous to Exclusion (e). The court found that coverage could not apply because of this exclusion, noting that it would be improper to turn bonds into credit insurance. *Flagstar Bank, FSB v. Fed. Ins. Co.,* No. 05-70950, 2006 U.S. Dist. LEXIS 83825, at *33-40.

E.D. Mich. 1993. A bank employee created false loans and funded old loans with the proceeds of new loans. The loan exclusion was found to be inapplicable because the fraudulent loans were not made at the request of a customer and the loans were being paid. *Peoples State Bank v. Am. Cas. Co. of Reading, Pa.,* 818 F. Supp. 1073, 1077-78.

S.D. Miss. 2012. An executive vice president of the bank was discovered to have created fictitious loans through a variety of fraudulent actions, including forged signatures, unauthorized withdrawals and releases of collateral, that were then used to pay off a customer's legitimate loan. When the bank discovered the executive's actions, it issued a new, legitimate loan to the customer. The court determined that the bank's claim was excluded because there was no loan loss, since the customer "remains legitimately indebted to the Bank, albeit on the basis of new loan documents," and the bank suffered no pecuniary loss. *BankInsure, Inc. v. Peoples Bank of the South,* 866 F. Supp. 2d 577, 587-88.

D.N.J. 1983. The insured bank made loans secured by certificates of deposit, which turned out to be worthless. The court noted that the parties did not dispute that the loan exclusion was generally applicable to the transactions at issue. The court stated that the issue was whether the bank can prove its right to recover under one of the enumerated insuring agreements. *Liberty Nat'l Bank v. Aetna Life & Cas. Co.,* 568 F. Supp. 860, 866-67.

S.D.N.Y. 1984. An insured sustained losses when it invested in certificates of deposit for a company that closed due to insolvency. The insured claimed that a certificate of deposit is not in the nature of a loan under the bond. The court held that deposits are, in effect, loans, and the exclusion applied. *IBM Poughkeepsie Emps. Fed. Credit Union v. Cumis Ins. Soc'y, Inc.,* 590 F. Supp. 769, 775-77.

S.D. Ohio 1990. Where insured bank sustained losses due to the misrepresentation of a mortgage company on the bank's purchase of mortgages, the fact that the bank did not make the loans did not take the transaction outside the loan exclusion. In reaching its decision, the court found that "the actual cause of [the bank's] loss was its inability to collect on the loans it purchased" from the mortgage company. The loss resulted directly or indirectly from the default or non-payment of an extension of credit. Thus, the loan loss exclusion precluded coverage.

Liberty Sav. Bank, F.S.B. v. Am. Cas. Co. of Reading, Pa., 754 F. Supp. 559, 561-63.

S.D. Ohio 1954. The insured bank engaged in a procedure where it would credit customer's account upon receiving bills of lading. The bank customer obtained credits to account by presenting fictitious papers. The court held that the loan exclusion did not apply to bar coverage. The court stated that a loan of money was a contract requiring a meeting of the minds. The court reasoned that no meeting of the minds was present where the insured bank expected a return of its money in the same manner that it received in previous transactions. *Nat'l Bank of Paulding v. Fid. & Cas. Co.,* 131 F. Supp. 121, 123-24.

D.S.D. 1969. The insured bank made a loan secured by a mechanic's lien on real property. The insured later discovered that the mechanic's lien waiver was forged. The court determined that the loan loss exclusion would preclude coverage under the bond; however, a special rider obtained by the insured provided an exception to the loan exclusion where the insured issued a loan in reliance upon a mortgage, deed or other like instrument that proved to be defective by reason of trick, fraud or false pretenses. The court concluded that the insured relied upon the forged mechanic's lien in issuing the loan and, thus, the insured's losses were covered by operation of the special rider. *First Fed. Sav. & Loan Ass'n v. Aetna Ins. Co.,* 303 F. Supp. 272, 273-74.

E.D. Va. 1975. The case involved a claim for loss sustained by an insured when a car dealer was allowed to draw against deposits which ultimately were dishonored. The court found coverage under Insuring Agreement (B) and held that the "loan loss" exclusion was not applicable. This exclusion was intended to cover check kiting. The court concluded that there was no evidence that there were two accounts in different banks and, therefore, the exclusion was not applicable. The court held that, assuming that the exclusion was applicable, the exception to the exclusion was met, as payments and withdrawals were made to the customer while he was in the office of the insured. *Clarenden Bank & Trust v. Fid. & Deposit Co. of Md.,* 406 F. Supp. 1161, 1173-74.

Ala. 1970. The loan exclusion was held applicable to a transaction involving a loan by a bank based upon fraudulent invoices. *Fid. & Cas. Co. v. Bank of Commerce,* 234 So. 2d 871, 877-78.

Conn. Super. Ct. 2005. Bank customer took advantage of a computer error that allowed her to continue withdrawing funds on a line of credit after she had exhausted it. When the customer was unable to repay those funds, the bank suffered a loss and sought recovery from its insurer. The insurer denied coverage based on the loan loss exclusion. The court agreed and dismissed the insured's argument that the loss resulted not from a loan but from the customer's fraud of continuing to take money from the bank that she was not entitled to. It concluded that the bank, through the computer error, "assumed" a creditor relationship with the dishonest customer. The fact that the bank did not intend this result had no significance. *First New England Federal Credit Union v. Cuna Mutual Group,* No. CV03520148, 2005 Conn. Super. LEXIS 1086, at *1-8.

Fla. Dist. Ct. App. 1985. A loan exclusion was held inapplicable to an agreement to reduce a customer's obligation to the insured between the insured and the customer who caused the loss. *NCNB Nat'l Bank of Fla. v. Aetna Cas. & Sur. Co.,* 477 So. 2d 579, 583.

Ill. Ct. App. 1998. The loan exclusion was inapplicable to a check kiting scheme. A loan implies an agreement, and there was no meeting of the minds between the insured and the customer involved in the check kiting scheme. *Oxford Bank & Trust v. Hartford Acc. & Indem. Co.,* 698 N.E.2d 204, 213-14.

Iowa 1986. A customer obtained loans based on misrepresentations to the insured bank. When the customer defaulted on his loans, the insured was unable to recoup its losses and made a claim under the bond. The court determined that the loan exclusion bars recovery for losses resulting from default on a loan even where loan was obtained under false pretenses. Thus, the exclusion barred recovery for the insured's losses. *Gateway State Bank v. N. River Ins. Co.,* 387 N.W.2d 344, 347-48.

Iowa 1980. The court determined that the loan exclusion applied where the insured renewed loans to customer with questionable credentials on the strength of a forged or altered instrument. The exclusion was applicable because the insured failed to show that its losses resulted from the alteration of the document, rather than the loans already in default. *First Nat'l Bank, Colfax v. Hartford Acc. & Indem. Co.,* 295 N.W.2d 425, 430.

Kan. 2010. The Kansas Supreme Court affirmed the lower court's holding that the insured bank's honoring of check overdrafts constituted loans, even if the bank claimed that the employee who authorized the overdrafts lacked authority to do so. However, the court did not decide "as a matter of law" whether the loan loss exclusion precluded coverage under Insuring Agreement (A). *Nat'l Bank of Andover v. Kan. Bankers Sur. Co.,* 225 P.3d 707, 723-24, 730-31.

La. Ct. App. 1976. The insured bank loaned customer $75,000 and accepted a $100,000 "international cashiers draft" for collection, allowing a deposit of $175,000 to customer's checking account with the understanding that $100,000 would be kept in account until draft paid. A few days later, customer signed new note for $175,000. Five weeks later, the bank was advised that payment had been stopped on the draft. The customer had withdrawn all but $65,000 from its checking account. The trial court granted summary judgment, and the appellate court reversed because there was a factual dispute as to whether or not a loan was made to the customer. *Sugarland State Bank v. Aetna Ins. Co.,* 330 So. 2d 336, 338.

La. Ct. App. 1972. A customer made an unsecured loan from the insured bank. The bank later requested collateral, which was furnished in the form of third person notes, which the customer assigned to the bank. It was later discovered that some of these notes involved fraud and forgery. The loan exclusion was held applicable. *Allen State Bank v. Travelers Indem. Co.,* 270 So. 2d 270, 273-74.

Minn. Ct. App. 1989. The insured claimed losses for a customer's deposit of fraudulent sales slips showing fictitious credit card sales into the customer's account and subsequent withdrawal from that account. The court held that the sales slips bought by the insured created a debtor/creditor relationship as to the insured and the customer. The sales slips, therefore, were evidence of loans between the customer and the insured. *Suburban Nat'l Bank v. Transam. Ins. Co.,* 438 N.W.2d 119, 121-22.

N.Y. S. Ct. App. Div. 1958. Bank made car loans to customers of a car dealer who would assign the sales contract to the bank. Many of the sales contracts were fictitious. The insured sought coverage under a bond. The court found that an early version of the loan loss exclusion did not apply because the transactions did not involve loans. It reasoned that a conditional sales agreement is not usually considered a loan. *Johnstown Bank v. Am. Surety Co. of New York,* 174 N.Y.S.2d 385, 387-88.

Ohio Ct. App. 1965. The loan exclusion was held applicable to a transaction involving loans by the insured bank which were secured by certificates of title obtained through false representations. *Union Banking Co. v. USF&G,* 213 N.E.2d 191, 198.

Wis. 1973. The insured bank made a loan to the customer based on a pledge of securities. The securities were later returned to the customer on his false representation that he owned other securities which he would send to the bank as new collateral. The court held that the loan exclusion was applicable. *Racine Cnty. Nat'l Bank v. Aetna Cas. & Sur. Co.,* 203 N.W.2d 145, 148-49.

SECONDARY SOURCES

Samuel J. Arena, Jr. & Jason W. Glasgow, *"On Premises" Coverage: The Bad Exchange Scam* (unpublished paper presented at the Fall 2010 Meeting of the Fidelity & Surety Law Committee of the ABA).

Stephen J. Beatty, *From Wall Street to Main Street: Employee Dishonesty Claims, the Trading Loss Exclusion, and Other Matters* (unpublished paper presented at 1989 Annual Meeting of the Surety Claims Institute, June 22, 1989).

Byrne A. Bowman, *Defenses, Including Prior Knowledge* (unpublished paper presented at 1987 International Association of Defense

Counsel Surety Trial College Mid-Year Surety Trial Practice Program, New York, N.Y., Jan. 24, 1987).

Michael D. Feiler, *Ponzi Schemes: Claims, Coverage Issues and Quantification of Losses* (unpublished paper presented at Surety Claims Institute, June 2009).

Karen Kohler Fitzgerald, *The Loan Exclusion: Allocating the Business Risks to the Banker*, in FINANCIAL INSTITUTION BONDS 293 (Duncan L. Clore ed., 1998).

David D. Gilliss et al., *Securities: The Warehouse Lending Scam—Is Your Bank Loan All Wet?* (unpublished paper presented at the Fall 2010 Meeting of the Fidelity & Surety Law Committee of the ABA).

Bruce Gillman, *The Loan Exclusion. Employee Dishonesty and Officers and Directors Liability Under the Bankers Blanket Bond—A Natural Combination* (unpublished paper presented at 1984 Annual Meeting of the Surety Claims Institute, Lake of the Ozarks, Mo., June 22, 1984).

Jason Glasgow & Elizabeth F. Staruck, *The Bubble Burst: The Fraudulent Mortgage Rider in the Current Mortgage Crisis*, XVI FID. L.J. 179 (2010).

James A. Knox & Karen Kohler Fitzgerald, *The Loan Exclusion: The Predominant Risk Allocator*, in FINANCIAL INSTITUTION BONDS 197 (Duncan L. Clore ed., 1995).

James A. Knox, *The Loan and Uncollected Funds Exclusions*, in FINANCIAL INSTITUTION BONDS 197 (Duncan L. Clore & Harvey Koch eds., 1992).

Edgar L. Neel, *Financial Institution and Fidelity Coverage for Loan Losses*, 21 TORT & INS. L.J. 590 (1986).

Susan Koehler Sullivan & Teresa Jones, *The Question of Causation in Loan Loss Cases*, XI FID. L.J. 97 (2005).

David E. Wood, *Risk Allocation for Forged Checks: When is a Check "Finally Paid" Under the Uncollected Funds Exclusion?*, VIII FID. L.J. 127 (2002).

F. Safe Deposit Box

    (f) loss of Property contained in customers' safe deposit boxes, except when the Insured is legally liable therefor and the loss is covered under Insuring Agreement (A);

COMMENT

This clear and unambiguous exclusion was last revised in the 1980 version of the Bankers Blanket Bond, Standard Form No. 24. The 1980 form substituted the phrase "except when" for the phrase "unless the" so as to provide a simpler, more easily read text. The exclusion removes from coverage loss of property contained in a customer's safe deposit box, "except when" the insured is legally liable for the loss and the loss is covered under Insuring Agreement (A). The safe deposit box exclusion has been in the Bankers Blanket Bond since the earliest forms. In 2004, the language "the Insured is legally liable therefor and the loss is" was removed.

ANNOTATIONS

NONE

SECONDARY SOURCES

NONE

G. Travelers' Checks

    (g) loss through cashing or paying forged or altered travelers' checks or travelers' checks bearing forged

endorsements, except when covered under Insuring Agreement (A); or loss of unsold travelers' checks or unsold money orders placed in the custody of the Insured with authority to sell, unless (a) the Insured is legally liable for such loss and (b) such checks or money orders are later paid or honored by the drawer thereof, except when covered under Insuring Agreement (A);

COMMENT

In 1969, the word "cashing" was added to this exclusion. Additional changes in the language of this exclusion came in the 1980 version of the Bankers Blanket Bond, Standard Form No. 24 and were editorial in nature. These changes resulted in a more streamlined and simpler text. In 2004, the second clause of the exclusion was revised to read, "or loss of unsold travelers' checks or unsold money orders in the custody of the Insured with authority to sell, unless (a) the Insured, by Written contract, has agreed to indemnify the drawer of the travelers checks or money orders for such loss and (b) such checks or money orders are later paid or honored by said drawer."

Except when the loss is covered under Insuring Agreement (A) (Fidelity), the following losses are excluded by operation of Exclusion (g): (1) loss through cashing or paying forged or altered travelers' checks or travelers' checks bearing forged endorsements; and (2) loss of unsold travelers' checks or unsold money orders placed in the custody of the insured with authority to sell, unless the insured is legally liable for such loss and such checks or money orders are later paid or honored by the drawer.

ANNOTATIONS

NONE

SECONDARY SOURCES

Toni Scott Reed, *Coverage Under Insuring Agreements (D) and (E): Has the Insured Satisfied All Required Elements* (unpublished paper at the Midwinter 2010 Meeting of the American Bar Association, FSLIC).

H. Employee

(h) loss caused by an Employee, except when covered under Insuring Agreement (A) or when covered under Insuring Agreement (B) or (C) and resulting directly from misplacement, mysterious unexplainable disappearance or destruction of or damage to Property;

COMMENT

This exclusion was added in the 1980 version of the Bankers Blanket Bond, Standard Form No. 24. In its original form, this exclusion limited the bond's coverage for employee-caused loss to the coverage provided under Insuring Agreement (A), and it excluded from coverage under the bond "loss caused by an Employee, except when covered under Insuring Agreement (A)."

In 1986, with the introduction of the Financial Institution Bond, Standard Form No. 24, this exclusion was supplemented with a second clause to the carve-out language of the exclusion. The 1986 version of this exclusion, with the supplementary language set forth in italics, provides for the exclusion of:

(h) loss caused by an Employee, except when covered under Insuring Agreement (A) *or when covered under Insuring Agreement (B) or (C) and resulting directly from misplacement, mysterious unexplainable disappearance or destruction of or damage to Property.*

The carve-out was added to make it clear that, while loss caused by the dishonesty of an employee was limited to that coverage provided by Insuring Agreement (A) (Fidelity), the bond also provided coverage for certain employee-related property losses otherwise covered by Insuring Agreement (B) (On Premises) or Insuring Agreement (C) (In Transit). Coverage for such employee-related property losses often was added to the bond by rider prior to its inclusion by way of a carve-out to this exclusion.

The 2004 version of the exclusion was revised to read:

> (h) loss caused by an Employee, except when covered under Insuring Agreement (A) *or when covered under Insuring Agreement (B) or (C) and resulting directly from unintentional acts of the Employee causing mysterious unexplainable disappearance, misplacement, destruction of or damage to Property.*

ANNOTATIONS

4th Cir. 1965 (S.C.). The insured misrepresented financial statements to deceive the insurance commissioner of the bank, which was considering the grant of a loan to the insured. The stockholders, who owned seventy-five percent of the insured's stock, were effectively the sole stockholders and the only directors of the closely held insured. The bond was intended to protect the corporation from the fraud or dishonesty of employees, not to protect its creditors from the fraud or dishonesty of the stockholders and directors. Here, the individuals were not "Employees" of the corporation, thus, the exclusion was inapplicable. *Kerr v. Aetna Cas. & Sur. Co.*, 350 F.2d 146, 154-55.

7th Cir. 2009 (Ill.). The court affirmed the district court's finding that the bank's losses were covered under the insuring agreement, and determined that the employee exclusion did not apply. The bank suffered $307,000 of losses as a result of a customer cashing worthless checks. The insurer argued that the employee exclusion precluded coverage because the bank's employees failed to follow bank policy. The court disagreed with the insurer's reading of the exclusion and stated that "[the customer's] on premises fraud was the actual and direct cause of the bank's loss; the bank employees' *failure to prevent* the loss does not trigger Exclusion (h)." *First State Bank of Monticello v. Ohio Cas. Ins. Co.*, 555 F.3d 564, 571-72.

7th Cir. 2007 (Wis.). The insured bank lost approximately $1.7 million after it extended credit to a used-car dealership. The credit was partially based on the dealership's providing the bank with signed leases.

However, the dealership's president forged signatures on leases that were either fictitious or altered. The insurer argued that had the employees properly investigated the collateral, they would have realized that the leases were forged. However, the court explained that that is an overbroad reading of the employee exclusion because bank employees are "intermediaries in every forger-related bank loss." Exclusions "do not operate as complete cancellations of coverage granted in the insuring agreements," which is what would occur under the insurer's reading of the exclusion. *First Nat'l Bank of Manitowoc v. Cincinnati Ins. Co.*, 485 F.3d 971, 980-81.

8th Cir. 1994 (Mo.). The insured bank sustained losses from cashing customer's checks and checks drawn by the customer's employees to third parties. The customer's employees signed the checks with the names of other persons and presented the checks with forged endorsements. The insured's employees never enforced the bank's policy of requiring endorsement by the presenter of third-party checks. The customer declared bankruptcy and sued the bank for the wrongful check-cashing transactions. The Eighth Circuit concluded that the "Employee" exclusion applied because the insured's losses resulted directly from the acts of employees of the insured. Thus, the "Employee" exclusion precluded coverage under the bond. *Empire Bank v. Fid. & Deposit Co. of Md.*, 27 F.3d 333, 335-36.

S.D. Miss. 2012. An executive vice president of the bank was discovered to have conducted fraudulent transactions where he forged signatures, made unauthorized withdrawals, and released collateral. The insurer argued that as the loss resulted "from theft, and not from misplacement ... or damage to property, then exclusion (h) bars coverage . . . ." The court held that the exclusion "unambiguously excludes coverage under the insuring agreement for losses caused by an employee unless the loss is caused by the 'misplacement, mysterious unexplainable disappearance or destruction of or damage to Property.'" The bank's claim fell within the Employee exclusion, which precluded coverage. *BankInsure v. Peoples Bank of the S.*, 866 F. Supp. 2d 577, 580.

W.D. Mo. 1993. The employee exclusion was applicable because the insured's losses were caused by the insured's employees' failure to comply with the insured's own internal policies and procedures. *Empire Bank v. Fid. & Deposit Co. of Md.,* 828 F. Supp. 675, 678-80.

D. Vt. 2001. The insured assigned its rights under the bond to a customer who obtained a verdict in his favor on the claims of fraudulent misrepresentation, negligent misrepresentation, and negligent failure to disclose against two employees of the insured. The court found that the language of the bond, including the section headings and plain meaning of the terms used in the bond, and Exclusion (h) necessarily precluded the determination that the customer's losses were direct losses as required by the bond. The insured is covered for losses caused by its employee's dishonesty, not for injuries arising from its employee's tortious conduct. *Patrick v. St. Paul Fire & Marine Ins.,* No. 1:99CV314, 2001 WL 828251, at *3.

Minn. 1976. The court held that the insured's losses arising from allegedly fraudulent acts of the bank were not covered under the bond. The directors of the bank knew of the questionable transactions and the facts surrounding them. The court concluded that the acts of the directors constituted the acts of the bank. *Farmers & Merch. State Bank of Pierz v. St. Paul Fire & Marine Ins. Co.,* 242 N.W.2d 840, 843-44.

SECONDARY SOURCES

Samuel J. Arena, Jr. & Jason W. Glasgow, *"On Premises" Coverage: The Bad Exchange Scam* (unpublished paper presented at the at the Fall 2010 Meeting of the American Bar Association, FSLIC).

Cole S. Kain, *Alter Ego Defense*, VII FID. L.J. 217 (2001).

John R. Riddle, *Defense Cost Coverage Under Financial Institution Bonds and the Interplay between Fidelity Bonds and D&O and E&O Policies* (unpublished paper presented at the Surety & Fidelity Claims Institute Annual Meeting, June 2011).

I. Trading Loss

(i) **loss resulting directly or indirectly from trading, with or without the knowledge of the Insured, whether or not represented by any indebtedness or balance shown to be due the Insured on any customer's account, actual or fictitious, and notwithstanding any act or omission on the part of any Employee in connection with any account relating to such trading, indebtedness, or balance, except when covered under Insuring Agreements (D) or (E);**

COMMENT

The trading loss exclusion was added to the 1980 version of the Bankers Blanket Bond, Standard Form No. 24. The 1980 revisions saw an adoption of the language of the Stockbrokers Bankers Blanket Bond, Standard Form No. 14. Prior to its addition to the bond form, this exclusion had been added with some frequency by way of a rider. The term "trading" was not separately defined. This exclusion was not modified when the Financial Institution Bond, Standard Form No. 24 was introduced in 1986.

By its clear and unambiguous terms, this exclusion includes within its scope loss resulting directly or indirectly from trading, with or without the insured's knowledge, except to the extent such loss is covered under Insuring Agreement (D) (Forgery or Alteration) or Insuring Agreement (E) (Securities). Trading loss resulting from employee dishonesty is excluded from coverage. In 2004, Insuring Agreement (A) (Fidelity) was added to Insuring Agreements (D) and (E) as carve-outs to the exclusion.

ANNOTATIONS

2d Cir. 1989 (N.Y.). The insured's employee induced investors to invest money based on employee's misrepresentations that he would follow a conservative investment strategy. The strategy was reckless, and the insured sustained losses. The insured's receiver sued the insurer for coverage under the bond. In reversing the trial court, the Second Circuit held that the losses resulted from bad trades. The exclusion's purpose is to "exempt from coverage losses caused by market forces, misjudgments of those forces by buyers and sellers of securities, or various errors or omissions... in the course of trading." Thus, the losses were not covered by operation of the "trading" exclusion. *Glusband v. Fittin Cunningham & Lauzon, Inc.*, 892 F.2d 208, 211-12.

2d Cir. 1978 (N.Y.). A mutual fund sought recovery for losses resulting from the acts of its president who was bribed to knowingly acquire securities at manipulated prices. Reversing the trial court, the Second Circuit noted that where the insured is a regulated investment company and not a broker, the fraudulent purchase of securities by an employee "may well be considered" outside the contemplated meaning of trading. Moreover, the bond at issue was a "statutory bond," which must be read to afford coverage for the "larceny and embezzlement" of a company officer. Thus, the court concluded that the trading loss exclusion was inapplicable, and the insurer was liable to the insured on the bond. *Index Fund, Inc. v. Ins. Co. of N. Am.*, 580 F.2d 1158, 1161-63.

3d Cir. 1954 (Pa.). A securities broker sought to recover for losses incurred when an employee made unauthorized use of a customer "mark-up account" to buy and sell securities. The Third Circuit determined that the trading loss exclusion was applicable to such transactions; the term "trading" is not to be equated solely with authorized trading; and although protection against such losses may be of predominant importance to a securities broker, the clause cannot be ignored within the bond without doing violence to the plain meaning of the insurance contract. The court made passing mention of the insurer's assertion that such coverage is available at a "substantially higher premium." *Roth v. Md. Cas. Co.*, 209 F.2d 371, 373-74.

4th Cir. 1938 (N.C.). A brokerage subsidiary sought recovery for a variety of losses, among which were included funds that an employee wrongfully misappropriated to finance a series of securities trades which she carried out through another broker. The trading losses exclusion was held inapplicable because none of the transactions involved use of the insured's name or credit and the insured had no liability thereon. The loss resulted solely from the dishonest use of the insured's funds, and coverage was determined to exist. *In re Schluter, Green & Co.*, 93 F.2d 810, 812-13.

6th Cir. 1990 (Ohio). The insured made a claim for losses arising out of lost repurchase agreements. The transactions involving the repurchase agreements were handled in a sloppy fashion. Upon reconciling the statements for the repurchase agreements, it was discovered that some of the securities underlying the repurchase agreements were missing. The Sixth Circuit determined that the insured's losses were not market losses, and, thus, the "trading" exclusion was inapplicable to bar coverage. *First Fed. Sav. & Loan Ass'n of Toledo v. Fid. & Deposit Co. of Md.*, 895 F.2d 254, 260-61.

7th Cir. 1989 (Wis.). The insured sought coverage for losses it suffered as a result of the malfeasance of a former employee of the insured's title company subsidiary. The court found that the exclusion precluded the insured from recover, as the losses resulted from dishonest employee's issuance of fraudulent policies. *Cont'l Corp. v. Aetna Cas. & Sur. Co.*, 892 F.2d 540, 543-47.

8th Cir. 1985 (Neb.). An insured grain trading business sustained losses due to poor trades. An employee of the grain trading business forged the company's books to make the company look more profitable. In the meantime, the employee tried to improve the company's profitability in hopes that eventually the company would recoup the losses. The employee made bad trades, and the insured's loss worsened. The Eighth Circuit determined that the trading exclusion applied to the losses despite the fact that the insured was not a commodity brokerage house. The court relied on the trial court's consideration of the caption to the rider for the trading exclusion, the exclusion's endorsement, and extrinsic evidence to support its decision. *Lincoln Grain, Inc. v. Aetna Cas. & Sur. Co.*, 756 F.2d 75, 76-78.

9th Cir. 1979 (Cal.). A mutual fund sought to recover for losses resulting from the acquisition of securities at manipulated prices upon the recommendation of a bribed employee of the insured's independent investment advisor. The Ninth Circuit affirmed the judgment for the insurer and determined that: (1) the term "trading" is not ambiguous; is not commonly understood to apply only to the activities of stockbrokers;

SECTION 2 — EXCLUSIONS

and the exclusionary language could have been waived for an additional premium which the insured declined; and (2) statutory mandates of a fidelity bond, with which the trading loss exclusion is arguably in conflict, extend solely to the officers and employees of the mutual fund, not to the employees of an independent investment advisor. *Research Equity Fund, Inc. v. Ins. Co. of N. Am.,* 602 F.2d 200, 203-05.

9th Cir. 1974 (Cal.). The trustee of a bankrupt municipal bond broker sought recovery for a variety of losses including the repurchase of depressed or delinquent issues for the personal benefit of controlling shareholders or in consequence of customer sales induced by fraudulent misrepresentations. The Ninth Circuit affirmed summary judgment for insurer and determined that the repurchase losses came within the trading loss exclusion and, to the extent customer monies were wrongfully diverted to payment of the insured's operating expenses, these are not direct losses, but third-party liabilities for which no coverage is afforded. *Bass v. Am. Ins. Co.,* 493 F.2d 590, 591-93.

D.D.C. 1962. A stock brokerage sought recovery for losses resulting from customer's short check given to procure a stock purchase for its account. After first concluding that the employee's carelessness in accepting the check did not rise to the level of dishonest or fraudulent within the meaning of the bond, the trading loss exclusion was held applicable and precluded recovery for the customer's admitted fraud. While there may be a technical distinction in the securities business between trading for one's own account and a purchase transacted for a customer's account, the term employed in the bond should not be given such restricted meaning, "but the same meaning it has in any mercantile business, namely, the buying and selling of commodities—in the instant case, the buying and selling of securities on a customer's account." *Sade v. Nat'l Sur. Corp.,* 203 F. Supp. 680, 685-86.

E.D. La. 2011. The insured sought recovery under the insurer's commercial crime policy for losses suffered as a result of the insured's investments in the Bernard Madoff Ponzi scheme. Although the insured argued that the losses were not a result of its investment in the Ponzi scheme, but rather by Madoff's actions, the court determined that the losses were "sufficiently connected to the investment in the Madoff Ponzi scheme as to fall under the indirect provision of the Trading Loss

Exclusion of the insurance policy." *Methodist Health Sys. Found., Inc. v. Hartford Fire Ins. Co.,* 834 F. Supp. 2d 493, 497.

W.D. Mo. 1984. A customer fraudulently used the securities account of his employer for his own securities transactions. The court determined that the exclusion applied to deny recovery. The court reasoned that the historical context of the exclusion, adoption of the clause from stockbroker's bonds, and discussions by the American Bankers Association publication indicate that a reasonable banker would understand the "trading" exclusion to bar recovery for losses resulting from the legal and illegal buying and selling of securities. *Shearson/Express, Inc. v. First Cont'l Bank & Trust Co.,* 579 F. Supp. 1305, 1311-13.

S.D.N.Y. 1967. The insured stockbroker sought to recover for more than $1.2 million worth of short checks given by a corporate customer to procure delivery of various stocks. The trading loss exclusion was held applicable and judgment entered for the insurer on all of a variety of issues. Trading "means the operation of the usual occupation of buying and selling stocks," and even though the purchase by the insured had been completed, collection from the customer was still "an inherent part of the completion of the transaction." *Sutro Bros. & Co. v. Indem. Ins. Co. of N. Am.,* 264 F. Supp. 273, 289.

Del. Ch. 2010. The insureds alleged that the millions of dollars they invested in what was later determined to be Bernard Madoff's Ponzi scheme was stolen by an agent of the insured. The court stated that the purpose of the trading loss exclusion was to "exempt from coverage losses caused by market forces, misjudgments of those forces by buyers and sellers of securities, or various errors or omissions." The court concluded that the trading loss exclusion did not apply, because Madoff stole the insureds' money; he did not lose it through "reckless, improvident, or even dishonest trading." *Mass. Mut. Life Ins. Co. v. Certain Underwriters at Lloyd's of London,* No. 4791-VCL, 2010 WL 2929552, at *13-14.

La. Ct. App. 1970. A customer claiming to have been misled into unsuitable investments sought recovery against municipal bond broker. The municipal bond broker later impleaded its insurer seeking indemnification for its defense costs and potential accountability to the plaintiff. The broker prevailed on the primary claim because no customer relationship existed, and the trading loss exclusion was held applicable to preclude any recovery against the insurer. In reaching its decision, the court found that, irrespective of employee fraud or dishonesty being at the root of the alleged loss, the claimed loss was at least the indirect result of trading and rejected "the premise that there can be no trading unless it is authorized, legally executed and honestly accomplished." *Hepler v. Fireman's Fund Ins. Co.,* 239 So. 2d 669, 677-79.

N.J. Super. Ct. App. Div. 1993. The insured made a claim for recovery of losses arising out of mortgages and a mortgage pool. The insured argued in a prior action that the mortgage pools were "securities," and in this action, it contended that the mortgage pools were not securities and, therefore, not subject to the "trading loss" exclusion. The court determined that the doctrine of judicial estoppel precluded the insured's inconsistent positions, and the court declined to address the applicability of the exclusion. *N.J. Sav. & Loan Ass'n v. Fid. & Deposit Co. of Md.,* 660 A.2d 1287, 1298-99.

N.Y. 1964. A brokerage firm sought recovery for losses resulting from the acknowledged fraud of one of its customers on whose behalf various purchase and separate short sale commitments were entered. The court reversed the judgment for the insured, following a line of cases in which trading was given its generally accepted meaning and not a restricted application to transactions for the broker's own account. *Condon v. Nat'l Sur. Corp.,* 254 N.Y.S.2d 620, 625.

SECONDARY SOURCES

Mark S. Gamell, *The Impact of the Securities Laws on the Financial Institution Bond* (unpublished paper presented at 1994 Annual Meeting of the Surety Claims Institute, June 22-24, 1994).

John T. Harris & David R. Glissman, *Fidelity Exposure for Repo Losses: A Billion Dollar Time Bomb?* (unpublished paper presented at 1986 Annual Meeting of the Surety Claims Institute, Jan. 1, 1986).

Mark Johnson & Peter Haley, *Securities Fraud and the Financial Institution Bond* (unpublished paper presented at the 2011 Midwinter Meeting of the American Bar Association, FSLIC Session).

William P. Sullivan, Jr., *The Trading Exclusion in the Brokers Blanket Bond* (unpublished paper presented at Meeting of ABA Tort and Insurance Practice Section, Fidelity and Surety Law Committee, Aug. 12, 1979).

Robert K. Tucker, *Insuring Agreement (A) and Coverage Exclusions Under the Stockbroker's Blanket Bond* (unpublished paper presented at Meeting of ABA Tort and Insurance Practice Section, Fidelity and Surety Law Committee, August 7, 1988).

J. Teller's Cash Shortage

(j) **shortage in any teller's cash due to error, regardless of the amount of such shortage, and any shortage in any teller's cash which is not in excess of the normal shortage in the teller's cash in the office where such shortage shall occur shall be presumed to be due to error;**

COMMENT

This exclusion first appeared in the 1941 version of the Bankers Blanket Bond, Standard Form No. 24. In the 1980 version of that bond, the word "assumed" was changed to the word "presumed" in the last clause of the bond to "shall be presumed to be due to error." The Financial Institution Bond, Standard Form No. 24, introduced in 1986, included the 1980 version of Exclusion (j). The language of Exclusion (j) in the 2004 version of Form 24 was significantly reduced to "shortage in any teller's cash due to error." The clear and unambiguous language of this exclusion is based on the rationale that teller error is a normal business risk that should be borne by the financial institution. This exclusion has resulted in no reported decisions.

ANNOTATIONS

NONE

SECONDARY SOURCES

NONE

K. Credit, Debt, Charge Cards

(k) loss resulting directly or indirectly from the use or purported use of credit, debit, charge, access, convenience, identification or other cards
  (1) in obtaining credit or funds, or
  (2) in gaining access to automated mechanical devices which, on behalf of the Insured, disburse Money, accept deposits, cash checks, drafts or similar written instruments or make credit card loans, or
  (3) in gaining access to point of sale terminals, customer-bank communication terminals, or similar electronic terminals of electronic funds transfer systems,
  whether such cards were issued, or purport to have been issued, by the Insured or by anyone other than the Insured, except when covered under Insuring Agreement (A);

COMMENT

This exclusion was added in the 1980 version of the Bankers Blanket Bond, Standard Form No. 24. Prior to its incorporation in the bond form as Exclusion (k), it was added by rider. The scope of the exclusion was clarified in 1986 with the introduction of the Financial Institution Bond, Standard Form No. 24 when the words "or purported use" were added to the initial clause of the exclusion. Thus, under the 1986 language, financial institutions could no longer argue that a card actually had to have existed for the exclusion to apply. Under the 1980 language, such an argument could have prevailed where the fraud involved card numbers, but no card existed and, therefore, there was no actual "use" of a card. Other than this revision, the language was not changed. The 2004 version of the exclusion eliminated "identification" from the list of specific types of cards governed by the exclusion, and capitalized "written" in subpart (2).

Under this exclusion, unless the loss is covered under Insuring Agreement (A) (Fidelity), all loss resulting from the use or purported use of credit, debt, charge, access, convenience, identification, or other cards in connection with the exclusions enumerated in subparagraphs (1), (2) and (3) is excluded regardless of whether the cards were issued or even purportedly issued by the insured or anyone else.

ANNOTATIONS

S.D.N.Y. 1991. The insured bank incurred losses when the credit card sales drafts deposited by a merchant proved uncollectible. The court noted that the credit card exclusion may be ambiguous regarding schemes where the authorization codes and numbers of the credit cards serve as the basis for fraud. The court subsequently declined to address the applicability of the exclusion to the matter before the court. *Broadway Nat'l Bank v. Progressive Cas. Ins. Co.*, 775 F. Supp. 123, 128-129.

SECONDARY SOURCES

Samuel J. Arena, Jr., and Jason W. Glasgow, *"On Premises" Coverage: The Bad Exchange Scam* (unpublished paper presented at the 2010 FSLIC Fall Program).

Gilbert J. Schroeder, *Claims Under Financial Institution & Commercial Fidelity Bonds for Losses Due to Credit Card Chargebacks* (unpublished paper presented at the 2003 FSLC Fall Program).

SECTION 2 — EXCLUSIONS   305

L. Automated Mechanical Devices

(l)   loss involving automated mechanical devices which, on behalf of the Insured, disburse Money, accept deposits, cash checks, drafts or similar written instruments or make credit card loans, unless such automated mechanical devices are situated within an office of the Insured which is permanently staffed by an Employee whose duties are those usually assigned to a bank teller, even though public access is from outside the confines of such office, but in no event shall the Underwriter be liable for loss (including loss of Property)
  (1) as a result of damage to such automated mechanical devices from vandalism or malicious mischief perpetrated from outside such office, or
  (2) as a result of failure of such automated mechanical devices to function properly, or
  (3) through misplacement or mysterious unexplainable disappearance while such Property is located within any such automated mechanical devices, except when covered under Insuring Agreement (A);

COMMENT

Exclusion (l) was added in the 1980 version of the Bankers Blanket Bond. Prior to its incorporation into the bond form as Exclusion (l), it was added by rider. This exclusion was not changed when the Financial Institution Bond was introduced in 1986. In 2004, the language of Exclusion (l) was revised by capitalizing "written" and deleting "from vandalism or malicious mischief" from subpart (1). The 2011 version of the exclusion revised the language of subpart (3) from "while such Property is" to "of Property."

Under the exclusion, there is no coverage for loss involving automated mechanical devices that perform certain enumerated functions on behalf of the insured financial institution, unless they are located within an office of the insured financial institution and are permanently staffed by an employee who functions as a bank teller. It is the employee's job functions, and not the employee's title, that is determinative. Once the "office of the Insured" test is met, the carve-out to this exclusion applies regardless of whether public access to the automated mechanical device is from inside or outside the confines of the "office of the Insured." Exclusion (l) also enumerates additional circumstances involving automated mechanical devices, which in no event will fall within the coverage of the bond.

ANNOTATIONS

NONE

SECONDARY SOURCES

NONE

M. Extortion

(m) loss through the surrender of Property away from an office of the Insured as a result of a threat
   (1) to do bodily harm to any person, except loss of Property in transit in the custody of any person acting as messenger provided that when such transit was initiated there was no knowledge by the Insured of any such threat, or
   (2) to do damage to the premises or property of the Insured, except when covered under Insured Agreement (A);

COMMENT

The 1980 version of the Bankers Blanket Bond incorporated this exclusion. For many years this exclusion has been added to the bond by rider. The exclusion makes it clear that unless the dishonesty of an employee is involved, the policy gives no coverage for extortion losses whether the threat be made to person or property. Limited extortion coverage can be purchased separately and added by rider. Since the underwriters started attaching extortion exclusion riders to the bond, there have been no reported cases allowing coverage for extortion losses.

In 2004, Exclusion (m) was amended to exclude "loss resulting directly or indirectly from surrender of property away from an office of the insured as a result of:

(1) kidnapping,
(2) payment of ransom,
(3) threats of bodily harm to any person, except the custodian of the property, or of damage to the premises or property of the Insured, or
(4) actual disappearance, damage, destruction, confiscation, or theft of property intended as ransom or extortion payment while held or conveyed by a person duly authorized by the Insured to have custody of such property, except when covered under Insuring Agreement (A)."

ANNOTATIONS

NONE

SECONDARY SOURCES

NONE

N. Erroneous Entry

   (n) loss resulting directly or indirectly from payments made or withdrawals from a depositor's account involving erroneous credits to such account, unless such payments or withdrawals are physically received by such depositor or representative of such depositor who is within the office of the Insured at the time of such payment or withdrawal, or except when covered under Insuring Agreement (A);

COMMENT

This exclusion expressly allocates primary risk of loss resulting from erroneous credits to a deposit account to the bank. Unless employee dishonesty is involved, there is no coverage for payments or withdrawal of funds erroneously credited to a depositor's account unless the depositor or his representative is present on the insured's premises at the time of the withdrawal and the payments or withdrawals are physically received. The word "physically" was added in the 1980 revisions, which stresses the intention of the underwriter to exclude coverage arising from erroneous credits unless the depositor physically receives the withdrawal or payment while on the bank's premises. This provision has been interpreted by one court to apply to circumstances where the "erroneous credit" arose from the bank's acceptance for deposit of checks which contained fraudulent or unauthorized endorsements. The 2004 and 2011 versions of Exclusion (n) do not include the "unless such payments or withdrawals are physically received by such depositor or representative of such depositor who is within the office of the Insured at the time of such payment or withdrawal" exception to the exclusion.

ANNOTATIONS

7th Cir. 1991 (Ill.). A bank filed a declaratory judgment action seeking determination of whether the Financial Institution Bond covered potential loss as a result of allowing customer to wrongfully deposit misappropriated checks. A customer of the bank misappropriated more than $100,000 in checks that had been drawn to the order of his employer by endorsing the checks with a rubber stamp that read "for deposit only" and his account number. The checks were then deposited into his personal account at the bank. The lower court granted summary judgment for the insured. On appeal, the court reversed, holding the on premises loss provision did not provide coverage because the checks were stolen from the customer's premises and, thus, the theft did not take place on the premises of the insured. In addition, the amount that the customer's employee received while on the premises of the insured did not exceed the insured's $10,000 deductible. The court held that the exception to the exclusion required that the account holder must be physically present in the bank when he receives the money in order for the exception to apply. *Alpine State Bank v. Ohio Cas. Ins. Co.*, 941 F.2d 554, 560-61.

N.D. Ill. 2004. The insured bank sought recovery after it made payment on two stolen checks. A man entered the bank claiming he was an employee of BBI Enterprises, Ltd. ("BBI"). He opened an account in the name of BBI and deposited two checks drawn on the account of Lear Corporation and made payable to BBI. The bank did not require the depositor to endorse the checks, and instead, a bank employee endorsed the checks with a stamp. When the checks cleared two days later, the depositor telephoned the bank and requested payment of $400,200.00 to another account holder at the bank. The bank honored the request and transferred the sum. It was later discovered that the deposited checks were stolen and actually issued to a company similarly named. In addition to finding that the loss was not covered under the "on premises" insuring agreement, the court held that Exclusion (n) precluded coverage because the bank "erroneously credited the account when it accepted checks for deposit without requiring and verifying an endorsement for [the depositor] at the time of presentment." The court rejected the insured's argument that funds deposited under false pretenses could not be "erroneously" deposited. *Private Bank & Trust Co. v. Progressive Cas. Ins. Co.*, No. 03 C 6031, 2004 WL 1144048, at *5-6.

SECONDARY SOURCES

Mark S. Gamell & Joseph G. Perry, *The Potential Income Exclusion and Principal Other Exclusions and Definitions*, in FINANCIAL INSTITUTION BONDS 471, 492-96 (Duncan L. Clore ed., 3d ed. 2008).

O. Uncollected Funds

    (o) loss resulting directly or indirectly from payments made or withdrawals from a depositor's account involving items of deposit which are not finally paid for any reason, including but not limited to Forgery or any other fraud, except when covered under Insuring Agreement (A);

COMMENT

This exclusion was the second half of Exclusion (e) in the 1969 version of the Bankers Blanket Bond standard form. The 1980 version treated it separately and stressed that, unless employee dishonesty is involved, all losses arising from the drawing on uncollected funds where the depositor does not physically receive the payment on the premises of the insured are excluded. The 1986 Financial Institution Bond removed an exception to the application of the exclusion where funds are received by a depositor on the bank's premises. The current exclusion is broader in application as it applies equally to claims arising from items which are not finally paid, even if the depositor receives payment or withdraws the deposited funds while on the premises of the bank.

This provision is commonly referred to as the "uncollected funds exclusion" or the "check kiting exclusion." While the exclusion is intended to preclude coverage for loss resulting from a check kiting scheme, the plain language is broader in its application. Until an item of deposit is "finally paid," any loss resulting from payments or withdrawals from the account on which an item of deposit is not finally paid is excluded from coverage. While most courts applying this exclusion have abstained from an analysis of, or reference to, the Uniform Commercial Code, an analysis of the state's law regarding when an instrument is "finally paid" may impact the application of this exclusion. Most states address this issue through the adoption of Section 4-215 of the Uniform Commercial Code, which discusses when an item is "finally paid." Since the revisions in the 1986 Financial Institution Bond, courts have acknowledged that, while a check kiting loss is clearly excluded from coverage, the application of Exclusion (o) applies to all circumstances where the loss arises from the deposit of an item which is not "finally paid."

ANNOTATIONS

5th Cir. 1996 (Miss.). The insured's loss involved a check kiting scheme as well as forged checks negotiated on a fully funded trust account. The court held that checks included in the check kiting scheme were excluded, finding that Exclusion (o) is meant generally, though not exclusively, to prohibit coverage for losses due to a check kiting scheme.

Because certain checks were fraudulently negotiated without sufficient funds to support them, the very definition of a check kite, Exclusion (o) applied. Court held, however, that forged checks negotiated on a trust account that had sufficient funds did not fall within exclusion. *USF&G v. Planters Bank & Trust Co.,* 77 F.3d 863, 867-68.

5th Cir. 1992 (Tex.). A savings and loan association brought action against the insurer on savings and loan blanket bond arising from the customer's check kiting scheme. On appeal, the court reversed the lower court's summary judgment decision in favor of insured on the grounds that the loan exclusion precluded coverage. In a lengthy footnote, the court discusses the distinction between the loan exclusion and the uncollected funds exclusion, finding that, where the bank advanced funds in reliance on a customer's representations regarding his ability and willingness to pay repeated overdrafts, the loan exclusion clause, rather than the uncollected funds exclusion clause, applied. *First Tex. Sav. Ass'n v. Reliance Ins. Co.,* 950 F.2d 1171, 1174-78 & n.6.

7th Cir. 1984 (Wisc.). The insured obtained coverage for loss resulting from a check kiting scheme. The court found that the exception to the exclusion was unambiguous and that the "only way losses from uncollected funds merited coverage was if the depositor was physically within the office of the insured at the time the bank makes payments out of the account." *Bradley Bank v. Hartford Acc. & Indem. Co.,* 737 F.2d 657, 659-61.

9th Cir. 1986 (Cal.). The court applied an exclusion provision similar to Exclusion (o) to preclude coverage for loss suffered from deposits that were credited to the customer's account, but were not collected because the endorsements on the checks were forged. The bank's argument that the exclusion applied only to check kiting losses was rejected. *Mitsu Mfrs. Bank v. Fed. Ins. Co.,* 795 F.2d 827, 829-30.

N.D. Cal. 1986. An action brought by the insured to collect for losses sustained when credit card sales drafts proved uncollectible. The court held that the uncollected funds exclusion is not limited to losses incurred through check kiting, but also applied when loss resulted from credit card sales drafts which were uncollected by reason of a fraud perpetrated on the insured. The on premises exception to the uncollected funds exclusion was held not to apply because the insured did not make an irrevocable commitment to pay checks drawn against the depositor's account until after the depositor had left the premises. Any sight postings done while the depositor was on the premises were expressly revocable under the bank card merchant agreement entered into between the depositor and the bank. That agreement allowed the bank to debit an account at any time for the amount of authorized credit card sales drafts erroneously credited to the account. *Bay Area Bank v. Fid. & Deposit Co. of Md.,* 629 F. Supp. 693, 695-96.

N.D. Ill. 1992. The insured bank brought claim against its insurer on a Financial Institution Bond for losses resulting from check kiting, unpaid overdrafts and certain intrabank transfers of funds. The insurer moved for summary judgment on the grounds that Exclusions (o) and (e) precluded coverage. The court held that the exception in Exclusion (o) regarding application of Insuring Agreement (A) applied because the scheme involved an employee of the bank. The court went on to find that whether the employee had the manifest intent to cause a loss was a question of fact and denied the motion. *Affiliated Bank/Morton Grove v. Hartford Acc. & Indem. Co.,* No. 91-C-4446, 1992 WL 91761, at *9.

D. Kan. 1982. The insured under a blanket bond sought recovery of loss resulting from a check kiting scheme. The court held that all losses suffered by the insured resulted from the insured crediting uncollected items of deposit to depositor's account. The exception to this exclusion was held not to apply when the withdrawals were made during bookkeeping functions or computer data processing procedures that would normally occur after normal banking hours. "The plain meaning and common sense interpretation of this provision refers to payments or withdrawals in cash or by a negotiable instrument such as a cashier's check to the depositor or his representative over the counter within the bank." *Sec. Nat'l Bank of Kansas City v. Cont'l Ins. Co.,* 586 F. Supp. 139, 146.

D. Neb. 1992. A bank sought coverage under Insuring Agreement (D) of the Financial Institution Bond for loss incurred when the bank accepted a certified check for deposit. After crediting customer's account for the "certified check," the bank was advised that the "certifying" bank did not in fact certify the check and that the drawee was not a customer of that bank. The court held that Exclusion (o) precluded coverage even though plaintiff argued that Exclusion (o) applied only to non-certified items. Although Exclusion (o) is typically directed at excluding coverage for check kiting schemes, the language of the exclusion specifically excludes coverage for losses of any kind involving items of deposit that are not finally paid. The reason that an item of deposit is not finally paid has no significance under the exclusion. *Ralston Bank v. Kan. Banker Sur. Co.,* 794 F. Supp. 896, 898.

N.D.N.Y. 2010. The insured sought coverage for a loss due to a check kiting scheme. The court held that the bond's uncollected funds exclusion was unambiguous and excluded coverage for the insured's loss. It was undisputed that the customer's cashier check was an item of deposit, that it was not finally paid, or that the loss arose from the payment of funds involving that unpaid item. Additionally, the court rejected the insured's argument that the uncollected funds exclusion conflicted with the bond's counterfeiting exclusion. *Adirondack Trust Co. v. St. Paul Mercury Ins. Co.,* No. 1:09-cv-1313, 2010 WL 2425915, at *2-4.

S.D.N.Y. 1991. The bank sued the insurer on a Financial Institution Bond for losses sustained when credit card sales drafts deposited by merchant customer proved uncollectible. The district court held that the credit card sale slips were "items of deposit" within meaning of the uncollected funds exclusion. *Broadway Nat'l Bank v. Progressive Cas. Ins. Co.,* 775 F. Supp. 123, 128-29.

D. Or. 2001. A securities brokerage firm sought coverage under a Financial Institution Bond for losses resulting from forgeries and alterations on checks. The insurer moved for summary judgment as to certain checks contending that Exclusion (o) precluded coverage. The insurer based its argument on an Oregon statute which allowed a bank to "charge back" a customer's account for dishonored items only before settlement of the item received by the bank was final. Because the bank's actions in debiting plaintiff's account were taken pursuant to the statute, insurer argued that the exclusion applied. The court disagreed and denied the motion finding that Exclusion (o) applied only when the loss was not finally paid. The court examined each check in question, finding that the items were in fact "finally paid" and, thus, the exclusion did not apply. *Bidwell & Co. v. Nat'l Union Fire Ins. Co. of Pitt., Pa.,* No. CV-00-89-HU, 2001 WL 204843, at *7-8.

Cal. Ct. App. 2002. The bank accepted a fraudulent foreign check for deposit and incurred a loss as a result thereof. The court found that an exclusion provision identical to Exclusion (o) was unambiguous and precluded coverage as the loss resulted from withdrawals from the customer's account before the fraudulent check was finally paid. The court rejected the bank's argument that the customer did not "deposit" the funds into his account because the bank informed the customer that they could not make a deposit of a foreign currency check. The court found that where the bank accepted the check and ultimately gave the customer credit in his account for the check, a deposit occurred. *Pac. Bus. Bank v. St. Paul Mercury Ins. Co.,* No. B150853, 2002 WL 31521730, at *7-8.

Fla. Dist. Ct. App. 1985. The insured sought to recover losses sustained as a result of a depositor's check kiting scheme. The depositor maintained three checking accounts and one savings account at the same bank. Because of the size of his accounts, the bank allowed the deposits to be credited without any hold pending collection. The court held that the uncollected funds exclusion applied. "It appears to us that the loss incurred here is the result of payments of funds uncollected and uncollectible because, upon presentation for payment to the bank upon which the items were drawn, there were insufficient funds." The court also held that the exception to the uncollected funds exclusion did not apply because there was no direct showing that the depositor authorized specific payments while actually on the premises. *NCNB Nat'l Bank of Fla. v. Aetna Cas. & Sur. Co.,* 477 So. 2d 579, 581-83.

Ill. App. Ct. 1998. Exclusion (o) is inapplicable when coverage under Insuring Agreement (A) (Employee Dishonesty) is applicable. *Oxford Bank & Trust v. Hartford Acc. & Indem. Co.,* 698 N.E.2d 204, 214.

N.Y. 1996. The bank made a claim under its Financial Institution Bond for loss resulting from the robbery of its messenger while the property was in transit. The court held that Exclusion (o) and the in-transit coverage provision were mutually exclusive. Exclusion (o) clearly and explicitly addresses losses due to uncollected funds, whereas the "in-transit provision" addresses loss due to bank property being physically lost, stolen or destroyed while in transit. *Flushing Sav. Bank v. Hartford Fire Ins. Co.,* 234 A.D.2d 108, 109.

SECONDARY SOURCES

Samuel J. Arena, Jr. & David M. Burkholder, *Insuring Agreement (B)— On Premises, in* FINANCIAL INSTITUTION BONDS 259, 305-08 (Duncan L. Clore ed., 3d ed. 2008).

Mark S. Gamell & Joseph G. Perry, *The Potential Income Exclusion and Principal Other Exclusions and Definitions, in* FINANCIAL INSTITUTION BONDS 471, 496-99 (Duncan L. Clore ed., 3d ed. 2008).

Scott L. Schmookler, *Insuring Agreement D, in* FINANCIAL INSTITUTION BONDS 313, 352-54 (Duncan L. Clore ed., 3d ed. 2008).

Scott L. Schmookler & Sandra M. Stone, *Check Fraud Claims: The Interplay of Financial Institution Bonds and the Uniform Commercial Code,* (unpublished paper at the 2005 Mid-Winter Meeting of the American Bar Association, FSLC).

Gary J. Valeriano, *Handling Forgery Claims and Articles 3 and 4 of the Uniform Commercial Code, in* HANDLING FIDELITY BOND CLAIMS 223, 267-69 (Michael Keeley & Sean Duffy eds., 2d ed. 2005).

David E. Wood, *Risk Allocation for Forged Checks: When Is a Check "Finally Paid" Under the Uncollected Funds Exclusion?,* VIII FID. L.J. 127 (2002).

P. Counterfeiting

    (p) loss resulting directly or indirectly from counterfeiting, except when covered under Insuring Agreements (A), (E) or (F);

COMMENT

Unless employee dishonesty is involved and coverage implicated under Insuring Agreement (A), coverage for losses due to counterfeiting is restricted to (1) loss resulting from the bank's receipt of counterfeit money (Insuring Agreement (F)) and (2) loss resulting from the bank's acceptance of or reliance upon a Certificated Security; Document of Title; deed, mortgage or other instrument conveying title to or creating or discharging a lien upon property; or a Certificate of Origin or Title (Insuring Agreement (E)).

The 2004 and 2011 versions of the Financial Institution Bond include Insuring Agreement (D) in the exceptions to the counterfeiting exclusion in order to incorporate coverage for "desktop published checks" into the bond.

ANNOTATIONS

NONE

SECONDARY SOURCES

Scott L. Schmookler, *Insuring Agreement D, in* FINANCIAL INSTITUTION BONDS 313, 347-51 (Duncan L. Clore ed., 3d ed. 2008).

Q. Tangible Personal Property

(q) loss of any tangible item of personal property which is not specifically enumerated in the paragraph defining Property and for which the Insured is legally liable, if such property is specifically insured by other insurance of any kind and in any amount obtained by the Insured, and in any event, loss of such property occurring more than 60 days after the Insured shall have become aware that it is liable for the safekeeping of such property, except when covered under Insuring Agreements (A), or (B)(2);

COMMENT

Unless employee dishonesty is involved or a loss to the bank's property is incurred during robbery, vandalism, or other similar conduct, the loss of tangible personal property, which is not expressly enumerated in the definition of "Property," is not covered if the bank or other party obtained insurance on the property (in any amount). Even if the insured has not obtained insurance covering the loss or damage to the item, the loss is not covered if the loss occurred more than sixty days after the insured became aware that it was liable for the safekeeping of the property.

The definition of "Property" is broader than those items "specifically enumerated" as it also defines "Property" generally as "tangible items of personal property which are not hereinbefore enumerated." Exclusion (q) limits the bond's coverage, generally, to loss of the items of personal property which are expressly enumerated in the definition of "Property."

The word "chattel" used in the 1969 version of the Bankers Blanket Bond was changed to "tangible personal property" in the current version. In the 1980 version, the word "obtained" in reference to acquiring insurance on the property replaced the word "effected."

In earlier versions, the exclusion's application was limited where the insurance on the property was obtained by a party other than the bank. In those circumstances, the coverage provided under the bond was excess.

In 2004, the exclusion for tangible "nonenumerated" property was re-written to be consistent with the revised ownership condition. The 2004 and 2011 versions of the Exclusion (q) exclude the following:

> (q) loss of any tangible item of personal property which is not specifically enumerated in the paragraph defining Property if such property is insured by other insurance of any kind and in any amount obtained by the Insured, and in any event, loss of such property occurring more than 60 days after the Insured shall have become aware that it owns, holds or is responsible for such property, except when covered under Insuring Agreements (A) or (B)(2);

ANNOTATIONS

NONE

SECONDARY SOURCES

NONE

R. Property in Mail or With Carrier for Hire

    (r) loss of Property while
        (1) in the mail, or
        (2) in the custody of any Transportation Company, unless covered under Insuring Agreement (C) except when covered under Insuring Agreement (A);

COMMENT

    Unless employee dishonesty is involved, loss of property while in the mail or in the custody of an organization that provides its own or leased vehicles for transportation or that provides freight forwarding or air express services is not covered under the bond unless coverage is applicable under Insuring Agreement (C) (In Transit). This exclusion was modified in the 1986 Financial Institution Bond. The prior Bankers Blanket Bond did not use the term "Transportation Company." Instead, it excluded loss of property while in the mail "or with a carrier for hire (other than an armored motor vehicle), except when covered under Insuring Agreement (A)." Since Insuring Agreement (C) provides coverage under certain circumstances where property is lost while being transported by a carrier other than an armored vehicle, the current exclusion is slightly narrower. The revision also provides more clarity and specificity regarding the scope of the exclusion.

    In the 2004 revision to the Financial Institution Bond, Exclusion (r) was modified by adding a subsection (3) for loss of property "while located on the premises of any Messenger or Transportation Company." Subsection (3) is also included in the 2011 version of the bond.

According to commentary explaining the change, subsection (3) was added to foreclose claims asserting that money stolen by an ATM servicer was "in transit" even though it was transferred to the servicer, stored at its premises, and stolen by the servicer.[9]

ANNOTATIONS

NONE

SECONDARY SOURCES

David K. Kerr, *The Potential Income and Principal Other Exclusions*, in FINANCIAL INSTITUTION BONDS 215, 223-24 (Duncan L. Clore ed., 1995).

S. Potential Income

(s) potential income, including but not limited to interest and dividends, not realized by the Insured;

COMMENT

This exclusion was first incorporated as a standard exclusion in the 1980 Bankers Blanket Bond. It emphasizes the underwriter's intention to cover only out of pocket loss and not the loss of potential income or lost earning potential in any form. As is evidenced from the cases annotated below, there is a split of authority on the application of the exclusion where the bank's claim involves fictitious or otherwise covered loans used to pay, in part, interest on prior fictitious or fraudulent loans. Insurers have consistently asserted that the exclusion evidences the intent under the bond to calculate an insured's loss as the net amount of funds which were taken from or otherwise lost by the

---

[9] Surety Association of America, Form & Rider Filing Letter, Financial Institution Bond, Standard Form No. 24 § IV (Dec. 24, 2003) (mistakenly referencing Exclusion (y)).

bank. This measure is simply the net amount of the money pocketed by the defalcator or his intended beneficiary less any recoveries received by the bank. Certain jurisdictions have allowed a bank to also recover the full principal balance of a fictitious loan even if part of the principal balance represents disbursements to satisfy the principal and interest on prior outstanding loans. This clearly is an expansion of the underwriter's intent under the plain language of the exclusion.

ANNOTATIONS

4th Cir. 1987 (N.C.). A bank brought an action to recover total outstanding principal lost through an employee's ongoing fraudulent loan scheme. The employee had initially made false loans to obtain money for personal use and, when those loans became due, paid the interest by making new loans. The insurer claimed that interest paid on prior loans should be subtracted from loss as potential income because that money represented a return on the bank's own money. The court held that the insured was liable for all of the outstanding principal balance of the notes, excluding only the recovery of interest accrued but not yet paid. *St. Paul Fire & Marine Ins. Co. v. Branch Bank & Trust Co.,* 834 F.2d 416, 417-18.

5th Cir. 1987 (La.). The insured under a comprehensive dishonesty, disappearance and destruction policy sought recovery of lost profits sustained when two employees surreptitiously submitted a bid on behalf of their individual companies deliberately underbidding their employer. The employees were awarded a five-year contract as a result. The court held that the potential income exclusion excluded coverage for loss of future profits or future income flow resulting from fraudulent or dishonest acts of employees. The court reversed and remanded on the issue of whether other losses allegedly sustained by the employee, including travel expenses, salaries, telephone services and secretarial assistance, were also excluded under the policy. *Diversified Grp., Inc. v. Van Tassel,* 806 F.2d 1275, 1278.

6th Cir. 2012 (Ohio). An insured bank sued to recover under its fidelity policy for a bank employee's theft of money from brokerage accounts of customers. The insurer argued that recovery for lost interest was excluded by the policy. The court disagreed: "The exclusion speaks to lost interest not realized by the insured, not to interest payments owed to customers. The interest payments owed to First Defiance's customers were not income to First Defiance; they were unpaid liabilities." *First Defiance Fin. Corp. v. Progressive Cas. Ins. Co.,* 688 F.3d 265, 272.

7th Cir. 1987 (Ill.). The insured, a manufacturer of sealant, brought action under comprehensive crime insurance policy for loss of income as a result of an employee's leak of a trade secret to a competitor. The insured argued that the trade secret should be treated like property and that the lost income from the theft of the trade secret was the "actual liquidated value" of the stolen trade secret. The court held that loss of income suffered by the insured was loss of potential income rather than loss analogous to theft of property and, as such, was expressly excluded from coverage by the potential income exclusion. *U.S. Gypsum Co. v. Ins. Co. of N. Am.,* 813 F.2d 856, 858-59.

8th Cir. 1990 (Iowa). A bank brought an action against an insurer under the banker's fidelity bond where insurer denied coverage under the bond for bank losses resulting from fraudulent loan and commodity/cattle schemes involving two bank clients. False financial statements, falsified loan documents and elaborate withdrawal methods were used to conceal the nature of the transactions. Although the court held that the bank sustained losses under the bond when loan proceeds were transferred to third parties, the court also held that the future interest claimed by the insured was excluded by potential income exclusion. The court held that, although the bank restructured the loan debt, sustaining a loss of future interest, the payments were not yet due and, therefore, not realized, falling squarely within the potential income exclusion. The court further held that the potential income exclusion is not ambiguous with regard to the treatment of future interest, and therefore, the court construed the provision according to its plain meaning. *First Am. State Bank v. Cont'l Ins. Co.,* 897 F.2d 319, 329.

S.D. Ga. 2007. The insured bank submitted a loss of $1,452,010.94 involving thirty-nine fraudulent loans issued by a branch vice-president. It was determined that the vice president had depleted the insured's loan proceeds checking accounts by $884,000 over the course of his scheme. The remaining $568,010.94 of the claimed loss constituted accrued interest on fraudulent loans that were capitalized or rolled over as principal into new fraudulent loans. The district court agreed with the insurer "that the 'direct loss' is determined by calculating the amount of the theft (the 'cash-out-the-door'), and that the satisfaction of old notes with new fraudulent loans was merely 'bookkeeping.'" Additionally, the lost time value of money and income the bank would have earned had the loans been legitimate were potential income and excluded by the bond. *Citizens Bank & Trust Co. v. St. Paul Mercury Ins. Co.,* No. CV305-167, 2007 WL 4973847, at *3-5.

N.D. Ill. 2006. Insured automobile dealers sought coverage under commercial crime policy for losses incurred due to dishonest activities of former employee. Dishonest employee received kickbacks in scheme whereby he sold insureds' cars to accomplice wholesalers for less than the cars' worth and bought cars from accomplice wholesalers for more than cars' worth. The insurer moved for summary judgment arguing that a portion of the insured's claimed loss was excluded as unrealized income. The court denied the motion. For transactions in which the insureds overpaid for cars, the court held that the insureds' loss was covered to the extent that they paid "an ascertainable amount greater than they would have paid in an arm's length transaction." For cars in which the insureds undersold, the court held that summary judgment was inappropriate because neither party presented information about "how the amount received for a car compares to the prices initially paid for the car." *Patrick Schaumburg Autos., Inc. v. Hanover Ins. Co.,* 452 F. Supp. 2d 857, 875.

E.D. La. 1994. After a successful suit on Bankers Blanket Bond, a question arose as to how recoveries by the insured of both principal and interest losses were to be applied. The parties questioned whether the recoveries obtained by the insured must be applied first to principal on the underlying loans to offset the surety's liability under the bond or whether they should be applied to accrued interest not covered under the bond. The court held that the potential income exclusion was not determinative of the manner in which recovery should be applied. The sureties were not bound to pay the insured for loss of income that was earned but not received. The court concluded that the funds actually collected and received by the insured on the underlying loans could not be used to offset an uncovered loss of accrued interest. The court further held that, even if the potential income exclusion had some bearing on the question of how to apply recoveries, the exclusion would not apply to the funds recovered by the insured because such income is both accrued and received, or "realized." *First Nat'l Bank of Louisville v. Lustig,* 847 F. Supp. 1322, 1323-24.

D. Minn. 1990. The bank brought an action against the insurer on a Bankers Blanket Bond to recover for losses arising out of an employee's alleged misconduct in connection with the renewal of loans. The insurer argued that insured was not entitled to recover for the loss of accrued interest based on the potential income exclusion because the term "realized" indisputably means "to convert into money." The insured argued that many banks in the United States customarily report utilizing the accrual basis of accounting and that, therefore, under this practice, the term "realized" may mean the recognition of revenue by a seller of goods for services. The court held that both definitions offered by the parties were reasonable and that the precise interpretation of the potential income exclusion would be left to the jury. *Mid-Am. Bank of Chaska v. Am. Cas. Co. of Reading, Pa.,* 745 F. Supp. 1480, 1485.

S.D. Miss. 2011. The insurer and insured bank disagreed over whether the district court's prior summary judgment ruling included accrued interest in the insured's covered loss. The district court held that the claimed accrued interest was excluded as potential income under Exclusion (s). Interest that had accrued but not been paid when the loan went into default was unrealized and thus only "potential income." *Peoples Bank of the S. v. BancInsure, Inc.,* No. 3:09CV217TSL-FKB, 2011 WL 10099621, at *1-2.

D. Neb. 2009. The insured bank submitted a claim to recover its losses after a mortgage servicing contractor failed to remit over $12 million in loan payments that it had collected. After the insured filed a breach of contract lawsuit, the insurer concluded that the bank's claim was covered and paid the policy limit. The parties then submitted cross motions for summary judgment on the insured's claim for prejudgment interest. The court rejected the insurer's argument that prejudgment interest was barred by the potential income exclusion. *Tierone Bank v. Hartford Cas. Ins. Co.,* No. 4:08CV3156, 2009 WL 2709296, at *25.

D.N.J. 1990. A savings and loan association brought an action seeking a declaratory judgment that the surety was obligated to indemnify it under savings and loan blanket bond and for bad faith damages. The insured argued that it was entitled to recover costs, prejudgment interest and attorney's fees after the court held in its favor. The surety argued that prejudgment interest was excluded by Exclusion (s). The court found a distinction between interest that accrues, or could have been earned, between the time that a loss is suffered and a claim is paid, and the interest that accrues between the time that a claim is wrongfully denied and recovery is had under the contract. The court held that the purpose of the exclusionary section was to limit the bounds of insurance coverage as opposed to limiting the insurer's liability in the event of a lawsuit. The court, therefore, held that the insured was entitled to an award of prejudgment interest. *Oritani Sav. & Loan Ass'n. v. Fid. & Deposit Co. of Md.,* 744 F. Supp. 1311, 1318-19.

M.D. Tenn. 1982. The employee of a bank established 161 fictitious installment loans in a scheme to embezzle funds from bank. Each loan included unearned interest and a $25 loan origination fee. The majority of the claim was settled but the parties submitted the issue of the loan origination fee to the court for determination. Judgment was entered for the insured because the bond did not include a potential income exclusion. "In the case of a blanket fidelity bond with a clause excluding potential income, the underwriter stands in the shoes of the unfaithful employee and a recovery is limited to the amount that went into his hands. However, without the exclusion of potential income, the underwriter stands in the shoes of each fictitious borrower at date of discovery. Therefore, recovery is for unpaid principal, accrued interest, and the loan origination fee." *United S. Bank v. Glen Falls Ins. Co.,* 548 F. Supp. 355, 356-57.

S.D. W. Va. 1994. A bank brought an action against its insurer on a Financial Institution Bond seeking interest on the amount owed under the bond for the period between notice of loss and receipt of payment from the insurer. Seventeen months passed between notice of loss and receipt of payment from the insurer. The court held that the insured effectively discharged its claim against insurer for interest on the amount owed by the insurer under the bond by accepting settlement on the principal amount of the loss. The court also noted that Exclusion (s) specifically excluded interest but relied primarily on state law. *Bank One, W. Va. v. USF&G,* 869 F. Supp. 426, 429.

Iowa 1988. A bank brought an action on a Bankers Blanket Bond arising from an employee's embezzlement scheme. The court held that the "loss" under the bond refers to the actual depletion of the bank funds by the employee's dishonesty rather than the face amount of the notes. Thus, the court held that the "loss" does not include that portion of the outstanding notes that represents interest payments made to cover prior embezzlements. *Am. Trust & Sav. Bank v. USF&G,* 418 N.W.2d 853, 854-55.

Mass. App. Ct. 1992. The bank brought an action against its insurer on a Financial Institution Bond arising from losses sustained as a result of manipulation by an employee of a check proofing and transit system. The court upheld the trial court's award of statutory prejudgment interest, finding that the exclusion refers to interest that might have been earned on the stolen money between the time of the theft and presentation to the insurer of a proof of loss. The exclusion does not include the period between the wrongful refusal of an insurer to pay a proper claim and ultimate recovery after litigation. *Cambridge Trust Co. v. Commercial Union Ins. Co.,* 591 N.E.2d 1117, 1121-22.

Tenn. Ct. App. 1981. A bank sued a former employee and its fidelity bond insurer to recover for loss of embezzled funds. The bank employee had embezzled funds from bank over a period of years by forging signatures to interest bearing promissory notes and pocketing the proceeds. When the notes came due, the employee created new notes that he used to pay interest due on old notes, to pay off some notes in full and to obtain additional funds. The insurer conceded coverage for the portion of loss relating to funds retained by the employee but denied coverage for interest, citing the exclusion. The court agreed that the exclusion applied to interest outstanding on unrepaid funds. However, the court held that the insured's loss included amounts borrowed by the employee in the form of new notes, the proceeds of which were used to pay off old loans, even though that amount essentially resulted in the payment of interest on the old notes to the bank. In addition, the court upheld trial court's award of prejudgment interest on common law grounds. *Bank of Huntington v. Smothers,* 626 S.W.2d 267, 270-71.

SECONDARY SOURCES

William T. Bogaert & Andrew F. Caplan, *Computing the Amount of Compensable Loss Under the Financial Institution Bond,* 33 TORT & INS. L.J. 807 (1998).

Bradford R. Carver, *Loss and Causation, in* HANDLING FIDELITY BOND CLAIMS 363, 367-68 (Michael Keeley & Sean Duffy eds., 2d ed. 2005).

David T. DiBiase & David J. Billings, *"Loss? What Loss?": Unique Claims on Crime Policies/Fidelity Bonds,* XIV FID. L.J. 271 (2008).

Mark S. Gamell & Joseph G. Perry, *The Potential Income Exclusion and Principal Other Exclusions and Definitions, in* FINANCIAL INSTITUTION BONDS 471, 500-511 (Duncan L. Clore ed., 3d ed. 2008).

Benjamin D. Lentz, *Profit and the Potential Income Exclusion,* 19 FORUM 694 (1984).

Edgar L. Neel, *Financial Institution and Fidelity Coverage for Loan Losses,* 21 TORT & INS. L.J. 590 (1986).

Scott L. Schmookler, *How Much Was That? Quantification of Losses in Ponzi Schemes,* (unpublished paper at the 2012 Mid-Winter Meeting of the American Bar Association, FSLC).

D.M. Studler et al., *Income Exclusion—Is There More To It?,* XIII FID. L.J. 197 (2007).

T. Damages Other Than Direct Compensatory Damages

(t) damages of any type for which the Insured is legally liable, except compensatory damages, but not multiples thereof, arising directly from a loss covered under this bond;

COMMENT

In prior versions of the Financial Institution Bond, this exclusion did not expressly address compensatory damage awards which were multiplied. The 1986 version clarified that multiplied damage awards under RICO, antitrust statutes, consumer protection statutes, and other similar statutes are neither completely compensatory (including the multiple of the compensatory damage award) nor completely punitive (including the basis for the multiplied award). If a damage award includes a compensatory component plus either punitive damages or trebled damages, only the basis of the award (and not the multiple thereof or additional punitive damages) may be covered under the bond. The 1986 bond also moved the word "direct," which, in the prior version, modified "compensatory." The revision provides that covered compensatory damages must arise "directly from" a covered loss. The significance of this change is that the damage must not only be direct to the insured, but must also arise directly from a loss covered under the bond.

At least one court has used the language of Exclusion (t) to exclude coverage for indirect claims of third parties asserting liability against the bank based on the dishonest conduct of the bank's employee. There is also a large body of cases establishing that indirect claims of third parties are not direct loss to the insured and, therefore, are not covered under the bond. Other courts have reached this conclusion based on the requirement of the various insuring agreements that the loss result "directly" from a covered loss.

In the 2004 and 2011 revised bond forms, this exclusion was substantively changed to exclude "damages of any type for which the insured is legally liable, unless the insured establishes that the act or acts which gave rise to the damages involved conduct which would have caused a covered loss to the insured in a similar account in the absence of such damages." Thus, the damages exclusion was re-written to remove the exception for compensatory damages but to allow recovery for an otherwise covered loss which would exist independently of the damage award. This change reflects the principle that a Financial Institution Bond is not a liability policy. Only when the insured suffers a covered loss is indemnity owed. The fact that damages are awarded against the insured, however, should not remove coverage when it would have existed independently of the damage award.

ANNOTATIONS

N.Y. App. Div. 1998. The insured brokerage firm was sued by investors and other third parties after an employee of the brokerage firm engaged in an insider trading scheme that caused third-party losses. The brokerage firm settled with the plaintiffs and then sought indemnity under its fidelity bond. The appeals court affirmed summary judgment for the insurer, holding that the bond's exclusion of all damages except "direct compensatory damages" clearly excluded the firm's settlement payments to third parties. The court explained that the insured's loss "arises in part from a settlement with third parties, but the settlement was not the direct result of the employee's dishonest conduct; the employee's dishonesty only caused pricing irregularities in the stock, which, themselves, caused losses to the customers, which then led to litigation concluding in settlement." *Aetna Cas. & Sur. Co. v. Kidder, Peabody & Co.*, 676 N.Y.S.2d 559, 563-64.

SECONDARY SOURCES

Mark S. Gamell & Joseph G. Perry, *The Potential Income Exclusion and Principal Other Exclusions and Definitions,* in FINANCIAL INSTITUTION BONDS 471, 511-19 (Duncan L. Clore ed., 3d ed. 2008).

U. Costs, Fees and Expenses

(u) all fees, costs and expenses incurred by the Insured
   (1) in establishing the existence of or amount of loss covered under this bond, or
   (2) as a party to any legal proceeding whether or not such legal proceeding exposes the Insured to loss covered by this bond;

COMMENT

Exclusion (u) was designated Exclusion (v) in the 1980 standard form Bankers Blanket Bond. The language of the exclusion has been changed to additionally delete from coverage fees, costs, and expenses incurred by the insured in the defense of any legal proceeding. This change is intended to bring the language of the exclusion in line with the more restrictive coverage for defense costs provided in General Agreement F of the 1986 bond.

ANNOTATIONS

N.D. Ill. 1992. A bank and a holding company were insureds under a Financial Institution Bond. On an insurer's motion to strike and dismiss portions of the complaint, the court granted the motion in its entirety on the grounds that a count seeking attorneys' fees and consequential damages for breach of the terms of the bond was excluded by exclusions (u) and (v). The court held that these exclusions clearly exclude coverage for attorney's fees and consequential damages. *Beverly Bancorp., Inc. v. Cont'l Ins. Co.,* No. 92C4823, 1992 WL 345420, at *3.

S.D. Miss. 2010. The insured bank filed suit against its insurer to recover under its Financial Institution Bond for losses caused by a borrower and his attorney. The bank sought to recover the attorneys' fees and expenses that it incurred in connection with litigation as a portion of its covered loss. The insurer moved for partial summary judgment as to a portion of the bank's claim for attorneys' fees and expenses, arguing that they were barred by Exclusions (u) and (v) of the policy. The district court held that it was not persuaded that the bank's attorneys' fees and expenses were not covered by Insuring Agreement (T), which provided coverage for "[r]easonable expenses incurred and paid by the Insured in preparing any valid claim for loss caused by any dishonest or fraudulent act or acts of any of the Insured's Employees, which loss exceeds the Single Loss Deductible Amount applicable to Insuring Agreement (T)." *Peoples Bank of the S. v. BancInsure, Inc.,* 753 F. Supp. 2d 649, 661.

SECONDARY SOURCES

Gilbert J. Schroeder, *Court Costs and Attorneys' Fees, in* FINANCIAL INSTITUTION BONDS 237 (Duncan L. Clore ed., 1995).

V. Indirect or Consequential Loss

(v)   indirect or consequential loss of any nature;

COMMENT

Exclusion (v) reinforces the language of the insuring agreements that coverage is provided only for direct losses to the insured. Thus, losses sustained by third parties but claimed against the insured are not covered. In 2004, the phrase "including, but not limited to, fines, penalties, multiple or punitive damages" was added to Exclusion (v).

ANNOTATIONS

2d Cir. 2000 (N.Y.). FDIC, as receiver of a bank, brought claim on a fidelity bond, claiming that dishonest acts of a trustee caused loss to the bank. The trustee of the bank failed to inform the bank of a construction manager's fraud in soliciting bribes and demanding kickbacks from subcontractors on a real estate venture funded by the bank. On appeal, the court upheld summary judgment in favor of FDIC, holding, among other things, that the fraudulent non-disclosure resulted directly in loss to the bank because the bank would not have continued funding but for the non-disclosure. Thus, the amounts claimed constituted a "direct loss" to the insured. The court considered Exclusion (v), along with language in coverage part A, in reaching its conclusion. *FDIC v. Nat'l Union Fire Ins. Co. of Pitt., Pa.,* 205 F.3d 66, 76.

D. Conn. 2002. A trustee for a bankrupt payroll administration company sought coverage for losses sustained when director misappropriated customer funds that company held in trust for IRS. The court granted insurer's motion for summary judgment on grounds that bankrupt company did not sustain a direct loss of money or property. The court further held that the policy expressly excluded coverage for indirect losses such as payment of damages resulting from the insured's legal liability to third parties caused by an employee's dishonesty. *Finkel v. St. Paul Fire & Marine Ins. Co.,* No. 3:00CV1194 (AHN), 2002 WL 1359672, at *4-8.

N.D. Ill. 1992. A bank and a holding company were insureds under a Financial Institution Bond. On the insurer's motion to strike and dismiss portions of the complaint, court granted the motion in its entirety on the grounds that a count seeking attorney's fees and consequential damages for breach of the terms of the bond was excluded by exclusions (u) and (v). The court held that these exclusions clearly exclude coverage for attorney's fees and consequential damages. *Beverly Bancorp., Inc. v. Cont'l Ins. Co.,* No. 92 C 4823, 1992 WL 345420, at *3.

D. Mass. 2003. The insurer filed a declaratory judgment action to determine whether it was responsible to indemnify insured for diversion of contributions. The court held that this was not a direct loss and, therefore, did not specifically reach whether exclusion applied. The court did note, however, that the exclusion "reinforces the conclusion that the policy meant to insure . . . only against immediate harm from employee dishonesty but not for any obligations 'insured' might have to others as a result of that dishonesty." *Fireman's Fund Ins. Co. v. Special Olympics Int'l, Inc.,* 249 F. Supp. 2d 19, 27-28.

D. Minn. 2005. A securities broker sued to recover under its fidelity bond for its registered representative's actions in connection with pledged accounts. The broker's customer pledged assets in several accounts as security for a loan from a third party, and the insured signed an agreement that the assets could not be removed from the accounts without the consent of the lender. The customer had the assets liquidated and wired to "Baltic Bank" in payment for certificates of deposit issued by "Baltic Bank," which turned out to be a shell controlled by the customer. In effect, the customer removed the pledged assets without the lender's consent. The lender sued the insured, and the insured settled with the lender for $7 million and submitted a claim on its fidelity bond alleging employee dishonesty. The insurer argued that the broker's loss was excluded as indirect or consequential because the broker suffered the loss when it settled the lender's lawsuit, not when the registered representative initiated the wire transfer. The district court rejected the insurer's argument, holding that the loss occurred when the wire transfer was completed, not years later when the insured settled with the lender, and the indirect or consequential loss exclusion did not bar the claim. *RBC Dain Rauscher, Inc. v. Fed. Ins. Co.,* 370 F. Supp. 2d 886, 889-90.

D.N.J. 1990. A savings and loan association brought an action against its insurer on a savings and loan blanket bond. The court held that savings and loan was entitled to recover attorney's fees incurred in connection with collection actions brought against responsible parties, but not attorney's fees incurred in connection with current action. The court held that the fees relating to the collection actions should not be characterized as "consequential damages," but as general damages flowing directly from the insurer's breach of contract. These fees were costs incurred in mitigating losses that, if carrier had paid loss, would not have accrued to insured. *Oritani Sav. & Loan Assoc. v. Fid. & Deposit Co. of Md.,* 744 F. Supp. 1311, 1320-22.

D. Utah. 2008. The insured sought coverage for its liability to third party financial institutions that unknowingly purchased fraudulently-obtained mortgages from the insured and then demanded that the insured buy back the mortgages under warranty clauses in the purchase agreements. The court followed a "direct means direct" approach and held that the insured's liability to the third party financial institutions was not a direct loss to the insured. The court found support for following the "direct means direct" standard in the bond's exclusion of "indirect or consequential loss of any nature." *Direct Mortg. Corp. v. Nat'l Union Fire Ins. Co. of Pa.,* 625 F. Supp. 2d 1171, 1177-78.

N.Y. App. Div. 1993. Drexel Burnham Lambert Group ("Drexel") commenced a lawsuit seeking coverage for losses sustained through the fraud and dishonesty of Michael Milkin and Dennis Levine against insurers that had issued multiple bankers and brokers blanket bonds. Drexel alleged that by reason of the dishonest activities of these former employees, criminal and civil claims were made against Drexel as a result of which Drexel sustained and continued to sustain losses which were covered under the employee dishonesty coverage provisions of the bonds. The court granted the insurer's motions to dismiss on various grounds, including exclusions for losses resulting from the purchase and sale of securities, losses resulting from violation of securities acts, exemplary, punitive or consequential damages or consequential loss. The court held, in part, that the blanket bond's exclusion for "consequential damages" was applicable in that the fraud was committed not against Drexel, but against members of the investing public, against companies they manipulated and against federal regulatory agencies.

The court held that the bond covered loss to the insured, not losses sustained by the outside world and claimed against the insured. *Drexel Burnham Lambert Grp., Inc. v. Vigilant Ins. Co.,* 595 N.Y.S.2d 999, 1007.

SECONDARY SOURCES

Mark S. Gamell & Joseph G. Perry, *The Potential Income Exclusion and Principal Other Exclusions and Definitions, in* FINANCIAL INSTITUTION BONDS 471, 511-19 (Duncan L. Clore ed., 3d ed. 2008).

Scott L. Schmookler, *Insuring Agreement D, in* FINANCIAL INSTITUTION BONDS 313, 347-51 (Duncan L. Clore ed., 3d ed. 2008).

W. Securities Violation

(w) loss resulting from any violation by the Insured or by any Employee
- **(1) of law regulating (i) the issuance, purchase or sale of securities, (ii) securities transactions upon security exchanges or over the counter market, (iii) investment companies, or (iv) investment advisers, or**
- **(2) of any rule or regulation made pursuant to such law, unless it is established by the Insured that the act or acts which caused the said loss involved fraudulent or dishonest conduct which would have caused a loss to the Insured in a similar amount in the absence of such laws, rules or regulations;**

COMMENT

Exclusion (w) precludes coverage for any loss resulting from a violation of the securities laws or from a violation of any rule or regulation made pursuant to such laws unless the acts that caused the loss involved fraudulent or dishonest conduct which would have caused a loss in the absence of such laws, rules, or regulations. The exclusion does not specifically restrict the exception to acts covered by Insuring Agreement (A), but rather excepts acts which "involved fraudulent or dishonest conduct" generally. Because losses arising from securities violations likely arise in the context of claims by third parties, which typically are not covered as indirect losses, it is not surprising that there are few cases construing this exclusion.

ANNOTATIONS

N.Y. App. Div. 1993. Drexel Burnham Lambert Group ("Drexel") commenced a lawsuit, as debtor in possession, in New York Supreme Court seeking coverage for losses sustained through the fraud and dishonesty of Michael Milkin and Dennis Levine against insurers that had issued multiple bankers and brokers blanket bonds. Drexel alleged that by reason of the dishonest activities of these former employees, criminal and civil claims were made against Drexel as a result of which Drexel sustained and continued to sustain losses which were covered under the employee dishonesty coverage provisions of the bonds. The court granted the insurer's motions to dismiss on various grounds including Exclusion (w). The court held, in part, that the exclusion for losses resulting from trading and the purchase and sale of securities and for violations of security laws and regulations was "the heart" of plaintiff's claims and thus excluded. *Drexel Burnham Lambert Grp., Inc. v. Vigilant Ins. Co.*, 595 N.Y.S.2d 999, 1007.

SECONDARY SOURCES

David K. Kerr, *The Potential Income and Principal Other Exclusions, in* FINANCIAL INSTITUTION BONDS 215, 225-26 (Duncan L. Clore ed., 1995).

X. Failure of Financial Institution

(x) **loss resulting directly or indirectly from the failure of a financial or depository institution, or its receiver or liquidator, to pay or deliver, on demand of the Insured,**

funds or Property of the Insured held by it in any capacity, except when covered under Insuring Agreements (A) or (B)(1)(a);

COMMENT

Exclusion (x) was new to the 1986 version of the Financial Institution Bond and has received no attention by the courts. This exclusion excludes direct loss caused by the failure of a financial or depositary institution to return funds or property to the insured unless the property is lost due to robbery, burglary, misplacement, mysterious unexplainable disappearance and damage thereto or destruction thereof, while the property is lodged or deposited within the insured's offices or premises located anywhere or if the loss is caused by employee dishonesty. One commentator suggests that the exclusion shows that the underwriters do not intend to cover losses caused as a result of another financial institution's failure to pay or deliver over funds or property of the insured which could be lost as a result of fire, theft, or liquidation of the other financial institution that should be covered by the other institution's insurance portfolio and, thus, operates, like Exclusion (q), as another insurance provision.[10] This exclusion is most likely to be involved in circumstances where an insured claims money or property withheld by other financial institutions, a situation typically occurring when the other institution is defunct. Thus, the exclusion has been dubbed the "failure of financial institutions" exclusion.

ANNOTATIONS

NONE

SECONDARY SOURCES

James F. Crowder, Jr., *On Premises Coverage, in* FINANCIAL INSTITUTION BONDS 119 (Duncan L. Clore ed., 1995).

---

10 James F. Crowder, Jr., *On Premises Coverage, in* FINANCIAL INSTITUTION BONDS 119, 123 (Duncan L. Clore ed., 1995).

David K. Kerr, *The Potential Income and Principal Other Exclusions, in* FINANCIAL INSTITUTION BONDS 215, 226 (Duncan L. Clore ed., 1995).

Y. Uncertified Securities

(y) loss involving any Uncertificated Security except an Uncertificated Security of any Federal Reserve Bank of the United States or when covered under Insuring Agreement (A);

COMMENT

There are no reported decisions construing Exclusion (y), likely due to its very specific application. "Uncertificated Security" is defined as a "share, participation or other interest in property of or an enterprise of the issuer or an obligation of the issuer, which is: (1) not represented by an instrument and the transfer of which is registered upon books maintained for that purpose by or on behalf of the issuer; (2) of a type commonly dealt in on securities exchanges or markets; and (3) either one of a class or series or by its terms divisible into a class or series of shares, participations, interests or obligations." The exclusion includes two exceptions for uncertificated securities issued by any Federal Reserve Bank and for losses resulting from employee dishonesty.

In the 2004 revision to the standard form Financial Institution Bond, Exclusion (y) was deleted and replaced with an exclusion for "loss resulting directly or indirectly from accepting checks payable to an organization for deposit into an account of a natural person." According to one commentator, the new Exclusion (y) reflects the standard banking principle that organizations do not make payments by endorsing checks made to the organization over to individuals.[11]

---

11 Mark S. Gamell & Joseph G. Perry, *The Potential Income Exclusion and Principal Other Exclusions and Definitions, in* FINANCIAL INSTITUTION BONDS 471, 521 (Duncan L. Clore ed., 3d ed. 2008).

ANNOTATIONS

NONE

SECONDARY SOURCES

Mark S. Gamell & Joseph G. Perry, *The Potential Income Exclusion and Principal Other Exclusions and Definitions*, in FINANCIAL INSTITUTION BONDS 471 (Duncan L. Clore ed., 3d ed. 2008).

David K. Kerr, *The Potential Income and Principal Other Exclusions*, in FINANCIAL INSTITUTION BONDS 215, 224-25 (Duncan L. Clore ed., 1995).

Z. Civil, Criminal or Legal Proceeding

(z) damages resulting from any civil, criminal or other legal proceeding in which the Insured is alleged to have engaged in racketeering activity except when the Insured establishes that the act or acts giving rise to such damages were committed by an Employee under circumstances which result directly in a loss to the Insured covered by Insuring Agreement (A). For the purposes of this exclusion, "racketeering activity" is defined in 18 United States Code 1961 et seq., as amended.

COMMENT

Exclusion (z) precludes coverage for damages assessed in a legal proceeding in which the insured is charged with violating the Racketeer Influenced and Corrupt Organizations Act, 18 U.S.C. §1961-1968 (Supp. 1991). Unlike Exclusion (w), this exclusion specifically excepts losses covered by Insuring Agreement (A). Considering the nature of RICO claims, a claim for violation of the statute is likely to involve circumstances that would involve employee dishonesty and, therefore, the exclusion has limited applicability. There are no reported decisions construing the exclusion.

ANNOTATIONS

NONE

SECONDARY SOURCES

David K. Kerr, *The Potential Income and Principal Other Exclusions*, in FINANCIAL INSTITUTION BONDS 327-28 (Duncan L. Clore ed., 1995).

Kevin M. Solan, *RICO and the Surety*, 25 TORT & INS. L.J. 785 (1990).

AA. Theft, Disappearance or Destruction of Confidential Information

(aa) loss resulting directly or indirectly from the theft, disappearance or destruction of confidential information including, but not limited to, trade secrets, customer lists, and intellectual property.

COMMENT

Exclusion (aa) was added in the 2004 version of the Financial Institution Bond, Standard Form No. 24. The exclusion was added to exclude losses resulting from, among other things, an Employee's theft of personal customer information that would allow the Employee to fraudulently commit an electronic transfer. To date, no case law has interpreted this exclusion.

ANNOTATIONS

NONE

SECONDARY SOURCES

NONE

BB. Dishonest or Fraudulent Acts of an Employee

(bb) **loss resulting directly or indirectly from the dishonest or fraudulent acts of an Employee of any Insured, or any director or officer of an Insured who is not in collusion with such Employee, knows, or knew at any time, of any dishonest or fraudulent act committed by such Employee at any time, whether in the employment of the Insured or otherwise, whether or not of the type covered under Insuring Agreement (A), against the Insured or any other person or entity and without regard to whether knowledge was obtained before or after the commencement of this bond. Provided, however, that this exclusion does not apply to loss of any Property already in transit in the custody of such Employee at the time such knowledge was obtained or to loss resulting directly from dishonest or fraudulent acts occurring prior to the time such knowledge was obtained.**

COMMENT

An Exclusion (bb) was added with the 2004 revision of the Financial Institution Bond and in that form, the exclusion applied to "loss resulting directly or indirectly from the Intentional damage or destruction of property by an Employee." The addition of Exclusion (bb) was a response to the deletion of Insuring Agreement (A)'s financial benefit requirement. It was intended to preclude coverage for instances of employee sabotage where the employee intends to cause a loss but not to benefit himself or another person.

In the 2011 revision to the bond, the financial benefit requirement was restored, making the above-referenced intentional action exclusion unnecessary. The exclusion was replaced with the exclusion set forth above to exclude loss caused by an employee's dishonest or fraudulent acts when the insured or any non-colluding officer or director of the insured has knowledge of any fraudulent or dishonest act previously committed by the Employee. The 2011 revision to Exclusion (bb) bolsters the bond's automatic termination provision to unambiguously exclude loss caused by a known fraudulent or dishonest employee, even in situations where the insured knew of the employee's prior bad acts before the issuance of the bond. Several court decisions had held that the automatic termination provision was not triggered when the insured's knowledge of a dishonest or fraudulent act pre-dated the bond. The broad language of Exclusion (bb) should address the concern that those cases raised for insurers.

ANNOTATIONS

NONE

SECONDARY SOURCES

Patrick Q. Hustead & Angela J. Lee, *Automatic Termination Provision in Fidelity and Financial Institution Bonds*, (unpublished paper at the 2012 Fall Meeting of the American Bar Association, FSLC).

SECTION 3 — DISCOVERY*

DISCOVERY

Section 3. This bond applies to loss first discovered by the Insured during the Bond Period. Discovery occurs when the Insured first becomes aware of facts which would cause a reasonable person to assume that a loss of a type covered by this bond has been or will be incurred, regardless of when the act or acts causing or contributing to such loss occurred, even though the exact amount or details of loss may not then be known. Discovery also occurs when the Insured receives notice of an actual or potential claim in which it is alleged that the Insured is liable to a third party under circumstances which, if true, would constitute a loss under this bond.

COMMENT

When discovery occurs continues to be an important issue in bond claims due to the very fact-based and sometimes inconsistent analysis applied by various courts. While the more recent forms of the bond make clear that an objective standard of discovery is to be applied, the facts of each case deemed important by the court direct the outcome of the analysis. The revisions to the bond language have been necessary to make clear that the use of a subjective standard is not the intent of the parties.

At least until the addition of a definition of discovery to the Bankers Blanket Bond in 1980, courts struggled in their efforts to interpret and apply the discovery of loss requirements of fidelity bonds, often reaching inconsistent results. The early cases were far from uniform in their choice of the appropriate standard for determining when discovery of loss occurs and in their application of the type of standard chosen. Courts often utilized tests combining both objective and subjective elements, usually requiring the insured to draw reasonable inferences, but only from the facts of which it actually had knowledge. A disturbing

---

* By Toni Scott Reed, Strasburger & Price, LLP, Dallas, Texas. Many thanks to my partners Michael Keeley and Duncan Clore as the chapter is based upon earlier ones written by the two of them.

number of older cases, while paying lip service to an objective standard, ultimately imposed a subjective standard and determined the date of discovery based solely upon the insured's subjective beliefs, without any apparent regard to the reasonableness of those conclusions and without imposing any duty to make reasonable inquiry. These cases claimed to find support in the United States Supreme Court's seminal decision in *American Surety Co. v. Pauly*,[1] in which the Court applied a standard which contained both subjective and objective elements. While the influence of *Pauly* has been significant in the case law, unfortunately for bond insurers, the United States Supreme Court's adoption of a clearly objective standard for discovery in *Guaranty Co. of North America v. Mechanics' Savings Bank & Trust Co.*,[2] handed down only four years after *Pauly*, has been largely overlooked in the case law.

The propensity of some judicial decisions to espouse an objective standard but apply a subjective interpretation to the facts was particularly problematic for insurers, since such cases increasingly led to confusion in the standard to be applied and allowed disingenuous insureds to avoid the timely notice and proof of loss provisions of the bond by simply characterizing beliefs as mere suspicions. As a result, when the Surety Association of America revised the Bankers Blanket Bond, Standard Form No. 24 in 1980, it included, for the first time, a definition of discovery that clearly set forth insurers' intent that an objective standard, based upon the assumptions of a reasonable person, was to be applied. When read in conjunction with the bond's notice provision, requiring notice at "the earliest practicable moment," the bond's discovery definition clearly is intended to counteract those decisions allowing insureds to delay providing their insurers notice due to their subjective doubts about an employee's dishonesty.

In the 1986 standard form bond, the discovery definition was moved to Section 3 with a few minor changes in wording to further emphasize the original intent of the bond's drafters to require early notice of a loss. The word "first" was added before "becomes aware" to underscore that discovery does not require that the insured have complete knowledge and that discovery is intended to occur, and notice must be given, at the first moment possible. The words "of a type" were added to the phrase "loss covered by this bond" to remove any argument that discovery has not

---

1   170 U.S. 133, 145-49 (1898).
2   183 U.S. 402, 420-21 (1902).

occurred unless the insured recognizes that a potential loss is covered. Finally, the phrase "regardless of when the act or acts causing or contributing to such loss occurred" was added to make it abundantly clear that the events causing the loss need not occur during the bond period and to avoid potential arguments by insureds that knowledge of past dishonest conduct or of past loss causing events may trigger discovery. This version of the definition of discovery was retained in the 2004 and 2011 standard form bonds.

Under the current definition, discovery occurs: (1) when the insured "first" becomes "aware" of facts which would cause a reasonable person to "assume" that a covered loss has been or will be incurred, and (2) relates to each and every act causing or contributing to the loss, "regardless of when such acts occurred even though the exact amount or details of loss may not be known." Significantly, the definition utilizes the term "becomes aware" as contained in the United States Supreme Court's decision in *Mechanics'*, rather than the term "knowledge," as found in *Pauly*. Also of note, the definition requires that the insured only "assume a loss has been or will be incurred," rather than actually "believe a loss has occurred," a decidedly lesser standard. This is significant because most reported decisions prior to adoption of the definition required that the insured "believe" a loss has occurred as opposed to simply "assume" a loss has or will be incurred. Further, no longer can an insured contend that discovery did not occur until it uncovers all of the details of the loss. The discovery definition now strongly implies that only the core elements of a covered loss need be discovered to trigger discovery of loss, *e.g.* that a loss may have occurred due to employee dishonesty.

Although cases decided since adoption of the discovery definition often continue to cite *Pauly* and other pre-definition cases injecting subjective elements into the determination of when discovery of loss takes place, the discovery definition appears to be having its intended effect. The overwhelming majority of recent cases conclude that the new definition sets forth a purely objective test based upon the assumptions of a reasonable person. A number of courts have further imposed a duty of inquiry, such as required by *Mechanics,* upon an insured based upon the conduct expected of a reasonable person.[3] These courts have recognized

---

3   *See, e.g.,* Royal Trust Bank v. Nat'l Union Fire Ins. Co. of Pitt., Pa., 788 F.2d 719, 721-22 (11th Cir. 1986); Utica Mut. Ins. Co. v. Fireman's Fund

that if a reasonable person would have investigated further upon becoming aware of facts indicating the possibility that a loss had or will be incurred, then a duty of inquiry exists. As noted by one recent court, "[t]he law will charge a person with notice and knowledge of whatever he would have learned, upon making such inquiry as it would have been reasonable to expect him to make under the circumstances."[4] While it is still too soon to tell whether all courts will impose a duty of inquiry on insureds as appears to be mandated by the discovery definition, it is clear that insurers now have a contractual basis for arguing that such a duty should be imposed.

ANNOTATIONS

U.S. 1902. Under a bank employee fidelity bond providing that "the employer shall at once notify the company, on his becoming aware of said employee being engaged in speculation or gambling . . . ," the Court concluded that the phrase "to be aware" is not the same as "to have knowledge." The obvious meaning of "becoming aware," as used in the bond, is "to be informed of" or "to be apprised of" or "to be put on one's guard in respect to." In analyzing the intent of the fidelity bond's notice provision, the Court found that the term "awareness" contemplated notice to the insurer whenever there was reason for an inquiry concerning dishonesty. The Court concluded that it was the duty of the insured either to have made a prompt investigation or to have promptly notified the insurer of the knowledge it possessed once the bank received reports of speculation by the employee. *Guar. Co. of N. Am. v. Mechs.' Sav. Bank & Trust Co.*, 183 U.S. 402, 419-22.

U.S. 1898. A bank employee fidelity bond requiring notice of loss "as soon as practicable after such act shall have come to the knowledge of the employer" obligates the insured to provide notice upon knowledge, not simply suspicion, of the existence of such facts as would justify a careful and prudent man in charging another with fraud or dishonesty. *Am. Sur. Co. v. Pauly*, 170 U.S. 133, 145-49.

Ins. Co., 748 F.2d 118, 122 (2nd Cir. 1984); Boston Mut. Life Ins. Co. v. Fireman's Fund Ins. Co., 613 F. Supp. 1090, 1093-95.

4   *Royal Trust Bank*, 788 F.2d at 721.

1st Cir. 1997 (Mass.). The court upheld a summary judgment precluding coverage under a standard form Financial Institution Bond, which defined Discovery as occurring "when the insured receives notice of an actual or potential claim in which it is alleged that the insured is liable to a third party under circumstances which, if true, would constitute a loss." The court specifically found that the insured failed to provide timely notice of a potentially covered loss given the insured's "discovery" of lawsuits and counterclaims that, six months prior to notice, alleged knowing acts of dishonesty and fraud. *FDIC v. Ins. Co. of N. Am.*, 105 F.3d 778, 782-83.

1st Cir. 1990 (Mass.). Tolling of the discovery period under a fidelity bond, as an equitable remedy to protect innocent investors, is inapplicable under the principle of adverse domination and control absent a genuine issue of fact. *J.I. Corp. v. Fed. Ins. Co.*, 920 F.2d 118, 119.

1st Cir. 1966 (Mass.). An insured discovered a loss within the meaning of a Bankers Blanket Bond when a customer made a written demand for checks improperly cashed. The insured thus was not required to give notice when it learned of unlawful conduct by telephone. *Aetna Cas. & Sur. Co. v. Guar. Bank & Trust Co.*, 370 F.2d 276, 280-81.

2d Cir. 1984 (N.Y.). The fidelity bond at issue required notice "as soon as practicable." Applying what it termed an "objective" test, the Second Circuit held that the insured's knowledge of the facts underlying its claim, and its duty to inquire, vitiated the insured's claim of a good faith belief in its employee's honesty. *Utica Mut. Ins. Co. v. Fireman's Fund Ins. Co.*, 748 F.2d 118, 122.

2d Cir. 1935 (N.Y.). Fidelity bond required that proof of loss be filed within thirty days after discovery of any default causing a loss and not within thirty days after discovery of sufficient details of any default entitling the insured to swear to a claim. *Pub. Warehouses of Matanzas, Inc. v. Fid. & Deposit Co. of Md.*, 77 F.2d 831, 832-33.

2d Cir. 1927 (N.Y.). Discovery under a fidelity bond occurs "only on actually learning of the thefts," which thereby invokes an insured's duty to give notice. *Mass. Bonding & Ins. Co. v. Norwich Pharmacal Co.*, 18 F.2d 934, 937.

3d Cir. 2011 (N.J.). The court affirmed summary judgment on commercial crime policy for the insurer on the basis of pre-loss discovery/termination. The policy at issue defined discovery for termination purposes as when the insured "first becomes aware of facts which would cause a reasonable person to assume that a loss of a type covered by this bond . . . has been or will be incurred." Discovery occurred when the insured, an armored car company, learned of the disappearance of money in its care and custody, which was all that was required for a covered loss. *Diebold Inc. v. Cont'l Cas. Co.*, 430 F. App'x 201, 206-07.

3d Cir. 2000 (N.J.). In interpreting a Savings and Loan Blanket Bond that limited coverage to losses discovered by the insured during the bond period, and defined "discovery" as occurring when the insured became aware of facts that would cause a reasonable person to assume that a covered loss had been incurred, the court found that the trier of fact had to make determinations as to subjective and objective components by identifying the totality of facts and information the insured actually knew during the relevant time period, and reaching conclusions that a reasonable person could draw from those facts. Cautioning that the discovery threshold is low, the court found a genuine issue of material fact and reversed a summary judgment granted in favor of the insurer and based on the trial court's conclusion that the insured possessed little more than mere suspicions of employee dishonesty or fraud. *RTC v. Fid. & Deposit Co. of Md.*, 205 F.3d 615, 631-35.

3d Cir. 1981 (N.J.). In a rescission action seeking a declaration that the bond was void *ab initio*, the court held that the bank's knowledge of a loss, which it believed was not covered under the bond, would not justify rescission when, as a matter of law, there was insufficient evidence of employee dishonesty to impose a duty of disclosure in the application process. The court reasoned that its conclusion was proper since "mere suspicion of wrong-doing" fails to give rise to the insured's obligation to provide notice of a loss. *Fid. & Deposit Co. of Md. v. Hudson United Bank*, 653 F.2d 766, 774-76.

3d Cir. 1937 (Pa.). Notice under a fidelity bond must be given after discovery of any default or dishonest act and not after dishonesty is suspected. There is a vast difference between suspicion, be it mere or real, and positive discovery that justifies affirmative action. *Hunt v. Fid. & Deposit Co. of Md.*, 92 F.2d 75, 77.

4th Cir. 1993 (S.C.). Under a fidelity bond defining discovery as "awareness of facts which would cause a reasonable party to assume that a loss covered by the bond had been or would be incurred, even though the exact amount or details of the loss may not then be known," the Fourth Circuit upheld the propriety of a jury instruction that used the language of the bond. The court thus concluded, under the totality of evidence, that it was reasonable for a jury to determine that discovery occurred well before the insured provided notice. *First Sav. Bank, FSB v. Am. Cas. Co.*, No. 92-1320, 1993 U.S. App. LEXIS 2049, at *11-16.

4th Cir. 1979 (S.C.). Knowledge of facts that constitute dishonesty as a matter of law also constitutes discovery of loss within the meaning of the bond. *C. Douglas Wilson & Co. v. Ins. Co. of N. Am.*, 590 F.2d 1275, 1278-79.

5th Cir. 1995 (La.). Under the 1980 Bankers Blanket Bond, discovery of loss does not occur until the insured discovers facts showing that dishonest acts occurred and the insured appreciates the significance of those facts. Suspicion of loss is not enough. Although affirming a jury finding that discovery occurred within the bond period, the court refused to adopt the FDIC's argument that it had unlimited time to investigate and add later losses caused by unrelated acts as long as it could find some act or omission within the bond period committed by the same actor. Court held that later losses would be covered only if the loss arose out of the same pattern of conduct or scheme that was originally discovered. *FDIC v. Fid. & Deposit Co. of Md.*, 45 F.3d 969, 974-75.

5th Cir. 1985 (Tex.). The court held that a bank officer's knowledge of another's dishonest and fraudulent acts, which the officer gained as a result of access to financial records, was imputable to the bank. The court noted that it is a well-established rule in Texas that, under a Bankers Blanket Bond, an insured is not bound to give notice until he has acquired knowledge of some specific fraudulent or dishonest act. The court further commented that, although there is no uniformity as to whether actual or constructive knowledge is required, there is agreement that an insured is under no obligation to act when it merely suspects wrongdoing, although an insured's subjective knowledge should at least be considered. *City State Bank in Wellington v. USF&G*, 778 F.2d 1103, 1107-10.

5th Cir. 1972 (Tex.). Bank directors' knowledge of irregularities and violations of bank policy is not sufficient to require notice under Bankers Blanket Bonds. Notice is not required until the insured acquires knowledge of some specific fraudulent or dishonest act which might give rise to liability under the bonds. *FDIC v. Lott*, 460 F.2d 82, 86-87.

5th Cir. 1970 (Tex.). For the purpose of providing notice required by a Bankers Blanket Bond and an Excess Bank Employee Dishonesty Blanket Bond, the term "loss" means the date fraudulent misconduct "came to light," and not when the insured discovers that an employee's purchase of notes fail to conform to standards. *FDIC v. Aetna Cas. & Sur. Co.*, 426 F.2d 729, 738-39.

5th Cir. 1918 (Ala.). The existence of mere suspicion of misconduct did not require notice under a fidelity bond. Insured must be informed of the conduct of the employee and of the intent accompanying the conduct in order to be aware that the employee was guilty of larceny or embezzlement. *USF&G v. Walker*, 248 F. 42, 43-44.

6th Cir. 1990 (Tenn.). Suspicion that a bank would incur a loss covered by a Bankers Blanket Bond, which grew from concerns over the financial viability of the bank and not from knowledge that dishonest acts were committed, is not enough to invoke coverage. "[D]iscovery of loss does not occur until the insured discovers facts showing that dishonest acts occurred and appreciates the significance of those facts." *FDIC v. Aetna Cas. & Sur. Co.*, 903 F.2d 1073, 1079.

6th Cir. 1975 (Ohio). "Discovery of loss," within a policy provision requiring that proof of loss be filed within four months of discovery, does not occur until the insured has had a reasonable time to discover the extent and amount of loss. *Russell Gasket Co. v. Phoenix of Hartford Ins. Co.*, 512 F.2d 205, 208-09.

6th Cir. 1934 (Mich.). Knowledge that a loss has been or will be sustained fixes the critical date from which the time for giving notice begins to run. *USF&G v. Barber*, 70 F.2d 220, 224.

6th Cir. 1932 (Tenn.). When a bond requires "written notice of any loss hereunder as soon as possible after the insured shall learn of such loss," then "loss" refers to a condition in which the insured would be subject to a claim or demand from which "liability might arise," and not to an adjudicated liability. *Nat'l City Bank v. Nat'l Sec. Co.*, 58 F.2d 7, 8-9.

7th Cir. 1980 (Ill.). Discovery of loss under a bond occurs when the insured knew or should have known that the acts of an employee were dishonest or fraudulent. Thus, inferences that may reasonably be drawn from undisputed facts present a jury question and make entry of summary judgment inappropriate. *Cent. Nat'l Life Ins. Co. v. Fid. & Deposit Co. of Md.*, 626 F.2d 537, 548-49.

7th Cir. 1956 (Ill.). Notice under a bond given one day after a meat packing plant discovered employee theft complied with the terms of the bond. Although insured began investigation of inventory losses, insured's suspicions were merely gestating during the period it was investigating the cause of the loss and prompt notice followed viable knowledge of the specific culprits. *B. Constantino & Sons Co. v. New Amsterdam Cas. Co.*, 234 F.2d 902, 903-04.

8th Cir. 1993 (S.D.). Bank officers' collusion to divert funds for personal use cannot be imputed to its board of directors for the purposes of determining discovery under a fidelity bond when the officers' interests are adverse to that of the bank. Moreover, absent the board of directors' knowledge of the "true nature" of the fraudulent activities, a state agency's criticism of banking practices and subsequent accounting measures were not sufficient, as a matter of law, to charge the bank with discovery of a covered loss. As stated, "[n]either negligence nor any failure to discover what by due diligence might have been discovered will bar an insured from recovering the loss." *First Dakota Nat'l Bank v. St. Paul Fire & Marine Ins. Co.*, 2 F.3d 801, 807-08.

8th Cir. 1988 (Neb.). Coverage under fidelity and employee bonds was precluded on summary judgment when evidence belied insured's argument that bank examiner's investigation concerned collectability, not fraudulent or illegal conduct, and the record resoundingly implicated the insured's knowledge of covered acts before a fidelity bond became effective. Simply, "[a]lthough [the insured] correctly points out that mere suspicions do not constitute 'discovery,' an insured cannot disregard known facts." *First Sec. Sav. v. Kan. Bankers Sur. Co.*, 849 F.2d 345, 349-50.

8th Cir. 1982 (Mo.). The court affirmed a summary judgment and held that the insurer properly disclaimed coverage under a Bankers Blanket Bond when the insured failed to provide timely notice while having knowledge of facts that would lead a reasonable person to conclude that a loss occurred. *Columbia Union Nat'l Bank v. Hartford Acc. & Indem. Co.*, 669 F.2d 1210, 1213-14.

8th Cir. 1979 (Ark.). Discovery of fraud or dishonesty occurs when the insured actually becomes aware of sufficient facts that would lead a reasonable person to believe that an insured loss has occurred. Mere suspicion of an insured loss is not sufficient to trigger the notice requirement. The test of discovery under the bond, which insures against the negligent release of escrow documents based on false misrepresentations, must relate to a reasonable person's subsequent awareness of facts, which would convert his negligent appreciation of facts into actual knowledge of the alleged dishonesty. *Perkins v. Clinton State Bank*, 593 F.2d 327, 333-35.

8th Cir. 1971 (Mo.). In determining when discovery has occurred, the trier of fact must find the pertinent underlying facts known to the insured and must further determine the conclusions that reasonably can be drawn by the insured as a result of those facts. Suspicion alone does not satisfy the test of discovery. *USF&G v. Empire State Bank*, 448 F.2d 360, 365-66.

8th Cir. 1932 (Neb.). Notice requirements under a fidelity bond must be strictly complied with, such that the insured's delay in giving notice is not justified by asserting a lack of detailed information. Rather, notice should be given when insured has reasonable grounds for believing that the terms of the bond have been violated. *Am. Sur. Co. of N.Y. v. Bankers Sav. Ass'n*, 59 F.2d 577, 579-80.

8th Cir. 1907 (Mo.). Notice is not required on mere rumor of irregularity or suspicion of dishonesty. Likewise, absolute or complete knowledge of an accomplished crime is not necessary before the insured is required to act. Notice, however, is required upon knowledge of facts as would justify a careful and prudent man to believe that a crime has been committed. *Aetna Indem. Co. v. J.R. Crowe Coal & Mining Co.*, 154 F. 545, 549.

9th Cir. 2005 (Cal.). Summary judgment for the insurers affirmed because losses were not discovered during their bond period in Financial Institution Bonds. Insured's knowledge that principal had violated its conflict-of-interest policy by making purchases from insured's customers and writing down customers' loans was insufficient to give rise to discovery because Insured did not know during the policy period that loans would result in covered losses. *FDIC v. Fid. & Deposit Co. of Md.*, 132 F. App'x 139, 141-42.

9th Cir. 2001 (Idaho). Insured oil company could recover from its fidelity insurer under theft policy for loss attributable to theft by its employees only if it first discovered the loss after the inception date of the crime policy. A loss is discovered once an insured has obtained facts that would cause a reasonable person to charge that there had been dishonesty or fraud resulting in loss. The insured must have discovered facts showing that dishonest acts occurred, and it must have appreciated the significance of those facts; suspicion of loss is not enough. *Gulf USA Corp. v. Fed. Ins. Co.*, 259 F.3d 1049, 1058-60.

9th Cir. 1992 (Cal.). The court reversed a district court's grant of summary judgment on the issue of discovery, reasoning that it was a fact issue and that the "court took over the jury's function to decide that the relevant facts would inform the ordinary, reasonable and sensible employer that dishonesty had occurred...." Knowledge of the insured's branch manager could be imputed to the insured for purposes of discovery. *Mercedes-Benz of N. Am. v. Hartford Acc. & Indem. Co.*, Nos. 89-56011, 89-56012, 1992 U.S. App. LEXIS 19825, at *4-7.

9th Cir. 1991 (Cal.). The FDIC argued that the definition of discovery under a fidelity bond should be narrowly interpreted as an exclusion to coverage, thereby placing the burden on the insurer to prove discovery. The court disagreed, stating that "a reasonable insured would not construe the language of the bond as requiring the *insurer* to prove facts within the personal knowledge of the insured," and held that the term was a limitation defining the scope of coverage. Nevertheless, the court reversed a summary judgment granted in favor of the insurer on the basis that the insured met its burden of proving a genuine issue of material fact regarding discovery of employee dishonesty covered under the bond. *FDIC v. N.H. Ins. Co.*, 953 F.2d 478, 483-85.

9th Cir. 1991 (Cal.). Equitable tolling is inapplicable to extend the discovery period under fidelity bonds when examiners and regulators, who were investigating and overseeing the thrift, had the ability, independently or through the FSLIC, to uncover the illegal activity of individuals controlling the bank. The FSLIC's failure to seek reformation of bonds or charge the insured with knowledge thus cannot invoke the adverse-domination doctrine. *Cal. Union Ins. Co. v. Am. Diversified Sav. Bank*, 948 F.2d 556, 565-66.

9th Cir. 1981 (Cal.). Under a Savings and Loan Blanket Bond requiring the insured to provide notice of a loss "at the earliest practicable moment after discovery of any loss," the court found that discovery of both the dishonesty and the loss were necessary prerequisites to the insured's obligation. *Fid. Sav. & Loan Ass'n v. Aetna Life & Cas. Co.*, 647 F.2d 933, 937-38.

9th Cir. 1912 (Cal.). The words in a fidelity bond do not mean that notice shall be given upon the mere discovery of facts sufficient to create a suspicion of a loss, but they do mean that notice is to be given upon obtaining definite knowledge or receiving credible information sufficient to justify the insured in preferring charges. *Nat'l Sur. Co. v. W. Pac. Ry. Co.*, 200 F. 675, 682-84.

10th Cir. 1994 (Utah). The language of the 1980 Bankers Blanket Bond "clearly ties coverage to discovery of *possible loss* and does not require actual loss." Discovery requires that the insured have more than "mere suspicion" of a possible loss, and the test is that of the objectively reasonable person. A cease and desist order by the savings and loan regulator supported a finding of discovery under one of the bonds at issue, but the court remanded the issue of discovery under another bond to determine the proper application of the adverse-domination theory. *FDIC v. Oldenburg*, 34 F.3d 1529, 1542-43.

10th Cir. 1991 (Okla.). Bank examiners' discovery of a check kiting scheme perpetrated by the chairman of the board was not precluded from coverage under a fidelity bond even though other bank officers had knowledge of the scheme. The evidence supported a determination that the bank officers were participants in the scheme, insofar as the officers acted to promote the chairman's interests over the interests of the bank, and the court accordingly held that their knowledge could not be imputed to the bank's board of directors for the purposes of determining discovery. *Adair State Bank v. Am. Cas. Co.*, 949 F.2d 1067, 1073-75, *overruled on other grounds*, *Stauth v. Nat'l Union Fire Ins. Co. of Pitt., Pa.*, 236 F.3d 1260 (2001).

10th Cir. 1966 (N.M.). Insured is not required to give notice under an employee fidelity bond of merely suspicious conduct, but only knowledge that justifies a careful and prudent man in charging another with fraud or dishonesty. *Hidden Splendor Mining Co. v. Gen. Ins. Co. of Am.*, 370 F.2d 515, 517.

10th Cir. 1941 (N.M.). An insured is not required to give notice under a fidelity bond based merely on suspicious behavior; rather, an insured's notice obligation arises only upon knowledge which would justify a careful and prudent man in charging another with fraud or dishonesty. *Am. Emp'rs' Ins. Co. v. Raton Wholesale Liquor Co.*, 123 F.2d 283, 285.

11th Cir. 1986 (Fla.). Section 4 of the 1980 Bankers Blanket Bond, read together with a rider excluding losses known to the insured before the bond inception date, was interpreted as precluding recovery because the insured should have discovered the check kiting scheme prior to the beginning of the bond period had the bank officers paid closer attention to computer records and reports that were received regularly. The court held that a duty of inquiry arises when one has sufficient knowledge of dishonest acts, but lacks direct knowledge of fraud. The court thus upheld a jury verdict and the propriety of a jury instruction regarding the insured's knowledge, and rejected the insured's argument that "actual discovery" was required to defeat coverage. *Royal Trust Bank v. Nat'l Union Fire Ins. Co.*, 788 F.2d 719, 721-22.

D. Ariz. 2009. The court granted the insured's motion for summary judgment that the loss was not discovered during the prior policy period because the policy only allowed discovery to be made by the insured's risk manager. During the prior policy period, the insured's risk manager knew only that the loss and principal were being investigated. *Eaglepitcher Mgmt. Co. v. Zurich Am. Ins. Co.*, 640 F. Supp. 2d 1109, 1118-20.

D. Ariz. 1994. The court held that, as a matter of law, non-colluding officers knew of dishonest and/or fraudulent acts, which thereby terminated coverage under the bond, despite bank officers' testimony that prior to the inception date of the policy, they did not believe the bank president's intentions concerning an illegally collateralized loan. *RTC v. Aetna Cas. & Sur. Co.*, 873 F. Supp. 1386, 1390-93.

D. Colo. 2008. District court denied insurer's motion for summary judgment on discovery where insured's 100% shareholder knew of his own fraud prior to alleged discovery date. His knowledge was not imputed to insured under sole-actor or alter-ego doctrines because insured had seven-member board of directors. Insured's non-colluding officer did not discover loss when he questioned other principals concerning loss and was advised that they were doing nothing illegal. *FDIC v. St. Paul Cos.*, 634 F. Supp. 2d 1213, 1220-21.

D. Conn. 1997. Summary judgment was granted to an insurer arguing untimely notice when a savings bank waited over two years to provide notice under a Financial Institution Bond even though it was aware of facts constituting discovery of a loss. Discovery occurred when the bank directors, who were not acting in collusion with the dishonest employee, learned of fraudulent acts at a special board of directors' meeting. *Cmty. Sav. Bank v. Fed. Ins. Co.*, 960 F. Supp. 16, 20.

D.D.C. 1980. Under the terms of a crime policy, notice must be given upon either discovery of loss or discovery of an occurrence that may give rise to a claim for loss. Loss cannot be discovered until it exists. Loss based upon claim made by a third party against the insured does not exist until third party demands indemnification from the insured. *Fid. & Deposit Co. of Md. v. President & Dirs. of Georgetown Coll.*, 483 F. Supp. 1142, 1147.

S.D. Fla. 2012. District court denied summary judgment on discovery in Financial Institution Bond case as a result of disputed facts known to insured. The court noted signs of fraud in business records for substantial period of time, regular opportunities to observe signs of fraud, the fact that the signs of fraud were such that reasonable person would have investigated records, and knowledge by numerous employees of facts concerning underlying claims. *ABCO Premium Fin. LLC v. Am. Int'l Group, Inc.*, No. 11-23020, 2012 U.S. Dist. LEXIS 111833, at *28-29, *aff'd*, No. 12-14780, 2013 U.S. App. LEXIS 7092 (11th Cir. Apr. 9, 2013).

S.D. Fla. 2011. The court denied summary judgment on grounds that the insured bank's knowledge prior to closure of the bank by the FDIC was insufficient to establish discovery for claim later pursued by the FDIC. The insured knew during policy period that the loan giving rise to the loss had almost no documentation and was deemed a total loss by the OCC almost as soon as it had been made. The OCC believed that the loan was fraudulent; the loan proceeds had been wired in a circuitous manner; the loan documentation failed to specify the loan principals or proceed recipients; one of the loan principals had withheld information from federal examiners; the loan's credit analysis was deficient; and no security interest had been perfected for the loan. Court held that discovery requires only "enough information to assume that the employee has acted fraudulently or dishonestly." Under these facts, the court could not say that no reasonable person could assume that a covered loss had occurred. *St. Paul Mercury Ins. Co. v. FDIC*, No. 08-21192, 2011 U.S. Dist. LEXIS 32908, at *10-11, *18-19.

Bankr. N.D. Ga. 1995. The court held that actual knowledge of employee theft is not required to trigger an insured's notice requirement. Bank officers' knowledge of "seemingly corrupt" and "highly irregular" loans based on false documents gave rise to the insured's duty to provide notice under an employee fidelity policy because "no reasonable person" would ignore suspicions given the wrongdoer's inadequate response upon confrontation. *Ellenberg v. Certain Underwriters at Lloyd's (In re Prime Commercial Corp.)*, 187 B.R. 785, 802-05.

N.D. Ill. 1995. The court dismissed plaintiff's action seeking coverage under an unidentified fidelity bond because the alleged wrongdoing was not discovered within one year of the end of the policy period as expressly required. The court recognized that discovery provisions are given a literal construction and that diligent attempts to discover loss, difficulty of discovering loss, and intentional concealment of loss by a dishonest employee do not excuse a failure to comply with the discovery clause. The court distinguished cases establishing the "domination and control" exception, finding that a dishonest employee at issue was clearly not in a managerial position. *Willow Mgmt. Co. v. Am. States Ins.*, No. 94 C 6994, 1995 U.S. Dist. LEXIS 467, at *6-9.

N.D. Ill. 1990. In fidelity bond case, the insurer argued that discovery occurred prior to the inception date of policy, which defined discovery as occurring "when the insured becomes aware of facts which would cause a reasonable person to assume that a loss covered by the bond has been or will be incurred...." The court, however, found the evidence concerning the president's "opinion" of the dishonest employee to be inconclusive. Although the court agreed that the evidence clearly gave rise to suspicion, the court held that summary judgment should be denied. *In re Conticommodity Serv., Inc., Sec. Litig.*, 733 F. Supp. 1555, 1578-79, *rev'd on other grounds*, 63 F.3d 438 (5th Cir. 1995).

E.D. Ky. 1989. Insurer was denied summary judgment because of an affidavit filed by the insured, "attesting that the Board did not know or suspect the dishonesty of [the employees] prior to July, 1986.... Therefore, the date of discovery cannot be determined by the court as a matter of law." *FDIC v. Reliance Ins. Corp.*, 716 F. Supp. 1001, 1002-03.

W.D. La. 2007. Discovery occurred as of the date the principal confessed to her fraud, though the amount or extent of the loss was uncertain. The court ultimately held that suit was untimely under a policy provision requiring that suit be filed within two years of discovery by a "proprietor, partner, officer or Insurance Representative of any Insured of loss or an occurrence which may become a loss...."

Magnolia Mgmt. Corp. v. Fed. Ins. Co., No. 06-0447, 2007 WL 4124496, at *14-22.

E.D. La. 1997. Court held that company became aware of facts that would cause a reasonable person to assume that a loss covered under a commercial crime policy had occurred even though exact amount or details were not known. Discovery requires both the insured's actual knowledge of an employee's dishonest acts and an appreciation of their significance. In order to constitute discovery within the terms of a policy, the insured must obtain facts of a dishonest act that would lead a reasonable person to infer that a loss has been suffered. Insurer argued that discovery date could not be definitively determined. Court held that no reasonable jury could find that discovery had occurred after policy period. The definitive discovery date was therefore immaterial. *USF&G v. Maxicare Health Plans*, No. 96-2457, 1997 U.S. Dist. LEXIS 12045, at *11-18.

E.D. La. 1994. In a coverage dispute under a 1980 Bankers Blanket Bond, the insurer argued that discovery required the insured to prove the existence of a loss and more than mere suspicion of covered conduct directly causing the loss. The court, however, found that the express bond language made no such requirement and accordingly disagreed that Louisiana adopted such a "discovery" standard. *FDIC v. Fid. & Deposit Co. of Md.*, No. 92-2109, 1994 U.S. Dist. LEXIS 462996, at *4-8.

E.D. La. 1994. An insured sought coverage under successive bonds issued by two different insurers for a loss discovered two months after the latter bond expired. Creatively, the insured argued that it had "constructive notice" of facts that would cause a reasonable person to assume that a loss occurred, and asserted "impossibility" for its failure to give timely notice. Rather than rejecting the argument on legal grounds, the court held that there was insufficient evidence to prove the bank's awareness of dishonesty prior to the termination of the bond. The court's holding was supported by an adoption of the objective test, but the court cited, with seeming approval, the subjective standard adopted by *Pauly* and its progeny. *Fountainebleau Cmty. Bank v. Fid. & Deposit Co. of Md.*, No. 93-4220, 1994 U.S. Dist. LEXIS 3880, at *7-9, *13-18.

D. Md. 1969. Court held that insured's officer-directors dominated insured such that they were its alter ego. Officer-directors' knowledge of their own dishonesty, which pre-dated bond period, constituted discovery outside of bond period such that recovery was precluded. *Phoenix Sav. & Loan, Inc. v. Aetna Cas. & Sur. Co.*, 302 F. Supp. 832, 837.

D. Mass. 1998. In FDIC's action to recover under a Bankers Blanket Bond for employee dishonesty, the court rejected the insured's argument that notice is triggered by proof of an illicit financial benefit. Rather, the court held that discovery occurs when the insured is "'aware of facts' sufficient to 'cause a reasonable person to *assume*' that a loss had occurred." Moreover, the court found that, assuming that the insured's premise regarding discovery was proper, the only reasonable inference to be drawn from the facts known by the insured was that discovery occurred well before the inception date of the policy. *FDIC v. Underwriters of Lloyd's of London Fid. Bond Number 834/FB9010020*, 3 F. Supp. 2d 120, 146-47.

D. Mass. 1996. The court concluded that there was no issue of a material fact to preclude summary judgment in favor of the insurer when the insured had an awareness of facts and had "assumed" that a loss covered by a Financial Institution Bond occurred. *FDIC v. Ins. Co. of N. Am.*, 928 F. Supp. 54, 62-63, *aff'd*, 105 F.3d 778 (1st Cir. 1997).

D. Mass. 1985. The bond's prescribed cut-off period for notice and for filing suit began at the time the insured "becomes aware of any act or circumstance indicating a probable claim." The bond also stated that coverage terminated when "the insured becomes aware of any act of the employee which is or could be made the basis of a claim." "Discovery," however, was not defined by the bond. The district court, sitting without a jury, held that "becoming aware" and "discovery" refer to a state of mind and require application of a subjective standard. Nevertheless, the court imposed a duty of inquiry once suspicion of fraudulent conduct is aroused. Thus, the court ruled that the insured violated the bond requirement of ten days' notice, and submission of a proof of loss within ninety days, following discovery of the loss. *Boston Mut. Life Ins. Co. v. Fireman's Fund Ins. Co.*, 613 F. Supp. 1090, 1093-96.

E.D. Mich. 1993. The court denied an insurer summary judgment based on its finding of a material fact question concerning whether discovery occurred prior to the inception of the policy or more than thirty days prior to notice. The fact issue to be resolved was whether a bank teller's knowledge could be imputed to a corporate entity when the bank teller held the position of vice president in charge of installment loans and was the principal employee that unwittingly accepted the fraudulent transactions. The court further found genuine issues of material fact as what the employee knew and when she knew it. *Peoples State Bank v. Am. Cas. Co.*, 818 F. Supp. 1073, 1076.

D. Minn. 1990. After the court examined the term discovery, which was defined in accordance with the 1980 Bankers Blanket Bond, it ruled that the provision must be read to require that third-party claims be reasonable because a contrary holding would result in policyholders providing notice every time a frivolous lawsuit was filed. The court also found that a fact issue existed with respect to discovery, despite the testimony of several bank employees who confirmed knowledge of dishonest acts, because the evidence could not conclusively establish the insured's discovery of fraud more than two years before filing its action in connection with the bond. *Mid-Am. Bank of Chaska v. Am. Cas. Co.*, 745 F. Supp. 1480, 1483-84.

S.D. Miss. 2012. The court denied an insurer's motion for summary judgment because a fact issue existed as to date of discovery. The insured bank knew about a shortage in vault cash. However, neither the bank's auditor nor the insurer's adjustor believed that the shortage was unusual or unreasonable. Also, the insured's records showed that its dual-control policy was not being followed, but the bank had no knowledge of this failure. The court held that an insured must appreciate the significance of the facts for discovery to occur. The insured did not know—and thus could not appreciate—that its dual-control policies were not being followed, and imputation could not satisfy the knowledge requirement. *FDIC v. Denson*, 908 F. Supp. 2d 792, 803-05.

W.D. Mo. 1989. Insurer was entitled to summary judgment because bankruptcy trustee for the insured failed to present any evidence of the insured's "subjective conclusions" related to discovery of the employee's defalcation. The court held that facts must not only be known, but their significance must be "necessarily appreciated" before there is discovery of employee misconduct. *Block v. Granite State Ins. Co.*, No. 87-0658-CV-W-6, 1989 U.S. Dist. LEXIS 13388, at *6-9.

D. Mont. 1990. Court held that the insured failed to comply with the notice requirements under a fidelity bond when non-colluding directors learned of fraudulent conduct nearly two years prior to giving notice under a fidelity bond. The court adopted an objective test concerning discovery and rejected the insured's argument that the facts learned as a result of a federal investigation and giving rise to the bond claim were more than merely suspicion. *FSLIC v. Aetna Cas. & Sur. Co.*, 785 F. Supp. 867, 868-70.

M.D.N.C. 1959. To constitute discovery under a fidelity bond there must be facts known which lead a reasonable person to an assumption that a shortage exists. The facts must be viewed as they would have been by a reasonable person at the time discovery is asserted, not as they appear in light of subsequently acquired knowledge. *Wachovia Bank & Trust Co. v. Mfr. Cas. Ins. Co.*, 171 F. Supp. 369, 375-76.

D.N.J. 2010. Discovery occurred as of the date the insured filed a federal lawsuit alleging that the principal had defrauded it. *Omega Advisors, Inc. v. Fed. Ins. Co.*, No. 10-912, 2010 U.S. Dist. LEXIS 125934, at *19-20.

D.N.J. 2006. Court granted summary judgment for the insurer, concluding that discovery occurred before policy period because (1) the insured had received two customer complaints that the principal had engaged in conflicts of interest and an inquiry letter from the NASD concerning alleged securities fraud by the principal, and (2) the principal's supervisor and the insured's compliance director had learned via news media of the principal's arrest for securities fraud. *Inv. Ctr. v. Great Am. Ins.*, No. 04-CV-6204, 2006 U.S. Dist. LEXIS 21625, at *7-9.

D.N.J. 1996. In a case involving the rescission of a fidelity bond, the court recognized that discovery does not occur until "a bank has sufficient knowledge of specific dishonest acts to justify a careful and prudent person in charging another with dishonesty or fraud," and held that a fact issue precluded an insurer that argued discovery occurred outside the bond period from obtaining summary judgment. Nevertheless, the court agreed to rescind the bond due to fraudulent misrepresentations made during the application process. *FDIC v. Moskowitz*, 946 F. Supp. 322, 332-33.

D.N.J. 1994. When a regulator seeks coverage under a fidelity bond, in its capacity as the receiver for the insured, it is irrelevant whether and when the regulator discovers a loss. The court applied an objective test with respect the meaning of discovery under a 1986 Bankers Blanket Bond and held that there was a fact issue regarding what the insured's board of directors knew and when they knew it that precluded summary judgment. *RTC v. Moskowitz*, No. 93-2080, 1994 U.S. Dist. LEXIS 15259, at *12-15.

D.N.J. 1977. Knowledge that the amount of loans was excessive and documentation poor did not require notice. Notice is not required when the insured merely suspects or has reason to suspect the wrongdoing. Notice is required when the insured acquires knowledge of some specific fraudulent or dishonest act which might involve the bonding company in liability for the misconduct. *Midland Bank & Trust Co. v. Fid. & Deposit Co. of Md.*, 442 F. Supp. 960, 971-72.

D.N.J. 1971. Time to give notice began when insured had knowledge of all facts upon which its claim was based. *Essex Cnty. State Bank v. Fireman's Fund Ins. Co.*, 331 F. Supp. 931, 939-40.

S.D.N.Y. 2004. The court granted summary judgment for insurer on late-notice grounds where insured acknowledged in its proof of loss that discovery had occurred over two years before filing suit. The insured knew as of the discovery date set forth in its proof of loss that it had been the victim of fraud and that the fraud had resulted in a loss. It also knew or should have known that the customers who had perpetrated the fraud were not who they purported to be. *Wall St. Disc. Corp. v. Hartford Fire Ins. Co.*, No. 03-4936, 2004 U.S. Dist. LEXIS 7718, at *18-19.

N.D. Ohio 1964. Where one has actual knowledge of facts that, without more, constitute dishonesty as a matter of law, it follows that one has actual knowledge of dishonesty as a matter of law. The knowledge or discovery of dishonesty does not depend upon knowledge or discovery of the full scope and exact details of the entire affair. Knowledge arises when the insured knows or has reasonable cause or opportunity to know that there has been dishonesty. Knowledge can arise either by knowledge derived from known facts or from reasonable inferences of fact. *City Loan & Sav. Co. v. Emp'rs Liab. Assurance Corp.*, 249 F. Supp. 633, 658-59.

W.D. Okla. 1973. Discovery under a Comprehensive Dishonesty, Disappearance and Destruction Policy means that time when the insured gains sufficient factual knowledge, not merely suspicion, which would justify a careful and prudent man in charging another with dishonesty. Knowledge is what a reasonable person should have concluded from known facts. *Alfalfa Elec. Coop., Inc. v. Travelers Indem. Co.*, 376 F. Supp. 901, 906-08.

D. Or. 1992. Insured's director caused insured to make a loan to entity in which he held an undisclosed interest. Insurer claimed that notice was untimely because insured had discovered loss when it first developed concerns as to loan's potential profitability, borrower's compliance with loan agreement, and value of collateral. In granting insured's partial motion for summary judgment, the court disagreed that there was a question of fact regarding the insured's discovery of loss. The court held that discovery of loss occurs when an insured has "acquired knowledge of some specific fraudulent or dishonest act which might involve the defendant in liability for the misconduct"; therefore, insured's concerns did not constitute discovery of fraud or dishonesty, but were instead only mere suspicion of problems with loan's credit administration. *Interstate Prod. Credit Ass'n v. Fireman's Fund Ins. Co.*, 788 F. Supp. 1530, 1535-37.

E.D. Pa. 1995. Court granted summary judgment for fidelity insurer on the grounds that the insured did not timely notify the insurer of a loss after discovery or timely bring action thereafter. Even if the wrongdoer convinced the insured that he would repay the money wrongfully taken, it did not change the objective fact that a wrongful action had been discovered. *Northwood Nursing & Convalescent Homes, Inc. v. Cont'l Ins. Co.*, 902 F. Supp. 79, 82-84.

E.D. Pa. 1993. Under a discovery bond, covering losses discovered during the policy period, but sustained at any time, the court held that the adverse-domination theory applied to toll discovery because the corporate entity was controlled by the very individuals engaged in fraudulent conduct. *In re Lloyd Sec., Inc.*, 153 B.R. 677, 683-85.

D.P.R. 1991. Unless it is otherwise provided in a Savings and Loan Blanket Bond, "it seems that even the strongest suspicion does not amount to knowledge nor discovery of dishonesty, and that nothing short of actual discovery of dishonesty or positive breach of an imperative condition by the insured employee will terminate the bond as to the defaulting employee." *FDIC v. CNA Cas. of P.R.*, 786 F. Supp. 1082, 1089.

M.D. Tenn. 1990. The court held that discovery of dishonesty occurs in connection with a Bankers Blanket Bond "only when the insured has knowledge which would justify a careful and prudent man in charging another with fraud or dishonesty." The court also noted that irregularities and discrepancies in accounts, if as consistent with the integrity of the employee as their dishonesty, does not constitute discovery even though dishonest acts may later be found to exist. *FDIC v. St. Paul Fire & Marine Ins. Co.*, 738 F. Supp. 1146, 1162.

N.D. Tex. 1997. Court denied insurer's summary judgment under a Bankers Blanket Bond because a fact issue existed as to when discovery occurred. Court held that discovery of loss does not occur until the insured discovers facts showing that dishonest acts occurred and appreciates the significance of those facts. Mere suspicion of loss is not enough. *FDIC v. Fid. & Deposit Co. of Md.*, No. 3:95-CV-1094-R, 1997 U.S. Dist. LEXIS 24375, at *4-8.

D. Utah 2010. The court denied the insurer's motion for summary judgment because there was a fact issue regarding when discovery occurred. The insured learned before the policy period that the principals had extended speculative loans in violation of the insured's policies. However, it was unclear to what extent the policies were actually enforced, and it was not certain until the policy period which loans would result in losses. *Transwest Credit Union v. CUMIS Ins. Soc'y, Inc.*, No. 2:09-297, 2010 U.S. Dist. LEXIS 99245, at *6, *10.

E.D. Va. 1963. The court held that the bond required notice at the earliest practicable moment after discovery of loss as a condition precedent to recovery, and that insured had failed to give such notice where it had notified insurer approximately nine months after discovery of loss. The court reasoned that "loss" as used in the bond means the date the fraud was discovered by the insured—not the date the insured was called upon to make the loss good. "Loss" refers to a condition in which the insured would be subject to a claim or demand "out of which a legal liability might arise"—not to an adjudicated liability. *Mount Vernon Bank & Trust Co. v. Aetna Cas. & Sur. Co.,* 224 F. Supp. 666, 670.

Cal. Ct. App. 1987. Fidelity bond did not require the insured to give notice upon discovery of a potential loss or of an occurrence that may give rise to a claim, but only to give notice after "the discovery of any loss." The court thus held that no loss occurred until the insured settled the lawsuit against it by paying $55,000, and time for giving notice began to run on that date. *Downey Sav. & Loan Ass'n v. Ohio Cas. Ins. Co.,* 234 Cal. Rptr. 835, 843-44.

Cal. Ct. App. 1985. Real estate investment trust sued insurer for bad faith failure to pay an employee dishonesty claim under a bond. The covered employee was the president of the trust, who fraudulently misrepresented facts relating to a loan acquired by the trust. The misrepresentations were discovered by the insured well in advance of the default on the loan. A jury found the insurer liable for bad faith and breach of contract. On appeal, having found that the bond did not define "discovery," the court, in deciding whether suit had been timely filed, held that discovery in loan transactions takes place when the loan goes into default, and not, as urged by the insurer, when the insured discovers the fraudulent acts which caused the loss. *Pac.-S. Mortg. Trust v. Ins. Co. of N. Am.,* 212 Cal. Rptr. 754, 759-60.

Cal. Ct. App. 1983. A group of mutual funds made a claim under a fidelity bond for employee dishonesty involving the former president of the funds. The bond provided that coverage attached only for loss "discovered not later than one year from the end of the policy period." The policy period terminated in September 1971, but the insureds admitted that their first notice of the covered employee dishonesty came in early 1973. The court of appeal, reversing summary judgment for the insurer, held that (1) equitable tolling principles extended the time to discover losses caused by the covered employees because these employees adversely dominated and controlled the insured entities; (2) the tolling period extended far enough to permit recovery under the policies; and (3) permitting recovery enhances the goals of the Investment Company Act of 1940. *Admiralty Fund v. Peerless Ins. Co.*, 191 Cal. Rptr. 753, 759-60.

Cal. Ct. App. 1981. Discovery of loss occurs under a fidelity bond when the insured learns of the dishonest or fraudulent acts committed by an employee. Knowledge of the acts which are alleged to be fraudulent or dishonest is discovery of loss. Insured's understanding of the nature of the acts is not relevant. *USLIFE Sav. & Loan Ass'n v. Nat'l Sur. Corp.*, 171 Cal. Rptr. 393, 399.

Cal. Ct. App. 1931. "Discovers a loss," within the context of a fidelity bond, means actual knowledge, and the opportunity to investigate and means of knowledge without actual knowledge do not require the insured to give notice. *Pac. Coast Adjustment Bureau v. Indem. Ins. Co. of N. Am.*, 2 P.2d 218, 219-20.

Cal. Ct. App. 1919. Notice is not required under a fidelity bond upon mere suspicion, but notice must be given when insured knows or had every opportunity of knowing of default. *L.A. Athl. Club v. USF&G*, 183 P. 174, 177.

Colo. App. 1978. Discovery of loss occurred in connection with a Bankers Blanket Bond when the bank learned of the employee's fraudulent conduct, not when the bank learned that the loan would not be repaid. *First Nat'l Bank of Fleming v. Md. Cas. Co.*, 581 P.2d 744, 745.

Conn. 1990. The court held that employees' knowledge of fraudulent conduct which is sufficient to trigger an insured's obligation to provide notice under a fidelity policy is properly imputed to the principal when the circumstances in a given case give rise to an express or implied obligation, born out of the employees' authority or control or to report fraudulent activity. The court thus concluded that the insurer was precluded from its obligations under a bond for a second, more substantial loss caused by employee dishonesty when the insured's store manager and bookkeeper knew of the clerk's dishonest conduct but failed to provide the store owner or the insurer with notice of the initial loss. The bond stated that coverage "shall not apply to any employee from ... the time the insured or any [non-colluding] partner or officer thereof ... shall have knowledge" of the employee committing fraudulent or dishonest acts. *E. Udolf, Inc. v. Aetna Cas. & Sur. Co.*, 573 A.2d 1211, 1213-15.

Fla. Dist. Ct. App. 2003. In an action seeking coverage under an employee dishonesty endorsement attached to a comprehensive policy, the court strictly enforced the policy in accordance with its terms. The endorsement at issue unambiguously obligated the insurer to pay for covered losses discovered within ninety days after the policy expired. Here, however, the insured failed to discover the loss for more than two years. *Fireman's Fund Ins. Co. v. Levine & Partners, P.A.*, 848 So. 2d 1186, 1187.

Ga. App. 1996. Adopting an objective standard for when discovery under an insurance policy covering employee dishonesty occurs, the court found a genuine issue of material fact and reversed the summary judgment held in the insurer's favor. Although the court found that the car dealership's officer-in-charge of operations had knowledge supporting suspicion of wrongdoing in the used car department, it could not find that the officer discovered, as a matter of law, a loss falling within the coverage period. *Boomershine Pontiac-GMC Truck, Inc. v. Globe Indem. Co.*, 466 S.E.2d 915, 917-19.

Ill. App. 1995. Under a Public Employee's Bond, stating that cancellation would occur upon discovery of any covered act that created liability for the insurer, the court was persuaded that an objective standard should be applied to determine when discovery occurred. The court then held that a material fact issue prevented summary judgment in favor of a taxpayer complaining of illegal expenditures. *Kinzer v. Fid. & Deposit Co. of Md.*, 652 N.E.2d 20, 27-29.

Ind. App. 1995. The court refused to find that the discovery period of an unidentified fidelity policy was equitably tolled by the adverse-domination doctrine. Mere stock ownership in a company does not establish domination as officers and other employees of the corporation are primarily responsible for the day-to-day operations of the organization. *Mut. Sec. Life Ins. Co. v. Fid. & Deposit Co. of Md.*, 659 N.E.2d 1096, 1102-03.

Ind. App. 1931. The insured is not required to give notice until it has actual knowledge of a loss under the bond. *Fletcher Sav. & Trust Co. v. Am. Sur. Co.*, 175 N.E. 247, 251-52.

Iowa 1979. Discovery requires that the insured have actual knowledge of the improper conduct and that the insured knew or should have known that such conduct was dishonest or fraudulent. *FDIC v. Nat'l Sur. Corp.*, 281 N.W.2d 816, 820-21.

Kan. App. 1989. The court held that discovery acts as a limitation to coverage. Discovery is determined by the trier of fact deciding what the insured subjectively knew, and then deciding what subjective conclusions reasonably can be drawn by the insured as a result. The court thus found that, although one insurer was excused from its obligation to provide coverage, the subsequent insurer's obligation was triggered under a 1980 Bankers Blanket Bond. Simply put, discovery occurred during the subsequent insurer's bond period when the insured received knowledge that a lawsuit, which arose out of a former employee's fraudulent conduct, would be filed. Discovery of a loss could not reasonably be concluded from an investigatory meeting held prior to the inception of the subsequent policy. *Home Life Ins. Co. v. Clay*, 773 P.2d 666, 677-78.

Ky. 1906. An insured is not bound to report its suspicions to its insurer, even though such suspicions may be strong enough to justify, in the opinion of the insured, the discharge of the employee. After suspicion is aroused, it ought to pursue its inquiries with reasonable diligence, and when satisfied that defalcation exists, and the extent, or the substantial extent, of it, notice of the fact ought to be given promptly. *Fid. & Guar. Co. v. W. Bank*, 94 S.W. 3, 5-6.

La. App. 1997. Court held, with respect to the two crime policies at issue, that the claim was not covered due to the insured's late notice. The insured discovered the loss when it was served with a lawsuit alleging that misrepresentations were made by one of its salesmen, but waited until a final judgment was rendered to provide notice. Since discovery occurred in the first policy period, the loss cannot be discovered again. *Newpark Res., Inc. v. Marsh & McLennan*, 691 So. 2d 208, 212-13.

La. App. 1938. With respect to a fidelity bond, an insured is not required to give notice of suspicions. Rather, insured must give notice when it has knowledge of fraudulent or dishonest conduct on the part of its employee that might involve the liability of the insurer. *Inter-City Express Lines, Inc. v. Hartford Acc. & Indem. Co.*, 178 So. 280, 282.

Me. 2002. The court held that the "ordinary standards of objective reasonableness" applied to the insured's discovery of employee dishonesty, which arose out of the president's violation of internal procedure concerning personal use of company credit cards. Thus, the court found that the insured's proof of loss was untimely filed and affirmed a judgment in favor of the insurer. *Acadia Ins. Co. v. Keiser Indus., Inc.*, 793 A.2d 495, 498-99.

Mass. 1935. The language in a fidelity bond cannot reasonably be construed to mean that the giving of notice may be deferred until such time as the insured had not only discovered but was actually able to prove that loss had occurred. Rather, discovery of loss must mean knowledge of loss that is derived from known facts or reasonable inferences of fact. *Gilmour v. Standard Sur. & Cas. Co.*, 197 N.E. 673, 675-76.

Minn. 1957. An insured is not obligated to give notice of a loss under a Bankers Blanket Bond "until he is justified in believing that a loss has occurred through dishonesty rather than through errors consistent with integrity." That does not mean, however, that an insured may wait to provide notice until the extent of the loss is determined. *Prior Lake State Bank v. Nat'l Sur. Corp.*, 80 N.W.2d 612, 616.

Minn. 1910. Though the insured may have suspicions of irregularities or fraud, he is not bound to assume that an employee is guilty of acts of dishonesty until he has acquired the knowledge of such specific acts that could trigger an insurer's liability under an employee fidelity bond. *Gamble-Robinson Co. v. Mass. Bonding & Ins. Co.*, 129 N.W. 131, 132.

Miss. 1921. To be aware of a loss sustained by reason of acts constituting larceny or embezzlement, the insured must have knowledge of facts which would constitute the crime and not be based upon mere inferences or suspicions arising from unexplained irregularities or discrepancies in the books or accounts of the employee. To be aware of such loss with sufficient certainty to justify the charge of larceny or embezzlement may, and probably will, require considerable time for investigation after a well-founded suspicion of wrongdoing has been aroused. *Md. Cas. Co. v. Hall*, 88 So. 407, 409.

Mo. 1966. To constitute discovery in accordance with the terms of the bond, there must be facts known which would lead a reasonable person to assume that the insured has suffered a loss by reason of its handling of its customer's account. The time of discovery is when the insured reasonably has knowledge of a loss and recognizes that the customer suffered a loss for which the customer intends to hold the insured responsible. *Jefferson Bank & Trust Co. v. Cent. Sur. & Ins. Corp.*, 408 S.W.2d 825, 831-32.

Mo. Ct. App. 1998. In a coverage dispute involving commercial crime policies, an employee's undisclosed knowledge of his own fraudulent conduct will not be imputed to his employer to target when discovery occurs and thereby whether notice is timely provided. The term "you," as used in the policies, refers not to an employee but to the insured named in the policy declarations. *Se. Bakery Feeds, Inc. v. Ranger Ins. Co.*, 974 S.W.2d 635, 639.

Mont. 1924. Insured is not required to give notice under an employee fidelity bond upon suspicion. Notice is required when insured has knowledge of the existence of such facts as would justify a careful and prudent man in charging another with the acts for which the claim is made. *Outlook Farmers' Elevator Co. v. Am. Sur. Co.*, 223 P. 905, 911.

Neb. 1989. Insured's action was dismissed due to its failure to assert that discovery occurred prior to termination of the bond. Although the petition implied that the bank had some knowledge of employee dishonesty, the Nebraska Supreme Court held that the insured lacked knowledge of specific acts of wrongdoing until after the bond expired. *First Sec. Bank & Trust v. N.H. Ins. Co.*, 441 N.W.2d 188, 195-96.

N.J. 1978. Discovery of a loss occurs when the insured "learns of facts or obtains knowledge which would justify a careful and prudent person in charging another with dishonesty or fraud." Mere suspicions of irregularities or improper conduct do not trigger an insured's obligation under the policy. *Nat'l Newark & Essex Bank v. Am. Ins. Co.*, 385 A.2d 1216, 1224.

N.Y. App. 1992. Insured argued that discovery of loss, under a Comprehensive Dishonesty, Disappearance and Destruction Policy, occurs only when the insured has obtained facts from which the extent and the amount of the loss reasonably can be estimated. Rejecting the insureds position, the court held that discovery of loss occurs once an insured has obtained facts sufficient to cause a reasonable person to recognize there has been dishonesty or fraud resulting in loss. The court also noted that the time of discovery must be determined according to "an objective test," that is, what a reasonable insured would conclude from the information available. *Commodore Int'l, Ltd. v. Nat'l Union Fire Ins. Co. Pitt., Pa.*, 591 N.Y.S.2d 168, 169-170.

N.Y. App. 1934. Discovery occurs under a fidelity bond when the insured acquires knowledge of facts from which the conclusion of fraud and dishonesty reasonably follow. *Charles W. Schreiber Travel Bureau v. Standard Sur. & Cas. Co.*, 269 N.Y.S. 804, 806-07.

N.Y. Sup. 1993. A contentious coverage dispute erupted in the wake of the securities scandal perpetrated by Michael Milken and Dennis Levine. Drexel Burnham, the insured, sought coverage against its insurers and artfully avoided pleading an affirmative date of discovery. Insured had discovered dishonesty in 1986, but asserted claims on bonds for years 1986-1990. Court held that discovery had occurred in 1986, thus precluding claims on bonds covering subsequent years. The court reasoned that "discovery is not a gradual awakening"; it can be made only once. *Drexel Burnham Lambert Group, Inc. v. Vigilant Ins. Co.*, 595 N.Y.S.2d 999, 1006-07.

N.C. 1926. Notice to the bonding company of suspicion is not required. *Forest City Bldg. & Loan Ass'n. v. Davis*, 133 S.E. 530, 533, *modified on other grounds*, 138 S.E. 338 (1927).

Okla. 1932. Time for giving notice to insurer on a terminated bond did not begin until officers of the insured discovered that embezzlement had occurred during the term of the prior bond. *Am. Sur. Co. v. State*, 12 P.2d 212, 214-15.

Or. App. 2000. Court reversed and remanded a judgment in favor of an insurer when it found a material fact question as to when a manufacturer discovered a loss. Although an insured is not obligated to know all of the details concerning a loss for there to be discovery, the insured is deemed to have discovered a loss only when there is sufficient knowledge justifying a reasonable person to believe that a covered loss has taken place. An insured's knowledge that a company policy has been violated does not necessarily amount to discovery. *Nike, Inc. v. Nw. Pac. Indem. Co.*, 999 P.2d 1197, 1203-04.

Pa. 1934. Discovery occurred when bank president learned of employee fraud and received a demand for payment from its customer. So far as the insured was concerned, the loss, in the sense of a claim out of which a legal liability might arise, was discovered at that time and not upon receipt of a written demand made several months later. *Gentile v. Am. Bank & Trust Co.*, 172 A. 303, 305.

Pa. 1928. Court affirmed judgment for insurer based on its finding that the insured discovered the loss and failed to give notice for over two years. The court held that notice cannot be delayed while the insured seeks to determine the extent of loss that will not be reimbursed by the employee. *Morrelville Deposit Bank v. Royal Indem. Co.*, 144 A. 424, 425.

Pa. App. 1936. Discovery under a fidelity bond occurs when the insured has actual knowledge that a default has occurred. *Thomas Holme Bldg. & Loan Ass'n v. New Amsterdam Cas. Co.*, 188 A. 374, 376-77.

Tenn. App. 1984. The bond at issue required notice as soon as practicable and proof of loss within four months after "knowledge or discovery of an occurrence which may give rise to a claim for loss." The

Appellate court held that notice and proof of loss requirements are conditions precedent to recovery under Tennessee law. The insured did not give notice as soon as practicable, despite knowing of an occurrence that might give rise to a loss, and prerequisites to coverage may not be excused by the insured's failure to know the amount of the loss. *Griffith Motors, Inc. v. Compass Ins. Co.*, 676 S.W.2d 555, 558.

Tenn. App. 1965. The word "discovery" means "the knowledge of facts and circumstances sufficient to satisfy persons of ordinary prudence that a loss has occurred." *World Secret Serv. Ass'n v. Travelers Indem. Co.*, 396 S.W.2d 848, 849.

Tenn. App. 1937. "Discovery of fraud or of default" means the knowledge of facts and circumstances sufficient to satisfy persons of ordinary prudence that default or conversion had been committed. *Nashville & Am. Trust Co. v. Aetna Cas. & Sur. Co.*, 110 S.W.2d 1041, 1046.

Tex. App. 1984. Coverage under a fidelity bond is terminated when the insured gains knowledge of facts sufficient to infer that employee dishonesty has occurred, but insurer was held liable only for loss on loans discovered before termination. *Fid. & Cas. Co. v. Cent. Bank*, 672 S.W.2d 641, 644-45.

Tex. App. 1944. Irregularities revealed by an insurance examiner's report did not show any loss due to dishonesty or bad faith and were not sufficient to trigger a board's duty to inquire. The bond requires notice of losses due to dishonesty and bad faith and not merely a warning to prevent possible future losses. *Bd. of Ins. Comm'r of Tex. v. Allied Underwriters*, 180 S.W.2d 990, 995.

Utah App. 1991. In a coverage dispute under a bond that included a rider defining discovery in the same manner adopted under the 1980 Bankers Blanket Bond, the court held that "discovery" applied to the notice provision, but not to the loss sustained provision. Rejecting respected law addressing the meaning of discovery, the court rationalized its holding on its conclusion that "sustained loss" refers to "actual rather than possible losses." *Home Sav. & Loan v. Aetna Cas. & Sur. Co.*, 817 P.2d 341, 354-58.

Vt. 1940. The court reversed and rendered judgment for insurer having found that discovery of loss means knowledge of loss derived from known facts or reasonable inferences of fact and that notice cannot be delayed until the extent of loss is ascertained. *Brown v. Md. Cas. Co.*, 11 A.2d 222, 223-24.

Wash. 1966. Fidelity bond required notice after insured acquired actual knowledge of shortage. Knowledge that employee was tardy in making deposits was not sufficient to constitute knowledge of dishonesty. *Tradewell Stores, Inc. v. Fid. & Cas. Co.*, 410 P.2d 782, 784-85.

Wash. 1935. Notice is not required until discovery of dishonesty. *Hansen v. Am. Bonding Co.*, 48 P.2d 653, 656.

Wis. 1912. Notice is required upon actual knowledge and not mere constructive notice. *First Nat'l Bank v. USF&G*, 137 N.W. 742, 745.

SECONDARY SOURCES

Paul Briganti, *Inside the Mind of the Reasonable Person: Determining When Discovery of Loss Has Occurred Under a Fidelity Bond in the Third Circuit,* 46 VILL. L. REV. 801 (2001).

Duncan L. Clore, *Discovery of Loss: The Contractual Predicate to the Claim, in* FINANCIAL INSTITUTION BONDS 193 (Duncan L. Clore ed., 3d ed. 2008).

Duncan L. Clore & Michael Keeley, *Discovery of Loss: The Contractual Predicate to the Claim*, *in* FINANCIAL INSTITUTION BONDS 193 (Duncan L. Clore ed., 3d ed. 2008).

Duncan L. Clore & John Tomaine, *Discovery of Loss*, *in* HANDLING FIDELITY BOND CLAIMS 385 (Michael Keeley & Timothy M. Sukel, eds., 1999).

Paul R. Devin & Allen N. David, *Discovery Under Fidelity Bonds: The Emerging Concept of the Insured's Duty of Inquiry*, 21 TORT & INS. L.J. 543 (1986).

David T. DiBiase, *Notice Requirements*, in EMPLOYEE DISHONESTY: CLAIMS, BOND COVERAGES AND CAVEATS (Charles W. Franklin ed. 1983).

Edward Etcheverry, *Discovery, Notice, Proof of Loss, and Suit Limitations*, in COMMERCIAL CRIME POLICY 12 (Gil J. Schroeder ed., 1996).

Edward Etcheverry & Guy W. Harrison, *Employee Dishonesty—When Does Your Bond "Automatically Terminate"?*, VI FID. L.J. 71 (2000).

Edward G. Gallagher, *Discovery and Termination*, in LOAN LOSS COVERAGE UNDER FINANCIAL INSTITUTION BONDS 263 (Gilbert J. Schroeder & John J. Tomaine eds., 2007).

Peter C. Haley, *Clause (E): The Continued Importance of Defined Terms and Causation Requirements*, in FINANCIAL INSTITUTION BONDS 253 (Duncan L. Clore ed., 2d. ed. 1998).

Peter C. Haley, *The Power of Defined Terms & Causation Theories Under Insuring Agreement (E) of the Financial Institution Bond*, 31 TORT & INS. L.J. 609 (1996).

Michael Keeley & Toni Scott Reed, *"Superpowers" of Federal Regulators: How The Banking Crisis Created an Entire Genre of Bond Litigation*, 31 TORT & INS. L.J. 817 (1996).

M.A.L., Annotation, *Suspicion, or Reasons for Suspicion, of Wrongdoing by Officer or Employee Covered by Fidelity Bond or Policy as Requiring Obligee to Comply with Conditions of Bond with Respect to Notice of Discovery or Knowledge of Loss*, 129 A.L.R. 1411 (1940).

John M. McCormick, *Frauds of the Insured, Imputation of Knowledge and Impleading the Employee in Fidelity Cases*, 4 THE FORUM 204 (1969).

G. Wayne Murphy, *Allegations, Assertion and Charges as Discovery of Loss*, 12 THE FORUM 986 (1977).

Andrew M. Reidy & Barbara M. Tapscott, *The Pitfalls of Fidelity Insurance: Banks Seeking Coverage for Employee Fraud Face Four Hurdles: Timely Notice, Discovery, Termination & Manifest Intent*, 18 NAT. L.J. 137 (1996).

Scott L. Schmookler & Bruce Robbibaro, *Discovery by the Risk Manager: The Effect of Noise Reducing Headphones on Fidelity Coverage*, XVII FID. L.J. 171 (2011).

Paul D. Schoonover, *Discovery, Notice and Automatic Cancellation under Revised Form 24*, 16 THE FORUM 962 (1981).

Karen Wildau & Marlo Orlin Leach, *What Did They Know and When Did They Know It, Who Are "They" Anyway, and What Difference Does It Make—Imputation Under The Financial Institution Bond and Its Implication for Coverage*, III FID. L.J. 1 (1997).

SECTION 4 — LIMIT OF LIABILITY*

Aggregate Limit of Liability

The Underwriter's total liability for all losses discovered during the Bond Period shown in Item 2. of the Declarations shall not exceed the Aggregate Limit of Liability shown in Item 3. of the Declarations. The Aggregate Limit of Liability shall be reduced by the amount of any payment made under the terms of this bond.

Upon exhaustion of the Aggregate Limit of Liability by such payments:

    (a) The Underwriter shall have no further liability for loss or losses regardless of when discovered and whether or not previously reported to the Underwriter; and

    (b) The Underwriter shall have no obligation under General Agreement F to continue the defense of the Insured, and upon notice by the Underwriter to the Insured that the Aggregate Limit of Liability has been exhausted, the Insured shall assume all responsibility for its defense at its own cost.

The Aggregate Limit of Liability shall not be increased or reinstated by any recovery made and applied in accordance with subsections (a), (b) and (c) of Section 7. In the event that a loss of Property is settled by the Underwriter through the use of a lost instrument bond, such loss shall not reduce the Aggregate Limit of Liability.[1]

---

* By Thomas J. Vollbrecht and Jason Tarasek, Hammargren & Meyer, P.A., Minneapolis, Minnesota.

[1] The only substantive change in the 2004 revision to the bond is as follows:

The Aggregate Limit of Liability shall be reinstated by any net recovery received by the Underwriter during the Bond Period and before the Aggregate Limit of Liability is exhausted. Recovery from reinsurance and/or indemnity of the Underwriter shall not be deemed a recovery as used herein. In the event that a loss of Property is settled by the Underwriter through the use of a lost instrument bond, such loss shall not reduce the Aggregate Limit of Liability, but any payment

Single Loss Limit of Liability

Subject to the Aggregate Limit of Liability, the Underwriter's liability for each Single Loss shall not exceed the applicable Single Loss Limit of Liability shown in Item 4. of the Declarations. If a Single Loss is covered under more than one Insuring Agreement or Coverage, the maximum payable shall not exceed the largest applicable Single Loss Limit of Liability.

Single Loss Defined

Single Loss means all covered loss, including court costs and attorneys' fees incurred by the Underwriter under General Agreement F, resulting from

- (a) any one act or series of related acts of burglary, robbery or attempt thereat, in which no Employee is implicated, or
- (b) any one act or series of related unintentional or negligent acts or omissions on the part of any person (whether an Employee or not) resulting in damage to or destruction or misplacement of Property, or
- (c) all acts or omissions other than those specified in (a) and (b) preceding, caused by any person (whether an Employee or not) or in which such person is implicated; or
- (d) any one casualty or event not specified in (a), (b) or (c) preceding.

COMMENT

Section 4 of the bond serves two over-arching purposes: (1) to set and define the insurer's total potential liability for all losses discovered during the bond period—that is, the aggregate limit of liability; and (2) to set and define the insurer's potential liability under each insuring

---

under the lost instrument bond shall reduce the Aggregate Limit of Liability under this Bond.

agreement for a single loss discovered during the bond period—that is, the single loss limit of liability. In recognition of these two purposes, the cases in this annotation are divided into two categories: (1) cases involving the cumulation of policy periods where losses extend over multiple policy periods; and (2) cases involving the insurer's liability for multiple losses caused by a single person.

A. Non-cumulation

Courts deciding whether an insured may cumulate successive policies typically attempt to determine whether the parties clearly expressed their intent through unambiguous policy language on the issue of whether each bond renewal constitutes a separate contract or one continuous contract. In the absence of an ambiguity, courts generally conclude that—despite an insured's payment of annual premiums—the bond constitutes one continuous contract that limits the insured's total potential recovery to the aggregate limit of liability for a single policy period. When concluding that only one contract exists, courts often point to the absence of a definitive end date as evidence of the parties' intent to enter one continuous contract.

B. Single loss/occurrence.

When weighing whether one occurrence or multiple occurrences exist, courts typically focus upon the underlying cause of the loss. If a loss is caused by one employee, who employed one method to engage in a continuous pattern of wrongdoing, courts are likely to conclude that only one occurrence exists. If there are multiple employees, multiple methods and/or significant temporal gaps in the series of wrongful acts, courts are more likely to conclude that multiple occurrences exist.

OUTLINE OF ANNOTATIONS

A. Non-Cumulation
 1. Cases Disallowing Recovery under Successive Policies
 2. Cases Allowing Recovery under Successive Policies

B. Single Loss/Occurrence
   1. Cases Finding a Single Loss/Occurrence.
   2. Cases Finding Multiple Losses/Occurrences.

ANNOTATIONS

A. Non-Cumulation

1. Cases Disallowing Recovery under Successive Policies.

2d Cir. 2001 (N.Y.). Fidelity bond contained provision limiting liability to a set amount "regardless of the . . . number of premiums . . . paid." The court found that the clause non-ambiguously limited the insurer's liability to one bond penalty although losses were incurred in four successive years. *Scranton Volunteer Fire Co. v. USF&G,* 450 F.2d 775, 776-77.

8th Cir. 1960 (Mo.). Fidelity bond was not for a definite, fixed period and provided that bond periods would not be cumulative. Despite regular renewal payments, the court noted: "[i]t has generally been held that where the bond is for an indefinite term, the date it begins to run being the only date given, the fact that the premiums were paid annually does not make the relation a series of separate yearly contracts." *Mass. Bonding & Ins. Co. v. Julius Seidel Lumber Co.,* 279 F.2d 861, 868.

11th Cir. 2009 (Fla.). Non-cumulation clause and limit-of-liability clause limited insured's recovery to policy limit even though employee's acts of theft occurred over 13 years and spanned multiple policies. *PBSJ Corp. v. Fed. Ins. Co.,* 347 F. App'x 532, 535-36.

D.C. Cir. 1951. Rejecting the obligee's argument that it was victimized by employee's four discrete acts of theft during four discrete periods, the court found that obligee could only recover for one annual policy period. "Where, as here, in addition to the continuous term of the bond, there was language in the bond or its attachments which militated against a finding of cumulative liability, the courts have consistently held liability to be limited, in the aggregate, to the amount stated in the bond (i.e., non-cumulative)." *Columbia Hosp. for Women and Lying-in Asylum v. USF&G,* 188 F.2d 654, 657.

M.D. La. 1974. The original bond was for a period of one year and contained no provision regarding cumulative liability; however, each renewal certificate provided that liability was limited to the face amount of the original bond. Because the obligee paid each annual premium and was aware of the restrictive language in the renewal certificates, its recovery for losses over three years was limited to $50,000, rather than the $150,000 claimed. *Parish of East Baton Rouge v. Fid. & Cas. Co. of N.Y.,* 373 F. Supp. 440, 444.

D.C. 2007. Because bonds were continuous, not cumulative, surety's liability was capped at face amount of bonds. Annual premiums were installment payments reflecting that the longer the bond remained in effect, the greater the risk assumed by the surety, and the more the bond should cost. *May v. Cont'l Cas. Co.,* 936 A.2d 747, 752-53.

Fla. Dist. Ct. App. 1995. Although employee's embezzlement occurred over four years, coverage was available under only one policy in light of non-cumulation provision, particularly its clear statement that recovery was limited to the higher of two consecutive policies. *Reliance Ins. Co. v. Treasure Coast Travel Agency, Inc.,* 660 So. 2d 1136, 1137-38.

Ill. App. Ct. 1973. Coverage under blanket bond that replaced position security bond was continuous where all instruments stated that the insurer's liability was not cumulative. When bond is for an indefinite term, annual premium payments do not convert it into separate annual contracts. *Santa Fe Gen. Office Credit Union v. Gilberts,* 299 N.E.2d 65, 73.

La. 1983. Presence of non-cumulation clause, absence of specific termination date and absence of separate renewal certificates supported holding that there was only one continuous bond. The court also held that the insured received the protection for which he bargained and rejected his argument that the non-cumulation provision should be deemed void as against public policy. *Guste v. Aetna Cas. & Sur. Co.,* 429 So. 2d 106, 110.

La. Ct. App. 1961. Bond and all subsequent bonds held cancelled upon first discovery of employee dishonesty, despite employee restitution of those funds. Issuance of a certificate of continuation of original bond did not create a separate contract affording coverage for subsequent embezzlements. "It is obvious that the parties intended to create one bond, subject to annual renewal." *Emp'rs Liab. Assurance Corp. v. S. Produce Co., Inc.,* 129 So. 2d 247, 249.

Md. App. 1970. Bond issued for definite term that was periodically renewed by certificates that adopted the original bond's terms and provided that the premium was accepted for the renewal and shall not be cumulative, limited surety's liability to amount stated in original bond. *Comm'rs of Leonardtown v. Fid. & Cas. Co. of N.Y.,* 270 A.2d 788, 790-91.

Minn. Ct. App. 1997. Because policy unambiguously limited recovery on claims arising from misconduct occurring over several years to the policy limit and included an unambiguous non-cumulation clause, insured's recovery was limited to one policy period. *Landico, Inc. v. Am. Family Mut. Ins. Co.,* 559 N.W.2d 438, 441.

N.Y. 2001. Court applied non-cumulation clause and held that "what plaintiff would characterize as separate policy periods are simply three-year premium terms." *Shared-Interest Mgmt. v. CNN Fin'l Ins. Gp.,* 283 A.D.2d 136, 139.

N.C. 1980. Payment of annual premiums did not create separate and distinct cumulative contracts but only one contact with maximum liability fixed by the principal amount of the bond because bond is for an indefinite period without a specified termination date. *Town of Scotland Neck v. W. Sur. Co.,* 271 S.E.2d 501, 504-05.

N.D. 1993. Coverage was limited to the policy limits of one term because "[t]he combination of the provision against cumulation of coverage and... provision [that] extend[ed] coverage to prior losses, indicates the intention that the policies constitute one continuous and noncumulative contract." *Kavaney Realtor & Developer, Inc. v. Travelers Ins. Co.,* 501 N.W.2d 335, 342.

Pa. Super. Ct. 2006. In light of non-cumulation clause, annual fidelity bonds covering several years were a continuous bonding scheme with a single limit for employee dishonesty, rather than multiple contracts, even though original bond was renewed on annual basis and parties did not complete provision on cancellation of prior insurance. *Reliance Ins. Co. v. IRPC, Inc.,* 904 A.2d 912, 916-17.

Pa. Super Ct. 1998. Bond was ambiguous because phrase "aggregate and non-cumulative" stands "in isolation" rather than explicitly identifying the losses that were to be aggregated. "In every case that we have located in which such a clause was found to be unambiguous, the clause stated that the surety would pay no more than the maximum amount stated in the bond no matter how many times the bond was renewed or for how many years it was in effect." Nonetheless, the insured's admission that the bond covered multiple years within a single, aggregate and non-cumulative policy limit established that liability was limited to the fixed sum of the original bond. *Penn. Twp. v. Aetna Cas. & Sur. Co.,* 719 A.2d 749, 754.

Pa. Super Ct. 1981. Even though each of three fidelity bonds designated a different insurer, all contained an express non-cumulation provision that operated to limit recovery to a single bond limit. Furthermore, by accepting each yearly bond, plaintiff (through termination/cancellation clause) agreed to terminate the prior bond. *Eddystone Fire Co. No. 1 v. Cont'l Ins. Cos.,* 425 A.2d 803, 806.

Va. 1990. Express non-cumulation clause that "liability could not cumulate from year to year or period to period" explicitly limited liability regardless of the number of years that coverage was in effect. *Graphic Arts Mut. Ins. Co. v. C.W. Warthen Co., Inc.,* 397 S.E.2d 876, 877-78.

Va. 1988. Policy expressly limited maximum liability to single occurrence coverage under one policy even though losses in both policy periods exceeded the coverage limit. *White Tire Distrib., Inc. v. Penn. Nat'l Mut. Cas. Ins. Co.,* 367 S.E.2d 518, 519-20.

Vt. 1958. Express non-cumulation clause in bond and in continuation certificates limited liability to a single policy. *Town of Troy v. Am. Fid. Co.,* 143 A.2d 469, 476.

2. Cases Allowing Recovery under Successive Policies

4th Cir. 2001 (S.C.). The non-cumulation provision was ambiguous because it did not expressly preclude coverage for an "occurrence" occurring over a period of time covered by successive policies. Further, a cancellation of prior insurance provision was not completed. Consequently, the court allowed recovery under each of two consecutive policy periods for the acts of one employee that spanned both periods. *Spartan Iron & Metal Corp. v. Liberty Ins. Corp.,* 6 F. App'x 176, 181.

8th Cir. 1983 (N.D.). Bankruptcy trustee bond held to be separate contract for each year despite limiting language in continuation certificates because there was no evidence that the obligee (the bankruptcy judge) knew or approved of the non-cumulation provision in the renewal certificates. Court affirmed that bond constitutes a separate and distinct contract unless the parties expressly intend that renewal of a policy shall constitute one continuous contract. *Endeco, Inc. v. Fid. and Cas. Co. of N.Y.,* 718 F.2d 879, 881-82.

9th Cir. 2000 (Cal.). The court concluded that coverage was available through each of a series of successive policies. "[A]n insurer will be liable up to the policy limit for each separate period, unless it can show clear intent by the parties to enter into a single continuous insurance contract." Finding that the policy was ambiguous as to whether an "occurrence" is a single act or series of act, the court found ruled that it must be construed "in favor of liability." *Karen Kane, Inc. v. Reliance Ins. Co.,* 202 F.3d 1180, 1188.

N.D. Ala. 1963. Because each succeeding bond expressly terminated and cancelled the prior bond, the court held that each bond was "separate and distinct" and, therefore, the non-cumulation clause was meaningless. *White Dairy Co. v. St. Paul Fire & Marine Ins. Co.,* 222 F. Supp. 1014, 1016-17.

N.D. Ill. 2008. Insurer's annual renewal of employee dishonesty policy created three separate one-year policies even though policies all had same policy number because each policy had different provisions and discrete policy periods. Prior loss provision related only to losses during period of *immediately* prior policy. *Am. Auto Guardian, Inc. v. Acuity Mut. Ins. Co.,* 548 F. Supp. 2d 624, 630.

Cal. Ct. App. 1995. Rejecting insurer's contention that non-cumulation provision and prior loss provision demonstrated the parties' intent that there be one continuous contract, the court held that those clauses were ambiguous such that coverage was available under each policy. The court found that non-cumulation has several possible meanings and that other policy provisions indicated an intent that renewals constitute separate and distinct contracts. *A.B.S. Clothing Collection, Inc. v. Home Ins. Co.,* 41 Cal. Rptr. 2d 166, 171.

Fla. Dist. Ct. App. 1978. Despite non-cumulation clause, court held that a renewal of a fidelity policy or bond created a separate and distinct contract for the period of time covered by such renewal. *City of Miami Springs v. Travelers Indem. Co.,* 365 So. 2d 1030, 1032.

Ga. 2004. Non-cumulation clause was ambiguous as to whether limit applied to policy period or to aggregated period under original and renewal policies. *Sherman & Hemstreet, Inc. v. Cincinnati Ins. Co.,* 594 S.E.2d 648, 650.

Ga. Ct. App. 2003. Finding non-cumulation clause ambiguous, the court allowed recovery under successive policies. *Cincinnati Ins. Co. v. Sherman & Hemstreet, Inc.,* 581 S.E.2d 613, 616.

Iowa 1994. Court held non-cumulation clause ambiguous because it could be construed as either limiting coverage to the single policy limit for the entire three-year period, or as providing separate protection for each of those three years. *Cincinnati Ins. Co. v. Hopkins Sporting Goods, Inc.,* 522 N.W.2d 837, 839-40.

Kan. Ct. App. 1990. Finding ambiguity, applying doctrine of reasonable expectations and ruling that a reasonable insured would expect that policy limits would renew upon renewal of policy, court held that insured was entitled to recover the limits of liability for each period of insurance. Court also noted that numerous cases have addressed this issue over roughly a century, such that insurer knew this question would arise as to its policy, yet it failed to address the problem with unambiguous policy language. *Penalosa Coop. Exch. v. Farmland Mut. Ins. Co.,* 789 P.2d 1196, 1200.

Minn. 1979. Court held non-cumulation provision ambiguous on ground that policy provisions limiting "total" liability and "annual" liability were contradictory. *Columbia Heights Motors, Inc. v. Allstate Ins. Co.,* 275 N.W.2d 32, 36.

Wyo. 1984. Because bond was renewed annually, providing coverage of $5,000 each year for losses occurring during policy period, plaintiff was entitled to recover $25,000 for misappropriations over a five-year period. *W. Sur. Co. v. Town of Evansville,* 675 P.2d 258, 264-65.

B. Single Loss/Occurrence

1. Cases Allowing Recovery as Only One Loss/Occurrence

5th Cir. 2008 (Miss.). Employee's embezzlement through repeated, related acts over a decade constituted a single occurrence. *Madison Materials Co., Inc. v. St. Paul Fire & Marine Ins. Co.,* 523 F.3d 541, 544-45.

5th Cir. 1977 (La.). Broker's employee incurred trading losses speculating in commodities market. Court held that loss was single loss even though it was the product of more than one act. *Howard, Weil, Labouisse, Friedrichs, Inc. v. Ins. Co. of N. Am.,* 557 F.2d 1055, 1059-60.

7th Cir. 1970 (Ill.). Rejecting argument that non-reduction of liability clause reinstated coverage limit after each loss, and reversing district court, court held that multiple thefts (94 transactions) by one person constituted one loss. *Roodhouse Nat'l Bank v. Fid. & Deposit Co. of Md.,* 426 F.2d 1347, 1351.

8th Cir. 1971 (Ark.). Real estate developer obtained loans through fraudulent notes and mortgages, causing losses in excess of $600,000. Court limited liability to $25,000 (face amount of bond), rejecting insured's argument that non-reduction of liability clause reinstated coverage limit after each loss. *Benton State Bank v. Hartford Acc. & Indem. Co.,* 452 F.2d. 5, 7-8.

9th Cir. 2009 (Ariz.). Fact that one employee was guilty of multiple embezzlements did not mean that there were multiple occurrences under policy. New policy year did not trigger the beginning of a new occurrence. *Superstition Crushing, LLC v. Travelers Cas. and Sur. Co. of Am.,* 360 F. App'x 844, 846.

10th Cir. 1984 (Okla.). Applying rule that "an occurrence is determined by the cause or causes of the resulting injury," court found that employee's act of embezzling 40 checks was part of a continuation of one act of dishonesty. As such, there was one occurrence and a single loss. *Bus. Interiors, Inc. v. Aetna Cas. & Sur. Co.,* 751 F.2d 361, 363.

11th Cir. 2013 (Fla.). Retroactive date endorsement precluded coverage for any loss occurring in part before retroactive date of April 24, 2009. Fraudulent scheme commenced in March 2007, and majority of losses were incurred before the retroactive date. Court held all losses to be from one occurrence and, hence, barred recovery under the retroactive date endorsement. *ABCO Premium Fin., LLC v. Am. Int'l Grp., Inc.,* 518 F. App'x 601, 603-04.

W.D. Ark. 1969. Exceptions to non-reduction of liability clause in brokers blanket bond limited insurer's liability to one bond penalty even though there were multiple losses caused by one employee. *SEC v. Ark. Loan & Thrift Corp.,* 297 F. Supp. 73, 82.

D. Colo. 2004. Because cause of loss was one employee's dishonesty, there was only one occurrence. *Wausau Bus. Ins. Co. v. US Motels Mgmt. Inc.,* 341 F. Supp. 2d 1180, 1183-84.

N.D. Ill. 1968. Court held that Non-Reduction of Liability clause limited coverage to one bond penalty regardless of the number of acts committed by one employee, noting that use of the plural "acts" demonstrated insurer's intent to limit its liability. *Fed. Sav. & Loan Ins. Assoc. v. Aetna Ins. Co.,* 279 F. Supp. 161, 163-64.

E.D. Mo. 1997. Even though theft was accomplished through 46 separate counterfeit documents, acts were part of "one common scheme to defraud" and, therefore, constituted a single loss. *Citizens Bank of Newburg v. Kan. Bankers Sur. Co.*, 971 F. Supp. 1301, 1304.

D. Nev. 2011. Only one occurrence existed even though controller stole money in different ways. *APMC Hotel Mgmt, LLC v. Fid. & Deposit Co. of Md.*, No. 2:09-cv-2100-LDG-VCF, 2011 WL 5525966, at *6-7.

N.D. Ill. 1993. Even though loss occurred over several years, the entire loss constituted one occurrence subject to the per-occurrence limit. *Diamond Transp. Sys., Inc. v. Travelers Indem. Co.*, 817 F. Supp. 710, 712.

Bankr. N.D. Ohio 1988. Finding policy phrase "all acts or omissions" and definition of "single loss" as "all loss" unambiguous, court held that all acts of fraud by employee constituted a single loss. *In re Baker & Getty Fin. Servs., Inc.*, 93 B.R. 559, 569.

E.D. Pa. 1998. Noting that inquiry is whether there "was but one proximate, uninterrupted, and continuing cause which resulted in all of the injuries and damage," court held that losses from the dishonest acts of one employee involving two separate customers constituted one occurrence. *Omni Servs. Grp., Inc. v. Hartford Ins. Co.*, 2 F. Supp. 2d 714, 719.

S.D. Tex. 1996. Policy neither limited an occurrence to the coverage period nor distinguished between an act versus a series of acts. Thefts constituted a series of acts that policy defined as one occurrence. *Bethany Christian Church v. Preferred Risk Mut. Ins. Co.*, 942 F. Supp. 330, 335.

N.D. Tex. 1994. Series of acts by employee constituted a single occurrence of theft even though losses resulted from theft committed by employee over a period of years. *Potomac Ins. Co. of Ill. v. Lone Star Web, Inc.*, No. 3:93-CV-2122-H, 1994 WL 494784, at *2-3.

Ariz. 2008. Employee's embezzlement over the course of five years was a "series of acts" and, therefore, one occurrence. *Emp'rs Mut. Cas. Co. v. DGG & CAR, Inc.*, 183 P.3d 513, 515-16.

Cal. Ct. App. 2002. Multiple acts of fraud by employee constituted one occurrence because there was no evidence that acts were not part of the same scheme. *Pasternak v. Boutris,* 121 Cal. Rptr. 2d 493, 509-10.

Fla. Dist. Ct. App. 1995. Employee's acts of embezzlement over four years constituted one occurrence. *Reliance Ins. Co. v. Treasure Coast Travel Agency, Inc.,* 660 So. 2d 1136, 1137-38.

Ga. 2004. Loss was one occurrence because it was a series of embezzlements by one employee. *Sherman & Hemstreet, Inc. v. Cincinnati Ins. Co.,* 594 S.E.2d 648, 650-51.

Ill. App. Ct. 1999. Court denied recovery where insured failed to prove number of occurrences or that any occurrence exceeded the deductible. *Reedy Indus., Inc. v. Hartford Ins. Co.,* 715 N.E.2d 728, 732.

La. Ct. App. 1996. Finding that aim of employee's scheme was solely to steal money, court held that employee's multiple acts constituted one occurrence. *Jefferson Parish Clerk of Court Health Ins. Trust Fund v. Fid. & Deposit Co. of Md.,* 673 So. 2d 1238, 1245.

N.C. Ct. App. 1996. There was only one occurrence even though loss occurred through employee's embezzlement accomplished through the writing of twenty-four checks. *Christ Lutheran Church v. State Farm Fire & Cas. Co.,* 471 S.E.2d 124, 125-26.

Wash. Ct. App. 2001. Even though theft was accomplished through different methods involving several employees, there was only one occurrence pursuant to policy language defining occurrence as a series of related acts. *Valley Furniture & Interiors, Inc. v. Transp. Ins. Co.,* 26 P.3d 952, 955.

2. *Cases Allowing Recovery as Multiple Losses/Occurrences*

4th Cir. 2001 (S.C.). The policy definition of "occurrence" was ambiguous because it did not "affirmatively indicate whether a 'series of acts' includes acts occurring outside the policy term." *Spartan Iron & Metal Corp. v. Liberty Ins. Corp.,* 6 F. App'x 176, 178.

5th Cir. 2001 (Tex.). Reading the "involving one or more employees" clause of the "occurrence" definition as signifying a group conspiracy, the court held that the acts of two employees independently stealing from the insured constituted separate occurrences. *Ran-Nan, Inc. v. Gen. Acc. Ins. Co. of Am.,* 252 F.3d 738, 740.

9th Cir. 2000 (Cal.). The definition of "occurrence" was ambiguous because it could either refer to the entire conspiracy or each act of theft within the conspiracy and was silent as to whether the term encompassed acts within a single policy period or across multiple periods. In light of such ambiguity, the court held that coverage was available under each policy. *Karen Kane, Inc. v. Reliance Ins. Co.,* 202 F.3d 1180, 1188.

D. Haw. 1985. Because policy provided limit "per loss," court found that "it must have been contemplated that there could be more than one loss." The court held, therefore, that acts of officers and directors constituted multiple losses. *Okada v. MGIC Indem. Corp.,* 608 F. Supp. 383, 388.

N.D. Ill. 1989. Two banks, the majority of whose stock was held by the same bank holding company, suffered losses as a result of the fraud of a customer of each bank. The banks asserted that they suffered a single loss subject to one deductible ever though each bank was insured by a different bond. Court held that each bank had a separate claim under its own policy, such that each bank had to satisfy its own deductible. *M.G. Bancorporation, Inc. v. Reliance Ins. Co.,* No. 87 C 10470, 1989 WL 20774, at *6-7.

D. Kan. 1985. Series of loan swap transactions were separate occurrences because they happened at separate times, with separate borrowers, separate collateral and for separate purposes. *N. River Ins. Co. v. Huff,* 628 F. Supp. 1129, 1133-34.

D. Md. 2005. Various acts of embezzlement were not separate occurrences just because employee used different means to accomplish the separate acts of embezzlement. Definition of "series of acts" was ambiguous, however, as to acts occurring outside policy term, requiring construction in insured's favor, particularly because insured paid different premiums in successive periods to account for varied levels of coverage for different property. *Glaser v. Hartford Cas. Ins. Co.*, 364 F. Supp. 2d 529, 538.

E.D. Wis. 2009. Series of thefts over six-month period was more than one "occurrence" although thefts were committed by same person because each theft was the result of a separate action that required a new decision by the thief. *Basler Turbo Conversions, LLC v. HCC Ins. Co.*, 601 F. Supp. 2d 1082, 1091-92.

Conn. 2000. Found definition of occurrence to be ambiguous and held that separate acts of embezzlements constituted multiple occurrences because employee could have stopped stealing at any time. *Shemitz Lighting, Inc. v. Hartford Fire Ins. Co.,* No. CV960052970, 2000 WL 1781840, at *7.

Iowa 1963. Because rider contained a clause making it subject to a non-reduction of liability clause, insurer's liability was renewed after each loss and each of nine forgeries were compensable up to the policy limit. *Humboldt Trust & Sav. Bank v. Fid. & Cas. Co.*, 122 N.W.2d 358, 359-60.

Mass. 1980. Found definition of occurrence to be ambiguous when it was undefined and held insurer separately liable for each act of embezzlement. *Slater v. USF&G,* 400 N.E.2d 1256, 1261-62.

Minn. 1996. Held that two occurrences occurred because employee used two separate methods to embezzle. *Am. Commerce Ins. Brokers, Inc. v. Minn. Mut. Fire & Cas. Co.,* 551 N.W.2d 224, 231.

Miss. 1999. Court allowed insured's recovery for each of bookkeeper's acts misappropriating monies on 175 separate occasions over the course of five years. *Universal Underwriters Ins. Co. v. Buddy Jones Ford, Lincoln-Mercury, Inc.,* 734 So. 2d 173, 178.

N.J. 1994. Submission of twenty-seven fraudulent credit applications by dealership's finance manager were separate occurrences entitling insured to recover coverage limit for each fraudulent act even though acts were similar and were only committed by one person. *Auto Lenders Acceptance Corp. v. Gentilini Ford, Inc.,* 854 A.2d 378, 397.

Or. Ct. App. 2003. Court held that "occurrence" definition and liability limitation applied separately to each policy period. Consequently, insurer was liable to pay coverage limits for two consecutive policy periods for series of thefts committed by same employee during both periods. *Robben & Sons Heating, Inc. v. Mid-Century Ins. Co.*, 74 P.3d 1141, 1145.

SECONDARY SOURCES

Dolores A. Parr & D.M. Studler, *Limits of Liability: Attempts to Go Beyond the Outer Limits*, X FID. L.J. 129 (2004).

Tracey Santor, Armen Shahinian & Andrew S. Kent, *Limits of Liability, in* HANDLING FIDELITY BOND CLAIMS 319 (Michael Keeley & Sean Duffy, eds., 2d. ed. 2005).

H.D. Warren, Annotation, *Extent of Liability on Fidelity Bond Renewed from Year to Year*, 7 A.L.R.2d 946 (1949).

SECTION 5 — NOTICE/PROOF—LEGAL PROCEEDINGS AGAINST UNDERWRITER*

Section 5.

(a) At the earliest practicable moment, not to exceed 30 days, after discovery of loss, the Insured shall give the Underwriter notice thereof.

(b) Within 6 months after such discovery, the Insured shall furnish to the Underwriter proof of loss, duly sworn to, with full particulars.

(c) Lost Certificated Securities listed in a proof of loss shall be identified by certificate or bond numbers if such securities were issued therewith.

(d) Legal proceedings for the recovery of any loss hereunder shall not be brought prior to the expiration of 60 days after the original proof of loss is filed with the Underwriter or after the expiration of 24 months from the discovery of such loss.

(e) If any limitation embodied in this bond is prohibited by any law controlling the construction hereof, such limitation shall be deemed to be amended so as to equal the minimum period of limitation provided by such law.

(f) This bond affords coverage only in favor of the Insured. No suit, action or legal proceedings shall be brought hereunder by any one other than the named Insured.

COMMENT

This section of the Financial Institution Bond has remained essentially unchanged since 1980, except that in 2004, the phrase "limitation period" was substituted for the word "limitation" and the phrase "period of limitation" in subsection (e). Much of the substance of this section has been in the standard form Financial Institution Bond since 1969 or earlier. The substance as well as the language of this section has for many years also appeared, in whole or in part, in many other forms of fidelity policies.

---

* By Armen Shahinian, Andrew S. Kent, and Scott W. Lichtenstein, Wolff & Samson PC, West Orange, New Jersey and New York, New York.

Courts in the majority of jurisdictions view the language of this section as unambiguous, reasonable, and enforceable. In such jurisdictions, courts have has generally focused upon determining the date of "discovery of loss" as defined in Section 3 of the standard form bond under the unique facts and circumstances of each case, as discussed in Chapter 3, Section 3 of this book.

Section 5(a) of the Financial Institution Bond contains the notice provision. It requires that notice be provided to the insurer at "the earliest practicable moment" after discovery of loss, and it specifies an outer limit of thirty days for such notice. Section 5(b) then requires that the insured's proof of loss be filed within six months of such discovery of loss.

Courts in most jurisdictions addressing the effect of the insured's failure to timely provide notice and a proof of loss recognize that the notice and proof of loss provisions are conditions precedent to recovery. In these jurisdictions, any failure to comply with such provisions will act as a complete bar to recovery. The rationale for this interpretation is that the parties knowingly contracted for these terms, and the notice and proof of loss provisions are integral to the contract. In the view of these courts, extra-contractual common law rules which were developed to protect unsophisticated purchasers of liability insurance, such as the so-called "notice-prejudice rule" (discussed below), should not be applied to relieve sophisticated parties, such as financial institutions, from the express terms of their bargains. In so holding, courts strictly enforcing the conditions of coverage under the bond take notice of the fact that its terms were developed through years of experience and negotiations between the insurance and banking industries.

Courts in a minority of jurisdictions, however, have applied the notice-prejudice rule in cases involving fidelity bonds. In general, this rule provides that, regardless of any policy provision conditioning coverage upon the receipt of timely notice, the insurer must show that it has been prejudiced by the late notice before it is relieved of liability.

Courts in jurisdictions adhering to the minority view have undercut the plain meaning and purpose of the notice and proof of loss provisions, which appear in the Conditions and Limitations section of the standard form bond. Courts in these jurisdictions have determined that the notice and proof of loss provisions do not create conditions precedent to coverage. These courts view the purpose of notice provisions as protecting insurers against stale claims, where the lapse of time has destroyed opportunities to investigate, mitigate, and/or recover loss. In cases where late notice cannot be shown to have actually created such problems, such courts view late notice as inconsequential and, hence, an insufficient basis to find a forfeiture of coverage. In such jurisdictions, the ultimate burden of proving prejudice rests with the insurer. However, courts in several of those jurisdictions recognize a rebuttable presumption of prejudice due to late notice, placing upon the insured the obligation to introduce at least some evidence of the absence of prejudice before the insurer becomes required to prove that actual prejudice resulted from delayed notice of the claim.

While application of the notice-prejudice rule may be appropriate in liability insurance cases involving coverage sold to unsophisticated consumers, in Financial Institution Bond cases, where the parties are both sophisticated business entities, this protection afforded to unsophisticated lay persons is unnecessary. Moreover, the particular risks assumed by a fidelity insurer, which assumes exposure to loss caused to its insured by the secret and dishonest acts of its employees, render it of central importance to the parties' relationship that the insured demonstrate candor at all times and provide prompt, full disclosure of loss and proof thereof. Additionally, because under the Financial Institution Bond and similar "discovery policies" coverage and the notice requirement are both triggered by the insured's discovery of loss, a court's failure to require strict adherence to the notice requirement could permit an opportunistic insured to manipulate the alleged date of discovery and seek to obtain coverage where none exists.

Some jurisdictions find that application of the notice-prejudice rule is dependent upon whether the subject policy is an "occurrence" policy or a "claims-made policy." "Occurrence" policies provide coverage for insurable events that occur during the policy period. Because third-party liability claims may be asserted long after the period of the events giving rise to a claim, an insurer under an occurrence policy assumes a "tail" of potential liability that may extend for years after the expiration of its policy. Claims-made policies, in contrast, afford coverage for claims made (and sometimes also reported) to the insurer during the policy period, regardless of when the insurable event occurred. Once that period for claims and claims-reporting has expired, the insurer under a claims-made policy may "close its books" on the policy, with the knowledge that its potential liability under that policy has come to an end. The insurer's ability to close its books on a claims-made policy is viewed as central to the insurer's bargain and its ability to determine an appropriate premium for that policy. Courts are less prone to apply the notice-prejudice rule to deprive insurers under claims made policies of the benefit of that bargain. Discovery policies, such as the Financial Institution Bond, are analogous to claims made policies in that discovery policies permit the insurer to close its books on a policy period if, within thirty days after the expiration of such period, notice of loss is not provided. Thus, in jurisdictions limiting application of the notice-prejudice rule to occurrence policies, the rule should be viewed as inapplicable to discovery policies such as the Financial Institution Bond.

Statutes in certain states may have an impact upon enforcement of the Financial Institution Bond's proof of loss requirement. Section 3407 of New York's Insurance Law, for example, which applies to claims for "loss or damage to property under any contract of insurance," requires that the insured be given written notice of the insurer's desire for a written proof of loss and be furnished with "a suitable blank form or forms." That statute further provides that "[i]f the insured shall furnish proofs of loss within sixty days after the receipt of such notice and such form or forms, or within any longer period of time specified in such notice, such insured shall be deemed to have complied with the provisions of such contract of insurance relating to the time within which proofs of loss are required." Section 1136 of Puerto Rico's Insurance Code, in contrast, only requires insurers to provide blank proof of loss forms "upon written request[.]" Local law should be consulted regarding the existence of such statutes and/or their applicability or inapplicability to fidelity claims.

Statutes in some jurisdictions may also have an impact upon the enforceability of the Financial Institution Bond's twenty-four month suit-limitation clause. Maryland Insurance Article—Section 12-104, for example, negates the enforceability of contractual limitations periods in insurance policies if less than the applicable statute of limitation, which in Maryland is three years. Local law should be consulted for the presence of such statutes and whether, or the extent to which, they may apply to claims under fidelity policies.

Courts in a minority of jurisdictions, while purporting to enforce suit limitation periods in insurance contracts, have ignored and effectively rewritten their plain language by tolling the running of such limitation periods from the time an insured first gives notice of a loss or claim until the date that the insurer expressly denies coverage. This approach is completely unjustified when applied to Financial Institution Bond claims brought by sophisticated parties, and essentially substitutes the court's own ideas of fairness for the parties' unambiguous agreement that the suit limitation shall run from the date of the insured's discovery of loss, and not from the date of the insurer's denial of coverage. Indeed, the Financial Institution Bond expressly contemplates that the insured may file a lawsuit against the insurer beginning "60 days after the original proof of loss is filed," i.e., without waiting for the insurer to expressly admit or deny coverage. Of course, a fidelity insurer, like any other defendant in a lawsuit, may under unusual facts be estopped from defending on the basis of the timeliness of suit, such as where such defendant actively lulls the plaintiff into inactivity until after the limitation period has passed. The availability of such a remedy of estoppel is more than adequate to prevent injustice against a sophisticated Financial Institution Bond claimant.

Finally, in cases where a financial institution is placed into receivership by federal regulators, a federal statute may act to extend the bond's twenty-four month suit limitation as it concerns lawsuits brought by such a receiver. Similar extensions of contractual limitations periods in favor of trustees or receivers exist under bankruptcy law and many state receivership statutes. However, courts appear to agree that such statutes will not act to revive claims for which suit was already time-barred prior to the appointment of such a receiver or trustee.

OUTLINE OF ANNOTATIONS

A. Earliest Practicable Moment
B. Discovery of Loss
C. Written Notice Thereof
D. Effect of Failure to Give Notice or Delay in Giving Notice
   1. Notice-Prejudice Rule Applied / Limitations Provision not Treated as Condition Precedent
      (a) Insured required to disprove or rebut presumption of prejudice
      (b) Insurer required to prove prejudice
   2. Notice-Prejudice Rule Not Applied / Compliance with Notice Provision Construed as Condition Precedent
E. Proof of Loss, Duly Sworn to, with Full Particulars

F. Effect of Failure to Provide Proof of Loss or Delay in Providing Proof of Loss
G. Time for Commencement of Legal Proceedings
H. Law Prohibiting or Tolling Contractual Limitation of Bond
I. Effect of Failure to Commence Legal Proceedings Within Contractual Limitation of Bond
J. Suits, Actions, and Legal Proceedings Commenced By Party Other Than Insured
K. Waiver and Estoppel

ANNOTATIONS

A. **Earliest Practicable Moment**

U.S. 1902. Notice should be given as soon as reasonably practicable under the circumstances of the case. *Fid. & Deposit Co. of Md. v. Courtney*, 186 U.S. 342, 347-48.

1st Cir. 1966 (Mass.). The "earliest practicable moment" for insured to give notice to surety company was on November 29, 1961, when written demand was made by bank's customer, whose employee had wrongfully withdrawn funds which employee was charged with depositing at bank; insured was not required to give notice on November 28, 1961, when it learned of such unlawful conduct by telephone. *Aetna Cas. & Sur. Co. v. Guar. Bank & Trust Co.*, 370 F.2d 276, 280-81.

2d Cir. 1984 (N.Y.). "As soon as practicable" means that notice must be given within a reasonable time of discovery. Notice given six months after discovery of loss was not "as soon as practicable." *Utica Mut. Ins. Co. v. Fireman's Fund Ins. Cos.*, 748 F.2d 118, 121.

4th Cir. 1905 (S.C.). Notice under a Bank Employee Fidelity Bond should be given as soon as reasonably practicable under the circumstances of the case. *Fid. & Cas. Co. v. Bank of Timmonsville*, 139 F. 101, 104.

5th Cir. 1987 (Miss.). The court held that "as soon as practicable" meant within a reasonable time. If notice is so late that it is unreasonable or prejudices the insurer, then coverage will be defeated. *State v. Richardson*, 817 F.2d 1203, 1207.

7th Cir. 1952 (Ind.). Time for giving notice is something less than the time for filing proof of loss. All circumstances must be considered to determine what is a "reasonable time" for filing notice of loss. Prejudice to the bonding company is one of the factors to be considered. Unexplained delay of nine months and twelve days after insured learned of the loss meant that notice was not given "within a reasonable time" as required by bond. *Muncie Banking Co. v. Am. Sur. Co.*, 200 F.2d 115, 119-20.

7th Cir. 1937 (Ill.). Immediate notice under an Individual Fidelity Bond means such notice as is reasonable under the circumstances. *Hartford Acc. & Indem. Co. v. Swedish Methodist Aid Ass'n*, 92 F.2d 649, 652.

8th Cir. 1907 (Mo.). Immediate notice under an Employee Dishonesty Bond means such notice as reasonable diligence, under all circumstances of the case, dictates after knowledge of facts requiring it are obtained. *Aetna Indem. Co. v. J. R. Crowe Coal & Mining Co.*, 154 F. 545, 549-50.

9th Cir. 1912 (Cal.). Immediate notice means no more than that degree of promptness which is reasonable under the circumstances. *Nat'l Sur. Co. v. W. Pac. R. Co.*, 200 F. 675, 681-82.

10th Cir. 1985 (N.M.). In June of 1982, insured became aware of potential liability to a third party. Report of investigation commenced in August of 1982 by insured's general counsel and accountants resulted in report issued on September 30th confirming potential liability of insured. Notice given to insurer on October 1 substantially complied with the notice requirement of the Banker's Special Bond requiring prompt notice. *Wells Fargo Bus. Credit v. Am. Bank of Commerce*, 780 F.2d 871, 874-75.

D. Kan. 1982. Notice given seventeen days after discovery of loss was not given at the earliest practicable moment after discovery of loss, as required by the bond. The court's determination was based upon the purely subjective test advocated by the plaintiff bank. *Sec. Nat'l Bank v. Cont'l Ins.*, 586 F. Supp. 139, 148-50.

S.D.N.Y. 1974. Under a Blanket Crime Policy and 3-D Policy, "[a]s soon as practicable" was held to mean within a reasonable time in light of all the circumstances. *U. S. Smelting Ref. & Mining Co. v. Aetna Cas. & Sur. Co.*, 372 F. Supp. 489, 491.

Fla. Dist. Ct. App. 1970. Failure to give notice for six months after discovery of loss does not comply with terms of the bond requiring notice at the earliest practicable moment. *Miami Nat'l Bank v. Pa. Ins. Co.*, 240 So. 2d 832, 833.

Ind. App. 1937. Under an Employee Fidelity Bond requiring that the insured give notice within a reasonable time after discovery of loss, a delay of eleven days in giving notice was held not unreasonable. *Fid. & Deposit Co. of Md. v. Mesker*, 11 N.E.2d 528, 531-32.

Ind. App. 1931. "As soon as possible" means that the insured shall give notice of any loss under the bond within a reasonable time, having in view all of the facts and circumstances of the particular case. *Fletcher Sav. & Trust Co. v. Am. Sur. Co.*, 175 N.E. 247, 251-52.

Iowa 1902. Under a Building and Loan Employee Fidelity Bond, the requirement that notice be given "immediately" required that notice be given without unnecessary or inexcusable delay under all the circumstances. Delay of six to eight days or longer, with no prejudice to bonding company, does not violate terms of bond as a matter of law. *Perpetual Bldg. & Loan Ass'n v. USF&G*, 92 N.W. 686, 688-89.

Ky. 1938. Under an Employee Fidelity Bond, a delay of over two years after discovery of loss was held not to comply with a provision which required notice at the "earliest practicable moment," and not later than five days after such discovery. *Jellico Grocery Co. v. Sun Indem. Co.*, 114 S.W.2d 83, 85-86.

Ky. 1912. "Immediate notice" means that the insured shall promptly (considering the probability of the loss and the probability of escape by the defaulting employee) give notice to the bonding company. Delay of fourteen days in giving notice complies with requirement, even though insured attempted to recover from the defaulting employee in the period between discovery and notice to the bonding company. *Emp'rs Liab. Assurance Corp. v. Stanley Deposit Bank*, 149 S.W. 1025, 1026-27.

Ky. 1906. Unless lapse of time is so long as to be obviously in noncompliance with the contract, the question of whether notice is timely is one for the jury. *Fid. & Guar. Co. of N.Y. v. W. Bank*, 94 S.W. 3, 5.

La. 1927. Employee Fidelity Bond was held to require notice "at the earliest practicable moment." Irregularities were discovered on March 15, 1915. The employee admitted shortages in his accounts on April 30, 1915, and requested time to pay. On May 3, 1915, employee stated he was unable to raise the money. Notice given to the bonding company at that time was held to be timely, following rule that notice must be given as soon as practicable under all the circumstances. *People's State Bank v. USF&G*, 113 So. 779, 780-81.

La. App. 1937. When insured had knowledge of possible discrepancies in January, notice given on May 25 was not "immediate" notice, no matter how liberally that word is interpreted. *George J. Ricau & Co. v. Indem. Ins. Co.*, 173 So. 217, 221-22.

Mich. Ct. App. 1970. Prejudice to the rights of the bonding company is a necessary element in determining if there has been unreasonable delay. A delay of seven months and eight days constitutes a prima facie failure to give notice "as soon as practicable." *Grand Rapids Auctions, Inc. v. Hartford Acc. & Indem. Co.*, 178 N.W.2d 812, 815.

Minn. 1925. Immediate notice under a Bank Employee Fidelity Bond means notice within a reasonable time. The court affirmed a jury finding that delay from November 20, 1922 to December 14, 1922 was unreasonable. *Farmers & Merchs. State Bank v. Fid. & Deposit Co. of Md.*, 204 N.W. 33, 34-35.

Minn. 1910. Employee Fidelity Bond requiring immediate notice obligated insured to give notice within a reasonable time. Delay from August 3, when shortages in accounts were discovered, until September 28, during which time an investigation occurred, was unreasonable. *Gamble-Robinson Co. v. Mass. Bonding & Ins. Co.*, 129 N.W. 131, 133-34.

Neb. 1989. In order to state a cause of action for recovery under a Bankers Blanket Bond, the insured must plead that it provided notice at the earliest practicable moment after discovery of the loss. *First Sec. Bank & Trust v. N.H. Ins. Co.*, 441 N.W.2d 188, 191.

N.H. 1920. Bond required that insured give immediate notice. Whether notice given three months after discovery of default complied with terms of bond was a jury question. *Guar. Trust Co. v. USF&G*, 112 A. 247, 249.

N.Y. Sup. Ct. 1964. Insured's failure to give notice of loss for six months breached provisions of Stevedore Operations Indemnity Policy requiring notice "as soon as may be practicable." *Am. Stevedores, Inc. v. Sun Ins. Office, Ltd.*, 248 N.Y.S.2d 487, 489.

N.C. 1934. Notice given three or four days after discovery of dishonesty complied with Bank Fidelity Bond provision requiring that the insured give "immediate written notice" after such discovery. *Hood v. Davidson*, 177 S.E. 5, 8-9.

N.C. 1926. Employee Fidelity Bond provision requiring insured to provide notice "immediately after becoming aware of any act or omission which may be made the basis of a claim hereunder" held to require that notice be given within a reasonable time after discovery and in good faith; whether requirements of provision were met was a jury question. *Forest City Bldg. & Loan Ass'n v. Davis*, 133 S.E. 530, 533.

N.C. 1913. Delay of five days was not a failure to give immediate notice, as required by Employee Fidelity Bond. *Dixie Fire Ins. Co. v. Am. Bonding Co.*, 78 S.E. 430, 433.

N.C. 1901. "Immediate notice" under a Bank Employee Fidelity Bond means that notice must be given in a reasonable time with due diligence under the circumstances, including the necessity of conducting an investigation. *Bank of Tarboro v. Fid. & Deposit Co. of Md.*, 38 S.E. 908, 910-11.

Ohio 1912. Under a Bank Employee Fidelity Bond, "[a]t the earliest practicable moment" was held to mean that notice should be given as soon as it would be practicable to give it, considering everything that would affect the minds and conduct of the bank officials. Jury finding of timely notice upheld where directors learned of misconduct on

November 30, 1904, and notice was given on January 15, 1905. *Rankin v. USF&G*, 99 N.E. 314, 317-18.

Ohio Ct. App. 1978. Under a Deputy Registrar's Blanket Position Bond, a letter which insured sent to surety fifteen months after insured's discovery of defalcation, did not constitute substantial compliance with terms of bond requiring notice within a reasonable time of such discovery; surety was entitled to summary judgment against insured. *State of Ohio v. Safeco Ins. Co.*, 396 N.E.2d 794, 788-89.

Pa. 1928. Insured discovered a loss in January 1921, and did not give notice to the bonding company until May 1923, and therefore failed to comply with bond provision requiring that the insured give notice "as soon as possible after the insured learns that a loss has been sustained." Notice could not be delayed while insured sought to determine extent of loss which would not be reimbursed by employee. *Morrelville Deposit Bank v. Royal Indem. Co.*, 144 A. 424, 425-26.

Tenn. Ct. App. 1984. Under an Employee Dishonesty Commercial Blanket Policy requiring that insured, upon "knowledge or discovery of loss or of an occurrence which may give rise to a claim for loss," give notice "as soon as practicable," insured was required to give notice when it became or should have become aware of facts which would suggest to a reasonably prudent person that the event for which coverage is sought might reasonably be expected to produce a claim against the insurer. Notice which was given nine months after discovery did not comply. *Griffith Motors, Inc. v. Compass Ins. Co.*, 676 S.W.2d 555, 558.

Wash. 1935. When insured bank went into voluntary liquidation on April 15, 1932, its books did not disclose certain losses, which were only discovered when State Supervisor of Banking took charge of the bank on June 1, 1932. Notice given within ten days after discovery thereof constituted notice "at earliest practical moment." *Hansen v. Am. Bonding Co.*, 48 P.2d 653, 656.

Wash. 1902. When insured discovered defalcation on August 20, whether notice given on October 3 complied with bond provision requiring insured to "immediately give notice" was a question for the jury. *Remington v. Fid. & Deposit Co. of Md.*, 67 P. 989, 991-92.

W. Va. 1920. Default was discovered on November 7, 1917 and was discussed at a board meeting on November 21. Notice was given on December 3, 1917. Trial court held that insured had failed to comply with condition of bond requiring "immediate notice." Supreme Court did not "entirely agree" with trial court's conclusion, but held that notice condition had been waived. *Piedmont Grocery Co. v. Hawkins*, 104 S.E. 736, 738-39.

Wis. 1974. Notice given by insured fifteen months after its discovery of a forgery did not comply with bond provision requiring notice at "earliest practicable movement." *State Bank v. Capitol Indem. Corp.*, 214 N.W.2d 42, 44-47.

B. Discovery of Loss

U.S. 1902. Bank Fidelity Bond provided "that the employer shall at once notify the company, on his becoming aware of said employee being engaged in certain dishonest acts." To be aware is not the same as to have knowledge. The obvious meaning of "becoming aware," as used in the bond, is "to be informed of" or "to be apprised of" or "to be put on one's guard in respect to." *Guar. Co. of N. Am. v. Mechs.' Sav. Bank & Trust Co.*, 183 U.S. 402, 416-24.

U.S. 1898. Under a Bank Employee Fidelity Bond, "[a]s soon as practicable after such act shall have come to the knowledge of the employer" was held to mean that the insured "had knowledge—not simply suspicion—of the existence of such facts as would justify a careful and prudent man in charging another with fraud or dishonesty." *Am. Sur. Co. v. Pauly*, 170 U.S. 133, 147.

1st Cir. 1997 (Mass.). Discovery of loss was held to have occurred, at the latest, when the bank was served with legal pleadings alleging facts that, if true would constitute a loss under a Financial Institution Bond. *FDIC v. Ins. Co. of N. Am.*, 105 F.3d 778, 782.

1st Cir. 1966 (Mass.). Insured bank discovered loss within meaning of the bond on November 29, 1961, when written demand was made by bank's customer, whose employee had wrongfully withdrawn funds which employee was charged with depositing at bank; bank was not required to give notice on November 28, 1961, when it learned of such unlawful conduct by telephone. *Aetna Cas. & Sur. Co. v. Guar. Bank & Trust Co.*, 370 F.2d 276, 280-81.

2d Cir. 1984 (N.Y.). A loss is discovered once an insured is in full possession of the information necessary for it to determine that a loss has occurred. Whether discovery has occurred is determined by an objective test, based upon the conclusions that a reasonable person would draw from the facts known to the insured. Insured discovered loss when it received report confirming that investment manager had purchased bonds at above-market rates in violation of IRS rules, that insured would experience related tax problems, and that excess commissions had been paid to broker. *Utica Mut. Ins. Co. v. Fireman's Fund Ins. Cos.*, 748 F.2d 118, 120.

2d Cir. 1927 (N.Y.). Under an Employee Fidelity Bond requiring notice within ten days of discovery of loss, insurer argued that insured could have, with reasonable diligence, discovered defalcations much earlier than it did, based upon documents which existed in insured's possession for more than two years. Contrasting "discovery" with "the duty to make it," the Court held that the district judge should have allowed the jury to decide whether insured should have made discovery some time earlier than it did. *Mass. Bonding & Ins. Co. v. Norwich Pharmacal Co.*, 18 F.2d 934, 936.

3d Cir. 2000 (N.J.). Savings and Loan Blanket Fidelity Bond, which defined "discovery" to occur "when the Insured becomes aware of facts which would cause a reasonable person to assume that a loss covered by the bond has or will be incurred, even though the exact amount or details of the loss may have not then been known," is satisfied when the insured has sufficient facts showing that a dishonest act occurred, and the insured appreciates the significance of those facts. The insured's mere suspicion of wrongdoing does not suffice. *RTC v. Fid. & Deposit Co. of Md.*, 205 F.3d 615, 630-31.

3d Cir. 1937 (Pa.). Under an Employee Fidelity Bond requiring that notice be given to the surety after the insured's discovery of an employee's default or dishonest act, notice was not required when the insured's president's personal use of company funds aroused suspicions of vice-president, as vice-president had reason to believe in the possible honesty of the president's actions. Whether notice did not become due until an investigation commenced by vice-president confirmed his suspicions was a jury question. Judgment for insurer notwithstanding the verdict was reversed and case remanded for new trial. *Hunt v. Fid. & Deposit Co. of Md.*, 92 F.2d 75, 76-77.

5th Cir. 1995 (La.). When insured bank's loss resulted from a number of loans made by a rogue employee to persons with whom the employee had an undisclosed business relationship, insurer claimed that the bank failed to prove that the loss resulting from two particular loans, which loans were discovered later on and were not listed on the bank's Proof of Loss forms, were discovered within the bond's effective period. The Court held because the loans arose out of the same pattern of conduct or scheme that was originally discovered, that the later-discovered loans were part of the same loss discovered during the bond period. *FDIC v. Fid. & Deposit Co. of Md.*, 45 F.3d 969, 974-75.

5th Cir. 1972 (Tex.). Insured bank's president's knowledge of his own fraudulent acts would not be imputed to the insured, and bank directors' knowledge of irregularities and violations of bank policy was not sufficient to trigger bond provision requiring notice "within 100 days after a discovery by any director or officer not in collusion with the person in default," where directors believed that such irregularities and violations would be corrected. Notice is not required until insured has acquired knowledge of some specific fraudulent or dishonest act which might give rise to liability of the bonding company for the misconduct. *FDIC v. Lott*, 460 F.2d 82, 87-88.

5th Cir. 1970 (Tex.). Insured bank's employee fraudulently participated in the purchase of notes that failed to comply with applicable law. The bank "discovered" its loss—and became obligated to give notice to the surety—when the bank uncovered the employee's fraudulent conduct, and not earlier, when the bank's cashier noticed defects in the notes, which might have given rise to suspicions of wrongdoing. *FDIC v. Aetna Cas. & Sur. Co.*, 426 F.2d 729, 738-39.

5th Cir. 1918 (Ala.). Under an Employee Fidelity Bond requiring notice at the earliest practical moment after discovery of an act which would give rise to liability thereunder, insured bank's mere suspicion of misconduct by its president, who directed cashier to expropriate funds for his personal use, did not require notice. Insured must be informed of the conduct of the employee and of the intent accompanying the conduct in order to be aware that he was guilty of larceny or embezzlement. *USF&G v. Walker*, 248 F. 42, 43.

6th Cir. 1975 (Ohio). Insured's receipt of telephone call indicating that insured's employee was stealing insured's valuable records did not automatically commence time for filing proof of loss, because insured was entitled to investigate what were extensive, complicated, and difficult facts. Under Ohio law, "discovery of loss" does not occur until insured has had a reasonable time to discover extent and amount of loss. *Russell Gasket Co. v. Phoenix of Hartford Ins. Co.*, 512 F.2d 205, 209.

6th Cir. 1934 (Mich.). Under a "fidelity schedule bond" requiring notice within ten days of discovery of a loss, insured bank was not required to give notice of overdrafts when it had reason to believe that depositor was assumed to be in excellent financial condition. Notice was due only when insured bank had knowledge that a loss had been or would be sustained. *USF&G v. Barber*, 70 F.2d 220, 223-24.

7th Cir. 1980 (Ill.). Although employer had unquestionably discovered loss resulting from employee's actions outside the time periods for giving notice, filing proof of loss, and commencing an action, the fidelity bond required, in addition, that the employer have knowledge that the employee's actions were "dishonest or fraudulent." Whether the employer knew at that time that the employee's actions were "dishonest or fraudulent" was a question of fact. Summary judgment in favor of the insurer reversed. *Central Nat'l Life Ins. Co. v. Fid. & Deposit Co. of Md.*, 626 F.2d 537, 548-49.

7th Cir. 1956 (Ill.). Insured meat packing company began investigation of inventory losses in July of 1952, discovered employee stealing meat on September 17, 1952, and provided fidelity insurer with notice the next day. Held that insured complied with terms of Blanket Position Bond requiring notice no later than 15 days after discovery of fraudulent or dishonest acts, as insured's suspicions were "merely gestating" during the investigation period, and notice was given following discovery of the specific culprits. *B. Constantino & Sons Co. v. New Amsterdam Cas. Co.*, 234 F.2d 902, 903-04.

7th Cir. 1937 (Ill.). Insured gave notice under fidelity bond of its principal's defalcations 10 weeks after the insured obtained knowledge thereof. This late notice did not bar the insured's related claim for losses resulting from the principal's act of altering the face value of checks without the issuer's knowledge, which acts were discovered the day before notice was given, and occurred before insured obtained any knowledge of principal's dishonesty. *Hartford Acc. & Indem. Co. v. Swedish Methodist Aid Ass'n*, 92 F.2d 649, 650-53.

8th Cir. 1993 (S.D.). Insured did not become aware of facts sufficient to cause a reasonable person to assume that a loss covered by the fidelity bonds had been incurred when it received a report from a state board criticizing the insured's overpayment for the purchase of certain leasing companies. Moreover, the insured's employees' knowledge of their own acts could not be imputed to the insured. *First Dakota Nat'l Bank v. St. Paul Fire & Marine Ins. Co.*, 2 F.3d 801, 805-08.

8th Cir. 1992 (Mo.). Knowledge available to insured of its president's defalcation did not arise above mere suspicion and therefore did not constitute "discovery" of a loss within fidelity bond's policy period. Although it was known that money had been transferred to president's account, there was only a suspicion that the transfer was fraudulent in nature, and an outside investigator made no accusations against president. *Block v. Granite State Ins. Co.*, 963 F.2d 1127, 1130-31.

8th Cir. 1982 (Mo.). Insured bank's discovery of potential loss occurred not when trustee of bankrupt company filed complaint against the insured bank, but when insured bank became aware that funds which were being transferred into and then out of one of its accounts were payable to bankrupt's creditors. An actual written demand from the trustee was not necessary to supply insured with facts which would lead a reasonable person to believe that a loss had been suffered. *Columbia Union Nat'l Bank v. Hartford Acc. & Indem. Co.*, 669 F.2d 1210, 1212.

8th Cir. 1979 (Ark.). Insured bank discovered potential loss when it received a letter from an attorney indicating that insured bank may have breached its fiduciary duty to the attorney's client by prematurely releasing escrow documents as a result of a fraud perpetuated upon the insured bank. *Perkins v. Clinton State Bank*, 593 F.2d 327, 333.

8th Cir. 1971 (Mo.). In determining when discovery has taken place, the trier of fact must find the pertinent underlying facts known to the insured and must further determine subjective conclusions reasonably drawn therefrom by the insured. Suspicion alone does not satisfy the test of discovery. Although insured bank knew that loan was made upon inappropriate collateral to a corporation controlled by person with poor personal reputation and poor credit, district court could have found that the bank only discovered that related losses resulted from employee dishonesty when additional investigation confirmed the bank's initial suspicions. *USF&G v. Empire State Bank*, 448 F.2d 360, 366.

8th Cir. 1932 (Neb.). Insured discovered accounting irregularities and confronted employee in charge of the accounts. The employee admitted certain misapplications of funds and delivered a note to the insured in the amount of the irregularities. Under an Employee Fidelity Bond requiring notice within fifteen days of discovery of loss, insured was obligated to immediately provide notice to insurer upon finding a similar note in its files, which likely meant that employee had attempted to cover up other defalcations. Insured had reasonable grounds to believe terms of bond had been violated, and notice became due even if insured did not have detailed information as to the loss sustained. *Am. Sur. Co. v. Bankers Sav. Ass'n of Omaha*, 59 F.2d 577, 578-80.

8th Cir. 1907 (Mo.). Bond insuring against employee's fraudulent or dishonest acts required that insured provide notice of such acts "immediately after the occurrence of such act shall have come to the knowledge of the employer." Insured was not obligated to provide notice based upon irregular and anxious behavior of employee on the day he was approached regarding an accounting and bookkeeping deficiency. Insured was only required to give notice based upon knowledge of facts as would justify a careful and prudent man in believing a crime to have been committed. *Aetna Indem. Co. v. J. R. Crowe Coal & Mining Co.*, 154 F. 545, 549.

9th Cir. 2001 (Idaho). "Discovery of loss" occurs when an insured discovers facts that would cause a reasonable person to assume a loss had been or would be incurred. Factual issues regarding when insured discovered that certain acquisitions involved loss by theft made summary judgment inappropriate. *Gulf USA Corp. v. Fed. Ins. Co.*, 259 F.3d 1049, 1058.

9th Cir. 1912 (Cal.). Insured's employee knowingly deposited $250,000 with a bank that was insolvent. Under an Employee Fidelity Bond requiring the insured to give notice upon discovery that a loss has been sustained, or of facts indicating that a loss has probably been sustained, the insured was not required to give notice upon becoming aware that the bank had closed its doors. Notice was required when the insured obtained definite knowledge or received credible information sufficient to justify charging another with fraud or culpable negligence, such as when it learned that the bank had been insolvent at the time the deposits were made, and that the employee knew of the insolvency. *Nat'l Sur. Co. v. W. P. Ry. Co.*, 200 F. 675, 682.

10th Cir. 1991 (Okla.). Where the employees of an insured bank participated in another employee's defalcations, the participating employees' knowledge of the insurer's losses were not imputed to the bank, and therefore, the losses were not "discovered" until FDIC examiners reported the losses to the bank's board of directors. *Adair State Bank v. Am. Cas. Co.*, 949 F.2d 1067, 1072-75.

10th Cir. 1966 (N.M.). Employee Fidelity Bond required insured to give notice to surety within 15 days of discovery of a fraudulent or dishonest act. Insured received reports from its accountant showing that former president's "sale" of assets to the insured was never authorized and, although the president was paid, no instruments of conveyance existed in the insured's files. Although insured was not obligated to give notice of merely suspicious conduct, it had "discovered" the fraud, and was required to give notice, before the date on which it confirmed that the former president could not explain the reports. *Hidden Splendor Mining Co. v. Gen. Ins. Co. of Am.*, 370 F.2d 515, 518-19.

10th Cir. 1941 (N.M.). Under Employee Fidelity Bond requiring that the insured give notice as soon as possible after becoming aware of an act by an employee which might be made the basis of a claim, insured was not required to give notice when checks remitted by its collection agent were returned for insufficient funds. The insured was not required to give notice of suspicious behavior. Rather, insured complied with notice requirements by giving notice once insured learned that collection agent had actually used the funds for his own purposes. *Am. Emp'rs' Ins. Co. v. Raton Wholesale Liquor Co.*, 123 F.2d 283, 285.

D. Colo. 2008. Financial institution bond provision requiring notice of loss thirty days after discovery of loss was not triggered by notice to the directors of the insured who were themselves involved in the fraud; however, report of possible loss to an honest officer was sufficient to trigger the limitations period. *FDIC v. St. Paul Cos.*, 634 F. Supp. 2d 1213, 1223.

D.D.C. 1980. Blanket crime policy required that "upon knowledge or discovery of loss or an occurrence which may give rise to a claim for loss, the insured shall: (a) give notice thereof as soon as practicable . . . and . . . (b) file detailed proof of loss, duly sworn to, with the company with four months after discovery of loss . . ." The Court read this provision as requiring that proof of loss be filed only within four months of discovery of loss, and not merely upon discovery of an occurrence which may give rise to a claim for loss. *Fid. & Deposit Co. of Md. v. President and Dirs. of Georgetown Coll.*, 483 F. Supp. 1142, 1146-47.

Bankr. N.D. Ga. 1995. Under an Employee Theft Policy requiring notice within sixty days of an officer of insured obtaining knowledge of or discovering a loss or an occurrence which could lead to a loss, notice requirement was triggered when officers knew that majority shareholder had been dishonest with respect to transactions that ultimately became losses, even if such knowledge did not amount to actual confirmation of theft or fraud. The failure of the insured to inquire promptly, or the failure of the employee to respond promptly in a manner that would cause a reasonable and prudent person to put aside his suspicion of fraud, triggers the duty to notify the surety under a policy requiring notice upon discovery of an "occurrence which may become a loss" for theft or fraud. *In re Prime Commercial Corp.*, 187 B.R. 785, 804.

D. Mass. 1985. Provider of group insurance discovered that third-party administrator had expropriated premiums from group insurance policies due to the provider. Provider initiated "lockbox" procedures to keep premiums out of administrator's possession in order to avoid future expropriations. The insured was required, under the bond, to give notice upon "[d]iscovery by the Insured of any act or circumstance indicating a probable claim hereunder." Predicting that the Massachusetts Supreme Judicial Court would adopt a standard for "discovery" that would include "conscious disregard of recognized uncertainty about whether a known act is or is not fraudulent," the Court found that "discovery" had occurred when insured's executives discussed at a meeting the fact that the aforementioned "lockbox" procedures were not effective, and that notice was not timely given thereafter. *Boston Mut. Life Ins. v. Fireman's Fund Ins.*, 613 F. Supp. 1090, 1100.

D. Kan. 1982. Insured bank had knowledge of a check kiting scheme, as employees knew full well that customer routinely drew on account in excess of available funds. Because "discovery" occurred upon acquiring knowledge which would have justified a careful and prudent person in charging the customer with a check kiting scheme, bank failed to comply with bond provision requiring notice "at the earliest practicable moment after discovery of any loss." *Sec. Nat'l Bank v. Cont'l Ins.*, 586 F. Supp. 139, 150.

W.D. La. 2007. Insured's discovery of loss—which commenced period within which insured could commence lawsuit under an Executive Protection Policy—occurred when insured obtained written confession from bookkeeper. The court rejected the insured's argument that its discovery of the loss was extended because an investigation was required to determine the extent of the loss. *Magnolia Mgmt. Corp. v. Fed. Ins. Co.*, No. 06-0447, 2007 WL 4124496, *5-8.

M.D.N.C. 1959. Loss was not discovered within effective period of Bank Employee Fidelity Bond when bank employees founds books and records out of balance, but did not make a detailed examination leading to the discovery of a shortage until days after the bond's effective period expired. The facts known at the time the policy expired would not lead a reasonable person to an assumption that a shortage existed, as opposed to a mere clerical error. The facts must be viewed as they would have been by a reasonable person at the time discovery is asserted to have occurred, and not as they appear in light of subsequently-acquired knowledge. *Wachovia Bank & Trust Co. v. Mfrs. Cas. Ins. Co.*, 171 F. Supp. 369, 375.

D.N.J. 1977. Under fidelity bond requiring notice at the "earliest practicable moment after discovery of any loss hereunder," insured bank's receipt of a state Department of Banking report condemning certain loans made under the bank's new ship-loan program may have given bank notice that the loans were excessive and the related documentation poor, but did not require notice. Notice is not required when the insured only knows of insufficient business procedures, irregularities, or account deficiencies, or merely suspects or has reason to suspect the wrongdoing. Bank only "discovered" a loss when it obtained counsel to investigate the loan program, learned incriminating facts, and acquired knowledge of a specific, fraudulent act. *Midland Bank & Trust Co. v. Fid. & Deposit Co. of Md.*, 442 F. Supp. 960, 971-73.

W.D. Okla. 1973. Insured held to have "discovered" alleged dishonesty of its manager when it authorized certain investment decisions from which loss resulted—including making pledges of collateral—and learned of unauthorized loans. Knowledge is what a reasonable person should have concluded from known facts. *Alfalfa Elec. Coop., Inc. v. Travelers Indem. Co.*, 376 F. Supp. 901, 906.

N.D. Ohio 1964. Insured bank's discovery of several acts of dishonesty by branch manager triggered notice obligation under bond requiring notice "at the earliest practical moment, and at all events not later than 15 days after discovery of any fraudulent or dishonest act on the part of any Employee," irrespective of whether insured only later learned that such dishonesty resulted in a loss. *City Loan & Sav. Co. v. Emp'rs' Liab. Assurance Corp., Ltd.*, 249 F. Supp. 633, 655-58.

D. P.R. 1991. Fidelity insurer moved for summary judgment on multiple grounds, including defense that insured financial institution failed to comply with provision requiring that notice be given "at the earliest practicable moment after discovery of any loss hereunder." Motion denied, with the court holding that whether the information possessed by the employer amounts to actual knowledge of the wrongdoing is a question for the jury. Nothing short of actual discovery of dishonesty or positive breach of an imperative condition by the insured employee will terminate the bond as to the defaulting employee. *FDIC v. CNA Cas.*, 786 F. Supp. 1082, 1088-89.

E.D. Va. 1963. Under Bankers Blanket Bond requiring notice at the earliest practical moment following discovery of loss, notice became due when insured bank discovered forgeries on government issued bonds—even though bank believed a release between the bond payee and the forger settled the dispute. The word "loss" refers to a condition in which the insured would be subject to a claim or demand "out of which a legal liability might arise," and not to an adjudicated liability. *Mount Vernon Bank & Trust Co. v. Aetna Cas. & Sur. Co.*, 224 F. Supp. 666, 670.

Cal. Ct. App. 1981. Insured discovered loss prior to the issuance of the bond, when it had knowledge of the fraud and dishonest acts committed by its employees. The fact that plaintiff did not understand the dishonest or fraudulent nature of these acts did not delay the "discovery" such that it occurred within the bond period. Discovery occurs when the insured acquires knowledge of a fraudulent or dishonest act resulting in loss. *USLIFE Sav. & Loan Ass'n v. Nat'l Sur. Corp.*, 115 Cal. App. 3d 336, 346.

Cal. Ct. App. 1931. Under an Employee Fidelity Bond requiring that written notice be given to the insurer "[w]hen the Assured discovers a loss hereunder," insured bank was not charged with giving notice as soon as it discovered branch manager drawing upon funds for personal use. Because the branch manager repaid each draw except the very last, it did not occur to the bank until the very end that what was occurring was fraudulent. The phrase "discovers a loss" required actual knowledge of fraud—not merely an opportunity to investigate and means of knowledge. *Pac. Coast Adjustment Bureau v. Indem. Ins. Co. of N. Am.*, 2 P.2d 218, 220.

Cal. Ct. App. 1919. Under an Employee Fidelity Bond requiring that insured sports club provide notice "promptly after becoming aware of any act which may be made the basis of a claim," notice is not required upon a mere suspicion, but notice must be given when insured knows or had every opportunity of knowing of default. But in this case the insured knew, or had every opportunity of knowing, all the facts when it became obvious to employees of sports club that employee was helping himself to enormous amounts of cigars, liquor, and other items, and the failure of the insured to give prompt notice was a breach of a material condition of the bond. *Los Angeles Athl. Club v. USF&G*, 183 P. 174, 175-77.

Ga. Ct. App. 1989. Insured public board's suspicions as to misappropriations by chairman did not rise to "knowledge or discovery of loss of a loss" triggering notice provisions of fidelity bond until the board received an audit report confirming those suspicions. The fact that the chairman was prosecuted at an earlier time did not provide the requisite level of knowledge, given that the chairman had been acquitted. *USF&G v. Macon-Bibb Cnty. Econ. Opp. Council, Inc.*, 381 S.E.2d 539, 540.

Ky. 1906. The insured is not bound to report suspicions to the bonding company, even though they are strong enough to justify, in the opinion of the insured, the discharge of an employee. After suspicion is aroused, the insured ought to pursue its inquiries with reasonable diligence, and when satisfied that a defalcation exists, and the extent, or the substantial extent, of it, notice of the fact ought to be given promptly to the bonding company. *Fid. & Guar. Co. v. W. Bank*, 94 S.W. 3, 6.

La. Ct. App. 1997. Insured's subsidiary was sued by a customer alleging misrepresentation and fraud. After a jury verdict was entered against the subsidiary, the insured learned that its agent failed to add subsidiary in the blanket crime policy the insured had obtained. The appellate court sustained the trial judge's grant of a directed verdict in favor of the agent, on the grounds that the loss sustained by the insurer had been discovered under a different, prior policy in effect when the action against the subsidiary had commenced, and rejected the insured's assertion that it did not truly discover the loss until a final judgment was entered against the subsidiary. *Newpark Res., Inc. v. Marsh & McLennan of La., Inc.*, 691 So. 2d 208, 211-13.

La. Ct. App. 1938. Under fidelity bond requiring insured to give "immediate notice" "[u]pon the discovery . . . of any dishonest act on the part of any employee," insured was required to give notice of knowledge of fraudulent or dishonest conduct on the part of its employee which might involve the liability of the bonding company, but not of mere suspicions of such conduct; in this instance, such knowledge was acquired upon receiving an auditor's report confirming the loss *Inter-City Express Lines, Inc. v. Hartford Acc. & Indem. Co.,* 178 So. 280, 282-83.

Mass. 1935. Insured insurance business's obligation to give notice under bond was not triggered during a period of time when the insured knew that its agent was not timely remitting premiums collected on behalf of the insured. Although insured could not prolong giving notice until it could prove the existence of a fraud giving rise to these losses, acts creating mere suspicion of fraudulent activity do not give rise to discovery of a loss. *Gilmour v. Standard Sur. & Cas. Co.*, 197 N.E. 673, 676.

Mass. App. Ct. 2009. Affirming trial court's determination that insured, the Department of State Treasurer, did not discover "loss or a situation that may result in loss" at the time when the state Attorney General was notified of suspicious deposits prompting its investigation of insured's employee. The trial court declined to attribute the Attorney General's knowledge to the insured, and accepted testimony that the insured did not know of the loss until the media identified the employee as someone under suspicion. *Hanover Ins. Co. v. Treasurer & Receiver Gen.*, 910 N.E.2d 921, 930.

Minn. 1957. Bankers Blanket Bond required that insured initiate legal proceedings within 12 months of discovery of loss. The court upheld a special referee's finding that the insured did not discover the loss until after the bank's auditor began his examination of accounting irregularities. While an insured cannot wait to give notice until the extent of loss is known, notice is not due until the insured is justified in believing that a loss has occurred through dishonesty rather than through errors consistent with integrity. *Prior Lake State Bank v. Nat'l Sur. Corp.*, 80 N.W.2d 612, 618.

Minn. 1910. When insured company received account reports from travelling salesman indicating the salesman's indebtedness to the insured, it was not obligated to give notice of claim under bond, as an insured is not obligated to give notice of irregularities or suspicions of fraud. However, given insured's lack of diligence in investigating salesman's claims that there were sufficient credits and discounts forthcoming to balance the account, notice was appropriately deemed untimely when the insured ultimately determined that the salesman had collected an account which was not reported. *Gamble-Robinson Co. v. Mass. Bonding & Ins. Co.*, 129 N.W. 131, 132-34.

Miss. 1921. Under bond requiring notice to the insurer within ninety days of insured becoming "aware of a loss sustained by reason of acts constituting larceny or embezzlement," insured's discovery of unexplained irregularities or discrepancies in the books or accounts of an employee did not trigger the insured's obligation to give notice, as in order to justify a charge of larceny or embezzlement, the insured would have required considerable time for investigation after its suspicions were aroused. *Md. Cas. Co. v. Hall*, 88 So. 407, 408-09.

Mo. 1966. Bank sought to recover under Bankers Blanket Bond when it was adjudicated liable to a third party for allowing the unauthorized deposit of checks. The bank's discovery of its loss occurred not when the checks were originally presented for deposit, nor when the third party began requesting information with respect to the checks without voicing an intent to assert a claim against the bank, but when the third party demanded reimbursement for the checks, at which time the insured must reasonably have known and recognized that the third party had suffered a loss and that the customer intended to attempt to hold the insured liable for such loss. *Jefferson Bank & Trust Co. v. Cent. Sur. & Ins. Corp.*, 408 S.W.2d 825, 829-33.

Mo. Ct. App. 1998. Under a Commercial Crime Policy, the named insured was required to have discovered the wrongdoing within the policy period in order to qualify for coverage. The insured's employees' knowledge of their own fraud would not be imputed to the insured. However, where the insured's discovery of the wrongdoing occurred one year after the policies expired, the loss was not covered. *Se. Bakery Feeds, Inc. v. Ranger Ins. Co.*, 974 S.W.2d 635, 637-41.

Mont. 1924. Insured's manager bought and sold options and futures in violation of insured's bylaws. The insured was entitled to rely on the manager's fidelity, and was not required to give notice based upon its suspicion, upon the manager's departure, that recoverable losses had occurred. Notice was required when insured had knowledge of the existence of such facts as would justify a careful and prudent man in charging another with the acts for which the claim is made. *Outlook Farmers' Elevator Co. v. Am. Sur. Co.*, 223 P. 905, 912.

N.J. 1978. Insured sought coverage for loss resulting from manager's fraudulent handling of large, collateralized loans. The insured insisted that its discovery of the loss did not occur until it had obtained sufficient details about the manager's wrongdoing. However the trial court appropriately determined that discovery occurred a year earlier, when the insured had extensive knowledge of the excessive loans, the wrongful release of collateral, and confusing, illegible collateral loan cards. "Discovery" of the loss occurs when the insured learns of facts or obtains knowledge which would justify a careful and prudent person in charging another with dishonesty or fraud. *Nat'l Newark & Essex Bank v. Am. Ins. Co.*, 385 A.2d 1216, 1225.

N.Y. App. Div. 2011. Policy required insured to provide notice of loss at the earliest practical moment after discovery of the loss by the Corporate Risk Manager. Insured had no Corporate Risk Manager, but maintained that the chief actuary of its parent company, its "de facto corporate risk manager," learned of the loss in May 2003. The Court held that "discovery" took place in July 2002, when the insured's legal department learned of the subject loss, and that their knowledge was imputed to the chief actuary. *Hudson Ins. Co. v. M.J. Oppenheim*, 81 A.D.3d 427, 427-28.

N.Y. App. Div. 1934. Insured corporation's secretary's discovery of missing cash in cashier drawer did not necessarily lead to conclusion of employee dishonesty, rather than carelessness, and therefore did not trigger obligation to give notice to fidelity insurer within ten days "after the Employer shall have become aware of any fraudulent or dishonest act on the part of the Employee." The operative test, whether insured acquired knowledge of facts from which the conclusion of dishonesty and fraud reasonably would follow, was a jury question. *Charles W. Schreiber Travel Bureau v. Standard Sur. & Cas. Co.*, 240 A.D. 279, 280-82.

N.C. 1926. Bond required insured bank to notify insurer "immediately after becoming aware of any act or omission which may be made the basis of a claim hereunder." After employee left bank in August, an audit which had been commenced earlier in July revealed shortages in the employee's account. Whether the bank had acted reasonably in notifying the insurer in September was an issue properly submitted to the jury, which returned a verdict in the insured's favor. *Forest City Bldg. & Loan Ass'n v. Davis,* 133 S.E. 530, 533.

Okla. 1932. Bond required that loss be discovered within the bond period or 18 months after the termination thereof, and that notice of loss be submitted forty-five days after such discovery. Although insured learned that employee's account was short slightly before the bond expired, the notice requirement was only triggered when the insured later obtained definite information that an actual defalcation had occurred. *Am. Sur. Co. v. State,* 12 P.2d 212, 214-16.

Or. Ct. App. 2000. The Court reversed a grant of summary judgment in favor of the insured, on the grounds that there was a genuine issue of material fact as to whether insured discovered its loss outside of the suit limitations period (when the insured filed a criminal complaint against its employee and provided the insurer with a proof of loss) or whether the insured discovered its loss inside the bond's suit limitations period (when the employee was indicted and the insured gained more knowledge of its employee's intentional scheme). The factual issue was whether, when the insured filed the complaint and proof of loss, it merely knew that the employee had violated company policies, or whether it had knowledge of the employee's intentional scheme to defraud. *Nike, Inc. v. N.W. Pac. Indem. Co.,* 999 P.2d 1197, 1203-04.

Pa. 1934. Under a Bank Employee Fidelity Bond, the court held that discovery occurred when bank president learned of fraud perpetuated by employee upon customer, and customer demanded payment from the bank. So far as the insured was concerned, the loss, in the sense of a claim out of which a legal liability might arise, was discovered at that time, and not later, when the customer made a formal written demand for payment. *Gentile v. Am. Bank & Trust Co.,* 172 A. 303, 304-05.

Pa. Super. Ct. 1936. Insured reported accounting irregularities in its books to the State in July 1933. In September, a report was delivered from the State confirming that the losses were due to embezzlement by a bank employee. Given that the insured was obligated to notify the surety when it became satisfied that a default had taken place, but was not obligated to give notice of mere suspicions, the court declined to reverse a jury verdict which found that the insured discovered its loss only upon receiving the report. *Thomas Holme Bldg. & Loan Ass'n v. New Amsterdam Cas. Co.,* 188 A. 374, 376-77.

Tenn. Ct. App. 1965. Insured's knowledge of employee's mishandling of funds—including writing checks to himself in large amounts—was sufficient to justify trial court's finding that insured "discovered" a loss under fidelity bond, notwithstanding testimony by insured's principals that no knowledge of an actual defalcation was obtained until a later date. The word "discovery" means the knowledge of facts and circumstances sufficient to satisfy persons of ordinary prudence that a loss has occurred. *World Secret Serv. Ass'n v. Travelers Indem. Co.,* 396 S.W.2d 848, 849.

Tenn. Ct. App. 1937. Although hospital manager knew of nurse's misappropriation of funds, because he was a participant in the misappropriation, his knowledge would not be imputed to the hospital and did not trigger the hospital's obligation to give notice to its fidelity insurer. However, the hospital's receiver became obligated to give notice immediately upon learning of the embezzlement, because "discovery of fraud or of default," which triggered the notice requirement under the bond, meant the insured's knowledge of facts and circumstances sufficient to satisfy persons of ordinary prudence that default or conversion had been committed. *Nashville & Am. Trust Co. v. Aetna Cas. & Sur. Co.,* 110 S.W.2d 1041, 1045-46.

Tex. App. 1944. Irregularities revealed in report of insurance examiner did not show any loss due to dishonesty or bad faith and were not sufficient to put board on inquiry notice. The fidelity bonds at issue required notice of losses due to dishonesty and bad faith, and not merely a warning to prevent possible future losses. *Bd. of Ins. Comm'rs v. Allied Underwriters,* 180 S.W.2d 990, 993-96.

Vt. 1940. Trial court erred in allowing jury to determine whether notice was timely given under policy. Although insured's initial discovery of inventory shortages may not have given rise to anything more than suspicion, testimony at trial clearly demonstrated that upon discovering subsequent shortages, insured believed that misappropriations had occurred, and was therefore obligated to comply with the bond's notice provisions. *Brown v. Md. Cas. Co.,* 11 A.2d 222, 224-25.

Wash. 1966. Knowledge that employee was tardy in making deposits was not sufficient to trigger insured's obligation to give notice upon acquiring "knowledge or discovery of loss or of an occurrence which may give rise to a claim for loss." *Tradewell Stores, Inc. v. Fid. & Cas. Co.,* 410 P.2d 782, 783-85.

Wash. 1935. In action against Bankers Blanket Bond by insured bank, for losses caused by former president making fictitious loans, the court held that notice was not due until bank acquired actual knowledge of the former president's dishonesty through an audit which disclosed unpaid and uncollectible loans which did not identify interested parties. *Hansen v. Am. Bonding Co.,* 48 P.2d 653, 656.

Wis. 1912. Officers of insured bank were not obligated under bond to notify bonding company of check kiting activity which they might have discovered had they made a critical examination of the bank's books from time to time. Notice is required upon actual knowledge and not mere constructive notice. *First Nat'l Bank of Crandon v. USF&G,* 137 N.W. 742, 745.

C. Written Notice Thereof

D.N.J. 1993. Information which insured submitted to insurer in order to renew directors and officers liability policies did not satisfy policy's requirement that insured submit "notice" of the basis of a claim during the policy period. As the purpose of notice under a claims-made policy is to invoke coverage, the requirement of "notice" must be construed as requiring more than coincidental transmission of information. *Am. Cas. Co. v. Continisio,* 819 F. Supp. 385, 398-99.

SECTION 5 — NOTICE/PROOF—LEGAL PROCEEDINGS AGAINST UNDERWRITER   421

La. Ct. App. 1937. Under an Employee Fidelity Bond, a letter to agent for new bonding company who once but no longer was agent for prior bonding company, which incidentally mentioned prior bonding company but did not indicate that it was intended to be notice to prior bonding company or its successor of any loss, and did not state dates or details of loss, did not constitute written notice to prior bonding company. *George J. Ricau & Co., Inc. v. Indem. Ins. Co. of N. Am.*, 173 So. 217, 219-22.

N.J. 1978. Notice need not include a statement of facts which could reasonably be read to require bonding company to admit or deny liability. The purpose of notice of loss provision is to allow insurer to commence an investigation and protect its interests. Letter which informs bonding company of discovery of seriously under-margined accounts and investigation by the insured is sufficient notice of loss even though letter also stated "we have no tangible evidence of defalcation, mysterious disappearance, kiting operation or other purported act." *Nat'l Newark & Essex Bank v. Am. Ins. Co.*, 385 A.2d 1216, 1223-26.

Pa. 1934. Statement provided by insured tax collector to surety under Tax Collector Official Bond merely showed a shortage in the insured's accounts, without any indication as to whether the shortage was due to a cause which would give rise to the surety's liability under the bond. Although the Court held that this did not constitute formal notice under the bond, the surety's subsequent investigation and conduct waived any requirement for further notice. *Nanty-Glo Borough v. Am. Sur. Co.*, 175 A. 536, 536-38.

D. Effect of Failure to Give Notice or Delay in Giving Notice

    1. Notice-Prejudice Rule Applied / Limitations Provision Not Treated as Condition Precedent

        (a) Insured required to disprove or rebut presumption of prejudice

5th Cir. 1979 (Fla.). Under an Errors and Omissions Insurance Policy, insured's failure to comply with the terms of condition of policy regarding notice does not prevent recovery, but insured must prove that failure to comply did not prejudice insurer. *United States v. United Bonding Ins. Co.*, 422 F.2d 277, 280.

N.D. Cal. 1963. Evidence showing that insurer on forgery bond was prejudiced by the failure of the insured to comply with the notice provision of the bond was not rebutted by insured. Therefore, the bonding company was not liable. However, the court did not specifically require the insurer to prove prejudice, or require the insured to rebut a presumption of prejudice, but instead found that under either test, the insurer would prevail. *St. Paul Fire & Marine Ins. Co. v. Bank of Stockton*, 213 F. Supp. 716, 722.

Conn. 2008. Insured sued insurer under business insurance contract providing employee dishonesty and business interruption coverage. On appeal from a jury verdict in favor of the insured, the court held that the trial court's failure to instruct the jury on the insurer's special defense of late notice of claim—including the insured's burden of proving that any such late notice did not prejudice the insurer—was harmful error. The court held that the jury should have been instructed that if it found that the insured had delayed notifying the insurer, and that the delay was unexcused and unreasonable, such a delay would constitute a failure to comply with the policy's notice condition and would excuse the insurer from liability, unless the jury found that the insured had proven by a fair preponderance of the evidence that the insurer had suffered no material prejudice due to the late notice. *Nat'l Pub. Co., Inc. v. Hartford Fire Ins. Co.*, 949 A.2d 1203, 1210-13.

Fla. Dist. Ct. App. 1970. Failure to give notice as required by the terms of the bond raises presumption of prejudice to the bonding company. Insured failed to rebut presumption of prejudice and could not recover. *Miami Nat'l Bank v. Pa. Ins. Co.*, 240 So. 2d 832, 833.

N.Y. Sup. Ct. 1964. Under a Stevedore Operations Indemnity Policy, failure to give notice as required by policy voided the contract in absence of mitigating circumstances justifying or excusing the delay. *Am. Stevedores, Inc. v. Sun Ins. Office, Ltd.*, 248 N.Y.S.2d 487, 488.

Wis. 1979. Interpreting a statute which provided that an insured's notice is not deemed untimely and preclusive of recovery if the notice is furnished as soon as reasonably possible within one year of the time notice is required by the terms of the insurance policy, the court concluded that where notice was given after that one-year period expired, the insured carried the burden of rebutting the presumption that the insurer was prejudiced by the late notice. *Gerrard Realty Corp. v. Am. States Ins. Co.*, 277 N.W.2d 863, 871.

    (b) Insurer required to prove prejudice

8th Cir. 1999 (Minn.). Under a Corporate Crime Policy, untimely notice was held to have prejudiced the insurer and defeated coverage because the insurer could not assert its subrogation rights against the banks that paid on the dishonest employee's misappropriated checks within a time limit set by the U.C.C. *Winthrop & Weinstein, P.A. v. Travelers Cas. & Sur. Co.*, 187 F.3d 871, 874-75.

10th Cir. 1998 (Kan.). Pursuant to Kansas law, untimely notice does not defeat coverage under a fidelity bond absent prejudice to the insurer. *Nat'l Union Fire Ins. Co. of Pitt., Pa. v. FDIC*, 160 F.3d 657, 657-58.

10th Cir. 1994 (Utah). The court predicted that the Utah Supreme Court would hold that under a Bankers Blanket Bond, timely notice was not a condition precedent to coverage. Accordingly, the insurer could only deny coverage if it could show it had suffered "substantial prejudice" from the delay in terms of its ability to investigate, settle, or defend the claims at issue. *FDIC v. Oldenburg*, 34 F.3d 1529, 1546-47.

D. Kan. 1982. Upon failure of insured to give timely notice, the insurer is discharged from liability upon a showing of substantial prejudice. Insured bank's late notice to bonding company of check kiting scheme was prejudicial to the surety particularly because within the period of the delay, insured bank increased its loss by paying checks it was not legally obligated to pay. *Sec. Nat'l Bank v. Cont'l Ins. Co.*, 586 F. Supp. 139, 148.

E.D. La. 1995. Where there was doubt as to the prejudice caused by later notice under a Financial Institution Bond, the insurer could not avoid coverage. Under Louisiana law, an insurer seeking to avoid coverage based on untimely notice must show prejudice if the bond does not make notice an express condition precedent to coverage. *RTC v. Gaudet*, 907 F. Supp. 212, 216-17.

E.D. La. 1990. The court opined that notice provisions exist to provide insurers an opportunity to investigate claims, and not to serve as escapes from coverage. Therefore, an insurer must show prejudice in order to avoid coverage. *FDIC v. Aetna Cas. & Sur. Co.*, 744 F. Supp. 729, 733.

D.N.J. 1994. Surety would have to show "appreciable prejudice" before denying claim based upon insured's failure to comply with provision requiring that notice be given "as soon as practicable" after discovery of loss under the policy. *RTC v. Moskowitz*, 868 F. Supp. 634, 639-40.

E.D. Pa. 1995. Under an Employee Crime Policy, the court found that the insurer must show that the insured's late notice prejudiced the insurer. Where the insurer showed that a three-year delay prevented the insurer from avoiding other losses and prevented adequate investigation, prejudice was found. *Northwood Nursing & Convalescent Home, Inc. v. Cont'l Ins. Co.*, 902 F. Supp. 79, 81-86.

D. Utah 2013. The court applied a Utah statute providing that failure to give notice under an "insurance policy" does not bar recovery thereunder if the insurer fails to show it was prejudiced by the failure, such that insurer under a credit union bond was required to show that it was prejudiced by insured's failure to give notice within sixty days of discovering loss. *Transw. Credit Union v. CUMIS Ins. Soc'y, Inc.*, No. 2:09-cv-297, 2013 WL 411485, at *1-3.

Mich. Ct. App. 1970. Trial court improperly charged jury that notice was timely as a matter of law, where insurer alleged that loss had been discovered eight to nine months before notice was given. Bonding company is entitled to reasonable notice, and failure to give it would release bonding company from liability. However, prejudice to the bonding company is a necessary element in determining if there has been unreasonable delay. *Grand Rapids Auctions, Inc. v. Hartford Acc. & Indem. Co.*, 178 N.W.2d 812, 815.

Miss. 1951. Under a Fidelity Blanket Position Bond, the court held that in absence of a provision that insured's giving of notice is a condition precedent to recovery, the insured's failure to give notice within the required period of time does not preclude recovery unless the failure has resulted in prejudice to the rights of the bonding company. *Hartford Acc. & Indem. Co. v. Hattiesburg Hardware Stores, Inc.*, 49 So. 2d 813, 819.

Miss. 1934. Bond required notice within ten days of insured discovering defalcations by employees, but did not provide that failure to give such notice relieved the insurer, nor did the bond make such notice the essence of the bond. Absent showing of prejudice to insurer, insured's failure to comply with notice provision of bond would not defeat recovery thereunder. *Fid. & Deposit Co. of Md. v. Merchs. & Marine Bank*, 151 So. 373, 375.

Mo. Ct. App. 1931. Where Employee Fidelity Bond did not provide that the giving of notice was a condition precedent to recovery thereunder, surety could not argue that the insured was precluded from recovery as a result of failing to give timely notice. *People's Bank v. Aetna Cas. & Sur. Co.*, 40 S.W.2d 535, 541-42.

N.C. 1913. Insured's failure to comply with indemnity bond's notice provision did not defeat recovery, because noncompliance with provision was not expressly made a ground for forfeiture. The court did not expressly address the issue of prejudice. *Dixie Fire Ins. Co. v. Am. Bonding Co.*, 78 S.E. 430, 433.

N.C. Ct. App. 1984. Under an Embezzlement Insurance Policy, an unexcused delay in notifying the insurer of a loss or claim does not relieve the insurer of liability if the delay does not materially prejudice the insurer and the insured acted in good faith. The court opined that delay in filing proof is less likely to prejudice the insurer in the case of embezzlement than in the case of a loss under a general liability policy. *B & H Supply Co., Inc. v. Ins. Co. of N. Am.*, 311 S.E.2d 643, 647.

Tenn. Ct. App. 1978. Compliance with notice provision was held not to be a condition precedent, because the bond did not expressly provide that compliance was a condition precedent. Bonding company has burden of proving that notice is defective. *Union Planters Corp. v. Harwell*, 578 S.W.2d 87, 90.

2. Notice-Prejudice Rule Not Applied / Compliance with Notice Provision Construed as Condition Precedent

U.S. 1902. Failure to comply with condition requiring notice defeated bank's recovery against a teller's bond for defalcations. *Guar. Co. of N. Am. v. Mechs.' Sav. Bank & Trust Co.*, 183 U.S. 402, 416-24.

1st Cir. 1997 (Mass). Bank first provided written notice to the insurer approximately five months after the latest date discovery of loss could have occurred. The insurer was not required to prove that it was prejudiced by such late notice, as the "notice-prejudice" rule, developed under the common law to protect laypersons purchasing liability policies, was inapplicable to a Financial Institution Bond, the terms of which had evolved through years of negotiations between sophisticated parties in the banking and insurance industries. *FDIC v. Ins. Co. of N. Am.*, 105 F.3d 778, 786.

1st Cir. 1990 (Mass.). Where the court found the terms of the insurance policy to be unambiguous, denial of coverage was deemed appropriate when the insured failed to give notice in the specified period of time. *J.I. Corp. v. Fed. Ins. Co.*, 920 F.2d 118, 120.

2d Cir. 1984 (N.Y.). Compliance with the notice requirement set forth in an insurance contract is a condition precedent to recovery under New York law, and therefore, failure by the insured to comply with notice provisions in fidelity bond precluded the insured from recovering thereunder. The insurer was not required to show that the lack of timely notice was prejudicial. *Utica Mut. Ins. Co. v. Fireman's Fund Ins. Cos.*, 748 F.2d 118, 122.

2d Cir. 1935 (N.Y.). Time for filing proof of loss is a condition precedent to liability. Bond required filing proof of loss within thirty days after discovery of default. Proof of loss was not filed until eighty five days after discovery. Insurer was entitled to dismissal of insured's complaint. *Public Warehouses of Matanzas v. Fid. & Deposit Co. of Md.*, 77 F.2d 831, 831-33.

4th Cir. 1933 (N.C.). Compliance with notice provision of Employee Fidelity Bond held to be condition to liability. *Fid. & Cas. Co. v. Hoyle*, 64 F.2d 413, 416.

4th Cir. 1930 (N.C.). Compliance with notice provision of Bank Employee Fidelity Bond is condition precedent to liability of the bonding company. *Nat'l City Bank v. Nat'l Sec. Co.,* 37 F.2d 550, 552.

5th Cir. 1972 (Tex.). Savings and Loan Blanket Bond required that proof of loss be filed within 100 days after discovery of loss. Failure of insured to file proof of loss for nearly two years after discovery is a bar to claim. Compliance with proof of loss provision is condition precedent to recovery. *Abilene Sav. Ass'n v. Westchester Fire Ins. Co.,* 461 F.2d 557, 559.

5th Cir. 1957 (La.). The court noted that stipulations for notice "are usually enforced literally and as conditions," but did not decide whether insured was discharged from liability on grounds of inadequate notice because the district court granted summary judgment in favor of insurer on other grounds. *J.S. Fearing, Inc. v. Emp'rs Mut. Liab. Ins. Co.,* 242 F.2d 609, 611.

5th Cir. 1954 (Tex.). Insured's undisputed failure to file proof of loss as required by 3-D Policy was an appropriate basis for district court granting summary judgment in favor of insurer, as filing proof of loss was made an "unequivocal condition" in bond. *Lawson v. Am. Motorists Ins. Corp.,* 217 F.2d 724, 726-27.

5th Cir. 1934 (Fla.). Compliance with notice provision of fidelity bond is condition to bonding company's liability on the bond. *Murray v. Am. Sur. Co.,* 69 F.2d 147, 149.

6th Cir. 1994 (Ohio). Court rejected proposition that the Ohio Supreme Court would abandon the traditional Ohio rule that an insured's unreasonable delay in giving notice will relieve the surety of liability, irrespective of whether the surety has been prejudiced. *Am. Emp'rs Ins. Co. v. Metro Reg'l Trans. Auth.,* 12 F.3d 591, 592-98.

6th Cir. 1932 (Tenn.). Compliance with notice provision of Bank Employee Fidelity Bond is condition precedent to liability of the bonding company. *Nat'l City Bank v. Nat'l Sec. Co.,* 58 F.2d 7, 8.

7th Cir. 1952 (Ind.). Compliance with notice provision of bond is condition precedent to liability of bonding company. *Munice Banking Co. v. Am. Sur. Co.*, 200 F.2d 115, 118.

8th Cir. 1932 (Neb.). Compliance with notice provision of Employee Fidelity Bond is condition to recovery under the bond. *Am. Sur. Co. v. Bankers Sav. Ass'n*, 59 F.2d 577, 580.

9th Cir. 1954 (Ariz.). Under a Blanket Position Bond, the court held that absent waiver or estoppel, compliance with conditions governing proof of loss is condition precedent to liability. *Alianza Hispano-Americana v. Hartford Acc. & Indem. Co.*, 209 F.2d 578, 578.

10th Cir. 1966 (N.M.). The court held that failure to comply with provision requiring notice "at the earliest practicable moment and at all events not later than fifteen days after discovery of any fraudulent act" precluded recovery by the insured thereunder. *Hidden Splendor Mining Co. v. Gen. Ins. Co.*, 370 F.2d 515, 518-520.

D.C. Cir. 1938. Given that it is of utmost importance that the surety receive prompt notice under a fidelity bond so that it may take all proper steps to reduce its loss, most fidelity bonds require notice of default within a certain time period, and compliance with such terms is "indispensable to fix liability," irrespective of whether the surety can show that it was prejudiced. *U.S. Shopping Bd. Merch. Fleet Corp. v. Aetna Cas. & Sur. Co.*, 98 F.2d 238, 241-42.

D. Conn. 1997. Notice provisions are a condition precedent to coverage, and the insurer need not show prejudice where notice is not timely given. *Cmty. Sav. Bank v. Fed. Ins. Co.*, 960 F. Supp. 16, 21.

D. Colo. 2008. Precedential Colorado caselaw did not apply "notice prejudice" rule to claims against fidelity bonds, and therefore, court would not overrule such caselaw on the basis that the Colorado Supreme Court might do so in the future. *FDIC v. St. Paul Cos.*, 634 F. Supp. 2d 1213, 1224.

D. Md. 1969. Compliance with notice provision of Savings and Loan Blanket Bond is condition precedent to recovery. *Phoenix Sav. & Loan, Inc. v. Aetna Cas. & Sur. Co.*, 302 F. Supp. 832, 837.

D. Mass. 1998. Where the insured failed to provide timely notice under a Bankers Blanket Bond, the insurer did not need to show prejudice in order to deny coverage. Summary judgment in favor of the insurer in such a case is appropriate where the only reasonable inference to be drawn from the undisputed historical facts is that discovery of the loss occurred outside the notice period. *FDIC v. Underwriters of Lloyd's of London Fid. Bond Number 834/FB9010020,* 3 F. Supp. 2d 120, 146.

D. Mass. 1996. Noting that notice provisions allow insurers to properly investigate claims before the evidentiary trail grows cold, the court held that where notice was given more than thirty days after the insured had sufficient facts to raise more than a suspicion of loss, notice under the bond was untimely and the insurer did not have to show prejudice in order to deny claim. *FDIC v. Ins. Co. of N. Am.,* 928 F. Supp. 54, 59.

D. Mass. 1985. As a result of insurance company's failure to give notice to fidelity insurer as required by bond, insurance company could not recover thereunder. *Boston Mut. Life Ins. Co. v. Fireman's Fund Ins. Co.,* 613 F. Supp. 1090, 1096-98.

D. Mont. 1990. Fidelity insurer was not required to demonstrate that insured's failure to provide timely notice caused substantial prejudice to insurer. Montana law recognizes that timely notice of discovery is a condition precedent to recovery under a surety bond containing a notice clause. *FSLIC v. Aetna Cas. & Sur. Co.,* 785 F. Supp. 867, 871.

N.D. Ohio 1964. Failure to give notice for over two years after discovery of dishonest acts precluded recovery. *City Loan & Sav. Co. v. Emp'rs' Liab. Assurance Corp.,* 249 F. Supp. 633, 655.

W.D. Okla. 1973. Under a Comprehensive Dishonesty, Disappearance, and Destruction Policy, compliance with notice provision was held to be a condition precedent to liability of bonding company under Oklahoma law. *Alfalfa Elec. Coop., Inc. v. Travelers Indem. Co.,* 376 F. Supp. 901, 908.

Cal. Ct. App. 1919. Compliance with notice provision is condition precedent to liability of bonding company, and insured cannot argue that the provision is immaterial such that a violation thereof does not avoid the policy. *Los Angeles Athl. Club v. USF&G,* 183 P. 174, 177.

Colo. 1957. Court affirmed trial court's judgment in favor of insurer, stating that not only did insured asserting claim under Dishonesty Bond fail to produce direct and positive proof of loss due to dishonesty of employee, but insured also failed to give timely notice to insurer of claim. *Pueblo Athl. Club v. Am. Bonding. Co.*, 307 P.2d 813, 815.

Ky. 1956. Notice and proof of loss must be given within the time limits fixed in the policy. Insured was not entitled to jury instruction that provision requiring notice within 15 days after discovery of loss was complied with by giving notice within a reasonable period of time. *Shatz v. Am. Sur. Co.*, 295 S.W.2d 809, 816.

Ill. App. Ct. 1983. Although failure to give notice of loss to insurer for certain length of time may, as a matter of law, constitute failure to give notice as "soon as possible" under the bond, factual questions as to when loss was discovered and when notice was delivered prevented summary judgment. *Mortell v. Ins. Co. of N. Am.*, 458 N.E.2d 922, 928-29.

La. Ct. App. 1937. Failure to comply with notice provision precludes recovery. Statute which provided that notice by insured could be made to any authorized agent of insurer did not absolve insured of obligation to comply with bond requirement that notice be made by registered mail. *George J. Ricau & Co., Inc. v. Indem. Ins. Co. of N. Am.*, 173 So. 217, 219-20.

Mass. 1935. Compliance with notice provision is a condition precedent to the liability of the bonding company. *Gilmour v. Standard Sur. & Cas. Co.*, 197 N.E. 673, 676.

Mich. 1954. Fidelity insurer was entitled to judgment on the basis of record showing that insured did not give notice of employee misconduct to insurer until 34 days after loss was discovered, in violation of policy provision requiring that insured notice of loss at the earliest practical moment, not exceeding 15 days after discovery of loss. *Cont'l Studios v. Am. Auto Ins. Co.*, 64 N.W.2d 615, 618.

Minn. 1929. Failure to give notice of loss within time provided by bond precludes recovery. Failure to give notice of prior loss does not preclude recovery of subsequent losses, for which timely notice was given.

SECTION 5 — NOTICE/PROOF—LEGAL PROCEEDINGS AGAINST UNDERWRITER 431

Citizens State Bank of St. Paul v. New Amsterdam Cas. Co., 224 N.W. 451, 453.

Minn. 1910. Unreasonable delay in providing notice to surety discharged surety's liability under bond requiring that the insured give notice immediately upon discovering employee dishonesty or fraud. *Gamble-Robinson Co. v. Mass. Bonding & Ins. Co.*, 129 N.W. 131, 133-34.

Mo. Ct. App. 1998. Trial court erred in holding, on motion for summary judgment by insured, that the notice-prejudice rule, which is applicable to untimely notice under "occurrence" policies, applied to commercial crime policy. *Se. Bakery Feeds, Inc. v. Ranger Ins. Co.*, 974 S.W.2d 635, 641.

Ohio 1926. Compliance with notice provision of bond is a condition precedent to the liability of the bonding company. Insured's failure to comply with notice provision relieves surety of liability under the policy. *Kornhauser v. Nat'l Sur. Co.*, 150 N.E. 921, 922.

Ohio Ct. App. 1978. Compliance with provisions of a Deputy Registrar's Blanket Position Bond governing notice and proof of loss is condition precedent to liability of surety. Surety demonstrated, as a matter of law, that insured failed to comply with these provisions. *State of Ohio v. Safeco Ins. Co.*, 396 N.E.2d 794, 798.

Pa. 1934. Insured's failure to give notice within period specified in bond voids the contract and the court is required to enforce the forfeiture of the contract. *Gentile v. Am. Bank & Trust Co.*, 172 A. 303, 305.

Pa. 1928. Insured's failure to comply with indemnity policy's notice provision entitled insurer to judgment in its favor, notwithstanding verdict in favor of insured. *Morrelville Deposit Bank v. Royal Indem. Co.*, 144 A. 424, 425-26.

S.C. 1935. Compliance with notice provision is condition precedent to liability of bonding company. *Planter's Sav. Bank of Greer v. Am. Sur. Co.*, 181 S.E. 222, 224.

Tenn. Ct. App. 1984. Compliance with notice provision in an Employee Dishonesty Commercial Blanket Bond was held to be a condition precedent to coverage. Although the notice provision at issue contained a forfeiture clause, the Court wrote that compliance with a notice clause is a condition precedent, even if the policy does not contain a forfeiture clause and the insurer had not been prejudiced by delay in notice. *Griffith Motors, Inc. v. Compass Ins. Co.*, 676 S.W.2d 555, 557.

Tenn. Ct. App. 1965. Bond promised indemnity, "provided, however, that within 10 days after discovery, the insured shall give the underwriter notice of loss." The words "provided however" are words of art for creation of a condition precedent so that the failure to give notice as provided by the bond releases the bonding company. *World Secret Serv. Ass'n v. Travelers Indem. Co.*, 396 S.W.2d 848, 851.

Tenn. Ct. App. 1937. Insured's failure to comply with fidelity bond provision requiring that insured give notice within ten days after discovering loss released the insurer from liability. *Nashville & Am. Trust Co. v. Aetna Cas. Sur. Co.*, 110 S.W.2d 1041, 1046.

Vt. 1940. Where bond provision provides that notice is to be given within a certain time period after discovery, failure to comply with such provision releases surety from its bond obligations. *Brown v. Md. Cas. Co.*, 11 A.2d 222, 224.

Wis. 1974. Compliance with notice provision is a condition precedent in fact to liability, whether or not its importance is emphasized by further language that noncompliance works a forfeiture. *State Bank of Viroqua v. Capitol Indem. Corp.*, 214 N.W.2d 42, 45-46.

E. Proof of Loss, Duly Sworn to, with Full Particulars

U.S. 1902. Bond requires a full statement of all items of claimed misappropriation on which the right to recover on the bond was based. *Fid. & Deposit Co. of Md. v. Courtney*, 186 U.S. 342, 349.

2d Cir. 1935 (N.Y.). Insured was not required to follow instructions on back of proof of loss form requiring itemized statements. Such instructions cannot enlarge the terms of the bond, and are advisory only.

The insured is required only to give the information which it has. *Public Warehouses v. Fid. & Deposit Co. of Md.*, 77 F.2d 831, 833.

2d Cir. 1927 (N.Y.). Proof of loss provision will not be construed to require the impossible. Proof of loss was sufficient when it stated the amount of embezzlements on a month-by-month basis by comparing amount of postage stamps taken by employee with the amount of stamps actually used for postage, rather than individually stating each theft of such stamps in terms of amount or time. *Mass. Bonding & Ins. Co. v. Norwich Pharmacal Co.*, 18 F.2d 934, 936.

4th Cir. 1934 (N.C.). A surety cannot escape liability if an employer is unable to show the exact time and manner of an embezzlement. Moreover, estoppel does not arise as a result of erroneous statements made by insured in proof of loss, unless, as a result of such statement, the insurer admits a liability that it would not otherwise have admitted, or is misled by the erroneous statement into changing its position. *Fid. & Deposit Co. of Md. v. People's Bank*, 72 F.2d 932, 939.

5th Cir. 1938 (Ga.). Where bond required insured to "file" proof of loss within ninety days after date it gave notice, and proof of loss was mailed within that time period, but was not received by bonding company until one day after time period expired, insured had substantially complied with the proof of loss provision. *Franklin Sav. & Loan Co. v. Am. Emp'rs Ins. Co.*, 99 F.2d 494, 497-98.

5th Cir. 1917 (Ala.). Bond's requirement that the insured file an "itemized statement of loss" was held to require an "enumeration of the things claimed to have been lost," and was fulfilled when the insured set forward the total amount the insured claimed to have lost as a result of its employee's dishonesty. Insured was not required to describe the money lost, or to state the exactly when or how the employee's dishonest acts were committed. *Md. Cas. Co. v. First Nat'l Bank*, 246 F. 892, 901.

6th Cir. 2002 (Ohio). The court affirmed the district court's award of sanctions against a bank that had asserted an employee dishonesty claim under a Financial Institution Bond after a bank employee acted in excess of his authority when increasing a borrower's line of credit. The bank submitted a proof of loss form, but failed to disclose information establishing the employee's "manifest intent" to harm the bank as required to recover under the bond. When the insurer moved for summary judgment, the bank produced an affidavit alleging for the first time that, two years earlier, the employee orally admitted to increasing the credit line "to get back at the bank" for denying the employee a bonus. The court declined to consider the affidavit because it contradicted the bank's prior interrogatory responses, and concluded that the bank's lawsuit lacked a colorable basis because in failing to disclose in its proof of loss form the particulars of the employee's alleged admission of intent, the bank failed to comply with "a clear condition precedent to filing suit." *First Bank v. Hartford Underwriters Ins. Co.*, 307 F.3d 501, 521.

7th Cir. 1953 (Ill.). Under a Brokers Blanket Bond, the court held that if the proof is itemized to the extent that is reasonably possible under the circumstances and is sufficient for the bonding company to ascertain the nature of the different items upon which the claim is based, it is sufficient. The court recognized that when employee dishonesty is discovered, it is normally impossible for an employer to include each item of the loss without further investigation. *Irwin Jacobs & Co. v. Fid. & Deposit Co. of Md.*, 202 F.2d 794, 799-800.

9th Cir. 1991 (Cal.). The FSLIC, as receiver of the insured. brought suit under fidelity bond for losses which were discovered by the FSLIC's attorneys after the bond's termination date. However, the FSLIC's complaint alleged that these losses were discovered by the insured's employees during the bond's effective period, but were not reported due to the employees' wrongful misconduct and concealment. Held, that the FSLIC met its burden of demonstrating that there was an issue of fact in dispute regarding whether the loss was discovered within the term of the bond. The court noted that the evidence submitted by the FSLIC—including a grand jury indictment reciting specific facts showing when the insured's employee's discovered the loss—did not have to be in a form that would be admissible at trial in order to defeat a motion for summary judgment. *FDIC v. N.H. Ins. Co.*, 953 F.2d. 478, 485.

D.D.C. 1980. Insured under a blanket crime policy discovered and gave notice of a "possible" fidelity loss due to claim that Insured expected might be asserted against it by a third party. After two years, third party finally served insured with formal demand letter. Insured then attempted to provide the insurer with completed proof of loss form, but insurer denied claim based on insured's failure to provide a completed proof of loss form within four months of discovery of loss, as required by the policy. On the parties' cross-motions for summary judgment, the court held for the insured, noting that the policy only required a detailed proof of loss within four months after discovery of "loss." With respect to third-party claims, "loss" does not accrue until the third party demands compensation from the insured, and that because the insured had provided a completed proof of loss form within four months of such a third party demand, proof of loss was timely. *Fid. & Deposit Co. of Md. v. President and Dir. of Georgetown Coll.*, 483 F. Supp. 1142, 1146-47.

E.D. Ky. 1989. After submitting an initial proof of loss in March 1987, and after bond coverage terminated in June 1987, the insured filed an amended proof of loss in July 1988. The amended proof of loss added the name of another employee who committed fraudulent acts, and claimed additional losses of over $1.1 million. Insurer moved to dismiss the losses included in the amendment on the grounds that (a) this was an entirely new claim, and (b) that the insured failed to fulfill the "full particulars" requirement of the original proof of loss. The insured countered that all losses contained in the amended proof of loss were identified in the original proof of loss and based on the same set of circumstances. Held, the insured met its obligation to supply "full particulars" by filing an original proof of loss which was sufficient to enable to the insurer to intelligently prosecute its claim. Additionally, under Kentucky law, the amendment related back to the original proof of loss, and could not be rejected on the grounds that it was filed after the expiration of the notice period. *FDIC v. Reliance Ins. Co.*, 716 F. Supp. 1001, 1003.

D. Mass. 2010. When insured bank's former employee mistakenly received direct deposit of insured's CEO's pay and, instead of returning the funds, the employee sought to recover his own pay, insured submitted proof of loss indicating that it was making a claim for employee dishonesty. However, because insured left blank the section of proof of loss form providing for other claims, including "Mysterious Disappearance/Misplacement," the court declined to address the insured's argument that it was, alternatively, entitled to coverage for misplacement. *FundQuest, Inc. v. Travelers Cas. & Sur. Co.*, 715 F. Supp. 2d 202, 210.

S.D.N.Y. 1974. Under a Blanket Crime Policy and 3-D Policy, proof of loss with supporting papers which adequately notifies bonding company of the factual basis of insured's claim (the loss of more than six tons of gold and silver) was adequate. *U.S. Smelting Ref. & Mining Co. v. Aetna Cas. & Sur. Co.*, 372 F. Supp. 489, 491-92.

D. Nev. 1968. Under a 3-D Policy and Blanket Crime Policy excluding certain classes of employees, proof of loss with respect to a claim under this provision should identify the employee or employees charged with the loss. Fear of suit for defamation does not justify failure to comply with proof of loss requirement. On the other hand, if the bond also provides coverage for loss caused by unidentifiable employees, it was sufficient for insured's proof of loss to state the amount of the loss occurring as a result of "various employees." *Mapes Casino, Inc. v. Md. Cas. Co.*, 290 F. Supp. 186, 192.

E.D. Wis. 1945. Proof of loss which states nature and amount of claim is sufficient. Where bond purchased by insurance company requiring the filing of a "affirmative proof of loss, itemized and duly sworn to," liquidator of insured insurance company complied by filing a claim listing a specific amount of funds which were collected from insured's customers and then misapplied, thus allowing bonding company to pay or adjust claim without further expense if it chose to do so. *Duel v. Nat'l Sur. Corp.*, 64 F. Supp. 961, 968.

Ariz. Ct. App. 1971. Insured under certain fidelity policies learned of unspecified facts that caused it to terminate two employees and to engage a CPA firm to audit its books. The CPAs produced an audit report after approximately sixty days, describing in detail the thefts committed and false ledger entries made by the two subject employees. The insured notified its insurer of the possibility of a loss, kept the insurer "continuously advised of the progress of the investigation," and also provided the insurer with a copy of the audit report within days of receiving same. It was only several months later, however, that the insured completed and returned a sworn proof of loss form, by attaching the prior audit report to the signed form. On these facts, the court held that the insured had substantially complied with the policies' proof of loss requirement. *Md. Cas. Co. v. Clements*, 487 P.2d 437, 442-43.

Cal. Ct. App. 1919. Insured complied, as fully as it could under the circumstances, with fidelity bond provision requiring it to provide an "itemized claim," by submitting all information as to the nature and amount of its employee's misappropriations possessed by the witnesses thereto. *Los Angeles Athl. Club v. USF&G*, 183 P. 174, 175.

Ind. Ct. App. 1931. Bond provision requiring that insured file "itemized" proof of loss requires that proof of loss be itemized to the extent then reasonably possible under the circumstances. Insured would not be required to provide the exact dates and exact amounts embezzled. It would be sufficient to show that an amount of funds were embezzled between certain dates. *Fletcher Sav. & Trust Co. v. Am. Sur. Co.*, 175 N.E. 247, 255.

Mo. 1941. In a filing proof of loss, insured provided total loss claimed and method of embezzlement. Insured offered to provide additional information and permitted inspection of books and records. Insured substantially complied with proof of loss provision even though it could not provide dates of each loss. *Lemay Ferry Bank v. New Amsterdam Cas. Co.*, 149 S.W.2d 328, 330-31.

N.Y. Sup. Ct. 1975. Under a 3-D Policy, the proof of loss stated that a specific employee had stolen property. At trial, insured contended that property was stolen by unidentified employees. Held, that although the insured should not be rigidly bound by the statements contained in the proof of loss, the entire proof of loss in this case was fallacious, and did not comply with the terms of the policy. *Kaplan Jewelers, Inc. v. Ins. Co. of N. Am.*, 383 N.Y.S.2d 127, 130.

N.C. 1926. Insured is not required to include every specific item in its proof of loss. Insured is required to furnish a verified statement sufficient to enable bonding company to ascertain the nature of the different items upon which the claim is based. *Forest City Bldg. & Loan Ass'n v. Davis*, 133 S.E. 530, 533, *modified on other grounds,* 138 S.E. 338, 338-39.

Neb. 1989. The court rejected insured bank's contention that provision in fidelity bond requiring the bank to provide proof of loss within six months of discovery of loss was contrary to public policy. Moreover, because insured did not discover loss within policy's time period, the court affirmed the trial court's dismissal of the insured's claim. *First Sec. Bank & Trust v. N.H. Ins. Co.*, 441 N.W.2d 188, 196.

Neb. 1989. Bankers blanket bond required insured to furnish insurer with proof of loss within six months after discovery of loss. The court granted summary judgment in favor of the insurer on the grounds that the loss described in the insured's first proof of loss was clearly discovered outside the policy period. The court also noted, in relevant part, that a second proof of loss, which added additional transactions not described in the first proof of loss and increased the insured's claim by $2 million, did not amend and relate back to the first proof of loss, and, on its own, constituted a new and untimely proof of loss. *First Sec. & Sav. v. Aetna Cas. & Sur. Co.*, 445 N.W.2d 596, 598.

Or. 1973. Under a Crime Policy requiring insured to file a signed and sworn proof of loss, and providing that no coverage could be obtained without complying with all requirements of the policy, the court held that substantial, as distinguished from strict, compliance with proof of loss provision was all that was required of the insured. The insured's failure to sign the proof of loss under oath was not a failure to substantially comply with policy requirements, because what the insured submitted fulfilled the purpose of a proof of loss. *Sutton v. Fire Ins. Exch.*, 509 P.2d 418, 419-20.

Tex. App. 1967. Under a Burglary Policy, the court held that substantial compliance with proof of loss provision is all that is required. Insured is not bound by statements made in proof of loss where bonding company could have requested additional information and was not prejudiced by statements in the proof of loss. *Great Cent. Ins. Co. v. Cook*, 422 S.W.2d 801, 808-09.

Tex. App. 1941. Surety paid bank's claim under fidelity bond for loss covered by teller's breach of good faith, and sought, as bank's subrogee, to recover from stock brokers the money embezzled by the teller. The court held that the surety's rights were not limited to the items shown in the bank's proof of loss. *Fenner v. Am. Sur. Co.*, 156 S.W.2d 279, 288.

F. Effect of Failure to Provide Proof of Loss or Delay in Providing Proof of Loss

D.C. Cir. 1964. Failure to file proof of loss within period of ninety days after discovery of loss as provided by Employee Fidelity Bond precluded recovery thereunder. *Ace Van & Storage Co. v. Liberty Mut. Ins. Co.*, 336 F.2d 925, 926-27.

D.N.J. 1994. The court held that an insurer would have to show appreciable prejudice before denying coverage due to a late proof of loss. *RTC v. Moskowitz*, 868 F. Supp. 634, 642.

W.D. Okla. 1973. Under a Comprehensive Dishonesty, Disappearance, and Destruction Policy, compliance with proof of loss provision is condition precedent to liability of bonding company. *Alfalfa Elec. Coop., Inc. v. Travelers Indem. Co.*, 376 F. Supp. 901, 909.

Ala. 1970. Compliance with proof of loss provision is a condition precedent to the right to bring suit, but failure to comply does not void the policy or work a forfeiture of the claim in the absence of an express provision that failure to file a proof of loss works a forfeiture. *Am. Fire & Cas. Co. v. Burchfield*, 232 So. 2d 606, 610.

Ariz. Ct. App. 1971. In holding that insured complied in substance with fidelity policies' proof of loss requirements, the Court noted that, under Arizona law, the failure to timely comply with a proof of loss requirement would not result in a forfeiture of coverage unless it appeared that the insurer was prejudiced by that failure. The court also observed that no specific form need be utilized in order to satisfy the policies' proof of loss requirement. *Md. Cas. Co. v. Clements*, 487 P.2d 437, 443.

Conn. 1929. Compliance with proof of loss provision is not a condition precedent to liability in the absence of an express provision making compliance a condition precedent. *Elberton Cotton Mills, Inc. v. Indem. Ins. Co. of N. Am.*, 145 A. 33, 35.

Ga. Ct. App. 1929. In the absence of an explicit provision making compliance with the proof of loss provision a condition precedent to liability, the failure to comply with the provision does not work a forfeiture. However, insured must bring suit within time provided. *People's Loan & Sav. Co. v. Fid. & Cas. Co.*, 147 S.E. 171, 172.

Kan. 1998. Under Kansas law, an insurer must prove prejudice before denying coverage based on a late filing of proof of loss. The same would be true for untimely notice of loss. *Nat'l Union Fire Ins. Co. of Pitt., Pa. v. FDIC*, 957 P.2d 357, 365.

Me. 2002. Under an Employee Dishonesty Policy, the insured's filing proof of loss one year after discovery of an employee's wrongdoing was sufficient to defeat coverage. The court concluded that the trial court's determination that the delay prejudiced the insurer was correct, as surety had lost the opportunity to recoup its losses. *Acadia Ins. Co. v. Keiser Indus., Inc.*, 793 A.2d 495, 498-99.

G. Time for Commencement of Legal Proceedings

6th Cir. 1996 (Ohio). Crime policy provided that insured could not bring a legal action thereunder until ninety days after insured filed its proof of loss. The policy further prohibited insured from bringing a legal action thereunder more than twelve months from the date insured discovered the loss. Insured discovered the loss on June 30, 1990, and brought suit nearly fifteen months later. The court held that the insured's action was untimely, and rejected the insured's contention that the policy's twelve-month limitations period was tolled until ninety days after the insured filed its proof of loss. *Friendly Farms v. Reliance Ins. Co.*, 79 F.3d 541, 544-45.

8th Cir. 1996 (S.D.). Insured filed suit under a standard savings and loan blanket bond almost twenty-five months after discovery of the loss, and approximately eight months after denial of coverage. The district court held that the bond's two-year suit limitation clause was tolled during the insurer's fifteen month investigation, following "a minority of courts that have used the concept of tolling to enlarge a contractual time limitations." The court of appeals reversed, explaining: "A court must not impose its own concept of fairness under the guise of construing a

SECTION 5 — NOTICE/PROOF—LEGAL PROCEEDINGS AGAINST UNDERWRITER   441

contract. Where the parties make by agreement a fixed, unqualified limitation that no suit or action on the policy shall be sustainable unless commenced within twenty-four months after discovery of the loss, the parties are bound to their contract as written." *FDIC v. Hartford Acc. & Indem. Co.*, 97 F.3d 1148, 1151.

E.D. Tenn. 1936. The time for bringing suit runs from the discovery of loss and not from three months from the filing of the proof of loss. *Holland v. Fuller,* 14 F. Supp. 688, 693.

Ga. Ct. App. 2009. Insured sought to recover under commercial crime policy containing two-year-limitations period. The Court affirmed summary judgment in favor of the insurer, on the grounds that the insured had brought suit more than two years after the latest date of loss given in the insured's notice of loss. *Bickerstaff Imports, Inc. v. Sentry Select Ins. Co.*, 682 S.E.2d 365, 368.

Fla. 1917. Under bond providing that no action to recover from the surety any claim under said bond should be brought "unless commenced within a period of 12 months after the date the employer shall have given notice of claim," the time for filing begins to run from the time the proof of loss with itemized statement of claim is filed, not from the time notice is given. *Nat'l Sur. Co. v. Williams,* 77 So. 212, 220-21.

Ky. Ct. App. 1977. Provision of employee dishonesty bond providing that no legal proceedings be brought against surety more than 15 months after presentation of claim is enforced to require dismissal of lawsuit brought 6 months after that deadline. Insured claimed that after paying the premium, it did not receive a copy of the bond and was unaware of the contractual limitations period until after that period had passed. Held that a purchaser of a bond may be presumed to have received a copy thereof, and that the insured failed to overcome the presumption. *U.S. Fire Ins. Co. v. Am. Turners of Louisville, Inc.*, 557 S.W.2d 905, 907.

Ky. Ct. App. 1971. Where bond provided that suit must be brought within one year after discovery of loss, the limitation period ran from date of discovery of loss and not from expiration of "no suit" period stated in bond. *Ashland Fin. Co. v. Hartford Acc. & Indem. Co.*, 474 S.W.2d 364, 366.

H. Law Prohibiting or Tolling Contractual Limitation of Bond

5th Cir. 2007 (Tex). Because commercial crime policy barred action against surety sooner than ninety days from the date insured submitted proof of loss, or later than two years from the time loss was discovered, the contractual limitations period was void pursuant to Texas law. Nevertheless, the four-year statute of limitations had run, barring the insured's claim. *Admin. Servs. of N. Am., Inc. v. Hartford Fid. & Bonding Co.*, 245 F. App'x 384, 385-86.

7th Cir. 1938 (Ind.). Blanket bonds conditioned on the honest and faithful discharge of the duties of bank officers were required to be procured by Indiana state statute, and therefore qualified as "statutory and official bonds" governed by the Indiana statute of limitations rather than the shorter limitations period specified in the bonds. *Hack v. Am. Sur. Co.*, 96 F.2d 939, 943.

8th Cir. 1994 (S.D.). Standard Savings and Loan Blanket Bond was "fidelity insurance" for purposes of statute that restricted the enforceability of contractual limitations periods in insurance policies, but authorized contractual limitations of not less than two years in "surety and fidelity" policies, and therefore, the bond's two-year limitation provision was enforceable. The court rejected the argument that 12 U.S.C. § 1821(d)(14) controlled the time limitations on actions brought by the RTC, because the argument was first raised on appeal, the action was not "brought" by the RTC but by the bank prior to the RTC becoming appointed receiver, and the applicable two-year contractual limitation period had expired before the action was commenced by the bank. *RTC v. Hartford Acc. & Indem. Co.*, 25 F.3d 657, 658-59.

8th Cir. 1965 (Mo.). Missouri state statute rendering null and void "[a]ll parts of any contract or agreement . . . which either directly or indirectly limit or tend to limit the time in which any suit or action may be instituted" applied to the limitations period prescribed by the terms of a "policy of Fidelity and Indemnity Insurance." *Lumberman's Mut. Cas. Co. v. Norris Grain Co.*, 343 F.2d 670, 683-85.

9th Cir. 1991 (Cal.). The FDIC, as receiver of the insured, filed a lawsuit for coverage under a fidelity bond after the bond's 24-month limitations period had already expired. Held, that the FIRREA, which provides a six-year statute of limitations applicable actions brought by the FDIC as conservator or receiver, applied to the FDIC's pending claim against the fidelity insurer. *FDIC v. N.H. Ins. Co.*, 953 F.2d. 478, 486-87.

N.D. Ind. 2007. Commercial crime policy, which employee pension benefit plan was required to obtain pursuant to ERISA, qualified as an "official bond" under Indiana law, and therefore, two-year contractual limitations provision in policy was void. *Ind. Reg'l Counsel of Carpenters Pension Trust Fund v. Fid. & Deposit Co.*, No. 2:06-CV-32 PS, 2007 WL 683795, at *3-5.

D. Del. 2011. Insured discovered loss more than 24 months prior to the commencement of legal proceedings against the insurer. The court noted that, because the insured was placed into bankruptcy prior to the running of the suit-commencement-deadline under the bond, the time period during which the bankruptcy trustee may file suit was tolled under 11 U.S.C. § 108(a) until 2 years after an order for relief in the bankruptcy case. The court found that the trustee's cross-claim against the insurer was untimely under that standard, but that triable issues of fact existed as to whether the insurer had waived and/or was estopped from asserting defenses based upon untimely suit. *Arrowood Indem. Co. v. Hartford Fire Ins. Co.*, 774 F. Supp. 2d 636, 654-55.

W.D. La. 2007. Provision in Executive Protection Policy requiring that lawsuit be commenced no later than the expiration of two years from the discovery of loss was valid under Louisiana statute prohibiting suit limitations of less than twenty-four months after the "inception of the loss." *Magnolia Mgmt. Corp. v. Fed. Ins. Co.*, No. 06-0447, 2007 WL 4124496, at *11-13.

E.D. Mich. 2008. Provision in business insurance policy providing coverage for employee dishonesty, which required that a lawsuit be commenced within 12 months from the date of discovery of loss, appeared to violate Michigan Office of Financial and Insurance Services rule prohibiting shortened limitation of action clauses. However, the rule did not apply to the contract at issue, which was already in effect when the rule was published. *Livonia Volkswagen, Inc. v. Universal*

Underwriters Grp., No. 06-13619, 2008 U.S. Dist. LEXIS 25519, at *15-16.

W.D. Okla. 1973. Provision of a Comprehensive Dishonesty, Disappearance, and Destruction Policy governing time for filing suit was a condition precedent to coverage and liability and not a limitation upon existing legal remedies. Even if provision were a limitation upon right to bring action, two-year limitation was authorized for this type of policy under Oklahoma law. *Alfalfa Elec. Coop., Inc. v. Travelers Indem. Co.*, 376 F. Supp. 901, 911.

D. S.D. 1991. Insured contended that fidelity bond's two-year limitations period was void, pursuant to a South Dakota state statute prohibiting limitations clauses contained in "a contract," but expressly permitting limitations periods of two years or more prescribed by "a surety contract." The insurer countered that the fidelity bond was a "surety contract," and that the fidelity bond's two-year limitations period was not voided by the statute. Held, that a fidelity bond is not a surety contract, and that the statute therefore voided fidelity bond's limitations period. *First Fed. Bank, F.S.B. v. Hartford Acc. & Indem. Co.*, 762 F. Supp. 1352, 1353-54.

W.D. Wis. 2009. Wisconsin statute setting one-year statute of limitations for claims against "fire-insurance" policies—rather than general six-year statute of limitations—was interpreted by court to apply to claim against multi-part insurance policy providing employee dishonesty coverage, and therefore, policy's more generous two-year limitations period was enforceable. *Ward Mgmt. Co. v. Westport Ins. Corp.*, 598 F. Supp. 2d 923, 925-27.

Ill. App. Ct. 2001. Insured, under a "financial institution crime bond insurance policy," gave insurer written notice of a possible loss of substantial funds, for which the insured acted as custodian. Insurer responded by letter requesting proof of loss with full particulars within six months of the date of discovery of the loss. One month later, insured was placed into receivership pursuant to Illinois' Corporate Fiduciary Act, which tolls any limitation period fixed by statute, rule, or agreement, for six months. Six months and ten days into the receivership, the insured filed a proof of loss. Held, questions of fact as to whether insured timely complied with proof of loss requirement within the tolled six month period, warranted reversing trial court's award of summary judgment to insurer. *Indep. Trust Corp. v. Kan. Bankers Sur. Co.*, 954 N.E.2d 401, 407.

Ind. 1913. Bond guaranteeing against loss caused by bank cashier's fraud or dishonesty was executed in compliance with Indiana banking law, and therefore, a lawsuit against the surety for breach of the bond was subject to state statute of limitations rather than bond's 12-month suit limitations clause. It would violate statutory law and public policy to allow the parties to contract around the statute requiring the bond. *USF&G v. Poetker*, 102 N.E. 372, 375-76.

Md. 2010. Commercial crime policy requiring that lawsuit be brought within three years from discovery of loss violated a Maryland Statute voiding surety contract provisions that set shorter limitations period than that provided for under state law, which was three years from the date an action accrues. The court concluded that the statute in question did not intend to permit effectively shortening the otherwise applicable three-year period by setting an earlier accrual period. Because the policy prohibited the insured from filing suit prior to filing a proof of loss, the insured's cause of action did not accrue until that was accomplished, and the statutory three-year limitation period did not begin to run until that time. *St. Paul Travelers v. Millstone*, 987 A.2d 116, 123.

Minn. 1957. Parties may limit the time within which an action may be brought to a period less than that fixed by the general statute of limitations, provided the limitation is not unreasonably short, but such provisions are not favored and are construed strictly against the party invoking them. *Prior Lake State Bank v. Nat'l Sur. Corp.*, 80 N.W.2d 612, 616.

Miss. 1972. Provision of Employee Fidelity Bond requiring that action be brought within one year after discovery of loss was in conflict with Section 724 of the Mississippi Code and therefore null and void. *Latham v. USF&G*, 267 So. 2d 895, 897.

N.J. 1978. In determining that suit for coverage under Bankers Blanket Bond was timely, the court determined that the time for filing suit under the bond is tolled from the date notice of loss is given to the date the bonding company formally denies coverage of the claim. *Nat'l Newark & Essex Bank v. Am. Ins. Co.*, 385 A.2d 1216, 1224.

I. Effect of Failure to Commence Legal Proceedings Within Contractual Limitation of Bond

2d Cir. 1915 (N.Y.). Insured failed to comply with provision of bond which made it a condition precedent that suit be brought within twelve months from filing of claim, and therefore, the insured was barred from recovering against the bond. *United States v. Fid. & Deposit Co. of Md.*, 224 F. 866, 869.

6th Cir. 1956 (Mich.). Failure to comply with provision of Blanket Position Bond requiring that suit not be brought after the expiration of fifteen months from discovery of fraudulent and dishonest acts bars suit on the bond. *Goosen v. Indem. Ins. Co.*, 234 F.2d 463, 465.

6th Cir. 1927 (Ohio). Failure to bring suit within twelve months after discovery of any act of larceny or embezzlement bars suit on the bond. *Reynolds v. Detroit Fid. & Deposit Co. of Md.*, 19 F.2d 110, 114.

D. Del. 2011. Insured discovered loss more than 24 months prior to the commencement of legal proceedings against the insurer. The court observed that while under Delaware law an insurer must demonstrate prejudice before it can disclaim coverage on the basis of noncompliance with a notice of loss provision, it was unlikely that a Delaware court would require a showing of prejudice where the issue is the failure to timely file suit. Nevertheless, the court declined to grant summary judgment in favor of the insurer, finding triable issues of fact as to whether the insurer had waived and/or was estopped from asserting defenses based upon untimely suit and failure to submit a proof of loss. *Arrowood Indem. Co. v. Hartford Fire Ins. Co.*, 774 F. Supp. 2d 636, 654-56.

S.D.N.Y. 1978. Provision of a Stockholders' Blanket Bond requiring that suit be commenced with two years from discovery of loss is not unreasonable. Failure of insured to commence suit within two years from discovery of loss bars action upon the bond. *Redington v. Hartford Acc. & Indem. Co.,* 463 F. Supp. 83, 86.

W.D. Okla. 1973. Under a Comprehensive Dishonesty, Disappearance, and Destruction Policy, insured's failure to comply with provision of policy relating to filing of suit barred recovery against the surety, where policy provided that bringing suit within limitations period was a condition precedent to coverage and liability. *Alfalfa Elec. Coop., Inc. v. Travelers Indem. Co.,* 376 F. Supp. 901, 911.

D. Or. 2003. Insured filed suit in June 2003 seeking to recover from Employee Dishonesty policy for former employee's acts of embezzlement over a thirteen-year period duration. The court upheld a suit-limitations provision requiring that lawsuits be brought within two years after the date on which the direct physical loss or damage occurred, limiting the insured's recovery to coverage for the 2001-2002 policy period. The court rejected the insured's argument that the "notice-prejudice" rule should apply to suit limitation provisions. *Harrington v. Am. Econ. Ins. Co.*, No. 03-712-MO, 2003 U.S. Dist. LEXIS 26033, at *12-13.

E.D. Tenn. 1988. The court declined to literally apply a blanket bond provision that "legal proceedings for recovery of any loss hereunder shall not be brought prior to the expiration of sixty days after such proof of loss is filed . . . nor after the expiration of twenty-four months from the discovery of such loss." The court instead alternatively applied an accrual approach, a waiver approach, and a tolling approach in finding that the insured's claims under the bond were timely. *FSLIC v. Aetna Cas. & Sur. Co.*, 701 F. Supp. 1357, 1361-62.

E.D. Tenn. 1936. Failure to bring suit within one year of discovery of loss as required by the bond, is a bar to the action. *Holland v. Fuller,* 14 F. Supp. 688, 693.

Ill. App. Ct. 1909. Failure to bring suit within 365 days of termination of coverage as provided by the bond is a bar to the claim. *E. Liverpool China Co. v. Ill. Sur. Co.,* 152 Ill. App. 89, 91.

Ky. Ct. App. 1977. Action against bonding company was barred by failure of insured to commence legal proceedings within fifteen months of the presentation of claim, as required by the terms of the bond. *U.S. Fire Ins. Co. v. Am. Turners of Louisville, Inc.*, 557 S.W.2d 905, 907.

Mass. 1886. Compliance with provision of a Bank Employee Fidelity Bond requiring that suit be commenced with twelve months after breach of the condition is valid, but the provision is subject to implied qualification that commencing a lawsuit within that period would be possible. *Eliot Nat'l Bank v. Beal*, 6 N.E. 742, 744.

Minn. 1938. Provision of blanket schedule bond requiring insured to bring suit within one year of the discovery of the wrongful or felonious act upon which liability is predicated was reasonable, and failure to comply with that provision barred recovery under the policy. *Hayfield Farmers Elevator & Merc. Co. v. New Amsterdam Cas. Co.*, 282 N.W. 265, 269.

N.Y. Gen. Term. 1890. Failure to give notice prior to commencing action, and failure to commence action within time provided by the contract, is a bar to the claim. *Better v. Prudential Ins. Co.*, 11 N.Y.S. 70, 71.

Tenn. Ct. App. 1959. Failure of insured to bring suit within three years of the cancellation of bond, as provided by the bond, is a bar to the claim. *State v. Evans*, 334 S.W.2d 337, 345.

J. Suits, Actions, and Legal Proceedings Commenced by Party Other Than Insured.

5th Cir. 1980 (Fla.). Lender sought to recover directly from blanket fidelity bond obtained by borrower, relying on Florida's strong policy of affording rights to third-party beneficiaries of liability insurance contracts. In determining that the lender was not a covered party, the court relied on policy language providing that only the insured (or entities permitted to be covered by the insured) were afforded coverage under the bond. *Everhart v. Drake Mgmt. Inc.*, 627 F.2d 686, 690-91.

5th Cir. 1969 (Fla.). Insured insurance broker managed a "pool" of participating insurance companies that insured crops against hail damage. The pool collected premiums from the participants, paid the participants' losses, and remitted excesses to the participants at the end of the year. Held, that the participants in the pool did not have standing to assert claims against a fidelity bond issued to the insurance broker managing the pool. *Am. Empire Ins. Co. v. Fid. & Deposit Co. of Md.*, 408 F.2d 72, 74-77.

8th Cir. (Iowa) 1987. Plaintiff sought to recover from a fidelity bond issued to bank against whom plaintiff obtained a judgment. On the fidelity insurer's motion for summary judgment, the court held that an Iowa statute providing a judgment creditor a direct right of action against a policy insuring the legal liability of the judgment debtor does not apply to a fidelity bond, because a fidelity bond does not insure the legal liability of the insured. *Anderson v. Emp'rs Ins. Co.*, 826 F.2d 777, 779.

D. Del. 2011. Insurer received notices of claim from both its insured and a third party, Royal, which was identified in a rider to the bond as a joint loss payee. Insurer sought summary judgment against Royal on the basis that bond provided that no suit may be brought under the bond by any one other than the named insured. The court denied the motion, citing to evidence that in the court's view raised triable issues of fact as to whether the parties had intended that Royal be a third-party beneficiary under the bond. *Arrowood Indem. Co. v. Hartford Fire Ins. Co.*, 774 F. Supp. 2d 636, 658.

M.D. Fla. 1995. Victim of fraud perpetuated by bank's employee secured an arbitration award against the bank, and sought to collect from the bank's fidelity insurer. The court held that the victim did not have a right of action against the fidelity bond as a third-party beneficiary, as the bond clearly provided that the insurer would not be liable for losses sustained by parties other than the insured unless the insured included those losses in its proof of loss. The court further rejected the victim's claim that Florida law, which allows for direct actions by third-party beneficiaries against liability policies, should apply to fidelity insurance. *Gasslein v. Nat'l Union Fire Ins. Co. of Pitt., Pa.*, 918 F. Supp. 373, 376-77.

D. Kan. 1993. Plaintiff alleged that it was injured by security broker's fraudulent acts, and filed action directly against security broker's fidelity insurer. Applying Arkansas law, the court granted the fidelity insurer's motion for summary judgment. The bond made clear that it only provided coverage in favor of the security broker. The court rejected the Plaintiff's argument that despite such bond language, a direct right of action against the bond was implied from the fact that the Arkansas Code required securities dealers in Arkansas to post a surety bond, and authorized direct suits against those bonds. In this instance, the insured was permitted to post a fidelity bond in lieu of a surety bond, and unlike a surety bond, no third-party coverage was provided by the fidelity bond. *Sch. Emp. Credit Union v. Nat'l Union Fire Ins. Co. of Pitt., Pa.*, 839 F. Supp. 1477, 1480.

S.D.N.Y. 1984. Receiver of limited partnership sought to recover from indemnity bonds issued to general partner of the limited partnership. The surety moved to dismiss the receiver's claim against the bonds, on the ground that the general partner was the only party afforded coverage under the bonds. The court denied the motion, finding that the receiver had sufficiently alleged third-party beneficiary status, despite the fact that the terms of the bond did not make that status apparent, as the circumstances under which the bond was written could lead to the conclusion that the receiver was an intended third-party beneficiary. *Glusband v. Fitin Cunningham Lauzon, Inc.*, 582 F. Supp. 145, 152-53.

Bankr. E.D. Pa. 1987. Trustee of debtor mortgage company had standing to seek recovery under fidelity bonds issued to debtor for losses resulting from the fraudulent conduct of the debtor's officers and employees. Even if most of the losses caused by the fraudulent conduct affected only creditors and/or investors of the debtor, such losses would appear to constitute at least indirect losses to the debtor, given the debtor's potential liability for such claims. Moreover, trustee had standing, as representative for the estate, to bring claims which would benefit creditors and/or investors, as well as indirectly benefit the estate. *Leedy Mortg. Co., Inc. v. Burnhope*, 76 B.R. 440, 450.

Iowa 1994. The plaintiff asserted claims against fidelity bonds issued to parties against whom the plaintiff had obtained judgments. The court held that Iowa's direct action statute, which provided a right of action to a judgment creditor against any policy insuring the legal liability of a judgment debtor, did not provide the plaintiff with a right of action against the fidelity bonds, because the fidelity bonds did not insure the legal liability of the insured. *Ctrl. Nat'l Ins. Co. v. Ins. Co. of N. Am.*, 522 N.W.2d 39, 42-43.

Kan. 1970. Plaintiff obtained judgment against corporation and its former president for breach of contract and fraudulent representations made by president and other employees of the corporations. Plaintiff attempted to bring garnishment action against the corporation's fidelity insurer. The court held that the Blanket Honesty Bond was for the protection of the corporation alone, and unlike a liability policy, did not provide coverage for liability attaching to the insured. *Ronnau v. Caranvan Int'l Corp.*, 468 P.2d 118, 120-21.

La. Ct. App. 1993. Plaintiff brought action seeking damages for insured bank's alleged illegal fraudulent acts in the course of financial dealings with plaintiff. After settling claims against the bank and its employees, plaintiff proceeded with claims against bank's fidelity insurer. Held: (1) plaintiff could not maintain action against fidelity insurer under Louisiana's "oblique action" statute; (2) plaintiff could not maintain action under fidelity bond, as bond clearly stated that it provided coverage only in favor of the insured bank, and that no one other than insured could maintain an action thereunder; and (3) the bond did not vest plaintiff with rights as a third party beneficiary. *Killingsworth v. United Merc. Bank*, 623 So. 2d 1384, 1385-87.

Neb. 1976. Plaintiff obtained a judgment against insured bank as a result of bank employee's dishonesty, and then brought garnishment action against the bank's fidelity insurer. Distinguishing fidelity insurance from liability insurance, the court held that under the language of the bond, the insurer assumed no obligation to respond to the liability of the insured to third persons. *Foxley Cattle Co. v. Bank of Mead*, 244 N.W.2d 205, 208-09.

N.Y. 1980. Plaintiff engaged agent to manage its property, and agent agreed to obtain a fidelity bond covering the employees responsible for managing plaintiff's money. Plaintiff sued agent's fidelity insurer to recover funds that went missing. In dismissing plaintiff's complaint, the court held that the fidelity bond against which plaintiff sought to recover was not a liability policy, and therefore, Section 167 of New York's Insurance Law, which provided a direct right of action against a "contract or policy insuring against liability," did not provide plaintiff with a right of action against the fidelity insurer. *175 E. 74th Corp. v. Hartford Acc. & Indem. Co.*, 416 N.E.2d 584, 590-91.

N.Y. 1975. Plaintiff, the New York Stock Exchange, required its members to carry blanket bonds, and purchased excess insurance coverage in addition to its members' bonds. Plaintiff sued its excess insurer, alleging that when one of its members went bankrupt, the excess insurer corrupted a witness in the bankruptcy proceedings in order to induce the primary insurer to settle for less than the amount of primary coverage, thereby allowing the excess liability insurer to avoid liability. The court held that plaintiff's claims for tortious interference with plaintiff's third-party rights under the primary policy stated a valid cause of action, noting that plaintiff had alleged facts that, if proven, could render plaintiff an intended third parties of the bonds. *Newin Corp. v. Hartford Acc. & Indem. Co.*, 333 N.E.2d 163, 167.

Md. 1989. Clients of property manager asserted claims directly against manager's fidelity insurer for alleged misappropriations by manager's shareholders. Although the court noted the general rule that a third party "may not predicate a claim against the fidelity insurer solely on the fact that the dishonesty rendered the insured legally liable to the third party," the court remanded to determine whether the HUD regulations pursuant to which the fidelity bond was posted extended coverage to the plaintiffs. *Three Garden Village Ltd P'ship v. USF&G*, 567 A.2d 85, 93-95.

N.M. 1987. Plaintiff alleged that escrow company misappropriated funds deposited with the company by plaintiff, and asserted action directly against the company's fidelity insurer. The court held that under New Mexico law, plaintiff was entitled to maintain a direct action against the fidelity bond, pursuant to an established three-prong test: (1) the bond was required by state statute, (2) the benefit of the bond inured to the public, and (3) notwithstanding the difference between fidelity and liability insurance, nothing in the language of the statute negated the idea of joining the fidelity insurer. *Anchor Equities, Ltd. v. Pac. Coast Am.*, 737 P.2d 532, 534.

Wash. Ct. App. 1991. Clients of bankrupt escrow agent sued agent's fidelity insurer in order to recover against fidelity bond, which agent was required to post under Washington's Escrow Agent Registration Act. The court held that coverage under the bond only ran in favor of the insured agent, as neither the bond nor the act provided the clients standing to assert a claim against the bond. However, the court held that the clients did have standing because the escrow agent assigned to the clients its rights under the bond. *Estate of K.O. Jordan v. Hartford Acc. & Indem. Co.*, 813 P.2d 1279, 1280-82, *rev'd on other grounds*, 844 P.2d 403 (Wash. 1993) (reversing the appellate court's determination that there had been no covered "loss" within the meaning of the bond).

K. Waiver and Estoppel

3d Cir. 1947 (Pa.). Substantial evidence supported jury's conclusion that bonding company had waived bond's proof of loss provision. Evidence included statement by bonding company representative that insured could not file a proof of loss until it knew amount of loss. *Du Bois Nat'l Bank v. Hartford Acc. & Indem. Co.,* 161 F.2d 132, 136.

3d Cir. 1932 (N.J.). Bonding company had actual notice of items in claim and cooperated with insured to reduce loss. The court held that the filing of formal proof of loss was waived. *New Amsterdam Cas. Co. v. Basic Bldg. & Loan Ass'n,* 60 F.2d 950, 952.

5th Cir. 1954 (Tex.). By accepting documentation provided by insured upon discovering the loss, investigating the claim, and denying the claim on the merits, insured waived the bond's proof of loss requirement. *New Amsterdam Cas. Co. v. W.D. Felder & Co.,* 214 F.2d 825, 830.

5th Cir. 1934 (Fla.). Employee fidelity bond was canceled on May 25, 1930, and by its terms covered only losses which were sustained prior to said date, and discovered before the expiration of one year thereafter. Bank failed on February 2, 1931. Receiver discovered losses sued for on April 10, 1931, and notified bonding company on June 10, 1931. The bonding company denied liability "because of the cancellation of our bond and the expiration of the time limit for the discovery of the claim." After suit was filed, bonding company defended based on late notice. The court held that there was no waiver or estoppel in connection with the notice requirement. There was no waiver because bonding company did not know date of discovery until after suit was filed. There was no estoppel because time for giving notice had expired before the date notice was given and receiver was not misled. *Murray v. Am. Sur. Co.*, 69 F.2d 147, 148-49.

5th Cir. 1929 (Ala.). After receiving late notice from insured, bonding company failed to object, and induced the insured to further document the claim. The court held that these actions waived the requirement of timely notice. *Am. Sur. Co. v. Blount Cnty. Bank*, 30 F.2d 882, 883-84, *cert. denied*, 280 U.S. 561.

6th Cir. 2002 (Ohio). The court found "meritless" a bank's argument that its insurer had waived a Financial Institution Bond's six month proof of loss provision, noting that the bank had "never" supplied a "proof of loss with full particulars," and the insurer, in claim-related correspondence had expressly "reserved all rights and defenses[.]" *First Bank v. Hartford Underwriters Ins. Co.*, 307 F.3d 501, 521.

6th Cir. 1996 (Ohio). Insurer under crime policy did not waive, and was not estopped from asserting, policy's limitations provision as a result of continuing to investigate insured's claim and making settlement offer to insured after the limitations period expired. Nothing the insurer did led the insured to delay in bringing an action under the policy. Moreover, none of the acts giving rise to the alleged waiver or estoppel took place within the limitations period. *Friendly Farms v. Reliance Ins. Co.*, 79 F.3d 541, 545.

6th Cir. 1927 (Ohio). After discussing ways that the bonding company could have waived the bond's suit limitation, the court held that there was no evidence in the record showing any such conduct by bonding company. The court stated that in the absence of conduct creating an estoppel, a waiver must be supported by an agreement founded on valuable consideration. *Reynolds v. Detroit Fid. & Sur. Co.*, 19 F.2d 110, 113.

7th Cir. 1953 (Ill.). Fidelity insurer's denial of claim on grounds that insured's employee's acts were not "dishonest" within the meaning of the bond was held to waive the bond's proof of loss requirement. *Irving Jacobs & Co. v. Fid. & Deposit Co. of Md.*, 202 F.2d 794, 800.

8th Cir. 1996 (S.D.). The court of appeals rejected the argument that the insurer had waived or should be estopped from asserting defenses based upon a standard savings and loan blanket bond's two-year suit limitation clause. The insurer expressly denied the claim within the two year period, and did nothing to lull the insured into inaction. The insurer's statements that it would consider additional information if the bank believed that any facts were misstated or omitted from the insurer's analysis did not create a waiver or estoppel, but "were simply good faith expressions of a willingness to consider corrected information if necessary." *FDIC v. Hartford Acc. & Indem. Co.*, 97 F.3d 1148, 1152.

8th Cir. 1935 (Iowa). Bank advised bonding company of "possibility of liability under the bond in connection with acts of its cashier." Bonding company made investigation. Later, the bank failed and receiver filed proofs of loss. The bonding company's adjuster continued its investigation without objection to the insufficiency and untimeliness of notice or proof of loss and said to examiner in charge that loss which was shown to be result of dishonest act of cashier would be paid. The court held that there was sufficient evidence to justify a jury's conclusion that notice and proof of loss were timely submitted, and further, there was "substantial evidence" that bonding company had waived the requirement. *Fid. & Deposit Co. of Md. v. Bates*, 76 F.2d 160, 167-68.

10th Cir. 1960 (Colo.). Insurer's oral offer of settlement prior to expiration of time for filing suit, which insured rejected, followed by written offer made by insurer after the limitations period expired, which insured also rejected, was held to estop the bonding company from asserting the bond's strict limitation's period. *Home Indem. Co. v. Midwest Auto Auction, Inc.*, 285 F.2d 708, 711.

D.C. Cir. 1970. Time for filing proof of loss could be waived orally or by conduct despite a provision in the policy stating that the terms of the policy could not be waived except by endorsement signed by an authorized representative of company. *Imperial Ins., Inc. v. Emp'r's Liab. Assurance Corp.*, 442 F.2d 1197, 1202.

D.C. Cir. 1964. Conduct by bonding company after receiving late proof of loss, including holding a conference with the insured and issuing a memo indicating that the matter would continue to be investigated, and continuing to conference with the insured despite having received a late proof of loss, was held not to constitute waiver or estoppel. *Ace Van & Storage Co. v. Liberty Mut. Ins. Co.*, 336 F.2d 925, 926-27.

D.C. Cir. 1938. The insured discovered its loss in 1922 but did not give notice until 1928, the bonding company investigated claim and denied liability based in part on lack of notice. The court held that there was no waiver of the notice requirement by the bonding company. *U.S. Shipping Bd. Merch. Fleet Corp. v. Aetna Cas. & Sur. Co.*, 98 F.2d 238, 243.

D. Del. 2011. Insurer received notices of claim from both its insured and a third party identified in a rider to the bond as a joint loss payee. Both submitted notices of loss to insurer in 2002. Insurer responded by sending a proof of loss form to the third party only. In 2003, insurer closed its file on the third party's claim due to inactivity, and took no further action as to either claimant. Five years later, the third party provided insurer with a proof of loss. Both the third-party and the trustee of the insured's bankruptcy estate commenced legal proceedings against insurer. Although both insured and the third party had failed to comply with the bond's proof of loss provision and filed suit out of time, the Court declined to grant summary judgment in favor of insured, finding triable issues of fact as to whether insurer had waived and/or was estopped from asserting defenses based upon untimely suit and failure to submit a proof of loss. *Arrowood Indem. Co. v. Hartford Fire Ins. Co.*, 774 F. Supp. 2d 636, 655.

S.D. Ill. 1959. Acts of bonding company in receiving late proof of loss and denying liability on the grounds that no covered loss had occurred, held not to be a waiver as a matter of law, as the acts alleged to constitute a waiver occurred after the insured's deadline for filing proof of loss had already expired. *Oakley Grain & Supply Co. v. Indem. Ins. Co. of N. Am.*, 173 F. Supp. 419, 421.

W.D. La. 2008. Neither insurer's agreement to re-open file and reconsider additional documentation supporting insured's claim, nor the insurer's pattern of extending documentation deadlines in connection with its reconsideration of the claim, waived insurer's right to rely on two-year contractual limitations period. *Korean War Veterans Assn. v. Fed. Ins. Co.*, No. 07-0690, 2008 U.S. Dist. LEXIS 4682, at *6-14.

E.D. Mich. 2008. Insurer's two-year exchange with insured, involving numerous requests for additional documentation, was not a waiver of business insurance policy's one-year suit limitation provision. Insured failed to allege in its complaint that insurer made false representations or concealed facts that caused insured to delay in filing its lawsuit, and correspondence sent by insurer always included full reservation of rights. *Livonia Volkswagen, Inc. v. Universal Underwriters Grp.*, No. 06-13619, 2008 U.S. Dist. LEXIS 25519, at *17-20.

E.D. Mich. 1934. After insured provided notice, insured and bonding company agreed that "without further preliminaries a suit at law should be constituted to determine the question of liability." The court held that the bonding company waived "the necessity of a formal proof of claim." *Thomas v. Standard Acc. Ins. Co.*, 7 F. Supp. 205, 207.

S.D.N.Y. 1978. Surety did not waive protection of bond's limitations provision merely because it did not promptly assert the defense upon receiving the claim. Moreover, the doctrine of laches barred the claimant from arguing that the surety was estopped from invoking the limitations provision, because the claimant had waited seven months to commence an action after the surety disclaimed liability under the policy. *Redington v. Hartford Acc. & Indem. Co.*, 463 F. Supp. 83, 86.

D. Nev. 1968. Denial of liability on grounds other than those relating to defects in notice or timeliness of proof of loss was held to waive defects in notice or timeliness of proof of loss. *Mapes Casino, Inc. v. Md. Cas. Co.*, 290 F. Supp. 186, 191-92.

W.D. Okla. 1973. Insured gave notice that it had tentatively discovered a discrepancy in amount of its securities and other funds, had fired an employee, and promised a complete audit. Six months later, and after the time for filing the proof of loss had expired, the insured requested that the bonding company extend the period for filing proof of loss. The extension was granted with a reservation of rights. The proof of loss was subsequently filed and rejected. The court held that there was no waiver or estoppel in connection with the proof of loss requirement. *Alfalfa Elec. Coop., Inc. v. Travelers Indem. Co.*, 376 F. Supp. 901, 910-11.

Ark. 1915. Unconditional denial of liability was held to waive timely notice under bond. *Equitable Sur. Co. v. Bank of Hazen*, 181 S.W. 279, 281.

Del. 1964. The court recognized rule that denial of liability during period in which proof of loss may be filed will constitute a waiver of a bond's proof of loss requirement. However, a mere request for more information would not be construed as a waiver. A statement by the bonding company's agent that the company "was not going to do anything about this claim" could be construed as a denial of liability. *Standard Acc. Ins. Co. v. Ponsell's Drug Store, Inc.*, 202 A.2d 271, 274.

Ga. Ct. App. 2009. Summary judgment in favor of insurer affirmed where no factual issue existed as to whether insurer waived commercial crime policy's two-year limitations period. While waiver might occur when insurer never denies liability but continuously discussed loss with insured with a view toward negotiation and settlement, mere negotiations which are not calculated to induce reliance on the part of the insured do not constitute a waiver. Here, insurer consistently rejected insured's claim, and never lead insured to believe that limitations period would be expanded. *Bickerstaff Imports, Inc. v. Sentry Select Ins. Co.*, 682 S.E.2d 365, 368.

Ga. Ct. App. 1936. Failure to complain of sufficiency of notice held to waive timely compliance. Statement by bonding company that other insurance would have to be exhausted before it could be called upon to pay loss was held to present fact issue as to whether bonding company waived limitation on filing suit. *Am. Sur. Co. v. Peoples Bank*, 189 S.E. 414, 418-19.

Ga. Ct. App. 1933. Prior to expiration of time for filing proof of loss, insured asked that matter be held in abeyance. The bonding company did not insist on proof being filed, and attempted to negotiate settlement both before and after deadline for filing proof of loss. The court held that proof of loss requirement was waived. *Knights of the Ku Klux Klan v. Fid. & Deposit Co. of Md.*, 169 S.E. 514, 518.

SECTION 5 — NOTICE/PROOF—LEGAL PROCEEDINGS AGAINST UNDERWRITER 459

Ill. App. Ct. 1961. After expiration of time for giving notice and filing proof of loss, local agent of bonding company met with insured, requested that the insured sign a proof of loss, and said that the loss would be taken care of. The court held that the bonding company waived both requirements. *Royal Loan Corp v. Am. Sur. Co.*, 173 N.E.2d 17, 19-20.

Iowa 1906. Insured attempted to file two proofs of loss, one under bond before it was increased, and one under increased bond. Bonding company retained first proof of loss until time limit expired, and then returned it to insured, demanding new one. After insured filed second proof of loss, bonding company denied liability because of want of authority on the part of the agent who granted the increase. The court held that the conduct of the insurer after receipt of first proof of loss was a waiver of "any further proofs," and denial of liability was further waiver. *T. M. Sinclair & Co. v. Nat'l Sur. Co.*, 107 N.W. 184, 188.

Kan. 1927. Insurer's denial of liability on grounds other than the insured's failure to timely file a proof of loss was held to waive the bond's proof of loss requirement. *Docking v. Nat'l Sur. Co.*, 252 P. 201, 205.

Kan. 1918. Insurer's denial of liability on grounds other than the insured's failure to timely file a proof of loss was held to waive the bond's proof of loss requirement. *Del. State Bank v. Colton*, 170 P. 992, 993.

La. 1938. Action of agent in leading insured to believe that notice to agent was sufficient was held to waive bond provision requiring notice to the bonding company "at its home office." *Inter-City Express Lines, Inc. v. Hartford Acc. & Indem. Co.*, 178 So. 280, 282-83.

La. Ct. App. 1963. Investigation and denial of claim was held to constitute waiver of notice and proof of loss requirement, despite fact that material furnished to bonding company conclusively showed that claim was not timely. *Standard Brass & Mfg. Co. v. Md. Cas. Co.*, 153 So. 2d 475, 479-80.

Mass. 1951. Upon receiving insured's notice of loss, bonding company acknowledged the notice and stated that the claim was being turned over to the company's claim department. The bonding company later advised the insured that it would write to the insured when the investigation was complete. The insured never filed a proof of loss and after the time for filing had expired, the bonding company denied liability. The court held that as a result of the first letter, bonding company was estopped from asserting failure to comply with the notice requirement. However, it was not estopped from asserting failure to timely file proof of loss, because denial of liability occurred after the time for filing the proof of loss had expired. *Star Fastener, Inc. v. Emp'rs' Ins. Co.*, 96 N.E.2d 713, 714.

Mass. 1945. Insurer's receipt of unsworn statement of loss without objection, and its subsequent denial of liability on the ground that insured's loss was not covered by the bond, were held to constitute a waiver of bond's proof of loss requirement. *Fuller v. Home Indem. Co.*, 60 N.E.2d 1, 4-5.

Mass. 1931. Insurer's acceptance of insured's notice by letter, with stated objection, was held to waive bond requirement that notice be made by registered letter or telegram. However, insurer's denial of liability was held not to waive proof of loss requirements. *Fitchburg Sav. Bank v. Mass. Bonding & Ins. Co.*, 174 N.E. 324, 329.

Mich. 1957. Insurer's receipt of actual notice of claim within time for giving notice and filing proof of loss, and insurer's subsequent denial of liability under bond, on grounds other than timeliness, was held to waive the insurer's objections based upon timeliness of notice. *Masters v. Mass. Bonding & Ins. Co.*, 84 N.W.2d 462, 466.

Mich. 1927. Insurer's investigation of claim, without reference to insured's late notice, and insurer's general denial of liability, were held to waive bond's notice and proof of loss requirements as a matter of law. *Farmers' Produce Co. v. Aetna Cas. & Sur. Co.*, 213 N.W. 685, 690.

Mich. 1909. Insurer's acceptance of insured's proof of loss, without objection, held to waive timely notice under bond, as well as other affirmative defenses available to insurer based upon insurer's knowledge of the facts at that time. *Crystal Ice Co. v. United Sur. Co.*, 123 N.W. 619, 621.

SECTION 5 — NOTICE/PROOF—LEGAL PROCEEDINGS AGAINST UNDERWRITER 461

Minn. 1933. Without using the words "waiver" or "estoppel," the court held that in view of insurer's denial of liability under the bond, the surety could not assert that insured failed to comply with notice and proof of loss requirements, even though insurer also denied liability on the basis that the bond had been terminated and that the time for discovering loss had passed and further reserved its rights and defenses. *Cary v. Nat'l Sur. Co.*, 251 N.W. 123, 192-93.

Minn. 1925. Insured sent letter to insurer's local agent requesting the forms necessary to submit an itemized proof of loss. Insurer's and agent's conduct, including sending blank forms to insured after the date on which proof of loss was due, justified jury's conclusion that the insurer waived the bond's requirement that proof of loss be submitted within ninety days after insured became aware of defalcation. *Ceylon Farmers' Elevator Co. v. Fid. & Deposit Co. of Md.*, 203 N.W. 985, 986-87.

Mo. 1929. Insurer's admission of liability for certain items in claim after deadline for filing proof of loss, and its ultimate denial of liability on grounds other than proof of loss provision, were held to extend insured's time for filing proof of loss by implication, and were further held to waive insurer's defense based upon insured's late proof of loss. *Exch. Bank of Novinger v. Turner,* 14 S.W.2d 425, 432-33.

Mo. Ct. App. 1931. After insured gave defective and late notice, bonding company made full investigation, did not object to sufficiency of notice, and denied liability on the merits. The court upheld the jury's decision that notice was timely, and held that any defect in notice was waived as a matter of law. *People's Bank v. Aetna Cas. & Sur. Co.*, 40 S.W.2d 535, 542.

Mo. Ct. App. 1908. By accepting late notice without objection, and causing insured to go to additional trouble and expense to prove its loss, insurer waived defense based upon insufficiency of notice. *Roark v. City Trust, Safe Deposit & Sur. Co.,* 110 S.W. 1, 3.

N.C. Ct. App. 1984. Independent agent who sold and serviced embezzlement policy waived insurer's right to insist upon a timely sworn proof of loss, by failing to furnish or mention a proof of loss form when he began handling the insured's claim, and only providing a proof of loss form to the insured much later. *B & H Supply Co., Inc. v. Ins. Co. of N. Am.,* 311 S.E.2d 643, 647.

N.Y. App. Div. 2012. Letter agreement between insurer and insured did not toll two-year contractual limitations period, as it contained no language tolling or extending the limitations period, nor did insured offer evidence of bad-faith behavior to support an estoppel argument. *Sterling Nat'l Bank v. Travelers Cas. & Sur. Co. of Am.,* 93 A.D.3d 543, 543.

Okla. 1966. Conduct of bonding company in not denying liability, but insisting that it could not pay the claim until the accused employee admitted the defalcation, was sufficient to lead the insured to believe that the technical requirements of the policy were not being insisted upon, and was held to be a waiver of proof of loss requirement and suit limitation. *Hartford Acc. & Indem. Co. v. Luper,* 421 P.2d 811, 815-16.

Okla. 1939. After receiving insured's notice, agent for bonding company had insured's books audited. At a meeting, agent for bonding company said: "We can just let this matter ride and when we can determine the exact amount of the shortage, we will get together on it." Thereafter, proof of loss forms were sent to insured but never filed. Jury finding of waiver upheld. *Md. Cas. Co. v. Tucker,* 96 P.2d 80, 83.

Pa. 1934. Surety under Tax Collector Official Bond waived the bond's requirements that the insured file a notice and proof of claim. After being notified merely that there were shortages in the insured's accounts (which, the court held, did not constitute formal notice under the bond because the surety was not notified that the shortages were due to conduct giving rise to the surety's liability under the bond) the surety undertook a year-long investigation during which it asked the insured's indulgence despite requests by the insured to settle, and did not request any additional notice or proof of loss. *Nanty-Glo Borough v. Am. Sur. Co.,* 175 A. 536, 537-38.

Tex. App. 1969. Insurer waived bond's requirement that proof of loss be filed within 100 days of discovery of loss by stating that it would advise insured if anything needed to be done in connection with the claim, in absence of which statement insured would have filed proof of loss within the 100-day period. *Comm. Standard Ins. Co. v. J.D. Hufstedler Truck Co.*, 443 S.W.2d 54, 55.

W. Va. 1920. When surety denies liability only on grounds other than those relating to notice, it is held to have treated the notice it received as sufficient or waived notice, and will be estopped from later denying liability based up late or insufficient notice. *Piedmont Grocery Co. v. Hawkins,* 104 S.E. 736, 739.

Wis. 1974. Insurer's investigation of claim and denial of liability did not estop insurer from raising lack of timely notice as a defense, because it did not deny coverage until after the insured's time for providing notice had already expired, and therefore, did not mislead the insured into postponing giving notice. *State Bank v. Capital Indem. Corp.,* 214 N.W.2d 42, 44.

SECONDARY SOURCES

Duncan L. Clore, *Discovery of Loss: The Contractual Predicate to the Claim, in* FINANCIAL INSTITUTION BONDS 193 (Duncan L. Clore, ed., 3d ed. 2008).

Edward F. Donohue, III, *How a Bank Failure Affects Insurance Coverage*, 47 TORT TRIAL & INS. PRAC. L.J. 591, 655 (2012).

J. Michael Dorman & James E. Essig, Annotation, *Special Commentary: Limitation of actions under § 2(d)(14) of Federal Institutions Reform, Recovery, and Enforcement Act of 1989 (FIRREA) (12 U.S.C.A. § 1821(d)(14)) in actions brought by Federal Deposit Insurance Corporation as receiver*, 126 A.L.R. Fed. 1 (1995).

K.A.D., Annotation, *Validity, Construction, and Application of Provision of Fidelity Bond as to Giving Notice of Loss or Claim within Specified Time after Close of Bond Year*, 149 A.L.R. 945 (1944).

Jacqueline Lewis et al., *Recent Developments in Fidelity and Surety Law*, 35 TORT & INS. L.J. 327 (2000).

M.A.L., Annotation, *Suspicion, or Reasons for Suspicion, of Wrongdoing by Officer or Employee Covered by Fidelity Bond or Policy as Requiring Obligee to Comply with Conditions of Bond with Respect to Notice of Discovery or Knowledge of Loss*, 129 A.L.R. 1411 (1940).

Charles C. Marvel, Annotation, *Modern Status of Rules Requiring Liability Insurer to Show Prejudice to Escape Liability Because of Insured's Failure or Delay in Giving Notice of Accident or Claim, or in Forwarding Suit Papers*, 32 A.L.R.4th 141 (1984).

Richard S. Mills & Frederick M. Zauderer, *At the Apex of the Arc of the Pendulum: Does FDIC v. INA Spell the Beginning of the End of the Notice Prejudice Rule in Fidelity Cases?*, IV FID. L. ASS'N J. 127 (1998).

Sam H. Poteet, Jr., Jeffrey S. Price & Michael J. Sams, *What Happens when the Insured Fails? Analyzing the Impact on Coverage Under the Financial Institution Bond and the Commercial Crime Policy*, XV FID. L.J. 57 (2009).

Armen Shahinian & Scott D. Baron, *The Notice Defense to Financial Institution Bond Claims Dissected: No Showing of Prejudice From Late Notice Should Be Required*, II FID. L. ASS'N J. 1 (1996).

Scott L. Schmookler & Bruce Robbibaro, *Discovery by the Risk Manager: The Effect of Noise-Reducing Headphones on Fidelity Coverage*, XVII FID. L. J. 171 (2011).

Joel P. Williams, *Time (And Time Again?): Contractual Limitations Periods*, FOR THE DEFENSE (March 2008).

William H. Woods & Jonathan M. Bryan, *Conditions to Recovery: Presentation of the Insured's Claim*, in FINANCIAL INSTITUTION BONDS 613 (Duncan L. Clore, ed., 3d ed. 2008).

L.C. Warden, Annotation, *Effect of Failure to Give Notice, or Delay in Giving Notice or Filing of Proofs of Loss, upon Fidelity Bond or Insurance*, 23 A.L.R.2d 1065 (1952).

SECTION 6 — VALUATION*

Section 6. Any loss of Money, or loss payable in Money, shall be paid, at the option of the Insured, in the Money of the country in which the loss was sustained or in the United States of America dollar equivalent thereof determined at the rate of exchange at the time of payment of such loss.

Securities

The Underwriter shall settle in kind its liability under this bond on account of a loss of any securities or, at the option of the Insured, shall pay to the Insured the cost of replacing such securities, determined by the market value thereof at the time of such settlement. In case of a loss of subscription, conversion or redemption privileges through the misplacement or loss of securities, the amount of such loss shall be the value of such privileges immediately preceding the expiration thereof. If such securities cannot be replaced or have no quoted market value, or if such privileges have no quoted market value, their value shall be determined by agreement or arbitration.

If the applicable coverage of this bond is subject to a Deductible Amount and/or is not sufficient in amount to indemnify the Insured in full for the loss of securities for which claim is made hereunder, the liability of the Underwriter under this bond is limited to the payment for, or the duplication of, so much of such securities as has a value equal to the amount of such applicable coverage.

Books of Account and Other Records

In case of loss of, or damage to, any books of account or other records used by the Insured in its business, the Underwriter shall be liable under this bond only if such books or records are actually reproduced and then for not more than the cost of the blank books, blank pages or other materials plus the cost of labor for the actual transcription or

---

* By Dolores A. Parr, Zurich North America Surety, Baltimore, Maryland.

copying of data which shall have been furnished by the Insured in order to reproduce such books and other records.

Property other than Money, Securities or Records

In case of loss of, or damage to, any Property other than Money, securities, books of account or other records, or damage covered under Insuring Agreement (B)(2), the Underwriter shall not be liable for more than the actual cash value of such Property, or of items covered under Insuring Agreement (B)(2). The Underwriter may, at its election, pay the actual cash value of, replace or repair such property. Disagreement between the Underwriter and the Insured as to the cash value or as to the adequacy of repair or replacement shall be resolved by arbitration.

COMMENT

The rules for valuation are clear. Most likely because nearly all losses sustained by financial institutions are money losses and the valuation provision for securities is clear, this section has not resulted in much litigation. This section also provides for arbitration if there is a dispute as to the value of securities or property, which prevents litigation between an insurer and its insured when the only issue involved is the valuation of the securities or property. Further, if the loss consists of securities, the matter is usually resolved by obtaining a lost instrument bond.

The paragraph for books of account and other records clearly states that the underwriter's liability for books of account and other records is limited to the cost of the materials on which the records are stored and the cost of the labor for the transcription of the data. If the loss involves property other than money, securities, books of account, or other records, the carrier is liable for the actual cash value of the missing property, with disputes being resolved by arbitration.

OUTLINE OF ANNOTATIONS

A. Cases under Financial Institution Bonds
B. Cases under Crime Policies

ANNOTATIONS

A. Cases Under Financial Institution Bonds

D.D.C. 1980. Insurer under Stockbrokers Blanket Bond satisfied liability to insured—who sustained loss through mysterious unexplainable disappearance of securities—by issuing lost instrument bonds and obtaining duplicate securities from the issuing agents. *Bellamark, Neuhauser & Barrett, Inc. v. Hanover Ins. Co.*, 531 F. Supp. 4, 11.

N.Y. App. Div. 2012. Insureds sought recovery of the amounts they were supposed to have held in their accounts per their account statements from Madoff immediately before Madoff's admission that he was involved in a Ponzi scheme. The court held that "loss" meant money the insureds invested, less money they received. It did not include assets that never actually existed. *Jacobson Family Invs., Inc. v. Nat'l Union Fire Ins. Co. of Pitt., Pa.*, 955 N.Y.S.2d 338, 347.

Wash. Ct. App. 1982. On a claim for a loss involving fraudulent loans under the 1969 Bankers Blanket Bond Standard Form No. 24, the insured's measure of actual loss was the aggregate outstanding balance due on the fraudulent loan loss. *Puget Sound Nat'l Bank v. St. Paul Fire & Marine Ins. Co.*, 645 P.2d 1122, 1130.

B. Cases Under Crime Policies

3d Cir. 2002 (Pa.). Nurses employed by the insured falsified clinical test results for new drugs for pharmaceutical companies, requiring the insured to replicate the studies at no cost to the sponsors. The court held that the nurses' actions constituted a loss of property, and the loss was subject to the valuation provisions of the crime policy. It further held that the valuation language did not limit the insured's recovery where there was no real market for the product, which was produced at a fixed price for one consumer. *Scirex Corp. v. Fed. Ins. Co.*, 313 F.3d 841, 851.

S.D. Fla. 1997. Insured's employee misappropriated mobile telephone serial and identification numbers and sold the lists to third parties. The third parties used the numbers, resulting in significant charges to the insured for unauthorized telephone usage. The court held that the lists were not tangible property with intrinsic value and thus were not covered under the insured's crime policy. *Peoples Tel. Co., Inc. v. Hartford Fire Ins. Co.*, 36 F. Supp. 2d 1335, 1339.

N.D. Ga. 1991. Insured's employee stole architectural plans belonging to the insured. The court held that the plans were tangible property. However, the court also held that the value of the plans—whether it be the cost of the paper and ink with which they were printed or something else—was a question of fact. *State Farm Fire & Cas. Ins. Co. v. White*, 777 F. Supp. 952, 955.

Ill. App. Ct. 1995. Under a commercial crime policy that provided coverage for the failure of city employees to perform their duties faithfully, the insurer sought to recover funds spent for city sponsored events through an account that had not been properly approved and for which appropriations had not been authorized. The loss was found to be covered under the bond. However, the court held that the loss must be set off by profits generated by the illegal expenditures so that the insured would not have an "undeserved windfall." *Kinzer v. Fid. & Deposit Co. of Md.*, 652 N.E.2d 20, 25.

SECONDARY SOURCES

Martin J. McMahon, Annotation, *Computation of Net "Loss" for which Fidelity Insurer Is Liable*, 5 A.L.R.5th 152 (1993).

Joseph G. Perry & Bruce C. King, *Currency Valuation Losses: The Fidelity Insurer's Liability for Exchange Rate Differentials* (unpublished paper presented at 1999 ABA Fidelity and Surety Law Committee Annual Mid-Winter CLE Meeting in New York, N.Y., Jan. 22, 1999).

Steven D. Roland, *Valuation Issues Involving Product Theft under Commercial Crime Policies: Cutting Edge Issues in Fidelity Bond Underwriting and Claims Handling* (unpublished paper presented at 1998 ABA Annual Meeting in Toronto, Ontario, Aug. 3, 1998).

SECTION 7 — ASSIGNMENT—SUBROGATION—RECOVERY—COOPERATION*

Section 7.

(a) In the event of payment under this bond, the Insured shall deliver, if so requested by the Underwriter, an assignment of such of the Insured's rights, title and interest and causes of action as it has against any person or entity to the extent of the loss payment.

(b) In the event of payment under this bond, the Underwriter shall be subrogated to all of the Insured's rights of recovery therefor against any person or entity to the extent of such payment.

(c) Recoveries, whether effected by the Underwriter or by the Insured, shall be applied net of the expense of such recovery first to the satisfaction of the Insured's loss which would otherwise have been paid but for the fact that it is in excess of either the Single or Aggregate Limit of Liability, secondly, to the Underwriter as reimbursement of amounts paid in settlement of the Insured's claim, and thirdly, to the Insured in satisfaction of any Deductible Amount. Recovery on account of loss of securities as set forth in the second paragraph of Section 6. or recovery from reinsurance and/or indemnity of the Underwriter shall not be deemed a recovery as used herein.

(d) Upon the Underwriter's request and at reasonable times and places designated by the Underwriter the Insured shall
  (1) submit to examination by the Underwriter and subscribe to the same under oath; and
  (2) produce for the Underwriter's examination all pertinent records; and
  (3) cooperate with the Underwriter in all matters pertaining to the loss.

(e) The Insured shall execute all papers and render assistance to secure to the Underwriter the rights and causes of action provided for herein. The Insured shall

---

* By Dolores A. Parr, Zurich North America Surety, Baltimore, Maryland.

do nothing after discovery of loss to prejudice such rights or causes of action.

COMMENT

This section first appeared in the 1980 form of the Financial Institution Bond. The 1969 form of the Bankers Blanket Bond only set forth the order in which recoveries were to be applied. In the 1969 form, the only reference to an assignment was the last sentence of this section, which provided that "the Insured shall execute all necessary papers to secure to the underwriter the rights herein provided for." The 1986 form is much clearer than the 1969 form and also sets forth the insured's duty to cooperate throughout the life of a claim.

Paragraph (a) specifically requires that the insured assign its rights against third parties. Paragraph (b) refers to common law subrogation rights. Paragraph (c) provides for the division of recoveries between the insured and the insurer when the insurer has paid a loss. Paragraph (e) provides that the insured shall do nothing after discovery of loss to prejudice any rights or causes of action. It captures the "circle of indemnity" theory of suretyship, so that the insurer should be able to argue successfully that the insured's release of a wrongdoer against whom the insured had a right of recovery releases the insurer.

Earlier editions devoted much time to the compensated-surety/balancing-of-equities defense, which prevented a compensated surety from recovering against another person or entity who negligently contributed to the loss on the theory that the surety was paid to assume the risk. This defense is most often asserted by financial institutions in connection with claims asserted against them by insurance carriers who pay employee dishonesty claims and then seek recovery against the financial institutions who accepted checks with forgeries or alterations. The compensated-surety or superior-equities defense has not been asserted as frequently in recent years. It is still a viable defense when the insurer seeks to recover against financial institution directors and officers whose negligence contributed to a loss. Most of the annotations in this edition relate to more recent decisions.

An important provision of Section 7 is the requirement that the insured cooperate with the bond insurer. Perhaps to highlight its significance, it was moved to a new separate Section 8 in the 2004 and

2011 forms. Few cases discuss the Financial Institution Bond's cooperation provision. The same type of cooperation clause is found in fire policies and other forms of commercial fidelity insurance, however, and cases construing other policies are helpful in determining cooperation issues under the Financial Institution Bond. The cooperation clause strengthens the insurer's ability to conduct a thorough investigation and can be a very powerful tool when dealing with an insured who does not want to provide the information necessary for an insurer to investigate a claim.

OUTLINE OF ANNOTATIONS

A. Assignment
B. Subrogation
C. Salvage
D. Compensated Surety—Balancing of Equities
E. Impairment of Subrogation Rights
F. Cooperation
   1. Cases under Financial Institution Bonds
   2. Cases under Crime Policies
   3. Cases under Other Policies

ANNOTATIONS

A. Assignment

5th Cir. 1965 (Ga.). Insurer paid loss under Bankers Blanket Bond and, by assignment, sued the bank that held funds from forged checks. Defendant argued election of remedies barred enforcement of assignment. The court held that suing as assignee of bank and depositor was not consistent, but alternative. *Citizens and S. Nat'l Bank v. Am. Sur. Co.*, 347 F.2d 18, 22-23.

N.D. Ga. 2013. The court held that the Mandatory Victim Restitution Act (MVRA), 18 U.S.C. § 3663A (2012) *et seq.*, allows a victim to assign its restitution rights. Based on the assignment documents, the insurers were entitled to all restitution paid in the criminal proceedings, despite the insured's argument that its losses exceeded the amount of the settlement with the insurers. *United States v. Smith*, No. 12-14307, 2013 U.S. App. LEXIS 9325, at *6.

D.N.J. 2010. After paying the insured's employee dishonesty loss, the insurer received assignment of a civil judgment by way of restitution entered against the employee in connection with the thefts. The employee subsequently filed for bankruptcy and did not list the insurer in his schedules. He later filed an amended schedule listing another insurance company with a similar name and that other company's address. The insurer had no notice of the bankruptcy until after the employee was discharged. The district court held that since the insurer was not scheduled as a creditor and did not have notice of the bankruptcy proceeding in time to file a timely objection to discharge of its claim, the discharge did not bar its claim. *In Re: Korman Lumber Mut. Ins. Co. v. Korman (In re Korman)*, No. 09-3276, 2010 U.S. Dist. LEXIS 17602, at *18.

Cal. Ct. App. 1978. Employee was found to be a constructive trustee of property purchased with embezzled funds. Insurer was subrogated to insured's rights against employee, including right to enforce constructive trust and have benefit of profit from sale of trust property. Insured's assignment to fidelity insurer of its claims against employee produced same conclusion. *Haskel Eng'g & Supply Co. v. Hartford Acc. & Indem. Co.*, 144 Cal. Rptr. 189, 192-94.

N.Y. Sup. Ct. 1985. Insured sustained a loss when its officer received unauthorized salary payments over a five-year period. As subrogee and assignee of insured's rights, insurer sought recovery from insured's auditors for negligence and breach of contract for their failure to detect the apparent embezzlement. Auditors moved to dismiss the suit based on the doctrine of superior equities. The court agreed that superior equities barred the insurer's subrogation action, but that the undisputed assignment to insurer allowed the suit to proceed. *Hartford Acc. & Indem. Co. v. Peat, Marwick, Mitchell & Co.*, 494 N.Y.S.2d 821, 822.

Wis. 1978. Fidelity bond insurer was a secured creditor by assignment from its insured and could enforce rights to purchase price of stock when it received its insured's rights to participate in a note secured by the stock. Argument of estoppel against insurer's enforcement of its assignment rights did not succeed. *Kornitz v. Commercial Land Title Ins. Co.*, 260 N.W.2d 680, 685.

B. Subrogation

4th Cir. 1965 (N.C.). After paying an employee dishonesty claim under a crime policy, the insurer brought an action against the bank where the embezzled funds were deposited. The bank was held liable to insurer under Uniform Fiduciaries Act, N.C. Gen. Stat. § 32-6 (1950). The court found bank guilty of "actual knowledge" or "bad faith" within terms of Act. *Md. Cas. Co. v. Bank*, 340 F.2d 550, 556.

6th Cir. 1975 (Ohio). Insurer's subrogation rights were not prejudiced by acts of insured. *Russell Gasket Co. v. Phoenix of Hartford Ins. Co.*, 512 F.2d 205, 209.

9th Cir. 1977 (Cal.). Insurer settled a loss under Bankers Blanket Bond, and, by subrogation, sued a party to the scheme that had defrauded the bank. The Ninth Circuit reversed grant of summary judgment against insurer because state law allowed the imposition of independent tort liability upon a third party by an insurer. *Cmty. Nat'l Bank v. Fid. & Deposit Co.*, 563 F.2d 1319, 1322.

S.D. Ala. 2009. The court would not enter an open-ended default judgment against a principal in an action that the insurer commenced against the principal when the insurer had made a partial payment but the insured had not yet completed its investigation of the loss. *Pa. Nat'l Mut. Cas. Ins. Co. v. Edmonds*, No. 09-0089, 2009 U.S. Dist. LEXIS 36764, at *6-7.

E.D. Ark. 2012. The insured assigned its rights against the dishonest employee after the insurer paid the loss. The court found that the insurer was a "victim" within the meaning of 18 U.S.C. § 3663A (2012) and that restitution should be paid to the insurer pursuant to 18 U.S.C. § 3664. *United States v. Sorensen*, No. 4:09-cr-163 4, 2012 U.S. Dist. LEXIS 143805, at *4.

M.D. Fla. 2007. The dishonest employee used properly signed corporate checks to pay her personal credit card debts. The court dismissed the subrogated insurer's claim against the bank that issued the credit card. The court did not think that it was unusual commercial standards to process the checks without contacting the employer. The court noted that given the huge volume of checks the bank processed each month, the employer was in a much better position to have detected or prevented the fraud. The court held that the bank was a holder in due course of the checks and did not handle them negligently. *Travelers Cas. & Sur. Co. v. Citibank (S.D.), N.A.*, 64 U.C.C. Rep. Serv. 2d (Callaghan) 99, 109.

S.D. Fla. 1980. Fidelity bond insurer could not obtain a declaratory judgment that any judgment obtained in a separate action against a debtor for indemnification of the fidelity company would not be dischargeable in a bankruptcy action. *In re Harris*, 7 B.R. 284, 288-89.

S.D. Fla. 1970. Surety, compelled by court to pay bank losses, was granted indemnity judgment against loan officer who approved unauthorized loans. *Miami Nat'l Bank v. Pa. Ins. Co.*, 314 F. Supp. 858, 867.

S.D. Ind. 2011. The insured claimed that the dishonest employee overpaid commissions to other employees. In the action that the insurer filed against the insured, the insured filed a third party complaint against the allegedly dishonest employee and ten other employees who allegedly received the overpayments. The court dismissed the complaint against all of the employees except the allegedly dishonest employee because the claims against her arose from the same set of facts that the insured would have to prove to recover under the policy. The third party claims against the other employees were too attenuated from the coverage dispute to support supplemental jurisdiction. *The College Network v. Cincinnati Ins. Co.*, No. 1:10-cv-0370, 2011 U.S. Dist. LEXIS 19073, at *9.

D. Kan. 2012. The insurer paid the insured and sued the former employee for fraud. The employee argued that the complaint was barred by the two year statute of limitations for fraud. The court held that the two year statute of limitations started running when the injury became reasonably ascertainable. In the context of a fidelity bond, an allegedly dishonest employee is not an insured. *CUMIS Ins. Soc'y, Inc. v. Keilig*, No. 11-1115, 2012 U.S. Dist. LEXIS 7199, at *8.

D. Kan. 1995. Insurer who sought to rescind a bank's fidelity bond also sought to implead third party defendants before the subrogation claim accrued. The court held that the insurer could maintain its subrogation claims even though it had not yet sustained a loss. *Nat'l Union Fire Ins. Co. v. FDIC*, 887 F. Supp. 262, 264.

M.D. La. 2006. The husband of the dishonest employee was held to be jointly liable for the stolen funds because the funds were deposited in a joint account and used for the benefit of the "community" under Louisiana law. *Fid. & Deposit Co. v. Bizette*, 415 F. Supp. 2d 673, 674-75.

M.D. La. 1993. The court held that the insurer was entitled to the insured's rights of recovery only to the extent of the payment made by the insurer. The insurer is not entitled to a credit or reduction of the jury verdict by the estimated value of the security. *FDIC v. Fid. & Deposit Co.*, 827 F. Supp. 385, 389.

E.D. Mich. 2008. Insured's settlement with employee prior to resolution of claim under crime policy breached the subrogation provision in crime policy. *Livonia Volkswagen, Inc. v. Universal Underwriters Grp.*, No. 06-13619, 2008 U.S. Dist. LEXIS 25519, at *21.

D. Minn. 2010. Insurer reimbursed its insured for loss related to a fraudulently altered check and sought recovery under UCC theory against the drawee bank. The bank asserted that its agreement with the insured varied the liability under the UCC. The court agreed that the agreement between the bank and the insured controlled. The court granted summary judgment for the bank. *Cincinnati Ins. Co. v. Wachovia Bank, N.A.*, No. 08-CV-2734, 2010 U.S. Dist. LEXIS 70670, at *24.

D. Minn. 2010. The dishonest employee perpetrated a kickback scheme, in which the insured overpaid for shipping. After paying the loss, the insurer sued the employee and other parties to the scheme, including the shipping company. The court dismissed the shipping company based on the limitations clause in the bills of lading. *Hartford Fire Ins. Co. v. Clark*, 727 F. Supp. 2d 765, 779.

Bankr. E.D. Mo. 2010. Insurer paid $150,000 limit of liability. The employee had embezzled $314,327. The employee and her husband filed for bankruptcy and the insured filed a complaint objecting to their discharge. The issues were the amount to be excepted from discharge and whether the discharge exception should also apply to the husband. The court found that only the claim against the employee was nondischargeable because the husband did not know of his wife's activities. *Acuity v. Rodenbaugh (In re Rodenbaugh)*, 431 B.R. 473, 478.

D.N.J. 1975. Insurer on stockbroker's blanket bond was entitled to subrogation. However, no recovery would be allowed until there was a loss by insurer. *Fid. & Cas. Co. v. First Nat'l Bank in Fort Lee*, 397 F. Supp. 587, 590.

W.D.N.Y. 2010. The crime insurer paid loss its insured sustained when copper cathodes that the insured had purchased were discovered to be missing from shipment. Insurer sued the shipping company and various shipping agents for breach of contract, *inter alia.* The court dismissed the breach of contract claim because the bill of lading required suit in Japan for any action brought against the carrier, but denied the defendants motion to dismiss the other claims. *Luvata Buffalo, Inc. v. MOL Mitsui O.S.K. Lines, Ltd.*, No. 08-CV-0701, 2010 U.S. Dist. LEXIS 141250, at *19.

W.D.N.Y. 2010. The crime insurer paid a loss sustained by the insured for a missing a shipment of copper cathodes. The crime insurer then sued as subrogee and assignee of the insured, as well as in its own right, for contribution or indemnity from the ocean marine insurer. The court held that the crime insurer had standing to assert the claims and rejected the ocean marine insurer's arguments that, having been paid, the insured had nothing to assign or to which the crime insurer could be subrogated. *Luvata Buffalo, Inc. v. Lombard Gen. Ins. Co. of Can.*, No. 08-CV-00034, 2010 U.S. Dist. LEXIS 19334, at *22.

E.D.N.Y. 1979. Bank's insurer has no claim under the Federal Tort Claims Act that failure of U.S. agencies to effectively regulate caused bank's losses. However, a showing that the regulatory agencies acted arbitrarily and capriciously or exceeded their regulatory authority and actually managed the insured bank might cause liability. *In re Franklin Nat'l Bank Sec. Litig.*, 478 F. Supp. 210, 216.

E.D.N.Y. 1978. Bank's insurers had no subrogation claim against United States by reason of its regulation of bank, but allegation that the involvement of the United States was so pervasive as to result in the United States and its agencies essentially running the bank could support claim. *In Re Franklin Nat'l Bank Sec. Litig.*, 445 F. Supp. 723, 734.

E.D.N.Y. 1977. Bank's insurer had a claim for relief against insured's directors. Provision in bond excluding losses caused by directors is no defense to indemnity claim against directors. *FDIC v. Nat'l Sur. Co.*, 434 F. Supp. 61, 63-64.

Bankr. N.D. Ohio 2012. After the insurer paid an employee dishonesty loss and recovered a judgment against the employee, the employee filed for bankruptcy. The insurer filed a proceeding to declare the debt nondischargeable. The court thought that the largely conclusory allegations of the complaint did not include facts that would establish that the debt arose out of the debtor's fraud, embezzlement, or malicious injury to the employer's property. *Cent. Mut. Ins. Co. v. Starr (In re Starr)*, No. 11-16958, 2012 Bankr. LEXIS 630, at *7-8.

W.D. Okla. 1976. Subrogation rights were not effective against brokerage firm with whom officer of insured had invested embezzled funds in a margin account. *Hartford Acc. & Indem. Co. v. Merrill Lynch, Pierce, Fenner & Smith, Inc.*, 74 F.R.D. 357, 360.

Bankr. E.D. Pa. 2012. The bankruptcy debtor aided the dishonest employee by signing legal documents and checks and receiving mail in exchange for gifts and other benefits from the dishonest employee. The debtor had no direct contact with the insured. After paying the insured and settling with the dishonest employee, the insurer filed an adversary proceeding against the debtor, asserting claims under RICO and for fraud. The insurer also sought to have its claim declared nondischargeable. The court found that the evidence did not support the insurer's claims. *Hartford Fire Ins. Co. v. Lewis (In re Lewis)*, 478 B.R. 645, 669.

E.D. Pa. 1984. Motions to dismiss by third-party defendants were denied, because the insurer, if liable to its insured, would be legally subrogated to any rights its insured would have against such third-party defendants. Though the insurer had not paid a claim to its insured and the actions brought by each were different, they shared facts that would substantially overlap, therefore allowing the third-party claim by insurer to go forward. *Gen. Acc. Ins. Co. of Am. v. Fid. & Deposit Co.*, 598 F. Supp. 1223, 1230.

E.D. Tenn. 2011. The insurer paid an embezzlement loss and sued the former employee as subrogee of the insured. The insurer asserted claims for breach of fiduciary duty, fraud, conversion and unjust enrichment. The defendant moved to dismiss the complaint. The insurer voluntarily dismissed the breach of fiduciary duty claim, but the court dismissed the fraud and unjust enrichment claims because the insurer did not allege particular misrepresentations upon which the insured relied and did not allege that the insured willingly conferred a benefit on the defendant. *Travelers Cas. & Sur. Co. of Am. v. Pascarella*, No. 1:10-cv-157, 2011 U.S. Dist. LEXIS 87696, at *20.

Bankr. E.D. Tenn. 2006. The insured and insurer agreed to share recovery on a pro rata basis. The insured filed bankruptcy proceedings and the insurer sought to recover its pro rata share, which the insured had collected and failed to pay to the insurer prior to filing bankruptcy. The court held that the fidelity insurer's claim for its share of recovery from the dishonest employee was barred because the insurer did not file a timely proof of claim. *In re Lay Packing Co., Inc.; Fid. & Deposit Co. of Md. v. Hendon (In re Lay Packing Co.)*, 350 B.R. 420, 428.

Cal. Ct. App. 2009. The insurer paid an employee dishonesty loss and sued the employee. The employee argued that a restitution order entered in criminal proceedings arising out of the same theft barred the insurer's civil suit. The court held that the employer, and the insurer as its assignee, was entitled to a civil judgment as well as to the benefit of the restitution order, but that payments on the principal amount of the civil judgment (but not interest or costs) would be credited on the restitution obligation and vice versa. There could be no duplicate recovery, but the insurer could recover and enforce a judgment. *Vigilant Ins. Co. v. Chiu*, 96 Cal. Rptr. 3d 54, 57.

Cal. Ct. App. 1977. Having paid part of savings and loan association's loss, insurer was partially subrogated to the extent of its payment. *Bank of the Orient v. Super. Court S.F. Cnty.*, 136 Cal. Rptr. 741, 745.

Cal. Ct. App. 1967. Fidelity bond insurer sued bank that paid checks in violation of its rules and contrary to purpose indicated on face of checks. The court held that the bank was liable because it was not innocent party in cause of loss and employee was not negligent. *Pac. Indem. Co. v. Sec. First Nat'l Bank*, 56 Cal. Rptr. 142, 156-58.

Fla. 2000. An insurer under a fidelity bond may assert a claim against its insured's independent auditor for professional malpractice. *KPMG Peat Marwick v. Nat'l Union Fire Ins. Co.*, 765 So. 2d 36, 37.

Ill. App. Ct. 2006. Subrogated insurer obtained a judgment against the bank in whose ATM the dishonest employee deposited stolen checks. The checks were for deposit at the employee's account in another bank. The checks, which contained forged endorsements, were also endorsed "For Deposit Only." The court held that U.C.C. § 3-206 imposes liability for conversion on a depository bank that accepts a check with a restrictive endorsement if the proceeds are not credited in accordance with the endorsement. The bank that owned the ATM was found to be the depository bank. *Interior Crafts, Inc. v. Leparski*, 853 N.E.2d 1244, 1249.

Ind. App. Ct. 2006. The dishonest employee deposited checks into an account that he opened at defendant bank. The checks were endorsed with a stamp with the employer's name and "for deposit only. The court held that checks deposited more than three years before the date on which the suit was filed were barred by the statute of limitations. The court also found that the bank had a defense under U.C.C. § 3-405(b) because the dishonest employee had been entrusted with responsibility for the checks and the bank did not fail to exercise ordinary care in paying the instrument. *Auto-Owners Ins. Co. v. Bank One*, 852 N.E.2d 604, 610, *aff'd*, 879 N.E.2d 1086 (Ind. 2008).

Iowa 1965. Subrogating insurer was given a lien on property granted to the wife of the dishonest employee in divorce settlement agreement.

A fraudulent conveyance was involved. *Travelers Indem. Co. v. Cormaney*, 138 N.W.2d 50, 55-56.

La. Ct. App. 2007. The insurer and insured sued the dishonest employee and her husband to recover embezzled funds. The husband argued that he did not have any knowledge of or connection to the embezzlement. The court affirmed the judgment against the husband and wife, finding that the funds were deposited into a joint account and benefited both spouses. *Lafayette Ins. Co. v. Pennington*, 966 So. 2d 136, 138.

Mo. Ct. App. 1966. Insurer on stockbroker's bond paid loss and sued insured's customer in conversion. The court held that loss was due to conversion, which was covered by bond. Therefore, insurer was not a volunteer when it made its payment and was entitled to recovery through subrogation. *Fireman's Fund Ins. Co. v. Tripp*, 402 S.W.2d 577, 581.

Nev. 1966. Insurer, having paid loss, was entitled to subrogation to all insured's rights against bank, unimpaired by any doctrine of weighing equities or consideration of fact that insurer was compensated. *Fed. Ins. Co. v. Toiyabe Supply Co.*, 409 P.2d 623, 627.

N.J. Super. Ct. App. Div. 2008. The Court agreed that the insurer was entitled to any recovery of compensatory damages up to the amount of its payment. The court stated, "subrogation substitutes the insurer in the place of the insured, thus giving the insurer all the rights of the person for whom the insurer is substituted." The court affirmed the trial court judgment, including the compensatory damages awarded to the insurer. *Dimmerman v. First Union Nat'l Bank*, No. A-6334-05T2, 2008 N.J. Super. Unpub. LEXIS 3053, at *11.

N.Y. App. Div. 2011. Insured's settlement of claims against other parties did not violate the subrogation provision because insurer was subrogated to the insured's rights only after payment of the claim. *Gould Investors, L.P. v. Travelers Cas. & Sur. Co. of Am.*, 920 N.Y.S.2d 395, 397.

Or. 1977. Constructive trust imposed on embezzled funds and traceable proceeds in favor of subrogated dishonesty bond insurer. *Lane Cnty. Escrow Serv., Inc. v. Smith*, 560 P.2d 608, 614.

C. Salvage

7th Cir. 1940 (Ill.). Where insured made a partial recovery of stolen funds before payment of loss, insurer was entitled to credit *pro tanto*, and the insured was not entitled to apply the funds to an uncovered obligation of the principal debtor. *City Trust & Sav. Bank of Kankakee N. Ill. v. Lloyds Underwriting Members*, 109 F.2d 110, 111.

10th Cir. 1998 (Utah). Trial court denied insurer's request that anticipated future recoveries be offset against loss sustained by insured on dishonest loans. A judgment was entered for the FDIC for the limit of liability under fidelity bond. The appellate court held that the insurer was entitled to a credit for any recoveries that were obtained after the trial. *FDIC v. United Pac. Ins. Co.*, 152 F.3d 1266, 1275.

10th Cir. 1994 (Utah). In a dispute over the application of recoveries to loan losses that resulted from employee dishonesty, the court held that FDIC was entitled to recover administrative expenses incurred in settling claims with third parties. Settlements were recoveries, and the cost of obtaining such recoveries should be deducted from the amount of recoveries that apply against the loss. The court also held that the collateral source rule did not apply to exclude evidence of a settlement with a separate party relating to loss on the same loan. The collateral source rule should not prevent an insurer under a fidelity bond from receiving credit for a settlement with a separate party. *FDIC v. United Pac. Ins. Co.*, 20 F.3d 1070, 1081-82.

M.D. La. 1993. With regard to a loan loss covered under a Financial Institution Bond, recovery must first be applied to satisfy the insured's covered loss in excess of the amount paid under the bond. When the loss involves fraudulently made loans, any payments received on the loans after discovery must be applied to the principal amount of the loan, not to interest. *FDIC v. Fid. & Deposit Co.*, 827 F. Supp. 385, 389.

Cal. Ct. App. 1971. This case involved both uncovered and covered loss in excess of the policy limits, with the issue being how to apply salvage recoveries. The court prorated between that part of the loss that would be covered if there was no policy limit and that part of the loss that was not within the terms of the policy. Consequently, it was held that the insured should receive towards the uncovered loss that proportion of the salvage which the uncovered loss bore to the entire loss. Until the excess covered loss was reimbursed, the insured should receive the balance of the salvage as well. Thereafter, the carrier would receive the covered loss percentage while the insured received the uncovered loss percentage until the entire loss was fully reimbursed. *Gradon-Murphy Oldsmobile v. Ohio Cas. Ins. Co.*, 93 Cal. Rptr. 684, 689.

Conn. Super. Ct. 2011. The insurer commenced a suit as the insured's assignee against the allegedly dishonest employee. The employee filed a third party complaint against the insured, claiming that the disputed expenditures were authorized. The court dismissed the third party complaint because if the expenditures were authorized, the insurer had no claim against the employee and, if unauthorized, the employee had no claim against the insured. *Travelers Cas. & Sur. Co. v. Stanfield*, No. CV085019329, 2011 Conn. Super. LEXIS 2126, at *4.

D.C. 2001. In a dispute over the interpretation of a settlement agreement in which the insured and insurer were to share recovery, the insured claimed that it was entitled to recover non-covered loss before any recovery was paid to the insurer. The court held that the non-covered losses were taken into consideration in the settlement agreement, and recoveries were to be shared as set forth in the agreement. The "make whole" doctrine, which provides that the insurer cannot exercise a right of reimbursement or subrogation until the insured's entire loss has been compensated, can be altered by contract. *Dist. No. 1-Pac. Coast Dist., Marine Eng'rs' Beneficial Ass'n v. Travelers Cas. & Sur. Co.*, 782 A.2d 269, 276.

Iowa 1997. Insurer paid state tax department for loss resulting from the embezzlement of one of the department's employees. The state then seized assets to satisfy the tax debts of the employee. The court held that the insurer could not have its liability on the covered direct loss reduced by amount collected on non-covered tax debt and that the insured state tax department had not breached the crime policy's subrogation clause by collecting the delinquent taxes. *Lumbermens Mut. Cas. Co. v. State*, 564 N.W.2d 431, 435-36.

La. Ct. App. 2009. A dishonest employee admitted as part of a plea bargain that he had stolen approximately $25,000 and agreed to pay restitution to the aggrieved party. The insured recovered all but the $1,000 deductible from its insurer. When the employee contested the restitution order ordering him to pay restitution to the insurer, the court found that the plea agreement only applied to the aggrieved party, i.e., the employer. The court held that the insurer was not entitled to restitution. *State v. Green*, 28 So. 3d 1105, 1110.

Wash. Ct. App. 2009. The insurer sued a collection agency whose checks to the insured were diverted by the insured's dishonest employee. The court held that the collection agency did not owe a contractual or common law duty to the insured to indemnify the insured for the loss or to issue payments in a different way or to inspect the endorsements on its checks. Insurer, therefore, had no right of recovery against the collection agency. *Fid. & Deposit Co. v. Dally*, 201 P.3d 1040, 1045.

D. Compensated Surety—Balancing of Equities

6th Cir. 1988 (Ohio). Insurer brought a subrogation action against insured's directors and officers to recover amounts paid in settlement of claims under a fidelity bond. The court held that a fidelity insurer, in the absence of fraud, bad faith, or evidence that the individual directors derived a benefit from the defaulting employee's dishonesty, may not recover from the insured's officer and directors. *Home Indem. Co. v. Shaffer*, 860 F.2d 186, 188-89.

11th Cir. 1985 (Fla.). Insurer settled a claim and took the bank's written assignment of rights. The insurer sought to recover by way of the assignment and subrogation allegedly negligent against third-party defendant bank directors. The district court entered summary judgment for the directors, concluding that the insurer did not have a cause of action in subrogation. The Eleventh Circuit certified two questions on appeal to the Supreme Court of Florida: (1) whether an assignment and subrogation action required an insurer to establish superior equities against the directors to recover; and (2) whether an insurer's status as a paid surety established the superior equities in favor of directors charged with mere negligence. As to the first question, the court advised that the insurer's right of subrogation did require a showing of superior equities and that the written assignment by the bank did nothing to change that requirement. On the second question, the court stated that equitable principles would require the insurer to show bad faith, actual knowledge, or fraud on the part of the directors to maintain a subrogation action. The court affirmed the district court's grant of summary judgment for the directors. *Dixie Nat'l Bank of Dade Cnty. v. Emp'rs Commercial Union Ins. Co. of Am.*, 759 F.2d 826, 827-28.

N.D. Cal. 2006. The insurer paid an employee dishonesty loss involving 49 forged or altered checks, and the insured employer assigned its rights to the insurer. The insurer sued the depository credit union and drawee bank. The court dismissed the complaint based on the bank's argument that the superior equities doctrine is still the law in California and that the insurer had not alleged any fault or negligence by the bank. That is, even though the insured could have recovered under the U.C.C. because the items were not properly payable, the insurer, who was paid a premium to take the risk of employee dishonesty, cannot similarly recover against an "innocent" third party. *Travelers Cas. & Sur. Co. of Am. v. Wells Fargo Bank, N.A.*, No. C 06-03531, 2006 U.S. Dist. LEXIS 76049, at *6.

C.D. Ill. 1989. No recovery may be had by right of subrogation in the absence of fraud, bad faith, or other evidence indicating that the bank officers derived a personal benefit from the defaulting employee's dishonesty or that the officers actually discovered the conduct causing the loss. *Emp'rs Ins. of Wausau v. Doonan*, 712 F. Supp. 1368, 1369.

M.D. La. 1984. Insurer who had sustained a loss under a fidelity bond sought to recover contribution and indemnity under insured's D&O policy. The insurer's loss was upon a fraudulent credit card deposit scheme, which the bank's officers and directors negligently failed to discover. The court granted the D&O insurer's motion for summary judgment because the D&O insurer was not primarily or actually responsible for the debt. Therefore, the relationship of co-debtors *in solido* did not exist as alleged by the fidelity insurer. *Fid. Nat'l Bank v. Aetna Cas. & Sur. Co.*, 584 F. Supp. 1039, 1046.

E.D. Mo. 1983. Insurer under Bankers Blanket Bond was sued by bank and filed third-party claims against two bank officers. The court denied a motion to dismiss filed by the officers, reasoning that the bank had a cause of action for negligence against its officers, and the insurer would "step into the shoes" of the bank if it paid a loss. Further, the court found that, "[d]enying subrogation would confuse the bank as a corporate entity with its agents." *Mfr. Bank & Trust Co. v. Transam. Ins. Co.*, 568 F. Supp. 790, 792-93.

E.D. Tenn. 1988. Fidelity bond insurer brought third party claim against directors and officers of the insured bank. The court held that a "fidelity bond insurer may only sue active wrongdoing bank officials when the level of wrongdoing, be it negligence or fraud, is equal to or greater than the level of wrongdoing covered by the bond in question." Thus, if a fidelity bond insurer has paid a claim based on employee dishonesty, it may not maintain an action against the insured's directors and officers for any lesser wrongdoing, such as simple negligence or gross negligence. *FSLIC v. Aetna Cas. & Sur. Co.*, 696 F. Supp. 1190, 1194.

Cal. Ct. App. 1970. Equities of subrogating insurer were held to be inferior to those of the purchaser of tires as to insured's employee who stole tires. Compensated fidelity bond insurer did not stand in shoes of its insured. *Fed. Ins. Co. v. Allen*, 92 Cal. Rptr. 125, 126.

Cal. Ct. App. 1963. Fidelity bond insurer's equities found superior to those of bank that took forged checks from embezzler. *Hartford Acc. & Indem. Co. v. All Am. Nut Co.*, 34 Cal. Rptr. 23, 26-27.

Wis. 1978. Lack of ordinary care by directors and officers of insured bank held not to give fidelity insurer an equitable position superior to that of the officers and directors. The insurer's subrogation claim against the directors and officers was denied. *First Nat'l Bank v. Hansen*, 267 N.W.2d 367, 371.

E. Impairment of Subrogation Rights

2d Cir. 1981 (N.Y.). Insurer under brokers blanket bond could not recover by subrogation from insured's employee where insured had taken responsibility for employee's defense and had not informed employee that by terms of settlement he might be open to liability to insurer. *H.S. Equities, Inc. v. Hartford Acc. & Indem. Co.*, 661 F.2d 264, 269.

9th Cir. 2005 (Cal). The court, interpreting Section 7 of the bond to require the insurer to demonstrate prejudice from the insured's actions in order to be discharged by impairment of the insurer's subrogation rights, found that the FDIC's sale of collateral for substantially less than it was appraised for impaired the insurer's subrogation rights. *FDIC v. Fid. & Deposit Co.*, Nos. 03-55752, 03-55876, 2005 U.S. App. LEXIS 8933, at *8-9.

S.D. Miss. 2012. The dishonest employee created loans to bank customers without their knowledge or consent. The employee used some of the proceeds to pay off prior fraudulent loans, some to make payments on legitimate loans, and some for himself. In a declaratory judgment action commenced by the insurer, the court rejected the insurer's argument that the insured's workout agreement with two of the customers involved in the transactions prejudiced the insurer's subrogation rights so as to bar recovery for those transactions. *BancInsure, Inc. v. Peoples Bank of the S.*, 866 F. Supp. 2d 577, 588-89.

D.N.J. 1977. Insurer argued that by settlement between insured and third party for less than claimed loss, it was released by prejudice to its rights. Court held insurer is not subrogated to rights of insured until insurer has reimbursed insured's total loss. An insurer, therefore, cannot complain of settlement by insured, which released its rights against another to mitigate its loss. *Midland Bank & Trust Co. v. Fid. & Deposit Co.*, 442 F. Supp. 960, 973.

Ind. Ct. App. 2011. The insured and its employee had a settlement agreement, which provided that the insured would not sue the former employee, but also provided that the agreement would not impair or affect insurer's subrogation rights. When the insurer sued the employee, the employee alleged a breach of the settlement agreement. Court held that there was no breach of the settlement agreement because the settlement agreement explicitly permitted suit by the subrogated insurer even though the insured itself could not have sued. *Jinkins v. Jet Credit*

Union, No. 49A02-1006-PL-666, 2011 Ind. App. Unpub. LEXIS 1127, at *19-20.

Kan. 1989. Insured settled with the alleged wrongdoer. The insurer argued that the settlement released it from any liability under the bond by creating a complete "circle of indemnity," as well as by violating the terms of the bond. The court held that the insurer did not possess an independent claim for indemnification or subrogation and was limited to its insured's rights against the alleged wrongdoer. After denial of liability by the insurer, the insured may enter into a settlement with a third party without prejudicing its rights against the insurer. *First Hays Bancshares, Inc. v. Kan. Bankers Sur. Co.*, 769 P.2d 1184, 1189.

Kan. Ct. App. 1988. Insured refused to allow insurer to use the insured's name in a negligent supervision suit against the insured's directors and officers. The court held that Section 7 does not require the insured to allow its name to be used in a subrogation action, nor did the insured's refusal prejudice the insurer's subrogation action. *Fid. & Deposit Co. v. Shawnee State Bank*, 766 P.2d 191, 185-86.

F. Cooperation

1. Cases under Financial Institution Bonds

6th Cir. 2002 (Ohio). Insured who failed to file adequate proof of loss commenced an action against the insurer for bad faith failure to pay claim. The court held that there was no colorable basis to file suit when the insured had never provided information to insurer that its claim was covered. The insured's suit against the insurer for failure to pay a claim was held to be made in bad faith because the insured had failed to file adequate proof of loss or to provide any information that might have substantiated the claim. *First Bank of Marietta v. Hartford Underwriters Ins. Co.*, 307 F.3d 501, 524.

2. Cases under Crime Policies

D.D.C. 2007. Employee embezzled funds over several policy periods. The insured obtained substantial restitution from the employee, applied it to losses from the earlier years, and made policy limit claims on the last two annual policies. The insured did not supply the documentation requested by the insurer and sued on the last two policies. The court granted summary judgment for the insurer. The policies required a signed, sworn proof of loss containing information requested by the insurer within sixty days of the request. The insurer offered time extensions, but the insured never provided the documents. *MDB Commc'ns, Inc. v. Hartford Cas. Ins. Co.,* 479 F. Supp. 2d 136, 145.

S.D.N.Y. 2010. Insured failed to provide a signed, sworn proof of loss. Its failure to provide the documents requested by the insurer was a breach of the policy's proof of loss and cooperation provisions. *Schupak Group, Inc. v. Travelers Cas. and Sur. Co. of Am.,* 716 F. Supp. 2d 262, 269.

Ind. Ct. App. 2006. The insured claimed over $41.3 million loss due to its employee's alleged theft of computer hardware and software. The policy required the insured to provide documents and to submit to examination under oath at the insurer's request. The insurer requested documents and scheduled an examination under oath. The insured failed to comply. The court held that the insured's breach of the cooperation provision barred the insured's claim without proof of prejudice. *Knowledge A-Z, Inc. v. Sentry Ins.,* 857 N.E.2d 411, 420-423.

Mass. App. Ct. 2009. The insured provided 300 boxes of unorganized records in support of its employee dishonesty claim. The court found that the insured had not breached the cooperation provision because it had turned over its pertinent documents. *Hanover Ins. Co. v. Treasurer and Receiver Gen.,* 910 N.E.2d 921, 929.

Mo. Ct. App. 2003. Insured failed to present its owner/employee for examination under oath. Insurer denied the claim, invoking the bond's cooperation provision. The court, reversing summary judgment for the insured, held that until employee was found to be the alter ego of the insured, it cannot be found that the insured refused to cooperate. *E. Attucks Cmty. Hous. Inc. v. Old Republic Sur. Co.,* 114 S.W.3d 311, 327.

N.Y. App. Div. 2011. The insured's failure to advise the insurer of the restitution it had received from the dishonest employee and the insured's objection to the insurer's stated intent to interview the employee were held to be a breaches of the cooperation clause. *Conference Assocs., Inc. v. Travelers Cas. and Sur. Co. of Am.*, 914 N.Y.S.2d 310, 311.

3. Cases under Other Policies

S.D. Ohio 2013. An insurer may properly void a homeowner's insurance policy and deny coverage when an insured delays and fails to fully cooperate with an insurer's thorough fire investigation, despite the insured's partial cooperation and promise of additional cooperation in the future. The court found that the cooperation provision was a condition precedent of recovery under the policy. *Joseph v. State Farm Fire & Cas. Co.*, No. 2:11-cv-794, 2013 U.S. Dist. LEXIS 24511, at *18-19.

SECONDARY SOURCES

Robert J. Berens & Sandra M. Stone, *An Insurer's Claim against a Financial Institution for Allowing an Employee to Negotiate Checks Payable and Delivered to the Insured*, XIII FID. L.J. 227 (2007).

Bradford R, Carver & D.M. Studler, *The Auditor's Responsibility to Detect Fraud: Recently Issued SAS No. 82 and Its Potential Effect on Fidelity Claims*, IV FID. L.J. 89 (1998).

John V. Church, Gail Speilberger & Gerald Carozza, *Insured's Duty to Cooperate*, in COMMERCIAL CRIME POLICY 611-639 (Randall I. Marmor & John J. Tomaine, eds., 2d ed. 2005).

Michael R. Davisson & Susan Koehler Sullivan, *20—Subrogation and Mitigation*, in HANDLING FIDELITY BOND CLAIMS 573-620 (Michael Keeley and Timothy Sukel eds. 1999).

Robert J. Donovan & Sam H. Poteet, Jr., *Impairment of Subrogation Rights: What are the Insured's Duties and Obligations to the Fidelity Carrier?* (unpublished paper presented at ABA Fidelity and Surety Law Committee Annual Mid-Winter CLE Meeting in New York, N.Y., Jan. 22, 1999).

Edward G. Gallagher, *Barriers to the exercise of the Fidelity Insurer's Subrogation Rights with Emphasis on Conflicts Involving Federal Forfeiture Statues*, I FID. L.J. 37 (1995).

C. David Hailey, *Who's On First—The Fidelity Insurer's Rights to First Recoveries*, XI FID. L.J. 121 (2004).

Judy J. Hlafcsak, *The Nature and Extent of Subrogation Rights of Fidelity Insurers Against Officers and Directors of Financial Institutions,* 47 U. PITT. L. REV. 727-47 (1986).

Michael Keeley & Sean Duffy, *Investigating the Employee Dishonesty Claim: Interviewing Witnesses, Obtaining Documents & Other Important Issues*, in HANDLING FIDELITY BOND CLAIMS 153, 196 (Michael Keeley & Sean Duffy, eds., 2d ed. 2005).

James A. Knox & Mark Kriegel, *Recovery of Loss, in* FINANCIAL INSTITUTION BONDS 711-73 (Duncan Clore, ed., 3d ed. 2008).

Harvey C. Koch, Ashley L. Belleau & Patrick J. Collins, *Effecting Recovery and Subrogation in Specialized Situations*, XVIII FID. L.J. 235 (2012).

Randall Marmor, *Liability of Payee for Accepting Fraudulent checks in Payment of a Fiduciary's Personal Debt*, XII FID. L.J. 49 (2006).

Roger W. Rizk, *Bank Directors' Liability to Fidelity Insurers: How Bad is Bad Faith*, 19 FORUM 481 (1984).

Gil Schroeder, *Handling the Complex Fidelity or Financial Institution Bond Claim: The Liability of the Insured's Officers and Directors and Their D&O Carrier*, 21 TORT & INS. L.J. 269-95 (1986).

Gregory R. Veal, *Subrogation: The Duties and Obligations of the Insured and Rights of the Insurer Revisited*, 28 TORT & INS. L.J. 69 (1992).

Michael J. Weber & Robert K. Grennan, *ATMs and Check Fraud: Life after Interior Crafts and the Depositary Bank's Obligation to Honor Restrictive Indorsements*, XIII FID. L.J. 133 (2007).

Mark E. Wilson, *Banking Industry Standards Relevant to Coverage and Recoveries under the Revised Uniform Commercial Code*, V FID. L.J. 79 (1999).

Richard S. Wisner & Scott O. Reed, *Salvage and Subrogation Rights, in* FINANCIAL INSTITUTION BONDS 257-70 (Harvey C. Koch ed., 1989).

SECTION 8 — LIMIT OF LIABILITY*

LIMIT OF LIABILITY UNDER THIS BOND AND PRIOR INSURANCE

Section 8. With respect to any loss set forth in subsection (c) of Section 4. of this bond which is recoverable or recovered in whole or in part under any other bonds or policies issued by the Underwriter to the Insured or to any predecessor in interest of the Insured and terminated or canceled or allowed to expire and in which the period for discovery has not expired at the time any such loss thereunder is discovered, the total liability of the Underwriter under this bond and under such other bonds or policies shall not exceed, in the aggregate, the amount carried hereunder on such loss or the amount available to the Insured under such other bonds or policies, as limited by the terms and conditions thereof, for any such loss if the latter amount be the larger.

If the coverage of this bond supersedes in whole or in part the coverage of any other bond or policy of insurance issued by an Insurer other than the Underwriter and terminated, canceled or allowed to expire, the Underwriter, with respect to any loss sustained prior to such termination, cancellation or expiration and discovered within the period permitted under such other bond or policy for the discovery of loss thereunder, shall be liable under this bond only for that part of such loss covered by this bond as is in excess of the amount recoverable or recovered on account of such loss under such other bond or policy, anything to the contrary in such other bond or policy notwithstanding.

COMMENT

The language of this provision has been substantially the same for many years. Since the Financial Institution Bond is written on a discovery basis almost universally and there is no tail within which to discover loss, once the bond terminates there is almost never an issue as

---

*   By Dolores A. Parr, Zurich North America Surety, Baltimore, Maryland.

to whether a financial institution's prior insurance is liable for a loss. This provision does not affect many claims under the Financial Institution Bond and does not appear to have been litigated in situations involving the standard form Financial Institution Bond.

ANNOTATIONS

10th Cir. 1992 (Utah). Insured brought a suit against the insurer for insurer's failure to pay the full million dollar limit of liability for loss due to employee dishonesty under a Commercial Crime Bond. The loss occurred over several bond periods in which coverage was written by different carriers with different limits of liability. The bond contained the superseded suretyship provision. The court held that the insured could not recover any more than the prior limit of liability for the loss that occurred during that period. *Brigham Young Univ. v. Lumbermens Mut. Cas. Co.*, 965 F.2d 830, 834-35.

SECONDARY SOURCES

NONE

SECTION 9 — OTHER INSURANCE OR INDEMNITY*

Section 9. Coverage afforded hereunder shall apply only as excess over any valid and collectible insurance or indemnity obtained by the Insured, or by one other than the Insured on Property subject to exclusion (q) or by a Transportation Company, or by another entity on whose premises the loss occurred or which employed the person causing the loss or the messenger conveying the Property involved.

COMMENT

This section contains a typical "other insurance clause," noting that the bond is excess over any other valid and collectible insurance. The substitution of the broader reference to a "Transportation Company," in place of the formerly used "an armored motor vehicle company," appears to be in recognition of the widespread use of freight forwarding and air express companies. Section 9 is otherwise unchanged from the prior form. Exclusion (q) deals with any tangible items of personal property not specifically enumerated in the definition of "Property" for which the insured is legally liable and on which the insured has obtained insurance.

There are no cases or secondary sources addressing this section. However, there are many cases addressing similar "other insurance" provisions in other types of insurance policies. These cases generally find that where the "other insurance" clauses are similar, the insurance companies are required to satisfy the insured loss on a pro rata basis.[1]

This provision was moved to Section 10 in the 2011 form, but was not changed in substance.

---

* By Lisa D. Sparks, Wright, Constable & Skeen, LLP, Baltimore, Maryland.

[1] *See, e.g.,* First Defiance Fin. Corp. v. Progressive Cas. Ins. Co., 688 F.3d 265, 273 (6th Cir. 2012) (covered risks did not overlap so pro rata rule for multiple excess clauses did not apply); First Nat'l Ins. Co. v. FDIC, 977 F. Supp. 1051, 1058-59 (S.D. Cal. 1977); Rader v. Johnson, 97 S.W.2d 280, 285 (Miss. Ct. App. 1995); Universal Underwriters Ins. Co. v. Allstate Ins. Co., 638 A.2d 1220, 1223-24 (Md. App. 1994); Aetna Cas. & Sur. Co. v. Cont'l Ins. Co., 429 S.E.2d 406, 409 (N.C. 1993).

ANNOTATIONS

NONE

SECONDARY SOURCES

NONE

SECTION 10 — OWNERSHIP*

(1986 Form) Section 10. This bond shall apply to loss of Property (1) owned by the Insured, (2) held by the Insured in any capacity, or (3) for which the Insured is legally liable. This bond shall be for the sole use and benefit of the Insured named in the Declarations.

(2011 Form) Section 11. This bond shall apply to loss of Property (a) owned by the Insured, (b) held by the Insured in any capacity, or (c) owned and held by someone else under circumstances which make the Insured responsible for the Property prior to the occurrence of the loss. This bond shall be for the sole use and benefit of the Insured named in the Declarations.

COMMENT

This Ownership provision first appeared as a separate section in the 1980 standard form bond and was carried over verbatim into the 1986 standard form bond. As noted in the Surety Association of America's Statement of Change in connection with the 1980 form, this section combined concepts found in several places in the 1969 form.

This section describes the property that is potentially covered by the bond. The intent of this section is to preclude coverage for anyone except a named insured. It is on this section, as well as others in the bond, that the insurers can rely to assert that the bond is not subject to claims or suits by a non-insured.

Coverage for indirect third-party claims is limited by certain provisions in the bond. Before the 1980 form, courts were split on whether coverage under fidelity bonds extended to third parties. After the 1980 revisions, the majority of courts have consistently held that standard forms of fidelity bonds are not contracts for the benefit of third parties. The Ownership provision is one of several in the bond to review when the insured is faced with an indirect third-party claim. The phrase "legally liable" contained in the 1980 and 1986 forms was not intended to extend coverage to losses resulting from the imposition of tort liability through a third-party action. Instead the phrase "legally liable" extends coverage to property which, prior to its theft or misappropriation, was the

---

* By Seth Mills and Kevin Mekler, Mills Paskert Divers, Tampa, Florida.

legal responsibility of the insured. Additionally, this language was intended to prevent the insured from acting as a volunteer by reimbursing a third party for its otherwise uncovered loss(es), and subsequently seeking reimbursement under the bond on the theory that it was legally liable for the third party's property.

The modification made to the 2011 form further clarifies the intent of the prior "legally liable" language by expressly stating that if the property is owned or held by someone other than the insured, coverage only extends if the circumstances make the insured responsible for the property prior to the occurrence of the loss. However, there are few references in case law to the revised language in the 2011 form at this time.

Additionally, the last line of this provision provides further insight regarding the intent to limit coverage under the bond to direct losses sustained by the insured. The "sole use and benefit of the Insured" language contained in this provision is also used in other bond provisions, riders, and endorsements. The majority of courts apply this sentence in furtherance of its stated purpose; that is, limiting the coverage to the insured identified in the declarations, not third parties.

ANNOTATIONS

5th Cir. 1998 (Tex.). The Fifth Circuit held that the embezzlement by the insured's employee of funds in a customer's personal bank account (not managed by the insured) did not amount to employee dishonesty as defined in the commercial crime policy. The policy contained an "Interest Covered" provision that limited coverage to property (1) that the insured owned or held, or (2) for which the insured was legally liable. The court observed that the plain language of the "Interest Covered" provision, which requires that the employer/insured have some interest in the misappropriated property, forecloses the argument that the policy insures any vicarious liability arising from an employee's dishonesty. Therefore, the court concluded that the customer's separate bank accounts were too tenuous to trigger the policy's "legally liable" provision. *Lynch Props., Inc. v. Potomac Ins. Co.*, 140 F.3d 622, 629-30.

9th Cir. 2000 (Cal.). The insured sought recovery of amounts it paid to settle its vicarious liability to third parties resulting from the fraudulent conduct of an employee. The policy provided coverage for "direct losses of Money . . . caused by Theft or forgery by any Employee." The "Ownership" section of the policy stated that coverage applied to property "owned by the Insured or for which the Insured is legally liable." The court held that the policy provided coverage for direct loss of property by the insured but did not provide indemnity arising from its liability for its employees' tortious conduct. In addition, the court held that the "Ownership" provision defines the insured's interest in the property but does not create liability coverage. *Vons Cos., Inc. v. Fed. Ins. Co.*, 212 F.3d 489, 491-92.

10th Cir. 2000 (Okla.). The Tenth Circuit held that a Commercial Crime Policy permitted recovery for acts of employee dishonesty that had not yet resulted in a loss to the insured's bankruptcy estate but for which the estate was potentially liable. The policy covered "compensatory damages arising directly from a loss covered under this insurance" and defined "interests covered" as property that "you own or hold" or "for which you are legally liable." The court held that payment of the claims was not a condition of coverage. The court stated that the policy provided indemnity from liability and not just indemnity from loss, so that the insurer was required to pay claims as soon as they were established by creditors of the bankruptcy estate. *Nelson v. ITT Hartford Fire Ins. Co.*, No. 99-6275, 2000 WL 763772, at *2.

M.D. Florida 1995. A victim of securities fraud obtained an arbitration award against an insured and subsequently sued fidelity insurer seeking coverage for the arbitration award. Although the type of bond is not specifically identified, the bond expressly stated "this Bond is for the use and benefit only of the Insured." The court held that the plaintiff could not maintain a suit against the insurer because: (1) the plaintiff was neither a party to the bond nor a named insured, and (2) the bond is not a liability insurance policy. *Gasslein v. Nat'l Union Fire Ins. Co. of Pitt., Pa.*, 918 F. Supp. 373, 376.

S.D. Miss. 1998. Company's general agent and its shareholders brought suit against company and its insurer. Among other provisions, the court analyzed the language of the bond's "Ownership" provision, which stated that "this Bond shall be for the sole use and benefit of the Insured named in the Declarations hereof." The court compared the facts of the claim to the policy language and concluded that the plaintiffs were not insured under the "clear and unambiguous terms of the bond." Court granted summary judgment for insurer on all claims dependent upon coverage afforded only to the named insured. *Nationalcare Corp., Inc. v. St. Paul Prop. & Cas. Ins. Co.*, 22 F. Supp. 2d 558, 565-67.

D.N.J. 2011. The court held that insured failed to state a claim for relief under a Financial Institution Bond when the claim asserted was expressly precluded by the language of the bond. The insured alleged that an employee of its agent embezzled funds belonging to the agent, which resulted in the agent's inability to make required payments to third parties. The insured made the required payments to third parties and sought coverage under its Financial Institution Bond. The insured argued that it was legally liable for the payments. The court found the insured's argument unpersuasive because the insured's agency agreement did not establish liability for the funds prior to the embezzlement. *N.J. Title Ins. Co. v. Nat'l Union Fire Ins. Co. of Pitt., Pa.*, No. 11-CV-0630(DMC)(JAD), 2011 WL 6887130, at *5-7.

Bankr. D.N.J. 2006. The court dismissed claims asserted by joint loss payees under theories of breach of contract, promissory estoppel, equitable estoppel, implied contract, and misrepresentation. The policy contained an "Ownership" provision that limited coverage to property (1) owned by the insured, (2) held by the insured in any capacity, or (3) for which the insured was legally liable. The court focused on the difference between fidelity bonds and liability insurance and recognized that fidelity bonds are a form of first-party coverage, indemnifying the obligee for its loss, and are not a form of third-party coverage, indemnifying the insured for its liability to third persons. Ultimately, the court concluded that the express language of the bond confirmed that coverage was "only" for the named insured and "provided no rights or benefits to any other person or organization." *In re Tri-State Armored Servs., Inc.*, No. 01-11917/JHW, 2006 WL 4452993, at *6-7.

SECONDARY SOURCES

Paul R. Devin & R. Alan Fryer, *Third-Party Claims Against the Insured*, in HANDLING FIDELITY BOND CLAIMS 359 (Michael Keeley & Timothy M. Sukel eds., 1999).

David T. DiBiase & David J. Billings, *Direct Still Means Direct*, (unpublished paper presented at the ABA Tort & Insurance Practice Section, Fidelity & Surety Law Committee Fall Meeting in Hartford, CT, November 7, 2012).

Lawrence R. Fish, *Ownership of Property—Interest Covered: Where Are We Now?*, in COMMERCIAL CRIME POLICY 10-1 (Gilbert J. Schroeder ed., 1997).

Edward G. Gallagher & Christopher R. Ward, *Claims by Persons Other Than the Insured*, in HANDLING FIDELITY BOND CLAIMS 523 (Michael Keeley & Sean Duffy eds., 2d ed. 2005).

Scott L. Schmookler, *The Compensability of Third-Party Losses Under Fidelity Bonds*, VII FID. L.J. 115 (2001).

James W. Smirz, *Ownership of Property; Interests Covered*, in FIDELITY BONDS (Gilbert J. Schroeder ed., 1991).

Karen Wildau, *Evolving Law of Third-Party Claims Under Fidelity Bonds: When Is Third-Party Recovery Allowed?*, 25 TORT & INS. L.J. 92, 99 (1989).

SECTION 11 — DEDUCTIBLE AMOUNT*

Section 11. The Underwriter shall be liable hereunder only for the amount by which any single loss, as defined in Section 4, exceeds the Single Loss Deductible amount for the Insuring Agreement or Coverage applicable to such loss, subject to the Aggregate Limit of Liability and the applicable Single Loss Limit of Liability.

The Insured shall, in the time and in the manner prescribed in this bond, give the Underwriter notice of any loss of the kind covered by the terms of this bond, whether or not the Underwriter is liable therefor, and upon the request of the Underwriter shall file with it a brief statement giving the particulars concerning such loss.

(1986 version)

Section 13. The Underwriter shall be liable hereunder only for the amount by which any single loss, as defined in Section 4., exceeds the Single Loss Deductible amount for the Insuring Agreement or Coverage applicable to such loss, subject to the Aggregate Limit of Liability and the applicable Single Loss Limit of Liability.

If the loss involved Employee dishonesty, or if the amount of the potential loss exceeds the amount set forth in Item 6. of the Declarations, the Insured shall, in the time and in the manner prescribed in this bond, give the Underwriter notice of any loss of the kind covered by the terms of this bond, even if the amount of loss does not exceed the Single Loss Deductible, and upon the request of the Underwriter shall file with it a brief statement giving the particulars concerning such loss.

(2004 version)

---

* By William T. Bogaert and Stefan R. Dandelles, Wilson Elser Moskowitz Edelman & Dicker LLP, Boston Massachusetts and Chicago, Illinois, and Camilla Conlon, ACE North American Professional Risk Claims, Chicago, Illinois.

COMMENT

This section was re-numbered to Section 13 in 2004 as a result of the addition of new Sections 8 (Cooperation) and 9 (Anti-Bundling) in the 2004 form. The first paragraph of this section was carried over verbatim from the 1986 form, which itself was revised to accommodate the new concepts in the 1986 form of the single loss limit of liability, the single loss deductible, and the aggregate limit of liability.

The second paragraph of this section was modified in 2004 to limit the notice provision to matters involving employee dishonesty or those that exceed a pre-determined quantum threshold. The 2011 form makes only a minor modification to the second paragraph to track more closely the wording of Insuring Agreement (A). In addition, the section is again renumbered to Section 12 due to the 2011 form's elimination of the previous Section 10.

Section 13 provides that an insurer will only be liable for an amount that exceeds the deductible amount. This means that an insurer will pay for a single loss if it exceeds the deductible amount, but only up to the limit of the policy. Applying the specific facts at issue on a case-by-case basis to the definition of single loss is key in determining whether a single deductible and limit will apply to a given loss or whether potentially multiple deductibles and limits will be triggered, subject of course to any aggregate limit of liability.

ANNOTATIONS

Ohio Ct. App. 1996. The court of appeals found that the trial court incorrectly applied the deductible provision in the Bankers Blanket Bond by subtracting the $25,000 deductible amount from the total of the insured's loss, which included interest on a judgment. The court held that the deductible should have been applied to the first $25,000 of loss so that the judgment, along with interest on the judgment, were based on the amount in excess of the $25,000 deductible. *Bank One, Steubenville v. Buckeye Union Ins. Co.*, 683 N.E.2d 50, 55.

SECONDARY SOURCES

Bradford R. Carver, *Loss and Causation, in* HANDLING FIDELITY BOND CLAIMS 363 (Michael Keeley & Sean Duffy eds., 2d ed. 2005).

SECTION 12 — TERMINATION OR CANCELLATION*

Section 12. This bond terminates as an entirety upon occurrence of any of the following: (a) 60 days after the receipt by the Insured of a written notice from the Underwriter of its desire to cancel this bond, or (b) immediately upon the receipt by the Underwriter of a written notice from the Insured of its desire to cancel this bond, or (c) immediately upon the taking over of the Insured by a receiver or other liquidator or by State or Federal officials, or (d) immediately upon the taking over of the Insured by another institution, or (e) upon exhaustion of the Aggregate Limit of Liability, or (f) immediately upon expiration of the Bond Period as set forth in Item 2 of the Declarations.

This bond terminates as to any Employee or partner, officer, or employee of any Processor—(a) as soon as the Insured, or any director or officer not in collusion with such person, learns of any dishonest or fraudulent act committed by such person at any time, whether in the employment of the Insured or otherwise, whether or not of the type covered under Insuring Agreement (A), against the Insured or any other person or entity, without prejudice to the loss of any Property then in transit in the custody of such person, or (b) 15 days after the receipt by the Insured of a Written notice from the Underwriter of its desire to cancel this bond as to such person.

Termination of the bond as to any Insured terminates liability for any loss sustained by such Insured which is discovered after the effective date of such termination.

COMMENT

The Termination or Cancellation provision of the Financial Institution Bond consists of two parts. The first sets forth six ways in which a bond may be automatically terminated in its entirety: (1) sixty days after receipt by the insured of written notice of cancellation from

---

* By Michael R. Davisson, Sedgwick LLP, Los Angeles, California, with assistance from Ira Steinberg of the same firm.

the insurer; (2) immediately upon receipt by the insurer of written notice of cancellation from the Insured; (3) immediately upon the taking over of the Insured by a receiver or liquidator or by state or federal officials; (4) immediately upon the taking over of the Insured by another institution; (5) immediately upon exhaustion of the bond limit; or (6) immediately upon expiration of the policy period.

The second part of the Termination or Cancellation provision concerns the automatic termination of the Financial Institution Bond as to any specific employee when the insured learns of any dishonest or fraudulent acts committed by the employee, or when any director or officer not in collusion with the dishonest employee learns of such an act. The dishonest act sufficient for termination need not have been performed while in the employ of the insured, and also need not be of a type covered by the bond for termination to occur.

During the savings and loan crisis in the 1980s, the provision for automatic termination in the event of government takeover received substantial judicial scrutiny. During that era, federal regulators were generally rebuffed in their arguments that automatic termination provisions violated public policy. However, the Termination or Cancellation provision of the bond has not fared as well in situations where the insured is bankrupt or insolvent. In such situations, courts have sometimes held that anti-termination provisions in the bankruptcy code supersede the termination provisions of the bond. Litigation of these issues has subsided in recent years, however. Surprisingly, coverage litigation over the first part of the Termination or Cancellation provision has not, as yet, increased, despite the financial and real estate crisis that began in 2008.

On the other hand, the provision for automatic termination as to specific employees has been consistently and sometimes hotly litigated, and has received notable attention from a number of courts. This provision of the bond is intended to protect insurers from the moral hazard of the insured's decision to continue to employ persons that are known by the insured to be dishonest. As noted above, in this part of the Termination or Cancellation provision, automatic termination is triggered by knowledge of dishonest acts, whenever occurring and whether or not such acts would give rise to a covered loss under the bond. Litigation about this provision is generally fact intensive, and sometimes involves proof of both objective and subjective elements concerning the employee's conduct, as well as evidence regarding the insured's awareness of the conduct. Accordingly, some of the more frequently litigated issues include: (1) who must learn of the prior dishonest conduct; (2) whether such knowledge is imputable to the insured; (3) whether a director or officer who learns of the dishonest conduct was in collusion with the dishonest employee; (4) what facts must be known in order to terminate coverage; (5) whether the prior conduct was sufficiently "dishonest" to terminate coverage; and (6) when the insured had knowledge of the conduct sufficient to trigger the termination provision.

The Termination or Cancellation provision was moved to Section 14 in the 2004 standard form Financial Institution Bond. The 2004 form, though used less frequently than the 1986 form, reflects the continuing evolution of the Termination or Cancellation provision, and differs from the 1986 form in two key ways. First, the 2004 form substitutes "change in control" for the phrase "taking over the insured by another institution," and in doing so provides additional clarification as to the application of that provision. The 2004 form also makes explicit the exclusion of liability for any loss caused by an employee after coverage for that employee was terminated. The 2011 form made no changes to the 2004 version other than correcting a typographical error and moving the provision to Section 13.

OUTLINE OF ANNOTATIONS

A. Termination or Cancellation of the Bond in Its Entirety
B. Termination of the Bond as to Any Employee

ANNOTATIONS

A. Termination or Cancellation of the Bond in Its Entirety

4th Cir. 1993 (N.C.). Action by bankruptcy trustee on a Securities Dealer Blanket Bond. The court granted the trustee's motion for summary judgment, and the insurer appealed, arguing that summary judgment was erroneously granted because the bond automatically terminated upon takeover by a receiver or liquidator. The court held that the trustee's rights under the bond constituted property of the estate under Section 541 of the Bankruptcy Code, and the automatic termination provision contained in Section 12(c) of the bond was ineffective by virtue of Section 541(c)(l)(B) of the bankruptcy code. *In re Waddell Jenmar Sec., Inc.*, No. 92-2158, 1993 U.S. App. LEXIS 9535, at *8-10.

5th Cir. 1993 (Tex.). The court held that a Savings and Loan Blanket Bond terminated when the Texas Savings and Loan Commissioner issued a cease and desist order and the thrift voluntarily placed itself under the Commissioner's supervisory control. The court noted that a takeover does not have to be in the form of a receivership or liquidation in order to trigger the automatic termination provision, nor does a takeover have to be hostile or involuntary. The court affirmed the district court's declaratory judgment that the insurer had no liability under the bond. *U.S. Fire Ins. Co. v. FDIC*, 981 F.2d 850, 851-52.

5th Cir. 1988 (La.). In an action seeking a declaratory judgment that a Savings and Loan Blanket Bond terminated immediately upon appointment of the FHLB as conservator for the insured, the court held that under Louisiana law, the plain meaning of the bond controls. Therefore, Section 12 of the bond terminated coverage automatically upon commencement of the conservatorship, with or without notice to the FHLB. *Sharp v. FSLIC*, 858 F.2d 1042, 1044-48.

6th Cir. 1993 (Tenn.). A Bankers Blanket Bond and Excess Blanket Bond provided that the bonds would be canceled in their entirety immediately upon the taking over of the insured by another institution. During the period covered by the bonds, the bank was declared insolvent and its voting stock was purchased by another bank at a foreclosure sale. After the foreclosure sale, but before the merger, a loss to the insured as a result of acts of its president was discovered and was claimed under the bonds. The insurer denied the claim and the insured brought suit. The Sixth Circuit held that the takeover of the insured occurred when the purchasing bank assumed management control, and further that the purchasing bank assumed management control when officers of the purchasing institution fired the insured bank's president, announced management plans to the board of directors of the insured bank, and the insured's board approved the merger. *First Am. Nat'l Bank v. Fid. & Deposit Co. of Md.*, 5 F.3d 982, 984-86.

6th Cir. 1990 (Tenn.). The FDIC brought an action against the insurer claiming coverage under Bankers Blanket Bonds after the insurer denied the FDIC's request to purchase an additional discovery period provided for in the bonds. The insurer informed the FDIC that it was not entitled to purchase the additional discovery period because of a provision that the additional period could not be purchased by any government official or agency, and returned the unearned premium. The court held that sections 12 and 13 of the bonds, regarding automatic termination and purchase of an additional discovery period, were not void as contrary to public policy, and were valid and enforceable absent a clear manifestation of public policy to the contrary. *FDIC v. Aetna Cas. & Sur. Co.*, 903 F.2d 1073, 1077-80.

9th Cir. 1991 (Cal.). The FSLIC filed a complaint to recover under a Savings and Loan Blanket Bond for losses sustained due to defalcations of two principal officers and directors of a failed thrift. The district court granted summary judgment to the insurers, holding that coverage automatically terminated upon the thrift's takeover by federal officials. On appeal, the court held that under California law, the bond's automatic termination provision does not violate public policy. *Cal. Union Ins. Co. v. Am. Diversified Sav. Bank*, 948 F.2d 556, 559-63.

9th Cir. 1991 (Cal.). The court found that an automatic termination provision in a fidelity bond was clear and unambiguous, and required termination of the bond immediately upon takeover of the bank by the FSLIC. The court also held that, for purposes of the automatic termination provision, there was no meaningful difference between being taken over by a receiver or liquidator, on the one hand, and a conservator on the other. *RTC v. Fid. & Deposit Co. of Md.*, No. 90-56157, 1992 U.S. App. LEXIS 1592, at *1-3.

10th Cir. 1992 (Okla.). The insured was placed into receivership triggering termination of the bond in its entirety. The policy provided that the bank receive all proofs of loss before termination in the entirety is triggered in order for there to be coverage. Just before the bond terminated upon the appointment of a receiver the insured submitted letters to the insurer claiming they had discovered a covered loss. They did not submit a proof of loss before termination. After holding that the termination provision did not violate public policy the court held that the loss was not covered because irrespective of the loss letters no proof of loss was submitted before termination as a whole. Since the insurer required proofs of loss to be submitted before termination it evinced an intent of the parties to make time of the essence with respect to notice before termination and precluded coverage for the loss irrespective of whether the insured "substantially complied" with the policy by submitting loss letters before termination. *FDIC v. Kan. Bankers Sur. Co.*, 963 F.2d 289, 292-95.

11th Cir. 2002 (Ga.). An insured bank was acquired by another corporation. Two months after acquisition, the corporation notified the insurer of the claim under a Financial Institution Bond. The trial court granted judgment for the corporation, holding that the "takeover" provision of the bond was ambiguous. The Eleventh Circuit reversed, holding that the takeover provision was plain and unambiguous, such that the purchase by the corporation of 100 percent of the bank's stock constituted a takeover, thereby immediately terminating coverage. *Am. Cas. Co. v. Etowah Bank*, 288 F.3d 1282, 1285-88.

11th Cir. 1992 (Fla.). Appeal of judgment entered in favor of bankruptcy trustee on Securities Dealer Blanket Bond. The court held that the Bankruptcy Code anti-termination provision, 11 U.S.C. § 541(c)(l)(B), applies to a liquidation proceeding under the Securities Investor Protection Act of 1970, 15 U.S.C. §§ 78aaa-78111, to invalidate a clause that purported to terminate liability under the bond automatically upon the takeover of the insured by a receiver or other liquidator. *In re Gov't Sec. Corp.*, 972 F.2d 328, 330-31.

D. Colo. 2008. A fidelity bond issued to a financial institution terminated under the termination provision of the bond when the FDIC took over the insured as its receiver. The court held that if the insured discovered a fidelity loss before termination of the bond, the FDIC could step into the shoes of the insured to pursue coverage for such loss under the bond. *FDIC v. St. Paul Cos.*, 634 F. Supp. 2d 1213.

M.D. Ga. 1967. A Bankers Blanket Bond provided for three methods by which it could be terminated or canceled: (a) by the underwriter; (b) by the insured; or (c) by the appointment of a receiver. The courts also recognized cancellation by mutual assent. Under circumstances of this case it made no difference which of the four methods the termination occurred, since the result was the same: according to the terms of the bond, discovery had to be made prior to the termination. Moreover, even if it had been established that the bonding company had knowledge that the bank was insolvent and initiated cancellation for that reason, validity of cancellation would not be affected in view of bonding company's reservation of the right to cancel. *Hartford Acc. & Indem. Co. v. Hartley*, 275 F. Supp. 610, 615-20.

N.D. Ill. 1989. The FSLIC filed a complaint against the insurer claiming a wrongful denial of its claim under a Savings and Loan Blanket Bond (Form 22). The insurer asserted the bond's automatic termination provision as one defense. The court rejected the FSLIC's argument that the automatic termination provision was unenforceable because it was contrary to the statutory rights and duties of the FSLIC as conferred by Congress. However, the court denied summary judgment for the insurer, finding an issue of fact with respect to whether the insurer waived its right to rely on Section 11(c), providing for termination in the entirety upon takeover by a liquidator or receiver, by billing the insured's agent for unpaid premium with full knowledge of the FSLIC receivership. *FSLIC v. Transam. Ins. Co.*, 705 F. Supp. 1328, 1334-38.

E.D. La. 1994. The insurer issued a Savings and Loan Blanket Bond to a savings and loan which subsequently entered into a consent agreement with the FHLBB in which it agreed to the appointment of a conservator, receiver or other legal custodian. Seven months later, the FDIC was appointed receiver of the savings and loan. The bond provided for termination immediately upon takeover of the insured by state or federal officials. In its motion for summary judgment, the insurer argued that the bond automatically terminated either on the date of the consent agreement or on the date of the FDIC's appointment as receiver. The court denied the motion, finding that a genuine issue of material fact existed with respect to the date of the takeover. *FDIC v. Fid. & Deposit Co. of Md.*, No. 92-2109, 1994 WL 117790, at *2-3.

S.D.N.Y. 2001. Whether under New York or English law, the termination provision of a firm's fidelity insurance policy, providing that the policy automatically terminated upon appointment of receiver, did not operate to preclude coverage of investors' fraud claims against the insured (regardless of whether the claims were filed after the receiver's appointment) because, prior to the appointment, the insurer had received notice of SEC fraud complaint. The court reached the conclusion because the SEC notice contained a description of circumstances that could give rise to future claims, the investors' claims were based on same facts giving rise to SEC action, and the policy tied coverage to discovery of loss or potential loss rather than the filing of claim. *SEC v. Credit Bancorp, Ltd.*, 147 F. Supp. 2d 238, 251-53.

D.R.I. 1992. Insurer issued a Small Loan Companies Blanket Bond which provided that the bond could be canceled upon thirty days' written notice or immediately upon the taking over of the insured by a receiver. The bond also provided a twelve month discovery tail following the date of cancellation. The insurer gave notice of cancellation to insured, but not to the Rhode Island Department of Business Regulation as required by state law. Twenty months after the notice of cancellation, the insured was declared insolvent and placed in receivership. The receiver filed a claim under the bond. The court held that because notice was not given to the State Department of Business Regulation, the bond remained in effect until the receivership was established, and thus, the receiver's claim was timely. *Paradis v. Aetna Cas. & Sur. Co.*, 796 F. Supp. 59, 61-63.

N.D. Tex. 1997. Prior to the appointment of a receiver state regulators appointed a "supervisory agent" with limited powers over the insured pursuant to two agreements between the insured and state regulators. The insurer brought a motion for summary judgment arguing that the termination provision was triggered at the appointment of the supervisory agent prior to the appointment of a receiver. The court denied the motion, finding that a genuine issue of fact existed with respect to if and when the appointment and empowerment of the supervisory agent constituted a takeover under the termination provision. *FDIC v. Fid. & Deposit Co. of Md.*, No. 3:95-CV-1094, 1997 WL 560616, at *4-5.

Ill App. Ct. 2011. An insured subject to the Illinois Corporate Fiduciary Act sought coverage under its fidelity bond for misappropriation of funds by corporate officers. The insurer denied coverage on the ground that discovery of loss occurred after the bond terminated upon appointment of a receiver for the insured. The court held that a provision in the Corporate Fiduciary Act applied to toll the termination provision in the bond for six months after appointment of the receiver. *Indep. Trust Corp. v. Kan. Bankers Sur. Co.*, 954 N.E.2d 401, 405-07.

Ind. Ct. App. 1995. A liquidator brought suit on a Financial Institution Bond to recover for losses allegedly resulting from employee misconduct. Summary judgment was granted in favor of the bonding company on grounds that claim was barred by the automatic termination of coverage upon takeover of the insured by state or federal officials. The court noted that the termination provision was not void as against public policy. The court also held that a rider providing that: "[n]o cancellation or termination of this policy or bond, as an entirety, whether by or at the request of the Insured or the Underwriter, shall take effect prior to the expiration of thirty days after written notice of such termination or cancellation has been filed with [the] Indiana Department of Insurance" was not applicable to an automatic termination following takeover by state or federal officials, even if the insured consented to the takeover. *Mut. Sec. Life Ins. Co. v. Fid. & Deposit Co. of Md.*, 659 N.E.2d 1096, 1098-1104.

Tex. 1984. A stockbroker doing business as limited partnership sued under a stockbrokers blanket fidelity bond for losses resulting from fraudulent misappropriation by an employee. Insurer denied coverage on the ground that the bond terminated when the insured was taken over by another business entity which purchased a substantial part of the insured's assets and took over most of its business. The loss was discovered during the policy period and two months after the execution of the purchase agreement, but while the insured was still doing business and winding up its affairs prior to final closing. The blanket bond provided that it "shall be terminated or canceled as an entirety . . . immediately upon the taking over of the Insured by another business entity." On appeal, the Texas Supreme Court held that the takeover clause was ambiguous. The court also held that because the insured was a partnership still doing business at the time the loss was discovered, there could be no "takeover" until all partnership business had been completely terminated and the partnership had ceased to exist. *Kelly Assocs., Ltd. v. Aetna Cas. & Sur. Co.*, 681 S.W.2d 593, 594-97.

B. Termination of the Bond as to Any Employee

4th Cir. 1979 (S.C.). Where insured mortgage broker, prior to the effective date of fidelity policies, discovered during the course of a routine audit that the vice president was falsely certifying pre-advances for certain HUD/FHA loans, the bonding companies were held not liable for losses sustained by insured because of vice president's false certifications of letters of credit after effective date of policies. *C. Douglas Wilson & Co. v. Ins. Co. of N. Am.*, 590 F.2d 1275, 1276-80.

4th Cir. 1970 (Md.). Insurer denied claim on the grounds that the bond terminated as to the two dishonest directors that caused the loss. The insurer argued that while normally the knowledge of an employee acting outside the scope of their agency is not imputed to their employer, the exception for individuals who are alter-egos of a company should apply and therefore the dishonest officers' knowledge could be imputed the insured in this case. The court held that the insurer failed to establish as a matter of law that the officers were alter-egos of the insured and thus whether their knowledge of their defalcations was imputable to the insured corporation. *Phoenix Sav. & Loan, Inc. v. Aetna Cas. & Sur. Co.*, 427 F.2d 862, 866-74.

5th Cir. 1992 (La.). A bank brought suit under a Bankers Blanket Bond (1980 Form), claiming damages for losses incurred as a result of the acts of a former loan officer, who had issued fraudulent credit reports in connection with proposed loans. The court held that it was error to incorporate the restrictive definition of dishonest or fraudulent acts from Insuring Agreement (A) into the automatic termination clause. The court noted that the only reasonable interpretation of the automatic termination clause is that knowledge of dishonest acts falling short of those triggering coverage under Insuring Agreement (A) may nonetheless terminate coverage under the bond. *First Nat'l Bank of Louisville v. Lustig*, 961 F.2d 1162, 1168.

5th Cir. 1985 (Tex.). The court held that a Bankers Blanket Bond (1969 Form 24) terminated by its own terms before it was renewed due to the bank vice president's knowledge of the bank president's dishonest and fraudulent acts relating to improper use of bank funds. The court reasoned that since the bank was wholly owned by the vice president his knowledge of the president's activity of using funds to finance his side business barred the claim made under the Bankers Blanket Bond for losses resulting from the dishonest activity of the president. *City State Bank v. USF&G*, 778 F.2d 1103, 1106-1111.

5th Cir. 1981 (La.). A bank's president made fictitious loans to allow use of bank funds for political contributions, the purpose of which was to gain business for the bank. The evidence showed that the board of directors of the insured bank had knowledge or information of prior fraudulent or dishonest activities of bank president. Finding for the insurer, the court held that a bond provision precluding coverage after knowledge of an employee's dishonesty was valid. *Cent. Progressive Bank v. Fireman's Fund Ins. Co.*, 658 F.2d 377, 378-82.

5th Cir. 1972 (Tex.). That president of insured bank was controlling shareholder and actually ran the bank did not justify imputing his knowledge of his own fraudulent acts to insured bank so as to terminate liability under Bankers Blanket Bonds where there was no showing that other directors neglected their duties and responsibilities or that other directors knew of actions of president. *FDIC v. Lott*, 460 F.2d 82, 86-88.

5th Cir. 1970 (Tex.). The court held that an insured under Bankers Blanket Bond is not bound to give notice when it merely suspects or has reason to suspect wrongdoing, but only when it has acquired knowledge of some specific fraudulent or dishonest act. Thus, the insured bank was not required to give notice to the bonding company at the time it discovered that real estate notes it purchased did not conform to the type authorized for purchase by a national bank, even if it did have reason to suspect wrongdoing, where it had not yet discovered the fraudulent conduct of a director in connection with such purchase. Knowledge of directors acting adversely to interest of insured bank could not be imputed to insured bank for purposes of precluding coverage on ground that the insured bank had ratified the acts of the directors. *FDIC v. Aetna Cas. & Sur. Co.*, 426 F.2d 729, 738-39.

5th Cir. 1966 (Fla.). Bond provision terminating coverage upon knowledge that the insured's employee had committed any fraudulent or dishonest act was reasonable and valid. *St. Joe Paper Co. v. Hartford Acc. & Indem. Co.*, 359 F.2d 579, *amended* 376 F.2d 33, 35.

5th Cir. 1957 (La.). Provision that fidelity bond was deemed canceled as to any employee upon discovery of dishonesty was valid. Such a clause should be enforced in the absence of ambiguity in the plain, ordinary and popular sense of the language used. Only if any of the terms are of doubtful meaning should the construction most favorable to the insured be adopted. *J.S. Fraering, Inc. v. Emp'rs Mut. Liab. Ins. Co.*, 242 F.2d 609, 610-13.

6th Cir. 1982 (Mich.). Bonding company denied coverage based on the insured's knowledge of an employee's unauthorized purchase of stock for a customer's account for a prior employer. The court held that the termination provision was ambiguous because the language implied that there would be prior coverage for employee who was hired with knowledge of dishonest conduct. However, the court refused to construe the ambiguity against the bonding company due to prior course of conduct between the bonding company and the insured whereby the insured had twice contacted bonding company prior to employment of individuals with blemished past for purposes of determining whether coverage could be obtained. *William C. Roney & Co. v. Fed. Ins. Co.*, 674 F.2d 587, 588-92.

8th Cir. 1993 (S.D.). First Dakota National Bank, after buying failed American State Bank, sued its fidelity insurer for losses allegedly caused by dishonest former employees of American, seeking recovery under two fidelity bonds. The insurer contended that American was aware of dishonest acts by the subject employees as of a given date, which terminated coverage for such employees thereafter. The court held that the knowledge of the two dishonest officers themselves could not be imputed to the bank because their interests were adverse to those of the bank, and there was insufficient evidence that a non-colluding officer learned of a loss "covered under the bond" as of the given date. *First Dakota Nat'l Bank v. St. Paul Fire & Marine Ins. Co.*, 2 F.3d 801, 806-08.

8th Cir. 1991 (Mo.). A securities broker appealed the district court's order denying coverage under a Brokers Blanket Bond (Form 14) for losses sustained because of an employee's fraud. The Eighth Circuit affirmed the district court's denial of coverage based upon the automatic termination provision where prior to the time of the fraud that gave rise to the claim under the bond, the broker had knowledge of at least four previous complaints by its clients alleging fraud and misrepresentation with respect to the same employee. *Newhard, Cook & Co. v. Ins. Co. of N. Am.*, 929 F.2d 1355, 1357-58.

8th Cir. 1975 (Mo.). The court found that an insured bank, which knew that its president was part owner of a livestock company, knew that the president had previously used his position as bank officer to give the livestock company immediate credit on checks deposited but not yet collected, that this practice had been criticized by comptroller of the currency, and that the president had made arrangements with another bank to cover checks drawn on the livestock company's account on the day they arrived at that bank. Thus, the court concluded that the insured had knowledge of the dishonest and fraudulent acts of the bank president, thereby terminating Bankers Blanket Bond as to the president prior to the instant loss, precluding coverage. *First Nat'l Bank v. Transam. Ins. Co.*, 514 F.2d 981, 984-88.

8th Cir. 1971 (S.D.). Even though the employees' acts underlying their dishonest conduct were not hidden or concealed, no other employees understood the true nature of the acts. Accordingly, the termination provision did not apply as the insured lacked sufficient knowledge of dishonest or fraudulent conduct to trigger it. *Gen. Fin. Corp. v. Fid. & Cas. Co. of N.Y.*, 439 F.2d 981, 987.

8th Cir. 1970 (Ark.). Insured's branch manager's knowledge that an employee had previously committed tire theft was imputed to insured and barred coverage as to that employee. *Ritchie Grocer Co. v. Aetna Cas. & Sur. Co.*, 426 F.2d 499, 500-04.

10th Cir. 1994 (Utah). The FDIC, in its corporate capacity, sued fidelity insurers to recover on two Savings and Loan Blanket Bonds for losses caused by alleged fraud and negligence of former officers and directors of a failed savings and loan. Both bonds provided for termination of coverage as to any employee upon learning of any dishonest act committed by such person. The court held that automatic termination provisions would apply only if a non-colluding person learned of the dishonest acts prior to the latest date of the relevant transactions in the case. *FDIC v. Oldenburg*, 34 F.3d 1529, 1548-49.

10th Cir. 1991 (Okla.). Where bank officer was aware of check kiting scheme by bank's chairman and withheld such information from her monthly reports, such actions constituted collusion with the chairman and did not trigger automatic termination of policy. Alternatively, court held that applying the automatic termination provision would be contrary to the legislative intent of Oklahoma insurance statutes. *Adair State Bank v. Am. Cas. Co.*, 949 F.2d 1067, 1075-76.

10th Cir. 1970 (Okla.). Evidence supported finding that directors of insured bank did not have notice of fraudulent acts of bank president-director, who recycled overdrafts and covered overdrafts in commercial accounts by fictitious drafts granting fictitious loans, by reason of directors' examination of national bank examiner's report disapproving officer's holding bookkeepers' turn-backs, and that directors should not have had notice of fraud by reason of contents of bank's records. Directors thus had notice only of a practice not necessarily in accord with best banking practices, and fraud was not "disclosed" until insured bank's chairman was advised by bank president of his check cycling, which was thereupon verified by national bank examiners. *First Nat'l Bank v. Sec. Mut. Cas. Co.*, 431 F.2d 1025, 1027-29.

10th Cir. 1966 (N.M.). The court held that when the insured's officials had reason to believe that president had committed fraud but failed to notify its fidelity carrier within fifteen days as required under the bond, the insured was precluded from recovery. The court noted that discovery of an employee's fraudulent act occurs when the insured is in possession of knowledge that would justify a careful and prudent man in charging another with fraud or dishonesty. *Hidden Splendor Mining Co. v. Gen. Ins. Co. of Am.*, 370 F.2d 515, 516-20.

10th Cir. 1936 (Okla.). The insured's secretary-treasurer procured blanket position bonds to protect against misappropriation by employees. The secretary-treasurer certified in the bond application that the insured had no knowledge of employees' infidelity. The secretary-treasurer's knowledge that he and two others had embezzled money from the company was not imputable to the company since the board of directors had made the decision to secure bonds and his act in submitting applications was merely ministerial. Accordingly the insured was not precluded from recovering under the bond. *Md. Cas. Co. v. Tulsa Indus. Loan & Inv. Co.*, 83 F.2d 14, 16-17.

D. Ariz. 1994. The RTC brought an action to recover on a fidelity bond issued to a savings and loan association. Losses were sustained when the insured's president approved an illegal loan. The bond contained a provision terminating coverage as to any employee when one or more non-colluding insureds, directors or officers learned of any dishonest or fraudulent act committed by the employee. Testimony by the insured's CFO and vice-president revealed that both knew that the president had authorized the illegal loan and suspected that the president had not been truthful about how the loan would be handled. The court found that this evidence was sufficient to implicate the termination provision and granted summary judgment for the insurer. *RTC v. Aetna Cas. & Sur. Co.*, 873 F. Supp. 1386, 1390-93.

D. Conn. 1997. Insured savings institution sought coverage for loan losses allegedly caused by loans the President recommended to the Board without disclosing his interest in the entities receiving the loans. The district court entered summary judgment in favor of insurer based upon evidence that, prior to the initiation of the bond period, non-colluding members of the insured's board learned of the president's dishonesty with respect to the first of the nine loans, but, because "the loan was performing . . . did not take action." Thus, the court also ruled coverage was barred under a section of the bond that required the insured to provide notice to the insurer at the earliest practicable moment, not to exceed thirty days after discovery of the loss. *Cmty. Sav. Bank v. Fed. Ins. Co.*, 960 F. Supp. 16, 20-21.

Bankr. N.D. Ga. 1995. A Chapter 7 bankruptcy trustee brought action to recover under employee fidelity policy for losses suffered by debtor-insured arising from employee theft. The policy contained provisions (1) requiring the insured to notify the insurer no later than sixty days after an officer of the insured obtained knowledge or discovered a loss or an occurrence which may become a loss; and (2) immediately terminating coverage as to any employee upon discovery by the insured, or its non-colluding partners or officers, of theft or other fraudulent or dishonest acts by said employee. The court held that the termination provision validly limited coverage because leaving a demonstrably dishonest person in a position to cause losses through dishonesty increases the risk beyond the point that the insurer believes it can make a profit on the premium charged. Accordingly the court granted summary judgment for the insured. *In re Prime Commercial Corp.*, 187 B.R. 785, 802-08.

M.D. Ga. 1967. Knowledge of partner who had sole and complete management of operations of insured unincorporated bank as to his own misappropriation was imputable to insured bank at time partner made application for Bankers Blanket Bond, even though application provided that such knowledge as any officer signing for bank may have in respect to his own personal acts and conduct is not imputable to bank. *Hartford Acc. & Indem. Co. v. Hartley*, 275 F. Supp. 610, 618-20.

D. Idaho 2010. The insured credit union sought coverage for the embezzlement of an employee. Several years prior to the discovery of the embezzlement it was discovered that the employee had made an unauthorized attempt to modify the due date of the loan at issue. The insurer argued that the bond terminated as to the employee when the unauthorized modifications were initially discovered. The court agreed with the insurer's broad definition of "dishonest or fraudulent," holding that it did not require a covered or criminal or act, or even an intent to cause harm, but also held that the issue of dishonesty was a question of fact. *Pioneer Fed. Credit Union v. CUMIS Ins. Soc'y, Inc.*, Case No. 08-00496 (Sept. 8, 2010).

N.D. Ill. 1990. The issuer of a fidelity bond moved for summary judgment based upon a bond provision stating that the bond "shall be terminated or canceled as to any Employee . . . as soon as the insured shall learn of any dishonest or fraudulent act on the part of such Employee." A rider to the bond stated that "[d]ishonest or fraudulent acts as used in this Insuring Agreement shall mean only dishonest or fraudulent acts committed by such Employee with the manifest intent: (a) to cause the insured to sustain such loss; and (b) to obtain financial benefit for the employee . . . ." The court held that a dishonest or fraudulent act as used in the termination clause meant an act causing a covered loss, not just any dishonest act. Thus, a belief by one employee that another was dishonest did not invoke the termination clause; only learning of a dishonest act causing a covered loss could do so. Thus, the court denied the motion. *In re Conticommodity Servs., Inc. Sec. Litig.*, 733 F. Supp. 1555, 1577-79.

E.D. La. 1993. A bank brought an action against its insurer under a Bankers Blanket Bond, claiming damages for losses allegedly caused by a former loan officer who issued fraudulent reports in connection with proposed loans. The district court held that a clause of the bond. terminating coverage for employee dishonesty when insured bank "learned" of the particular employee's dishonest or fraudulent act, applied when the bank had actual knowledge of facts which would cause a reasonable person in the bank's position to infer that the employee had committed dishonest acts. *First Nat'l Bank v. Lustig*, 150 F.R.D. 548, 550.

D. Mass. 1985. Suit was brought by an insured against a fidelity insurer seeking to recover on a Fidelity Name Schedule Bond for losses resulting from the dishonest acts of an administrator. The court held that due to its failure to give notice as required by the bond, the insured could not recover. The court also held that the notice provision of the bond could be invoked by the fidelity insurer upon proof that some person in authority for the insured had knowledge fifteen days before written notice was given of the act of the employee which indicated a probable claim of fraud by the employee. *Boston Mut. Life Ins. Co. v. Fireman's Fund Ins. Co.*, 613 F. Supp. 1090, 1093-1107.

S.D. Miss. 2012. Where a bank had access to sufficient information to determine that a vault under an employee's charge was short cash but did not appreciate the fact that a dishonest or fraudulent act was occurring, the court would not impute knowledge to the bank based on the contents of written records so as to trigger the termination provision. According to the court, knowledge under the termination provision required an appreciation that dishonest or fraudulent acts were occurring and could not be based on mere imputed knowledge of wrongdoing. *FDIC v. Denson*, 908 F. Supp. 2d 792, 804-06.

D.N.J. 1993. Sportswear company sought recovery under comprehensive dishonesty, disappearance, and destruction policy for inventory and cash losses resulting from an employee's dishonesty. Defendant insurer moved for summary judgment, claiming it was not liable under the policy based upon plaintiff insured's prior knowledge of employee dishonesty, and the motion was granted. The court concluded that the New Jersey Supreme Court would find enforceable a clause that excluded fidelity coverage for an employee if the insured learned of a dishonest act by that employee prior to policy inception, and found that plaintiff had sufficient information of the employee's dishonest and fraudulent acts while the application was pending to trigger that clause of the policy. *Cooper Sportswear Mfg. Co. v. Hartford Cas. Ins. Co.*, 818 F. Supp. 721, 723-25.

D.N.J. 1977. The court held that the mere fact that board of directors of the insured bank may have had knowledge, by virtue of state banking department reports of examination, that the amount of ship loans was excessive and their documentation poor, was not by itself sufficient to warrant a conclusion by the board that the bank president and an attorney-director were guilty of dishonest acts. Accordingly the insured lacked knowledge sufficient to trigger termination and the court found that it could recover under the bond. *Midland Bank & Trust Co. v. Fid. & Deposit Co. of Md.*, 442 F. Supp. 960, 971-73.

Bankr. S.D.N.Y. 1992. Securities Dealer Blanket Bond issuer moved for summary judgment on complaint by Chapter 7 Trustee of securities brokerage firm. The court granted summary judgment in favor of the insurer, concluding that the stockbroker-employee's trading for his own account, though a violation of company policy, did not qualify as dishonest or fraudulent acts within the meaning of the employee dishonesty coverage provision bond. Further, the court held that even if such acts had qualified as dishonest or fraudulent for purposes of coverage under the bond, coverage terminated pursuant to the automatic termination provision of the bond by virtue of the insured's knowledge of such trading by the employee on a prior occasion. Despite such knowledge, the insured had permitted the employee to continue his brokerage activities after the first violation because the employee made up for the loss. The court found that the insured's decision to condone the prior violation did not bind the insurer. *In re J.T. Moran Fin. Corp.*, 147 B.R. 335, 339-41.

M.D.N.C. 1959. Knowledge of inefficient business procedure or irregularities and discrepancies in accounts, if it is as consistent with integrity of bank employees as with their dishonesty, does not constitute a discovery of dishonesty within Bankers Blanket Bond termination provision. *Wachovia Bank & Trust Co. v. Mfrs. Cas. Ins. Co.*, 171 F. Supp. 369, 375-77.

N.D. Ohio 1964. A finance company's actual discovery in 1956 of its branch manager's specific acts of dishonesty thereafter voided coverage under a fidelity bond issued in 1957, and further precluded recovery on any prior bonds due to non-compliance with requirement that notice of dishonesty be given within fifteen days of discovery, although knowledge of amount of loss through dishonesty was not acquired until later. *City Loan & Sav. Co. v. Emp'rs Liab. Assur. Corp.*, 249 F. Supp. 633, 655-58.

W.D. Okla. 1973. A "Comprehensive Dishonesty, Disappearance and Destruction Policy-Form B" provided that coverage was terminated as to any employee immediately upon discovery by the insured of any fraudulent or dishonest act on the part of such employee. The court held that the insured had discovered its manager's dishonesty so as to terminate coverage no later than April, where board of directors of the insured had authorized loan transactions nearly identical to that for which claim asserted in February, March and April. *Alfalfa Elec. Coop., Inc. v. Travelers Indem. Co.*, 376 F. Supp. 901, 911-14.

Bankr. W.D. Penn. 1994. An insurer filed a motion for summary judgment for dismissal of claims by the insured on a fidelity policy which contained a provision for automatic termination upon discovery by the insured of fraudulent or dishonest acts by an employee. The insured's president, majority shareholder and director completed the policy application, but failed to disclose that he had engaged in embezzlement. The insurer argued that because the president knew he was guilty of embezzlement at the time the application was prepared, his knowledge was imputed to the insured and coverage was vitiated. However, the policy application provided that "[s]uch knowledge as any officer signing for the Applicant may now have in respect to his own personal acts or conduct, unknown to the Applicant, is not imputable to the Applicant." The court denied the insurer's motion for summary judgment, holding that this language reflected an intent that the knowledge of the individual who provides the information for the application will not be imputed to the insured. *In re Mechem Fin., Inc.,* 167 B.R. 799, 802-03.

D.P.R. 1991. The FDIC brought an action against an insurer on a Savings and Loan Blanket Bond seeking indemnification for alleged fraudulent acts of an employee of an insured failed bank. The insurer filed a motion for summary judgment, asserting the automatic termination provision as a defense, among others. The court denied the insurer's motion for summary judgment. The court noted that unless the bond provides otherwise, even the strongest suspicion does not amount to knowledge or discovery of an employee's dishonesty. Nothing short of actual discovery of dishonesty or positive breach of an imperative condition by the employee would terminate the bond as to the defaulting employee. Accordingly the court denied the insurer's motion for summary judgment. *FDIC v. CNA Cas. Co. of P.R.*, 786 F. Supp. 1082, 1087-89.

M.D. Tenn. 1990. The FDIC, as receiver for a failed bank, filed an action against the bank's insurer on a Bankers Blanket Bond for damages due to defalcations by the bank's president. The court held that knowledge by junior officers of amounts embezzled under the guise of "executive committee fees" did not constitute knowledge of dishonest acts. The court noted that an officer's suspicion that payments are dishonest is not sufficient to constitute discovery of dishonesty under a fidelity bond; discovery of dishonesty exists only where the officers have "knowledge which would justify a careful and prudent man in charging another with fraud or dishonesty." *FDIC v. St. Paul Fire & Marine Ins. Co.*, 738 F. Supp. 1146, 1161-62.

W.D. Wash. 2005. A supermarket brought a claim under a commercial crime policy for loss due to a robbery which was assisted by an employee. The employee had disclosed a prior conviction for grand theft auto on his employment application but the employee's supervisor claimed he had never read the application and thus did not know about the conviction. The insurer denied the claim under a termination provision which terminated coverage for an employee "upon discovery" of any theft or dishonest act. The insured claimed the employee's supervisor did not have actual knowledge of the conviction the termination provision did not apply. The court held that the phrase "discovery" was ambiguous as to whether it required actual knowledge and therefore interpreted it in favor of the insured, holding that actual knowledge was required for the termination provision to operate. Lastly, the court held that knowledge of the bookkeeper that accepted the application could not be imputed to the supervisor for purposes of the termination provision. *Akin Foods, Inc. v. Am. & Foreign Ins. Co.*, No. C04-2195, 2005 WL 2090678, at *3-4.

E.D. Wis. 2011. Court held that the termination provision did not apply where the insured was aware of an employee's dishonest or fraudulent conduct before the policy incepted. The court based its conclusion on the finding that the language "as soon as the Insured . . . learns of any dishonest or fraudulent act," being phrased in the present tense, implied that the termination provision only applied to dishonesty discovered during the policy period. The court further reasoned that the provision did not apply to dishonest acts discovered before the bond incepted because it would be illogical for a bond to "terminate" without ever having been active. *Waupaca Northwoods, LLC v. Travelers Cas. & Sur. Co. of Am.*, No. 10-C-459, 2011 WL 1563278, at *1-5.

E.D. Wis. 1945. A fidelity bond provided that it was canceled as to any employee immediately upon discovery by the insured, or by any partner or officer thereof not in collusion with such employee, of any fraudulent or dishonest act on the part of such employee. The court held that this provision had no application where evidence showed that every officer and employee of insured, with respect to employee's acts, was in collusion with him. *Duel v. Nat'l Sur. Corp.*, 64 F. Supp. 961, 966-68.

Ariz. Ct. App. 1971. The court held that different rules apply in determining whether acts prior to coverage of a fidelity bond were dishonest so as to preclude coverage for employee by a termination clause, and in determining dishonesty after issuance of bond so as to come within coverage of bond. It noted that in determining an insured employer's knowledge of prior acts, the question usually is not whether in light of all facts, including the employee's subjective intent, the employee's acts were in fact dishonest, but rather whether, based upon the facts known to the employer, the employer should reasonably have perceived the dishonesty. In the case of coverage, a different standard applies. *Md. Cas. Co. v. Clements*, 487 P.2d 437, 441-47.

Cal. 1959. Bookkeeper, who prior to the issuance of a fidelity bond had taken $20 from petty cash drawer contrary to his employer's instructions and replaced cash with duplicate freight bill to cover shortage and paid money back to employer when questioned, was guilty of fraudulent misappropriation. As such, the court held that the employer was not entitled to recover from bonding company for a subsequent misappropriation by same employee during effective period of fidelity bond. *Ciancetti v. Indem. Ins. Co. of N. Am.*, 335 P.2d 1048, 1049-50.

Conn. 1990. A store manager and bookkeeper discovered that an employee had embezzled $6,000. They arranged for the employee to repay the amount, which she did. The store owner was not notified of the employee's theft. The store brought an action on its fidelity bond two years later when the employee was again caught embezzling funds. Denying coverage, the court held the store manager's and the bookkeeper's knowledge of the employee's prior embezzlements terminated coverage pursuant to automatic termination provision of employee fidelity policies. *E. Udolf, Inc. v. Aetna Cas. & Sur. Co.*, 573 A.2d 1211, 1213-16.

Conn. Super. Ct. 2009. The court held that a termination provision did not apply to dishonesty discovered by the insured prior to the inception of the bond. The termination provision at issue provided: "This insurance is cancelled as to any 'employee': (a) Immediately upon discovery by: (1) You; or (2) Any of your partners, officers or directors not in collusion with the 'employee;' . . . of any dishonest act committed by that 'employee' whether before or after becoming employed by you." The court held the provision was ambiguous because it referred to "cancellation" not "coverage," and because the phrase "[i]mmediately upon discovery" did not make clear that coverage could terminate based on the discovery of dishonest acts that occurred before the policy incepted. Though so limiting the termination provision exposed the insurer to additional risk, the court held that the burden is on the insurer to explicitly state in the bond that there would be no coverage irrespective of whether the dishonesty is discovered during or prior to the inception of the bond. *C.A. White v. Travelers Cas. & Sur. Co. of Am.*, No. CV0850L35515, 2009 Conn. Super. LEXIS 989, at *9-33.

Ga. Ct. App. 1995. An insurer sought a declaratory judgment that its fidelity bond was terminated as to ten allegedly dishonest employees of the insured bank. The bond contained a provision terminating coverage "as to any employee . . . as soon as the insured or any director or officer not in collusion with such person, learns of any dishonest or fraudulent act committed by such person." The court held that the termination provision did not apply to the employees collectively, but instead as individuals. As such, the insurer was required to show prior knowledge of dishonest acts with respect to each of the ten allegedly dishonest employees, considered individually. *Banca Nazionale Del Lavoro v. Lloyd's*, 458 S.E.2d 142, 142-44.

Ill. App. Ct. 1995. At issue was a Public Employees' Bond containing provision canceling coverage as to any employee immediately upon discovery of any act that would constitute a liability under the bond. The court held that the cancellation provision was governed by a subjective standard, and was triggered when the insured had actual knowledge that its employees were involved in the unauthorized expenditure of funds. *Kinzer v. Fid. & Deposit Co. of Md.*, 652 N.E.2d 20, 27-30.

Iowa 1968. Knowledge of managing agent of insured bank, who was also active in management of insurance agency partially owned by insured bank, that he had been embezzling insured bank's funds was not imputable to insured bank and did not preclude recovery under Bankers Blanket Bond obtained by him. *Mechanicsville Trust & Sav. Bank v. Hawkeye-Security Ins. Co.*, 158 N.W.2d 89, 91-92.

Kan. Ct. App. 2005. Applying broad definition of "dishonest" and "fraudulent," the Court held that a bond terminated as to an employee when her employer discovered that she had surreptitiously raised her personal credit limit in violation of bank policy. The Court rejected the insured's argument that the employee's actions were a simple violation of bank policy and held that by imposing substantial discipline on the employee after discovering what she had done, the bank evidenced actual knowledge of the dishonesty of the employee's conduct. *Troy State Bank v. BancInsure, Inc.*, 109 P.3d 203, No. 92,115, 2005 Kan. App. Unpub. LEXIS 120, at *2-16.

La. 1969. Where employee whose defalcations brought about loss to insured had previously been confined in penitentiary for theft, and official of insured obtained employee's parole and gave him employment, insured could not recover on blanket crime policy in view of provision that bond shall not apply from and after the time the insured shall have knowledge or information that an employee has committed any fraudulent or dishonest act before or after date of employment by insured. *Verneco, Inc. v. Fid. & Cas. Co. of N.Y.*, 219 So. 2d 508, 510-11.

La. Ct. App. 1969. A Blanket Crime Policy provided for termination of coverage as to an employee from the time that the insured or any partner or officer thereof not in collusion had knowledge of any fraudulent or dishonest act by such employee. The court held that where the allegedly dishonest employee eight years earlier was short in his accounts, voluntarily reported the discrepancies, expressed the desire to straighten them out, and gave his own check to make appropriate adjustments, the employee's shortage was not a "fraudulent or dishonest act" such as to terminate coverage under bond. *Salley Grocer Co. v. Hartford Acc. & Indem. Co.*, 223 So. 2d 5, 6-10.

La. Ct. App. 1961. Fidelity bond was canceled under termination provision providing for termination upon discovery by employer of any act which "may be made basis of any claim" upon employer's discovery of bookkeeper's dishonesty several years prior to time claim was made, even though bookkeeper made restitution of funds embezzled on prior occasion. *Emp'rs' Liab. Assur. Co. v. S. Produce Co.*, 129 So. 2d 247, 248-49.

Me. 2002. The chairman of the board of the insured became aware that the insured's president made unauthorized personal uses of a corporate credit card. The chairman did not notify the insurer of the president's acts. The insured and president agreed that the president would stop using the credit card and repay the charges, but would keep his job. However, the president instead continued his unauthorized use of the credit card and was subsequently terminated. The court of appeals held the chairman's knowledge of the president's unauthorized use and non-payment of the debt triggered an obligation to notify the insurer as well as the automatic termination provision because the insured was aware of a dishonest act at the time the initial unauthorized charges were discovered. Moreover, the late notification by the president prejudiced the insurer. *Acadia Ins. Co v. Keiser Indus., Inc.*, 793 A.2d 495, 498-99.

Miss. 1969. Employer was under no obligation to volunteer information with respect to his knowledge of a re-employed employee's previous defalcation, and employer's knowledge thereof did not preclude coverage for subsequent defalcations by same employee, where evidence showed that issuance of one-man fidelity bond for such employee had been a condition precedent to employee's re-employment and was a transaction entirely between the employee and the bonding company. *St. Paul Fire & Marine Ins. Co. v. Comer*, 227 So. 2d 859, 861-62.

Miss. 1934. The insured bank made a claim under a Bankers Blanket Bond for unauthorized loans by an officer. The court, applying the termination provision, held that if other employees knew about the unauthorized loans, the bond terminated at that time. If the loan was not then known to other employees at the time it was made, then the bond terminated when the board subsequently approved loan. *Fid. & Deposit Co. v. Merchs. & Marine Bank*, 151 So. 373.

N.J. Super. Ct. Law Div. 1993. Mere suspicions by savings and loan about irregularities or improper conduct in its contractor's servicing of mortgages did not trigger the bond's automatic cancellation clause. Moreover, the fact that dishonesty should have been suspected in hindsight was insufficient to trigger termination. Accordingly, the termination provision was not triggered despite the fact that the insured received a letter pointing out irregularities with certain transactions. *N. Jersey Sav. & Loan Ass'n v. Fid. & Deposit Co. of Md.*, 660 A.2d 1287, 1296-98.

N.Y. App. Div. 2012. A bank brought a claim under a fidelity bond for losses caused an employee that forged the signatures of bank officers in order to authorize a number of loans. During the course of discovery the insurer found out that two years prior to the loss at issue the same employee had been reprimanded for forging signatures on credit extensions and renewals for non-performing loans. The employee was not fired at the time because the forgeries did not cause any loss as the loans were already non-performing before the employee forged the necessary signatures to extend or renew the credit. The insurer denied the claim on the ground that coverage was terminated with respect to that employee when the forgeries were discovered. The insured claimed that the termination provision did not apply since the earlier forgeries did not cause any actual loss. However, the court rejected this claim, holding that the termination provision applies to any dishonest act, irrespective of whether the dishonest act caused a financial loss. Additionally, the court held that coverage was excluded under the exclusion for "circumstances known to plaintiff prior to the inception of the bond." *Capital Bank & Trust Co. v. Gulf Ins. Co.*, 91 A.D.3d 1251, 1251-54.

N.C. Ct. App. 2004. The insured made a claim under a fidelity bond to recover for an employee's embezzlement. Prior to the inception of the bond the insured learned that the employee had been convicted of embezzling funds from a former employer. As a result the fidelity bond carrier denied the claim on the grounds that coverage for the employee had terminated at the point that the insured learned of the employee's prior embezzlement conviction. The insured contended that the termination provision didn't apply since it learned of the embezzlement conviction before the bond incepted. The Court held that the termination provision was ambiguous as to whether it applied to knowledge acquired before inception and therefore interpreted the bond in favor of the insured, holding that the provision did not apply to dishonest or fraudulent acts discovered before inception. *Home Sav. Bank v. Colonial Am. Cas. & Sur. Co.*, 598 S.E.2d 265, 267-70.

Tex. Ct. App. 1984. A bank brought suit to recover under a Bankers Blanket Bond (Form 24) for loan losses resulting from dishonest acts of a former bank president. That bank president, as a member of the insured's loan committee, approved loans to a borrower with whom he was a partner in trading securities without disclosing this relationship to the directors. The court held that coverage terminated as to the bank president when the board of directors became aware of facts from which they could infer the dishonesty, and therefore the insurer was only liable for loss on loans made before coverage terminated. In addition, renewal of the fidelity bond did not reinstate coverage for the bank president because coverage had already been terminated as to him. *Fid. & Cas. Co. of N.Y. v. Cent. Bank of Houston,* 672 S.W.2d 641, 644-47, 690.

Tex. Ct. App. 1962. Where employer knew that his employee had misappropriated $500 of the employer's funds before fidelity bond was issued covering such employee, and bond provided that it terminated as to future acts of any employee immediately upon discovery by insured of any fraudulent or dishonest act on part of an employee, subsequent misappropriation by that employee was excluded from coverage under the bond. *Larson v. Peerless Ins. Co.*, 362 S.W.2d 863, 864.

Utah Ct. App. 1991. In 1982, the insured replaced its Savings and Loan Blanket Bond issued by F&D with a similar bond issued by Aetna. The insured truthfully stated in the Aetna application that it had incurred no insurable losses over the $5,000 deductible within the past five years. At the time the sale of the Aetna bond was completed, an action by second mortgage loan recipients was pending that involved a Home Savings employee whom it had learned was engaged in fraudulent and dishonest acts and had fired in December 1981. The court held that neither Aetna nor F&D were liable for losses caused by dishonest acts by the dishonest employee that occurred after the December 1981 discovery, but *both* were liable for such acts prior to that time that were discovered within their successive bond periods. *Home Sav. & Loan v. Aetna Cas. & Sur. Co.*, 817 P.2d 341, 348-58.

SECONDARY SOURCES

David E. Bordon, *Current Issues and Positions Taken by the RTC and FDIC in Litigation Arising Under the Standard Forms 22 and 24*, in 2 FINANCIAL INSTITUTION BONDS, § T (ABA, 1992).

Michael Keeley & Toni Scott Reed, *"Superpowers" of Federal Regulators: How the Banking Crisis Created an Entire Genre of Bond Litigation*, 31 TORT & INS. L.J. 817 (1996).

Michael B. McGeehon & Martin J. O'Leary, *Termination of Coverage*, in HANDLING FIDELITY BOND CLAIMS 445 (Michael Keeley & Timothy Sukel, eds., 1999).

Maura Z. Pelleteri, Amy S. Malish & Andrea Mittleider, *Severing Ties: Application of the Termination Clause in Fidelity Bonds* (2010) (presented at 21st Annual Surety & Fidelity Claims Conference).

Hugh E. Reynolds, Jr. & James Dimos, *Symposium: The Restatement of Suretyship: Fidelity Bonds and the Restatement,* 34 WM. & MARY L. REV. 1249 (1993).

Sandra M. Stone & Barry F. MacEntee, *Defining Employee Dishonesty Within the Framework of the Automatic Termination Provision and the Fidelity Insuring Agreement,* XVII FID. L.J. 143 (2011).

Susan Koehler Sullivan & Teresa Schoenhaar, *Conditions to Recovery: Termination or Cancellation, in* FINANCIAL INSTITUTION BONDS 679-710 (Duncan Clore ed., 3rd ed. 2008).

Annotation, *Federal Deposit Insurance Corporation May Not Recover Under Insolvent Thrift's Fidelity Bond,* 14 INS. LIT. RPTR. 170 (1992).

Annotation, *Fiduciary Insurance and Financial Institutions in the Post— FIRREA Era,* 14 INS. LIT. RPTR. 40 (1992).

Annotation, *Bankers Blanket Bond's Termination of Coverage Upon FDIC Takeover Did Not Violate Public Policy,* 12 INS. LIT. RPTR. 349 (1990).

Chapter 4

Important Riders and Miscellaneous Topics

SECTION 1 — A CONCISE HISTORY OF THE FINANCIAL INSTITUTION BOND, STANDARD FORM NO. 24*

A. Introduction and Background

The United States insurance industry has offered financial institution bond coverage for almost a century. Over the decades, coverages, exclusions, definitions, and conditions have evolved for many reasons. Market forces and customer demand, in particular, have played a prominent role. The loss history of fidelity insurers and court decisions that restrict or expand coverage have also led to bond form revisions. But, perhaps the most significant factor contributing to the evolution of financial institution bond coverage is the change in how financial institutions deliver their product and service to customers. Operations and business practices can create new exposures and risks that must be addressed directly, either by providing coverage for the new risk or excluding it. In recent years, technology has been a prominent factor in driving how financial institutions conduct business. This article will trace the development of the Financial Institution Bond, Standard Form No. 24 as affected by the various factors noted above, and will provide an update regarding the most recent changes to Form 24 since 2004.[1]

---

* By Robert J. Duke, Surety & Fidelity Association of America, Washington, D.C.
[1] There are several published articles on the history of fidelity coverage, and particularly the Financial Institution Bond. This article builds on the works by these practitioners, particularly by providing an update regarding developments after 2004. *See* Robert J. Duke, *A Brief History of the Financial Institution Bond, in* FINANCIAL INSTITUTION BONDS 1 (Duncan L. Clore ed., 3d ed. 2008); Edward G. Gallagher & Robert J. Duke, *A Concise History of Fidelity Insurance, in* HANDLING FIDELITY BOND CLAIMS 1

This article will also examine some of the recent developments of financial institution bond coverage as affected by technology.

1. Fidelity Bonds—Early and Ancient Developments

Financial Institution Bonds, which insure the honesty of the institution's employees and provide coverage for other crime risks, were developed in the beginning of the twentieth century. However, the history of Financial Institution Bonds begins with the history of surety bonds, which is centuries old.

A surety bond is a three-party agreement by which one party—the surety—guarantees the obligation owed by a second party—the principal—to a third party—the obligee.[2] Suretyship is an ancient concept that has existed for thousands of years. Principles of suretyship were referenced in the eleventh century in the Magna Carta.[3]

Surety bonds provide the benefit of financial security in the event that a certain obligation is not performed. One such obligation that has

---

(Michael Keeley & Sean Duffy eds., 2d ed. 2005); Edward G. Gallagher, *A Concise History of the Financial Institution Bond Standard Form No. 24, 1986 Edition*, in ANNOTATED FINANCIAL INSTITUTION BONDS 5 (Michael Keeley ed., 2d ed. 2004); Edward G. Gallagher et. al., *A Brief History of the Financial Institution Bond*, in FINANCIAL INSTITUTION BONDS 1 (Duncan L. Clore ed., 2d ed. 1998); Robin V. Weldy, *History of the Bankers Blanket Bond and the Financial Institution Bond Standard Form No. 24 with Comments on the Drafting Process*, in ANNOTATED BANKERS BLANKET BOND 3 (Harvey C. Koch ed., 2d Supp. 1988); Robin V. Weldy, *History of Financial Institution Bonds*, in BANKERS AND OTHER FINANCIAL INSTITUTION BONDS 1 (American Bar Association 1979); Robin V. Weldy, *A Survey of Recent Changes in Financial Institution Bonds*, 12 FORUM 895 (1977); John F. Fitzgerald, *Comments on Current Changes in Financial Institution Blanket Bonds*, AMERICAN BAR ASSOCIATION SECTION OF INSURANCE NEGLIGENCE AND COMPENSATION LAW PROCEEDINGS 89 (1969); Robert A. Babcock, *History of Fidelity Coverage*, in COMMERCIAL BLANKET BOND ANNOTATED 1 (William F. Haug ed. 1985); Francis L. Kenney, Jr., *A Dissertation on Fidelity and Surety Law*, 1962 INS. L.J. 763.

2   John B. Fitzgerald et. al., PRINCIPALS OF SURETYSHIP 1.3 (2d ed. 2003).
3   Magna Carta of 1215 ch. 9 ("Neither we nor our bailiffs will seize for any debt any land or rent, so long as the chattles of the debtor are sufficient to repay the debt; nor will those who have gone surety for the debtor be distrained so long as the principal debtor is himself able to pay the debt.").

been secured by bonds over the years is an employee's obligation to remain faithful and honest to her employer. Thus, fidelity protection was provided by way of a surety bond. In the late 1800s and early 1900s, as a means to enhance their employment prospects, household servants in England would offer to provide a fidelity bond to their employers.[4] Professional individual sureties would conduct a background check of the individual and would pay the employer for his losses caused by the employee's dishonesty.[5] During the industrial revolution corporate sureties moved onto the scene and soon replaced individual sureties in securing the honesty of employees in various commercial enterprises.[6] As commercial activity expanded, obtaining a separate bond for each employee became cumbersome.[7] Corporate sureties developed fidelity bonds that covered the dishonest acts of multiple employees: name schedule bonds and position schedule bonds. Thus began the progression of fidelity bonds from a three-party surety product to the form it takes today, a two-party insurance agreement.

2. *Early Developments in Financial Institution Bonds—the Birth of Form 1*

The rapid growth of the banking industry in the early 1900s, which required the hiring of many yet largely inexperienced employees, exposed banks' need for employee dishonesty and other coverages.[8] Insurers responded to the demand by providing various types of "honesty insurance." Unfortunately, the banking community had more problems than just unfaithful employees. Beset by robbery, theft, and other perils, a bank had to purchase a number of separate bonds and policies to be

---

4 David A. Lewis, *History of Fidelity Coverage: Types of Commercial Crime Policies,* in COMMERCIAL CRIME POLICY 1 (Gilbert J. Schroeder ed., 1st ed. 1997).
5 *Id.*
6 *Id.*
7 Robert A. Babcock, *History of Fidelity Coverage,* in COMMERCIAL BLANKET BOND ANNOTATED 1 (William F. Haug ed., 1985).
8 Edward G. Gallagher et. al., *A Brief History of the Financial Institution Bond,* in FINANCIAL INSTITUTION BONDS 6 (Duncan L. Clore ed., 2d ed. 1998).

fully covered.[9] Insurance regulation at the time prohibited United States companies from offering multiple coverages under a single policy.[10] Then, in 1912, the New York State Commissioner of Insurance permitted insurers to combine various types of unrelated coverages for financial institutions into a single bond.[11] Four years later, the Surety Association of America (now called the Surety & Fidelity Association of America),[12] with the assistance of the American Bankers Association, developed the "Bankers Blanket Bond," the first standard form multiple-line insurance against certain commercial risks and the forerunner of the modern "Financial Institution Bond."[13]

The first Bankers Blanket Bond, Form 1, was a two-party agreement that protected banks against employee dishonesty, loss of property on the premises and in transit through robbery or theft, loss by false pretenses, and other risks.[14] The employee dishonesty coverage under Form 1 indemnified the insured against loss "through any dishonest act of any of the employees wherever committed directly or by collusion with others."[15] Initially, only certain underwriting syndicates offered Form 1, and then only to preferred risks. The purpose of this limitation was to develop reliable loss ratios.[16] After Form 1 proved profitable, the syndicates dissolved and individual companies began underwriting the bonds.

The SFAA's efforts to develop Form 1 likely were the result of a desire to develop a competing product to the insurance policy developed by Lloyd's of London, which offered coverage for employee dishonesty, theft, burglary, fire, and disappearance in transit—all under a single policy.[17] In fact, apparently to encourage such institutions to buy the

---

9 Robin V. Weldy, *History of the Bankers Blanket Bond and the Financial Institution Bond Standard Form No. 24 with Comments on the Drafting Process*, in ANNOTATED BANKERS BLANKET BOND 1, 3 (Harvey C. Koch ed., 2d Supp. 1988).
10 Gallagher, *supra* note 8, at 7.
11 *Id.*
12 Hereinafter SFAA.
13 Weldy, *supra* note 9, at 4.
14 Gallagher, *supra* note 8, at 7.
15 SAMUEL J. ARENA, JR. et al., THE "MANIFEST INTENT" HANDBOOK 4 (American Bar Association 2002).
16 Weldy, *supra* note 9, at 4.
17 Gallagher, *supra* note 9, at 7.

new Form 1, the SFAA developed a special rider, which provided superseded suretyship with a discovery period of up to five years for bonds substituted for Lloyd's coverage.[18] Thus, even from the beginning, the development of the Financial Institution Bond was spurred by competitive considerations.

3. *Form 2 to Form 24*

In 1920, the SFAA introduced Bankers Blanket Bond, Standard Form No. 2.[19] Form 2 provided coverage for employee dishonesty, on premises "robbery, burglary, larceny ... theft, hold-up or destruction," and in-transit "robbery, larceny ... theft or hold-up."[20] Form 2 contained an amended "Superseded Suretyship Rider" and a "Teller's Short, Misplacement Rider."[21]

On the whole, Form 2 represented a pullback in coverage compared to Form 1. Indemnity provided under Form 1 "is granted to the bank in the ordinary transaction of its business. It need not have been the victim of burglary, robbery or hold-up, or fire: it need not have suffered from the dishonest or criminal acts of its clerks."[22] A commentator observed that coverage under the Lloyd's form or Form 2 was not as broad.[23] One noteworthy limitation of coverage occurred in the language of the "Loss Insured" provision. Form 1 had covered "any loss." However, industry analysts recognized that such language could be broadly construed to include not only direct losses, but also indirect or consequential losses, such as insolvency, bad debts, or a change in the value of securities.[24]

---

18 Minutes of Committee on Bankers Blanket Bonds, November 17, 1915 (on file at SFAA). A superseded surety rider typically provided coverage for losses sustained during the period of time the superseded bond would have been in effect, if losses were discovered after the cancelled bond's cut-off period for presenting claims had expired. *See, e.g., Commercial Casualty Ins. Co. v. Hartford Accident & Indem. Co.*, 2 N.E.2d 517, 521 (N.Y. 1936).
19 Weldy, *supra* note 9, at 4.
20 The Surety & Fidelity Association of America, Bankers Blanket Bond, Standard Form No. 2 (1920) [hereinafter Form 2].
21 Gallagher, *supra* note 8, at 9-10.
22 Towner Rating Bureau, *Bankers Blanket Bonds: Analysis of American Forms and Lloyds H.A.N.(C) Form*, at 4 (Aug. 4, 1920).
23 *Id.*
24 Gallagher, *supra* note 8, at 10 (citing Towner Rating Bureau, *supra* note 21, at 4.

Form 2 consequently narrowed the scope of coverage by insuring only "direct" loss.[25]

Form 2 introduced a number of other limiting changes. For example, the definition of "money" under "Property Insured" contained in Form 1, which had included losses of intangible assets, was narrowed by Form 2 to refer only to tangible assets that could be taken and carried away: "currency, coin, bullion, bank notes (signed or unsigned), Federal Reserve notes and uncancelled United States Postage and revenue stamps."[26]

A commentator characterized Form 2's coverage as primarily guaranteeing the safety of the insured's premises and the honesty of its employees.[27] Notably, coverage under Form 1, which had extended to "negligence in the ordinary administration of the bank's affairs"[28] had created significant loss experience. Again, the shift from Form 1 to Form 2 appears to have been driven by loss experience that required a re-evaluation of what exposures can be underwritten profitably and prudently.

During the 1920s and 1930s, surety underwriters experimented with different types of bond forms, introducing separate blanket bonds for stockbrokers, mutual savings banks, savings and loan associations, and other types of financial institutions.[29] Competitive considerations were at play. For example, the minutes of the Bankers Blanket Bond Committee that was involved in the drafting of Form 5 reflect that Form 5 was adopted "[i]n order to meet London Lloyd's competition on a new form of Bankers Blanket Bond offered by them to Savings Banks."[30] Other than Forms 1 and 2, additional forms of Bankers Blanket Bonds were Forms 7 and 8, introduced in 1923.[31] By 1924, the SFAA had developed a wide variety of financial institution bonds: Form 5 (for

---

25 Form 2.
26 *Id.*
27 *Id.*; Towner Rating Bureau, *supra* note 22, at 4.
28 *Id.*
29 Weldy, *supra* note 9 at 4.
30 Minutes of the Bankers Blanket Bond Committee, May 31, 1922 (on file at SFAA).
31 Gallagher, *supra* note 8, at 12 (citing Robin V. Weldy, *The Evolution of the Financial Institution Bond: A New Perspective* at 1 (unpublished paper submitted at the International Association of Defense Counsel mid-winter program on January 26, 1991)).

savings banks); Form 6 (for Federal Reserve Banks); Form 9 (for War Finance Corporation Banks); Form 10 (for Federal Home Loan Land Banks); Forms 12, 13, and 14 for stockbrokers; and Form 16 (for Building and Loan Associations).[32] During the 1920s and 1930s, the earliest versions of the Forgery Insuring Agreement and the Securities Insuring Agreement were offered as riders to the basic bond.

After the release of new forms and coverages, the SFAA made a number of "adjustments" under its various forms based on loss experience and competitive conditions.[33] For example, in a report dated March 16, 1934, the Bankers Blanket Bond Subcommittee on Revision reported various recommended revisions to the financial institution forms, including: an insertion of a provision which limits the underwriter's liability to the penalty of the bond regardless of the number of years the bond remains in force, a reduction of the discovery period to three months in cases where the bond is superseded by a bond written by the same insurer, and an exclusion of coverage for aircraft-related losses.[34] In addition, the SFAA modified the existing cancellation clause in all bankers and brokers bonds so that, where an insured institution was taken over by a receiver, liquidator, or regulatory agency, coverage would cease.[35] The idea was to stop any accumulation of liability in case the bond was reinstated in favor of the receiver, liquidator, or similar entities.[36]

B. The Form 24

In March of 1941, the SFAA introduced Bankers Blanket Bond Standard Form No. 24.[37] The stated "primary purpose" of Form 24 was to "provide superior coverage adapted to the special requirements of

---

32 *Id.* at 12 n.45 (citing Robin V. Weldy, *supra* note 30, at 1).
33 *Id.* at 13 (citing Dean P. Felton, *The History of the Financial Institution Bond* (1991) (unpublished manuscript available from Mr. Felton)).
34 Report of Bankers Blanket Bond Subcommittee on Revision, March 16, 1934 (on file at SFAA).
35 *Id.*
36 Gallagher, *supra* note 8, at 14.
37 Weldy, *supra* note 9, at 4; The Surety & Fidelity Association of America, Financial Institution Bond, Standard Form No. 24 (Special Form) (Mar. 1941).

those financial institutions which conduct the greatest volume and variety of banking transactions."[38] Form 24 afforded the following coverage:

(a) fidelity losses;

(b) loss of property while in the Insured's offices resulting from robbery, larceny, burglary, theft, false pretenses, hold up, misplacement, mysterious unexplainable disappearance and damage or destruction to Property as defined in the bond;

(c) loss of Property while in transit sustained through robbery, larceny, theft, hold up, mysterious unexplainable disappearance;

(d) loss resulting from check forgery and forgery of similar instruments;

(e) forgery of or on securities, promissory notes or resulting from guaranteeing or witnessing of signatures; and

(f) misplacement or unexplainable disappearance.

Under Form 24, the coverage pendulum swung in the opposite direction, from restricted coverage to broad coverage. Form 24 offered expanded coverage compared to Form 8 by adopting a broad definition of property and broad forgery protection.[39] Perhaps the most significant change was the inclusion of the word "criminal" in the fidelity insuring agreement; thus, covered losses included not only dishonest and fraudulent acts, but also criminal acts.[40] This ultimately had the effect of making losses for violations of federal or state banking statutes covered under Form 24.

1. Form 24's Subsequent Revisions up to 1986

The SFAA introduced revisions to Form 24 in 1946, 1951, 1969, 1980, and 1986 to clarify insuring agreements, add commonly used riders, and generally ensure that the bond conformed to the current

---

38 *Compare* The Surety & Fidelity Association of America, Bankers Blanket Bond Standard Form No 24 (Special Form) Adopted 3/7/41 *with* Bankers Blanket Bond, Standard Form No. 8—Revised (on file at SFAA).
39 *Id.*
40 Bankers Blanket Bond, Standard Form No. 24 (Special Form) (March 1941).

SECTION 1 — A CONCISE HISTORY OF THE FINANCIAL INSTITUTION BOND 541

banking practices of the day.[41] In the years after its introduction, the SFAA adopted a number of changes to Form 24.[42]

Among the changes made in the 1946 form, was adding loss through vandalism and malicious mischief to the Premises Insuring Clause.[43] The 1946 form included an optional rider to include coverage on attorneys as employees.[44] Many of the changes in the 1951 form involved the incorporation of revisions that formerly were available by rider: the broader definition of employee that includes attorneys, a broadened in-transit coverage, and counterfeit currency coverage.[45]

Prior to 1954, Form 24 was in a "Loss Sustained" form, which required the insured to establish the date when a loss occurred, and the relevant coverage was the particular coverage applicable on that date. In 1954, by rider, the SFAA converted Form 24 and several other bond forms to "Loss Discovery" forms.[46] Under the "Loss Discovery" forms, the coverage available on the date of the discovery of the loss was the applicable coverage, but there was no coverage for losses discovered after the termination or cancellation of the bond. However, for an additional premium, an insured could obtain a twelve-month discovery period effective after the bond's cancellation.[47]

During the years between the 1951 revision and the 1969 revision, judicial construction of Form 24 precipitated a number of changes in the bond language. For example, as noted above, the fidelity insuring agreement in Form 24 applied to losses arising from dishonest, fraudulent, and criminal acts. However, a decision by the Illinois Court

---

41 Weldy, *supra* note 9, at 4.
42 An in-depth treatment of the changes in Form 24 in the 1951 and 1969 editions can be found in John Fitzgerald, *Comments on Current Changes in Financial Institution Bonds, Negligence and Compensation Law Proceedings* (ABA Section of Insurance 1969). This section will highlight a few key revisions and address the revisions in the 1980 and 1986 forms.
43 The Surety & Fidelity Association of America, Analysis of Changes in Bankers Blanket Bonds Standard Forms Nos. 2 and 24 Revised to March 1, 1946.
44 *Id.*
45 The Surety & Fidelity Association of America, Analysis of Changes in Bankers Blanket Bonds Standard Forms Nos. 2 and 24 Revised to June, 1951.
46 Gallagher, *supra* note 8, at 17; The Surety & Fidelity Association of America, Discovery Rider, SR 5506, September 1954.
47 *Id.*

of Appeal prompted the SFAA to delete the word "criminal" from the fidelity coverage.[48]

In *Home Indemnity Co. v. Reynolds & Co.*,[49] the Home Indemnity Company issued Brokers Blanket Bonds to Reynolds & Company, a broker and dealer in stocks and commodities. The insured's salesmen sold securities in violation of an Illinois statute that prohibited the sale of unregistered securities. The issue before the court was whether the acts of the salesmen were dishonest or criminal under the terms of the fidelity insuring agreement of the insured's bonds.[50] The court held that the violation of the Illinois statute, although not dishonest or fraudulent, was "criminal" as that term was used in the bond. The court reasoned that the word "criminal" must appear in the bonds for some purpose. It must refer to acts of employees which violate public laws, as distinguished from those acts generally characterized as fraudulent or dishonest.[51] Thus, the court's interpretation of "criminal" expanded coverage beyond that originally intended: criminal acts by employees involving theft and embezzlement. As a result, the word "criminal" ultimately was eliminated in the fidelity insuring agreement of the 1969 form.

Similarly, in response to a decision by the Missouri Supreme Court, the SFAA amended the On Premises Insuring Agreement, which had provided coverage for money and securities in the possession of the insured's customer under certain conditions.[52] In *Brugioni v. Maryland Casualty Co.*,[53] the insured bank's customer was robbed on the insured's parking lot. The customer sought to collect directly against the surety, arguing that the customer was a third-party beneficiary of the bond issued by the surety. Even though the customer was not a named insured and contributed "nothing directly" to the premium payment, the court concluded that he was a third-party beneficiary of the bond and could sue

---

48 Gallagher, *supra* note 8, at 17.
49 187 N.E.2d 274 (Ill. App. Ct. 1962).
50 The bonds insured against: "(A) Any loss through any dishonest, fraudulent or criminal act of any of the Employees, committed anywhere and whether committed along or in collusion with others, including loss of Property through any such act of any of the Employees." *Id.* at 280 (quoting bond language).
51 *Id.* at 280-81.
52 Gallagher, *supra* note 8, at 18.
53 382 S.W.2d 707 (Mo. 1964).

the surety directly.[54] In response to the holding in *Brugioni* and "[t]o avoid the implication of any third party coverage to customers or representatives of the Insured," the 1969 form's On Premises Insuring Agreement provided that a loss by a customer will be covered only if, at the option of the insured, it is included in the insured's proof of loss.[55] Members of the SFAA drafting committee expressed concern that the adverse case law would open the way to third-party action under the bond.

To address this same concern, Section 4 of Form 24 also was amended to state:

> This bond is for the use and benefit only of the Insured named in the Declarations and the Underwriter shall not be liable for loss sustained by anyone other than the Insured unless the Insured, in its sole discretion and at its option, includes such loss in the Insured's proof of loss.[56]

The 1969 Form 24 also contained a revised and expanded Loan Exclusion and a new Check Kiting Exclusion to address a series of check kiting cases that held that the bond covered losses incurred due to a check kiting scheme. For example, in *Hartford Accident & Indemnity Co. v. FDIC*,[57] a customer deposited checks in the insured bank and then withdrew cash equal to the amount of the checks before the insured presented the checks for collection. The checks bounced and the advanced funds could not be retrieved from the customer. Resulting losses were so severe that the insured was ultimately taken over by the FDIC.

The FDIC then sought to recover the check kiting losses from the surety that had issued the insured's fidelity coverage as a loss through "false pretenses."[58] The bond at issue covered loss of property "through robbery, burglary, common-law or statutory larceny, theft, false pretenses, hold up . . . ." In response to the FDIC's action, the insurer claimed that the advance of funds on the uncollected checks was

---

54 *Id.* at 712-13.
55 The Surety & Fidelity Association of America, Analysis of Changes, Bankers Blanket Bond, Standard Form No. 24, Revised to April 1969.
56 *Id.*
57 204 F.2d 933 (8th Cir. 1953) (applying Missouri law).
58 *Id.* at 935.

equivalent to a loan, and therefore subject to the loan loss exclusion of the bond.[59]

The court disagreed, explaining that it saw no difference between a robbery and an advancement of funds based upon a customer's misrepresentation that a check was valid. In either example, the court reasoned, the person who received the funds from the insured would be obligated to reimburse the bank. Therefore, if one were a loan loss, the other would be also, which leads to an "unsound" result.[60] The existence of an obligation to reimburse the bank does not make the transaction a loan. Construing the passing of a bad check as obtaining money by "false pretenses," the court concluded that the loss was covered by the bond.[61]

To counter the courts' limited construction of the loan loss exclusion, the SFAA expanded the exclusion to refer to both "loans" and other similar transactions "in the nature of" a loan. In addition, the loan loss exclusion was amended to add a check kiting exclusion.[62]

In the ten years from 1969 to 1979, the SFAA developed a number of riders to amend the standard bond language that eventually were incorporated into the 1980 revision of Form 24.[63] The revisions were made to address broad judicial interpretation of the form and reflect changes in the nature of the banking industry.

Perhaps the most significant revision was to add an intent requirement to the employee dishonesty insuring agreement, Insuring

---

59 Id. at 935-36.
60 Id. at 936.
61 Id. at 936-37.
62 The Surety & Fidelity Association of America, Analysis of Changes, Bankers Blanket Bond, Standard Form No. 24, Revised to April 1969.
63 The 1980 Form 24 incorporated several riders. These were: SR 6019 (Definition of Dishonesty and Exclusions), SR 5538 (Joint Insured Rider), SR 5524d ((D) Aggregate Deductible), SR 5791e ((E) Aggregate Deductible, SR 5527b (Misplacement Coverage)), SR 5653c (Deductible— Not (D) or (E)), SR 5887c (Credit Card Exclusion), SR 5936c (Extortion Exclusion), SR 6030a (Trading Loss Exclusion), SR 6064 (Uncollected Funds Exclusion), SR 6015 (Notice of Merger), SR 6014a (Notice of Change of Control), SR 5923b (60 Day Cancellation Rider), SR 6059 (Effective Time Rider), and SR 5886c (Automated Teller Machine Rider). The Surety & Fidelity Association of America, Statement of Change, Bankers Blanket Bond, Standard Form No. 24, Revised to July, 1980. This article addresses a few of these riders.

Agreement (A). First by Rider SR 6019 and then by revising the 1980 standard form bond, coverage under the fidelity insuring agreement was limited to dishonest acts committed by an employee with the "manifest intent" to cause the insured to sustain a loss and to obtain a financial benefit. Prior to the revision, the fidelity insuring agreement covered loss "through any dishonest act." Case law had developed over the years such that courts sometimes found coverage for reckless or even merely negligent conduct.[64]

For example, in *Mortgage Corp. of New Jersey v. Aetna Casualty and Surety Co.*,[65] the insured mortgage company's employee was responsible for preparing progress reports on which the insured relied when disbursing construction loan funds. The employee's responsibilities included visiting the job sites to determine the extent of work in progress. Inclement weather intervened, however, and the insured's employee relied upon the representations of the borrower/builder, rather than brave the elements to personally verify the project's progress. The borrower's representations, unfortunately, proved to be false, and the borrower defaulted on its loans. The insured sought to recover under its Brokers Blanket Bond, which provided coverage for "[a]ny loss through any dishonest, fraudulent or criminal act" of the insured's employees.

The insurer argued that there should be no fidelity coverage because the insured's employee did not profit from his acts and did not intend to harm his employer. The court rejected these arguments. The court adopted an expansive interpretation of "dishonest" conduct and concluded:

> Under the admitted facts [the employee] palpably was faithless to his trust and deceived his employer; it matters not that his conscious deceptions may not have been accompanied by intent to cause actual monetary loss to his employer and may have been induced by motives of personal comfort or convenience rather than personal profit or gain for, in any event, his conduct was morally as well as legally wrongful.[66]

---

64 *See* Frank L. Skillern, *The Insuring Agreements, Section 1—Insuring Agreement (A)—Fidelity, in* ANNOTATED BANKERS BOND (Frank L. Skillern ed., 1st ed. 1980).
65 115 A.2d 43 (N.J. 1955).
66 *Id.* at 48.

Under the revised language, the requirement that the employee must have intended to cause a loss was made explicit—the intent that the *Aetna* court found unnecessary. In addition to correcting a judicial misinterpretation, the revision reflects a desire to cover what can be prudently and effectively underwritten. It reflects the philosophy that coverage under Form 24 should be for losses that are caused by intentionally circumventing sound banking practices and internal controls. Form 24 should not be a protection against bad (or negligent) banking practices.

Rider SR 6019 also added four exclusions:

> (i) Potential income ... including but not limited to interest and dividends, not realized by the Insured because of a loss covered under this bond.
>
> (ii) All damages of any type for which the Insured is legally liable, except compensatory damages arising from a loss covered under this bond.
>
> (iii) All costs, fees and other expenses incurred by the Insured in establishing the existence of or amount of loss covered under this bond.
>
> (iv) Loss resulting from payments made or withdrawals from a depositor's account involving funds erroneously credited to such account ....[67]

These exclusions were incorporated into the 1980 Form 24.[68]

The general purpose of the first three exclusions was to exclude consequential damages.[69] The first exclusion, the potential income exclusion, emphasizes that the surety does not guarantee the profits of the financial institution.[70] One commentator likened the coverage under Form 24 to coverage under mercantile policies by which the wholesale cost of lost goods is used determine the amount of the loss.[71] In the context of a bank and a fraudulent loan transaction, the loss is the amount

---

67 The Surety & Fidelity Association of America, Rider SR 6019.
68 The Surety & Fidelity Association of America, Statement of Change, Bankers Blanket Bond, Standard Form No. 24, Revised to July, 1980.
69 Robin V. Weldy, *A Survey of Recent Changes in Financial Institutions Bonds*, 12 THE FORUM 895, 898 (1977).
70 *Id.*
71 *Id.*

that is actually handed over to the customer, the principal loan amount, and not the interest which represents the profit to the bank.[72]

The consequential damages exclusion was simply a "restatement of a traditionally non-covered area" intended to "emphasize that the surety is not responsible for any punitive or exemplary damages assessed against an insured institution by reason of tortious or dishonest conduct of an employee involving a third party."[73] The audit fees exclusion was an exclusion of a specific kind of consequential loss.[74]

In addition, to emphasize that Form 24 covered only direct loss, SR 6019 revised the fidelity insuring agreement so that coverage was for loss "resulting directly from" the dishonest acts. This change also was incorporated into the 1980 form.

The 1980 form also incorporated riders SR 6014a (Notice of Change of Control) and SR 6015 (Notice of Merger).[75] These riders were drafted to account for the changing banking environment in which merger activity was more commonplace. The 1969 Form 24 permitted coverage of the acts of employees of banks that had been acquired by the insured bank without any requirement to immediately notify the underwriter.[76] Prior to the 1970s, mergers were not a common event and consequently, increased risk under Form 24 was not an issue.[77] However, competitive pressures in the banking industry led to the increasing practice of the acquisition of one institution by another institution.[78]

In an environment of increased merger and acquisition activity, underwriters needed a mechanism by which they were aware of the risks related to taking on an acquired bank and had the opportunity to underwrite it. One rider (SR 6015) modified General Agreement B of the Bankers Blanket Bond to require sixty-days' notice to the underwriter of any merger, consolidation, or purchase of assets of another institution, and the underwriter's written agreement to provide coverage for the

---

72 *Id.*
73 *Id.*
74 *Id.*
75 The Surety & Fidelity Association of America, Statement of Change, Bankers Blanket Bond, Standard Form No. 24, Revised to July, 1980.
76 Gallagher, *supra* note 8, at 24.
77 *Id.*
78 Weldy, *supra* note 69, at 899-900.

additional risks.[79] Rider SR 6014a added a new General Agreement titled "Notice of Change of Control" and required the insured to notify the underwriter within thirty days after a change of control. Failure to give notice results in the lack of coverage for any loss in which the transferee is implicated.[80]

Rider SR 6030a, which was incorporated into the 1980 Form 24, created an exclusion for trading losses. This exclusion is another illustration of revisions in coverage to account for changing banking practices and significant fidelity losses. In the 1970s, underwriters noted increased trading activity on a "very large scale" often involving "transactions in the volatile foreign exchange market."[81] Losses as a result of such exposure were significant. To address the exposure, SR 6030a excluded loss from trading "with or without the knowledge of the Insured, in the name of the Insured or otherwise, whether or not represented by any indebtedness or balance shown to be due the Insured on any customer's account, actual or fictitious, and notwithstanding any act or omission on the part of any Employee in connection with any account relating to such trading, indebtedness, or balance."[82] Recognizing that certain banks may have a need for trading coverage, a buy-back of the coverage was available.[83]

The 1980 Form 24 also included revisions that were not previously made by rider but first appeared in the 1980 form. The 1980 Form 24 included a new definition of "Forgery," which excluded signing one's own name, and defining "Counterfeit" as an imitation which is intended to deceive and be taken as an original. In addition, new definitions of several financial instruments were added based largely on the Uniform Commercial Code.[84]

Under the 1969 Form 24, the receiver or governmental entity taking over the insured had a right to purchase a one-year discovery period. This right was deleted in the 1980 Form 24, with the FDIC's knowledge and acceptance.[85]

---

79 The Surety & Fidelity Association of America, Statement of Change, Bankers Blanket Bond, Standard Form No. 24, Revised to July, 1980.
80 *Id.*
81 Weldy, *supra*, note 69, at 899.
82 *Id.* (quoting Rider SR 6030a).
83 *Id.*
84 Gallagher, *supra* note 8, at 28.
85 *Id.*

Section 4 of the 1969 form was changed to add an "objective" definition of discovery. That is, the 1980 form provided that discovery occurs when the insured learns of facts which would cause a reasonable person to believe a loss has been or will be incurred. In the case of third-party claims, discovery occurs when the insured receives notice of a claim which, if true, would create a covered loss.

The 1980 form made extensive changes to Insuring Agreement (E). The 1969 form had added a definition of "securities, documents or other written instruments." The 1980 revision eliminated the phrase (and its definition) and substituted a list of specific instruments which would be covered. The 1980 form also required that the insured have relied on an original bill of lading whereas the 1969 form allowed coverage based on carbon copies.

2. 1986 Form 24

The 1986 version of Form 24 was referred to as "Financial Institution Bond," rather than "Bankers Blanket Bond." The new term was adopted for two primary reasons. First, the term "blanket" had been an issue in certain claims. Several reported cases contained statements that indicated that "blanket" implies broad coverage.[86] Second, the bond was intended to be used by insureds other than banks (savings banks and savings and loans).[87] Thus, the broader term of "financial institution" was more appropriate in light of this more expansive use.

The 1986 form provided for a definite term (rather than continuous) and an aggregate limit of liability that applies to the bond term.[88] Payments made by the surety reduce the aggregate liability until it is exhausted, at which time the bond automatically terminates, and the insurer may tender back to its insured a defense of any lawsuits.[89]

The 1986 form established a threshold of $2,500 for employee dishonesty loses involving loan transactions. The SFAA determined that setting a threshold was necessary because loan officers are frequently the

---

[86] Weldy, *supra* note 9, at 6; *see, e.g.*, *Provident Trust Co. v. Nat'l. Sur. Co.*, 44 F. Supp. 514, 516 (W.D. Pa. 1942) (The designation of the bond by the defendant, as a 'Bankers Blanket Bond,' indicates that it was to have a broad coverage.")

[87] Weldy, *supra* note 9, at 6.

[88] *Id.*

[89] *Id.*

recipients of small favors from the borrower, which are a financial benefit but do not necessarily, indicate a dishonest act.[90] A benefit of $2,500 provides indicia of dishonesty. Thus, coverage for employee dishonesty involving loan losses must satisfy three criteria: (1) a bribe or kickback of at least $2,500; (2) an intent by the employee to cause a loss to the employer; and (3) the employee's intent to personally profit.

The on premises coverage was amended so that false pretenses and larceny must be committed by a person on bank premises, although the property could be located in some other location.[91] The securities insuring agreement was expanded to include uncertificated securities issued by a Federal Reserve Bank.[92]

The 1986 form added a definition of "Loan." The term was defined to mean an actual extension of credit by the financial institution. Thus, the creation of bogus paperwork by a loan officer when no actual borrower exists is not a "Loan" and would not be subject to the $2,500 financial benefit threshold.[93]

The 1986 form contained two substantially modified General Agreements. First, the 1986 form replaced the Warranty General Agreement of the 1980 bond with a new General Agreement titled "Representation of Insured." This provision was strengthened to explicitly give the Underwriter the right to rescind the bond.

The 1986 Bond stated:

> The Insured represents that the information furnished in the application for this bond is complete, true and correct. Such application constitutes part of this bond.
>
> Any misrepresentation, omission, concealment or any incorrect statement of a material fact, in the application or otherwise, shall be grounds for the rescission of this Bond.[94]

When read in conjunction with the consideration clause, which states, in relevant part, that the underwriter enters the agreement "in reliance upon

---

[90] *Id.* at 7.
[91] *Id.* at 7.
[92] Weldy, *supra* note 9, at 7.
[93] *Id.*
[94] The Surety & Fidelity Association of America, Financial Institution Bond, Standard Form No. 24, Revised to January 1986.

all statements made and information furnished to the Underwriter by the Insured," the underwriter's right to rescind the bond is strengthened.[95]

Second, the 1986 form modified the General Agreement formerly titled "Court Costs and Attorneys' Fees." Under the prior provision, the insured was required to give "prompt" notice to the underwriter of a legal proceeding. The underwriter had to indemnify the insured for court costs and reasonable attorneys' fees incurred and paid by the insured in defending a lawsuit. However, the underwriter could elect to defend the insured.[96] The modified General Agreement F, titled "Notice of Legal Proceedings Against Insured—Election to Defend" required notice within thirty days (rather than "prompt" notice). In addition, it strengthened the language regarding the underwriter's election to defend by stating that the underwriter could defend at its "sole option." Any judgment and attorneys' fees and costs would be a loss covered under the bond. However, if the underwriter elects not to defend, or the insured gives late notice, a judgment or settlement against the insured does not determine the existence of bond coverage, and the underwriter is not liable for any of the insured's legal expenses.[97]

In addition to the revisions discussed above, the 1986 form added the following definitions:
- Certified Security;
- Instruction;
- Loan;
- Statement of Uncertificated Security;
- Transportation Company;
- Uncertificated Security; and
- Withdrawal Order.

The 1986 form modified or added certain exclusions to "Conditions and Limitations." For example, the "Securities—Law—Violation Exclusion," denoted (w), and the "Racketeer Influenced and Corrupt Organizations Act ("RICO") Exclusion," denoted (z), were new to the 1986 form.

---

95 Weldy, *supra* note 9, at 7.
95 The Surety & Fidelity Association of America, Bankers Blanket Bond, Standard Form No. 24, Revised to July 1980.
96 *Id.*
97 *Id.*

3. *2004 Form 24*

In 2004, Form 24 underwent a substantial change for three general reasons. First, the SFAA recognized that the emergence of electronic commerce would affect some banks in how they transact business with their customers. Electronic transactions may present exposures that are not readily compatible with the terms and conditions under the 1986 Form 24. The SFAA concluded that the standard form should be directed largely to paper transactions since many banks will continue to transact business traditionally and non-electronically. Banks that desire coverage for losses from electronic transactions may obtain this additional coverage by rider, subject to appropriate underwriting and pricing. Second, the bond was revised to provide greater clarity and correct misinterpretations of the bond by some courts. Third, the SFAA made some changes to take technology into account, such as desktop publishing software. In other words, many of the same reasons that drove revisions of financial institution coverage over previous decades are the same reasons that drove the 2004 revisions.

The most significant revision in the 2004 form was the revision of the intent standard in Insuring Agreement (A). The SFAA revised the description of the required intent from "manifest intent" to "active and conscious purpose." The change was made because some courts had misinterpreted the meaning of "manifest intent."[98] Those courts applied a tort concept of intent and found that the employee intended the natural and probable consequences of her acts or intended a result substantially certain to occur. The drafters of the language intended a stricter standard of intent, closer to purposeful conduct. "Active and conscious purpose" was meant to restore that standard. As a practical matter, "active and conscious purpose" was intended to be the same as "manifest intent" as that term should be interpreted.

Under the 2004 form, the double coverage trigger of intent to cause the insured loss and to obtain financial benefit was now deleted for most employee dishonesty losses. The revised Form 24 generally had a single coverage trigger of "active and conscious purpose" to cause the insured a loss. By eliminating the requirement of a financial benefit, the SFAA noted that an exposure to loss caused by intentional damage by an

---

98 For a thorough treatment of judicial interpretation of "manifest intent," see Samuel J. Arena, Jr. et al., THE "MANIFEST INTENT" HANDBOOK (2002).

employee is created. Coverage for such a loss was not intended and an exclusion addressing this type of loss was developed. In addition, to foreclose the argument that "loss" includes employee benefits intentionally paid to the employee, Insuring Agreement (A) explicitly stated that such benefits are not included in the meaning of "loss." Salary and other benefits that are paid unintentionally because of an embezzlement scheme are contemplated as a covered loss.

The drafters observed that the inclusion of Insuring Agreement (A) losses involving trading by rider was quite routine. Fidelity coverage involving trading was made applicable to practically all bonds. Therefore, the drafters concluded that the coverage was common enough to add it to the base form. Thus, the 2004 form provided trading loss coverage as a part of the standard policy and contained an amended trading loss exclusion.

Although the double trigger (intent to cause a loss and obtain financial gain) was deleted generally, the revised Insuring Agreement (A) maintained the double coverage trigger for loan losses. In addition, the double trigger applied to losses from "trading."

With respect to loans and trading, the "financial benefit" provision was revised to ensure that bonuses or other compensation that were generated as part of the dishonest scheme are not considered to be a financial benefit. The phrase "financial benefit" was revised to "improper financial benefit." Also, the phrase regarding benefits "earned in the normal course of employment" was replaced by benefits "received by an Employee." The purpose of the change was to strengthen the effect of the language, which is to preclude an argument that wages, salaries, or commissions generated through a dishonest scheme are not earned during the *normal* course of employment and, therefore, are not excluded from the meaning of an "improper financial benefit." The intent is that any employee benefit received by the employee is excluded from the meaning of "improper financial benefit." For example, claimants have incorrectly argued that since a bonus was generated as a result of making fraudulent loans and making fraudulent loans was not a duty of employment, then the bonus was an improper financial benefit. On the other hand, a kickback from the customer receiving the fraudulent loan would be an example of an improper financial benefit.

The revised Insuring Agreement (B) does not provide coverage for vandalism or malicious mischief. This revision incorporated Rider SR 6263 into the policy. The covered property is limited to the enumerated items set forth in the "Property" definition. The intent of the coverage is to avoid duplication of coverage with ISO property coverages and insure only those items that are not covered under ISO forms. The enumerated items generally are not covered under the ISO property forms. Similarly, the revised Insuring Agreement (B) does not cover loss or damage to the office or interior of the office, which previously was covered under Insuring Agreement (B)(2)(b). The reason for the deletion was that such coverage is afforded by ISO property policies.

The revised Insuring Agreement (B) requires that the perpetrator be "physically" present on the premises "at the time the Property was surrendered." The revised language explicitly emphasizes the point that the intent of Insuring Agreement (B) was to cover losses entirely attributable to face-to-face transactions.

Clause (a) of Insuring Agreement (C) was revised so that the custodian of "Property" must be a "Messenger" (a newly defined term) or a "Transportation Company." The last paragraph clarifies that Insuring Agreement (C) covers property "only while the property is being conveyed." Thus, the covered property must be in transit and not parked or stored at the Transportation Company's premises. Sureties had experienced claims under the in transit coverage when the property was not actually "in transit" and on the premises of the Transportation Company.

The 2004 form contained revisions to prevent claims for the same loss made under Insuring Agreements (D) and (E). Insuring Agreement (D) was revised so that the coverage it provides is exclusive of the coverage provided in Insuring Agreement (E). Insuring Agreement (D) covers loss caused by a payment or transfer by the bank on the faith of a forged or altered "Negotiable Instrument" or other enumerated item. The transaction under Insuring Agreement (D) is a direction to pay and not an application for or extension of a loan. Losses in connection with a loan made on the faith of forged documents would be covered under Insuring Agreement (E) only. Under prior versions of Form 24, Insuring Agreement (E) had an explicit requirement that the insured have actual physical possession of the forged or altered document, but Insuring Agreement (D) contained no such explicit requirement. This difference created the likelihood that an insured that did not have possession of the document would attempt to make an Insuring Agreement (D) claim despite facts that suggested that Insuring Agreement (E) was more appropriate. By adding the possession requirement to Insuring Agreement (D), the 2004 form forecloses this scenario.

Insuring Agreement (D) also incorporated Rider SR 6253 which addresses coverage for forged desktop published checks. Recent advances in technology enabled a criminal to produce a phony check using desktop publishing software. A legitimate check can be scanned or otherwise inputted into a computer and then altered as to the payee and amount. An imitation of a legitimate check can then be printed with the altered data. Often, it is very difficult to distinguish between the imitation and a legitimate check drawn on the account. Insuring Agreement (D) protected the insured against certain forgery losses, but Exclusion (p) of the 1986 form excludes losses resulting from counterfeiting. "Counterfeiting" is not a defined term. There was some question whether a "desktop published check" is a product of counterfeiting. Insuring Agreement (D) and Exclusion (p) were revised to clearly provide coverage. The last paragraph of Insuring Agreement (D) was revised to state that a reproduction of a handwritten signature shall be treated the same as a handwritten signature. This revision expands the type of reproductions beyond mechanical reproductions because the forged signature of a desktop published check may be produced by a laser printer, which may not necessarily constitute a mechanical reproduction.

Under Insuring Agreement (E), "Instruction to a Federal Reserve Bank" and "Statement of Uncertificated Security of any Federal Reserve Bank" were removed from the list of enumerated documents. The SFAA reviewed the list of documents under Insuring Agreement (E) and concluded that, unlike the other enumerated items, these items do not represent ownership or convey an interest in something of value. As such, the SFAA questioned whether banks lend funds or extend credit solely on the good faith reliance of these documents. Further, the definition of "Statement" does not specify that it must come directly from the issuer of the security. Relying on a Statement that did not come directly from the issuer appears to be bad banking practice.

Insuring Agreement (G) (Fraudulent Mortgages) was added to Form 24 in 2004. Experience indicated that this coverage was added to the policy by rider often enough to warrant its inclusion in the standard form.

General Agreement C was revised as a "Change of Ownership" provision rather than "Change of Control." The revised General Agreement establishes a bright line of a change of ownership of more than ten percent of the stock that will trigger the insured's notice requirements. As a related change, the termination section was revised to include a provision that the policy terminates upon a "Change in Control." This is a defined term which also sets a bright line of a change in ownership of over fifty percent of the stock. The revision incorporates the meaning of "taking over" as set forth in *American Casualty Co. of Reading, Pennsylvania v. Etowah Bank.*[99]

The 2004 form included a new General Agreement G that provides coverage for the ERISA bonding obligations of the insured's directors and employees acting as fiduciaries or handling money of the insured's own ERISA plans. The policy's deductible becomes effective after losses exceed the statutory minimum limit. (No deductible is permitted for coverage required under ERISA.)[100]

The 2004 form also included several new definitions in response to company claim activity, case law, or to clarify that the base Form 24 coverage extends only to paper transactions, summarized as follows:

- A new definition of "Original" was added and a new definition of "Written" was added.
- "Written" was inserted into a number of definitions to assure that coverage is not provided for electronic transactions.
- A new definition of "Electronic Data Processor" was added and included in the current definition of "Employee." The language was tightened to include only processors of checks presented to the insured by a customer or another financial institution. Processors of "other accounting records" were deleted from the definition. The purpose of this change was to prevent the types of arguments put forward in several cases trying to obtain coverage for thefts by third parties with business relationships with the insured by arguing that they were processing "other accounting records."[101]
- The definition of "Employee" was revised to track the definition in the mercantile coverage, which "codifies" the case law requirement that an employee be under the insured's direction

---

[99] 288 F.3d 1282 (11th Cir 2002).
[100] 29 U.S.C. § 1112 (2006); 29 C.F.R. § 2580.412-11 (2013).
[101] For an example of an attempted claim that a third party providing inventory information was a "processor," *see Humboldt Bank v. Gulf Ins. Co.*, 323 F. Supp. 2d 1027, 1036 (N.D. Cal. 2004).

SECTION 1 — A CONCISE HISTORY OF THE FINANCIAL INSTITUTION BOND

and control. The definition also incorporated the exception in Exclusion (d) of the 1986 form that effectively provided coverage for directors while performing duties normally performed by employees.
- The definition of "Evidence of Debt" was revised to state that the instrument evidencing the debt must be executed "or purportedly executed" by a customer of the insured. The addition of the phrase, "or purportedly executed," forecloses an argument that a forged instrument that is not actually signed by the customer is not an Evidence of Debt.
- The definition of "Forgery" was revised to limit forgeries to handwritten signatures or reproductions of handwritten signatures (such as facsimile signatures or printed signatures). Under the revised definition, electronic or digital signatures, such a series of hashes or symbols, are explicitly not forgeries. In addition, the definition specifically states that a Forgery includes affixing the name of an organization as an endorsement to a check and with intent to deceive. This revision reflected the common practice of an organization endorsing a check by stamping the name of the organization on the back of the check, rather than using a handwritten signature.
- The enumerated items of "Property" are set forth in a revised definition. "Books of account... on tangible media," has replaced "books of account... recorded electronically." The revision clarifies that the books of account must be stored on a disc or tape. The revision is also consistent with how electronic books are described in Insuring Agreement (C).

The 2004 form also revised and added certain exclusions. Among the more notable changes are the following:

- Under the 1986 form, Exclusion (h) had excluded loss caused by an employee except when covered under Insuring Agreement (A), or Insuring Agreements (B) or (C) and resulting from misplacement or destruction of the property. To make explicit that intentional acts of an employee should be covered only under Insuring Agreement (A), the exception for Insuring Agreements (B) and (C) losses in the employee exclusion was revised to pertain to "unintentional" acts of the employee.

- Since limited trading loss coverage was added to Insuring Agreement (A), that Insuring Agreement was added to the exception in the trading loss exclusion.
- Exclusion (r) of the 2004 form excludes loss of property on the premises of a "Messenger" or "Transportation Company." There had been several claims alleging that money stolen by an ATM servicer was "in transit" even though it was transferred to the servicer, stored at its premises and stolen by the servicer. The new exclusion forecloses such a claim which was never intended to be covered by the bond.
- Exclusion (t) of the 1986 form was an exclusion for damages for which the insured is legally liable. Several provisions of the bond were revised, including Exclusion (t) to remove any suggestion that the legal liability of the insured has any effect on the obligations of the underwriter. The bond is not a liability policy, and indemnity is owed to the insured only if and when the insured itself has suffered a covered loss. The fact that damages are awarded against the insured, however, should not remove coverage which would have existed independently of those damages. The damages exclusion was revised to remove the exception for compensatory damages but allow recovery for an otherwise covered loss that would exist independently of the damage award.

Finally, in 2004 certain conditions of Form 24 were revised as follows:

Section 4: Under the 1986 form, reinstatement of the aggregate limit by recoveries was not permitted. Section 4 was revised to allow reinstatement from net recoveries if the aggregate limit has not been exhausted and the recoveries are received prior to the termination of the bond.

Section 6: The "Valuation" condition was amended to state that interest, fees, payments, recoveries, or credits the Insured receives in the fraudulent transaction are a credit reducing the loss. A loss under the bond should be measured by the net detriment to the Insured.

Section 7: In the 1986 form, the cooperation obligation was contained in the condition pertaining to the recovery of losses.

In the 2004 form, the "Assignment—Subrogation—Recovery—Cooperation" section was divided into two conditions to clarify that the duty to cooperate is not limited to recovery of losses. Subsection (d) of the Conditions and Limitations section of the 1986 form was removed and became Section 8, "Cooperation."

Section 9: The mistaken decision in *Omnisource Corp. v. CNA Transcontinental Insurance Co.*[102] led a number of banks to believe erroneously that coverage can be claimed based on forgery to a document not covered by the bond if the forged document is "bundled" with a covered document. A new Section 9 was added to correct this misconception. The forgery must be on the covered document.

Section 12: As noted above, the inclusion of property "for which the Insured is legally liable" in the "Ownership" section has led to claims that the legal liability of the insured is covered. The "Ownership" section is amended to "codify" cases, such as *Lynch Properties Inc. v. Potomac Ins. Co.*,[103] which correctly hold that the insured must be responsible for the property prior to the events giving rise to the loss.

4. 2011 Form 24

In 2010, the SFAA embarked on a massive revision project involving its primary Financial Institution Bond standard forms: Form 14, Form 15, Form 24, and Form 25. Many of the revisions were intended to achieve greater consistency of the forms' terms and provisions. In addition, Form 24's Insuring Agreement (A) was revised to restore the "manifest intent" language that was used in prior editions.

As noted above, Insuring Agreement (A) was revised in the 2004 edition of Form 24 such that the description of the intent required for a covered act was changed from "manifest intent" to "active and conscious purpose." The change was made in the 2004 form in light of the fact that some judicial decisions misinterpreted the meaning of "manifest intent." Thus, alternative phrasing was selected to convey what was always intended—a conscious object to cause the result.

However, after being available in the market for several years, it became apparent to the SFAA that the market did not accept the new

---

[102] 949 F. Supp. 681 (N.D. Ind. 1996).
[103] 140 F.3d 622 (5th Cir. 1998).

language.[104] Therefore, the SFAA returned to the "manifest intent" language in the 2011 form, even though the intent of coverage is the same—the employee must act with the actual subjective or specific intent to cause his or her employer a loss. In addition to restoring the "manifest intent" language, the double coverage trigger of "manifest intent" to cause the insured a loss and to obtain financial benefit was restored. Likewise, because the 2011 form has a double trigger, "there is no longer a possibility of a claim for loss caused by intentional damage by an employee (e.g. sabotage)."[105] Thus, the "sabotage exclusion" was deleted from Form 24.

Other revisions in the form sought to improve the organization to make the form's terms more consistent with the other Financial Institution Bonds, where possible. These revisions are summarized as follows:

- Insuring Agreement (B) was revised so that the covered Property may be lodged or deposited in premises and offices located anywhere, unless the insured and Underwriter agree to exclude particular premises or offices.
- Insuring Agreement (D) in the 1986 form included as an enumerated item an instruction "directed to the Insured." This phrase was dropped in the 2004 edition of Form 24. After reconsideration, the phrase was added back to Form 24 because good banking practice dictates that Property is transferred on the faith of an instruction only if it is directed to the insured.[106]
- Insuring Agreement (E)(2) in Form 24 relates to signature guarantees. "Guarantee" is an enumerated item and a defined term. The definition refers to a debt owed to the insured. It would seem unlikely that the insured would guarantee the signature on an obligation owed to the insured. A broader

---

[104] The Surety & Fidelity Association of America, STATEMENT OF CHANGE, FINANCIAL INSTITUTION BOND, STANDARD FORM NO. 14 (REVISED TO MAY 1, 2011), FINANCIAL INSTITUTION BOND, STANDARD FORM NO. 15 (REVISED TO MAY 1, 2011), FINANCIAL INSTITUTION BOND, STANDARD FORM NO. 24 (REVISED TO MAY 1, 2011), FINANCIAL INSTITUTION BOND, STANDARD FORM NO. 25 (REVISED TO MAY 1, 2011).
[105] *Id.*
[106] *Id.*

meaning was intended. Therefore, the term was revised to remove the limit of debts owed to the insured.
- The "Representation of Insured" General Agreement was revised by deleting "intentional." The key factor (absent a contrary law) in determining whether an insurer can rescind the bond is whether the fact that was concealed, misstated, or omitted was material, irrespective of whether the concealment or misstatement was intentional.[107] The provision was restructured so that the materiality requirement clearly applies to an omission, concealment, and incorrect statement. In addition, considering that "misrepresentation" is part of the larger category of "incorrect statement," "misrepresentation" was redundant and has been deleted.
- Attorneys were deleted from the definition of "Employee." Generally, attorneys are independent contractors. Sound underwriting practice requires that insurers have an opportunity to underwrite independent contractors before they are added as "Employees." Therefore, attorneys were deleted from the definition. Attorneys can be added to the definition by rider, giving the insurer an opportunity to underwrite.
- The condition for losses discovered too late to claim under a prior loss-sustained policy was deleted from Form 24. This condition contemplated coverage written on a loss-sustained basis with a discovery period following the policy period. Such coverage has not been written for Form 24 insureds for many years, and therefore, SFAA deleted the condition as unnecessary.
- A set off condition was added in the "Valuation" section. In addition, the "Books of Account and Other Records" section was updated to reflect how records are maintained in the current technological environment (i.e. no paper books).
- A phrase was added to the "Assignment—Subrogation—Recovery" section to address the order of payment of recoveries. In particular, a provision was added to make explicit that reimbursement for losses not covered under the bond are paid last out of recoveries. This provision was in Form 25 and was added to Form 24 for consistency.

---

107 *Id.*; *See, e.g., Hanover Ins. Co. v. Treasurer and Receiver General*, 910 N.E.2d 921 (Mass. App. Ct. 2009).

- The "Deductible Amount" section—was revised to track the language in Form 25.

C. Technology and Coverage Developments

1. Computer Crime Policy

Technology changes constantly, creating new exposures for the insured and providing fraudsters with new ways to steal. Even as early as 1980, questions arose regarding whether the traditional coverages under the Financial Institution Bond effectively addressed exposures created by technology and automation.[108] For over thirty years, the United States and London insurance markets have developed products to address the new exposures created by technology.[109] A big exposure for banks is a hacker's ability to impersonate the account holder virtually, "enter" the bank through the bank's computer system and provide fraudulent instructions to the bank's system to transfer funds. In 1981, Lloyds of London introduced the Electronic and Computer Crime Policy.[110] In 1983, the SFAA introduced the Computer Systems Rider for the standard form Financial Institution Bond.[111] The rider provided coverage for:

> Loss resulting directly from a fraudulent
> (1) entry of data into, or
> (2) change of data elements or programs within a Computer System listed in the schedule . . .

---

[108] Steven A. Balmer, *The History and Development of the Surety Association of America Computer Crime Policy for Financial Institutions*, at A-11, presented at the meeting of the American Bar Association Fidelity & Surety Committee Tort & Insurance Practice Section (August 4, 1996) (on file at SFAA) (hereinafter *Computer Crime Policy History*).

[109] *Id.* at A-1.

[110] *Id.* at A-11.

[111] *Id.* at A-12.

After a number of revisions to the rider, the SFAA introduced a stand-alone Computer Crime Policy for Financial Institutions in 1993.[112] The policy offered seven coverages:

(1) Computer Systems Fraud (which was the coverage offered by the rider);
(2) Data Processing Service Operations;
(3) Voice Initiated Transfer Fraud;
(4) Telefacsimile Transfer Fraud;
(5) Destruction of Data or Programs by Hacker;
(6) Destruction of Data or Programs by Virus; and
(7) Voice Computer system Fraud.

The Computer Crime Policy has not been revised significantly since 1993. Looking ahead, however, more changes for the Computer Crime Policy are likely on the horizon. When the policy was developed initially, the "computer" that was contemplated was a mainframe into which communication took place over wires. The advent of internet banking over mobile devices stretches what is meant by a "computer." The process of ensuring that the terms and coverages reflect current technology and practices is a continuous process that calls for ongoing revisions of the policy.

2. *Fraudulent Transfer Instructions*

The creation of the Fraudulent Transfer Instructions Rider is a good example of the need to make revisions to address evolving technology. The SFAA introduced the rider (SR 6271) in 2004. The rider provides coverage for loss caused by fraudulent transfer instructions that were submitted to the bank employee either by fax or telephone. These coverages were provided previously by two separate riders: Telefacsimile Transfer Fraud (SR 6195) and Voice Initiated Transfer Fraud (SR 6184). In addition, SR 6271 recognizes that the bank employee may receive the instructions by some other electronic means, such as electronic mail.

---

112 Arthur Lambert provides a more comprehensive treatment of the development of the Computer Crime Policy in Chapter 4, Section 2 of this book.

3. Remote Deposit Capture/Check Images

In some cases, evolving technology does not necessarily create new exposures, but the terms of coverage for existing exposures must be modified to reflect new technologies. For example, Insuring Agreement (D) of Form 24 provides coverage for forged or altered instruments that are an "Original." "Original" is defined as "the first rendering or archetype and does not include photocopies or electronic transmissions even if received and printed." The federal Check Clearing for the 21st Century Act, 12 U.S.C. 5001, et seq. ("Check 21 Act"), which became effective October 28, 2004, required banks and others to accept "substitute checks" in place of original checks. The Check 21 Act defines a "substitute check" as follows:

> The term "substitute check" means a paper reproduction of the original check that—
> (A) contains an image of the front and back of the original check;
> (B) bears a MICR line containing all the information appearing on the MICR line of the original check, except as provided under generally applicable industry standards for substitute checks to facilitate the processing of substitute checks;
> (C) conforms, in paper stock, dimension, and otherwise, with generally applicable industry standards for substitute checks; and
> (D) is suitable for automated processing in the same manner as the original check.

The exposure for forgery and alteration remain. However, a substitute check would not be an "Original" as defined in Form 24. The SFAA developed a rider (SR 6274) that amended the definition of "Original" to include, for purposes of Insuring Agreement (D) only, a substitute check as defined in the Check 21 Act.

Similarly, technology exists that facilitates the use of an image of a check in the check clearing process. Through remote deposit capture, a bank customer is able to deposit his or her check by electronically transferring an image of the check to the bank with a device provided by the bank or even with a smart phone.[113] Images are then exchanged from

---

[113] *See* Lisa Valentine, *Time to Expand RDC*, ABA Banking Journal (Nov. 2012).

the depository bank ultimately to the payor bank. According to CheckImage Collaborative, paper checks are transitioning to electronic images, with approximately seventy percent of all institutions now receiving images.[114] Again, the "Original" requirement in Form 24 would not accommodate these images. The SFAA is in the process of developing a rider that, for the purposes of forgery and alteration coverage under Insuring Agreement (D), would include such images as "Originals."

D. Conclusion

Since its introduction in the United States almost a century ago, financial institution coverage has undergone numerous changes and revisions. These revisions were not made for their own sake, but were in response to competitive pressures, erroneous court decisions, as well as evolving banking practices, often driven by technology. Whatever the change and whatever the decade, these same factors have been in play. In addition, underscoring these factors has been the form drafters' determination as to what risks and exposures can be underwritten prudently, effectively, and profitably. It remains to be seen what the next iteration of financial institution bonds will look like. The new exposures created by developing technologies likely will play a central role. The revisions certainly will be a reflection of outside forces, whether in the courtroom or marketplace, which is exactly how it should be. It yields a product that is responsive to the needs of the financial services industry and is a product that insurers are willing to provide.

---

114 The CheckImage Collaborative was founded by the Electronic Check Clearing House Organization (ECCHO) and the Retail Payments Office (RPO) of the Federal Reserve Bank of Atlanta and is comprised of representatives of trade and financial organizations from across the country. *see* http://www.checkimagecentral.org/aboutus (last visited May 28, 2013).

SECTION 2 — ELECTRONIC FRAUD INSURING AGREEMENT RIDERS*

COMPUTER SYSTEMS FRAUD

Loss resulting directly from fraudulent
(1) Entry of Electronic Data or computer Program into, or
(2) Change of Electronic Data or Computer Program within
any Computer System operated by the Insured, whether owned or leased; or any Computer System identified in the application for this policy; or a Computer System first used by the Insured during the Policy Period, as provided by General Agreement A; provided that the entry or change causes
(i) Property to be transferred, paid or delivered,
(ii) an account of the Insured, or of its customer, to be added, deleted, debited or credited, or
(iii) an unauthorized account or a fictitious account to be debited or credited.

COMMENT

By the 1970s, technology had changed the methods by which financial institutions maintained their records, transacted their business, executed transactions, and communicated with customers. This evolution continues even now, as financial institutions have moved beyond paper transaction documents presented in person or couriered to the bank, punch cards, tape drives, and dedicated "dumb" network terminals, to web-based systems accessible by personal computer, tablet, or smartphone.

The SFAA sought to keep bond coverage in tandem with the technological changes hinted at during the 1970s by offering, at first, discrete additional riders and, ultimately, a standalone computer crime

---

* By Arthur N. Lambert, Daniel W. White, and Victor B. Kao of Frenkel Lambert Weiss Weisman & Gordon LLP, New York, New York.

policy. From about 1977 on, the precursor to the current Computer Systems Fraud Rider was drafted, and redrafted, and made available to banks, as a rider, supplementing the coverage provided to them by their Form 24 bond. At the time, it appears that conventional banks were the most interested in using computers and getting coverage for associated risks.

The Computer Systems Fraud Rider or Insuring Agreement in essentially its present form was drafted in 1991 to 1993, and arose out of the SFAA's efforts to draft its Computer Crime Policy. After considering the suggestion that the riders be eliminated, on April 9, 1993, the Financial Institutions Revision Subcommittee stated that the SFAA's "consensus was to leave the free standing riders in the marketplace for those companies who wish to use them" noting, however, that the riders should conform to the coverage being provided under the Computer Crime Policy. The same subcommittee earlier took pains to make clear that the Computer Crime Policy and the Financial Institution Bond are "mutually exclusive as to the risks that they cover" and that the Computer Crime Policy was designed to work in conjunction with a number of SFAA standard products.

The December 1993 edition of the Computer Crime Policy For Financial Institutions has seven insuring agreements embracing the technological side of coverage. In addition to computer systems fraud, there are insuring agreements for data processing service operations, voice initiated transfer fraud,[1] telefacsimile transfer fraud,[2] destruction of data or programs by hacker, destruction of data or programs by virus, and voice computer systems fraud. Here, as before, the SFAA issued different riders with these insuring agreements to be used with different Financial Institution Bond forms. The insuring agreements, whether in the Computer Crime Policy or as a rider, are substantially identical, and any differences between the policy and riders will not be covered for purposes of this discussion.

The insuring agreement includes as "fraudulent entry" entries made in good faith by the employee of the insured, acting in good faith from a software vendor or secure instructions.

The Computer Crime Policy provides coverage for voice initiated transfer fraud as follows:

---

[1] This coverage is offered by Rider SR 6187b for use with Form 23.
[2] This coverage is offered by Rider SR 7000 for use with Form 23.

3. **VOICE INITIATED TRANSFER FRAUD**
Loss resulting directly from the Insured having, in good faith, transferred Funds from a Customer's account through a Computer System covered under the terms of Insuring Agreement 1 [Computer Systems Fraud] in reliance upon a fraudulent voice instruction transmitted by telephone which was purported to be from
   (1) an officer, director, partner or employee of a Customer of the Insured who was authorized by the Customer to instruct the Insured to make such transfer,
   (2) an individual person who is a Customer of the Insured, or
   (3) an employee of the Insured in another office of the Insured who was authorized by the Insured to instruct other employees of the Insured to transfer Funds,
and was received by an employee of the Insured specifically designated to receive and act upon such instructions, but the voice instruction was not from a person described in (1), (2) or (3) above,

provided that:
   (i) such voice instruction was electronically recorded by the Insured and required password(s) or code word(s) given; and
   (ii) if the transfer was in excess of the amount shown on the Declarations Page as the verification callback amount for this Insuring Agreement, the voice instruction was verified by a call-back according to a prearranged procedure.

The Computer Crime Policy provides coverage for telefacsimile transfer fraud as follows:

4. **TELEFACSIMILE TRANSFER FRAUD**
Loss resulting directly from the Insured having, in good faith, transferred or delivered Funds, Certificated Securities or Uncertificated Securities through a Computer system covered under the terms of Insuring Agreement 1 in

SECTION 2 — ELECTRONIC FRAUD INSURING AGREEMENT RIDERS

reliance upon a fraudulent instruction received through a Telefacsimile Device, and which instruction
- **(1)** purports and reasonably appears to have originated from
  - **(a)** a Customer of the Insured,
  - **(b)** another financial institution, or
  - **(c)** another office of the Insured

  but, in fact, was not originated by the Customer or entity whose identification it bears and
- **(2)** contains a valid test code which proves to have been used by a person who was not authorized to make use of it, and
- **(3)** contains the name of a person authorized to initiate such transfer;

provided that, if the transfer was in excess of the amount shown in the Declarations Page as the verification call-back amount for this Insuring Agreement, the instruction was verified by a call-back according to a prearranged procedure.

As used in this Insuring Agreement, Customer means an entity or individual which has a written agreement with the Insured authorizing the Insured to rely on Telefacsimile Device instructions to initiate transfers and has provided the Insured with the names of persons authorized to initiate such transfers, and with which the Insured has established an instruction verification mechanism.

Coverage for fraudulent transfer instructions is offered by Rider 6271b (for Forms 14, 24, and 25), which adds an insuring agreement that provides:

FRAUDULENT TRANSFER INSTRUCTIONS
Loss resulting directly from the Insured having, in good faith, transferred Money on deposit in a Customer's account, or a Customer's Certificated Securities, in reliance upon a fraudulent instruction transmitted to the Insured via telefacsimile, telephone, or electronic mail; provided, however that
- (1) The fraudulent instruction purports, and reasonably appears, to have originated from:

a. such Customer,
b. an Employee acting on instructions of such Customer; or
c. another financial institution acting on behalf of such Customer with authority to make such instructions; and

(2) The sender of the fraudulent instruction verified the instruction with the password, PIN, or other security code of such Customer; and

(3) The sender was not, in fact, such Customer, was not authorized to act on behalf of such Customer, and was not an Employee of the Insured; and

(4) The instruction was received by an Employee of the Insured specifically authorized by the Insured to receive and act upon such instructions; and

(5) For any transfer exceeding the amount set forth in item 8 of this Rider [which is "The amount of any single transfer for which verification via callback will be required"], the Insured verified the instruction via a call back to a predetermined telephone number set forth in the Insured's Written agreement with such Customer or other verification procedure approved in writing by the Underwriter, and

(6) The Insured preserved a contemporaneous record of the call back, if any, and of the instruction which verifies use of the authorized password, PIN or other security code of the Customer.

* * *

As used in this Rider, Customer means a natural person or entity which has a Written agreement with the Insured authorizing the Insured to transfer Money on deposit in an account or Certificated Securities in reliance upon instructions transmitted to the Insured via the means utilized to transmit the fraudulent instruction.

Whether one of these technology-based coverages is provided by standalone policy or a rider, the interplay, if any, between the definitions and exclusions set forth in the main bond and the ancillary coverage provision should be noted in the analysis of the claim. In particular, a

SECTION 2 — ELECTRONIC FRAUD INSURING AGREEMENT RIDERS   571

specific set of facts that does not satisfy one technology-based coverage might be presented as, for example, a broader Insuring Agreement (D) claim, depending upon the filtering structure of the relevant bond or rider.

In fact, a telling aspect of many of the situations that have led to litigation involving these technology-based coverages is that, by and large, there is no single technology employed; a faxed instruction will call for telephone verification, for example. Given the multiple technologies that would be employed in any such fraudulent transaction, any given set of claim facts would likely be presented to the attention of the full range of technology coverages provided to that Insured.

In light of the dearth of cases involving these aforementioned insuring agreements, we also address cases arising under relevant provisions of proprietary financial institution bonds and commercial crime policies.

OUTLINE OF ANNOTATIONS

A. Definition of a Covered "Computer System"
B. Definition of a Covered "Instruction"
C. Fraudulent Activity from Authorized Users
D. Determining Whether a Requisite "Direct Loss" Has Occurred
E. Wire Transfers from Home Equity Lines of Credit[3]
F. Interaction with Other Bond Provisions and/or Exclusions

ANNOTATIONS

A. Definition of a Covered "Computer System"

3d Cir. 2004 (Pa.). The insured bank's claim was that the rider covered losses arising from the bank's software vendor's allegedly fraudulent

---

[3] A number of recent decisions determine claims arising out of faxed instructions to banks, fraudulently directing the bank wire transfer funds to an overseas account, drawing down on a customer's Home Equity Line of Credit account, and including telephone verification procedures. Because these cases involve several potential coverages, they are addressed in a group.

production of data. However, the Third Circuit noted that this fraudulent data was only entered on the vendor's own computer system; the vendor did not have any access to the insured's computer system; and the vendor only provided the data to the insured in hard copy. Only after receiving the hard copy did the insured choose to put the fraudulent data into its own computer system. There was no coverage, as this constituted neither fraudulent entry of data on a computer system operated by the insured, nor entries on a covered computer system made on "instruction from a software contractor," as required by the rider. *Hudson United Bank v. Progressive Cas. Ins. Co.*, 112 F. App'x 170, 176.

B. Definition of a Covered "Instruction"

W.D. Mo. 2010. An insured bank's employees executed an international wire transfer, only to later discover that the faxed wire request was fraudulent. The carrier argued that the faxed wire request was not a covered written instruction as required by the forgery coverage in Insuring Agreement D, and that the only applicable insuring agreement was the "Telefacsimile, Email and Voice Instruction Transactions Coverage," included in the bond as "Insuring Agreement K." The court disagreed, finding that the fax instructions were a "writing" or "written" for purposes of the bond. The court also found that the language in the bond did not indicate that the "Telefacsimile, Email and Voice Instruction Transactions Coverage" was the only coverage meant to apply. The court held that the loss was covered under the "written instructions" provision of Insuring Agreement D. *Mo. Bank and Trust Co. of Kansas City v. OneBeacon Ins. Co.*, 2010 WL 4386536, at *2, *6.

N.D. Tex. 2009. The insured's agent submitted false insurance applications, which caused the insured to issue checks to that agent, who then deposited the checks in his own personal bank account. The court granted summary judgment for the insurer under the "Computer Fraud" insuring agreement because that the insured had not shown how a computer caused the transfer of funds from the insured's bank account, which meant that it had met the agreement's direct loss requirement. Similarly, the applicable definitions of "fraudulent instructions" and "wire funds transfer fraud" excluded instructions as described in the separate forgery/alteration insuring agreement, precluding coverage for losses resulting from the falsified insurance applications under the disputed policies' "Funds Transfer Fraud" provisions. *Great Am. Ins. Co. v. AFS/IBEX Fin. Serv., Inc.*, No. 3:07-CV-924-O, 2008 WL 2795205, at *14-15.

Pa. Com. Pl. Ct. 2001. The company had electronically transmitted debit and credit card authorizations to the insured bank in connection with fraudulent transactions which ultimately caused the bank to sustain a loss. The insured sought coverage under the "Electronic Funds Transfer" and "Computer Systems Fraud" coverage in its Financial Institution Bond, but the court found that the purpose of those insuring agreements "was to protect the Bank from someone breaking into the electronic fund transfer system and pretending to be an authorized representative or altering the electronic instructions to divert monies from the rightful recipient." In contrast, the instructions at issue were never altered and were not a covered "fraudulent electronic instruction or advice" instructions as defined in the bond. The acts at issue were intended and authorized by the bank's customer so there was no coverage under either "Electronic Funds Transfer" or the "Computer Systems Fraud" provisions. *Northside Bank v. Am. Cas. Co. of Reading*, 60 Pa. D. & C.4th 95, 101-02.

C. Fraudulent Activity from Authorized Users

N.J. Super. Ct. App. Div. 2005. This case involved multiple insuring agreements, including those offering coverage for computer fraud, facsimile transfer, and voice-initiated transfers. The insured sought coverage for costs of defense and settlement of a lawsuit arising from fraudulent acts committed by an investment advisor. The court, however, dismissed the insured's complaint as to computer coverage because the exclusion for losses "by reason of the input of Electronic Data [. . .] by a customer or other person who had authorized access to the customer's authentication mechanism," clearly and unambiguously precluded coverage for fraud committed by customers or other authorized persons, such as the investment advisor. Similarly, the court dismissed the complaint as to the facsimile transfer agreement because the agreement unambiguously limited coverage to situations where an unauthorized person was posing as a customer or authorized person.

However, the court found that the voice transfer agreement did not require that an imposter or hacker commit the fraud and remanded that part of the dispute for further proceedings. *Morgan Stanley Dean Witter & Co. v. Chubb Grp. of Ins. Cos.*, No. A-4124-03T2, 2005 WL 3242234, at *2-5.

N.Y. Sup. Ct. 2013. The insured brought a claim under the computer system fraud rider for losses arising from fraudulent claims made by medical providers directly into the insured's computer system. Seeing the terms of the rider as unambiguous, the court found that the rider did not provide coverage for losses arising from users utilizing their authorized computer system privileges to commit fraud. *Universal Am. Corp. v. Nat'l Union Fire Ins. Co. of Pitt., Pa.*, 959 N.Y.S.2d 849, 853.

D. Determining Whether a Requisite "Direct Loss" Has Occurred

6th Cir. 2012 (Ohio). The insured sought coverage for losses allegedly arising from a hacker's use of a store's wireless network to access customer credit card and checking account information that was later used for fraudulent transactions, under the rider of "Blanket Crime Policy," which contained a "direct loss" requirement similar to that in the computer systems fraud rider. The court found that the policy's "direct loss" language called for a proximate cause inquiry. The court also notably found that the exclusion for "any loss of proprietary information, Trade Secrets, Confidential Processing Methods, or other confidential information of any kind," did not clearly preclude coverage of the claimed loss—even if it was due to misuse of sensitive customer information—since that information was "owned or held by many, including the customer, the financial institution, and the merchants to whom the information is provided in the ordinary stream of commerce." *Retail Ventures, Inc. v. Nat'l Union Fire Ins. Co. of Pitt., Pa.*, 691 F.3d 821, 832-33.

E.D. La. 2011. Insured sought coverage under multiple provisions of a commercial crime policy for losses arising from the infamous Madoff Ponzi scheme. In particular, the insured claimed under the insuring agreement which covered "loss from damage to 'money,' 'securities' and 'other property' following and directly related to the use of any computer

SECTION 2 — ELECTRONIC FRAUD INSURING AGREEMENT RIDERS   575

to fraudulently cause a transfer of that property." The insured claimed that Madoff's use of computers to generate false documents and mislead investors created a covered loss under that specific agreement by inducing the fund in which the insured had invested to invest in Madoff. The court found that the insured had not shown that a covered "direct loss" due to use of a computer had taken place. *Methodist Health Sys. Found., Inc. v. Hartford Fire Ins. Co.*, 834 F. Supp. 2d 493, 495.

W.D. Wash. 2011. An insured credit card processor claimed that losses arising from fraudulent merchant activity involving "chargeback credits" were covered by a computer fraud insuring agreement. The fraudster caused funds to be deducted from the insured's reserve account, which triggered the insured's obligation to use its own funds to replenish that reserve account. The court, however, found that the insured did not suffer a loss until after the insured's bank was unable to recover chargeback credits arising from the fraudulent activity. As such, the loss did not fit the insuring agreement's "direct loss" requirement. *Pinnacle Processing Grp., Inc. v. Hartford Cas. Ins. Co.*, No. C10-1126-RSM, 2011 WL 5299557, at *7.

E. Wire Transfers from Home Equity Lines of Credit

E.D. Mich. 2013. This case involved a fax from a fraudster posing as a customer requesting a wire transfer of funds from the customer's HELOC to a bank in South Korea. The signature on the fax matched that on file for the customer and the bank verified the call to a recently fraudulently changed telephone number. On cross motions for summary judgment, the court rejected the application of the loan exclusion and found coverage under Insuring Agreement (D). *Bank of Ann Arbor v. Everest Nat'l Ins. Co.*, No. 12-cv-11252, 2013 WL 665067, at *3-4.

Cal. Ct. App. 2012. The insured received a telephone call requesting a change to the telephone number associated with an account. Five days later, a fraudulent wire transfer request form was faxed, directing the wiring of money from the customer's home equity line of credit ("HELOC") to an overseas account. The insured complied with the request. The filtering exclusion stated that any claim involving fraudulent facsimile instructions was excluded unless covered under the

"Funds Transfer" coverage, which required the implementation of a "callback verification procedure" or other alternate security procedures. The insurer also had explicitly warned the insured about the requirements for these procedures and even sent a fraud warning regarding a similar HELOC wire transfer fraud scheme. The court ultimately found there was no coverage for the claim, as the funds transfer exclusion was conspicuous, plain, and clear, and the insured had not complied with security procedure requirements. *Universal City Studios Credit Union v. Cumis Ins. Soc'y, Inc.*, 145 Cal. Rptr. 3d 650, 652-59.

F. Interaction with Other Bond Provisions and/or Exclusions

D. Colo. 2008. The FDIC, as receiver for an insured bank, claimed coverage under the fidelity and computer systems fraud provisions in the insured's Financial Institution Bond for losses arising from manipulation of customer accounts. The court found that knowledge of those losses could reasonably be imputed to the insured more than thirty days prior to when the insured gave notice of the loss to the insurer, as almost 7 months elapsed between the time an honest member of the board of directors received word of the scheme from individuals who were not involved in the fraud and the time the insurer received notice. This, in turn, violated the notice conditions of the bond, and the loss was therefore not covered. *FDIC v. St. Paul Cos.*, 634 F. Supp. 2d 1213, 1222-1225.

D. Minn. 2006. A forged or unauthorized check was issued. A stop payment order was then issued and honored. Two weeks later, an impersonator submitted a wire transfer request by telephone, verified with a wire transfer authorization code, which was honored that same day. The parties agreed that the wire transfer, standing alone, would not be covered under Insuring Agreement (D). The issue here was whether to view the initial check, for which payment was stopped, and the wire transfer request, "as one continuous fraud or whether each constitutes a separate event." The court decided that the wire transfer fraud and the check "may be construed as one act" and "were part of the same fraudulent conduct." The court went so far as to say that "it is possible that the check could have been 'altered' by a telephonic wire transfer request." *First Integrity Bank, N.A. v. Ohio Cas. Ins. Co.,* No. 05-2761 (MJD/RLE), 2006 WL 1371674, at *3.

SECONDARY SOURCES

John J. McDonald, Joel T. Wiegert & Jason W. Glasgow, *Computer Fraud and Funds Transfer Fraud Coverages*, XIV FID. L.J. 109 (2008).

SECTION 3 — RETROACTIVE DATE RIDER*

        RETROACTIVE DATE—_____
                                      month   day   year
This bond does not cover loss sustained by the Insured resulting directly or indirectly from acts or events occurring prior to the Retroactive Date noted above.

COMMENT

The Retroactive Date Rider provides the insurer with the ability to limit its exposure under a Financial Institution Bond for losses that occurred, in whole or in part, prior to the date the bond was issued or renewed. The language of the Retroactive Date Rider will vary depending upon the facts and circumstances necessitating the use of the rider, the flexibility of the insurer and Insured, and other underwriting considerations. However, the Retroactive Date Rider will provide a clear and ascertainable window for discovery by an insured. There are a limited number of cases addressing the Retroactive Date Rider. However, the cases addressing the application of the Retroactive Date Rider hold that the rider may bar coverage claims, depending on the specific policy language modified by the rider. The court's analysis on this issue is influenced by state law decisions regarding contract interpretation, and statutory insurance schemes. Thus, the analysis may vary depending upon jurisdiction.

ANNOTATIONS

11th Cir. 2013 (Fla.). The Eleventh Circuit held that a retroactive date rider precluded coverage for a Ponzi scheme that did not occur in its entirety subsequent to the retroactive date enumerated in the policy rider. The court relied upon the plain language of the rider that modified the sections of the Financial Institution Bond and excess policy for discovery and single loss, to require that all acts or omissions causing or contributing to a single loss must occur after the retroactive date for coverage. The court held that the loss suffered by the insured was not a claim covered by the plain language of the bond/policy because the

---

*   By Seth Mills and Kevin Mekler, Mills Paskert Divers, Tampa, Florida.

fraudulent scheme began prior to the retroactive date. *ABCO Premium Fin., LLC v. Am. Int'l Grp., Inc.,* No. 12-14780, 2013 WL 1442517, at *7-8.

9th Cir. 2000 (Cal.). Summary judgment entered in favor of the insurer on claim asserted by insured seeking coverage for losses related to a Ponzi scheme that commenced in July 29, 1989. The policy at issue contained a retroactive date rider that stated coverage will not extend to any loss arising out of or in any way involving a transaction that occurs prior to the retroactive date of December 1, 1989. The court held that despite the insured's argument that the entire Ponzi scheme did not arise out of the initial loan, the scheme started with the initial loan and was therefore barred in its entirety by the plain language of the retroactive date rider. *Royalty Mgmt. Corp. v. Lloyd's of London,* 166 F.3d 1218.

SECONDARY SOURCES

NONE

SECTION 4 — CAUSATION*

The Underwriter, in consideration of an agreed premium, and in reliance upon all statements made and information furnished to the Underwriter by the Insured in applying for this bond, and subject to the Declarations, Insuring Agreements, General Agreements, Conditions and Limitations, and other terms hereof, agrees to indemnify the Insured for:
  Loss resulting directly from . . . .

COMMENT

Throughout the last fifty years, Financial Institution Bonds have implemented varying causation standards. Before 1980, Financial Institution Bonds typically covered losses "through" employee dishonesty.[1] In 1980, the fidelity industry implemented changes to "strengthen the concept of coverage for direct loss only."[2] It did so by substituting a new definition of dishonesty for the "loss-through" standard, and by implementing the indirect loss[3] and consequential damage exclusions.[4]

---

* By Scott L. Schmookler, Gordon & Rees, L.L.P., Chicago, Illinois and Michael Maillet, Chubb Group of Insurance Companies.

1 See Financial Institution Bond, Standard Form No. 24 (revised to April 1969), *reprinted in* STANDARD FORMS OF THE SURETY ASSOCIATION OF AMERICA; Comprehensive Dishonesty Disappearance and Destruction Policy (revised to March 1940), *reprinted in* STANDARD FORMS OF THE SURETY ASSOCIATION OF AMERICA (Surety Ass'n of America).

2 Statement of Changes, Financial Institution Bond, Standard Form No. 24 (revised to April 1980); *see also* Robin Weldy, *A Survey of Recent Changes in Financial Institution Bonds*, 12 FORUM 895 (1977).

3 Financial Institution Bond, Exclusions, § 2(w) (bond excludes coverage for "indirect and consequential loss of any nature"); Commercial Crime Policy, General Exclusions, § A(3) ("We will not pay for . . . [l]oss that is an indirect result of any act or 'occurrence' covered by this insurance . . . .").

4 Financial Institution Bond, Exclusions, § 2(u) (bond excludes coverage for "damages of any type for which the Insured is legally liable, except direct compensatory damages arising from a loss covered under this bond"); *see also* Commercial Crime Policy, General Exclusions, § A(3)(a) ("We will not pay for loss that is an indirect result of any act of 'occurrence' covered

These revisions had a substantial impact on claims arising from third-party losses and claims arising from the extension of credit against fictitious or worthless collateral. Courts addressing these types of claims under post-1980 bonds incorporating the "resulting directly from" standard have generally held that the bond does not cover amounts paid to settle a liability or loss incurred where an insured extends credit against fictitious or worthless collateral. Conversely, courts often have reached the opposite conclusion when interpreting policies incorporating a broader causation standard.

A. Third-Party Losses

Because pre-1980 bonds covered losses "through" Employee dishonesty[5] and did not define the term "through," a split of authority arose over the compensability of losses resulting from an insured's vicarious liability to a third party. Although courts generally recognized that the "through" standard required proof of a causal connection between purportedly dishonest conduct and the claimed loss, they disagreed as to whether it provided coverage for indirect losses resulting from an employee's fraudulent misconduct.

Although recognizing that losses resulting from an insured's vicarious liability for an employee's misconduct constitute an indirect loss, a majority of courts refused to inject a direct loss requirement into fidelity bonds and found the "through" standard broad enough to encompass indirect losses. These courts reasoned that the "through" standard was sufficiently broad to cover both direct and indirect losses, meaning that claims based upon an insured's vicarious liability to a third party were, subject to other defenses, covered under fidelity bonds. A minority of courts rejected the notion that fidelity bonds must cover

---

by this insurance, including, but not limited to, loss resulting from . . . [p]ayment of damages of any type for which you are legally liable. But, we will pay compensatory damages arising from a loss covered under this insurance.").

5 *See* Financial Institution Bond, Standard Form No. 24 (revised to April 1969), *reprinted in* STANDARD FORMS OF THE SURETY ASSOCIATION OF AMERICA; Comprehensive Dishonesty Disappearance and Destruction Policy (revised to March 1940), *reprinted in* STANDARD FORMS OF THE SURETY ASSOCIATION OF AMERICA (Surety Ass'n of America).

indirect losses simply because they did not exclude such losses, holding that the inherent nature of coverage afforded by fidelity bonds prohibited coverage for indirect losses.

The SFAA's 1980 revisions to Financial Institution Bond, Standard Form No. 24, and the corresponding revisions to the Commercial Crime Policy, resolved the split of authority relating to coverage for indirect losses. By substituting a new definition of dishonesty for the "through" standard, and by incorporating the indirect loss[6] and the consequential damage exclusions, the fidelity industry reinforced the concept that fidelity bonds only cover direct loss.

These revisions eliminated coverage for losses resulting from an insured's liability to a third party in three respects. First, the revisions reaffirmed that fidelity bonds are not liability policies and do not provide indemnity for losses resulting from an insured's liability to a third party. Second, the definition of dishonesty limited coverage to losses resulting from dishonest conduct committed with the manifest intent to cause the insured a loss, which typically is not the employee's intent when defrauding a third party. Third, the substitution of the "resulting directly" standard for the "through" standard, and the incorporation of the indirect loss and consequential damage exclusions, obviated coverage for indirect losses, including an insured's liability to a third party.

B. No Coverage For Extensions of Credit Against Fictitious or Worthless Collateral

It is well established that a financial institution bond "is not a form of credit insurance" and does not protect an insured when it simply makes a bad business deal. The failure to follow sound business practices and verify the authenticity is a business risk taken by the insured, not an insured risk covered by the bond. To this end, Financial Institution Bonds exclude coverage for losses "resulting from the complete or partial non-payment of or default on any Loan whether such Loan was procured in good faith or through trick, artifice, fraud or false pretenses...." While this exclusion does not apply to claims under Insuring Agreements (D) and (E), these insuring agreements do not provide blanket coverage for all loan losses.

---

6   Financial Institution Bond, Exclusions, § 2(w); Commercial Crime Policy, General Exclusions, § A(3).

In contrast to Insuring Agreement A (which covers a loss due to employee dishonesty, regardless of how the employee perpetrates the fraud), Insuring Agreements (D) and (E) cover only certain enumerated risks, subject to certain conditions. Accordingly, the methodology used by the wrongdoer to perpetrate the fraud will, in many instances, dictate whether the claim is covered.

Insuring Agreement (D) and Insuring Agreement (E) cover loss "resulting directly from" a forgery or alteration on a qualifying document. By adopting the "resulting directly" standard, these insuring agreements draw a distinction "between the 'risk of authentication' (forgery and counterfeiting) against which the bank could not reasonably protect itself and the credit risk posed by worthless collateral."[7] The latter is not covered because a bank can investigate the assertions made therein through credit checks, appraisals, title searches, financial statements, and the like.

Courts generally have enforced this allocation of risk and drawn a strict distinction between claims involving the extension of credit against fictitious or worthless collateral and claims involving the extension of credit against legitimate collateral having value. Because Insuring Agreements (D) and (E) only cover loss "resulting directly" from a qualifying impairment on a qualifying document, courts have held that a claim is not covered unless the insured proves that it sustained an economic loss as a direct result of the defect.

OUTLINE OF ANNOTATIONS

A. Cases Interpreting the Causation Standard
   1. Interpreting "Resulting Directly From"
   2. Bonds/Policies Incorporating Other Causation Standards
B. Third-Party Loss Cases
   1. Direct Loss Bonds/Policies
   2. Pre-1980 Bonds/Policies
C. Fictitious Collateral Cases
   1. Direct Loss Bonds/Policies
   2. Pre-1980 Bonds/Policies

---

7 Liberty Nat'l Bank v. Aetna, 568 F. Supp. 860, 863 (D.N.J. 1983).

D. Compensability of Loan and Check Losses
   1. Direct Loss Bonds/Policies
   2. Pre-1980 Bonds/Policies

ANNOTATIONS

A. Cases Interpreting the Causation Standard

1. Interpreting "Resulting Directly From"

3d Cir. 2002 (Pa.). Court equated "resulting directly from" standard with proximate causation. *Scirex Corp. v. Fed. Ins. Co.*, 313 F.3d 841, 849-50.

3d Cir. 2000 (N.J.). "Loss resulting directly" standard in a Financial Institution Bond covers losses that would not have occurred "but for" the dishonest conduct. *RTC v. Fid. & Deposit Co. of Md.*, 205 F.3d 615, 655.

3d Cir. 1992 (Pa.). Court held that "resulted directly from" equated to "proximately caused by" and therefore, the insured need only prove that forgery was a "substantial factor" causing the bank's loss. *Jefferson Bank v. Progressive Cas. Ins. Co*, 965 F.2d 1274, 1281.

5th Cir. 1992 (La.). Loss resulting directly standard does not require insured to rule out all reasons for loss. In the context of a loan loss, the bank is required to demonstrate that it would not have approved the loan in the absence of the employee's fraud. *First Nat'l Bank of Louisville v. Lustig*, 961 F.2d 1162, 1168.

6th Cir. 2012 (Ohio). Predicted that Ohio Supreme Court would apply a proximate cause standard to determine whether plaintiffs sustained loss "resulting directly from" the "theft of Insured property by Computer Fraud." *Retail Ventures, Inc. v. Nat'l Union Fire Ins. Co. of Pitt., Pa.*, 691 F.3d 821, 831-32.

6th Cir. 2012 (Mich.). Court refused to apply a proximate causation analysis to determine if loss resulted directly from a covered peril, subscribing to a "direct is direct" approach. *Tooling, Mfg. & Techs. Ass'n v. Hartford Fire Ins. Co.*, 693 F.3d 665, 676.

6th Cir. 2007 (Tenn.). Court held that "resulted directly" standard incorporates the overlapping concept of proximate cause and efficient cause. *Union Planters Bank, N.A. v. Cont'l Cas. Co.*, 478 F.3d 759, 764.

7th Cir. 2009 (Ill.). Court refused to equate "direct loss" with proximate causation and calling proximate cause approach "misdirected." *First State Bank of Monticello v. Ohio Cas. Ins. Co.*, 555 F.3d 564, 571.

7th Cir. 1989 (Wis.). The court rejected the insured's attempt to use "but for" causation to establish coverage. *Cont'l Corp. v. Aetna Cas. & Sur. Co.*, 892 F.2d 540, 549.

9th Cir. 2000 (Cal.). Interpreting a commercial crime policy that covered "direct loss," court held that "direct means direct" and rejected application of proximate causation standard. *Vons Cos. v. Fed. Ins. Co.*, 212 F.3d 489, 492.

E.D. Ark. 2004. "Resulting directly from" standard is the equivalent to proximate causation. *Pine Bluff Nat'l Bank v. St. Paul Mercury Ins. Co.*, 346 F. Supp. 2d 1020, 1030.

D. Minn. 1990. Court applied a proximate causation analysis when determining whether bank's loan loss resulted directly from employee dishonesty. *Mid-America Bank of Chaska v. Am. Cas. Co. of Reading, Pa.*, 745 F. Supp. 1480, 1485.

D. Or. 2001. "Resulting directly from" standard represents a standard proximate cause analysis. *Bidwell & Co. v. Nat'l Union Fire Ins. Co. of Pitt., Pa.*, No. CV-00-89-HU, 2001 WL 204843, at *10.

N.D. Tex. 1996. Direct loss requirement in a commercial crime policy designed to limit coverage for immediate harm from employee dishonesty and does not refer to insured's liability to a third party. *Lynch Prop., Inc. v. Potomac Ins. Co.*, 962 F. Supp. 956, 962 (N.D. Tex. 1996).

Ill. App. 2004. Phrase "resulting directly from" is clear and unambiguous. Proximate causation analysis too broad to capture accurately the intent behind the phrase "loss resulting directly from." *RBC Mortg. Co. v. Nat'l Union Fire Ins. Co of Pitt., Pa.*, 349 Ill. App. 3d 706, 736-37.

Ka. 2007. Court overruled district court's decision to equate "resulting directly from" standard with "but for" causation and held that insured must establish a direct nexus between theft and loss. *Citizens Bank v. Kansas Bankers Sur. Co.*, 149 P.3d 25, 2007 Kan. App. LEXIS 1, at *1 (reversing *Citizens Bank v. Kansas Bankers Sur. Co.*, 2007 Kan. App. Unpub. LEXIS 524 (Kan. Ct. App., Jan. 5, 2007) without issuing new opinion).

Ka. App. 1990. Phrase "direct loss" is not difficult for the jury to understand and therefore jury did not need definition of the term. *Southgate Bank v. Fid. & Deposit Co. of Md.*, 794 P.2d 310, 315.

Mont. 2006. In the context of a policy covering "direct loss . . . resulting from dishonest acts," the term "direct loss" means all losses proximately caused by employee's dishonesty. *Frontline Processing Corp. v. Am. Econ. Ins. Co.*, 149 P.3d 906, 911.

N.J. 2004. Court applied proximate cause test to determine whether insured had, in the context of a commercial crime policy, suffered a direct loss. *Auto Lenders Acceptance Corp. v. Gentilini Ford, Inc.*, 854 A.2d 378, 386-87.

Wash. App. 1990. Trial court properly instructed jury to apply proximate causation standard when determining whether loss "resulted directly" from employee dishonesty. Court defined proximate causation to mean a cause which, in a direct sequence, unbroken by any independent cause produces the injury complained of and without which such injury would not have happened. *Hanson PLC v. Nat'l Union Fire Ins. Co. of Pitt., Pa.*, 794 P.2d 66, 74.

Wis. App. 2003. "Resulting directly from" standard incorporated into Financial Institution Bond, Standard Form No. 24 does not equate to proximate causation and requires proof that the loss occurred as a direct result of employee dishonesty. *Tri City Nat'l Bank v. Fed. Ins. Co.*, 674 N.W.2d 617, 625.

2. Bonds/Policies Incorporating Other Causation Standards

4th Cir. 1938 (N.C.). Bankers Blanket Bond covering loss "through any dishonest or criminal act" covered insured's liability to customers for loss suffered by customers when employee improperly used customers' money and securities. *In Schluter, Green & Co.*, 93 F.2d 810, 812-14.

6th Cir. 1934 (Mich.). The court held that where the insured bank takes a deed to property as collateral for an otherwise covered loss, the fact that the collateral proves insufficient does not prevent recovery on the bond to that extent. *USF&G v. Barber*, 70 F.2d 220, 224-27.

7th Cir. 2007 (Wis.). Financial Institution Bond covering loss "by reason of" its extension of credit against forged documents only required proof that the bank extended credit in reliance upon the documents and would not have approved the loans absent the forged documents. *First Nat'l Bank of Manitowoc v. Cincinnati Ins. Co.*, 485 F.3d 971, 980.

B. Third-Party Loss Cases

1. Direct Loss Bonds/Policies

1st Cir. 2003 (Mass.). Insured's liability for loss suffered by a third-party as a result of employee's dishonesty did not constitute a direct loss covered by a commercial crime policy. *Fireman's Fund Ins. Co. v. Special Olympics Int'l, Inc.*, 346 F.3d 259, 264.

5th Cir. 1980 (Fla.). Lender could not recover under a Bankers Blanket Bond issued to a borrower because the bond did not cover a loss sustained by a third-party and the lender sought to recover a loss it sustained after the borrower defaulted on a loan. *Everhart v. Drake Mgmt., Inc.*, 627 F.2d 686, 690-91.

6th Cir. 2012 (Ohio). Bank's liability to repay customers for loss customers suffered after employee embezzled money held in brokerage account constituted a loss "resulting directly from" employee dishonesty. *First Defiance Fin. Corp. v. Progressive Cas. Ins. Co.*, 688 F.3d 265, 270-271.

6th Cir. 1997 (Ky.). Financial Institution Bond did not cover insured's liability to a third party, even though that liability arose as a result of employee's fraudulent misrepresentations to the third party because the employee did not intend to cause the insured to suffer a loss. *Peoples Bank & Trust Co. of Madison County v. Aetna Cas. & Sur. Co.*, 113 F.3d 629, 635-36

7th Cir. 2011 (Wis.). Mortgage banker's liability to repurchase loan induced by employee dishonesty did not constitute a "direct financial loss" within the meaning of a Financial Institution Bond because the banker did not suffer a loss until it received and honored a repurchase demand. *Universal Mortg. Corp. v. Württembergische Versicherung AG*, 651 F.3d 759, 764.

7th Cir. 1989 (Wis.). The court held that losses claimed by an insured could not include indemnification of expenses incurred in settling a racketeering conspiracy case filed against the insured by a competitor because the bond provided coverage only for losses resulting directly from the dishonest or fraudulent acts of an employee of the insured. The court rejected the insured's contention that it could recover its costs on the ground that it would not have incurred the cases but for employee dishonesty. *Cont'l Corp. v. Aetna Cas. & Sur. Co.*, 892 F.2d 540, 546-48.

8th Cir. 1990 (Ark.). Although Financial Institution Bond limited coverage to loss "resulting directly" from employee dishonesty, the court interpreted the bond to cover a loss sustained by a third party because the public policy reflected in Arkansas Securities Act required fidelity bond sold to brokerage firm to cover losses sustained by firm's customers. *Foster v. Nat'l Union Fire Ins. Co. of Pitt., Pa.*, 902 F.2d 1316, 1319.

8th Cir. 1990 (Iowa). Employee induced third parties to borrow money from the insured and thereafter lend that amount to a co-conspirator. Insured's liability to third parties constituted a loss resulting directly from employee dishonesty because the bank was vicariously liable to the third parties. *First Am. State Bank v. Cont'l Ins. Co.*, 897 F.2d 319, 325-26.

8th Cir. 1987 (Iowa). Bankers Blanket Bond is not a form of liability insurance and therefore did not cover judgment entered against insured and was not subject to garnishment, even though judgment was based upon employee's embezzlement of grain from the judgment creditors. *Anderson v. Emp'rs Ins. of Wausau*, 826 F.2d 777, 779-80.

9th Cir. 2002 (Cal.). Fidelity bond issued to title company did not cover amount title company was required to contribute to make up deficiencies in title company's escrow account. *United Gen. Title ins. Co. v. Am. Int'l Grp., Inc.*, 51 F. App'x 224, 226.

9th Cir. 2000 (Cal.). Amounts paid to settle two lawsuits which alleged that insured was vicariously liable for employee's fraud on a third party did not constitute a "direct loss" under a commercial crime policy. *Vons Cos. Ins., v. Fed. Ins. Co.*, 212 F.3d 489, 492-93.

9th Cir. 2000 (Cal.). Bank's liability to customer stemming from an unauthorized withdrawal from a customer account did not constitute a loss resulting directly from a fraud on the premises of the insured. *Cal. Korea Bank v. Va. Sur. Co.*, No. 98-56778, 98-56806, 2000 U.S. App. LEXIS 12306, at *4-5.

9th Cir. 1997 (Cal.). Phrase "loss resulting directly from" is not equivalent to "proximately caused by." Bond only covered direct loss from criminal acts and therefore only covered money improperly disbursed from the bank. *United Sec. Bank v. Fid. & Deposit Co. of Md.*, No. 96-16331, 1997 U.S. App. LEXIS 27965, at *3

N.D. Cal. 1986. In the context of a loss arising from uncollected funds, court refused to apply California's concurrent causation doctrine to a Financial Institution Bond, concluding that to treat losses through fraud as being attributable to an independent and concurrent cause separate from losses through withdrawal of uncollected funds would be to rewrite the bond. *Bay Area Bank v. Fid. & Deposit Co. of Md.*, 629 F. Supp. 693, 698.

D. Conn. 2002. Commercial crime policy did not cover insured's liability to reimburse customers from money embezzled from trust accounts because the payment of a liability is not a loss resulting directly from employee dishonesty. *Finkel v. St. Paul Fire & Marine Ins. Co.*, No. 00 CV 1194, 2002 WL 1359672, at *24.

N.D. Ill. 2012. Firm's liability of money stolen by an employee from a third party's bank account did not constitute a loss resulting directly from employee dishonesty. *Sperling & Slater, P.C. v. Hartford Cas. Ins. Co.*, No. 12 C 761, 2012 U.S. Dist. LEXIS 181944, at *11-12.

D. Kan. 1993. Although Arkansas statute required securities broker and their agents to post bond which authorized direct suits thereon by third parties, that statute did not provide implied direct action on a fidelity bond because a fidelity bond is a form of first-party coverage and it does not cover insured's liability to a third party. *Sch. Emps. Credit Union v. Nat'l Union Fire Ins. Co. of Pitt., Pa.*, 839 F. Supp. 1477, 1480.

E.D. Ky. 1990. Fidelity bond issued to a city does not cover loss suffered by the public as a result of police officer's performance of his duties because the bond was only intended to cover loss to the city. *Thornsberry v. W. Sur. Co.*, 738 F. Supp. 209, 211-212.

E.D. Mich. 2008. Insured's liability for money stolen from escrow account represented a loss resulting directly from employee dishonesty because insured held the money at the time of its theft. *Phillip R. Seaver Title Co. v. Great Am. Ins. Co.*, No. 08-CV-11004, 2008 U.S. Dist. LEXIS 78568, at *9.

E.D. Mich. 1992. Amounts paid to settle lawsuits alleging that partnership was liable for employee's dishonest acts triggered fidelity bond issued to stock broker because the complaints alleged that the broker was liable for employee's fraudulent acts. *Manley, Bennett, McDonald & Co. v. St. Paul Fire & Marine Ins. Co.*, 807 F. Supp. 1287, 1288-89.

D. Minn. 2005. Stock broker suffered loss when its registered representative initiated unauthorized wire transfer of funds from client's account (rather than when broker settled secured lender's lawsuit) and thus, the loss did not fall within indirect loss exclusion. *RBC Dain Rauscher, Inc. v. Fed. Ins. Co.*, 370 F. Supp. 2d 886, 890.

D. Minn. 2001. The insured bank was sued by a customer and his creditor after a loan officer embezzled funds using the customer's line of credit. The court held that there was a genuine issue of fact as to whether the employee's misconduct occurred in connection with the embezzlement or whether it was an unrelated act intended to benefit the bank as his employer. *First Nat'l Bank of Fulda v. BancInsure, Inc.*, No. 00-2002 DDA/FLN, 2001 WL 1663872, at *3.

W.D. Mo. 1993. Bank's claimed loss did not result directly from a forgery, but resulted directly from bank's failure to follow proper procedures because bank's procedures required it to reject transaction and loss occurred solely because bank violated procedure and accepted check for deposit. *Empire Bank v. Fid. & Deposit Co of Md.*, 828 F. Supp. 675, 679.

Bank. N.D. Ohio. 1988. Liability arising after employee falsely represented that he had authority to sell large blocks of insured's stock at a discount (in order to defraud investors) was a loss "resulting directly from" employee dishonesty because the employee's conduct contemporaneously caused the insured to sustain a loss. *In re Baker & Getty Fin. Servs., Inc.*, 93 B.R. 559, 564.

W.D. Tenn. 2009. Insured could not recover under commercial crime policy because it could not prove that it owned, held, or was legally liable for stolen property. *Loeb Props. v. Fed. Ins. Co.*, 663 F. Supp. 2d 640, 646-49.

N.D. Tex. 1996. Insured's liability to customer for loss sustained by the customer after an employee embezzled money from the customer (by issuing checks on the customer's bank account) was not a direct loss covered by a commercial crime policy. *Lynch Props., Inc. v. Potomac Ins. Co.*, 752 F. Supp. 956, 964.

D. Utah. 2008. Bank's liability to repurchase loan induced by employee dishonesty did not constitute a loss resulting directly from employee dishonesty because the bank did not suffer a loss until it received and honored a repurchase demand. *Direct Mortg. Corp. v. Nat'l Union Fire Ins. Co. of Pitt., Pa.*, 625 F. Supp. 2d 1171, 1177-78.

W. Va. 1985. Direct action statute did not authorize suit against Financial Institution Bond carrier because the bond limited coverage to loss "resulting directly" from employee dishonesty and did not cover liability incurred by the insured. *Commercial Bank of Bluefield v. St. Paul Fire. & Marine Ins. Co.*, 336 S.E.2d 552, 559.

W.D. Wash. 2011. Insured that sustained chargeback losses as a result of fraudulent credit card transactions processed through its computer system by several retail merchants did not suffer a direct loss because the loss did not occur until it was unable to recover the chargeback funds from the merchant banks, bank deducted funds from insured's reserve account and insured fulfilled its contractual obligation to replace those deducted funds. *Pinnacle Processing Grp., Inc. v. Hartford Cas. Ins. Co.*, No. C10-1126-RSM, 2011 U.S. Dist. LEXIS 128203, at *13.

Cal. Ct. App. 2007. Insured's liability for stolen game piece did not constitute a direct loss within the meaning of a commercial crime policy because the insured did not own the game piece, hold the game piece and, aside from tort liability, was not legally liable for the game piece. *Simon Mktg., Inc. v. Gulf Ins. Co.*, 149 Cal. App. 4th 616, 625-26.

Del. Ch. 2010. Interpreting Massachusetts law, court held that insured could only recover defense costs expended defending suits for loss of property owned or held by insured. *Mass. Mut. Life Ins. Co. v. Certain Underwriters at Lloyd's of London*, No. 4791-VCL, 2010 Del. Ch. LEXIS 156, at *64-72.

Ill. App. 2004. Insured's liability to repurchase loans is not a loss "resulting directly from" employee dishonesty, even though the employee induced the lender to approve the loan by concealing fraudulent financial information, the insured approved and funded the claimed loans and sold the loans before it discovered the employee's dishonesty. *RBC Mortg. Co. v. Nat'l Union Fire Ins. Co of Pitt., Pa.*, 812 N.E.2d 728, 735.

Ill. App. 1990. Insured's liability to a third party for a loss sustained by the third party as a result of employee's dishonest acts was covered under a commercial crime policy covering loss "through any fraudulent or dishonest act or acts committed by any of the Employees...."

Northbrook Nat'l Ins. Co. v. NEHOC Adver. Serv., Inc., 554 N.E.2d 251, 254-55.

Ill. App. 1983. Trial court did not err in finding that bond covered liability to indemnify customer of commodity merchant for loss customer suffered when salesmen stole money customer deposited with commodity merchant. *Mortell v. Ins. Co. of. N. Am.*, 458 N.E.2d 922, 930-31.

Iowa 1999. Insured's liability for potential damage suffered by a third-party after insured's employee failed to account for a key did not qualify a "loss caused to the Insured" covered under a public employee blanket bond. *City of Burlington v. W. Sur. Co.*, 599 N.W.2d 469, 472.

Iowa 1994. Direct action statute did not authorize suit against commercial crime carrier because the policy limited coverage to loss "resulting directly" from employee dishonesty and did not cover liability incurred by the insured. *Cen. Nat'l Ins. Co. v. Ins. Co. of N. Am.*, 522 N.W.2d 39, 42-43.

Ka. 2007. Bank's liability to a third-party arising deposit of fiduciary funds into personal and business bank accounts did not constitute a loss of property resulting directly from theft on the premises of the insured. *Citizens Bank v. Kan. Bankers Sur. Co.*, 149 P.3d 25, 30-31.

La. App. 1994. Commercial crime policy issued to police department did not cover liability to state for amounts state paid on fraudulent invoices because the policy limited coverage to direct losses. State could not, therefore, pursue a direct claim on the policy pursuant to Louisiana's direct action statute. *State ex rel. Dept. of Transp. & Dev. v. Acadia Parish Police Jury*, 631 So. 2d 611, 614.

Md. 1989. Fidelity bonds are a form of first-party coverage indemnifying the insured for its loss and not a form of third-party coverage indemnifying the insured for its liability to third persons. *Three Garden Village v. USF&G*, 567 A.2d 85, 93.

Mass App. 2007. Theft from a bank account maintained by a non-insured third party did not result in a direct loss to the insured, even if the insured is liable to the third party. *Atlas Metals Prods. Co. v. Lumbermans Mut. Cas. Co.*, 63 Mass. App. Ct. 738, 743-45.

Mich. App. 1992. Insured's liability to repay commissions improperly received were not covered under a commercial crime policy because the repayment of commissions did not cause the insured a loss. *Bralko Holding, Ltd. v. Ins. Co. of N. Am.*, 483 N.W.2d 929, 930-31.

Mont. 2006. Addressing a certified question from the United States District Court for the District of Montana, the court held that "direct loss" within the context of a business owner's policy means all losses proximately caused by an employee's dishonesty. Distinguishing cases involving liability to a third party, the court held that the insured was entitled to recover costs incurred to investigate the extent of an employee dishonesty and remedy the discovered damages. *Frontline Processing Corp. v. Am. Economy Ins. Co.*, 149 P.3d 906, 911.

N.J. 2004. Employee fraudulently induced lender to approve automobile loans based upon fraudulent financial information. Auto dealer's liability to lender for loss sustained by the lender was a direct loss within the scope of a commercial crime policy. *Auto Lenders Acceptance Corp. v. Gentilini Ford, Inc.*, 854 A.2d 378, 387.

N.Y. App. 2003. Addressing a policy that covered theft of client funds while in the possession of the insured, the court held that the insured could only recover the amount embezzled and could not recover fees, interest and costs caused by the theft. *Ernst & Young LLP v. Nat'l Union Fire Ins. Co. Pitt., Pa.*, 758 N.Y.S.2d 304, 305.

N.Y. App. 1998. Security broker's liability for loss sustained by the third parties as a result of an insider trading scheme constituted an indirect loss not covered by a Financial Institution Bond. *Aetna Cas. & Sur. Co. v. Kidder, Peabody & Co. Inc.*, 676 N.Y.S.2d 559, 560-561 (N.Y. App. Div. 1998).

N.Y. Sup. Ct. 2010. Commodities futures merchant's payment of a loss suffered on personal trades conducted by a broker constituted a "direct financial loss" within the meaning of a Financial Institution Bond. *N.H. Ins. Co. v. MF Global, Inc.*, 108 A.D.3d 463, 467.

N.Y. Sup. Ct. 1995. Commodities broker's settlement of a claim brought to recover a loss due to an employee's unauthorized trades did not constitute a loss resulting directly from employee dishonesty. Court held that payment of a liability constitutes an indirect loss outside the scope of coverage. *Cont'l Bank, N.A. v. Aetna Cas. & Sur. Co.*, 626 N.Y.S.2d 385, 387-88.

N.Y. App. Div. 1993. Insured's liability to third parties as a result of employee's insider trading scheme was not a loss "resulting directly from" employee dishonesty because insured suffered a loss (i.e., the payment of a liability) solely as a result of its vicarious liability for the employee's conduct. *Drexel Burnham Lambert Grp., Inc. v. Vigilant Ins. Co.*, 595 N.Y.S.2d 999, 1009-10.

Pa. Commer. Ct. 1981. In the context of a commercial crime policy covering loss "through" employee dishonesty, mere proof that employee accepted a kickback was insufficient to establish a covered loss. Insured had to prove that it suffered a loss as a result of the kickback. *Commw. of Pa. v. Ins. Co. of N. Am.*, 436 A.2d 1067, 1070.

Vt. 2001. Customer who obtained a judgment against the insured for loss sustained by the customer as a result of an employee's embezzlement scheme could not (even with an assignment) recover on a commercial crime policy because the embezzlement scheme did not cause the insured a direct loss and insured's liability represented an indirect loss. *Patrick v. St. Paul Fire & Marine Ins. Co.*, No. 1:99CV314, 2001 U.S. Dist. LEXIS 26434, at *7.

Wash. 1993. Employee's embezzlement of third-party's money in a trust account resulted in a loss within the meaning of a commercial crime policy and Escrow Agent Registration Act. *Estate of K.O. Jordan v. Hartford Acc. & Idem. Co.*, 844 P.2d 403, 408-10.

Wash. App. 1999. The court dismissed a garnishment because it held that a loss under fidelity coverage occurs when an employee has misappropriated property from the insured, not when an employee has misappropriated property from a third party. *Fireman's Fund Ins. Co. v. Puget Sound Escrow Closers, Inc.*, 979 P.2d 872, 876-77.

Wis. App. 2008. Insured's liability to a customer, for whom it oversaw a bank account, did not constitute a direct loss covered by a commercial crime policy because the insured did not have physical possession of the customer's money and was not a bailee of the customer's money. *Meriter Health Servs. v. Travelers Cas. & Sur. Co. of Am.*, 758 N.W.2d 112, 115-18.

Wis. App. 2003. Insured's liability to repurchase loans constituted an indirect loss and did not "result directly from" employee dishonesty, even though employee colluded with third parties to obtain the loans from mortgage companies and insured's liability to repurchase the loans was due, in part, to employee's dishonesty. Because loss arose only after the borrowers defaulted on the loans and the mortgage companies demanded that the insured repurchase the loans, the insured suffered an indirect loss. *Tri City Nat'l Bank v. Fed. Ins. Co.*, 674 N.W.2d 617, 626.

2. *Pre-1980 Bonds/Policies*

1st Cir. 1966 (Mass.). Although the court recognized that Bankers Blanket Bond did not cover judicially imposed liability, it held that bond covered settlement of claims brought against the bank for loss sustained by the third party as a result of wrongful cashing of checks because settlements were a determination of total loss, not a judicially imposed liability. *Aetna Cas. & Sur. Co. v. Guar. Bank & Trust Co.*, 370 F.2d 276, 280-81.

Kan. 1970. Financial Institution Bond covering loss "through any fraudulent or dishonest act or acts committed by any of the Employees . . ." did not cover insured's potential liability to a third-party, even if that liability arose from dishonesty by an employee. *Ronnau v. Caravan Int'l Corp.*, 468 P.2d 118, 120-24.

Minn. 1976. Court held that Bankers Blanket Bond covering loss "by reason of" employee dishonesty was broad enough to cover insured's liability to a third-party, but only if the liability arose as a result of undisclosed dishonesty. The bond did not cover liability incurred as a result of the conduct disclosed to and approved by bank's board of directors. *Farmers & Merchs. State Bank of Pierz v. St. Paul Fire & Marine Ins. Co.*, 242 N.W.2d 840, 843-44.

Neb. 1976. Judgment creditor could not garnish Bankers Blanket Bond covering loss "by reason of" employee dishonesty because the bond did not cover an insured's liability to the creditor, even if that liability arose as a result of employee's fraudulent scheme to sell property he did not own. *Foxley Cattle Co. v. Bank of Mead*, 244 N.W.2d 205, 207-09.

Neb. 1981. Financial Institution Bond covering loss "through any fraudulent or dishonest act or acts committed by any of the Employees . . ." did not cover insured's potential liability to a bank customer for loss sustained by the customer as a result of a loan officer's fraudulent representations. *Omaha Bank for Coops. v. Aetna Cas. & Sur. Co.*, 301 N.W.2d 564, 566-69.

N.Y. 1980. Commercial crime policy covering loss "through" fraudulent and dishonest acts is not governed by the New York direct action statute because it does not cover insured's liability to a third party. *175 E. 74th Corp. v. Hartford Acc. & Ind. Co.*, 416 N.E.2d 584, 587-88.

C. Fictitious or Worthless Collateral Cases

1. Direct Loss Bonds/Policies

3d Cir. 2002 (Pa.). Interpreting policy that covered "direct loss caused by fraudulent or dishonest acts," court held that expenses incurred conducting studies were a direct loss caused by employee dishonesty because the employee's dishonesty (failing to follow protocols and deceptive record keeping) rendered the studies worthless. *Scirex Corp. v. Fed. Ins. Co.*, 313 F.3d 841, 849-50.

3d Cir. 1992 (Pa.). Loss resulted from the extension of credit against mortgage bearing a forged notary signature "resulted directly from" was "proximately caused by" forgery because collateral existed, the forgery precluded the bank from recording and enforcing the mortgage, and the bank could have, absent a forgery, enforced mortgage. *Jefferson Bank v. Progressive Cas. Ins. Co*, 965 F.2d 1274, 1280-85.

5th Cir. 2004 (Tex.). Bank suffered a loss resulting directly from its extension of credit on faith of a stolen certificate of deposit because the certificate of deposit existed and, absent the theft thereof, the insured could have recouped its loss by enforcing the certificate of deposit. *Brady Nat'l Bank v. Gulf Ins. Co.*, 94 F. App'x 197, 202-04.

6th Cir. 2007 (Mich.). Loss sustained under a warehouse line of credit did not result directly from a forgery because the underlying loans did not occur and therefore mortgages would not (even if legitimately executed) have been enforceable. *Flagstar Bank, FSB v. Fed. Ins. Co.*, 260 F. App'x 820, 821-22.

6th Cir. 2007 (Ohio). Loss sustained under a warehouse line of credit resulted directly from insured acting upon forged mortgage notes because the insured could have recovered its loss if the forged mortgage notes bore legitimate signatures. *Union Planters Bank, N.A. v. Cont'l Cas. Co.*, 478 F.3d 759, 764-65.

7th Cir. 2007 (Wis.). Bank suffered a loss "by reason of" its extension of credit against forged documents where it extended credit in reliance upon the documents and would not have approved the loans absent the forged documents. *First Nat'l Bank of Manitowoc v. Cincinnati Ins. Co.*, 485 F.3d 971, 977-80.

9th Cir. 2010 (Mt.). Loss allegedly sustained after a bank approved a loan based upon forged stock certificates was not covered by a Financial Institution Bond because the stock certificates were worthless and the bank would have sustained the same loss regardless of the alleged forgery. *Bank of Bozeman v. BancInsure, Inc.*, 404 F. App'x 117, 119.

11th Cir. 2011 (Fla.). Bank that approved loan based upon forged guarantee established a loss covered under a Financial Institution Bond because it could have enforced the guarantee and obtained a money judgment against a solvent guarantor absent the forgery. Thus, the guaranty would have had value to the insured if not forged. *Beach Cmty. Bank v. St. Paul Mercury Ins. Co.*, 635 F.3d 1190, 1194-97.

E.D. Ark. 2004. Bank suffered a loss resulting directly from the extension of credit on faith of forged leases because the underlying lease transactions existed and the insured could have enforced the leases if they bore legitimate signatures. *Pine Bluff Nat'l Bank v. St. Paul Mercury Ins. Co.*, 346 F. Supp. 2d 1020, 1029-33.

N.D. Ind. 1996. Insured suffered a loss resulting directly from forgery because underlying collateral existed and would have reimbursed the loss absent a forgery. *Omnisource Corp. v. CNA/Transcon. Ins. Co.*, 949 F. Supp. 681, 682-91.

E.D. Ky. 2011. Bank's loss did not result directly from a forgery, but rather from bank's acceptance of collateral that was nearly worthless regardless of whether the signatures on the assignment documents were legitimate. *Forcht Bank, N.A. v. BancInsure, Inc.*, No. 10-259-JBC, 2011 U.S. Dist. LEXIS 118141, at *8, *aff'd*, 514 F. App'x 586 (6th Cir. 2013).

D. Minn. 2013. Court held that loss did not directly result from forged guaranty because the guaranty was worthless due to the fact that the guarantor was insolvent at the time the bank made the loan. Even if the guaranty was authentic, "the loss nevertheless would have occurred because the assets purportedly represented did not exist." Court examined Pine Bluff and expressly disagreed with its analysis. *BancInsure, Inc. v. Highland Bank*, No. 11-cv-2497 (SRN/JSM), slip op. at 12-14.

D. Or. 2011. Court held that bank established loss resulting directly from extension of credit on faith of a forged document because the document would have been enforceable absent a forgery, the loans were not based upon fictitious or fraudulent collateral, and alleged guarantors had, at the time of the loan, significant assets. *Columbia Cmty. Bank v. Progressive Cas. Ins. Co.*, No. 10-817-AA, 2011 U.S. Dist. LEXIS 64004, at *6-14.

S.D.N.Y. 1990. Loss sustained after the insured extended credit against fictitious bills of lading did not directly result from extension of credit on faith of forged documents because even if the signatures had been identifiable and genuine, the bills of lading represented non-existent or previously completed transactions, and thus, the insured would have suffered the same loss. *French Am. Banking Corp. v. Flota Mercante Grancolombiana, S.A.*, 752 F. Supp. 83, 90-91.

W.D. Tenn. 1997. Bank did not suffer loss resulting directly from extension of credit against forged document when it approved a loan based upon a forged letter purporting to memorialize the borrower's entitlement to a bonus because the borrower was not entitled to a bonus and the insured would have sustained the same loss, even if the letter had been genuine. *KW Bancshares, Inc. v. Syndicates of Underwriters at Lloyd's*, 965 F. Supp. 1047, 1053-55.

Ga. App. 2000. Bank did not suffer loss resulting directly from extension of credit against forged document when it approved a loan based upon a forged assignment of a bank account because the bank account did not exist, and therefore, the bank would have been unable to recoup its loss by enforcing the assignment. *Georgia Bank & Trust v. Cincinnati Ins. Co.*, 245 Ga. App. 687, 688-90.

Minn. App. 2012. Loss allegedly sustained after a bank approved a loan based upon forged stock certificates was not covered by a Financial Institution Bond because the stock certificates were worthless and the bank would have sustained the same loss regardless of the alleged forgery. *Alerus Fin. v. St. Paul Mercury Ins. Co.*, No. A11-680, 2012 WL 254484, at *14-17.

Va. 1986. On review of a summary judgment entered in the favor of the insurer under a Bankers Blanket Bond, the court agreed that the insured suffered a loss as a result of the insolvency of the maker of the note and not because the note was altered in amount. *Va. Capital Bank v. Aetna Cas. & Sur. Co.*, 343 S.E.2d 81, 84.

2. *Pre-1980 Bonds/Policies*

4th Cir. 1962 (Va.). Bank was not entitled to recover under a Bankers Blanket Bond after it approved a loan based upon forged documents because the loss was not caused by the forgery. The loss resulted because of the insolvency of the borrower and failure of the collateral. *Piedmont Fed. Sav. & Loan Ass'n v. Hartford Acc. Ind. Co.*, 307 F.2d 310, 313-15.

D.N.J. 1983. Bank did not suffer loss resulting directly from extension of credit against forged document when it approved a loan based upon fictitious certificates of deposit because the bank could not enforce the certificates of deposit and would have sustained the same loss, even if certificates had been legitimately executed. *Liberty Nat'l Bank v. Aetna Life & Cas. Co.*, 568 F. Supp. 860, 864-67.

D. Compensability of Loan and Check Losses

1. Direct Loss Bonds/Policies

3d Cir. 2000 (N.J.). A genuine issue of material fact existed on issue on whether the bank suffered a loss resulting directly from employee dishonesty where bank officers concealed check kiting scheme and the concealment led the insured to exclude loan from a sale, which in turn resulted in the insured being put in the unfavorable position of having to deal with a delinquent account that was certain to result in a significant loan loss. *RTC v. Fid. & Deposit Co. of Md.*, 205 F.3d 615, 654-57.

2d Cir. 2000 (N.Y.). Bank suffered a loss "resulting directly from" employee dishonesty because loan officer fraudulently induced the bank to approve the claimed loans by concealing that borrower was accused of illegal acts. That the value of the bank's collateral decreased due to a downturn in the real estate market did not break the causal connection because the employee's dishonesty occurred prior to the approval of the loan and the bank would not have approved the loan had it known the concealed allegations. *FDIC v. Nat'l Union Fire. Ins. Co. of Pitt., Pa.*, 205 F.3d 66, 76-77.

5th Cir. 1997 (N.J.). Bank induced to enter into mortgage swap transactions based upon fraudulent documents was not entitled to recover under Fraudulent Mortgages Rider because the fraud did not impair the value of the swap documents. *FDIC v. Firemen's Ins. Co. of Newark, N.J.*, 109 F.3d 1084, 1088.

5th Cir. 1995 (La.). The FDIC produced sufficient evidence from which jury could conclude that the bank suffered a loss resulting directly from employee dishonesty because evidence introduced at trial proved that loan officer had a personal relationship with the borrower and the bank would not have approved the claimed loans if the loan officer had not concealed that relationship. *FDIC v. Fid. & Deposit Co. of Md.*, 45 F.3d 969, 976.

5th Cir. 1992 (La.). Bank suffered a loss resulting directly from employee dishonesty because it was fraudulently induced to approve loans based upon fraudulent loan proposals, which concealed material information about the borrower. *First Nat'l Bank of Louisville v. Lustig*, 961 F.2d 1162, 1167-68.

5th Cir. 1932 (Tex.). A jury question was raised as to whether the alleged acts of fraud or dishonesty were the cause of loss to the insured bank. *Shaw v. Metro. Cas. Ins. Co. of N.Y.*, 62 F.2d 133, 134.

8th Cir. 1983 (Ark.). Insured did not suffer a loss resulting directly from overdrafts because upon discovery of the overdrafts, it created a loan to cover the overdrafts and sold that loan to another bank. The insured's potential exposure to repurchase the loan was not covered and thus, district court properly directed a verdict for the insurer. *Bank of Mulberry v. Fireman's Fund Ins. Co.*, 720 F.2d 501, 502-03.

8th Cir. 1934 (Neb.). The court held that dishonesty in the abstract cannot be compensated in damages. In a suit to recover on a fidelity bond, the dishonesty must have resulted in pecuniary loss. Proof that money was missing and that the cashier was in a critical position with regard to the money was held insufficient evidence of loss. *Am. Employer's Ins. Co. v. Roundup Coal Mining Co.*, 73 F.2d 592, 593-94.

9th Cir. 1986 (Cal.). Bank's crediting of checks to depositor's account and allowing subsequent withdrawal of those funds proximately caused loss sustained by depository bank and thus, was within scope of an exclusion precluding coverage for loss "resulting from" uncollected items. *Mitsui Mfrs. Bank v. Fed. Ins. Co.*, 795 F.2d 827, 830-31.

N.D. Cal. 2012. Insured's claimed loss was not caused by the allegedly forged signature on the Account Control Agreement, but by the fact that alleged borrower lied about his securities. Even if the signature on the agreement was genuine, insured would have suffered the same loss because it had made the loan based on nonexistent collateral. *Valley Cmty. Bank v. Progressive Cas. Ins. Co.*, 854 F. Supp. 2d 697, 707-10.

E.D. La. 2011. Customer that invested in a hedge fund that invested in Madoff's Ponzi scheme did not suffer a loss resulting directly from employee dishonesty. Direct loss was borne by the hedge fund. That the customer could not recoup its investment did not constitute a direct loss. *Methodist Health Sys. Found. v. Hartford Fire Ins. Co.*, 834 F. Supp. 2d 493, 496-97.

D. Minn. 2004. Unauthorized use of a trade secret did not constitute a loss directly caused by a theft because the insured was not deprived of its use of the trade secret. Loss of the exclusive use of a trade secret was not a direct loss caused by theft. *Cargill, Inc. v. Nat'l Union Fire Ins. Co. of Pitt., Pa.*, No. A03-187, 2004 WL 51671, at *11-12.

D. Minn. 1990. Question of fact existed as to whether bank suffered a loss resulting directly from employee's fraudulent concealment of past-due loans. That the bank approved and disbursed the loan proceeds before the employee's alleged misrepresentation did not prevent recovery because the insured renewed the loans based upon the employee's dishonesty. *Mid-America Bank of Chaska v. Am. Cas. Co. of Reading, Pa.*, 745 F. Supp. 1480, 1484-85.

D. Or. 2001. Securities broker suffered a loss "resulting directly from" a forged check because it accepted forged checks from a client, negotiated the checks, and credited the client's account. That the loss did not manifest until the insured's bank detected the forgery and exercised its right of set off (based upon a breach of transfer warranties) did not break causal chain because deposit of checks proximately caused breach of transfer warranties and triggered claim for set off. *Bidwell & Co. v. Nat'l Union Fire Ins. Co. of Pitt., Pa.*, No. CV-00-89-HU, 2001 WL 204843, at *9-11.

D.P.R. 2004. Employee's manipulation of internal records did not cause loss "resulting directly and solely from employee dishonesty" where the insured could not demonstrate that the employee misappropriated its assets. Write-off of accounts did not constitute a loss "resulting directly and solely from employee dishonesty." *Oriental Fin. Grp. v. Fed. Ins. Co.*, 309 F. Supp. 2d 216, 222-27.

S.D. W. Va. 1973. Upon entry of a valid judgment, insured's liability for loss sustained by another bank that purchased fraudulent loans could trigger liability under a Financial Institution Bond covering loss "through" employee dishonesty because liability arose as a result of employee's dishonesty. *First Nat'l Bank of W. Hamlin v. Md. Cas. Co.*, 354 F. Supp. 189, 194-95.

Ill. App. 1971. Insured suffered loss "through fraudulent or dishonest acts" because employee concealed shortage and shortage could only have been caused by employee embezzlement. *Daniel Grocer Co. v. New Amsterdam Cas. Co.*, 266 N.E.2d 365, 368-69.

La. App. 1983. Employee dishonesty policy did not cover insured's liability to a customer for a loss sustained by the customer after an employee set the customer's property on fire to conceal theft. *Gulf Build. Servs. v. Travelers Ind. Co.*, 435 So. 2d 477, 478-79.

Va. 1986. Bank did not suffer a loss "through" its extension of credit on faith of a forged or altered document because note was enforceable under Virginia law. If the bank was unable to collect on the note, the loss would arise from the maker's insolvency or another cause unrelated to the enforceability of the note and thus, would not be incurred "through the Insured's having . . . given any value . . . on the faith of . . . written instruments which prove to have been . . . raised or otherwise altered." *Va. Cap. Bank v. Aetna Cas. & Sur. Co.*, 343 S.E.2d 81, 83-84.

   2.   *Pre-1980 Bonds/Policies*

5th Cir. 1981 (La.). Jury's finding that bank suffered a loss "through" employee dishonesty and verdict in favor of insurer were not inconsistent because insurer had defenses unrelated to causation. *Central Progressive Bank v. Fireman's Fund Ins. Co.*, 658 F.2d 377, 381-82.

5th Cir. 1966 (Tex.). An insurer raised as a defense the fact that the insured could have settled its claim and avoided loss under the policy by early action to rescind the contract in question with its aggrieved customers. However, the court held that the insured was not required to make such a decision at its peril, particularly when the insured's position was uncertain and the insurer was given the option to participate in the settlement negotiations, but refused. *Nat'l Sur. Corp. v. Rauscher, Pierce & Co.*, 369 F.2d 572, 576-78.

5th Cir. 1934 (Tex.). Bank suffered a direct loss from a dishonest act when the bank president secretly procured loans from bank through straw men not qualified for loans. *Md. Cas. Co. v. Am. Trust Co.*, 71 F.2d 137, 139.

7th Cir. 1979 (Ill.). Bank suffered a loss "through" employee dishonesty after the bank's president approved unsecured loans to a small circle of friends, relatives, and business associates based upon false documentation. *First Nat'l Bank Co of Clinton, Ill. v. Ins. Co. of N. Am.*, 606 F.2d 760, 768-69.

7th Cir. 1971 (Ind.). The insured claimed a loss resulting from acts by its vice president and cashier in failing to properly handle NSF checks. Court held that evidence was sufficient to sustain the district court's finding that the employee's actions were dishonest from the beginning and that the insured "suffered a loss as a result of the dishonest acts." *Citizens State Bank v. TransAmerica Ins. Co.*, 452 F.2d 199, 203-04.

8th Cir. 1971 (Mo.). An insured bank officer made two loans: one to a corporation that the officer knew was in bad financial condition, for which the officer received a payment; and the other to a different corporation, from which the officer received a payment after he had resigned from the bank. The court held that the insured's loss on the first loan was covered by the bond, but the loss on the second one was not because the bank continued extending additional credit to this borrower long after the officer's employment had terminated. *U.S. Fire & Guar. Co. v. Empire State Bank*, 448 F.2d 360, 364-65.

D. Or. 1968. The court held: (1) a bank may claim for loss of forged or counterfeit securities under Insuring Clause E, irrespective of whether it has a remedy against third parties for the loss; i.e., the cause of the loss is the false writing, rather than the bank's refusal or failure to exercise its salvage remedies; and (2) a bank's negligence (unless it rises to discovery of fraud, or bad faith) is not such an intervening cause as to displace the forged or counterfeit signatures as the cause of the loss in question. *Citizens Bank of Or. v. Am. Ins. Co.*, 289 F. Supp. 211, 214.

E.D. Va. 1969. A bank's negligence in failing to detect or discover a loss was held not to be a defense; i.e., it is not the effective cause of a loss due to fraud or dishonesty by its employees. The court reasoned that "[n]either negligence nor any failure to discover what by diligence might have been discovered; nothing, short of actual discovery by the Bank of dishonesty ... will defeat claims for loss caused by that dishonesty, unless it is otherwise provided in the [policy]." *Arlington Trust Co. v. Hawkeye Sec. Ins. Co.*, 301 F. Supp. 854, 858.

Colo. 1935. The court found that an insured must establish a direct cash loss, instead of an uncertain book shortage, and must trace the cash shortage to the dishonest act. The court noted that "[b]efore liability attaches under the bond, a loss due to the 'dishonest act' of an employee or employees must be already established." *Am. Sur. Co. v. Capitol Bldg. & Loan Ass'n*, 50 P.2d 792, 794.

Ind. App. 1980. The bank was held to have no claim for alteration or forgery because the alteration of the number line did not constitute a material alteration of the check; i.e., it was as if the check did not show the number. Thus, the bank's loss was held to have occurred not because of a "forgery or alteration," but rather because the purchaser negligently issued the check in the amount shown and wrongfully stopped payment after the bank had credited the farmer's account with the amount of the check. *St. Paul Fire & Marine Ins. Co. v. State Bank of Salem*, 412 N.E.2d 103, 113.

Iowa 1980. A bank consolidated and renewed various loans to a contractor, allegedly based on the contractor's purported settlement with an owner showing that a substantial amount of funds were due. In fact, the owner had already paid the contractor, who kept the funds and did not repay the bank. The purported settlement agreement was a photocopy of a copy, and the bank had, by its own investigation, determined that at least a portion of the funds said to be owing to its customer/contractor had already been paid, or was not owed. Nevertheless, the bank made a loan. The bank made a claim against the insurer after discovering that funds were not owed. However, the court held that because the bank conducted an independent investigation, the bank did not extend credit on the faith of the false settlement agreement within the meaning of Insuring Clause E. *First Nat'l Bank, Colfax v. Hartford Acc. & Indem. Co.*, 295 N.W.2d 425, 428-29.

La. App. 1999. An insured sought recovery under a commercial crime policy for loss attributed to embezzlements to which its employee had confessed. The evidence at trial was held to have failed to corroborate the fact or amount of the thefts, or when the alleged dishonesty occurred, so the insurer prevailed. The court held that the insured must prove the dishonest acts took place during the policy term and directly caused the loss. *Provincial Hotels, Inc. v. Mascair*, 734 So. 2d 136, 139.

La. App. 1972. A bank advanced loans on an unsecured basis. Subsequently the borrower pledged as collateral third-party notes that were allegedly forged. The court held that there was no coverage under Insuring Clause (E) because "the real cause of the loss sustained by the [bank] in this case was [the borrower's] failure to repay the loan and not any fraud perpetrated on the bank at the time the loan was made." *Allen State Bank v. Traveler's Indem. Co.*, 270 So. 2d 270, 273.

La. Ct. App. 1969. The court held that a claimed loss must (a) be "actually suffered" by the insured and (b) result from the proven fraud or dishonesty of the insured's employees. A mere discrepancy in an employee's accounts is not sufficient to establish dishonesty within the intents of the bond because "every man is presumed to be honest until the contrary is established." *Salley Grocer Co., Inc. v. Hartford Acc. & Indem. Co.*, 223 So. 2d 5, 8-9.

Mich. 1927. The court held that the question of causation is for the jury and may be proven by circumstantial evidence, based on "preponderance of the evidence test" rather than "beyond a reasonable doubt." *Farmers' Produce Co. v. Aetna Cas. & Sur. Co.*, 213 N.W. 685, 687.

Tex. App. 1975. Loss on loans secured by forged stock certificates delivered to the insured as collateral after the loans were made and when the borrower could not repay the insured were held not "through" forged documents. The term "through" was held to be defined as: "by means of, in consequence of, by reason of, by the intermediary of, and because of." *Tex. Nat'l Bank v. Fid. & Deposit Co. of Md.*, 526 S.W.2d 770, 774.

SECONDARY SOURCES

John W. Bassett, *Direct Loss Under the Fidelity Insuring Agreement of the Financial Institution Bond*, DEF. COUNS. J. 487 (1987).

Lisa Block & Dirk E. Ehlers, *Aetna v. Kidder Peabody: Trend or Anomaly?*, in AMERICAN BAR ASSOCIATION'S 1999 SURVEY: TOP TEN LIST OF MOST VEXING FIDELITY CLAIMS ISSUES (1999).

Joseph J. Brenstrom, *Third Party Losses: Causational Approach to Resolving Claims on Fidelity Bonds and Other Common Crime Coverages Based Upon Losses To An Insured Arising out of Claims Against the Insured By Third Parties* (unpublished paper presented at the annual meeting of the Surety Claims Institute, Miami, Florida in June, 1997).

Bradford R. Carver, *Loss and Causation*, in HANDLING FIDELITY BOND CLAIMS (Michael Keeley & Timothy M. Sukel eds., 2005).

Duncan L. Clore, *Suits Against Financial Institutions: Coverage and Considerations*, 20 FORUM 83 (1984).

Paul R. Devin & R. Allan Fryer, *Third-Party Claims Against the Insured*, in HANDLING FIDELITY BOND CLAIMS (Michael Keeley and Timothy M. Sukel eds., 1999).

Christopher Franklin, *Legal Liability for Third Party Losses under Commercial Crime Policies* (unpublished paper presented at the Fidelity and Surety Annual Mid-Winter Meeting of the Fidelity and Surety Law Committee of TIPS in New York, New York, January 27, 1995).

Lawrence R. Fish, *Ownership of Property—Interest Covered*, in COMMERCIAL CRIME POLICY, (Gilbert J. Schroeder, ed., 1996).

Mark S. Gamell, *Third Party Claims and Losses under the Financial Institution Bond*, in I FID. L.J. 75 (1995).

Peter C. Haley, *How to Combine Fact-Finding and Legal Research in the Investigation of a Clause (E) Claim*, in HANDLING FIDELITY BOND CLAIMS (Michael Keeley & Timothy M. Sukel eds., 2005).

Peter C. Haley, *Paradigms of Proximate Cause*, 36 TORT & INS. L.J. 147 (2000).

Peter C. Haley, *Clause (E): The Continued Importance of Defined Terms and Causation Theories*, in Financial Institution Bonds (Duncan L. Clore ed., 1998).

Stephen M. Kranz, Patricia H. Thompson, & Ashley M. Daugherty, *Can Direct mean Direct? Untangling the Web of Causation in Fidelity Coverage*, XVI FID. L.J. 153 (2010).

John F. Kruger & Linda Sorensen, *Causation in Fidelity Cases*, 12 FORUM 420 (1976).

John A. Nocera, *Third Party Claims Under Fidelity Bonds* (unpublished paper presented at Surety Claims Institute Annual Meeting in Williamsburg, Virginia, June, 1995).

Maura Z. Pelleteri, *Causation in Loan Loss Cases*, in LOAN LOSS COVERAGE UNDER FINANCIAL INSTITUTION BONDS (Gilbert Schroeder & John J. Tomaine eds., 2007).

Scott L. Schmookler, *Third Party Claims and Losses under the Financial Institution Bond*, in I FID. L.J. 75 (1995).

Scott L. Schmookler, *The Compensability of Third-Party Losses Under Fidelity Bonds*, VII FID. L.J. 115 (2001).

Scott L. Schmookler, *The Compensability of Warehouse Lending Losses*, in LOAN LOSS COVERAGE UNDER FINANCIAL INSTITUTION BONDS (Gilbert Schroeder & John J. Tomaine eds., 2007).

Susan Sullivan & Teresa Jones, *The Question of Causation in Loan Loss Cases*, XI FID. L.J. 97 (2005).

Bradford A. Thomas, *Analysis of Direct Losses and Indirect Losses Under the Modern Financial Institution Bonds Fidelity Coverage and Exclusions* (unpublished paper presented at the Southern Surety and Fidelity Claims Conference, April 1990).

Karen Wildau, *Evolving Law of Third-Party Claims Under Fidelity Bonds: When Is Third-Party Recovery Allowed?*, 25 TORT & INS. L.J. 92 (1989).

SECTION 5 — LOSS*

> The Underwriter, in consideration of an agreed premium, and in reliance upon all statements made and information furnished to the Underwriter by the Insured in applying for this bond, and subject to the Declarations, Insuring Agreements, General Agreements, Conditions and Limitations, and other terms hereof, agrees to indemnify the Insured for:
> Loss resulting directly from . . . .

COMMENT

All insuring agreements of the standard form Financial Institution Bond begin with the phrase "Loss resulting directly from," followed by the relevant coverage description. No recovery is possible under these insuring agreements without an insured showing it has a legally cognizable interest in assets which were misappropriated, or were measurably lessened in value, as a direct result of facts both (a) covered by an insuring agreement and (b) established by the insured.

The word "loss" has been interpreted by most courts in a common-sense way. The net financial impact on the insured is the focus of the vast majority of loss determinations. The movement of money between accounts at the insured institution, absent other facts, is not a covered loss. Nor is the taking of money in which the insured has no legally cognizable ownership or custodial interest. An embezzlement accomplished by the creation of non-existent "loans" to fictitious persons (absent other facts) engenders no greater recovery than a simple hand-in-till embezzlement. A loss that might be sustained in the future is, in virtually all cases, not compensable until actually sustained. And loss involving an employee's actions that create a liability of the insured to a third party, but not a loss of the insured's own assets, or those it holds in trust, only rarely results in a covered claim.

Nonetheless, the complex fact patterns of many bond claims make it difficult to craft legal rules that apply in all cases. Some courts have allowed recovery in a very limited class of cases where an employee directly caused the insured to incur liability to a third party. And difficult loss determinations often involve claims which allege a series of

---

* By Peter C. Haley, Nielsen, Haley & Abbott, San Rafael, California.

loan transactions which were partly legitimate and partly fictitious; the timing of recoveries by insureds also engenders loss calculations which can vary considerably.

As a result, the following important questions must be asked regarding any alleged "loss" under the Financial Institution Bond:

(1) What is the nature of the asset or property that constitutes the alleged "loss?"
(2) When was the alleged "loss" discovered?
(3) When was it sustained?
(4) What was the value of the subject matter of the alleged "loss" when it was discovered and when it was sustained?
(5) Did the insured receive anything of value in connection with the events causing the alleged "loss?"
(6) Did the insured recoup any of its alleged "loss" from any source?

These questions are required because "loss" is an undefined term; because the bond excludes recoveries for certain kinds of "loss" because "money" and "property" are protean terms that insureds continuously attempt to manipulate; because the legal concepts of "ownership" and "control" must be tightly tied to the historical facts of the subject claim; and because "loss" scenarios often play out over periods of time that do not precisely coincide with the relevant policy period or periods involved in the claim.

ANNOTATIONS

1st Cir. 1998 (Mass.). A diversion of funds by the company's officer for his own gain fell under the authorized representative exclusion of a commercial crime policy and did not constitute a direct loss because the policy did not restrict the scope of the exclusion to acts benefiting the company; the exclusion encompassed all acts resulting from the officer's power to divert funds. *Stop & Shop Cos. v. Fed. Ins. Co.,* 136 F.3d 71, 75-76.

2d Cir. 1981 (N.Y.). The court reversed summary judgment for a fidelity insurer on an insured's claim for attorneys' fees and litigation expenses to settle lawsuits brought against it by customers of its brokerage company based upon waiver of the policy's notice requirements. But it held that the insured could not add to its recovery any portion of the other losses from the lawsuits, including the sum of money paid by it in settlement of the suits. When a fidelity insured recovers a portion of its losses, it must apply the recovery to the items of loss for which the fidelity insurer is liable. Because the insurer had no liability for the margin violations underlying part of the settlement payment, and because the remainder of the settlement did not arise from the employee's misconduct, the insurer had no liability for the settlement. *H.S. Equities, Inc. v. Hartford Acc. & Indem. Co.*, 661 F.2d 264, 269-71.

3d Cir. 2013. Summary judgment for insurer reversed because there was a genuine dispute of fact whether the insured investment firm owned, held or was legally liable for any of the embezzled funds. *Marion v. Hartford Fire Ins. Co.*, No. 12-1553, 2013 U.S. App. Lexis 9825, at *10-14.

4th Cir. 1987 (N.C.). The insurer refused to pay the amount of an employee dishonesty claim that represented proceeds from outstanding loans previously paid to the bank as interest due on earlier loans. The court held that the bank was entitled to this amount, less the amount of funds recovered from the dishonest employee, because if the bank had not made loans to the dishonest employee, it would have allocated the funds to honest borrowers, who would have repaid the principal with interest. *St. Paul Fire & Marine Ins. Co. v. Branch Bank & Trust Co.*, 834 F.2d 416, 417-18.

5th Cir. 1998 (Tex.). An insured's replacement of funds embezzled from a third party's account managed by the insured did not constitute loss under a commercial crime policy because the funds embezzled did not belong to the insured. The embezzlement caused a direct loss to the third party, but the replacement of the third party's funds by the insured represented an indirect loss, and the intent of the policy was to provide coverage only for a direct loss to the insured from acts of employee dishonesty. *Lynch Props., Inc. v. Potomac Ins. Co. of Ill.*, 140 F.3d 622, 627-29.

5th Cir. 1980 (Fla.). The insured sustained no loss when employees took permanent investment funds and deposited them to a general account of insured; the insured merely experienced a 'shifting of liabilities.'" *Everhart v. Drake Mgmt., Inc.,* 627 F.2d 686, 691-92.

5th Cir. 1975 (Fla.). The court held that unauthorized transfers from one corporate trust account to another corporate trust account does not in and of itself constitute loss compensable under a corporate blanket bond. A bonding company's liability is premised on whether the allegedly dishonest transfer fulfilled any legitimate obligation of the insured. The burden of proving the legitimacy of the inter-corporate transfer is on the party relying on its validity. *Fid. & Deposit Co. of Md. v. USAFO S Hail Pool, Inc.,* 523 F.2d 744, 754-64.

5th Cir. 1969 (Fla.). The court held that a bonding company is not liable under a fidelity bond until the insured has suffered a proven loss. *Am. Empire Ins. Co. of South Dakota v. Fid. & Deposit Co. of Md.,* 408 F.2d 72, 75-77.

5th Cir. 1966 (Tex.). In an action on a brokerage blanket bond, where the broker rejected the bond purchasers' demand for rescission of the sale of bonds and later settled an action brought by the purchasers' by agreeing to repurchase the bonds in ten installments at seventy-five percent of face value, the court rejected defendant's argument that all loss would have been avoided by accepting the proposed rescission. The court held that accepting rescission under these circumstances would have put the insured in the position of choosing at its peril between taking the safe way out by returning to the pre-sale status or simply relinquishing its coverage bond by insisting in good faith on its rights to defend the suit. Finally, the court refused to deduct from the loss the profits made by the insured on the subject transactions. *Nat'l Sur Corp. v. Rauscher, Pierce & Co.,* 369 F.2d 572, 577-79.

7th Cir. 1994 (Ind.). The court stated that a "loss" as defined by the bond does not include bookkeeping or theoretical loss unaccompanied by actual withdrawals of cash or other penuiary loss. *Cincinnati Ins. Co. v. Star Fin. Bank,* 35 F.3d 1186, 1191-92.

8th Cir. 2010 (Wis.). Insured cannot recover loss alleging employee dishonesty due to overpayments based on inflated time records submitted by employee. The "loss" was a financial benefit earned in the normal course of employment and could not characterized as "stolen" money. *R & J Enterprises v. General Cas. Ins. Co.,* 627 F.3d 723.

8th Cir. 1983 (Mo.). The insured attempted to recover under a Mortgage Bankers Blanket Bond for loss it sustained in executing a loan under a forged Veteran's Administration certificate of commitment. After executing the certificate of commitment, the insured assigned the loan to the G.N.M.A. The insured was forced to repurchase the loan once the forgery was discovered. Following the borrower's default, the insured purchased the mortgaged property at its own foreclosure sale for the amount of the loan plus incurred interest and expenses. Later, the insured sold the property for an amount below the purchase price. The court held that although the insured's purchase of the mortgaged property at the foreclosure sale extinguished the debt owed by the mortgagor, this was only a "paper transaction." It further held that the insured had suffered a loss in the amount of the price that it paid to repurchase the loan, less the fair market value of the property when the insured bought it at the foreclosure sale. *Regional Inv. Co. v. Haycock,* 723 F.2d 38, 40-42.

8th Cir. 1971 (Mo.). When the bank's officers dishonestly made the loans in question, the insurer was obligated to indemnify the insured for all losses incident to the covered loan transactions, including loss attributable to depreciation of collateral pledged to the bank in connection with one of the transactions. *U.S. Fire & Guar. Co. v. Empire State Bank,* 448 F.2d 360, 366-67.

8th Cir. 1971 (Mo.). Court held that the insured could recover kickbacks received by its employee for referring potential customers to other lending agencies, even though the kickbacks were not paid from the company's funds and no diminution of assets had occurred. The court noted that an employee is required at all times to act in his employer's best interest, and when by culpable conduct he fails to do so and the employee profits, a loss to the insured occurs and liability attaches under the bond. *Boston Sec., Inc. v. United Bonding Ins. Co.,* 441 F.2d 1302, 1303-04.

9th Cir. 1997 (Cal.). A fidelity bond did not provide coverage for expenses incurred after the insured's employees violated an IRS levy, because the policy limited coverage to loss resulting directly from employee dishonesty. Only the plain meaning interpretation of the term "direct loss" applied,"- not the broader term "proximately caused loss." *United Sec. Bank v. Fid. & Deposit Co. of Md.*, No. 96-1, 6331, 1997 U.S. App. LEXIS 27965, at *2-3.

9th Cir. 1986 (Cal.). After two of the insured's employees perpetrated a complex fraud involving fictitious shipments of equipment to dealers and the sale of equipment to unauthorized foreign purchasers, the court found the provision in the policy concerning replacement costs ambiguous and held that the proper measure of the insured's loss was the stipulated fair market value of its equipment. Prejudgment interest also was allowed. *James B. Lansing Sound, Inc. v. Nat'l Union Fire Ins. Co. of Pitt.*, 981 F.2d 1549, 1569-71.

9th Cir. 1975 (Cal.). A savings and loan association that survived a merger brought an action against the insurer that had issued a bond to it and against the insurer that had issued a bond to the merged association to recover attorneys' fees and costs incurred subsequent to merger in defending suits based upon allegedly fraudulent acts committed by employees of the merged association prior to the merger. The court held that the surviving association's acquisition of liabilities of the merged association did not amount to a new loss under the bond. *Fid. Sav. & Loan Ass'n v. Republic Ins. Co.*, 513 F.2d 954, 956.

10th Cir. 1998 (Utah). FIB insurer was allowed to offset net recoveries relating to covered loan loss of the failed, insured bank, pursuant to the recovery provisions of the FIB, even though the insurer itself did not pursue those recoveries. *FDIC v. United Pacific Ins. Co.*, 152 F.3d 1266, 1274-75.

10th Cir. 1994 (Utah). An FIB loss is calculated as of the date a dishonest employee disbursed loan funds, and an FIB insurer cannot assert the defense that the value of unliquidated collateral exceeds the claimed loss. Once recoveries are made on that collateral, the insurer is entitled to them under the recovery provisions of the FIB. *FDIC v. United Pacific Ins. Co.*, 20 F.3d 1070, 1079-80.

10th Cir. 1992 (Utah). A fidelity insurer, sued on a fidelity policy in connection with a loss of artwork stolen from a university, was not liable for money spent by the university to recover some of the missing artwork. The rider in the policy limited the insurer's liability to the amount of loss remaining "after deducting the net amount of all reimbursement and recovery." To make the insurer liable for the recovery cost would require deducting a negative "net amount." The court held that only a positive amount should come into play as a deduction. *Brigham Young Univ. v. Lumbermens Mut. Cas. Co.,* 965 F.2d 830, 835-36.

D.D.C. 1980. The court held that where a loss is suffered by a third party, but the insured is obligated to pay the third party, loss to the insured accrues when the third party demands such compensation from the insured. *Fid. & Deposit Co. of Md. v. President & Directors of Georgetown Co.,* 483 F. Supp. 1142, 1146-47.

M.D. Fla. 1979. Employees of the insured misappropriated funds. The insurer denied coverage on the ground that there was no "loss" under the bond because the misappropriated funds were used to pay legitimate corporate expenses. The court held that the insurer had not met its burden of showing that the funds were used for legitimate corporate purposes, in part because the insured was insolvent at the time such expenses were incurred, and state law prohibited the insured from incurring such expenses in its insolvent condition. *Fid. & Deposit Co. of Md. v. USA FORM HailPool, Inc.,* 465 F. Supp. 478, 484-90.

D. Md. 1985. In an action under a Commercial Blanket Fidelity Bond, the court held that the insured bears the initial burden of proving the existence of a loss by demonstrating how the missing funds were spent and that this burden was not met by showing only that the insured was put into receivership. *Towne Mgmt. Corp. v. Hartford Acc. & Indem. Co.,* 627 F. Supp. 170, 175.

D. Mass. 2010. Fundquest brought suit to recover moneys mistakenly paid to one of its employees. The court held that the employee's silence, while employed at the insured, after receiving the money constituted employee dishonesty, and also held that Traveler's was limited to applying one deductible for the entire claim. *Fundquest, Inc. v. Travelers Cas. and Sur. Co.*, 715 F. Supp. 2d 202, 205-06

D. Mass. 2003. An employee diverted donations as part of a fraudulent fund-raising campaign. Coverage was properly denied under two crime insurance policies. The organization did not suffer a direct loss covered under the policies. On motion for summary judgment, the court held that the insured did not suffer a direct loss unless the insured's assets, and not those of a third party, decreased because of the offending employee's wrongful conduct. Because the donors suffered the loss, and not the organization, the insurer did not have a duty to indemnify its insured. *Fireman's Fund Ins. Co. v. Special Olympics, Inc.*, 249 F. Supp., 2d 19, 26-28; *aff'd*, 346 F.3d 259 (1st Cir. 2003).

W.D. Mich. 2011. Auto dealer did not incur a "Loss" under crime policy when employees used funds received on vehicle sales to pay current expenses rather than paying Chrysler Financial as required by the dealer's contract with Chrysler Financial. *Coopersville Motors, Inc., v. Federated Mut. Ins. Co.*, 771 F. Supp. 2d 796, 800-01.

W.D. Mo. 1984. A bank sought recovery under a 1980 edition of a Form 24 Bankers Blanket Bond, alleging that a bank employee embezzled funds held in a trust account. The uncontradicted testimony established that the bank did not suffer any loss because the bank did not own an interest in the trust account. *Shearson/Am. Express, Inc. v. First Cont'l Bank & Trust Co.*, 579 F. Supp. 1305, 1313-14.

D.N.J. 2011. An auto dealership could not recover for loss sustained by its failure to receive bonus monies that were not earned because the dealership's employees had submitted bogus customer satisfaction surveys as the basis for the bonus. *Jack Daniels Motors, Inc. v Universal Underwriters Ins. Co.*, No. 11-1379., 2011 WL 346500, at *2.

S.D.N.Y. 1978. Court held that "[t] here is no requirement to balance losses against past profits." It further noted that "[a]ll that is required is that such losses be due to the fraud or dishonest acts of the employee." *H.S. Equities. Inc. v. Hartford Acc. & Indem. Co.*, 464 F. Supp. 83, 88, *rev'd on other grounds*, 661 F.2d 264 (2d Cir. 1981).

D. Or. 1992. A production credit association made bad loans to a cattle company that resulted in a loss. The fidelity bond covered the dishonesty of the director of the association, who controlled the cattle corporation and who had failed to disclose the corporation's fraudulent procurement of the loans and loan extensions. The insurer was liable for interest on earlier loans paid out of the proceeds of later loans. The bond provision excluding from coverage loss of potential income not realized by the insured due to covered loss did not apply to such loss items. *Interstate Prod. Credit Ass'n v. Fireman's Fund ins. Co.*, 788 F. Supp. 1530, 1539-40.

D. Or. 1968. The court held that an insured bank that loans money to a borrower with forged or counterfeited stock certificates as collateral for the loan at the request of and through another bank, in accordance with a long established inter-relationship of accommodation between those banks, has sustained a loss under the bond without regard to the insured's possible remedy against the makers of the note. *Citizens Bank of Or. v. Am. Ins. Co.*, 289 F. Supp. 211, 213.

E.D. Pa. 1971. Where the insured's employee used company funds to cover previous shortages in other customers' accounts and where such embezzlement is continuing, the principal has suffered a loss recoverable under a commercial blanket bond the bond. *John B. White, Inc. v. Providence Wash. Ins. Co.*, 329 F. Supp. 300, 303.

D.S.C. 1981. After a borrower defaulted in the interest payments on an allegedly fraudulent mortgage arranged by the insured credit union's employee, the credit union discovered that the value of the loan exceeded the value of the property. The court held that the net amount of loss included attorneys' fees and foreclosure expenses incurred by the insured in pursuit of recovery against the borrower. *MBAFB Fed. Credit Union v. Cumis Ins. Soc'y, Inc.*, 507 F. Supp. 794, 797-99.

W.D. Tenn. 2009. The insured did not sustain a covered "Loss" when its employee's stole the personal funds of the insured's CEO from a checking account the insured did not own and over which it did not have control. *Loeb Props., Inc., v Fed. Ins. Co.*, 663 F. Supp. 2d 640, 647-48.

E.D. Va. 1969. Where the insured bank attempted to mitigate losses by consolidating loans and taking additional security, the bank was not barred from collecting net losses from the bonding company up to the authorized limits of the bond. *Arlington Trust Co. Hawkeye-Sec. Ins. Co.,* 301 F. Supp. 854, 859.

Cal. Ct. App. 2007. The insured transferred money to a company to pay advertising costs. An employee of that company which also had money from other advertisers in its account stole $24 million from that account. The insured settled with the unpaid vendors for $10.6 million. The court held that the loss of the insured was not limited to the $10.6 in settlement funds, because all entities that placed funds in that account were tenants in common of interests in their respective funds. *Sears, Roebuck & Co. v. Nat'l Union Fire Ins. Co. Of Pitt., Pa.,* No. B187280, 2007 WL 2876149, at *4-5, *9.

Del. Chancery Ct. 2010. Several fund entities insured by Lloyd's which both directly and indirectly provided money to Bernard Madoff and his companies, sought coverage relating to Madoff's embezzlements. One Plaintiff was held to have stated a valid indemnity claim because it directly provided funds to Madoff. After an extended discussion of conditions under which insureds may assert fidelity claims for loss of money and property for which they are legally liable, the court ordered further proceedings relating to claims involving third-party actions against the insureds. *Mass. Mut. Life Ins. Co. v. Certain Underwriters at Lloyd's Of London,* No. C.A. No. 4791-VCL, 2010 WL 2929552, at *2, *5, *7, *14-18.

Ga. Ct. App. 1985. A fidelity insurer issued a life insurance company blanket bond to an insurance company. A general agent of the insured submitted fraudulent life insurance applications; the insured's losses consisted of commissions paid this employee, as well as advances for office expense and other items. Although one section of the fidelity bond exempted the insurer from liability for loss sustained through failure of any general agent to repay money advanced by the company, the court held that the insured could include office expense allowance and related items advanced to the dishonest employee in connection with the insured's business of selling life insurance as part of net loss. *Fid. & Deposit Co. v. Sun L Ins. Co.,* 329 S.E.2d 517, 520.

Ill. Ct. App. 1979. In the case of successive bonds, the date of "loss" is the date the dishonest acts occurred, not when the insured was required to settle liability based on the acts in question. Also, prejudgment interest is recoverable. *Reserve Ins. Co. v. Gen. Ins. Co. of Am.,* 395 N.E.2d 933, 936-38.

Iowa 1988. An employee of the insured bank embezzled funds from the bank by forging hundreds of notes purporting to be loan agreements with bank customers. To conceal the embezzlement, the employee paid off these notes as they became due, in part with funds obtained from newly forged notes. At the time the employee's misconduct was discovered, the face amount of the outstanding notes was $4 million, of which over $2 million represented interest payments on prior fraudulent notes. The court held that the insured bank could not recover the portion of the outstanding notes representing prior interest payments. The court held that "loss" under the bond refers to the actual depletion of bank funds caused by the employee's dishonest act, not to the eventual personal liability of the employee to the bank. The court reasoned that allowing the bank to recover the prior interest payments would, in effect, allow the bank to profit from the employee's misconduct. *Am. Trust & Sav. Bank v. U.S. Fire & Guar. Co.,* 418 N.W.2d 853, 855-56.

Kan. 1970. In a garnishment action by a judgment creditor of the insured against a bonding company, the court held that a creditor cannot recover because debts incurred for regular business liabilities are outside the scope of the bond and do not constitute loss under the bond. *Ronnau v. Caravan Int'l Corp.,* 468 P.2d 118, 121-23.

La. Ct. App. 1976. In an action by an insured bank against a bonding company, the court found that the insured could maintain the action even though the directors of the bank paid the sums missing to the bank as payments on loans to be repaid, because the insured has sustained a loss under the bond. *Sugarland State Bank v. Aetna Ins. Co.,* 330 So. 2d 336, 338.

Minn. 1992. The majority shareholder of the insured bank, who was also an officer of the bank, financed the purchase of stock with a personal loan from another bank. After that bank threatened to call the personal loan, the officer sold certificates of deposit of the insured bank without recording the liability on the insured's books, and deposited the funds in the bank that had threatened to call the personal loan. He later transferred these funds to the insured bank and used them to repay personal loans he had obtained from the insured bank. The court held that this series of transactions did not cause a loss to the insured bank because the officer had merely moved money between accounts at the insured bank. The court held that bookkeeping losses are not actual losses, and are not recoverable under the bond. *TransAmerica Ins. Co. v. FDIC,* 489 N.W.2d 224, 229-30.

Miss. 1968. In an action on a commercial blanket bond the court held that a loss of trust funds occurs when a misappropriation is made by the insured's employee. The insurer's liability is not conditioned on first requiring the employer to reimburse the trust fund for the missing sums. *Am. Nat'l Ins. Co. v. U.S. Fire & Guar. Co.,* 215 So. 2d 245, 248-49.

N.C. Ct. App. 1984. The court allowed a setoff, from the amount for which a fidelity insurer was liable, for amounts of money collected from a dishonest employee after discovery of the employee's embezzlement. The insurer had received such funds after waiving a proof of loss to allow the insured to collect the loss without filing a claim; since the court could not separate the waiver from the collections it facilitated, equity required the crediting of the insurer's liability. *B & H Supply Co. v. Ins. Co. of N. Am.,* 311 S.E.2d 643, 648-49.

N.D. 1979. A defaulting employee embezzled funds prior to expiration of bond. After expiration, employee transferred new funds to old accounts to cover up original losses. The insurer denied a substantial part of the claim on the theory that when the employee replaced the original funds, the first loss was nullified, and the real loss occurred after expiration of the policy, when the employee took new funds to replace the original embezzled funds. However, there was an ambiguity in the policy as to when the loss occurred, at the time of the original embezzlement, or when later funds were taken to replace the earlier funds. The insurer was presumed to know that ambiguities should be resolved in favor of coverage. Therefore, coverage existed. *Corwin Chrysler-Plymouth, Inc. v. Westchester Fire Ins. Co.,* 279 N.W.2d 324, 327.

Tenn. Ct. App. 1981. The court rejected an insurer's contention that an insured bank had suffered no actual loss with respect to embezzled funds used to pay off previously-created fictitious notes and the interest thereon. The officer's purpose in obtaining the funds had no bearing on the bank's loss; the actual loss suffered by the bank consisted of the principal balance due on the unpaid notes, plus accrued interest. If the officer created a new note to pay off an old note, payment on the old note would come out of the general funds of the bank. When those funds reentered the bank as payment of an old note, they reentered the bank's general fund and lost any interest character they might have had at the time of payment. *Bank of Huntingdon v. Smothers*, 626 S.W.2d 267, 270.

Va. 1986. The insured sought recovery under a Bankers Blanket Bond for loss it sustained when an insolvent maker and endorser were unable to pay off a note that had been raised in amount by a third-party wrongdoer. The court held that the insured was a holder in due course and could enforce the note in its altered form. No loss is incurred by paying value for a valid and enforceable instrument. The grant of the insurer's motion for summary judgment was appropriate. *Va. Capital Bank v. Aetna Cas. & Sur. Co.*, 343 S.E.2d 81,83.

Wash. Ct. App. 1982. A bank obtained two fidelity bonds from the insurer, insuring against losses due to dishonest or fraudulent acts of employees. One employee obtained fraudulent loans from the bank by making the loans to fictitious customers. In refusing to reduce the bank's recovery by the amount of the fraudulently obtained funds used to cancel any prior fraudulent indebtedness, the court held that when a fidelity insured recovers a portion of its losses, it does not have to apply the recovery to the items of loss for which the fidelity insurer is liable. *Puget Sound Nat'l Bank v. St. Paul Fire & Marine Ins. Co.*, 645 P.2d 1122, 1129.

W. Va. 1985. The court held that without a "misappropriation" of the insured's property, a "loss" under an Employee Fidelity Insurance Policy will not result—despite the presence of damages sustained by a third party as a result of a fraudulent misrepresentation and a judgment against the insured. *Commercial Bank of Bluefield v. St. Paul Fire & Marine Ins. Co.*, 336 S.E.2d 552, 556-58.

Wis. Ct. App. 2008. Hospital's fidelity claim was properly denied because it was based on the theft by a hospital employee of dues paid to the hospital by on-staff physicians. The hospital did not own or control the account from which the funds were taken. *Meriter Health Sys., Inc. v. Traveler's Cas. & Sur. Co. of Am.*, 758 N.W. 2d 112, 116.

SECONDARY SOURCES

Samuel J. Arena, Jr. & Marianne Johnston, *Determining the Amount of Loan Losses and the Potential Income Exclusion, in* LOAN LOSS COVERAGE (Gilbert J. Schroeder & John J. Tomaine, eds. 2007)

William T. Bogaert & Kerry Evenson, *Loss and Causation Under the Financial Institution Bond, in* FINANCIAL INSTITUTION BONDS 577 (Duncan L. Clore, ed., 3d ed. 2008).

SECTION 6 — CONSTRUCTION AND INTERPRETATION*

To determine what it covers, a Financial Institution Bond must be construed or interpreted. This is easy when there is no dispute about what the bond covers. Instead of disputing the scope of coverage, the real dispute may be whether the loss that the insured alleges actually occurred. On many occasions, however, the parties disagree as to what the bond covers; they construe or interpret it differently. Then it becomes essential to understand the rules of interpretation and construction that a court would use to decide the question. These rules can have a decisive effect on the outcome.

A. The Rules of Interpretation

The interpretation of a Financial Institution Bond is a question of law.[1] The bond is a contract, so the general rules of contract interpretation apply.[2] Although the rules of construction are based on state law, they are fairly uniform across state jurisdictions. A court's objective is to ascertain what the agreement was between the parties and enforce it accordingly.[3] But because the bond is a type of insurance, rules peculiar to the construction of insurance contracts may also apply.[4]

The court's primary objective is to effectuate the true intent of the parties,[5] as manifested when they formed the contract, inferred if possible solely from the written terms of the contract.[6] This task "is significantly guided by the principle that a contract should be construed to give it effect as a rational business instrument and in a manner that

---

* By James A. Knox, Jr., Christensen & Ehret, LLP, Chicago, Illinois.
1   Universal City Studios Credit Union v. CUMIS Ins. Society, Inc., 208 Cal. App. 4th 730, 737-38 (Ct. App. 2012); Aldridge Elec., Inc. v. Fid. & Dep. Co. of Md., No. 04 C 4021, 2008 U.S. Dist. LEXIS 85090, at *9-10 (N.D. Ill. Sept. 10, 2008).
2   *Id.* at 626.
3   Bank of Ann Arbor v. Everest Nat'l Ins. Co., No. 12-11251, 2013 U.S. Dist. LEXIS 24999, at *7 (E.D. Mich. Feb. 25, 2013).
4   Fireman's Fund Ins. Co. v. Special Olympics Int'l, 249 F. Supp. 2d 19, 26 (D. Mass. 2001), *aff'd,* 346 F.3d 259 (1st Cir. 2003); Am. Cas. Co. v. Etowah Bank, 288 F.3d 1282, 1284 (11th Cir. 2002); FDIC v. Firemen's Ins. Co., 109 F.3d 1084, 1087 (5th Cir. 1997).
5   *Lynch,* 140 F.3d at 625-26.
6   *Universal City,* 208 Cal. App. 4th at 738.

will carry out the intent of the parties."[7] For example if the purpose of the insurance is to cover only loss resulting directly from employee dishonesty, that purpose will govern the interpretation.[8]

No single term is construed in a vacuum to determine if it is ambiguous.[9] Rather, the bond is construed as a whole, with due regard to the risk undertaken, the subject matter that is insured, and the purposes of the entire contract.[10] "[N]o one phrase, sentence, or part of [the bond] should be isolated from its setting and considered apart from the other provisions."[11] Thus, the entire contract is examined, including the relation of all of its parts to each other, in order to arrive at an objective and reasonable construction.[12] As stated by one court: "It is axiomatic that a contract should be interpreted so as to harmonize all of its provisions and all of its terms, which terms should be given effect if it is possible to do so."[13]

For example, although the term "abstraction or removal" did not necessarily require dishonesty, fraud, or a criminal act if considered in isolation, it had to be read with the rest of the bond. And since every other coverage did require dishonesty, fraud, or a criminal act, so did abstraction or removal.[14] In another case, where the insurer's interpretation of the bond's limits allowed all other bond terms to have meaning but the insured's interpretation did not, the insurer's interpretation controlled because under the assumption that parties to an insurance contract do not intend to create meaningless provisions, only the insurer's interpretation was reasonable.[15] The bond was, therefore,

---

7 Commerce Bank & Trust v. St. Paul Mercury Ins. Co., No. 04-1264B, 2005 Mass. Super. LEXIS 692, at *8 (Mass. Super. Ct. May 31, 2005).
8 *Aldridge*, 2008 U.S. Dist. LEXIS 85090, at *9.
9 Home Sav. & Loan v. Aetna Cas. & Sur. Co., 817 P.2d 341, 366-67 (Utah Ct. App. 1991).
10 *Aldridge*, 2008 U.S. Dist. LEXIS 85090, at*9.
11 *Lynch*, 140 F.3d at 626; *see also* Traders State Bank v. Cont'l Ins. Co., 448 F.2d 280, 283 (10th Cir. 1971).
12 *Home Sav.*, 817 P.2d at 366-67.
13 *Id.* at 367.
14 Hamiltonian Fed. Sav. & Loan Assoc. v. Reliance Ins. Co., 527 S.W.2d 440, 443 (Mo. Ct. App. 1975).
15 United Ass'n Union Local No. 290 v. Fed. Ins. Co., No. 07-1521, 2008 U.S. Dist. LEXIS 62746, at *15 (D. Or. Aug. 11, 2008).

unambiguous, and the court could not go to the next step of construing the ambiguity against the insurer.[16]

Courts assume the parties intended for the words and phrases of a bond to be construed in accordance with their plain meaning, if possible.[17] A Financial Institution Bond "is construed according to the plain and ordinary meaning of its terms, like any other contract."[18] As another court stated, the words "are to be understood in their ordinary and popular sense . . . unless used by the parties in a technical sense, or unless a special meaning is given them by usage."[19]

B. Resolving Ambiguities

If after applying the foregoing initial interpretive principles, the words of a bond are still susceptible to more than one reasonable interpretation, an ambiguity may exist.[20] However, courts do not search for ambiguity.[21] They avoid adopting a strained or absurd interpretation.[22] Mere disagreement over meaning does not render a term ambiguous.[23] Particularly when dealing with a defined term, a court should not resort to extrinsic definitions.[24]

If application of the plain and ordinary meaning rule does not readily yield an unambiguous interpretation, the court may resort to rules of construction. These rules are not always so enlightening—it has been said "that there is a canon to support every possible result."[25] Nevertheless, they can be useful.

---

16 *Id.*
17 *Bank of Ann Arbor*, 2013 U.S. Dist. LEXIS 24999, at *7.
18 PrivateBank & Trust Co. v. Progressive Cas. Ins. Co., 2004 U.S. Dist. LEXIS 8938, at *8 (N.D. Ill. May 17, 2004).
19 Cal. Union Ins. Co. v. Am. Diversified Sav. Bank, 948 F.2d 556, 560 (9th Cir. 1991) (quoting CAL. CIVIL CODE § 1644 (West 1985)).
20 *PrivateBank & Trust*, 2004 U.S. LEXIS 8938, at *9.
21 *Id.*
22 *Cal. Union*, 948 F.2d at 560.
23 *Lynch*, 140 F.3d at 626.
24 Alpine State Bank v. Ohio Casualty Ins. Co., 941 F.2d 554, 560 (7th Cir. 1991).
25 RICHARD A. POSNER, THE FEDERAL COURTS: CRISIS AND REFORM 276 (1985).

The following are some of the more frequent construction rules relied on by the courts. If inconsistent, specific provisions in a contract control over general ones.[26] Exclusions may be read narrowly.[27] Under the principle of ejusdem generis, a general term must take its meaning from the specific terms with which it appears. A court recently invoked this to narrowly construe an exclusion's reference to "other confidential information of any kind."[28]

Similarly, if a particular word is obscure or of doubtful meaning taken by itself, its meaning may be clarified by reference to associated words. A court once used this doctrine to construe a bond's reference to statutory larceny as not extending to telephone fraud.[29] The bond's other related coverages—robbery, larceny, burglary, theft, and hold-up—all imported a crime of taking property right from where it was located. Thus, statutory larceny likewise had to be limited to schemes perpetrated by persons present at the location of the property.

Courts do strive to follow the language of the bond itself. That is, they follow the "four corners rule" of contract interpretation, which requires that the court initially look to the language of the contract alone, and not to extrinsic evidence, to determine if the contract is ambiguous. An agreement reduced to writing must be presumed to speak the intention of the parties who signed it. It speaks for itself, and the intention with which it was executed must be determined from its wording, not changed by extrinsic evidence, absent a facial ambiguity.[30]

If and only if there is an ambiguity in the text of the bond—more than one reasonable interpretation even after application of the ordinary rules of construction—courts take different approaches. They may allow extrinsic evidence—underwriting, statements made during negotiations of terms, trade usage, etc. This may or may not reveal what the parties really intended. Or courts may, and all too often do, invoke the doctrine

---

26 Exchange State Bank v. Kan. Bankers Sur. Co., 177 P.3d 1284, 1285 (Kan. Ct. App. 2008) (applying willful extension of credit exclusion).
27 Fed. Ins. Co. v. United Cmty. Banks, Inc., No. 2:08-cv-0128-RWS, 2010 U.S. Dist. LEXIS 101646, at *30-31 (N.D. Ga. Sept. 27, 2010).
28 Retail Ventures, Inc. v. Nat'l Union Fire Ins. Co., 691 F.3d 821, 833 (6th Cir. Ohio 2012).
29 Kean v. Maryland Cas. Co., 223 N.Y.S. 373 (App. Div. 1927).
30 *Aldridge*, 2008 U.S. Dist. LEXIS 85090, at *11.

of contra proferentem.[31] This doctrine dictates that the ambiguity be construed in favor of the insured and against the insurer as drafter of the policy.[32]

C. Against Contra Proferentem

Although some courts still apply this doctrine, other courts have come to realize that contra proferentem is a rule of absolute last resort.[33] It should not be applied when the question may be resolved by extrinsic evidence.[34] It is meant primarily for cases "where the written contract is standardized and between parties of unequal bargaining power."[35] Even then, it does not allow a court to adopt an unreasonable interpretation or construe an unclear term in an implausible and harmful way.[36]

As another court explained, the doctrine "does not bar the use of oral testimony to disambiguate a written contract," but "is a tie-breaker, used to resolve cases in which the written contract remains ambiguous even after oral evidence has been admitted."[37] Besides, "English does not contain words for all complex economic arrangements; whenever the language lacks a one-to-one mapping of words to ideas (or words to things) there is a potential for ambiguity and confusion."[38] That does not mean the insured should always win. If every possible ambiguity was resolved in favor of the insured, "the cost of insurance would skyrocket and policies would become even longer, more complex, and less digestible, as insurers tried to define every term (and then define the words used in the definitions)."[39] Thus, contra proferentem "is the last

---

31 *United Cmty. Banks, Inc.*, 2010 U.S. Dist. LEXIS 101646, at *30-31 (N.D. Ga. Sept. 24, 2010) (The bond should be read as a layman would read it. Hence, if the bond would be confusing to a layman, the bond is ambiguous, and it will be construed against the drafter.).
32 *Aldridge*, 2008 U.S. Dist. LEXIS 85090, at *10.
33 *See, e.g.*, French Am. Banking Corp. v. Flota Mercante Grancolombiana, S.A., 752 F. Supp. 83, 90 (S.D.N.Y. 1990).
34 New Jersey v. Merrill Lynch & Co., 640 F.3d 545, 550 (3d Cir. 2011).
35 Yellowbook Inc. v. Brandeberry, 708 F.3d 837, 847 (6th Cir. 2013).
36 *Id.*
37 Residential Mktg. Grp., Inc. v. Granite Inv. Grp., 933 F.2d 546, 549 (7th Cir. 1991).
38 Hall v. Life Ins. Co. of N. Am., 317 F.3d 773, 775 (7th Cir. 2003).
39 *Id.* at 776 (emphasis original).

rule to be resorted to, and never to be applied except when other rules of interpretation fail."[40]

Resort to the rule should also be "limited by the degree of sophistication of the contracting parties or the degree to which the contract was negotiated."[41] "The argument for contra proferentem is pretty feeble when the policyholder is a sophisticated commercial enterprise rather than an individual consumer."[42] Nevertheless, some courts construe ambiguities in favor of sophisticated insureds if the policy was issued with little or no negotiation of its terms.[43]

Be that as it may, the standard form Financial Institution Bond is different. It was not drafted by insurers unilaterally. It was drafted jointly by representatives of the banking and surety industries; that is, the American Bankers Association and the SFAA.[44] The rule of construction of an ambiguity against the insurer is not applicable because the terms of the standard bond were negotiated between parties with relatively equal bargaining power.[45] In effect, the bond is "an arms-length, negotiated contract between sophisticated business entities," and, therefore, the

---

40 Quad Constr., Inc. v. William A. Smith Contracting Co., 534 F.2d 1391, 1394 (10th Cir. 1976).
41 New Jersey v. Merrill Lynch & Co., 640 F.3d 545, 550 (3d Cir. 2011) (citing 11 WILLISTON ON CONTRACTS § 32:12, at 480-81 (4th ed. 1999)); Cummins, Inc. v. Atl. Mut. Ins. Co., 867 N.Y.S. 2d 81, 83 (App. Div. 2008) (doctrine of contra proferentem inapplicable where parties, both sophisticated entities, had equal bargaining power in drafting agreement).
42 Farmers Auto. Ins. Ass'n v. St. Paul Mercury Ins. Co., 482 F.3d 976, 977-78 (7th Cir. 2007) (citing F.S. Smithers & Co. v. Federal Ins. Co., 631 F.2d 1364, 1368 (9th Cir. 1980)); see also Beanstalk Group, Inc. v. AM General Corp., 283 F.3d 856, 858-59 (7th Cir. 2002); Eagle Leasing Corp. v. Hartford Fire Ins. Co., 540 F.2d 1257, 1260-61 (5th Cir. 1976).
43 *Farmers*, 482 F. 3d at 977-78; Minn. Sch. Bds. Assoc. Ins. Trust v. Employers Ins. Co., 331 F.3d 579, 581-82 (8th Cir. 2003).
44 Shearson/American Express, Inc. v. First Cont'l Bank & Trust Co., 579 F. Supp. 1305, 1309 (W.D. Mo. 1984).
45 Sharp v. Fed. Savings & Loan Ins. Corp., 858 F.2d 1042, 1046 (5th Cir. 1988); Commerce Bank & Trust v. St. Paul Mercury Ins. Co., No. 04-1264B, 2005 Mass. Super. LEXIS 692, at *7-8 (Mass. Super. Ct. May 31, 2005).

public policy considerations in favor of coverage that govern, for instance, certain types of liability insurance, do not apply.[46]

Moreover, even when a term of the bond is drafted solely by the insurer, the fact remains that an insurer and a financial institution are both sophisticated business entities dealing at arm's length. The financial institution is capable of understanding the terms of an industry-wide bond form (along with any custom terms) and negotiating for different terms if desired. As one court explained, "The general rule of construing terms against the drafter and in favor of coverage is not controlling in a dispute between established and experienced parties as it would be between a sophisticated organization and an unsophisticated, private party."[47]

D. About the Annotations

The annotations below have been divided into categories of coverage issues and then further into cases finding the coverage unambiguous, ambiguous, controlled (or not) by statute, or controlled by the fact that the language had been jointly drafted.

OUTLINE OF ANNOTATIONS

A. Employee Dishonesty
   1. Unambiguous
   2. Ambiguous or Construed Against Insurer
   3. Statutory Considerations
   4. Employee Benefit Definition
     (a) Unambiguous
     (b) Ambiguous or construed against insurer
     (c) Joint drafting considerations
   5. Employee Definition
     (a) Unambiguous

---

[46] *Commerce Bank & Trust,* 2005 Mass. Super. LEXIS 692, at *7 (citing FDIC v. Ins. Co. of N. Am., 105 F.3d 778, 785 (1st Cir. 1997)) (holding that notice prejudice rule does not apply to financial institution bonds).

[47] First McHenry Corp. v. BancInsure, Inc., No. 10 C 50256, 2011 U.S. Dist. LEXIS 64589, at *12 (N.D. Ill. June 17, 2011).

        (b) Ambiguous or construed against insurer
        (c) Statutory Considerations
    B. On Premises (including Loan Exclusion)
        1. Unambiguous
        2. Ambiguous or Construed Against Insurer
        3. Joint Drafting
    C. In Transit
    D. Forgery, Counterfeit, Alteration, and Similar Coverages
        1. Unambiguous
        2. Ambiguous or Construed Against Insurer
        3. Joint Drafting
    E. Fraudulent Mortgage
    F. Computer and Funds Transfer Fund
        1. Unambiguous
        2. Ambiguous or Construed Against Insurer
    G. Trading Exclusion
        1. Unambiguous
        2. Ambiguous or Construed Against Insurer
        3. Statutory Considerations
        4. Joint Drafting
    H. Miscellaneous Terms
        1. Unambiguous
        2. Ambiguous or Construed Against Insurer
    I. Discovery
        1. Unambiguous
        2. Ambiguous
        3. Statutory Considerations
    J. Notice and Proof of Loss
        1. Unambiguous
        2. Ambiguous or Construed Against Insurer
        3. Joint Drafting
        4. Statutory
    K. Limitations
        1. Unambiguous
        2. Ambiguous or Construed Against Insurer
        3. Statutory Considerations
    L. Loss
        1. Unambiguous
        2. Ambiguous or Construed Against Insurer

3. Statutory Considerations
4. Third-Party Liability
   (a) Unambiguous
   (b) Ambiguous or construed against insurer
   (c) Statutory considerations
M. Single Loss, Prior Loss, and Limits Issues
   1. Unambiguous
   2. Ambiguous or Construed Against Insurer
   3. Statutory Considerations
N. Termination as to Employee
   1. Unambiguous
   2. Ambiguous or Construed Against Insurer
O. Termination, Takeover, and Merger
   1. Unambiguous
   2. Ambiguous or Construed Against Insurer
   3. Joint Drafting

ANNOTATIONS

A. **Employee Dishonesty**

1. Unambiguous

3d Cir. 2000 (N.J.). The term "manifest intent" in a fidelity bond's definition of employee dishonesty is unambiguous and requires proof the employee had a purpose or desire to obtain a financial benefit for himself or a third party and to cause the insured to sustain a loss. *RTC v. Fid. & Deposit Co. of Md.*, 205 F.3d 615, 643.

6th Cir. 1997 (Ky.). A battery of interpretative canons applies to insurance contracts when the language is ambiguous or self-contradictory. Otherwise, the contract is read according to its plain meaning, character, and intent. *Peoples Bank & Trust Co. v. Aetna Cas. & Sur. Co.*, 113 F.3d 629, 636.

10th Cir. 1994 (Utah). Manifest intent can be inferred if a particular result is substantially certain to follow from the employee's act. *FDIC v. Oldenburg,* 34 F.3d 1529, 1539.

D.N.J. 1991. Insurance contracts are contracts of adhesion. If policy supports two meanings, the one sustaining coverage will be applied. Even if not ambiguous, policy will be interpreted in accordance with the objectively reasonable expectations of the average insured. These rules extend to fidelity bonds issued to banks. However, it would unduly strain employee dishonesty definition to construe it as including acts undertaken by employee with a pure heart and no dishonest motive or intent to cause loss to insured and gain a financial benefit for himself. Nor can insured reasonably expect to recover in such a case. *Oritani Sav. & Loan Ass'n v. Fid. & Deposit Co. of Md.,* 821 F. Supp. 286, 291.

Ill. App. Ct. 1983. Definition of "dishonest or fraudulent acts" imposed by amendment to brokers blanket bond did not render coverage illusory. Amendment was part of an industry-wide response to confusion created by undefined dishonesty terms. Insured was experienced and sophisticated; the amendment was unambiguous and had to be given effect as written. Officer did not gain anything from unauthorized trading except commission and thus exclusion to sub-definition of financial benefit applied. *Mortell v. Ins. Co. of N. Am.,* 458 N.E.2d 922, 929-30.

2. Ambiguous or Construed Against Insurer

4th Cir. 1930 (W. Va.). If bond is fairly and reasonably susceptible of two constructions, one favorable to the bank and the other favorable to insurer, the former, if consistent with the object for which the bond was given, must be adopted. *Brandon v. Holman,* 41 F.2d 586, 588.

4th Cir. 1915 (W. Va.). "Fraud and dishonesty" extend beyond acts which would be criminal. The words are to be given broad signification and "taken more strongly against the surety company." *Citizens Trust & Guar. Co. v. Globe & Rutgers Fire Ins. Co.,* 229 F. 326, 330.

5th Cir. 1978 (Fla.). Bankers Blanket Bond is to be broadly construed and any ambiguity is construed against insurer. *Eglin Nat'l Bank v. Home Indem. Co.,* 583 F.2d 1281, 1285.

7th Cir. 1979 (Ill.). Dishonest and fraudulent as terms in a fidelity bond have a broader meaning than they do in criminal law and include acts showing a want of integrity or breach of trust. *First Nat'l Bank Co. v. Ins. Co. of N. Am.,* 606 F.2d 760, 768.

7th Cir. 1971 (Ind.). Words "dishonest and fraudulent" used in reference to conduct covered by a Bankers Blanket Bond are to be given broad meaning. *Citizens State Bank v. Transamerica Ins. Co.,* 452 F.2d 199, 203.

E.D. Pa. 1995. An insurance policy must be read as a whole and construed according to the plain meaning of its terms. Clear and unambiguous language is given effect, not rewritten to mean something other than what it says. "Manifest intent" as used in fidelity bond means the employee must have a subjective intent to cause loss but the employee would have this intent if she desired the loss to result from her actions or knew it was substantially certain to result from her actions. *Good Lad Co. v. Aetna Cas. & Sur. Co.,* No. 92-5678, 1995 U.S. Dist. LEXIS 9456, at *13-16, *aff'd without op.,* 1996 U.S. App. LEXIS 15068 (3d Cir. May 9, 1996).

D.P.R. 1991. Fidelity bonds are subject to the rules of construction applicable to insurance policies generally. Construing "fraud or dishonesty" broadly against the insurer, those words extend beyond criminal acts. *FDIC v. CNA Cas. of P.R.,* 786 F. Supp. 1082, 1087.

Ill. App. Ct. 1998. An insurance policy's construction presents a question of law suitable for disposition by summary judgment. *Oxford Bank & Trust v. Hartford Acc. & Indem. Co.,* 698 N.E.2d 204, 208.

N.J. 1978. The words dishonest or fraudulent in a Bankers Blanket Bond are given broad scope and taken most strongly against the insurer. *Nat'l Newark & Essex Bank v. Am. Ins. Co.,* 385 A.2d 1216, 1224.

N.J. 1955. Construction of the terms of a fidelity bond is a matter of law unless it depends upon disputed extrinsic facts. "Fraud and dishonesty" are broadly interpreted. *Mortgage Corp. of N.J. v. Aetna Cas. & Sur. Co.,* 115 A.2d 43, 36.

3. Statutory Considerations

8th Cir. 1990 (Iowa). Statute governed Bankers Blanket Bond and required that it be liberally construed. *First Am. State Bank v. Cont'l Ins. Co.*, 897 F.2d 319, 325-26.

S.D. Iowa 2005. An Iowa statute required fidelity coverage for state banks and did not include manifest intent or direct loss requirements, unlike the fidelity bond at issue. The bond stated it was not statutory but the court applied the statute anyway. However, the manifest intent and direct loss requirements were consistent with the statute, not mere surplusage, and therefore could be applied, although a substantial certainty test would be used to determine intent. *Kan. Bankers Sur. Co. v. Farmers State Bank,* 408 F. Supp. 2d 751, 755-56.

Tex. 1935. A fidelity bond required by statute to protect a state bank against embezzlement, wrongful abstraction, or willful misapplication by the bank's employees will be given a more liberal construction than a contract involving only the rights and obligations of a surety. Court held bank could recover from its fidelity insurer a dividend declared by directors and officers that was partially converted by them instead of being paid in full to the shareholders; the dividend was not the act of the bank itself. *First State Bank of Temple v. Metro. Cas. Ins. Co.,* 79 S.W.2d 835, 839-40.

Wash. 1993. Ambiguous terms in fidelity bonds are to be construed in favor of coverage. If a bond is given pursuant to statute, the statute is considered part of the bond. Conditions repugnant to the statute will be treated as surplusage, and statutory provisions not expressed in the bond will be inserted. A standard dictionary may be used to define undefined terms as used in an insurance policy. A "fraudulent act" is synonymous with a deceitful act. An act is "dishonest" if it involves a breach of trust. *Estate of Jordan v. Hartford Acc. & Indem. Co.,* 844 P.2d 403, 408-13.

4. Employee Benefit Definition

(a) Unambiguous

3d Cir. 2000 (N.J.). "Golden handcuff" bonuses, even if "one time only" in nature, unambiguously were "normal course" of employment benefits excluded from the financial benefit definition. *RTC v. Fid. & Deposit Co. of Md.,* 205 F.3d 615, 646, 649-50.

5th Cir. 2003 (Tex.). If a policy term has a definite and certain meaning, it is not ambiguous. *Performance Autoplex II Ltd. v. Mid-Continent Cas. Co.,* 322 F.3d 847, 857-59.

8th Cir. 2010 (Iowa). Insured overpaid employee as a result of his dishonest time records. Bond unambiguously excluded this as employee benefits earned in the normal course of employment. The payments were not unearned and therefore outside the exclusion; the word "earned" referred merely to employee benefits as a generic category. *R & J Enterprizes v. Gen. Cas. Co. of Wis.,* 627 F.3d 723, 727-28.

M.D. Ala. 1997. An ambiguous policy must be construed in favor of insured and exclusions will be interpreted as narrowly as possible. However, clear language will be enforced as written; court will not defeat express provision by making a new contract for the parties. Thus, where only financial benefit to employee was increased commissions, exclusion of commissions from definition of financial benefit applied and fidelity claim based on improper administration of fleet sales program by car dealer's employee was not covered. *Auburn Ford Lincoln Mercury, Inc. v. Universal Underwriters Ins. Co.,* 967 F. Supp. 475, 478, *aff'd without op.*, 130 F.3d 444 (11th Cir. 1997).

N.D. Ill. 1986. Ambiguities are resolved in favor of coverage and exclusions must be narrowly construed. However, if there is no ambiguity in the terms of an insurance contract, the court's construction should favor neither party. A fidelity bond excluded commissions from a definition of the financial benefit a dishonest employee had to manifestly intend to obtain for coverage to arise. That exclusion extended to all types of commissions, including those not earned in the normal course of employment. However, coverage could arise if the employee intended both to cause loss to the insured and financially benefit third parties. *Hartford Acc. & Indem. Ins. Co. v. Wash. Nat'l Ins. Co.,* 638 F. Supp. 78, 81, 85.

S.D.N.Y. 1986. Although ambiguity is construed against insurer, court will not indulge in forced or strained construction to create ambiguity or impose a liability the insurer did not assume. *Morgan, Olmstead, Kennedy & Gardner, Inc. v. Fed. Ins. Co.,* 637 F. Supp. 973, 976-77, *aff'd without op.,* 833 F.2d 1003 (2d Cir. 1986).

Ga. Ct. App. 1985. Fidelity bond exclusion of losses arising from commission advances was unambiguous. *Fid. & Deposit Co. of Md. v. Sun Life Ins. Co.,* 329 S.E.2d 517, 520.

Md. Ct. Spec. App. 2003. Bond required that dishonest employee manifestly intend to gain a financial benefit but excluded salaries. Exclusion was unambiguous and applied to overpayment that employee fraudulently induced. *ABC Imaging of Wash. v. Travelers Indem. Co.,* 820 A.2d 628, 632-35.

Mich. Ct. App. 2012. To have meaning, salary exclusion of financial benefit definition extends to dishonestly gained salary but controller's secret duplicate paychecks to herself did not fall within exclusion; employer must at least know it is paying for a purportedly job-related duty. *Amerisure Ins. Co. v. Debruyn Produce Co.,* 825 N.W.2d 666, 670-71.

Tex. App. 1997. Courts strive to give effect to an insurance policy as the written expression of the parties' intent. Only if the policy remains ambiguous despite the rules of interpretation should courts construe it against the insurer. Fidelity coverage protects the employer against actions such as embezzlement or selling the employer's property for personal gain. Courts strive for uniformity in construing insurance terms, especially when the term at issue is identical across the jurisdictions. *Dickson v. State Farm Lloyds,* 944 S.W.2d 666, 668.

(b) Ambiguous or construed against insurer

Ala. 2002. Unambiguous provisions, including exclusions, cannot be defeated by making a new contract for the parties. *Cincinnati Ins. Co. v. Tuscaloosa County Parking & Transit Auth.,* 827 So. 2d 765, 767-68.

(c) Joint drafting considerations

Cal. Ct. App. 2002. Financial Institution Bond's definition of fraudulent or dishonest acts, including financial benefit definition, was the carefully crafted product of negotiation between the banking industry and fidelity insurers. The financial benefit definition was unambiguous in clearly limiting the extent of coverage. Its use of the word "however" did not make the definition into an exclusion such that the insurer had the burden of proving it applied. Insured's failure to produce evidence the accused employees received a financial benefit in excess of $2,500 precluded coverage. *Mortgage Assocs. v. Fid. & Deposit Co. of Md.,* 129 Cal. Rptr. 2d 365, 369.

5. Employee Definition

(a) Unambiguous

1st Cir. 1993 (Mass.). When there is no ambiguity in the language at issue, it will be interpreted according to its ordinary meaning. Language is ambiguous only if it is fairly susceptible to more than one construction. When the intention of the parties as to who are employees is expressed in a fidelity policy, that intention will be given effect. Accused individual was not an employee of the two insureds; they did not control him; he controlled them. That the insureds may have had a theoretical right of control was insufficient to make him an employee. Employee definition was unambiguous in materially limiting the scope of coverage; it could not be tortured into having a broader meaning. *Bird v. Centennial Ins. Co.,* 11 F.3d 228, 232-33.

5th Cir. 1976 (Ala.). Function of insurance contract is to specify the risks assumed and define the extent of coverage provided for them. Contract is typically one of adhesion, requiring any doubts or ambiguity to be resolved in favor of coverage. However, intent of parties remains the lodestar and once that intent has been ascertained it is strictly applied. Promoters who obtained control of and looted assets of life insurer were not employees under fidelity bond defining employees as persons in service of insured and subject to its control. *First Nat'l Life Ins. Co. v. Fid. & Deposit Co. of Md.,* 525 F.2d 966, 969.

6th Cir. 1977 (Ohio). There was no ambiguity in a savings and loan blanket bond. In offering coverage only by separate rider for non-employee agents, insurer demonstrated an intent to limit its fidelity coverage to employees as ordinarily understood. Right to control is hallmark of employment relationship. Insurer's exposure could not be expanded by construing the bond to cover persons performing services for it but not subject to its control. Part-time appraiser was not a covered employee. *Third Fed. Sav. & Loan Ass'n v. Fireman's Fund Ins. Co.,* 548 F.2d 166, 170-72.

8th Cir. 2011 (Mo.). Officer-shareholder exclusion extended to loss caused by officers and "others." Term "others" was not defined but it had to be construed in reference to its antecedent; it therefore included other employees, not just non-employees. The word when used as a pronoun, is indefinite and draws its meaning from its context. The exclusion unambiguously included loss caused by an owner acting in collusion with other employees. *Tactical Stop-Loss, LLC v. Travelers Cas. & Sur. Co. of Am.,* 657 F.3d 757, 761.

8th Cir. 1989 (Minn.). Ambiguities must be resolved in favor of the insured, but the allegations of a complaint against the insured would not have constituted a valid and collectible employee dishonesty loss under the bond so there was no attorney fees coverage available. The complaint did not allege the elements of "manifest intent" but did allege that the accused employee controlled the bank, so he did not qualify as an employee and knowledge of his acts had to be imputed to the bank. *Red Lake County State Bank v. Employer's Ins. of Wausau,* 874 F.2d 546, 549.

8th Cir. 1966 (Mont.). Unambiguous contract is accepted as written without resort to any rules of interpretation. Interpretation and construction are questions of law. Commercial blanket bond covered dishonest agent even if there was no written agency agreement. *Standard Title Ins. Co. v. United Pac. Ins. Co.,* 364 F.2d 287, 289-90.

9th Cir. 1999 (Cal.). To ascertain meaning of insurance policy, court looks to its plain language as a whole and the context. Ambiguous exclusions are construed narrowly against the insurer. They must be conspicuous, plain, and clear but need not be grammatically perfect. Court concluded tax service and its officers and employees were all authorized representatives of the insured within exclusion and therefore held that there was no coverage. *Stanford Univ. Hosp. v. Fed. Ins. Co.,* 174 F.3d 1077, 1083.

9th Cir. 1990 (Cal.). The insured's accused principals were not employees. The insured did not have the right to control them, as the unambiguous employee definition required. *Cal. Union Ins. Co. v. Am. Diversified Sav. Bank,* 948 F.2d 556, 566.

Bankr. N.D. Ga. 1995. The construction of an insurance policy is a question of law for the court. The words in the policy are given their ordinary, everyday meaning. The court construed the term "employee" to exclude a director who made improper loans because the employer did not control the director as required by the fidelity bond at issue. *Ellenberg v. Certain Underwriters at Lloyds (In re Prime Commercial Corp),* 187 B.R. 785, 797-98.

S.D. Fla. 2012. Insurance agent's employee defrauded the insured, a premium finance company. Bond unambiguously covered the perpetrator as an employee of the insured only if he was authorized to perform data processing services. That he was an insurance agent did not preclude coverage because the capitalization of the "E" in the "non-Employee" exclusion called for incorporation of the employee definition. *ABCO Premium Finance, LLC v. Am. Int'l Group, Inc.,* No. 1:11-cv-23020, 2012 U.S. Dist. LEXIS 111833, at *16.

D. Kan. 1994. An insurance contract is construed against the insurer as drafter if ambiguous but not if it is clear. The test is not what the insurer intends but what a reasonably prudent insured would understand the language to mean. Exclusions are construed narrowly. *Lyons Fed. Sav. & Loan v. St. Paul Fire & Marine Ins. Co.,* 863 F. Supp. 1441, 1448.

D. Mass. 1986. When the terms of a contract are plain and unambiguous, its construction is a matter of law to be decided by the court. Blanket bond claim for loss as a result of insolvency of bank that issued certificates of deposit ("CDs") to insured was not covered. The bond's definition of employee did not extend either to a corporate money broker advising the insured, nor to the bank that issued the CDs. *Mass Cuna Corporate Cent. Fed. Credit Union v. Cumis Ins. Soc'y,* No. 84-2050-W, 1986 U.S. Dist. LEXIS 27809, at *9, *17.

SECTION 6 — CONSTRUCTION AND INTERPRETATION 641

S.D.N.Y. 1984. Definition of "employee" in credit union discovery bond was unambiguous. *IBM Poughkeepsie Emps. Fed. Credit Union v. Cumis Ins. Soc'y,* 590 F. Supp. 769, 774-75 (S.D.N.Y. 1984).

E.D.N.Y. 1977. Insurer prevails in dispute involving construction of policy only if it shows interpretation favoring it is the only reasonable reading. Conversely, insured prevails if any reasonable interpretation permits coverage. Court assumes a clause is included in a policy rider to accomplish a purpose. A construction that would neutralize a particular clause will not be adopted if the policy can be construed to give effect to that and every other provision. Rider limited insurer's liability for fraud by service contractor. Exception for money disbursed by servicing contractor in accordance with instructions by insured did not apply. *Hudson City Sav. Inst. v. Hartford Acc. & Indem. Co.,* 440 F. Supp. 41, 42-43.

S.D. Ohio 2005. Policy did not cover embezzlement by president and sole shareholder of insured brokerage; president was not employee because insurer did not direct and control him as employee definition required. *Lutz v. St. Paul Fire & Marine Ins. Co.,* No. 1:03-CV-750, 2005 U.S. Dist. LEXIS 21065, at *10-11.

E.D. Pa. 1998. When insurance policy language is plain and unambiguous, it must be given its plain and ordinary meaning. Commercial crime policy's definition of employee was unambiguous. In an outsourcing arrangement, accused person engaged insured to provide payroll processing for companies controlled by accused. Accused used arrangement to abscond with funds insured advanced to fund payrolls. Court held accused was not the insured's employee; he was not in the insured's "service" and insured had no right to fire, discipline, or control him. Court rejected insured's reasonable expectations argument as well. *Omni Servs. Group v. Hartford Ins. Co.,* 2 F. Supp. 2d 714, 717-18.

E.D. Va. 2007. Parties agreed crime policy was plain and unambiguous. *Carytown Jewelers, Inc. v. St. Paul Travelers Cos., Inc.,* No. 3:06 CV 312, 2007 U.S. Dist. LEXIS 3620, at *15-16.

Ariz. Ct. App. 1985. The rules of construction applicable to insurance contracts generally apply to fidelity bonds. The bond will be enforced according to its terms when those terms are clear and unambiguous. The requirement that the insured have right to govern and direct employees as a condition to coverage was unambiguous. The court would not indulge in forced construction to fasten a liability the insurer did not contract to assume. *Emp'rs Admin. Serv. v. Hartford Acc. & Indem. Co.,* 709 P.2d 559, 562-64.

Ind. Ct. App. 2003. Insured mortgage lender issued check to title company to fund home loan at closing. Title company was to return check if closing did not occur but title company converted check. Court held loss did not result from employee dishonesty nor was otherwise covered for several reasons, including that title company did not meet definition of employee as a "data processor" of check because check was made payable to title company and deposited in its account. *Utica Mut. Ins. Co. v. Precedent Cos.,* 782 N.E.2d 470, 475.

Mass. Super. 1998. The interpretation of an insurance contract is generally a question of law for the court. A contract term will be construed according to its plain and ordinary meaning. A fidelity policy's definition of employee was not ambiguous in requiring that the insured employer have a right of control. An employee is one who is at all times bound to obedience and subject to direction and supervision as to details; one who is only responsible for the accomplishment of an agreed result is not. An attorney acting on behalf of the insured was not an employee. His yearly retainer was not salary. He did not qualify as a director or trustee of the insured merely because the insured entrusted him with funds. *S. New Eng. Conference Ass'n of Seventh-Day Adventists v. Fed. Ins. Co.,* No. 96-1148-A, 1998 Mass. Super. LEXIS 700, at *10-14.

Mo. Ct. App. 2003. A fidelity bond must be read as a whole to determine the parties' intent. The contract is enforced as written, unless that would violate public policy. Giving terms their plain and ordinary meaning, terms are not ambiguous merely because the parties disagree over how to interpret them. An ambiguity arises when a duplicity, indistinctness, or uncertainty in the meaning of the words makes them reasonably open to different constructions. However, if a term is defined, and that definition is itself unambiguous, the definition will control. The bond's definition of employee, in requiring that the insured have the right to direct and control the employee, was unambiguous and would exclude a person who was the insured's "alter ego" even if the insured's board had a technical right of control, but there was a fact issue whether the person completely dominated the insured as required. *E. Attucks Cmty. Hous. v. Old Republic Sur. Co.,* No. WD 61142, 2003 Mo. App. LEXIS 936, at *17-20.

N.J. Super. Ct. App. Div. 2006. A policy clearly covered the insured corporation against employee theft but also was clear in providing no coverage if the theft was committed by "you or one of your partners." One owner alleged that the other owner as president had taken the insured's property. The accused owner was not an employee despite the salary he received as an officer; the corporation was in effect a partnership. *Sys. Design Concepts, Inc. v. CNA Ins. Co.,* No. A-5834-04T3, 2006 N.J. Super. Unpub. LEXIS 2989, at *3, 15.

N.J. Super. Ct. App. Div. 2000. Generally, fidelity bonds are broadly construed but that principle is customarily limited to cases involving the acts of a true employee. Bond's definition of an employee as being a person whom the insured had the right to direct and control was unambiguous. Although president's wife owned the stock and was the insured's sole director, in reality the president owned and controlled the insured so there was no possibility his thefts from insured were covered. *Hartford Fire Ins. Co. v. Conestoga Title Ins. Co.,* 746 A.2d 460, 461.

Tenn. Ct. App. 1978. It was harmless error to instruct jury that insurance contracts are strictly construed against the insurer, though that is not the rule. Insurance contracts are construed just like any other contract, by plain meaning with no application of strictness in favor of either party, unless ambiguity is found, in which case it is resolved against drafter. The determination of whether an ambiguity exists and the resolution of that ambiguity is a task for the judge, not the jury. The blanket bond at issue was not ambiguous. Ambiguous terms should not be confused with ambiguous facts. Court upheld verdict that person on leave of absence was still an employee. *Union Planters Corp. v. Harwell,* 578 S.W.2d 87, 92.

(b) Ambiguous or construed against insurer

5th Cir. 1970 (Tex.). In construing fidelity bonds, courts follow liberal rules applicable to insurance contracts but bond must be read as a whole and cannot be enlarged by construction beyond its actual terms. Exception to director exclusion applied on basis that accused director was performing acts within the scope of an employee's usual duties in purchasing notes as authorized by board. *FDIC v. Aetna Cas. & Sur. Co.*, 426 F.2d 729, 736.

8th Cir. 1971 (S.D.). Majority shareholder and president was specifically excluded from bond by endorsement. That suggested president was covered absent the endorsement. At insured's request, insurer cancelled endorsement. If there was ambiguity, court was guided in its interpretation by the parties' conduct. Bond covered loss from loans made by president to a company he controlled while insured was insolvent. *Gen. Fin. Corp. v. Fid. & Cas. Co. of N.Y.*, 439 F.2d 981, 984.

8th Cir. 1967 (Iowa). If language of fidelity bond is unambiguous, court should give effect to it in harmony with its plain meaning. Court rejected insurer's surety defense. Obligee need not warn surety of risk if facts are equally accessible to both. Insured's president was employee; court rejected alter-ego defense. *Wooddale, Inc. v. Fid. & Deposit Co. of Md.*, 378 F.2d 627, 630.

9th Cir. 1992 (Cal.). A written contract must be read as a whole and every part must be interpreted with reference to the whole. In construing a fidelity bond, the court held that the president, director, and sole shareholder of the insured was an "employee" because the bond defined that term to include officers and did not specify that the insured had to have a right of control. *FDIC v. N.H. Ins. Co.*, No. 90-55865, 1992 U.S. App. LEXIS 2372, at *8-10.

9th Cir. 1991 (Cal.). Applying federal law because FSLIC was suing in its corporate capacity as receiver of failed thrift, the court recited familiar canons of construction and concluded accused officer was an employee under plain meaning of bond's broad definition. *FDIC v. N.H. Ins. Co.*, 953 F.2d 478, 482.

9th Cir. 1991 (Or.). Fidelity bond defined directors as employees while (1) employed in, at, or by any of the insured's offices, or (2) when performing acts within the scope of usual duties of an officer or employee. Court concluded that first alternative could not be limited in scope to services normally performed by officers or employees as that would render the second alternative superfluous. Court held accused director was an employee. *Interstate Prod. Credit Ass'n v. Fireman's Fund Ins. Co.,* 944 F.2d 536, 538-39.

10th Cir. 1969 (Okla.). Fidelity bond as surety contract must be liberally construed against surety under statute. Director exclusion did not exclude directors who also served as officers and received salary. *Ins. Co. of N. Am. v. Greenberg,* 405 F.2d 330, 333.

D. Del. 2011. Alter-ego defense was not available under bond as worded because it did not expressly require the employee to be under the direction and control of the insured. *Arrowood Indem. Co. v. Hartford Fire Ins. Co.,* 774 F. Supp. 2d 636, 651.

D.N.J. 2012. Loan servicer sold insured credit union's mortgages and pocketed proceeds, concealing fraud from credit union. The definition that made servicer an employee only while performing certain services extended to this conduct. Court used a "but for" analysis to hold this extended coverage to the servicer while committing the fraud—but for the concealment while servicing, there would have been no opportunity to commit the fraud. *Sperry Assoc. Fed. Credit Union v. Cumis Ins. Soc., Inc.,* No. 10-00029, 2012 U.S. Dist. LEXIS 26839, at *19-29.

S.D. W. Va. 2011. Policy covered loss caused by a fiduciary, including an employee benefit administrator. Exclusion of loss caused by independent contractor did not apply even if employee benefit administrator who committed fraud was an independent contractor. Court did not address requirement that fiduciary be a natural person. *Guyan Int'l, Inc. v. Travelers Cas. & Sur. Co.,* No. 3:10-1244, 2011 U.S. Dist. LEXIS 142828, at *13-15.

Wash. Ct. App. 1982. Ambiguous exclusion is construed strictly against insurer. Bank directors were covered as employees because they were acting within the scope of employees' usual duties when they engaged in fraudulent insurance premium financing scheme. *Puget Sound Nat'l Bank v. St. Paul Fire & Marine Ins. Co.,* 645 P.2d 1122, 1126.

(c) Statutory considerations

Or. Ct. App. 2010. A crime bond with an ERISA endorsement had to be construed with reference to ERISA but did not incorporate ERISA. Thus, it did not have to cover all persons who must be bonded under ERISA. It is the ERISA fund's responsibility to buy a compliant policy. Dishonest administrators of the insured's investment advisor fell within the independent contractor exception to coverage. The coverage grant was not illusory in referring to administrators who are neither employees nor independent contractors. *Employers-Shopmens Local 516 Pension Trust v. Travelers Cas. & Sur. Co. of Am.,* 235 P.3d 689, 700.

B. On Premises (including Loan Exclusion)

1. Unambiguous

5th Cir. 1970 (Tex.). When language is clear and unambiguous, the rules of construction do not apply. Advance in exchange for note secured by warehouse receipts was loan within exclusion and thus there was no on premises coverage. Nor were the warehouse receipts counterfeit. They were genuine and valuable at time of issuance, not worthless imitations. *Md. Cas. Co. v. State Bank & Trust Co.,* 425 F.2d 979, 982.

6th Cir. 2004 (Tenn.). Gambler used forged cashier's checks to obtain credit from casino. Casino made an on premises claim for "wrongful abstraction" but court applied an exclusion of loss by surrender of money or securities in any exchange or purchase. The policy's money order coverage did not apply either as cashier's checks are not "money orders." Casino drafted policy so any ambiguities were construed against it. *Harrah's Entertainment, Inc. v. Ace Am. Ins. Co.,* 100 F. App'x 387, 390-93.

7th Cir. 1984 (Wis.). Bankers Blanket Bond was unambiguous in excluding loss from payments made on depositor's account unless depositor was in office of insured at time payments were made. Court rejected insured's ambiguity argument holding that the only reasonable construction of "within the office of the insured" was that the account holder be physically present in the bank at the time of the withdrawal. *Bradley Bank v. Hartford Acc. & Indem. Co.,* 737 F.2d 657, 660-61.

D. Kan. 1982. Uncollected funds exclusion would not be construed against insurer; it plainly and unambiguously excluded loss from credit given on uncollected check deposits where depositor did not withdraw funds over the counter. *Sec. Nat'l Bank of Kan. City v. Cont'l Ins. Co.,* 586 F. Supp. 139, 146.

E.D. Wis. 2012. Telephone fraud inducing bank to issue cashier's checks to ignorant messenger did not occur by physical presence on premises within unambiguous coverage of bond. *Bankmanagers Corp. v. Fed. Ins. Co.,* No. 11-cv-871, 2012 U.S. Dist. LEXIS 129647, at *19.

Del. Super. Ct. 1982. Clear and unambiguous words and phrases in insurance policies should be given their ordinary, usual meaning. *Kirkwood Holding Co. v. Home Fed. Sav. & Loan Ass'n,* No. 80C-SE-12, 1982 Del. Super. LEXIS 871, at *3, 7.

Minn. Ct. App. 2008. Insured incurred loan losses as a result of accepting fictitious collateral. Insurer's robbery coverage defined robbery to include an obviously unlawful act as witnessed by the person from whom property was taken. The policy did not define "obviously unlawful" but the court found plain meaning. Hindsight did not count. Obviousness requires immediate clarity and transparency. The act may have been unlawful but this was not obvious at the time, so there was no coverage. *Sela v. St. Paul Travelers Cos.,* No. A07-0411, 2008 Minn. App. Unpub. LEXIS 202, at *7-9.

Minn. Ct. App. 1989. In interpreting a contract, the terms must be given their plain, ordinary, and popular meaning. *Suburban Nat'l Bank v. Transamerica Ins. Co.,* 438 N.W.2d 119, 121-22.

Mo. Ct. App. 1975. A savings and loan blanket bond is designed to protect the insured against risks of dishonesty, external or internal. The bond is not broad insurance against business risks. The meaning of its terms is ascertained from the parties' intent and the purpose of the contract. The coverage for abstraction or removal of property from the premises was not ambiguous. All the other terms in that coverage involved dishonest or criminal acts. An abstraction or removal therefore must be dishonest as well. A loss due to mere negligence is not covered. *Hamiltonian Fed. Sav. & Loan Ass'n v. Reliance Ins. Co.,* 527 S.W.2d 440, 443-44.

N.Y. City Civ. Ct. 1967. A Bankers Blanket Bond is not broad insurance against the risk of loss in banking operations. No degree of construction can broaden the coverage beyond what a reasonable reading would permit. The bond is primarily designed to protect against risks of dishonesty, which may be external—robbery, burglary, larceny, theft, holdup, or counterfeiting—or internal—embezzlement, forgery, or employee defalcation. Coverage in this context includes loss of property through misplacement, but the bond did not cover loss from bank's failure to give heed to a prior assignment, resulting in its having to pay proceeds twice, even if notice of assignment was misplaced. *Metro. Sav. & Loan v. Hanover Ins. Co.,* 286 N.Y.S.2d 129, 131, 134.

Tex. Civ. App. 1978. On premises coverage of Bankers Blanket Bond was unambiguous in covering only loss of specific tangible property physically taken from the premises of the bank as a direct result of a covered crime. Bond did not cover liability of bank for negligence and breach of contract to depositor in allowing his business associate to wrongfully withdraw funds. *White Rock Nat'l Bank v. U.S. Fire Ins. Co.,* 562 S.W.2d 268, 274.

Wis. 1973. Doctrine of strict construction against insurer does not apply unless ambiguity exists. Not one but all the rules of construction must be considered. Loan-loss exclusion of Bankers Blanket Bond was unambiguous in precluding recovery for loss resulting from false pretenses when borrower induced bank to return securities he pledged as collateral and failed to deliver substitute collateral as promised. Although the transaction had many steps, on the whole it was a loan. *Racine Cnty. Nat'l Bank. v. Aetna Cas. & Sur. Co.,* 203 N.W.2d 145, 149.

2. Ambiguous or Construed Against Insurer

2d Cir. 2012 (N.Y.). Crooks used false pretenses to induce insured's cashier to deliver cash in person. Crime policy defined robbery as "the unlawful taking of insured property . . . by violence, threat of violence or other overt felonious act committed in the presence and cognizance of [an employee] . . . ." Although no robbery or other openly criminal act had occurred, "overt" modified "act," not "felonious." "Overtly" should have been used if it was intended to modify "felonious." The remainder of the definition did not eliminate the ambiguity. The taking was both felonious (as a larceny by trick) and overt (as an open taking of the money). Applying contra proferentem, the court found coverage. *Vam Check Cashing Corp. v. Fed. Ins. Co.,* 699 F.3d 727, 730-31, 733.

7th Cir. 1970 (Ill.). If fidelity insurer does not intend to insure a risk inherent in the insured's business, it should specifically exclude such risk. Ambiguities will be resolved in the insured's favor. Money intentionally placed by teller in wrong area was "misplaced" within meaning of on premises coverage and thus theft of the money by an office equipment mover was covered. *Bremen State Bank v. Hartford Acc. & Indem. Co.,* 427 F.2d 425, 427-28.

8th Cir. 1965 (Iowa). If insurance policy is ambiguous it should be construed to effectuate intention of parties in manner most favorable to insured. Bond was not inescapably clear and unambiguous in its use of terms "false pretenses" as used in coverage and "loan" as used in exclusion and thus check kiting loss was covered. "False pretenses" could be defined by criminal law, common law, or common understanding. As for "loan," the allowable dubiety was even more obvious. It could be either limited to the understanding of a banker or it could extend to every possible financial obligation to a bank. *Indem. Ins. Co. of N. Am. v. Pioneer Valley Sav. Bank,* 343 F.2d 634, 647.

8th Cir. 1965 (Neb.). Allowing credit on worthless checks was not a loan. The bond's false pretenses coverage applied, for it was as least as broad as the crime of that name. *United States ex rel. First Cont'l Nat'l Bank & Trust Co. v. W. Contracting Corp.,* 341 F.2d 383, 388.

M.D. La. 1975. Check-kiting exclusion was not ambiguous, but it did not exclude loss arising when bank credited deposit to wrong account and funds were withdrawn by wrongdoer through checks written off premises. No uncollected funds loss was involved. Definition of property as including money and evidence of debt was broad enough to include credit represented by deposit at issue. Loss of property misplaced while on premises occurred. Although misplacement occurred through modern, computerized banking techniques, it was as real as if bank had put cash in wrong pigeon-hole. *Aetna Cas. & Sur. Co. v. La. Nat'l Bank,* 399 F. Supp. 54, 56.

N.D. Miss. 1995. Unambiguous uncollected-funds exclusion in Financial Institution Bond was not limited in scope to check kiting losses, but it did not extend to cashing of forged checks by perpetrator on the premises of the bank. *USF&G v. Planters Bank & Trust Co.,* No. 4:92CV240-S-D, 1995 U.S. Dist. LEXIS 21673, at *6-8.

W.D. Mo. 1969. Bank settled suits against it arising from promoter's failure to disclose that stock bank issued as transfer agent was unfunded. Promoter's conduct was false pretenses under either technical definition of criminal statute or broad ordinary meaning of term. Term was not ambiguous but if it was, it would be construed against insurer as a "compensated surety." Court assumed insurer was familiar with the long-standing rules of construction and that the premiums it charged for its exceedingly broad on premises coverage took this into account. *Merchants-Produce Bank v. USF&G,* 305 F. Supp. 957, 966-67.

E.D. Va. 1975. Insurer failed to prove insured bank participated in drafting negotiations between Surety Association of America and American Bankers Association, so court would construe any ambiguities in bond against insurer. Bond did not define forgery, but unauthorized endorsements were not forgeries. However, deposit of worthless checks was intended to deceive and thus constituted false pretenses. Inclusion of "rights" and "evidence of indebtedness" extended definition of property to intangible property. Revision of term "money" did not limit property to tangible items. Loan and uncollected-funds exclusions excluded check kiting, but loss did not involve transfers between banks and therefore was not check kiting. False pretenses coverage applied because loss occurred on premises when bank sight-posted checks deposited at bank, although funds were not withdrawn until later. *Clarendon Bank & Trust v. Fid. & Deposit Co. of Md.,* 406 F. Supp. 1161, 1165, 1169, 1172.

D. Wyo. 1974. In construing insurance contract, court must ascertain intention of parties as expressed. Coverage is determined not by what the insurer intended its words to mean but by what a reasonable person in the insured's position would understand them to mean. Doubts will be resolved against insurer. The term "blanket bond" indicates broad coverage. Deposit was "lodged" in night depository from which it was stolen and therefore loss was covered. *W. Nat'l Bank v. Hawkeye-Sec. Ins. Co.,* 380 F. Supp. 508, 511-12.

Minn. 1975. Airplane highjacker forced insured airline to pay cash ransom by landing plane at terminal and obtaining cash on credit from a bank. Court found crime policy ambiguous and construed it in favor of insured, holding loss was a "wrongful abstraction" that occurred "on premises." *Nw. Airlines v. Globe Indem. Co.,* 225 N.W.2d 831, 837.

N.Y. Sup. Ct. 1968. Court construed customer's failure to repay check kiting overdraft as a loss of "money" which blanket bond's list of covered property. Court looked to penal code to conclude a "larceny by false pretenses" had occurred within the bond's on premises coverage. Loan exclusion as interpreted did not extend to an overdraft. *Liberty Nat'l Bank & Trust Co. v. Travelers Indem. Co.,* 295 N.Y.S.2d 983, 986.

Tex. Civ. App. 1977. If the meaning of a policy term is doubtful it is construed against the insurer. An impersonator stole cash he had induced the insured bank to deliver to a customer's office. The customer's office qualified as "any office or premises located anywhere." *Purolator Sec. v. Citizens Nat'l Bank of Waco,* 546 S.W.2d 935, 939.

3. *Joint Drafting*

3d Cir. 1992 (N.J.). Insured claimed wire fraud loss caused by off-site telephone caller was a "false pretenses" committed "on premises." However, drafting history of 1980 bond revision confirmed that person committing false pretenses had to be physically "present" on premises of bank. Average bank would not reasonably expect otherwise. The court would not strain to find coverage in favor of sophisticated and powerful insureds with significant bargaining power and expertise in drafting insurance contracts. It was unreasonable to construe "present" as including "constructive" presence. *Oritani Sav. & Loan Ass'n v. Fid. & Deposit Co. of Md.,* 989 F.2d 635, 638-42.

7th Cir. 2009 (Ill.). A bond that contains no ambiguity is to be construed according to the plain and ordinary meaning of its terms, just as would any other contract. Standard Financial Institution Bonds are drafted by sophisticated parties (representatives of the banking and insurance industries); the traditional rule of construing any ambiguity in favor of coverage does not apply. The bond, once known as a Bankers Blanket Bond, is a unique instrument with a long history. Nearly every term has been developed in response to and tested by case law. Form 24 descends from Form 1, issued in 1916 by the Surety Association of America and the American Bankers Association to compete with a Lloyd's form. It is important to determine the version under consideration and whether it has been modified in any respect. Cases interpreting other versions may be unhelpful. *First State Bank of Monticello v. Ohio Cas. Ins. Co.,* 555 F.3d 564, 568-70.

M.D. Ala. 1974. That blanket bond may have resulted from joint efforts of Surety Association of America and American Bankers Association did not deprive bank of rule that ambiguities must be construed against insurer absent evidence insured bank or association acting for it negotiated bond at issue. *Shoals Nat'l Bank v. Home Indem. Co.,* 384 F. Supp. 49, 54-55, *aff'd without op.,* 515 F.2d 1182 (5th Cir. 1974).

E.D. La. 1970. Although bond resulted from joint efforts of Surety Association of America and American Bankers Association, there was no need to apply any rule of construction as the bond was not ambiguous. The false pretenses coverage extended to check kiting and the loan exclusion did not extend to money advanced in good faith on worthless checks. *Nat'l Bank of Commerce v. Fid. & Cas. Co. of N.Y.,* 312 F. Supp. 71, 74-75, *aff'd,* 437 F.2d 96 (5th Cir. 1971).

W.D. Wis. 1983. Had the terms of an uncollected funds exclusion been ambiguous, the rule of construction in favor of the drafter still would not have applied because the bond was a product of negotiation between the Surety Association of America and the American Bankers Association.

Bradley Bank v. Hartford Acc. & Indem. Co., 557 F. Supp. 243, 249, *aff'd,* 737 F.2d 657 (7th Cir. 1984).

C. In Transit

10th Cir. 1976 (Colo.). Words of Bankers Blanket Bond should be interpreted according to their ordinary and obvious meaning absent a showing of ambiguity. Intention of in-transit coverage was to cover cash in transit except in the mail or possession of carrier for hire. A messenger who was not an employee of the insured was "any other person or persons acting as messenger." Further, "delivery at destination" (precluding coverage) did not occur when cash letter was delivered to employee of receiving bank outside premises of bank nor when that employee was robbed in bank's outside mall. *United Bank of Pueblo v. Hartford Acc. & Indem. Co.,* 529 F.2d 490, 493-94.

C.D. Cal. 2007. No in-transit loss occurred within bond's Clause (C) coverage. The insured's loss of ATM cash did not occur while the cash was in an armored car, on the move, ready for delivery, or in the process of delivery. Loss occurred while contractor was counting the money in its office. Court looked in part to Black's Law Dictionary which defines "transit" as "transportation of goods or persons from one place to another" or "passage; the act of passing." *Palm Desert Nat'l Bank v. Fed. Ins. Co.,* 473 F. Supp. 2d 1044, 1048-49.

D. Forgery, Counterfeit, Alteration, and Similar Coverages

1. Unambiguous

3d Cir. 2005 (N.J.). Fraudulent check endorsements were not forged under bond and statutory definitions of forgery; perpetrator's signing of his own name was not a forgery and the signing of a company name was not a forgery because the company had an actual legal existence. *Lusitania Sav. Bank, FSB v. Progressive Cas. Ins. Co.,* No. 04-3503, 2005 U.S. App. LEXIS 13331, at *6-9.

5th Cir. 2002 (Tex.). A fidelity bond covering loss by forgery of checks and the like did not cover loss involving forged invoices. The invoices were not "drawn upon [the insured]." That phrase had a single legal meaning in its commercial paper context, even if had other meanings in other contexts. *Travelers Cas. & Sur. Co. v. Baptist Health Sys.*, 313 F.3d 295, 298-99.

5th Cir. 1976 (La.). Special interpretation rules apply only when there is an ambiguity. The term "loan" in a Bankers Blanket Bond is not a term of art but has a plain and broad meaning. Loan exclusion applied to advances bank made to customers on deposit of drafts. *Calcasieu-Marine Nat'l Bank v. Am. Emp'rs Ins. Co.*, 533 F.2d 290, 296.

6th Cir. 2013 (Ky.). Forgery coverage unambiguously did not apply to assignment of worthless life insurance policy that happened to be forged. *Forcht Bank, NA v. BancInsure, Inc.*, No. 11-6328, 2013 U.S. App. LEXIS 3193, at *15.

7th Cir. 2012 (Wis.). Court consulted bond form's drafting history to conclude that a fraudulent certificate of origin did not qualify as a counterfeit, because no valid certificate existed with the same VIN number. Nearly every bond term has been developed in reaction to court interpretations of prior bond versions. As a result, certain terms have nuanced meanings. A document is not counterfeit unless it imitates an existing genuine original. *N. Shore Bank FSB v. Progressive Cas. Ins. Co.*, 674 F.3d 884, 887-88.

8th Cir. 1969 (Mo.). Ambiguities are construed in favor of insured but unnatural meaning is not forced from plain words. Loan exclusion applied to bank's advances in exchange for assignments of notes. *Twin Cities Fed. Sav. & Loan Ass'n v. Transamerica Ins. Co.*, 413 F.2d 494, 497-98.

8th Cir. 1961 (Mo.). Blanket bond is complex because banking is complex. This need not equate with ambiguity. The terms forgery and counterfeit did not apply to chattel mortgages describing autos borrower did not own or possess. *State Bank of Poplar Bluff v. Md. Cas. Co.*, 289 F.2d 544, 547-48.

8th Cir. 1960 (Mo.). Loan exclusion unambiguously applied to loan loss induced by borrower's misrepresentations. *Cmty. Fed. Sav. & Loan Ass'n v. Gen. Cas. Co.*, 274 F.2d 620, 624-25.

9th Cir. 2010 (Mont.). Participating banks did not have physical possession of documents in advance of funding. The term "authorized representative" did not extend to the lead bank and its attorney. *Bank of Bozeman v. BancInsure, Inc.*, 404 F. App'x 117, 117-19.

9th Cir. 2005 (Cal.). Gambler obtained cash by presenting check to insured casino for deposit and signing withdrawal receipts. Court found exclusion of loss from fraudulently induced disbursements unambiguously applied. Broker's summary of coverage did not justify any belief that coverage was broader. *Bell Gardens Bicycle Casino v. Great Am. Ins. Co.*, 124 F. App'x 551, 552-53.

10th Cir. 2011 (Okla.). Bank argued Insuring Agreement (E)'s punctuation, layout, and similarity to Insuring Agreement (D) created an ambiguity as to whether the forgery or alteration requirement applied to every type of covered document, including a guaranty. Court found no ambiguity. *First Nat'l Bank of Davis, Okla. v. Progressive Cas. Ins. Co.*, 415 F. App'x 867, 870.

N.D. Cal. 2012. Court held a forged account control agreement was part of a "security agreement" despite an anti-bundling clause, but went on to hold that the forgery did not cause the loss; it was caused by nonexistent collateral, so there was no coverage. *Valley Cmty. Bank v. Progressive Cas. Ins. Co.*, No. C-11-574, 2012 U.S. Dist. LEXIS 22072, at *9-14, *24-25.

D. Kan. 1992. Fidelity bonds are interpreted liberally like other insurance policies, not under the strict rules of suretyship. Forgery coverage unambiguously required proof that original checks were forged. *RTC v. Cont'l Cas. Co.*, 799 F. Supp. 77, 82-83.

D. Kan. 1991. If a term has a plain meaning, that meaning will apply. Construction site reports were not "withdrawal orders" within bond's forgery coverage. Coverage of documents that "create or discharge a lien" did not apply to documents that merely evidenced that work was done. Checks tendered with forged lien waivers were not counterfeits either. *First Fed. Sav. Bank of Newton v. Cont'l Cas. Co.*, 768 F. Supp. 1449, 1453, 1455-56.

D. Minn. 2005. Bank possessed only faxes of forged documents in advance of loan funding. Court found no coverage. In treating a mechanically reproduced facsimile signature the same as a handwritten signature, the bond referred only to a signature produced by a mechanical or photographic process. *BancInsure, Inc. v. Marshall Bank, N.A.,* 400 F. Supp. 2d 1140, 1143-44.

D.N.J. 1983. Neither the loan exclusion nor the forgery and counterfeit coverages are ambiguous; there was no coverage of a loan loss caused by undervalued or nonexistent collateral, even if fictitious certificates of deposit were forged. *Liberty Nat'l Bank v. Aetna Life & Cas. Co.,* 568 F. Supp. 860, 866.

S.D.N.Y. 1990. Court applied bond's forgery definition in concluding that illegible scribbles were not forgeries. Rule of construing ambiguities against insurer did not apply and bond was product of joint drafting between surety and banker associations. Drafting history also showed bond's definition of counterfeit was unambiguous. Bills of lading referring to nonexistent shipments were not imitations of authentic originals and thus were not counterfeits. *French Am. Banking Corp. v. Flota Mercante Grancolombiana, S.A.,* 752 F. Supp. 83, 94, *aff'd,* 925 F.2d 603 (2d Cir. 1991).

D.N.D. 2008. A buyer's bill with false information was not counterfeit; it did not imitate a genuine existing document. The bond's counterfeit definition as construed by national case law applied, not dictionary definitions offered by the insured. *Dakota West Credit Union v. CUMIS Ins. Soc'y, Inc.,* 532 F. Supp. 2d 1110, 1115-17.

E.D. Pa. 1990. Bond unambiguously did not cover involving mortgages bearing forged notary signatures. Rider covering "mortgages, deeds of trust or like instruments pertaining to realty" could not be stretched to include title insurance documents. General terms following an enumeration of specific terms are construed with reference to the specific terms. *Jefferson Bank v. Progressive Cas. Ins. Co.,* No. 90-584, 1990 U.S. Dist. LEXIS 15558, at *12-13.

Cal. Ct. App. 1978. The definition of counterfeit is unambiguous. The bond did not cover loss arising from false representations in genuinely executed invoices. *Hinkson v. Fireman's Fund Ins. Co.,* 146 Cal. Rptr. 669, 672.

Cal. Ct. App. 1972. Phrase "on the faith of" in securities coverage meant "in reliance upon." Even if bond was a contract of adhesion, bank could not demonstrate a contrary reasonable expectation. *Cont'l Bank v. Phoenix Ins. Co.,* 101 Cal. Rptr. 392, 394.

Colo. 1961. Bond's coverage of documents "counterfeited or forged as to the signature" unambiguously did not extend to false invoices. *USF&G v. First Nat'l Bank of Ft. Morgan,* 364 P.2d 202, 204-05.

Iowa 1986. The cardinal principle of contract construction is that the intent of the parties controls. Except in cases of ambiguity, this is determined by what the contract states. A security agreement was not counterfeit as it was not an imitation; nor was it forged, as the obligor signed his own name. *Gateway State Bank v. N. River Ins. Co.,* 387 N.W.2d 344, 346-48.

Iowa 1980. No amount of liberal construction would allow a photocopy of a photocopy to qualify as an original within a bond's securities coverage. *First Nat'l Bank, Colfax v. Hartford Acc. & Indem. Co.,* 295 N.W.2d 425, 429.

Me. 1961. Loan exclusion unambiguously excluded coverage on basis of a loan made on a false trust receipt. *Depositors Trust Co. v. Md. Cas. Co.,* 174 A.2d 288, 292.

Minn. 1989. Interpretation of a bond is a question of law as applied to the facts presented. The bond insures against certain risks of dishonesty, external and internal, but it does not insure good management or against the risk of loss inherent in banking operations. *Nat'l City Bank of Minneapolis v. St. Paul Fire & Marine Co.,* 447 N.W.2d 171, 177, 179.

Minn. Ct. App. 1989. Bond's forgery definition was not ambiguous. When agent signed his own name as authorized for a corporation, it was not a forgery on the basis that the corporation was "another." *Empire State Bank v. St. Paul Fire & Marine Ins. Co.,* 441 N.W.2d 811, 812-13.

Ohio Ct. App. 1965. A certificate of title was a "document or other written instrument" within a bond's securities coverage. Duplicates genuinely signed by state officer on being told the originals were lost were not forgeries or counterfeits. *Union Banking Co. v. USF&G,* 213 N.E.2d 191, 193, 195, 197-98.

Pa. Super. Ct. 1989. Securities coverage unambiguously required the bank to physically possess originals before it extended credit, not copies. *Hamilton Bank v. Ins. Co. of N. Am.,* 557 A.2d 747, 750-51.

Wis. 1964. Court referred to the commercial meaning of the term instrument in concluding that unsigned copies of false invoices and assignment of nonexistent accounts were neither counterfeit nor forged. *First Am. State Bank v. Aetna Cas. & Sur. Co.,* 130 N.W.2d 824, 826-27.

Wis. Ct. App. 2008. An exclusion of computer fraud by an authorized representative applied. The insured argued it did not authorize an adjuster to steal so he was not an authorized representative, but the court found this circular; it would abrogate the exclusion. A construction giving reasonable meaning to every term is better than one that leaves a term useless. *Milwaukee Area Tech. College v. Frontier Adjusters of Milwaukee,* 752 N.W.2d 396, 400-02.

    2. *Ambiguous or Construed Against Insurer*

2d Cir. 1978 (N.Y.). Term "forgery" was ambiguous and therefore bond covered checks signed by president without authority. Insurer could have excluded unauthorized signatures from its definition of forgery. *Filor, Bullard & Smyth v. Ins. Co. of N. Am.,* 605 F.2d 598, 602.

5th Cir. 2012 (La.). Bond's "on the faith of" requirement was met by bank's proof it possessed originals before it extended credit, despite never looking at the documents. If higher burden of review or verification was intended, it should have been expressly specified. *Peoples State Bank v. Progressive Cas. Ins. Co.,* 478 F. App'x 858, 859.

5th Cir. 2010 (Tex.). The policy defined forgery so neither the UCC definition nor criminal law applied. The policy definition was ambiguous as applied. It excluded a signature of one's own name in whole or in part, but the endorsements at issue (of an insurance agency in the depositor's name) did not have that character. The reference to a signature of one's own name "in part" meant a signature of both the signer's own name and the name of another. *Great Am. Ins. Co. v. AFS/IBEX Financial Serv., Inc.,* 612 F.3d 800, 805-06.

5th Cir. 2008 (Tex.). Unauthorized signature coverage plainly did not apply to an employee's conversion of customer checks. The employee was listed and had a signature on file in the records for the accounts at issue. *Citibank Texas, N.A. v. Progressive Cas. Ins. Co.,* 522 F.3d 591, 596-97.

5th Cir. 1974 (Fla.). Conflict between uncollected funds exclusion and forgery coverage of Bankers Blanket Bond created ambiguity. Bond covered loss when forged check was returned for insufficient funds but bank paid second check drawn on account. *First Nat'l Bank of Miami v. Ins. Co. of N. Am.,* 495 F.2d 519, 522.

5th Cir. 1970 (Fla.). "Counterfeit or forged" is read disjunctively, and thus, a false stock certificate with a genuine signature was counterfeit. *Am. Nat'l Bank & Trust Co. of S. Pasadena v. Fid. & Cas. Co.,* 431 F.2d 920, 922-23.

5th Cir. 1970 (Tex.). Term "document or other written instrument" clearly covered a false telegram. *Snyder Nat'l Bank v. Westchester Fire Ins. Co.,* 425 F.2d 849, 852.

5th Cir. 1969 (Fla.). Court rejected joint drafting argument and found bond ambiguous. A reinvestment advice was a "document or other written instrument" within forged securities coverage. *First Nat'l Bank of Ft. Walton Beach v. USF&G,* 416 F.2d 52, 56-57.

6th Cir. 1977 (Mich.). Words will not be rejected as superfluous if they reasonably can be given meaning. Terms "documents and other written instruments," extended coverage beyond "securities." *Union Inv. Co. v. Fid. & Deposit Co. of Md.,* 549 F.2d 1107, 1110.

6th Cir. 1971 (Ky.). Forgery exclusion in Bankers Blanket Bond rider was unambiguous and applied to false pretenses claim based on customer deceiving teller into cashing altered check. Alteration with intent to defraud was forgery under state law. *Am. Nat'l Bank & Trust Co. of Bowling Green v. Hartford Acc. & Indem. Co.,* 442 F.2d 995, 999.

8th Cir. 1969 (Mo.). Words connected by an "or" generally have separate meanings. Thus "securities, documents or other written instruments" covered more than securities. *Am. Ins. Co. v. First Nat'l Bank in St. Louis,* 409 F.2d 1387, 1390.

9th Cir. 1967 (Idaho). In an exclusion of losses from "counterfeit or forged" documents, counterfeit could not mean the same thing as forged. *United Pac. Ins. Co. v. Idaho First Nat'l Bank,* 378 F.2d 62, 69.

N.D. Ill. 2009. Construing a bond against the insurer, the court found that advance requests with purported invoices attached were security agreements and thus covered documents to consider along with the invoices, which were altered. The court refused to consider joint drafting evidence. *Metro Fed. Credit Union v. Fed. Ins. Co.,* 607 F. Supp. 2d 870, 874, 878-79.

E.D. Mich. 2005. Bond covered loan losses caused by reliance on fraudulent finance documentation but required bank to have written procedures for verifying the collateral. Court found ambiguity in the phrases "physically verify the existence of the underlying property" and "original financial documentation" and denied insurer's dispositive motion. *Citizens Banking Corp. v. Gulf Ins. Co.,* No. 03-CV-74044, 04-CV-70459, 2005 U.S. Dist. LEXIS 47762, at *14-19.

D. Minn. 2012. Using agency law analysis, court construed the term "authorized representative" as used in Insuring Agreement (E) as extending to equipment lessor in possession of original guaranty because (1) the bank consented to this; (2) the borrower acted for the bank; and (3) the bank disbursed funds only after reviewing entire package including certified copy of guaranty. *BancInsure, Inc. v. Highland Bank,* No. 11-cv-2497, 2012 U.S. Dist. LEXIS 171545, at *11-19.

D. Minn. 2006. A check was not forged but related to an unauthorized wire transfer. The undefined term "alter" was ambiguous. It means "to make different in some particular, as size, style, course, or the like; modify." It was possible the check was "altered" by the telephonic wire transfer request. *First Integrity Bank v. Ohio Cas. Ins. Co.*, No. 05-2761, 2006 U.S. Dist. LEXIS 3042, at *12.

Cal. Ct. App. 1969. The term "securities" as the caption of a bond's securities coverage did not restrict the meaning of the term "written instrument." It included a guaranty. The term "any customer" was ambiguous and had to be construed against the insurer. *Jones v. Fireman's Fund Ins. Co.*, 76 Cal. Rptr. 97, 100-01.

Ill. App. Ct. 1989. Although a power-of-attorney was forged it was not an enumerated document. However, a note was forged. Construing the note and the power-of-attorney as a single instrument, the bank suffered a covered loss as a result of a forged evidence of debt or negotiable instrument. *Cmty. State Bank v. Hartford Ins. Co.*, 542 N.E.2d 1317, 1319-21.

N.Y. Sup. Ct. App. Div. 1986. As policy was originally drafted by insurer, it must be construed in favor of insured. *William Iselin & Co. v. Fireman's Fund Ins. Co.*, 501 N.Y.S.2d 846, 849-51, *modified*, 508 N.E.2d 9323 (N.Y. App. Div. 1987).

3. *Joint Drafting*

2d Cir. 1967 (N.Y.). Discovery was allowed against the Surety Association of America on the meaning of the term "deposit" in Savings and Loan Blanket Bond. When an insurer is responsible for the wording of a policy, drafting history may be relevant with respect to disputed terms. *In re Sur. Ass'n of Am.*, 388 F.2d 412, 415-16.

9th Cir. 1986 (Cal.). Uncollected funds exclusion was not limited to check kiting and applied to cashing of checks that proved uncollectible because of forged endorsements. Cases construing prior versions of the exclusion did not apply. The exclusion was revised specifically to make it clear that it was not limited to check kiting. *Mitsui Mfrs. Bank v. Fed. Ins. Co.*, 795 F.2d 827, 829-31.

Cal. 1971. Citing Webster's, court concluded a treaty of reinsurance, taken as security for a loan, was forged and counterfeit. Separate opinion pointed out bond was drafted in cooperation with the American Bankers

Association. *Century Bank v. St. Paul Fire & Marine Ins. Co.,* 482 P.2d 193, 194-95.

E. Fraudulent Mortgage

5th Cir. 1997 (Tex.). Fraudulent mortgages rider unambiguously only covered losses where the defect in the document was caused by a signature obtained by fraud. *FDIC v. Firemen's Ins. Co. of Newark,* 109 F.3d 1084, 1087-89.

8th Cir. 2008 (Minn.). The word "defective" established that a bond's fraudulent mortgage coverage did not apply to a loss resulting from fraudulent inducement as opposed to fraud as to the nature and terms of the document being signed. Lost mortgage coverage did not apply either since no document already lost to the true owner had been pledged. *Ohio Savings Bank v. Progressive Cas. Ins. Co.,* 521 F.3d 960, 963-65.

D. Neb. 2008. Purchaser was fraudulently induced to sign deeds of trust assigned to insured but coverage required proof "that the signature is invalid or defective because the signatory was tricked or defrauded as to the nature of the document signed." This was unambiguous and enforceable as written. *TierOne Bank v. Hartford Fire Ins. Co.* No. 4:07CV3199, 2008 U.S. Dist. LEXIS 99262, at *12-18.

F. Computer and Funds Transfer Fraud

1. Unambiguous

N.D. Cal. 2013. Imposter inducing wire transfer out of depositor's account did not qualify as a "customer" within bond definition. Actual depositor only entered into general deposit agreement and never actually agreed to wire transfer procedures under which coverage for impersonation of a customer could have arisen. *First Nat'l Bank of N. Cal. v. St. Paul Mercury Ins. Co.,* No. 4:11-cv-6631, 2013 U.S. Dist. LEXIS 1045, at *11-14.

E.D. La. 2011. Insured who invested in hedge fund did not suffer direct computer fraud loss when hedge fund invested in a second hedge fund that was defrauded by a third hedge fund's Ponzi scheme. Direct meant immediate or proximate, not remote, and the third fund's fraud was too remote to be a direct cause of the insured's loss. *Methodist Health Sys. Found., Inc., v. Hartford Fire Ins. Co.,* No. 10- 3292, 2011 U.S. Dist. LEXIS 71258, at *6-8.

N.J. Super. Ct. App. Div. 2005. The insured agreed to hold securities in an account for its customer subject to computer instructions by authorized users. Authorized users ordered a liquidation by computer, fax, and voice after an entity offering to buy the account instructed the customer to cease trading. The would-be buyer sued the insured. The insured settled and made a claim under its Electronic Computer Crime Policy. Applying rules of construction, the court found no ambiguity. No facsimile coverage existed; that coverage was limited to loss caused by an imposter and none was involved. No computer systems coverage existed due to an exclusion of loss from authorized input of data by a customer. But voice initiated transfer coverage arguably applied. *Morgan Stanley Dean Witter & Co. v. Chubb Group of Ins. Cos.,* No. A-4124-03T2, 2005 N.J. Super. Unpub. LEXIS 798, at *7-9.

N.Y. Sup. Ct. 2013. Fraudulent health claims made through a computer system by authorized users did not cause loss resulting directly from a fraudulent entry of electronic data into the insured's computer system. Coverage unambiguously applied only to hacking—loss as a result of access by an unauthorized user. The title of the coverage—"Computer Systems Fraud"—helped show this. There was no intent to cover all fraud that happened to be processed by computer. *Universal Am. Corp. v. Nat'l Union Fire Ins. Co. of Pitt., Pa.,* 959 N.Y.S.2d 849, 862-64.

2. *Ambiguous or Construed Against Insurer*

6th Cir. 2012 (Ohio). Direct loss requirement of crime policy was ambiguous as to computer fraud coverage of insured's liability to customers and others as a result of hacker theft of credit card and other customer information. Confidential information exclusion applied only to bank's own information, not to customers' information. A broader interpretation would swallow the other terms in the exclusion. They referred to the insured's own secret business information so "confidential information" had to refer to that too. *Retail Ventures, Inc. v. Nat'l Union Fire Ins. Co. of Pitt., Pa.*, 691 F.3d 821, 831-33.

8th Cir. 2012 (Mo.). Fax with forged signature qualified as a "written instruction or advice" under Insuring Agreement (D) but not as an "electronic record" within exception. An electronic record had to be "retrievable in perceivable form" under bond's definition. Court consulted dictionary to distinguish between "retrievable" and "retrieved" and concluded fax had lost electronic record status because it had been "retrieved." This did not turn separate fax coverage with an unmet callback condition into a nullity. The overlap was not complete and the bond recognized loss could be covered under more than one insuring agreement. *Mo. Bank & Trust Co. of K.C. v. OneBeacon Ins. Co.*, 688 F.3d 943, 947, 949.

Conn. Super. Ct. 2011. Law firm agreed by e-mail to collect a debt and wired amount of fraudulent check to client. Check did not clear and court found policy ambiguous and upheld firm's computer fraud claim despite absence of computer funds transfer by holding the e-mails proximately caused the loss. Money exclusions did not apply because the check was not money. No exchange occurred though firm deducted a sum from the wire transfer. *Owens, Schine & Nicola, P.C. v. Travelers Cas. & Sur. Co. of Am.*, No. CV095024601, 2011 Conn. Super. LEXIS 1572, at *6, *25-28.

N.J. Super. Ct. App. Div. 2005. "Customer voice initiated transfers" coverage arguably applied. The term funds in that coverage was undefined and ambiguous. It is often defined broadly enough to include securities, so the court would adopt that meaning to foster coverage. *Morgan Stanley Dean Witter & Co. v. Chubb Group of Ins. Cos.*, No. A-4124-03T2, 2005 N.J. Super. Unpub. LEXIS 798, at *10-12.

G. Trading Exclusion

1. Unambiguous

3d Cir. 1954 (Pa.). To give an exclusion meaning, it must withdraw something from the coverage. Trading exclusion excluded dishonest trading unambiguously; trading loss coverage was available at a higher premium. *Roth v. Md. Cas. Co.,* 209 F.2d 371, 373-74.

E.D. La. 2011. The insured's investment in a mutual fund was trading, which simply meant buying and selling of commodities, including securities. Thus, a trading loss exclusion applied. An entrustment exclusion also applied, as the insured did not have to be the one who made voluntary delivery of funds to the entity that caused the loss; that entity could be twice removed from the insured. *Methodist Health Sys. Found., Inc., v. Hartford Fire Ins. Co.,* No. 10- 3292, 2011 U.S. Dist. LEXIS 71258, at *9-13.

Mass. 1927. Bond's trading exclusion was unambiguous and was not restricted to brokers' own trading. Evidence that term had a special or restrictive meaning was rejected. *Harris v. Nat'l Sur. Co.,* 155 N.E. 10, 11.

N.Y. App. Div. 1985. Language of fidelity bond's trading exclusion was unambiguous and applied to that part of the insured's claim relating to the short sale of government treasury notes. *Flushing Nat'l Bank v. Transamerica Ins. Co.,* 491 N.Y.S.2d 793, 793-94.

2. Ambiguous or Construed Against Insurer

7th Cir. 1938 (Ill.). Bond was ambiguous. Trading loss exclusion did not extend to dishonest trading by employees. *Paddleford v. Fid. & Cas. Co. of N.Y.,* 100 F.2d 606, 613.

9th Cir. 1988 (Cal.). Trading exclusion was ambiguous as to losses involving both trading and employee dishonesty. Construing it against insurer, it did not exclude an insured's loss as a result of employee's wrongful retention of trading proceeds or theft of actual bonds. *Ins. Co. of N. Am. v. Gibralco, Inc.,* 847 F.2d 530, 534.

3. Statutory Considerations

2d Cir. 1978 (N.Y.). If bond is statutory, it also must be read in conjunction with the statute. Fraudulently priced purchase of securities by employee was not within trading exclusion. Statute also precluded enforcement of exclusion. *Index Fund v. Ins. Co. of N. Am.,* 580 F.2d 1158, 1162-63.

9th Cir. 1979 (Cal.). As statute did not require coverage for actions of investment adviser in recommending overpriced securities, trading exclusion would be enforced. *Research Equity Fund v. Ins. Co. of N. Am.,* 602 F.2d 200, 204.

4. *Joint Drafting*

W.D. Mo. 1984. Trading exclusion applied to an employee's use of forged guaranties to make it appear the bank stood behind his securities trading. American Bankers Association materials showed knowledge of the exclusion's history and meaning. Even if the exclusion was ambiguous, it would not be construed against the insurer because the bond form was the result of the combined efforts of the Surety Association of America and the American Bankers Association. Statute requiring bonding did not negate exclusion either; state had approved bond forms. *Shearson/Am. Express v. First Cont'l Bank & Trust Co.,* 579 F. Supp. 1305, 1309, 1311-12.

H. Miscellaneous Terms

1. *Unambiguous*

N.D. Ill. 2012. Exclusion of property lost after transfer off premises on basis of unauthorized instructions had plain meaning and applied to secretary's theft from partner's personal bank account. *Sperling & Slater, P.C. v. Hartford Cas. Ins., Co.,* No. 12-cv-761, 2012 U.S. Dist. LEXIS 125897, at *28-29.

D. Utah 2012. Missing endorsement exclusion unambiguously applied to all checks with missing endorsements. *Cyprus Fed. Credit Union v. Cumis Ins. Soc.,* No. 2:10CV00550, 2012 U.S. Dist. LEXIS 75643, at *6.

2. *Ambiguous or Construed Against Insurer*

E.D. La. 1989. Recoveries section of bond applied to recoveries made by bank before insurers paid loss. The doctrine of contra proferentem did not apply because the language was clear and had been drafted by a joint effort of the American Bankers Association and the Surety Association of America. *First Nat'l Bank of Louisville v. Lustig*, No. 87-5488, 88-1682, 89-202, 1989 U.S. Dist. LEXIS 14191, at *3-5.

E.D. Pa. 1992. Plain language of application required insured to list all losses, not just employee dishonesty losses. No alternative meaning could be ascribed. *Fid. Fed. Sav. & Loan Ass'n v. Felicetti*, No. 92-0643, 1992 U.S. Dist. LEXIS 15150, at *10-11.

Cal. Ct. App. 2007. The broader meaning of the term "arising out of" does not apply when there is an "independent act or intervening cause" separate from the insured's activities. *Sears Roebuck & Co. v. Nat'l Union Fire Ins. Co. of Pitt., Pa.*, No. B187280, 2007 Cal. App. Unpub. LEXIS 8084, at *19-21.

D.C. 2001. Absent ambiguity a contract speaks for itself and binds the parties without the necessity of extrinsic evidence. Plain bond language entitled insurer to portion of insured's recovery before insured could apply it to losses not covered. *Dist. No. 1–Pac. Coast Dist., Marine Eng'rs' Beneficial Ass'n v. Travelers Cas. & Sur. Co.*, 782 A.2d 269, 273-74.

Ga. Ct. App. 1970. Attorneys' fees provision of Savings and Loan Blanket Bond was not ambiguous in covering only defense costs, not costs of an affirmative suit by insured. *Rossville Fed. Sav. & Loan Ass'n v. Ins. Co. of N. Am.*, 174 S.E.2d 204, 207.

I. Discovery

1. Unambiguous

1st Cir. 1990 (Mass.). The discovery and notice provisions of a fidelity policy were unambiguous in providing no coverage for any losses not discovered within sixty days of policy termination. Court rejected insured's argument that the policy should be construed as an occurrence-type policy requiring actual prejudice, rather than a claims made-type policy requiring none. *J.I. Corp. v. Fed. Ins. Co.*, 920 F.2d 118, 119-20.

3d Cir. 2011 (N.J.). A literal construction of the term "Risk Management Department" so as to limit the operation of the discovery condition could not be adopted as it would produce an absurd result. The knowledge of a risk manager for the subcontractor would be imputed. *Diebold Inc. v. Cont'l Cas. Co.,* 430 F. App'x 201, 208.

5th Cir. 1981 (La.). Absent conflict with statute or public policy, bond term unambiguously limiting coverage to dishonest or fraudulent acts discovered during the policy term is enforceable. *Cent. Progressive Bank v. Fireman's Fund Ins. Co.,* 658 F.2d 377, 380.

6th Cir. 2008 (Tenn.). Under plain language of policies, insured could not recover even if insurers were not prejudiced by late discovery of loss. *Stewart's Wholesale Elec. Supply, Inc. v. FCCI Ins. Group,* No. 07-5895, 2008 U.S. App. LEXIS 11933, at *6.

8th Cir. 1979 (Ark.). To avoid frustration of intent, terms of Bankers Blanket Bond should be considered in context of whole agreement. Discovery and notice provisions should be construed in a manner consistent with the coverage. *Perkins v. Clinton State Bank,* 593 F.2d 327, 335.

9th Cir. 2001 (Idaho). Where a word or phrase used in an insurance contract has a settled legal meaning, that meaning must be given even though other interpretations are possible. *Gulf USA Corp. v. Fed. Ins. Co.,* 259 F.3d 1049, 1057-58.

9th Cir. 1991 (Cal.). Discovery provision could not be construed as an exclusion; insurer did not have burden of proving loss was not discovered in bond period. *FDIC v. N.H. Ins. Co.,* 953 F.2d 478, 482-83.

9th Cir. 1980 (Cal.). Term "losses discovered" in endorsement terminating coverage for losses discovered after a certain date was not ambiguous. Insured's interpretation that it extended to any losses occurring before the date, even if not discovered until after the date, was totally unreasonable. *F.S. Smithers & Co. v. Fed. Ins. Co.,* 631 F.2d 1364, 1367.

D. Md. 2008. Court explained difference between occurrence, claims made, and discovery based policies. Discovery policies enable an insurer to predict its exposure; they must be strictly enforced. *Gray & Assoc., LLC v. Travelers Cas. & Sur. Co. of Am.,* No. CCB-07-2216, 2008 U.S. Dist. LEXIS 23903, at *10-11, *14-15.

D.N.J. 2010. The bond clearly defined all loss involving a single employee as a single loss, so there was no later discovery of a separate loss when the insured learned more facts. *Omega Advisors, Inc. v. Fed. Ins. Co.,* No. 10-912, 2010 U.S. Dist. LEXIS 125934, at *20-22.

Cal. Ct. App. 1985. The term "discovery of the loss" in fidelity bond was not ambiguous. It plainly meant when the insured discovered it suffered a loss, not when it discovered it had a potential loss. *Pacific-Southern Mortgage Trust Co. v. Ins. Co. of N. Am.,* 212 Cal. Rptr. 754, 758.

Cal. Ct. App. 1981. Discovery clause of fidelity bond was not ambiguous. Discovery occurred when insured acquired knowledge of any fraudulent or dishonest act resulting in loss, not when it developed a later understanding of previously known facts or a later recognition of coverage under the bond. *USLIFE Sav. & Loan Ass'n v. Nat'l Sur. Corp.,* 171 Cal. Rptr. 393, 398.

Mo. Ct. App. 1998. Fidelity bond clause requiring insured to discover covered losses no later than one year from end of policy was unambiguous. Dishonest employee's knowledge did not count as discovery of loss. *S.E. Bakery Feeds v. Ranger Ins. Co.,* 974 S.W.2d 635, 639.

2. *Ambiguous*

10th Cir. 1991 (Okla.). Absent definition of "collusion" in discovery provision of Bankers Blanket Bond, the term must be given its plain and ordinary meaning. Further, as bond was required by broadly worded statute, statute must be read into it. Knowledge of president and others could not be imputed to insured as they effectively colluded in employee's scheme by allowing checks to be honored and overdrafts to accrue. *Adair State Bank v. Am. Cas. Co. of Reading, Pa.,* 949 F.2d 1067, 1072-75.

D.D.C. 1980. Ambiguous blanket crime policy is construed against insurer as party that selected language. Insured did not have to give notice within four months of discovery of occurrence that might give rise to claim for loss but could give notice within four months of loss that occurred at time third party made demand on insured. *Fid. & Deposit Co. of Md. v. President & Dirs. of Georgetown Coll.*, 483 F. Supp. 1142, 1146-47.

S.D. Fla. 2011. Discovery of loss does not require knowledge of wrongdoing by a particular employee, so long as a reasonable person would assume an employee dishonesty loss had occurred. Facts that later prove untrue can support such an assumption. *St. Paul Mercury Ins. Co. v. FDIC*, No. 08-21192, 2011 U.S. Dist. LEXIS 32908, at *12-13, *16-18.

D. Kan. 1989. A policy is not ambiguous absent doubtful and conflicting meanings gleaned from natural and reasonable interpretations. Policy in effect when employee committed the dishonest acts covered acts discovered within that policy's discovery period. *Koch Indus. v. Nat'l Union Fire Ins. Co. of Pitt., Pa.*, No. 89-1158-K, 1989 U.S. Dist. LEXIS 15703, at *18, *32-33.

D. Minn. 1990. Provisions limiting time within which an insured can bring an action are disfavored and strictly construed against insurer. *Mid-Am. Bank of Chaska v. Am. Cas. Co. of Reading, Pa.*, 745 F. Supp. 1480, 1483, 1485.

S.D. Miss. 2012. Under the Fifth Circuit's interpretation of the discovery clause, insured had to appreciate its shortage was a result of its teller's dishonesty; suspicion was not enough. *FDIC v. Denson*, No. 3:11CV498, 2012 U.S. Dist. LEXIS 159672, at *34-36.

Cal. Ct. App. 1978. Successive Brokers Blanket Bonds were ambiguous as to when loss was discovered, and thus, both would be construed as covering the loss. *Cont'l Ins. Co. v. Morgan, Olmstead, Kennedy & Gardner*, 148 Cal. Rptr. 57, 66.

Utah Ct. App. 1991. A contract will be construed against drafter only if extrinsic evidence fails to clarify intent of parties. However, there usually is no resort to extrinsic evidence to construe insurance contracts because they are on standard forms; the language is not negotiated. Court held loss was not discovered until it was established by final judgment in favor of investors. Court also excused insured's failure to disclose loan problems in application. Ambiguities in applications will be construed against insurer. *Home Sav. & Loan v. Aetna Cas. & Sur. Co.*, 817 P.2d 341, 347-48, 353.

3. Statutory Considerations

Cal. Ct. App. 1983. Discovery provisions in fidelity insurance policies are strictly enforced so that neither difficulty in discovering insured's losses nor employee concealment excuses an insured mutual fund's failure to discover a loss within the bond's discovery period. However, insured claimed it could not discover employees' fraudulent acts because they adversely dominated it. Denying coverage in this circumstance would defeat the statutory purpose of protecting the shareholders of the mutual fund from such losses. *Admiralty Fund v. Peerless Ins. Co.*, 191 Cal. Rptr. 753, 756, 759.

J. Notice and Proof of Loss

1. Unambiguous

D. Mass. 1994. Unambiguous exclusionary provisions must be applied in accord with their ordinary meaning. Notice provision was drafted by government. It straightforwardly made timely notice a condition precedent to coverage. Court declined to extend statute that had been construed to require liability insurers show prejudice as a result of late notice. Fidelity insurance is not liability insurance. *United States v. Nat'l Grange Mut. Ins. Co.*, No. 92-12813-MAP, 1994 U.S. Dist. LEXIS 13321, at *9-10.

2. Ambiguous or Construed Against Insurer

10th Cir. 1994 (Utah). Contract interpretation begins with an examination of the contract itself. Its terms should be harmonized to the extent possible. Any legitimate ambiguities are usually construed against the insurer. Insured discovered loss when government issued cease and desist orders. However, as bond did not expressly condition coverage upon timely notice, or forfeit it absent notice, insurer was not discharged by late notice absent a showing of prejudice. *FDIC v. Oldenburg,* 34 F.3d 1529, 1542, 1545-46.

N.D. Ill. 1987. Proof-of-loss requirement must be construed reasonably; loss need only be itemized to extent reasonably possible under the circumstances. *Premier Elec. Constr. Co. v. USF&G,* No. 80 C 6689, 1987 U.S. Dist. LEXIS 5588, at *4-5.

Ala. 1970. Court would not read into policy that failure to file proof of loss would work a forfeiture. *Am. Fire & Cas. Co. v. Burchfield,* 232 So. 2d 606, 610-11.

3. Joint Drafting

1st Cir. 1997 (Mass.). The Financial Institution Bond is more like a claims-made policy than an occurrence policy. It is the latest in a long line of forms written specifically for sophisticated financial institutions through negotiation between the banking industry and the fidelity industry. The bond has evolved from a surety instrument to a type of insurance, for most purposes, but it continues to retain certain surety characteristics and is not liability insurance. It is not subject to the doctrine of contra proferentem. For these reasons, the notice prejudice rule does not apply. *FDIC v. Ins. Co. of N. Am.,* 105 F.3d 778, 785-86.

Wis. 1974. The form of the blanket bond is the result of negotiations between the Surety Association of America and the American Bankers Association. The bond is not a contract of adhesion and the rule of interpretation against an insurer does not apply. The bond's requirement that notice be given at the earliest practical moment after discovery of a loss is a condition precedent. No showing of prejudice is necessary. *State Bank of Viroqua v. Capitol Indem. Corp.,* 214 N.W.2d 42, 43-44, 47.

4. Statutory

5th Cir. 1972 (Tex.). Savings and loan blanket bond was unambiguous. The parties were on equal terms and should be held to the obligations they assumed. Failure to furnish timely proof of loss barred coverage. Statute requiring notice periods be reasonable did not preclude the defense. *Abilene Sav. Ass'n v. Westchester Fire Ins. Co.,* 461 F.2d 557, 562.

K. Limitations

1. Unambiguous

NONE

2. Ambiguous or Construed Against Insurer

D. Conn. 2013. A bank as loss payee had standing to sue and a limitations provision was ambiguous in that it did not specify an accrual event, whether loss, knowledge or notice. *Known Litigation Holdings, LLC v. Navigators Ins. Co.,* No. 3:12-cv-269, 2013 U.S. Dist. LEXIS 38429, at *13-20, 22.

3. Statutory Considerations

8th Cir. 1954 (Ark.). Fidelity bond was contract of suretyship, but compensated surety is not entitled to strict construction in its favor. However, bond was not ambiguous. Insurer was discharged under statute exonerating surety when employer failed to sue employee within thirty days of notice to do so by surety. *Madison Cty. Farmers Ass'n v. Am. Emp'rs Ins. Co.,* 209 F.2d 581, 583-85.

N.D. Ind. 2007. Contractual limitations provision of ERISA bond could not be enforced; bond was an official bond under Indiana law. *Indiana Regional Council of Carpenters Pension Trust Fund v. Fid. & Deposit Co. of Md.,* No. 2:06-CV-32 PS, 2007 U.S. Dist. LEXIS 15429, at *18-20.

D. Mass. 1985. Fidelity bond was not a surety bond but an insurance policy. The bond's one-year limitations provision was unenforceable as a statute required the insured be given at least two years to sue. *Luso-Am. Credit Union v. Cumis Ins. Soc'y,* 616 F. Supp. 846, 848-49.

Fla. Dist. Ct. App. 2003. Term requiring that loss be discovered within ninety days of termination was unambiguous and did not impermissibly shorten statute of limitations for suit on bond. *Fireman's Fund Ins. Co. v. Levine & Partners, P.A.,* 848 So. 2d 1186, 1187-88.

Ind. Ct. App. 1984. Public Official Blanket Bond's contractual limitation period could not be enforced because it was shorter than statute allowed. Public officials do not have the power to contract away the rights of the public under statutory bonds. *State v. Lidster,* 467 N.E.2d 47, 49.

Md. 2010. Maryland statute barring contractual shortening of time to sue on crime policy applied in spite of endorsement matching statute in giving the insured three years to sue. Policy ran time to sue from discovery of loss, but statute ran it from date insured was called upon to perform, i.e., the date the proof of loss was filed. *St. Paul Travelers v. Millstone,* 987 A.2d 116, 126.

L. Loss

1. Unambiguous

6th Cir. 2010 (Mich.). Plain reading of policy terms revealed parties did not intend to insure agency. Applying dictionary definitions of direct loss, the insured's loss as a result of its failure to receive commissions from agency was not immediate in character. It was indirect and not covered either. *Tooling, Mfr. & Tech. Assoc. v. Hartford Fire Ins. Co.,* 693 F.3d 665, 677.

9th Cir. 2002 (Cal.). Fidelity coverage covered only loss of "tangible property" and that term unambiguously meant only things that could be touched, seen, and smelled—not trade secrets. *Avery Dennison Corp. v. Allendale Mut. Ins. Co.,* 310 F.3d 1114, 1116-17.

10th Cir. 1994 (Okla.). Although bond did not expressly state that insured had to suffer actual loss as a condition to recovery, court construed it to require actual loss because otherwise the insured did not have an insurable interest. To allow it to recover more than its actual loss, would convert bond into an illegal wagering contract. *Spears v. St. Paul Ins. Co. (In re Ben Kennedy and Assoc.),* 40 F.3d 318, 319-20.

S.D. Ga. 2007. The fidelity policy phrase "loss resulting directly from" is not ambiguous. It bars recovery for indirect interest losses. A cash-out-the-door method would be used to measure the reduction of the loss as a result of the employee's partial repayments. *Citizens Bank & Trust Co. v. St. Paul Mercury Ins. Co.*, No. cv 305-167, 2007 U.S. Dist. LEXIS 96529, at *11-13.

N.D. Ill. 2006. A commercial crime policy's undefined terms of "direct loss," "indirect loss," and "inability to realize income" were not ambiguous and should be given their plain and ordinary meanings. *Patrick Schaumburg Autos., Inc. v. Hanover Ins. Co.*, 452 F. Supp. 2d 857, 870-72.

N.D. Ill. 1992. Financial institution bond clearly excluded coverage of insured's attorney fees and consequential damages and court enforced exclusion as written. *Beverly Bancorp. v. Cont'l Ins. Co.*, No. 92 C 4823, 1992 WL 345420, at *6-7.

N.D.N.Y. 2001. Fidelity bond's clear definition of property and exclusion of indirect loss precluded insured from recovering business opportunities lost as a result of employee's diversion of work to insured's competitors. *Benchmark Printing, Inc. v. Am. Mfrs. Mut. Ins. Co.*, No. 00-CV-0865, 2001 U.S. Dist. LEXIS 619, at *7.

N.Y. App. Div. 2012. Policy could not be construed to cover "loss" of fictitious gains reported by investment manager engaged in Ponzi scheme. Loss meant real money invested, less real money received. *Jacobson Family Inv., Inc. v. Nat'l Union Fire Ins. Co. of Pitt., Pa.*, 955 N.Y.S.2d 338, 346.

N.Y. Sup. Ct. App. Div. 2003. Bond's endorsement unambiguously limited its coverage to client property, as defined, lost as a direct result of employee dishonesty. *Ernst & Young LLP. v. Nat'l Union Fire Ins. Co. of Pitt., Pa.*, 758 N.Y.S.2d 304, 305.

Ohio Ct. App. 1993. As fidelity bond did not define the term "loss," it would be given its plain and ordinary meaning unless ambiguous, in which case it would be construed in favor of the insured. Insured could recover losses arising from employee's diversion of customer funds and creation of fictitious loans. Potential income exclusion did not apply when fictitious loans were used to pay interest on pre-existing loans. *First Nat'l Bank of Dillonvale v. Progressive Cas. Ins. Co.,* 640 N.E.2d 1147, 1148, 1150-51.

Tex. Civ. App. 1975. In construing fidelity bonds, courts follow the liberal rules applicable to insurance contracts rather than the strict rules of suretyship. The bank's securities claim was not covered. Although the stock certificates were forged, the bank suffered no loss by receiving them when it renewed loans. It had already advanced its funds; no new money was advanced. *Tex. Nat'l Bank v. Fid. & Deposit Co. of Md.,* 526 S.W.2d 770, 774.

   2. Ambiguous or Construed Against Insurer

3d Cir. 2002 (Pa). Nurses' falsification of records was dishonest even if sending patients home was not. Cost of replicating studies rendered worthless by this conduct was direct loss because direct meant proximate. However, insurer was liable for only one occurrence because same nurses were guilty of same misconduct in all four clinical trials. It was a "series of related acts," the nurses themselves drew no distinction. *Scirex Corp. v. Fed. Ins. Co.,* 313 F.3d 841, 849-50.

9th Cir. 1989 (Or.). The bond's definition of "money" was not ambiguous; it did not extend to a loan loss. However, the term "securities" was construed to cover intangible as well as tangible interests, including the insured's loss, as it involved the use of checks and mortgages, both of which were included in the definition. *Portland Fed. Emps. Credit Union v. Cumis Ins. Soc'y,* 894 F.2d 1101, 1103-04.

10th Cir. 1994 (Utah). The liberal rules of interpretation applicable to insurance contracts apply to fidelity bonds, rather than the strict rules of suretyship. Manifest intent means apparent or obvious intent and exists when a particular result is substantially certain to follow from the employee's conduct; recklessness may suffice. The bonds at issue did not define loss. A loan loss occurs when the funds are disbursed, without regard to possible remedies or the value of the bank's security; if and when the security is realized, it is treated as a recovery under the bond. *FDIC v. United Pac. Ins. Co.,* 20 F.3d 1070, 1079-81.

D. Mass. 2010. Employee did not alert employer that it was depositing its CEO's salary into employee's account and continued receiving that salary after he quit. Fidelity insurer paid part of loss incurred before employee quit, but court also found coverage of loss incurred afterwards. Employee committed acts causing loss while still an employee and did nothing after to add to the loss. Policy's single loss definition figured in the analysis. If that definition was ambiguous, the intent of the parties could be interpreted by their own actions, and the insurer had treated the claim as presenting a single loss. *Fundquest, Inc. v. Travelers Cas. & Sur. Co.,* 715 F. Supp. 2d 202, 207, 209.

D. Minn. 1990. Court found potential income exclusion was ambiguous in excluding income not realized by the insured—"realized" could reasonably mean either conversion into money or recognition of income on an accrual basis. *Mid-Am. Bank of Chaska v. Am. Cas. Co. of Reading, Pa.*, 745 F. Supp. 1480, 1484-85.

S.D.N.Y. 1987. Insurance policies, such as a fidelity bond, are construed most favorably to the insured and most strictly against the insurer. The "acts covered" section of the bond was broad enough to include attorneys' fees incurred in the underlying action. *Glusband v. Fittin Cunningham Lauzon, Inc.,* No. 80 Civ. 7387, 1987 U.S. Dist. LEXIS 1867, at *8-9.

E.D.N.C. 1986. The court applied the rules of contract interpretation to a fidelity bond's potential income exclusion. Interest received when employee refinanced fictitious loans was realized income and therefore exclusion did not apply. Even if that interpretation could lead to highly inequitable results, insurer did not offer any contrary evidence and the exclusion's plain language permitted the interpretation. *St. Paul Fire & Marine Ins. Co. v. Branch Banking & Trust Co.,* 643 F. Supp. 648, 651, *aff'd*, 834 F.2d 416 (4th Cir. 1987).

D. Or. 1968. Reading the entire contract, any ambiguities must be construed against insurer. Advance of money on basis of forged stock certificate gave rise to covered "loss" without regard to insured's possible remedies against maker of note. *Citizens Bank v. Am. Ins. Co.,* 289 F. Supp. 211, 213-14.

Mont. 2006. The term "direct loss" in a fidelity policy included consequential damages proximately caused by the alleged dishonesty. *Frontline Processing Corp. v. Am. Eco. Ins. Co.,* 149 P.3d 906, 911.

N.Y. App. Div. 1968. List of covered property included "money" and customer's failure to repay overdrafts was a loss of money. *Liberty Nat'l Bank & Trust Co. v. Travelers Indem. Co.,* 295 N.Y.S.2d 983, 985-86.

Or. Ct. App. 1988. Insurer asserted exclusion limiting coverage of the loss of valuable records to the cost of copying the records. The court held the exclusion did not apply; it was not unreasonable to construe it as referring only to physical documents, not the value they might represent. *Kelch v. Indus. Indem. Co.,* 763 P.2d 402, 404.

 3. *Statutory Considerations*

Iowa 1988. If a statute applies, it will be read into the bond. The term "loss" as defined in statute included all losses incurred until all of the employee's accounts had been fully settled. This meant a loss includes interest accrued up to suit against the insurer. *Am. Trust & Sav. Bank v. USF&G,* 418 N.W.2d 853, 854-55.

 4. *Third-Party Liability*

  (a) Unambiguous

5th Cir. 1998 (Tex.). The true intent of the parties is paramount. Each term should be given effect, none rendered a nullity. No one phrase, sentence, or section should be considered in isolation. A uniform interpretation is desirable if similar policies are being construed in other jurisdictions. *Lynch Props. v. Potomac Ins. Co. of Ill.,* 140 F.3d 622, 625-29.

5th Cir. 1969 (Fla.). Policy terms that are clear and unambiguous and not illegal by statute or against public policy will be enforced as written. Fidelity bond is not for benefit of third party. It covers only loss insured itself suffers as a result of defalcation by its employee. *Am. Empire Ins. Co. v. Fid. & Deposit Co. of Md.,* 408 F.2d 72, 76-77.

SECTION 6 — CONSTRUCTION AND INTERPRETATION   679

7th Cir. 1989 (Wis.). Construction of an insurance policy is a question of law. An issue of fact arises only if there is ambiguity and extrinsic evidence is offered. Words will be given their common and ordinary meaning. An exclusion is as much an operative component of a policy as the insuring clause itself and entitled to equal enforcement as written. Claim on blanket bond issued to title insurer involved underlying claims that titles were not as represented in title policies. Claim was not covered because exclusion of loss from liability under contract or purported contract of insurance included loss from dishonest employee's issuance of such policies. *Cont'l Corp. v. Aetna Cas. & Sur. Co.,* 892 F.2d 540, 543-45.

5th Cir. 1980 (Fla.). Principal consideration in construction of blanket fidelity bond is the parties' intention as revealed by the language of the bond. Bond covered only loss suffered by insured, and thus, bank could not recover loan loss from borrower's fidelity insurer. *Everhart v. Drake Mgmt.,* 627 F.2d 686, 690-91.

D. Conn. 2002. Giving words their natural and ordinary meaning, not ignoring or distorting words but giving every word effect if reasonably possible, an insurance policy will be enforced as written if it is plain and unambiguous. A fidelity policy covers only direct loss to the insured; it does not cover loss resulting from liability to third parties as such loss is indirect. *Finkel v. St. Paul Fire & Marine Ins. Co.,* No. 3:00cv1194, 2002 U.S. Dist. LEXIS 11581, at *8-12.

D. Kan. 1993. A fidelity bond is not a surety bond or liability policy; it provides first party coverage to the insured only and a third party has no rights even if dishonesty by an employee of the insured has made the insured legally liable to the third party. *Sch. Emps. Credit Union v. Nat'l Union Fire Ins. Co. of Pitt., Pa.,* 839 F. Supp. 1477, 1480, *aff'd,* 1995 U.S. App. LEXIS 8254 (10th Cir. Apr. 7, 1995).

E.D. Ky. 2011. An employee stole from a client by causing client's bank to make payment to the client's ex-employee. No coverage existed because no direct loss of the insured's own funds or funds in its use and custody occurred; the liability to the client was indirect. The plain meaning of "use" required a more custodial relationship to the funds.

Monroe Guar. Ins. Co. v. Radwan Brown & Co., No. 09-247, 2011 U.S. Dist LEXIS 30263, at *4.

E.D. Pa. 2012. Where officer ran Ponzi scheme by selling fake CDs and stealing the induced deposits, no coverage arose. The money never belonged to the insured. The insured's loss theory was inconsistent with the nature of fidelity insurance and the bond language. Fidelity bonds indemnify against first-party loss; they do not cover injuries sustained by third parties. *Marion v. Hartford Fire Ins. Co.,* No. 06-4666, 2012 U.S. Dist. LEXIS 10606, at *16.

D. Utah 2008. The court rejected the insured's argument that a settlement with loan purchasers was covered because a proximate cause standard applied. The bond required the loss to be direct and direct meant direct. *Direct Mortgage Corp. v. Nat'l Union Fire Ins. Co. of Pitt., Pa.,* No. 2:06-cv-534, 2008 U.S. Dist. LEXIS 60695, at *7-11.

Colo. App. 2012. Bank's liability to investors was not bank's own "direct financial loss" within fidelity coverage. Black's Law Dictionary defines "direct" to mean "free from extraneous influence." That plus fact that this was a fidelity policy and not a liability policy meant it should not be construed as a liability policy. *Abady v. Certain Underwriters at Lloyd's London,* No. 2012 COA 173, 2012 Colo. App. LEXIS 1650, at *11-14.

Ill. App. Ct. 2004. Mortgage company's settlement with third party was a consequential loss that did not result directly from its employee's fraudulent acts; proximate cause standard did not apply to determine what is a direct loss under a fidelity bond. *RBC Mtg. Co. v. Nat'l Union Fire Ins. Co. of Pitt., Pa.,* 812 N.E.2d 728, 737.

Iowa 1999. A fidelity bond is not a liability policy; it does not cover loss suffered by a third party. Instead, fidelity insurance is direct insurance procured by the insured in favor of itself. *City of Burlington v. W. Sur. Co.,* 599 N.W.2d 469, 472.

Kan. 1970. Coverage of "loss for which the insured is legally liable" is not ambiguous. It did not extend rights under fidelity bond to third parties. *Ronnau v. Caravan Int'l Corp.,* 468 P.2d 118, 122.

Kan. Ct. App. 2007. The bond covers theft of property from a bank by a physically present thief. It does not cover a bank's loss when the proceeds of a theft are deposited by a thief's employee to the bank and the bank becomes liable to a third party from whom the funds are stolen. The Financial Institution Bond was created jointly by the banking and insurance industry (parties with relatively equal bargaining power) so the rule of construction against the insurer when an ambiguity is found does not apply. *Citizens Bank, N.A. v. Kan. Bankers Sur. Co.*, No. 95,136, 2007 Kan. App. Unpub. LEXIS 524, at *9.

Mass. App. Ct. 2005. Employee dishonesty policy covered only direct losses of the insured's covered property. It did not cover insured's reimbursement of client for theft by insured's employee. *Atlas Metals Prod. Co., Inc. v. Lumbermans Mut. Cas. Co.*, 829 N.E.2d 257, 261-262.

Mich. Ct. App. 2008. The fidelity coverage of a property policy did not cover the insured's liability to third parties defrauded by employees of the insured. *First Mountain Mortgage Corp. v. Citizens Ins. Co.*, No. 04-001170-CK, 2008 Mich. App. LEXIS 2017, at *7.

Mich. Ct. App. 1992. Fidelity bond indemnifies insured against loss from want of fidelity by its employees; it does not insure against liability to third parties or otherwise benefit third parties. *Koerber v. Alter*, 483 N.W.2d 929, 930.

Minn. Ct. App. 2004. Fidelity policy did not cover settlement of third-party claims and excluded losses arising from trade secret theft alleged. *Cargill, Inc. v. Nat'l Union Fire Ins. Co.*, No. A03-187, 2004 WL 51671, at *29-31, *41-42.

Miss. Ct. App. 2005. Fidelity policy provided first-party coverage only and did not cover insured's liability for fraud on third party by allowing customer to buy vehicles in third-party's name using altered power-of-attorney. *Watson Quality Ford, Inc. v. Great River Ins. Co.*, 909 So. 2d 1196, 1199-1200.

N.M. 1980. Blanket fidelity bond in favor of state unambiguously did not cover third-parties' loss from conversion of livestock by employees at state livestock board. *N.M. Livestock Board v. Dose*, 607 P.2d 606, 610-11.

N.Y. App. Div. 1998. Insured settled third-party claims against stockbroker arising from employee's illegal disclosures of insider information to customers. Fidelity bond did not cover settlement; employee did not intend to cause the employer a loss. Clear exclusion of any damage other than direct compensatory damages also applied. Both the history of fidelity bonds generally and the specific drafting history of the bond form at issue (which included securities industry participation) demonstrated there was never an intent to cover third parties from the consequences of unauthorized trading by an employee. *Aetna Cas. & Sur. Co. v. Kidder, Peabody & Co.,* 676 N.Y.S.2d 559, 563-65.

N.Y. Sup. Ct. 1993. Stockbroker sought to recover from its fidelity insurers cost of proposed settlement of securities fraud claims against it. Court held fidelity bonds were not liability policies and dismissed suit. Insured could not plead repeated discovery of fraud as discovery can occur only once. *Drexel Burnham Lambert Group v. Vigilant Ins. Co.,* 595 N.Y.S.2d 999, 1006, 1010-11.

Wis. Ct. App. 2008. The insured hospital's employee stole funds from a bank account in the name of the medical staff and funded by annual dues. The insured did not own, hold, or have legal liability for the account. The word "owned" was undefined but unambiguous; it means belonging to oneself. Possession and control of personal property such as money gives rise to a presumption of ownership. The insured did not own the account because it did not exercise possession or control over it, i.e., did not have signatory authority and did not deposit money into it or decide how deposited funds were to be spent. Moreover, the policy covered only direct loss of covered property, not liability to a third party. *Meriter Health Services, Inc. v. Travelers Cas. & Sur. Co. of Am.,* 758 N.W.2d 112, 116.

Wis. Ct. App. 2003. Bond language was product of joint drafting and could not be construed against insurer. Losses did not result until borrowers defaulted and mortgagees sued bank; such indirect losses are not covered. *Tri City Nat'l Bank v. Fed. Ins. Co.,* 674 N.W.2d 617, 621-22.

SECTION 6 — CONSTRUCTION AND INTERPRETATION

(b) Ambiguous or construed against insurer

Fla. Dist. Ct. App. 1980. Fidelity bond was ambiguous as to meaning of "loss" and had to be construed liberally in favor of insured. Bond covered insured's settlement of suit for damages caused by employee's dishonest or fraudulent acts directed against third persons. *Southside Motor Co. v. Transam. Ins. Co.,* 380 So. 2d 470, 471.

(c) Statutory considerations

8th Cir. 1990 (Ark.). Although stockbroker's fidelity bond by its own terms excluded third-party claims, statute requiring bond was liberally construed by court to allow third-party claims as a matter of public policy to protect the investing public. *Foster v. Nat'l Union Fire Ins. Co. of Pitt.,* 902 F.2d 1316, 1320.

M. Single Loss, Prior Loss, and Limits Issues

1. *Unambiguous*

5th Cir. 2008 (Miss.). Embezzlement over ten years was only one occurrence and policies could not be stacked. The definition of occurrence as a series of acts was not ambiguous. Non-cumulation clause was also plain and would be enforced as written. Insured could only collect limits of policy in effect when the thefts were discovered. *Madison Materials Co. v. St. Paul Fire & Marine Ins. Co.,* 523 F.3d 541, 544-45.

6th Cir. 1964 (Ky.). Complex character of bond does not automatically render it ambiguous. Securities coverage with lower limit covered loss, but there was no higher limit forgery coverage available as forged car loans and leases pledged by borrower were not "advices and instructions directed to bank." *Liberty Nat'l Bank & Trust Co. v. Nat'l Sur. Corp.,* 330 F.2d 697, 700.

6th Cir. 1934 (Mich.). Fidelity bond was unambiguous. There was only one ongoing bond, and thus, only a single limit could be recovered; coverage in prior years could not be stacked, no matter how long bond was in force or how many premiums paid. *USF&G v. Barber,* 70 F.2d 220, 226.

7th Cir. 1970 (Ill.). "Non-reduction of liability" provision did not reinstate limits for each forgery committed by same person. Although language favoring insurer was not absolutely clear, no other purpose was evident and insured's only argument was that language was a nullity. Insurer's interpretation had a basis in sensible insurance practices. When banks engage in multiple transactions with any one person, insurers encourage banks to scrutinize reliability and solvency of that person by limiting coverage. *Roodhouse Nat'l Bank v. Fid. & Deposit Co. of Md.,* 426 F.2d 1347, 1351.

9th Cir. 1996 (Cal). The term "loss sustained" was unambiguous. The insured sustained loss when the money was stolen. *Lincoln Tech. Inst. v. Fed. Ins. Co.,* No. 94-16369, 1996 U.S. App. LEXIS 2155, at *7-9.

9th Cir. 1991 (Cal.). Court held only reasonable interpretation of "loss" as used in bond was that it meant the event creating liability, not the ensuing judgment. *First Am. Title Ins. Co. v. St. Paul Fire & Marine Ins. Co.,* 951 F.2d 1134, 1136-37.

10th Cir. 1992 (Utah). Court looks at all parts of a fidelity bond in relation to each other, giving an objective and reasonable construction to the whole, avoiding a construction that neutralizes any one provision. Court concluded bond unambiguously referred only to bonds issued by same insurer; its reference to a discovery period was to that of the prior bond, as the discovery provision of current bond was in a third section. The insured's interpretation would render clear terms meaningless. *Brigham Young Univ. v. Lumbermens Mut. Cas. Co.,* 965 F.2d 830, 834-36.

10th Cir. 1990 (Okla.). Courts interpreting fidelity bonds follow the liberal rules applicable to insurance contracts, not the strict rules of suretyship. However, if the policy is complete and unambiguous then its plain language is enforced. Loss occurred when insured extended credit, not when it discovered collateral was counterfeit after customer defaulted. *United Bank & Trust Co. v. Kan. Bankers & Sur. Co.,* 901 F.2d 1520, 1522.

10th Cir. 1971 (Kan.). A contract should be interpreted as a harmonious whole. Every word should be given meaning in context. Retroactive extension clause of Bankers Blanket Bond provided not double coverage but coverage for a loss if it would have been covered by the prior bond. *Traders State Bank v. Cont'l Ins. Co.*, 448 F.2d 280, 283.

D.C. Cir. 1951. Courts are not free to rewrite clear contract language. Blanket position bond had a continuous term, not an annual one and express provision against cumulation limited coverage to amount stated in bond regardless of years bond had been in effect. *Columbia Hosp. for Women & Lying-In Asylum v. USF&G*, 188 F.2d 654, 659-60.

D. Ariz. 1994. Insurer correctly applied lower limits to a claim because by the clear meaning of the term, "loss" occurs when the insured parts with money due to fraud and loss at issued predated increase of limits. The doctrine of reasonable expectations had no play. *Lincoln Technical Inst. of Ariz. v. Fed. Ins. Co.*, 927 F. Supp. 376, 378-79.

E.D. Ark. 1971. A blanket bond rider limiting liability under the securities coverage was enforced as written as it was not ambiguous. *Benton State Bank v. Hartford Acc. & Indem. Co.*, 338 F. Supp. 674, 679-80, *aff'd*, 452 F.2d 5 (8th Cir. 1971).

S.D. Fla. 2012. A retroactive date endorsement unambiguously ruled out coverage of a loss that occurred in part before the date. *ABCO Premium Finance, LLC v. Am. Int'l Group, Inc.*, No. 1:11-cv-23020, 2012 U.S. Dist. LEXIS 111833, at *33-34.

S.D. Fla. 2008. Provisions relating to the policy period, termination of prior policies, the discovery period, and liability for prior losses, when read together, covered losses sustained during the earlier policy periods, but only under the current policy and subject to its limits. *PBSJ Corp. v. Fed. Ins. Co.*, No. 07-22248-CIV, 2009 U.S. App. LEXIS 2169, at *6-7.

N.D. Ill. 2008. Coverage could not be stacked for embezzlement by checks written over three years. Each policy unambiguously limited coverage to loss discovered within a year of termination and also covered loss sustained during the immediately preceding policy period. The insured's attempt to "extend recovery backward by cobbling together prior loss provisions calls for a wholly illogical reading of the policies."

The insurer was only liable for the losses occurring in the second and third policy periods. *Am. Auto Guardian, Inc. v. Acuity Mut. Ins. Co.,* 548 F. Supp. 2d 624, 627-30.

N.D. Ill. 2008. Employee used different schemes to steal from the insured's profit sharing plan. Court found policy's standard occurrence definition unambiguous. There was not one occurrence for each scheme, nor one for each theft from the eighty-three individual plan participants. Under the policy definition and under the cause theory of occurrence, multiple acts of theft by the same employee had to be treated as a single occurrence, even if the employee was using different methods to carry out the theft. *Aldridge Elec., Inc. v. Fid. & Deposit Co. of Md.,* No. 04 C 4021, 2008 U.S. Dist. LEXIS 85090, at *18-19.

N.D. Ill. 1968. Ambiguities are construed against insurer as drafter but policy must be construed as a whole, giving effect to each provision and not perverting language under guise of construction to create a right not intended by parties. Term "any" in "any loss" was synonymous with "all." Single loss limit applied to single officer's multiple defalcations. *FSLIC v. Aetna Ins. Co.,* 279 F. Supp. 161, 162-63.

D. Md. 2013. Only the last of the insurer's three policies covered any part of a loss occurring over many years; the policy covered only loss sustained during its period and the period of the preceding policy. The last policy's reference to "this insurance" meant "this policy," not successive policies. Similarly, "prior insurance" meant only the immediately preceding policy, not a prior carrier's program. This did not upset the meaning of other conditions. It was consistent with the one year discovery window that each policy provided. Extrinsic evidence could not be considered. *Emcor Group v. Great Am. Ins. Co.,* No. 1:12-cv-142, 2013 U.S. Dist. LEXIS 43346, at *39-41, *43-44, *81-82.

D. Mass. 1988. Either the insured could recover up to the limit of a fidelity policy for each dishonest act by an employee or a single limit applied regardless of the number of acts. In providing only the latter, policy was not ambiguous. Nothing about the policy's structure, content, manner of printing, or marketing reasonably justified expectations of any more coverage, especially as the insured was sophisticated and discussed the limit with its broker. Reading the policy as a whole, it did not matter that the coverage section did not itself make reference to the policy limit; the limit was prominently displayed on the first page of the policy. There was also no ambiguity in the provision imposing an aggregate limit for any loss caused by any one employee resulting from single act or any number of acts. *Waltham Precision Instruments v. Fed. Ins. Co.,* No. 87-0732-MA, 1988 U.S. Dist. LEXIS 1729, at *10-15.

E.D. Mich. 2009. Insured's employee in collusion with three different third parties embezzled in excess of single policy limit over several years. The court found the single loss definition and prior loss provisions were unambiguous. The supervisor was integral to the entire scheme; without her it could not have been carried out. Only a single loss under one policy occurred. *Hartman & Tyner, Inc. v. Fed. Ins. Co.,* No. 08-cv-12461, 2009 U.S. Dist. LEXIS 90004, at *11-13.

W.D. Mo. 2005. Policy issued to a doctor's professional corporation had a prior coverage provision which unambiguously precluded coverage of loss sustained during the prior policy unless the insured was covered during that period. There was no prior coverage because the prior policy insured only the doctor, not the corporation. *Travelers Indem. Co. v. Vas-Nes, P.C.,* No. 03-5120, 2005 U.S. Dist. LEXIS 28897, at *4-5.

D. Nev. 2010. Embezzlement over three policy periods gave rise to only one occurrence under only the one policy in force when the loss was discovered (the last of the three). The prior policies had terminated and their discovery windows had closed before the loss was discovered. The last policy did not, by its use of the term occurrence or otherwise, suggest that coverage was limited to the policy period such that the other polices could somehow also apply. *APMC Hotel Mgt., LLC v. Fid. & Deposit Co. of Md.,* No. 5:07-cv-00652, 2011 U.S. Dist. LEXIS 131638, at *21.

E.D.N.Y. 2012. Servicing contractor's principal sold 189 of the insured credit union's loans over five years and stole the proceeds. Bond unambiguously excluded loss to extent principal caused it outside of his loan servicing capacity; his company was not an employee of the credit union except in that capacity. Independent contractor exclusion reinforced this interpretation. Only a single loss occurred in that the principal had directed all of the misconduct. Alternatively, only a single loss occurred because the fraud involved a series of related acts. *Suffolk Fed. Credit Union v. CUMIS Ins. Soc., Inc.,* No. 10-CV-0001, 2012 U.S. Dist. LEXIS 178198, at *24-26, *36-39.

S.D. W. Va. 2009. Bookkeepers dishonest payments to herself by way of 293 checks over time was a single occurrence. Definition of occurrence as "all loss caused by, or involving, one or more employees, whether the result of a single act or a series of acts" was unambiguous. That she was guilty of multiple torts or crimes did not matter. *Beckley Mech., Inc. v. Erie Ins. Co.,* No. 5:07-cv-00652, 2009 U.S. Dist. LEXIS 30881, at *11.

Ariz. 2008. A series of thefts by an employee over multiple policy periods had to be treated as a single occurrence under policy in force at time of discovery. In referring to "all loss," the policy did not create an ambiguity as to whether it meant "each loss" or "all losses." Nor did loss mean each theft in a series of thefts. Nor was the occurrence definition meant only to prevent the insured from claiming an occurrence for each employee or each act involved in a single theft. The policy covered loss, not acts, so the number of employees or acts was irrelevant. The policy did not provide illusory coverage by treating unrelated thefts by multiple employees as a single occurrence. The phrase "series of acts" was not ambiguous as meaning either a series of thefts or a series of acts leading up to a theft. Only acts from which loss results—acts of theft—were part of the occurrence. *Emp'rs Mut. Cas. Co. v. DGG & CAR, Inc.,* 183 P.3d 513, 519.

Ariz. Ct. App. 1971. Fidelity bond was clear in limiting insurers' liability for loss committed by colluding employees to single limit; there was not a separate limit available for each employee. *Md. Cas. Co. v. Clements,* 487 P.2d 437, 445.

Cal. Ct. App. 1995. Successive fidelity policies were construed against insurer such that insured could recover loss from an ongoing embezzlement up to the limit of each policy. "Any one occurrence" defined as a series of acts could mean either the entire theft over time or the multiple steps in each theft. The wording also suggested there could be more than one occurrence. *A.B.S. Clothing Collection v. Home Ins. Co.,* 41 Cal. Rptr. 2d 166, 170, 173-74.

Ill. App. Ct. 1999. Insured with inventory loss failed to present evidence as to number of occurrences and which, if any, were in excess of deductible. Occurrence defined as a single act or series of acts is not ambiguous. *Reedy Indus. v. Hartford Ins. Co.,* 715 N.E.2d 728, 732-33.

Ill. App. Ct. 1991. A fidelity policy should be construed like any other contract—in its entirety, with each part harmonized. Single policy limit applying to all losses in which an employee was concerned or implicated applied to independently initiated fraud by two employees because they colluded in perpetuating and concealing the fraud. *Purdy Co. of Ill. v. Transp. Ins. Co.,* 568 N.E.2d 318, 322-23.

La. 1983. Courts are not free to rewrite a commercial contract entered into at arm's length by fully competent parties. Fidelity bond unambiguously was a single continuous contract limiting the maximum liability of the insurer to the amount stated in the bond, regardless of the extent of losses over the years it was in force and despite annual billing for premiums, where no renewal certificates were issued and the bond did not terminate on a specified date. *State ex rel. Guste v. Aetna Cas. & Sur. Co.,* 429 So. 2d 106, 110-11.

Mo. 1968. Liability of fidelity insurer for loss partly occurring under prior bond was unambiguously limited to amount of later bond. *State v. Hanover Ins. Co.,* 431 S.W.2d 141, 143.

Mo. Ct. App. 2007. Each check written in an ongoing embezzlement was not a separate occurrence. The policies' definition of occurrence as "all loss caused by or involving, one or more employees, whether the result of a single act or series of acts" was unambiguous. *Thornburgh Insulation, Inc. v. J.W. Terrill, Inc.,* 236 S.W.3d 651, 656.

N.Y. Sup. Ct. App. Div. 1997. Single loss discovery and notice provisions of fidelity bond were unambiguous in requiring that all dishonest transactions in which a particular employee is involved be considered a single loss. *Bank Saderat Iran N.Y. Agency v. Nat'l Union Fire Ins. Co. of Pitt., Pa.,* 665 N.Y.S.2d 79, 83-84.

Pa. 2007. Insured suffered loss over consecutive years. Insurer issued bond and renewed it annually during those years. Court affirmed insurer had entered into a single continuous bonding scheme with a single limit of insurance. The bond's unambiguous non-cumulation clause was enforceable without any need to cancel the prior coverage at the end of each period; the coverage by its terms expired at the end of each period. *Reliance Ins. Co. v. IRPC, Inc.*, 904 A.2d 912, 916-17.

Pa. Super. Ct. 1981. Court will enforce clear terms. Insurers' liability under continuous bond was not cumulative. *Eddystone Fire Co. v. Cont'l Ins. Co.*, 425 A.2d 803, 805.

2. Ambiguous or Construed Against Insurer

4th Cir. 2001 (S.C.). Successive fidelity policies were ambiguous as they did not indicate whether an "occurrence" defined in part as "a single act or series of acts" included acts occurring outside the policy term. Prior insurance and non-cumulation clauses were also ambiguous. The insured could recover up to the limit of each policy. *Spartan Iron & Metal Corp. v. Liberty Ins. Corp.*, 6 F. App'x 176, 178, 181.

5th Cir. 1977 (La.). Only single deductible of Brokers Blanket Bond could be applied to loss resulting from multiple acts that were part of a single ongoing trading spree because only single loss could be recovered under another clause of bond. Any other construction would render the deductible provision ambiguous when losses resulted from two or more acts. *Howard, Weil, Labouisse, Friedrichs, Inc. v. Ins. Co. of N. Am.*, 557 F.2d 1055, 1059-60.

9th Cir. 2000 (Cal.). Occurrence and prior loss provisions of successive fidelity policies were held ambiguous and construed against insurer. Insured could recover loss from an ongoing embezzlement up to the limit of each policy, except that a limitations defense barred recovery on the earliest policy. *Karen Kane, Inc. v. Reliance Ins. Co.*, 202 F.3d 1180, 1185, 1187.

E.D. Mo. 2005. Fidelity coverage of commercial insurance policy had limits of $5000 and a deductible of $1000 for each occurrence. Forgery coverage covered loss resulting from a single act or any number of acts but fidelity coverage did not have same term. Court found this created an ambiguity such that an employee's ongoing fraud involving multiple invoices was covered as a loss for each invoice, not a single loss for the whole scheme. *Acid Piping Tech., Inc. v. Great Northern Ins. Co.,* No. 4:04CV1667, 2005 U.S. Dist. LEXIS 27110, at *7-10.

D.R.I. 2011. Various combinations of employees and others pilfered from the insured over a decade. The court found the crime policies' definition of "single loss" was ambiguous and contradicted a clause stating there was no aggregate limit. Employees acting independently could have caused multiple losses even if they conspired with the same outside person. *R.I. Resource Recovery Corp. v. Travelers Indem. Co.,* No. 10-294, 2011 U.S. Dist. LEXIS 58007, at *7, 11.

Ga. 2004. Consecutive policies had single occurrence limits and defined occurrence as "all loss caused by, or involving, one or more employees whether the result of a single act or a series of acts." Policies also provided that limits did not cumulate from year to year or period to period. Insured suffering embezzlement loss over two policy periods could recover limit under renewal policy in addition to a single limit (not three limits as insured contended) under first policy. Insurer had stipulated there were two policies. *Sherman & Hemstreet, Inc. v. Cincinnati Ins. Co.,* 594 S.E.2d 648, 650-52.

Ill. App. Ct. 1979. Construing bond liberally in favor of coverage, loss was sustained when dishonest acts were committed, not when insured finally had to meet its obligation under a contract surety bond issued by the dishonest employee. *Reserve Ins. Co. v. Gen. Ins. Co.,* 395 N.E.2d 933, 938-39.

Iowa 1994. Non-cumulation clause was ambiguous and thus insured could recover up to the limits of policy each year it was in force. *Cincinnati Ins. Co. v. Hopkins Sporting Goods,* 522 N.W.2d 837, 840-41.

Ohio Ct. App. 1993. A fidelity policy limited coverage to losses sustained in the policy period and defined occurrence as an act or series of related acts. These terms were ambiguous as applied to forgeries of checks, some of which were not negotiated until after the policy terminated. Inasmuch as the forgeries themselves occurred during the policy period, the policy covered the entire resulting loss. *G & S Mgmt. Co. v. Commercial Union Ins. Cos.,* No. 92AP-1429, 1993 Ohio App. LEXIS 2836, at *6-8.

Or. Ct. App. 2003. Employee's embezzlements in successive policy periods made insurer liable for limits of both policies in spite of single occurrence provision. Funds in insured's bank account were "money" within the meaning of that term as used in policy. Checks stolen by employee and used to withdraw funds from account were "securities." *Robben & Sons Heating, Inc. v. Mid-Century Ins. Co.,* 74 P.3d 1141, 1145.

Pa. Super. Ct. 1998. Court held aggregate and non-cumulation provisions of a fidelity bond were ambiguous but limited recovery to single aggregate limit based on extrinsic evidence as to the intent of the parties. *Penn Township v. Aetna Cas. & Sur. Co.,* 719 A.2d 749, 753-54.

3. Statutory Considerations

Ill. App. Ct. 1973. Blanket bond and its predecessor were unambiguous and therefore court was not authorized to use canons of construction but had to enforce agreement in accordance with its terms. Bond renewed annually over period of embezzlement was not cumulative and insured could recover only single limit. Credit union statute was part of bond but did not require accumulation of limits from year to year. *Santa Fe Gen. Office Credit Union v. Gilberts,* 299 N.E.2d 65, 74-76.

N. Termination as to Employee

1. Unambiguous

5th Cir. 1957 (La.). Proof of loss and deemed cancellation clauses were enforceable and unambiguous, and therefore, there was no room for construction in favor of insured, precluding coverage. *J.S. Fraering, Inc. v. Employers Mut. Liab. Ins. Co.,* 242 F.2d 609, 611, 613.

6th Cir. 1982 (Mich.). Bond provided it terminated as to an employee as soon as insured learned of dishonest or fraudulent acts by that employee. It did not specify if this included acts committed before the employee was hired. Manner in which parties treat an executory contract with ambiguous terms is given great weight. If this resolves the ambiguity, it takes precedence over construing policy against insurer. Insured had previously contacted insurer as to whether individuals with similarly suspect records would be covered if hired. This showed it understood automatic termination clause applied if insured knew of prior misconduct by employee when it hired him. *William C. Roney & Co. v. Fed. Ins. Co.,* 674 F.2d 587, 590-91.

La. Ct. App. 1968. Provision terminating coverage of employee from time insured has knowledge of any dishonest or fraudulent act committed by employee at any time was enforceable and not contra bonos mores. *Verneco, Inc. v. Fid. & Cas. Co. of N.Y.,* 207 So. 2d 828, 830, *aff'd,* 219 So. 2d 508 (La. 1969).

N.Y. App. Div. 2012. The termination clause was broad; it applied to acts whether the bond covered them or not. The bond did not define dishonest or fraudulent acts, but the ordinary meaning of those terms in the context of a fidelity bond includes acts that demonstrate a want of integrity, breach of trust, or moral turpitude affecting the official fidelity or character of the employee. *Capital Bank & Trust Co. v. Gulf Ins. Co.,* 937 N.Y.S.2d 463, 465-66.

2. *Ambiguous or Construed Against Insurer*

6th Cir. 2005 (Ohio). In referring to insured corporation as "you," primary commercial crime policy was ambiguous and manager's knowledge could not be imputed so as to effect cancellation as to dishonest president. *Century Bus. Serv., Inc. v. Utica Mut. Ins. Co.,* 122 F. App'x 196, 201.

W.D. Wash. 2005. Court found the term "discovery" as applied to a termination issue to be ambiguous. Coverage was not canceled as to the employee unless one of the specified officials had actual knowledge of his prior conviction. *Akins Foods, Inc. v. Am. & Foreign Ins. Co.,* No. C04-2195, 2005 U.S. Dist. LEXIS 36765, at *9-12.

E.D. Wis. 2011. Insurer asserted coverage terminated as to an employee "as soon as" an officer became aware of an incident before policy inception. Court found the clause ambiguous. It could refer only to knowledge first acquired after the inception of the policy. *Waupaca Northwoods v. Travelers Cas. & Sur. Co. of Am.,* No. 10-C-459, 2011 U.S. Dist. LEXIS 44467, at *10-13.

Conn. Super. Ct. 2009. Clause terminating coverage as to employee on discovery by the insured of "any dishonest act committed by that 'employee' whether before or after becoming employed by you" was ambiguous and would be construed so as not to apply to discovery occurring before the policy period. *C.A. White, Inc. v. Travelers Cas. & Sur. Co. of Am.,* No. CV0850L35515, 2009 Conn. Super. LEXIS 989, at *30-33.

N.C. Ct. App. 2004. Bank knew when it hired officer that he had been convicted of embezzlement at another firm. Court held bond's termination as to employee clause was ambiguous in that it could be read either as (1) terminating if the bank learned at any time of a dishonest act by the employee, or (2) terminating only if the bank acquired such knowledge after the bond became effective. Court construed bond against insurer. *Home Sav. Bank v. Colonial Am. Cas. & Sur. Co.,* 598 S.E.2d 265, 270.

Pa. Super. Ct. 1956. Insured's failure to notify insurer on learning of dishonest acts by employee during prior employment did not cancel coverage for that employee under deemed cancellation clause, as clause was ambiguous and had to be construed against insurer as to whether it referred only to dishonesty while employed by the insured or dishonesty at any time. *N.E. Lincoln-Mercury v. Century Indem. Co.,* 124 A.2d 420, 422.

O. Termination, Takeover, and Merger

1. Unambiguous

9th Cir. 1990 (Cal.). The termination provisions of a 3-D policy were clear and unambiguous. *Cal. Union Ins. Co. v. Am. Diversified Sav. Bank,* 948 F.2d 556, 559-560, 564-65.

11th Cir. 2002 (Fla.). Bank's acquisition of all the insured bank's stock was a takeover terminating Financial Institution Bond. Context established that term was not limited to regulatory takeovers of failed banks. While a contract should be interpreted so every section has a function, construing takeover in this manner would not leave separate term relating to change in control superfluous. *Am. Cas. Co. v. Etowah Bank,* 288 F.3d 1282, 1285-87.

N.D. Ill. 2013. Insurer's termination clause unambiguously closed discovery window when insured obtained replacement coverage. *Midway Truck Parts, Inc. v. Federated Ins. Co.,* No. 11 CV 9060, 2013 U.S. Dist. LEXIS 20554, at *7-8.

N.D. Ill. 1989. Clause partially terminating coverage upon a change in control was not ambiguous. Clause totally terminating coverage upon takeover by receiver was enforceable, as bond was on form specified by FSLIC. *FSLIC v. Transamerica Ins. Co.,* 705 F. Supp. 1328, 1334, 1336-37.

Fla. Dist. Ct. App. 1960. Rules of construction do not overcome plain language. Where insurer complied with terms of cancellation of fidelity bond, it did not matter if insured never received actual notice. *Graves v. Iowa Mut. Ins. Co.,* 123 So. 2d 351, 353.

   2. *Ambiguous or Construed Against Insurer*

W.D. Pa. 2012. Exclusion of employees of merged, consolidated, or purchased entity did not define its terms. Consulting law dictionary, court found terms referred to a total acquisition of a target company that ceases to exist. Asset purchase at issue was not total so exclusion did not apply. *K2 Settlement, LLC v. Certain Underwriters at Lloyd's, London,* No. 11-0191, 2012 U.S. Dist. LEXIS 170832, at *14-17.

Tex. 1984. The term "takeover" in Brokers Blanket Bond's termination clause was ambiguous, and therefore, coverage did not terminate when insured sold substantially all of its assets to another company but was to some extent still winding up its affairs prior to a final closing date at the time the loss was discovered. *Kelly Assocs., Ltd. v. Aetna Cas. & Sur. Co.,* 681 S.W.2d 593, 596-97.

   3. *Joint Drafting*

5th Cir. 1988 (La.). Notice to the Federal Home Loan Board was not required to terminate a Savings and Loan Blanket Bond upon takeover of a bank by the government. The notice clause applied only to voluntary terminations by the insured or insurer. No definition of "whether," as used in the bond's termination section, reasonably supported a different reading. Sound underwriting reasons lay behind the section as drafted. Even if it was ambiguous, it would not be construed in favor of the insured because the bond form was a joint effort of insurers and insureds and was required by the FSLIC itself. Neither drafting history nor Surety Association of America's analysis reveal any substantial doubt about its meaning. *Sharp v. FSLIC*, 858 F.2d 1042, 1044-47.

SECONDARY SOURCES

Michele L. Fenice & Adam P. Friedman, *The Rule of Contra Proferentem and the Interpretive Impact of Making Changes to Standard Fidelity Bond Forms*, XII FID. L.J. 125 (2006).

Theresa Gooley & Greg Veal, *Enforceability of Statutory Fidelity Bonds* (unpublished paper presented at American Bar Association Fidelity & Surety Law Committee Meeting, Jan. 23, 2009).

Sam H. Poteet, Jr. & H. Rowan Leathers, III, *Financial Institution Bond, Standard Form 24—Common Law or Statutory Bond? and Consequences of Such a Decision on Surety Defenses Such as Manifest Intent and Notice Requirements* (Unpublished paper presented at the Third Annual Conference of the Southern Fidelity & Surety Association, Atlanta, Georgia (May 1992)).

Michael B. Rappaport, *The Ambiguity Rule and Insurance Law: Why Insurance Contracts Should Not Be Construed Against the Drafter*, 30 GA. L. Rev. 171, 211 (1995),

Timothy M. Sukel & Toni Scott Reed, *Interpretation, Construction and Reformation of the Commercial Crime Policy*, COMMERCIAL CRIME POLICY Ch. 2 (Fid. & Sur. Law Comm. ABA 1996)

Jeffrey E. Thomas, *The Role of Ambiguity in Insurance Policy Interpretation, in* NEW APPLEMAN ON INSURANCE: CURRENT CRITICAL ISSUES IN INSURANCE LAW (2006).

SECTION 7 — RETALIATORY LITIGATION*

COMMENT

Fidelity claims often are based on allegations that an employee committed a crime or engaged in other dishonest conduct. Such allegations can be harmful to the employee's reputation. As a result, such accusations can be fertile grounds for defamation claims by the allegedly dishonest employees.

The term "retaliatory litigation" was first coined in the fidelity context in 1970.[1] The term refers to suits by former employees against insured-employers and others, including the insurer-bonding company, to recover damages for defamation arising from fidelity claims. Generally, defamation claims are governed by the law of the state where the publication occurs. In the fidelity context, publication occurs where the defamatory communication is received. The cases generally hold that a qualified or conditional privilege attaches to communications between the insured and the insurer relative to fidelity claims. The privilege is founded on the common interest of the insured and insurer in the subject matter of the communications. In some jurisdictions, the basis for the privilege may be codified. The common interest giving rise to the privilege stems from the insured's contractual obligation to provide notice and submit proof of an employee dishonesty claim to the insurer and the insurer's concomitant obligation to investigate those allegations to determine coverage.

Otherwise defamatory communications are protected if made without malice (which requires a good faith investigation), but only to the extent necessary to fulfill the purpose for which the qualified privilege was created. In the fidelity context, that means an insured's false accusations published to its insurer regarding an employee's alleged dishonesty are conditionally privileged, but only to the extent required for the insured to present and prove the claim and only if made without reckless disregard for the truthfulness of the information communicated.

---

* By Carol A. Pisano and Richard S. Mills, McElroy, Deutsch, Mulvaney & Carpenter, LLP, New York, New York and Ben Zviti, Managing Director, Counsel, Travelers, Bond & Financial Product Claim, New York, New York.

[1] Douglas M. Reimer, *Fidelity Claims and Retaliatory Litigation*, 5 FORUM 321 (1970).

Although there is no case law on the subject, an insurer's communication to third parties of its insured's allegations will presumably be privileged if the insurer made the communication in furtherance of its claim investigation and did not exceed what was required to make a coverage determination. To maintain the qualified privilege, the accusations cannot be republished by either the insured or the insurer to third parties that have no valid interest in the substance of the communication.

If a communication is protected by a qualified privilege, it is afforded a presumption of truth. In other words, once a qualified privilege is established, the burden shifts to the employee bringing the retaliatory suit to prove that the communication was false. In addition, to defeat a qualified or conditional privilege, the allegedly defamed employee also bears the burden of proving that the publication of the defamatory material was motivated by malice. Malice or bad faith will be inferred from an improper investigation of the incident by the insured before submitting a claim. Truth, however, is an absolute defense to a defamation cause of action. If truthful, even excessive communications maliciously made that go beyond what is necessary to present or investigate a claim will not give rise to defamation liability.

Even if truthful, however, such conduct may be actionable as a tort. For example, as privacy statutes and common law breach of privacy and similar tort claims have developed, the term "retaliatory litigation" must be considered in a broader context. It is commonplace in the investigation of fidelity claims for the insurer to request a copy of the employee's personnel file. Such files can contain sensitive and confidential information. Thus, another potential retaliatory claim may arise as a result of an alleged invasion of the employee's privacy.

The primary elements of an invasion-of-privacy claim are (1) that the information communicated is of a type and nature that a reasonable person would expect it to be kept confidential, and (2) the information is conveyed to a third party having no legitimate interest in receiving the information. There is little doubt that personnel files often contain information that reasonable people would consider private. While an insurer has an undeniably legitimate interest in receiving such information as part of its fidelity claim investigation, employees may argue, probably unsuccessfully, that certain information contained in such files is of questionable value to claim investigation.

Other potential retaliatory causes of action include false light claims—publicizing something that casts an individual in a false light—and tortious interference claims, including tortious interference with contractual relationships and even prospective business relationships.

OUTLINE OF ANNOTATIONS

A. Choice of Law in Connection with Defamation Suits
B. Qualified Privilege Between an Insured and Insurer
C Absolute Privilege for Communications Between an Insured and Its Insurer
D. Truth as a Defense
E. The Doctrine of Compelled Self-Publication
F. Retaliatory Litigation Based on Other Causes of Action
G. Litigation Against the Insurer and/or Its Employees
H. Fear of Retaliatory Litigation Does Not Excuse Compliance with Policy Conditions

A. Choice of Law in Connection with Defamation Suits

COMMENT

Virtually all fidelity claims involve the submission of a proof of loss with the insurer, and subsequent written and oral communications between the insured and the insurer to facilitate the investigation and analysis of the claim. The location where the proof of loss and other defamatory information is received is generally deemed to be the place of publication. The reported decisions have held that the law of the state where publication occurs governs in a defamation suit stemming from the filing of a fidelity claim.

ANNOTATIONS

2d Cir. 1957 (N.Y.). An employer filed a proof of loss alleging that an employee misappropriated cash. The proof of loss was completed and filed in New York, but the alleged misappropriation occurred in Pennsylvania. In a defamation suit by the employee against the employer and its insurer, the court held that the law of New York, where the proof of loss was published, governed whether the publication was qualifiedly privileged. However, the court applied the law of Pennsylvania in holding that the proof of loss charged the employee with the crime of embezzlement. *DeRonde v. Gaytime Shops,* 239 F.2d 735, 738.

10th Cir. 1939 (Colo.). A bus company submitted a claim to its insurer alleging a loss of money due to discrepancies in a former employee's accounts. The insurer paid the claim. When the employee could not secure alternate employment due to his inability to obtain another bond, he sued the employer for libel. The claim was submitted via letters mailed by the employer's auditor from Nebraska, based on instructions and information sent by the employer from Colorado, and the letters were received by the bonding company in Missouri. "Under the weight of authority," Missouri law governed the dispute because the insurer received the defamatory information there. *Interstate Transit Lines v. Crane,* 100 F.2d 857, 862.

B. Qualified Privilege Between an Insured and Insurer

COMMENT

Common law recognizes a privilege for communications between an insured and its insurer in connection with fidelity claims involving employees. In some states, the privilege is based on a statute. In others, it is inferred from the contractual relationship between the insured and the insurer, which gives rise to a common interest of both parties in information relevant to the claim. The privilege attaches only to the extent that the information published is necessary to support and evaluate the claim. The privilege can be overcome by proof of malice. The burden of proving malice is on the employee alleging defamation. A party can prove malice through evidence showing ill will, bad faith (or an absence of good faith), or reckless disregard for whether the statements were true or false.

ANNOTATIONS

2d Cir. 1957 (N.Y.). An employer filed a proof of loss charging an employee with misappropriating cash. The employee sued the employer and its insurer for defamation. The law of New York recognizes a qualified privilege between the insured and the fidelity insurer with respect to an employer's publication of a defamatory statement concerning an employee in a proof of loss. However, the privilege can be destroyed by a showing of malice, which is determined by whether the publication was motivated by personal ill will or made with a wanton and reckless disregard for its truth. Evidence that an officer of the insured signed a proof of loss "without knowledge of the facts and having made no effort to ascertain them" was sufficient to warrant submission of the question of malice to the jury and to sustain the jury's finding of actual malice. *DeRonde v. Gaytime Shops,* 239 F.2d 735, 738-39.

10th Cir. 1939 (Colo.). A bus company submitted a claim to its bonding company alleging discrepancies in the accounts of a former employee. When the employee was unable to obtain another bond because of the claim, he sued the employer for libel. The court held that a claim submitted to a bonding company and all communications between an insured and the bonding company concerning the claim are qualifiedly privileged. However, a qualified privilege can be defeated by evidence that the insured acted with actual malice in filing the claim. The burden to prove malice is on the employee and can be established by proof of indifference to the truth and repetition of the defamatory remarks. Evidence that the employer failed to properly investigate the facts before submitting the claim was sufficient to raise a jury question and to support the jury's verdict that the employer acted with malice. *Interstate Transit Lines v. Crane,* 100 F.2d 857, 859-63.

Bankr. Ga. 1995. Georgia, pursuant to statute (O.C.G.A. § 51-5-7(2)-(3)(2013)), recognizes a qualified privilege for reporting a claim to a fidelity insurer. To be eligible for the privilege, the statements made in connection with the claim must be "made in good faith in the performance of a legal or moral private duty" or be "made with a good faith intent on the part of the speaker to protect his interest in a matter in which it is concerned." Because the privilege is qualified, it can be overcome by proof of malice or the absence of good faith. The court presumed that most states recognize such a privilege. *In re Prime Commercial Corp.,* 187 B.R. 785, 803.

Ala. 1941. An employer submitted a fidelity claim alleging that an employee wrongfully abstracted the employer's funds. The employee sued the employer for libel. The court held that the contractual relationship between an insured and its fidelity insurer gives rise to a qualified privilege with regard to statements made in the course of presenting a fidelity claim. Statements that are qualifiedly privileged are presumed to be true and to have been made without malice. Because of this presumption, the burden is on the employee to prove both that statement was false and that the employer acted in bad faith or with malice in submitting the claim. False statements made in good faith, under an honest but mistaken belief in their truth, are conditionally privileged. Good faith requires a bona fide inquiry before a claim for dishonesty is made. To remain protected, defamatory statements made in support of a claim cannot be broader than necessary to support coverage. *Ripps v. Herrington,* 1 So. 2d 899, 902-03.

Ala. 1933. An employer filed a proof of loss alleging that a former employee committed larceny, embezzlement, and other dishonest acts. In a libel suit by the employee against the employer, the court held that the filing of a proof of loss is qualifiedly privileged to the extent that the statements made therein are pertinent and material to the claim. Once the privilege attaches, the burden of proof shifts to the employee to demonstrate that the employer was motivated by malice. An employer can rebut evidence of malice by showing that it had probable cause to charge the employee with dishonesty, or acted on the advice of counsel. *Interstate Elec. Co. v. Daniel,* 151 So. 463, 466-67.

Ariz. 1937. An employer submitted a fidelity claim alleging that an employee misappropriated money and property. The bonding company reported the allegations to the employee, who sued the employer and the corporate officers that submitted the claim for libel. Because statements made in connection with a fidelity claim are qualifiedly privileged, the employee was required to prove that the statements were maliciously made. After a trial, the jury returned a verdict in favor of the corporate officers, but against the employer. The employer appealed. On appeal, the judgment was reversed. The appellate court concluded that a holding in favor of the corporate officers established lack of malice, and since the officers did not act maliciously, neither did the corporate defendant. *Rosenzweig & Sons v. Jones,* 72 P.2d 417, 418-20.

Cal. Ct. App. 1987. A bank officer filed a proof of loss alleging that an employee received a gratuity in exchange for approving a loan. The employee sued the bank for libel, alleging that the bank falsely accused him of committing a crime. The bank argued that its publication of the proof of loss was absolutely privileged pursuant to a California statute because the bank was required by federal regulation to report known or suspected violations of the United States Code to its bonding company. The lower court agreed with the bank. On appeal, the portion of the statute relied upon by the bank was held to be inapplicable. Because the bank did not plead or argue the existence of a qualified privilege, that issue was not considered by the appellate court. *Prevost v. First W. Bank,* 239 Cal. Rptr. 161, 164-66.

Fla. 1908. A company submitted a claim alleging that its former secretary-treasurer failed to account for money. The individual that was the subject of the claim sued for defamation. Although the court did not label it as such, it recognized a qualified privilege with respect to information communicated "to only those who have a right, duty, or interest in the subject of the publication," but only if the communication is "made without malice in a manner and on an occasion to properly serve the right, duty, or interest, and not to needlessly injure another." The court found that such an interest exists between the parties to a fidelity bond because "[e]mployers have a right and interest in the way in which [employees] discharge their duties towards the employers; and indemnity companies have an interest in the business conduct of those for whom indemnity bonds have been given." However, the qualified privilege is negated if the allegedly defamed individual can prove that the information published concerning him was both false and maliciously made. *Briggs v. Brown,* 46 So. 325, 330-31.

Iowa 1906. A former employee alleged that he was defamed in a letter sent by his former employer to the company that issued the employee's "faithful performance" bond. The court held that while such communications are privileged, the "privilege in such cases is not absolute, but qualified and will not avail as a defense where actual malice is shown." Malice is usually a jury question and may be proven based on "the face of the alleged libel itself" or "from the facts and circumstances which surround and characterize it." *Sunley v. Metro. Life Ins. Co.,* 109 N.W. 463, 464.

N.Y. 1982. An insured sued its fidelity insurer and its former employee, whom it accused of dishonesty in a claim submitted to the insurer. The employee sought to allege a counterclaim for libel. The court held that although the statement of claim and letters submitted to the fidelity insurer were defamatory, "since the communications were made in conjunction with the plaintiff's claim under its fidelity coverage, a matter in which the plaintiff had a definite interest and a corresponding duty, the statements were qualifiedly or presumptively privileged." Thus, the employee was required to plead and prove actual malice. Because he did so in proposed amended counterclaims, the proposed pleading was legally sufficient, and his motion to serve the amended counterclaims was granted. *T.R. Am. Chem., Inc. v. Seaboard Sur. Co.,* 456 N.Y.S. 608, 618-19.

N.Y. App. 1970. An employer submitted letters in support of a fidelity claim. The letters contained accusations that a former employee embezzled funds. The court held that the letters were qualifiedly privileged because they were submitted in connection with the claim, pursuant to the instructions of the bonding company, and were required by the terms of the bond. Because of the qualified privilege, the burden was on the allegedly defamed employee to establish actual malice by evidentiary facts as distinguished from conclusory allegations. *Gallagher v. Albert Co.,* 315 N.Y.S.2d 99, 100.

Or. 1958. In a conversation with the agent who had written a fidelity bond that covered city employees, the defendants allegedly accused the plaintiff (a city employee) of being a thief. Because the communication was conditionally privileged, the city employee was required to prove malice. The question of malice is usually a jury question. Malice can be established by facts demonstrating repetition of the defamatory statements. *Phelan v. Beswick,* 326 P.2d 1034, 1036.

Or. App. 1987. A car dealership submitted a claim alleging that another dealership shirked its responsibility to provide good title to an automobile. In the defamation suit that ensued, the defendant argued that the complaint alleged facts that established a qualified privilege, and thus, should be dismissed for failing to state a cause of action. The lower court granted the motion, but on appeal, the complaint was reinstated. The appellate court held that in order to establish a qualified privilege, the fact that a defamatory statement is part of a bond claim is not sufficient. It must also be shown that the bond claimant reasonably believed that it was necessary to convey all of the information that was included with the claim to the bonding company. Because the complaint was silent on that issue, the defendant had to plead and prove this fact as an affirmative defense. *Greenfield v. Ollikala,* 736 P.2d 599, 601.

Tex. App. 1978. An employer sued its bonding company and two former employees, alleging a loss caused by employee dishonesty. The former employees counterclaimed for libel. The court recognized the existence of a qualified privilege for statements contained in a fidelity proof of loss, but noted that the privilege can be negated by a showing of malice. Malice can be inferred from evidence that the employer knew or should have known that the statements were false, or acted with reckless disregard for their truth or falsity. However, where the statements contained in the proof of loss were made after a thorough investigation by the employer, and only after receiving the opinion of an independent auditor, neither malice nor ill will were supported by the evidence. *Roegelein Provision Co. v. Mayen,* 566 S.W.2d 1, 11-12.

C. Absolute Privilege for Communications Between an Insured and Its Insurer

COMMENT

The law does not recognize an absolute privilege over the contents of a proof of loss submitted to or other communications between an insured and its fidelity insurer.

ANNOTATIONS

Cal. Ct. App. 1987. A bank officer filed a proof of loss alleging that an employee received a gratuity in exchange for approving a loan. The employee sued the bank for libel, alleging that the bank had falsely accused him of committing a crime. The bank argued that its publication of the proof of loss was absolutely privileged pursuant to a California statute because the bank was required by federal regulation to report known or suspected violations of the United States Code to its insurer. The court held that the portion of the statute relied upon by the bank was inapplicable. Because the bank did not plead or argue the existence of a qualified privilege, that issue was not considered by the appellate court. *Prevost v. First W. Bank,* 239 Cal. Rptr. 161, 164-66.

Fla. 1940. The insured submitted a proof of loss alleging that a former employee had misappropriated money. The insured knew that the statements contained in the proof of loss were false when it made the statements. Under these circumstances, "express malice will be conclusively presumed." The conclusive presumption of malice precluded the insured from defending the employee's defamation suit on the basis of a qualified privilege. Therefore, the insured attempted to argue that its statements in the proof of loss were protected under the absolute privilege that is usually afforded to statements made in the course of judicial proceedings. The insured argued that its statements were the basis for a claim against its fidelity insurer that the insured "intended, if necessary, to [and actually did] enforce in a court of law." The court flatly refused to extend this privilege under these circumstances. *Merriman v. Lewis,* 194 So. 349, 350-52.

Iowa 1906. A former employee alleged that he was defamed in a letter sent by his former employer to the bonding company that had issued the employee's "faithful performance" bond. The court held that while such communications are privileged, the "privilege in such cases is not absolute, but qualified and will not avail as a defense where actual malice is shown." *Sunley v. Metro. Life Ins. Co.,* 109 N.W. 463, 464.

D. Truth as a Defense

COMMENT

Truth is a complete defense to a defamation suit. Unlike the defense of qualified privilege, where the allegedly defamed individual bears the burden of proving that the defamatory statement was false, the publisher of an allegedly defamatory statement bears the burden of proving that the statement was true.

ANNOTATIONS

Minn. 1952. An employer published an article stating that it had received a check from its insurer to cover a deficit in funds caused by a former employee. In a subsequent libel suit by the former employee, the employer argued that the facts alleged in the complaint established the defense of truth, and, therefore, that the complaint should be dismissed. The lower court dismissed the complaint, but was reversed on appeal. The appellate court held that because the complaint did not concede that there was a "deficit in funds," as the publication expressly stated, the employer could not demonstrate "the truth of the published article in its entirety." Therefore, the defense of truth was not established. *Gadach v. Benton Cnty. Coop.,* 53 N.W.2d 230, 233-34.

Tex. App. 1977. A former secretary-treasurer for a union brought an action for libel against the union alleging that the union had falsely accused him of misappropriating union funds in a proof of loss submitted to the union's insurer. The employee also sued the insurer, alleging that it had libeled him when it approved and paid the claim. The court held that the allegations concerning the former secretary-treasurer's misappropriations were true, and truth was a complete defense to the causes of action against both the union and the insurer. The court noted that the defense of truth does not require proof that the allegedly libelous statement is literally true in every detail; rather, substantial truth is sufficient. *Downer v. Amalgamated Meatcutters & Butcher Workmen of N. Am.,* 550 S.W.2d 744, 747.

E. The Doctrine of Compelled Self-Publication

COMMENT

In the law of defamation, publication occurs when a defamatory statement is published to someone other than the person defamed. The doctrine of compelled self-publication recognizes a cause of action for damages flowing from a defamed person's own republication of the defamation under circumstances where the republication is foreseeable by the original publisher.

ANNOTATIONS

Tex. App. 1980. A bank submitted a proof of loss to its bonding company alleging a loss stemming from the dishonesty of its former president. The allegations of the proof of loss were made with knowledge that they were false. Thus, the bank was properly held liable for defamation. In calculating damages, the court held that it was permissible to include loss flowing from the former president's own republication of the defamation by reporting it to a prospective employer, because disclosure of the bond claim to prospective employers was foreseeable. *First State Bank of Corpus Christi v. Ake,* 606 S.W.2d 696, 701-02.

F. Retaliatory Litigation Based on Other Causes of Action

ANNOTATIONS

Ga. App. 1983. A bank filed a claim with its fidelity insurer alleging that a former employee misappropriated $8,000 when she failed to have her uncle co-sign two $4,000 promissory notes for which she had already taken the funds from the bank. After the bonding company paid the claim, the former employee sued the bank for libel. The bank and the employee settled all claims between them, including the dispute over the two $4,000 notes. Later, the insurer, wishing to recover on its loss, asked the bank for the notes. The bank relinquished the notes to the insurer. The insurer then commenced an action against the employee on the notes. In the insurer's action, the employee impleaded the bank, alleging malicious injury from the bank's assignment of the two notes. The lower court granted judgment to the employee. On appeal, it was held that the insurer had no basis for recovery against the employee on the theory of assignment or equitable subrogation; once the bank had settled with the employee, the bank had no rights to assign to the insurer. Since the insurer could not recover from the employee, the employee did not have a viable claim against the bank. *Bank of Danielsville v. Seagraves,* 305 S.E.2d 790, 793-95.

G. Litigation Against the Insurer and/or Its Employees

ANNOTATIONS

2d Cir. 1957 (N.Y.). A bonding company received a proof of loss in which the insured charged an employee with misappropriating cash. The employee sued the employer and the insurer for defamation. The suit against the insurer was based solely on its receipt of the proof of loss. The matter proceeded to trial, but was discontinued against the insurer before a verdict was rendered. Presumably, the employee was unable to prove that in the course of its investigation, the bonding company made a malicious republication of the employer's allegedly defamatory statements. *DeRonde v. Gaytime Shops,* 239 F.2d 735, 737.

Tex. App. 1977. The former secretary-treasurer of a union alleged that the union's insurer libeled him by approving and paying the union's claim, which alleged that the secretary-treasurer had misappropriated union funds. The employee sued the insurer and the union. The court affirmed summary judgment for the insurer because the union's allegations were proven true. The court mentioned, but did not weigh, the evidence against the insurer, which consisted solely of its check and a cover letter stating that the check was in payment of the amount alleged in the proof of loss. *Downer v. Amalgamated Meatcutters & Butcher Workmen of N. Am.,* 550 S.W.2d 744, 745.

H. Fear of Retaliatory Litigation Does Not Excuse Compliance with Policy Conditions

ANNOTATIONS

N.D. Ga. 1995. The Trustee of a Chapter 7 debtor sued to recover under a fidelity policy for losses caused by employee theft. The insurer sought to defeat coverage on the basis of late notice. Acting on the advice of counsel that it would be exposed to a defamation suit by the employee, the insured had failed to provide the insurer with timely notice of "an occurrence which may become a loss." The court stated that although Georgia recognizes a privilege for reporting a claim to a fidelity insurer, the privilege is qualified; therefore, an insured's concern regarding a possible defamation suit is justified. Nonetheless, the court held that such fear does not excuse the insured's failure to give timely notice of "an occurrence which may become a loss," when it contractually bound itself to do so. *In re Prime Commercial Corp.,* 187 B.R. 785, 800-03.

SECONDARY SOURCES

JOHN ALAN APPLEMAN & JEAN APPLEMAN, INSURANCE LAW AND PRACTICE §§ 8901, 8902, 8915, 8920 (1981 & Supp. 1992).

William T. Bogaert & Daniel E. Tranen, *Retaliatory Litigation,* in HANDLING FIDELITY BOND CLAIMS 541 (Michael Keeley & Sean Duffy eds., 2d ed. 2005).

Andrew F. Caplan & Robert Donovan, The Ethical Investigation of Fidelity Claims: Protecting Privacy, X FID L.J. 63 (2004).

Donald Paul Duffala, Annotation, *Defamation: Loss of Employer's Qualified Privilege to Publish Employee's Work Record or Qualification,* 24 A.L.R.4th 144 (1983).

Jane Landes Foster, *Retaliatory Litigation,* in ANNOTATED FINANCIAL INSTITUTION BOND 571 (Michael Keeley ed., 2d ed. 2004).

Mark P. Gergen, *A Grudging Defense of the Role of the Collateral Torts in Wrongful Termination Litigation,* 74 TEX. L. REV. 1693 (1996).

Cole S. Kain & Cynthia A. Mellon, *Potential Conflicts Between Fidelity Insurers and Insureds: Parallel Proceedings, Interviewing Witnesses and Actions Against Third Parties*, V FID L.J. 1, 27-31 (1999).

Kristine Cordier Karnezis, Annotation, *Libel and Slander: Privileged Nature of Communications Between Insurer and Insured*, 85 A.L.R.3d 1161 (1978).

Richard E. Kaye, *Cause of Action by Former Employee Against Former Employer for Defamation*, 27 CAUSES OF ACTION 2d 305 (2005 & Supp. 2013).

Michael Keeley & Sean Duffy, *Investigating the Employee Dishonesty Claim: Interviewing Witnesses, Obtaining Documents and Other Important Issues, in* HANDLING FIDELITY BOND CLAIMS 153 (Michael Keeley & Sean Duffy eds., 2d ed. 2005).

Harvey C. Koch, *Retaliatory Litigation, in* HANDLING FIDELITY BOND CLAIMS 483 (Michael Keeley & Timothy M. Sukel eds. 1999).

Toni Scott Reed, *Legal, Ethical, and Practical Considerations for an Insurer's Witness Interviews in the Context of a Fidelity Bond or Commercial Crime Policy Claim Investigation*, VII FID L.J. 1, 26 (2001).

Douglas M. Reiner, *Fidelity Claims and Retaliatory Litigation*, 5 FORUM 321 (1970).

Patricia H. Thompson & Michael A. Shafir, *An Insured's Guide to Effective Claims Investigation, Presentation, and Resolution, in* FINANCIAL INSTITUTION BONDS 775, 805-06 (Duncan L. Clore ed., 3rd ed. 2008).

Mary Cullen Yager & Deborah J. Mackay, *Defamation Concerns Regarding Disclosure of Proof of Loss to Alleged Dishonest Employee and Witnesses* (unpublished paper submitted at the ABA-TIPS Fid. & Sur. Law Comm. Annual Mid-Winter Meeting, N.Y., NY January 25, 2002).

RESTATEMENT (SECOND) OF TORTS § 594-96 (1977 & Supp. 2012).

Appendix—Bond Forms

Exhibit 1
FINANCIAL INSTITUTION BOND, STANDARD FORM NO. 24
(Revised January, 1986) 717

Exhibit 2
STATEMENT OF CHANGE, FINANCIAL INSTITUTION BOND,
STANDARD FORM NO. 24
(Revised January, 1986) 733

Exhibit 3
FINANCIAL INSTITUTION BOND, STANDARD FORM NO. 24
(Revised May, 2011) 741

Exhibit 4
SFAA ELECTRONIC FILING LETTER FOR FINANCIAL INSTITUTION
BOND, STANDARD FORM NO. 24
(Revised May, 2011) 759

Exhibit 5
FINANCIAL INSTITUTION BOND, STANDARD FORM NO. 24
(Revised April 1, 2004) 771

Exhibit 6
SFAA FILING LETTER FOR FINANCIAL INSTITUTION BOND,
STANDARD FORM NO. 24
(Revised April 1, 2004) 789

Exhibit 7
COMPUTER CRIME POLICY FOR FINANCIAL INSTITUTIONS
(Edition December, 1993) 799

The forms appearing in this Appendix are copyrighted by The Surety Association of America. Use of these forms requires the prior written approval of the Surety Association of America.

Exhibit 8
FRAUDULENT TRANSFER INSTRUCTIONS RIDER
(Revised May, 2011) 813

Exhibit 9
RETROACTIVE DATE RIDER/ENDORSEMENT
(Revised May, 2011) 817

Exhibit 10
BANKERS BLANKET BOND, STANDARD FORM NO. 24
(Revised July, 1980) 821

Exhibit 11
STATEMENT OF CHANGE, BANKERS BLANKET BOND,
STANDARD FORM NO. 24 837
(Revised July, 1980)

The forms appearing in this Appendix are copyrighted by The Surety Association of America. Use of these forms requires the prior written approval of the Surety Association of America.

Exhibit 1

FINANCIAL INSTITUTION BOND,
STANDARD FORM NO. 24

(Revised January, 1986)

FINANCIAL INSTITUTION BOND
Standard Form No. 24, Revised to January, 1986

Bond No.

(Herein called Underwriter)

DECLARATIONS

Item 1. Name of Insured (herein called Insured):

Principal Address:

Item 2. Bond Period: from 12:01 a.m. on _____ to 12:01 a.m. on _____
(MONTH, DAY, YEAR)   (MONTH, DAY, YEAR)

Item 3. The Aggregate Liability of the Underwriter during the Bond Period shall be
$

Item 4. Subject to Sections 4 and 11 hereof,
the Single Loss Limit of Liability is $
and the Single Loss Deductible is $

Provided, however, that if any amounts are inserted below opposite specified Insuring Agreements or Coverage, those amounts shall be controlling. Any amount set forth below shall be part of and not in addition to amounts set forth above. (If an Insuring Agreement or Coverage is to be deleted, insert "Not Covered.")

Amount applicable to:	Single Loss Limit of Liability	Single Loss Deductible
Insuring Agreement (D)—FORGERY OR ALTERATION	$	$
Insuring Agreement (E)—SECURITIES	$	$
Optional Insuring Agreements and Coverages:	$	$

If "Not Covered" is inserted above opposite any specified Insuring Agreement or Coverage, such Insuring Agreement or Coverage and any other reference thereto in this bond shall be deemed to be deleted therefrom.

Item 5. The liability of the Underwriter is subject to the terms of the following riders attached hereto:

TSB 5018d

Item 6. The Insured by the acceptance of this bond gives notice to the Underwriter terminating or canceling prior bond(s) or policy(ies) No.(s)
such termination or cancellation to be effective as of the time this bond becomes effective.

The Underwriter, in consideration of an agreed premium, and in reliance upon all statements made and information furnished to the Underwriter by the Insured in applying for this bond, and subject to the Declarations, Insuring Agreements, General Agreements, Conditions and Limitations and other terms hereof, agrees to indemnify the Insured for:

INSURING AGREEMENTS

FIDELITY

(A) Loss resulting directly from dishonest or fraudulent acts committed by an Employee acting alone or in collusion with others.

Such dishonest or fraudulent acts must be committed by the Employee with the manifest intent.
(a) to cause the Insured to sustain such loss; and
(b) to obtain financial benefit for the Employee or another person or entity.

However, if some or all of the Insured's loss results directly or indirectly from Loans, that portion of the loss is not covered unless the Employee was in collusion with one or more parties to the transactions and has received, in connection therewith, a financial benefit with a value of at least $2,500.

As used throughout this Insuring Agreement, financial benefit does not include any employee benefits earned in the normal course of employment, including: salaries, commissions, fees, bonuses, promotions, awards, profit sharing or pensions.

ON PREMISES

(B) (1) Loss of Property resulting directly from
    (a) robbery, burglary, misplacement, mysterious unexplainable disappearance and damage thereto or destruction thereof, or
    (b) theft, false pretenses, common-law or statutory larceny, committed by a person present in an office or on the premises of the Insured.
while the Property is lodged or deposited within offices or premises located anywhere.

(2) Loss of or damage to
    (a) furnishings, fixtures, supplies or equipment within an office of the Insured covered under this bond resulting directly from larceny or theft in, or by burglary or robbery of, such office, or attempt thereat, or by vandalism or malicious mischief, or
    (b) such office resulting from larceny or theft in, or by burglary or robbery of such office or attempt thereat, or to the interior of such office by vandalism or malicious mischief,
provided that
    (i) the Insured is the owner of such furnishings, fixtures, supplies, equipment, or office or is liable for such loss or damage, and
    (ii) the loss is not caused by fire.

TSB 5018d

IN TRANSIT

(C) Loss of Property resulting directly from robbery, common-law or statutory larceny, theft, misplacement, mysterious unexplainable disappearance, being lost or made away with, and damage thereto or destruction thereof, while the Property is in transit anywhere in the custody of
- (a) a natural person acting as a messenger of the Insured (or another natural person acting as messenger or custodian during an emergency arising from the incapacity of the original messenger), or
- (b) a Transportation Company and being transported in an armored motor vehicle, or
- (c) a Transportation Company and being transported in a conveyance other than an armored motor vehicle provided that covered Property transported in such manner is limited to the following:
  - (i) records, whether recorded in writing or electronically, and
  - (ii) Certificated Securities issued in registered form and not endorsed, or with restrictive endorsements, and
  - (iii) Negotiable Instruments not payable to bearer, or not endorsed, or with restrictive endorsements.

Coverage under this Insuring Agreement begins immediately upon the receipt of such Property by the natural person or Transportation Company and ends immediately upon delivery to the designated recipient or its agent.

FORGERY OR ALTERATION

(D) Loss resulting directly from
- (1) Forgery or alteration of, on or in any Negotiable Instrument (except an Evidence of Debt), Acceptance, Withdrawal Order, receipt for the withdrawal of Property, Certificate of Deposit or Letter of Credit,
- (2) transferring, paying or delivering any funds or Property or establishing any credit or giving any value on the faith of any written instructions or advices directed to the Insured and authorizing or acknowledging the transfer, payment, delivery or receipt of funds or Property, which instructions or advices purport to have been signed or endorsed by any customer of the Insured or by any banking institution but which instructions or advices either bear a signature which is a Forgery or have been altered without the knowledge and consent of such customer or banking institution. Telegraphic, cable or teletype instructions or advices, as aforesaid, exclusive of transmissions of electronic funds transfer systems, sent by a person other than the said customer or banking institution purporting to send such instructions or advices shall be deemed to bear a signature which is a Forgery.

A mechanically reproduced facsimile signature is treated the same as a handwritten signature.

SECURITIES

(E) Loss resulting directly from the Insured having, in good faith, for its own account or for the account of others.
- (1) acquired, sold or delivered, or given value, extended credit or assumed liability, on the faith of, any original
  - (a) Certificated Security,
  - (b) Document of Title,
  - (c) deed, mortgage or other instrument conveying title to, or creating or discharging a lien upon, real property,
  - (d) Certificate of Origin or Title
  - (e) Evidence of Debt.

TSB 5018d

(f) corporate, partnership or personal Guarantee,
(g) Security Agreement,
(h) Instruction to a Federal Reserve Bank of the United States, or
(i) Statement of Uncertified Security of any Federal Reserve Bank of the United States

which (i) bears a signature of any maker, drawer, issuer, endorser, assignor, lessee, transfer agent, registrar, acceptor, surety, guarantor, or of any person signing in any other capacity which is a Forgery, or
(ii) is altered, or
(iii) is lost or stolen;

(2) guaranteed in writing or witnessed any signature upon any transfer, assignment, bill of sale, power of attorney, Guarantee, endorsement or any items listed in (a) through (h) above;

(3) acquired, sold or delivered, or given value, extended credit or assumed liability, on the faith of any item listed in (a) through (d) above which is a Counterfeit.

Actual physical possession of the items listed in (a) through (i) above by the Insured, its correspondent bank or other authorized representative, is a condition precedent to the Insured's having relied on the faith of such items.

A mechanically reproduced facsimile signature is treated the same as a handwritten signature.

COUNTERFEIT CURRENCY

(F) Loss resulting directly from the receipt by the Insured, in good faith, of any Counterfeit Money of the United States of America, Canada or of any other country in which the Insured maintains a branch office.

GENERAL AGREEMENTS

NOMINEES

A. Loss sustained by any nominee organized by the Insured for the purpose of handling certain of its business transactions and composed exclusively of its Employees shall, for all the purposes of this bond and whether or not any partner of such nominee is implicated in such loss, be deemed to be loss sustained by the Insured.

ADDITIONAL OFFICES OR EMPLOYEES–CONSOLIDATION MERGER OR PURCHASE OF ASSETS–NOTICE

B. If the Insured shall, while this bond is in force, establish any additional offices, other than by consolidation or merger with, or purchase or acquisition of assets or liabilities of, another institution, such offices shall be automatically covered hereunder from the date of such establishment without the requirement of notice to the Underwriter or the payment of additional premium for the remainder of the premium period.

If the Insured shall, while this bond is in force, consolidate or merge with, or purchase or acquire assets or liabilities of, another institution, the Insured shall not have such coverage as is afforded under this bond for loss which
(a) has occurred or will occur in offices or premises, or
(b) has been caused or will be caused by an employee or employees of such institution, or
(c) has arisen or will arise out of the assets or liabilities acquired by the Insured as a result of such consolidation, merger or purchase or acquisition of assets or liabilities unless the Insured shall

TSB 5018d

(i) give the Underwriter written notice of the proposed consolidation, merger or purchase or acquisition of assets or liabilities prior to the proposed effective date of such action and
(ii) obtain the written consent of the Underwriter to extend the coverage provided by this bond to such additional offices or premises, Employees and other exposures, and
(iii) upon obtaining such consent, pay to the Underwriter an additional premium.

CHANGE OF CONTROL—NOTICE

C. When the Insured learns of a change in control, it shall give written notice to the Underwriter.

As used in this General Agreement, control means the power to determine the management or policy of a controlling holding company or the Insured by virtue of voting stock ownership. A change in ownership of voting stock which results in direct or indirect ownership by a stockholder or an affiliated group of stockholders of ten percent (10%) or more of such stock shall be presumed to result in a change of control for the purpose of the required notice.

Failure to give the required notice shall result in termination of coverage for any loss involving a transferee, to be effective upon the date of the stock transfer.

REPRESENTATION OF INSURED

D. The Insured represents that the information furnished in the application for this bond is complete, true and correct. Such application constitutes part of this bond.

Any misrepresentation, omission, concealment or any incorrect statement of a material fact, in the application or otherwise, shall be grounds for the rescission of this bond.

JOINT INSURED

E. If two or more Insureds are covered under this bond, the first named Insured shall act for all Insureds. Payment by the underwriter to the first named Insured of loss sustained by any Insured shall fully release the Underwriter on account of such loss. If the first named Insured ceases to be covered under this bond, the Insured next named shall thereafter be considered as the first named Insured. Knowledge possessed or discovery made by any Insured shall constitute knowledge or discovery by all Insureds for all purposes of this bond. The liability of the Underwriter for loss or losses sustained by all Insureds shall not exceed the amount for which the Underwriter would have been liable had all such loss or losses been sustained by one Insured.

NOTICE OF LEGAL PROCEEDINGS AGAINST INSURED–ELECTION TO DEFEND

F. The Insured shall notify the Underwriter at the earliest practicable moment, not to exceed 30 days after notice thereof, of any legal proceeding brought to determine the Insured's liability for any loss, claim or damage, which, if established, would constitute a collectible loss under this bond. Concurrently, the Insured shall furnish copies of all pleadings and pertinent papers to the Underwriter.

The Underwriter, at its sole option, may elect to conduct the defense of such legal proceeding, in whole or in part. The defense by the Underwriter shall be in the Insured's name through attorneys selected by the Underwriter. The Insured shall provide all reasonable information and assistance required by the Underwriter for such defense.

TSB 5018d

If the Underwriter elects to defend the Insured, in whole or in part, any judgment against the Insured on those counts or causes of action which the Underwriter defended on behalf of the Insured or any settlement in which the Underwriter participates and all attorneys' fees, costs and expenses incurred by the Underwriter in the defense of the litigation shall be a loss covered by this bond.

If the Insured does not give the notices required in subsection (a) of Section 5 of this bond and the first paragraph of this General Agreement, or if the Underwriter elects not to defend any causes of action, neither a judgment against the Insured, nor a settlement of any legal proceeding by the Insured, shall determine the existence, extent or amount of coverage under this bond for loss sustained by the Insured, and the Underwriter shall not be liable for any attorneys' fees, costs and expenses incurred by the Insured.

With respect to this General Agreement, subsections (b) and (d) of Section 5 of this bond apply upon the entry of such judgment or the occurrence of such settlement instead of upon discovery of loss. In addition, the Insured must notify the Underwriter within 30 days after such judgment is entered against it or after the Insured settles such legal proceeding, and, subject to subsection (e) of Section 5, the Insured may not bring legal proceedings for the recovery of such loss after the expiration of 24 months from the date of such final judgment or settlement.

CONDITIONS AND LIMITATIONS

DEFINITIONS

Section 1. As used in this bond:

(a) Acceptance means a draft which the drawee has, by signature written thereon, engaged to honor as presented.

(b) Certificate of Deposit means an acknowledgment in writing by a financial institution of receipt of Money with an engagement to repay it.

(c) Certificate of Origin or Title means a document issued by a manufacturer of personal property or a governmental agency evidencing the ownership of the personal property and by which ownership is transferred.

(d) Certificated Security means a share, participation or other interest in property of or an enterprise of the issuer or an obligation of the issuer, which is:
  (1) represented by an instrument issued in bearer or registered form;
  (2) of a type commonly dealt in on securities exchanges or markets or commonly recognized in any area in which it is issued or dealt in as a medium for investment; and
  (3) either one of a class or series or by its terms divisible into a class or series of shares, participations, interests or obligations.

(e) Counterfeit means an imitation which is intended to deceive and to be taken as an original.

(f) Document of Title means a bill of lading, dock warrant, dock receipt, warehouse receipt or order for the delivery of goods, and also any other document which in the regular course of business or financing is treated as adequately evidencing that the person in possession of it is entitled to receive, hold and dispose of the document and the goods it covers and must purport to be issued by or addressed to a bailee and purport to cover goods in the bailee's possession which are either identified or are fungible portions of an identified mass.

(g) Employee means
  (1) an officer or other employee of the Insured, while employed in, at, or by the Insured's offices or premises covered hereunder, and a guest student pursuing studies or duties in any of said offices or premises;
  (2) an attorney retained by the Insured and an employee of such attorney while either is performing legal services for the Insured;

APPENDIX—BOND FORMS 723

(3) a person provided by an employment contractor to perform employee duties for the Insured under the Insured's supervision at any of the Insured's offices or premises covered hereunder;
(4) an employee of an institution merged or consolidated with the Insured prior to the effective date of this bond; and
(5) each natural person, partnership or corporation authorized by the Insured to perform services as data processor of checks or other accounting records of the Insured (not including preparation or modification of computer software or programs), herein called Processor. (Each such Processor, and the partners, officers and employees of such Processor shall, collectively, be deemed to be one Employee for all the purposes of this bond, excepting, however, the second paragraph of Section 12. A Federal Reserve Bank or clearing house shall not be construed to be a processor.)

(h) Evidence of Debt means an instrument, including a Negotiable Instrument, executed by a customer of the Insured and held by the Insured which in the regular course of business is treated as evidencing the customer's debt to the Insured.

(i) Forgery means the signing of the name of another person or organization with intent to deceive; it does not mean a signature which consists in whole or in part of one's own name signed with or without authority, in any capacity, for any purpose.

(j) Guarantee means a written undertaking obligating the signer to pay the debt of another to the Insured or its assignee or to a financial institution from which the Insured has purchased participation in the debt, if the debt is not paid in accordance with its terms.

(k) Instruction means a written order to the issuer of an Uncertificated Security requesting that the transfer, pledge, or release from pledge of the Uncertificated Security specified be registered.

(l) Letter of Credit means an engagement in writing by a bank or other person made at the request of a customer that the bank or other person will honor drafts or other demands for payment upon compliance with the conditions specified in the Letter of Credit.

(m) Loan means all extensions of credit by the Insured and all transactions creating a creditor relationship in favor of the Insured and all transactions by which the Insured assumes an existing creditor relationship.

(n) Money means a medium of exchange in current use authorized or adopted by a domestic or foreign government as a part of its currency.

(o) Negotiable Instruments means any writing
    (1) signed by the maker or drawer; and
    (2) containing any unconditional promise or order to pay a sum certain in Money and no other promise, order, obligation or power given by the maker or drawer; and
    (3) is payable on demand or at a definite time; and
    (4) is payable to order or bearer.

(p) Property means Money, Certificated Securities, Uncertificated Securities by any Federal Reserve Bank of the United States, Negotiable Instruments, Certificates of Deposit, Documents of Title, Acceptances, Evidences of Debt, Security Agreements, Withdrawal Orders, Certificates of Origin or Title, Letters of Credit, insurance policies, abstracts of title, deeds and mortgages on real estate, revenue and other stamps, tokens, unsold state lottery tickets, books of account and other records whether recorded in writing or electronically, gems, jewelry, precious metals in bars or ingots, and tangible items of personal property which are not hereinabove enumerated.

(q) Security Agreement means an agreement which creates an interest in personal property or fixtures and which secures payment on performance of an obligation.

(r) Statement of Uncertificated Security means a written statement of the issuer of an Uncertificated Security containing:
    (1) A description of the Issue of which the Uncertificated Security is a part;
    (2) the number of shares or units:
        (a) transferred to the registered owner;

TSB 5018d

(b) pledged by the registered owner to the registered pledgee;
(c) released from pledge by the registered pledgee;
(d) registered in the name of the registered owner on the date of the statement; or
(e) subject to pledge on the date of the statement;
(3) the name and address of the registered owner and registered pledgee;
(4) a notation of any liens and restrictions of the issuer and any adverse claims to which the Uncertificated Security is or may be subject or a statement that there are none of those liens, restrictions or adverse claims; and
(5) the date:
(a) the transfer of the shares of units to the new registered owner of the shares or units was registered;
(b) the pledge of the registered pledgee was registered, or
(c) of the statement, if it is a periodic or annual statement.

(s) Transportation Company means any organization which provides its own or leased vehicles for transportation or which provides freight forwarding or air express services.

(t) Uncertificated Security means a share, participation or other interest in property of or an enterprise of the issuer or an obligation of the issuer, which is:
(1) not represented by an instrument and the transfer of which is registered upon books maintained for that purpose by or on behalf of the issuer;
(2) of a type commonly dealt in on securities exchanges or markets; and
(3) either one of a class or series or by its terms divisible into a class or series of shares, participations, interests or obligations.

(u) Withdrawal Order means a non-negotiable instrument, other than an Instruction, signed by a customer of the Insured authorizing the Insured to debit the customer's account in the amount of funds stated therein.

EXCLUSIONS

Section 2. This bond does not cover:

(a) loss resulting directly or indirectly from forgery or alteration, except when covered under Insuring Agreements (A), (D), (E) or (F);

(b) loss due to riot or civil commotion outside the United States of America and Canada; or loss due to military, naval or usurped power, war or insurrection unless such loss occurs in transit in the circumstances recited in Insuring Agreement (C), and unless, when such transit was initiated, there was no knowledge of such riot, civil commotion, military, naval or usurped power, war or insurrection on the part of any person acting for the Insured in initiating such transit;

(c) loss resulting directly or indirectly from the effects of nuclear fission or fusion or radioactivity; provided, however, that this paragraph shall not apply to loss resulting from industrial uses of nuclear energy;

(d) loss resulting directly or indirectly from any acts of any director of the Insured other than one employed as a salaried, pensioned or elected official or an Employee of the Insured, except when performing acts coming within the scope of the usual duties of an Employee, or while acting as a member of any committee duly elected or appointed by resolution of the board of directors of the Insured to perform specific, as distinguished from general, directorial acts on behalf of the Insured;

(e) loss resulting directly or indirectly from the complete or partial nonpayment of, or default upon, any Loan or transaction involving the Insured as a lender or borrower, or extension of direct, including the purchase, discounting or other acquisition of false or genuine accounts, invoices, notes, agreements or Evidences of Debt, whether such Loan, transaction or extension was procured in good faith or through trick, artifice, fraud or false pretenses, except when covered under Insuring Agreements (A), (D) or (E);

(f) loss of Property contained in customers' safe deposit boxes, except when the Insured is legally liable therefor and the loss is covered under Insuring Agreement (A);

(g) loss through cashing or paying forged or altered travelers' checks or travelers' checks bearing forged endorsements, except when covered under Insuring Agreement (A); or loss of unsold travelers' checks or unsold money orders placed in the custody of the Insured with authority to sell, unless (a) the Insured is legally liable for such loss and (b) such checks or money orders are later paid or honored by the drawer thereof, except when covered under Insuring Agreement (A);

(h) loss caused by an Employee, except when covered under Insuring Agreement (A) or when covered under Insuring Agreement (B) or (C) and resulting directly from misplacement, mysterious unexplainable disappearance or destruction of or damage to Property;

(i) loss resulting directly or indirectly from trading, with or without the knowledge of the Insured, whether or not represented by any indebtedness or balance shown to be due the Insured on any customer's account, actual or fictitious, and notwithstanding any act or omission on the part of any Employee in connection with any account relating to such trading, indebtedness, or balance, except when covered under Insuring Agreements (D) and (E);

(j) shortage in any teller's cash due to error, regardless of the amount of such shortage, and any shortage in any teller's cash which is not in excess of the normal shortage in any teller's cash in the office where such shortage shall occur shall be presumed to be due to error;

(k) loss resulting directly or indirectly from the use or purported use of credit, debit, charge, access, convenience, identification or other cards
    (1) in obtaining credit or funds, or
    (2) in gaining access to automated mechanical devices which, on behalf of the Insured, disburse Money, accept deposits, cash checks, drafts or similar written instruments or make credit card loans, or
    (3) in gaining access to point of sale terminals, customer-bank communication terminals, or similar electronic terminals of electronic funds transfer systems,

whether such cards were issued, or purport to have been issued, by the Insured or by anyone other than the Insured, except when covered under Insuring Agreement (A);

(l) loss involving automated mechanical devices which, on behalf of the Insured, disburse Money, accept deposits, cash checks, drafts or similar written instruments or make credit card loans, unless such automated mechanical devices are situated within an office of the Insured which is permanently staffed by an Employee whose duties are those usually assigned to a bank teller, even though public access is from outside the confines of such office, but in no event shall the Underwriter be liable for loss (including loss of Property)
    (1) as a result of damage to such automated mechanical devices from vandalism or malicious mischief perpetrated from outside such office, or
    (2) as a result of failure of such automated mechanical devices to function properly, or
    (3) through misplacement or mysterious unexplainable disappearance while such Property is located within any such automated mechanical devices, except when covered under Insuring Agreement (A);

(m) loss through the surrender of Property away from an office of the Insured as a result of a threat
    (1) to do bodily harm to any person, except loss of Property in transit in the custody of any person acting as messenger provided that when such transit was initiated there was no knowledge by the Insured of any such threat, or
    (2) to do damage to the premises or property of the Insured, except when covered under Insuring Agreement (A);

(n) loss resulting directly or indirectly from payments made or withdrawals from a depositor's account involving erroneous credits to such account, unless such payments or withdrawals are physically received by such depositor or representative of such depositor who is within the office of the Insured at the time of such payment or withdrawal, or except when covered under Insuring Agreement (A);

(o) loss resulting directly or indirectly from payments made or withdrawals from a depositor's account involving items of deposit which are not finally paid for any reason, including but not limited to Forgery or any other fraud, except when covered under Insuring Agreement (A);

TSB 5018d

(p) loss resulting directly or indirectly from counterfeiting, except when covered under Insuring Agreements (A), (E) or (F);

(q) loss of any tangible item of personal property which is not specifically enumerated in the paragraph defining Property and for which the Insured is legally liable, if such property is specifically insured by other insurance of any kind and in any amount obtained by the Insured, and in any event, loss of such property occurring more than 60 days after the Insured shall have become aware that it is liable for the safekeeping of such property, except when covered under Insuring Agreements (A) or (B)(2);

(r) loss of Property while
    (1) in the mail, or
    (2) in the custody of any Transportation Company, unless covered under Insuring Agreement (C) except when covered under Insuring Agreement (A);

(s) potential income, including but not limited to interest and dividends, not realized by the Insured;

(t) damages of any type for which the Insured is legally liable, except compensatory damages, but not multiples thereof, arising directly from a loss covered under this bond;

(u) all fees, costs and expenses incurred by the Insured
    (1) in establishing the existence of or amount of loss covered under this bond, or
    (2) as a party to any legal proceeding whether or not such legal proceeding exposes the Insured to loss covered by this bond;

(v) indirect or consequential loss of any nature;

(w) loss resulting from any violation by the Insured or by any Employee
    (1) of law regulating (i) the issuance, purchase or sale of securities, (ii) securities transactions upon security exchanges or over the counter market, (ii) investment companies, or (iv) investment advisers, or
    (2) of any rule or regulation made pursuant to any such law, unless it is established by the Insured that the act or acts which caused the said loss involved fraudulent or dishonest conduct which would have caused a loss to the Insured in a similar amount in the absence of such laws, rules or regulations;

(x) loss resulting directly or indirectly from the failure of a financial or depository institution, or its receiver or liquidator, to pay or deliver, on demand of the Insured, funds or Property of the Insured held by it in any capacity, except when covered under Insuring Agreements (A) or (B)(1)(a);

(y) loss involving any Uncertificated Security except an Uncertificated Security of any Federal Reserve Bank of the United States or when covered under Insuring Agreement (A);

(z) damages resulting from any civil, criminal or other legal proceeding in which the Insured is alleged to have engaged in racketeering activity except when the Insured establishes that the act or acts giving rise to such damages were committed by an Employee under circumstances which result directly in a loss to the Insured covered by Insuring Agreement (A). For the purposes of this exclusion, "racketeering activity" is defined in 18 United States Code 1961 et seq., as amended.

DISCOVERY

Section 3. This bond applies to loss discovered by the Insured during the Bond Period. Discovery occurs when the Insured first becomes aware of facts which would cause a reasonable person to assume that a loss of a type covered by this bond has been or will be incurred, regardless of when the act or acts causing or contributing to such loss occurred, even though the exact amount or details of loss may not then be known.

Discovery also occurs when the Insured receives notice of an actual or potential claim in which it is alleged that the Insured is liable to a third party under circumstances which, if true, would constitute a loss under this bond.

LIMIT OF LIABILITY

Section 4.

Aggregate Limit of Liability

The Underwriter's total liability for all losses discovered during the Bond Period shown in Item 2 of the Declarations shall not exceed the Aggregate Limit of Liability shown in Item 3 of the Declarations. The Aggregate Limit of Liability shall be reduced by the amount of any payment made under the terms of this bond.

Upon exhaustion of the Aggregate Limit of Liability by such payments:
   (a) The Underwriter shall have no further liability for loss or losses regardless of when discovered and whether or not previously reported to the Underwriter, and
   (b) The Underwriter shall have no obligation under General Agreement F to continue the defense of the Insured, and upon notice by the Underwriter to the Insured that the Aggregate Limit of Liability has been exhausted, the Insured shall assume all responsibility for its defenses at its own cost.

The Aggregate Limit of Liability shall not be increased or reinstated by any recovery made and applied in accordance with subsections (a), (b) and (c) of Section 7. In the event that a loss of Property is settled by the Underwriter through the use of a lost instrument bond, such loss shall not reduce the Aggregate Limit of Liability.

Single Loss Limit of Liability

Subject to the Aggregate Limit of Liability, the Underwriter's liability for each Single Loss shall not exceed the applicable Single Loss Limit of Liability shown in Item 4 of the Declarations. If a Single Loss is covered under more than one Insuring Agreement or Coverage, the maximum payable shall not exceed the largest applicable Single Loss Limit of Liability.

Single Loss Defined

Single Loss means all covered loss, including court costs and attorneys' fees incurred by the Underwriter under General Agreement F, resulting from
   (a) any one act or series of related acts of burglary, robbery or attempt thereat, in which no Employee is implicated, or
   (b) any one act or series of related unintentional or negligent acts or omissions in damage to or destruction or misplacement of Property, or
   (c) all acts or omissions other than those specified in (a) and (b) preceding, caused by any person (whether an Employee or not) or in which such person is implicated, or
   (d) any one casualty or event not specified in (a), (b) or (c) preceding.

NOTICE/PROOF—LEGAL PROCEEDINGS AGAINST UNDERWRITER

Section 5.
   (a) At the earliest practicable moment, not to exceed 30 days, after discovery of loss, the Insured shall give the Underwriter notice thereof.
   (b) Within 6 months after such discovery, the Insured shall furnish to the Underwriter proof of loss, duly sworn to, with full particulars.
   (c) Lost Certificated Securities listed in a proof of loss shall be identified by certificate or bond numbers if such securities were issued therewith.

TSB 5018d

(d) Legal proceedings for the recovery of any loss hereunder shall not be brought prior to the expiration of 60 days after the original proof of loss is filed with the Underwriter or after the expiration of 24 months from the discovery of such loss.

(e) If any limitation embodied in this bond is prohibited by any law controlling the construction hereof, such limitation shall be deemed to be amended so as to equal the minimum period of limitation provided by such law.

(f) This bond affords coverage only in favor of the Insured. No suit, action or legal proceedings shall be brought hereunder by any one other than the named Insured.

VALUATION

Section 6. Any loss of Money, or loss payable in Money, shall be paid, at the option of the Insured, in the Money of the country in which the loss was sustained or in the United States of America dollar equivalent thereof determined at the rate of exchange at the time of payment of such loss.

Securities

The Underwriter shall settle in kind its liability under this bond on account of a loss of any securities or, at the option of the Insured, shall pay to the Insured the cost of replacing such securities, determined by the market value thereof at the time of such settlement. In case of a loss of subscription, conversion or redemption privileges through the misplacement or loss of securities, the amount of such loss shall be the value of such privileges immediately preceding the expiration thereof. If such securities cannot be replaced or have no quoted market value, or if such privileges have no quoted market value, their value shall be determined by agreement or arbitration.

If the applicable coverage of this bond is subject to a Deductible Amount and/or is not sufficient in amount to indemnify the Insured in full for the loss of securities for which claim is made hereunder, the liability of the Underwriter under this bond is limited to the payment for, or the duplication of, so much of such securities as has a value equal to the amount of such applicable coverage.

Books of Account and Other Records

In case of loss of, or damage to, any books of account or other records used by the Insured in its business, the Underwriter shall be liable under this bond only if such books or records are actually reproduced and then for not more than the cost of the blank books, blank pages or other materials plus the cost of labor for the actual transcription or copying of data which shall have been furnished by the Insured in order to reproduce such books and other records.

Property other than Money, Securities or Records

In case of loss of, or damage to, any Property other than Money, securities, books of account or other records, or damage covered under Insuring Agreement (B)(2), the Underwriter shall not be liable for more than the actual cash value of such Property, or of items covered under Insuring Agreement (B)(2). The Underwriter may, at its election, pay the actual cash value of, replace or repair such property. Disagreement between the Underwriter and the Insured as to the cash value or as to the adequacy of repair or replacement shall be resolved by arbitration.

TSB 5018d

ASSIGNMENT—SUBROGATION—RECOVERY—COOPERATION

Section 7.
    (a)   In the event of payment under this bond, the Insured shall deliver, if so requested by the Underwriter, an assignment of such of the Insured's rights, title and interest and causes of action as it has against any person or entity to the extent of the loss payment.
    (b)   In the event of payment under this bond, the Underwriter shall be subrogated to all of the Insured's rights of recovery therefor against any person or entity to the extent of such payment.
    (c)   Recoveries, whether effected by the Underwriter or by the Insured, shall be applied net of the expense of such recovery first to the satisfaction of the Insured's loss which would otherwise have been paid but for the fact that it is in excess of either the Single or Aggregate Limit of Liability, secondly, to the Underwriter as reimbursement of amounts paid in settlement of the Insured's claim, and thirdly, to the Insured in satisfaction of any Deductible Amount. Recovery on account of loss of securities as set forth in the second paragraph of Section 6 or recovery from reinsurance and/or indemnity of the Underwriter shall not be deemed a recovery as used herein.
    (d)   Upon the Underwriter's request and at reasonable times and places designated by the Underwriter the Insured shall
            (1)   submit to examination by the Underwriter and subscribe to the same under oath; and
            (2)   produce for the Underwriter's examination all pertinent records; and
            (3)   cooperate with the Underwriter in all matters pertaining to the loss.
    (e)   The Insured shall execute all papers and render assistance to secure to the Underwriter the rights and causes of action provided for herein. The Insured shall do nothing after discovery of loss to prejudice such rights or causes of action.

LIMIT OF LIABILITY UNDER THIS BOND AND PRIOR INSURANCE

Section 8. With respect to any loss set forth in sub-section (c) of Section 4 of this bond which is recoverable or recovered in whole or in part under any other bonds or policies issued by the Underwriter to the Insured or to any predecessor in interest of the Insured and terminated or canceled or allowed to expire and in which the period for discovery has not expired at the time any such loss thereunder is discovered, the total liability of the Underwriter under this bond and under such other bonds or policies shall not exceed, in the aggregate, the amount carried hereunder on such loss or the amount available to the Insured under such other bonds or policies, as limited by the terms and conditions thereof, for any such loss if the latter amount be the larger.

If the coverage of this bond supersedes in whole or in part the coverage of any other bond or policy of insurance issued by an Insurer other than the Underwriter and terminated, canceled or allowed to expire, the Underwriter, with respect to any loss sustained prior to such termination, cancellation or expiration and discovered within the period permitted under such other bond or policy for the discovery of loss thereunder, shall be liable under this bond only for that part of such loss covered by this bond as is in excess of the amount recoverable or recovered on account of such loss under such other bond or policy, anything to the contrary in such other bond or policy notwithstanding.

OTHER INSURANCE OR INDEMNITY

Section 9. Coverage afforded hereunder shall apply only as excess over any valid and collectible insurance or indemnity obtained by the Insured, or by one other than the Insured on Property subject to exclusion (q) or by a Transportation Company, or by another entity on whose premises the loss occurred or which employed the person causing the loss or the messenger conveying the Property involved.

TSB 5018d

OWNERSHIP

Section 10. This bond shall apply to loss of Property (1) owned by the Insured, (2) held by the Insured in any capacity, or (3) for which the Insured is legally liable. This bond shall be for the sole use and benefit of the Insured named in the Declarations.

DEDUCTIBLE AMOUNT

Section 11. The Underwriter shall be liable hereunder only for the amount by which any single loss, as defined in Section 4, exceeds the Single Loss Deductible amount for the Insuring Agreement or Coverage applicable to such loss, subject to the Aggregate Limit of Liability and the applicable Single Loss Limit of Liability.

The Insured shall, in the time and in the manner prescribed in this bond, give the Underwriter notice of any loss of the kind covered by the terms of this bond, whether or not the Underwriter is liable therefor, and upon the request of the Underwriter shall file with it a brief statement giving the particulars concerning such loss.

TERMINATION OR CANCELLATION

Section 12. This bond terminates as an entirety upon occurrence of any of the following:—(a) 60 days after the receipt by the Insured of a written notice from the Underwriter of its desire to cancel this bond, or (b) immediately upon the receipt by the Underwriter of a written notice from the Insured of its desire to cancel this bond, or (c) immediately upon the taking over of the Insured by a receiver or other liquidator of by State or Federal officials, or (d) immediately upon the taking over of the Insured by another institution, or (e) immediately upon exhaustion of the Aggregate Limit of Liability, or (f) immediately upon expiration of the Bond Period as set forth in Item 2 of the Declarations.

This bond terminates as to any Employee or any partner, officer or employee of any Processor—(a) as soon as any Insured, or any director or officer not in collusion with such person, learns of any dishonest or fraudulent act committed by such person at any time, whether in the employment of the Insured or otherwise, whether or not of the type covered under Insuring Agreement (A), against the Insured or any other person or entity, without prejudice to the loss of any Property then in transit in the custody of such person, or (b) 15 days after the receipt by the Insured of a Written notice from the Underwriter of its desire to cancel this bond as to such person.

Termination of the bond as to any Insured terminates liability for any loss sustained by such Insured which is discovered after the effective date of such termination.

In witness whereof, the Underwriter has caused this bond to be executed on the Declarations Page.

TSB 5018d

Exhibit 2

STATEMENT OF CHANGE,
FINANCIAL INSTITUTION BOND,
STANDARD FORM NO. 24

(Revised January, 1986)

STATEMENT OF CHANGE
FINANCIAL INSTITUTION BOND, STANDARD FORM NO. 24
Revised to January 1986

The Surety Association of America, after discussion with the American Bankers Association, has revised the Bankers Blanket Bond, Standard Form No. 24 to January 1986. Other than editorial amendments, the changes are as follows:

DECLARATIONS PAGE

The name of this bond has been changed from Bankers Blanket Bond to Financial Institution Bond. The numerical identification - Form No. 24 remains the same. Item 3 of the Declarations is now used to show the Aggregate Liability of the Underwriter during the Bond Period. Item 4 is now used to show the Single Loss Limit of Liability and the Single Loss Deductible for the basic bond and individual insuring agreements. In the prior version of the bond, space was provided to list offices or premises not covered. The new Financial Institution Bond covers all offices and premises of the insured unless specifically excluded by rider.

AGGREGATE LIABILITY OF UNDERWRITER

An important feature of the Financial Institution Bond is the provision to limit the liability of the underwriter over the life of the bond to a predetermined dollar amount. This fixed amount is shown in Item 3 of the Declarations Page as the Aggregate Liability of the Underwriter. All claims paid by the underwriter during the bond period are applied against the Aggregate Limit, and upon exhaustion of that limit the bond is automatically canceled.

Section 4 of the bond contains the operative language for both the Aggregate Liability of the Underwriter, applicable to the bond as a whole, and the Single Loss Limit of Liability, applicable to the individual insuring agreements.

CONSIDERATION CLAUSE

The Consideration Clause has been amended by making reference to the fact that the underwriter has issued the bond in reliance on the statements and information supplied by the insured in the bond application. The Consideration Clause should be studied together with the Representation of Insured General Agreement.

INSURING AGREEMENTS

INSURING AGREEMENT (A) covers loss resulting from dishonest or fraudulent acts of Employees. Changes include:
* * Loss resulting from Loan (now a defined term) activity is covered only if the employee involved acts in collusion with another party to the transaction and has himself received a financial benefit of at least $2,500.00.

COPYRIGHT THE SURETY ASSOCIATION OF AMERICA, USED BY PERMISSION

INSURING AGREEMENT (B) covers loss of Property caused by specified perils which occur on the premises of the Insured or on other premises. Changes include:
* * Rider SR 6127, to amend Insuring Agreement (B) of the 1980 edition of the Bankers Blanket Bond, has been withdrawn.
* * False pretenses and larceny must be committed by a person on the bank premises, although the Property may be located "within offices or premises located anywhere."
* * Because Uncertificated Securities of any Federal Reserve Bank of the United States have been added to the definition of Property, coverage runs to these items.

INSURING AGREEMENT (C) covers loss caused by specified perils which occur during transit by a messenger or Transportation Company (now a defined term). Changes Include:
* * The reference to "designated" messenger has been removed.
* * Records, specified securities and specified Negotiable Instruments are now covered while being transported by a Transportation Company in a conveyance other than an armored mother vehicle. All Property is covered while in an armored motor vehicle.
* * In the event that the underwriter receives late notice or elects not to defend the insured, it is not liable for legal fees of the insured. Nor does any judgment against the insured determine the existence of bond coverage.

CONDITIONS AND LIMITATIONS

DEFINITIONS are unchanged except for the following revised or new definitions.
* * Certified Security, (d), replaced the prior definition of Security.
* * Employee, (g), is modified by incorporating a portion of existing rider SR 6127 into part (5).
* * Forgery, (i), now also makes reference to a signature which consists in whole or in part of one's own name.
* * Instruction, (k), is a new definition and relates back to sub-part (h) of the Securities Insuring Agreement.
* * Loan, (m), is a new definition and relates to the Fidelity Insuring Agreement and exclusion (e).
* * Property, (p), contains the phrase Certificated Securities and the phrase Uncertificated Securities of any Federal Reserve Bank of the United States.
* * Statement of Uncertificated Security, (r), is new and relates back to part (i) of the Securities Insuring Agreement.
* * Transportation Company, (s), is new and relates back to the In Transit Insuring Agreement and exclusion (r).
* * Uncertificated Security, (t), is new and relates back to the definition of Property.
* * Withdrawal Order, (u), is newly defined although the term has been in prior editions of the bond.
* * The definition of Security in the prior bond was not carried over to this edition.

EXCLUSIONS are unchanged except for the following. Titles given to the exclusions are informal, and have no legal significance.
* * Loan exclusion, (e), is simplified because Loan is a now defined term.
* * Acts-of-employees exclusion, (h), is an incorporation of a portion of existing rider SR 6127.
* * Plastic-card exclusion, (k), is modified by reference to "purported use" of cards, and by making reference to obtaining funds.
* * Uncollected-funds exclusion, (o), is modified by the deletion of the "on-premises" exception to the exclusion.
* * Carrier-for-hire exclusion, (r), now refers to Transportation Company. The prior designation was (s).

** Damages-other exclusion, (t) is modified by expanding it to exclude multiple compensatory damages. Other editorial changes were made. The prior designation was (u).
** Fees-and-costs exclusion, (u), is modified by reference to legal proceedings. The prior designation was (v).
** Securities-law-violation exclusion, (w), is new to this bond. It has been in the Stockbrokers Blanket Bond for many years.
** Failure-to-deliver exclusion, (x), is new. It excludes loss caused by the failure of a financial or depository institution to return funds or property to the insured. Certain exceptions to the exclusion exist.
** Uncertificated-security exclusion, (y), is new. Uncertificated securities issued by a federal reserve bank are covered under the bond. Other such securities are not.
** Racketeer Influenced and Corrupt Organizations Act exclusion, (z), is new. The bond does not cover damages resulting solely from violation of the Act. It does cover loss resulting directly from dishonest acts.
** Exclusion (s) relating to Insuring Agreement (C) has been replaced by exclusion (r).

INSURING AGREEMENT (D) covers loss caused by Forgery of specified instruments. The change is:
** The term "Withdrawal Order" now appears in initial capitals because the term has been defined in the Definitions section.

INSURING AGREEMENT (E) covers loss caused by the Forgery of a signature on specified instruments, the counterfeiting of specified instruments, and specified other perils. Changes included:
** Two additional instruments have now been added to the list in the Agreement. The instruments are those designated as (h) and (i) relating to Uncertificated Securities issued by a Federal Reserve Bank of the United States. An Instruction (now a defined term) to a Federal Reserve Bank or a Statement of Uncertificated Security (now a defined term) of any Federal reserve Bank are now covered as provided by the terms of the Agreement.
** The term Security, item (a) on the list in the prior version of the Agreement, is now Certificated Security (a defined term).
** The term "or otherwise acted upon" has been removed.

INSURING AGREEMENT (F), covering loss caused by counterfeit currency, has been expanded to cover the currency of any country in which the insured maintains a branch office.

GENERAL AGREEMENTS

GENERAL AGREEMENT A has minor editorial change.

GENERAL AGREEMENT B has minor editorial change and the following:
** Purchase or acquisition of assets or liabilities of another institution requires prior notification to the underwriter. The prior edition referred only to assets.
** The 60 day limitation has been removed. Now the reference is to "notice...prior to the proposed effective date of such action."

GENERAL AGREEMENT C has minor editorial change and the following:
** A change of power to determine the management of a controlling bank holding company must be reported to the underwriter. The prior edition referred only to the power to determine the management of the insured.
** The 30 day time limit for the giving of notice has been removed.
** The reference to the names of owners and total number of shares has been removed.

GENERAL AGREEMENT D is now entitled Representation of the Insured and is substantially different from the General Agreement it replaces. Changes include:

** The insured represents that information furnished in the application is complete, true and correct.

** The application is stated to constitute part of the bond.

GENERAL AGREEMENT E is unchanged.

GENERAL AGREEMENT F is now entitled Notice of Legal Proceeding Against Insured - Election to Defend and is substantially different from the General Agreement it replaces. Changes include:

** Notification of legal proceeding must be given to the underwriter at the earliest practical moment, not to exceed 30 days.

** The underwriter need not indemnify the insured against court costs and attorneys' fees. The underwriter, at its option, may elect to conduct the defense of the insured.

** In the event that the underwriter or elects to defend the insured, any judgment or settlement, and legal expenses, shall be a loss covered under the bond.

Many of the remaining sections of the bond have only editorial changes. However the following may be noted.

DISCOVERY—Section 3

In the prior edition of the bond, this was section 4. New language points out that discovery occurs when the insured discovers loss, regardless of when the acts causing the loss occurred.

LIMIT OF LIABILITY—Section 4

This section contains the operative language for the aggregate limit of liability. All payments made under the terms of the bond reduce the aggregate liability of the underwriter as set forth in Item 3 of the Declarations. Upon exhaustion of the aggregate the underwriter has no further obligation to the insured.

In the event a loss is settled through the use of a lost instrument bond, that loss will not reduce the aggregate amount.

This section also includes language setting forth the Single Loss limit of liability, similar to that of the prior edition of the bond.

NOTICE/PROOF—LEGAL PROCEEDING AGAINST UNDERWRITER—Section 5

The name of this section has been modified to avoid confusion with General Agreement F which has a somewhat similar name. Otherwise the section is unchanged except for editorial revision necessary because of the changes in General Agreement F.

Sections 6, 7, 8, 9, 1 and 11 are unchanged except for minor editing necessary for proper referencing.

TERMINATION OR CANCELLATION—Section 12

This section is modified by the inclusion of parts (e) and (f) in the first paragraph. These two provisions state that the bond is automatically canceled upon either the exhaustion of the Aggregate Limit of Liability, or the expiration of the Bond Period.

The second paragraph contains new language relating to the type of and time of prior dishonest acts of an employee which cause automatic cancellation of fidelity coverage for that employee.

* * * * * * * * *

Note that the Rights After Termination section of the prior edition of the bond has not been carried over to the Financial Institution Bond.

THIS STATEMENT IS INTENDED TO BE INFORMATIVE ONLY. THE TERMS AND PROVISIONS OF THE BOND AND RIDERS WILL GOVERN ANY QUESTION ARISING IN CONNECTION THEREWITH.

(November 1985)

Exhibit 3

FINANCIAL INSTITUTION BOND, STANDARD FORM NO. 24

(Revised May, 2011)

APPENDIX—BOND FORMS 741

FINANCIAL INSTITUTION BOND
Standard Form No. 24, Revised to May, 2011

Bond No.

(Herein called Underwriter)

DECLARATIONS

Item 1. Name of Insured (herein called Insured):

Principal Address:

Item 2. Bond Period: from 12:01 a.m. on _____ to 12:01 a.m. on _____
(MONTH, DAY, YEAR)   (MONTH, DAY, YEAR)

Item 3. The Aggregate Liability of the Underwriter during the Bond Period shall be
$

Item 4. Subject to Sections 4 and 12 hereof,
the Single Loss Limit of Liability applicable to each of Insuring Agreements (A), (B), (C) and (F) is $
and the Single Loss Deductible applicable to each of Insuring Agreements (A), (B), (C) and (F) is $

If coverage is provided under the following Insuring Agreements or Coverages, the applicable Single Loss Limit of Liability and Single Loss Deductible shall be inserted below:

	Single Loss Limit of Liability	Single Loss Deductible
Insuring Agreement (D)—FORGERY OR ALTERATION	$	$
Insuring Agreement (E)—SECURITIES	$	$
Insuring Agreement (G)—FRAUDULENT MORTGAGES	$	$
Optional Insuring Agreements and Coverages:	$	$

If "Not Covered" is inserted above opposite any specified Insuring Agreement or Coverage, or if no amount is inserted, such Insuring Agreement or Coverage and any other reference thereto in this bond shall be deemed to be deleted.

Copyright, The Surety & Fidelity Association of America, 2011   TSB 5018f

ANNOTATED FINANCIAL INSTITUTION BOND

Item 6. The amount of anticipated loss which the Insured must report to the Underwriter pursuant to Section 12 is:

Item 7. For the purposes of Insuring Agreement B, Property lodged or deposited in the following offices and premises is not covered:

Item 8. The Insured by the acceptance of this bond gives notice to the Underwriter terminating or canceling prior bond(s) or policy(ies) No.(s)
Such termination or cancelation to be effective as of the time this bond becomes effective.

The Underwriter, in consideration of an agreed premium, and in reliance upon all statements made and information furnished to the Underwriter by the Insured in applying for this bond, and subject to the Declarations, Insuring Agreements, General Agreements, Conditions and Limitations and other terms hereof, agrees to indemnify the Insured for:

INSURING AGREEMENTS

FIDELITY

(A) Loss resulting directly from dishonest or fraudulent acts committed by an Employee, acting alone or in collusion with others. Such dishonest or fraudulent acts must be committed by the Employee with the manifest intent:
    (1) to cause the Insured to sustain such loss; and
    (2) to obtain an improper financial benefit for the Employee or another person or entity.
However, if some or all of the Insured's loss results directly or indirectly from:
    (a) Loans, that portion of the loss involving any Loan is not covered unless the Employee also was in collusion with one or more parties to the Loan transactions and has received, in connection therewith, an improper financial benefit with a value of at least $2500; or
    (b) trading, that portion of the loss is not covered unless the Employee also has received, in connection therewith, an improper financial benefit.
As used in this Insuring Agreement, an improper financial benefit does not include any employee benefits received in the course of employment, including but not limited to: salaries, commissions, fees, bonuses, promotions, awards, profit sharing or pensions.
As used in this Insuring Agreement, loss does not include any employee benefits (including but not limited to: salaries, commissions, fees, bonuses, promotions, awards, profit sharing or pensions) intentionally paid by the Insured.

ON PREMISES

(B) (1) Loss of items enumerated in the definition of Property resulting directly from:
    (a) robbery, burglary, misplacement, mysterious unexplainable disappearance and damage thereto or destruction thereof, or
    (b) theft, false pretenses, common-law or statutory larceny, committed by a person physically present in an office or on the premises of the Insured at the time the enumerated items of Property are surrendered,

while such enumerated items of Property are lodged or deposited within offices or premises located anywhere, except those offices set forth in Item 7 of the Declarations.

(2) Loss of or damage to furnishings, fixtures, supplies or equipment within an office of the Insured covered under this bond resulting directly from larceny or theft in, or burglary or robbery of, such office, or attempt thereat, provided that:

(a) the Insured is the owner of such furnishings, fixtures, supplies, equipment, or office or is liable for such loss or damage, and

(b) the loss is not caused by fire.

IN TRANSIT

(C) Loss of Property resulting directly from robbery, common-law or statutory larceny, theft, misplacement, mysterious unexplainable disappearance, and damage thereto or destruction thereof, while the Property is in transit anywhere in the custody of:

(1) a Messenger, or
(2) a Transportation Company and being transported in an armored motor vehicle, or
(3) a Transportation Company and being physically (not electronically) transported in other than an armored motor vehicle, provided that covered Property transported in such manner is limited to the following:

(a) Books of account and other records stored on tangible media, including magnetic tapes, disks and computer drives as well as paper, but not including any of the other items listed in the definition of Property, however stored, and

(b) Certificated Securities issued in registered form and not endorsed, or with restrictive endorsements, and

(c) Negotiable Instruments not payable to bearer, and either not endorsed or with restrictive endorsements.

Coverage under this Insuring Agreement begins immediately upon the receipt of such Property by the Messenger or Transportation Company and ends immediately upon delivery to the designated recipient or its agent, but only while the Property is being conveyed.

FORGERY OR ALTERATION

(D) Loss resulting directly from the Insured having, in good faith, paid or transferred any Property in reliance on any Written, Original:

(1) Negotiable Instrument (except an Evidence of Debt),
(2) Certificate of Deposit,
(3) Letter of Credit,
(4) Withdrawal Order,
(5) receipt for the withdrawal of Property, or
(6) instruction or advice directed to the Insured and purportedly signed by a customer of the Insured or by a banking institution

which (a) bears a handwritten signature which is a Forgery; or (b) is altered, but only to the extent the Forgery or alteration causes the loss.

Actual physical possession of the items listed in (1) through (6) above by the Insured is a condition precedent to the Insured's having relied on the items.

A reproduction of a handwritten signature is treated the same as the handwritten signature. An electronic or digital signature is not treated as a reproduction of a handwritten signature.

SECURITIES

(E) Loss resulting directly from the Insured having, in good faith, for its own account or for the account of others,

(1) acquired, sold or delivered or given value, extended credit or assumed liability, on the faith of, any Written, Original:
    (a) Certificated Security,
    (b) Document of Title,
    (c) deed, mortgage or other instrument conveying title to, or creating or discharging a lien upon, real property,
    (d) Certificate of Origin or Title,
    (e) Certificate of Deposit,
    (f) Evidence of Debt,
    (g) corporate, partnership or personal Guarantee, or
    (h) Security Agreement
which (i) bears a handwritten signature which is material to the validity or enforceability of the security, which is a Forgery, or (ii) is altered, but only to the extent the Forgery or alteration causes the loss or (iii) is lost or stolen;

(2) guaranteed in writing or witnessed any signature upon any transfer, assignment, bill of sale, power of attorney, guarantee, endorsement or any items listed in (a) through (h) above; or

(3) acquired, sold or delivered, or given value, extended credit or assumed liability, on the faith of any item listed in (a) through (e) above which is a Counterfeit, but only to the extent the Counterfeit causes the loss.

Actual physical possession of the items listed in (a) through (h) above by the Insured, its correspondent bank or other authorized representative, is a condition precedent to the Insured's having relied on the faith of such items.

A reproduction of a handwritten signature is treated the same as the handwritten signature. An electronic or digital signature is not treated as a reproduction of a handwritten signature.

COUNTERFEIT MONEY

(F) Loss resulting directly from the receipt by the Insured, in good faith, of any Counterfeit Money of the United States of America, Canada or of any other country in which the Insured maintains a branch office.

FRAUDULENT MORTGAGES

(G) Loss resulting directly from the Insured's having, in good faith and in the normal course of business in connection with any Loan, accepted or received or acted upon the faith of any Written, Original:
    (1) real property mortgages, real property deeds of trust or like instruments pertaining to realty, or
    (2) assignments of such mortgages, deeds of trust or instruments
which prove to have been defective by reason of the signature thereon of any person having been obtained through trick, artifice, fraud or false pretenses or the signature on the recorded deed conveying such real property to the mortgagor or grantor of such mortgage or deed of trust having been obtained by or on behalf of such mortgagor or grantor through trick, artifice, fraud or false pretenses.

GENERAL AGREEMENTS

NOMINEES

A. This bond does not indemnify any Insured for loss sustained by a proprietorship, partnership or corporation which is owned, controlled or operated by an Insured and not named as an Insured hereunder unless:
    (1) such loss is sustained by a nominee organized by an Insured for the purpose of handling certain of its business transactions and composed exclusively of its Employees; and
    (2) such Insured is not a holding company.

If the conditions of (1) and (2) are met, loss sustained by the nominee shall, for all the purposes of this bond and whether or not any partner of such nominee is implicated in such loss, be deemed to be loss sustained by the Insured.

ADDITIONAL OFFICES OR EMPLOYEES—CONSOLIDATION, MERGER OR PURCHASE OF ASSETS—NOTICE

B. If the Insured shall, while this bond is in force, establish any additional offices, other than by consolidation or merger with, or purchase or acquisition of assets or liabilities of, another institution, such offices shall be automatically covered hereunder from the date of such establishment without the requirement of notice to the Underwriter or the payment of additional premium for the remainder of the premium period.

If the Insured shall, while this bond is in force, consolidate or merge with, or purchase or acquire assets or liabilities of, another institution, the Insured shall not have such coverage as is afforded under this bond for loss which:
    (1) has occurred or will occur in offices or premises, or
    (2) has been caused or will be caused by an employee or employees of such institution, or
    (3) has arisen or will arise out of the assets or liabilities
acquired by the insured as a result of such consolidation, merger or purchase or acquisition of assets or liabilities unless the Insured shall (i) give the Underwriter Written notice of the proposed consolidation, merger or purchase or acquisition of assets or liabilities prior to the proposed effective date of such action, and (ii) obtain the Written consent of the Underwriter to extend the coverage provided by this bond to such additional offices or premises, employees and other exposures, and (iii) upon obtaining such consent, pay to the Underwriter an additional premium.

CHANGE OF OWNERSHIP—NOTICE

C. When an Insured learns of a change in ownership by a single stockholder, partner or member, or by a group of affiliated stockholders, partners or members, of more than ten percent (10%) of its voting stock or total ownership interest, or of the voting stock or total ownership interest of a holding company or parent corporation which itself owns or controls the Insured, it shall give Written notice to the Underwriter, as soon as practicable but not later than within thirty (30) days. Failure to give the required notice shall result in termination of coverage for any loss involving a transferee of such stock or ownership interest, effective upon the date of the stock transfer or transfer of ownership interest.

REPRESENTATION OF INSURED

D. The Insured represents that the information furnished in the application for this bond is complete, true and correct. Such application constitutes part of this bond.

Any omission, concealment or incorrect statement, in the application or otherwise, shall be grounds for the rescission of this bond, provided that such omission, concealment or incorrect statement is material.

JOINT INSURED

E. Only the first named Insured can submit a claim under this bond, and shall act for all Insureds. Payment by the Underwriter to the first named Insured of loss sustained by any Insured shall fully release the Underwriter on account of such loss. If the first named Insured ceases to be covered under this bond, the Insured next named shall thereafter be considered as the first named Insured. Knowledge possessed or discovery made by any Insured shall constitute knowledge or discovery by all Insureds for all purposes of this bond. The liability of the Underwriter for loss or losses sustained by all Insureds shall not exceed the amount for which the Underwriter would have been liable had all such loss or losses been sustained by one Insured.

NOTICE OF LEGAL PROCEEDINGS AGAINST INSURED– ELECTION TO DEFEND

F. The Insured shall notify the Underwriter at the earliest practicable moment, not to exceed 30 days after notice thereof, of any legal proceeding brought to determine the Insured's liability for any loss, claim or damage, which, if established, would constitute a collectible loss under this bond. Concurrently, the Insured shall furnish copies of all pleadings and pertinent papers to the Underwriter.

The Underwriter, at its sole option, may elect to conduct the defense of such legal proceeding, in whole or in part. The defense by the Underwriter shall be in the Insured's name through attorneys selected by the Underwriter. The Insured shall provide all reasonable information and assistance required by the Underwriter for such defense.

If the Underwriter elects to defend the Insured, in whole or in part, any judgment against the Insured on those counts or causes of action which the Underwriter defended on behalf of the Insured or any settlement in which the Underwriter participates and all attorneys' fees, costs and expenses incurred by the Underwriter in the defense of the litigation shall be a loss covered by this bond.

If the Insured does not give the notices required in subsection (a) of Section 5. of the Conditions and Limitation of this bond and in the first paragraph of this General Agreement, or if the Underwriter elects not to defend any causes of action, neither a judgment against the Insured, nor a settlement of any legal proceeding by the Insured, shall determine the existence, extent or amount of coverage under this bond for loss sustained by the Insured, and the Underwriter shall not be liable for any attorneys' fees, costs and expenses incurred by the Insured.

With respect to this General Agreement, subsections (b) and (d) of Section 5. of the Conditions and Limitation of this bond apply upon the entry of such judgment or the occurrence of such settlement instead of upon discovery of loss. In addition, the Insured must notify the Underwriter within 30 days after such judgment is entered against it or after the Insured settles such legal proceeding, and, subject to subsection (e) of Section 5., the Insured may not bring legal proceedings for the recovery of such loss after the expiration of 24 months from the date of such final judgment or settlement.

INSURED'S ERISA PLANS

G. If any Employee or director of the Insured is required to provide a bond to a health, welfare or pension plan subject to the Employee Retirement Income Security Act of 1974 (ERISA) (hereinafter the Plan), the majority of whose beneficiaries are Employees or former Employees of the Insured, the Plan shall be deemed an Insured under this bond for the purposes of Insuring Agreement (A) only and subject, in addition to all other terms and conditions of this bond, to the following:

(1) the deductible required by Section 12 of the Conditions and Limitations of this bond shall be applicable to a loss suffered by the Plan only after the Plan has received from the Underwriter
    (a)   the lesser of $500,000 or 10% of the assets of the Plan at the beginning of the fiscal year of the Plan in which the loss is discovered, if the Plan does not hold "employer securities" within the meaning of section 407(d)(1) of ERISA; or
    (b)   the lesser of $1,000,000 or 10% of the assets of the Plan at the beginning of the fiscal year of the Plan in which the loss is discovered, if the Plan holds "employer securities" within the meaning of section 407(d)(1) of ERISA,
(2) notwithstanding Section 3 of the Conditions and Limitations of this bond, loss suffered by the Plan is covered if discovered during the term of this bond or within one year thereafter, but if discovered during said one year period, the loss payable under this bond shall be reduced by the amount recoverable from any other bond or insurance protecting the assets of the Plan against loss through fraud or dishonesty; and
(3) if more than one Plan subject to ERISA is an Insured pursuant to this General Agreement, the Insured shall purchase limits sufficient to provide the minimum amount of coverage required by ERISA for each Plan and shall distribute any payment made under this bond to said Plans so that each Plan receives the amount it would have received if insured separately for the minimum coverage which ERISA required it to have.

CONDITIONS AND LIMITATIONS

DEFINITIONS

Section 1. As used in this bond:
    (a)   Certificate of Deposit means a Written acknowledgment by a financial institution of receipt of Money with an engagement to repay it.
    (b)   Certificate of Origin or Title means a Written document issued by a manufacturer of personal property or a governmental agency evidencing the ownership of the personal property and by which ownership is transferred.
    (c)   Certificated Security means a share, participation or other interest in property of or an enterprise of the issuer or an obligation of the issuer, which is:
        (1)   represented by a Written instrument issued in bearer or registered form;
        (2)   of a type commonly dealt in on securities exchanges or markets or commonly recognized in any area in which it is issued or dealt in as a medium for investment; and
        (3)   either one of a class or series or by its terms divisible into a class or series of shares, participations, interests or obligations.
    (d)   Change in Control means a change in ownership of more than fifty percent (50%) of the voting stock or ownership interest of the Insured, or of a parent corporation or holding company which controls the Insured.
    (e)   Counterfeit means a Written imitation of an actual, valid Original which is intended to deceive and to be taken as the Original.
    (f)   Document of Title means a Written bill of lading, dock warrant, dock receipt, warehouse receipt or order for the delivery of goods, and also any other Written document which in the regular course of business or financing is treated as adequately evidencing that the person in possession of it is entitled to receive, hold and dispose of the document and the goods it covers and must purport to be issued by or addressed to a bailee and purport to cover goods in the bailee's possession which are either identified or are fungible portions of an identified mass.
    (g)   Electronic Data Processor means a natural person, partnership or corporation with the Insured's Written authorization to perform services as data processor of checks presented to the Insured by a customer or another financial institution. A Federal Reserve Bank or clearinghouse shall not be an Electronic Data Processor.

(h) Employee means:
 (1) a natural person while in the service of the Insured whom the Insured has the right to direct and control in the performance of his or her duties and
  (i) whom the Insured directly compensates by wages, salaries or commissions, or
  (ii) who is compensated by an employment agency which is paid by the Insured for providing the person's services for work at or in the Insured's offices or premises covered hereunder;
 (2) a member of the Board of Directors of the Insured, or a member of an equivalent body, when performing acts coming within the scope of the usual duties of a person described in paragraph (h)(1) above or while acting as a member of any committee duly elected or appointed by resolution of the board of directors or equivalent body to perform specific, as distinguished from general, directorial acts on behalf of the Insured;
 (3) an employee of an institution merged or consolidated with the Insured prior to the effective date of this bond, but only as to acts while an employee of such institution which caused said institution to sustain a loss which was not known to the Insured or to the institution at the time of the merger or consolidation; and
 (4) an Electronic Data Processor, provided, however, that each such Electronic Data Processor, and the partners, officers and employees of such Electronic Data Processor shall, collectively, be deemed to be one Employee for all the purposes of this bond, excepting, however, the Employee termination provisions of Section 13.
(i) Evidence of Debt means a Written instrument, including a Negotiable Instrument, executed, or purportedly executed, by a customer of the Insured and held by the Insured which in the regular course of business is treated as evidencing the customer's debt to the Insured.
(j) Forgery means:
 (1) affixing the handwritten signature, or a reproduction of the handwritten signature, of another natural person without authorization and with intent to deceive; or
 (2) affixing the name of an organization as an endorsement to a check without authority and with the intent to deceive.
 Provided, however, that a signature which consists in whole or in part of one's own name signed with or without authority, in any capacity, for any purpose is not a Forgery. An electronic or digital signature is not a reproduction of a handwritten signature or the name of an organization.
(k) Guarantee means a Written undertaking obligating the signer to pay the debt of another, to the Insured or its assignee or to a financial institution from which the Insured has purchased participation in the debt, if the debt is not paid in accordance with its terms.
(l) Letter of Credit means a Written engagement by a bank made at the request of a customer, that the bank will honor drafts or other demands for payment upon compliance with the conditions specified in the Letter of Credit.
(m) Loan means all extensions of credit by the Insured and all transactions creating a creditor relationship in favor of the Insured and all transactions by which the Insured assumes an existing creditor relationship.
(n) Messenger means an Employee while in possession of the Insured's Property away from the Insured's premises and any other natural person acting as custodian of the Property during an emergency arising from the incapacity of the original Employee.
(o) Money means a medium of exchange in current use authorized or adopted by a domestic or foreign government as a part of its currency.
(p) Negotiable Instrument means any writing:
 (1) signed by the maker or drawer; and
 (2) containing any unconditional promise or order to pay a sum certain in Money and no other promise, order, obligation or power given by the maker or drawer; and
 (3) payable on demand or at a definite time; and
 (4) payable to order or bearer.

(q) Original means the first rendering or archetype and does not include photocopies or electronic transmissions even if received and printed.
(r) Property means Money, Certificated Securities, Negotiable Instruments, Certificates of Deposit, Documents of Title, Evidences of Debt, Security Agreements, Withdrawal Orders, Certificates of Origin or Title, Letters of Credit, insurance policies, abstracts of title, deeds and mortgages on real estate, revenue and other stamps, tokens, unsold state lottery tickets, books of account and other records stored on tangible media, gems, jewelry, precious metals in bars or ingots (which are collectively the enumerated items of property), and tangible items of personal property which are not hereinbefore enumerated.
(s) Security Agreement means a Written agreement which creates an interest in personal property or fixtures and which secures payment or performance of an obligation.
(t) Transportation Company means any organization which regularly provides its own or leased vehicles for transportation of its customers' property or which provides freight forwarding or air express services.
(u) Withdrawal Order means a Written, non-negotiable instrument, signed by a customer of the Insured authorizing the Insured to debit the customers account in the amount of funds stated therein.
(v) Written means expressed through letters or marks placed upon paper and visible to the eye.

EXCLUSIONS

Section 2. This bond does not cover:
(a) loss resulting directly or indirectly from Forgery or alteration, except when covered under Insuring Agreements (A), (D), or (E);
(b) loss due to riot or civil commotion outside the United States of America and Canada; or loss due to military, naval or usurped power, war or insurrection unless such loss occurs in transit in the circumstances recited in Insuring Agreement (C), and unless, when such transit was initiated, there was no knowledge of such riot, civil commotion, military, naval or usurped power, war or insurrection on the part of any person acting for the Insured in initiating such transit;
(c) loss resulting directly or indirectly from the effects of nuclear fission or fusion, radioactivity, or chemical or biological contamination;
(d) loss resulting directly or indirectly from any acts of any person who is a member of the Board of Directors of the Insured or a member of any equivalent body by whatsoever name known, except when covered under Insuring Agreement (A);
(e) loss resulting directly or indirectly from the complete or partial nonpayment of, or default upon, any Loan or transaction involving the Insured as a lender or borrower, or extension of credit, including but not limited to the purchase, discounting or other acquisition of false or genuine accounts, invoices, notes, agreements or Evidences of Debt, whether such Loan, transaction or extension was procured in good faith or through trick, artifice, fraud or false pretenses, except when covered under Insuring Agreements (A), (E) or (G);
(f) loss of Property contained in customers' safe deposit boxes, except when covered under Insuring Agreement (A);
(g) loss through cashing or paying forged or altered travelers' checks, or travelers' checks bearing forged endorsements, except when covered under Insuring Agreement (A); or loss of unsold travelers' checks or unsold money orders in the custody of the Insured with authority to sell, unless (1) the Insured, by Written contract, has agreed to indemnify the drawer of the travelers checks or money orders for such loss and (2) such checks or money orders are later paid or honored by said drawer;
(h) loss caused by an Employee, except when covered under Insuring Agreement (A), or when covered under Insuring Agreements (B) or (C) and resulting directly from unintentional

acts of the Employee causing mysterious unexplainable disappearance, misplacement, destruction of or damage to Property;

(i) loss resulting directly or indirectly from trading, with or without the knowledge of the Insured, whether or not represented by any indebtedness or balance shown to be due the Insured on any customer's account, actual or fictitious, and notwithstanding any act or omission on the part of any Employee in connection with any account relating to such trading, indebtedness, or balance, except when covered under Insuring Agreements (A), (D) or (E);

(j) shortage in any teller's cash due to error;

(k) loss resulting directly or indirectly from the use, or purported use, of credit, debit, charge, access, convenience or other cards:

(1) in obtaining credit or funds, or

(2) in gaining access to automated mechanical devices which, on behalf of the Insured, disburse Money, accept deposits, cash checks, drafts or similar Written instruments or make credit card loans, or

(3) in gaining access to point of sale terminals, customer-bank communication terminals, or similar electronic terminals of electronic funds transfer systems,

whether such cards were issued, or purport to have been issued, by the Insured or by anyone other than the Insured, except when covered under Insuring Agreement (A);

(l) loss involving automated mechanical devices which, on behalf of the Insured, disburse Money, accept deposits, cash checks, drafts or similar Written instruments or make credit card loans, unless such automated mechanical devices are situated within an office of the Insured which is permanently staffed by an Employee whose duties are those usually assigned to a bank teller, even though public access is from outside the confines of such office, but in no event shall the Underwriter be liable for loss (including loss of Property)

(1) as a result of damage to such automated mechanical devices perpetrated from outside such office, or

(2) as a result of failure of such automated mechanical devices to function properly, or

(3) through misplacement or mysterious unexplainable disappearance of Property located within any such automated mechanical devices, except when covered under Insuring Agreement (A);

(m) loss resulting directly or indirectly from surrender of property away from an office of the Insured as a result of:

(1) kidnapping,

(2) payment of ransom,

(3) threats of bodily harm to any person, except the custodian of the property, or of damage to the premises or property of the Insured, or

(4) actual disappearance, damage, destruction, confiscation or theft of Property intended as a ransom or extortion payment while held or conveyed by a person duly authorized by the Insured to have custody of such Property,

except when covered under Insuring Agreement (A);

(n) loss resulting directly or indirectly from payments made or withdrawals from a depositor's account involving erroneous credits to such account, except when covered under Insuring Agreement (A);

(o) loss resulting directly or indirectly from payments made or withdrawals from a depositor's account involving items of deposit which are not finally paid, for any reason, including but not limited to Forgery or any other fraud, except when covered under Insuring Agreement (A);

(p) loss resulting directly or indirectly from counterfeiting, except when covered under Insuring Agreements (A), (D), (E) or (F);

(q) loss of any tangible item of personal property which is not specifically enumerated in the paragraph defining Property if such property is insured by other insurance of any kind and in any amount obtained by the Insured, and in any event, loss of such property occurring more

than 60 days after the Insured shall have become aware that it owns, holds or is responsible for such property, except when covered under Insuring Agreements (A) or (B)(2);
(r) loss of Property while
    (1) in the mail, or
    (2) in the custody of any Transportation Company, unless covered under Insuring Agreement (C), or
    (3) while located on the premises of any Messenger or Transportation Company
    except when covered under Insuring Agreement (A);
(s) potential income, including but not limited to interest and dividends, not realized by the Insured;
(t) damages of any type for which the Insured is legally liable, unless the Insured establishes that the act or acts which gave rise to the damages involved conduct which would have caused a covered loss to the Insured in a similar amount in the absence of such damages;
(u) all fees, costs and expenses incurred by the Insured:
    (1) in establishing the existence of or amount of loss covered under this bond, or
    (2) as a party to any legal proceeding whether or not such legal proceeding exposes the Insured to loss covered by this bond;
(v) indirect or consequential loss of any nature including, but not limited to, fines, penalties, multiple or punitive damages;
(w) any loss resulting from any violation by the Insured or by any Employee:
    (1) of law regulating (i) the issuance, purchase or sale of securities, (ii) securities transactions upon any security exchange or over the counter market, (iii) investment companies, or (iv) investment advisers, or
    (2) of any rule or regulation made pursuant to any such law,
    unless it is established by the Insured that the act or acts which caused the said loss involved fraudulent or dishonest conduct which would have caused a loss to the Insured in a similar amount in the absence of such laws, rules or regulations;
(x) loss resulting directly or indirectly from the failure of a financial or depository institution, or its receiver or liquidator, to pay or deliver, on demand of the Insured, funds or Property of the Insured held by it in any capacity, except when covered under Insuring Agreements (A) or (B)(1)(a);
(y) loss resulting directly or indirectly from the Insured's accepting checks payable to an organization for deposit into an account of a natural person;
(z) damages resulting from any civil, criminal or other legal proceeding in which the Insured is alleged to have engaged in racketeering activity except when the Insured establishes that the act or acts giving rise to such damages were committed by an Employee under circumstances which result directly in a loss to the Insured covered by Insuring Agreement (A). For the purposes of this exclusion, "racketeering activity" is defined in 18 United States Code 1961 et seq., as amended.
(aa) loss resulting directly or indirectly from the theft, disappearance or destruction of confidential information including, but not limited to, trade secrets, customer lists, and intellectual property.
(bb) loss resulting directly or indirectly from the dishonest or fraudulent acts of an Employee if any Insured, or any director or officer of an Insured who is not in collusion with such Employee, knows, or knew at any time, of any dishonest or fraudulent act committed by such Employee at any time, whether in the employment of the Insured or otherwise, whether or not of the type covered under Insuring Agreement (A), against the Insured or any other person or entity and without regard to whether knowledge was obtained before or after the commencement of this bond. Provided, however, that this exclusion does not apply to loss of any Property already in transit in the custody of such Employee at the time such knowledge was obtained or to loss resulting directly from dishonest or fraudulent acts occurring prior to the time such knowledge was obtained.

DISCOVERY

Section 3. This bond applies to loss first discovered by the Insured during the Bond Period. Discovery occurs when the Insured first becomes aware of facts which would cause a reasonable person to assume that a loss of a type covered by this bond has been or will be incurred, regardless of when the act or acts causing or contributing to such loss occurred, even though the exact amount or details of the loss may not then be known. Discovery also occurs when the Insured receives notice of an actual or potential claim in which it is alleged that the Insured is liable to a third party under circumstances which, if true, would constitute a loss under this bond.

LIMIT OF LIABILITY

Section 4.

Aggregate Limit of Liability

The Underwriter's total liability for all losses discovered during the Bond Period shown in Item 2. of the Declarations shall not exceed the Aggregate Limit of Liability shown in Item 3. of the Declarations. The Aggregate Limit of Liability shall be reduced by the amount of any payment made under the terms of this bond.

Upon exhaustion of the Aggregate Limit of Liability by such payments:
(a) the Underwriter shall have no further liability for loss or losses regardless of when discovered and whether or not previously reported to the Underwriter; and
(b) the Underwriter shall have no obligation under General Agreement F to continue the defense of the Insured, and upon notice by the Underwriter to the Insured that the Aggregate Limit of Liability has been exhausted, the Insured shall assume all responsibility for its defense at its own cost.

The Aggregate Limit of Liability shall be reinstated by any net recovery received by the Underwriter during the Bond Period and before the Aggregate Limit of Liability is exhausted. Recovery from reinsurance and/or indemnity of the Underwriter shall not be deemed a recovery as used herein. In the event that a loss of Property is settled by the Underwriter through the use of a lost instrument bond, such loss shall not reduce the Aggregate Limit of Liability, but any payment under the lost instrument bond shall reduce the Aggregate Limit of Liability under this bond.

Single Loss Limit of Liability

Subject to the Aggregate Limit of Liability, the Underwriter's liability for each Single Loss shall not exceed the applicable Single Loss Limit of Liability shown in Item 4. of the Declarations. If a Single Loss is covered under more than one Insuring Agreement or Coverage, the maximum amount payable shall not exceed the largest applicable Single Loss Limit of Liability.

Single Loss Defined

Single Loss means all covered loss, including court costs and attorneys' fees incurred by the Underwriter under General Agreement F, resulting from:
(a) any one act or series of related acts of burglary, robbery or attempt thereat, in which no Employee is implicated, or
(b) any one act or series of related unintentional or negligent acts or omissions on the part of any person (whether an Employee or not) resulting in damage to or destruction or misplacement of Property, or
(c) all acts or omissions other than those specified in (a) and (b) preceding, caused by any person (whether an Employee or not) or in which such person is implicated, or

TSB 5018f   Copyright, The Surety & Fidelity Association of America, 2011

(d) any one casualty or event not specified in (a), (b) or (c) preceding.

NOTICE/PROOF—LEGAL PROCEEDINGS AGAINST UNDERWRITER

Section 5.
   (a) At the earliest practicable moment, not to exceed 30 days, after discovery of loss, the Insured shall give the Underwriter notice thereof.
   (b) Within 6 months after such discovery, the Insured shall furnish to the Underwriter proof of loss, duly sworn to, with full particulars.
   (c) Lost Certificated Securities listed in a proof of loss shall be identified by certificate or bond numbers if such securities were issued therewith.
   (d) Legal proceedings for the recovery of any loss hereunder shall not be brought prior to the expiration of 60 days after the original proof of loss is filed with the Underwriter or after the expiration of 24 months from the discovery of such loss.
   (e) If any limitation period embodied in this bond is prohibited by any law controlling the construction hereof, such limitation period shall be deemed to be amended so as to equal the minimum limitation period allowed by such law.
   (f) This bond affords coverage only in favor of the Insured. No suit, action or legal proceedings shall be brought hereunder by any one other than the first named Insured.

VALUATION

Section 6.
   The value of any loss for purposes of coverage under this bond shall be the net loss to the Insured after crediting any receipts, payments or recoveries, however denominated, received by the Insured in connection with the transaction giving rise to the loss. If the loss involves a Loan, any interest or fees received by the Insured in connection with the Loan shall be such a credit.

Money

Any loss of Money, or loss payable in Money, shall be paid, at the option of the Insured, in the Money of the country in which the loss was sustained or in the United States of America dollar equivalent thereof determined at the rate of exchange at the time of payment of such loss.

Securities

The Underwriter shall settle in kind its liability under this bond on account of a loss of any securities or, at the option of the Insured, shall pay to the Insured the cost of replacing such securities, determined by the market value thereof at the time of such settlement. In case of a loss of subscription, conversion or redemption privileges through the misplacement or loss of securities, the amount of such loss shall be the value of such privileges immediately preceding the expiration thereof. If such securities cannot be replaced or have no quoted market value, or if such privileges have no quoted market value, their value shall be determined by agreement or arbitration.

If the applicable coverage of this bond is subject to a Deductible Amount and/or is not sufficient in amount to indemnify the Insured in full for the loss of securities for which claim is made hereunder, the liability of the Underwriter under this bond is limited to the payment for, or the duplication of, so much of such securities as has a value equal to the amount of such applicable coverage.

Books of Account and Other Records

In case of loss of, or damage to, any books of account or other records used by the Insured in its business, the Underwriter shall be liable under this bond only if such books or records are actually reproduced and then for not more than the cost of the blank books, blank pages or other materials, including electronic media, plus the cost of labor for the actual transcription or copying of data which shall have been furnished by the Insured in order to reproduce such books and other records.

Property other than Money, Securities or Records

In case of loss of, or damage to, any Property other than Money, securities, books of account or other records, or damage covered under Insuring Agreement (B)(2), the Underwriter shall not be liable for more than the actual cash value of such Property, or of items covered under Insuring Agreement (B)(2). The Underwriter may, at its election, pay the actual cash value of, replace or repair such property. Disagreement between the Underwriter and the Insured as to the cash value or as to the adequacy of repair or replacement shall be resolved by arbitration.

Set-Off

Any loss covered under this bond shall be reduced by a set-off consisting of any amount owed to the Employee (or to his or her assignee) causing the loss if such loss is covered under Insuring Agreement (A).

ASSIGNMENT—SUBROGATION—RECOVERY—COOPERATION

Section 7.
    (a) In the event of payment under this bond, the Insured shall deliver, if so requested by the Underwriter, an assignment of such of the Insured's rights, title and interest and causes of action as it has against any person or entity to the extent of the loss payment.
    (b) In the event of payment under this bond, the Underwriter shall be subrogated to all of the Insured's rights of recovery therefor against any person or entity to the extent of such payment.
    (c) Recoveries, whether effected by the Underwriter or by the Insured, shall be applied, net of the expense of such recovery, first to the satisfaction of the Insured's loss which would otherwise have been paid but for the fact that it is in excess of either the Single or Aggregate Limit of Liability, secondly, to the Underwriter as reimbursement of amounts paid in settlement of the Insured's claim, thirdly, to the Insured in satisfaction of any Deductible Amount, and fourthly, to the Insured for any loss not covered by this bond. Recovery on account of loss of securities as set forth in the third paragraph of Section 6 or recovery from reinsurance and/or indemnity of the Underwriter shall not be deemed a recovery as used herein.
    (d) The Insured shall execute all papers and render assistance to secure to the Underwriter the rights and causes of action provided for herein. The Insured shall do nothing after discovery of loss to prejudice such rights or causes of action.

COOPERATION

Section 8. Upon the Underwriter's request and at reasonable times and places designated by the Underwriter, the Insured shall
    (a) submit to examination by the Underwriter and subscribe to the same under oath; and
    (b) produce for the Underwriter's examination all pertinent records; and
    (c) cooperate with the Underwriter in all matters pertaining to any claim or loss.

ANTI-BUNDLING

Section 9. If any Insuring Agreement requires that an enumerated type of document be altered or Counterfeit, or contain a signature which is a Forgery or obtained through trick, artifice, fraud or false pretenses, the alteration or Counterfeit or signature must be on or of the enumerated document itself not on or of some other document submitted with, accompanying or incorporated by reference into the enumerated document.

OTHER INSURANCE OR INDEMNITY

Section 10. Coverage afforded hereunder shall apply only as excess over any valid and collectible insurance or indemnity obtained by the Insured, or by one other than the Insured, on Property subject to exclusion (q), or by a Transportation Company, or by another entity on whose premises the loss occurred or which employed the person causing the loss.

COVERED PROPERTY

Section 11. This bond shall apply to loss of Property (a) owned by the Insured, (b) held by the Insured in any capacity, or (c) owned and held by someone else under circumstances which make the Insured responsible for the Property prior to the occurrence of the loss. This bond shall be for the sole use and benefit of the Insured named in the Declarations.

DEDUCTIBLE AMOUNT

Section 12. The Underwriter shall be liable hereunder only for the amount by which any single loss, as defined in Section 4., exceeds the Single Loss Deductible for the Insuring Agreement or Coverage applicable to such loss, subject to the Aggregate Limit of Liability and the applicable Single Loss Limit of Liability.

If the loss involves a dishonest or fraudulent act committed by an Employee, or if the amount of the potential loss exceeds the amount set forth in Item 6. of the Declarations, the Insured shall, in the time and in the manner prescribed in this bond, give the Underwriter notice of any loss of the kind covered by the terms of this bond, even if the amount of the loss does not exceed the Single Loss Deductible, and upon the request of the Underwriter shall file with it a brief statement giving the particulars concerning such loss.

TERMINATION OR CANCELLATION

Section 13. This bond terminates as an entirety upon occurrence of any of the following:
(a) 60 days after the receipt by the Insured of a Written notice from the Underwriter of its desire to cancel this bond;
(b) immediately upon the receipt by the Underwriter of a Written notice from the Insured of its desire to cancel this bond;
(c) immediately upon the taking over of the Insured by a receiver or other liquidator or by State or Federal officials;
(d) immediately upon a Change in Control of the first named Insured;
(e) immediately upon exhaustion of the Aggregate Limit of Liability; or
(f) immediately upon expiration of the Bond Period as set forth in Item 2. of the Declarations.

If there is a Change in Control of an Insured other than the first named Insured, this bond immediately terminates as to that Insured only.

This bond terminates as to any Employee, or any partner, officer or employee of any Electronic Data Processor, (a) as soon as any Insured, or any director or officer of an Insured who is not in collusion with such person, learns of any dishonest or fraudulent act committed by such person at any time, whether in the employment of the Insured or otherwise, whether or not of the type covered under Insuring Agreement (A), against the Insured or any other person or entity, without prejudice to the loss of any Property then in transit in the custody of such person, or (b) 15 days after the receipt by the Insured of a Written notice from the Underwriter of its desire to cancel this bond as to such person.

Termination of this bond as to any Insured terminates liability for any loss sustained by such Insured which is discovered after the effective date of such termination. Termination of this bond as to any Employee, or any partner, officer or employee of any Electronic Data Processor, terminates liability for any loss caused by a fraudulent or dishonest act committed by such person after the date of such termination.

In witness whereof, the Underwriter has caused this bond to be executed on the Declarations Page.

Exhibit 4

SFAA ELECTRONIC FILING LETTER FOR FINANCIAL INSTITUTION BOND, STANDARD FORM NO. 24

(Revised May, 2011)

APPENDIX—BOND FORMS

Enclosed for filing are the policy forms and related riders for revised Financial Institution Bonds, Standard Form (SF) Nos. 14 (TSB 5062c), 15 (TSB 5867b), 24 (5018f) and 25 (5174c). These Financial Institution Bond forms cover loss resulting from employee dishonesty and other crime risks. Different types of financial institutions are eligible insureds under the different forms. The Surety & Fidelity Association of America ("SFAA") prepared these revised forms and Riders. The policy numbers and eligible insureds for each of the four standard form policies included in this filing are:

SF No.	New Policy No.	Replaced Policy No.	Eligible Insureds
14	TSB 5062c	TSB 5062b	Stock Brokers and Investment Banks
15	TSB 5867b	TSB 5867a	Finance and Small Loan Cos., Mortgage Bankers and Brokers, and Real Estate Investment Trusts
24	TSB 5018e	TSB 5018f	Banks and Savings & Loans
25	TSB 5174c	TSB 5174b	Insurance Cos. and Reinsurance Cos.

This filing replaces the 1987 SF No. 14, 1990 SF No, 15, 2004 SF No. 24 and 2008 SF No, 25 currently filed with your Department. This filing does not contain any manual rules or loss costs, The filings for the corresponding rules and loss costs are submitted under separate cover letters.

The revisions contained in these forms can be placed in three categories. First, many of the revisions in the Form 14 and Form 15 are a continuation of the changes made to the Form 24 (2004 edition) and the Form 25 (2008 edition) ("Follow-On Revisions"). Second, some of the revisions in all four forms seek to improve the organization of the forms and make the forms' terms more consistent where possible ("Improvement Revisions"). Last, Insuring Agreement (A) of the Form 24 and Form 25 have been revised to restore the "manifest intent" language that was used in prior editions ("Insuring Agreement (A) Revisions"). These three categories of revisions will be addressed in turn.

Follow On Revisions (Form 14 and Form 15)

In 2003, SFAA filed an updated, revised edition of Standard Form No. 24 with an effective date of April 1, 2004. In 2007, SFAA filed a revised Standard Form No. 25 (effective date January 1, 2008). The revised Form 25 incorporates many of the changes made to the Form 24. A predominant reason for the revisions was to provide greater clarity, correct misinterpretations of the bond by some courts and make changes to take current technology into account. In addition, the revisions were intended so that the forms contemplate primarily paper transactions. In recent years electronic commerce and communications have significantly impacted virtually all businesses, but different companies and industries have reacted differently. Electronic transactions present exposures that are not readily compatible with the terms and conditions of the prior forms. SFAA concluded that the standard form should be directed largely to paper transactions since many Insureds will continue to transact business traditionally and non-electronically. Insureds that desire coverage for losses from electronic transactions may obtain this additional coverage by rider, but Insureds that do not need or desire such coverage will not be forced to purchase it.

SFAA is continuing its revision process with regard to its other Financial Institution Bonds and intends to keep the different forms as consistent as possible. Therefore, the revised Form 14 and Form 15 implement many of the same changes made in the 2004 edition of Form 24 and 2008 edition of the Form 25.

We highlight and explain certain revisions.

I. Insuring Agreements

Insuring Agreement (A) The Form 14 specifically references loans and trading, as these activities are conducted by securities and investment institutions. (Trading refers to trading activities in the Insured's account, rather than in a customer's account, which is excluded by Exclusion (i)). Trading is not referenced in the Form 15 because trading is not an activity typically conducted by a small loan company or mortgage broker.

With respect to these activities, the "financial benefit" provision has been revised in the Form 14 and Form 15 to ensure that bonuses or other compensation that were generated as a result of the dishonest scheme are not included as financial benefit. "Financial benefit" has been revised to "improper financial benefit." Also, the phrase regarding benefits "earned in the normal course of employment" is replaced by benefits "received" by the Employee. The purpose of the change is to strengthen the effect of the language, to preclude an argument that wages, salaries or commissions generated through a dishonest scheme were not in the normal course of employment and therefore not excluded from the meaning of a "financial benefit." The intent is that any employee benefit received by the employee should be excluded from the meaning of improper financial benefit. For example, claimants could argue that since a bonus was generated as a result of making an improper loan, and making improper loans was not a duty of employment, then the bonus was an improper financial benefit. However, the intent of the provision is to exclude such a bonus. A kickback from the customer receiving a fraudulent loan is an example of an improper financial benefit.

Note that although Insuring Agreement (A) generally requires the improper financial benefit to go to the Employee or another person or entity, the benefit with respect to the specific activities (Loans or trading) must go to the Employee.

Insuring Agreement (B) The revised Insuring Agreement (B) does not provide coverage for vandalism or malicious mischief. This revision incorporates Rider SR 6263 into the policy. The covered Property is limited to the enumerated items set forth in the Property definition. The reason for this change is to avoid duplication of coverage with Insurance Services Office (ISO) property coverages and insure only those items that are not covered under standard property insurance forms. The enumerated items generally are not covered under the ISO property forms.

The revised Insuring Agreement (B) does not cover loss or damage to the office or interior of the office, which previously was covered under paragraph B(2)(b). The reason for the deletion was that such coverage is afforded by ISO property policies.

The revised Insuring Agreement (B) requires that the perpetrator be "physically" present on the premises "at the time the Property was surrendered." The intent of Insuring Agreement (B) is to cover losses entirely attributable to face-to-face transactions.

Insuring Agreement (C) Clause (1) was revised so that the custodian of Property must be a Messenger (a defined term, which also incorporates the person acting as a custodian in the event of an emergency).

Clause (3) excludes coverage for any property being transmitted electronically. Clause (3)(a) elaborates on the meaning of "records" as books of account and other records but not any other items enumerated in the definition of property.

APPENDIX—BOND FORMS 761

The last paragraph clarifies that Insuring Agreement C covers property "only while the property is being conveyed." Thus the covered property must be in transit and not stored at the Transportation Company's premises.

Insuring Agreement (D) Insuring Agreement (D) of the Form 14 was revised so that the coverage it provides is exclusive of the coverage provided in Insuring Agreement (E). Insuring Agreement (D) covers loss caused by the Insured making a payment or transfer on the faith of a forged or altered document of a type enumerated in the Insuring Agreement. The types of documents enumerated in Insuring Agreement D are ones directing the Insured to make a payment or transfer. The format of Insuring Agreement (D) under the Form 14 was revised so that the enumerated items are presented as a list, similar to the Form 24 and Form 25. Insuring Agreement D now requires actual possession of the forged or altered document. Although reliance on a Written Original implies a requirement of possession, the provision sets forth the requirement explicitly.

Insuring Agreement (D) in the Form 15 is largely unchanged. Unlike the types of businesses covered under the other forms, a mortgage broker or small loan company does not maintain accounts from which Property is paid or transferred. The main Forgery exposure for a Form 15 insured is loss caused by the Forgery of checks issued or purportedly issued by the Insured.

Insuring Agreement (E) Insuring Agreement E covers losses in loan or purchase transactions involving certain forged, altered or counterfeit documents. "Instruction to a Federal Reserve Bank" and "Statement of Uncertificated Security of any Federal Reserve Bank" have been removed from the list of items in the Form 14. Unlike the other enumerated items, these items do not represent ownership or convey an interest in something of value. The Statement is only the issuer's representation of any interests in an uncertificated security at a single point in time. Further, the definition of Statement does not specify that it must come directly from the issuer of the security. Relying on a Statement that did not come directly from the issuer appears to be a bad business practice. The same change was made in the 2004 edition of Form No. 24.

With respect to both the Form 14 and Form 15, the forgery or alteration must have caused the loss. Although reliance on a Written Original implies a requirement of possession of the instrument, the provision sets forth the requirement explicitly.

Both Insuring Agreements D and E require a handwritten signature or a reproduction of a handwritten signature, and explicitly state that an electronic or digital signature is not treated as a handwritten signature.

II. General Agreements

General Agreement A General Agreement A of the Form 14 (Nominees) was revised to incorporate the Holding Company Rider (SR5955) and reworded for clarification. The Form 15 did not have a Nominees General Agreement. Therefore, no similar revision was needed.

General Agreement C General Agreement C of the Form 14 and General Agreement B of the Form 15 were revised as a "Change of Ownership" provision rather than "Change of Control." The revised General Agreement establishes a bright line of a change of ownership. If there is a change by a single owner or group of owners of 10% of the ownership interest of the Insured or its parent, that will trigger the insured's notice requirements. The General Agreement also was modified to include other organizational forms recognizing that Form 14 and Form 15 Insureds may not necessarily be corporations.

As a related change, the Termination Condition has been revised to include a provision that the policy terminates upon a "Change in Control." This is a defined term which also sets a bright line of a change in ownership of over 50% of the ownership interest of the Insured or its parent. The revision incorporates the meaning of "taking over" as set forth in *American Casualty Company of Reading, Pennsylvania v. Etowah Bank*, 288 F.3d 1282 (11th Cir 2002).

General Agreement G A new General Agreement G of the Form 14 and General Agreement F of the Form 15 add coverage for the ERISA bonding obligations of the Insured's directors and employees acting as fiduciaries or handling money of the Insured's own ERISA plans. The policy's deductible becomes effective only after losses exceed the statutory minimum bond limit required by ERISA. The General Agreement will eliminate the need for an ERISA Rider under those circumstances, but it does not meet the ERISA bonding requirement when the Insured or its employees are handling funds of other employers' plans.

III. Definitions

The definitions of "acceptance," "instruction," "statement of uncertificated security," and "uncertificated security" are deleted because the terms are no longer used in Form 14. ("Instruction" is a term still used in the Form 14, but as an undefined term.) Similarly, the definition of "acceptance" has been deleted from the Form 15.

"Written" is inserted into a number of definitions to assure that coverage under the basic Form 14 and Form 15 is not provided for electronic transactions.

In addition, the following definitions have significant changes;

The definition of Counterfeit now "codifies" the case law requirement that there be an actual, valid original that the counterfeit document is imitating.

The definition for Electronic Data Processor has been added to the Form 14 to pertain explicitly only to a data processor of checks. The term is not used in the Form 15 because mortgage brokers and small loan companies are not involved in check processing.

The definition of Employee is re-written to minimize the use of "employee" in the definition of "Employee." It also borrows language from the mercantile coverages to "codify" the case law requirement that an Employee be under the Insured's direction and control. The definition also incorporates the current exception in the exclusion for acts of directors, which effectively allows coverage for directors while performing duties normally performed by employees, and it clarifies that coverage for employees of institutions acquired by the Insured through merger or consolidation is limited to losses they caused the acquired institution and which were unknown at the time of the merger. A person provided by an employment contractor was incorporated into subsection (1) of the definition.

The definition of Forgery is re-written to limit forgeries to handwritten signatures or reproductions of handwritten signatures (such as facsimile signatures or printed signatures). Electronic or digital signatures are explicitly not forgeries. In addition, the definition specifically states that a forgery includes affixing the name of an organization as an endorsement to a check without authority and with intent to deceive.

Loan is now defined in the Form 14 because loan losses have been added to Insuring Agreement (A).

Member is defined in the Form 14 to reflect that the Insured may be a limited liability company.

A new definition of Messenger is added. A Messenger must be an Employee or a custodian in the event of an emergency arising out of the incapacity of the Employee.

A new definition of Original is added.

The enumerated items of Property are more clearly specified. "Books of account . . , on tangible media," has replaced "books of account . . . recorded electronically." The revision clarifies that the books of account must be stored on a disc or tape or other tangible device. The revision is also consistent with how electronic records are described in Insuring Agreement (C).

A new definition of Written is added.

IV. Exclusions

Substantive changes were made in the following Exclusions:

Form 14 Exclusion (c) and Form 15 Exclusion (d) -- Chemical and biological contamination is added to the nuclear exclusion, and the exception for the industrial use of nuclear energy is deleted.

Form 14 Exclusion (d) and Form 15 Exclusion (e) -- The exception was removed from the directors exclusion because it was incorporated into the definition of Employee.

Form 14 Exclusion (h) and Form 15 Exclusion (h) -- If an Employee of the Insured intentionally loses or destroys property, the loss should be covered, if it is covered at all, under Insuring Agreement (A). The exception for Insuring Agreements (B) and (C) losses in the Employee Exclusion, therefore, inserts "unintentional" before "acts of the Employee."

Form 14 Exclusion (m) and Form 15 Exclusion (m) -- The exclusion has been revised to explicitly exclude losses resulting from kidnap, ransom or extortion unless a dishonest employee is involved. Coverage for such losses is available under a Kidnap Ransom policy.

Form 14 Exclusion (r) and Form 15 Exclusion (g) -- Loss of property while on the premises of a Transportation Company or Messenger (i.e. while no longer in transit) is excluded, but an exception is provided for if the loss is caused by the dishonesty of the Insured's Employee.

Form 14 Exclusion (t) and Form 15 Exclusion (l) -- The bond is not a liability policy, and indemnity is owed the Insured only if and when the Insured itself has suffered a covered loss. Several provisions of the bond are re-written to remove any suggestion that the legal liability of the Insured has any effect on the obligations of the Underwriter. The fact that damages are awarded against the Insured, however, should not remove coverage which would have existed independently of those damages. The damages exclusion is re-written to remove the exception for compensatory damages but to allow recovery for an otherwise covered loss which would exist independently of the damage award.

Form 14 Exclusion (v) and Form 15 Exclusion (n) -- The consequential damage exclusion gives as examples fines, multiple or punitive damages or the Insured's liability to others.

Form 14 Exclusion (w) and Form 15 Exclusion (w) -- Because non-bank Insureds sometimes perform bank-like functions, the exclusion for accepting a check payable to a corporation for deposit into the account of an individual was imported from Form 24.

Form 14 Exclusion (bb) and Form 15 Exclusion (y) -- Losses related to the theft, disappearance and destruction of confidential information are excluded. This is an exclusion that is common on company forms.

Form 14 Exclusion (cc) and Form 15 Exclusion (v) -- Fidelity bonds do not cover loss caused by an Employee that the Insured knows is dishonest. The termination provision automatically terminates coverage for such an Employee. However, a court misinterpreted the termination provisions and held that termination could be caused only by knowledge obtained after commencement of the policy. This exclusion reiterates that coverage is never provided for loss caused by the act of an Employee known to be dishonest at the time of the act. Condition 13 is also revised accordingly.

Form 15 did not have an exclusion for loss of tangible property not specifically enumerated that is typically covered by property insurance policies. The other Financial Institution Bond forms have such an exclusion. Exclusion (x) was added to the Form 15.

V. Conditions

The Condition for losses discovered too late to claim under a prior loss sustained policy (Condition 8) is deleted because coverage for Form 14 and Form 15 Insureds has been written on a discovery basis for many years. This condition contemplates coverage written on a loss sustained basis with a discovery period following the policy period. Such coverage is no longer written for Form 14 and Form 15 Insureds. Revisions to the other policy conditions are:

Section 4 (Form 14 and Form 15) The current bond forms do not allow reinstatement of the aggregate limit by recoveries. Section 4 is changed to allow reinstatement from net recoveries if the aggregate limit has not been exhausted and the recoveries are received prior to the termination of the bond. It also adds a clarification that a loss settled with a lost instrument bond does not reduce the aggregate limit until a payment is made under the lost instrument bond.

Section 6 (Form 14 and Form 15) A loss under the bond should be measured by the net detriment to the Insured. Any interest, fees, payments, recoveries or credits the Insured receives in the fraudulent transaction should reduce the amount claimed. In addition, the Valuation Condition is amended to state that such recoveries or receipts from interest or fees on a loan involved in the loss are a credit reducing the loss.

Section 7 (Form 14 and Form 15) The Assignment – Subrogation – Recovery – Cooperation Condition has been divided into two Conditions to clarify that the duty to cooperate is not limited to recovery of losses. Subsection (d) of the Condition is moved to a new Cooperation Condition 8.

Section 9 (Form 14 and Form 15) The mistaken decision in *Omnisource Corp. v. CNA Transcontinental Ins. Co.*, 949 F. Supp. 681 (N.D. Ind. 1996) led a number of Insureds to believe erroneously that coverage can be claimed based on forgery to a document not covered by the bond if the forged document is "bundled" with a covered document. A new Condition 9 is added to correct this misconception.

Section 11 (Form 14 and Form 15) The inclusion of property "for which the Insured is legally liable" in the Ownership Condition has led to claims that the legal liability of the Insured is covered.

This condition is amended to "codify" cases, such as *Lynch Properties Inc. v. Potomac Ins. Co.* 140 F3d 622 (5th Cir. 1998), which correctly hold that the Insured must be responsible for the property prior to the events giving rise to the loss. In addition, the condition is renamed, "Covered Property."

Section 12 (Form 14 and Form 15) The Insured's obligation to notify the Underwriter of losses within the deductible is reduced to instances of employee dishonesty and losses in excess of an agreed-upon amount.

Improvement Revisions (Form 14, Form 15, Form 24 and Form 25)

As noted above, some of the revisions in all four forms seek to improve the organization of the forms and make the forms' terms more consistent where possible. Each section of the forms is addressed in turn.

I. Declarations

Only the Form 24 had a provision that addressed the cancellation of prior bonds. Such a provision is particularly useful when an entity mergers with or takes over another entity and new bonds are issued. A bright line is established as to when coverage under the old bond ends and when coverage under the replacement bond begins. Therefore, all forms now contain an item addressing cancellation of prior bonds.

In addition, the scope of Property covered under Insuring Agreement B has been made consistent. The forms follow the coverage in the Form 24 Insuring Agreement (B) that covers Property lodged or deposited "anywhere". However, insurers should have the opportunity to underwrite the locations and exclude certain office and premises. Therefore, Insuring Agreement (B) will be amended accordingly. The Declaration are amended to include an Item that permits the insurer to name certain offices and premises that are not covered.

II. Insuring Agreements

Insuring Agreement (A) - Insuring Agreement (A) of the Form 25 contains the phrase "that portion of the loss involving any Loan transaction." The Form 24 and the other forms, as revised, refer only to "involving any Loan." The word "transaction" appears to be surplusage and therefore was deleted from the Form 25 Insuring Agreement(A),

Insuring Agreement (B) - As noted above, Insuring Agreement (B) has been revised so that the covered Property may be lodged or deposited in premises and offices located anywhere, unless the Insured and Underwriter agree to exclude particular premises or offices.

Insuring Agreement (D) and (E) (enumerated items) - The enumerated types of documents in Insuring Agreements (D) and (E) vary from bond to bond based on the business of the Insureds.

a. Insuring Agreement (E) for Forms 14 and 15 did not have Certificates of Deposit in the enumerated items. For consistency, Certificate Of Deposit was added to the list of enumerated items.
b. Among the enumerated items in Insuring Agreement (D) is Negotiable Instruments. Forms 14 and 24 carve out Evidence of Debt. Forms 15 and 25 have no such exception. For the sake of consistency, the exception as to an Evidence of Debt is added to Forms 15 and 25 because loss involving a forged Evidence of Debt would be covered under Insuring Agreement (E).

c. Insuring Agreement (D) in the Form 14 and the 1986 edition of the Form 24 included as an enumerated item an instruction "directed to the Insured." This phrase was dropped in the 2004 edition of the Form 24. After reconsideration, the phrase has been added back to the Form 24. Good banking practice dictates that Property is transferred on the faith of an instruction only if it is directed to the Insured.
d. A major principle regarding the revisions of. Insuring Agreements (D) and (E) was to avoid an overlap of coverage by having Insuring Agreement (E) focus on credit transactions and Insuring Agreement (D) focus on a payment or transfer on the faith of a forged or altered instrument. Currently, a policy loan is an enumerated item in Insuring Agreement (D) of Form 25. Recognizing that a policy loan is a credit transaction, this item has been moved to Insuring Agreement (E).

Insuring Agreement (E) - Insuring Agreement (E) of Forms 14, 15 and 25 have been revised to track the requirement in Form 25 that the forged signature must be "material to the validity or enforceability of the security."

Insuring Agreement (E)(2) in Form 24, Form 25 and Form 14 relates to signature guarantees. "Guarantee" is an enumerated item and a defined term. The definition refers to a debt owed to the Insured. It would seem unlikely that the Insured would guarantee the signature on an obligation owed to the Insured. A broader meaning is intended. Therefore, the term has been revised to remove the limit of debts owed to the insured.

III. General Agreements

General Agreement A (Form 15) and General Agreement (B) (Form 14) - In the Additional Offices or Employees General Agreement, SFAA amended "employees" in the last paragraph to a lower case term so that it is not limited by the definition of "Employee". This revision is consistent with the Additional Offices or Employees General Agreement in Form 24 and Form 25.

General Agreement C (Form 15 and Farm 25) and General Agreement D (Form 14 and Form 24) - The Representation of Insured General Agreement has been revised. "Intentional" has been deleted from the Form 24 General Agreement and the Form 25 General Agreement to be consistent with the provisions in the other forms. The key factor (absent a contrary law) in determining whether an insurer may be able to rescind the bond is whether the fact that was concealed, misstated or omitted was material, whether or not the concealment or misstatement was intentional. The provision has been restructured in all forms so that the materiality requirement clearly applies to an omission, concealment and incorrect statement. In addition, considering that "misrepresentation" is part of the larger category of "incorrect statement", "misrepresentation" is redundant and has been deleted.

IV. Definition

Employee – All four forms include within the definition of Employee "a member of the Board of Directors of the insured, or a member of an equivalent body." Form 14, Form 24 and Form 25 included attorneys within the definition of Employee. Generally, attorneys are independent contractors. Sound underwriting practice requires that insurers have an opportunity to underwrite independent contractor before they are added as "Employees". Therefore, attorneys have been deleted from the definition in the Form 24 and Form 14. Attorneys can be added to the definition by rider, giving the insurer an opportunity to underwrite. The exception to this approach involves the Form 25. Insurance companies may have employee attorneys that defend third parties in liability actions. However, such employees are not subject to the direction and control of the insured because, as attorneys, they must exercise independent judgment on behalf of their clients. Thus they cannot fall within the first paragraph of the definition. Therefore, attorneys must be in the Form 25's definition of Employee.

Letter of Credit – The Form 15 did not include a definition of Letter of Credit. However, the term is used in the definition of Property. Therefore, the term is now defined in the Form 15. In the prior definition, a Letter of Credit could be issued by a bank or "other person." As a best practice, a Letter of Credit on which value is provided should be issued only by a bank. As to all four forms, the phrase, "or other person" has been deleted.

Security Agreement – This term was not defined in the Form 14. However, the term is used in the definition of Property. Therefore, the definition has been added to the Form 14.

V. Exclusions

Exclusion (a) – "Forgery" has been capitalized to indicate that the defined term is intended.

Exclusion (d) (Form 24, Form 25 and Form 14) and Exclusion (e) (Form 15) – The Directors exclusion has been revised to be consistent in all four forms. In addition, the revised language contemplates organizational forms in addition to a corporation.

Exclusion (e) (Form 25) – Because policy loans has been moved from the list of items in Insuring Agreement (D) to the list of items in Insuring Agreement (E), Insuring Agreement (D) has been stricken from the loan loss exclusion's exceptions.

Exclusion (q) (Form 24), Exclusion (j) (Form 25) and Exclusion (q) (Form 14) - The exclusion for loss of tangible unenumerated property starts 60 days after the Insured "becomes aware" it has the property in the Form 24 and after the Insured "takes possession" in the Form 14 and Form 25. This exclusion has been revised so that the phrase "becomes aware" is used in all three forms. Whether and when an insured "takes possession" of tangible property can be less clear than when an insured is aware it has the property. In addition, in the case of a very large insured, an insured may become aware it has the property well after it has come into possession of the property. Lastly, for the sake of consistency, this exclusion was added as Exclusion (x) in the Form 15.

VI. Conditions

The Condition for losses discovered too late to claim under a prior loss sustained policy has been deleted from the Form 24. (The Condition had already been deleted in the 2008 version of the Form 25.) As noted above in the discussion regarding the changes to the Form 14 and Form 15, this condition contemplates coverage written on a loss sustained basis with a discovery period following the policy period. Such coverage has not been written for Form 24 insureds for many years.

Valuation Condition - A set off condition has been added to Forms 24 and 15 so that all forms have it. In addition, the Books of Account provision has been updated to reflect how records are maintained in the current technological environment (i.e. no paper books).

Anti Bundling Condition –"Counterfeit" has been capitalized so that it refers to the defined term (just as "Forgery" refers to a defined term).

Assignment – Subrogation – Recovery Condition – A phrase has been added to the Condition in the Form 24, Form 14 and Form 15, which addresses the order of payment of recoveries. In particular, a provision has been added to make explicit that reimbursement for losses not covered under the bond are paid last out of recoveries. This provision is in the Form 25 and has been added for consistency.

Deductible Amount Condition – The condition in the Form 24 has been revised to track the language in the Form 25.

Insuring Agreement (A) Revisions

As explained in our filing of the Form 24 (2004 edition) and Form 25 (2008 edition), the description of the intent required for a covered act was revised from "manifest intent" to "active and conscious purpose." The change was made in light of the fact that some judicial decisions misinterpreted the meaning of "manifest intent". Thus, alternative phrasing was selected to convey what was always intended -- a conscious object to cause the result.

The revised forms have been available for use for several years. However, it is apparent that the market has not accepted the new language, even though "active and conscious purpose" has the same meaning as "manifest intent". SFAA has decided to reinstate the "manifest intent" formulation that has been accepted as the standard in the marketplace.

In addition to restoring the "manifest intent" language to the Form 24 and Form 25, the double coverage trigger of "manifest intent" to cause the Insured a loss and to obtain financial benefit has been restored. Likewise, because there is now a requirement to have intended to cause a loss and obtain a benefit, there is no longer a possibility of a claim for loss caused by intentional damage by an employee (e.g. sabotage). Thus, Exclusion (bb) has been deleted from the Form 24 and Exclusion (w) has been deleted from the Form 25.

Riders

As a result of the revisions, many provisions are in different locations or under new headings. As a result, SFAA needed to revise some riders to incorporate the new cross-references or terms. Other riders are withdrawn because their provisions were incorporated into the bond forms or the provisions are no longer needed. A list of the revised riders and the changes to each is attached. We have also enclosed a list of riders that have not been revised but can still be used with the revised Standard Forms, a list of riders that are withdrawn for use with the revised Standard Forms, and copies of prior editions of each Standard Form and each changed Rider with the changes shown by redlining.

We request that this filing of the 2011 editions of Standard Form Nos. 14, 15, 24 and 25 and related riders become effective on May 1, 2011. Please feel free to contact me at (202) 778-3630 if you have any questions. If you prefer e-mail, my e-mail address is rduke@surety.org. Your consideration is appreciated.

Exhibit 5

FINANCIAL INSTITUTION BOND, STANDARD FORM NO. 24

(Revised April 1, 2004)

FINANCIAL INSTITUTION BOND
Standard Form No. 24, Revised to April 1, 2004

Bond No.

(Herein called Underwriter)

DECLARATIONS

Item 1. Name of Insured (herein called Insured):

Principal Address:

Item 2. Bond Period: from 12:01 a.m. on   to 12:01 a.m. on
                            (MONTH, DAY, YEAR)   (MONTH, DAY, YEAR)

Item 3. The Aggregate Limit of Liability of the Underwriter during the Bond Period shall be
$

Item 4. Subject to Sections 4 and 13 hereof,
the Single Loss Limit of Liability applicable to each of Insuring Agreements (A), (B), (C) is $ and (F) is $ and the Single Loss Deductible applicable to each of Insuring Agreements (A), (B), (C) and (F) is $
If coverage is provided under the following Insuring Agreements or Coverages, the applicable Single Loss Limit of Liability and Single Loss Deductible shall be inserted below:

	Single Loss Limit of Liability	Single Loss Deductible
Insuring Agreement (D)—FORGERY OR ALTERATION	$	$
Insuring Agreement (E)—SECURITIES	$	$
Insuring Agreement (G) —FRAUDULENT MORTGAGES	$	$
Optional Insuring Agreements and Coverages:		
	$	$

If "Not Covered" is inserted above opposite any specified Insuring Agreement or Coverage, or if no amount is inserted, such Insuring Agreement or Coverage and any other reference thereto in this bond shall be deemed to be deleted therefrom.

Item 5. The liability of the Underwriter is subject to the terms of the following riders attached hereto. All of the terms and conditions of this bond apply to such riders except to the extent the rider explicitly provides otherwise.

Copyright, The Surety & Fidelity Association of America, 2004   TSB 5018e

Item 6.	The amount of anticipated loss which the Insured must report to the Underwriter pursuant to Section 13 is:
Item 7.	The Insured by the acceptance of this bond gives notice to the Underwriter terminating or canceling prior bond(s) or policy(ies) No.(s) Such termination or cancelation to be effective as of the time this bond becomes effective.

The Underwriter, in consideration of an agreed premium, and in reliance upon all statements made and information furnished to the Underwriter by the Insured in applying for this bond, and subject to the Declarations, Insuring Agreements, General Agreements, Conditions and Limitations and other terms hereof, agrees to indemnify the Insured for:

INSURING AGREEMENTS

FIDELITY

(A) Loss resulting directly from dishonest or fraudulent acts committed by an Employee, acting alone or in collusion with others, with the active and conscious purpose to cause the Insured to sustain such loss. However, if some or all of the Insured's loss results directly or indirectly from:
 (1) Loans, that portion of the loss is not covered unless the Employee also was in collusion with one or more parties to the Loan transactions and has received, in connection therewith, an improper financial benefit with a value of at least $2500; or
 (2) trading, that portion of the loss is not covered unless the Employee also has received, in connection therewith, an improper financial benefit.
As used in this Insuring Agreement, an improper financial benefit does not include any employee benefits received in the course of employment, including: salaries, commissions, fees, bonuses, promotions, awards, profit sharing or pensions.
As used in this Insuring Agreement, loss does not include any employee benefits, including: salaries, commissions, fees, bonuses, promotions, awards, profit sharing or pensions, intentionally paid by the Insured.

ON PREMISES

(B) (1) Loss of items enumerated in the definition of Property resulting directly from:
  (a) robbery, burglary, misplacement, mysterious unexplainable disappearance and damage thereto or destruction thereof, or
  (b) theft, false pretenses, common-law or statutory larceny, committed by a person physically present in an office or on the premises of the Insured at the time the enumerated items of Property are surrendered.
 while such enumerated items of Property are lodged or deposited within offices or premises located anywhere.
 (2) Loss of or damage to furnishings, fixtures, supplies or equipment within an office of the Insured covered under this bond resulting directly from larceny or theft in, or burglary or robbery of, such office, or attempt thereat, provided that:
  (a) the Insured is the owner of such furnishings, fixtures, supplies, equipment, or office or is liable for such loss or damage, and
  (b) the loss is not caused by fire.

TSB 5018e   Copyright, The Surety & Fidelity Association of America, 2004

IN TRANSIT

(C) Loss of Property resulting directly from robbery, common-law or statutory larceny, theft, misplacement, mysterious unexplainable disappearance, and damage thereto or destruction thereof, while the Property is in transit anywhere in the custody of
  (1) a Messenger, or
  (2) a Transportation Company and being transported in an armored motor vehicle, or
  (3) a Transportation Company and being physically (not electronically) transported in other than an armored motor vehicle, provided that covered Property transported in such manner is limited to the following:
    (a) Books of account and other records stored on tangible media, including magnetic tapes, disks and computer drives as well as paper, but not including any of the other items listed in the definition of Property, however stored, and
    (b) Certificated Securities issued in registered form and not endorsed, or with restrictive endorsements, and
    (c) Negotiable Instruments not payable to bearer, and either not endorsed or with restrictive endorsements.

Coverage under this Insuring Agreement begins immediately upon the receipt of such Property by the Messenger or Transportation Company and ends immediately upon delivery to the designated recipient or its agent, but only while the Property is being conveyed.

FORGERY OR ALTERATION

(D) Loss resulting directly from the Insured having, in good faith, paid or transferred any Property in reliance on any Written, Original
  (1) Negotiable Instrument (except an Evidence of Debt),
  (2) Certificate of Deposit,
  (3) Letter of Credit,
  (4) Withdrawal Order,
  (5) receipt for the withdrawal of Property, or
  (6) instruction or advice purportedly signed by a customer of the Insured or by a banking institution

which (a) bears a handwritten signature of any maker, drawer or endorser which is a Forgery; or (b) is altered, but only to the extent the Forgery or alteration causes the loss.

Actual physical possession of the items listed in (1) through (6) above by the Insured is a condition precedent to the Insured's having relied on the items.

A reproduction of a handwritten signature is treated the same as the handwritten signature. An electronic or digital signature is not treated as a reproduction of a handwritten signature.

SECURITIES

(E) Loss resulting directly from the Insured having, in good faith, for its own account or for the account of others,
  (1) acquired, sold or delivered or given value, extended credit or assumed liability, on the faith of, any Written, Original
    (a) Certificated Security,
    (b) Document of Title,
    (c) Deed, mortgage or other instrument conveying title to, or creating or discharging a lien upon, real property,
    (d) Certificate of Origin or Title,
    (e) Certificate of Deposit
    (f) Evidence of Debt,

(g) Corporate, partnership or personal Guarantee, or
(h) Security Agreement,
which (i) bears a handwritten signature of any maker, drawer, issuer, endorser, assignor, lessee, transfer agent, registrar, acceptor, surety, guarantor, or of any other person whose signature is material to the validity or enforceability of the security, which is a Forgery, or (ii) is altered, or (iii) is lost or stolen;
(2) guaranteed in writing or witnessed any signature upon any transfer, assignment, bill of sale, power of attorney, Guarantee, endorsement or any items listed in (a) through (h) above; or
(3) acquired, sold or delivered, or given value, extended credit or assumed liability, on the faith of any item listed in (a) through (e) above which is a Counterfeit.

Actual physical possession of the items listed in (a) through (h) above by the Insured, its correspondent bank or other authorized representative, is a condition precedent to the Insured's having relied on the faith of such items.

A reproduction of a handwritten signature is treated the same as the handwritten signature. An electronic or digital signature is not treated as a reproduction of a handwritten signature.

COUNTERFEIT CURRENCY

(F) Loss resulting directly from the receipt by the Insured, in good faith, of any Counterfeit Money of the United States of America, Canada or of any other country in which the Insured maintains a branch office.

FRAUDULENT MORTGAGES

(G) Loss resulting directly from the Insured's having, in good faith and in the normal course of business in connection with any Loan, accepted or received or acted upon the faith of any Written, Original
(1) real property mortgages, real property deeds of trust or like instruments pertaining to realty, or
(2) assignments of such mortgages, deeds of trust or instruments
which prove to have been defective by reason of the signature thereon of any person having been obtained through trick, artifice, fraud or false pretenses or the signature on the recorded deed conveying such real property to the mortgagor or grantor of such mortgage or deed of trust having been obtained by or on behalf of such mortgagor or grantor through trick, artifice, fraud or false pretenses.

GENERAL AGREEMENTS

NOMINEES

A. This bond does not indemnify any Insured for loss sustained by a proprietorship, partnership or corporation which is owned, controlled or operated by an Insured and not named as an Insured hereunder unless:
(1) such loss is sustained by a nominee organized by an Insured for the purpose of handling certain of its business transactions and composed exclusively of its Employees; and
(2) such Insured is not a holding company.

If the conditions of (1) and (2) are met, loss sustained by the nominee shall, for all the purposes of this bond and whether or not any partner of such nominee is implicated in such loss, be deemed to be loss sustained by the Insured.

ADDITIONAL OFFICES OR EMPLOYEES—CONSOLIDATION, MERGER OR PURCHASE OF ASSETS—NOTICE

B. If the Insured shall, while this bond is in force, establish any additional offices, other than by consolidation or merger with, or purchase or acquisition of assets or liabilities of, another institution, such offices shall be automatically covered hereunder from the date of such establishment without the requirement of notice to the Underwriter or the payment of additional premium for the remainder of the premium period.

If the Insured shall, while this bond is in force, consolidate or merge with, or purchase or acquire assets or liabilities of, another institution, the Insured shall not have such coverage as is afforded under this bond for loss which:
   (1) has occurred or will occur in offices or premises, or
   (2) has been caused or will be caused by an employee or employees of such institution, or
   (3) has arisen or will arise out of the assets or liabilities

acquired by the insured as a result of such consolidation, merger or purchase or acquisition of assets or liabilities unless the Insured shall (i) give the Underwriter Written notice of the proposed consolidation, merger or purchase or acquisition of assets or liabilities prior to the proposed effective date of such action, and (ii) obtain the Written consent of the Underwriter to extend the coverage provided by this bond to such additional offices or premises, employees and other exposures, and (iii) upon obtaining such consent, pay to the Underwriter an additional premium.

CHANGE OF OWNERSHIP—NOTICE

C. When an Insured learns of a change in ownership by a single stockholder, or by a group of affiliated stockholders, of more than ten percent (10%) of its voting stock, or of the voting stock of a holding company or parent corporation which itself owns or controls the Insured, it shall give Written notice to the Underwriter, as soon as practicable but not later than within thirty (30) days. Failure to give the required notice shall result in termination of coverage, effective upon the date of the stock transfer, for any loss involving a transferee of such stock interest.

REPRESENTATION OF INSURED

D. The Insured represents that the information furnished in the application for this bond is complete, true and correct. Such application constitutes part of this bond.
Any intentional misrepresentation, omission, concealment or incorrect statement of a material fact, in the application or otherwise, shall be grounds for the rescission of this bond.

JOINT INSUREDS

E. Only the first named Insured can submit a claim under this bond, and shall act for all Insureds. Payment by the Underwriter to the first named Insured of loss sustained by any Insured shall fully release the Underwriter on account of such loss. If the first named Insured ceases to be covered under this bond, the Insured next named shall thereafter be considered as the first named Insured. Knowledge possessed or discovery made by any Insured shall constitute knowledge or discovery by all Insureds for all purposes of this bond. The liability of the Underwriter for loss or losses sustained by all Insureds shall not exceed the amount for which the Underwriter would have been liable had all such loss or losses been sustained by one Insured.

NOTICE OF LEGAL PROCEEDING AGAINST INSURED—ELECTION TO DEFEND

F. The Insured shall notify the Underwriter at the earliest practicable moment, not to exceed 30 days after notice thereof, of any legal proceeding brought to determine the Insured's liability for any loss, claim or damage, which, if established, would constitute a collectible loss under this bond. Concurrently, the Insured shall furnish copies of all pleadings and pertinent papers to the Underwriter.

The Underwriter, at its sole option, may elect to conduct the defense of such legal proceeding, in whole or in part. The defense by the Underwriter shall be in the Insured's name through attorneys selected by the Underwriter. The Insured shall provide all reasonable information and assistance required by the Underwriter for such defense.

If the Underwriter elects to defend the Insured, in whole or in part, any judgment against the Insured on those counts or causes of action which the Underwriter defended on behalf of the Insured or any settlement in which the Underwriter participates and all attorneys' fees, costs and expenses incurred by the Underwriter in the defense of the litigation shall be a loss covered by this bond.

If the Insured does not give the notices required in subsection (a) of Section 5. of this bond and in the first paragraph of this General Agreement, or if the Underwriter elects not to defend any causes of action, neither a judgment against the Insured, nor a settlement of any legal proceeding by the Insured, shall determine the existence, extent or amount of coverage under this bond for loss sustained by the Insured, and the Underwriter shall not be liable for any attorneys' fees, costs and expenses incurred by the Insured.

With respect to this General Agreement, subsections (b) and (d) of Section 5. of this bond apply upon the entry of such judgment or the occurrence of such settlement instead of upon discovery of loss. In addition, the Insured must notify the Underwriter within 30 days after such judgment is entered against it or after the Insured settles such legal proceeding, and, subject to subsection (e) of Section 5., the Insured may not bring legal proceedings for the recovery of such loss after the expiration of 24 months from the date of such final judgment or settlement.

INSURED'S ERISA PLANS

G. If any Employee of the Insured is required to provide a bond to a health, welfare or pension plan subject to the Employee Retirement Income Security Act of 1974 (ERISA) (hereinafter the Plan), the majority of whose beneficiaries are Employees or former Employees of the Insured, the Plan shall be deemed an Insured under this bond for the purposes of Insuring Agreement (A) only and subject, in addition to all other terms and conditions of the bond, to the following:

(1) The deductible required by Section 13 of the Conditions and Limitations of this bond shall be applicable to a loss suffered by the Plan only after the Plan has received from the Underwriter the lesser of $500,000 or ten percent (10%) of the assets of the Plan at the beginning of the fiscal year of the Plan in which the loss is discovered;

(2) Notwithstanding Section 3 of the Conditions and Limitations of this bond, loss suffered by the Plan is covered if discovered during the term of this bond or within one year thereafter, but if discovered during said one year period, the loss payable under this bond shall be reduced by the amount recoverable from any other bond or insurance protecting the assets of the plan against loss through fraud or dishonesty;

(3) If more that one plan subject to ERISA is an Insured pursuant to this General Agreement, the Insured shall purchase limits sufficient to provide the minimum amount of coverage required by ERISA for each Plan and shall distribute any payment made under this bond to said Plans so that each Plan receives the amount it would have received if insured separately for the minimum coverage which ERISA required it to have; and

(4) For purposes of this General Agreement only, a director of the Insured shall be deemed an Employee.

CONDITIONS AND LIMITATIONS

DEFINITIONS

Section 1. As used in this bond:
(a) Certificate of Deposit means a Written acknowledgment by a financial institution of receipt of Money with an engagement to repay it.
(b) Certificate of Origin or Title means a Written document issued by a manufacturer of personal property or a governmental agency evidencing the ownership of the personal property and by which ownership is transferred.
(c) Certificated Security means a share, participation or other interest in property of or an enterprise of the issuer or an obligation of the issuer, which is:
    (1) represented by a Written instrument issued in bearer or registered form;
    (2) of a type commonly dealt in on securities exchanges or markets or commonly recognized in any area in which it is issued or dealt in as a medium for investment; and
    (3) either one of a class or series or by its terms divisible into a class or series of shares, participations, interests or obligations.
(d) Change in Control means a change in ownership of more than fifty percent (50%) of the voting stock of the Insured, or of a parent corporation or holding company which controls the Insured.
(e) Counterfeit means a Written imitation of an actual, valid Original which is intended to deceive and to be taken as the Original.
(f) Document of Title means a Written bill of lading, dock warrant, dock receipt, warehouse receipt or order for the delivery of goods, and also any other Written document which in the regular course of business or financing is treated as adequately evidencing that the person in possession of it is entitled to receive, hold and dispose of the document and the goods it covers and must purport to be issued by or addressed to a bailee and purport to cover goods in the bailee's possession which are either identified or are fungible portions of an identified mass.
(g) Electronic Data Processor means a natural person, partnership or corporation with the Insured's Written authorization to perform services as data processor of checks presented to the Insured by a customer or another financial institution. A Federal Reserve Bank or clearinghouse shall not be an Electronic Data Processor.
(h) Employee means:
    (1) a natural person while in the service of the Insured whom the Insured has the right to direct and control in the performance of his or her duties and
        (i) whom the Insured directly compensates by wages, salaries or commissions, or
        (ii) who is compensated by an employment agency which is paid by the Insured for providing the person's services for work at or in the Insured's offices or premises covered hereunder;
    (2) an attorney retained by the Insured, and an employee of such attorney, while performing legal services for the Insured;
    (3) a director of the Insured when performing acts coming within the scope of the usual duties of an employee, or while acting as a member of any committee duly elected or appointed by resolution of the board of directors of the Insured to perform specific, as distinguished from general, directorial acts on behalf of the Insured;
    (4) an employee of an institution merged or consolidated with the Insured prior to the effective date of this bond, but only as to acts while an employee of such institution which caused said institution to sustain a loss which was not known to the Insured or to the institution at the time of the merger or consolidation; and
    (5) an Electronic Data Processor, provided, however, that each such Electronic Data Processor, and the partners, officers and employees of such Electronic Data Processor

shall, collectively, be deemed to be one Employee for all the purposes of this bond, excepting, however, the Employee termination provisions of Section 14.

(i) Evidence of Debt means a Written instrument, including a Negotiable Instrument, executed, or purportedly executed, by a customer of the Insured and held by the Insured which in the regular course of business is treated as evidencing the customer's debt to the Insured.

(j) Forgery means:

(1) affixing the handwritten signature, or a reproduction of the handwritten signature, of another natural person without authorization and with intent to deceive; or

(2) affixing the name of an organization as an endorsement to a check without authority and with the intent to deceive.

Provided, however, that a signature which consists in whole or in part of one's own name signed with or without authority, in any capacity, for any purpose is not a Forgery. An electronic or digital signature is not a reproduction of a handwritten signature or the name of an organization.

(k) Guarantee means a Written undertaking obligating the signer to pay the debt of another, to the Insured or its assignee or to a financial institution from which the Insured has purchased participation in the debt, if the debt is not paid in accordance with its terms.

(l) Letter of Credit means a Written engagement by a bank or other person, made at the request of a customer, that the bank or other person will honor drafts or other demands for payment upon compliance with the conditions specified in the Letter of Credit.

(m) Loan means all extensions of credit by the Insured and all transactions creating a creditor relationship in favor of the Insured and all transactions by which the Insured assumes an existing creditor relationship.

(n) Messenger means an Employee while in possession of the Insured's Property away from the Insured's premises and any other natural person acting as custodian of the Property during an emergency arising from the incapacity of the original Employee.

(o) Money means a medium of exchange in current use authorized or adopted by a domestic or foreign government as a part of its currency.

(p) Negotiable Instrument means any writing:

(1) signed by the maker or drawer; and

(2) containing any unconditional promise or order to pay a sum certain in Money and no other promise, order, obligation or power given by the maker or drawer; and

(3) is payable on demand or at a definite time; and

(4) is payable to order or bearer.

(q) Original means the first rendering or archetype and does not include photocopies or electronic transmissions even if received and printed.

(r) Property means Money, Certificated Securities, Negotiable Instruments, Certificates of Deposit, Documents of Title, Evidences of Debt, Security Agreements, Withdrawal Orders, Certificates of Origin or Title, Letters of Credit, insurance policies, abstracts of title, deeds and mortgages on real estate, revenue and other stamps, tokens, unsold state lottery tickets, books of account and other records stored on tangible media, gems, jewelry, precious metals in bars or ingots, (which are collectively the enumerated items of Property), and tangible items of personal property which are not hereinbefore enumerated.

(s) Security Agreement means a Written agreement which creates an interest in personal property or fixtures and which secures payment or performance of an obligation.

(t) Transportation Company means any organization which regularly provides its own or leased vehicles for transportation of its customers' property or which provides freight forwarding or air express services.

(u) Withdrawal Order means a Written, non-negotiable instrument, signed by a customer of the Insured authorizing the Insured to debit the customer's account in the amount of funds stated therein.

(v) Written means expressed through letters or marks placed upon paper and visible to the eye.

APPENDIX—BOND FORMS 779

EXCLUSIONS

Section 2. This bond does not cover:
   (a)   loss resulting directly or indirectly from forgery or alteration, except when covered under Insuring Agreements (A), (D), or (E);
   (b)   loss due to riot or civil commotion outside the United States of America and Canada; or loss due to military, naval or usurped power, war or insurrection unless such loss occurs in transit in the circumstances recited in Insuring Agreement (C), and unless, when such transit was initiated, there was no knowledge of such riot, civil commotion, military, naval or usurped power, war or insurrection on the part of any person acting for the Insured in initiating such transit;
   (c)   loss resulting directly or indirectly from the effects of nuclear fission or fusion, radioactivity, or chemical or biological contamination;
   (d)   loss resulting directly or indirectly from any acts of any director of the Insured, except when covered under Insuring Agreement (A);
   (e)   loss resulting directly or indirectly from the complete or partial nonpayment of, or default upon, any Loan or transaction involving the Insured as a lender or borrower, or extension of credit, including the purchase, discounting or other acquisition of false or genuine accounts, invoices, notes, agreements or Evidences of Debt, whether such Loan, transaction or extension was procured in good faith or through trick, artifice, fraud or false pretenses, except when covered under Insuring Agreements (A), (E) or (G);
   (f)   loss of Property contained in customers' safe deposit boxes, except when covered under Insuring Agreement (A);
   (g)   loss through cashing or paying forged or altered travelers' checks, or travelers' checks bearing forged endorsements, except when covered under Insuring Agreement (A); or loss of unsold travelers' checks or unsold money orders in the custody of the Insured with authority to sell, unless (a) the Insured, by Written contract, has agreed to indemnify the drawer of the travelers checks or money orders for such loss and (b) such checks or money orders are later paid or honored by said drawer;
   (h)   loss caused by an Employee, except when covered under Insuring Agreement (A), or when covered under Insuring Agreements (B) or (C) and resulting directly from unintentional acts of the Employee causing mysterious unexplainable disappearance, misplacement, destruction of or damage to Property;
   (i)   loss resulting directly or indirectly from trading, with or without the knowledge of the Insured, whether or not represented by any indebtedness or balance shown to be due the Insured on any customer's account, actual or fictitious, and notwithstanding any act or omission on the part of any Employee in connection with any account relating to such trading, indebtedness, or balance, except when covered under Insuring Agreements (A), (D) or (E);
   (j)   shortage in any teller's cash due to error;
   (k)   loss resulting directly or indirectly from the use, or purported use, of credit, debit, charge, access, convenience or other cards
      (1)   in obtaining credit or funds, or
      (2)   in gaining access to automated mechanical devices which, on behalf of the Insured, disburse Money, accept deposits, cash checks, drafts or similar Written instruments or make credit card loans, or
      (3)   in gaining access to point of sale terminals, customer-bank communication terminals, or similar electronic terminals of electronic funds transfer systems,
whether such cards were issued, or purport to have been issued, by the Insured or by anyone other than the Insured, except when covered under Insuring Agreement (A);
   (l)   loss involving automated mechanical devices which, on behalf of the Insured, disburse Money, accept deposits, cash checks, drafts or similar Written instruments or make credit card loans, unless such automated mechanical devices are situated within an office of the Insured which is permanently staffed by an Employee whose duties are those usually assigned to a

bank teller, even though public access is from outside the confines of such office, but in no event shall the Underwriter be liable for loss (including loss of Property)
    (1) as a result of damage to such automated mechanical devices perpetrated from outside such office, or
    (2) as a result of failure of such automated mechanical devices to function properly, or
    (3) through misplacement or mysterious unexplainable disappearance while such Property is located within any such automated mechanical devices, except when covered under Insuring Agreement (A);

(m) loss resulting directly or indirectly from surrender of property away from an office of the insured as a result of
    (1) kidnaping,
    (2) payment of ransom,
    (3) threats of bodily harm to any person, except the custodian of the property, or of damage to the premises or property of the Insured, or
    (4) actual disappearance, damage, destruction, confiscation or theft of property intended as a ransom or extortion payment while held or conveyed by a person duly authorized by the Insured to have custody of such property,

except when covered under Insuring Agreement (A);

(n) loss resulting directly or indirectly from payments made or withdrawals from a depositor's account involving erroneous credits to such account, except when covered under Insuring Agreement (A);

(o) loss resulting directly or indirectly from payments made or withdrawals from a depositor's account involving items of deposit which are not finally paid, for any reason, including but not limited to Forgery or any other fraud, except when covered under Insuring Agreement (A);

(p) loss resulting directly or indirectly from counterfeiting, except when covered under Insuring Agreements (A), (D), (E) or (F);

(q) loss of any tangible item of personal property which is not specifically enumerated in the paragraph defining Property if such property is insured by other insurance of any kind and in any amount obtained by the Insured, and in any event, loss of such property occurring more than 60 days after the Insured shall have become aware that it owns, holds or is responsible for such property, except when covered under Insuring Agreements (A) or (B)(2);

(r) loss of Property while
    (1) in the mail, or
    (2) in the custody of any Transportation Company, unless covered under Insuring Agreement (C), or
    (3) while located on the premises of any Messenger or Transportation Company
except when covered under Insuring Agreement (A);

(s) potential income, including but not limited to interest and dividends, not realized by the Insured;

(t) damages of any type for which the Insured is legally liable, unless the Insured establishes that the act or acts which gave rise to the damages involved conduct which would have caused a covered loss to the Insured in a similar amount in the absence of such damages;

(u) all fees, costs and expenses incurred by the Insured
    (1) in establishing the existence of or amount of loss covered under this bond, or
    (2) as a party to any legal proceeding whether or not such legal proceeding exposes the Insured to loss covered by this bond;

(v) indirect or consequential loss of any nature including, but not limited to, fines, penalties, multiple or punitive damages;

(w) loss resulting from any violation by the Insured or by any Employee
    (1) of law regulating (i) the issuance, purchase or sale of securities, (ii) securities transactions upon any security exchange or over the counter market, (iii) investment companies, or (iv) investment advisers, or

(2) of any rule or regulation made pursuant to any such law,
unless it is established by the Insured that the act or acts which caused the said loss involved fraudulent or dishonest conduct which would have caused a loss to the Insured in a similar amount in the absence of such laws, rules or regulations;

(x) loss resulting directly or indirectly from the failure of a financial or depository institution, or its receiver or liquidator, to pay or deliver, on demand of the Insured, funds or Property of the Insured held by it in any capacity, except when covered under Insuring Agreements (A) or (B)(1)(a);

(y) loss resulting directly or indirectly from accepting checks payable to an organization for deposit into an account of a natural person;

(z) damages resulting from any civil, criminal or other legal proceeding in which the Insured is alleged to have engaged in racketeering activity except when the Insured establishes that the act or acts giving rise to such damages were committed by an Employee under circumstances which result directly in a loss to the Insured covered by Insuring Agreement (A). For the purposes of this exclusion, "racketeering activity" is defined in 18 United States Code 1961 et seq., as amended.

(aa) loss resulting directly or indirectly from the theft, disappearance or destruction of confidential information including, but not limited to, trade secrets, customer lists, and intellectual property.

(bb) loss resulting directly or indirectly from the intentional damage or destruction of property by an Employee.

DISCOVERY

Section 3. This bond applies to loss first discovered by the Insured during the Bond Period. Discovery occurs when the Insured first becomes aware of facts which would cause a reasonable person to assume that a loss of a type covered by this bond has been or will be incurred, regardless of when the act or acts causing or contributing to such loss occurred, even though the exact amount or details of the loss may not then be known. Discovery also occurs when the Insured receives notice of an actual or potential claim in which it is alleged that the Insured is liable to a third party under circumstances which, if true, would constitute a loss under this bond.

LIMIT OF LIABILITY

Section 4.

Aggregate Limit of Liability

The Underwriter's total liability for all losses discovered during the Bond Period shown in Item 2. of the Declarations shall not exceed the Aggregate Limit of Liability shown in Item 3. of the Declarations. The Aggregate Limit of Liability shall be reduced by the amount of any payment made under the terms of this bond.

Upon exhaustion of the Aggregate Limit of Liability by such payments:

(a) The Underwriter shall have no further liability for loss or losses regardless of when discovered and whether or not previously reported to the Underwriter; and

(b) The Underwriter shall have no obligation under General Agreement F to continue the defense of the Insured, and upon notice by the Underwriter to the Insured that the Aggregate Limit of Liability has been exhausted, the Insured shall assume all responsibility for its defense at its own cost.

The Aggregate Limit of Liability shall be reinstated by any net recovery received by the Underwriter during the Bond Period and before the Aggregate Limit of Liability is exhausted.

Recovery from reinsurance and/or indemnity of the Underwriter shall not be deemed a recovery as used herein. In the event that a loss of Property is settled by the Underwriter through the use of a lost instrument bond, such loss shall not reduce the Aggregate Limit of Liability, but any payment under the lost instrument bond shall reduce the Aggregate Limit of Liability under this Bond.

Single Loss Limit of Liability

Subject to the Aggregate Limit of Liability, the Underwriter's liability for each Single Loss shall not exceed the applicable Single Loss Limit of Liability shown in Item 4. of the Declarations. If a Single Loss is covered under more than one Insuring Agreement or Coverage, the maximum payable shall not exceed the largest applicable Single Loss Limit of Liability.

Single Loss Defined

Single Loss means all covered loss, including court costs and attorneys' fees incurred by the Underwriter under General Agreement F, resulting from
(a) any one act or series of related acts of burglary, robbery or attempt thereat, in which no Employee is implicated, or
(b) any one act or series of related unintentional or negligent acts or omissions on the part of any person (whether an Employee or not) resulting in damage to or destruction or misplacement of Property, or
(c) all acts or omissions other than those specified in (a) and (b) preceding, caused by any person (whether an Employee or not) or in which such person is implicated, or
(d) any one casualty or event not specified in (a), (b) or (c) preceding.

NOTICE/PROOF—LEGAL PROCEEDINGS AGAINST UNDERWRITER

Section 5.
(a) At the earliest practicable moment, not to exceed 30 days, after discovery of loss, the Insured shall give the Underwriter notice thereof.
(b) Within 6 months after such discovery, the Insured shall furnish to the Underwriter proof of loss, duly sworn to, with full particulars.
(c) Lost Certificated Securities listed in a proof of loss shall be identified by certificate or bond numbers if such securities were issued therewith.
(d) Legal proceedings for the recovery of any loss hereunder shall not be brought prior to the expiration of 60 days after the original proof of loss is filed with the Underwriter or after the expiration of 24 months from the discovery of such loss.
(e) If any limitation period embodied in this bond is prohibited by any law controlling the construction hereof, such limitation period shall be deemed to be amended so as to equal the minimum limitation period allowed by such law.
(f) This bond affords coverage only in favor of the Insured. No suit, action or legal proceedings shall be brought hereunder by any one other than the first named Insured.

VALUATION

Section 6.
The value of any loss for purposes of coverage under this bond shall be the net loss to the Insured after crediting any receipts, payments or recoveries, however denominated, received by the Insured in connection with the transaction giving rise to the loss. If the loss involves a

Loan, any interest or fees received by the Insured in connection with the Loan shall be such a credit.

Money

Any loss of Money, or loss payable in Money, shall be paid, at the option of the Insured, in the Money of the country in which the loss was sustained or in the United States of America dollar equivalent thereof determined at the rate of exchange at the time of payment of such loss.

Securities

The Underwriter shall settle in kind its liability under this bond on account of a loss of any securities or, at the option of the Insured, shall pay to the Insured the cost of replacing such securities, determined by the market value thereof at the time of such settlement. In case of a loss of subscription, conversion or redemption privileges through the misplacement or loss of securities, the amount of such loss shall be the value of such privileges immediately preceding the expiration thereof. If such securities cannot be replaced or have no quoted market value, or if such privileges have no quoted market value, their value shall be determined by agreement or arbitration.

If the applicable coverage of this bond is subject to a Deductible Amount and/or is not sufficient in amount to indemnify the Insured in full for the loss of securities for which claim is made hereunder, the liability of the Underwriter under this bond is limited to the payment for, or the duplication of, so much of such securities as has a value equal to the amount of such applicable coverage.

Books of Account and Other Records

In case of loss of, or damage to, any books of account or other records used by the Insured in its business, the Underwriter shall be liable under this bond only if such books or records are actually reproduced and then for not more than the cost of the blank books, blank pages or other materials plus the cost of labor for the actual transcription or copying of data which shall have been furnished by the Insured in order to reproduce such books and other records.

Property other than Money, Securities or Records

In case of loss of, or damage to, any Property other than Money, securities, books of account or other records, or damage covered under Insuring Agreement (B)(2), the Underwriter shall not be liable for more than the actual cash value of such Property, or of items covered under Insuring Agreement (B)(2). The Underwriter may, at its election, pay the actual cash value of, replace or repair such property. Disagreement between the Underwriter and the Insured as to the cash value or as to the adequacy of repair or replacement shall be resolved by arbitration.

ASSIGNMENT— SUBROGATION— RECOVERY

Section 7.
    (a)   In the event of payment under this bond, the Insured shall deliver, if so requested by the Underwriter, an assignment of such of the Insured's rights, title and interest and causes of action as it has against any person or entity to the extent of the loss payment.
    (b)   In the event of payment under this bond, the Underwriter shall be subrogated to all of the Insured's rights of recovery therefor against any person or entity to the extent of such payment.

(c) Recoveries, whether effected by the Underwriter or by the Insured, shall be applied, net of the expense of such recovery, first to the satisfaction of the Insured's loss which would otherwise have been paid but for the fact that it is in excess of either the Single or Aggregate Limit of Liability, secondly, to the Underwriter as reimbursement of amounts paid in settlement of the Insured's claim, and thirdly, to the Insured in satisfaction of any Deductible Amount. Recovery on account of loss of securities as set forth in the third paragraph of Section 6 or recovery from reinsurance and/or indemnity of the Underwriter shall not be deemed a recovery as used herein.

(d) The Insured shall execute all papers and render assistance to secure to the Underwriter the rights and causes of action provided for herein. The Insured shall do nothing after discovery of loss to prejudice such rights or causes of action.

COOPERATION

Section 8. Upon the Underwriter's request and at reasonable times and places designated by the Underwriter, the Insured shall
   (a) submit to examination by the Underwriter and subscribe to the same under oath; and
   (b) produce for the Underwriter's examination all pertinent records; and
   (c) cooperate with the Underwriter in all matters pertaining to any claim or loss.

ANTI-BUNDLING

Section 9. If any Insuring Agreement requires that an enumerated type of document be altered or counterfeit, or contain a signature which is a Forgery or obtained through trick, artifice, fraud or false pretenses, the alteration or counterfeit or signature must be on or of the enumerated document itself not on or of some other document submitted with, accompanying or incorporated by reference into the enumerated document.

LIMIT OF LIABILITY UNDER THIS BOND AND PRIOR INSURANCE

Section 10. With respect to any loss set forth in sub-section (c) of Section 4. of this bond which is recoverable or recovered in whole or in part under any other bonds or policies issued by the Underwriter to the Insured or to any predecessor in interest of the Insured and terminated or canceled or allowed to expire and in which the period for discovery has not expired at the time any such loss thereunder is discovered, the total liability of the Underwriter under this bond and under such other bonds or policies shall not exceed, in the aggregate, the amount carried hereunder on such loss or the amount available to the Insured under such other bonds or policies, as limited by the terms and conditions thereof, for any such loss if the latter amount be the larger.

If the coverage of this bond supersedes in whole or in part the coverage of any other bond or policy of insurance issued by an Insurer other than the Underwriter and terminated, canceled or allowed to expire, the Underwriter, with respect to any loss sustained prior to such termination, cancelation or expiration and discovered within the period permitted under such other bond or policy for the discovery of loss thereunder, shall be liable under this bond only for that part of such loss covered by this bond as is in excess of the amount recoverable or recovered on account of such loss under such other bond or policy, anything to the contrary in such other bond or policy notwithstanding.

OTHER INSURANCE OR INDEMNITY

Section 11. Coverage afforded hereunder shall apply only as excess over any valid and collectible insurance or indemnity obtained by the Insured, or by one other than the Insured on Property subject

TSB 5018e   Copyright, The Surety & Fidelity Association of America, 2004 to exclusion (q), or by a Transportation Company, or by another entity on whose premises the loss occurred or which employed the person causing the loss.

COVERED PROPERTY

Section 12. This bond shall apply to loss of Property (1) owned by the Insured, (2) held by the Insured in any capacity, or (3) owned and held by someone else under circumstances which make the Insured responsible for the Property prior to the occurrence of the loss. This bond shall be for the sole use and benefit of the Insured named in the Declarations.

DEDUCTIBLE AMOUNT

Section 13. The Underwriter shall be liable hereunder only for the amount by which any single loss, as defined in Section 4., exceeds the Single Loss Deductible for the Insuring Agreement or Coverage applicable to such loss, subject to the Aggregate Limit of Liability and the applicable Single Loss Limit of Liability.

If the loss involves Employee dishonesty, or if the amount of the potential loss exceeds the amount set forth in Item 6. of the Declarations, the Insured shall, in the time and in the manner prescribed in this bond, give the Underwriter notice of any loss of the kind covered by the terms of this bond, even if the amount of the loss does not exceed the Single Loss Deductible, and upon the request of the Underwriter shall file with it a brief statement giving the particulars concerning such loss.

TERMINATION OR CANCELATION

Section 14. This bond terminates as an entirety upon occurrence of any of the following:
(a) 60 days after the receipt by the Insured of a Written notice from the Underwriter of its desire to cancel this bond;
(b) immediately upon the receipt by the Underwriter of a Written notice from the Insured of its desire to cancel this bond;
(c) immediately upon the taking over of the Insured by a receiver or other liquidator or by State or Federal officials;
(d) immediately upon a Change in Control of the first named Insured;
(e) immediately upon exhaustion of the Aggregate Limit of Liability; or
(f) immediately upon expiration of the Bond Period as set forth in Item 2. of the Declarations.

If there is a Change in Control of an Insured other than the first named Insured, this bond immediately terminates as to that Insured only.

This bond terminates as to any Employee, or any partner, officer or employee of any Electronic Data Processor, (a) as soon as any Insured, or any director or officer of an Insured who is not in collusion with such person, learns of any dishonest or fraudulent act committed by such person at any time, whether in the employment of the Insured or otherwise, whether or not of the type covered under Insuring Agreement (A), against the Insured or any other person or entity, without prejudice to the loss of any Property then in transit in the custody of such person, or (b) 15 days after the receipt by the Insured of a Written notice from the Underwriter of its desire to cancel this bond as to such person.

Termination of this bond as to any Insured terminates liability for any loss sustained by such Insured which is discovered after the effective date of such termination. Termination of this bond as to any Employee, or any partner, officer or employee of any Electronic Data Processor, terminates liability for any loss caused by a fraudulent or dishonesty act committed by such person after the date of such termination.

In witness whereof, the Underwriter has caused this bond to be executed on the Declarations Page.

Exhibit 6

SFAA FILING LETTER FOR FINANCIAL INSTITUTION BOND, STANDARD FORM NO. 24

(Revised April 1, 2004)

APPENDIX—BOND FORMS 789

The Surety Association of America

1101 CONNECTICUT AVENUE, NW, SUITE 800, WASHINGTON, DC 20036   TEL: (202) 463-0600 – FAX: (202) 463-0606
website: http://www.surety.org
E-mail: information@surety.org

LYNN M. SCHUBERT
President

EDWARD G. GALLAGHER
General Counsel
SETH MONES
Vice President of Public Affairs
and Government Relations
ROBERT J. DUKE
Director-Underwriting
BARBARA FINNEGAN REIFF
Director of Regulatory Affairs
SEAN P. FOLEY
Senior Statistical Analyst

December 24, 2003

Honorable David Parsons, Commissioner of Insurance
Alabama Department of Insurance
201 Monroe Street, Suite 1700
Montgomery, AL 36130-3351

RE: Financial Institution Bond, Standard Form No. 24
Form and Rider Filing
Reference Filing Number: SAA-F-241

Dear Commissioner Parsons:

Enclosed for filing are the policy forms and related endorsements for the revised Financial Institution Bond, Standard Form No. 24 (Form 24). The Form 24 covers loss incurred by employee dishonesty and other crime risks. It may be used by commercial banks, savings and loan associations and other similar entities. The Surety Association of America ("SAA") provided the banking industry with drafts of the proposed Form 24 and received valuable advice from members of the American Bankers Association.

This filing replaces the Form 24 currently fled with your Department (Form TSB 5018d). This filing does not contain any manual rules or loss costs. The filings for the corresponding rules and loss costs are submitted under separate cover letters.

This form filing applies to all bonds and policies written on and after April 1, 2004.

The Form 24 was last revised by SAA in 1986. SAA has made several revisions to the Form 24 included in this filing. There are two general reasons for the revisions: to develop an approach to address the exposure related to electronic banking transactions and to clarify existing provisions of the form. First, SAA recognized that the emergence of electronic commerce would affect some banks in how they transact business with their customers. Electronic transactions present exposures that are not readily compatible with the terms and conditions of the current Form 24. SAA concluded that the standard form should be directed largely to paper transactions since many banks will continue to transact business traditionally and non-electronically. Banks that desire coverage for losses from electronic transactions may obtain this additional coverage by rider. This filing includes a new rider to provide coverage for electronic transfers. The second reason for the revision project is to provide greater clarity, correct misinterpretations of the bond by some courts and make changes to take current technology into account (e.g. desktop publishing software).

I.   **Insuring Agreements**

Insuring Agreement A   The intent standard has been revised from "manifest intent" to "active and conscious purpose." The change was made in light of the fact that some judicial decisions misinterpreted the meaning of "manifest intent." In those cases courts applied a tort concept of intent and found that the employee intended the natural and probable consequences of his acts or intended a result substantially certain to occur. The drafters of the language intended a stricter meaning of a conscious object to cause the result. "Active and conscious purpose" is meant to restore that standard.

In the revised draft, the double coverage trigger of "manifest intent" to cause the Insured loss and to obtain financial benefit no longer applies for most employee dishonesty losses. The revised Form 24 generally has a single coverage trigger of "active and conscious purpose" to cause the Insured a loss. By eliminating the requirement of a financial benefit, staff noted that an exposure to loss caused by intentional damage by an employee is created. Coverage for such a loss was not intended and Exclusion (bb) addressing this type of loss was developed. In addition, in order to foreclose the argument that "loss" includes employee benefits intentionally paid to the Employee, Agreement A explicitly states that such benefits are not included in the meaning of "loss." Salary and other benefits that are paid unintentionally because of an embezzlement scheme are contemplated as a covered loss.

The revised Insuring Agreement A maintains the double coverage trigger for Loan losses. In addition, the double trigger applies to losses from Trading. In making this revision, and amending the Trading Loss exclusion, the revised Form 24 provides Trading Loss coverage as a part of the standard policy. It previously was available only by rider.

With respect to Loans and Trading, the "financial benefit" provision has been revised to ensure that bonuses or other compensation that were generated as part of the dishonest scheme are not included as financial benefit. "Financial benefit" has been revised to "improper financial benefit." Also, the phrase regarding benefits "earned in the normal course of employment" is replaced by benefits "received by an Employee." The purpose of the change is to strengthen the effect of the language, which is to preclude an argument that wages, salaries or commissions generated through a dishonest scheme is not in the normal course of employment and therefore not excluded from the meaning of an "improper financial benefit." The intent is that any employee benefit received by the employee should be excluded from the meaning of improper financial benefit. For example, claimants have argued that since a bonus was generated as a result of making fraudulent loans, and making fraudulent loans were not a duty of employment, then the bonus was an improper financial benefit. However, the intent of the provision is to exclude the bonus. A kickback from the customer receiving the fraudulent loan would be an example of improper financial benefit.

Insuring Agreement B The revised Insuring Agreement B does not provide coverage for vandalism or malicious mischief. This revision incorporates Rider SR 6263 into the policy. The covered Property is limited to the enumerated items set forth in the Property definition. The intent of the coverage is to avoid duplication of coverage with ISO property coverages and insure only those items that are not covered under ISO forms. The enumerated items generally are not covered under the ISO property forms.

The revised Insuring Agreement B does not cover loss or damage to the office or interior of the office, which previously was covered under B(2)(b). The reason for the deletion was that such coverage is afforded by ISO property policies.

The revised Insuring Agreement B requires that the perpetrator be "physically" present on the premises "at the time the Property was surrendered." The intent of Insuring Agreement B is to cover losses entirely attributable to face-to-face transactions.

APPENDIX—BOND FORMS 791

Insuring Agreement C. Clause (a) was revised so that the custodian of Property must be a Messenger (a defined term, which also incorporates the person acting as a custodian in the event of an emergency).

Clause (c) excludes coverage for any property being transmitted electronically. Clause (c)(i) elaborates on the meaning of "records" as books of account and other records but not any other items enumerated in the definition of property.

The last paragraph clarifies that Insuring Agreement C covers property "only while the property is being conveyed." Thus the covered property must be in transit and not parked or stored at the Transportation Company's premises.

Insuring Agreement D   Insuring Agreement D was revised so that the coverage it provides is exclusive of the coverage provided in Insuring Agreement E. Insuring Agreement D covers loss caused by a payment or transfer by the bank on the faith of a forged or altered Negotiable Instrument or other enumerated item. The transaction under Insuring Agreement D is a direction to pay and not an application for or extension of a loan.

Insuring Agreement D incorporates Rider SR 6253 which addresses coverage for forged desktop published checks.

Insuring Agreement D includes a provision which requires actual possession of the forged or altered document. Although reliance on a Written Original implies a requirement of possession, the provision sets forth the requirement explicitly.

Insuring Agreement E   Losses in connection with a loan made on the faith of forged documents would be covered under Insuring Agreement E only. "Instruction to a Federal Reserve Bank" and "Statement of Uncertificated Security of any Federal Reserve Bank" have been removed from the list of enumerated documents. Unlike the other enumerated items, these items do not represent ownership or convey an interest in something of value. The Statement is only the issuer's representation of any interests in an uncertificated security at a single point in time. Further, the definition of Statement does not specify that it must come directly from the issuer of the security. Relying on a Statement that did not come directly from the issuer appears to be bad banking practice. Discussions with the banking industry indicates that banks do not rely on these documents.

Insuring Agreement F   No changes were made to Insuring Agreement F, except the title so that it more accurately describes the coverage.

Insuring Agreement G   Insuring Agreement G, Fraudulent Mortgages, was added to the Form 24. Experience indicates that this coverage is added to the policy by rider often enough to warrant its inclusion in the standard form.

II.   General Agreements

General Agreement C   General Agreement C was revised as a "Change of Ownership" provision rather than "Change of Control." The revised General Agreement establishes a bright line of a change of ownership of more than 10% of the stock that will trigger the insured's notice requirements. As a related change, the Termination Condition has been revised to include a provision that the policy terminates upon a "Change in Control." This is a defined term which also sets a bright line of a change in ownership of over 50% of the stock. The revision incorporates the meaning of "taking over" as set forth in *American Casualty Company of Reading, Pennsylvania v. Etowah Bank*, 288 F.3d 1282 (11th Cir 2002).

Insuring Agreement G   A new General Agreement G adds coverage for the ERISA bonding obligations of the Insured's directors and employees acting as fiduciaries or handling money of the Insured's own ERISA plans. It will eliminate the need for an ERISA Rider under those circumstances but does not meet the ERISA bonding requirement when the Insured or its employees are handling funds of other employer's plans. Most insureds under Form 24 are exempt from the ERISA bonding requirement unless the regulated institution is itself the fiduciary. See 29 U.S.C. § 1112 (a)(2) (2000). The policy's deductible becomes effective after losses exceed the statutory minimum limit required by ERISA.

III. Definitions

"Written" is inserted into a number of definitions to assure that coverage under the basic Form 24 is not provided for electronic transactions. In addition the following definitions have significant changes:

(e) The definition of Counterfeit now "codifies" the case law requirement that there be an actual, valid original that the counterfeit document is imitating.

(g) A new definition of Electronic Data Processor is added based on language in the current definition of Employee. The language is tightened to include only processors of checks presented to the Insured by a customer or another financial institution. Processors of "other accounting records" were deleted from the definition. The purpose of this change is to prevent the types of arguments put forward in several recent cases trying to obtain coverage for thefts by third parties with business relationships with the Insured by arguing that they were processing "other accounting records."

(h) The definition of Employee is re-written to minimize the use of "employee" in the definition of "Employee." It also borrows language from the mercantile coverages to "codify" the case law requirement that an Employee be under the Insured's direction and control. The definition also incorporates the current exception in Exclusion (d) which effectively allows coverage for directors while performing duties normally performed by employees, and it clarifies that coverage for employees of institutions acquired by the Insured through merger or consolidation is limited to losses they caused the acquired institution and which were unknown at the time of the merger.

(i) The definition of Forgery is re-written to limit forgeries to handwritten signatures or reproductions of handwritten signatures (such as facsimile signatures or printed signatures). Electronic or digital signatures are explicitly not forgeries. In addition, the definition specifically states that a forgery includes affixing the name of an organization as an endorsement to a check and with intent to deceive.

(o) A new definition of Messenger is added. A Messenger must be an Employee or a custodian in the event of an emergency arising out of the incapacity of the Employee.

(r) A new definition of Original is added.

(s) The enumerated items of Property are more clearly specified. "Books of account . . . on tangible media," has replaced "books of account . . recorded electronically." The revision clarifies that the books of account must be stored on a disc or tape. The revision is also consistent with how electronic records are described in Insuring Agreement C.

(y) a new definition of Written is added.

IV. Exclusions

Substantive changes were made in the following Exclusions:

(c) Chemical and biological contamination are added to the nuclear exclusion, and the exception for the industrial use of nuclear energy is deleted.

(d) The exception was removed from the directors exclusion because it is incorporated into the definition of Employee.

(g) A travelers check which is never negotiated should not be a loss to the Insured or to the drawer of the check, and the exception to the travelers check exclusion for unsold checks in the custody of the Insured is modified to clarify that the drawer must have honored the check.

(h) If an Employee of the Insured intentionally loses or destroys property, the loss should be covered, if it is covered at all, under Insuring Agreement (A). The exception for (B) and (C) losses in the Employee Exclusion, therefore, inserts "unintentional" before "acts of the Employee."

(i) Since limited trading loss coverage is added to Insuring Agreement (A), that Insuring Agreement is added to the exception in the trading loss exclusion.

(j) The exclusion for shortage of teller's cash is limited by removing the presumption that any shortage not in excess of the normal shortage for the office involved is due to error. The exclusion is intended for honest errors and the Insured should not be foreclosed from proving that a "normal" shortfall was caused by dishonesty.

(m) The exclusion has been revised to explicitly exclude losses resulting from kidnap, ransom or extortion. Coverage for such losses is available under a Kidnap Ransom policy.

(n) An erroneous credit to an account, which is not the result of employee dishonesty, is poor banking practice which the bond is not designed to cover. This is the reason for the erroneous credit exclusion, and there is no logical reason for an exception if the withdrawal is received on the Insured's premises rather than made by check. This exception to the exclusion is, therefore, deleted.

(p) Insuring Agreement (D) is added to the exceptions to the counterfeiting exclusion to incorporate into the bond the coverage for "desktop published checks" previously available by rider.

(q) The exclusion for tangible "nonenumerated" property is re-written to be consistent with the revised Ownership Condition.

(t) The bond is not a liability policy, and indemnity is owed the Insured only if and when the Insured itself has suffered a covered loss. Several provisions of the bond are re-written to remove any suggestion that the legal liability of the Insured has any effect on the obligations of the Underwriter. The fact that damages are awarded against the Insured, however, should not remove coverage which would have existed independently of those damages. The damages exclusion is re-written to remove the exception for compensatory damages but to allow recovery for an otherwise covered loss which would exist independently of the damage award.

(v) The consequential damage exclusion gives as examples multiple or punitive damages or the Insured's liability to others.

(y) Exclusion (y) for uncertificated securities is deleted and replaced with an exclusion for loss of property on the premises of a messenger or transportation company. There have been several claims alleging that money stolen by an ATM servicer was "in transit" even though it was transferred to the servicer, stored at its premises and stolen by the servicer. The new exclusion forecloses such a claim which was never intended to be covered by the bond.

(aa) Exclusion (aa) excludes losses related to the theft, disappearance and destruction of confidential information. This is an exclusion that is common on company forms.

V. Conditions

Section 4   The current bond does not allow reinstatement of the aggregate limit by recoveries. Section 4 is changed to allow reinstatement from net-recoveries if the aggregate limit has not been exhausted and the recoveries are received prior to the termination of the bond. It also adds a clarification that a loss settled with a lost instrument bond does not reduce the aggregate limit until a payment is made under the lost instrument bond.

Section 6   A loss under the bond should be measured by the net detriment to the Insured. Any interest, fees, payments, recoveries or credits the Insured receives in the fraudulent transaction should reduce the amount claimed. Insureds often claim that interest received on a fraudulent loan should not reduce the amount lost. The Valuation Condition is amended to state that such recoveries or receipts are a credit reducing the loss.

Section 7   The Assignment – Subrogation – Recovery – Cooperation Condition has been divided into two Conditions to clarify that the duty to cooperate is not limited to recovery of losses. Subsection (d) of the Condition is moved to a new Cooperation Condition 8.

Section 9   The mistaken decision in *Omnisource Corp. v. CNA Transcontinental Ins. Co.,* 949 F. Supp. 681 (N.D. Ind. 1996) led a number of Insureds erroneously to believe that coverage can be claimed based on forgery to a document not covered by the bond if the forged document is "bundled" with a covered document. A new Condition 9 is added to correct this misconception.

Section 12   The inclusion of property "for which the Insured is legally liable" in the Ownership Condition has led to claims that the legal liability of the Insured is covered. The Ownership Condition is amended to "codify" cases, such as *Lynch Properties Inc. v. Potomac Ins. Co.,* 140 F3d 622 (5th Cir. 1998), which correctly hold that the Insured must be responsible for the property prior to the events giving rise to the loss.

Section 13.   The Insured's obligation to notify the Underwriter of losses within the deductible is reduced to instances of employee dishonesty and computer theft.

VI. Electronic Coverages

Insuring Agreement H, Fraudulent Transfer Instructions

Insuring Agreement H is new and provides coverage that currently is provided by two existing riders: Telefacsimile Transfer Fraud (SR 6195) and Voice Initiated Transfer Fraud (SR 6184a). In addition, Insuring Agreement H accommodates transfer instructions that are sent via electronic mail. The coverage provided by this rider contemplates that a bank employee will receive the instructions and act upon them. Only the transmission of the instruction is fully electronic. The transfer is effected with human intervention. The coverage requires the use of a password or PIN, and a call-back or other verification procedure for transfers exceeding a stipulated amount.

Insuring Agreement H contains two additional exclusions. First, the rider excludes loss that resulted directly or indirectly from an instruction transmitted by a person who ever had authorized access to the password. The rider does not cover a loss caused by the transmission of an instruction by a person who had authority to use the correct security code, but did not have authority for the particular transactions.

Such a loss could be prevented by the customer changing the security code whenever there is a change in authorization, and should, in any case, be placed on the customer in the insured's customer agreement. The internal controls of the Insured's customer are difficult to underwrite and losses that could be prevented through those controls should be excluded. Second, the rider excludes loss involving instructions to initiate an automated clearing house ("ACH") entry containing several items unless each item was verified and the instructions are encrypted or encoded, so that alteration would be apparent.

Existing Riders

As a result of the Form 24 revision, many provisions of the Form 24, although substantively the same compared to the 1986 revision, are in different locations or under new headings. As a result, SAA revised those existing riders that apply to the Form 24 to incorporate the new cross-references. In some cases, a rider applied to the Form 24 and other Financial Institution Bonds. For these instances, SAA deleted the reference to the Form 24 from the existing rider and created a new rider for the Form 24.

We note one substantive revision to rider SR-6110f. This rider changes the coverage from discovery basis to loss sustained basis. Under prior versions of this rider, coverage for loss was provided in circumstances where the insured would have recovered under the prior policy except for the fact that "at the time of discovery of such loss, the period for discovery of loss under all bonds and policies of insurance which afford coverage applicable to such loss and for which the coverage of this bond is substituted, has expired." SR 6110f does not contain this provision. SAA believes that if the insured desires-coverage for losses incurred prior to the effective date of the current policy, but discovered during the current policy's term, then such coverage is provided by the Form 24 as drafted, without the need for a rider.

We request that this filing of the policy form and related endorsements of the Form 24 become effective on April 1, 2004. Please feel free to contact me if you have any questions. If you prefer e-mail, my e-mail address is rdukeasuretv.org. Your consideration is appreciated.

Respectfully,

Robert J. Duke

Enclosures

Exhibit 7

COMPUTER CRIME POLICY FOR FINANCIAL INSTITUTIONS

(Edition December, 1993)

APPENDIX—BOND FORMS

COMPUTER CRIME POLICY FOR FINANCIAL INSTITUTIONS
Edition of December, 1993

Policy No.

(Herein called Company)

DECLARATIONS

Item 1. Name of Insured (herein called Insured):

Principal Address:

Item 2. Policy Period: from 12:01 a.m. on _____ to 12:01 a.m. _____
(MONTH, DAY, YEAR) (MONTH, DAY, YEAR)

Item 3. The Aggregate Limit of Liability of the Company during the Policy Period shall be
$

Item 4. Subject to Sections 4 and 10 hereof, the Single Loss Limit of Liability and Single Loss Deductible applicable to individual Insuring Agreements are as follows:

Insuring Agreements	Single Loss Limit of Liability	Single Loss Deductible
1. Computer Systems Fraud	$	$
2. Data Processing Service Operations	$	$
3. Voice Initiated Transfer Fraud	$	$
4. Telefacsimile Transfer Fund	$	$
5. Destruction of Data or Programs by Hacker	$	$
6. Destruction of Data or Programs by Virus	$	$
7. Voice Computer System Fraud	$	$

Insuring Agreement 1 is mandatory; all others are optional. If Not Covered" is inserted above opposite any specified optional Insuring Agreement, such Insuring Agreement and any other reference thereto in this policy shall be deemed to be deleted therefrom.

Item 5.
Voice Initiated Transfer Fraud
Under the terms of the Voice Initiated Transfer Fraud Insuring Agreement, the Insured must place a verification call-back for each transfer in excess of $_____

Telefacsimile Transfer Fraud
Under the terms of the Telefacsimile Transfer Fraud Insuring Agreement, the Insured must place a verification call-back for each transfer in excess of $_____

Copyright, The Surety Association of America, 1997   TSB 6189

Item 6. The liability of the Company is subject to the terms of the following endorsements attached hereto:

Item 7. The Insured by the acceptance of this policy gives notice to the Company terminating or canceling prior policy(ies) No.(s)
such termination or cancelation to be effective as of the time this policy becomes effective.

The Company, in consideration of an agreed premium, and in reliance upon all statements made and information furnished to the Company by the Insured in applying for this policy, and subject to the Declarations, Insuring Agreements, General Agreements, Conditions and Limitations and other terms hereof, agrees to indemnify the Insured for:

INSURING AGREEMENTS

1. **COMPUTER SYSTEMS FRAUD**
   Loss resulting directly from a fraudulent
   (1) entry of Electronic Data or Computer Program into, or
   (2) change of Electronic Data or Computer Program within
   any Computer System operated by the Insured, whether owned or leased; or any Computer System identified in the application for this policy; or a Computer System first used by the Insured during the policy period, as provided by General Agreement A;
   provided the entry or change causes
   (i) property to be transferred, paid or delivered,
   (ii) an account of the Insured, or of its customer, to be added, deleted, debited or credited, or
   (iii) an unauthorized account or a fictitious account to be debited or credited.
   In this Insuring Agreement, fraudulent entry or change shall include such entry or change made by an employee of the Insured acting in good faith
   (a) on an instruction from a software contractor who has a written agreement with the Insured to design, implement or service programs for a Computer System covered by this Insuring Agreement, or
   (b) on an instruction transmitted by Tested telex or similar means of Tested communication identified in the application for this policy purportedly sent by a customer, financial institution, or automated clearing house.

2. **DATA PROCESSING SERVICE OPERATIONS**
   Loss sustained by a Client of the Insured resulting directly from a fraudulent
   (1) entry of Electronic Data or a Computer Program into, or
   (2) change of Electronic Data or a Computer Program within a Computer System covered under the terms of Insuring Agreement 1, or
   (3) entry or change of Electronic Data during electronic transmission or physical transit from the Insured to its Client,
   provided that the entry or change causes
   (i) property to be transferred, paid or delivered,
   (ii) an account of the Client, or a customer of the Client, to be added, deleted, debited or credited, or
   (iii) an unauthorized account or a fictitious account to be debited or credited,
   and for which loss the Insured is legally liable to the Client as a provider of data processing services for such Client.
   In this Insuring Agreement, fraudulent entry or change shall include such entry or change made by an employee of the Insured acting in good faith

Copyright, The Surety Association of America, 1997

APPENDIX—BOND FORMS 801

 (a) on an instruction from a software contractor who has a written agreement with the Insured to design, implement or service programs for a Computer System covered by this Insuring Agreement, or
 (b) on an instruction transmitted by Tested telex or similar means of Tested communication identified in the application for this policy purportedly sent by a customer, financial institution, or automated clearing house.
In this Insuring Agreement, Client means an entity for whom the Insured serves as data processor under the terms of a written agreement.

3. **VOICE INITIATED TRANSFER FRAUD**
Loss resulting directly from the Insured having, in good faith, transferred Funds from a Customer's account through a Computer System covered under the terms of Insuring Agreement 1 in reliance upon a fraudulent voice instruction transmitted by telephone which was purported to be from
 (1) an officer, director, partner or employee of a Customer of the Insured who was authorized by the Customer to instruct the Insured to make such transfer,
 (2) an individual person who is a Customer of the Insured, or
 (3) an employee of the Insured in another office of the Insured who was authorized by the Insured to instruct other employees of the Insured to transfer Funds,
and was received by an employee of the Insured specifically designated to receive and act upon such instructions, but the voice instruction was not from a person described in (1), (2) or (3) above, provided that
 (i) such voice instruction was electronically recorded by the Insured and required password(s) or code word(s) given; and
 (ii) if the transfer was in excess of the amount shown on the Declarations Page as the verification call-back amount for this Insuring Agreement, the voice instruction was verified by a call-back according to a prearranged procedure.
As used in this Insuring Agreement, Customer means an entity or individual which has a written agreement with the Insured authorizing the Insured to rely on voice instructions to initiate transfers and has provided the Insured with the names of persons authorized to initiate such transfers, and with which the Insured has established an instruction verification mechanism.

4. **TELEFACSIMILE TRANSFER FRAUD**
Loss resulting directly from the Insured having, in good faith, transferred or delivered Funds, Certificated Securities or Uncertificated Securities through a Computer System covered under the terms of Insuring Agreement 1 in reliance upon a fraudulent instruction received through a Telefacsimile Device, and which instruction.
 (1) purports and reasonably appears to have originated from
  (a) a Customer of the Insured,
  (b) another financial institution, or
  (c) another office of the Insured
  but, in fact, was not originated by the Customer or entity whose identification it bears and
 (2) contains a valid test code which proves to have been used by a person who was not authorized to make use of it, and
 (3) contains the name of a person authorized to initiate such transfer;
provided that, if the transfer was in excess of the amount shown on the Declarations Page as the verification call-back amount for this Insuring Agreement, the instruction was verified by a call-back according to a prearranged procedure.
As used in this Insuring Agreement, Customer means an entity or individual which has a written agreement with the Insured authorizing the Insured to rely on Telefacsimile Device instructions to initiate transfers and has provided the Insured with the names of persons

Copyright, The Surety Association of America, 1997

authorized to initiate such transfers, and with which the Insured has established an instruction verification mechanism.

5. **DESTRUCTION OF DATA OR PROGRAMS BY HACKER**
   Loss resulting directly from the malicious destruction of, or damage to, Electronic Data or Computer Programs owned by the Insured or for which the Insured is legally liable while stored within a Computer System covered under the terms of Insuring Agreement 1.

   The liability of the Company shall be limited to the cost of duplication of such Electronic Data or Computer Programs from other Electronic Data or Computer Programs which shall have been furnished by the Insured. In the event, however, that destroyed or damaged Computer Programs cannot be duplicated from other Computer Programs, the Company will pay the cost incurred for computer time, computer programmers, consultants or other technical specialists as is reasonably necessary to restore the Computer Programs to substantially the previous level of operational capability.

6. **DESTRUCTION OF DATA OR PROGRAMS BY VIRUS**
   Loss resulting directly from the malicious destruction of, or damage to, Electronic Data or Computer Programs owned by the Insured or for which the Insured is legally liable while stored within a Computer System covered under the terms of Insuring Agreement 1 if such destruction or damage was caused by a computer program or similar instruction which was written or altered to incorporate a hidden instruction designed to destroy or damage Electronic Data or Computer Programs in the Computer System in which the computer program or instruction so written or so altered is used.

   The liability of the Company shall be limited to the cost of duplication of such Electronic Data or Computer Programs from other Electronic Data or Computer Programs which shall have been furnished by the Insured.

   In the event, however, that destroyed or damaged Computer Programs cannot be duplicated from other Computer Programs, the Company will pay the cost incurred for computer time, computer programmers, consultants or other technical specialists as is reasonably necessary to restore the Computer Programs to substantially the previous level of operational capability.

   Special Condition:
   Under this Insuring Agreement, "Single Loss" means all covered costs incurred by the Insured between the time destruction or damage is discovered and the time the Computer System is restored to substantially the previous level of operational capability. Recurrence of destruction or damage after the Computer System is restored shall constitute a separate "Single Loss."

7. **VOICE COMPUTER SYSTEM FRAUD**
   Loss resulting directly from charges for voice telephone long-distance toll calls which were incurred due to the fraudulent use or fraudulent manipulation of an Account Code or System Password required to obtain access to a Voice Computer System owned or leased by the Insured, installed on the Insured's premises, whose System Administration is performed and controlled by the Insured; provided, however, that the unauthorized access was not made possible by

   (1) failure to incorporate a System Password feature or failure to change the System Password at least once every 30 days thereafter, or

   (2) failure to have a call-disconnect feature in operation to automatically terminate a caller's access to the Voice Computer System after not more than three unsuccessful attempts to input an Account Code.

Special Condition:
Under this Insuring Agreement, "Single Loss" means loss resulting from toll call charges made only on telephone lines directly controlled by one Voice Computer System and only toll call charges occurring for a period of not more than 30 days inclusive of the date on which the first such toll call charge was made.

GENERAL AGREEMENTS

A. **CONSOLIDATION, MERGER, OR PURCHASE OF ASSETS OR COMPUTER SYSTEMS OF ANOTHER INSTITUTION—NOTICE**
If the Insured consolidates or merges with another institution, or purchases or acquires the assets, liabilities or Computer System(s) of another institution, the Insured shall not have the coverage provided by this policy unless the Insured
   (i) gives the Company written notice of the proposed consolidation, merger, purchase or acquisition prior to the proposed effective date of such action, and
   (ii) obtains the written consent of the Company to extend the coverage provided by this policy, and
   (iii) pays to the Company any additional premium which may be due.

B. **REPRESENTATION OF INSURED**
The Insured represents that the information furnished in the application for this policy is complete, true and correct. Such application constitutes part of this policy. Any misrepresentation, omission, concealment or incorrect statement of a material fact, in the application or otherwise, shall be grounds for the rescission of this policy.

C. **JOINT INSURED**
If two or more Insureds are covered under this policy, the first named Insured shall act for all insureds. Payment by the Company to the first named Insured for loss sustained by any Insured shall fully release the Company on account of such loss. If the first named Insured ceases to be covered under this policy, the Insured next named shall thereafter be considered as the first named Insured. Knowledge possessed or discovery made by any Insured shall constitute knowledge or discovery by all Insureds for all purposes of this policy. The liability of the Company for loss or losses sustained by all Insureds shall not exceed the amount for which the Company would have been liable had all such loss or losses been sustained by one Insured.

D. **NOTICE OF LEGAL PROCEEDINGS AGAINST INSURED—ELECTION TO DEFEND.**
The Insured shall notify the Company at the earliest practicable moment, not to exceed 30 days after notice thereof, of any legal proceeding brought to deter-mine the Insured's liability for any loss, claim damage, which, if established, would constitute a collectible loss under this policy. Concurrently, the Insured shall furnish copies of all pleadings and pertinent papers to the Company.
The Company at its sole option, may elect to conduct the defense of such legal proceeding, in whole or in part. The defense by the Company shall be in the Insured's name through attorneys selected by the Company. The Insured shall provide all reasonable information and assistance required by the Company for such defense.
If the Company elects to defend the Insured, in whole or in part, any judgment against the Insured on those counts or causes of action which the Company defended on behalf of the Insured or any settlement in which the Company participates and all attorneys' fees, costs and expenses incurred by the Company in the defense of the litigation shall be a loss covered by this policy.
If the Insured does not give the notices required in subsection (a) of Section 5 of this policy and in the first paragraph of this General Agreement, or if the Company elects not to defend

Copyright, The Surety Association of America, 1997

any causes of action, neither a judgment against the Insured, nor a settlement of any legal proceeding by the Insured, shall determine the existence, extent or amount of coverage under this policy for loss sustained by the Insured, and the Company' shall not be liable for any attorneys' fees, costs and expenses incurred by the Insured.

With respect to this General Agreement, subsections (b) and (g) of Section 5 of this policy apply upon the entry of such judgment or the occurrence of such settlement instead of upon discovery of loss. In addition, the Insured must notify the Company within 30 days after such judgment is entered against it or after the Insured settles such legal proceeding, and, subject to subsection (h) of Section 5, the Insured may not bring legal proceedings for the recovery of such loss after the expiration of 24 months from the date of such final judgment or settlement.

CONDITIONS AND LIMITATIONS

Section 1. **DEFINITIONS**

As used in this Policy:

(a) Account Code means a confidential and protected string of characters which identifies or authenticates a person and permits that person to gain access to a Voice Computer System for the purpose of making toll calls or utilizing voice mail box messaging capabilities or other similar functional features of the System;

(b) Certificated Security means a share, participation or other interest in the property, of or an enterprise of, the issuer or an obligation of the issuer, which is:
  (1) represented by an instrument issued in bearer or registered form;
  (2) of a type commonly dealt in on securities exchanges or markets or commonly recognized in any area in which it is issued or dealt in as a medium for investment, and
  (3) either one of a class or series or by its terms divisible into a class or series of shares, participations, interests or obligations;

(c) Computer Program means a set of related electronic instructions which direct the operations and functions of a computer or devices connected to it which enable the computer or devices to receive, process, store or send Electronic Data;

(d) Computer System means
  (1) computers with related peripheral components, including storage components wherever located,
  (2) systems and applications software,
  (3) terminal devices, and
  (4) related communication networks

  by which Electronic Data are electronically collected, transmitted, processed, stored and retrieved;

(e) Electronic Data means facts or information converted to a form usable in a Computer System by Computer Programs and which is stored on magnetic tapes or disks, or optical storage disks or other bulk media;

(f) Funds means Money on deposit in an account;

(g) Money means a medium of exchange in current use authorized or adopted by a domestic or foreign government as a part of its currency;

(h) System Administration means the performance of security functions including but not limited to defining authorized persons to access a Voice Computer System and adding, changing and deleting Account Codes or passwords in connection therewith; and invoking or revoking a System option which directs telephone call routing or which adds, moves or drops telephone lines or which performs any other similar activity allowed by a hardware or software-based System option that has been incorporated by a manufacturer or vendor into a System or any component thereof provided said System option is not intended for the sole use of such manufacturer or vendor;

(i) System Maintenance means the performance of hardware and software installation, diagnostics and corrections and similar activities that are performed in the usual custom and practice by a

Copyright, The Surety Association of America, 1997

APPENDIX—BOND FORMS 805

(j)   manufacturer or vendor to establish or maintain the basic operational functionality of a Voice Computer System or any component thereof;

(j)   System Password means a confidential and protected string of characters which identifies or authenticates a person and permits that person to gain access to a Voice Computer System or any portion thereof for the purpose of performing System Administration or System Maintenance activities;

(k)   Telefacsimile Device means a machine capable of sending or receiving a duplicate image of a document by means of electronic impulses transmitted through a telephone line and which reproduces the duplicate image on paper;

(l)   Tested means a method of authenticating the contents of a communication by placing a valid test key on it which has been agreed upon by the Insured and a customer, automated clearing house, or another financial institution for the purpose of protecting the integrity of the communication in the ordinary course of business;

(m)   Uncertificated Security means a share, participation or other interest in property of, or an enterprise of, the issuer or an obligation of the issuer, which is:
- (1) not represented by an instrument and the transfer of which is registered upon books maintained for that purpose by or on behalf of the issuer,
- (2) of a type commonly dealt in on securities exchanges or markets, and
- (3) either one of a class or series or by its terms divisible into a class or series of shares, participations, interests or obligations;

(n)   Voice Computer System means a Computer System installed in one location which functions as a private branch exchange (PBX), voice mail processor, automated call attendant or provides a similar capability used for the direction or routing of telephone calls in a voice communications network.

Section 2.   **EXCLUSIONS**

This policy does not cover:

(a)   any loss of the type or kind covered by the Insured's financial institution bond, regardless of any deductible amount or limit of liability;

(b)   loss caused by a director or employee of the Insured or by a person in collusion with any director or employee of the Insured; (Collusion shall include the willful withholding of knowledge from the Insured by any director or employee that a fraudulent act by a person not an employee has been or will be perpetrated against the insured.);

(c)   loss resulting directly or indirectly from entry or change of Electronic Data or Computer Programs in a Computer System, unless covered under Insuring Agreement 1 or 2;

(d)   loss resulting directly or indirectly from the Insured having transferred Funds in reliance on the validity of a voice instruction, unless covered under Insuring Agreement 1 or 3;

(e)   loss resulting directly or indirectly by the Insured having transferred or delivered Funds, Certificated Securities or Uncertificated Securities in reliance on an instruction received through a Telefacsimile Device, unless covered under Insuring Agreement 4;

(f)   loss resulting directly or indirectly from theft of confidential information;

(g)   loss resulting directly or indirectly from payments made or withdrawals from a depositor's account involving items of deposit which are not finally paid for any reason;

(h)   potential income, including but not limited to interest and dividends;

(i)   damages of any type for which the Insured is legally liable, except compensatory damages, but not multiples thereof, arising directly from a loss covered under this policy;

(j)   loss resulting directly or indirectly from the assumption of liability by the Insured by contract unless the liability arises from a loss covered by this policy and would be imposed on the Insured regardless of the existence of the contract;

(k)   any fees, costs and expenses incurred by the Insured
- (1) in establishing the existence of or amount of loss covered under this policy, or
- (2) as a party to any legal proceeding whether or not such legal proceeding exposes the Insured to loss covered by this policy;

Copyright, The Surety Association of America, 1997

(l) indirect or consequential loss of any nature;
(m) the cost of duplication of Electronic Data or Computer Programs, unless covered under Insuring Agreement 5 or 6;
(n) loss involving a Voice Computer System, unless covered under Insuring Agreement 7;
(o) loss involving automated mechanical devices which, on behalf of the Insured, disburse money, accept deposits, cash checks, drafts or similar written instruments or make credit card loans;
(p) loss resulting directly or indirectly from
   (1) written instructions or advices, or
   (2) telegraphic or cable instructions or advices;
   unless the instructions or advices are Tested and the loss is covered under Insuring Agreement 1 or 2;
(q) loss resulting directly or indirectly from negotiable instruments, securities, documents or other written instruments which bear a forged signature, or are counterfeit, altered or otherwise fraudulent and which are used as source documentation in the preparation of Electronic Data or manually keyed into a data terminal;
(r) loss resulting directly or indirectly from the fraudulent preparation, or fraudulent modification of Computer Programs unless covered under Insuring Agreement 1 or 2;
(s) loss resulting directly or indirectly from
   (1) mechanical failure, faulty construction, error in design, latent defect, fire, wear or tear, gradual deterioration, electrical disturbance or electrical surge which affects a Computer System, or
   (2) failure or breakdown of electronic data processing media, or
   (3) error or omission in programming or processing;
(t) loss due to riot or civil commotion or loss due to military, naval or usurped power, war or insurrection;
(u) loss resulting directly or indirectly from the effects of nuclear fission or fusion or radioactivity; provided, however, that this exclusion shall not apply to loss resulting from industrial uses of nuclear energy;
(v) loss as a result of a threat
   (1) to do bodily harm to any person, or
   (2) to do damage to the premises or property of the Insured, or
   (3) to Computer System operations;
(w) loss resulting directly or indirectly from the use of a telephone credit, debit, charge, identification or similar card to gain access to the Insured's Voice Computer System;
(x) loss resulting directly or indirectly from the use or purported use of credit, debit, charge, access, convenience, customer identification or other cards;
(y) loss resulting directly or indirectly from the input of Electronic Data into a Computer System terminal device either on the premises of a customer of the Insured or under the control of such customer by a person who had authorized access to the customer's authentification mechanism.

Section 3.   DISCOVERY

This policy applies to loss discovered by the Insured during the Policy Period. Discovery occurs when the Insured first becomes aware of facts which would cause a reasonable person to assume that a loss of a type covered by this policy has been or will be incurred, regardless of when the act or acts causing or contributing to such loss occurred, even though the exact amount or details of loss may not then be known.

Discovery also occurs when the Insured receives notice of an actual or potential claim in which it is alleged that the Insured is liable to a third party under circumstances which, if true, would constitute a loss under this policy.

Section 4.   LIMIT OF LIABILITY

Aggregate Limit of Liability

The Company's total liability for all losses discovered during the Policy Period shown in Item 2 of the Declarations shall not exceed the Aggregate Limit of Liability shown in Item 3 of the Declarations. The Aggregate Limit of Liability shall be reduced by the amount of any payment made under the-terms of this policy.
Upon exhaustion of the Aggregate Limit of Liability by such payments:
(a) The Company shall have no further liability for loss or losses regardless of when discovered and whether or not previously reported to the Company; and
(b) The Company shall have no obligation under General Agreement D to continue the defense of the Insured, and upon notice by the Company to the Insured that the Aggregate Limit of Liability has been exhausted, the Insured shall assume all responsibility for its defense at its own cost.
The Aggregate Limit of Liability shall not be increased or reinstated by any recovery made and applied in accordance with subsections (a), (b) and (c) of Section 7. In the event that a loss is settled by the Company through the use of a lost instrument bond, such loss shall not reduce the Aggregate Limit of Liability.

Single Loss Limit of Liability
Subject to the Aggregate Limit of Liability, the Company's liability for each Single Loss shall not exceed the applicable Single Loss Limit of Liability shown in Item 4 of the Declarations. If a Single Less is covered under more than one Insuring Agreement, the maximum payable shall not exceed the largest applicable Single Loss Limit of Liability.
All loss or series of losses involving the fraudulent or destructive acts of one individual, or involving fraudulent or destructive acts in which one individual is implicated, whether or not that individual is specifically identified, shall be treated as a Single Loss and subject to the Single Loss Limit of Liability.
A series of losses involving unidentified individuals but arising from the same method of operation shall be deemed to involve the same individual and in that event shall be treated as a Single Loss and subject to the Single Loss Limit of Liability.

Section 5. NOTICE/PROOF—LEGAL PROCEEDINGS AGAINST COMPANY
(a) At the earliest practicable moment, not to exceed 30 days, after discovery of loss, the Insured shall give the Company notice thereof.
(b) Within 6 months after such discovery, the Insured shall furnish to the Company proof of loss, duly sworn to, with full particulars.
(c) This policy affords coverage only in favor of. the Insured. No suit, action or legal proceedings shall be brought hereunder by any one other than the named Insured.
(d) Proof of loss for claim under the Voice Initiated Transfer Fraud Insuring Agreement must include electronic recordings of such voice instructions and the verification call-back, if such call-back was required.
(e) Proof of loss for claim under the Telefacsimile Transfer Fraud Insuring Agreement must include a copy of the document reproduced by the Telefacsimile Device.
(f) Certificated Securities listed in a proof of loss shall be identified by certificate or bond numbers if such securities were issued therewith.
(g) Legal proceedings for the recovery of any loss here-under shall not be brought prior to the expiration of 60 days after the original proof of loss is filed with the Company or after the expiration of 24 months from the discovery of such loss.
(h) If any limitation embodied in this policy is prohibited by any law controlling the construction hereof, such limitation shall be deemed to be amended so as to equal the minimum period of limitation provided by such law.

Section 6. **VALUATION**
Any loss of Money, or loss payable in Money, shall be paid, at the option of the Insured, in the Money of the country in which the loss was sustained or in the United States of America dollar equivalent thereof determined at the rate of exchange at the time of payment of such loss.

Securities
The Company shall settle in kind its liability under this policy on account of any securities or, at the option of the Insured, shall pay to the Insured the cost of replacing such securities, determined by the market value thereof at the time of such settlement. In the case of loss of subscription, conversion or redemption privileges through the loss of securities, the amount of such loss shall be the value of such privileges immediately preceding the expiration thereof. If such securities cannot be replaced or have no quoted market value, or if such privileges have no quoted market value, their value shall be determined by agreement or arbitration.

If the applicable coverage of this policy is subject to a Deductible Amount and/or is not sufficient in amount to indemnify the Insured in full for the loss of securities for which claim is made hereunder, the liability of the Company under this policy is limited to the payment for, or the duplication of, so much of such securities as has a value equal to the amount of such applicable coverage.

Section 7. **ASSIGNMENT—SUBROGATION—RECOVERY—COOPERATION**
(a) In the event of payment under this policy, the Insured shall deliver, if so requested by the Company, an assignment of such of the Insured's rights, title and interest and causes of action as it has against any person or entity to the extent of the loss payment.
(b) In the event of payment under this policy, the Company shall be subrogated to all of the insured's rights of recovery therefor against any person or entity to the extent of such payment.
(c) Recoveries, whether effected by the Company or by the Insured, shall be applied net of the expense of recovery:
   * * first to the satisfaction of the Insured's loss which would otherwise have been paid but for the fact that it is in excess of either the Single or Aggregate Limit of Liability,
   * * second, to the Company as reimbursement of amounts paid in settlement of the Insured's claim, and
   * * third, to the Insured in satisfaction of any Deductible Amount.

Recovery from reinsurance and/or indemnity of the Company shall not be deemed a recovery as used herein.
(d) Upon the Company's request and at reasonable times and places designated by the Company the Insured shall
   (1) submit to examination by the Company and subscribe to the same under oath, and
   (2) produce for the Company's examination all pertinent records, and
   (3) cooperate with the Company in all matters pertaining to the loss.
(e) The Insured shall execute all papers and render assistance to secure to the Company the rights and causes of action provided for herein. The Insured shall do nothing after discovery of loss to prejudice such rights or causes of action.

Section 8. **OTHER INSURANCE OR INDEMNITY**
Coverage afforded hereunder shall apply only as excess over any valid and collectible insurance or indemnity obtained by the Insured, or by one other than the Insured. However, this policy does not provide excess indemnity for losses covered by the Insured's financial institution bond.

Section 9. **OWNERSHIP**
This policy shall apply to loss of Money, Certificated and Uncertificated Securities, Electronic Data, Computer Programs and other property
(1) owned by the Insured,
(2) held by the Insured in any capacity, or

(3) for which the Insured is legally liable because of all-covered by this policy.
This policy shall be for the sole use and benefit of the Insured named in the Declarations.

Section 10. **DEDUCTIBLE AMOUNT**
The Company shall be liable hereunder only in the event a Single Loss, as described in Section 4, exceeds the Single Loss Deductible amount for the Insuring Agreement applicable to such loss, subject to the Aggregate Limit of Liability and the applicable Single Loss Limit of Liability.

Section 11. **TERMINATION OR CANCELATION**
This policy terminates as an entirety upon occurrence of any of the following:
- **(a)** 60 days after the receipt by the Insured of a written notice from the Company of its desire to cancel this policy, or
- **(b)** immediately upon the receipt by the Company of a written notice from the Insured of its desire to cancel this policy, or
- **(c)** immediately upon the taking over of the Insured by a receiver or other liquidator or by State or Federal officials, or
- **(d)** immediately upon the taking over of the Insured by another institution, or
- **(e)** immediately upon exhaustion of the Aggregate Limit of Liability, or
- **(f)** immediately upon expiration of the Policy Period as set forth in Item 2 of the Declarations.

Termination of the policy as to any Insured terminates liability for any loss sustained by such Insured which is discovered after the effective date of such termination.

In witness whereof, the Company has caused this policy to be executed on the Declarations page.

Copyright, The Surety Association of America, 1997

Exhibit 8

FRAUDULENT TRANSFER INSTRUCTIONS RIDER

(Revised May, 2011)

RIDER

To be attached to and form part of Financial Institution Bond, Standard Form No. , No. in favor of

1. It is agreed that the following Insuring Agreement is added to the above Bond:

FRAUDULENT TRANSFER INSTRUCTIONS

Loss resulting directly from the Insured having, in good faith, transferred Money on deposit in a Customer's account, or a Customer's Certificated Securities, in reliance upon a fraudulent instruction transmitted to the Insured via telefacsimile, telephone, or electronic mail; provided, however that
    (1) The fraudulent instruction purports, and reasonably appears, to have originated from:
        (a) such Customer,
        (b) an Employee acting on instructions of such Customer; or
        (c) another financial institution acting on behalf of such Customer with authority to make such instructions; and
    (2) The sender of the fraudulent instruction verified the instruction with the password, PIN, or other security code of such Customer; and
    (3) The sender was not, in fact, such Customer, was not authorized to act on behalf of such Customer, and was not an Employee of the Insured; and
    (4) The instruction was received by an Employee of the Insured specifically authorized by the Insured to receive and act upon such instructions; and
    (5) For any transfer exceeding the amount set forth in item 8 of this Rider, the Insured verified the instruction via a call back to a predetermined telephone number set forth in the Insured's Written agreement with such Customer or other verification procedure approved in writing by the Underwriter; and
    (6) The Insured preserved a contemporaneous record of the call back, if any, and of the instruction which verifies use of the authorized password, PIN or other security code of the Customer.

2. As used in this Rider, Customer means a natural person or entity which has a Written agreement with the Insured authorizing the Insured to transfer Money on deposit in an account or Certificated Securities in reliance upon instructions transmitted to the Insured via the means utilized to transmit the fraudulent instruction.

3. It shall be a condition precedent to coverage under this Insuring Agreement that the Insured assert any available claims, offsets or defenses against such Customer, any financial institution or any other party to the transaction.

4. The following additional Exclusions are added to the Bond applicable only to this Insuring Agreement:

FRAUDULENT TRANSFER INSTRUCTIONS RIDER
FOR USE WITH FINANCIAL INSTITUTION BOND,
STANDARD FORM Nos 14, 24 and 25.
REVISED TO MAY, 2011

Copyright, The Surety & Fidelity Association of America, 2011   SR 6271b

(a) loss resulting directly or indirectly from a fraudulent instruction if the sender, or anyone acting in collusion with the sender, ever had authorized access to such Customer's password, PIN or other security code; and

(b) loss resulting directly or indirectly from the fraudulent alteration of an instruction to initiate an automated clearing house (ACH) entry, or group of ACH entries, transmitted as an electronic message, or as an attachment to an electronic message, sent via the Internet, unless:
- (1) each ACH entry was individually verified via the call back procedure without regard to the amount of the entry; or
- (2) the instruction was formatted, encoded or encrypted so that any alteration in the ACH entry or group of ACH entries would be apparent to the Insured.

5. Liability of the Underwriter under this Insuring Agreement shall be a part of, not in addition to, the Aggregate Limit of Liability of this Bond.

6. For purposes of this Insuring Agreement, all loss or losses involving one natural person or entity, or one group of natural persons or entities acting together, shall be a Single Loss without regard to the number of transfers or the number of instructions involved. A series of losses involving unidentified natural persons or entities but arising from the same method of operation shall be deemed to involve the same natural person or entity and shall be treated as Single Loss.

7. The Single Loss Limit of Liability and Single Loss Deductible applicable to loss under this Insuring Agreement are set forth in the Declarations.

8. The amount of any single transfer for which verification via a call back will be required is: $_____

9. This rider shall become effective as of 12:01 a.m. on _____.

Copyright, The Surety & Fidelity Association of America, 2011   SR 6271b

Exhibit 9

RETROACTIVE DATE RIDER/ENDORSEMENT

(Revised May, 2011)

RIDER/ENDORSEMENT

To be attached to and form part of Financial Institution Bond, No.
or Computer Crime Policy for Financial Institutions, No.
in favor of

It is agreed that:

RETROACTIVE DATE — _____
                                     month   day   year

This bond does not cover loss sustained by the Insured resulting directly or indirectly from acts or events occurring prior to the Retroactive Date noted above.

This rider/endorsement shall become effective when the bond/policy becomes effective.

Accepted:

RETROACTIVE DATE RIDER/ENDORSEMENT
FOR USE WITH FINANCIAL INSTITUTION BONDS, STANDARD FORMS NOS. 14, 15, 24, AND 25 AND EXCESS BANK EMPLOYEE DISHONESTY BOND. STANDARD FORM NO. 28 AND COMPUTER CRIME POLICY FOR FINANCIAL INSTITUTIONS.

REVISED MAY, 2011

Exhibit 10

BANKERS BLANKET BOND,
STANDARD FORM NO. 24

(Revised July, 1980)

BANKERS BLANKET BOND
Standard Form No. 24, Revised to July, 1980

Bond No.

(Herein called Company)

DECLARATIONS

Item 1. Name of Insured (herein called Insured):

Principal Address:

Item 2. Bond Period: from 12:01 a.m. on _____ to 12:01 a.m. on the effective date
(MONTH, DAY, YEAR)
of the termination or cancellation of this bond, standard time at the Principal Address as to each of said dates.

Item 3. Limit of Liability and Deductible Amount–
Subject to Sections 3 and 11 hereof,
the Limit of Liability is $ _____ and the Deductible Amount is $ _____
(INSERT AMOUNT) (INSERT AMOUNT)
Provided, however, that if any amounts are inserted below opposite specified Insuring Agreements or Coverage, those amounts shall be controlling. Any amount set forth below shall be part of and not in addition to amounts set forth above. (If an Insuring Agreement or Coverage is to be deleted, insert "Not Covered.")

Amount applicable to:	Limit of Liability	Deductible
Insuring Agreement (D)—FORGERY OR ALTERATION	$	$
Insuring Agreement (E)—SECURITIES	$	$
Misplacement, Mysterious Unexplainable Disappearance Coverage in Insuring Agreement B)—ON PREMISES	$	$

If "Not Covered" is inserted above opposite any specified Insuring Agreement or Coverage, such Insuring Agreement or Coverage and any other reference thereto in this bond shall be deemed to be deleted therefrom.

Item 4. Offices or Premises Covered—All the Insured's offices or premises in existence at the time this bond becomes effective are covered under this bond except the offices or premises located as follows:

Item 5. The liability of the Underwriter is subject to the terms of the following riders attached hereto:

Item 6. The Insured by the acceptance of this bond gives notice to the Underwriter terminating or canceling prior bond(s) or policy(ies) No.(s)
such termination or cancellation to be effective as of the time this bond becomes effective.

The Underwriter, in consideration of an agreed premium, subject to the Declarations, Insuring Agreements, General Agreements, Conditions and Limitations and other terms hereof, agrees to indemnify the Insured for:

INSURANCE AGREEMENTS

FIDELITY

(A) Loss resulting directly from dishonest or fraudulent acts of an Employee committed alone or in collusion with others.

Dishonest or fraudulent acts as used in this Insuring Agreement shall mean only dishonest or fraudulent acts committed by such Employee with the manifest intent
  (a) to cause the Insured to sustain such loss, and
  (b) to obtain financial benefit for the Employee or for any other person or organization intended by the Employee to receive such benefit, other than salaries, commissions, fees, bonuses, promotions, awards, profit sharing, pensions or other employee benefits earned in the normal course of employment.

ON PREMISES

(B) (1) Loss of Property resulting directly from
  (a) robbery, burglary, misplacement, mysterious unexplainable disappearance and damage thereto or destruction thereof, or
  (b) theft, false pretenses, common law or statutory larceny, committed by a person present in an office or on the premises of the Insured,
while the Property is lodged or deposited within offices or premises located anywhere.
(2) Loss of a damage to
  (a) furnishings, fixtures, supplies or equipment with an office of the Insured covered under this bond resulting directly from larceny or theft in, or by burglary or robbery of, such office, or attempt thereat, or by vandalism or malicious mischief, or
  (b) such office resulting from larceny or theft in, or by burglary or robbery of such office or attempt thereat, or to the interior of such office by vandalism or malicious mischief,
provided that,
  (i) the Insured is the owner of such furnishings, fixtures, supplies, equipment, or office or is liable for such loss or damage, and
  (ii) the loss is not caused by fire.

IN TRANSIT

(C) Loss of Property resulting directly from robbery, common-law or statutory larceny, theft, misplacement, mysterious unexplainable disappearance, being lost or otherwise made away with, and damage thereto or destruction thereof, while the Property is in the custody of a person designated by the Insured to act as its messenger (or a person acting as messenger or custodian during an emergency arising from the incapacity of such designated messenger) and while the Property is in transit anywhere, such transit to begin immediately upon receipt of such Property by said messenger and to end immediately upon delivery to the designated recipient or its agent.

FORGERY OR ALTERATION

(D) Loss resulting directly from

(1) Forgery or alteration of, on or in any Negotiable Instrument (except as Evidence of Debt), Acceptance, withdrawal order, receipt for the withdrawal of Property, Certificate of Deposit or Letter of Credit.

(2) transferring paying or delivering any funds or Property or establishing any credit or giving any value on the faith of any written instructions or advices directed to the Insured and authorizing or acknowledging the transfer, payment, delivery or receipt of funds or Property, which instructions or advices purport to have been signed or endorsed by any customer of the Insured or by any banking institution but which instructions or advices either bear a signature which is a Forgery or have been altered without the knowledge and consent of each customer or banking institution. Telegraphic, cable or teletype instructions or advices as aforesaid. exclusive of transmissions of electronic funds transfer systems, sent by a person other than the said customer or banking institution purporting to send such instructions or advices shall be deemed to bear a signature which is a Forgery.

A mechanically reproduced facsimile signature is treated the same as a handwritten signature.

SECURITIES

(E) Loss resulting directly from the insured having, in good faith, for its own account or for the account of others.

(1) acquired, sold or delivered, or given value, extended credit or assumed liability, on the faith of, or otherwise acted upon, any original.

    (a) Security,
    (b) Document of Title,
    (c) deed, mortgage or other instrument conveying title tom, or creating or discharging a lien upon, real property,
    (d) Certificate of Origin or Title,
    (e) Evidence of Debt,
    (f) corporate, partnership or personal Guarantee, or
    (g) Security Agreement

which

    (i) bears a signature of any maker, drawer, issuer, endorser, assignor, lessee, transfer agent, registrar, acceptor, surety, guarantor, or of any person signing in any other capacity which is a Forgery, or
    (ii) is altered, or
    (iii) is lost or stolen;

(2) guaranteed in writing or witnessed any signature upon any transfer, assignment, bill of sale, power of attorney, Guarantee, endorsement or any items listed in (a) through (g) above.

(3) acquired, sold or delivered, or given value, extended credit or assumed liability, on the faith of, or otherwise acted upon, any item listed in (a) through (d) above which is a Counterfeit.

Actual physical possession of the items listed in (a) through (g) above by the Insured, its correspondent bank or other authorized representative, is a condition precedent to the Insured's having relied on the faith of, or otherwise acted upon, such items.

A mechanically reproduced facsimile signature is treated the same as a handwritten signature.

(F) Loss resulting directly from the receipt by the Insured, in good faith, of any Counterfeit or altered Money of the United States of America or Canada.

GENERAL AGREEMENTS

NOMINEES

A. Loss sustained by any nominee organized by the Insured for the purpose of handling certain of its business transactions and composed exclusively of its officers, clerks or other employees shall, for all the purposes of this bond and whether or not any partner of such nominee is implicated in such loss, be deemed to be loss sustained by the Insured.

ADDITIONAL OFFICES OR EMPLOYEES—CONSOLIDATION, MERGER OR PURCHASE OF ASSETS NOTICE

B. If the Insured shall, while this bond is in force, establish any additional offices, other than by consolidation or merger with, or purchase of assets of, another institution, such offices shall be automatically covered hereunder from the date of such establishment without the requirement of notice to the Underwriter or the payment of additional premium for the remainder of the premium period.

If the Insured shall, while this bond is in force, consolidate or merge with, or purchase assets of, another institution, the Insured shall not have such coverage as is afforded under this bond for loss which
    (a) has occurred or will occur in offices or premises, or
    (b) has been caused or will be caused by an employee or employees of an institution, or
    (c) has arising or will arise out of the assets acquired by the Insured as a result of such consolidation, merger or purchase of assets; unless the insured shall
        (i) give the Underwriter written notice of the proposed consolidation, merger or purchase of assets at least 60 days prior to the proposed effective date of the consolidation, merger or purchase of assets, and
        (ii) obtain the written consent of the Underwriter to extend the coverage provided by this bond to such additional offices or premises, Employees and other exposures and
        (iii) pay to the Underwriter an additional premium computed pro rata from the date of such consolidation, merger or purchase of assets to the end of the current premium period.

CHANGE OF CONTROL—NOTICE

C. When the Insured learns of a transfer of its outstanding voting stock which results in a change in control of the Insured, it shall within 30 days give written notice to the Underwriter setting forth
    (a) the names of the transferors and transferees (or the names of the beneficial owners if the shares are registered in another name), and
    (b) the total number of shares owned by the transferors and the transferees (or the beneficial owners), both immediately before and after the transfer, and
    (c) the total number of outstanding shares of voting stock.

As used in this General Agreement, control means the power to determine the management or policy of the Insured by virtue of voting stock ownership. A change in ownership of voting stock which results in direct or indirect ownership by a stockholder or an affiliated group of stockholders of ten per cent (10%) or more of the outstanding voting stock of the Insured shall be presumed to result in a change of control for the purpose of the required notice.

Failure to give the required notice shall result in termination of coverage of this bond, effective upon the date of stock transfer, for any loss in which any transferee is implicated.

WARRANTY

D. No statement made by or on behalf of the Insured, whether contained in the application or otherwise, shall be deemed to be a warranty of anything except that it is true to the best of the knowledge and belief of the person making the statement.

JOINT INSURED

E. If two or more Insureds are covered under this bond, the first named Insured shall act for all Insureds. Payment by the Underwriter to the first named Insured of loss sustained by any Insured shall fully release the Underwriter on account of such loss. If the first named Insured ceases to be covered under this bond, the Insured next named shall thereafter be considered as the first named Insured. Knowledge possessed or discovery made by any Insured shall constitute knowledge or discovery by all Insureds for all purposes of this bond. The liability of the Underwriter for loss or losses sustained by all Insureds shall not exceed the amount for which the Underwriter would have been liable had all such loss or losses been sustained by one Insured.

COURT COSTS AND ATTORNEYS' FEES

F. The Underwriter shall indemnify the Insured against court costs and reasonable attorneys' fees incurred and paid by the Insured in defending any suit or legal proceeding brought against the Insured to enforce the Insured's liability or alleged liability on account of any loss, claim or damage which, if established against the Insured, would constitute a collectible loss under this bond in excess of any Deductible Amount.

The Insured shall promptly give notice to the Underwriter of the institution of any such suit or legal proceeding and at the request of the Underwriter shall furnish it with copies of all pleadings and other papers therein. At the Underwriter's election the Insured shall permit the Underwriter to conduct the defense of such suit or legal proceeding, in the Insured's name, through attorneys of the Underwriter's selection. In such event, the Insured shall give all reasonable information and assistance which the Underwriter shall deem necessary to the defense of such suit or legal proceeding.

If the amount of the Insured's liability or alleged liability is greater than the amount recoverable under this bond, or if a Deductible Amount is applicable, or both, the liability of the Underwriter under this General Agreement is limited to the proportion of court costs and attorneys' fees incurred and paid by the Insured or by the Underwriter that the amount recoverable under this bond bears to the total of such amount plus the amount which is not so recoverable. Such indemnity shall be a part of the Limit of Liability for the applicable Insuring Agreement or Coverage.

If the Underwriter pays court costs and attorneys' fees in excess of its proportionate share of such costs and fees, the Insured shall promptly reimburse the Underwriter for such excess.

CONDITIONS AND LIMITATIONS

DEFINITIONS

Section 1. As used in this bond:
  (a) Acceptance means a draft which the drawee has, by signature written thereon, engaged to honor as presented.

(b) Certificate of Deposit means an acknowledgment in writing by a financial institution of receipt of Money with an engagement to repay it.

(c) Certificate of Origin or Title means a document issued by a manufacturer of personal property or a governmental agency evidencing the ownership of the personal property and by which ownership is transferred.

(d) Counterfeit means an imitation which is intended to deceive and to be taken as an original.

(e) Document of Title means a bill of lading, dock warrant, dock receipt, warehouse receipt or order for the delivery of goods, and also any other document which in the regular course of business or financing is treated as adequately evidencing that the person in possession of it is entitled to receive, hold and dispose of the document and the goods it covers and must purport to be issued by or addressed to a bailee and purport to cover goods in the bailee's possession which are either identified or are fungible portions of an identified mass.

(f) Employee means
   (1) an officer or other employee of the Insured, while employed in, at, or by any of the Insured's offices or premises covered hereunder, and a guest student pursuing studies or duties in any of said offices or premises;
   (2) an attorney retained by the Insured and an employee of such attorney while either is performing legal services for the Insured;
   (3) a person provided by an employment contractor or perform employee duties for the Insured under the Insured's supervision at any of the Insured's offices or premises covered hereunder;
   (4) an employee of an institution merged or consolidated with the Insured prior to the effective date of this bond; and
   (5) each natural person, partnership or corporation authorized by the Insured to perform services as data processor of checks or other accounting records of the Insured, herein called Processor. (Each such Processor, and the partners, officers and employees of such Processor shall, collectively, be deemed to be one Employee for all the purposes of this bond, excepting, however, the second paragraph of Section 12. A Federal Reserve Bank or clearing house shall not be construed to be a processor.)

(g) Evidence of Debt means an instrument, including a Negotiable Instrument, executed by a customer of the Insured and held by the Insured which in the regular course of business is treated as evidencing the customer's debt to the Insured.

(h) Forgery means the signing of the name of another with intent to deceive; it does not include the signing of one's own name with or without authority, in any capacity, for any purpose.

(i) Guarantee means a written undertaking obligating the signer to pay the debt of another to the Insured or its assignee or to a financial institution from which the Insured has purchased participation in the debt. If the debt is not paid in accordance with its terms.

(j) Letter of Credit means an engagement in writing by a bank or other person made at the request of a customer that the bank or other person will honor drafts or other demands for payment upon compliance with the conditions specified in the Letter of Credit.

(k) Money means a medium of exchange in current use authorized or adopted by a domestic or foreign government as a part of its currency.

(l) Negotiable Instrument means any writing
   (1) signed by the maker or drawer; and
   (2) containing an unconditional promise or order to pay a sum certain in Money and no other promise, order, obligation or power given by the maker or drawer; and
   (3) is payable on demand or at a definite time, and
   (4) is payable to order or bearer.

(m) Property means Money, Securities, Negotiable Instruments, Certificates of Deposit, Documents of Title, Acceptances, Evidences of Debt, Security Agreements, withdrawal orders, Certificates of Origin or Title, Letters of Credit, insurance policies, abstracts of title, deeds and mortgages on real estate, revenue and other stamps, tokens, unsold state lottery tickets, books of

account and other records whether recorded in writing or electronically, gems, jewelry, precious metals in bars and ingots, and tangible items of personal property which are not hereinbefore enumerated.
    (n)   Security means an instrument which
           (1)   is issued in bearer or registered form; and
           (2)   is of a type commonly dealt in upon securities exchanges or markets or commonly recognized in any area in which it is issued or dealt in as a medium for investment; and
           (3)   is either one of a class or series or by its terms is divisible into a class or series of instruments; and
           (4)   evidences a share, participation or other interest in property or in an enterprise or evidences an obligation of the issuer.
    (o)   Security Agreement means an agreement which creates an interest in personal property or fixtures and which secures payment or performance of an obligation.

EXCLUSIONS

Section 2. This bond does not cover:
    (a)   loss resulting directly or indirectly from Forgery or alteration, except when covered under Insuring Agreements (A), (D), (E) or (F);
    (b)   loss due to riot or civil commotion outside the United States of America and Canada; or loss due to military, naval or usurped power, war or insurrection unless such loss occurs in transit in the circumstances recited in Insuring Agreement (C), and unless, when such transit was initiated, there was no knowledge of such riot, civil commotion, military, naval or usurped power, war or insurrection on the part of any person acting for the Insured in initiating such transit;
    (c)   loss resulting directly or indirectly from the effects of nuclear fission or fusion or radioactivity; provided, however, that this paragraph shall not apply to loss resulting from industrial uses of nuclear energy;
    (d)   loss resulting directly or indirectly from any acts of any director of the Insured other than one employed as a salaried, pensioned or elected official or an Employee of the Insured, except when performing acts coming within the scope of the usual duties of an Employee, or while acting as a member of any committee duly elected or appointed by resolution of the board of directors of the Insured to perform specific, as distinguished from general, directorial acts on behalf of the Insured;
    (e)   loss resulting directly or indirectly from the complete or partial non-payment of, or default upon, any loan or transaction in the nature of a loan or extension of credit, whether involving the Insured as a lender or as a borrower, including the purchase, discounting or other acquisition of false or genuine accounts, invoices, notes, agreements or Evidences of Debt, whether such loan or transaction was procured in good faith or through trick, artifice, fraud or false pretenses, except when covered under Insuring Agreements (A), (D) or (E);
    (f)   loss of Property contained in customers' safe deposit boxes, except when the Insured is legally liable therefor and the loss is covered under Insuring Agreement (A);
    (g)   loss through cashing or paying forged or altered travelers' checks or travelers' checks bearing forged endorsements, except when covered under Insuring Agreement (A); or loss of unsold travelers' checks or unsold money orders placed in the custody of the Insured with authority to sell, unless (a) the Insured is legally liable for such loss and (b) such checks or money orders are later paid or honored by the drawer thereof, except when covered under Insuring Agreement (A);
    (h)   loss caused by an Employee, except when covered under Insuring Agreement (A):
    (i)   loss resulting directly or indirectly from trading, with or without the knowledge of the Insured, whether or not represented by any indebtedness or balance shown to be due the Insured on any customer's account, actual or fictitious, and notwithstanding any act or omission on the part of any Employee in connection with any account relating in such trading, indebtedness, or balance, except when covered under Insuring Agreements (D) or (E);

(j) shortage in any teller's cash due to error, regardless of the amount of such shortage; and any shortage in any teller's cash which is not in excess of the normal shortage in the tellers' cash in the office where such shortage shall occur shall be presumed to be due to error.

(k) loss resulting directly or indirectly from the use of credit, debit, charge, access, convenience, identification or other cards
    (1) in obtaining credit, or
    (2) in gaining access to automated mechanical devices which, on behalf of the Insured, disburse Money, accept deposits, cash checks, drafts or similar written instruments or make credit card loans, or
    (3) in gaining access to point of sale terminals, customer-bank communication terminals, or similar electronic terminals of electronic funds transfer systems,

whether such cards were issued, or purport to have been issued, by the Insured or by anyone other than the Insured, except when covered under Insuring Agreement (A);

(l) loss involving automated mechanical devices which, on behalf of the Insured, disburse Money, accept deposits, cash checks, drafts or similar written instruments or make credit card loans, unless such automated mechanical devices are situated within an office of the Insured which is permanently staffed by an Employee whose duties are those usually assigned to a bank teller, even though public access is from outside the confines of such office, but in no event shall the Underwriter be liable for loss (including loss of Property)
    (1) as a result of damage to such automated mechanical devices from vandalism or malicious mischief perpetrated from outside such office, or
    (2) as a result of failure of such automated mechanical devices to function properly, or
    (3) through misplacement or mysterious unexplainable disappearance while such Property is located within any such automated mechanical devices,

except when covered under Insuring Agreement (A);

(m) loss through the surrender of Property away from an office of the Insured as a result of a threat
    (1) to do bodily harm to any person, except loss of Property in transit in the custody of any person acting as messenger provided that when such transit was initiated there was no knowledge by the Insured of any such threat, or
    (2) to do damage to the premises or property of the Insured,

except when covered under Insuring Agreement (A);

(n) loss resulting directly or indirectly from payments made or withdrawals from a depositor's account involving erroneous credits to such account, unless such payments or withdrawals are physically received by such depositor or representative of such depositor who is within the office of the Insured at the time of such payment or withdrawal, or except when covered under Insuring Agreement (A);

(o) loss resulting directly or indirectly from payments made or withdrawals from a depositor's account involving items of deposit which are not finally paid for any reason, including but not limited to Forgery or any other fraud, unless such payments or withdrawals are physically received by such depositor or representative of such depositor who is within the office of the Insured at the time of such payment of withdrawal, or except when covered under Insuring Agreement (A);

(p) loss resulting directly or indirectly from counterfeiting, except when covered under Insuring Agreements (A), (E) or (F);

(q) loss of any tangible item of personal property which is not specifically enumerated in the paragraph defining Property and for which the Insured is legally liable, if such property is specifically insured by other insurance of any kind and in any amount obtained by the Insured, and in any event, loss of such property occurring more than 60 days after the Insured shall have become aware that it is liable for the safekeeping of such property, except when covered under Insuring Agreements (A) or (B)(2);

(r) loss or loss of Property in or from an office of premises listed in Item 4 of the Declarations;

(s) loss of Property while in the mail or with a carrier for hire (other than an armored motor vehicle company), except when covered under Insuring Agreement (A);

(t)   potential income, including but not limited to interest and dividends, not realized by the Insured;
(u)   damages of any type for which the Insured is legally liable, except direct compensatory damages arising from a loss covered under this bond;
(v)   costs, fees and other expenses incurred by the Insured in establishing the existence of or amount of loss covered under this bond;
(w)   indirect or consequential loss of any nature.

LIMIT OF LIABILITY/NON-ACCUMULATION OF LIABILITY

Section 3. The total liability of the Underwriter under this bond on account of loss, including court costs and attorneys' fees,
(a)   caused by any one act of burglary, robbery or attempt threat, in which no Employee is implicated, or
(b)   with respect to any one unintentional or negligent act of omission on the part of any person (whether an Employee or not) resulting in damage to or destruction or misplacement of Property, or
(c)   other than those specified in (a) and (b) preceding, caused by all acts or omissions by any person (whether an Employee or not) or all acts of omissions in which such person is implicated, or
(d)   other than those specified in (a), (b) and (c) preceding, resulting from any one casualty or event, is limited to the Limit of Liability stated in Item 3 of the Declarations of this bond or amendment thereto or to the amount of the applicable coverage, if such amount be smaller, without regard to the total amount of such loss.

Subject to the foregoing, payment of loss shall not reduce liability for other losses whenever sustained.

Regardless of the number of years this bond shall continue in force and the number of premiums which shall be payable or paid, the liability of the Underwriter shall not be cumulative in amounts from year to year or from period to period.

If any loss is covered under more than one Insuring Agreement or Coverage the maximum payable for such loss shall not exceed the largest amount available under any one Insuring Agreement or Coverage.

DISCOVERY

Section 4. This bond applies to loss discovered by the Insured during the bond period. Discovery occurs when the Insured becomes aware of facts which would cause a reasonable person to assume that a loss covered by the bond has been or will be incurred, even though the exact amount or details of loss may not then be known.

Notice to the Insured or an actual or potential claim by a third party which alleges that the Insured is liable under circumstances which, if true, would create a loss under this bond constitutes such discovery.

NOTICE/PROOF—LEGAL PROCEEDINGS

Section 5.
(a)   At the earliest practicable moment, not to exceed 30 days, after discovery of loss, the Insured shall give the Underwriter notice thereof.
(b)   Within 6 months after such discovery, the Insured shall furnish to the Underwriter proof of loss, duly sworn to, with full particulars.
(c)   Lost Securities listed in a proof of loss shall be identified by certificate or bond numbers if the Securities were issued therewith.

(d) Legal proceedings for the recovery of any loss hereunder shall not be brought, prior to the expiration of 60 days after the original proof of loss is filed with the Underwriter or after the expiration of 24 months from the discovery of such loss, except that the action or proceeding to recover hereunder on account of any judgment against the Insured in any suit mentioned in General Agreement F, or to recover attorneys' fees paid in any such suit, shall be brought within 24 months from the date upon which the judgment and such suit shall become final.

(e) If any limitation embodied in this bond is prohibited by any law controlling the construction hereof, such limitation shall be deemed to be amended so as to equal the minimum period of limitation provided by such law.

(f) This bond affords coverage only in favor of the Insured. No suit, action or legal proceedings shall be brought hereunder by any one other than the named insured.

VALUATION

Section 6.

Any loss of Money, or loss payable in Money, shall be paid, at the option of the Insured, in the Money of the country in which the loss was sustained or in the United States of America dollar equivalent thereof determined at the rate of exchange at the time of payment of such loss.

Securities

The Underwriter shall settle in kind its liability under this bond on account of a loss of any securities or, at the option of the Insured, shall pay to the Insured the cost of replacing such Securities, determined by the market value thereof at the time of such settlement. In case of a loss of subscription, conversion or redemption privileges through the misplacement or loss of Securities, the amount of such loss shall be the value of such privileges immediately preceding the expiration thereof. If such Securities cannot be replaced or have no quoted market value, of if such privileges have no quoted market value, their value shall be determined by agreement or arbitration.

If the applicable coverage of this bond is subject to a Deductible Amount and/or is not sufficient in amount to indemnify the Insured in full for the loss of Securities for which claim is made hereunder, the liability of the Underwriter under this bond is limited to the payment for, or the duplication of, so much of such Securities as has a value equal to the amount of such applicable coverage.

Books of Account and Other Records

In case of loss of, or damage to, any books of account or other records used by the Insured in its business, the Underwriter shall be liable under this bond only if such books or records are actually reproduced and then for not more than the cost of the blank books, blank pages or other materials plus the cost of labor for the actual transcription or copying of data which shall have been furnished by the Insured in order to reproduce such books and other records.

Property other than Money, Securities or Records

In case of loss of, or damage to, any Property other than Money, Securities, books of account or other records, or damage covered under Insuring Agreement (B)(2), the Underwriter shall not be liable for more than the actual cash value of such Property, or of items covered under Insuring Agreement (B)(2). the Underwriter may, at its election, pay the actual cash value of, replace or repair such property. Disagreement between the Underwriter and the Insured as to the cash value or as to the adequacy of repair or replacement shall be resolved by arbitration.

ASSIGNMENT—SUBROGATION—RECOVERY—COOPERATION

Section 7.
(a) In the event of payment under this bond, the Insured shall deliver, if so requested by the Underwriter, an assignment of such of the Insured's rights, title and interest and causes of action as it has against any person or entity to the extent of the loss payment.

(b) In the event of payment under this bond, the Underwriter shall be subrogated to the Insured's rights of recovery therefor against any person or entity to the extent of such payment.

(c) Recoveries, whether effected by the Underwriter or by the Insured, shall be applied net of the expense of such recovery first to the satisfaction of the Insured's loss in excess of the amount paid under this bond, secondly, to the Underwriter as reimbursement of amounts paid in settlement of the Insured's claim, and thirdly, to the Insured in satisfaction of any Deductible Amount, Recovery on account of loss of Securities as set forth in the second paragraph of Section 6 or recovery from reinsurance and/or indemnity of the Underwriter shall not be deemed a recovery as used herein.

(d) Upon the Underwriter's request and at reasonable times and places designated by the Underwriter the Insured shall
   (1) submit to examination by the Underwriter and subscribe to the same under oath; and
   (2) produce for the Underwriter's examination all pertinent records; and
   (3) cooperate with the Underwriter in all matters pertaining to the loss.

(e) The Insured shall execute all papers and render assistance to secure to the Underwriter the rights and causes of action provided for herein. The Insured shall do nothing after discovery of loss to prejudice such rights or causes of action.

LIMIT OF LIABILITY UNDER THIS BOND AND PRIOR INSURANCE

Section 8. With respect to any loss set forth in subsection (c) of Section 3 of this bond which is recoverable or recovered in whole or in part under any other bonds or policies issued by the Underwriter to the Insured or to any predecessor in interest of the Insured and terminated or canceled or allowed to expire and in which the period for discovery has not expired at the time any such loss thereunder is discovered, the total liability of the Underwriter under this bond and under such other bonds or policies shall not exceed, in the aggregate, the amount carried hereunder on such loss or the amount available to the Insured under such other bonds or policies, as limited by the terms and conditions thereof, for any such loss if the latter amount be the larger.

If the coverage of this bond supersedes in whole or in part the coverage of any other bond or policy of insurance issued by an Insurer other than the Underwriter and terminated, canceled or allowed to expire, the Underwriter, with respect to any loss sustained prior to such termination, cancellation or expiration and discovered within the period permitted under such other bond or policy for the discovery of loss thereunder, shall be liable under this bond only for that part of such loss covered by this bond as is in excess of the amount recoverable or recovered on account of such loss under such other bond or policy, anything to the contrary in such other bond or policy notwithstanding.

OTHER INSURANCE OR INDEMNITY

Section 9. Coverage afforded hereunder shall apply only as excess over any valid and collectible insurance or indemnity obtained by the Insured, or by one other than the Insured on Property subject to exclusion (g) or by an armored motor vehicle company, or by another entity on whose premises the loss occurred or which employed the person causing the loss or the messenger conveying the Property involved.

OWNERSHIP

Section 10. This bond shall apply to loss of Property (1) owned by the Insured, (2) held by the Insured in any capacity, or (3) for which the Insured is legally liable. This bond shall be for the sole use and benefit of the Insured named in the Declarations.

DEDUCTIBLE AMOUNT

Section 11. The underwriter shall be liable hereunder only for the amount by which any loss exceeds the Deductible Amount for the Insuring Agreement or Coverage applicable to such loss, subject to the Limit of Liability for such Agreement or Coverage.

The Insured shall, in the time and in the manner prescribed in this bond, give the Underwriter notice of any loss of the kind covered by the terms of this bond, whether or not the Underwriter is liable therefor, and upon the request of the Underwriter shall file with it a brief statement giving the particulars concerning such loss.

TERMINATION OR CANCELLATION

Section 12. This bond shall be deemed terminated or canceled as an entirety—(a) 60 days after the receipt by the Insured of a written notice from the Underwriter of its desire to terminate or cancel this bond, or (b) immediately upon the receipt by the Underwriter of a written request from the Insured to terminate or cancel this bond, or (c) immediately upon the taking over of the Insured by a receiver or other liquidator or by State or Federal officials, or (d) immediately upon the taking over of the Insured by another institution. The Underwriter shall, on request, refund to the Insured the unearned premium, computed pro rata, if this bond be terminated or canceled or reduced by notice from, or at the instance of, the Underwriter, or if the terminated or canceled as provided in subsection (c) or (d) of this paragraph. The Underwriter shall refund to the Insured the unearned premium computed at short rates if this bond be terminated or canceled or reduced by notice from, or at the instance of, the Insured.

This bond shall be deemed terminated or canceled as to any Employee or any partner, officer or employee of any Processor—(a) as soon as any Insured, or any director or officer not in collusion with such person, shall learn of any dishonest or fraudulent act committed by such person at any time against the Insured or any other person or entity without prejudice to the loss of any Property then in transit in the custody of such person, or (b) 15 days after the receipt by the Insured of a written notice from the Underwriter of its desire to terminate or cancel this bond as to such person.

Termination of the bond as to any Insured terminates liability for any loss sustained by such Insured which is discovered after the effective date of such termination.

RIGHTS AFTER TERMINATION OR CANCELLATION

Section 13. At any time prior to the termination or cancellation of this bond as an entirety, whether by the Insured or the Underwriter, the Insured may give to the Underwriter notice that it desires under this bond an additional period of 12 months within which to discover loss sustained by the Insured prior to the effective date of such termination or cancellation and shall pay an additional premium therefor.

Upon receipt of such notice from the Insured, the Underwriter shall give its written consent thereto; provided, however, that such additional period of time shall terminate immediately
  (a) on the effective date of any other insurance obtained by the Insured, it successor in business or any other party replacing in whole or in part the insurance afforded by this bond, whether or not such other insurance provides coverage for loss sustained prior to its effective date, or

(b) upon any takeover of the Insured's business by any State or Federal official or agency, or by any receiver or liquidator, acting or appointed for this purpose.

without the necessity of the Underwriter giving notice of such termination. In the event that such additional period of time is terminated, as provided above, the Underwriter shall refund any unearned premium.

The right to purchase such additional period for the discovery of loss may not be exercised by any State or Federal official or agency, or by any receiver or liquidator, acting or appointed to take over the Insured's business for the operation or for the liquidation thereof or for any other purpose.

In witness whereof, the Underwriter has caused this bond to be executed on the Declarations Page.

Exhibit 11

STATEMENT OF CHANGE,
BANKERS BLANKET BOND,
STANDARD FORM NO. 24

(Revised to July, 1980)

STATEMENT OF CHANGE
BANKERS BLANKET BOND, STANDARD FORM NO. 24
Revised to July, 1980

The Surety Association of America, in collaboration with the American Bankers Association, has revised the Bankers Blanket Bond to July, 1980. Other than editorial amendments, the changes are as follows:

DECLARATIONS PAGE

The Declarations Page has been modified to allow the insertion of the Deductible Amount in Item 3. Thus, certain deductible riders are no longer necessary when the bond is issued. Specific language dealing with Insuring Agreements (D) and (E) and misplacement coverage has been inserted.

GENERAL COMMENT

Provisions of the following riders have been included in this Bond:

1.	SR 6019—Definition of Dishonesty and Exclusions	8.	SR 5936c—Extortion Exclusion
2.	SR 5538—Joint Insured Rider	9.	SR 6030a—Trading Loss Exclusion
3.	SR 5524d—(D) Aggregate Deductible	10.	SR 6064—Uncollected Funds Exclusion
4.	SR 5791e—(E) Aggregate Deductible	11.	SR 6015—Notice of Merger
5.	SR 5527b—Misplacement Coverage	12.	SR 6014a—Notice of Change of Control
6.	SR 5653c—Deductible - Not (D) or (E)	13.	SR 5923b—60 Day Cancellation Rider
7.	SR 5887c—Credit Card, etc., Exclusion	14.	SR 6059—Effective Time Rider
		15.	SR 5886c—Automated Teller Machine Rider

INSURING AGREEMENTS

INSURING AGREEMENT (A) covers dishonest or fraudulent acts of Employees. This Insuring Agreement is an incorporation of rider SR 6019, which was originally promulgated in April, 1976. Language in the prior edition of the bond dealing with Property held by the Insured has been relocated to a new Ownership Section.

INSURING AGREEMENT (B), On Premises, has been modified as follows:
* * The Agreement has been broken down into outline form and now clearly requires that "false pretenses" and similar crimes must be committed on bank premises, although the Property may be located "within offices or premises anywhere."
* * Language specifically covering property of a bank customer has been eliminated. Coverage for customer property still exists under the Ownership Section if the bank is liable for the loss.
* * Language relating to "subscription, conversion redemption or deposit privileges" has been eliminated. In the Valuation Section, however, there is still reference to loss of subscription, conversion or redemption privileges. No adequate definition of a "deposit privilege" was found, and the term was deleted.
* * The parenthetical phrase "(or is supposed to be)" has been eliminated. This language was placed in the bond over 40 years ago for competitive purposes and serves no real purpose.

** The phrase "occurring with or without negligence or violence" has been eliminated from Agreements (B) and (C) as it adds nothing to the coverage. Also, the colloquial expression "hold-up" has been removed from both Agreements.

** A new exclusion, (r), deletes coverage for non-covered offices listed in Item 4 of the Declarations Page. New exclusion (s) deals with property in the mail or with a carrier for hire.

INSURING AGREEMENT (C), In Transit, has been modified as follows:

** The language describing the messenger now requires that the messenger be a "designated" messenger rather than "any person... acting as messenger."

** Provision for emergency situations caused by the unexpected incapacity of the messenger has been inserted into this Agreement.

** It is now clear that transit coverage ceases when Property is delivered to the agent of the recipient, even if that agent is not within the office of the recipient.

INSURING AGREEMENT (D), Forgery or Alteration, has been rewritten in Uniform Commercial Code terminology.

** The laundry list of negotiable instruments has been eliminated and a short reference is made to "any Negotiable Instrument." Certain other paper instruments remain in the list in addition to negotiable instruments. An Evidence of Debt is specifically eliminated from Agreement (D) because coverage exists in Agreement (E).

** Language referring to the fictitious payee has been deleted from this Insuring Agreement because the Uniform Commercial Code treats the signature of a fictitious person as a forgery. Thus, specific reference is unnecessary.

** The defined term Forgery is used in Insuring Agreement (D) to describe those signatures or endorsements which give rise to covered loss.

** Specific statement is made that transmissions through an electronic funds transfer system shall not be considered the same as a message sent through a telegraph system for coverage purposes.

INSURING AGREEMENT (E), Securities, has been largely rewritten. The following changes have been made:

** Specific reference by name is made to those paper instruments which are covered under this Agreement and most are defined in Uniform Commercial terms in the definitions section. This is in contrast to the 1969 edition of the bond in which securities were simply defined as negotiable or non-negotiable instruments having transferable value.

** It is made clear that the Securities Insuring Agreement now runs to specified counterfeits as well as forgeries. The definitions of forgery and counterfeit are now in the definitions section.

** This is no reference in the new Insuring Agreement to carbon copies of instruments. The instruments must be "original."

** Much of the language dealing with the "whether or not" situations has been eliminated due to the fact that it adds nothing to the coverage.

** Old Insuring Agreement (F) entitled Redemption of United States Savings Bonds has been absorbed by new Insuring Agreement (E). Savings bonds fall into the category of covered instruments if they have been either counterfeit or bear a forged signature.

** The exclusionary language relating to Insuring Agreement (D) has been removed because the two Agreements now cover different instruments.

INSURING AGREEMENT (F), Counterfeit Currency, has been shortened by the elimination of language dealing with the United States of America or Canadian Statutes. The word "Counterfeit" is defined in the Definitions Section.

APPENDIX — BOND FORMS

GENERAL AGREEMENTS

GENERAL AGREEMENTS A and D unchanged.

GENERAL AGREEMENT B, Additional Offices or Employees, has been rewritten similar to the rider calling for notice of consolidation or merger which was promulgated in 1976. Employees or offices acquired prior to the effective date of the bond are treated in the new definition of Employee discussed below.

GENERAL AGREEMENT C, Change of Control-Notice, is an incorporation of the Change of Control Rider which has been in use for several years. It requires that the Insured give to the underwriter notice of a change of control within thirty days after such change. Failure to give this notice of change results in failure of coverage for any loss in which the transferee of stock or voting rights is involved.

GENERAL AGREEMENT E, Joint Insured, is new to this bond. It is, however, essentially the existing Joint Insured Rider which has been slightly rewritten and inserted into the bond as a new General Agreement. The concept is not new. Several portions of the Rider have been relocated to other appropriate parts of the bond.

GENERAL AGREEMENT F, Court Costs and Attorney's Fees, has been simplified. The mathematical formula for determining the proportion of fees to be borne by the underwriter is set forth in the third paragraph of this Agreement. In addition, to editorial changes, the Agreement makes it clear that any expense payable under this General Agreement is part of the limit of liability of the applicable Insuring Agreement and not in addition to that limit. This is in contrast to the former approach.

DEFINITIONS

There are a number of definitions new to the Bond. Most were modeled on definitions found in the Uniform Commercial Code. Other revised or new definitions include:

** EMPLOYEE now has as part of its definition language relating to "temporary" employees acquired through a temporary placement agency. Also, reference is made to employees of an institution which was merged with the Insured before the effective date of the bond. The phrase "or premises" was inserted after the word "office" here and in other sections.

** FORGERY now means the imitation of a signature and does not, under any circumstances, include the signing of one's own name. In other words, mere unauthorized signatures are not covered under this bond.

** The definition of PROPERTY has been considerably shortened. The use of the defined term Negotiable Instruments in this definition makes it unnecessary to list all of the negotiable instruments covered. The reference to property owned by a predecessor in the interest has been removed because of new General Agreement B, and reference to bailment situations has been removed because of the new Ownership Section. Unsold state lottery tickets are specifically named. Many items of personal property are no longer individually referred to because of the new catch-all phrase, "tangible items of personal property not hereinbefore enumerated." Precious metals must now be in "bars or ingots" rather than "in any form."

EXCLUSIONS

Several existing exclusions have been incorporated into the revised bond. These are:
1. trading loss exclusion—now (i)
2. credit card, etc., exclusion—now (k)
3. automated teller machine exclusion—now (l)

840 ANNOTATED FINANCIAL INSTITUTION BOND

4. extortion exclusion—now (m)
5. erroneous entry exclusion—now (n)
6. uncollected funds exclusion—now (o)
7. indirect and consequential loss exclusions—now (t), (u), (v), and (w)

The erroneous entry exclusion and the uncollected funds exclusion now make reference to funds "physically received by such depositor." Exclusion (h) is a concrete expression of an existing exclusion. Only Insuring Agreement (A) is intended to cover wrongful acts of employees. Thus, exclusion (h) limits coverage for employee acts to Agreement (A).

* * * * * * * * * *

Many of the remaining sections of the bond have only editorial changes. However, the following may be noted.

LIMIT OF LIABILITY/NON-ACCUMULATION OF LIABILITY—Section 3

This section, and several others following, reflect the effort of the drafters to organize the bond in more logical fashion. Little is new in this Section, except that the provision that one loss shall not be covered under more than one Insuring Agreement is now clearly set forth.

DISCOVERY—Section 4

An explanation of "discovery" based on the perceptions of a reasonable person has been inserted. The insured is not relieved from the duty of notification simply because details of the loss are unknown. Discovery also occurs when a third party alleges that the insured is liable for loss which would be covered under the bond, if the allegation is true. Thus, the insured is required to notify the surety at the commencement (or earlier) of a suit, not after judgment.

NOTICE/PROOF—LEGAL PROCEEDINGS—Section 5

New material in this section includes a requirement that notice of loss be submitted within thirty days after discovery of loss. Also, lost securities must be identified by certificate number, if so identifiable.

VALUATION—Section 6

This section has been extensively edited for the sake of clarity. However, the only change of any substance is the provision that the Underwriter shall be liable for only the replacement of lost securities up to an amount equal to the dollar amount of coverage applicable to the loss.

ASSIGNMENT—SUBROGATION—RECOVERY—COOPERATION—Section 7

Language found here is essentially that of the Salvage Section of the 1969 bond. New requirements call for employees of the Insured to give depositions or produce pertinent records. The carrier's equitable right of subrogation is specifically called for in this section.

OWNERSHIP—Section 10

This new sections pulls together concepts found in several places in the 1969 bond. Here it is stated that insured property may be owned by the Insured, held by the Insured, or for which the Insured is liable. It is stated that the bond is for the sole use and benefit of the Insured.

DEDUCTIBLE AMOUNT—Section 11

This new section is derived from the old deductible rider. Provision for the reporting of loss less than the Deductible Amount has been retained.

TERMINATION OR CANCELLATION—Section 12

The sixty day cancellation rider has been incorporated into this section. In the second paragraph it is made clear that a dishonest or fraudulent act committed at any time against anyone will terminate coverage for an individual employee. The final paragraph is borrowed from the Joint Insured Rider.

RIGHTS AFTER TERMINATION OR CANCELLATION—Section 13

Note that any additional period for discovery which may have been purchased by the Insured will automatically terminate in the event of a takeover by a governmental entity. Further, the right to purchase the additional period is not offered to any official body.

* * * * * * * * * *

**THIS STATEMENT IS INTENDED TO BE INFORMATIVE ONLY.
THE TERMS AND PROVISION OF THE BOND AND RIDERS WILL GOVERN
ANY QUESTION ARISING IN CONNECTION THEREWITH**

Table of Cases

The following is an alphabetical listing of all cases annotated in this book. Although the cases that were annotated were shepardized, the subsequent history of the cases was not cited at the end of the individual annotations. As a result, the following list also does not include the subsequent history of the case. As always is prudent, a case should be shepardized before it is relied upon. Additionally, although this book generally follows *The Bluebook*,[1] editorial discretion was used, when deemed appropriate. Thus, for instance, although *The Bluebook* requires citation to a specific date for an electronic data base case citation, such a requirement did not seem necessary for purposes of this book. Thus, the reader hopefully will understand why the electronic data base citations that follow do not include the complete date.

175 Check Cashing Corp. v. Chubb Pac. Indem. Group,
  464 N.Y.S.2d 118 (N.Y. App. Div. 1983)..................................228

175 E. 74th Corp. v. Hartford Acc. & Indem. Co.,
  416 N.E.2d 584 (N.Y. 1980) 452, 597

A.B.S. Clothing Collection, Inc., v. Home Ins. Co.,
  41 Cal. Rptr. 2d 166 (Cal. Ct. App. 1995)..........................384, 688

Abady v. Certain Underwriters at Lloyd's London,
  No. 2012 COA 173, 2012 Colo. App. LEXIS 1650
  (Colo. App. 2012)..680

ABC Imaging of Wash., Inc. v. Travelers Indem. Co. of Am.,
  820 A.2d 628 (Md. Ct. Spec. App. 2003)............................49, 637

ABCO Premium Fin., LLC v. Am. Int'l Grp., Inc.,
  518 F. App'x 601 (11th Cir. 2013)...386

---

1   THE BLUEBOOK: A UNIFORM SYSTEM OF CITATION (Columbia Law Review Association et al. eds., 19th ed. 2010).

ABCO Premium Fin., LLC v. Am. Int'l Grp., Inc.,
　No. 12-14780, 2013 WL 1442517 (11th Cir. 2013) 579

ABCO Premium Fin. LLC v. Am. Int'l Group, Inc.,
　No. 11-23020, 2012 U.S. Dist. LEXIS 111833
　(S.D. Fla. 2012) 355, 640, 685

Abilene Sav. Ass'n v. Westchester Fire Ins. Co.,
　461 F.2d 557 (5th Cir. 1972) 427, 673

Acadia Ins. Co. v. Keiser Indus., Inc.,
　793 A.2d 495 (Me. 2002) 368, 440, 529

Ace Van & Storage Co. v. Liberty Mut. Ins. Co.,
　336 F.2d 925 (D.C. Cir. 1964) 439, 456

Acid Piping Tech., Inc. v. Great Northern Ins. Co.,
　No. 4:04CV1667, 2005 U.S. Dist. LEXIS 27110
　(E.D. Mo. 2005) 691

Acuity v. Rodenbaugh (In re Rodenbaugh),
　431 B.R. 473 (Bankr. E.D. Mo. 2010) 477

Adair State Bank v. Am. Cas. Co.,
　949 F.2d 1067 (10th Cir. 1991) 38, 353, 409, 518, 669

Adirondack Trust Co. v. St. Paul Mercury Ins. Co.,
　No. 1:09-cv-1313, 2010 WL 2425915 (N.D.N.Y. 2010) 104, 313

Admin. Servs. of N. Am., Inc. v. Hartford Fid. & Bonding Co.,
　245 F. App'x 384 (5th Cir. 2007) 442

Admiralty Fund v. Peerless Ins. Co.,
　191 Cal. Rptr. 753 (Cal. Ct. App. 1983) 365, 671

Aetna Cas. & Sur. Co. v. Commercial State Bank,
　13 F.2d 474 (E.D. Ill. 1926) 13

Aetna Cas. & Sur. Co. v. Cont'l Ins. Co.,
　429 S.E.2d 406 (N.C. 1993) 495

Aetna Cas. & Sur. Co. v. Guar. Bank & Trust Co.,
    370 F.2d 276 (1st Cir. 1966) 345, 397, 404, 596

Aetna Cas. & Sur. Co. v. Kidder, Peabody & Co.,
    676 N.Y.S.2d 559 (N.Y. App. Div. 1998) 35, 201, 328, 682

Aetna Cas. & Sur. Co. v. Kidder, Peabody & Co. Inc.,
    246 A.D.2d 202 (N.Y. App. 1998) 594

Aetna Cas. & Sur. Co. v. La. Nat'l Bank,
    399 F. Supp. 54 (M.D. La. 1975) 69, 650

Aetna Cas. & Sur. Co. v. S. Brokerage Co.,
    443 S.W.2d 45 (Tex. 1969) 202

Aetna Indem. Co. v. J.R. Crowe Coal & Mining Co.,
    154 F. 545 (8th Cir. 1907) 351, 398, 408

*Affiliated Bank/Morton Grove v. Hartford Accident &
    Indem. Co.*,
    No. 9 C 4446, 1992 WL 91761
    (N.D. Ill. 1992) 27, 41, 243, 282, 312

Akin Foods, Inc. v. Am. & Foreign Ins. Co.,
    No. C04-2195, 2005 WL 2090678
    (W.D. Wash. 2005) 525

Akins Foods, Inc. v. Am. & Foreign Ins. Co.,
    No. C04-2195, 2005 U.S. Dist. LEXIS 36765
    (W.D. Wash. 2005) 693

Alcona County v. Mich. Mun. League Liab. & Prop.,
    No. 292155, 2011 Mich. App. LEXIS 473
    (Mich. Ct. App. 2011) 18

Aldridge Elec., Inc. v. Fid. & Dep. Co. of Md.,
    No. 04 C 4021, 2008 U.S. Dist. LEXIS
    85090 (N.D. Ill. Sept. 10, 2008) 624, 625, 627, 628, 686

Alerus Fin. Nat'l Ass'n v. St. Paul Mercury Ins. Co.,
   No. A11-680, 2012 WL 254484
   (Minn. Ct. App. 2012) 107, 112, 130, 146, 600

Alfalfa Elec. Coop., Inc. v. Travelers Indem. Co.,
   376 F. Supp. 901 (W.D. Okla. 1973) 15, 362, 412, 429,
                                                            439, 444, 447, 458, 523

Alianza Hispano-Americana v. Hartford Acc. & Indem. Co.,
   209 F.2d 578 (9th Cir. 1954) 428

Allen State Bank v. Traveler's Indem. Co.,
   270 So. 2d 270 (La. Ct. App. 1972) 106, 115, 139, 287, 607

Alpine State Bank v. Ohio Cas. Ins. Co.,
   941 F.2d 554 (7th Cir. 1991) 72, 92, 122, 236, 309, 626

Am. Auto Guardian, Inc. v. Acuity Mut. Ins. Co.,
   548 F. Supp. 2d 624 (N.D. Ill. 2008) 384, 686

Am. Bonding & Trust Co. v. Burke,
   85 P. 692 (Colo. 1906) 173

Am. Bonding Co. of Baltimore v. Morrow,
   96 S.W. 613 (Ark. 1906) 172

Am. Bonding Co. of Baltimore v. Spokane Bldg. & Loan Soc.,
   130 F. 737 (9th Cir. 1904) 169

Am. Cas. Co. v. Continisio,
   819 F. Supp. 385 (D.N.J. 1993) 420

Am. Cas. Co. v. Etowah Bank,
   288 F.3d 1282 (11th Cir. 2002) 163, 510, 556, 624, 695

Am. Commerce Ins. Brokers, Inc. v. Minn. Mut. Fire & Cas. Co.,
   551 N.W.2d 224 (Minn. 1996) 390

Am. Empire Ins. Co. v. Fid. & Deposit Co. of Md.,
   408 F.2d 72 (5th Cir. 1969) 449, 613, 678

Am. Employer's Ins. Co. v. Roundup Coal Mining Co.,
 73 F.2d 592 (8th Cir. 1934) 602

Am. Emp'rs Ins. Co. v. Metro Reg'l Trans. Auth.,
 12 F.3d 591 (6th Cir. 1994) 427

Am. Emp'rs' Ins. Co. v. Raton Wholesale Liquor Co.,
 123 F.2d 283 (10th Cir. 1941) 353, 410

Am. Fire & Cas. Co. v. Burchfield,
 232 So. 2d 606 (Ala. 1970) 439, 672

Am. Ins. Co. v. First Nat'l Bank in St. Louis,
 409 F.2d. 1387 (8th Cir. 1969) 125, 660

Am. Nat'l Bank & Trust Co. of Bowling Green v. Hartford Acc. & Indem. Co.,
 442 F.2d 995 (6th Cir. 1971) 60, 267, 660

Am. Nat'l Bank & Trust Co. of S. Pasadena v. Fid. & Cas. Co. of N.Y.,
 431 F.2d 920 (5th Cir. 1970) 132, 659

Am. Nat'l Ins. Co. v. U.S. Fire & Guar. Co.,
 215 So. 2d 245 (Miss. 1968) 621

Am. Sav. Bank, F.S.B. v. Hartford Acc. & Indem. Co.,
 No. 88-3512, 1989 WL 76912 (9th Cir. 1989) 73

Am. Stevedores, Inc. v. Sun Ins. Office, Ltd.,
 248 N.Y.S.2d 487 (N.Y. Sup. Ct. 1964) 401, 422

Am. Sur. Co. of N.Y. v. Bankers Sav. Ass'n of Omaha,
 59 F.2d 577 (8th Cir. 1932) 351, 408, 428

Am. Sur. Co. v. Blount Cnty. Bank,
 30 F.2d 882, cert. denied, 280 U.S. 561 (5th Cir. 1929) 454

Am. Sur. Co. v. Capitol Bldg. & Loan Ass'n,
 50 P.2d 792 (Colo. 1935) 606

Am. Sur. Co. v. Peoples Bank,
    189 S.E. 414 (Ga. Ct. App. 1936) 458

Am. Sur. Co. v. State,
    12 P.2d 212 (Okla. 1932) 371, 418

Am. Trust & Sav. Bank v. USF&G,
    418 N.W.2d 853 (Iowa 1988).. 325, 620, 678

American Surety Co. v. Pauly,
    170 U.S. 133 (1898) .... v, 342, 344, 403

Amerisure Ins. Co. v. Debruyn Produce Co.,
    825 N.W.2d 666 (Mich. Ct. App. 2012).................................... 50, 637

Anchor Equities, Ltd. v. Pac. Coast Am.,
    737 P.2d 532 (N.M. 1987).. 452

Anderson v. Emp'rs Ins. Co.,
    826 F.2d 777 (8th Cir. 1987).. 449, 589

APMC Hotel Mgmt, LLC v. Fid. & Deposit Co. of Md.,
    No. 2:09-cv-2100-LDG-VCF, 2011 WL 5525966
    (D. Nev. 2011).. 387

APMC Hotel Mgt., LLC v. Fid. & Deposit Co. of Md.,
    No. 5:07-cv-00652, 2011 U.S. Dist. LEXIS 131638
    (D. Nev. 2010).. 687

Arlington Trust Co. v. Hawkeye Sec. Ins. Co.,
    301 F. Supp. 854 (E.D. Va. 1969)..................................... 16, 606, 619

Arrowood Indem. Co. v. Hartford Fire Ins. Co.,
    774 F. Supp. 2d 636 (D. Del. 2011) 443, 446, 449, 456, 645

Ashland Fin. Co. v. Hartford Acc. & Indem. Co.,
    474 S.W.2d 364 (Ky. Ct. App. 1971).. 441

Atkin v. Hill, Darlington, & Grimm,
    254 N.Y.S.2d 867 (N.Y. App. Div. 1964)....................................... 202

TABLE OF CASES

Atlas Metals Prod. Co., Inc. v. Lumbermans Mut. Cas. Co.,
829 N.E.2d 257 (Mass. App. Ct. 2005) 681

Atlas Metals Prods. Co. v. Lumbermans Mut. Cas. Co.,
63 Mass. App. Ct. 738 (Mass App. 2007) 594

Auburn Ford Lincoln Mercury, Inc. v. Universal Underwriters Ins. Co.,
967 F. Supp. 475 (M.D. Ala. 1997) 47, 636

Auto Lenders Acceptance Corp. v. Gentilini Ford, Inc.,
816 A.2d 1068 (N.J. Super. Ct. App. Div. 2003) 34

Auto Lenders Acceptance Corp. v. Gentilini Ford, Inc.,
854 A.2d 378 (N.J. 2004) 44, 390, 586, 594

Auto-Owners Ins. Co. v. Bank One,
852 N.E.2d 604, (Ind. App. Ct. 2006) 480

Avery Dennison Corp. v. Allendale Mut. Ins. Co.,
310 F.3d 1114 (9th Cir. 2002) 674

Avery Dennison Corp. v. Allendale Mut. Ins. Co.,
No. CV 99-09217CM, 2000 WL 33964136
(C.D. Cal. 2000) 252

B & H Supply Co., Inc. v. Ins. Co. of N. Am.,
311 S.E.2d 643 (N.C. Ct. App. 1984) 425, 462, 621

B. Constantino & Sons Co. v. New Amsterdam Cas. Co.,
234 F.2d 902 (7th Cir. 1956) 349, 407

Baltimore Bank & Trust Co. v. USF&G,
436 F.2d 743 (8th Cir. 1971) 143

Banca Nazionale Del Lavoro v. Lloyd's,
458 S.E.2d 142 (Ga. Ct. App. 1995) 527

BancInsure, Inc. v. BNC Nat'l Bank, N.A.,
263 F.3d 766 (8th Cir. 2001) 25

BancInsure, Inc. v. Highland Bank,
No. 11-cv-2497, 2012 U.S. Dist. LEXIS 171545
(D. Minn. 2012) 660

BancInsure, Inc. v. Highland Bank,
No. 11-cv-2497, slip op. (D. Minn. 2013) 599

BancInsure, Inc. v. Highland Bank,
No. 11-cv-2497, slip op. (D. Minn. 2013) 138

BancInsure, Inc. v. Marshall Bank, N.A.,
400 F. Supp. 2d 1140 (D. Minn. 2005) 236, 656

BancInsure, Inc. v. Marshall Bank, N.A.,
453 F.3d 1073 (8th Cir. 2006) 140

BancInsure, Inc. v. Peoples Bank of the S.,
866 F. Supp. 2d 577 (S.D. Miss. 2012) 487

BancInsure, Inc. v. U.K. Bancorporation Inc.,
830 F. Supp. 2d 294 (E.D. Ky. 2011) 169

Banco de San German, Inc. v. Md. Cas. Co.,
344 F. Supp. 496 (D.P.R. 1972) 15

Bank of Ann Arbor v. Everest Nat'l Ins. Co.,
No. 12-11251, 2013 U.S. Dist. LEXIS 24999
(E.D. Mich. 2013) 258, 624, 626

Bank of Ann Arbor v. Everest Nat'l Ins. Co.,
No. 12-11251, 2013 WL 665067
(E.D. Mich. 2013) 113, 243, 283, 575

Bank of Bozeman v. BancInsure, Inc.,
404 F. App'x 117 (9th Cir. 2010) 140, 598, 655

Bank of Cumberland v. Aetna Cas. & Sur. Co.,
956 F.2d 595 (6th Cir. 1992) 271

TABLE OF CASES

Bank of Dade v. Fid. & Deposit Co. of Md.,
483 F.2d 735 (5th Cir. 1973) 59, 72

Bank of Danielsville v. Seagraves,
305 S.E.2d 790 (Ga. App. 1983) 709

Bank of Huntington v. Smothers,
626 S.W.2d 267 (Tenn. Ct. App. 1981) 325, 622

Bank of Mead v. St. Paul Fire & Marine Ins. Co.,
275 N.W.2d 822 (Neb. 1979) 201

Bank of Mulberry v. Fireman's Fund Ins. Co.,
720 F.2d 501 (8th Cir. 1983) 602

Bank One, Steubenville v. Buckeye Union Ins. Co.,
683 N.E.2d 50 (Ohio Ct. App. 1996) 98, 503

Bank One, W. Va. v. USF&G,
869 F. Supp. 426 (S.D. W. Va. 1994) 325

Bank of the Orient v. Super. Court S.F. Cnty.,
136 Cal. Rptr. 741 (Cal. Ct. App. 1977) 480

Bank Saderat Iran N.Y. Agency v. Nat'l Union Fire Ins. Co. of Pitt., Pa.,
665 N.Y.S.2d 79 (N.Y. Sup. Ct. App. Div. 1997) 689

Bank of the Sw. v. Nat'l Sur. Co.,
477 F.2d 73 (5th Cir. 1973) 60, 79, 121, 277

Bank of Tarboro v. Fid. & Deposit Co. of Md.,
38 S.E. 908 (N.C. 1901) 401

BankInsure, Inc. v. Peoples Bank of the S.,
866 F. Supp. 2d 577 (S.D. Miss. 2012) 244, 284, 294, 487

Bankmanagers Corp. v. Fed. Ins. Co.,
712 F.3d 1163 (7th Cir. 2013) 72

Bankmanagers Corp. v. Fed. Ins. Co.,
   No. 11-871, 2012 U.S. Dist. LEXIS 129647
   (E.D. Wis. 2012) 198, 647

Basler Turbo Conversions, LLC v. HCC Ins. Co.,
   601 F. Supp. 2d 1082 (E.D. Wis. 2009) 390

Bass v. Am. Ins. Co.,
   493 F.2d 590 (9th Cir. 1974) 299

Bay Area Bank v. Fid. & Deposit Co. of Md.,
   629 F. Supp. 693 (N.D. Cal. 1986) 73, 312, 589

Bd. of Ins. Comm'r of Tex. v. Allied Underwriters,
   180 S.W.2d 990 (Tex. App. 1944) 372, 419

Beach Cmty. Bank v. St. Paul Mercury Ins. Co.,
   635 F.3d 1190 (11th Cir. 2011) 125, 144, 598

Beanstalk Group, Inc. v. AM General Corp.,
   283 F.3d 856 (7th Cir. 2002) 629

Beckley Mech., Inc. v. Erie Ins. Co.,
   No. 5:07-cv-00652, 2009 U.S. Dist. LEXIS 30881
   (S.D. W. Va. 2009) 688

Bell Gardens Bicycle Casino v. Great Am. Ins. Co.,
   124 F. App'x 551 (9th Cir. 2005) 655

Bellamark, Neuhauser & Barrett, Inc. v. Hanover Ins. Co.,
   531 F. Supp. 4 (D.D.C. 1980) 467

Benchmark Crafters, Inc. v. NW. Nat'l Ins. Co.,
   363 N.W.2d 89 (Minn. Ct. App. 1985) 34, 44, 50

Benchmark Printing, Inc. v. Am. Mfrs. Mut. Ins. Co.,
   No. 00-CV-0865, 2001 U.S. Dist. LEXIS 619
   (N.D.N.Y. 2001) 675

Benton State Bank v. Hartford Acc. & Indem. Co.,
    338 F. Supp. 674, *aff'd*, 452 F.2d 5 (8th Cir. 1971) (E.D.
    Ark. 1971) 685

Benton State Bank v. Hartford Acc. & Indem. Co.,
    452 F.2d. 5 (8th Cir. 1971) 386

Bethany Christian Church v. Preferred Risk Mut. Ins. Co.,
    942 F. Supp. 330 (S.D. Tex. 1996) 387

Better v. Prudential Ins. Co.,
    11 N.Y.S. 70 (N.Y. Gen. Term. 1890) 448

Beverly Bancorp., Inc. v. Cont'l Ins. Co.,
    No. 92C4823, 1992 WL 345420
    (N.D. Ill. 1992) 196, 329, 331, 675

Bickerstaff Imports, Inc. v. Sentry Select Ins. Co.,
    682 S.E.2d 365 (Ga. Ct. App. 2009) 441, 458

Bidwell & Co. v. Nat'l Union Fire Ins. Co. of Pitt., Pa.,
    No. CV-00-89-HU, 2001 WL 204843
    (D. Or. 2001) 99, 314, 585, 603

Bird v. Centennial Ins. Co.,
    11 F.3d 228 (1st Cir. 1993) 638

Bissinger & Co. v. Mass. Bonding & Ins. Co.,
    163 P. 592 (Or. 1917) 175

Block v. Granite State Ins. Co.,
    963 F.2d 1127 (8th Cir. 1992) 407

Block v. Granite State Ins. Co.,
    No. 87-0658-CV-W-6, 1989 U.S. Dist. LEXIS 13388
    (W.D. Mo. 1989) 360

Bloedow v. Nitschke,
    1 N.W.2d 762 (Wis. 1942) 177

Boomershine Pontiac-GMC Truck, Inc. v. Globe Indem. Co.,
466 S.E.2d 915 (Ga. App. 1996) 366

Boston Mut. Life Ins. Co. v. Fireman's Fund Ins. Co.,
613 F. Supp. 1090 (D. Mass. 1985) 344, 358, 411,
429, 521

Boston Sec., Inc. v. United Bonding Ins. Co.,
441 F.2d 1302 (8th Cir. 1971) 10, 614

Bradley Bank v. Hartford Acc. & Indem. Co.,
557 F. Supp. 243 (W.D. Wis. 1983) 65, 74, 653

Bradley Bank v. Hartford Acc. & Indem. Co.,
737 F.2d 657 (7th Cir. 1984) 311, 647

Brady Nat'l Bank v. Gulf Ins. Co.,
94 F. App'x. 197 (5th Cir. 2004) 192, 597

Bralko Holding, Ltd. v. Ins. Co. of N. Am.,
483 N.W.2d 929 (Mich. App. 1992) 594, 681

Brandon v. Holman,
41 F.2d 586 (4th Cir. 1930) 38, 633

Bremen State Bank v. Hartford Acc. & Indem. Co.,
427 F.2d 425 (7th Cir. 1970) 69, 649

Briggs v. Brown,
46 So. 325 (Fla. 1908) 703

Brigham Young Univ. v. Lumbermens Mut. Cas. Co.,
965 F.2d 830 (10th Cir. 1992) 494, 616, 684

Broadway Nat'l Bank v. Progressive Cas. Ins. Co.,
775 F. Supp. 123 (S.D.N.Y. 1991) 304, 313

Brown v. Md. Cas. Co.,
11 A.2d 222 (Vt. 1940) 373, 420, 432

Brugioni v. Md. Cas. Co.,
 382 S.W.2d 707 (Mo. 1964) 70, 542, 543

Bus. Interiors, Inc. v. Aetna Cas. & Sur. Co.,
 751 F.2d 361 (10th Cir. 1984) 386

C.A. White, Inc. v. Travelers Cas. & Sur. Co. of Am.,
 No. CV0850L35515, 2009 Conn. Super. LEXIS 989
 (Conn. Super. Ct. 2009) 526, 694

C. Douglas Wilson & Co. v. Ins. Co. of N. Am.,
 590 F.2d 1275 (4th Cir. 1979) 6, 347, 514

Cal. Kor. Bank v. Va. Sur. Co.,
 Nos. 98-56778, 98-56806, 2000 U.S. App. LEXIS 12306
 (9th Cir. 2000) 195, 589

Cal. Korea Bank v. Va. Sur. Co.,
 No. 98-56778, 2000 WL 713798 (9th Cir. 2000) 62, 102

Cal. Union Ins. Co. v. Am. Diversified Sav. Bank,
 948 F.2d 556 (9th Cir. 1991) 352, 509, 626, 640, 694

Calcasieu-Marine Nat'l Bank v. Am. Emp'rs Ins. Co.,
 533 F.2d 290 (5th Cir. 1976) 60, 137, 241, 276, 654

Cambridge Trust Co. v. Commercial Union Ins. Co.,
 591 N.E.2d 1117 (Mass. App. Ct. 1992) 325

Capital Bank & Trust Co. v Gulf Ins. Co.,
 91 A.D.3d 1251 (N.Y. App. Div. 2012) 19, 530

Capital Bank & Trust Co. v. Gulf Ins. Co.,
 937 N.Y.S.2d 463 (N.Y. App. Div. 2012) 693

Capitol Bank of Chicago v. Fid. & Cas. Co. of N.Y.,
 414 F.2d 986 (7th Cir. 1969) 134, 279

Cargill, Inc. v. Nat'l Union Fire Ins. Co. of Pitt., Pa.,
 No. A03-187, 2004 WL 51671 (Minn. Ct. App. 2004) 603, 681

Cary v. Nat'l Sur. Co.,
   251 N.W. 123 (Minn. 1933) 461

Carytown Jewelers, Inc. v. St. Paul Travelers Cos., Inc.,
   No. 3:06 CV 312, 2007 U.S. Dist. LEXIS 3620
   (E.D. Va. 2007) 641

Cen. Nat'l Ins. Co. v. Ins. Co. of N. Am.,
   522 N.W.2d 39 (Iowa 1994) 593

Cent. Mut. Ins. Co. v. Starr (In re Starr),
   No. 11-16958, 2012 Bankr. LEXIS 630
   (Bankr. N.D. Ohio 2012) 478

Cent. Nat'l Life Ins. Co. v. Fid. & Deposit Co. of Md.,
   626 F.2d 537 (7th Cir. 1980) 8, 349, 406

Cent. Progressive Bank v. Fireman's Fund Ins. Co.,
   658 F.2d 377 (5th Cir. 1981) 7, 515, 604, 668

Cent. Sch. Dist. v. Ins. Co. of N. Am.,
   391 N.Y.S.2d 492 (N.Y. App. Div. 1977) 80

Century Bank v. St. Paul Fire & Marine Ins. Co.,
   482 P.2d 193 (Cal. 1971) 662

Century Bank v. St. Paul Fire & Marine Ins. Co.,
   93 Cal. Rptr. 569 (Cal. 1971) 128

Century Bus. Serv., Inc. v. Utica Mut. Ins. Co.,
   122 F. App'x 196 (6th Cir. 2005) 693

Ceylon Farmers' Elevator Co. v. Fid. & Deposit Co. of Md.,
   203 N.W. 985 (Minn. 1925) 461

*Charles W. Schreiber Travel Bureau v. Standard Sur. &
   Cas. Co.*,
   240 A.D. 279 (N.Y. App. Div. 1934) 417

Charles W. Schreiber Travel Bureau v. Standard Sur. & Cas. Co.,
  269 N.Y.S. 804 (N.Y. App. 1934) 370

Charm Promotions, Ltd. v. Travelers Indem. Co.,
  489 F.2d 1092 (7th Cir. 1973) 230

Charter Bank NW v. Evanston Ins. Co.,
  791 F.2d 379 (5th Cir. 1986) 91, 101, 121, 266, 276

Christ Lutheran Church v. State Farm Fire & Cas. Co.,
  471 S.E.2d 124 (N.C. Ct. App. 1996) 388

Ciancetti v. Indem. Ins. Co. of N. Am.,
  335 P.2d 1048 (Cal. 1959) 526

Cincinnati Ins. Co. v. Hopkins Sporting Goods, Inc.,
  522 N.W.2d 837 (Iowa 1994) 384, 691

Cincinnati Ins. Co. v. Sherman & Hemstreet, Inc.,
  581 S.E.2d 613 (Ga. Ct. App. 2003) 384

Cincinnati Ins. Co. v. Star Fin. Bank,
  35 F.3d 1186 (7th Cir. 1994) 92, 193, 613

Cincinnati Ins. Co. v. Tuscaloosa Cnty. Parking & Transit Auth.,
  827 So. 2d 765 (Ala. 2002) 49, 637

Cincinnati Ins. Co. v. Wachovia Bank, N.A.,
  No. 08-CV-2734, 2010 U.S. Dist. LEXIS 70670
  (D. Minn. 2010) 476

Citibank Texas, N.A. v. Progressive Cas. Ins. Co.,
  522 F.3d 591 (5th Cir. 2008) 91, 189, 659

Citizens and S. Nat'l Bank v. Am. Sur. Co.,
  347 F.2d 18 (5th Cir. 1965) 472

Citizens Bank & Trust Co. v. St. Paul Mercury Ins. Co.,
   No. cv 305-167, 2007 U.S. Dist. LEXIS 96529
   (S.D. Ga. 2007) 675

Citizens Bank & Trust Co. v. St. Paul Mercury Ins. Co.,
   No. CV305-167, 2007 WL 4973847 (S.D. Ga. 2007) 322

Citizens Bank, N.A. v. Kan. Bankers Sur. Co.,
   149 P.3d 25, 2007 WL 45946 (Kan. Ct. App. 2007) 75, 586, 593

Citizens Bank, N.A. v. Kan. Bankers Sur. Co.,
   No. 95,136, 2007 Kan. App. Unpub. LEXIS 524
   (Kan. Ct. App. 2007) 681

Citizens Bank of Newburg v. Kan. Bankers Sur. Co.,
   971 F. Supp. 1301 (E.D. Mo. 1997) 387

Citizens Bank of Or. v. Am. Ins. Co.,
   289 F. Supp. 211 (D. Or. 1968) 145, 605, 618, 677

Citizens Banking Corp. v. Gulf Ins. Co.,
   No. 03-CV-74044, 04-CV-70459, 2005 U.S. Dist. LEXIS
   47762 (E.D. Mich. 2005) 660

Citizens Nat'l Bank of St. Petersburg v. Travelers Indem. Co.,
   296 F. Supp. 300 (M.D. Fla. 1967) 282

Citizens State Bank of Big Lake v. Capitol Indem. Corp.,
   No. C1-95-321, 1995 WL 421672, *at 2-3 (Minn. Ct. App.
   1995) 34, 43

Citizens State Bank of St. Paul v. New Amsterdam Cas. Co.,
   224 N.W. 451 (Minn. 1929) 430

Citizens State Bank v. Transamerica Ins. Co.,
   452 F.2d 199 (7th Cir. 1971) 9, 605, 634

Citizens Trust & Guar. Co. v. Globe & Rutgers Fire Ins. Co.,
   229 F. 326 (4th Cir. 1915) 633

TABLE OF CASES

City Bank & Trust Co. v. Commercial Cas. Co.,
176 So. 27 (La. Ct. App. 1937) 174

City of Burlington v. W. Sur. Co.,
599 N.W.2d 469 (Iowa 1999) 593, 680

City Loan & Sav. Co. v. Emp'rs Liab. Assurance Corp.,
249 F. Supp. 633 (N.D. Ohio 1964) 362, 412, 429, 523

City of Miami Springs v. Travelers Indem. Co.,
365 So. 2d 1030 (Fla. Dist. Ct. App. 1978) 384

City State Bank in Wellington v. USF&G,
778 F.2d 1103 (5th Cir. 1985) 348, 515

City Trust & Sav. Bank of Kankakee N. Ill. v. Lloyds Underwriting Members,
109 F.2d 110 (7th Cir. 1940) 482

Clarendon Bank & Trust v. Fid. & Deposit Co. of Md.,
406 F. Supp. 1161 (E.D. Va. 1975) 64, 97, 285, 651

Cmty. Fed. Sav. & Loan Ass'n v. Gen. Cas. Co.,
274 F.2d 620 (8th Cir. 1960) 654

Cmty. Nat'l Bank in Monmouth v. St. Paul Fire & Marine Ins. Co.,
399 F. Supp. 873 (S.D. Ill. 1975) 63, 282

Cmty. Nat'l Bank v. Fid. & Deposit Co.,
563 F.2d 1319 (9th Cir. 1977) 474

Cmty. Sav. Bank v. Fed. Ins. Co.,
960 F. Supp. 16 (D. Conn. 1997) 354, 428, 519

Cmty. State Bank v. Hartford Ins. Co.,
542 N.E.2d 1317 (Ill. App. Ct. 1989) 129, 661

Columbia Cmty. Bank v. Progressive Cas. Ins. Co.,
No. 10-817-AA, 2011 U.S. Dist. LEXIS 64004
(D. Or. 2011) 128, 145, 599

Columbia Heights Motors, Inc. v. Allstate Ins. Co.,
275 N.W.2d 32 (Minn. 1979) 385

Columbia Hosp. for Women and Lying-in Asylum v. USF&G,
188 F.2d 654 (D.C. Cir. 1951) 379, 685

Columbia Union Nat'l Bank v. Hartford Acc. & Indem. Co.,
496 F. Supp. 1263 (W.D. Mo. 1980) 64

Columbia Union Nat'l Bank v. Hartford Acc. & Indem. Co.,
669 F.2d 1210 (8th Cir. 1982) 189, 350, 407

Comm. Standard Ins. Co. v. J.D. Hufstedler Truck Co.,
443 S.W.2d 54 (Tex. App. 1969) 463

Commerce Bank & Trust v. St. Paul Mercury Ins. Co.,
No. 04-1264B, 2005 Mass. Super. LEXIS 692
(Mass. Super. Ct. May 31, 2005) 625, 629, 630

Commerce Bank & Trust v. St. Paul Mercury Ins. Co.,
No. 04-1264B, 2005 WL 4881101
(Mass. Super. Ct. 2005) 106, 268

Commercial Bank of Bluefield v. St. Paul Fire. & Marine Ins. Co.,
336 S.E.2d 552 (W. Va. 1985) 592, 622

Commercial Casualty Ins. Co. v. Hartford Accident & Indem. Co.,
2 N.E.2d 517 (N.Y. 1936) 537

Commodore Int'l, Ltd. v. Nat'l Union Fire Ins. Co. Pitt., Pa.,
591 N.Y.S.2d 168 (N.Y. App. 1992) 370

Comm'rs of Leonardtown v. Fid. & Cas. Co. of N.Y.,
270 A.2d 788 (Md. App. 1970) 381

Commw. of Pa. v. Ins. Co. of N. Am.,
    436 A.2d 1067 (Pa. Commer. Ct) 595

Condon v. Nat'l Sur. Corp.,
    254 N.Y.S.2d 620 (N.Y. 1964) 301

Conestoga Title Ins. Co. v. Premier Title Agency, Inc.,
    746 A.2d 462 (N.J. Super. Ct. App. Div. 2000) 228

Conference Assocs., Inc. v. Travelers Cas. and Sur. Co. of Am.,
    914 N.Y.S.2d 310 (N.Y. App. Div. 2011) 490

Cont'l Bank, N.A. v. Aetna Cas. & Sur. Co.,
    626 N.Y.S.2d 385 (N.Y. Sup. Ct. 1995) 35, 595

Cont'l Bank v. Aetna Cas. & Sur. Co.,
    No. 024780/91 (N.Y. Sup. Ct. Feb. 17, 1994) 4

Cont'l Bank v. Phoenix Ins. Co.,
    101 Cal. Rptr. 392 (Cal. Ct. App. 1972) 657

Cont'l Bank v. Phoenix Ins. Co.,
    24 Cal. App. 3d 909 (Cal. Ct. App. 1972) 139

Cont'l Cas. Co. v. Compass Bank,
    No. 04-0766-KD-C, 2006 U.S. Dist. LEXIS 13009
    (S.D. Ala. 2006) 38

Cont'l Corp. v. Aetna Cas. & Sur. Co.,
    892 F.2d 540 (7th Cir. 1989) 194, 298, 585, 588, 679

Cont'l Ins. Co. v. Morgan, Olmstead, Kennedy & Gardner,
    148 Cal. Rptr. 57 (Cal. Ct. App. 1978) 670

Cont'l Ins. Co. v. Morgan, Olmstead, Kennedy & Gardner, Inc.,
    83 Cal. App. 3d. 593 (Cal. Ct. App. 1978) 198

Cont'l Sav. Ass'n v. USF&G,
    762 F.2d 1239 (5th Cir. 1985) 7, 188, 192

Cont'l Studios v. Am. Auto Ins. Co.,
    64 N.W.2d 615 (Mich. 1954) 430

Cooper Sportswear Mfg. Co. v. Hartford Cas. Ins. Co.,
    818 F. Supp. 721 (D.N.J. 1993) 522

Coopersville Motors, Inc., v. Federated Mut. Ins. Co.,
    771 F. Supp. 2d 796 (W.D. Mich. 2011) 617

Corwin Chrysler-Plymouth, Inc. v. Westchester Fire Ins. Co.,
    279 N.W.2d 324 (N.D. 1979) 621

Crystal Ice Co. v. United Sur. Co.,
    123 N.W. 619 (Mich. 1909) 460

Ctrl. Nat'l Ins. Co. v. Ins. Co. of N. Am.,
    522 N.W.2d 39 (Iowa 1994) 451, 593

CUMIS Ins. Soc'y, Inc. v. Keilig,
    No. 11-1115, 2012 U.S. Dist. LEXIS 7199
    (D. Kan. 2012) 475

Cummins, Inc. v. Atl. Mut. Ins. Co.,
    867 N.Y.S. 2d 81 (App. Div. 2008) 629

Cyprus Fed. Credit Union v. Cumis Ins. Soc.,
    No. 2:10CV00550, 2012 U.S. Dist. LEXIS 75643
    (D. Utah 2012) 666

Cyprus Fed. Credit Union v. CUMIS Ins. Soc'y, Inc.,
    No. 2:10CV00550, 2012 WL 1952460 (D. Utah 2012) 65

Dakota W. Credit Union v. CUMIS Ins. Soc'y,
    532 F. Supp. 2d 1110 (D.N.D. 2008) 135, 220, 222, 656

Daniel Grocer Co. v. New Amsterdam Cas. Co.,
    266 N.E.2d 365 (Ill. App. 1971) 604

DeBaise v. Commercial Union Ins. Co.,
    53 Misc. 2d 45 (N.Y. Civ. Ct. 1967) 249

Del. State Bank v. Colton,
  170 P. 992 (Kan. 1918) 459

Delmar Bank of Univ. City v. Fid. & Deposit Co. of Md.,
  428 F.2d 32 (8th Cir. 1970) 93

Depositors Trust Co. v. Md. Cas. Co.,
  174 A.2d 288 (Me. 1961) 657

DeRonde v. Gaytime Shops,
  239 F.2d 735 (2d Cir. 1957) 700, 701, 709

Diamond Transp. Sys., Inc. v. Travelers Indem. Co.,
  817 F. Supp. 710 (N.D. Ill. 1993) 387

Dickson v. State Farm Lloyds,
  944 S.W.2d 666 (Tex. App. 1997) 51, 637

Diebold Inc. v. Cont'l Cas. Co.,
  430 F. App'x 201 (3d Cir. 2011) 346, 668

Dimmerman v. First Union Nat'l Bank,
  No. A-6334-05T2, 2008 N.J. Super. Unpub. LEXIS 3053 481

Direct Mortg. Corp. v. Nat'l Union Fire Ins. Co. of Pa.,
  625 F. Supp. 2d 1171 (D. Utah. 2008) 332, 591

Direct Mortgage Corp. v. Nat'l Union Fire Ins. Co. of Pitt., Pa.,
  No. 2:06-cv-534, 2008 U.S. Dist. LEXIS 60695
  (D. Utah 2008) 680

*Dist. No. 1-Pac. Coast Dist., Marine Eng'rs' Beneficial Ass'n v.
  Travelers Cas. & Sur. Co.,*
  782 A.2d 269 (D.C. 2001) 483, 667

Diversified Grp., Inc. v. Van Tassel,
  806 F.2d 1275 (5th Cir. 1987) 320

Dixie Fire Ins. Co. v. Am. Bonding Co.,
  78 S.E. 430 (N.C. 1913) 401, 425

Dixie Nat'l Bank of Dade Cnty. v. Emp'rs Commercial Union Ins. Co. of Am.,
  759 F.2d 826 (11th Cir. 1985) 485

Docking v. Nat'l Sur. Co.,
  252 P. 201 (Kan. 1927) 459

Downer v. Amalgamated Meatcutters and Butcher Workmen of N. Am.,
  550 S.W.2d 744 (Tex. Civ. App. 1977) 19, 707, 709

Downey Sav. & Loan Ass'n v. Ohio Cas. Ins. Co.,
  234 Cal. Rptr. 835 (Cal. Ct. App. 1987) 191, 364

Drexel Burnham Lambert Group, Inc. v. Vigilant Ins. Co.,
  595 N.Y.S.2d 999 (N.Y. App. Div. 1993) 202, 333, 334, 370, 595, 682

Du Bois Nat'l Bank v. Hartford Acc. & Indem. Co.,
  161 F.2d 132 (3d Cir. 1947) 453

Duel v. Nat'l Sur. Corp.,
  64 F. Supp. 961 (E.D. Wis. 1945) 436, 525

Duke v. Fid. & Deposit Co.,
  5 F.2d 305 (9th Cir. 1925) 169

E. Attucks Cmty. Hous. Inc. v. Old Republic Sur. Co.,
  114 S.W.3d 311 (Mo. Ct. App. 2003) 489

E. Attucks Cmty. Hous. v. Old Republic Sur. Co.,
  No. WD 61142, 2003 Mo. App. LEXIS 936
  (Mo. Ct. App. 2003) 643

E. Gadsden Bank v. USF&G,
  415 F.2d 357 (5th Cir. 1969) 277

E. Liverpool China Co. v. Ill. Sur. Co.,
  152 Ill. App. 89 (Ill. App. Ct. 1909) 447

E. Udolf, Inc. v. Aetna Cas. & Sur. Co.,
  573 A.2d 1211 (Conn. 1990) 366, 526

Eagle Indem. Co. v. Cherry,
  182 F.2d 298 (5th Cir. 1950) 8

Eagle Leasing Corp. v. Hartford Fire Ins. Co.,
  540 F.2d 1257 (5th Cir. 1976) 629

Eaglepitcher Mgmt. Co. v. Zurich Am. Ins. Co.,
  640 F. Supp. 2d 1109 (D. Ariz. 2009) 354

Eddystone Fire Co. No. 1 v. Cont'l Ins. Cos.,
  425 A.2d 803 (Pa. Super Ct. 1981) 382, 690

Eglin Nat'l Bank v. Home Indem. Co.,
  583 F.2d 1281 (5th Cir. 1978) 7, 633

Elberton Cotton Mills, Inc. v. Indem. Ins. Co. of N. Am.,
  145 A. 33 (Conn. 1929) 439

*Ellenberg v. Certain Underwriters at Lloyds (In re Prime
  Commercial Corp)*,
  187 B.R. 785, 797-98 (Bankr. N.D. Ga. 1995) 356, 640

Eliot Nat'l Bank v. Beal,
  6 N.E. 742 (Mass. 1886) 448

Emcor Group v. Great Am. Ins. Co.,
  No. 1:12-cv-142, 2013 U.S. Dist. LEXIS 43346
  (D. Md. 2013) 686

Empire Bank v. Fid. & Deposit Co. of Md.,
  27 F.3d 333 (8th Cir. 1994) 57, 294

Empire Bank v. Fid. & Deposit Co. of Md.,
  828 F. Supp. 675 (W.D. Mo. 1993) 295, 591

Empire of Carolina, Inc. v. Cont'l Cas. Co.,
  N.C. App. 675 (4th Cir. 1992 (N.C.) 247

Empire State Bank v. St. Paul Fire & Marine Ins. Co.,
 441 N.W.2d 811 (Minn. Ct. App. 1989) 130, 657

Emp'rs Admin. Servs., Inc. v. Hartford Acc. & Indem. Co.,
 709 P.2d 559 (Ariz. Ct. App. 1985) 231, 642

Emp'rs Ins. of Wausau v. Doonan,
 712 F. Supp. 1368 (C.D. Ill. 1989) 485

Emp'rs' Liab. Assurance Corp. of London, England v. Wasson,
 75 F.2d 749 (8th Cir. 1935) 168

Emp'rs Liab. Assurance Corp. v. S. Produce Co., Inc.,
 129 So. 2d 247 (La. Ct. App. 1961) 381, 528

Emp'rs Liab. Assurance Corp. v. Stanley Deposit Bank,
 149 S.W. 1025 (Ky. 1912) 399

Emp'rs Mut. Cas. Co. v. DGG & CAR, Inc.,
 183 P.3d 513 (Ariz. 2008) 387, 688

Emp'rs Reinsurance Corp. v. Landmark,
 547 N.W.2d 527 (N.D. 1996) 231

Emp'rs-Shopmens Local 516 Pension Trust v. Travelers Cas. and Sur. Co. of Am.,
 235 P. 3d 689 (Oregon Ct. App. 2009) 207, 646

Endeco, Inc. v. Fid. and Cas. Co. of N.Y.,
 718 F.2d 879 (8th Cir. 1983) 383

Equitable Sur. Co. v. Bank of Hazen,
 181 S.W. 279 (Ark. 1915) 458

Ernst & Young LLP v. Nat'l Union Fire Ins. Co. Pitt., Pa.,
 758 N.Y.S.2d 304 (N.Y. App. 2003) 594, 675

Essex County State Bank v. Fireman's Fund Ins. Co.,
 331 F. Supp. 931 (D.N.J. 1971) 14, 361

TABLE OF CASES

Estate of K.O. Jordan v. Hartford Acc. & Indem. Co.,
813 P.2d 1279 (Wash. Ct. App) 453

Estate of K.O. Jordan v. Hartford Accident & Indem. Co.,
844 P.2d 403 (Wash. 1993) 20, 37, 45,
52, 595, 635

Everhart v. Drake Mgmt. Inc.,
627 F.2d 686 (5th Cir. 1980) 448, 587, 613, 679

Exch. Bank of Novinger v. Turner,
14 S.W.2d 425 (Mo. 1929) 461

Exch. Nat'l Bank of Olean v. Ins. Co. of N. Am.,
341 F.2d 673 (2d Cir. 1965) 100, 131

Exchange State Bank v. Kan. Bankers Sur. Co.,
177 P.3d 1284 (Kan. Ct. App. 2008) 627

Exeter Banking Co. v. N.H. Ins. Co.,
438 A.2d 310 (N.H. 1981) 139, 201

F.S. Smithers & Co., Inc. v. Fed. Ins. Co.,
631 F.2d 1364 (9th Cir. 1980) 195, 629, 668

Farm Credit Bank of Tex. v. Fireman's Fund Ins. Co.,
822 F. Supp. 1251 (W.D. La. 1993) 14, 197

Farmers & Merchs. State Bank of Pierz v. St. Paul Fire & Marine Ins. Co.,
242 N.W.2d 840 (Minn. 1976) 200, 272, 295, 596

Farmers & Merchs. State Bank v. Fid. & Deposit Co. of Md.,
204 N.W. 33 (Minn. 1925) 400

Farmers Auto. Ins. Ass'n v. St. Paul Mercury Ins. Co.,
482 F.3d 976 (7th Cir. 2007) 629

Farmers Bank & Trust Co. of Winchester v. Transam. Ins. Co.,
674 F.2d 548 (6th Cir. 1982) 267, 278

Farmers' Produce Co. v. Aetna Cas. & Sur. Co.,
213 N.W. 685 (Mich. 1927) 460, 607

FDIC v. Aetna Cas. & Sur. Co.,
426 F.2d 729 (5th Cir. 1970) 8, 348, 405, 515, 644

FDIC v. Aetna Cas. & Sur. Co.,
744 F. Supp. 729 (E.D. La. 1990) 424

FDIC v. Aetna Cas. & Sur. Co.,
903 F.2d 1073 (6th Cir. 1990) 348, 509

FDIC v. Aetna Cas. & Sur. Co.,
947 F.2d 196 (6th Cir. 1992) 38, 167

FDIC v. CNA Cas. of P.R.,
786 F. Supp. 1082 (D.P.R. 1991) 15, 363, 413, 524, 634

FDIC v. Denson,
908 F. Supp. 2d 792 (S.D. Miss. 2012) 359, 521

FDIC v. Denson,
No. 3:11CV498, 2012 U.S. Dist. LEXIS 159672
(S.D. Miss. 2012) 670

FDIC v. Fid. & Deposit Co. of Md.,
827 F. Supp. 385 (M.D. La. 1993) 127, 134, 216, 220, 476, 482

FDIC v. Fid. & Deposit Co.,
Nos. 03-55752, 03-55876, 2005 U.S. App. LEXIS 8933
(9th Cir. 2005) 487

FDIC v. Fid. & Deposit Co. of Md.,
132 F. App'x 139 (9th Cir. 2005) 351

FDIC v. Fid. & Deposit Co. of Md.,
45 F.3d 969 (5th Cir. 1995) 6, 40, 347, 405, 601

FDIC v. Fid. & Deposit Co. of Md.,
No. 3:95-CV-1094, 1997 WL 560616 (N.D. Tex. 1997) 512

FDIC v. Fid. & Deposit Co. of Md.,
 No. 3:95-CV-1094-R, 1997 U.S. Dist. LEXIS 24375
 (N.D. Tex. 1997) 363

FDIC v. Fid. & Deposit Co. of Md.,
 No. 92-2109, 1994 U.S. Dist. LEXIS 462996 (E.D. La.
 1994)... 357

FDIC v. Fid. & Deposit Co. of Md.,
 No. 92-2109, 1994 WL 117790 (E.D. La. 1994) 511

FDIC v. Fireman's Ins. Co. of Newark, N.J.,
 109 F.3d 1084 (5th Cir. 1997)........................ 123, 152, 601, 624, 662

FDIC v. Hartford Acc. & Indem. Co.,
 97 F.3d 1148 (8th Cir. 1996)... 441, 455

FDIC v. Ins. Co. of N. Am.,
 105 F.3d 778 (1st Cir. 1997) 187, 345, 403, 426, 630, 672

FDIC v. Ins. Co. of N. Am.,
 928 F. Supp. 54 (D. Mass. 1996)... 358, 429

FDIC v. Kan. Bankers Sur. Co.,
 963 F.2d 289 (10th Cir. 1992)... 510

FDIC v. Lott,
 460 F.2d 82 (5th Cir. 1972).................................... 230, 348, 405, 515

FDIC v. Moskowitz,
 946 F. Supp. 322 (D.N.J. 1996)... 170, 361

FDIC v. N.H. Ins. Co.,
 953 F.2d 478 (9th Cir. 1991)......................... 352, 434, 443, 644, 668

FDIC v. N.H. Ins. Co.,
 No. 90-55865, 1992 U.S. App. LEXIS 2372 (9th Cir. 1992).......... 644

FDIC v. Nat'l Sur. Co.,
 434 F. Supp. 61 (E.D.N.Y. 1977).. 478

FDIC v. Nat'l Sur. Corp.,
281 N.W.2d 816 (Iowa 1979)... 17, 367

FDIC v. Nat'l Union Fire Ins. Co.,
No. 01-2524, 2003 WL 262502 (3d Cir. 2003).................................... 4

FDIC v. Nat'l Union Fire Ins. Co. of Pittsburgh, Pa.,
146 F. Supp. 2d 541 (D.N.J. 2001)... 28

FDIC v. Nat'l Union Fire Ins. Co. of Pittsburgh, Pa.,
205 F.3d 66 (2nd Cir. 2000)... 4, 5, 21, 330, 601

FDIC v. Nat'l Union Fire Ins. Co. of Pittsburgh, Pa.,
57 Fed. Appx. 965 (3d Cir. 2003) 22

FDIC v. Oldenburg,
34 F.3d 1529 (10th Cir. 1994) 3, 26, 38, 169, 353
423, 517, 632, 672

FDIC v. Reliance Ins. Corp.,
716 F. Supp. 1001 (E.D. Ky. 1989)... 356, 435

FDIC v. St. Paul Cos.,
634 F. Supp. 2d 1213 (D. Colo. 2008) 40, 232, 354, 410,
428, 510, 576

FDIC v. St. Paul Fire & Marine Ins. Co.,
738 F. Supp. 1146 (M.D. Tenn. 1990) 15, 48, 363, 524

FDIC v. St. Paul Fire & Marine Ins. Co.,
942 F.2d 1032 (6th Cir. 1991) 3, 24, 121

*FDIC v. Underwriters of Lloyd's of London Fid. Bond
Number 834/FB9010020,*
3 F. Supp. 2d 120 (D. Mass. 1998).................................. 170, 358, 429

FDIC v. United Pac. Ins. Co.,
152 F.3d 1266 (10th Cir. 1998).. 482, 615

FDIC v. United Pac. Ins. Co.,
   20 F.3d 1070 (10th Cir. 1994) 3, 26, 482, 615, 676

FDIC v. W. Sur. Co.,
   285 N.W. 909 (S.D. 1939) 176

Fed. Ins. Co. v. Allen,
   92 Cal. Rptr. 125 (Cal. Ct. App. 1970) 486

Fed. Ins. Co. v. Toiyabe Supply Co.,
   409 P.2d 623 (Nev. 1966) 481

Fed. Ins. Co. v. United Cmty. Banks, Inc.,
   No. 2:08-cv-0128-RWS, 2010 U.S. Dist.
   LEXIS 101646 (N.D. Ga. 2010) 41, 627

Fed. Sav. & Loan Ins. Assoc. v. Aetna Ins. Co.,
   279 F. Supp. 161 (N.D. Ill. 1968) 386, 686

Fed. Sav. & Loan Ins. Corp. v. Aetna Cas. & Sur. Co.,
   785 F. Supp. 867 (D. Mont. 1990) 39, 360, 429

Fenner v. Am. Sur. Co.,
   156 S.W.2d 279 (Tex. App. 1941) 439

Fid. & Cas. Co. v. Bank of Altenburg,
   216 F.2d 294 (8th Cir. 1954) 61, 273

Fid. & Cas. Co. v. Bank of Commerce,
   234 So. 2d 871 (Ala. 1970) 97, 114, 135, 286

Fid. & Cas. Co. v. Bank of Timmonsville,
   139 F. 101 (4th Cir. 1905) 397

Fid. & Cas. Co. v. Cent. Bank,
   672 S.W.2d 641 (Tex. App. 1984) 372, 530

Fid. & Cas. Co. v. First Nat'l Bank in Fort Lee,
   397 F. Supp. 587 (D.N.J. 1975) 477

Fid. & Cas. Co. v. Hoyle,
   64 F.2d 413 (4th Cir. 1933) 426

Fid. & Deposit Co. of Md. v. Bates,
   76 F.2d 160 (8th Cir. 1935) 455

Fid. & Deposit Co. of Md. v. Courtney,
   186 U.S. 342 (U.S. 1902) 397, 432

Fid. & Deposit Co. of Md. v. Hendon,
   350 B.R. 420 (Bankr. E.D. Tenn. 2006) 479

Fid. & Deposit Co. of Md. v. Hudson United Bank,
   653 F.2d 766 (3d Cir. 1981) 346

Fid. & Deposit Co. of Md. v. Merchs. & Marine Bank,
   151 So. 373 (Miss. 1934) 425, 529

Fid. & Deposit Co. of Md. v. Mesker,
   11 N.E.2d 528 (Ind. App. 1937) 399

Fid. & Deposit Co. of Md. v. People's Bank of Sanford,
   72 F.2d 932 (4th Cir. 1934) 6, 23, 433

Fid. & Deposit Co. of Md. v. President & Dirs. of Georgetown Coll.,
   483 F. Supp. 1142 (D.D.C. 1980) 355, 410, 435, 616, 670

Fid. & Deposit Co. of Md. v. Reliance Fed. Sav. & Loan Ass'n,
   795 F.2d 42 (7th Cir. 1986) 279

Fid. & Deposit Co. of Md. v. USA FORM HailPool, Inc.,
   465 F. Supp. 478 (M.D. Fla. 1979) 616

Fid. & Deposit Co. of Md. v. USAFO S Hail Pool, Inc.,
   523 F.2d 744 (5th Cir. 1975) 613

Fid. & Deposit Co. v. Bizette,
   415 F. Supp. 2d 673 (M.D. La. 2006) 476

Fid. & Deposit Co. v. Dally,
201 P.3d 1040 (Wash. Ct. App. 2009) 484

Fid. & Deposit Co. v. Kane,
206 S.W. 888 (Ky. Ct. App. 1918) 173

Fid. & Deposit Co. v. Shawnee State Bank,
766 P.2d 191 (Kan. Ct. App. 1988) 488

Fid. & Deposit Co. v. Sun L Ins. Co.,
329 S.E.2d 517 (Ga. Ct. App. 1985) 619, 637

Fid. & Guar. Co. v. W. Bank,
94 S.W. 3 (Ky. 1906) 367, 400, 414

Fid. Fed. Sav. & Loan Ass'n v. Felicetti,
813 F. Supp. 332 (E.D. Pa. 1993) 171

Fid. Fed. Sav. & Loan Ass'n v. Felicetti,
No. 92-0643, 1992 U.S. Dist. LEXIS 15150 (E.D. Pa. 1992) 667

Fid. Nat'l Bank v. Aetna Cas. & Sur. Co.,
584 F. Supp. 1039 (M.D. La. 1984) 485

Fid. Sav. & Loan Ass'n v. Aetna Life & Cas. Co.,
647 F.2d 933 (9th Cir. 1981) 10, 352

Fid. Sav. & Loan Ass'n v. Republic Ins. Co.,
513 F.2d 954 (9th Cir. 1975) 159, 196, 615

Fid. Trust Co. v. The Am. Sur. Co.,
268 F.2d 805 (3d Cir. 1959) 131

Fid. Trust Co. v. Am. Sur. Co. of N.Y.,
174 F. Supp. 630 (W.D. Penn. 1959) 149

Filor, Bullard & Smyth, Inc. v. Ins. Co. of N. Am.,
605 F.2d 598 (2d Cir. 1978) 89, 235, 658

Finkel v. St. Paul Fire & Marine Ins. Co.,
   No. 3:00CV1194 (AHN), 2002 WL 1359672
   (D. Conn. 2002).. 330, 590

Finkel v. St. Paul Fire & Marine Ins. Co.,
   No. 3:00cv1194, 2002 U.S. Dist. LEXIS 11581
   (D. Conn. 2002).. 679

Fireman's Fund Ins. Co. v. Levine & Partners, P.A.,
   848 So. 2d 1186 (Fla. Dist. Ct. App. 2003)............................ 366, 674

Fireman's Fund Ins. Co. v. Nat'l Bank for Coops.,
   849 F. Supp. 1347 (N.D. Cal. 1994).. 12

Fireman's Fund Ins. Co. v. Puget Sound Escrow Closers, Inc.,
   979 P.2d 872 (Wash. App. 1999) 595

Fireman's Fund Ins. Co. v. Special Olympics, Inc.,
   249 F. Supp. 617

Fireman's Fund Ins. Co. v. Special Olympics Int'l, Inc.,
   249 F. Supp. 2d 19 (D. Mass. 2003).............................. 331, 617, 624

Fireman's Fund Ins. Co. v. Special Olympics Int'l, Inc.,
   346 F.3d 259 (1st Cir. 2003) 20, 587

Fireman's Fund Ins. Co. v. Tripp,
   402 S.W.2d 577 (Mo. Ct. App. 1966) 481

First Am. Nat'l Bank v. Fid. & Deposit Co. of Md.,
   5 F.3d 982 (6th Cir. 1993)... 508

First Am. State Bank v. Aetna Cas. & Sur. Co.,
   130 N.W.2d 824 (Wis. 1964) 123, 658

First Am. State Bank v. Cont'l Ins. Co.,
   897 F.2d 319 (8th Cir. 1990).................................. 194, 321, 588, 635

First Am. Title Ins. Co. v. St. Paul Fire & Marine Ins. Co.,
   951 F.2d 1134 (9th Cir. 1991).. 684

First Am. Title Ins. Co. v. St. Paul Fire & Marine Ins. Co.,
  971 F.2d 215 (9th Cir. 1992) 188

First Bank of Marietta v. Hartford Underwriters Mut. Ins. Co.,
  997 F. Supp. 934 (S.D. Ohio 1998) 29, 42

First Bank v. Hartford Underwriters Ins. Co.,
  307 F.3d 501 (6th Cir. 2002) 434, 454, 488

First Dakota Nat'l Bank v. St. Paul Fire & Marine Ins. Co.,
  2 F.3d 801 (8th Cir. 1993) 9, 25, 40, 349, 407, 516

First Defiance Fin. Corp. v. Progressive Cas. Ins. Co.,
  688 F.3d 265 (6th Cir. 2012) 23, 321, 495, 587

First Defiance Fin. Corp. v. Progressive Cas. Ins. Co.,
  688 F. Supp. 2d 703 (N.D. Ohio 2010) 29

First Fed. Bank, F.S.B. v. Hartford Acc. & Indem. Co.,
  762 F. Supp. 1352 (D. S.D. 1991) 444

First Fed. Sav. & Loan Ass'n of Toledo v. Fid. & Deposit Co. of Md.,
  895 F.2d 254 (6th Cir. 1990) 68, 242, 277, 298

First Fed. Sav. & Loan Ass'n v. Aetna Ins. Co.,
  303 F. Supp. 272 (D.S.D. 1969) 285

First Fed. Sav. & Loan Ass'n v. Transamerica Ins. Co.,
  935 F.2d 1164 (10th Cir. 1991) 3, 26

First Fed. Sav. Bank of Newton v. Cont'l Cas. Co.,
  768 F. Supp. 1449 (D. Kan. 1991) 113, 127, 148, 258, 655

First Guar. Bank v. BancInsure, Inc.,
  No. 06-3497, 2007 U.S. Dist. LEXIS 30934
  (E.D. La. 2007) 41

First Hays Banshares, Inc. v. Kan. Bankers. Sur. Co.,
  769 P.2d 1184 (Kan. 1989) 17, 272, 488

First Integrity Bank, N.A. v. Ohio Cas. Ins. Co.,
  No. 05-2761, 2006 WL 1371674 (D. Minn. 2006) 98, 114, 576

First Integrity Bank v. Ohio Cas. Ins. Co.,
  No. 05-2761, 2006 U.S. Dist. LEXIS 3042 (D. Minn. 2006) 661

First McHenry Corp. v. BancInsure, Inc.,
  No. 10 C 50256, 2011 U.S. Dist. LEXIS 64589
  (N.D. Ill. 2011) 126, 630

First Mountain Mortgage Corp. v. Citizens Ins. Co.,
  No. 04-001170-CK, 2008 Mich. App. LEXIS 2017
  (Mich. Ct. App. 2008) 681

First Nat'l Bank & Trust Co. v. Cont'l Ins. Co.,
  510 F.2d 7 (10th Cir. 1975) 58, 62, 280

First Nat'l Bank and Trust Co. v. USF&G,
  347 F.2d 945 (10th Cir. 1965) 134

First Nat'l Bank of Bowie v. Fid. & Cas. Co. of N.Y.,
  634 F.2d 1000 (5th Cir. 1981) 7, 193

First Nat'l Bank Co. of Clinton, Ill. v. Ins. Co. of N. Am.,
  606 F.2d 760 (7th Cir. 1979) 9, 605, 634

First Nat'l Bank, Colfax v. Hartford Acc. & Indem. Co.,
  295 N.W.2d 425 (Iowa 1980) 129, 139, 287,
  606, 657

First Nat'l Bank of Davis v. Progressive Cas. Ins. Co.,
  415 F. App'x 867 (10th Cir. 2011) 94, 655

First Nat'l Bank of Davis v. Progressive Cas. Ins. Co.,
  No. CIV-09-546-F, 2010 U.S. Dist. LEXIS 141769
  (W.D. Okla. 2010) 145

First Nat'l Bank of Decatur v. Ins. Co. of N. Am.,
  424 F.2d 312 (7th Cir. 1970) 61, 242, 279

First Nat'l Bank of Dillonvale v. Progressive Cas. Ins. Co.,
  640 N.E.2d 1147 (Ohio Ct. App. 1993) 36, 44, 245, 676

First Nat'l Bank of Fleming v. Md. Cas. Co.,
  581 P.2d 744 (Colo. App. 1978) 365

*First Nat'l Bank of Fort Walton Beach v. United States Fid. &
  Guar. Co.*,
  274 F. Supp. 305 (N.D. Fla. 1967) 111

First Nat'l Bank of Fort Walton Beach v. USF&G,
  416 F.2d.52 (5th Cir. 1969) 124

First Nat'l Bank of Ft. Walton Beach v. USF&G,
  416 F.2d 52 (5th Cir. 1969) 659

First Nat'l Bank of Fulda, Minn. v. BancInsure, Inc.,
  No. Civ. 00-2002 DDA/FLN, 2001 WL 1663872
  (D. Minn. 2001) 27, 591

First Nat'l Bank of Louisville v. Lustig (Lustig II),
  96 F.3d 1554 (5th Cir. 1996) 23, 192

First Nat'l Bank of Louisville v. Lustig,
  847 F. Supp. 1322 (E.D. La. 1994) 323

First Nat'l Bank of Louisville v. Lustig (Lustig I),
  961 F.2d 1162 (5th Cir. 1992) 4, 23, 514, 584, 602

First Nat'l Bank of Louisville v. Lustig,
  No. 87-5488, 88-1682, 89-202, 1989 U.S. Dist. LEXIS
  14191 (E.D. La. 1989) 667

First Nat'l Bank of Manitowoc v. Cincinnati Ins. Co.,
  485 F.3d 971 (7th Cir. 2007) 125, 143, 294, 587, 598

First Nat'l Bank of Memphis v. Aetna Cas. & Sur. Co.,
  309 F.2d 702 (6th Cir. 1962) 91, 133, 278

First Nat'l Bank of Miami v. Ins. Co. of N. Am.,
  495 F.2d 519 (5th Cir. 1974) 101, 659

First Nat'l Bank of N. Cal. v. St. Paul Mercury Ins. Co.,
  No. 4:11-cv-6631, 2013 U.S. Dist. LEXIS 1045 (N.D. Cal.
  2013) 662

First Nat'l Bank of Northern Cal. v. St. Paul Mercury Ins. Co.,
  No. C 11-6631 PJH, 2013 WL 61026 (N.D. Cal. 2013) 110

First Nat'l Bank of S.C. v. Glens Falls Ins. Co.,
  304 F.2d 866 (4th Cir. 1962) 132

First Nat'l Bank of S. Md. v. USF&G,
  340 A.2d 275 (Md. 1975) 18

First Nat'l Bank of Sikestown v. Transamerica Ins. Co.,
  514 F.2d 981 (8th Cir. 1975) 9, 517

First Nat'l Bank v. Aetna Cas. & Sur. Co.,
  610 F.2d 424 (6th Cir. 1979) 124

First Nat'l Bank v. Cincinnati Ins. Co.,
  No. 03-C-241, 2005 U.S. Dist. LEXIS 42823
  (E.D. Wis. 2005) 141

First Nat'l Bank v. Hansen,
  267 N.W.2d 367 (Wis. 1978) 486

First Nat'l Bank v. Lustig,
  150 F.R.D. 548 (E.D. La. 1993) 521

First Nat'l Bank v. Sec. Mut. Cas. Co.,
  431 F.2d 1025 (10th Cir. 1970) 518

First Nat'l Bank v. Transam. Ins. Co.,
  514 F.2d 981 (8th Cir. 1975) 517

First Nat'l Bank of Crandon v. USF&G,
  137 N.W. 742 (Wis. 1912) 373, 420

First Nat'l Bank of West Hamlin v. Md. Cas. Co.,
354 F. Supp. 189 (S.D. W. Va. 1973) 16, 604

First Nat'l Ins. Co. v. FDIC,
977 F. Supp. 1051 (S.D. Cal. 1977) 495

First Nat'l Life Ins. Co. v. Fid. & Deposit Co. of Md.,
525 F.2d 966 (5th Cir. 1976) 230, 271, 638

First New England Federal Credit Union v. Cuna Mutual Group,
No. CV03520148, 2005 Conn. Super. LEXIS 1086 (Conn. Super. Ct. 2005) 286

First Philson Bank, N.A. v. Hartford Fire Ins. Co.,
727 A.2d 584 (Pa. Super. Ct. 1999) 44, 51, 245

First Sav. Bank, FSB v. Am. Cas. Co.,
No. 92-1320, 1993 U.S. App. LEXIS 2049 (4th Cir. 1993) 347

First Sav. Bank, FSB v. Am. Cas. Co. of Reading, Pa.,
No. 92-1320, 1993 WL 27403 (4th Cir. 1993) 275

First Sec. & Sav. v. Aetna Cas. & Sur. Co.,
445 N.W.2d 596 (Neb. 1989) 438

First Sec. Bank & Trust v. N.H. Ins. Co.,
441 N.W.2d 188 (Neb. 1989) 370, 401, 438

First Sec. Sav. v. Kan. Bankers Sur. Co.,
849 F.2d 345 (8th Cir. 1988) 350

First State Bank of Corpus Christi v. Ake,
606 S.W.2d 696 (Tex. App. 1980) 708

First State Bank of Monticello v. Ohio Cas. Ins. Co.,
555 F.3d 564 (7th Cir. 2009) 60, 72, 75, 293, 585, 652

First State Bank of Temple v. Metro. Cas. Ins. Co.,
  79 S.W.2d 835 (Tex. 1935) 635

First Tex. Sav. Ass'n v. Reliance Ins. Co.,
  950 F.2d 1171 (5th Cir. 1992) 58, 276, 311

First Thrift of Los Angeles v. Pac. Indem. Co.,
  212 P.2d 560 (Cal. Ct. App. 1949) 97

First Union Corp. v. USF&G,
  730 A.2d 278 (Md. Ct. Spec. App. 1999) 112, 115, 129, 233, 239

Fitchburg Sav. Bank v. Mass. Bonding & Ins. Co.,
  174 N.E. 324 (Mass. 1931) 460

Fitzgibbons Boiler Co. v. Employers' Liab. Assur. Corp.,
  105 F.2d 893 (2d Cir. 1939) 90, 108

Five Star Real Estate, LLC v. Kemper Cas. Ins. Co.,
  No. 258602, 2006 WL 1294238 (Mich. Ct. App. 2006) 33

Flagstar Bank, F.S.B. v. Fed. Ins. Co.,
  260 F. App'x 820 (6th Cir. 2008) 102, 143, 598

Flagstar Bank, FSB v. Fed. Ins. Co.,
  No. 05-70950, 2006 U.S. Dist. LEXIS 83825
  (E.D. Mich. 2006) 283

Fletcher Sav. & Trust Co. v. Am. Sur. Co.,
  175 N.E. 247 (Ind. App. 1931) 367, 399, 437

Flushing Nat'l Bank v. Transamerica Ins. Co.,
  491 N.Y.S.2d 793 (N.Y. App. Div. 1985) 665

Flushing Sav. Bank v. Hartford Fire Ins. Co.,
  234 A.D.2d 108 (N.Y. 1996) 315

Flushing Sav. Bank v. Hartford Fire Ins. Co.,
  650 N.Y.S.2d 727 (N.Y. App. Div. 1996) 84

Forcht Bank, N.A. v. BancInsure, Inc.,
No. 10-259-JBC, 2011 U.S. Dist. LEXIS 118141
(E.D. Ky. 2011) 599

Forcht Bank, N.A. v. BancInsure, Inc.,
No. 11-6328, 2013 WL 518405 (6th Cir. 2013) 101, 109, 267, 277

Forcht Bank, NA v. BancInsure, Inc.,
No. 11-6328, 2013 U.S. App. LEXIS 3193
(6th Cir. 2013) 142, 654

Forest City Bldg. & Loan Ass'n. v. Davis,
133 S.E. 530 (N.C. 1926) 371, 401, 418, 437

Fortunoff Silver Sales, Inc. v. Hartford Acc. & Indem. Co.,
459 N.Y.S.2d 866 (N.Y. App. Div. 1983) 229

Foster v. Nat'l Union Fire Ins. Co. of Pitt., Pa.,
902 F.2d 1316 (8th Cir. 1990) 588, 683

Fountainebleau Cmty. Bank v. Fid. & Deposit Co of Md.,
No. 93-4220, 1994 U.S. Dist. LEXIS 3880
(E.D. La. 1994) 357

Foxley Cattle Co. v. Bank of Mead,
244 N.W.2d 205 (Neb. 1976) 451, 597

Franklin Nat'l Bank v. St. Paul Fire & Marine Ins. Co.,
266 N.W.2d 718 (Minn. 1978) 66

Franklin Sav. & Loan Co. v. Am. Emp'rs Ins. Co.,
99 F.2d 494 (5th Cir. 1938) 433

*French Am. Bank Corp. v. Flota Mercante Grancolombiana
S.A.,*
609 F. Supp. 1352 (S.D.N.Y. 1985) 135

*French Am. Banking Corp. v. Flota Mercante
Grancolombiana S.A.,*
752 F. Supp. 83 (2nd Cir. 1991) 122, 237, 599, 628, 656

Friendly Farms v. Reliance Ins. Co.,
 79 F.3d 541 (6th Cir. 1996)..440, 454

Frontline Processing Corp. v. Am. Econ. Ins. Co.,
 149 P.3d 906 (Mont. 2006) 586, 594, 678

FSLIC v. Aetna Cas. & Sur. Co.,
 696 F. Supp. 1190 (E.D. Tenn. 1988) 486

FSLIC v. Aetna Cas. & Sur. Co.,
 701 F. Supp. 1357 (E.D. Tenn. 1988) 447

FSLIC v. Aetna Cas. & Sur. Co.,
 785 F. Supp. 867 (D. Mont. 1990) 360

FSLIC v. Aetna Ins. Co.,
 279 F. Supp. 161 (N.D. Ill. 1968)..686

FSLIC v. Transam. Ins. Co.,
 705 F. Supp. 1328 (N.D. Ill. 1989)...511, 695

FSLIC v. Transamerica Ins. Co.,
 661 F. Supp. 246 (C.D. Cal. 1987)...63

Fuller v. Home Indem. Co.,
 60 N.E.2d 1 (Mass. 1945)...460

FundQuest Inc. v. Travelers Cas. & Sur. Co.,
 715 F. Supp. 2d 202 (D. Mass. 2010)......................27, 436, 617, 677

G & S Mgmt. Co. v. Commercial Union Ins. Cos.,
 No. 92AP-1429, 1993 Ohio App. LEXIS 2836
 (Ohio Ct. App. 1993)..691

Ga. Bank & Trust v. Cincinnati Ins. Co.,
 538 S.E.2d 764 (Ga. Ct. App. 2000) 105, 146

Ga. Cas. & Sur. Co. v. Seaboard Sur. Co.,
 210 F. Supp. 644 (N.D. Ga. 1962) 230

TABLE OF CASES

Gadach v. Benton Cnty. Coop.,
  53 N.W.2d 230 (Minn. 1952) 707

Gallagher v. Albert Co.,
  315 N.Y.S.2d 99 (N.Y. App. 1970) 704

Gamble-Robinson Co. v. Mass. Bonding & Ins. Co.,
  129 N.W. 131 (Minn. 1910) 369, 400, 416, 431

Gasslein v. Nat'l Union Fire Ins. Co. of Pitt., Pa.,
  918 F. Supp. 373 (M.D. Fla. 1995) 449, 499

Gateway State Bank v. N. River Ins. Co.,
  387 N.W.2d 344 (Iowa 1986) 66, 199, 286, 657

Gen. Acc. Ins. Co. of Am. v. Fid. & Deposit Co.,
  598 F. Supp. 1223 (E.D. Pa. 1984) 479

Gen. Analytics Corp. v. CNA Ins. Cos.,
  86 F.3d 51 (4th Cir. 1996) 4, 22

Gen. Fin. Corp. v. Fid. & Cas. Co. of N.Y.,
  439 F.2d 981 (8th Cir. 1971) 10, 225, 230, 517, 644

Genisco Tech. Corp. v. Seaboard Sur. Co.,
  No. 90-55480, 1991 WL 78151 (9th Cir. 1991) 26

Gentile v. Am. Bank & Trust Co.,
  172 A. 303 (Pa. 1934) 371, 418, 431

George J. Ricau & Co. v. Indem. Ins. Co.,
  173 So. 217 (La. App. 1937) 400, 421, 430

Georgia Bank & Trust v. Cincinnati Ins. Co.,
  245 Ga. App. 687 (Ga. App. 2000) 600

Gerrard Realty Corp. v. Am. States Ins. Co.,
  277 N.W.2d 863 (Wis. 1979) 423

Gilmour v. Standard Sur. & Cas. Co.,
197 N.E. 673 (Mass. 1935) 368, 415, 430

Glaser v. Hartford Cas. Ins. Co.,
364 F. Supp. 2d 529 (D. Md. 2005) 390

Glenn Falls Indem. Co. v. Nat'l Floor & Supply Co.,
239 F.2d 412 (5th Cir. 1956) 8

Glusband v. Fitin Cunningham Lauzon, Inc.,
582 F. Supp. 145 (S.D.N.Y. 1984) 450

Glusband v. Fitten Cunningham Lauzon, Inc.,
No. 80 Civ. 7387, U.S. Dist. LEXIS 1867
(S.D.N.Y. 1987) 197

Glusband v. Fittin Cunningham & Lauzon, Inc.,
892 F.2d 208 (2nd Cir. 1989) 4, 21, 297

Glusband v. Fittin Cunningham Lauzon, Inc.,
No. 80 Civ. 7387, 1987 U.S. Dist. LEXIS 1867
(S.D.N.Y. 1987) 677

Good Lad Co. v. Aetna Cas. & Sur. Co.,
No. 92-5678, 1995 U.S. Dist. LEXIS 9456
(E.D. Pa. 1995) 634

Good Lad Co. v. Aetna Cas. & Sur. Co.,
No. 92-5678, 1995 WL 393964 (E.D. Pa. 1995) 30

Goosen v. Indem. Ins. Co.,
234 F.2d 463 (6th Cir. 1956) 446

Gordon v. Cont'l Cas. Co.,
166 A. 557 (Pa. 1933) 176

Gould Investors, L.P. v. Travelers Cas. & Sur. Co. of Am.,
920 N.Y.S.2d 395 (N.Y. App. Div. 2011) 481

Gradon-Murphy Oldsmobile v. Ohio Cas. Ins. Co.,
93 Cal. Rptr. 684 (Cal. Ct. App. 1971) 483

Grand Rapids Auctions, Inc. v. Hartford Acc. & Indem. Co.,
178 N.W.2d 812 (Mich. Ct. App. 1970).................................. 400, 424

Graphic Arts Mut. Ins. Co. v. C.W. Warthen Co., Inc.,
397 S.E.2d 876 (Va. 1990) 382

Graves v. Iowa Mut. Ins. Co.,
123 So. 2d 351 (Fla. Dist. Ct. App. 1960)...................................... 695

Gray & Assoc., LLC v. Travelers Cas. & Sur. Co. of Am.,
No. CCB-07-2216, 2008 U.S. Dist. LEXIS 23903
(D. Md. 2008) 669

Great Am. Bank of Fla. Keys v. Aetna Cas. & Sur. Co.,
662 F. Supp. 363 (S.D. Fla. 1986)... 196

Great Am. Ins. Co. v. AFS/IBEX Fin. Serv., Inc.,
No. 3:07-CV-924-O, 2008 WL 2795205 (N.D. Tex. 2009)........... 573

Great Am. Ins. Co. v. AFS/IBEX Financial Serv., Inc.,
612 F.3d 800 (5th Cir. 2010) 659

Great Am. Ins. Co. v. Langdeau,
379 S.W.2d 62 (Tex. 1964) 19

Great Am. Ins. Cos. v. Subranni (In re Tri-State Armored Servs.),
332 B.R. 690 (Bankr. D.N.J. 2005)... 170

Great Cent. Ins. Co. v. Cook,
422 S.W.2d 801 (Tex. App. 1967) 438

Green v. Interstate Cas. Co.,
256 F. 81 (5th Cir. 1919).. 167

Greenfield v. Ollikala,
736 P.2d 599 (Or. App. 1987)... 705

Gregoire v. Lowndes,
  342 S.E. 2d 264 (W. Va. 1986) 250

Griffith Motors, Inc. v. Compass Ins. Co.,
  676 S.W.2d 555 (Tenn. App. 1984) 372, 402, 432

Gross Veneer Co. v. Am. Mut. Ins. Co.,
  424 N.Y.S.2d 743 (N.Y. App. Div. 1980) 229

Guar. Trust Co. v. USF&G,
  112 A. 247 (N.H. 1920) 401

Guarantee Co. of North America v. Mechanics' Savings Bank & Trust Co.,
  183 U.S. 402 (U.S. 1902) .... v, 167, 342, 344, 403, 426

Gulf Build. Servs. v. Travelers Ind. Co.,
  435 So. 2d 477 (La. App. 1983) 604

Gulf USA Corp. v. Fed. Ins. Co.,
  259 F.3d 1049 (9th Cir. 2001) 168, 351, 409, 668

Guste v. Aetna Cas. & Sur. Co.,
  429 So. 2d 106 (La. 1983) 380, 689

Guyan Int'l, Inc. v. Travelers Cas. & Sur. Co.,
  No. 3:10-1244, 2011 U.S. Dist. LEXIS 142828 (S.D. W. Va. 2011) 645

H.S. Equities. Inc. v. Hartford Acc. & Indem. Co.,
  464 F. Supp. 83 (S.D.N.Y. 1978) 617

H.S. Equities, Inc. v. Hartford Acc. & Indem. Co.,
  661 F.2d 264 (2nd Cir. 1981) 187, 191, 487, 612

Hack v. Am. Sur. Co.,
  96 F.2d 939 (7th Cir. 1938) 442

Hall v. Life Ins. Co. of N. Am.,
  317 F.3d 773 (7th Cir. 2003) 628

Hamilton Bank v. Ins. Co. of N. Am.,
   557 A.2d 747 (Pa. Super. Ct. 1989) 142, 658

Hamiltonian Fed. Sav. & Loan Ass'n v. Reliance Ins. Co.,
   527 S.W.2d 440 (Mo. Ct. App. 1975) 69, 625, 648

Hanover Ins. Co. v. Treasurer & Receiver Gen.,
   910 N.E.2d 921 (Mass. App. Ct. 2009) 415, 489, 561

Hansen v. Am. Bonding Co.,
   48 P.2d 653 (Wash. 1935) 20, 373, 402, 420

Hanson PLC v. Nat'l Union Fire Ins. Co. of Pittsburgh, Pa.,
   794 P.2d 66 (Wash. Ct. App. 1990) 37, 586

Harrah's Entertainment, Inc. v. Ace Am. Ins. Co.,
   100 F. App'x 387 (6th Cir. 2004) 646

Harrington v. Am. Econ. Ins. Co.,
   No. 03-712-MO, 2003 U.S. Dist. LEXIS 26033 (D. Or. 2003) 447

Harris v. Nat'l Sur. Co.,
   155 N.E. 10 (Mass. 1927) 665

Hartford Acc. & Indem. Co. v. All Am. Nut Co.,
   34 Cal. Rptr. 23 (Cal. Ct. App. 1963) 486

Hartford Acc. & Indem. Co. v. FDIC,
   204 F.2d 933 (8th Cir. 1953) 62, 280, 543, 544

Hartford Acc. & Indem. Co. v. Hartley,
   275 F. Supp. 610 (M.D. Ga. 1967) 511, 520

Hartford Acc. & Indem. Co. v. Hattiesburg Hardware Stores, Inc.,
   49 So. 2d 813 (Miss. 1951) 425

Hartford Acc. & Indem. Co. v. Luper,
   421 P.2d 811 (Okla. 1966) 462

Hartford Acc. & Indem. Co. v. Merrill Lynch, Pierce, Fenner & Smith, Inc.,
74 F.R.D. 357 (W.D. Okla. 1976) 478

Hartford Acc. & Indem. Co. v. Peat, Marwick, Mitchell & Co.,
494 N.Y.S.2d 821 (N.Y. Sup. Ct. 1985) 473

Hartford Acc. & Indem. Co. v. Swedish Methodist Aid Ass'n,
92 F.2d 649 (7th Cir. 1937) 398, 407

Hartford Accident & Indem. Ins. Co. v. Wash. Nat'l Ins. Co.,
638 F. Supp. 78 (N.D. Ill. 1986) 47, 636

Hartford Fire Ins. Co. v. Clark,
727 F. Supp. 2d 765 (D. Minn 2010) 476

Hartford Fire Ins. Co. v. Conestoga Title Ins. Co.,
746 A.2d 460 (N.J. Super. Ct. App. Div. 2000) 228, 643

Hartford Fire Ins. Co. v. Lewis (In re Lewis),
478 B.R. 645 (Bankr. E.D. Pa. 2012) 478

Hartman & Tyner, Inc. v. Fed. Ins. Co.,
No. 08-cv-12461, 2009 U.S. Dist. LEXIS 90004
(E.D. Mich. 2009) 687

Haskel Eng'g & Supply Co. v. Hartford Acc. & Indem. Co.,
144 Cal. Rptr. 189 (Cal. Ct. App. 1978) 473

Hayfield Farmers Elevator & Merc. Co. v. New Amsterdam Cas. Co.,
282 N.W. 265 (Minn. 1938) 448

Heller Int'l Corp. v. Sharp,
974 F.2d 850 (7th Cir. 1992) 3, 25

Hepler v. Fireman's Fund Ins. Co.,
239 So. 2d 669 (La. Ct. App. 1970) 200, 301

TABLE OF CASES

Hidden Splendor Mining Co. v. Gen. Ins. Co. of Am.,
370 F.2d 515 (10th Cir. 1966) 353, 409, 428, 518

Highland Bank v. BancInsure, Inc.,
No. 10-4107, 2012 U.S. Dist. LEXIS 119940 (D. Minn. 2012) 138

Highland Bank v. BancInsure, Inc.,
No. 10-4107, 2012 WL 3656523 (D. Minn. 2012) 107

Hinkson v. Fireman's Fund Ins. Co.,
146 Cal. Rptr. 669 (Cal. Ct. App. 1978) 136, 657

Holland v. Fuller,
14 F. Supp. 688 (E.D. Tenn. 1936) 441, 447

Home Indem. Co. v. Midwest Auto Auction, Inc.,
285 F.2d 708 (10th Cir. 1960) 455

Home Indem. Co. v. Reynolds & Co.,
187 N.E.2d 274 (Ill. App. Ct. 1963) 17, 542

Home Indem. Co. v. Shaffer,
860 F.2d 186 (6th Cir. 1988) 484

Home Life Ins. Co. v. Clay,
773 P.2d 666 (Kan. App. 1989) 367

Home Sav. & Loan Ass'n v. Fid. & Deposit Co. of Md.,
742 F.2d 831 (4th Cir. 1984) 123

Home Sav. & Loan v. Aetna Cas. & Sur. Co.,
817 P.2d 341 (Utah Ct. App. 1991) 177, 203, 372, 531, 625, 671

Home Sav. Bank v. Colonial Am. Cas. & Sur. Co.,
598 S.E.2d 265 (N.C. Ct. App. 2004) 530, 694

Hood v. Davidson,
177 S.E. 5 (N.C. 1934) 401

Howard, Weil, Labouisse, Friedrichs, Inc. v. Ins. Co. of N. Am.,
  557 F.2d 1055 (5th Cir. 1977) 7, 225, 385, 690

HSBC USA Inc. v. Gulf Ins. Co.,
  Index No. 603413/04 (N.Y. Sup. Ct. 2006) 35

Hudson City Sav. Inst. v. Hartford Acc. & Indem. Co.,
  440 F. Supp. 41 (E.D.N.Y. 1977) 227, 641

Hudson Ins. Co. v. M.J. Oppenheim,
  81 A.D.3d 427 (N.Y. App. Div. 2011) 417

Hudson United Bank v. Progressive Cas. Ins. Co.,
  112 F. App'x 170 (3d Cir. 2004) 21, 45, 572

Hudson United Bank v. Progressive Cas. Ins. Co.,
  152 F. Supp. 2d 751 (E.D. Pa. 2001) 227

Hudson United Bank v. Progressive Cas. Ins. Co.,
  284 F. Supp. 2d 249 (E.D. Penn. 2003) 244

Humboldt Bank v. Gulf Ins. Co.,
  323 F. Supp. 2d 1027 (N.D. Cal. 2004) 242, 282, 556

Humboldt Trust & Sav. Bank v. Fid. & Cas. Co. of N.Y.,
  122 N.W.2d 358 (Iowa 1963) 199, 390

Hunt v. Fid. & Deposit Co. of Md.,
  92 F.2d 75 (3d Cir. 1937) 347, 405

Hunter v. USF&G,
  167 S.W. 692 (Tenn. 1914) 176

IBM Poughkeepsie Emps. Fed. Credit Union v. Cumis Ins. Soc'y, Inc.,
  590 F. Supp. 769 (S.D.N.Y. 1984) 69, 284, 641

Imperial Ins., Inc. v. Emp'r's Liab. Assurance Corp.,
  442 F.2d 1197 (D.C. Cir. 1970) 12, 246, 455

*In re Baker & Getty Fin. Servs., Inc. v. Nat'l Union Fire
   Ins. Co. of Pittsburgh, Pa.,*
   93 B.R. 559 (Bankr. N.D. Ohio 1988) 29, 198, 387, 591

In re Conticommodity Serv., Inc., Sec. Litig.,
   733 F. Supp. 1555 (5th Cir. 1995) (N.D. Ill. 1990) 356, 521

In Re Franklin Nat'l Bank Sec. Litig.,
   445 F. Supp. 723 (E.D.N.Y. 1978) 478

In re Franklin Nat'l Bank Sec. Litig.,
   478 F. Supp. 210 (E.D.N.Y. 1979) 478

In re Gov't Sec. Corp.,
   972 F.2d 328 (11th Cir. 1992) 510

In re Harris,
   7 B.R. 284 (S.D. Fla. 1980) 475

*In re J.T. Moran Fin. Corp. v. Nat'l Union Fire Ins. Co. of
   Pittsburgh, Pa.,*
   147 B.R. 335 (S.D. N.Y. 1992) 4, 29, 522

In re Leedy Mortgage Co.,
   76 B.R. 440 (Bankr. E.D. Pa. 1987) 43, 48, 450

In re Lloyd Sec., Inc.,
   153 B.R. 677 (E.D. Pa. 1993) 363

In re Lloyd Sec., Inc.,
   No. 91-1090S, 1992 WL 236162 (Bankr. E.D. Pa. 1992) 30

In re Lloyd Sec., Inc.,
   Nos. 90-0985S, 91-1090S, 1992 WL 119362 (Bankr. E.D.
   Pa. 1992) 171

In re Mechem Fin., Inc.,
   167 B.R. 799 (Bankr. W.D. Penn. 1994) 524

In re Payroll Express Corp.,
186 F.3d 196 (2d Cir. 1999) 167

In re Prime Commercial Corp.,
187 B.R. 785 (Bankr. N.D. Ga. 1995) 226, 356, 410, 520,
640, 702, 710

In re Schluter, Green & Co.,
93 F.2d 810 (4th Cir. 1938) 298, 587

In re Sur. Ass'n of Am.,
388 F.2d 412 (2d Cir. 1967) 661

In re Tri-State Armored Servs., Inc.,
No. 01-11917/JHW, 2006 WL 4452993 (Bankr. D.N.J.
2006) 500

In Re: Korman Lumber Mut. Ins. Co. v. Korman (In re Korman),
No. 09-3276, 2010 U.S. Dist. LEXIS 17602 (D.N.J. 2010) 473

Indem. Ins. Co. of N. Am. v. Pioneer Valley Sav. Bank,
343 F.2d 634 (8th Cir. 1965) 279, 649

Indep. Trust Corp. v. Kan. Bankers Sur. Co.,
954 N.E.2d 401 (Ill. App. Ct. 2001) 445, 513

Index Fund, Inc. v. Ins. Co. of N. Am.,
580 F.2d 1158 (2d Cir. 1978) 297, 666

Indiana Regional Council of Carpenters Pension Trust Fund v.
Fid. & Deposit Co. of Md.,
No. 2:06-CV-32 PS, 2007 U.S. Dist. LEXIS 15429
(N.D. Ind. 2007) 673

Ins. Co. of N. Am. v. Citizensbank of Thomasville,
491 So. 2d 880 (Ala. 1986) 32

Ins. Co. of N. Am. v. Gibralco, Inc.,
847 F.2d 530 (9th Cir. 1988) 665

Ins. Co. of N. Am. v. Greenberg,
  405 F.2d 330 (10th Cir. 1969) 11, 645

Ins. Co. of N. Am. v. Liberty Nat'l Bancorp.,
  No. 93-0624, 1996 U.S. Dist. LEXIS 22825 (W.D. Ky.
  1996) 197

Ins. Co. of N. America v. Liberty United Bancorp., Inc.,
  142 F.3d 434, No. 96-6502, 1998 U.S. App. LEXIS 3781
  (unpublished table opinion) (6th Cir. 1998) 24, 40

Inter-City Express Lines, Inc. v. Hartford Acc. & Indem. Co.,
  178 So. 280 (La. App. 1938) 368, 415, 459

Interior Crafts, Inc. v. Leparski,
  853 N.E.2d 1244 (Ill. App. Ct. 2006) 480

Interstate Elec. Co. v. Daniel,
  151 So. 463 (Ala. 1933) 702

Interstate Prod. Credit Ass'n v. Fireman's Fund Ins. Co.,
  788 F. Supp. 1530 (D. Or. 1992) 362, 618

Interstate Prod. Credit Ass'n v. Fireman's Fund Ins. Co.,
  944 F.2d 536 (9th Cir. 1991) 10, 645

Interstate Transit Lines v. Crane,
  100 F.2d 857 (10th Cir. 1939) 700, 701

Inv. Ctr. v. Great Am. Ins.,
  No. 04-CV-6204, 2006 U.S. Dist. LEXIS 21625 (D.N.J.
  2006) 360

Investors Trading Corp. v. Fid. and Deposit Co. of Md.,
  No. 3:02-CV-2176-P2004 U.S. Dist. LEXIS 25906, 2004
  WL 3045196 (N.D. Tex. 2004) 31

Irwin Jacobs & Co. v. Fid. & Deposit Co. of Md.,
  202 F.2d 794 (7th Cir. 1953) 434, 454

ITT Hartford Life Ins. Co. v. Pawson Assocs., Inc.,
No. 940361910S, 1997 WL 345345
(Conn. Super. Ct. 1997).. 32

J.I. Corp. v. Fed. Ins. Co.,
920 F.2d 118 (1st Cir. 1990) 345, 426, 667

J.S. Fearing, Inc. v. Emp'rs Mut. Liab. Ins. Co.,
242 F.2d 609 (5th Cir. 1957).. 427, 516, 692

Jack Daniels Motors, Inc. v Universal Underwriters Ins. Co.,
No. 11-1379., 2011 WL 346500 (D.N.J. 2011)............................... 617

Jacobson Family Invs., Inc. v. Nat'l Union Fire Ins. Co.,
No. 601325/10, 2012 N.Y. Misc. LEXIS 5752 (N.Y. App.
Div. 2012).. 181

Jacobson Family Invs., Inc. v. Nat'l Union Fire Ins. Co. of Pitt., Pa.,
955 N.Y.S.2d 338 (N.Y. App. Div. 2012).............................. 467, 675

James B. Lansing Sound, Inc. v. Nat'l Union Fire Ins. Co. of Pitt.,
981 F.2d 1549 (9th Cir. 1986).. 615

James B. Lansing Sound, Inc. v. Nat'l Union Fire Ins. Co. of Pittsburgh, Pa.,
801 F.2d 1560 (9th Cir. 1986).. 46

Jamie Brooke, Inc. v. Zurich-Am. Ins. Co.,
748 N.Y.S.2d 5 (N.Y. App. Div. 2002).. 51

Jefferson Bank & Trust Co. v. Cent. Sur. & Ins. Corp.,
408 S.W.2d 825 (Mo. 1966)....................................... 66, 200, 369, 416

Jefferson Bank v. Progressive Cas. Ins. Co.,
965 F.2d 1274 (3d Cir. 1992).......................... 142, 152, 275, 584, 597

Jefferson Bank v. Progressive Cas. Ins. Co.,
No. 90-584, 1990 U.S. Dist. LEXIS 15558 (E.D. Pa. 1990).......... 656

Jefferson Parish Clerk of Court Health Ins. Trust Fund v. Fid. & Deposit Co. of Md.,
   673 So. 2d 1238 (La. Ct. App. 1996) 388

Jefferson Pilot Fin. Ins. Co. v. Marsh USA, Inc.,
   582 S.E.2d 701 (N.C. 2003) 160

Jellico Grocery Co. v. Sun Indem. Co.,
   114 S.W.2d 83 (Ky. 1938) 399

Jinkins v. Jet Credit Union,
   No. 49A02-1006-PL-666, 2011 Ind. App.
   Unpub. LEXIS 11217 487

John B. White, Inc. v. Providence Wash. Ins. Co.,
   329 F. Supp. 300 (E.D. Pa. 1971) 618

Johnstown Bank v. Am. Sur. Co. of N.Y.,
   6 A.D.2d 4 (N.Y. App. Div. 1958) 67

Johnstown Bank v. American Surety Co. of New York,
   174 N.Y.S.2d 385 (N.Y. S. Ct. App. Div. 1958) 273, 288

Jones v. Fireman's Fund Ins. Co.,
   76 Cal. Rptr. 97 (Cal. Ct. App. 1969) 128, 661

Joseph Rosenbaum, M.D., Inc. v. Hartford Fire Ins. Co.,
   104 F.3d 258 (9th Cir. 1996) 207

Joseph v. State Farm Fire & Cas. Co.,
   No. 2:11-cv-794, 2013 U.S. Dist. LEXIS 24511 (S.D. Ohio
   2013) 490

K.W. Bancshares, Inc. v. Syndicates of Underwriters at Lloyd's,
   965 F. Supp. 1047 (W.D. Tenn. 1997) 111, 128, 239, 253, 600

K2 Settlement, LLC v. Certain Underwriters at Lloyd's, London,
   No. 11-0191, 2012 U.S. Dist. LEXIS 170832 (W.D. Pa.
   2012) 159, 695

Kan. Bankers Sur. Co. v. Farmers State Bank, Yale, IA
408 F. Supp. 2d 751 (S.D. Iowa 2005) 27, 41, 635

Kan. State Bank & Trust v. Emery Air Freight,
656 F. Supp. 200 (D. Kan. 1987) 82, 250

Kaplan Jewelers, Inc. v. Ins. Co. of N. Am.,
383 N.Y.S.2d 127 (N.Y. Sup. Ct. 1975) 437

Karen Kane, Inc. v. Reliance Ins. Co.,
202 F.3d 1180 (9th Cir. 2000) 383, 389, 690

Kavaney Realtor & Developer, Inc. v. Travelers Ins. Co.,
501 N.W.2d 335 (N.D. 1993) 381

Kean v. Maryland Cas. Co.,
223 N.Y.S. 373 (App. Div. 1927) 627

Kelch v. Indus. Indem. Co.,
763 P.2d 402 (Or. Ct. App. 1988) 678

Kelly Assocs., Ltd. v. Aetna Cas. & Sur. Co.,
681 S.W.2d 593 (Tex. 1984) 513, 695

Kerr v. Aetna Cas. & Sur. Co.,
350 F.2d 146 (4th Cir. 1965) 230, 293

Keystone Floor Prods., Inc. v. Home Ins. Co.,
No. 92-1988, 1992 WL 94918 (E.D. Pa. 1992) 30

Killingsworth v. United Merc. Bank,
623 So. 2d 1384 (La. Ct. App. 1993) 451

Kinzer v. Fid. & Deposit Co. of Md.,
652 N.E.2d 20 (Ill. App. 1995) 366, 468, 527

Kirkwood Holding Co. v. Home Fed. Sav. & Loan Ass'n,
No. 80C-SE-12, 1982 Del. Super. LEXIS 871
(Del. Super. Ct. 1982) 647

Klyn v. Travelers Indem. Co.,
  709 N.Y.S.2d 780 (N.Y. App. Div. 2000) 51

KMC Mgmt. Corp. v. Certain Underwriters,
  No. C7-00-1148, 2000 WL 1742096 (Minn. Ct. App. 2000) 82

Knights of the Ku Klux Klan v. Fid. & Deposit Co. of Md.,
  169 S.E. 514 (Ga. Ct. App. 1933) 458

Knowledge A-Z, Inc. v. Sentry Ins.,
  857 N.E.2d 411 (Ind. Ct. App. 2006) 489

Known Litigation Holdings, LLC v. Navigators Ins. Co.,
  No. 3:12-cv-269, 2013 U.S. Dist. LEXIS 38429
  (D. Conn. 2013) 673

Koch Indus., Inc. v. Nat'l Union Fire Ins. Co. of Pittsburgh, Pa.,
  No. 89-1158-K, 1989 U.S. Dist. LEXIS 15703
  (D. Kan. 1989) 13, 670

Koerber v. Alter,
  483 N.W.2d 929 (Mich. Ct. App. 1992) 681

Korean War Veterans Assn. v. Fed. Ins. Co.,
  No. 07-0690, 2008 U.S. Dist. LEXIS 4682 (W.D. La. 2008) 457

Kornhauser v. Nat'l Sur. Co.,
  150 N.E. 921 (Ohio 1926) 431

Kornitz v. Commercial Land Title Ins. Co.,
  260 N.W.2d 680 (Wis. 1978) 474

KPMG Peat Marwick v. Nat'l Union Fire Ins. Co.,
  765 So. 2d 36 (Fla. 2000) 480

Ks. Life Ins. Co. v. Am. Ins. Co.,
  12 F.3d 1102 (unpublished), 1993 WL 497073
  (8th Cir. 1993) 102

L.A. Athl. Club v. USF&G,
 183 P. 174 (Cal. Ct. App. 1919) 365, 414, 429, 437

Lafayette Ins. Co. v. Pennington,
 966 So. 2d 136 (La. Ct. App. 2007) 481

Landico, Inc. v. Am. Family Mut. Ins. Co.,
 559 N.W.2d 438 (Minn. Ct. App. 1997) 381

Lane Cnty. Escrow Serv., Inc. v. Smith,
 560 P.2d 608 (Or. 1977) 481

Larson v. Peerless Ins. Co.,
 362 S.W.2d 863 (Tex. Ct. App. 1962) 531

Latham v. USF&G,
 267 So. 2d 895 (Miss. 1972) 445

Lawson v. Am. Motorists Ins. Corp.,
 217 F.2d 724 (5th Cir. 1954) 427

Lawyers Sur. Corp. v. Am. Pub. Life Ins. Co.,
 540 S.W.2d 842 (Tex. Civ. App. 1976) 20

Leedy Mortg. Co., Inc. v. Burnhope,
 76 B.R. 440 (Bankr. E.D. Pa. 1987) 450

Lemay Ferry Bank v. New Amsterdam Cas. Co.,
 149 S.W.2d 328 (Mo. 1941) 437

Leucadia, Inc. v. Reliance Ins. Co.,
 864 F.2d 964 (2d Cir. 1988) 6

Liberty Nat'l Bank & Trust Co. of Louisville v. Nat'l Sur. Corp.,
 330 F.2d 697 (6th Cir. 1964) 109, 124, 253, 683

Liberty Nat'l Bank & Trust Co. v. Travelers Indem. Co.,
 295 N.Y.S.2d 983 (N.Y. App. Div. 1968) 67, 651, 678

Liberty Nat'l Bank v. Aetna Life & Cas. Co.,
  568 F. Supp. 860 (D.N.J. 1983).......................... 28, 42, 104, 134, 220,
  237, 284, 583, 601, 656

Liberty Sav. Bank v. Am. Cas. Co. of Reading, Pa.
  754 F. Supp. 559 (S.D. Ohio 1990).. 64, 285

Lincoln Grain, Inc. v. Aetna Cas. & Sur. Co.,
  756 F.2d 75 (8th Cir. 1985).. 298

Lincoln Tech. Inst. v. Fed. Ins. Co.,
  No. 94-16369, 1996 U.S. App. LEXIS 2155 (9th Cir. 1996).......... 684

Lincoln Technical Inst. of Ariz. v. Fed. Ins. Co.,
  927 F. Supp. 376 (D. Ariz. 1994)... 685

Livonia Volkswagen, Inc. v. Universal Underwriters Grp.,
  No. 06-13619, 2008 U.S. Dist. LEXIS 25519
  (E.D. Mich. 2008) 443, 457, 476

Loeb Props. v. Fed. Ins. Co.,
  663 F. Supp. 2d 640 (W.D. Tenn. 2009)................................. 591, 618

Lubin v. Cincinnati Ins. Co.,
  No. 09-2985, 2010 U.S. Dist. LEXIS 133794
  (N.D. Ga. 2010).. 181

Lumberman's Mut. Cas. Co. v. Norris Grain Co.,
  343 F.2d 670 (8th Cir. 1965)... 180, 442

Lumbermens Mut. Cas. Co. v. State,
  564 N.W.2d 431 (Iowa 1997)... 483

Lusitania Sav. Bank, FSB v. Progressive Cas. Ins. Co.,
  No. 04-3503, 2005 U.S. App. LEXIS 13331 (3d Cir. 2005).......... 653

Lusitania Sav. Bank, FSB, v. Progressive Cas. Ins. Co.,
  No. 04-3503, 2005 WL 1586618 (3d Cir. 2004)...................... 90, 235

Luso-Am. Credit Union v. Cumis Ins. Soc'y,
   616 F. Supp. 846 (D. Mass. 1985) 673

Lutz v. St. Paul Fire & Marine Ins. Co.,
   No. 1:03-CV-750, 2005 U.S. Dist. LEXIS 21065
   (S.D. Ohio 2005) 641

Luvata Buffalo, Inc. v. Lombard Gen. Ins. Co. of Can.,
   No. 08-CV-00034, 2010 U.S. Dist. LEXIS 19334
   (W.D.N.Y. 2010) 477

Luvata Buffalo, Inc. v. MOL Mitsui O.S.K. Lines, Ltd.,
   No. 08-CV-0701, 2010 U.S. Dist. LEXIS 141250
   (W.D.N.Y. 2010) 477

Luzerne Nat'l Bank v. Hanover Ins. Co.,
   49 Pa. D. & C.3d 399 (Pa. Ct. of Common Pleas 1988) 36

Lynch Properties, Inc. v. Potomac Ins. Co. of Ill.,
   962 F. Supp. 956 (N.D. Tex. 1996) 4, 31, 57, 585, 591

Lynch Props., Inc. v. Potomac Ins. Co.,
   140 F.3d 622 (5th Cir. 1998) 498, 559, 612, 624, 625, 626, 678

Lyndonville Sav. Bank & Trust Co. v. Peerless Ins. Co.,
   234 A.2d 340 (Ver. 1967) 68

Lyons Fed. Sav. & Loan v. St. Paul Fire & Marine Ins. Co.,
   863 F. Supp. 1441 (D. Kan. 1994) 196, 283, 640

M.G. Bancorporation, Inc. v. Reliance Ins. Co.,
   No. 87 C 10470, 1989 WL 20774 (N.D. Ill. 1989) 103, 389

Madison Cty. Farmers Ass'n v. Am. Emp'rs Ins. Co.,
   209 F.2d 581 (8th Cir. 1954) 673

Madison Materials Co., Inc. v. St. Paul Fire & Marine Ins. Co.,
   523 F.3d 541 (5th Cir. 2008) 385, 683

Magnolia Mgmt. Corp. v. Fed. Ins. Co.,
No. 06-0447, 2007 WL 4124496
(W.D. La. 2007) 357, 411, 443

*Manley, Bennett, MacDonald & Co. v. St. Paul Fire &
Marine Ins. Co.*,
No. 93-1664, 1994 U.S. App. LEXIS 20429
(6th Cir. 1994) 193

*Manley Bennett, McDonald & Co. v. St. Paul Fire &
Marine Ins. Co.*,
792 F. Supp. 1070 (E.D. Mich. 1992) 189

*Manley, Bennett, McDonald & Co. v. St. Paul Fire &
Marine Ins. Co.*,
807 F. Supp. 1287 (E.D. Mich. 1992) 590

Mapes Casino, Inc. v. Md. Cas. Co.,
290 F. Supp. 186 (D. Nev. 1968) 436, 457

Marion v. Hartford Fire Ins. Co.,
No. 06-4666, 2012 U.S. Dist. LEXIS 10606
(E.D. Pa. 2012) 680

Marion v. Hartford Fire Ins. Co.,
No. 12-1553, 2013 U.S. App. Lexis 9825 (3d Cir. 2013) 612

Marsh Inv. Corp. v. Langford,
554 F. Supp. 800 (5th Cir. 1982) 235

Marsh Inv. Corp. v. Langford,
721 F.2d 1011 (5th Cir. 1983) 121

Mass. Bonding & Ins. Co. v. Julius Seidel Lumber Co.,
279 F.2d 861 (8th Cir. 1960) 379

Mass. Bonding & Ins. Co. v. Norwich Pharmacal Co.,
18 F.2d 934 (2d Cir. 1927) 346, 404, 433

Mass Cuna Corporate Cent. Fed. Credit Union v. Cumis Ins. Soc'y,
   No. 84-2050-W, 1986 U.S. Dist. LEXIS 27809
   (D. Mass. 1986) 640

Mass. Mut. Life Ins. Co. v. Certain Underwriters at Lloyd's of London,
   No. 4791-VCL, 2010 Del. Ch. LEXIS 156 (Del. Ch. 2010) 592

Mass. Mut. Life Ins. Co. v. Certain Underwriters at Lloyd's of London,
   No. 4791-VCL, 2010 WL 2929552 (Del. Ch. 2010) 75, 300, 619

Masters v. Mass. Bonding & Ins. Co.,
   84 N.W.2d 462 (Mich. 1957) 460

May v. Cont'l Cas. Co.,
   936 A.2d 747 (D.C. 2007) 380

MBAFB Fed. Credit Union v. Cumis Ins. Soc'y, Inc.,
   507 F. Supp. 794 (D.S.C. 1981) 618

MBTA Employees Credit Union v. Employer's Mut. Liab. Ins. Co. of Wis.,
   374 F. Supp. 1299 (D. Mass. 1974) 95, 104

McKee v. State Farm Fire & Cas. Co.,
   145 Cal. App. 3d 772 (Cal. Ct. App. 1983) 248

Md. Cas. Co. v. Am. Trust Co.,
   71 F.2d 137 (5th Cir. 1934) 8, 605

Md. Cas. Co. v. Bank,
   340 F.2d 550 (4th Cir. 1965) 474

Md. Cas. Co. v. Bank of England,
   2 F.2d 793 (8th Cir. 1924) 168

Md. Cas. Co. v. Clements,
   487 P.2d 437 (Ariz. Ct. App. 1971) 16, 437, 439, 525, 688

Md. Cas. Co. v. First Nat'l Bank,
246 F. 892 (5th Cir. 1917) 433

Md. Cas. Co. v. Hall,
88 So. 407 (Miss. 1921) 369, 416

Md. Cas. Co. v. State Bank & Trust Co.,
425 F.2d 979 (5th Cir. 1970) 60, 132, 277, 646

Md. Cas. Co. v. Tucker,
96 P.2d 80 (Okla. 1939) 462

Md. Cas. Co. v. Tulsa Indus. Loan & Inv. Co.,
83 F.2d 14 (10th Cir. 1936) 519

MDB Commc'ns, Inc. v. Hartford Cas. Ins. Co.,
479 F. Supp. 2d 136 (D.D.C. 2007) 489

Mechanicsville Trust & Sav. Bank v. Hawkeye-Security Ins. Co.,
158 N.W.2d 89 (Iowa 1968) 527

Mercedes-Benz of N. Am. v. Hartford Acc. & Indem. Co.,
Nos. 89-56011, 89-56012, 1992 U.S. App. LEXIS 19825
(9th Cir. 1992) 351

Merch. & Farmers State Bank of Weatherford, Tex. v. Fid. &
Cas. Co. of N.Y.,
791 F.2d 1141 (5th Cir. 1981) 7

Merchants Bank & Trust Co. v. Cincinnati Ins. Co.,
No. 1:06cv561, 2008 WL 728332 (S.D. Ohio 2008) 105

Merchs.-Produce Bank v. USF&G,
305 F. Supp. 957 (W.D. Mo. 1969) 64, 197, 650

Merchs. Bank & Trust Co. v. Cincinnati Ins. Co.,
No. 1:06cv561, 2008 U.S. Dist. LEXIS 20151
(S.D. Ohio 2008) 127

Merchs. Nat'l Bank of Winona v. Transamerica Ins. Co.,
408 N.W.2d 651 (Minn. Ct. App. 1987) 130, 234, 254

Meriter Health Servs. v. Travelers Cas. & Sur. Co. of Am.,
758 N.W.2d 112 (Wis. App. 2008) 596, 623, 682

Merriman v. Lewis,
194 So. 349 (Fla. 1940) 706

Methodist Health Sys. Found., Inc., v. Hartford Fire Ins. Co.,
No. 10- 3292, 2011 U.S. Dist. LEXIS 71258
(E.D. La. 2011) 663, 665

Methodist Health Sys. Found., Inc. v. Hartford Fire Ins. Co.,
834 F. Supp. 2d 493 (E.D. La. 2011) 300, 575, 603

Metro Fed. Credit Union v. Fed. Ins. Co.,
607 F. Supp. 2d 870 (N.D. Ill. 2009) 113, 233, 258, 660

Metro. Sav. & Loan Ass'n v. Hanover Ins. Co.,
286 N.Y.S.2d 129 (N.Y. App. Div. 1967) 70, 648

Mfr. Bank & Trust Co. v. Transam. Ins. Co.,
568 F. Supp. 790 (E.D. Mo. 1983) 486

Mfr. Nat'l Bank of Troy v. USF&G,
156 N.E. 94 (N.Y. 1927) 70

Miami Nat'l Bank v. Pa. Ins. Co.,
240 So. 2d 832 (Fla. Dist. Ct. App. 1970) 399, 422

Miami Nat'l Bank v. Penn. Ins. Co.,
314 F. Supp. 858 (S.D. Fla. 1970) 13, 475

Mid-Am. Bank of Chaska v. Am. Cas. Co. of Reading, Pa.,
745 F. Supp. 1480 (D. Minn. 1990) 323, 359, 585, 603, 670, 677

Midland Bank & Trust Co. v. Fid. & Deposit Co. of Md.,
442 F. Supp. 960 (D.N.J. 1977) 14, 226, 231, 361, 412, 487, 522

Midway Truck Parts, Inc. v. Federated Ins. Co.,
No. 11 CV 9060, 2013 U.S. Dist. LEXIS 20554
(N.D. Ill. 2013) 695

Milwaukee Area Tech. College v. Frontier Adjusters of Milwaukee,
752 N.W.2d 396 (Wis. Ct. App. 2008) 658

Minn. Sch. Bds. Assoc. Ins. Trust v. Employers Ins. Co.,
331 F.3d 579 (8th Cir. 2003) 629

Mitsui Mfrs. Bank v. Fed. Ins. Co.,
795 F.2d 827 (9th Cir. 1986) 73, 311, 602, 661

Mo. Bank & Trust Co. v. OneBeacon Ins. Co.,
688 F.3d 943 (8th Cir. 2012) 110, 239, 664

Mo. Bank and Trust Co. of Kansas City v. OneBeacon Ins. Co.,
2010 WL 4386536 (W.D. Mo. 2010) 572

Monroe Guar. Ins. Co. v. Radwan Brown & Co.,
No. 09-247, 2011 U.S. Dist LEXIS 30263
(E.D. Ky. 2011) 679

Morgan, Olmstead, Kennedy & Gardner, Inc. v. Fed. Ins. Co.,
637 F. Supp. 973 (S.D.N.Y. 1986) 48, 637

Morgan Stanley Dean Witter & Co. v. Chubb Group of Ins. Cos.,
No. A-4124-03T2, 2005 N.J. Super. Unpub. LEXIS 798
(N.J. Super. Ct. App. Div. 2005). 663, 664

Morgan Stanley Dean Witter & Co. v. Chubb Grp. of Ins. Cos.,
No. A-4124-03T2, 2005 WL 3242234
(N.J. Super. Ct. App. Div. 2005) 574

Morrelville Deposit Bank v. Royal Indem. Co.,
144 A. 424 (Pa. 1928) 371, 402, 431

Mortell v. Ins. Co. of N. Am.,
458 N.E.2d 922 (Ill. App. Ct. 1983) 33, 43, 49, 191, 430, 593, 633

Mortgage Assocs., Inc. v. Fid. & Deposit Co. of Md.,
  129 Cal. Rptr. 2d 365 (Cal. Ct. App. 2002) 43, 638

Mortgage Corp. of New Jersey v. Aetna Casualty and Surety Co.,
  115 A.2d 43 (N.J. 1955) 545, 634

Mount Vernon Bank & Trust Co. v. Aetna Cas. & Sur. Co.,
  224 F. Supp. 666 (E.D. Va. 1963) 364, 413

Mt. Lodge Ass'n, v. Crum & Forster Indem. Co.,
  558 S.E.2d 336 (W. Va. App. 2001) 229

Mun. Sec., Inc. v. Ins. Co. of N. America,
  829 F.2d 7 (6th Cir. 1987) 24, 46

Muncie Banking Co. v. Am. Sur. Co.,
  200 F.2d 115 (7th Cir. 1952) 398, 428

Murray v. Am. Sur. Co.,
  69 F.2d 147 (5th Cir. 1934) 427, 454

Mut. Sec. Life Ins. Co. v. Fid. & Deposit Co. of Md.,
  659 N.E.2d 1096 (Ind. App. 1995) 367, 513

N.C. Nat'l Bank v. Lumbermen's Mut. Cas. Co.,
  335 F.2d 486 (4th Cir. 1964) 276

N.C. Nat'l Bank v. U.S. Cas. Co.,
  317 F.2d 304 (4th Cir. 1963) 131

N.E. Lincoln-Mercury v. Century Indem. Co.,
  124 A.2d 420 (Pa. Super. Ct. 1956) 694

N.H. Ins. Co. v. MF Global, Inc.,
  108 A.D.3d 463 (N.Y. Sup. Ct. 2010) 594

N.J. Sav. & Loan Ass'n v. Fid. & Deposit Co. of Md.,
  660 A.2d 1287 (N.J. Super. Ct. Law Div. 1993) 35, 51, 153,
                                                                  201, 301, 529

N.J. Title Ins. Co. v. Nat'l Union Fire Ins. Co. of Pitt., Pa.,
    No. 11-CV-0630(DMC)(JAD), 2011 WL 6887130
    (D.N.J. 2011) 500

N.M. Livestock Board v. Dose,
    607 P.2d 606 (N.M. 1980) 681

N.M. Sav. & Loan Ass'n v. USF&G,
    454 F.2d 328 (10th Cir. 1972) 11

N. River Ins. Co. v. Huff,
    628 F. Supp. 1129 (D. Kan. 1985) 389

N. Shore Bank FSB v. Progressive Cas. Ins. Co.,
    674 F.3d 884 (7th Cir. 2012) 133, 219, 654

N. Side "L" Fed. Credit Union v. Cumis Ins. Soc'y, Inc.,
    No. 87 C 7150, 1988 U.S. Dist. LEXIS 12010
    (N.D. Ill. 1988) 13

N.Y. Trust Co. v. Royal Indem. Co.,
    233 A.D. 408 (N.Y. App. Div. 1931) 70

Nanty-Glo Borough v. Am. Sur. Co.,
    175 A. 536 (Pa. 1934) 421, 462

Nashville & Am. Trust Co. v. Aetna Cas. & Sur. Co.,
    110 S.W.2d 1041 (Tenn. App. 1937) 372, 419, 432

Nationalcare Corp., Inc. v. St. Paul Prop. & Cas. Ins. Co.,
    22 F. Supp. 2d 558 (S.D. Miss. 1998) 156, 500

Nat'l Bank of Andover v. Kan. Bankers Sur. Co.,
    225 P.3d 707 (Kan. 2010) 245, 287

Nat'l Bank of Burlington v. Fid. & Cas. Co. of N.Y.,
    125 F.2d 920 (4th Cir. 1942) 224

Nat'l Bank of Commerce v. Fid. & Cas. Co. of N.Y.,
    312 F. Supp. 71 (E.D. La. 1970) 63, 73, 283, 652

Nat'l Bank of Pakistan v. Basham,
 531 N.Y.S.2d 250 (N.Y. App. Div. 1988) 36

Nat'l Bank of Paulding v. Fid. & Cas. Co.,
 131 F. Supp. 121 (S.D. Ohio 1954) 64, 244, 285

Nat'l City Bank of Minn. v. St. Paul Fire & Marine Ins. Co.,
 447 N.W.2d 171 (Minn. 1989) 141, 200, 220, 657

Nat'l City Bank v. Nat'l Sec. Co.,
 37 F.2d 550 (4th Cir. 1930) 427

Nat'l City Bank v. Nat'l Sec. Co.,
 58 F.2d 7 (6th Cir. 1932) 349, 427

Nat'l Newark & Essex Bank v. Am. Ins. Co.,
 385 A.2d 1216 (N.J. 1978) 19, 370, 417, 421, 446, 634

Nat'l Pub. Co., Inc. v. Hartford Fire Ins. Co.,
 949 A.2d 1203 (Conn. 2008) 422

Nat'l Sur. Co. v. First Nat'l Bank of Midland,
 431 S.W.2d. 353 (Tex. 1968) 202

Nat'l Sur. Co. v. W. Pac. Ry. Co.,
 200 F. 675 (9th Cir. 1912) 352, 398, 409

Nat'l Sur. Co. v. Williams,
 77 So. 212 (Fla. 1917) 441

Nat'l Sur. Corp. v. Rauscher, Pierce & Co.,
 369 F.2d 572 (5th Cir. 1966) 193, 604, 613

Nat'l Union Fire Ins. Co. of Pitt., Pa. v. FDIC,
 160 F.3d 657 (10th Cir. 1998) 423

Nat'l Union Fire Ins. Co. of Pitt., Pa. v. FDIC,
 957 P.2d 357 (Kan. 1998) 440

Nat'l Union Fire Ins. Co. v. City Sav. Bank,
  28 F.3d 376 (3rd Cir. 1994) 167

Nat'l Union Fire Ins. Co. v. FDIC,
  887 F. Supp. 262 (D. Kan. 1995) 476

NCNB Nat'l Bank v. Aetna Cas. & Sur. Co.,
  477 So. 2d 579 (Fla. Dist. Ct. App. 1985) 65, 286, 314

Nelson v. ITT Hartford Fire Ins. Co.,
  No. 99-6275, 2000 WL 763772 (10th Cir. 2000) 499

New Amsterdam Cas. Co. v. Basic Bldg. & Loan Ass'n,
  60 F.2d 950 (3d Cir. 1932) 453

New Amsterdam Cas. Co. v. W.D. Felder & Co.,
  214 F.2d 825 (5th Cir. 1954) 180, 453

New Jersey v. Merrill Lynch & Co.,
  640 F.3d 545 (3d Cir. 2011) 628, 629

Newhard, Cook & Co. v. Ins. Co. of N. Am.,
  929 F.2d 1355 (8th Cir. 1991) 517

Newin Corp. v. Hartford Acc. & Indem. Co.,
  333 N.E.2d 163 (N.Y. 1975) 452

Newpark Res., Inc. v. Marsh & McLennan of La., Inc.,
  691 So. 2d 208 (La. App. 1997) 368, 414

Nike, Inc. v. Nw. Pac. Indem. Co.,
  999 P.2d 1197 (Or. App. 2000) 371, 418

Northbrook Nat'l Ins. Co. v. NEHOC Adver. Serv., Inc.,
  554 N.E.2d 251 (Ill. App. 1990) 593

Northside Bank v. Am. Cas. Co. of Reading,
  60 Pa. D. & C.4th 95 (Pa. Com. Pl. Ct. 2001) 573

Northwood Nursing & Convalescent Homes, Inc. v. Cont'l Ins. Co.,
902 F. Supp. 79 (E.D. Pa. 1995).. 362, 424

Nw. Airlines, Inc. v. Global Indem. Co.,
225 N.W.2d 831 (Minn. 1975) 74, 651

Oakley Grain & Supply Co. v. Indem. Ins. Co. of N. Am.,
173 F. Supp. 419 (S.D. Ill. 1959) 456

Ohio Farmers Ins. Co. v. Clinton County Nat'l Bank,
220 N.E.2d 381 (Ohio 1966) 146

Ohio Sav. Bank v. Progressive Cas. Ins. Co.,
521 F.3d 960 (8th Cir. 2008) 143, 153, 662

Okada v. MGIC Indem. Corp.,
608 F. Supp. 383 (D. Haw. 1985) 389

Okla. Morris Plan Co. v. Sec. Mut. Cas. Co.,
455 F.2d 1209 (8th Cir. 1970) 156, 180

Old Colony Trust Co. v. Stumpel,
161 N.E. 173 (N.Y. 1928) 250

Omaha Bank for Coops. v. Aetna Cas. & Sur. Co.,
301 N.W.2d 564 (Neb. 1981) 19, 597

Omega Advisors, Inc. v. Fed. Ins. Co.,
No. 10-912, 2010 U.S. Dist. LEXIS 125934
(D.N.J. 2010) 360, 669

Ominsource Corp. v. CNA Ins. Co.,
949 F. Supp. 681 (N.D. Ind. 1996) 126, 559, 599

Omni Servs. Group v. Hartford Ins. Co.,
2 F. Supp. 2d 714 (E.D. Pa. 1998) 227, 387, 641

One Am. Corp. v. Fid. & Deposit Co. of Md.,
658 So. 2d 23 (La. Ct. App. 1995) 136

Oriental Fin. Group, Inc. v. Fed. Ins. Co.,
  598 F. Supp. 2d 199 (D.P.R. 2008) 31

Oriental Fin. Grp. v. Fed. Ins. Co.,
  309 F. Supp. 2d 216 (D.P.R. 2004) 31, 603

Oritani Sav. & Loan Ass'n v. Fid. & Deposit Co. of Md.,
  744 F. Supp. 1311 (D.N.J. 1990) 197, 324, 332

Oritani Sav. & Loan Ass'n v. Fid. & Deposit Co. of Md.,
  821 F. Supp. 286 (D.N.J. 1991) 28, 633

Oritani Sav. & Loan Ass'n v. Fid. & Deposit Co. of Md.,
  989 F.2d 635 (3d Cir. 1993) 59, 71, 652

Oscar Gruss & Son v. Lumbermens Mut. Cas. Co.,
  46 F.R.D. 635 (S.D.N.Y. 1969) 198

Outlook Farmers' Elevator Co. v. Am. Sur. Co.,
  223 P. 905 (Mont. 1924) 369, 417

Owens, Schine & Nicola, P.C. v. Travelers Cas. & Sur. Co. of Am.,
  No. CV095024601, 2011 Conn. Super. LEXIS 1572
  (Conn. Super. Ct. 2011) 664

Owens, Schine & Nicola, P.C. v. Travelers Cas. and Sur. Co. of Am.,
  No. CV095024601, 2010 WL 4226958 (Conn. Super. Ct. 2010) 248

Oxford Bank & Trust v. Hartford Accident & Indem. Co.,
  698 N.E.2d 204 (Ill. App. Ct. 1998) 16, 33, 244, 286, 314, 634

Pa. Nat'l Mut. Cas. Ins. Co. v. Edmonds,
  No. 09-0089, 2009 U.S. Dist. LEXIS 36764
  (S.D. Ala. 2009) 474

Pac.-S. Mortg. Trust v. Ins. Co. of N. Am.,
  212 Cal. Rptr. 754 (Cal. Ct. App. 1985) 364, 669

Pac. Bus. Bank v. St. Paul Mercury Ins. Co.,
 No. B150853, 2002 WL 31521730 (Cal. Ct. App. 2002) 314

Pac. Coast Adjustment Bureau v. Indem. Ins. Co. of N. Am.,
 2 P.2d 218 (Cal. Ct. App. 1931) 365, 413

Pac. Indem. Co. v. Hargreaves,
 98 P.2d 217 (Cal. Ct. App. 1940) 16

Pac. Indem. Co. v. Sec. First Nat'l Bank,
 56 Cal. Rptr. 142 (Cal. Ct. App. 1967) 480

Paddleford v. Fid. & Cas. Co. of N.Y.,
 100 F.2d 606 (7th Cir. 1938) 665

Palm Desert Nat'l. Bank v. Fed. Ins. Co.,
 473 F. Supp. 2d 1044 (C.D. Cal. 2007) 81, 653

Palm Hills Props., L.L.C. v. Cont'l Ins. Co.,
 No. 07-668-RET-SCR, 2008 WL 4303817 (M.D. La. 2008) 42, 47

Paradis v. Aetna Cas. & Sur. Co.,
 796 F. Supp. 59 (D.R.I. 1992) 512

Parish of East Baton Rouge v. Fid. & Cas. Co. of N.Y.,
 373 F. Supp. 440 (M.D. La. 1974) 380

Pasternak v. Boutris,
 121 Cal. Rptr. 2d 493 (Cal. Ct. App. 2002) 388

Patrick Schaumburg Autos., Inc. v. Hanover Ins. Co.,
 452 F. Supp. 2d 857 (N.D. Ill. 2006) 322, 675

Patrick v. St. Paul Fire & Marine Ins.,
 No. 1:99CV314, 2001 WL 828251 (D. Vt. 2001) 295

Patrick v. St. Paul Fire & Marine Ins. Co.,
 No. 1:99CV314, 2001 U.S. Dist. LEXIS 26434 (Vt. 2001) 595

PBSJ Corp. v. Fed. Ins. Co.,
  347 F. App'x 532 (11th Cir. 2009) 379

PBSJ Corp. v. Fed. Ins. Co.,
  No. 07-22248-CIV, 2009 U.S. App. LEXIS 2169
  (S.D. Fla. 2008) 685

Penalosa Coop. Exch. v. Farmland Mut. Ins. Co.,
  789 P.2d 1196 (Kan. Ct. App. 1990) 385

Penn. Twp. v. Aetna Cas. & Sur. Co.,
  719 A.2d 749 (Pa. Super Ct. 1998) 382, 692

Peoples Bank & Trust Co. of Madison Cnty. v. Aetna Cas. & Sur. Co.,
  113 F.3d 629 (6th Cir. 1997) 3, 24, 588, 632

Peoples Bank of the S. v. Bancinsure, Inc.,
  753 F. Supp. 2d 649 (S.D. Miss. 2010) 42, 48, 329

Peoples Bank of the S. v. BancInsure, Inc.,
  No. 3:09CV217TSL-FKB, 2011 WL 10099621
  (S.D. Miss. 2011) 323

People's Bank v. Aetna Cas. & Sur. Co.,
  40 S.W.2d 535 (Mo. Ct. App. 1931) 425, 461

People's Loan & Sav. Co. v. Fid. & Cas. Co.,
  147 S.E. 171 (Ga. Ct. App. 1929) 440

Peoples State Bank v. Am. Cas. Co. of Reading, Pa.,
  818 F. Supp. 1073 (E.D. Mich. 1993) 243, 284, 359

Peoples State Bank v. Progressive Cas. Ins. Co.,
  478 F. App'x 858 (5th Cir. 2012) 137, 658

People's State Bank v. USF&G,
  113 So. 779 (La. 1927) 400

Peoples Tel. Co., Inc. v. Hartford Fire Ins. Co.,
36 F. Supp. 2d 1335 (S.D. Fla. 1997)... 468

Performance Autoplex II LTC. v. Mid-Continent Cas. Co.,
322 F.3d 847 (5th Cir. 2003).. 46, 636

Perkins v. Clinton State Bank,
593 F.2d 327 (8th Cir. 1979).................................... 61, 350, 408, 668

Perpetual Bldg. & Loan Ass'n v. USF&G,
92 N.W. 686 (Iowa 1902).. 399

Phelan v. Beswick,
326 P.2d 1034 (Or. 1958).. 704

Philips Elecs., N.V. v. N.H. Ins. Co.,
692 N.E.2d 1268 (Ill. App. Ct. 1998).. 33

Phillip R. Seaver Title Co., Inc. v. Great Am. Ins. Co.,
No. 08-CV-11004, 2008 WL 4427582
(E.D. Mich. Sept. 30, 2008) 3

Phillip R. Seaver Title Co. v. Great Am. Ins. Co.,
No. 08-CV-11004, 2008 U.S. Dist. LEXIS 78568
(E.D. Mich. 2008) 590

Phoenix Sav. & Loan, Inc. v. Aetna Cas. & Sur. Co.,
302 F. Supp. 832 (D. Md. 1969) 358, 428

Phoenix Sav. & Loan, Inc. v. Aetna Cas. & Sur. Co.,
427 F.2d 862 (4th Cir. 1970).. 230, 271, 514

Piedmont Fed. Sav. & Loan Ass'n v. Hartford Acc. & Indem. Co.,
307 F.2d 310 (4th Cir. 1962)... 100, 600

Piedmont Grocery Co. v. Hawkins,
104 S.E. 736 (W. Va. 1920) 403, 463

TABLE OF CASES

Pine Bluff Nat'l Bank v. St. Paul Mercury Ins. Co.,
346 F. Supp. 2d 1020 (E.D. Ark. 2004) 112, 126, 144, 218,
222, 233, 281, 585, 598

Pinnacle Processing Grp., Inc. v. Hartford Cas. Ins. Co.,
No. C10-1126-RSM, 2011 U.S. Dist. LEXIS 128203
(W.D. Wash. 2011) 592

Pinnacle Processing Grp., Inc. v. Hartford Cas. Ins. Co.,
No. C10-1126-RSM, 2011 WL 5299557 (W.D. Wash. 2011) 575

Pioneer Fed. Credit Union v. CUMIS Ins. Soc'y, Inc.,
Case No. 08-00496 (Sept. 8, 2010) (D. Idaho 2010) 520

Pioneer Nat'l Trust Ins. Co. v. Am. Cas. Co. of Reading Pa.,
459 F.2d 963 (5th Cir. 1972) 231

Planter's Sav. Bank of Greer v. Am. Sur. Co.,
181 S.E. 222 (S.C. 1935) 431

Plaza Del Sol Nat'l Bank v. Firemen's Ins. Co.,
No. 78-073-B, 1979 U.S. Dist. LEXIS 12876 (D.N.M. 1979) 14

Portland Fed. Emps. Credit Union v. Cumis Ins. Soc'y,
894 F. 2d 1101 (9th Cir. 1990) 247, 280, 676

Potomac Ins. Co. of Ill. v. Lone Star Web, Inc.,
No. 3:93-CV-2122-H, 1994 WL 494784 (N.D. Tex. 1994) 387

Poultry Producers' Union v. Williams,
107 P. 1040 (Wash. 1910) 177

Premier Elec. Constr. Co. v. USF&G,
No. 80 C 6689, 1987 U.S. Dist. LEXIS 5588
(N.D. Ill. 1987) 672

Prevost v. First W. Bank,
239 Cal. Rptr. 161 (Cal. Ct. App. 1987) 703, 706

Prior Lake State Bank v. Nat'l Sur. Corp.,
80 N.W.2d 612 (Minn. 1957) 18, 368, 415, 445

Private Bank & Trust Co. v. Progressive Cas. Ins. Co.,
409 F.3d 814 (7th Cir. 2005) 57, 75

Private Bank & Trust Co. v. Progressive Cas. Ins. Co.,
No. 03 C 6031, 2004 WL 1144048 (N.D. Ill. 2004) 309

PrivateBank & Trust Co. v. Progressive Cas. Ins. Co.,
2004 U.S. Dist. LEXIS 8938 (N.D. Ill. May 17, 2004).................. 626

Progressive Cas. Ins. Co. v. First Bank,
828 F. Supp. 473 (S.D. Tex. 1993)....................................... 32, 39, 43

Provident Trust Co. v. Nat'l. Sur. Co.,
44 F. Supp. 514 (W.D. Pa. 1942) 549, 550, 551

Provident Trust Co. v. Nat'l Sur. Corp.,
138 F.2d 252 (3d Cir. 1943)... 90, 108

Provincial Hotels, Inc. v. Mascair,
734 So. 2d 136 (La. App. 1999).. 607

*Public Warehouses of Matanzas, Inc. v. Fid. & Deposit
Co. of Md.*,
77 F.2d 831 (2d Cir. 1935)... 345, 426, 433

Pueblo Athl. Club v. Am. Bonding. Co.,
307 P.2d 813 (Colo. 1957) 430

Puget Sound Nat'l Bank v. St. Paul Fire & Marine Ins. Co.,
645 P.2d 1122 (Wash. Ct. App. 1982) 467, 622, 646

Purdy Co. of Ill. v. Transp. Ins. Co., Inc.,
568 N.E.2d 318 (Ill. App. Ct. 1991).. 39, 689

Purolator Sec. v. Citizens Nat'l Bank of Waco,
546 S.W.2d 935 (Tex. Civ. App. 1977).. 651

Quad Constr., Inc. v. William A. Smith Contracting Co.,
534 F.2d 1391 (10th Cir. 1976) 629

Quick Serv. Box Co. v. St. Paul Mercury Indem. Co.,
95 F.2d 15 (7th Cir. 1938) 93

R & J Enterprizes v. Gen. Cas. Co. of Wis.,
627 F.3d 723 (8th Cir. 2010) 46, 614, 636

R.I. Resource Recovery Corp. v. Travelers Indem. Co.,
No. 10-294, 2011 U.S. Dist. LEXIS 58007
(D.R.I. 2011) 691

Racine Cnty. Nat'l Bank v. Aetna Cas. & Sur. Co.,
203 N.W.2d 145 (Wis. 1973) 68, 288, 648

Rader v. Johnson,
97 S.W.2d 280 (Miss. Ct. App. 1995) 495

Radiology Assocs., P.A. v. Aetna Cas. & Sur. Co.,
613 S.W.2d 106 (Ark. Ct. App. 1981) 228

Ralston Bank v. Kan. Bankers Sur. Co.,
794 F. Supp. 896 (D. Neb. 1992) 96, 236, 313

Ran-Nan, Inc. v. Gen. Acc. Ins. Co. of Am.,
252 F.3d 738 (5th Cir. 2001) 389

Rankin v. USF&G,
99 N.E. 314 (Ohio 1912) 402

RBC Dain Rauscher, Inc. v. Fed. Ins. Co.,
370 F. Supp. 2d 886 (D. Minn. 2005) 331, 590

RBC Dain Rauscher, Inc. v. Fed. Ins. Co.,
No. 03-2609, 2003 U.S. Dist. LEXIS 26475
(D. Minn. 2003) 190

RBC Mortg. Co. v. Nat'l Union Fire Ins. Co of Pitt., Pa.,
349 Ill. App. 3d 706 (Ill. App. 2004) 586

RBC Mortg. Co. v. Nat'l Union Fire Ins. Co of Pitt., Pa.,
812 N.E.2d 728 (Ill. App. 2004) 592, 680

Red Lake Cnty. State Bank v. Emp'rs Ins. of Wausau,
874 F.2d 546 (8th Cir. 1989) 26, 194, 639

Redington v. Hartford Acc. & Indem. Co.,
463 F. Supp. 83 (S.D.N.Y. 1978) 447, 457

Reedy Indus., Inc. v. Hartford Ins. Co.,
715 N.E.2d 728 (Ill. App. Ct. 1999) 388, 689

Regional Inv. Co. v. Haycock,
723 F.2d 38 (8th Cir. 1983) 614

Reliance Ins. Co. v. Capital Bancshares, Inc.,
912 F.2d 756 (5th Cir. 1990) 132, 219

Reliance Ins. Co. v. First Liberty Bank,
927 F. Supp. 448 (M.D. Ga. 1996) 94, 236

Reliance Ins. Co. v. IRPC, Inc.,
904 A.2d 912 (Pa. Super. Ct. 2006) 382, 690

Reliance Ins. Co. v. Treasure Coast Travel Agency, Inc.,
660 So. 2d 1136 (Fla. Dist. Ct. App. 1995) 380, 388

Remington v. Fid. & Deposit Co. of Md.,
67 P. 989 (Wash. 1902) 402

Republic Nat'l Bank v. Fid. & Deposit Co. of Md.,
894 F.2d 1255 (11th Cir. 1990) 138, 281

Research Equity Fund, Inc. v. Ins. Co. of N. Am.,
602 F.2d 200 (9th Cir. 1979) 10, 226, 299, 666

Reserve Ins. Co. v. Gen. Ins. Co.,
395 N.E.2d 933 (Ill. App. Ct. 1979) 16, 620, 691

TABLE OF CASES 919

Residential Mktg. Grp., Inc. v. Granite Inv. Grp.,
933 F.2d 546 (7th Cir. 1991) 628

Retail Ventures, Inc. v. Nat'l Union Fire Ins. Co. of Pitt., Pa.,
691 F.3d 821 (6th Cir. 2012) 574, 585, 627, 664

Reynolds v. Detroit Fid. & Deposit Co. of Md.,
19 F.2d 110 (6th Cir. 1927) 446, 454

Richardson Nat'l Bank v. Reliance Ins. Co.,
491 F. Supp. 121 (N.D. Tex. 1977) 128

Richland Trust Co. v. Fed. Ins. Co.,
494 F.2d 641 (6th Cir. 1974) 132

Ripps v. Herrington,
1 So. 2d 899 (Ala. 1941) 702

Ritchie Grocer Co. v. Aetna Cas. & Sur. Co.,
426 F.2d 499 (8th Cir. 1970) 517

Ritchie v. Capitol Indem. Corp.,
No. C11-1903RAJ, 2012 U.S. Dist. LEXIS 106804
(W.D. Wash. 2012) 32

Roark v. City Trust, Safe Deposit & Sur. Co.,
110 S.W. 1 (Mo. Ct. App. 1908) 461

Robben & Sons Heating, Inc. v. Mid-Century Ins. Co.,
74 P.3d 1141 (Or. Ct. App. 2003) 391, 692

Rock Island Bank v. Aetna Cas. & Sur. Co.,
706 F.2d 219 (7th Cir. 1983) 8, 25

Rockland-Atlas Nat'l Bank v. Mass. Bonding & Ins. Co.,
157 N.E.2d 239 (Mass. 1959) 129

Roegelein Provision Co. v. Mayen,
566 S.W.2d 1 (Tex. App. 1978) 705

Ronnau v. Caranvan Int'l Corp.,
   468 P.2d 118 (Kan. 1970) 451, 596, 620, 680

Roodhouse Nat'l Bank v. Fid. & Deposit Co. of Md.,
   426 F.2d 1347 (7th Cir. 1970) 61, 385, 684

Rosenzweig & Sons v. Jones,
   72 P.2d 417 (Ariz. 1937) 703

Rossville Fed. Sav. & Loan Assoc. v. Ins. Co. of N. Am.,
   174 S.E.2d 204 (Ga. Ct. App. 1970) 198, 667

Roth v. Md. Cas. Co.,
   209 F.2d 371 (3d Cir. 1953) 297, 665

Rothchild Inv. Corp. v. Travelers Cas. & Sur. Co.,
   No. 05-3041, 2006 U.S. Dist. LEXIS 30033
   (N.D. Ill. 2006) 190

Rothschild Inv. Corp. v. Travelers Cas. & Sur. Co.,
   No. 05 C 3041, 2006 WL 1236148 (N.D. Ill. 2006) 95, 103

Royal Loan Corp v. Am. Sur. Co.,
   173 N.E.2d 17 (Ill. App. Ct. 1961) 459

Royal Trust Bank v. Nat'l Union Fire Ins. Co. of Pitt., Pa.,
   788 F. 2d 719 (11th Cir. 1986) 343, 344, 354

Royalty Mgmt. Corp. v. Lloyd's of London,
   166 F.3d 1218 (9th Cir. 2000) 579

RTC v. Aetna Cas. & Sur. Co. of Ill.,
   25 F.3d 570 (7th Cir. 1994) 68, 137, 242, 279

RTC v. Aetna Cas. & Sur. Co.,
   873 F. Supp. 1386 (D. Ariz. 1994) 39, 354, 519

RTC v. Cont'l Cas. Co.,
   799 F. Supp. 77 (D. Kan. 1992) 655

RTC v. Fidelity & Deposit Co. of Maryland,
   205 F.3d 615 (3d Cir. 2000) 4, 22, 45, 346, 404,
                                                                      584, 601, 632, 636

RTC v. Fid. & Deposit Co. of Md.,
   No. 90-56157, 1992 U.S. App. LEXIS 1592 (9th Cir. 1991) 509

RTC v. Gaudet,
   907 F. Supp. 212 (E.D. La. 1995) 424

RTC v. Hartford Acc. & Indem. Co.,
   25 F.3d 657 (8th Cir. 1994) 442

RTC v. Moskowitz,
   868 F. Supp. 634 (D.N.J. 1994) 424, 439

RTC v. Moskowitz,
   No. 93-2080, 1994 U.S. Dist. LEXIS 15259
   (D.N.J. 1994) 361

Russell Gasket Co. v. Phoenix of Hartford Ins. Co.,
   512 F.2d 205 (6th Cir. 1975) 349, 406, 474

S. Nat'l Bank of N.C. v. United Pac. Ins. Co.,
   864 F.2d 329 (4th Cir. 1989) 59

S. Nat'l Bank of N.C. v. United Pac. Ins. Co.,
   864 F.2d 332-33 (4th Cir. 1989) 71

*S. New Eng. Conference Ass'n of Seventh-Day Adventists v.
   Fed. Ins. Co.,*
   No. 96-1148-A, 1998 Mass. Super. LEXIS 700
   (Mass. Super. 1998) 642

S. Sur. Co. v. Tyler & Simpson Co.,
   120 P. 936 (Okla. 1911) 175

Sade v. Nat'l Sur. Corp.,
   203 F. Supp. 680 (D.D.C. 1962) 12, 299

Salley Grocer Co. v. Hartford Acc. & Indem. Co.,
  223 So. 2d 5 (La. Ct. App. 1969) 528, 607

Santa Fe Gen. Office Credit Union v. Gilberts,
  299 N.E.2d 65 (Ill. App. Ct. 1973) 380, 692

*Sch. Emp. Credit Union v. Nat'l Union Fire Ins. Co.
  of Pitt., Pa.*,
  839 F. Supp. 1477 (D. Kan. 1993) 450, 590, 679

Schupak Group, Inc. v. Travelers Cas. and Sur. Co. of Am.,
  716 F. Supp. 2d 262 (S.D.N.Y. 2010) 489

Schwaber v. Hartford Acc. & Indem. Co.,
  No. 89-55736, 1991 U.S. App. LEXIS 14095
  (9th Cir. 1991) 195

Scirex Corp. v. Fed. Ins. Co.,
  313 F.3d 841 (3d Cir. 2002) 6, 468, 584, 597, 676

Scranton Volunteer Fire Co., v. USF&G,
  450 F.2d 775 (2d Cir. 2001) 379

Se. Bakery Feeds, Inc. v. Ranger Ins. Co.,
  974 S.W.2d 635 (Mo. App. 1998) 369, 416, 431, 669

Sears Roebuck & Co. v. Nat'l Union Fire Ins. Co. of Pitt., Pa.,
  No. B187280, 2007 Cal. App. Unpub. LEXIS 8084
  (Cal. Ct. App. 2007) 667

Sears, Roebuck & Co. v. Nat'l Union Fire Ins. Co. Of Pitt., Pa.,
  No. B187280, 2007 WL 2876149 (Cal. Ct. App. 2007) 619

Seattle Int'l Corp. v. Commerce & Indus. Ins. Co.,
  600 P.2d 612 (Wash. Ct. App. 1979) 229

*Sec. Investors Port. Corp. v. Nat'l Union Fire Ins. Co. (In re
  Waddell Jenmar Sec., Inc.)*
  No. 92-2158, 1993 U.S. LEXIS 9535 (4th Cir. 1993) 22, 508

Sec. Nat'l Bank of Kansas City v. Cont'l Ins. Co.,
586 F. Supp. 139 (D. Kan. 1982) 283, 312, 398, 411, 423, 647

SEC v. Ark. Loan & Thrift Corp.,
297 F. Supp. 73 (W.D. Ark. 1969) 386

SEC v. Credit Bancorp, Ltd.,
147 F. Supp. 2d 238 (S.D.N.Y. 2001) 170, 227, 512

Sela v. St. Paul Travelers Cos.,
No. A07-0411, 2008 Minn. (Minn. Ct. App. 2008) 647

Shared-Interest Mgmt. v. CNN Fin'l Ins. Gp.,
283 A.D.2d 136 (N.Y. 2001) 381

Sharp v. FSLIC,
858 F.2d 1042 (5th Cir. 1988) 508, 629, 696

Shatz v. Am. Sur. Co.,
295 S.W.2d 809 (Ky. 1956) 430

Shaw v. Metro. Cas. Ins. Co. of N.Y.,
62 F.2d 133 (5th Cir. 1932) 602

Shearson/Express, Inc. v. First Cont'l Bank & Trust Co.,
579 F. Supp. 1305 (W.D. Mo. 1984) 190, 300, 617, 629, 666

Shemitz Lighting, Inc. v. Hartford Fire Ins. Co.,
No. CV960052970, 2000 WL 1781840 (Conn. 2000) 390

Sherman & Hemstreet, Inc. v. Cincinnati Ins. Co.,
594 S.E.2d 648 (Ga. 2004) 384, 388, 691

Sherwood & Roberts-Kennewick, Inc. v. St. Paul Fire & Marine Ins. Co.,
322 F.2d 70 (9th Cir. 1963) 11

Shoals Nat'l Bank of Florence v. Home Indem. Co.,
  384 F. Supp. 49 (N.D. Ala. 1974) 63, 281, 652

Shoemaker v. Lumbermens Mut. Cas. Co.,
  176 F. Supp. 2d 449 (W.D. Pa. 2001) 30

Simon Mktg., Inc. v. Gulf Ins. Co.,
  149 Cal. App. 4th 616 (Cal. Ct. App. 2007)................................... 592

Skirlick v. Fid. & Deposit Co.,
  852 F.2d 1376 (D.C. Cir. 1988) 11

Slater v. USF&G,
  400 N.E.2d 1256 (Mass. 1980)... 390

Snyder Nat'l Bank v. Westchester Fire Ins. Co.,
  425 F.2d 849 (5th Cir. 1970).. 124, 659

Southgate Bank v. Fid. & Deposit Co. of Md.,
  794 P.2d 310 (Ka. App. 1990).. 586

Southgate State Bank & Trust Co. v. United Pac. Ins. Co.,
  588 P.2d 486 (Kan. Ct. App. 1979).. 199

Southside Motor Co. v. Transam. Ins. Co.,
  380 So. 2d 470 (Fla. Dist. Ct. App. 1980)..................................... 683

Spartan Iron & Metal Corp. v. Liberty Ins. Corp.,
  6 F. App'x 176 (4th Cir. 2001)..................................... 383, 388, 690

Spears v. St. Paul Ins. Co. (In re Ben Kennedy and Assoc.),
  40 F.3d 318 (10th Cir. 1994).. 674

Sperling & Slater, P.C. v. Hartford Cas. Ins., Co.,
  No. 12-cv-761, 2012 U.S. Dist. LEXIS 125897
  (N.D. Ill. 2012).. 666

Sperling & Slater, P.C. v. Hartford Cas. Ins. Co.,
  No. 12 C 761, 2012 U.S. Dist. LEXIS 181944
  (N.D. Ill. 2012).. 590

Sperry Assocs. Fed. Credit Union v. Cumis Ins. Soc'y, Inc.,
  No. 10-00029 (DRD), 2012 U.S. Dist. LEXIS 26839
  (D.N.J. 2012) 28, 645

St. Joe Paper Co. v. Hartford Acc. & Indem. Co.,
  359 F.2d 579 (5th Cir. 1966) 515

St. Lawrence Cnty. Nat'l Bank v. Am. Motorists Ins. Co.,
  544, 21 A.D.2d 702 (N.Y. App. Div. 1964) 67

St. Paul Fire & Marine Ins. Co. v. Bank of Stockton,
  213 F. Supp. 716 (N.D. Cal. 1963) 422

St. Paul Fire & Marine Ins. Co. v. Branch Bank & Trust Co.,
  834 F.2d 416 (4th Cir. 1987) 320, 612

St. Paul Fire & Marine Ins. Co. v. Branch Banking & Trust Co.,
  643 F. Supp. 648 (E.D.N.C. 1986) 677

St. Paul Fire & Marine Ins. Co. v. Comer,
  227 So. 2d 859 (Miss. 1969) 529

St. Paul Fire & Marine Ins. Co. v. Lefiore Bank & Trust Co.,
  181 So. 2d 913 (Miss. 1966) 146

St. Paul Fire & Marine Ins. Co. v. State Bank of Salem,
  412 N.E.2d 103 (Ind. Ct. App. 1980) 100, 106, 606

St. Paul Mercury Ins. Co. v. FDIC,
  No. 08-21192, 2011 U.S. Dist. LEXIS 32908 (S.D. Fla.
  2011) 355, 670

St. Paul Mercury Ins. Co. v. FDIC,
  No. 08-21192-CIV-GARBER, 2010 U.S. Dist. LEXIS
  30930 (S.D. Fla. 2011) 41

St. Paul Travelers v. Millstone,
  987 A.2d 116 (Md. 2010) 445, 674

Standard Acc. Ins. Co. v. Ponsell's Drug Store, Inc.,
   202 A.2d 271 (Del. 1964) 458

Standard Brass & Mfg. Co. v. Md. Cas. Co.,
   153 So. 2d 475 (La. Ct. App. 1963) 459

Standard Chartered Bank v. Milus,
   826 F. Supp. 310 (D. Ariz. 1990) 39

Standard Title Ins. Co. v. United Pac. Ins. Co.,
   364 F.2d 287 (8th Cir. 1966) 639

Stanford Univ. Hosp. v. Fed. Ins. Co.,
   174 F.3d 1077 (9th Cir. 1999) 83, 639

Star Fastener, Inc. v. Emp'rs' Ins. Co.,
   96 N.E.2d 713 (Mass. 1951) 460

Stargatt v. Avenell,
   434 F. Supp. 234 (D. Del. 1977) 12

State Bank of Kenmore v. Hanover Ins. Co.,
   267 N.Y.S.2d 672 (N.Y. App. Div. 1965) 136

State Bank of the Lakes v. Kan. Bankers Sur.,
   328 F.3d 906 (7th Cir. 2003) 133, 219

State Bank of the Lakes v. Kan. Bankers Sur. Co.,
   No. 98 C 3212, 1999 WL 674739 (N.D. Ill. 1999) 219

State Bank of Poplar Bluff v. Md. Cas. Co.,
   289 F.2d 544 (8th Cir. 1961) 93, 122, 654

State Bank of Viroqua v. Capitol Indem. Corp.,
   214 N.W.2d 42 (Wis. 1974) 403, 432, 463, 672

State ex rel. Dept. of Transp. & Dev. v. Acadia
   Parish Police Jury,
   631 So. 2d 611 (La. App. 1994) 593

State Farm Fire & Cas. Ins. Co. v. White,
  777 F. Supp. 952 (N.D. Ga. 1991) 468

State of Ohio v. Safeco Ins. Co.,
  396 N.E.2d 794 (Ohio Ct. App. 1978) 402, 431

State Street Bank & Trust v. USF&G,
  539 N.E.2d. 779 (Ill. App. Ct. 1989) 199

State v. Evans,
  334 S.W.2d 337 (Tenn. Ct. App. 1959) 448

State v. Green,
  28 So. 3d 1105 (La. Ct. App. 2009) 484

State v. Hanover Ins. Co.,
  431 S.W.2d 141 (Mo. 1968) 689

State v. Jay,
  10 N.E.2d 737 (Ind. Ct. App. 1937) 33

State v. Lidster,
  467 N.E.2d 47 (Ind. Ct. App. 1984) 674

State v. Richardson,
  817 F.2d 1203 (5th Cir. 1987) 398

Stauth v. Nat'l Union Fire Ins. Co. of Pitt., Pa.,
  236 F.3d 1260 (2001) 353

Sterling Nat'l Bank v. Travelers Cas. & Sur. Co. of Am.,
  93 A.D.3d 543 (N.Y. App. Div. 2012) 462

Stewart's Wholesale Elec. Supply, Inc. v. FCCI Ins. Group,
  No. 07-5895, 2008 U.S. App. LEXIS 11933
  (6th Cir. 2008) 668

Stop & Shop Cos. v. Fed. Ins. Co.,
  136 F.3d 71 (1st Cir. 1998) 83, 611

Suburban Nat'l Bank v. Transam. Ins. Co.,
   438 N.W.2d 119 (Minn. Ct. App. 1989) 66, 234, 288, 647

Suffolk Fed. Credit Union v. CUMIS Ins. Soc., Inc.,
   No. 10-CV-0001, 2012 U.S. Dist. LEXIS 178198
   (E.D.N.Y. 2012) 688

Suffolk Fed. Credit Union v. CUMIS Ins. Soc'y, Inc.,
   910 F. Supp. 2d 446 (E.D.N.Y. 2012) 96, 99, 232

Sugarland State Bank v. Aetna Ins. Co.,
   330 So. 2d 336 (La. Ct. App. 1976) 287, 620

Sunderland Roofing & Supply Co. v. USF&G,
   122 N.W. 25 (Neb. 1909) 174

Sunley v. Metro. Life Ins. Co.,
   109 N.W. 463 (Iowa 1906) 704, 706

Superstition Crushing, LLC v. Travelers Cas. and Sur. Co. of Am.,
   360 F. App'x 844 (9th Cir. 2009) 386

Susquehanna Bancshares, Inc. v. Nat'l Union Fire Ins. Co. of Pittsburgh, Pa.,
   659 A.2d 991 (Pa. Super. Ct. 1995) 36

Sutro Bros. & Co. v. Indem. Ins. Co. of N. Am.,
   264 F. Supp. 273 (S.D.N.Y. 1967) 300

Sutro Bros. & Co. v. Indem. Ins. Co. of N. Am.,
   386 F.2d 798 (2d Cir. 1967) 81

Sutton v. Fire Ins. Exch.,
   509 P.2d 418 (Or. 1973) 438

Sys. Design Concepts, Inc. v. CNA Ins. Co.,
   No. A-5834-04T3, 2006 N.J. Super.
   Unpub. LEXIS 2989 (N.J. Super. Ct. App. Div. 2006) 643

T. M. Sinclair & Co. v. Nat'l Sur. Co.,
    107 N.W. 184 (Iowa 1906) 459

T.R. Am. Chem., Inc. v. Seaboard Sur. Co.,
    456 N.Y.S. 608 (N.Y. 1982) 704

Tactical Stop-Loss, LLC v. Travelers Cas. & Sur. Co. of Am.,
    657 F.3d 757 (8th Cir. 2011) 639

Tenant Fin. Corp. v. Md. Cas. Co.,
    86 F.2d 789 (7th Cir. 1936) 109

Tex. Nat'l Bank of Dallas v. Fid. & Deposit Co. of Md.,
    526 S.W.2d 770 (Tex. Civ. App. 1975) 140, 607, 676

The College Network v. Cincinnati Ins. Co.,
    No. 1:10-cv-0370, 2011 U.S. Dist. LEXIS 19073
    (S.D. Ind. 2011) 475

Third Fed. Sav. & Loan Ass'n v. Fireman's Fund Ins.,
    548 F.2d 166 (6th Cir. 1977) 225, 278, 639

Thomas Holme Bldg. & Loan Ass'n v. New Amsterdam Cas. Co.,
    188 A. 374 (Pa. App. 1936) 371, 419

Thomas v. Standard Acc. Ins. Co.,
    7 F. Supp. 205 (E.D. Mich. 1934) 457

Thornburgh Insulation, Inc. v. J.W. Terrill, Inc.,
    236 S.W.3d 651 (Mo. Ct. App. 2007) 689

Thornsberry v. W. Sur. Co.,
    738 F. Supp. 209 (E.D. Ky. 1990) 590

Three Garden Village Ltd P'ship v. USF&G,
    567 A.2d 85 (Md. 1989) 452, 593

Tiarks v. First Nat'l Bank of Mobile,
    182 So. 2d 366 (Ala. 1966) 65, 135

Tierone Bank v. Hartford Cas. Ins. Co.,
   No. 4:08CV3156, 2009 WL 2709296 (D. Neb. 2009) 323

TierOne Bank v. Hartford Fire Ins. Co.,
   No. 4:07-CV-3199, 2008 WL 5170579 (D. Neb. 2008) 153

TierOne Bank v. Hartford Fire Ins. Co.
   No. 4:07CV3199, 2008 U.S. Dist. LEXIS 99262
   (D. Neb. 2008) 662

TIG Ins. Co. v. Privilege Care Mktg.,
   No. 03-03747, 2005 U.S. Dist. LEXIS 7428 (D.N.J. 2005) 170

Title Guar. & Sur. Co. v. Bank of Fulton,
   117 S.W. 537 (Ark. 1909) 172

Tooling, Mfg. & Techs. Ass'n v. Hartford Fire Ins. Co.,
   693 F.3d 665 (6th Cir. 2012) 585, 674

Torrance Nat'l Bank v. Aetna Cas. & Sur. Co.,
   251 F.2d 666 (9th Cir. 1958) 94, 122

Town of Scotland Neck v. W. Sur. Co.,
   271 S.E.2d 501 (N.C. 1980) 381

Town of Troy v. Am. Fid. Co.,
   143 A.2d 469 (Vt. 1958) 382

Towne Mgmt. Corp. v. Hartford Acc. & Indem. Co.,
   627 F. Supp. 170 (D. Md. 1985) 616

Traders State Bank v. Cont'l Ins. Co.,
   448 F.2d 280 (10th Cir. 1971) 625, 685

Tradewell Stores, Inc. v. Fid. & Cas. Co.,
   410 P.2d 782 (Wash. 1966) 373, 420

Transamerica Ins. Co. v. FDIC,
   465 N.W.2d 713 (Minn. Ct. App. 1991) 34

TransAmerica Ins. Co. v. FDIC,
  489 N.W.2d 224 (Minn. 1992) 621

Transw. Credit Union v. CUMIS Ins. Soc'y, Inc.,
  No. 2:09-cv-297, 2013 WL 411485 (D. Utah 2013) 424

Transwest Credit Union v. CUMIS Ins. Soc'y, Inc.,
  No. 2:09-297, 2010 U.S. Dist. LEXIS 99245
  (D. Utah 2010) 363

Travelers Cas. & Sur. Co. of Am. v. Pascarella,
  No. 1:10-cv-157, 2011 U.S. Dist. LEXIS 87696
  (E.D. Tenn. 2011) 479

Travelers Cas. & Sur. Co. of Am. v. Wells Fargo Bank, N.A.,
  No. C 06-03531, 2006 U.S. Dist. LEXIS 76049
  (N.D. Cal. 2006) 485

Travelers Cas. & Sur. Co. v. Baptist Health Sys.,
  313 F.3d 295 (5th Cir. 2002) 654

Travelers Cas. & Sur. Co. v. Citibank (S.D.), N.A.,
  64 U.C.C. Rep. Serv. 2d 475

Travelers Cas. & Sur. Co. v. Stanfield,
  No. CV085019329, 2011 Conn. Super. LEXIS 2126
  (Conn. Super. Ct. 2011) 483

Travelers Indem. Co. v. Cormaney,
  138 N.W.2d 50 (Iowa 1965) 481

Travelers Indem. Co. v. Vas-Nes, P.C.,
  No. 03-5120, 2005 U.S. Dist. LEXIS 28897
  (W.D. Mo. 2005) 687

Tri City Nat'l Bank v. Fed. Ins. Co.,
  674 N.W.2d. 617 (Wis. Ct. App. 2003) 37, 586, 596, 682

Troy State Bank v. BancInsure, Inc.,
  109 P.3d 203, No. 92,115, 2005 Kan. App.
  Unpub. LEXIS 120 (Kan. Ct. App. 2005) 17, 527

Twin Cities Fed. Sav. & Loan Ass'n v. Transamerica Ins. Co.,
  413 F.2d 494 (8th Cir. 1969) 654

U.S. Alliance Fed. Credit Union v. Cumis Ins. Soc'y, Inc.,
  No. 03 Civ. 10317 (PGG), 2009 U.S. Dist. LEXIS 83047
  (S.D.N.Y. 2009) 28

U.S. ex rel. First Cont'l Bank & Trust Co. v. W. Contracting Corp.,
  341 F.2d 383 (8th Cir. 1965) 280, 649

U.S. Fire Ins. Co. v. Am. Turners of Louisville, Inc.,
  557 S.W.2d 905 (Ky. Ct. App. 1977) 441, 448

U.S. Fire Ins. Co. v. FDIC,
  981 F.2d 850 (5th Cir. 1993) 508

U.S. Fire Ins. Co. v. First State Bank of El Paso,
  538 S.W.2d 209 (Tex. 1976) 74

U.S. Gypsum Co. v. Ins. Co. of N. Am.,
  813 F.2d 856 (7th Cir. 1987) 321

U.S. Shopping Bd. Merch. Fleet Corp. v. Aetna Cas. & Sur. Co.,
  98 F.2d 238 (D.C. Cir. 1938) 428, 456

U. S. Smelting Ref. & Mining Co. v. Aetna Cas. & Sur. Co.,
  372 F. Supp. 489 (S.D.N.Y. 1974) 399, 436

U.S. Trustee v. Tamm (In re Hokulani Square, Inc.),
  460 B.R. 763 (9th Cir. B.A.P. 2011) 247

Union Banking Co. v. USF&G,
  213 N.E.2d 191 (Ohio Ct. App. 1965) 137, 288, 658

TABLE OF CASES

Union Inv. Co. v. Fid. & Deposit Co.,
549 F.2d 1107 (6th Cir. 1977) 124, 659

Union Planters Bank, N.A. v. Cont'l Cas. Co.,
478 F.3d 759 (6th Cir. 2007) 585, 598

Union Planters Corp. v. Harwell,
578 S.W.2d 87 (Tenn. Ct. App. 1978) 425, 643

United Am. Bank in Memphis v. Aetna Cas. & Sur. Co.,
No. 84-2225, 1986 U.S. Dist. LEXIS 27619
(W.D. Tenn. 1986) 171

United Am. Fire Ins. Co. v. Am. Bonding Co. of Baltimore,
131 N.W. 994 (Wis. 1911) 177

United Ass'n Union Local No. 290 v. Fed. Ins. Co.,
No. 07-1521, 2008 U.S. Dist. LEXIS 62746
(D. Or. Aug. 11, 2008) 625, 626

United Bank & Trust Co. v. Kan. Bankers Sur. Co.,
901 F.2d 1520 (10th Cir. 1990) 138, 684

United Bank of Pueblo v. Hartford Acc. & Indem. Co.,
529 F.2d 490 (10th Cir. 1976) 80, 653

United Cmty. Banks, Inc.,
2010 U.S. Dist. LEXIS 101646 (N.D. Ga. Sept. 24, 2010) 628

United Gen. Title ins. Co. v. Am. Int'l Grp., Inc.,
51 F. App'x 224 (9th Cir. 2002) 589

United Pac. Ins. Co. v. Idaho First Nat'l Bank,
378 F.2d 62 (9th Cir. 1967) 62, 134, 267, 660

United S. Bank v. Glen Falls Ins. Co.,
548 F. Supp. 355 (M.D. Tenn. 1982) 324

United Sec. Bank v. Fid. & Deposit Co. of Md.,
 No. 96-16331, 1997 U.S. App. LEXIS 27965
 (9th Cir. 1997) 589, 615

United States v. Fid. & Deposit Co. of Md.,
 224 F. 866 (2d Cir. 1915) 446

United States v. Nat'l Grange Mut. Ins. Co.,
 No. 92-12813-MAP, 1994 U.S. Dist. LEXIS 13321
 (D. Mass. 1994) 671

United States v. Smith,
 No. 12-14307, 2013 U.S. App. LEXIS 9325 (N.D. Ga. 2013) 473

United States v. Sorensen,
 No. 4:09-cr-163 4, 2012 U.S. Dist. LEXIS 143805
 (E.D. Ark. 2012) 474

United States v. United Bonding Ins. Co.,
 422 F.2d 277 (5th Cir. 1979) 422

United Va. Factors Corp. v. Aetna Cas. & Sur. Co.,
 624 F.2d 814 (4th Cir. 1980) 59, 275

Universal Am. Corp. v. Nat'l Union Fire Ins. Co. of Pitt., Pa.,
 959 N.Y.S.2d 849 (N.Y. 2013) 574, 663

Universal Bank v. Northland Ins. Co.,
 8 F. App'x 784 (9th Cir. 2001) 110, 236

Universal Bank v. Northland Ins. Co.,
 8 F. App'x784 (9th Cir. 2001) 239

Universal City Studios Credit Union v. CUMIS Ins. Society, Inc.,
 208 Cal. App. 4th 730 (Ct. App. 2012) 624

Universal City Studios Credit Union v. Cumis Ins. Soc'y, Inc.,
 145 Cal. Rptr. 3d 650 (Cal. Ct. App. 2012) 576

TABLE OF CASES

Universal Mortg. Corp. v. Württembergische Versicherung AG,
651 F.3d 759 (7th Cir. 2011) 588

Universal Underwriters Ins. Co. v. Allstate Ins. Co.,
638 A.2d 1220 (Md. App. 1994) 495

Universal Underwriters Ins. Co. v. Buddy Jones Ford, Lincoln-Mercury, Inc.,
734 So. 2d 173 (Miss. 1999) 390

USF&G v. Bank of Batesville,
112 S.W. 957 (Ark. 1908) 172

USF&G v. Barber,
70 F.2d 220 (6th Cir. 1934) 349, 406, 587, 684

USF&G v. Boley Bank & Trust Co.,
144 P. 615 (Okla. 1914) 174

USF&G v. Citizens Bank of Tazewell,
718 F. Supp. 471 (W.D. Va. 1989) 32

USF&G v. Downey,
88 P. 451 (Colo. 1907) 173

USF&G v. Empire State Bank,
448 F.2d 360 (8th Cir. 1971) 194, 350, 408, 605, 614

USF&G v. First Nat'l Bank of Fort Morgan,
364 P.2d 202 (Colo. 1961) 122, 657

USF&G v. Macon-Bibb Cnty. Econ. Opp. Council, Inc.,
381 S.E.2d 539 (Ga. Ct. App. 1989) 414

USF&G v. Maxicare Health Plans,
No. 96-2457, 1997 U.S. Dist. LEXIS 12045
(E.D. La. 1997) 357

USF&G v. Planters Bank & Trust Co.,
77 F.3d 863 (5th Cir. 1996) 71, 311

USF&G v. Planters Bank & Trust Co.,
   No. 4:92CV240-S-D, 1995 U.S. Dist. LEXIS 21673
   (N.D. Miss. 1995) 650

USF&G v. Poetker,
   102 N.E. 372 (Ind. 1913) 445

USF&G v. Shull,
   43 F.2d 532 (10th Cir. 1930) 169

USF&G v. Walker,
   248 F. 42 (5th Cir. 1918) 348, 406

USLIFE Sav. & Loan Ass'n v. Nat'l Sur. Corp.,
   115 Cal. App. 3d 336 (Cal. Ct. App. 1981) 413

USLIFE Sav. & Loan Ass'n v. Nat'l Sur. Corp.,
   171 Cal. Rptr. 393 (Cal. Ct. App. 1981) 365, 669

Utica Mut. Ins. Co. v. Fireman's Fund Ins. Co.,
   748 F. 2d 118 (2nd Cir. 1984) 343, 345, 397, 404, 426

Utica Mut. Ins. Co. v. Precedent Cos.,
   782 N.E.2d 470 (Ind. 2003) 69, 80, 99, 228, 237, 642

Va. Capital Bank v. Aetna Cas. & Sur. Co.,
   343 S.E.2d 81 (Va. 1986) 600, 604, 622

Valley Cmty. Bank v. Progressive Cas. Ins. Co.,
   854 F. Supp. 2d 697 (N.D. Cal. 2012) 126, 141, 144, 602

Valley Cmty. Bank v. Progressive Cas. Ins. Co.,
   No. C-11-574, 2012 U.S. Dist. LEXIS 22072
   (N.D. Cal. 2012) 655

Valley Furniture & Interiors, Inc. v. Transp. Ins. Co.,
   26 P.3d 952 (Wash. Ct. App. 2001) 388

Vam Check Cashing Corp. v. Fed. Ins. Co.,
   699 F.3d 727 (2d Cir. 2012) 649

Verex Assurance, Inc. v. Gate City Mortgage Co.,
No. C-83-0506W, 1984 WL 2918 1984
(D. Utah Dec. 4, 1984) 4, 49

Verneco, Inc. v. Fid. & Cas. Co. of N.Y.,
207 So. 2d 828, *aff'd*, 219 So. 2d 508 (La. 1969)
(La. Ct. App. 1968) 693

Verneco, Inc. v. Fid. & Cas. Co. of N.Y.,
219 So. 2d 508 (La. 1969) 528

Vigilant Ins. Co. v. Chiu,
96 Cal. Rptr. 3d 54 (Cal. Ct. App. 2009) 479

Village of Plummer v. Anchor Cas. Co.,
61 N.W.2d 225 (Minn. 1953) 18

Vons Cos., Inc. v. Fed. Ins. Co.,
212 F.3d 489 (9th Cir. 2000) 499, 585, 589

W.A. Thomas Co. v. Nat'l Sur. Co.,
172 N.W. 697 (Minn. 1919) 174

W. Fid. Corp. v. Ins. Co. of N. Am.,
437 F.2d 752 (10th Cir. 1971) 11

W.H. Hodges & Co. v. Hartford Accident & Indem. Co.,
262 So. 2d 542 (La. Ct. App. 1972) 17

W. Nat'l Bank of Casper v. Hawkeye-Sec. Ins. Co.,
380 F. Supp. 508 (D. Wyo. 1974) 74, 651

W. Sur. Co. v. Town of Evansville,
675 P.2d 258 (Wyo. 1984) 385

Wachovia Bank & Trust Co. v. Mfrs. Cas. Ins. Co.,
171 F. Supp. 369 (M.D.N.C. 1959) 159, 360, 412, 523

Wall St. Disc. Corp. v. Hartford Fire Ins. Co.,
No. 03-4936, 2004 U.S. Dist. LEXIS 7718
(S.D.N.Y. 2004) 361

Waltham Precision Instruments v. Fed. Ins. Co.,
No. 87-0732-MA, 1988 U.S. Dist. LEXIS 1729
(D. Mass. 1988) 687

Ward Mgmt. Co. v. Westport Ins. Corp.,
598 F. Supp. 2d 923 (W.D. Wis. 2009) 444

Warren Deposit Bank v. Fid. & Deposit Co.,
74 S.W. 1111 (Ky. Ct. App. 1903) 173

Watson Quality Ford v. Great River Ins. Co.,
909 So. 2d 1196 (Miss. Ct. App. 2005) 50, 681

Waupaca Northwoods, LLC v. Travelers Cas. & Sur. Co. of Am.,
No. 10-C-459, 2011 WL 1563278 (E.D. Wis. 2011) 525

Waupaca Northwoods v. Travelers Cas. & Sur. Co. of Am.,
No. 10-C-459, 2011 U.S. Dist. LEXIS 44467
(E.D. Wis. 2011) 693

Wausau Bus. Ins. Co. v. US Motels Mgmt. Inc.,
341 F. Supp. 2d 1180 (D. Colo. 2004) 386

Webster Bank v. Travelers Cas. & Sur. Co.,
No. 960476078, 1999 Conn. Super. LEXIS 1218
(Conn. 1999) 188

Wells Fargo Bus. Credit v. Am. Bank of Commerce,
780 F.2d 871 (10th Cir. 1985) 398

White Dairy Co. v. St. Paul Fire & Marine Ins. Co.,
222 F. Supp. 1014 (N.D. Ala. 1963) 383

White Rock Nat'l Bank of Dallas v. U.S. Fire Ins. Co.,
562 S.W.2d 268 (Tex. Ct. App. 1978) 67, 203, 648

White Tire Distrib., Inc. v. Penn. Nat'l Mut. Cas. Ins. Co.,
367 S.E.2d 518 (Va. 1988) 382

Whitney Nat'l Bank v. Transam. Ins. Co.,
476 F.2d 632 (3d Cir. 1973) 131

William C. Roney & Co. v. Fed. Ins. Co.,
674 F.2d 587 (6th Cir. 1982) 516, 693

William H. Sill Mortgs., Inc. v. Ohio Cas. Ins. Co.,
412 F.2d 341 (6th Cir. 1969) 225

William Iselin & Co. v. Fireman's Fund Ins. Co.,
117 A.D.2d 86 (N.Y. App. Div. 1987) 123, 136

William Iselin & Co. v. Fireman's Fund Ins. Co.,
501 N.Y.S.2d 846 (N.Y. Sup. Ct. App. Div. 1986) 661

Williams Elecs. Games, Inc. v. Barry,
No. 97 C 3743, 2000 WL 106672 (N.D. Ill. 2000) 27

Williams v. Berube & Assocs.,
26 S.W.3d 640 (Tenn. Ct. App. 2000) 82

Willoughby v. Fid. & Deposit Co.,
85 P. 713 (Okla. 1906) 175

Willow Mgmt. Co. v. Am. States Ins.,
No. 94 C 6994, 1995 U.S. Dist. LEXIS 467 (N.D. Ill. 1995) 356

Winthrop & Weinstein, P.A. v. Travelers Cas. & Sur. Co.,
187 F.3d 871 (8th Cir. 1999) 423

Wolverine Brass Works v. Pac. Coast Cas. Co.,
146 P. 184 (Cal. Ct. App. 1914) 172

Wooddale, Inc. v. Fid. & Deposit Co. of Md.,
378 F.2d 627 (8th Cir. 1967) 226, 644

World Exch. Bank v. Commercial Cas. Ins. Co.,
 173 N.E. 902 (N.Y. 1930) 108

World Secret Serv. Ass'n v. Travelers Indem. Co.,
 396 S.W.2d 848 (Tenn. App. 1965) 372, 419, 432

Yellowbook Inc. v. Brandeberry,
 708 F.3d 837 (6th Cir. 2013) 628